An Actor Guide to the Talkies, 1965 through 1974

by

ANDREW A. AROS

(As conceived by Richard B. Dimmitt)

The Scarecrow Press, Inc.
Metuchen, N.J. & London
1977

Library of Congress Cataloging in Publication Data

Aros, Andrew A 1944-
An actor guide to the talkies, 1965 through 1974.

Includes index.
1. Moving-pictures--Catalogs. I. Dimmitt, Richard Bertrand. An actor guide to the talkies. II. Title.
PN1998.A6694 016.79143 77-21589
ISBN 0-8108-1052-2

Manufactured in the United States of America

FOR JOHN

INTRODUCTION

Every year film critics labor over their "ten best" lists, and every year it seems difficult to find ten films that were worthy of that distinction. However, with the passage of time, it is far simpler to look back on a particular year and single out the best, the typical, and the dross. For one reason or other, cinematic marvels achieve easier categorization that is often not apparent when the film is in general release.

The decade from 1965-1974 was one filled with memorable performances, new stars, new values, and a renaissance in film scholarship.

The "road" films that were so popular in the 40's and into the 50's with Bing Crosby, Bob Hope, and Dorothy Lamour took on an entirely new look and meaning in the late 60's. Rather than setting out on a new series of comic escapades on the Paramount soundstage, the new road films dealt with the counterculture, drugs, and a search for meaning amidst the urban landscape. In such films as _Blume in Love_, _Cisco Pike_, _Five Easy Pieces_, and the archetype, _Easy Rider_, modern man found himself a prisoner in a society from which there was no exit.

Musicals experienced a new boom as well. The musical is probably one of the most difficult genres of film to judge, since reality must often be suspended while songs are warbled in a fantasy setting. On Broadway, it is often a powerhouse performance that makes the tuner a success. But by the time it reaches the production stage in Hollywood, it is hardly discernible.

Given the standard Hollywood formula of big names, big numbers, and big money, it either falls apart at its musical seams, or else sets the box office on fire. Enough musical dinosaurs were brought to the silver screen to populate a primeval swamp--_On a Clear Day You Can See Forever_, _How to Succeed in Business Without Really Trying_, _Man of La Mancha_, _Hello Dolly_, and _Fiddler on the Roof._

The rock opera _Jesus Christ, Superstar_ was unable to resurrect itself or breathe life into the musical idiom, despite the vain attempts to overlook the music by almost constant camera gymnastics. _Godspell,_ set in contemporary New York City, fared worse, and even the unique rock musical western _Zachariah_ failed to pique the public's interest.

Money, it should be pointed out, is not the answer to making a musical a success. Star cost a small fortune, had a big name (Julie Andrews) around which the production revolved, and still came out on a loser financially and critically, as did lavish studio jobs on Song of Norway, The Great Waltz, and Paint Your Wagon.

A blatant example of miscasting occurred when Lucille Ball was chosen for the role in Mame, over Angela Lansbury, the musical's star on Broadway. While we still love Lucy, even love wasn't enough to overlook the obvious flaws in characterization.

On a more positive note, Liza Minnelli was superb as Sally Bowles in Cabaret, as was Barbra Streisand in Funny Girl, the film which propelled her to fame. Still, one of the most underrated performances was Shirley MacLaine's in Sweet Charity, a musical far ahead of its time. Camelot also remains an overlooked treasure, but did prove popular with the public despite critical dissent.

Disasters became the Grand Hotel of our age. Putting together an all-star cast and turning them loose in catastrophic situations made Earthquake, The Towering Inferno, and The Poseidon Adventure popular entertainments. Few will forget the suspense-heavy air of tension as Dean Martin piloted a damaged jumbo jet to safety in Airport. Far less memorable was the sequel, Airport 1975, or the cheapie programmer, Skyjacked.

Science fiction proved to be far different than the 50's preoccupation with atomic mutants, green men from Mars, and flying saucers. While Camille 2000 and Barbarella were journeys into sci-fi eroticism, back on earth, the highly successful Planet of the Apes and four sequels went through a time warp as complex as a subway map. Scientists battled the threat of human extinction in Andromeda Strain, fought off Blacula, Frogs, The Incredible Two-Headed Transplant, and the campy antics of the Abominable Dr. Phibes. 2001: A Space Odyssey, in which director Stanley Kubrick proved his cinematic genius, turned out to be a landmark film in the sci-fi field, followed by his futuristic classic, A Clockwork Orange.

Thrillers often seemed fixated on the supernatural. First there was Rosemary's Baby, The Mephisto Waltz, The Other, and The Stepford Wives. By the end of 1974, we had all been terrorized by the Exorcist which literally frightened the hell out of us.

It's a big step from Little Caesar to the Godfather, but the crime film has always had a certain attraction. To Francis Ford Coppola must certainly go the credit for bringing the Gone with the Wind of gangster epics, The Godfather (Parts I & II) to the screen. Bonnie and Clyde was clearly a triumph for Arthur Penn and his excellent cast, though the final death scene was far too violent for some tastes. Still, it's far less objectionable than the brutality of Death Wish, Dirty Harry, or Straw Dogs. Violence, which has always been big at the boxoffice, tended to fill studio coffers when buckets of blood, gouged eyes, cracked ribs, and loose teeth scattered in all directions. Kung-Fu films with such champions of the martial arts as Angela Mao and Bruce Lee became the new rage. Enter the Dragon was Bruce Lee's bid for stardom, but he died shortly thereafter and, like James Dean in the 50's, became a cult hero among the young.

The war which raged in Vietnam throughout most of the 60's was rarely encountered in the films of the time. Perhaps because the reality of the war was paraded nightly on the evening news, Hollywood chose to avoid its responsibility. The Ballad of the Green Berets showed the Vietnamese conflict, but it was World War II that received scrutiny. Catch-22 was a disappointing film at best, though it did have some moments of black comedy. Tora, Tora, Tora explained Pearl Harbor to a new generation, and to those who wanted to be reminded.

The Blue Max was a routine aerial adventure that tried to cram too much into its shaky plot. Even the star-ladden Battle of Britain had trouble getting into the air. Without a doubt, Patton was the crowning achievement of the blood and guts combat epics. Blessed with an intelligent script, inspired direction, and the masterful presence of George C. Scott, Patton rolled over its competition in the Oscar derby.

The western film remained the preserve of the macho hero, strong silent type, and "Marlboro" man. John Wayne, the undisputed king of the genre, capped a career with his portrayal of Sheriff Rooster Cogburn in True Grit, yet still found time to fight the Indians and cattle rustlers in Sons of Katie Elder, El Dorado, War Wagon, Chisum, and a score of others. One thing apparent to aficionados of the sagebrush saga is the age of those whom we are asked to believe, helped win and tame the West. William Holden (The Wild Bunch, Wild Rovers), James Stewart (Bandolero, Firecreek), Henry Fonda (The Rounders, Cheyenne Social Club), Dean Martin (The Ambushers), Burt Lancaster (Valdez Is Coming, Ulzana's Raid), and Kirk Douglas (A Gunfight) are well past fifty years, yet they continue to achieve results that younger men only dream of.

Is the western on its way to extinction? One can only ponder who will take the place of these movie giants once they have seen their last sunset. Of the new crop of actors, only Jan-Michael Vincent offers any possibilities of a career in this traditional genre. Filmmakers don't take the western as seriously as they once did. In fact, Lonesome Cowboys was a somewhat celebrated Andy Warhol vision of ranch life, and Mel Brooks' satiric Blazing Saddles also did well at the box office. The high cost of shooting in Hollywood gave rise to runaway productions, which were often shot in Spain and Italy. "Spaghetti" westerns were cheaply made films with an eye on a quick buck, and few realized that Clint Eastwood would emerge a star as a result of a Fistful of Dollars and For a Few Dollars More.

The social conscience of the 60's continued to examine the relationships of blacks and whites in such studio message films as Guess Who's Coming to Dinner, The Landlord, and In the Heat of the Night. By the 70's, a new surge of pride resulted in motion pictures aimed at black audiences such as Cotton Comes to Harlem, Cleopatra Jones, Super Fly, and Shaft.

Women's liberation was only timidly touched upon in such pictures as Up the Sandbox and Alice Doesn't Live Here Anymore, but there were monumental performances by actresses in this period among which were Elizabeth Taylor (Who's Afraid of Virginia Woolf?), Glenda Jackson (Women in Love); Maggie Smith (The Prime of Miss Jean Brodie), Gena Rowlands (A Woman Under the Influence), and Julie Christie (Darling). Male stars provided a number of equally memorable characterizations, including Dustin Hoffman (Little Big Man, The Graduate, Midnight Cowboy), Paul Newman and Robert Redford (Butch Cassidy and the Sundance Kid), Jon Voight (Midnight Cowboy), Jack Nicholson (Chinatown), Marlon Brando (Godfather) and Al Pacino (Godfather II).

Perhaps because of the dichotomy of male-female roles and the opened closets of gay liberation, homosexual lifestyles were explored in an understanding manner in Boys in the Band, Sunday Bloody Sunday, A Very Natural Thing, and with a more exploitative approach in Gay Deceivers, Killing of Sister George, The Fox, and Some of My Best Friends Are.

Love continued to triumph throughout such three-handkerchief weepies as Interlude, The Way We Were, Romeo and Juliet, Love Story, A Man and a Woman, and the lushly beautiful Elvira Madigan. On the other hand, films like The Happy Ending, Something for Everyone, and Two for the Road, left one wondering whether it was all worth the effort.

Screen comedy was made enjoyable by such personalities as Walter Matthau (Plaza Suite), Jack Lemmon (Odd Couple), Woody Allen (Play It Again, Sam), and Peter Bogdanovich's homage to the screwball comedy, What's Up, Doc?

The almost laughable sand and surf romances that lured youth to Beach Blanket Bingo and Wild on the Beach, relocated to ski slopes for Wild Wild Winter and the dragstrip for Red Line 7000 and Fireball 500. As times and tastes changed, contemporary topics such as drugs (Mary Jane, The Trip, Young Runaways), motorcycles (Wild Angels, Born Losers, Hell's Angels), demonstrations (Riot on the Sunset Strip, RPM), and even a political fantasy (Wild in the Streets) found their way to the screen.

Elvis Presley remained a stolid figure in almost all his films, and it was only through sheer charisma that translated into big box office that he managed to remain working almost constantly. His films have always been great fun and he remains an earnest and likeable personality.

With the British invasion begun by the Beatles, an entire cycle of semi-musicals emerged, with such groups as Herman's Hermits (Mrs. Brown You've Got a Lovely Daughter), the Dave Clark Five (Having a Wild Weekend), and Gerry and the Pacemakers (Ferry Cross the Mersey). These were intended less as film entertainment, than as an opportunity to see and hear one's favorites in a brief series of cute situations which usually lead into an excuse for a song.

With the success of the Beatles' Yellow Submarine and Help!, studios began to win back the youth market with such filmed concerts as Festival, Fillmore, Concert for Bangladesh, Wattstax, and Gimme Shelter. Only Woodstock captured the ethos of contemporary rock music, and served as a visual chronicle of a gathering of the tribes.

After timid exploitation films failed to live up to their lurid promises, filmgoers found an alternative in hard-core titles that appealed to "adult" interests in such films as High Rise, Boys in the Sand, Devil in Miss Jones, L. A. Plays Itself, and the celebrated Deep Throat.

With the high-speed chase through the streets of San Francisco, Bullitt set a precedent that was imitated in several other police dramas such as The French Connection, New Centurions, and Seven Ups.

While Hollywood remained the world's chief entertainment production center, countless talents abroad were discovered. Among some of the more prominent names are Sweden's Ingmar Bergman (Cries and Whispers), Jan Troell (The Immigrants), Bo Widerberg (Elvira Madigan), Italy's Federico Fellini (Fellini Satyricon, Amarcord), Michelangelo Antonioni (Blow Up), the late Luchino Visconti (The Damned, Death in Venice), and France's genius, François Truffaut (Day For Night).

There are countless other titles worthy of mention, but this brief introduction I trust has touched upon many of the best.

In addition, I wish to thank Mr. John C. Pearson for his assistance in researching particularly difficult and obscure titles. His patience and thoroughness is greatly appreciated.

Andrew A. Aros
Diamond Bar, California
February 1977

AN ACTOR GUIDE TO THE TALKIES, 1965-1974

1 THE ABDICATION. (Warner Bros.-1974). Cardinal Azzolino, Peter Finch; Queen Christina, Liv Ullmann; Chancellor, Cyril Cusack; Cardinal Barberini, Graham Crowden; The Dwarf, Michael Dunn; Father Dominic, Lewis Fiander; Queen Mother, Kathleen Byron; Magnus, James Faulkner; Ebba Sparre, Ania Marson; Charles, Richard Cornish; Christina's Father, Edward Underdown; Young Christina, Suzanne Huddart; Young Ebba, Debbie Nicholson; Altieri, Paul Rogers; Pinamonti, Harold Goldblatt; Carranza, Tony Steedman; Ginetti, Noel Trevarthen; Birgito, Franz Drago.

2 THE ABDUCTORS. (Joseph Brenner-1972). Ginger, Cheri Caffaro; Jason Varone, William Grannell; Ken Stanton, Richard Smedley; Jablon, Patrick Wright; Carter Winston, Jennifer Brooks; Brenda, Honey Well; Jane, Jeramie Rain; Rhonda, Ined Som; Mary Lou, Geri Bronson; Abductors, Rudy Hornish, Anthony Barone, Jay Rasummy, Doug Martin and Tony Vito; Mr. Whittington, Leo Tepp; Mr. Stuart, Eli Levine; Mr. Polsky, Berg Stone; Mr. Aronson, Stan Franklin; Mr. Byron, Jim Rankin.

3 THE ABOMINABLE DR. PHIBES. (American International-1971). Dr. Phibes, Vincent Price; Dr. Vesalius, Joseph Cotten; Rabbi, Hugh Griffith; Dr. Longstreet, Terry-Thomas; Vulnavia, Virginia North; Goldsmith, Audrey Woods; Nurse Allan, Susan Travers; Dr. Hargreaves, Alex Scott; Dr. Dunwoody, Edward Burnham; Dr. Kitaj, Peter Gilmore; Trout, Peter Jeffrey; Dr. Whitcombe, Maurice Kaufman; Schenley, Norman Jones; Waverley, John Cater; Crow, Derek Godfrey; Lem, Sean Bury; Ross, Walter Horsbrugh; Mrs. Frawley, Barbara Keogh; Police Officials, Dallas Adams, Alan Zipson.

4 ACCATONE! (Brandon-1968). Accattone (Vittorio), Franco Citti; Stella, Franca Pasut; Maddalena, Silvana Corsini; Ascenza, Paolo Guidi; Amore, Adriana Asti; Renato, Renato Capogna; Balilla, Mario Cipriana; Cartagine, Roberto Scaringella; Pio, Piero Morgia; The Neapolitan, Umberto Scaringella; A Prisoner, Elsa Morante; Nannina, Adele Cambria; Becchino, Polidor; Iaio, Danilo Alleva; Il Moicano, Luciano Conti; Piede D'Oro, Luciano Gonini; Intellectual, Gabriele Baldini.

5 ACCIDENT. (Cinema V-1967). Stephen, Dirk Bogarde; Charley,

Stanley Baker; Anna, Jacqueline Sassard; William, Michael York; Rosalind, Vivien Merchant; Francesca, Delphine Seyrig; College Provost, Alexander Knox; Laura, Ann Firbank; Bell, Harold Pinter; Police Sergeant, Brian Phelan; Plain Clothes Policeman, Terence Rigby; Man in Bell's Office, Freddie Jones; Secretary, Jill Johnson; T.V. Receptionist, Jane Hillary; Ted, Maxwell Findlater; Clarissa, Carole Caplin; Hedges, Nicholas Mosley.

6 ACE ELI AND RODGER OF THE SKIES. (20th Century-Fox-1973). Eli, Cliff Robertson; Rodger, Eric Shea; Shelby, Pamela Franklin; Hannah, Rosemary Murphy; Allison, Bernadette Peters; Sister Lite, Alice Ghostley; Rachel, Kelly Jean Peters; Mr. Parsons, Don Keefer; Wilma, Patricia Smith; Jake, Royal Dano; Dumb Dickie, Robert Hamm; Frank Savage, Herb Gatlin; Brother Watson, Arthur Malet; Betty Jo, Ariane Munker; Laura, Hope Summers; Abraham, Jim Boles; Harrison, Lew Brown; Jeffrey, Brent Hurst; Mrs. Parsons, Jan Simms; Leroy, Rodger Peck; Ann, Claudia Bryar; Mrs. Harrison, Dixie Lee; Linette, Felicity Van Runkle; Brother Foster, Pat O'Connor; Mortician, Bill Quinn; Gambler, Jerry Ayres; Sheriff, Hubert Brotten; Charlie, Gary L. Clothier; Bride, Penny Metropulos; Groom, John O'Connell.

7 ACE HIGH. (Paramount-1969). Cacopoulos, Eli Wallach; Cat Stevens, Terence Hill; Hutch Bessy, Bud Spencer; Thomas, Brock Peters; Drake, Kevin McCarthy; Harold, Steffan Zacharias; Paco Rosa, Livio Lorenzon; Thomas' Wife, Tiffany Hoyveld; Cangaceiro, Remo Capitani; Bank Cashier, Armando Bandini; Rick Boyd, Isa Foster.

8 ACROSS 110th STREET. (United Artists-1972). Captain Mattelli, Anthony Quinn; Lt. Pope, Yaphet Kotto; Nick D'Salvio, Anthony Franciosa; Jim Harris, Paul Benjamin; Joe Logart, Ed Bernard; Doc Johnson, Richard Ward; Gloria Roberts, Norma Donaldson; Henry J. Jackson, Antonio Fargas; Shevvy, Gilbert Lewis; Mrs. Jackson, Marlene Warfield; Lt. Reilly, Nat Polen; Lt. Hartnett, Tim O'Connor.

9 ACT OF THE HEART. (Universal-1970). Martha Hayes, Genevieve Bujold; Father Michael Ferrier, Donald Sutherland; Johane Foss, Monique Leyrac; Russell Foss, Bill Mitchell; Housekeeper, Suzanne Langlois; Adele, Sharon Acker; Diedrich, Ratch Wallace; Parks Commissioner, Jean Duceppe; Coach Ti-Jo, Gilles Vigneault; Choirmaster, Eric House.

10 ACT OF VENGEANCE. (American International-1974). Linda, Jo Ann Harris; Jack, Peter Brown; Nancy, Jennifer Lee; Karen, Lisa Moore; Teresa, Connie Strickland; Angie, Patric Estrin; Sgt. Long, Ross Elliot; Tom, Steve Kanaly; Bud, Tony Young; Tiny, Lada Edmund Jr.; John Pickard, Ninette Bravo, Stanley Adams, and Joan McCall.

11 THE ACTIVIST. (Regional-1969). Mike, Michael Smith; Lee,

Lesley Gilbrun; Prof. Williams, Tom Maier; Home Owner, Benbow Ritchie; His Wife, Patricia Ritchie; Steering Committee, Brian Murphy, Naome Gilbert, Ben Schwartz, Charles Goldman, Wendel Brunner.

12 ADALEN 31. (Paramount-1969). Kjell, Peter Schildt; His Mother, Kerstin Tidelius; His Father, Roland Hedlund; Anna, Marie de Geer; Her Mother, Anita Bjork; Her Father, Olof Bergstrom; Nisse, Jonas Bergstrom.

13 ADAM AT 6 A.M. (National General-1970). Adam Gaines, Michael Douglas; Jerri Jo Hopper, Lee Purcell; Harvey Gavin, Joe Don Baker; Inez Treadley, Grayson Hall; Mr. Hopper, Charles Aidman; Cleo, Marge Redmond; Mrs. Hopper, Louise Latham; Mavis, Carolyn Conwell; Van, Dana Elcar; Joyce, Meg Foster; Roger Gaines, Richard Derr; Mrs. Gaines, Ann Gwynn; Dr. Peters, Ned Wertheimer; Orville, Ed Call; Leroy, David Sullivan; Elwood, Butch Youngblood.

14 ADAM'S WOMAN. (Warner Bros.-1972). Adam, Beau Bridges; Bess, Jane Merrow; Dyson, James Booth; O'Shea, Andrew Keir; Duchess, Tracy Reed; Barrett, Peter O'Shaughnessy; Sir Philip, John Mills; Croydon, John Warwick; Muir, Harry Lawrence; Millie, Katy Wild; Nobby, Mark McManus; Cosh, Harold Hopkins; Fat Anne, Doreen Warburton; Matron, Clarissa Kaye; Chaplain, Peter Collingwood.

15 THE ADDING MACHINE. (Regional-1969). Mrs. Zero, Phyllis Diller; Zero, Milo O'Shea; Daisy Devore, Billie Whitelaw; Lt. Charles, Sydney Chaplin; Shrdlu, Julian Glover; Smithers, Raymond Huntley; Don, Phil Brown; Ethel, Libby Morris; Harry, Hugh McDermott; Mabel, Paddie O'Neil; Judy, Carol Cleveland; Joe, Kenny Damon; Detective, Bruce Boa; Jailers, John Brandon, Hal Galili, Tony Caunter; Judy's Lover, Bill Hutchinson; 2nd Apartment Girl, Helen Elliott; Jury Foreman, C. Denier Warren; Judee, Tommy Duggan; Apartment Tenants, John Bloomfield, Helena Stevens, Alan Surtees, Christine Pryor, Cal McCord, Shirley Cooklin, Anthony Harwood; Lawyer, Bill Nagy; District Attorney, Nicholas Stuart; and Gordon Sterne, Mike Reed, Lola Lloyd, George Margo, George Roderick, Janet Brown, Janie Baron, John Cook.

16 ADELAIDE. (Sigma III-1969). Elisabeth Hermann, Ingrid Thulin; Frederic Cournot, Jean Sorel; Adelaide Hermann, Sylvie Fennec; Governess, Faith Brook; Potier, Jacques Portet; Christian, Jean-Pierre Bernard; Janine, Joelle Bernard; Simone Gusin, Cynthia Grenier, and Robert Higgins.

17 ADIEU PHILLIPPINE. (New Yorker-1973). Liliane, Yveline Cery; Juliette, Stefania Sabatini; Michel, Jean-Claude Aimimi; Pachala, Vittorio Capriolo; Horatio, Davide Tonelli.

18 ADIOS GRINGO. (Trans-Lux-1968). Brent Landers, Montgomery

Wood; Lucy Tillson, Evelyn Stewart; Dr. Barfield, Roberto Camardiel; Tex Slaughter, Jesus Puente; Avery Ranchester, Max Dean; Clayton Ranchester, Peter Cross; Stan Clevenger, Grant Laramy; Murphy, Jean Martin; Maude Clevenger, Monique Saint Clare; Claude Servyll, Frank Pascal, Ramon Perez, Sterling Regell, Francisco Branna, Mimo Billi, Nelo Pazzafini.

19 ADIOS SABATA. (United Artists-1971). Sabata, Yul Brynner; Ballantine, Dean Reed; Escudo, Pedro Sanchez; Skimmel, Gerard Herter; September, Sal Borgese; Ocano, Franco Fantasia; Gitano, Joseph Persaud; Folgen, Gianni Rizzo; Manuel, Salvatore Billa; Juan, Massimo Carocci; Major, Antonio Gradoli.

20 THE ADOLESCENTS. (1967). Fiammetta, Micaela Esdra; Livia, Esmeralda Ruspoli; Genevieve, Genevieve Bujold; Louise, Louise Marleau; Bernard, Bernard Arcand; Marie-France, Marie-France de Chabaneix; Veronica, Veronique Duval; Daniele, Nadine Ballot; Marc, Marc Kalinoski; Michel, Michel Aracheguesne.

21 ADRIFT. (MPO-1971). Yanos, Rade Markovic; Zuzka, Milena Dravid; Anada, Paula Pritchett; Stutterer, Josef Kroner; Helmsman, Vlado Muller; Balthazar, Gustav Valach; Kristof, Ivan Darvas; Father-in-law, Jaroslav Marvan; Peter, Janko Boldis; Doctor, Dezso Kiraly.

22 THE ADVENTURERS. (Paramount-1970). Dax Xenos, Bekim Fehmiu; Marcel Campion, Charles Aznavour; Rojo, Alan Badel; Sue Ann Daley, Candice Bergen; Sergei Nikovitch, Thommy Berggren; Caroline de Boyne, Delia Boccardo; Fat Cat, Ernest Borgnine; Baron de Coyne, Rossano Brazzi; Deborah Hadley, Olivia de Havilland; Dania Leonardi, Anna Moffo; Amparo, Leigh Taylor-Young; Robert, Christian Roberts; El Lobo, Yorgo Voyagis; Jaime Xenos, Fernando Rey; John Ireland, Jorge Martinez de Hoyos, Sydney Tafler, Yolande Donlan, Angela Scoular, Milena Vucotic, Ferdy Mayne, Jaclyn Smith, Katharine Balfour, Roberta Donatelli, Peter Graves, John Frederick, Allan Cuthbertson, Zienia Merton, Roberta Haynes, Michael Balfour.

23 THE ADVENTURES OF BULLWHIP GRIFFIN. (Buena Vista-1967). Eric "Bullwhip" Griffin, Roddy McDowall; Arabella Flagg, Suzanne Pleshette; Judge Higgins, Karl Malden; Sam Trimble, Harry Guardino; Quentin Bartlett, Richard Haydn; Miss Irene Chesney, Hermione Baddeley; Jack Flagg, Bryan Russell; Captain Swain, Liam Redmond; Mr. Pemberton, Cecil Kellaway; Bandido Leader, Joby Baker; Mountain Ox, Mike Mazurki; Joe Turner, Alan Carney; Chief Executioner, Parley Baer; Referee, Arthur Hunnicutt; Timekeeper, Dub Taylor; Bandido, Pedro Gonzales-Gonzales.

24 THE ADVERSARY. (Belle-Kay-1970). Jimmy, Howard Lawrence; Johnny, Vic Campos; Pecky, Frank Mangiapane; Lisa, Stephanie Waxman; Timothy, Brian Roberts; Pinky, Marvin Davis; Carrie, Chris Assini; Muriel, Natalie Richards; Boxer, Ed Smith.

25 THE ADVERSARY. (Audio Brandon-1973). Siddhartha, Dhritiman Chatterjee; Krishna Rose, Joyshree Roy, Kalyan Chatterjee, Debral Roy.

26 AN AFFAIR OF THE HEART. (1967). Isabelle, Eva Ras; Ahmed, Siobadan Aligrudic; Friend, Ruzica Sokic; Seducer, Miodrag Andric; Experts, Dr. Aleksander Kostic and Dr. Zivolin Aleksic.

27 AFRICA--TEXAS STYLE! (Paramount-1967). Jim Sinclair, Hugh O'Brian; Wing Commander Hayes, John Mills; Karl Bekker, Nigel Green; John Henry, Tom Nardini; Fay Carter, Adrienne Corri; Hugo Copp, Ronald Howard; Sampson, Charles Malinda; Mr. Oyondi, Honey Wamala; Veterinary, Charles Hayes; Peter, Stephen Kikumu; Turk, Ali Twaha; Witch Doctor, Mohammed Abdullah; Girl at Airport, Hayley Mills.

28 AFRICAN SAFARI. (Crown International-1969). Documentary.

29 AFTER THE FOX. (United Artists-1966). Aldo Vanucci, Peter Sellers; Tony Powell, Victor Mature; Gina Romantica, Britt Ekland; Harry Granoff, Martin Balsam; Okra, Akim Tamiroff; Pollo, Paolo Stoppa; Siepi, Tino Buazzelli; Carlo, Mac Ronay; Mama Vanucci, Lidia Brazzi; Police Chief, Lando Buzzanca; Bikini Girl, Maria Grazia Buccella; Chief of Interpol, Maurice Denham; Tiberio Murgia, Francesco De Leone, Carlo Croccolo, Nino Musco, Pier Luigi Pizzi, Lino Mattera, Piero Gerlini, Daniele Vargas, Franco Sportelli, Giustino Durano, Mimmo Poli, Enzo Fiermonte, Roberto De Simoni, Angelo Spaggiari, David Lodge, Timothy Bateson; and as Himself, Vittorio De Sica.

30 AFTER YOU, COMRADE. (Continental-1967). Igor Strogoff, Jamie Uys; Granger J. Wellborne, Bob Courtney; Tanya Orloff, Reinet Maasdorp; Johnny Edwards, Angus Neill; Ed Sloane, Joe Stewardson; Anzonia, Arthur Swemmer; Italian Mayor, Frank Gregory; Italian Butcher, Mimmi Poli; Hostel Matron, Marjorie Gordon; Television Announcer, Emil Nofal; Yugoslav Mother, Sann De Lange; Austrian Farmer, Wilhelm Esterhuizen.

31 AGE OF CONSENT. (Columbia-1970). Bradley, James Mason; Cora, Helen Mirren; Nat, Jack MacGowran; Ma, Neva Carr-Glyn; Isabel, Andonia Katsaros; Hendricks, Michael Boddy; Ted, Harold Hopkins; Cooley, Slim DeGrey; Interviewer, Max Meldrum; Godfrey, Frank Thring; Meg, Clarissa Kaye; Grace, Judy McGrath; Edna, Lenore Caton; Susie, Diane Strachan; Ivy, Roberta Grant; Jasper, Prince Nial.

32 AGENT 008 3/4. (Continental-1965). Nicholas Whistler, Dirk Bogarde; Vlasta Simenova, Sylva Koscina; Colonel Cunliffe, Robert Morley; Simenova, Leo McKern; Josef, Roger Delgado.

33 AGENT FOR H. A. R. M. (Universal-1966). Adam Chance, Mark Richman; Jim Graff, Wendell Corey; Prof. Janos Steffanic, Carl Esmond; Ava Vestok, Barbara Bouchet; Malko, Martin Kosleck; Luis, Rafael Campos; Mid-Eastern Contact, Alizia Gur; Marian, Donna Michelle; Borg, Robert Quarry; Morgue Attendant, Robert Donner; Billy, Steve Stevens; Conrad, Marc Snegoff; Helgar, Horst Ebersberg; Schloss, Chris Anders; Manson, Ray Dannis; Police Lieutenant, Ronald Von; Police Officer, Robert Christopher.

34 THE AGONY AND THE ECSTASY. (20th Century-Fox-1965). Michelangelo, Charlton Heston; Pope Julius II, Rex Harrison; Contessina de Medici, Diane Cilento; Bramante, Harry Andrews; Duke of Urbino, Alberto Lupo; Giovanni de Medici, Adolfo Celi; Paris De Grassis, Venantino Venantini; Sangallo, John Stacy; Foreman, Fausto Tozzi; Woman, Maxine Audley; Raphael, Tomas Milian.

35 THE AGONY OF LOVE. (Boxoffice International-1966). Pat Barrington, Parker Garvey, Sam Taylor, R. A. Silverberg, Shannon Carse, Jay Edwards, Al Ward, Owen Hannifen, Betty Lavender, Tori Lambert, Helena Clayton, Oswald Fenwick, Morton Smith, Sherry Shannon, Joy Lowe, Ben Johns.

36 AIRPORT. (Universal-1970). Mel Bakersfeld, Burt Lancaster; Vernon Demerest, Dean Martin; Tanya Livingston, Jean Seberg; Gwen Meighen, Jacqueline Bisset; Patroni, George Kennedy; Ada Quonsett, Helen Hayes; D. O. Guerrero, Van Heflin; Inez Guerrero, Maureen Stapleton; Lt. Anson Harris, Barry Nelson; Cindy, Dana Wynter; Harry Standish, Lloyd Nolan; Sarah, Barbara Hale; Cy Jordan, Gary Collins; Peter Coakley, John Findlater; Jessie Royce Landis, Larry Gates, Peter Turgeon, Whit Bissell, Virginia Grey, Eileen Wesson, Paul Picerni, Robert Patten, Clark Howat, Lew Brown, Ilana Dowdling, Lisa Garritson, Jim Nolan, Patty Poulsen, Ena Hartman, Malila Saint Duval, Sharon Harvey, Albert Reed, Jodean Russo, Nancy Ann Nelson, Dick Winslow, Lou Wagner, Janis Hansen.

37 AIRPORT 1975. (Universal-1974). Alan Murdock, Charlton Heston; Chief Stewardess, Nancy Pryor, Karen Black; Joseph Petroni, George Kennedy; Pilot Stacy, Efrem Zimbalist Jr.; Mrs. Petroni, Susan Clark; Sister Ruth, Helen Reddy; Herself, Gloria Swanson; Janice Abbott, Linda Blair; Abbott's Mother, Nancy Olson; Small Plane Pilot Freeman, Dana Andrews; Stacy's Co-Pilot, Roy Thinnes; Talkative Passenger, Sid Caesar; Tipsy Mrs. Devaney, Myrna Loy; Rescue Pilot Alexander, Ed Nelson; TV Newsman, Larry Storch; Sister Beatrice, Martha Scott; Drinkers, Norman Fell, Jerry Stiller, Conrad Janis; Mrs. Freeman, Beverly Garland; Swanson's secretary,

Augusta Summerland; Col. Moss, Guy Stockwell; Navigator Julio, Erik Estrada; Steward, Ken Sansom; Junior Petroni, Brian Morrison; Stewardesses, Amy Farrell, Irene Tsu.

38 ALABAMA'S GHOST. (Ellman Enterprises-1973). Christopher Brooks, E. Kerrigan Scott, Turk Murphy Jazz Band.

39 ALEX IN WONDERLAND. (MGM-1970). Alex, Donald Sutherland; Beth, Ellen Burstyn; Amy, Meg Mazursky; Nancy, Glenna Sergent; Mother, Viola Spolin; Andre, Andre Philippe; Leo, Michael Lerner; Jane, Joan Delaney; Norman, Neil Burstyn; Lewis, Leon Frederick; Marlene, Carol O'Leary; Hal Stern, Paul Mazursky; Mr. Wayne, Moss Mabry; Themselves, Federico Fellini and Jeanne Moreau.

40 ALEXANDER. (Cinema V-1969). Alexander, Philippe Noiret; La Grande, Francoise Brion; Agathe, Marlene Jobert; Angele Sanguin, Antoinette Moya; Sanguin, Paul Le Person; Colibert, Pierre Richard; La Fringale, Jean Carmet.

41 ALF 'N' FAMILY. (Sherpix-1972). Alf Garnett, Warren Mitchell; Else Garnett, Dandy Nichols; Mike, Anthony Booth; Rita, Una Stubbs; Mike's Father, Liam Redmond; Bert, Bill Maynard; Sergeant, Brian Blessed; Fred, Sam Kydd; Valuation Officer, Frank Thornton; Girl at Wedding Party, Cleo Sylvestre; Ann Lancaster, Michael Robbins, Bob Grant, Edward Evans, Madge Brindley, Pat Coombes, Shelagh Fraser, Jack Jordan, Bill Ward, Leslie Noyes, Brenda Kempner.

42 ALFIE. (Paramount-1966). Alfie, Michael Caine; Ruby, Shelley Winters; Siddie, Millicent Martin; Gilda, Julia Foster; Annie, Jane Asher; Carla, Shirley Anne Field; Lily, Vivien Merchant; Woman Doctor, Eleanor Bron; Mr. Smith, Denholm Elliott; Harry, Alfie Bass; Humphrey, Graham Stark; Nat, Murray Melvin; Lofty, Sydney Tafler.

43 ALFRED THE GREAT. (MGM-1969). Alfred, David Hemmings; Guthrum, Michael York; Aelhswith, Prunella Ransome; Asher, Colin Blakely; Athelstan, Julian Glover; Rober, Ian McKellen; Ethelred, Alan Dobie; Buhrud, Peter Vaughan; Ivar, Julian Chagrin; Wulfstan, Barry Jackson; Freda, Vivien Merchant; Cedric, Christopher Timothy; Cuthbert, John Rees; Edwin, Andrew Bradford; Offa, Michael Billington; Bishop, Ralph Nossek; Olaf, David Glaisyer; Brother Thomas, Eric Brooks; Hadric, Keith Buckley; Sigurd, Trevor Jones; Eafa, Peter Plythe.

44 ALFREDO, ALFREDO. (Paramount-1973). Alfredo, Dustin Hoffman; Maria-rosa, Stefania Sandrelli; Carolina, Carla Gravina; Carolina's Mother, Clara Colosimo; Carolina's Father, Daniele Patella; Mariarosa's Mother, Danika La Loggia; Mariarosa's Father, Saro Urzi; Alfredo's Father, Luigi Baghetti; Oreste, Duilio Del Prete.

45 ALI. (New Yorker-1974). Brigitte Mira, El Hedi Ben Salem, Barbara Valentin, Irm Hermann, Peter Gauhe, Karl Scheydt, Rainer Werner Fassbinder, Marquard Bohn, Walter Sedlmayer, Doris Mattes, Liselotte Eder, Gusti Kreissl, Margit Symo, Elizabeth Bertram, Helga Ballhous, Elma Karlowa, Anita Bucher.

46 ALICE DOESN'T LIVE HERE ANYMORE. (Warner Bros.-1974). Alice Hyatt, Ellen Burstyn; David, Kris Kristofferson; Waitress Flo, Diane Ladd; Donald Hyatt, Billy Green Bush; Neighbor Bea, Lelia Goldoni; Ben Eberhart, Harvey Keitel; Ben's Wife Rita, Lane Bradbury; Restaurant Owner, Vic Tayback; Young Girl Audrey, Jodie Foster; Waitress Vera, Valerie Curtin; Bar Owner Jacobs, Murray Moston; Bartender, Harry Northrup; Alice's Son Tommy, Alfred Lutter; Young Alice, Mia Bendixsen.

47 ALICE IN THE CITIES. (1974). Phillip, Rudiger Vogeler; Alice, Yella Rottlander; Lisa, Elisabeth Kreutzer; Edda, Edda Kochl; The Girl, Didi Petrikat; The Agent, Ernest Bohm; The Car Salesman, Sam Presti; Girl at Ticket Counter, Lois Moran; Hans Hirschmuller, Sybille Baier, Mirko.

48 ALICE'S ADVENTURES IN WONDERLAND. (American National-1972). Alice, Fiona Fullerton; White Rabbit, Michael Crawford; Caterpillar, Ralph Richardson; Queen of Hearts, Flora Robson; March Hare, Peter Sellers; Mad Hatter, Robert Helpmann; Dormouse, Dudley Moore; Dodgson, Michael Jayston; Gryphon, Spike Milligan.

49 ALICE'S RESTAURANT. (United Artists-1969). Arlo Guthrie, Arlo Guthrie; Alice Brock, Pat Quinn; Ray Brock, James Broderick; Shelly, Michael McClanathan; Roger, Geoff Outlaw; Mari-chan, Tina Chen; Karin, Kathleen Dabney; Officer Obie, William Obanhein; Evangelist, Seth Allen; Blueglass, Monroe Arnold; Woody Guthrie, Joseph Boley; Lady Clerk, Vinnette Carroll; Marjorie Guthrie, Sylvia Davis; Jacob, Simm Landres; Eulalie Noble, Louis Beachner, MacIntyre Dixon, Rev. Dr. Pierce Middleton, Donald Marye, Shelley Plimpton, M. Emmet Walsh, Ronald Weyand, Eleanor Wilson, Simon Deckard, Thomas De Wolfe, Judge James Hannon, Graham Jarvis, John Quill, Frank Simpson, Pete Seeger, Lee Hays.

50 THE ALL-AMERICAN BOY. (Warner Bros.-1973). Vic Bealer, Jon Voight; Rodine, Carol Androsky; Drenna Valentine, Anne Archer; Rockoff, Gene Borkan; Larking, Ron Burns; Poppy, Rosalind Cash; Nola Bealer, Jeanne Cooper; Bett Van Daumee, Peggy Cowles; Lovette, Leigh French; Arty, Ned Glass; Ariel Van Daumee, Bob Hastings; Shereen Bealer, Kathy Mahoney; Jay David Swooze, Art Metrano; Magda, Jaye P. Morgan; Parker, Harry Northrup; Connie Swooze, Nancie Phillips; High Valentine, Jeff Thompson.

51 ALL MEN ARE APES. (Adelphia-1965). Mark Ryan, Grace Lynn, Steve Woods, Steve Vincent, Bonny Lee Noll, Mia Marlowe, Ted Teschner, Walter Teague, Tom O'Horgan, Wendy Winston, Jeanine Costa, Brigitta Batit, Bob Worms, Frank Geraci, Joe Boatner's Ink Spots, Sandi Brown.

52 ALL NEAT IN BLACK STOCKINGS. (National General-1969). Ginger, Victory Henry; Jill, Susan George; Dwyer, Jack Shepherd; Mother, Clare Kelly; Carole, Vanessa Forsyth; Old Gunge, Terence De Marney; Sis, Anna Cropper; Issur, Harry Towb; Babette, Jasmina Hamzavi; New Bird, Deirdre Costello; Jocasta, Nita Lorraine; First Bird, Rosalind Elliott; Hospital Sister, Anna Welsh; 1st Orderly, Geoffrey Reed; 2nd Orderly, Michael McKevitt; New Bird, Tanya Trude; Businessman, Eric Longworth; Pakistani, Shivendra Sinha; Suburban Housewife, Gwendolyn Watts; Young Bolke, Graham James; Toddler, Marc Bergman; Vicar, John Woodnutt; Man with Parrot, Andre Dakar; Cafe Waitress, Christine Pryor; Photographer, Malcolm Tierney; Car Salesman, Maurice Travers; New Mate, Larry Dann; Angry Householder, Neil Wilson; Nurse, Carmen Monroe.

53 ALL THE LOVING COUPLES. (U-M-1969). Kathy, Barbara Blake; Natalie, Lynn Cartwright; Mike Corey, Paul Comi; Dale, Scott Graham; Irv, Paul Lambert; Liz, Gloria Mannon; Thelma, Jackie Russell; Mitch, Norman Alden.

54 ALL THE OTHER GIRLS DO! (Harlequin International-1967). Giovenetta, Rosemarie Dexter; Gabrielle, Jacques Perrin; His Father, Folco Lulli; Giovenella's Mother, Gina Rovere; Giovenella's Father, Bice Valori; Mistress, Luisa Della Noce.

55 ALL THE RIGHT NOISES. (20th Century-Fox-1973). Len, Tom Bell; Val, Olivia Hussey; Joy, Judy Carne; Bernie, John Standing; Camera Operator, Roy Herrick; Ted, Edward Miggens; Jenny, Chloe Franks; Ian, Gareth Wright; Terry, Gordon Griffith; Len's Father, Robert Keegan; Laura, Lesley Down; Stage Manager, Peter Burton; Waitress, Chrissie Shrimpton; Stage hand, Stacy Davies; Conductor, Otto Diamont; First Musician, Roderick Jones; Second Musician, Larry Burns.

56 ALL THE WAY BOYS. (Avco Embassy-1973). Plata, Terence Hill; Salud, Bud Spencer; Mad Man, Cyril Cusack; Daveira, Michel Antoine; Mr. Ears, Rene Kolldehoff.

57 THE ALPHABET MURDERS. (MGM-1966). Hercule Poirot, Tony Randall; Amanda Beatrice Cross, Anita Ekberg; Hastings, Robert Morley; Japp, Maurice Denham; Duncan Doncaster, Guy Rolfe; Lady Diane, Sheila Allen; Franklin, James Villiers; Don Fortune, Julian Glover; Betty Barnard, Grazina Frame; "X," Clive Morton; Sir Carmichael Clarke, Cyril Luckham; Wolf, Richard Wattis; Sergeant, David Lodge; Cracknell, Patrick Newell; Judson, Austin Trevor; Miss Sparks, Alison Seebohm;

Dragbot, Windsor Davies; Mrs. Fortune, Sheila Reid; Miss Marple, Margaret Rutherford.

58 ALPHAVILLE. (Pathe Contemporary-1965). Lemmy Caution, Eddie Constantine; Natasha Von Braun, Anna Karina; Henry Dickson, Akim Tamiroff; Professor Von Braun, Howard Vernon; The Engineer, Laszlo Szabo; Asst. to Professor Von Braun, Michael Delahaye; Professor Eckel, Jean-Andre Fieschi; Professor Jeckel, Jean-Louis Comolli; Alpha 60, Itself.

59 ALVAREZ KELLY. (Columbia-1966). Alvarez Kelly, William Holden; Col. Tom Rossiter, Richard Widmark; Liz Pickering, Janice Rule; Major Albert Stedman, Patrick O'Neal; Charity Warwick, Victoria Shaw; Capt. Angus Ferguson, Roger C. Carmel; Sergeant Hatcher, Richard Rust; Captain Towers, Arthur Franz; Lt. Farrow, Donald Barry; John Beaurider, Duke Hobbie; Cpl. Peterson, Harry Carey Jr. ; McIntrye, Howard Caine; Ely Harrison, Mauritz Hugo; Gen. Kautz, G. B. Atwater; Capt. Williams, Robert Morgan; Capt. Webster, Paul Lukather; Mary Ann, Stephanie Hill; Melinda, Indus Arthur; Union Lt. , Clint Ritchie.

60 ALVIN PURPLE. (Bi-Jay-1974). Graeme Blundell, George Whaley, Penne Hackforth-Jones, Elli Maclure, Noel Ferrier, Jill Foster.

61 AMARCORD. (New World-1974). Titta's Mother, Pupella Maggio; Gradisca, Magali Noel; Titta's Father, Armando Brancia; Crazy Uncle, Ciccio Ingrassia; Pataca, Nandino Orfei; Lawyer, Luigi Rossi; Titta, Bruno Zanin.

62 AMAZING GRACE. (United Artists-1974). Grace, Moms Mabley; Forthwith Wilson, Slappy White; Welton J. Waters, Moses Gunn; Creola Waters, Rosalind Cash; Cousin Lincoln, Stepin Fetchit; Clarine, Butterfly McQueen; Annenberg, Jim Karen; Stokes, George Miles; William, Gary Boling; Mayor Scott, Dolph Sweet.

63 AMBUSH BAY. (United Artists-1966). 1st Sgt. Steve Corey, Hugh O'Brian; Sgt. Ernest Wartell, Mickey Rooney; PFC James Grenier, James Mitchum; Miyazaki, Tisa Chang; Sgt. William Maccone, Pete Masterson; Cpl. Alvin Ross, Harry Lauter; Cpl. Stanley Parrish, Greg Amsterdam; Pvt. Henry Reynolds, Jim Anauo; Pvt. George George, Tony Smith; Capt. Alonzo Davis, Clem Stadler; Amado Abello, Juris Sulit, Max Quismundo, Bruno Punzalan, Buff Fernandez, Joaquin Farjado, Limbo Lagdameo, Nonong Arceo.

64 THE AMBUSHERS. (Columbia-1967). Matt Helm, Dean Martin; Francesca Madeiros, Senta Berger; Sheila Sommers, Janice Rule; MacDonald, James Gregory; Jose Ortega, Albert Salmi; Quintana, Kurt Kasznar; Lovey Kravezit, Beverly Adams; Nassim,

David Mauro; Karl, Roy Jenson; Rocco, John Brascia; Linda, Linda Foster; The Slaygirls, Penny Brahms, Kyra Bester, Ulla Lindstrom, Lena Cederham, Yumiko Ishizuka, Suzanna Moore, Dee Duffy, Marilyn Tindall, Egidia Anabella Incontrera, Alena Johnston, Jann Watson, Karin Fedderson, Terri Hughes.

64a AN AMERICAN DREAM. (Warner Bros. -1966). Stephen Rojack, Stuart Whitman; Cherry McMahon, Janet Leigh; Lt. Roberts, Barry Sullivan; Barney Kelly, Lloyd Nolan; Arthur Kabot, Murray Hamilton; Sgt. Leznicki, J. D. Cannon; Ruta, Susan Denberg; Nicky, Les Crane; Johnny Dell, Warren Stevens; Eddie Ganucci, Joe De Santis; Detective O'Brien, Stacy Harris; Shago Martin, Paul Mantee; Ganucci's Lawyer, Harold Gould; Ord Long, George Takei; Freya, Kelly Jean Peters; Deborah Rojack, Eleanor Parker.

65 THE AMERICAN DREAMER. (EYR-1971). Dennis Hopper.

66 AMERICAN GRAFFITI. (Universal-1973). Curt, Richard Dreyfuss; Steve, Ron Howard; John, Paul Le Mat; Terry, Charlie Martin Smith; Laurie, Cindy Williams; Debbie, Candy Clark; Carol, Mackenzie Phillips; Disc Jockey, Wolfman Jack; Bob Falfa, Harrison Ford; The Pharoahs, Bo Hopkins, Manuel Padilla Jr., Beau Gentry; Herby & the Heartbeats, Flash Cadillac and the Continental Kids; Peg, Kathy Quinlan; Mr. Wolfe, Terry McGovern; Eddie, Tim Crowley; Girl, Jan Wilson; Jane, Kay Ann Kemper; Announcer, Caprice Schmidt; Budda, Jane Bellan; Vic, Joe Spano; Al, Chris Pray; Judy, Susan Richardson; Carhop #2, Donna Wehr; Holstein, Jim Bohan; Jeff Pazzuto, Ron Vincent; Ferber, Fred Ross; Girl in Studebaker, Jody Carlson; Balloon Girl, Cam Whitman; Gas Station Attendant, John Bracci; Wendy, Debbie Celiz; Bobbie, Lynne Marie Stewart; Kip Pullman, Ed Greenberg; Blonde in T-Bird, Suzanne Somers; Bozo, Gordon Analla; Girl in Dodge, Lisa Herman; Falfa's Girl, Debralee Scott; Man At Accident, Charles Dorsett; Kid at Accident, Stephen Knox; Dale, Bob Pasaak; Man, Joseph Miksak; Bum, George Meyer; Clerk, William Niven; Thief, James Cranna; Man, Del Close; Old Man, Charlie Murphy; Old Woman, Jan Dunn; Badass #1, Johnny Weissmuller Jr.; Mr. Gordon, Scott Beach; Hank, Al Nalbandian.

67 THE AMOROUS ADVENTURES OF MOLL FLANDERS. (Paramount-1965). Moll Flanders, Kim Novak; Jemmy, Richard Johnson; Lady Blystone, Angela Lansbury; Dutchy, Lilli Palmer; William, George Sanders; Squint, Leo McKern; The Count, Vittorio De Sica; The Elder Brother, Daniel Massey; The Younger Brother, Darren Nesbitt; The Mayor, Cecil Parker.

68 THE AMOROUS MR. PRAWN. (Medallion-1965). Joan Greenwood, Cecil Parker, Ian Carmichael, Robert Beatty, Dennis Price, Liz Fraser, Bridget Armstrong, Derek Nimmo, Narry Locke, Robert Nichols, Roddy McMillan, Patrick Jordan, Godfrey James, Gerald Sim, Geoffrey Bayldon, Eric Woodburn,

John Dunbar, Jack Stewart, Sandra Dorne, Finlay Currie, Eric Francis, Reg Lye, Michael Ripper, Drew Russell, Michael Hunt.

69 L'AMOUR. (Altura-1973). Michael, Michael Sklar; Donna, Donna Jordan; Jane, Jane Forth; Max, Max Delys; Patti, Patti D'Arbanville; Karl, Karl Lagerfeld; Coral, Coral Labrie; Peter, Peter Greenlaw; Corey, Corey Tippin.

70 L'AMOUR FOU. (New Yorker-1972). Claire, Bulle Ogier; Sebastien, Jean-Pierre Kalfon; Marta, Josee Destoop; Michele, Michele Moretti; Celia, Celia; Francoise, Francoise Godde; Maddly, Maddly Bomy; Puck, Liliane Bardam; Yves, Yves Beneyton; Michel, Michel Delahaye; TV Director, Andre S. Lebarthe; Didier, Didier Leon; Philippe, Clause Eric Richard; Denis Berry.

71 No entry.

72 AND HOPE TO DIE. (20th Century-Fox-1972). Charley, Robert Ryan; Tony, Jean-Louis Trintignant; Sugar, Lea Massari; Rizzio, Jean Gaven; Mattone, Aldo Ray; Pepper, Tisa Farrow; Paul, Daniel Breton Mastragos, Don Arres; Marjorette, Nadine Nabokov; Gypsy Chief, Andre Lawrence; Inspector, Jean Coutu; Lester, Jean-Marie Lemieux; Renner, Louis Aubert; Gypsy, Michel Maillot; MacCarthy, Mario Verdon.

73 AND NOW FOR SOMETHING COMPLETELY DIFFERENT. (Columbia-1972). Graham Chapman, John Cleese, Eric Idle, Terry Jones, Michael Palin, Carol Cleveland, Terry Gilliam, Connie Booth.

74 AND NOW MIGUEL. (Universal-1966). Miguel Chavez, Pat Cardi; George Perez, Guy Stockwell; Johnny, Clu Gulager; Blas Chavez, Michael Ansara; Padre de Chavez, Joe De Santis; Tomasita, Pilar Del Rey; Pedro, Peter Robbins; Gabriel, Buck Taylor; Eli, Edmund Hashim; Faustina, Emma Tyson; Bonafacio, Richard J. Brehm; Wool Buyer, Heil F. Waters; Ranger, James Hall; Shearer, J. Scott-Carroll; Priest, Father Ralph W. Pairon; Sister, Sister Katrina.

75 AND NOW THE SCREAMING STARTS. (Cinerama-1973). Dr. Pope, Peter Cushing; Henry, Herbert Lom; Dr. Whittle, Patrick Magee; Charles Ian Ogilvy; Catherine, Stephanie Beacham; Maitland, Guy Rolfe; Silas, Geoffrey Crutchley; Mrs. Luke, Rosalie Crutchley; Bridget, Janet Key; Aunt Edith, Gillian Lind; Sarah, Sally Harrison; Sir John, Lloyd Lamble; Constable, Norman Mitchell; Servant, Frank Forsyth.

76 AND SO TO BED. (Medallion-1965). Lilli Palmer, Hildegard Neff, Peter Van Eyck, Daliah Lavi, Angelo Santi, Paul Hubschmid, Nadja Tiller, Thomas Fritsch, Alexandra Stewart,

Martin Held, Peter Parten, Daniele Gaubert.

77 AND SOON THE DARKNESS. (Levitt-Pickman-1971). Jane, Pamela Franklin; Cathy, Michele Dotrice; Paul, Sandor Eles; Gendarme, John Nettleton; Schoolmistress, Clare Kelly; Madame Lassal, Hanna-Maria Pravda; Old Man, John Franklyn; Lassal, Claude Bertrand; Renier, Jean Carmet.

78 AND THERE CAME A MAN. (Brandon-1968). Intermediary, Rod Steiger; Bishop of Bergamo, Adolfo Celi; Signora Roncalli, Rita Bertocchi; Signor Roncalli, Pietro Gelmi; Uncle Xavier, Antonio Bertocchi; Angelo (age 4), Fabrizio Rossi; Angelo (age 7), Alberto Rossi; Angelo (age 10), Giovanni Rossi; Abbe Francois, Alfonso Orlando; Abbe Pierre, Antonio Ruttigni; Papal Secretary, Giorgio Fortunato; Drunken Priest, Ottone Candiani.

79 THE ANDERSON TAPES. (Columbia-1971). Anderson, Sean Connery; Ingrid, Dyan Cannon; Haskins, Martin Balsam; Delaney, Ralph Meeker; Angelo, Alan King; The Kid, Christopher Walken; Parelli, Val Avery; Spencer, Dick Williams; Everson, Garrett Morris; Pop, Stan Gottlieb.

80 ANDREI RUBLEV. (Columbia-1973). Andrei, Anatoll Solonitzine; Kiril, Ivan Lapikov; Daniel, Nikolai Grinko; Theophane, Nikolai Sergueiev; Simpleton, Irma Raouch; Boriska, Nikolai Bourliaiev; Grand Duke, Youri Nasarov.

81 THE ANDROMEDA STRAIN. (Universal-1971). Dr. Jeremy Stone, Arthur Hill; Dr. Charles Dutton, David Wayne; Dr. Mark Hall, James Olson; Dr. Ruth Leavitt, Kate Reid; Karen Anson, Paula Kelly; Jackson, George Mitchell; Major Manchek, Ramon Bieri; Dr. Robertson, Kermit Murdock; Grimes, Richard O'Brien; General Sparks, Peter Hobbs; Senator from Vermont, Eric Christmas.

82 ANDY. (Universal-1965). Andy, Norman Alden; Mrs. Cliadakis, Tamara Daykarhonova; Mr. Cliadakis, Zvee Scooler; Margie, Ann Wedgeworth; Bartender, Murvyn Vye; Sommerville, Al Nesor; Simovich, Warren Finnerty; Thelma, Sudie Bond.

83 ANGEL IN MY POCKET. (Universal-1969). Reverend Samuel D. Whitehead, Andy Griffith; Emery, Jerry Van Dyke; Racine, Kay Medford; Mary Elizabeth Whitehead, Lee Meriwether; Will Sinclair, Henry Jones; Axel Gresham, Edgar Buchanan; Art Shields, Gary Collins; Calvin Grey, Parker Fennelly; Norman Gresham, Jack Dodson; Lila Sinclair, Elena Verdugo; Rhoda, Margaret Hamilton; Nadine, Ruth McDevitt; Leonard Stone, Amber Smale, Buddy Foster, Todd Starke, Robert Hastings, Richard Van Fleet, Jim Boles, Steve Franken, Larry D. Mann, Al Checco, Margaret Ann Peterson, Peggy Mondo, Beverly Jean Powers, Joy Harmon, Benny Rubin, Herbie Faye, George Tapps, Eddie Quillan, Michael Barrier, Susan Seaforth, Athena Lord, Grace Albertson, Robert Lieb, Claudia Bryar, Tani Phelps,

Monti Margetts, Eve Bruce, Lynn Fields, Gloria Mills, Chela Bacigalupo, Anne Besant, Linda Carol, Jesslyn Fax, Stuart Nisbet, Ellen Corby, Kathryn Minner, Mary Gregory, Rufe Davis.

84 THE ANGEL LEVINE. (United Artists-1970). Morris Mishkin, Zero Mostel; Alexander Levine, Harry Belafonte; Fanny Mishkin, Ida Kaminska; Dr. Arnold Berg, Milo O'Shea; Sally, Gloria Foster; Welfare Lady, Barbara Ann Teer; Store Clerk, Eli Wallach; Lady in the store, Anne Jackson.

85 ANGEL UNCHAINED. (American International-1970). Angel, Don Stroud; Tremaine, Luke Askew; Pilot, Larry Bishop; Merilee, Tyne Daly; Magician, Neil Moran; Jackie, Jean Marie; Shotgun, Bill McKinney; Tom, Jordan Rhodes; Dave, Peter Laurence; Injun, Pedro Regas; Wendy, Linda Smith; Matty, Nita Michaels; Ray, J. Cosgrove Butchie; Hood, Rim Ryan; Duner, Alan Gibbs; Speed, Bud Ekins; Candy, Jerry Randall; Sheriff, Aldo Ray.

86 ANGELS DIE HARD. (New World-1970). Blair, Tom Baker; Tim, William Smith; Mel, R. G. Armstrong; Undertaker, Alan DeWitt; Nancy, Connie Nelson; Sheriff, Carl Steppling; Martin, Frank Leo; Piston, Gary Little-john; Naomi, Rita Murray; Dirty, Mike Angel; Houston, William Bonner; Monk, Michael Donovan O'Donnell; Tommy, Leslie Otis; Patsy, Dianne Turley; Shank, Beach Dickerson; Seed, Michael Stringer; Restaurant Owner, Richard Compton; His Wife, Bambi Allen.

87 ANGELS FROM HELL. (American International-1968). Mike, Tom Stern; Ginger, Arlene Martel; Smiley, Ted Markland; Speed, Stephen Oliver; Nutty Norman, Paul Bertoya; Tiny Tim, James Murphy; Bingham, Jack Starrett; George, Jay York; Dennis, Pepper Martin; Baney, Bob Harris; Clair, Saundra Gayle; Millie, Suzy Walters; Angry Annie, Luana Talltree; Jennifer, Susan Holloway; Louise, Judith Garwood; Buff, Susanne Sidney; Dude, Steve Rogers.

88 ANGELS HARD AS THEY COME. (New World-1971). Long John, Scott Glenn; The General, Charles Dierkop; Astrid, Gilda Texter; Monk, James Inglehart; Vicki, Janet Wood; Henry, Gary Besey; Brain, Brendan Kelly; Axe, Gary Littlejohn; Rings, Dennis Art; Louie, Marc Seaton; Lucifer, Larry Tucker; Clean Sheila, Neva Davis; Juicer, Don Carerra; Cheri, Cheri Latimer; Crab, John Taylor; Dr. Jagger, Hal Marshall; Magic, Steve Slauson.

89 THE ANGRY BREED. (Commonwealth United-1969). Gloria Patton, Jan Sterling; Deek Stacey, James MacArthur; Vance Patton, William Windom; Mori Thompson, Jan Murray; Johnny Taylor, Murray McLeod; Diane Patton, Lori Martin; April Wilde, Melody Patterson; Jade, Karen Malouf; Ginny Morris, Suzi Kaye.

90 THE ANIMALS. (Levitt-Pickman-1971). Chatto, Henry Silva; Pudge, Keenan Wynn; Alice, Michele Carey; Sheriff, John Anderson; Peyote, Joseph Turkel; Jamie, Pepper Martin; Cat, Bobby Hall; Karl, Peter Hellmann; Sheriff Lord, William Bryant; Emily, Peggy Stewart.

91 ANN AND EVE. (Chevron-1970). Anne, Gio Petre; Eve, Maria Liljedahl; Fisherman, Heinz Hopf; 2nd Fisherman, Ignae Pavkovic; Porter, Julian Mateos; Singer, Olivera Vuco; Francesco, Francisco Rabal.

92 ANNE OF THE THOUSAND DAYS. (Universal-1969). King Henry VIII, Richard Burton; Anne Boleyn, Genevieve Bujold; Queen Katherine, Irene Papas; Wolsey, Anthony Quayle; Cromwell, John Colicos; Thomas Boleyn, Michael Hordern; Elizabeth Boleyn, Katharine Blake; Norfolk, Peter Jeffrey; Fisher, Joseph O'Connor; Thomas More, William Squire; Mary Boleyn, Valerie Gearon; Mendoza, Vernon Dobtcheff; Smeaton, Gary Bond; Lord Percy, Terence Wilton; Weston, Denis Quilley; Kingston, Esmond Knight; Norris, T. P. McKenna; George Boleyn, Michael Johnson; Campeggio, Marne Maitland; Lady Kingston, Nora Swinburne; Bess, June Ellis; Prior Houghton, Cyril Luckham; Brereton, Brook Williams; Jane Seymour, Lesley Paterson; Willoughby, Kynaston Reeves; Baby Elizabeth, Amanda Jane Smythe; Princess Mary, Nicola Pagett.

93 THE ANNIVERSARY. (20th Century-Fox-1968). Mrs. Taggart, Bette Davis; Karen Taggart, Sheila Hancock; Terry Taggart, Jack Hedley; Henry Taggart, James Cossins; Tom Taggart, Christian Roberts; Shirley Blair, Elaine Taylor; Mr. Bird, Timothy Bateson; Headwaiter, Arnold Diamond; Albert Shepherd, Ralph Watson, Sally-Jane Spencer.

94 THE ANONYMOUS VENETIAN. (Allied Artists-1971). Enrico, Tony Musante; Valeria, Florinda Bolkan; House Owner, Toti Cal Monte; Factory Manager, Alessandro Grinfan; Waiter, Brizio Montinaro; South Technician, Giuseppe Bella.

95 ANTONIO DAS MORTES. (Grove-1970). Antonio das Mortes, Mauricio do Valle; Laura, Odete Lara; Teacher, Othon Bastos; Police Chief, Hugo Carvana; Colonel, Jofre Soares; Saint, Rosa Maria Penna; and the people of Milagres.

96 ANTONY AND CLEOPATRA. (Rank-1973). Antony, Charlton Heston; Cleopatra, Hildegard Neil; Enobarbus, Eric Porter; Octavius Caesar, John Castle; Lepidus, Fernando Rey; Alexas, Juan Luis Gallardo; Octavia, Carmen Sevilla; Pompey, Freddie Jones; Menas, Peter Arno; Varrius, Luis Barboo; Menecrates, Fernando Bilbao; Scarus, Warren Clarke; Soothsayer, Roger Delgado; Proculeius, Julian Glover; Canidius, Sancho Gracia; Eros, Garrick Hagan; Thidias, John Hallam; Messenger, Sergio Krumbel; Charmian, Jane Lapotaire; Guard, Jose Manuel Martin; Messenger, Joe Melia; Sentry, Manolo Otero; Iras,

Monica Peterson; Mardian, Emiliano Redondo; Ventidius, Aldo Sambrel; Soldier, Felipe Solano; Agrippa, Doug Wilmer.

97 ANY GUY CAN PLAY. (Golden Eagle-1968). Clayton, Edd Byrnes; Monetero, Gilbert Roland; The Bounty Hunter, George Hilton; Wapa, Kareen O'Hara; Pajondo, Pedro Sanchez; Backman, Gerard Herter.

98 ANY WEDNESDAY. (Warner Bros.-1966). Ellen Gordon, Jane Fonda; John Cleves, Jason Robards; Cass Henderson, Dean Jones; Dorothy Cleves, Rosemary Murphy; Miss Linsley, Ann Prentiss; Felix, Jack Fletcher; Girl in Museum, Kelly Jean Peters; Milkman, King Moody; Nurse, Monty Margetts.

99 ANYONE CAN PLAY. (Paramount-1968). Norma, Ursula Andress; Luisa, Virna Lisi; Esmerelda, Claudine Auger; Paola, Marisa Mell; Norma's Husband, Brett Halsey; Luisa's Husband, Jean-Pierre Cassel; Paola's Husband, Frank Wolff; Esmerelda's Husband, Marco Guglielmi; Thief, Vittorio Capriolo; Luisa's Lover, Franco Fabrizi; Psychiatrist, Luciano Salce; Blackmailers, Lando Buzzanca and Pietro Morfea; Traffic Cop, Mario Adorf; Esmerelda's Lover, Fred William; Contessa, Margherita Guzzinati; Luisa's Mother, Lio Zoppelli; Luisa's Second Lover, Stash De Rola; Playboy, Arthur Hansel.

100 ANZIO. (Columbia-1968). Dick Ennis, Robert Mitchum; Cpl. Rabinoff, Peter Falk; Sgt. Stimler, Earl Holliman; Richardson, Mark Damon; Movie, Reni Santoni; Doyle, Joseph Walsh; Andy, Thomas Hunter; Cellini, Giancarlo Giannini; General Marsh, Anthony Steel; General Starkey, Patrick Magee; General Howard, Arthur Franz; Emilia, Elsa Albani; Colonel Hendricks, Wayde Preston; Capt. Burns, Venantino Venantini; Anna, Annabella Andreoli; Marshal Kesselring, Wolfgang Preiss; General Van MacKensen, Tonio Selwart; Diana, Stefanella Giovannini; Assunta, Marcella Valeri; Pepe, Enzo Turco; Raffaella, Elisabeth Tompson; Hans (sniper), Wolf Hillinger; Neapolitan Street Hawker, Dante Maggio; MP, Tiberia Mitri; Neapolitan Girls, Vittoria Dal Verme, Giorgia Della Giusta, Carmen Scrapitta; General Lesly, Arthur Kennedy; General Carson, Robert Ryan.

101 APACHE UPRISING. (Paramount-1966). Jim Walker, Rory Calhoun; Janice MacKenzie, Corinne Calvet; Vance Buckner, John Russell; Charlie Russell, Lon Chaney; Jess Cooney, Gene Evans; Captain Gannon, Richard Arlen; Bill Gibson, Arthur Hunnicutt; Hoyt Taylor, Robert H. Harris; Toby Jack Saunders, De Forest Kelley; Jace Asher, George Chandler; and Johnny Mack Brown, Jean Parker, Abel Fernandez, Don Barry, Robert Carricart, Paul Daniel.

102 APARTMENT ON THE 13th FLOOR. (Hallmark-1973). Vincent Parra, Emma Cohen.

103 THE APPALOOSA. (Universal-1966). Matt Fletcher, Marlon Brando; Trini, Anjanette Comer; Chuy Medina, John Saxon; Lazaro, Emilio Fernandez; Squint Eye, Alex Montoya; Ana, Miriam Colon; Paco, Rafael Campos; Ramos, Frank Silvera; Priest, Larry D. Mann; Yaqui Woman, Argentina Brunetti.

104 APPASSIONATA. (PAC-1974). Dr. Emilio Rutelli, Gabriele Ferzetti; Eugenia, Ornella Muti; Nicola, Eleanora Giorgi; Elisa Rutelli, Valentina Cortese.

105 THE APPRENTICESHIP OF DUDDY KRAVITZ. (Paramount-1974). Duddy, Richard Dreyfuss; Yvette, Micheline Lanctot; Max, Jack Warden; Virgil, Randy Quaid; Uncle Benny, Joseph Wiseman; Friar, Denholm Elliott; Dingleman, Henry Ramer; Farber, Joe Silver; Grandfather, Zvee Scooler; Calder, Robert Goodier.

106 THE APRIL FOOLS. (National General-1969). Howard Brubaker, Jack Lemmon; Catherine Gunther, Catherine Deneuve; Ted Gunther, Peter Lawford; Potter Shrader, Jack Weston; Grace Greenlaw, Myrna Loy; Andre Greenlaw, Charles Boyer; Benson, Harvey Korman; Phyllis Brubaker, Sally Kellerman; Leslie Hopkins, Melinda Dillon; Don Hopkins, Kenneth Mars; Mimsy Shrader, Janice Carroll; Walters, David Doyle; Stanley Brubaker, Gary Dubin; Party Singer, Susan Barrett; Secretary, Dee Gardner; Doorman, Tom Ahearne.

107 ARABELLA. (Universal-1969). Arabella, Virna Lisi; Giorgio, James Fox; Princess Ilaria, Margaret Rutherford; Hotel Manager, Terry-Thomas; Duchess Moretti, Paola Borboni; Filberto, Antonio Cassagrande; Saverio, Giancarlo Giannini; Graziella, Milena Vukotic.

108 ARABESQUE. (Universal-1966). David Pollock, Gregory Peck; Yasmin Azir, Sophia Loren; Breshraavi, Alan Badel; Yussef, Kieron Moore; Sloane, John Merivale; Webster, Duncan Lamont; Jena, Carl Duering; Ragheeb, George Coulouris; Beauchamp, Ernest Clark; Lufti, Harold Kasket.

109 THE ARCH. (Cinema V-1972). Madam Tung, Lisa Lu; Captain Yang, Chiao-Hung; Wei-Ling, Chou-Hsuan; Chang, Li-Ying; Grandmother, Wen-Hsiu; Monk, Liang-Jui.

110 ARIZONA BUSHWHACKERS. (Paramount-1968). Lee Travis, Howard Keel; Jill Wyler, Yvonne De Carlo; Dan Shelby, John Ireland; Molly, Marilyn Maxwell; Tom Rile, Scott Brady; Mayor Joe Smith, Brian Donlevy; Sheriff Lloyd Grover, Barton MacLane; Ike Clanton, James Craig; Roy, Roy Rogers, Jr.; Curly, Reg Parton; Stage Driver, Montie Montana; Beshwhacker, Eric Cody; Narrator, James Cagney.

111 ARIZONA RAIDERS. (Columbia-1966). Audie Murphy,

Michael Dante, Ben Cooper, Buster Crabbe, Gloria Talbot.

112 ARNOLD. (Cinerama-1973). Karen, Stella Stevens; Robert, Roddy McDowall; Hester, Elsa Lanchester; Jocelyn, Shani Wallis; Evan Lyons, Farley Granger; Minister, Victor Buono; Governor, John McGiver; Constable Hooks, Bernard Fox; Douglas Whitehead, Patric Knowles; Dybbi, Jamie Farr; Arnold, Norman Stuart; Jonesy, Ben Wright; Flo, Wanda Bailey; Dart Players, Steve Marlo, Leslie Thompson.

113 ARNOLD'S WRECKING CO. (Cine Globe-1973). Arnold, Mike Ranshaw; Kenny, Steve De Souza; Rollo, Eddie Henderson; Mae, Shirley Kauffman; Officer Ace, Byron Schauer.

114 AROUND THE WORLD UNDER THE SEA. (MGM-1966). Dr. Doug Standish, Lloyd Bridges; Dr. Maggie Handford, Shirley Eaton; Dr. Craig Mosby, Brian Kelly; Dr. Phil Volker, David McCallum; Hank Stahl, Keenan Wynn; Dr. Orin Hillyard, Marshall Thompson; Dr. August Boren, Gary Merrill; Brinkman, Ron Hayes; Prof. Hamuru, George Shibata; Capt. of Diligence, Frank Logan; Sonar Man, Don Wells; Vice President, Donald Linton; Sup. Mining Barge, Jack Ewalt; Lt. Coast Guard, George De Vries; Officer, Tony Gulliver; Technician, Joey Carter; Secretary, Celeste Yarnall; Pilot, Paul Gray.

115 AROUSED. (Cambist-1968). Ginny, Janine Lenon; Johnny, Steve Hollister; Angela, Fleurette Carter; Ann, Joanna Mills; Louis, Tony Palladino; Gus, Ted Gelanza; Pat, Marlene Stevens.

116 THE AROUSERS. (New World-1972). Eddie Collins, Tab Hunter; Lauren, Cheri Latimer; Barbara, Nadyne Turney; Mrs. Cole, Isabel Jewell; Vickie, Linda Leider; Call Girl, Roberta Collins; Sherry, Kate McKeown; Lauren's Boyfriend, John Aprea; Brandy Herred, Angel Fox, Josh Green, Rory Guy, Sandy Kenyon.

117 THE ARRANGEMENT. (Warner Bros.-7 Arts-1969). Eddie Evangelos, Kirk Douglas; Gwen, Faye Dunaway; Florence Anderson, Deborah Kerr; Sam Anderson, Richard Boone; Arthur, Hume Cronyn; Michael, Michael Higgins; Charles, John Randolph Jones; Gloria, Carol Rossen; Thomna, Anne Hegira; Dr. Weeks, William Hansen; Finnegan, Charles Drake; Dr. Liebman, Harold Gould; Father Draddy, Michael Murphy; Uncle Joe, E. J. Andre; Judge Morris, Philip Bourneuf; Ellen, Dianne Hull.

118 ARRIVEDERCI, BABY! (Paramount-1966). Nick Johnson, Tony Curtis; Francesca de Rienzi, Rosanna Schiaffino; Parker, Lionel Jeffries; Gigi, Zsa Zsa Gabor; Baby, Nancy Kwan; Lady Fawcett, Fenella Fielding; Aunt Miriam, Anna Quayle; Conte de Rienzi, Warren Mitchell; Maximilian, Warren

Mitchell; Romeo, Mischa Auer; Captain O'Flannery, Noel Purcell; American Brasshat, Alan Gifford; German Brasshat, Joseph Furst; Butler, Monti De Lyle; French Inspector, Bernard Spear; Italian Dressmaker, Eileen Way; Head Waiter, Bruno Barnabe; Gypsy Baron, Gabor Baraker; Baby's Boy-friend, Tony Baron; Matron, Eunice Black; John Brandon, Windsor Davies, Franco De Rosa, Iole Marinelli, Miki Iveria, Henri Vidon, Raymond Young.

119 ARRUZA. (Avco Embassy-1972). Himself, Carlos Arruza; Narrator, Anthony Quinn.

120 THE ART OF LOVE. (Universal-1965). Casey, James Garner; Paul, Dick Van Dyke; Nikki, Elke Sommer; Laurie, Angie Dickinson; Madame Coco, Ethel Merman; Rodin, Carl Reiner; Carnot, Pierre Olaf; Chou Chou, Miiko Taka.

121 ASH WEDNESDAY. (Paramount-1973). Barbara Sawyer, Elizabeth Taylor; Mark Sawyer, Henry Fonda; Erich, Helmut Berger; David, Keith Baxter; Dr. Lambert, Maurice Teynac; Kate Sawyer, Margaret Blye; German Woman, Monique Van Vooren; Bridge Player, Henning Schlueter; Mario, Dino Mele; Mandy, Kathy Van Lypps; Murse Ilse, Dina Sassoli; Paolo, Carlo Puri; Comte D'Arnoud, Andrea Esterhazy; Simone, Jill Pratt; Silvana Del Campo, Irina Wassilchikoff; Viet Hartung, Muki Windisch-Graetz; Helga, Nadia Stancioff; Prince Von Essen, Rodolfo Lodi; Gregory De Rive, Raymond Vignale; Tony Gutierrez, Jose De Vega; Samantha, Samantha Starr.

122 THE ASPHYX. (Paragon-1973). Hugo, Robert Stephens; Giles, Robert Powell; Christina, Jane Lapotaire; President, Alex Scott; Clive, Ralph Arliss; Anna, Fiona Walker; Pauper, Terry Scully; Mason, John Lawrence; Vicar, David Gray; Warden, Tony Caunter; First Member, Paul Bacon.

123 THE ASSASSIN. (Toho-1973). Tetsuro Tanba.

124 THE ASSASSINATION BUREAU. (Paramount-1969). Ivan Dragomiloff, Oliver Reed; Sonya Winter, Diana Rigg; Lord Bostwick, Telly Savalas; General von Pinck, Curt Jurgens; Herr Weiss, Warren Mitchell; Monsieur Lucoville, Philippe Noiret; Monsieur Popescu, Kenneth Griffith; Cesare Spado, Clive Revill; Madame Otero, Beryl Reid; Mr. Muntzov, Vernon Dobtcheff; Eleanora, Anabella Incontrera; George Coulouris, Jess Conrad, Ralph Michael, Katherine Kath, Olaf Pooley, Eugene Deckers, George Murcell, Michael Wolf, Gordon Sterne, Peter Bowles, William Kendall, Jeremy Lloyd, Roger Delgado, Maurice Browning, Gerik Schjelderup, Clive Gazes, Frank Thornton, Milton Reid.

125 THE ASSASSINATION OF TROTSKY. (Cinerama-1972). Leon Trotsky, Richard Burton; Frank Jacson, Alain Delon; Gita, Romy Schneider; Natasha Trotsky, Valentina Cortese; Salazar,

Enrico Maria Salerno; Ruiz, Luigi Vannucchi; Felipe, Duilio Del Prete; Alfred Rosmer, Jean Desailly; Marguerite Rosmer, Simone Valere; Sheldon Harte, Carlos Miranda; Otto, Peter Chatel; Jim, Mike Forest; Seva, Marco Lucantoni; Roberto, Claudio Brook; Lou, Hunt Powers; Sam, Gianni Lofredo; Pedro, Pierangelo Civera.

126 ASSAULT ON A QUEEN. (Paramount-1966). Mark Brittain, Frank Sinatra; Rosa Lucchesi, Virna Lisi; Vie Rossiter, Tony Franciosa; Tony Moreno, Richard Conte; Eric Lauffnauer, Alf Kjellin; Linc Langley, Errol John; Captain, Murray Matheson; Master-at-Arms, Reginald Denny; Bank Manager, John Warburton; Doctor, Lester Matthews; Trench, Val Avery; First Officer, Gilchrist Stuart; Second Officer, Ronald Long; Third Officer, Lesley Bradley; Fourth Officer, Arthur E. Gould-Porter; Junior Officer, Laurence Conroy.

127 ASSIGNMENT K. (Columbia-1968). Philip Scott, Stephen Boyd; Toni Peters, Camilla Sparv; Harris, Michael Redgrave; Smith, Leo McKern; Hal, Jeremy Kemp; Paul Spiegler, Robert Hoffman; Martine, Jane Merrow; Inspector, Carl Mohner; Erika Herschel, Vivi Bach; Kramer, Werner Peters; Kurt, Dieter Geissler; George, John Alderton; Dr. Spiegler, Jan Werich; David, David Healey; Estelle, Ursula Howells; Howlett, Basil Dignam; Heinrich Herschel, Joachim Hansen; The Boffin, Geoffrey Bayldon; Mrs. Peters, Marthe Harell; Ski Instructress, Trudi Hochfilzer; Rolfe, Friedrich Von Thun; Maggi, Katharina Von Schell; Herbert Fuchs, Peter Capell, Heinz Leo Fisher, Karl Otto Alberty, Helmut Schneider, Friedrich Von Ledebur, Andrea Allen, Rosemary Reede, Mia Nardi, Jenny White, Olga Linden, Alexander Allerson, Alastair Hunter, Gert Widenhofen.

128 ASSIGNMENT TO KILL. (Warner Bros.-7 Arts-1969). Richard Cutting, Patrick O'Neal; Dominique Laurant, Joan Hackett; Curt Valayan, John Gielgud; Matt Wilson, Herbert Lom; Notary, Eric Portman; Walter Green, Peter Van Eyck; Inspector Ruff, Oscar Homolka; The Big Man, Leon Greene; Mr. Eversley, Kent Smith; Bohlen, Philip Ober; Mrs. Hennie, Fifi D'Orsay; Landlady, Eva Soreny; Felice Valayan, Cynthia Baxter.

129 THE ASTRO-ZOMBIES. (Gemini-1969). Holman, Wendell Corey; Dr. De Marco, John Carradine; Eric Porter, Tom Pace; Janine Norwalk, Joan Patrick; Juan, Rafael Campos; Satanna, Tura Stana; Franchot, William Bagdad; Tiros, Vincent Barbi; Chuck Edwards, Joe Hoover; Dr. Petrovich, Victor Izay; Mike Webber, Wally Moon; Thompson, John Hopkins; Foreign Agent, Egon Sirany; Ginger, Lynnette Lantz; Chauffeur, Vic Lance; Lynn, Janis Saul; Astro-Zombie, Rod Wilmoth.

130 ASYLUM. (Cinerama-1972). Bonnie, Barbara Parkins;

Walter, Richard Todd; Ruth, Sylvia Syms; Smith, Peter Cushing; Bruno, Barry Morse; Anna, Ann Firbank; Stebbins, John Franklyn-Robbins; Lucy, Britt Ekland; Barbara, Charlotte Rampling; George, James Villiers; Miss Higgins, Megs Jenkins; Byron, Herbert Lom; Dr. Rutherford, Patrick Magee; Dr. Martin, Robert Powell; Max, Geoffrey Bayldon.

131 ATRAGON. (American International-1965). Photographer, Tadao Takashima; Commander's Daughter, Yoko Fujiyama; Commander, Yu Fujiki; Kenji Sawara, Akemi Kita, Tetsuko Kobayashi, Akihiko Hirata, Hiroshi Koizumi, Jun Tazaki, Ken Uehara.

132 ATTACK ON THE IRON COAST. (United Artists-1968). Major James Wilson, Lloyd Bridges; Captain Owen Franklin, Andrew Keir; Sue Wilson, Sue Lloyd; Lt. Cdr. Donald Kimberley, Mark Eden; Sir Frederick Grafton, Maurice Denham; Lt. Forrester, Glyn Owen; Lt. Graham, Howard Pays; Captain Strasser, George Mikell; Lt. Smythe, Simon Prebble; Von Horst, Walter Gotell; 1st. Commando, Keith Buckley; 2nd Commando, Bill Henderson; 3rd Commando, Gavin Breck; Lt. Kramer, Michael Wolf; Cansley, John Welsh; Wren Officer, Joan Crane; Ernest Clark, Richard Shaw, Victor Beaumont, John Kelland, John Albineri, Mark Ward, Dick Haydon, John Golightly, Murray Evans, Robin Hawdon, Sean Barrett.

133 AU HASARD, BALTHAZAR. (Cinema Ventures-1970). Marie, Anne Wiazemsky; Gerard, Francoise Lafarge; Father, Philippe Asselin; Mother, Natalie Joyaut; Friend, Walter Green; Tramp, J. C. Guilbert; Merchant, Pierre Klossowski.

134 AU PAIR GIRLS. (Cannon-1973). Gabrielle Drake, Astrid Frank, Me Me Lay, Richard O'Sullivan, Ferdy Mayne, Julian Barnes, John Standing, John Le Mesurier, Rosalie Crutchley.

135 AN AUTUMN AFTERNOON. (New Yorker-1973). Michiko, Shima Iwashita; Kazuo, Shin-Ichiro Mikami; Mobuko, Kuniko Miyake; Koichi, Keiji Sada; Akiko, Mariko Okada; Shuhei, Chishu Ryu; Shuzo, Nobuo Nakamura; Susumum, Ryuji Kita; Sakuma, Eijiro Tohno; Miura, Teruo Yoshida.

136 AVANTI! (United Artists-1972). Wendell Armbruster, Jack Lemmon; Pamela Piggott, Juliet Mills; Carlo Carlucci, Clive Revill; J. J. Blodgett, Edward Andrews; Bruno, Gianfranco Barra; Arnold Trotta, Franco Angrisano; Mattarazzo, Pippo Franco; Armado Trotta, Franco Acampora; Anna, Giselda Castrini; Passport Officer, Rafaele Mottola; Cipriani, Lino Coletta; Dr. Fleischmann, Harry Ray; Maitre d', Guidarino Guidi; Barman, Giacomo Rizzo; Concierge, Antonino Faa'Di Bruno; Nurses, Yanti Sommer, Janet Agren; Rossi, Aldo Rendine; Hostess, Maria Rosa Sclauzero, Melu Valente.

137 THE AVENGER. (Medallion-1965). Steve Reeves, Cupia

Marlier, John Garko, Liana Orrei.

138 AWOL. (BFB-1973). Willy, Russ Thacker; Inga, Isabella Kaliff; Muhammed G., Glynn Turman; Sidney, Lenny Baker; Cupp, Dutch Miller; Sven, Stefan Ekman.

139 B.J. PRESENTS. (Maron-1971). B.J., Mickey Rooney; Carlotta, Luana Anders; Old Man, Keenan Wynn.

140 B.S. I LOVE YOU. (20th Century-Fox-1971). Paul, Peter Kastner; Marilyn/Michele, JoAnna Cameron; Harris, Richard B. Shull; Jane, Joanna Barnes; Paul's Father, John Gerstad; Car Rental Girl, mary Lou Mellace; Paul's Mother, Jeanne Sorel; Cab Driver, Joe Kottler; Travel Agent, Tom Ruisinger; Manuel, Frank Orsatti; Hippie, Barry Woloski.

141 THE BABY. (Scotia International-1973). Anjanette Comer, Ruth Roman, Mariana Hill, Suzan Zenor, David Manzy.

142 BABY LOVE. (Avco Embassy-1969). Amy Quayle, Ann Lynn; Robert Quayle, Keith Barron; Luci Thompson, Linda Hayden; Nick Quayle, Derek Lamden; Liz Thompson, Diana Dors; Mrs. Carmichael, Patience Collier; Harry Pearson, Dick Emery; Tessa Pearson, Sheila Steafel; Margo Pearson, Sally Stephens; Jeremy, Timothy Carlton; Jonathan, Christopher Witty; Man in Cinema, Vernon Dobtcheff; First Boy, Michael Lewis; Second Boy, Julian Barnes; Girl in Discotheque, Patsy Snell.

143 THE BABY MAKER. (National General-1970). Tish Gray, Barbara Hershey; Suzanne Wilcox, Collin Wilcox-Horne; Jay Wilcox, Sam Groom; Tad Jacks, Scott Glenn; Charlotte, Jeannie Berlin; Mrs. Culnick, Lili Valenty; Helena, Helena Kallianiotes; Dr. Sims, Robert Pickett; Sam, Paul Linke; Tish's Mother, Phyllis Coates; Tish's Grandmother, Madge Kennedy; George, Ray Hemphill; Frances, Brenda Sykes; Jimmy, Michael Geoffrey Horne; Stoned Young Man, Jeff Siggins; Toy Shop Owner, Charlie Wagenheim; Exotica, Bob Ennis; Woman Clerk, Mimi Doyle; Nurse, Patty Dietz; Child birth Instructress, Pat Hedruck; Single Wing Turquoise Bird Light Show; and Jonathan Green, Michael Scroggins, Samuel Francis, Allen Keesling, Charles Lippincott, Peter Mays, Jeffrey Perkins.

144 BABY THE RAIN MUST FALL. (Columbia-1965). Georgette Thomas, Lee Remick; Henry Thomas, Steve McQueen; Slim, Don Murray; Judge Ewing, Paul Fix; Mrs. Ewing, Josephine Hutchinson; Miss Clara, Ruth White; Mr. Tilman, Charles Watts; Miss Kate, Georgia Simmons; Mrs. Tillman, Carol Veazie; Catherine, Estelle Hemsley; Margaret Rose, Kimberly Block; Mrs. T. V. Smith, Zamah Cunningham; Counterman, George Dunn.

145 THE BABYSITTER. (Crown International-1969). Candy, Patricia Wymer; George, George E. Carey; Edith, Ann Bellamy; Julie, Cathy Williams; Laurence, Robert Tessier; Raymond, Ken Hooker; Kyle, Ted C. Frank; Inkie, James E. McLarty; Joan, Sheri Jackson; Doris, Ruth Noonan; Ben, Warren Rose; Aggie, Doris Rose; Frank, Charles Messenger; Lena, Mary Messenger; Richard, Paul Wilmuth; Dancer, Devon Blaine; Dancer, Kari Longacre.

146 BACCHANALE. (Amaro-1970). Ruth, Uta Erickson; M. C., Darcy Brown; Guitarist, Chuck Federico; Fag Hag, Lydia Burns; Louise, Pat Agers; In Coffin, Ron Babin; Guard, Richard Sherman; Lover, Stanley Carmel; Countess, Linda Joyce; Go-Go, Donny Lee; Harpie, LaRue Watts; Mourner, Steve Gould; Slave, Bobby Niles.

147 BACK DOOR TO HELL. (20th Century-Fox-1965). Jimmy Rodgers, Jack Nicholson, Joan Hackett, Anabelle Huggins, Conrad Maga, Johnny Monteiro, Joe Sison, Henry Duval.

148 THE BACK ROW. (Cedarlane-1973). Unnamed Protagonist, Casey Donovan; Kid from Montana, George Payne; Hippy, Robin Anderson; Sailor, David Knox; Cashier, Warren Carlton; Roommate, Robert Tristan; Student, Arthur Graham; Hard Hat, Chris Villette.

149 BACKFIRE. (Royal-1965). David Ladislas, Jean-Paul Belmondo; Olga Celan, Jean Seberg; Fehrman, Gert Frobe; Mario, Enrico Maria Salerno; The Countess, Renate Ewert; Hode, Jean-Pierre Marielle; Wolfgang Preiss, Diana Lorys, Fernando Rey, Michel Beaune, Roberto Camardiel, Xan Das Bolas, Peter Martinovitch, Margarita Gil, Fernando Sancho, Carmen Delirio.

150 BACKTRACK. (Universal-1969). Reese, Neville Brand; Ramrod, James Drury; Trampas, Doug McClure; Chad, Peter Brown; Riley, William Smith; Captain Parmalee, Philip Carey; Faraway, Royal Dano; Steve, Gary Clarke; Randy, Randy Boone; Belden, L. Q. Jones; Winnie, Carol Byron; Sheriff, Ross Elliot; Flake, Hal Baylor; Turnkey, George Savalas; Alvarez, Alberto Morin; Estrallita, Teresa Terry; Gaviota, Priscilla Garcia; The Yaqui Chief, Ruben Moreno; Mama Delores, Ida Lupino; Carmelita Flanagan, Rhonda Fleming; Captain Estrada, Fernando Lamas.

151 BAD CHARLESTON CHARLIE. (International Cinema-1973). Charlie, Ross Hagen; Thad, Kelly Thordsen; Claude, Hoke Howell; Ku Klux Klan Leader, Dal Jenkins; Lottie, Carmen Zapata; Police Chief, Mel Berger; Reporter, John Carradine; Sheriff, Ken Lynch; Promoter, John Dalk; Criminal, Tony Lorea.

152 BAD COMPANY. (New Yorker-1969). 1st Young Man,

Aristide; 2nd Young Man, Daniel Bart; The Woman, Dominique Jayr; Daniel, Jean-Pierre Leaud; Dumas, Gerard Zimmerman; Martinez, Henri Martinez; Photographer, Rene Gilson.

153 BAD GIRLS DON'T CRY. (Medallion-1965). Elsa Martinelli, Antonella Lualdi, Jean Claude Brialy, Laurent Terzieff, Franco Interlenghi, Anna Maria Ferrero.

154 BADGE 373. (Paramount-1973). Eddie Ryan, Robert Duvall; Maureen, Verna Bloom; Sweet William, Henry Darrow; Scanlon, Eddie Egan; Ruben, Felipe Luciano; Mrs. Caputo, Tina Cristiani; Rita Garcia, Marina Durell; Frankie Diaz, Chico Martinez; Ferrer, Jose Duval; Gigi Caputo, Louis Cosentino; Chico, Luis Avalos; Mrs. Diaz, Nubia Olivero; Assistant D. A., Sam Schact; Commissioner, Edward F. Carey; Superintendent, John Marriott; Reporter, Pete Hamill; Manuel, Joel Viega; Bouncer, Mark Tendler; Hans, Robert Weil; Rose Ann, Rose Ann Scamardella; Cop, Larry Appelbaum; Bus Driver, John McCurry; Patrolman, Bob Farley; Delivery Boy, Tracy Walter; Tugboat Crew, John Scanlon, Jimmy Archer, Ric Mancini, Mike O'Dowd; Sweet William's Hoods, Robert Miano, Pompie Pomposello, Hector Troy.

155 THE BALLAD OF CABLE HOGUE. (Warner Bros. -1970). Cable Hogue, Jason Robards; Hildy, Stella Stevens; Joshua, David Warner; Bowen, Strother Martin; Ben, Slim Pickens; Taggart, L. Q. Jones; Cushing, Peter Whitney; Quittner, R. G. Armstrong; Clete, Gene Evans; Jensen, William Mims; Mrs. Jensen, Kathleen Freeman; Claudia, Susan O'Connell; Powell, Vaughn Taylor; William, Felix Nelson.

156 THE BALLAD OF JOSIE. (Universal-1968). Josie Minick, Doris Day; Jason Meredith, Peter Graves; Arch Ogden, George Kennedy; Judge Tatum, Andy Devine; Charlie Lord, William Talman; Sheriff Fonse Pruitt, David Hartman; Doc, Guy Raymond; Annabelle Pettijohn, Audrey Christie; Deborah Wilkes, Karen Jensen; Widow Renfrew, Elisabeth Fraser; Jenny, Linda Meiklejohn; Elizabeth, Shirley O'Hara; Klugg, Timothy Scott; Bratsch, Don Stroud; Alpheus Minick, Paul Fix; Mooney, Harry Carey Jr.; Simpson, John Fiedler; Whit Minick, Robert Lowery; Luther Minick, Teddy Quinn.

157 A BALLAD OF LOVE. (Artkino-1966). The Girl, Victoria Fyodorova; The Boy, Valentin Smirnitsky.

158 BAMBOLE! (Royal-1965). Luisa, Virna Lisi; Giorgio, Nino Manfredi; Armenia, Alicia Bradet; Ulla, Elke Sommer; Massimo, Maurizio Arena; Valerio, Piero Focaccia; Giovanna, Monica Vitti; Husband, John Carlsen; Lover, Orazio Orlando; Peppe, De Simone; Beatrice, Gina Lollobrigida; Monsignor Arendi, Akim Tamiroff; Vencenzo, Jean Sorel.

159 BAMBOO GODS AND IRON MEN. (American International-1974). James Iglehart, Shirley Washington, Chiquito, Marissa Delgado, Eddie Garcia, Ken Metcalf, Joe Zucherro, Michael Boyet, Robert Rivera.

160 BAMBOO SAUCER. (World Entertainment-1968). Hank Peters, Dan Duryea; Fred Norwood, John Ericson; Anna Karachev, Lois Nettleton; Garson, Bob Hastings; Zagorsky, Vincent Beck; Ephram, Bernard Fox; Miller, Robert Dane; Dubovsky, Rico Cattani; Sam Archibald, James Hong; Rhodes, Bartlett Robinson; Gadyakoff, Nick Katurich; Joe Vetry, Bill Mims; Dorothy Vetry, Nan Leslie; Blanchard, Andy Romano.

161 BAMSE. (Chevron-1970). Barbro, Crynet Molvig; Christer, Folke Sundquist; Vera, Ulla Jacobsson; Chris, Bjorn Thambert; Lawyer, Henning Sjostrom.

162 BANANA PEEL. (Pathe Contemporary-1965). Cathy, Jeanne Moreau; Michel, Jean-Paul Belmondo; Lachard, Gert Frobe; Charlie, Claude Brasseur; Reynaldo, Jean-Pierre Marielle; Bontemps, Alain Cuny.

163 BANANAS. (United Artists-1971). Fielding Mellish, Woody Allen; Nancy, Louise Lasser; General Vargas, Carlos Montalban; Yolanda, Natividad Abascal; Esposito, Jacob Morales; Luis, Miguel Suarez; Sanchez, David Ortiz; Diaz, Rene Enriquez; Arroyo, Jack Axelrod; Howard Cosell, Howard Cosell; Roger Grimsby, Roger Grimsby; Don Dunphy, Don Dunphy; Mrs. Mellish, Charlotte Ray; Dr. Mellish, Stanley Ackerman; Priest, Dan Frazer; Dr. Feigen, Martha Greenhouse; Semple, Conrad Bain; Perez, Tigre Perez; Ambassador, Baron DeBeer; Judge, Arthur Hughes; Prosecutor, John Braden; J. Edgar Hoover, Dorthi Fox; Sharon, Dagne Crane; and Axel Anderson, Ted Chapman, Ed Barth, Nicholas Saunders, Eulogia Peraza, Norman Evans, Robert O'Connel, Robert Dudley, Marilyn Hengst, Ed Crowley, Beeson Carroll, Allen Garfield, Princess Fatosh, Dick Callinan.

164 BAND OF ASSASSINS. (Toho-1971). Toshiro Mifune, Isami Kondo, Keiju Kobayashi, Kinya Kitaoli, Rentaro Mikuni.

165 BAND OF OUTSIDERS. (Royal-1966). Odile, Anna Karina; Arthur, Claude Brasseur; Franz, Sami Frey; Mme. Victoria, Louisa Colpeyn; English Teacher, Chantal Darget; Ernest Menzer, Saniele Seghers, George Staquet.

166 BANDOLERO! (20th Century-Fox-1968). Mace Bishop, James Stewart; Dee Bishop, Dean Martin; Maria Stoner, Raquel Welch; Sheriff Johnson, George Kennedy; Roscoe Bookbinder, Andrew Prine; Pop Chaney, Will Geer; Babe, Clint Ritchie; Muncie Carter, Denver Pyle; Joe Chaney, Tom Heaton; Angel Munoz, Rudy Diaz; Robbie, Sean McClory; Cort Hayjack, Harry Carey; Jack Hawkins, Donald Barry;

Ossie Grimes, Guy Raymond; Frisco, Perry Lopez; Stoner, Jock Mahoney; Attendant, Dub Taylor; Bank Clerk, Big John Hamilton; Ross Harper, Bob Adler; Bath House Customer, John Mitchum; Bank Clerk, Joseph Patrick Cranshaw; Bartender, Roy Barcroft.

167 THE BANG BANG GANG. (Eden-1970). Tami, Jae Miller; Adam, Michael Kirkwood; Dallas, Revel Quinn; LeRoy, Mark Griffin; Chico, Edward Blessington; Lila, Bambi Allen.

168 THE BANG BANG KID. (Ajay-1968). Bear Bullock, Guy Madison; Gwenda Skaggel, Sandra Milo; Merriweather Newberry, Tom Bosley; Killer Kossock, Riccardo Garrone; Mayor Skaggel, Jose Maria Caffarel; Betsy Skaggel, Dianik Zurakowska; Hotchkiss, Giustino Durano.

169 BANG! BANG! YOU'RE DEAD! (American International-1967). Andrew Jessel, Tony Randall; Kyra Stanovy, Senta Berger; El Caid, Terry-Thomas; Mr. Casimir, Herbert Lom; Arthur Fairbrother, Wilfrid Hyde-White; Achmed, Gregoire Aslan; George Lillywhite, John Le Mesurier; Jonquil, Klaus Kinski; Samia Voss, Margaret Lee; Hotel Clerk, Emile Stemmler; Madame Bouseny, Helen Sanguineti; Martinez, Sanchez Francisco; Police Chief, William Sanguineti; Motorcycle Policeman, Hassan Essakali; Philippe, Keith Peacock; Export Manager, Burt Kwouk.

170 BANG THE DRUM SLOWLY. (Paramount-1973). Henry Wiggen, Michael Moriarty; Bruce Pearson, Robert De Niro; Cutch Schnell, Vincent Gardenia; Joe Jaros, Phil Foster; Katie, Ann Wedgeworth; Mr. Pearson, Patrick McVey; Piney Woods, Tom Ligon; Holly Wiggen, Heather Macrae; Tootsie, Selma Diamond; Team Owners, Barbara Babcock, Maurice Rosenfield; Ugly Jones, Andy Jarrell; Bradley Lord, Marshall Efron; Red Traphagen, Barton Heyman; Perry, Donny Burks; Diego, Hector Elias; Goose Williams, Tom Signorelli; Canada Smith, Jim Donahue; Aleck Olson, Nicolas Surovy; Horse, Danny Aillo; George, Hector Troy; Jonah, Tony Major; Dr. Loftus, Alan Manaon; Dr. Chambers, Ernesto Gonzales; Tegwar Players, Jack Hollander, Lou Girolami; Detective, Arnold Kapnick; Dutch's Wife, Jean David.

171 BANK SHOT. (United Artists-1974). Ballantine, George C. Scott; El, Joanna Cassidy; Lawyer Karp, Sorrell Booke; Chief FBI Agent, G. Wood; Streiger, Clifton James; Victor Karp, Robert Balaban; Mums, Bibi Osterwald; Herman X, Frank McRae; Stosh Gornik, Don Calfa; Painter, Liam Dunn.

172 BANNING. (Universal-1967). Mike Banning, Robert Wagner; Carol Lindquist, Anjanette Comer; Angela Barr, Jill St. John; Jonathan Linus, Guy Stockwell; Cynthia Linus, Susan Clark; Chris Patton, James Farentino; J. Pallister Young, Howard St. John; Harry Kalielle, Mike Kellin; Tommy Del Gaddo,

Gene Hackman; Richard Tyson, Sean Garrison; Doc Brewer, Logan Ramsey; Stuart Warren, Edmon Ryan; Senator Brady, Oliver McGowan; Maggi Andrews, Lucille Meredith; Tony, Bill Cort.

173 BARBARA. (Olympia-1970). Max, Jack Rader; Leslie, Nancy Boyle; Tom, Robert McLane; Barbara, Barbara; Franz, John Kuhner; Gemma, Melba LaRose Jr.; Zoltan, Bill Haislip; Sam, Myron Oglesby; Waitress, Erika Freeman; Supermom, Tequila Mockingbird; Frank, Will Gary; Laborer, Francisco Novaes; Fisherman, Robert Floria; Fisherman, Art Hill; Woman, Elsa Tresko; Doria, Ute Sielaff; Sentry, Victor Smith; Housewife, Marcia Mohr.

174 BARBARELLA. (Paramount-1968). Barbarella, Jane Fonda; Pygar, John Phillip Law; The Black Queen, Anita Pallenberg; Durand-Durand, Milo O'Shea; Dildano, David Hemmings; Professor Ping, Marcel Marceau; Mark Hand, Ugo Tognazzi; President of Earth, Claude Dauphin; Jean-Paul, Antonio Sabato; Pipe-Smoking Girl, Talitha Pol; Captain Sun, Serge Marquand; Captain Moon, Veronique Vendell; The Suicide Girl, Maria Theresa Orsini; The Twins, Catherine and Maria Therese Chevalier; The Black Queen's Messenger, Sergio Ferrero; The Revolutionary, Giancarlo Cobeli; The General, Nino Musco; The Female Revolutionary, Chantal Cachin; Romolo Valli, Franco Gula, Barbara Winner, and Carla Rousso.

175 THE BAREFOOT EXECUTIVE. (Buena Vista-1971). Steven Post, Kurt Russell; Francis X. Wilbanks, Joe Flynn; E. J. Crampton, Harry Morgan; Mertons, Wally Cox; Jennifer Scott, Heather North; Farnsworth, Alan Hewitt; Clifford, Hayden Rorke; Raffles, Raffles; Roger, John Ritter; Tom, Jack Bender; Dr. Schmidt, Tom Anfinsen; Network Executive, George N. Neise; Announcer, Ed Reimers; Advertising Executive, Morgan Farley; Sponsors, Glen Dixon, Robert Shayne, Tris Coffin; Network Executive, J. B. Douglas; Justice Department, Ed Prentiss; Jackhammer Man, Fabian Dean; Woman Shopper, Iris Adrian; Clatworthy, Jack Smith; Mrs. Crampton, Eve Brent; Mrs. Wilbanks, Sandra Gould; Father O'Leary, James Flavin; Policemen, Pete Renoudet, Judson Pratt, Vince Howard, Hal Baylor; Navigator, Bill Daily; Doorman, Dave Willock; TV Salesman, Anthony Teague; Reporter, Edward Faulkner.

176 BAREFOOT IN THE PARK. (Paramount-1967). Paul Bratter, Robert Redford; Corie Bratter, Jane Fonda; Victor Velasco, Charles Boyer; Mrs. Ethel Banks, Mildred Natwick; Harry Pepper, Herbert Edelman; Aunt Harriet, Mabel Albertson; Restaurant Proprietor, Fritz Feld; The Delivery Man, James Stone; Frank, Ted Hartley.

177 BARON BLOOD. (American International-1972). Alfred, Joseph Cotten; Eva, Elke Sommer; Karl, Massimo Girotti;

Peter, Antonio Cantafora; Fritz, Alan Collins; Inspector, Humi Raho; Christine, Rada Rassimov; Dortmundt, Dieter Tressler.

178 BARQUERO. (United Artists-1970). Travis, Lee Van Cleef; Remy, Warren Oates; Mountain Phil, Forrest Tucker; Marquette, Kerwin Mathews; Anna, Mariette Hartley; Nola, Marie Gomez; Sawyer, Armando Silvestre; Fair, John Davis Chandler; Pitney, Craig Littler; Happy, Ed Bakey; Poe, Richard Lapp; Steele, Harry Lauter; Driver, Brad Weston; Gibson, Thad Williams; Lopez, Armand Alzamora; Roland, Frank Babich; Hawk, Terry Leonard; Encow, Bennie Dobbins; Layeta, Rita Conde.

179 BARREN LIVES. (Pathe Contemporary-1969). The Father, Athila Iorio; The Mother, Maria Riberio; The Boy, Jofre Soares; The Policeman, Orlando Macedo; The Employer, Osmeninas Gilvan.

180 BARRIER. (1967). He, Jan Nowicki; She, Joanna Szczerbic; Doctor, Tadeusz Lomnicki; Girl Friend, Zdislaw Maklakiewicz; Eddy, Zygmunt Malanowicz; Marius, Andrzej Herder; Elegant, Gustaw Nehrebecki; Head Waiter, Ryszard Pietruski; Charlady, Maria Malicka; Lady of the House, Malgorzata Lorentowicz.

181 BARTLEBY. (Marion-1972). The Accountant, Paul Scofield; Bartleby, John McEnery; The colleague, Thorley Walters; Tucker, Colin Jeavons; Landlord, Raymond Mason; Tenant, Charles Kinross; First Client, Neville Barber; Office Boy, Robin Asquith; Tealady, Hope Jackman; Doctor, John Watson; Patient, Christine Dingle; Secretary, Rosalind Elliot; Clerk, Tony Parkin.

182 BATMAN. (20th Century-Fox-1966). Batman (Bruce Wayne), Adam West; Robin (Dick Grayson), Burt Ward; Catwoman (Kitka), Lee Meriwether; The Joker, Cesar Romero; The Penguin, Burgess Meredith; The Riddler, Frank Gorshin; Alfred, Alan Napier; Commissioner Gordon, Neil Hamilton; Chief O'Hara, Stafford Repp; Aunt Harriet Cooper, Madge Blake; Commodore Schmidlapp, Reginald Denny; Vice Admiral Fangschleister, Milton Frome; Bluebeard, Gil Perkins; Morgan, Dick Crockett; Quetch, George Sawaya.

183 BATTLE BENEATH THE EARTH. (MGM-1968). Commander Jonathan Shaw, Kerwin Mathews; Tila Yung, Viviane Ventura; Admiral Felix Hillebrand, Robert Ayres; Arnold Kramer, Peter Arne; Sgt. Marvin Mulberry, Al Mulock; General Chan Lu, Martin Benson; Kengh Lee, Peter Elliott; Sgt. Seth Hawkins, Earl Cameron; Major Frank Cannon, John Brandon; Lt. Cmdr. Vance Cassidy, Edward Bishop; Bill Nagy, Sarah Brackett, Paula Li Shiu, David Spencer, Michael McStay, Carl Jaffe, Norma West, Larry Cross, Bessie Love, Bee

Duffell, Martin Terry, Bill Hutchinson, Frank Lieberman, Roy Pattison, Chela Matthison.

184 BATTLE FOR THE PLANET OF THE APES. (20th Century-Fox-1973). Caesar, Roddy McDowall; Aldo, Claude Akins; Lawgiver, John Huston; Lisa, Natalie Trundy; Kolp, Severn Darden; Mandemus, Lew Ayres; Virgil, Paul Williams, MacDonald, Austin Stoker; Teacher, Noah Keen; Mutant Captain, Richard Eastham; Alma, France Nuyen; Mendez, Paul Stevens; Doctor, Heather Lowe; Cornelius, Bobby Porter; Jake, Michael Stearns; Soldier, Cal Wilson; Young Chimp, Pat Cardi; Jake's Friend, John Landis; Mutant on Motorcycle, Andy Knight.

185 THE BATTLE OF ALGIERS. (Allied Artists-1967). Colonel Mathieu, Jean Martin; Saari Kader, Yacef Saadi; Ali, Brahim Haggiag; Captain Dubeis, Tommaso Neri; Halima, Fawzia El Kader; Fathia, Michele Kerbash; Little Omar, Mohamed Ben Kassen.

186 THE BATTLE OF BRITAIN. (United Artists-1969). Senior Civil Servant, Harry Andrews; Sqn. Ldr. Canfield, Michael Caine; Air Vice Marshall Keith Park, Trevor Howard; Baron von Richter, Curt Jurgens; Sgt. Pilot Andy, Ian McShane; Group Captain Baker, Kenneth More; Air Chief Marshal Sir Hugh Dowding, Laurence Olivier; Group Captain Hope, Nigel Patrick; Flt. Lt.-Sqn. Ldr. Harvey, Christopher Plummer.

187 THE BATTLE OF LOVE'S RETURN. (Standard-1971). Abacrombie, Lloyd Kaufman; Dream Girl, Lynn Lowry; Loafer, Andy Kay; Crumb, Stanley Kaufman; Elderly Woman, Ida Goodcuff; Bridge Foreman, Jim Crispi; Det. Glass, Bernard Brown; Dr. Finger, Roderick Ghyka; Sgt., Bonnie Sacks; Preacher, Robert S. Walker.

188 BATTLE OF NERETVA. (American International-1972). Partisan Vlado, Yul Brynner; Martin, Sergei Bondarchuk; General Lohring, Curt Jurgens; Danica, Silva Koscina; Colonel Kranzer, Hardy Kruger; Captain Riva, Franco Nero; Senator, Orson Welles; Novak, Ljubisa Samardjic; Commander Ivan, Lojze Rozman; Nada, Milena Dravic; Nikola, Oleg Vidov; Stole, Bata Zivojinovic; Mad Bosko, Fabijan Sovagovic; Stipe, Boris Dvornik; Jordan, Pavle Vuisic; General Morelli, Anthony Dawson; Sergenat Mario, Howard Ross; Djuka, Charles Millot; Barbara Bold, Ralph Persson, Renato Rossini.

189 BATTLE OF THE AMAZONS. (American International-1973). Zeno, Lincoln Tate; Eraglia, Lucretia Love; Ilio, Robert Widmark; Sinade, Solvy Stubing; Valeria, Paola Tedesco; Melanippe, Mirta Miller; Erno, Benito Sefanelli; Antiope, Genia Woods; Filodos, Giancarlo Bastianoni; Turone, Luigi Ciavarro; Elperia, Pilar Clement; Fara, Sonia Ciuffi; Medonte, Riccardo Pizzuti; Medio, Marco Stefanelli; Artemio, Franco Ukmar.

190 BATTLE OF THE BULGE. (Warner Bros. -1965). Lieut. Col. Kiley, Henry Fonda; Col. Hessler, Robert Shaw; Gen. Grey, Robert Ryan; Col. Pritchard, Dana Andrews; Sgt. Duquesne, George Montgomery; Schumacher, Ty Hardin; Louise, Pier Angeli; Elena, Barbara Werle; Wolenski, Charles Bronson; Gen. Kohler, Werner Peters; Conrad, Hans Christian Blech; Lieut. Weaver, James MacArthur; Guffy, Telly Savalas.

191 THE BATTLE OF THE VILLA FIORITA. (Warner Bros. - 1965). Moira, Maureen O'Hara; Lorenzo, Rossano Brazzi; Darrell, Richard Todd; Margot, Phyllis Calvert; Michael, Martin Stephens; Debby, Elizabeth Dear; Donna, Olivia Hussey; Charmian, Maxine Audley; Lady Anthea, Ursula Jeans.

192 BAXTER. (National General-1973). Dr. Clemm, Patricia Neal; Roger Tunnell, Jean-Pierre Cassel; Chris Bentley, Britt Ekland; Mrs. Baxter, Lynn Carlin; Robert Baxter, Scott Jacoby; Nemo, Sally Thomsett; Mr. Rawling, Paul Eddington; Mr. Baxter, Paul Maxwell; Dr. Walsh, Ian Thomson; Mr. Fishie, Ronald Leigh-Hunt; Mrs. Newman, Frances Bennett; George, George Tovey.

193 BEACH BALL. (Paramount-1965). Edd Byrnes, Chris Noel, Robert Logan, Gail Gilmore, Aron Kincaid, Mikki Jamison, Don Edmonds, Brenda Benet, Anna Lavelle, James Wellman, The Supremes, The Four Seasons, The Righteous Brothers, The Hondells, The Walker Bros.

194 BEACH BLANKET BINGO. (American International-1965). Frankie Avalon, Annette Funicello, Deborah Walley, Harvey Lembeck, John Ashley, Jody McCrea, Donna Loren, Marta Kristen, Linda Evans, Timothy Carey, Donna Michelle, Mike Nader, Patti Chandler, The Hondells, Andy Romano, Allen Fife, Jerry Brutsche, John Macchia, Bob Harvey, Alberta Nelson, Myrna Ross, Don Rickles, Paul Lynde, Buster Keaton, Earl Wilson, Bobbi Shaw.

195 BEACH GIRLS AND THE MONSTERS. (U.S. Films-1965). Jon Hall, Sue Casey, Walker Edmiston, Arnold Lessing.

196 BEACH RED. (United Artists-1967). Captain MacDonald, Cornel Wilde; Sergeant Honeywell, Rip Torn; Egan, Burr De Benning; Cliff, Patrick Wolfe; Julia MacDonald, Jean Wallace; Colombo, Jaime Sanchez; Captain Sugiyama, Genki Koyama; Goldberg, Gene Blakely; Nakano, Norman Pak; Mouse, Dewey Stringer; Lieutenant Domingo, Fred Galang; Michio, Hiroshi Kiyama; Sgt. Lindstrom, Michael Parsons; Capt. Tanaka, Dale Ishimoto; Egan's Girl Friend, Linda Albertano; Susie, Jan Garrison; Michio Hazama, Masako Ohtsaki, Kiyoma Takezawa, George Bayot, John Allen, Ed Finlan, Bill Dunbar, Mike McMichael, Ernie Holt, Dennis Ullman, Jun Bona, Charles Weaver, Pat Whitlock, Rod Meir, Phil Beinke.

197 THE BEAR AND THE DOLL. (Paramount-1971). Felicia, Brigitte Bardot; Gaspard, Jean-Pierre Cassel; Ivan, Daniel Ceccaldi; Reginald, Xavier Gelin.

198 THE BEARS AND I. (Buena Vista-1974). Patrick Wayne, Chief Dan George, Andrew Duggan, Michael Ansara, Robert Pine, Val De Vargas, Hal Baylor.

199 THE BEAST MUST DIE. (Cinerama-1974). Tom Newcliffe, Calvin Lockhart; Dr. Christopher Lundgren, Peter Cushing; Bennington, Charles Gray; Pavel, Anton Diffring; Caroline Newcliffe, Marlene Clark; Davina Gilmore, Ciaran Madden; Paul Foote, Tom Chadbon; Jan Jarmokowski, Michael Gambon; Butler, Sam Mansaray; Pilot, Andrew Lodge; 1st Hunter, Carl Bohun; 2nd Hunter, Eric Carte.

200 BEAST OF BLOOD. (Marvin-1971). Bill, John Ashley; Myra, Celeste Yarnell; Ramu, Alfonso Carvajal; Laida, Lisa Belmonte; Razak, Bruno Punzalan; Dr. Lorca, Eddie Garcia; Angel Buenaventura, Beverly Miller, Johnny Long.

201 BEAU GESTE. (Universal-1966). Beau, Guy Stockwell; John, Doug McClure; Lt. De Ruse, Leslie Nielsen; Sgt. Major Dagineau, Telly Savalas; Boldini, David Mauro; Fouchet, Robert Wolders; Krauss, Leo Gordon; Rostov, Michael Constantine; Kerjacki, Malachi Throne; Beaujolais, Joe De Santis; Vallejo, X. Brands; Sergeant, Michael Carr; Platoon Sergeant, George Keymas; Surgeon, Patrick Whyte; Captain, Ted Jacques; Dancer, Ava Zamora; Legionnaires, Jeff Nelson, David Gross, Hal Hopper, Chuck Wood, Duane Grey, Vic Lundin.

202 THE BEAUTIFUL SWINDLERS. (Continental-1968). Nicole Karen, Jan Teulings, Arnold Gelderman, Gabriella Giorgelli, Beppo Mannaluolo, Guido Giuseppone, Jean-Pierre Cassel, Catherine Deneuve, Francis Blanche, Sacha Briquet, Jean-Louis Maury, Mie Hama, Ken Mitsuda.

203 BED AND BOARD. (Columbia-1971). Antoine, Jean-Pierre Leaud; Christine, Claude Jade; Kyoko, Hiroko Berghauer; Executive Secretary, Barbara Laage; Monsieur Darbon, Daniel Ceccaldi; Madame Darbon, Claire Duhamel; The "Sneerer," Pierre Fabre; Strangler, Claude Vega; American Customer, Bill Kearns; Tenor, Daniel Boulanger; Tenor's Wife, Silvana Blasi; Servant, Daniele Gerard; Bistro Landlord, Jacques Jouanneau; Housekeeper, Marie Irakane; Unknown Person, Serge Rousseau; Customer in Bistro, Pierre Maguelon; Mother of Young Violinist, Annick Asty; Pensioner, Rispal; String-Puller, Christian De Tiliere; "Hotel" Owner, Ada Lonati.

204 THE BED SITTING ROOM. (United Artists-1969). Penelope, Rita Tushingham; Lord Fortnum, Ralph Richardson; Inspector, Peter Cook; Sergeant, Dudley Moore; Mate, Spike Milligan; Bules, Michael Hordern; Plastic Mac, Roy Kinnear; Father,

Arthur Lowe; Allan, Richard Warwick; Mother, Mona Washbourne; Field Marshall Sgt. , Ronald Fraser; Ethyl, Dandy Nichols; BBC Man, Frank Thornton; Dwarf, Ron Moody; Patient, Gordon Rollings.

205 BEDAZZLED. (20th Century-Fox-1967). George Spiggott, Peter Cook; Stanley Moon, Dudley Moore; Margaret Spencer, Eleanor Bron; Lillian Lust, Raquel Welch; Inspector Clarke, Michael Bates; Irving Moses, Bernard Spear; Gluttony, Parnell McGarry; Sloth, Howard Goorney; Vanity, Alba; Envy, Barry Humphries; Avarice, Daniele Noel; Anger, Robert Russell; P. C. Roberts, Peter Hutchins; Priest, Max Faulkner; Cardinal, Martin Boddey; TV Announcer, John Steiner; Randolph, Robin Hawdon; Lord Dowdy, Michael Trubshawe; Seed, Eric Chitty; Mrs. Wisby, Evelyn Moore; Daphne, Robin Tolhurst; Shop Assistant, Anna Turner; St. Peter, Lockwood West.

206 THE BEDFORD INCIDENT. (Columbia-1965). Capt. Eric Finlander, Richard Widmark; Ben Munceford, Sidney Poitier; Ensign Ralston, James MacArthur; Lieut. Comdr. Chester Potter, Martin Balsam; Sonar Man 2nd Cl. , Wally Cox; Comdr. Wolfgang Schrepke, Eric Portman; Commander Allison, Michael Kane, Chief Pharmacits's Mate McKinley, Phil Brown; Lieutenant Bascombe, Gary Cockrell; Lt. Beekman, Brian Davies; Pharmacist's Mate Strauss, Warren Stanhope; Pharmacist's Mate Nerney, Donald Sutherland.

207 BEDKNOBS AND BROOMSTICKS. (Buena Vista-1971). Eglantine Price, Angela Lansbury; Emelius Browne, David Tomlinson; Mr. Jelk, Roddy McDowall; Bookman, Sam Jaffe; Col. Heller, John Ericson; Swinburne, Bruce Forsyth; General Teagler, Reginald Owen; Mrs. Hobday, Tessie O'Shea; Capt. Greer, Arthur E. Gould-Porter; Street Sweeper, Ben Wrigley; German Sergeants, Rick Traeger, Manfred Lating; Vendor, John Orchard; Paul, Roy Smart; Carrie, Cindy O'Callaghan; Charlie, Ian Weighall; Voice of secretary bird and lion, Lennie Weinrib.

208 BEEN DOWN SO LONG IT LOOKS LIKE UP TO ME. (Paramount-1971). Gnossos, Barry Primus; Kristin, Linda DeCoff; Heff, David Downing; Jack, Susan Tyrrell; Calvin, Philip Shafer; Fitzgore, Bruce Davison; Mojo, Zack Norman; Juan, Raul Julia.

209 BEFORE THE REVOLUTION. (New Yorker-1965). Adriana Asti, Francesco Barilli, Allen Midgette, Morando Morandini, Cecrope Barilli, Cristina Pariset, Emilia Borghi, Domenico Alpi, Iole Lunardi, Giuseppe Maghenzani.

210 BEFORE WINTER COMES. (Columbia-1969). Major Giles Burnside, David Niven; Janovic, Topol; Maria Holz, Anna Karina; Lt. Francis Pilkington, John Hurt; Brigadier-General

Bewley, Anthony Quayle; Cpt. Kamenev, Ori Levy; Sgt. Woody, John Collin; Count Derassy, Karel Stepanek; Kovacs, Guy Deghy; Komenski, Mark Malicz; Gertan Klauber, Hana-Maria Pravada, George Innes, Tony Selby, Hugh Futcher, Christopher Sandford, Colin Spaull, Larry Dann, Jeffrey Wickham, Alysoun Austin, John Savident, Constantin De Goguel, Jerry Tarrant, Josef Roubalik, David Carson, Albert Shepherd, Bruno Pantel, Hans Epskamp, Norah Minor, Lieselotte Quilling, Karin Schroeder, Hans Josef Schumm, Harry Kalenberg, Eduard Linkers, Peter Mathes.

211 THE BEGUILED. (Universal-1971). John McBurney, Clint Eastwood; Martha, Geraldine Page; Edwina, Elizabeth Hartman; Carol, Jo Ann Harris; Doris, Darleen Carr; Hallie, Mae Mercer; Amy, Pamelyn Ferdin; Abigail, Melody Thomas; Lizzie, Peggy Drier; Jane, Pattye Mattick.

212 BELATED FLOWERS. (Artkino-1972). Princess Priklonsky, Olga Zhizneva; Princess Marusya, Irina Lavrentyeva; Dr. Toporkov, Alexander Lazarev; Yegorushka Priklonsky, Valerie Zolotukhin.

213 BELIEVE IN ME. (MGM-1971). Remy, Michael Sarrazin; Pamela, Jacqueline Bisset; Alan, Jon Cypher; Stutter, Allen Garfield; Matthew, Kurt Dodenhoff; Nurse, Marcia Jean Kurtz; Clancy, Kevin Conway; Angel, Roger Robinson; Boy, Antonio Fargas; Physician, Milt Kamen; Ward Nurse, Susan Doukas; Sylvia, Suzannah Norstrand; Patient, Ultra Violet; Lecturer, William Abruzzi; David, Matthew Anton; Saleslady, Elizabeth Brown; Max, Tony Capodilupo; Michael, Tom Floral; Saleslady, Katherine Helmond; Manager, Tom Lacy; Margaret, Barbara Thurston; Dr. Markham, Larry Weber; Morgue Attendant, Jan Saint.

214 BELLE DE JOUR. (Allied Artists-1968). Severine Serizy, Catherine Deneuve; Pierre Serizy, Jean Sorel; Mme. Anais, Genevieve Page; Henri Husson, Michel Piccoli; Marcel, Pierre Clementi; Renee, Macha Meril; The Duke, Georges Marchal; Hyppolite, Francisco Rabal; Charlotte, Francoise Fabian; Mathilde, Marie Latour; Monsieur Adolphe, Francis Blanche; Asian Client, Iska Khan; Pallas, Muni; The Professor, Francois Maistre; Le Grele, Bernard Presson; Catherine, Dominique Dandrieux; Severine as a child, Brigitte Parmentier; Footman, Michel Charrel; Coachman, D. De Roseville; Professor Henri, Marcel Charvey; Intern, Pierre Marcay; Maid, Adelaide Blasquez; Barman, Marc Eyraud; Majordomo, Bernard Musson.

215 BEN. (Cinerama-1972). Danny Garrison, Lee Harcourt Montgomery; Cliff Kirtland, Joseph Campanella; Billy Hatfield, Arthur O'Connell; Beth Garrison, Rosemary Murphy; Eve Garrison, Meredith Baxter; Joe Greer, Kaz Garas; Kelly, Paul Carr; Reade, Richard Van Vleet; Engineer, Kenneth

Tobey; Ed, James Luisi; Carey, Lee Paul; Policeman, Norman Aldren; Henry Gray, Scott Garrett; Mrs. Gray, Arlen Stuart; George, Richard Drasin.

216 BENEATH THE PLANET OF THE APES. (20th Century-Fox-1970). Taylor, Charlton Heston; Brent, James Franciscus; Zira, Kim Hunter; Dr. Zaius, Maurice Evans; Nova, Linda Harrison; Mendez, Paul Richards; Fat Man, Victor Buono; Ursus, James Gregory; Caspay, Jeff Corey; Albina, Natalie Trundy; Minister, Thomas Gomez; Cornelius, David Watson; Negro, Don Pedro Colley; Skipper, Tod Andrews; Verger, Gregory Sierra; Gorilla Sergeant, Eldon Burke; Lucius, Lou Wagner.

217 BENJAMIN. (Paramount-1968). Countess de Valandry, Michele Morgan; Anne de Clecy, Catherine Deneuve; Benjamin, Pierre Clementi; Count Philippe, Michel Piccoli; Marion, Francine Berge; Celestine, Anna Gael; Victorine, Catherine Rouvel; Camille, Jacques Dufilho; Married Woman, Odile Versois.

218 BENJI. (Mulberry Square-1974). Dr. Chapman, Peter Breck; Henry, Christopher Connelly; Mary, Patsy Garrett; Riley, Tom Lester; Mitch, Mark Slade; Lt. Samuels, Herb Vigran; Linda, Deborah Walley; Benji, Higgins; Frances Bavier, Edgar Buchanan, Terry Carter, Allen Fiuzat, Cynthia Smith, Larry Swartz, J. D. Young, Erwin Hearne, Katie Hearne, Don Puckett, Ed DeLatte, Victor Raider-Wexler, Charles Starkey, Ben Vaughn, Joey Camp, Vicki Vanston, Jacqueline Ann Smith, Bill King, Robert Thomas.

219 BERSERK! (Columbia-1968). Monica Rivers, Joan Crawford; Frank Hawkins, Ty Hardin; Matilda, Diana Dors; Dorando, Michael Gough; Angela Rivers, Judy Geeson; Det. Sup't. Brooks, Robert Hardy; Commissioner Dalby, Geoffrey Keen; Harrison Liston, Sydney Tafler; Bruno, George Claydon; Lazlo, Philip Madoc; Miss Burrows, Ambrosine Phillpotts; Gaspar, Thomas Cimarro; Gustavo, Peter Burton; Bearded Lady, Golda Casimir; Skeleton Man, Ted Lune; Strong Man, Milton Reid; Wanda, Marianne Stone; Gypsy Fortune Teller, Miki Iveria; Emil, Howard Goorney; Det. Sgt. Hutchins, Reginald Marsh; Det. Constable Bradford, Bryan Pringle.

220 THE BEST HOUSE IN LONDON. (MGM-1969). Walter Leybourne/Benjamin Oakes, David Hemmings; Josephine Pacefoot, Joanna Pettet; Sir Francis Leybourne, George Sanders; Babette, Dany Robin; Count Pandolfo, Warren Mitchell; Home Secretary, John Bird; Sylvester Wall, William Rushton; Inspector Macpherson, Bill Fraser; Editor of "The Times," Maurice Denham; Chinese Trade Attache, Wolfe Morris; Headmistress, Martita Hunt; Charles Dickens, Arnold Diamond; Lord Tennyson, Hugh Burden; Oscar Wilde, John De Marco; Lord Alfred Douglas, George Reynolds; Lady Dilke,

Jan Holden; Algernon Charles Swinburne, Mike Lennox; Mr. Fortnum, Arthur Howard; Mr. Mason, Clement Freud; Dr. Livingstone, Neal Arden; Mr. Barrett, Walter Brown; Miss Elizabeth Barrett, Suzanne Hunt; Flora, Carol Friday; Phoebe, Marie Rogers; Tessie O'Shea, Avril Angers, Betty Marsden.

221 BETTER A WIDOW. (Universal-1969). Rosa Minniti, Virna Lisi; Tom Proby, Peter McEnery; Don Calogero Minniti, Gabriele Ferzetti; Massito, Lando Buzzanca; Baron Misceni, Jean Servais; The Prostitute, Agnes Spaak; Carmelo, Nino Terzo; Rosa's Governess, Carla Calo; Don Santo, Salvatore Fucile; Orchestra Conductor, Roy Bosier; Hotel Manager, Bruno Lauzi; Misceni's Chauffeur-Killer, Adriano Vitale; Francesco Leone, Oreste Palella, Luciano Taccone, Giorgio Cholet, Raniero Di Giovanbattista, Ivan Giovanni Scratuglia, Sebastiano Rossito, Salvatore Spadaro, Gaetano Tomaselli.

222 BEWARE OF THE BRETHREN. (Cinerama-1972). Birdie Wemys, Ann Todd; Minister, Patrick Magee; Kenny Wemys, Tony Beckley; Brigitte Lynch, Madeline Hinde; Paddy Lynch, Suzanna Leigh; Commissionaire, Percy Herbert; CID Inspector, David Lodge; Paul, Ronald Allen; Singer, Maxine Barrie; Prostitute, Jeannette Wild; Poolside Girl, Diana Chappell; Teenage Girl, Susanna East; Riverside Girl, Hani Borelle; Baptised Boy, Ian Kiddy; Child, Katherine McDonald; Congregation Members, Dee Shenderey, Brenda Kempner, Irving Lycett, James Watts.

223 BEWARE THE BLOB. (Jack H. Harris-1972). Robert Walker, Gwynne Gilford, Richard Stahl, Richard Webb, Godfrey Cambridge, Carol Lynley, Larry Hagman, Shelly Berman, Marlene Clark.

224 BEYOND ATLANTIS. (Dimension-1973). John Ashley, Patrick Wayne, Leigh Christian, George Nader.

225 BEYOND CONTROL. (Mishkin-1971). Jimmy, William Berger; Frank, Anthony Baker; Brigitte, Georgia Moll; Monica, Helga Anders; Christina, Grit Botcher; District Attorney, Willy Birgel.

226 BEYOND LOVE AND EVIL. (Allied Artists-1971). Xenia, Souchka; Zenoff, Lucas de Chabanieux; Yalo, Fred Saint-James; Young Man, Marc Coutant; Himself, Sabrina; Worlac, Serge Halsdorf; Ladies' Man, Michel Lablais; Initiator, Milarka Nervi; Panther Woman, Dorsi Thon; Driven-out woman, Nicole Huc; Lolita, Nadia Kempf; 25-year-old woman, Ursule Pauly.

227 BEYOND THE GREAT WALL. (Frank Lee International-1967). Lin Dai, Chao Lei, Hung Po, Chiang Kunang-chao, Li Ying, Chang Tsui-ying.

228 BEYOND THE LAW. (Grove-1968). Popcorn, Rip Torn; The Mayor, George Plimpton; Lt. Francis Xavier Pope, Norman Mailer; Det. Mickey Berk, Mickey Knox; Det. Rocco Gibraltar, Buzz Farber; Mary Pope, Beverly Bentley; Ilse Fuchs, Mara Lynn; Jose, Jose Torres; Irish, Tom Baker; Lee Ray Rogers, Lee Roscoe; Marcia Stillwell, Marcia Mason; Judy Grundy, Mary Wilson Price; Asst. District Attorney, Noel Parmentel; Jack Scott, Jack Richardson; Perry Fuchs, Harold Conrad; Joe Brown, Joe Shaw; Tom Finley, Tom Quinn; Detective, Roger Donahue; Grahr, Michael McClure; Wife-Killer, Edward Bonetti; Subway Arrestee, Peter Rosoff; John Francis, John Maloon; Detective Callahan, Jimmy Reardon; Buffalo, Tom Hickey; Buffalo's Brother, Bryan Hamill; Mario, Pedro Ortiz; Dolores, Dolores Elbert; Sylvia, Sylvia Allen.

229 BEYOND THE VALLEY OF THE DOLLS. (20th Century-Fox-1970). Kelly MacNamara, Dolly Read; Casey Anderson, Cynthia Myers; Petronella Danforth, Marcia McBroom; Ronnie (Z-Man) Barzell, John LaZar; Lance Rocke, Michael Blodgett; Harris Allsworth, David Gurian; Ashley St. Ives, Edy Williams; Roxanne, Erica Gavin; Susan Lake, Phyllis Davis; Emerson Thorne, Harrison Page; Porter Hall, Duncan McLeod; Randy Black, Jim Iglehart; Baxter Wolfe, Charles Napier; Otto, Henry Rowland; Matron, Princess Livingston; Disciple, Stan Ross; Vanessa, Lavelle Roby; Girl in Tub, Angel Ray; Blonde date, Veronica Erickson; Cat Woman, Haji; Red Head, Karen Smith; Art Director, Sebastian Brook; Photographer, Bruce V. McBroom; Boy in tub, Ian Sander; Assistant, Koko Tani; Cynthia, Samantha Scott; Makeup man, Heath Jobes; Fashion Models, Susan Reed, Ashley Phillips; Bay Boy, Robin Bach; Mother, Ceil Cabot; Hippy Boy, Frank Corsentino; Nurse, Lillian Martin; Marion Harrisburg, Joyce Rees; Strawberry Alarm Clock.

230 THE BIBLE ... IN THE BEGINNING. (20th Century-Fox-1966). Adam, Michael Parks; Eve, Ulla Bergryd; Cain, Richard Harris; Noah, John Huston; Nimrod, Stephen Boyd; Abraham, George C. Scott; Sarah, Ava Gardner; The Three Angels, Peter O'Toole; Hagar, Zoe Sallis; Lot, Gabriele Ferzetti; Lot's Wife, Eleonora Rossi Drago; Abel, Franco Nero; Noah's Wife, Pupella Maggio; Isaac, Alberto Lucantoni; Ishmael, Luciano Conversi; Abraham's Steward, Robert Rietty; Lot's Daughter, Adriana Ambesi, Grazia Maria Spina.

231 BIBLE. (Poolemar-1974). Adam, Bo White; Eve, Caprice Couselle; Bathsheba, Georgina Spelvin; David, Nicholas Flamel; Uriah, Robert Benes; Handmaiden, Nancy Wachter; Samson, Brahm van Zetten; Delilah, Gloria Grant; Mary, Bonnie Mathis; Angel, Dennis Wayne.

232 LES BICHES. (Jack H. Harris-1968). Paul Thomas, Jean-Louis Trintignant; Why, Jacqueline Sassard; Frederique,

Stephane Audran; Violetta, Nane Germon; Bookseller, Serge Bento; Robegue, Dominique Verdi; Riais, Pierre Attal; Filmmaker, Claude Chabrol.

233 BIG BAD MAMA. (New World-1974). Wilma McClatchie, Angie Dickinson; William J. Baxter, William Shatner; Fred Diller, Tom Skerritt; Billy Jean McClatchie, Susan Sennett; Polly McClatchie, Robbie Lee; Barney, Noble Willingham; Jane Kingston, Joan Prather; Rev. Johnson, William O'Connell; Sheriff, Ralph James; Dick Miller, Tom Signorelli, Royal Dano, John Wheeler, Sally Kirkland, Wally Berns, Shannon Christie, Michael Talbot, Rob Berger, Charles Pinney, Georgia Lee, Jay Brooks, Paul Linke, Mickey Fox, William F. Engle.

234 THE BIG BIRD CAGE. (New World-1972). Blossom, Pam Grier; Terry Rich, Anitra Ford; Carla, Candice Roman; Bull Jones, Teda Bracci; Mickie, Carol Speed; Karen, Karen McKevic; Django, Sid Haig.

235 THE BIG BOUNCE. (Warner Bros. -7 Arts-1969). Jack Ryan, Ryan O'Neal; Nancy Barker, Leigh-Taylor Young; Sam Mirakian, Van Heflin; Joanne, Lee Grant; Ray Ritchie, James Daly; Bob Rogers, Robert Webber; Joanne's Daughter, Cindy Eilbacher; Sam Turner, Noam Pitlik; Boy in Dune Buggy, Kevin O'Neal; Comancho, Victor Paul; Senator, Charles Cooper; Senator's Associate, Paul Sorensen; Girl in Bikini, Phyllis Davis.

236 THE BIG BUST-OUT. (New World-1973). Vonetta McGee, Monica Taylor, Linda Fox, Karen Carter, Gordon Mitchell, Christin Thorn, Tony Kendall, William Berger, Mara Krup, Giorgio Dolphin, Rebecca Mead, Miller Drake.

237 THE BIG CITY. (Edward Harrison-1967). Arati, Madhabi Mukherjee; Sobrata, Anil Chatterjee; Mukkerjee, Haradhan Banerjee; Father, Haren Chatterjee; Edith Simmons, Vicky Redwood; Sister, Jaya Bhaduri.

238 THE BIG CITY. (New Yorker-1971). Luzia, Anecy Rocha; Calunga, Antonio Pilanga; Jasao, Leonardo Vilar; Ignacio, Joel Barcelos.

239 THE BIG CUBE. (Warner Bros. -7 Arts-1969). Adriana, Lana Turner; Johnny, George Chakiris; Frederick, Richard Egan; Charles, Daniel O'Herlihy; Lisa, Karin Mossberg; Bibi, Pamela Rodgers; Lalo, Carlos East; Doctor, Augusto Benedico; Delacroix, Victor Junco; Stella, Norman Herrera; Dean, Pedro Galvan; Themselves, The Finks; Queen Bee, Regina Torne.

240 THE BIG DOLL HOUSE. (New World-1971). Collier, Judy Brown; Alcott, Roberta Collins; Grear, Pam Grier; Harrad,

Brooke Mills; Bodine, Pat Woodell; Harry, Sid Haig; Miss Dietrich, Christiane Schmidtmer; Lucian, Kathryn Loder; Fred, Jerry Franks; Dr. Phillips, Jack Davis; Ferina, Gina Stuart; Leyte, Letty Mirasol; Guard, Shirley De La Alas.

241 THE BIG GUNDOWN. (Columbia-1968). Jonathan Corbett, Lee Van Cleef; Cuchillo, Tomas Milian; Lizzie, Luisa Rivelli; Captain Segura, Fernando Sancho; The Widow, Nieves Navarro; Jess, Benito Stefanelli; Brokston, Walter Barnes; Brokston's Son-in-law, Angel Del Pozo; Rosita, Maria Granada; Jack, Lanfranco Ceccarelli; Jellicol, Roberto Camardiel; Hondo, Nello Pazzafini; Mitchell, Spartaco Conversi; Rocky, Romano Puppo; Chet, Tom Felleghi; Miller, Calisto Calisti; Dance, Antonio Casas; Nathan, Jose Torres.

242 A BIG HAND FOR THE LITTLE LADY. (Warner Bros.-1966). Meredith, Henry Fonda; Mary, Joanne Woodward; Henry Drummond, Jason Robards; Ballinger, Paul Ford; Benson Tropp, Charles Bickford; Doc Scully, Burgess Meredith; Otto Habershaw, Kevin McCarthy; Dennis Wilcox, Robert Middleton; Jesse Buford, John Qualen; Sam Rhine, James Kenny; Toby, Allen Collins; Pete, Jim Boles; Jackie, Gerald Michenaud; Mrs. Drummond, Virginia Gregg; Old Man in Saloon, Chester Conklin; Owney Price, Ned Glass; Mrs. Craig, Mae Clarke; Mr. Stribling, James Griffith; Sparrow, Noah Keene; Fleeson, Milton Selzer; Celie Drummond, Louise Glenn; Arthur, William Cort.

243 BIG JAKE. (National General-1971). Jacob McCandles, John Wayne; John Fain, Richard Boone; Martha McCandles, Maureen O'Hara; James McCandles, Patrick Wayne; Michael McCandles, Chris Mitchum; Sam Sharpnose, Bruce Cabot; Jeff McCandles, Bobby Vinton; O'Brien, Glenn Corbett; Pop Dawson, Harry Carey Jr.; Buck Duggan, John Doucette; Head of Lynching Party, Jim Davis; Bert Ryan, John Agar; John Goodfellow, Gregg Palmer; Will Fain, Robert Warner; Hank, Hank Worden; Billy Devries, Jeff Wingfield; Walt Devries, Everett Creach; Saloon Bully, Don Epperson; Saloon Brawler, Tom Hennesy; Stubby, Jerry Gatlin; Moses Brown, William Walker; Delilah, Virginia Capers; Little Jake McCandles, John Ethan Wayne; Kid Duffy, Dean Smith; Trooper, Jim Burke.

244 THE BIG MOUTH. (Columbia-1967). Gerald Clamson, Jerry Lewis; Thor, Harold J. Stone; Suzie Cartwright, Susan Day; Studs, Buddy Lester; Mr. Hodges, Del Moore; Moxie, Paul Lambert; Bambi Berman, Jeannine Riley; Fong, Leonard Stone; Rex, Charlie Callas; Bogart, Frank De Vol; Gunner, Vern Rowe; Lizard, Dave Lipp; Fancher, Vincent Van Lynn; Detective No. 1, Mike Mahoney; Detective No. 2, Walter Kray; FBI Agent, John Nolan; Specs, Eddie Ryder.

245 THE BIG T.N.T. SHOW. (American International-1966).

David McCallum, Roger Miller, Ray Charles and His Band, Joan Baez, Donovan, The Byrds, Petula Clark, The Lovin' Spoonful, The Ronettes, Ike and Tina Turner, Bo Diddley, The Modern Folk Quartet.

246 BIGFOOT. (Ellman Enterprises-1973). Rick, Chris Mitchum; Jasper B. Hawks, John Carradine; Joi Landis, Joi Lansing; Wheels, Lindsay Crosby; Chris, Judy Jordan; Sheriff Cyrus, James Craig; Elmer Briggs, John Mitchum; Peggy, Joy Wilkerson; Bigfoot, James Stellar; Mr. Bennett, Ken Maynard; Forest Ranger, Doodles Weaver; Nellie, Dorothy Keller; Hardrock, Jobie "Kid" Chissell; Slim, Nick Raymond; Mike, Sonny West; Deputy Hank, Walt Zachrich; Dum Dum, Ray Cantrell; Susy, Susy Marlin Crosby; Falling Star, Lois Red Elk; Bobbi, Jennifer Bishop; Cyclist, Holly Kamen; Henry, Walt Swanner; Billy, Billy Record; Mrs. Cummings, Carolyn Gilbert.

247 THE BIGGEST BUNDLE OF THEM ALL. (MGM-1968). Harry Price, Robert Wagner; Juliana, Raquel Welch; Cesare Celli, Vittorio De Sica; Professor Samuels, Edward G. Robinson; Benjamin Brownstead, Godfrey Cambridge; Davey Collins, Davy Kaye; Antonio Tozzi, Francesco Mule; Captain Giglio, Victor Spinetti; Teresa, Yvonne Sanson; Carlotta, Femi Benussi; Rosa, Paola Borboni; Andrea Aureli, Aldo Buffi Landi, Carlo Croccolo, Roberto De Simone, Piero Gerlini, Giulio Marchetti, Lex Monson, Giulio Donnini, Massimo Sarchielli, Gianna Dauro, Carlo Rizzi, Calisto Calisti, Clara Bindi, Milena Vucotic, Linda De Felice, Nino Vingelli, Nino Musco, The Counts.

248 BIJOU. (Poolemar-1972). Bill Harrison, Lydia Black, Tom Bradford, Cable, Peter Fisk, Michael Green, Cassandra Hart, Robert Lewis, Rocco Passalini, Bruce Williams.

249 BIKE BOY. (Andy Warhol-1967). Motorcyclist, Joe Spencer; His Buddy, Ed Wiener; Girl Cyclist, Vera Cruz; Woman in Kitchen, Ingrid Superstar; Woman in Doorway, Ann Wehrer; Woman at Party, Bridget Parker; Her Husband, Clay Bird; Woman on Couch, Viva; Girl Friend, Bettina Coffin; First Salesman, George Ann; Second Salesman, Bruce Ann.

250 BIKINI PARADISE. (Allied Artists-1967). Rachel, Janette Scott; Lt. Allison Fraser, Kieron Moore; Lt. Anthony Crane, John Baer; Harrier Pemproke, Kay Walsh; Commissioner Lighton, Alexander Knox; Maya, Anna Brazzou; Daphne, Sylvie Sorrente; Margarita, Margaret Nolan; Lisa, Michele Mahaut; Charlotte, Francine Welch; Julia, Pilar Clemens; Ingrid, Aida Power; Commissioner, Robert Beatty; Girl in Park, Shirley Faulls; Officer, Graham Sumner.

251 BILLIE. (United Artists-1965). Billie Carol, Patty Duke; Howard Carol, Jim Backus; Mike Benson, Warren Berlinger;

Agnes Carol, Jane Greer; Jean Matthews, Susan Seaforth; Mayor Davis, Billy de Wolfe; Coach Jones, Charles Lane; Matt Bullitt, Dick Sargent; Bob Mathews, Ted Bessell.

252 BILLION DOLLAR BRAIN. (United Artists-1967). Harry Palmer, Michael Caine; Leo Newbegin, Karl Maldin; General Midwinter, Ed Begley; Colonel Stok, Oscar Homolka; Anya, Francoise Dorleac; Colonel Ross, Guy Doleman; Dr. Eiwort, Vladek Scheybal; Basil, Milo Sperberg; Birkinshaw, Mark Elwes; G. P. O. Delivery Boy, Stanley Caine.

253 BILLY JACK. (Warner Bros-1971). Billy Jack, Tom Laughlin; Jean Roberts, Delores Taylor; Sheriff Cole, Clark Howat; Posner, Bert Freed; Barbara, Julie Webb; Deputy, Ken Tobey; Doctor, Victor Iaay; Kit, Debbie Schock; Martin, Stan Rice; Carol, Teresa Kelley; Maria, Katy Moffatt; Cindy, Susan Foster; Councilman, Paul Bruce; Sarah, Lynn Baker; Sunshine, Susan Sosa; Bernard, David Roya; Angela, Gwen Smith; Dinosaur, John McClure; Miss Eyelashes; Cissie Colpitts.

254 BILLY THE KID VS. DRACULA. (Embassy-1966). Chuck Courtney, John Carradine, Melinda Plowman, Virginia Christine, Walter Janovitz, Lennie Greer, Bing Russell, Roy Barcroft, Olive Carey, Richard Reeves, Marjorie Bennett, Harry Carey Jr.

255 BILLY TWO HATS. (United Artists-1974). Gregory Peck, Desi Arnaz Jr., Jack Warden, David Huddleston, Sian Barbara Allen, John Pearce, Dawn Little Sky, W. Vincent St. Cyr, Henry Medicine Hat, Zev Berlinsky, Antony Scott.

256 THE BIRD WITH THE CRYSTAL PLUMAGE. (UMC-1970). Sam, Tony Musante; Julia, Suzy Kendall; Monica, Eva Renzi; Morosini, Enrico Maria Salerno, Berto, Mario Adorf; Dover, Renato Romano; Ranieri, Umberto Rano.

257 THE BIRDS AND THE BEADS. (1973). Georgina Spelvin, Tina Russell.

258 BIRDS DO IT. (Columbia-1966). Melvin Byrd, Soupy Sales; Lt. Porter, Tab Hunter; Professor Wald, Arthur O'Connell; General Smithburn, Edward Andrews; Congresswoman Clanger, Doris Dowling; Claudine Wald, Beverly Adams; Sergeant Skam, Louis Quinn; Yellow Cab Driver, Frank Nastasi; Devlin, Burt Taylor; Arno, Courtney Brown; Clurg, Russell Saunders; Professor Nep, Julian Voloshin; Doorman, Bob Bersell; Curtis, Warren Day; Willie, Jay Laskay; Radar Operator, Burt Leigh.

259 BIRDS IN PERU. (Regional-1968). Adriana, Jean Seberg; Ranier, Maurice Ronet; The Husband, Pierre Brasseur; Madame Fernande, Danielle Darrieux; The Chauffeur, Jean-

Pierre Kalfon; Alejo, Michel Buades; Rita, Jackie Lombard; Bouncer, Pierre Koulak; Truck Driver, Henry Czarniak.

260 THE BIRDS, THE BEES AND THE ITALIANS. (Claridge-1967). Milena Zulian, Virna Lisi; Osvaldo Bisigato, Gastone Moschin; Gilda Bisigato, Nora Ricci; Toni Gasparini, Alberto Lionello; Ippolita Gasparini, Olga Villi; Lino Benedetti, Franco Fabrizi; Noemi Castellan, Beba Loncar; Giacinto Castellan, Gigi Ballista.

261 THE BIRTHDAY PARTY. (Continental-1968). Stanley, Robert Shaw; McCann, Patrick McGee; Meg, Dandy Nicholas; Goldberg, Sydney Tafler; Petey, Moultrie Kelsall; Lulu, Helen Fraser.

262 THE BISCUIT EATER. (Buena Vista-1972). Harve McNeill, Earl Holliman; Mr. Ames, Lew Ayres; Willie Dorsey, Godfrey Cambridge; Mrs. McNeill, Patricia Crowley; Charity Tomlin, Beah Richards; Lonnie McNeill, Johnny Whitaker; Text Tomlin, George Spell; Mr. Eben, Clifton James; Waiter, Mantan Moreland.

263 BITTER LOVE. (Alpherat-1974). Renata, Lisi Gastoni; Antonio, Leonard Mann.

264 BLACK BEAUTY. (Paramount-1971). Joe, Mark Lester; Hackenschmidt, Walter Slezak; Gervaise, Peter Lee Lawrence; Maria, Ursula Glas; Sam, Patrick Mower; Sir William, John Nettleton; Anne, Maria Rohm; Evans, Eddie Golden; Roger, Clive Geraghty; Muldoon, Johnny Hoey; Anna, Margaret Lacey.

265 THE BLACK BELLY OF THE TARANTULA. (MGM-1972). Inspector Tellini, Giancarlo Giannini; Anna Tellini, Stefania Sandrelli; Laura, Claudine Auger; Maria Zani, Barbara Bouchet; Woman with mole, Rosella Falk; Paolo Zani, Silvano Tranquilli; Mirta, Annabella Incontrera; Masseur, Ezio Marano; Jenny, Barbara Bach; Mario Giancarlo Prete; Amica Zani, Anna Saia; Waiter, Eugene Walter; Commissario Di Giacomo, Nini Vingelli; Entymologist, Daniele Dublini; Psychiatrist, Giuseppe Fortis; Informer, Guerrino Grovello; Director of Clinic, Fulvio Mingozzi; Policeman, Giorgio Dolfin; Client at the Beauty Parlor, Carla Manchini; Police Doctor, Amata Garbini.

266 BLACK BELT JONES. (Warner Bros. -1974). Jim Kelly, Gloria Hendry, Scatman Crothers, Alan Weeks, Eric Laneuville, Andre Phillipe, Vincent Barbi, Nate Esformes, Malik Carter, Mel Novak, Eddie Smith, Alex Brown, Clarence Barnes, Earl Brown, Esther Sutherland, Sid Kaiser, Doug Sides.

267 THE BLACK BUNCH. (Entertainment Pyramid-1973).

Gladys Bunker, Marshall Breedson, Evan Renshaw.

268 BLACK CAESAR. (American-International-1973). Rufus, D'Urville Martin; Tommy, Fred Williamson; Gibbs, Julius W. Harris; Helen, Gloria Hendry; Crawdaddy, Don Pedro Colley; McKinney, Art Lund; Cardoza, Val Avery; Mama Gibbs, Minnie Gentry; Joe, Philip Roye; Alfred, William Wellman Jr.; Bryant, James Dixon; Virginia, Myrna Hansen; Grossfield, Patrick McAllister; Motor, Cecil Alonzo; Sport, Allen Bailey; Tommy as boy, Omer Jeffrey; Joe as boy, Michael Jeffrey.

269 BLACK EYE. (Warner Bros.-1974). Stone, Fred Williamson; Miss Francis, Rosemary Forsyth; Cynthia, Teresa Graves; Diane Davis, Floy Dean; Dole, Richard Anderson; Talbot, Cyril Delevanti; Bowen, Richard X. Slattery; Avery, Larry Mann; Majors, Bret Morrison; Amy, Susan Arnold.

270 BLACK FANTASY. (Impact-1972). Jim Collier, Ellie Fascalini, Elena Hall, Hollis Hanson.

271 BLACK GIRL. (New Yorker-1969). The Maid, Mbissine Therese Diop; Madame, Anne-Marie Jelinck; Master, Robert Fontaine; Young Man, Momar Nar Sene; Boy With Mask, Ibrahima; Guests, Bernard Delbard, Nicole Donati, Raymond Lemery, Suzanne Lemery; and the voices of Toto Bissainthe, Robert Marcy, Sophie Leclerc.

272 BLACK GIRL. (Cinerama-1972). Earl, Brock Peters; Netta, Leslie Uggams; Mu' Dear, Claudia McNeil; Mama Rosie, Louise Stubbs; Norma, Gloria Edwards; Ruth Ann, Loretta Greene; Herbert, Kent Martin; Billie Jean, Peggy Pettit; Special Guest, Ruby Dee.

273 BLACK GOD, WHITE DEVIL. (New Yorker-1971). Manoel, Gerardo Del Rey; Rosa, Yona Magalhaes; Sebastian, Lydio Sylvia; Corisco, Othon Bestos; Antonio, Mauricio Do Valle; Dada, Sonia Dos Homildes.

274 THE BLACK GODFATHER. (Cinemation-1974). Jimmy Witherspoon, Rod Perry, Damu King, Dan Chastain, Diane Sommerfield, Tony Burton, Duncan McLeod, Kenny Bell, Cinque Attucks, Dion Jackson, Charles Lampkin, Katheryn Jackson, Tommy Scott, Ricardo Brown, John Alderman, Sue Woodson, Mary Vivian, Lee Pulford, Ernie Banks, Annie Green, Herb Jefferson Jr., Betsy Finley.

275 BLACK GUNN. (Columbia-1972). Gunn, Jim Brown; Capelli, Martin Landau; Judith, Brenda Sykes; Tomi, Luciana Paluzzi; Scott, Herbert Jefferson Jr.; Hopper, Jim Watkins; Sam, Vida Blue; Laurento, Stephen McNally; Winman, Keefe Brasselle; Larry, Timothy Brown; Rico, William Campbell; Seth, Bernie Casey; Adams, Gary Conway; Jimpy, Rick Ferrell;

Ray, Bruce Glover.

276 BLACK JACK. (American International-1972). Lynch, Georg Stanford Brown; Josh, Brandon DeWilde; Gen. Gobohare, Keenan Wynn; Sen. Recker, Tim O'Connor; Diver, Dick Gautier; President, James Daly; Maj. Reason, Robert Lansing; Capt. Breen, Larry Hovis; Penrat, Bernie Kopell; Corazza, Joseph Turkel; Roddenbery, Dub Taylor; Woody, Phil Vandervort.

277 BLACK JESUS. (Plaza-1971). Maurice Lalubi, Woody Strode; Commandant, Jean Servais; Thief, Franco Citti.

278 BLACK MAMA, WHITE MAMA. (American International-1973). Lee, Pam Grier; Karen, Margaret Markov; Ruben, Sid Haig; Densmore, Lynn Borden; Ernesto, Zaldy Zshornack; Logan, Laurie Burton; Capt. , Eddie Garcia; Juana, Alona Alegre; Rocco, Dindo Fernando; Vic, Vic Diaz; Ronda, Wendy Green; Jeanette, Lotis M. Key; Galindo, Alfonso Carvajal; Truck Driver, Bruno Punzalah; Luis, Ricardo Herrero; Alfredo, Jess Ramos.

279 THE BLACK MOSES OF SOUL. (Aquarius-1973). Isaac Hayes.

280 BLACK ON WHITE. (Audubon-1969). Barbara, Anita Sanders; Nino Segurino, Terry Carter.

281 BLACK PETER. (Billings-1971). Peter, Ladislav Jakim; Paula, Pavla Martinkova; Lada, Pavel Sedlacek; Peter's father, Jan Ostroll; Peter's mother, Bozena Matuskova; Cenda, Vladimir Puchholt; Zdenek, Zdenek Kulhanek.

282 BLACK RODEO. (Cinerama-1972). Guest Narrator, Woody Strode; Guest Appearance, Muhammad Ali.

283 BLACK SAMSON. (Warner Bros. -1974). Samson, Rockne Tarkington; Johnny Nappa, William Smith; Tina, Connie Strickland; Leslie, Carol Speed; Arthur, Michael Payne; Harry, Joe Tornatore; Joseph Nappa, Titos Vandis; Old Henry, Napoleon Whiting; Michael Briggs, John Alderman.

284 BLACK SPURS. (Paramount-1965). Santee, Rory Calhoun; Anna, Terry Moore; Sadie, Linda Darnell; Rev. Tanner, Scott Brady; Henderson, Bruce Cabot; Pete, Richard Arlen; Kile, Lon Chaney; Clare, Patricia Owens; Sam, Jerome Courtland.

285 A BLACK VEIL FOR LISA. (Commonwealth United-1969). Bulov, John Mills; Lisa, Luciana Paluzzi; Max, Robert Hoffmann; Marianne, Renata Kasche; Ostermeyer, Tullio Altamura; Mansfeld, Carlo Hintermann; Siegert, Enzo Fiermonte; Kruger, Loris Bazzocchio; Rabbit, Giuseppe Terranova; Olaf, Rodolfo Licari; Muller, Bernardino Solitari; Ursula, Vanna

Polverosi; Dr. Gross, Robert Van Daalen; Eric, Carlo Spadoni.

286 THE BLACK WINDMILL. (Universal-1974). Major Tarrant, Michael Caine; Harper, Donald Pleasence; Ceil, Delphine Seyrig; Chestermann, Clive Revill; McKee, John Vernon; Superintendent Wray, Joss Ackland; Mrs. Tarrant, Janet Suzman; Sir Julyan, Joseph O'Connor; Lady Julyan, Catherine Schell; Bateson, Denis Quilley.

287 BLACKBEARD'S GHOST. (Buena Vista-1968). Captain Blackbeard, Peter Ustinov; Steve Walker, Dean Jones; Jo Anne Baker, Suzanne Pleshette; Emily Stowecraft, Elsa Lanchester; Silky Seymour, Joby Baker; TV Commentator, Elliott Reid; Dean Wheaton, Richard Deacon; Virgil, Norman Grabowski; Motorcycle Cop, Kelly Thordsen; Pinetop Purvis, Michael Conrad; Croupier, Herbie Faye; Gudger Larkin, Hank Jones; Head Official, George Murdock; Teller, Ned Glass; Waiter, Gil Lamb; Bartender, Alan Carney; Charles, Ted Markland; Leon, Lou Nova; Edward, Charlie Brill; Herb Vigran, William Fawcett, Elsie Baker, Sara Taft, Betty Bronson, Kathryn Minner.

288 BLACKENSTEIN. (Exclusive International-1973). John Hart, Ivory Stone, Andrea King, Liz Renay, Roosevelt Jackson, James Cougar, Cardella Di Milo, Joe De Sue, Nick Bolin, Andy C.

289 BLACULA. (American International-1972). Blacula/Mamuwalde, William Marshall; Tina/Luva, Vonetta McGee; Michelle, Denise Nicholas; Gordon Thomas, Thalmus Rasulala; Lt. Peters, Gordon Pinsent; Dracula, Charles Macaulay; Nancy, Emily Yancy; Swenson, Lance Taylor Sr.; Bobby, Ted Harris; Billy, Rick Metzler; Skillet, Jitu Cumbuka; Barnes, Logan Field; Juanita Jones, Ketty Lester; Sam, Elisha Cook; Real Estate Agent, Eric Brotherson.

290 BLADE. (Joseph Green-1973). Blade, John Marley; Petersen, Jon Cypher; Maggie, Kathryn Walker; Powers, William Prince; Quincy, Michael McGuire; Spinelli, Joe Santos; Reardon, John Schuck; Freund, Peter White; Steiner; Keene Curtis; Connors, Karen Machon; Novak, Raina Barrett; Watson, Ted Lange; Fat Man, Marshall Efron; Sanchez, Arthur French; Debaum, Steve Landesberg; Kaminsky, James Cook; Melinda, Jeanne Lange; Bentley, Michael Pendry; Morgan, Vince Cannon; Examiner, Frederick Rolf; Attorney, Hugh Hurd; Producer, Eddie Lawrence; Caldwell, Jeri Miller.

291 BLAZING SADDLES. (Warner Bros. -1974). Cleavon Little, Gene Wilder, Slim Pickens, David Huddleston, Liam Dunn, Alex Karras, John Hillerman, George Furth, Claude E. Starrett Jr., Mel Brooks, Harvey Korman, Madeline Kahn, Carol Arthur, Charles McGregor, Robyn Hilton, Dom DeLuise,

Richard Collier, Don Megowan, Karl Lukas.

292 BLESS THE BEASTS & CHILDREN. (Columbia-1971). Teft, Bill Mumy; Cotton, Barry Robins; Shecker, Miles Chapin; Goodenow, Darel Glaser; Lally 1, Bob Kramer; Lally 2, Marc Vahanian; Sid Shecker, Jesse White; Wheaties, Ken Swofford; Camp Director, Dave Ketchum; Cotton's Mother, Elaine Devry; Hustler, Wayne Sutherlin; Hustler, Bruce Glover; Mr. Goodenow, William Bramley; Mrs. Goodenow, Vanessa Brown; Captain Cotton, Charles H. Gray; Mr. Teft, Vincent Van Lynn; Mom, June C. Ellis; Doctor, Frank Farmer; Young Shooter, Jess Smart.

293 BLINDFOLD. (Universal-1966). Dr. Bartholomew Snow, Rock Hudson; Victoria Vail, Claudia Cardinale; Fitzpatrick, Guy Stockwell; General Prat, Jack Warden; Harrigan, Brad Dexter; Smitty, Anne Seymour; Arthur Vincenti, Alejandro Rey; Captain Davis, Hari Rhodes; Michelangelo Vincenti, Vito Scotti; Lavinia Vincenti, Angela Clarke; Mario Vincenti, John Megna; Barker, Paul Comi; Lippy, Ned Glass; Homburg, Mort Mills; Homburg, Jack De Mave; Police Lieutenant, Robert Simon.

294 BLINDMAN. (20th Century-Fox-1972). Blindman, Tony Anthony; Candy, Ringo Starr; Pilar, Agneta Eckemyr; Domingo, Lloyd Battista; Sweet Mama, Magda Konopka; Mexican General, Raf Baldassarre; David Dreyer.

295 THE BLISS OF MRS. BLOSSOM. (Paramount-1968). Harriet Blossom, Shirley MacLaine; Robert Blossom, Richard Attenborough; Ambrose Tuttle, James Booth; Detective Sergeant Dylan, Freddie Jones; Dylan's Assistant, William Rushton; Dr. Taylor, Bob Monkhouse; Miss Reece, Patricia Routledge; Judge, John Bluthal; Doctor, Harry Towb; Art Dealer, Barry Humphries; Robert's Counsel, Michael Segal; Sandra Caron, Sheila Staefel, Clive Dunn, Frank Thornton, Geraldine Sherman, Julian Chagrin, John Cleese, Bruce Lacey, Tony Grey, Douglas Grey, Leslie Dwyer, Ronnie Brody, Bob Godfrey, John Mulgrew, Marjorie Gresley, Freddie Earle, Marianne Stone, Keith Smith; and The New Vaudeville Band.

296 BLOOD AND BLACK LACE. (Allied Artists-1965). Max Marian, Cameron Mitchell; Christina, Eva Bartok; Inspector Silvester, Thomas Reiner; Nicole, Arianna Gorini; Frank Scalo, Dante De Paolo; Peggy, Mary Arden; Marquis Richard Morell, Franco Rossel; Isabella, Lea Krugher; Tao-Li, Claude Dantes; Marco, Massimo Righi; Zanchin, Giuliano Raffaelli; Clarice, Harriette White Medin.

297 BLOOD AND LACE. (American International-1971). Mrs. Deere, Gloria Grahame; Ellie, Melody Patterson; Mullins, Milton Selzer; Tom, Len Lesser; Calvin, Vic Tayback; Bunch, Terri Messina; Walter, Ronald Taft; Pete, Dennis Christopher;

Ernest, Peter Armstrong; Jennifer, Maggie Corey; Nurse, Mary Strawberry; Edna, Louise Sherrill.

298 BLOOD BATH. (American International-1966). Sordi, William Campbell; The girl, Lori Saunders; Marrisa Mathes, Sandra Knight.

299 BLOOD BEAST FROM OUTER SPACE. (World Entertainment Corporation-1968). Jack Costain, John Saxon; Professor Morley, Maurice Denham; Ann Barlow, Patricia Haines; Det. Supt. Hartley, Alfred Burke; Major John Carson; Sergeant Hawkins, Jack Watson; Grant, Stanley Meadows; Lilbum, Warren Mitchell; Mrs. Lilbum, Marianne Stone; Thorburn, Aubrey Morris; Colonel Davy, Geoffrey Lumsden; Commander Savage, Ballard Berkeley; Joyce Malone, Barbara French; Private Higgins, Anthony Wager; Private Jones, David Gregory; Police Commissioner's Secretary, Tom Till; First R/T Soldier, Vincent Harding; Second R/T Soldier, Douglas Livingstone; Lieutenant, Romo Gorrara; TV Newscaster, John Sherlock; Medra, Robert Crewdson.

300 BLOOD FIEND. (Hemisphere-1968). Philippe Darvas, Christopher Lee; Dani Gireaux, Lelia Goldoni; Nicole Chapel, Jenny Till; Charles Marquis, Julian Glover; Inspector Micheaud, Ivor Dean; Madame Angele, Evelyn Laye.

301 BLOOD FOR DRACULA. (Bryanston-1974). Field hand, Joe Dallesandro; Dracula, Udo Kier; Count's Assistant, Arno Juerging; Lady Difiore, Maxime McKendry; Lord Difiore, Vittorio DeSica; Rubinia, Dominique Darell.

302 BLOOD FROM THE MUMMY'S TOMB. (American International-1972). Professor Julian Fuchs, Andrew Keir; Margaret Fuchs/Queen Tera, Valerie Leon; Corbeck, James Villiers; Dandridge, Hugh Burden; Berigan, George Coulouris; Tod Browning, Mark Edwards; Helen Dickerson, Rosalie Crutchley; Dr. Putnam, Aubrey Morris; Dr. Burgess, David Markham; Mrs. Caporal, Joan Young; Older Male Nurse, James Cossins; Young Male Nurse, David Jackson; Saturnine Young Man, Jonathan Burn; Youth in Museum, Graham James; Veronica, Tamara Ustinov; Nurses, Penelope Holt and Angela Ginders; Patient, Tex Fuller; Priests, Madina Luis, Omar Ammodi, Abdul Kader, Ahmed Osman, Oscar Charles, Soltan Lalani and Saad Ghazi.

303 BLOOD OF THE CONDOR. (Tricontinental-1973). Ignacio, Marcelino Yanahuava; Paulina, Benedicta Mendoza Huanca; Sixto, Vicente Salinas.

304 BLOOD ON THE ARROW. (Allied Artists-1965). Wade Cooper, Dale Robertson; Nancy Mailer, Martha Hyer; Clint Mailer, Wendell Corey; Tim, Dandy Curran; Segura, Paul Mantee; Kai-La, Robert Carricart; Jud, Ted De Corsia; Tex,

Elisha Cook; Mike, John Matthews; Charlie, Tom Reese; Capt. Stanhope, Boyce Wright.

305 THE BLOOD ROSE. (Allied Artists-1970). Frederic, Philippe Lemaire; Anne, Annie Duperey; Prof. Rohmer, Howard Vernon; Barbara, Elisabeth Tessier.

306 BLOODY MAMA. (American International-1970). Kate "Ma" Barker, Shelley Winters; Sam Pendlebury, Pat Hingle; Herman Barker, Don Stroud; Mona Gibson, Diane Varsi; Kevin Dirkman, Bruce Dern; Arthur Barker, Clint Kimbrough; Fred Barker, Robert Walden; Lloyd Barker, Robert De Niro; George Barker, Alex Nicol; Dr. Roth, Michael Fox; Moses, Scatman Crothers; Agent McClellan, Stacy Harris; Rembrandt, Pamela Dunlap.

307 BLOODY PIT OF HORROR. (Pacemaker-1967). Anderson, Mickey Hargitay; Edith, Louise Barret; Walter Brandt, Moa Thai, Femi Martin, Alfred Rice, Rita Klein, John Turner.

308 BLOW-UP. (MGM-1966). Thomas, David Hemmings; Jane, Vanessa Redgrave; Patricia, Sarah Miles; Herself, Verushka; Patricia's Artist Husband, John Castle; First Teenager, Jane Birkin; Second Teenager, Gillian Hills; Thomas' Assistant, Reg Wilkins; Thomas' Receptionist, Tsai Chin; Antique Shop Owner, Susan Broderick; Shopkeeper, Harold Hutchinson; Fashion Editor, Mary Khal; Themselves, The Yardbirds; Jane's Lover in Park, Ronan O'Casey; Models, Jill Kennington, Peggy Moffitt, Ann Norman, Rosaleen Murray, Melanie Hampshire.

309 BLUE. (Paramount-1968). Blue (Azul), Terence Stamp; Joanne Morton, Joanna Pettet; Doc Morton, Karl Malden; Ortega, Ricardo Montalban; Jess Parker, Anthony Costello; Carlos, Joe De Santis; Abe Parker, James Westerfield; Manuel, Stathis Giallelis; Xavier, Carlos East; Inez, Sara Vardi; Antonio, Robert Lipton; Rory Calvin, Kevin Corcoran; Helen Buchanan, Ivalou Redd; Alma Wishoff, Dorothy Konrad; Elizabeth Parker, Helen Kleeb; Jim Benton, Michael Bell; Settler, Wes Bishop; Mrs. Kramer, Marian Mason; Cantina Proprietress, Alma Bertrand; Sara Lambert, Sally Kirkland; Laurie Kramer, Peggy Lipton; Wes Lambert, Jerry Gatlin; Mexican Assassin, Michael Nader; Police Chief, William Shannon.

310 THE BLUE BEAST. (Toho-1965). Tatsuya Nakadai, Yoko Tsukasa, Koreya Senda, Keiko Awaji, Jun Tazaki, Ichiro Nakaya.

311 THE BLUE MAX. (20th Century-Fox-1966). Bruno Stachel, George Peppard; Count von Klugermann, James Mason; Countess Kaeti, Ursula Andress; Willi von Klugermann, Jeremy Kemp; Heidemann, Karl Michael Vogler; Elfie Heidemann,

Loni Von Friedl; Holbach, Anton Diffring; Rupp, Peter Woodthorpe; Kettering, Harry Towb; Ziegel, Derek Newark; Fabian, Derren Nesbitt; Field Marshal Von Lenndorf, Friedrich Ledebur; Crown Prince, Roger Ostime; Hans, Hugo Schuster; Pilots, Tim Parkes, Ian Kingsley, and Ray Browne; Baron von Richtofen, Carl Schell.

312 BLUE MONEY. (Crown International-1972). Jim Desalle, Alain-Patrick Chappuis; Lisa Desalle, Barbara Caron; Ingrid, Inga Maria; Mike, Jeff Gall; Fatman, Oliver Aubrey; Freddie, Steve Roberson; Lawyer, Alan Bouverat; Bernie, John Parker; Maria Arnold, Sandy Dempsey, Susan Draeger, Cindy Hopkins, Sunny Boyd.

313 BLUE MOVIE. (Andy Warhol-1969). Herself, Viva; Himself, Louis Waldon.

314 BLUE SEXTET. (Unisphere-1972). Jeff Ambler, John Damon; George Horner, Peter Clune; Tish Sumaki, Coco Sumaki; Liz Horner, Margaret Cahtell; Felicia Massey, Adrienne Jalbert; Bud Foster, Carey Poe; Pop Group, Paul Chin & the Dynasty; Indian Dancer, Bhaskar; Ghoul in Porno Film, Tony Rivers; Mark La Roche, Harry Skleros, Jacqueline Welter, James Skleros, Dorian Wayne.

315 BLUE SUMMER. (Monarch-1973). Tracy, Darcey Hollingsworth; Gene, Bo White; Bee, Lilly Bo Peep; Sparky, Joann Sterling; Regina, Melissa Evers; No Name, Chris Jordan; Margaret, Jacqueline Carol; Deborah, Any Mathieu; Liza, Shana McGran; Fred, Eric Edwards; Roger, Larry Lima; Gene's Mother, Sylvia Bernstein; Gene's Father, Hardy Harrison; Motorcyclist, Jeff Allen; Heavy, Joe Asaro; Preacher, Robert Joel; Ed, Mike Ledis.

316 BLUE SURFARI. (Excelsior-1970). Ricky Grigg, Greg Noll, Mike Benet, Sue Peterson, Miss Teenage Fair.

317 BLUE WATER, WHITE DEATH. (National General-1971). Peter Gimbel, Ron Taylor, Rodney Jonklaas, Stanton Waterman, Valerie Taylor, Peter A. Lake.

318 BLUEBEARD. (Cinerama-1972). Bluebeard, Richard Burton; Magdalena, Raquel Welch; Anne, Joey Heatherton; Elga, Virna Lisi; Brigitte, Nathalie Delon; Greta, Karin Schubert; Caroline, Agostina Belli; Prostitute, Sybil Danning; Sergio, Edward Meeks; Greta's Father, Jean Lefebvre; Violinist, Mathieu Carriere.

319 BLUES FOR LOVERS. (20th Century-Fox-1966). Ray Charles, himself; Steve Collins, Tom Bell; Peggy Harrison, Mary Peach; Gina Graham, Dawn Adams; David, Piers Bishop; Mrs. Babbidge, Betty McDowall; Margaret, Lucy Appleby; Duke Wade, Robert Lee Ross; Antonia, Monika Henreid;

and the Ray Charles Orchestra and the Raelets.

320 BLUME IN LOVE. (Warner Bros.-1973). Blume, George Segal; Nina, Susan Anspach; Elmo, Kris Kristofferson; Arlene, Marsha Mason; Mrs. Cramer, Shelley Winters; Analyst, Donald F. Muhich; Blume's Partner, Paul Mazursky; Cindy, Erin O'Reilly; Gloria, Anazette Chase.

321 THE BOATNIKS. (Buena Vista-1970). Ensign Garland, Robert Morse; Kate, Stefanie Powers; Harry Simmons, Phil Silvers; Max, Norman Fell; Charlie, Mickey Shaughnessy; Jason, Wally Cox; Cmdr. Taylor, Don Ameche; Lt. Jordan, Joey Forman; Pepe Galindo, Vito Scotti; Wagner, Tom Lowell; Chief Walsh, Bob Hastings; Garlotti, Sammy Jackson; Nutty Sailor, Joe E. Ross; Tina, Judy Jordon; Bert, Al Lewis; Chiyoko Kuni, Midori; Motorcycle Cop, Kelly Thordsen; Mr. Mitchell, Gil Lamb.

322 BOB & CAROL & TED & ALICE. (Columbia-1969). Carol Sanders, Natalie Wood; Bob Sanders, Robert Culp; Ted Henderson, Elliott Gould; Alice Henderson, Dyan Cannon; Horst, Horst Ebersberg; Emelio, Lee Bergere; Psychiatrist, Donald F. Muhich; Dean Sanders, Noble Lee Holderread Jr.; Phyllis, K. T. Stevens; Susan, Celeste Yarnall; Group Leader, Greg Mullavey; Oscar, Andre Philippe; Myrna, Diane Berghoff; Conrad, John Halloran; Toby, Susan Merin; Roger, Jeffrey Walker; Jane, Vicki Thal; Wendy, Joyce Easton; Howard, Howard Dayton; Alida, Alida Ihle; Dave, John Brent; Bert, Gary Goodrow; Sue, Carol O'Leary; Norma, Constance Egan.

323 BOB & DARYL & TED & ALEX. (Fanrow-1972). Danny DiCioccio, Anton Lewis, Don Sean, Ernie Likens.

324 THE BOBO. (Warner Bros.-7 Arts). Juan Bautista, Peter Sellers; Olimpia Segura, Britt Ekland; Carlos Matabosch, Rossano Brazzi; Francisco Carbonell, Adolfo Celi; Trinity, Hattie Jacques; Silvestre Flores, Ferdy Mayne; Pepe Gamazo, Kenneth Griffith; Eugenio Gomez, Alfredo Lettieri; Luis Castillo, John Wells; Pompadour Major, Marne Maitland; "Los Tarantos" Flamenco Company.

325 THE BODY STEALERS. (Allied Artists-1971). Armstrong, George Sanders; Matthews, Maurice Evans; Bob, Patrick Allen; Jim, Neil Connery; Baldwin, Robert Flemyng; Lorna, Lorna Wilde; Hindsmith, Alan Cuthbertson; Briggs, Carl Rigg; Julie, Hilary Dwyer; Joanna, Sally Faulkner; Bailes, Michael Culver; Paula, Carol Ann Hawkins; Mrs. Thatcher, Shelagh Fraser; Sally, Jan Miller.

326 BOEING BOEING. (Paramount-1965). Bernard Lawrence, Tony Curtis; Robert Reed, Jerry Lewis; Bertha, Thelma Ritter; Jacqueline Grieux, Dany Saval; Lise Bruner, Christiane Schmidtmer; Vicky Hawkins, Suzanna Leigh; Pierre, Lomax Study.

327 THE BOFORS GUN. (Regional-1968). Gunner Danny O'Rourke, Nicol Williamson; Gunner Flynn, Ian Holm; Lance-Bombardier Terry Evans, David Warner; Rowe, Richard O'Callaghan; Shone, Barry Jackson; Crawley, Donald Gee; Featherstone, John Thaw; Sgt. Walker, Peter Vaughan; Lieut. Pickering, Gareth Forwood; Cook Private Samuel, Geoffrey Hughes; German Painter, John Herrington; JAAFI Girl, Barbara Jefford.

328 LA BOHEME. (Warner Bros. -1965). Rodolfo, Gianni Raimondi; Marcello, Rolando Panerai; Schaunard, Gianni Maffeo; Benoit, Carol Badioli; Colline, Ivo Vinco; Alcindoro, Virgilio Carbonari; Mimi, Mirella Freni; Musetta, Adriana Martino; Parpignol, Franco Ricciardi; Sergeant, Giuseppe Morresi; The Orchestra and Chorus of La Scala, Milan.

329 LE BONHEUR. (Clover-1966). Francois, Jean-Claude Drouot; Therese, Claire Drouot; Gisou, Sandrine Drouot; Pierrot, Olivier Drouot; Emilie, Marie France Boyer.

330 LES BONNES FEMMES. (Robert and Raymond Hakim-1966). Jane, Bernadette Lafont; Rita, Lucile Saint-Simon; Jacqueline, Clothilde Joano; Ginette, Stephane Audran; Motorcyclist, Mario David; Cashier, Ave Ninchi; Young Playboy, Jean-Louis Maury; His Older Companion, Albert Dinan; Henri, Sacha Briquet; Andre, Claude Berri.

331 BONNIE AND CLYDE. (Warner Bros. -7 Arts-1967). Clyde Barrow, Warren Beatty; Bonnie Parker, Faye Dunaway; C. W. Moss, Michael J. Pollard; Buck Barrow, Gene Hackman; Blanche, Estelle Parsons; Sheriff Frank Hamer, Denver Pyle; Ivan Moss, Dub Taylor; Velma Davis, Evans Evans; Eugene Grizzard, Gene Wilder; Grocery Store Owner, James Stiver.

332 BONNIE'S KIDS. (General Film Corporation-1972). Ellie Thomas, Tiffany Bolling; Larry Evans, Steve Sandor; Myra Thomas, Robin Mattson; Ben Seamon, Scott Brady; Eddy, Alex Rocco; Frank McGuire, Max Showalter; Diana, Lenore Stevens; Charley Thomas, Leo Gordon; Digger, Timothy Brown; Paula Clark, Luanne Roberts; Muriel, Jane Greenspun; Miss Meadows, Diana Darrin; Brenda Desantis, Rodyn Wilton; Michael Desantis, Beau Marks; Waitress, Sharon Gless; Harry, Nick Courtland; Motel-Manager, James Lydon; Glen Stensel, John Baer, Larry Blake, and James Dunn.

333 BOOK OF NUMBERS. (Avco Embassy-1973). Blueboy Harris, Raymond St. Jacques; Kelly Simms, Freda Payne; Dave Greene, Philip Thomas; Pigmeat Goins, Hope Clarke; Makepeace Johnson, Willie Washington Jr.; Eggy, Doug Finell; Kid Flick, Sterling St. Jacques; Blip Blip, C. L. Williams; Billy Bowlegs, D'Urville Martin; Joe Gaines, Jerry Leon; Luis Antoine, Gilbert Greene; Carlos, Frank De Sal; Sister Clara Goode, Temie Mae Williams; Sister #2, Pauline

Herndon; Sister #3, Ethel Marie Crawford; Bus Station Prostitute, Mimi Lee Dodd; Mr. Booker, Charles F. Elyston; Mrs. Booker, Queen Esther Gent; Georgia Brown, Irma Hall; Didi, Chiquita Jackson; Honey, Katie Peters; Becky, Pat Peterson; Goons, Ray McDonald, and Charles Lewis.

334 BOOM! (Universal-1968). Flora Goforth, Elizabeth Taylor; Chris Flanders, Richard Burton; The Witch of Capri, Noel Coward; Blackie, Joanna Shimkus; Rudy, Michael Dunn; Dr. Lullo, Romolo Valli; Etti, Fernando Piazza; Simonetta, Veronica Wells; Manicurist, Claudye Ettori; Journalist, Howard Taylor; Sergio Carozzi, Giovanni Paganelli, Gens Block, Franco Pesci.

335 BOOTLEGGERS. (Howco International-1974). Othar Pruitt, Paul Koslo; Dewey Crenshaw, Dennis Fimple; Grandpa Pruitt, Slim Pickens; Grandma Pruitt, Betty Bluett; Silas Pruitt, Steve Ward; Rufus Woodall, Seamon Glass; Big-un-Woodall, Jim Clem; Sally Fannie Tatum, Taclyn Smith; Leola Gauldin, Darlye Ann Lindley; The Sheriff, Earl E. Smith.

336 BOOTS TURNER. (Rowland-Williams-1973). Terry Carter, Gwen Mitchell, Kyle Johnson, James Sikking, Art Lund.

337 BORA BORA. (American International-1970). Marita, Haydee Politoff; Robert, Corrado Pani; Susanne, Doris Kunstmann; Tehina, Rosine Copie; Mani, Antoine Coco Puputauki.

338 BORN FREE. (Columbia-1966). Joy Adamson, Virginia McKenna; George Adamson, Bill Travers; Kendall, Geoffrey Keen; Nuru, Peter Luckoye; Makkede, Omar Chambati; Sam, Bill Godden; Baker, Bryan Epsom; Ken, Robert Cheetham; James, Robert Young; Watson, Geoffrey Best; Indian Doctor, Surya Patel.

339 BORN LOSERS. (American International-1967). Billy Jack, Tom Laughlin; Vicky Barrington, Elizabeth James; Mrs. Shorn, Jane Russell; Danny Carmody, Jeremy Slate; Child, William Wellman Jr.; Cue Ball, Robert Tessier; Gangrene, Jeff Cooper; Crabs, Edwin Cook; Tex, Tex; Speechless, Paul Prokop; Lu Ann Crawford, Julie Cahn; Linda Prang, Susan Foster; Jodell Shorn, Janice Miller; Sheriff, Stuart Lancaster; Deputy, Jack Starett; District Attorney, Paul Bruce; Mr. Crawford, Robert Cleaves; Mrs. Prang, Ann Bellamy; Jerry Carmody, Gordon Hobar.

340 BORN TO WIN. (United Artists-1971). Jay Jay, George Segal; Pam, Karen Black; Veronica, Paula Prentiss; Billy Dynamite, Jay Fletcher; Danny, Robert De Niro; Cashier, Sylvia Syms; Stanley, Irving Selbst; Marlene, Marcia Jean Kurtz; The Greek, Hector Elizondo.

341 BORN WILD. (American International-1968). Tony, Tom

Nardini; Janet, Patty McCormack; Bruce, David Macklin; Raquel, Joanna Frank; Paco, Zooey Hall; Emmet, Sammy Vaughn; Jerry, Michael Wood; Din-Din, Keith Taylor; Johnny, Adolph Martinez; Ramon, Alberto Isaac; Mr. Simms, Russ Bender; Mr. Wilson, Arthur Peterson; The American Revolution.

342 BOROM SARRET. (New Yorker-1969). Cartman, Ly Abdoulaye; The Horse, Albourah.

343 BORSALINO. (Paramount-1970). Capella, Jean-Paul Belmondo; Siffredi, Alain Delon; Rinaldi, Michel Bouquet; Lola, Catherine Rouvel; Madame Escarguel, Francoise Christophe; Madame Rinaldi, Corinne Marchand; Boccace, Julien Guimoar; Marello, Arnoldo Foa; Ginette, Nicole Calfan; Siffredi's Mother, Laura Adani; Dancer, Christian de Tiliere; Mario, Mario David; Police Superintendent, Daniel Ivernel; Nono, Dennis Berry; Poli, Andre Bollet; Lidia, Helen Remy; Singer, Odette Piquet; Fernand, Lionel Vitrant; Accountant, Jean Aron; Spada, Pierre Koulak.

344 THE BOSTON STRANGLER. (20th Century-Fox-1968). Albert De Salvo, Tony Curtis; John S. Bottomly, Henry Fonda; Phillip J. DiNatale, George Kennedy; Julian Soshnick, Mike Kellin; Terence Huntley, Hurd Hatfield; Frank McAfee, Murray Hamilton; John Asgeirsson, Jeff Corey; Diane Cluny, Sally Kellerman; Edward W. Brooke, William Marshall; Peter Hurkos, George Voskovec; Mary Bottomly, Leora Dana; Carolyn Conwell, Jeanne Cooper, Austin Willis, Lara Lindsay, George Furth, Richard X. Slattery, William Hickey, Eve Collyer, Dwyda Donhowe, Alex Dreier, John Cameron Swayze, Shelly Burton, Elizabeth Baur, James Brolin, George Tyne, Dana Elcar, William Traylor, Isabella Hoops, Tom Aldredge, Marie Thomas, Gina Harding, Nancy Phillips, Enid Markey.

345 LE BOUCHER. (Cinerama-1971). Helene, Stephane Audran; Popual, Jean Yanne; Angelo, Antonio Passallia; Leon Hamel, Mario Beccaria; Pere Cahrpy, Pasquale Ferone; Police Inspector, Roger Rudel; Charles, William Gerrault.

346 BOUDU SAVED FROM DROWNING. (Pathe Contemporary-1967). Boudu, Michel Simon; Monsieur Lestingois, Charles Grandval; Madame Lestingois, Marcelle Hainia; Anne-Marie, Severine Lerczynska; Student, Jean Daste; Godin, Max Dalban; Vigour, Jean Gehret; Poet on Bench, Jacques Becker.

347 THE BOUNTY KILLER. (Embassy-1965). Dan Duryea, Rod Cameron, Audrey Dalton, Richard Arlen, Buster Crabbe, Fuzzy Knight, Johnny Mack Brown, Bob Steele, Bronco Billy Anderson.

348 BOXCAR BERTHA. (American International-1972). Boxcar

Bertha, Barbara Hershey; Big Bill Shelley, David Carradine; Rake Brown, Barry Primus; Von Morton, Bernie Casey; H. Buckram Sartoris, John Carradine; The McIvers, Victor Argo and David R. Osterhout; Tillie Stone, Ann Morell; Emeric Pressburger, Grahame Pratt; M. Powell, Chicken Holleman; Mrs. Mailler, Marianne Dole; Harvey Saunders, Harry Northup; Joe Dreft, Joe Reynolds.

349 BOY. (Grove-1970). Father, Fumio Watahabe; Boy, Tetsuo Abe; Mother, Akiko Koyama; Child, Tsuyoshi Kinoshita.

350 A BOY ... A GIRL. (Jack Hanson-1969). Boy, Dino Martin Jr.; Girl, Airion Fromer; Elizabeth, Karen Steele; Mr. Christian, Kerwin Mathews.

351 THE BOY CRIED MURDER. (Universal-1966). Clare, Veronica Hurst; Tom, Phil Brown; Jonathan, Fraser MacIntosh; Mike, Tim Barrett; Suzy, Beba Loncar; Col. Wetherall, Edward Steel; Mrs. Wetherall, Anita Sharpe-Bolster; Police Officer, Alex MacIntosh.

352 BOY, DID I GET A WRONG NUMBER. (United Artists-1966). Tom Meade, Bob Hope; Didi, Elke Sommer; Lily, Phyllis Diller; Pepe, Cesare Danova; Martha Meade, Marjorie Lord; Schwartz, Kelly Thordsen; Regan, Benny Baker; Doris Meade, Terry Burnham; Telephone Operator, Joyce Jameson; Newscaster, Harry Von Zell; Larry Meade, Kevin Burchett; Plympton, Keith Taylor; Newsboy, John Todd Roberts.

353 THE BOY FRIEND. (MGM-1971). Polly Browne, Twiggy; Tony Brockhurst, Christopher Gable; Madame Dubonnet, Moyra Fraser; Max, Max Adrian; Percy, Bryan Pringle; Rita, Glenda Jackson; Fay, Georgina Hale.

354 A BOY TEN FEET TALL. (Paramount-1965). Cocky Wainwright, Edward G. Robinson; Sammy, Fergus McClelland; Gloria von Imhoff, Constance Cummings; Lem, Harry H. Corbett; Spyros Dracondopolous, Paul Stassino; The Syrian, Zia Mohyeddin; Abu Lubaba, Orlando Martins; Heneker, John Turner; Aunt Jane, Zena Walker; District Commissioner Jack Gwillim; Cathie, Patricia Donahue; Bob, Jared Allen; Doctor, Guy Deghy.

355 THE BOY WHO CRIED WEREWOLF. (Universal-1973). Robert, Kerwin Mathews; Sandy, Elaine Devry; Ritchie, Scott Sealey; Sheriff, Robert J. Wilke; Jenny, Susan Foster; Harry, Jack Lucas; Brother Christopher, Bob Homel; Dr. Marderowin, George Gaynes; Monica, Loretta Temple; Deputy, Dave Cass; Duncan, Herold Goodwin; 1st Guard, Tim Haldeman; 2nd Guard, John Logan; Hippy Jesus Freak, Eric Gordon; First Werewolf, Paul Baxley.

356 THE BOYS IN THE BAND. (National General-1970). Donald,

Frederick Combs; Harold, Leonard Frey; Emory, Cliff Gorman; Bernard, Reuben Greene; Cowboy, Robert LaTourneaux; Hank, Laurence Luckinbill; Michael, Kenneth Nelson; Larry, Keith Prentice; Alan, Peter White.

357 BOYS IN THE SAND. (Poolemar-1971), Casey Donovan, Peter Fisk, Danny Di Cioccio, Tommy Moore.

358 THE BOYS OF PAUL STREET. (20th Century-Fox-1969). Nemecsek, Anthony Kemp; Boka, William Burleigh; Gerab, John Moulder-Brown; Csonakos, Robert Efford; Csele, Mark Colleano; Weisz, Gary O'Brien; Kolnay, Martin Beaumont; Barabas, Paul Bartlett; Leszik, Earl Younger, Richter, Gyorgy Vizi; Julien Holdaway, Peter Delmar, Miklos Jancso, Attila Nemethy, Imre Ebergenyi, Sandor Kentner, Andras Avar, Janos Pach, Istvan Seri, Orsolya Zeitler, Mari Torocsik, Sandor Pecsi, Laszlo Zokak, Laszlo Paal, Arpad Teri.

359 THE BRAIN. (Paramount-1969). The Brain, David Niven; Arthur, Jean-Paul Belmondo; Anatole, Bourvil; Scannapieco, Eli Wallach; Sofia, Silvia Monti; Bruno, Fernand Valois; Le Commanissaire, Raymond Gerome; Pochet, Jacques Balutin; Duboeuf, Jacques Ciron; Mazurel, Fernand Guiot; Man from fifth floor, Jean Le Poulain; Belgian with cold, Robert Dalban; Belgians, Raoul Del Frosse, Pierre Torrade, Paul Mercey; Chief Guard, Henri Genes; Guards, Yves Bersacq, Dominique Zardi; Superintendent Cummings, Tommy Duggan; Brain First Accomplice, Guy Delorme; Second Accomplice, Michael Garland.

360 BRAINSTORM. (Warner Bros. -1965). Jim Grayam, Jeffrey Hunter; Lorrie Benson, Anne Francis; Cort Benson, Dana Andrews; Dr. Larstadt, Viveca Lindfors.

361 BRANCHES. (New Line-1971). Bill, Bill Weidner; Girl, Connie Brady; Her other boy friend, Al Capogrossi; His side kick, Richard Perlmutter; Girl after Bill, Erica Saxe; Storyteller, Christian Larson.

362 BRAND X. (1970). Taylor Mead, Sally Kirkland, Frank Cavestani, Abbie Hoffman, Sam Shepard.

363 BRANDY IN THE WILDERNESS. (New Line-1971). Brandy, Michaux French; Simon, Stanton Kaye.

364 THE BRAZEN WOMEN OF BALZAC. (Globe-1971). Fabian, Joachim Hansen; Felicita, Edwige Fenech; Arabella, Angelica Ott; Eugenie, Michaela May; Sophie, Caterina Alt; Annette, Frances Fair; Manuel, Ivan Nessbeth; George, Sieghardt Rupp; Leuwenstam, Walter Buschoff.

365 BREEZY. (Universal-1973). Frank Harmon, William Holden; Breezy, Kay Lenz; Bob Henderson, Roger C. Carmel;

Betty, Marj Dusay; Paula, Joan Hotchkis; Marcy, Jamie Smith Jackson; Man in car, Norman Bartold; Overnight date, Lynn Borden; Nancy, Shelley Morrison; Bruno, Dennis Olivieri; Charlie, Eugene Peterson; Police Officer, Lew Brown; Doctor, Richard Bull; Norman, Johnie Collins III; Maitre 'd, Don Diamond; Veterinarian, Scott Holden; Real Estate Agent, Sandy Kenyon; Driver, Jack Kosslyn; Waitress, Mary Munday; Saleswoman, Frances Stevenson; Paula's escort, Buck Young; Dress Customer, Pricilla Morrill; Sir Love-a-Lot, Earle.

366 BREWSTER MCCLOUD. (MGM-1970). Brewster McCloud, Bud Cort; Louise, Sally Kellerman; Frank Shaft, Michael Murphy; Sheriff Weeks, William Windom; Suzanne, Shelley Duvall; Lecturer, Rene Auberjonois; Abraham Wright, Stacy Keach; Policeman Johnson, John Schuck; Daphne Heap, Margaret Hamilton; Hope, Jennifer Salt; Policeman Hines, Corey Fischer; Police Capt. Crandell, G. Wood; Policeman Breen, Bert Remsen; Breen's Wife, Angelin Johnson; Week's Aide, William Baldwin.

367 THE BRIDE WORE BLACK. (Lopert-1968). Julie Kohler, Jeanne Moreau; Corey, Jean-Claude Brialy; Robert Coral, Michel Bouquet; Fergus, Charles Denner; Bliss, Claude Rich; Holmes, Daniel Boulanger; Rene Morane, Michel Lonsdale; Miss Becker, Alexandra Stewart; Morane's Son, Christophe Brunot; David, Serge Rousseau; Charlie, Jacques Robiolles; Julie's Mother, Luce Fabiole; Mrs. Morane, Sylvine De Lannoy; Maid, Jacqueline Rouillard; Inspector Fabri, Van Doude; The Mechanic, Paul Pavel; The Plaintiff, Maurice Garell; Examining Magistrate, Gilles Queant; The Musicians, Frederique and Renaud Fontanarosa.

368 BRIDEGROOM, ET AL. (New Yorker-1969). James Powell, Lilith Ungerer, Rainer Werner Fassbinder, Peer Rabin, Irm Hermann, Kristin Peterson.

369 THE BRIDES OF FU MANCHU. (Seven Arts-1966). Fu Manchu, Christopher Lee; Mayland Smith, Douglas Wilmer; Marie Lentz, Marie Versini; Franz, Heinz Drache; Dr. Petrie, Howard Marion Crawford; Ling Tang, Tsai Chin; Sgt. Spicer, Kenneth Fortescue; Otto Lentz, Joseph Furst; Nikki Sheldon, Harald Leipnitz; Insp. Pierre Grimaldi, Roger Nanin; Merlin, Rupert Davies; Feng, Burt Kwouk; Assistant, Eric Young; Lotus, Poulet Tu; Abdul, Rulmaan Peer; Louise, Wendy Gifford; the Brides, Carole Gray, Lucille Soong, Dani Sheridan, Christine Rau, Daniele Defrere, Yvonne Ekman, Katarina Quest, Evelyne Dheliat, Janette Napper, Anje Langstraat, Grete-Lill Henden, Gaby Schar.

370 THE BRIDGE AT REMAGEN. (United Artists-1969). Lt. Phil Hartman, George Segal; Maj. Paul Kreuger, Robert Vaughn; Sgt. Angelo, Ben Gazzara; Maj. Barnes, Bradford Dillman; Brig. Gen. Shinner, E. G. Marshall; Gen Von Brock,

Peter Van Eyck; Corp. Jellicoe, Matt Clark; Col. Dent, Fritz Ford; Lt. Pattison, Tom Heaton; Corp. Grebs, Bo Hopkins; Pvt. Bissell, Robert Logan; Capt. Colt, Paul Prokop; Pvt. Slavek, Steve Sandor; Pvt. Glover, Frank Webb; Capt. Carl Schmidt, Hans Christian Blech; Joachim Hansen, Gunter Meisner, Richard Munch, Heinz Reincke, Sonja Zeimann, Vit Olmer, Rudolf Jelinek, Anna Gael.

371 THE BRIDGE IN THE JUNGLE. (United Artists-1971). Sleigh, John Huston; Gales, Charles Robinson; Angela, Katy Jurado.

372 THE BRIGAND OF KANDAHAR. (Columbia-1966). Ronald Lewis, Duncan Lamont, Catherine Woodville, Sean Lynch, Inigo Jackson, Oliver Reed, Yvonne Romain, Glyn Houston, Walter Brown, Jeremy Burnham.

373 BRIGHTY OF THE GRAND CANYON. (Feature Film Corp. of America-1967). Jim Owen, Joseph Cotten; Jake Irons, Pat Conway; Old Timer, Dick Foran; Theodore Roosevelt, Karl Swenson; Homer Hobbs, Dandy Curran.

374 BRING ME THE HEAD OF ALFREDO GARCIA. (United Artists-1974). Bennie, Warren Oates; Elita, Isela Vega; Quill, Gig Young; Sappensly, Robert Webber; Max, Helmut Dantine; El Jefe, Emilio Fernandez; Paco, Kris Kristofferson.

375 THE BROAD COALITION. (August-1972). William C. Reilly, Anita Morris, Sloan Shelton, Mary Cass, Jack Berns, George Harris, Thomas Murphy, Marybeth Ward, Jane Whitehill, Phyllicia Allen, Percy Simon, Lilly Lessing, Marcella Lowery.

376 THE BROKEN WINGS. (Continental-1968). Kahlil Gibran, Pierre Bordey; Mansour Bey Galib, Saladin Nader; Selma Karamy, Nidal Ash Kar; Ferris Affandi Karamy, Philip Akiki; Gibran's Friend, Joseph Gabrail Salim.

377 BRONCO BULLFROG. (New Yorker-1972). Del Quant, Del Walker; Irene Richardson, Anne Gooding; Jo Saville (Bronco Bullfrog), Sam Shepherd; Roy, Roy Haywood; Mrs. Richardson, Freda Shepherd; Del's Father, Dick Philpott; Chris, Chris Shepherd; Sgt. Johnson, Stuart Stones, Geoff, Geoff Wincott; Del's Uncle, J. Hughes Sr.; Parker's Friend, Trevor Oakley; Tina, Tina Syer.

378 BROTHER CARL. (New Yorker-1972). Carl, Laurent Terzieff; Lena, Gunnel Lindblom; Karen, Genevieve Page; Martin, Keve Hielm; Peter, Torsten Wahlund; Anna, Pernilla Ahlfeldt.

379 BROTHER JOHN. (Columbia-1971). John Kane, Sidney Poitier; Doc Thomas, Will Geer; Lloyd Thomas, Bradford

Dillman; Louisa MacGill, Beverly Todd; Orly Ball, Ramon Bieri; George, Warren J. Kemmerling; Henry Birkhardt, Paul Winfield.

380 BROTHER OF THE WIND. (Sun International-1973). Dick Robinson.

381 BROTHER ON THE RUN. (Southern Star-1973). Terry Carter, Gwenn Mitchell, Kyle Johnson, James Sikking, Diana Eden.

382 BROTHER SUN, SISTER MOON. (Paramount-1973). Francesco, Graham Faulkner; Clare, Judi Bowker; Pope Innocent III, Alec Guinness; Bernardo, Leigh Lawson; Paolo, Kenneth Cranham; Silvestro, Michael Feast; Giocondo, Nicholas Willatt; Pica, Valentina Cortese; Pietro di Bernardone, Lee Montague; Bishop Guido, John Sharp; Consul, Adolfo Celi; Deodato, Francesco Guerrieri.

383 No entry.

384 THE BROTHERHOOD. (Paramount-1969). Frank Ginetta, Kirk Douglas; Vince Ginetta, Alex Cord; Ida Ginetta, Irene Papas; Dominick Bertolo, Luther Adler; Emma Ginetta, Susan Strasberg; Jim Egan, Murray Hamilton; Don Peppino, Eduardo Cianelli; Pietro Rizzi, Joe De Santis; Carmela Ginetta, Connie Scott; Jake Rotherman, Val Avery; Cheech, Val Bisoglio; Sol Levin, Alan Hewitt; Vido, Barry Primus; Toto, Michele Cimarosa; Don Turridu, Louis Badolati.

385 THE BROTHERHOOD OF SATAN. (Columbia-1971). Doc, Strother Martin; Sheriff, L. Q. Jones; Ben, Charles Bateman; Nicky, Ahna Capri; Kiti, Geri Reischl; Priest, Charles Robinson; Tobey, Alvy Moore; Dame Alice, Helene Winston; Mildred, Joyce Easton; Billy Jo, Debi Storm; Stuart, Jeff Williams; Phyllis, Judy McConnell; Mike, Robert Ward; John Barclay, Patrick Sullivan Burke, Ysabel MacCloskey, Cicely Walper, Phyllis Coughlan, Anthony Joachim, Donald Journeaux, Elsie Moore, Lenore Shaenwise, Margaret Wheeler, Kevin McEveety, Alyson Moore, Sheila McEveety, Brian McEveety, Grant McGregor, Cindy Holden, Debbie Judith, Scott Aguilar, Jonathan Eisley, Robyn Grei, Linda Riffany.

386 BROTHERLY LOVE. (MGM-1970). Sir Charles Henry Arbuthnot Pinkerton Ferguson, Peter O'Toole; Hilary, Susannah York; Douglas Dow, Michael Craig; Brigadier Crieff, Harry Andrews; Dr. Maitland, Cyril Cusack; Rosie, Judy Cornwell; Jock Baird, Brian Blessed; Auctioneer, Robert Urquhart; Benny-the-Pole, Mark Malicz; Miss Mailer, Lennox Milne; Matron, Jean Anderson; Bank Lizzie, Marjorie Dalziel; Auntie Belle, Helena Gloag; Bun MacKenzie, Madeleine Christie; MacLachlan-Forbes, Roy Boutcher; Alex Smart, Peter Reeves; Storekeeper, Leonard Maguire; Alec, Paul Farrell; Miss Scott, Rona

Newton-John; Mr. Hutchinson, Ewan Roberts; Nurse, Frances de la Tour; Ambulance Driver, Patrick Gardiner; Hen Farmer, Alex McAvoy; Ginger-haired Farmer, John Malloy; Harry Jones, Geoff Golden, John Shedden, Bernadette Gallagher, Maura Keely, Clare Mullen, Eamonn Keane, Desmond Perry, Helen Norman, Wallace Campbell, Tom Irwin, Mary Larkin.

386a THE BROTHERS O'TOOLE. (CVD-1973). John Astin, Steve Carlson, Pat Carroll, Hans Conreid, Lee Meriwether, Allyn Joslyn, Richard Jury, Jesse White, Richard Erdman.

387 THE BRUTE AND THE BEAST. (American International-1968). Tom, Franco Nero; Jeff, George Hilton; Jason, Nino Castelnuovo; Brady, Lyn Shayne; Mr. Scott, John McDouglas; Mercedes, Rita Franchetti.

388 BRUTE CORPS. (General Film Corp. -1972). Ross, Paul Carr; Kevin, Joseph Kaufmann; Terry, Jennifer Billingsley; Wicks, Alex Rocco; McFarland, Michael Pataki; The Colonel, Charles Macaulay; Quinn, Roy Jensen; Hill, Felton Perry; Alvarez, Joseph Bernard; Ballard, Parker West; Cantina Owner, Paul Micale; Lupe, Edith Diaz; Beggar, Ramiro Jaloma.

389 THE BUBBLE. (Arch Obler-1967). Michael Cole, Deborah Walley, Johnny Desmond, Kassie McMahon, Barbara Eiler, Virginia Gregg, Victor Perrin, Olan Soule, Chester Jones.

390 BUCK AND THE PREACHER. (Columbia-1972). Buck, Sidney Poitier; Preacher, Harry Belafonte; Ruth, Ruby Dee; Deshay, Cameron Mitchell; Floyd, Denny Miller; Madam Esther, Nita Talbot; Sheriff, John Kelley; Headman, Tony Brubaker; Man who is shot, Bobby Johnson; Kingston, James McEachin; Cudjo, Clarence Muse; Sarah, Lynn Hamilton; Sam, Doug Johnson; Joshua, Errol John; Ken Menard, Pamela Jones, Drake Walker, Dennis Hines, Fred Waugh, Bill Shannon, Phil Adams, Walter Scott, John Howard, Enrique Lucero, Julie Robinson, Jose Carlo Ruiz, Jerry Gatlin, Ivan Scott, John Kennedy.

391 BUCKSKIN. (Paramount-1968). Chaddock, Barry Sullivan; Nora Johnson, Joan Caulfield; Rep Marlowe, Wendell Corey; Sheriff Tangley, Lon Chaney; Patch, John Russell; Sarah Cody, Barbara Hale; Doc Raymond, Barton MacLane; Frank Cody, Bill Williams; Townsman, Richard Arlen; Travis, Leo Gordon; Akii, Gerald Michenaud; Storekeeper Perkins, George Chandler; Sung Li, Aki Aleong; Jimmy Cody, Michael Larrain; Browdie, Craig Littler; Baker, James X. Mitchell; Corbin, Emile Meyer; Telegrapher, Robert Riordan; Bartender, Le Roy Johnson; Moni, Manuela Thiess.

392 BUDDHA. (Lopert-1965). Siddhartha, Kojiro Hong; Yashodhara, Charito Solis; Devadatta, Shintaro Katsu; Yashas, Machiko Kyo;

Kunala, Raizo Ichikawa; Usha, Fujiko Yamamoto; Upail, Keiza Kawasaki; Altashatru, Hiroshi Kawaguchi; Ananda, Katsuhiko Kabayashi; Auttami, Tamao Nakamura.

393 A BULLET FOR PRETTY BOY. (American International-1970). Floyd, Fabian Forte; Betty, Jocelyn Lane; Ruby, Astrid Warner; Ned, Michael Haynes; "Preacher," Adam Roarke; Hossler, Robert Glenn; Beryl, Anne MacAdams; Helen, Camilla Carr; Wallace, Jeff Alexander; Harvey, Desmond Dhooge; Huddy, Bill Thurman; Jack, Hugh Feagin; Mrs. Floyd, Jessie Lee Fulton; Mr. Floyd, James Harrell; William, Gene Ross; Bo, Ed Lo Russo; Charlie, Charlie Dell; Lester, Frank DeBenedett; Ben, Eddie Thomas; Seth, Ethan Allen; Sheriff, Troy K. Hoskins.

394 A BULLET FOR SANDOVAL. (Universal Marion-1970). Don Pedro Sandoval, Ernest Borgnine; Warner, George Hilton; Lucky Boy, Alberto De Mendozo; Padre, Leo Anchoriz; Sam, Antonio Pico; Guerico, Jose Manuel Martin; Jose, Manuel De Blas; Francisco, Manuel Miranda; Guadalupano, Gustavo Rojo.

395 A BULLET FOR THE GENERAL. (Avco Embassy-1969). El Chuncho, Gian Maria Volonte; Bill Tate, Lou Castel; El Santo, Klaus Kinski; Adelita, Martine Beswick; General Elias, Jaime Fernandez; Don Felipe, Andrea Checchi; Cirillo, Spartaco Conversi; Picaro, Joaquin Parra; Raimundo, Jose Manuel Martin; Guapo, Santiago Santos; Pedrito, Valentino Macchi.

396 BULLITT. (Warner Bros.-7 Arts-1968). Det. Lieut. Frank Bullitt, Steve McQueen; Walter Chalmers, Robert Vaughn; Cathy, Jacqueline Bisset; Detective Delgetti, Don Gordon; Weissberg, Robert Duvall; Captain Bennet, Simon Oakland; Captain Baker, Norman Fell; Dr. Willard, Georg Stanford Brown; Eddy, Justin Tarr; Detective Stanton, Carl Reindel; Ross, Felice Orlandi; Pete Ross, Victor Tayback; 1st Aide, Robert Lipton; Wescott, Ed Peck; Johnny Ross, Pat Renella; Hired Killer, Paul Genge; Killer, John Aprea; Desk Clerk, Al Checco; Phil, Bill Hickman.

397 BUMMER. (Entertainment Ventures-1973). Carol Speed, Connie Strickland, Dennis Burley, Kipp Whitman, David Buchanan, David Ankrum.

398 BUNNY LAKE IS MISSING. (Columbia-1965). Ann, Carol Lynley; Steven, Keir Dullea; Inspector Newhouse, Laurence Olivier; Wilson, Noel Coward; Ada Ford, Martita Hunt; Elvira, Anna Massey; Andrews, Clive Revill; Cook, Lucie Mannheim; Doll Maker, Finlay Currie.

399 BUNNY O'HARE. (American International-1971). Bunny O'Hare, Bette Davis; Bill Green, Ernest Borgnine; Detective Greeley, Jack Cassidy; R. J. Hart, Joan Delaney; Banker, Jay Robinson; Lulu, Reva Rose; Ad, John Astin; Commissioner

Dingle, Robert Foulk; Frank, Brayden Linden; Lola, Karen Mae Johnson; Rhett, Francis R. Cody; Elvira, Darra Lyn Tobin; Speed, Hank Wickham; State Trooper, David Cargo.

400 BUONA SERA, MRS. CAMPBELL. (United Artists-1969). Carla (Mrs. Campbell), Gina Lollobrigida; Shirley Newman, Shelley Winters; Phil Newman, Phil Silvers; Justin Young, Peter Lawford; Walter Braddock, Telly Savalas; Fritzie Braddock, Lee Grant; Gia, Janet Margolin; Lauren Young, Marian Moses; Rosa, Naomi Stevens; Vittorio, Philippe Leroy; Countess, Giovanna Galletti; Mayor, Renzo Palmer; Pete, Dale Cummings; Stubby, James Mishler.

401 THE BURGLARS. (Columbia-1972). Azad, Jean-Paul Belmondo; Abel Zacharia, Omar Sharif; Lena, Dyan Cannon; Ralph, Robert Hossein; Helene, Nicole Calfan; Renzi, Renato Salvatori; Mr. Tasco, Jose-Luis De Vallalonga; Madam Tasco, Myriam Colombi; The Caretaker, Raoul Delfosse; Malloch, Steve Eckardt; Johnny, Robert Duranton; Playboy, Daniel Verite; Restaurant Owner, Marc Arian.

402 THE BURMESE HARP. (Brandon-1967). Private Mizushima, Soji Yasui; Captain Inouye, Rentaro Mikuni; Old Woman, Taniye Kitabayashi; Defense Commander, Tatsuya Mihashi.

403 BURN. (United Artists-1970). Sir William Walker, Marlon Brando; Jose Dolores, Evaristo Marquez; Teddy Sanchez, Renato Salvatori; Shelton, Norman Hill; General Prado, Tom Lyons; Guarina, Wanani; Juanito, Joseph Persuad; Henry, Gianpiero Albertini; Jack, Carlo Palmucci; Lady Bella, Cecily Browne; Francesca, Dana Ghia; Ramon, Mauricio Rodriquez; English Major, Alejandro Obregon.

404 BURY ME AN ANGEL. (New World-1972). Dag, Dixie Peabody; Jonsie, Terry Mace; Bernie, Clyde Ventura; Killer, Stephen Wittaker; Maureen Math, Joanne Moore Jordan, Marie Denn, Dennis Peabody, Dianne Turley, Alan DeWitt, Janelle Pransky, Wayne Everett Chestnut, Dan Haggerty, Corky Williams, Beach Dickerson, David Atkins, Garry Littlejohn.

405 BUS RILEY'S BACK IN TOWN. (Universal-1965). Bus Riley, Michael Parks; Laurel, Ann-Margret; Judy, Janet Margolin; Slocum, Brad Dexter; Spencer, Crahan Denton; Mrs. Riley, Jocelyn Brando; Gussie, Kim Darby; Howie, Larry Storch; Paula, Mimsy Farmer; Carlotta, Brett Somers; Mrs. Nichols, Nan Martin; Mrs. Spencer, Ethel Griffies; Joy, Lisabeth Hush; Housewife, Alice Pearce; Benji, Chet Stratton; Stretch, David Carradine; Egg Foo, Marc Cavell; Mr. Griswald, Parley Baer.

406 THE BUSHBABY. (MGM-1970). Jackie Leeds, Margaret Brooks; Tembo, Louis Gossett; John Leeds, Donald Houston; Prof. "Cranky" Crankshaw, Laurence Naismith; The Hadj,

Marne Maitland; Tilison, Geoffrey Baildon; Ardsley, Jack Gwillim; Rev. Barlow, Noel Howlett; Policeman, Tommy Ansah; Bus Woman, Jumoke Debayo; Steward, Harold Goodwin; Gideon, Charles Hyatt; Police Sergeant, Willy Jonah; First Officer, Simon Lack; Barman, Victor Maddern; Policeman, Illario Pedro; Captain, Martin Wyldeck.

407 BUSHMAN. (American Film Institute-1971). Paul Eyam, Nzie Okpokam, Elaine Featherstone, Timothy Near, Jack Nance, Ann Scofield.

408 BUSTER AND BILLIE. (Columbia-1974). Buster Lane, Jan-Michael Vincent; Billie, Joan Goodfellow; Margie Hooks, Pamela Sue Martin; Jake, Clifton James; Whitey, Robert Englund; Mrs. Lane, Jessie Lee Fulton; Mr. Lane, J. B. Joiner; Warren, Dell C. Payne.

409 BUSTING. (United Artists-1974). Elliott Gould, Robert Blake, Allen Garfield, Antonio Fargas, Michael Lerner, Sid Haig, Ivor Francis, William Sylvester, Logan Ramsey, Richard X. Slattery, Margo Winkler, John Lawrence, Cornelia Sharp, Erin O'Reilly, Danny Goldman, Nick St. Nicholas, Ibycus, Howard Platt, Jack Knight, Mimi Doyle, Jessica Rains, Carl Eller, John Furlong, Kai Hernandez, Napoleon Whiting, Andy Stone, Dominique Pinassi, Ron Cummins, Elaine Partnow, Karen Anders, Dee Carroll.

410 THE BUSY BODY. (Paramount-1967). George Norton, Sid Caesar; Charley Barker, Robert Ryan; Margo Foster, Anne Baxter; Ma Norton, Kay Medford; Murray Foster, Jan Murray; Whittaker, Richard Pryor; Bobbi Brody, Arlene Golonka; Fred Harwell, Charles McGraw; Felix Rose, Ben Blue; Kurt Brock, Dom De Luise; Archie Brody, Bill Dana; Mike, Godfrey Cambridge; Willie, Marty Ingels; Mr. Fessel, George Jessel; Mrs. Fessel, Audrie Magee; First Cop, Mickey Deems; Woman No. 1, Choo Choo Collins; Mr. Merriwether, Paul Wexler; Marcia Woshikowski, Marina Koshetz; Board Members, Norman Bartold, Mike Wagner, Larry Gelman, Don Brodie.

411 BUTCH CASSIDY AND THE SUNDANCE KID. (20th Century-Fox-1969). Butch Cassidy, Paul Newman; The Sundance Kid, Robert Redford; Etta Place, Katharine Ross; Percy Garris, Strother Martin; Bike Salesman, Henry Jones; Sheriff Bledsoe, Jeff Corey; Woodcock, George Furth; Agnes, Cloris Leachman; Harvey Logan, Ted Cassidy; Marshall, Kenneth Mars; Macon, Donnelly Rhodes; Large Woman, Jody Gilbert; News Carver, Timothy Scott; Fireman, Don Keefer; Flat Nose Curry, Charles Dierkop; Bank Manager, Francisco Cordova; Photographer, Nelson Olmstead; Card Players, Paul Bryar and Sam Elliott; Bank Teller, Charles Akins; Tiffany's Salesman, Eric Sinclair.

412 BUTLEY. (American Film Theatre-1974). Alan Bates,

Jessica Tandy, Richard O'Callaghan, Susan Engel, Michael Byrne, Georgina Hale, Simon Rouse, John Savident, Oliver Maguire, Colin Haigh, Darien Angadi, Susan Woodridge, Lindsay Ingram, Patti Love, Belinda Low.

413 BUTTERFLIES ARE FREE. (Columbia-1972). Jill Tanner, Goldie Hawn; Don Baker, Edward Albert; Mrs. Baker, Eileen Heckart; Ralph Austin, Michael Glaser; Roy, Mike Warren; Jessica Rains, Paul Ryan, Charlene Jones, Sandra Vacey.

414 BWANA TOSHI. (Brandon-1970). Toshi, Kiyoshi Atsumi; Onishi, Tsutomu Shimoto; Hamisi Salehi, Bibi Agnes, Haide Gitaposta, Gilba Haide.

415 BYE BYE BRAVERMAN. (Warner Bros. -7 Arts-1968). Morroe Rieff, George Segal; Barnet Weiner, Jack Warden; Inez Braverman, Jessica Walter; Myra Mandelbaum, Phyllis Newman; Taxi Cab Driver, Godfrey Cambridge; Felix Ottensteen, Joseph Wiseman; Holly Levine, Sorrell Booke; Etta Rieff, Zohra Lampert; Max Ottensteen, Anthony Holland; Pilar, Susan Wyler; Custodian, Lieb Lensky; The Rabbi, Alan King.

416 C. C. AND COMPANY. (Avco Embassy-1970). C. C. Ryder, Joe Namath; Ann McCalley, Ann-Margret; Moon, William Smith; Pom Pom, Jennifer Billingsley; Eddie Ellis, Don Chastain; Pig, Teda Bracci; Rabbit, Mike Battle; Crow, Sid Haig; Lizard, Greg Mullavey; Capt. Midnight, Bruce Glover; Suicide Sam, Ted King; Sitting Bull, Gary Littlejohn; Kraut, Frank Noel; Eva, Kiva Kelly; Zit Zit, Jackie Rohr; Charlie Hopkins, Bob Keyworth; Wayne Cochran and the C. C. Rider.

417 CABARET. (Allied Artists-1972). Sally Bowles, Liza Minnelli; Brian Roberts, Michael York; Maximilian von Heune, Helmut Griem; Master of Ceremonies, Joel Grey; Fritz Wendel, Fritz Wepper; Natalia Landauer, Marisa Berenson; Fraulein Schneider, Elisabeth Neumann-Viertel; Fraulein Mayr, Sigrid von Richthofen; Fraulein Kost, Helen Vita; Bobby, Gerd Vespermann; Herr Ludwig, Ralf Wolter; Willi, Georg Hartmann; Elke, Ricky Renee; Cantor, Estrongo Nachama; Gorilla, Louise Quick; The Kit-Kat Dancers, Kathryn Doby, Inge Jaeger, Angelika Koch, Helen Velkovorska, Gitta Schmidt and Louise Quick.

418 CACTUS FLOWER. (Columbia-1969). Julian Winston, Walter Matthau; Stephanie Dickinson, Ingrid Bergman; Toni Simmons, Goldie Hawn; Harvey Greenfield, Jack Weston; Igor Sullivan, Rick Lenz; Senor Sanchez, Vito Scotti; Mrs. Durant, Irene Hervey; Georgia, Eve Bruce; Store Manager, Irwin Charone; Nephew, Matthew Saks.

419 CACTUS IN THE SNOW. (General Film Corp. -1971). Harley, Richard Thomas; Cissy, Mary Layne; Mrs. Sawyer,

Lucille Benson; Mr. Albert, Oscar Beregi; Pharmacist, Jan Burrell; Dolores, Ruby Dake; Mr. Harris, Joseph Di Reda; Drill Instructor, Hugh Fischer; Mr. Murray, Dennis Fimple; Seymour, Dan Halleck; Cal, Stan Kamber; Rhoda, Maggie King; Cab Driver, Tiger Joe Marsh; Joe, Gregory Mead; George, Christopher Mitchum; Valerie, Beatriz Monteil; Mrs. Harris, Tani Phelps.

420 CAGED VIRGINS. (Boxoffice International-1973). Marie Castel, Mireille D'Argent, Philippe Gaste, Dominique.

421 CAHILL, UNITED STATES MARSHALL. (Warner Bros.-1973). Cahill, John Wayne; Fraser, George Kennedy; Danny Cahill, Gary Grimes; Lightfoot, Neville Brand; Billy Joe Cahill, Clay O'Brien; Mrs. Green, Marie Windsor; Struther, Morgan Paull; MacDonald, Royal Dano; Ben Tildy, Scott Walker; Denver, Denver Pyle; Charlie Smith, Jackie Coogan; Pee Wee Simser, Rayford Barnes; Joe Meehan, Dan Kemp; Hank, Harry Carey Jr.; Sheriff Grady, Walter Barnes; Old Man, Paul Fix; Hard Case, Pepper Martin; Negro, Vance Davis; Boy, Ken Wolger; Undertaken, Hank Worden; Doctor, James Nusser; Deputy Gordine, Murray MacLeod; Deputy Jim Kane, Hunter von Leer.

422 CALIFORNIA SPLIT. (Columbia-1974). Bill Denny, George Segal; Charlie Waters, Elliott Gould; Barbara Miller, Ann Prentiss; Susan Peters, Gwen Welles; Lew, Edward Walsh; Sparkie, Joseph Walsh; Helen Brown, Bert Remsen; Lady on Bus, Barbara London; Reno Bar Maid, Barbara Ruick.

423 CALLIOPE. (Moonstone-1971). Groupie, Sherry Miles; Rock musician, Mark Gottlieb; Clerk, Sherry Bain; Boss, Marty Huston; Housewife, Dwen Van Dam; Husband, Lou Epton; Cultist, Diana Jones; Black Revolutionary, Shelly Fisher; Actress, Choo Choo Collins; Producer, Borah Silver; Snoopy Lady, Marjorie Bennett; Chauffeur, Stan Rose.

424 CAMELOT. (Warner Bros.-7 Arts). King Arthur, Richard Harris; Guenevere, Vanessa Redgrave; Lancelot Du Lac, Franco Nero; Mordred, David Hemmings; King Pellinore, Lionel Jeffries; Merlyn, Laurence Naismith; Dap, Pierre Olaf; Lady Clarinda, Estelle Winwood; Sir Lionel, Gary Marshal; Sir Dinaden, Anthony Rogers; Sir Sagramore, Peter Bromilow; Lady Sybil, Sue Casey; Tom of Warwick, Gary Marsh; King Arthur as a boy, Nicolas Beauvy.

425 THE CAMERONS. (1974). Shona Cameron, Lois Marshall; Donald Cameron, Joseph McKenna; Neil Cameron, Paul Kelly; Vicky, Elissa Watsman; Aunt Jane, Joan Fitzpatrick; Police Inspector, Bill Denniston; Police Sergeant, George McLennan; Mr. Cameron, Michael Elder; 1st Crook, Jake D'Arcy; 2nd Crook, Robin Lefevre; 3rd Crook, Peter Lincoln; Train Guard, Willy Joss.

426 CAMILLE 2000. (Audubon-1969). Marguerite Gautier, Daniele Gaubert; Armand Duval, Nino Castelnuovo; Prudence, Eleanora Rossi-Drago; DeVarville, Philippe Forquet; Gaston, Roberto Bisacco; Armand's Father, Massimo Serato; Olympe, Silvana Venturelli; Gody, Zachary Adams.

427 CAMPER JOHN. (Cinemation-1973). William Smith, Joe Flynn, Gene Evans, Barbara Luna.

428 CAN HEIRONYMUS MERKIN EVER FORGET MERCY HUMPPE AND FIND TRUE HAPPINESS? (Regional-1969). Heironymus Merkin, Anthony Newley; Polyester Poontang, Joan Collins; Good Time Eddie Filth, Milton Berle; The Presence, George Jessel; Fat Writer, Stubby Kaye; Uncle Limelight, Bruce Forsyth; Grandma, Patricia Hayes; Sharpnose, Victor Spinetti; Producer Ron, Rom Stern; Mercy Humppe, Connie Kreski; Filigree Fondle, Judy Cornwell; Fran, Berri Cornish; The Mask, Roy Desmond; Automation Bunny, Sally Douglas; Philip Bluster, Desmond Walter Ellis; Miss Maidenhead Fern, Gilly Frant; Marge, Isabel Hurll; Penelope, Rosaline Knight; Harriet, Aleta Morrison; Producer Peter, Louis Negin; Thumbelina, Tara Newley; Thaxted, Alexander Newley; Little Assistance, Margaret Nolan; The Red Cardinal, Julian Orchard; Bentley, Ronald Radd; Skinny Writer, Ronald Rubin.

429 CANCEL MY RESERVATION. (Warner Bros. -1972). Dan Bartlett, Bob Hope; Sheila Bartlett, Eva Marie Saint; John Ed, Ralph Bellamy; Reese, Forrest Tucker; Crazy Hollister, Anne Archer; Sheriff Tom Riley, Keenan Wynn; Chief Old Bear, Chief Dan George; Joe Little Cloud, Henry Darrow; Cactus Jones, Doodles Weaver; Mary Little Cloud, Betty Carr; Snagby, Herb Vigran; Yamamoto, Pat Morita; Willoughby Sparker, Gordon Oliver; Doc Morton, Buster Shaefer; Dr. Kaufman, Paul Bogart; Guest Stars, John Wayne, Flip Wilson, Bing Crosby, Johnny Carson.

430 THE CANDIDATE. (Warner Bros. -1972). Bill McKay, Robert Redford; Marvin Lucas, Peter Boyle; Senator Crocker Jarmon, Don Porter; Howard Klein, Allen Garfield; John J. McKay, Melvyn Douglas; Nancy McKay, Karen Carlson; Rich Jenkin, Quinn Redeker; Henderson, Morgan Upton; Paul Corliss, Michael Lerner; Starkey, Kenneth Tobey; David, Chris Prey; Neil Atkinson, Joe Miksak; Lynn, Jenny Sullivan; Pilot, Tom Dahlgren; Station Master, Gerald Hiken; Mabel, Leslie Allen; Groupie, Susan Demott; Boy in Commercial, Jason Goodrow; Jaime, Robert De Anda; Fleischer, Robert Goldsby; Wilson, Michael Barnicle; Large Girl, Lois Foraker; Watts Heckler, David Moody; Man in Urinal, George Meyer; Magazine Editor, Dudley Knight; As Themselves: Natalie Wood, Barry Sullivan, Senator Hubert H. Humphrey, Senator George McGovern, Senator John V. Tunney, Mayor Sam Yorty, Howard K. Smith, Van Amberg, Jesse Bimbaum, Senator Alan Cranston, Maury Green, Lu Hurley, Assemblyman Walter Karabian.

431 No entry.

432 CANDIDATE FOR MURDER. (Lester Schoenfeld Films-1968). Donald Edwards, Michael Gough; Helene Edwards, Erika Remberg; Kersten, Hans Borsody; Robert Vaughn, John Justin; Phillips, Paul Whitsun-Jones; Betty Conlon, Vanda Godsell; Police Inspector, Jerold Wells; Jacqueline, Annika Wills; Barman, Victor Charrington; Chauffeur, Ray Smith.

433 CANDY. (Cinerama-1968). Candy, Ewa Aulin; The Hunchback, Charles Aznavour; Grindl, Marlon Brando; McPhisto, Richard Burton; Dr. Krankeit, James Coburn; Dr. Dunlap, John Huston; General Smight, Walter Matthau; Emmanuel, Ringo Starr; Daddy/Uncle Jack, John Astin; Aunt Livia, Elsa Martinelli; Zero, Sugar Ray Robinson; Jonathan J. John, Enrico Maria Salerno; Nurse Bullock, Anita Pallenberg; Silvia, Lea Padovani; Lolita, Florinda Bolkan; Conchita, Marilu Tolo; Marquita, Nicoletta Machiavelli; 1st Hood, Umberto Orsini; The Cop, Joey Forman; The Sergeant, Fabian Dean; Miss Quimby, Peggy Nathan; Harold, Neal Noorlac; Luther, Peter Dane; 1st Weirdo, Tony Foutz; 2nd Weirdo, Tom Keyes; Girl, Micaela Pignatelli; Dr. Harris, Mark Salvage; 2nd Hood, Enzo Fiermonte; Members of the Living Theatre.

434 THE CANDY SNATCHERS. (GFC-1973). Tiffany Bolling, Ben Piazza, Susan Sennet, Brad David, Vincent Martorano.

435 CANDY STRIPE NURSES. (New World-1974). Candice Rialson, Robin Mattson, Maria Rojo, Kimberly Hyde, Roger Cruz, Rick Gates, Rod Haase, Don Keefer, Dick Miller, Stanley Ralph Ross, Monte Landis, Tom Baker, John David Garfield, Alma Baltran, Kendrew Lascelles, Michael Ross Verona, Elana Casey, John Hudson, Ruth Warshawski, June Christopher, Al Alu, Ray Galvin, Frank Lugo, Rick Garcia, Bill Erwin, Tara Strohmeier.

436 CANNIBAL GIRLS. (American International-1973). Cliff, Eugene Levy; Gloria, Andrea Martin; Reverend, Ronald Ulrich; Anthea, Randall Carpenter; Clarissa, Bonnie Neilson; Leona, Mira Pawluk; Sheriff, Bob McHeady; 1st Victim, Alan Gordon; 2nd Victim, Allan Price; 3rd Victim, Earl Pomerantz; Mrs. Wainwright, May Jarvis.

437 CANNON FOR CORDOBA. (United Artists-1970). Capt. Rod Douglas, George Peppard; Leonora, Giovanna Ralli; Cordoba, Raf Vallone; Andy, Pete Duel; Sgt. Harkness, Don Gordon; Peter, Nico Minardos; Brig. Gen. Pershing, John Russell; Sophia, Francine York; Harry, John Larch; Riggs, Charles Stainaker; Maj. Wall, John Clark; Lt. Guiterrez, Gabrielle Tinti; Svedborg, Hans Meyer.

438 THE CAPER OF THE GOLDEN BULLS. (Embassy-1967). Peter Churchman, Stephen Boyd; Grace Harvey, Yvette

Mimieux; Angela Tresler, Giovanna Ralli; Antonio Gonzales, Walter Slezak; Francois Morel, Vito Scotti; Philippe Lemoins, Clifton James; Paul Brissard, Lomax Study; Canalli, Tom Toner; Bendell, Henry Beckman; Ryan, Noah Keen; Carlos, Jay Novello; Mr. Shahari, Arnold Moss; Morchek, Leon Askin.

439 CAPRICE. (20th Century-Fox-1967). Patricia Fowler, Doris Day; Christopher White, Richard Harris; Stuart Clancy, Ray Walston; Matthew Cutter, Jack Kruschen; Sir Jason Fox, Edward Mulhare; Madame Piasco, Lilia Skala; Su Ling, Irene Tsu; Inspector Kapinsky, Larry D. Mann; Auber, Maurice Marsac; Butler, Michael (Prince) Romanoff; Mandy, Lisa Seagram; Barney, Michael J. Pollard; Swiss Innkeeper, Fritz Feld.

440 CAPRICIOUS SUMMER. (Sigma III-1968). Dura, Rudolf Hrusinsky; The Major, Vlastimil Brodsky; Durova, Mila Myslikova; The Abbe, Frantisek Rehak; Anna, Jana Drchalova; The Tightrope Walker, Jiri Menzel.

441 CAPTAIN APACHE. (Scotia Internationa. -1971). Capt. Apache, Lee Van Cleef; Maude, Carroll Baker; Griffin, Stuart Whitman; Moon, Percy Herbert; Rosita, Elisa Montes; Snake, Tony Vogel; O'Rourke, Charles Stalnaker; Sanchez, Charlie Bravo; Abigail, Faith Clift; Al, Dan Van Husen; Ben, D. Pollock; Gen Ryland, Hugh McDermott; Sheriff, George Margo; General, Jose Bodalo; Witch, Elsa Zabala; Maitre D', Allen Russell; Ezekiel, Luis Induni; Diablo, Vito Salier; Guitarist, Fernando Sanchez Pollack.

442 CAPTAIN KRONOS: VAMPIRE HUNTER. (Paramount-1974). Kronos, Horst Janson; Dr. Marcus, John Carson; Paul Durward, Shane Briant; Carla, Caroline Munro; Prof. Grost, John Cater; Sara Durward, Lois Daine; Lady Durward, Wanda Ventham; Kerro, Ian Hendry.

443 CAPTAIN MILKSHAKE. (Twi-National-1972). Paul Fredericks, Geoff Gage; Melissa Hamilton, Andrea Gagan; Thesp, David Korn; Anchovy, Ronald Barca; Evelyn, Evelyn King; Mrs. Fredericks, Belle Greer; Mrs. Randolph, Joanne Moore Jordan; Mrs. Hamilton, Darlene Conley; Uncle Jimson, James Ashton; Cabby, Stuart Lancaster; Mr. Toliver, Wally Starr; Priest, Buddy Pantsari; Lightning, Barry Leichtling; Frank, Rob Reece; Kip, Kip Winsett; Border Guards, Hal Neilsen and James Hourigan; Bubber, Paul Lagos; O. B., Edward O'Brien; Loose George, George Driver.

444 CAPTAIN NEMO AND THE UNDERWATER CITY. (MGM-1970). Capt. Nemo, Robert Ryan; Fraser, Chuck Connors; Helena, Nanette Newman; Mala, Luciana Paluzzi; Barnaby, Bill Fraser; Swallow, Kenneth Connor; Joab, John Turner; Lomax, Allan Cuthbertson; Philip, Christopher Hartstone;

Mate/Navigator, Vincent Harding; Engineer, Ralph Nosseck; Michael McGovern, Alan Barry, Anthony Bailey, Ann Patrice, Margot Ley, Patsy Snell.

445 LES CARABINIERS. (West End-1968). Venus, Genevieve Galea; Cleopatra, Catherine Ribero; Michelangelo, Marino Mase; Ulysses, Albert Juross; 1st Carabinier, Gerard Poirot; 2nd Carabinier, Jean Brassat; 3rd Carabinier, Alvaro Gheri.

446 CARAVAN TO VACCARES. (20th Century Fox-1974). Lila, Charlotte Rampling; Neil Bowman, David Birney; Duc de Croytor, Michel Lonsdale; Henri Dzerda, Marcel Bozzuffi; Stefan Zuger, Michael Bryant; Ricardo, Manitas de Plata; Ferenc, Serge Marquand; Cecile, Marianne Eggerick; Stella, Francoise Brion; 1st Guardian, Vania Vilers; Helicopter Pilot, Graham Hill; Ricardo, Jean-Pierre Cargol; Pierre, Jean-Pierre Castaldi; Waiter, Jean Michaux; Receptionist, Alan Scott; Gendarme; Jean-Yves Gauthier; Marcella Markham and Gordon Tanner.

447 CAREER BED. (Provocative-1972). Susan, Liza Duran; Emily, Honey Hunter; Bob, James David; Miss Reynolds, Merle Miller; Jack, John Cardoza; David, Donald Walters; Gerald, Stioge Glyspayne; Ross, Charles Carlton Buffum; Waiter, Lance Hirsch; Boris, Dennis Lord; Actor, Jeff Reed; Reporter, Gale McCarty; New Girl, Anna Welles.

448 CARESSED. (Brenner-1965). Robert Howay, Angela Gann, Lannie Beckman, Carol Pastinsky, Bob Silverman.

449 THE CAREY TREATMENT. (MGM-1972). Dr. Peter Carey, James Coburn; Georgia Hightower, Jennifer O'Neill; Captain Pearson, Pat Hingle; Nurse Angela Holder, Skye Aubrey; Evelyn Randall, Elizabeth Allen; Dr. Murphy, John Fink; Dr. J. D. Randall, Dan O'Herlily; Dr. David Tao, James Hong; Dr. Joshua Randall, Alex Dreier; Roger Hudson, Michael Blodgett; Sanderson, Regis Toomey; Walding, Steve Carlson; Janet Tao, Rosemary Edelman; Lydia Barrett, Jennifer Edwards; Dr. Jenkins, John Hillerman; Dr. Barr, Robert Mandan; Blaine, Warren Parker; Harvey William Randall, Robie Porter; Dr. Weston, Morgan Sterne; Karen Randall, Melissa Torme-March.

450 CARMEN, BABY. (Audubon-1967). Carmen, Uta Levka; Policeman, Claude Ringer; Medico, Carl Mohner; Dolores, Barbara Velentine; Baby Lucas, Walter Wiltz; Misty, Christiane Rucker; Magistrate, Michael Munzer; Darcy, Doris Pistek.

451 CARNAL KNOWLEDGE. (Avco Embassy-1971). Jonathan, Jack Nicholson; Susan, Candice Bergen; Sandy, Arthur Garfunkel; Bobbie, Anne-Margret; Louise, Rita Moreno; Cindy, Cynthia O'Neal; Jennifer, Carol Kane.

452 CARRY ON CABBY. (Governor-1967). Charlie Hawkins,

Sidney James; Peggy Hawkins, Hattie Jacques; Ted Watson, Kenneth Connor; "Pintpot" Tankard, Charles Hawtrey; Flo, Esma Cannon; Sally, Liz Fraser; Smiley Sims, Bill Owen; Len, Milo O'Shea; "Battleaxe," Judith Furse; Aristocratic Lady, Ambrosine Phillpotts; Renee Houston, Jim Dale, Amanda Barrie, Carole Shelley, Cyril Chamberlain, Norman Chappel, Peter Gilmore, Michael Ward, Noel Dyson, Michael Nightingale, Ian Wilson, Peter Byrne, Darryl Kavann, Peter Jesson, Don McCorkindale, Charles Stanley, Marion Collins, Frank Forsyth.

453 CARRY ON CAMPING. (American International-1972). Sid Boggle, Sidney James; Dr. Soper, Kenneth Williams; Joan Fussey, Joan Sims; Charlie Muggins, Charles Hawtrey; Bernie Lugg, Bernard Bresslaw; Peter Potter, Terry Scott; Babs, Barbara Windsor; Miss Haggerd, Hattie Jacques; Joshua Fiddler, Peter Butterworth; Jim Tanner, Julian Holloway; Harriet Potter, Betty Marsden; Anthea Meeks, Dilys Laye; Sally, Trisha Noble; Fanny, Sandra Caron.

454 CARRY ON CLEO. (Governor-1965). Mark Anthony, Sidney James; Cleo, Amanda Barrie; Julius Caesar, Kenneth Williams; Calpurnia, Joan Sims; Hengist, Kenneth Connor; Seneca, Charles Hawtrey; Horsa, Jim Dale; Gloria, Julie Stevens; Sergeant Major, Victor Maddern; Senna, Sheila Hancock; Bilius, David Davenport; Archimedes, Michael Ward.

455 CARRY ON DOCTOR. (American International-1972). Francis, Frankie Howerd; Charlie, Sidney James; Dr. Tinkle, Kenneth Williams; Barron, Charles Hawtrey; Dr. Kilmore, Jim Dale; Sandra, Barbara Windwor; Matron, Hattie Jacques; Chloe, Joan Sims; Nurse, Anita Harris; Ken, Bernard Bresslaw; Smith, Peter Butterworth; Sister Hoggett, June Jago; Mavis, Dilys Laye.

456 CARRY ON HENRY VIII. (American International-1972). Henry VIII, Sidney James; Sir Thomas Cromwell, Kenneth Williams; Marie of Normandy, Joan Sims; Sir Roger de Loggerley, Charles Hawtrey; Cardinal Wolsey, Terry Scott; Bettina, Barbara Windsor; Lord Hampton of Wick, Kenneth Connor; Sir Thomas, Julian Holloway; King Francis, Peter Gilmore; Duc de Pincenay, Julian Orchard; Gertan Klauber, David Davenport, William Mervyn, Margaret Nolan, Derek Francis, Bill Maynard, Norman Chappel, Douglas Ridley, Dave Prowse, Leon Greene, Brian Wilde, Monica Dietrich, Marjie Lawrence, Patsy Rowlands, Peter Butterworth, Billy Cornelius, Alan Curtis, David Essex, William McGuirk, John Clive, John Bluthal, Peter Rigby, Trevor Roberts, Peter Munt, Anthony Sagar, Jane Cardew, Valerie Shute.

457 CARRY ON SPYING. (Governor-1965). Desmond Simkins, Kenneth Williams; Harold Crump, Bernard Cribbins; Charlie Bind, Charles Hawtrey; Daphne Honeybutt, Barbara Windsor;

The Fat Man, Eric Pohlmann; The Chief, Eric Barker; Lila, Dilys Laye; Carstairs, Jim Dale; Cobley, Richard Wattis; Dr. Crow, Judith Furse; Milchmann, Victor Maddern; Prof. Stark, Frank Forsyth; Code Clerk, Gertan Klauber; Headwaiter, John Bluthal; Cigarette Girl, Jill Mai Meredith; Elderly Woman, Norah Gordon; Native Policeman, Norman Mitchell; Angela Ellison, Hugh Futcher, Tom Clegg, Renee Houston, Derek Sydney.

458 CASANOVA '70. (Embassy-1965). Maj. Andrea Rossi-Colombetti, Marcello Mastroianni; Gigliola, Virna Lisi; Noelle, Michele Mercier; Thelma, Marisa Mell; Count Ferreri, Marco Ferreri; Psychoanalyst, Enrico Maria Salerno; Addolorata, Yolanda Modio; Airline Stewardess, Seyna Seyn; Santina, Moira Orfei; Lion Tamer, Liana Orfei; Dolly Greenwater, Margaret Lee; Gen Greenwater, Frank Gregory; Chambermaid, Rosemarie Dexter.

459 THE CASE OF THE NAVES BROTHERS. (Europix International-1972). Joachim Naves, Raul Cortez; Sebastian Naves, Juca De Oliveira; Lieutenant, Anselmo Duarte; Joao Alamy Filko, John Herbert; Mother, Lila Abramo; Judge, Sergio Hingst; Cacilda Lamoza.

460 CASINO ROYALE. (Columbia-1967). Sir James Bond, David Niven; Evelyn Tremble (007), Peter Sellers; Vesper Lynd (007), Ursula Andress; Le Chiffre, Orson Welles; Mata Bond, Joanna Pettet; The Detainer (007), Daliah Lavi; Jimmy Bond (Dr. Noah), Woody Allen; Cooper (007), Terence Cooper; Moneypenny, Barbara Bouchet; Lady Fiona, Deborah Kerr; Ransome, William Holden; Le Grand, Charles Boyer; McTarry, John Huston; Smernov, Kurt Kasznar; Himself, George Raft; French Legionnaire, Jean-Paul Belmondo; Scottish Piper, Peter O'Toole; Angela Scoular, Gabriella Licudi, Tracey Crisp, Elaine Taylor, Jackie Bisset, Alexandra Bastedo, Anna Quayle, Stirling Moss, Derek Nimmo, Ronnie Corbett, Colin Gordon, Bernard Cribbins, Tracy Reed, John Bluthal, Geoffrey Bayldon, John Wells, Duncan Macrae, Graham Stark, Chic Murray, Jonathan Routh, Richard Wattis, Vladek Sheybal, Percy Herbert, Penny Riley, Jeanne Roland.

461 CAST A GIANT SHADOW. (United Artists-1966). David "Mickey" Marcus, Kirk Douglas; Magda Simon, Senta Berger; Emma Marcus, Angie Dickinson; Major Safir, James Donald; Ram Oren, Stathis Giallelis; Jacob Ibn Kader, Haym Topol; Mrs. Chaison, Ruth White; James MacAfee, Gordon Jackson; British Ambassador, Michael Hordern; British Immigration Officers on the Beach, Jeremy Kemp and Sean Barrett; Michael Shillo, Rina Ganor, Roland Barthrop, Vera Dolen, Robert Gardett, Michael Balston, Claude Aliotti, Samra Dedes, Michael Shagrir, Frank Lattimore, Ken Buckle, Rodd Dana, Robert Ross, Arthur Hansell, Don Sturkie; with Guest appearances by Yul Brynner, John Wayne, Frank Sinatra; Hillel

Rave, Shlomo Hermon.

462 THE CASTAWAY COWBOY. (Buena Vista-1974). Lincoln Costain, James Garner; Henrietta MacAvoy, Vera Miles; Bryson, Robert Culp; Booton MacAvoy, Eric Shea; Liliha, Elizabeth Smith; Kimo, Manu Tupou; Marrujo, Gregory Sierra; Captain Cary, Shug Fisher; Malakoma, Nephi Hannemann; Lito Capina, Ralph Hanalei, Kahana, Lee Wood, Luis Delgado, Buddy Joe Hooker, Patrick Sullivan Burke.

463 THE CASTLE. (Continental-1969). K., Maximilian Schell; Frieda, Cordula Trantow; Innkeeper's Wife, Trudik Daniel; Burgel, Helmut Qualtinger; Arthur, Franz Misar; Jeremiah, Johann Misar; Landlord, Hans Ernst Jager; Mayor, Friedfrich Maurer; Mizzi, Else Ehser; Olga, Iva Janzurova; Martha Wallner, George Lehn, Karl Hellmer, Ilse Kunkele, Benno Hoffmann, E. O. Fuhrmann, Leo Mally, Hans Possenbacher, Armand Ozory.

464 CASTLE KEEP. (Columbia-1969). Major Abraham Falconer, Burt Lancaster; Sgt. Orlando Rossi, Peter Falk; Capt. Lionel Beckman, Patrick O'Neal; Comte de Maldorais, Jean Pierre Aumont; Therese, Astrid Heeren; Cpl. Ralph Clearboy, Scott Wilson; Lt. Adam B. Amberjack, Tony Bill; Sgt. Juan De Vaca, Michael Conrad; Lt. Billy Byron Bix, Bruce Dern; Pfc. Alistair Benjamin, Al Freeman Jr.; James Patterson, Caterina Boratto, Karen Blanguernon, Maria Danube, Elizabeth Darius, Merja Allanen, Anne Marie Moscovenko, Elizabeth Teissier, Eye Tuuli, Bisera Vukotic, Jancika Kovac, Ernest Clark, Harry Baird, David Jones, Jean Gimello.

465 CASTLE OF EVIL. (United Pictures-1967). Matt Granger, Scott Brady; Sable, Virginia Mayo; Robert Hawley, David Brian; Carol Harris, Lisa Gaye; Dr. Corozal, Hugh Marlowe; Lupe, Shelley Morrison; Tunki, Ernest Sarracino; Electronic Man, William Thourlby; Machado, Natividad Vacio.

466 CASTLE OF PURITY. (Azteca-1974). Claudio Brook, Rita Macede, Arturo Beristain, Diana Bracho, Gladys Bermejo.

467 THE CAT. (Embassy-1966). Pete Kilby, Roger Perry; Martha Kilby, Peggy Ann Garner; Walt Kilby, Barry Coe; Toby, Dwayne Redlin; Bill Krim, George "Shug" Fisher; Art, Ted Darby; Jesse, John Todd Roberts; Sheriff Vern, Richard Webb; Mike, Les Bradley.

468 CAT AND MOUSE. (Evergreen-1970). Young Mahike, Lars Brandt; Older Mahike, Peter Brandt; Pilenz, Wolfgang Neuss; Tulla, Claudia Bremer; Klohse, Herbert Weisbach; Aunt, Ingrid van Bergen; Pilot, Michael Hinz; Lt.-Cmdr., Helmut Kircher.

469 THE CAT ATE THE PARAKEET. (KEP-1972). Philip Pine,

Robert Mantell, Madelyn Keen, Dawn Frame, Martin Margules, Sheila Brennan, Arthur Batanides, Paul Appleby, Jane Uhrig, Barbara Bartelme, Jeffery Caron, Barbara James, Scott Campbell, Bert Conway, Victor R. Schulte, Honeycomb.

470 CAT BALLOU. (Columbia-1965). Cat Ballou, Jane Fonda; Kid Shellen/Silvernose, Lee Marvin; Clay Boone, Michael Callan; Jed, Dwayne Hickman; Jackson Two-Bear, Tom Nardini; Frankie Ballou, John Marley; Sir Harry Percival, Reginald Denny; Sheriff Cardigan, Jay C. Flippen; Butch Cassidy, Arthur Hunnicutt; Sheriff Maledon, Bruce Cabot; Accuser, Burt Austin; Train Messenger, Paul Gilbert; Balladeers, Nat King Cole, Stubby Kaye.

471 CAT IN THE SACK. (Pathe Contemporary-1967). Claude, Barbara Ulrich; Claude, Claude Godbout.

472 No entry.

473 CATALINA CAPER. (Crown International-1968). Don Pringle, Tommy Kirk; Arthur Duval, Del Moore; Tad Duval, Peter Duryea; Fingers O'Toole, Robert Donner; Katrina, Ulla Stromstedt; Larry Colvis, Jim Begg; Anne Duval, Sue Casey; Tina Moss, Venita Wolf; Charlie Moss, Brian Cutler; Borman, Peter Mamakos; Angelo, Lyle Waggoner; Lakopolous, Lee Deane; Bob Draper, Mike Blodgett; Redhead, Bonnie Lomann; Brunette, Britt Nilsson; Blonde, Donna Russell; Sid, James Almanzar; Carol Connors, Little Richard, Adrian Teen Models, The Cascades.

474 CATCH MY SOUL. (Cinerama-1974). Othello, Richie Havens; Iago, Lance LeGault; Desdemona, Season Hubley; Cassio, Tony Joe White; Emilia, Susan Tyrrell; Delany Bramlett, Bonnie Bramlett, Raleigh Gardenshire, Wayne "Eagle" Waterhouse, The Family Lotus.

475 CATCH-22. (Paramount-1970). Capt. Yossarian, Alan Arkin; Col. Cathcart, Martin Balsam; Major Danby, Richard Benjamin; Capt. Nately, Art Garfunkel; Dr. Daneeka, Jack Gilford; Major Major, Bob Newhart; Chaplain Tappman, Anthony Perkins; Nurse Duckett, Paula Prentiss; Lt. Dobbs, Martin Sheen; Milo Minderbinder, Jon Voight; Gen. Dreedle, Orson Welles; Hungry Joe, Seth Allen; Capt. Orr, Robert Balaban; Gen. Dreedle's WAC, Susanne Benton; Capt. McWatt, Peter Bonerz; Sgt. Towser, Norman Fell; Aardvark, Chuck Grodin; Lt. Col. Korn, Buck Henry; Col. Moodus, Austin Pendleton; Nately's Whore, Gina Rovere; Luciana, Olympia Carlisli; Old Man, Marcel Dalio; Old Woman, Eva Matagliati; Father, Liam Dunn; Mother, Elizabeth Wilson; Brother, Richard Libertini; Snowden, Jonathan Korkes.

476 CATLOW. (MGM-1971). Catlow, Yul Brynner; Cowan,

Richard Crenna; Miller, Leonard Nimoy; Rosita, Daliah Lavi; Christina, Jo Ann Pflug; Merridew, Jeff Corey; Rio, Michael Delano; Recalde, Julian Mateos; Caxton, David Ladd; Mrs. Frost, Bessie Love.

476a THE CATS. (National Showmanship-1969). Marta, Eva Dahlbeck; Rike, Gio Petre; Jonny, Per Myrberg; Mirka, Monica Nielsen; Ragni, Lena Granhagen; Anna, Hjordis Petterson; Tora, Isa Quensel; Xenia, Ruth Kasdan; Klara, Inga Gill; Sally, Lena Hansson.

477 CAULDRON OF BLOOD. (Cannon-1971). Marchand, Jean-Pierre Aumont; Badulescu, Boris Karloff; Tania, Viveca Lindfors; Valerie, Rosenda Monteros; Shanghai, Milo Queseda; Elga, Dianik Zurakowska; Pablo, Ruben Rojo.

478 CAVE OF THE LIVING DEAD. (Trans-Lux-1966). Adrian Hoven, Carl Mohner, Karin Field, Erika Remberg, Wolfgang Preiss, Emmerich Schrenk, John Kitzmiller.

479 THE CAVERN. (20th Century-Fox-1965). American Private, John Saxon; Italian girl, Rosanna Schiaffino; American Captain, Larry Hagman; Canadian flyer, Peter L. Marshall; British general, Brian Aherne; Italian Soldier, Nino Castelnuovo; German soldier, Hans von Borsody.

480 CELEBRATION AT BIG SUR. (20th Century-Fox-1971). Joan Baez, Carol Ann Cisneros, David Crosby, Chris Ethridge, Mimi Farina, Joni Mitchell, Dorothy Morrison, Graham Nash, Julie Payne, Greg Reeves, John Sebastian, Steve Stills, Dallas Taylor, Neil Young, The Combs Sisters, Struggle Mountain Resistance Band, Christopher Ross, Don Sturdy, Lillian Roxon, Ron Martin, Ben Weaver, Peter Melchior, Dr. Francis X. Rigny, Kyle Lawton, Milan Melvin, Barry Adams, John Adams, Bob Cambridge, Patrick Cassidy, Fred Case, William S. Gay, Cynthia Harris, Jack Poet, Star, Yabo Yablonsky.

481 CESAR AND ROSALIE. (Cinema V-1972). Cesar, Yves Montand; Rosalie, Romy Schneider; David, Sami Frey; Antoine, Umberto Orsini; Lucie, Eva Marie Meineke; Michel, Bernard Le Coq; Carla, Gisella Hahn; Marite, Isabelle Hupper; Marcel, Henri-Jacques Huet; Albert, Pippo Merisi; Julien, Carlo Nell; Georges, Herve Sand.

482 CHAFED ELBOWS. (Impact-1967). Walter Dinsmore, George Morgan; His Mother and all other women, Elsie Downey; Doctor Sinfield and 34 other voices, Lawrence Wolfe.

483 CHAIN GANG WOMEN. (Crown International-1972). Mike Weed, Michael Stearns; Billy Harris, Robert Lott; Farmer's Wife, Barbara Mills; Ann, Linda York; Farmer, Ralph Campbell; Coleman, Wes Bishop; Willy, William B. Martin; Fat

Sam, Bruce Kemp; Gentry, Phil Hoover; Jones, Chuck Wells; Prison Guard, John Bliss; Larson, "Red" Schryver; Police Officer, James McLarty.

484 THE CHAIRMAN. (20th Century-Fox-1969). Dr. John Hathaway, Gregory Peck; Kay Hanna, Anne Heywood; Lt. General Shelby, Arthur Hill; Air Commodore Benson, Alan Dobie; The Chairman, Conrad Yama; Ting Ling, Zienia Merton; Alexander Shertov, Ori Levy; Yin, Eric Young; Chang Shou, Burt Kwouk; Colonel Gardner, Alan White; Professor Soong Li, Keye Luke; Francisca Tu, Mai Ling, Janet Key, Gordon Sterne, Robert Lee, Helen Horton, Keith Bonnard, Cecil Cheng, Lawrence Herder, Simon Cain, Anthony Chinn, Edward Cast.

485 A CHALLENGE FOR ROBIN HOOD. (20th Century-Fox-1969). Robin, Barrie Ingham; Friar Tuck, James Hayter; Little John, Leon Greene; Roger de Courtenay, Peter Blythe; Maid Marian, Gay Hamilton; Pie Merchant, Alfie Bass; "Lady Marian," Jenny Till; Sheriff of Nottingham, John Arnatt; Alan-a-Dale, Eric Flynn; Stephen, John Gugolka; Much, Reg Lye; Sir John, William Squire; Sir Jamyl de Penitone, Donald Pickering; Henry de Courtenay, Eric Woofe; Wallace, John Harvey; Will Scarlet, Douglas Mitchell; Justin, John Graham; Edwin, Arthur Hewlett; Dray Driver, Norman Mitchell.

486 THE CHALLENGES, A TRILOGY. (Selmier-1973). Francisco Rabal, Dean Selmier, Anuncion Balaguer, Teresa Rabal, Alfredo Mayo, Julia G. Caba, Barbara Deist, Fernando Polack, Julia Pena, Daysi Granados, Luis Suarez.

487 LA CHAMADE. (Lopert-1969). Lucille, Catherine Deneuve; Charles, Michel Piccoli; Antoine, Roger Van Hool; Diane, Irene Tunc; Johnny, Jacques Sereys; Claire, Philippine Pascal; Etienne, Amidou; Marianne, Monique Lejeune; Pauline, Louise Rioton; Destret, Matt Carney; Madeleine, Christiane Lasquin.

488 CHAMBER OF HORRORS. (Warner Bros.-1966). Jason Cravette, Patrick O'Neal; Anthony Draco, Cesare Danova; Harold Blount, Wilfrid Hyde-White; Marie Champlain, Laura Devon; Vivian, Patrice Wymore; Barbara Dixon, Suzy Parker; Senor Pepe de Reyes, Tun Tun; Inspector Strudwick, Philip Bourneuf; Mrs. Ewing Perryman, Jeanette Nolan; Madame Corona, Marie Windsor; Sgt. Albertson, Wayne Rogers; Judge Randolph, Vinton Hayworth; Dr. Cobb, Richard O'Brien; Gloria, Inger Stratton; Chun Sing, Berry Kroeger; Dr. Hopewell, Charles Seel; Barmaid, Ayllene Gibbons; Card Player, Tony Curtis.

489 THE CHAMPAGNE MURDERS. (Universal-1968). Christopher Balling, Anthony Perkins; Paul Wagner, Maurice Ronet; Jacqueline/Lydia, Stephane Audran; Christine Balling, Yvonne

Furneaux; Evelyn Wharton, Suzanne Lloyd; Denise, Catherine Sola; Paula, Christa Lang; Mr. Clarke, Henry Jones; Mr. Pfeifer, George Skaff; Michele, Marie-Ange Anies.

490 CHANDLER. (MGM-1972). Chandler, Warren Oates; Catherine, Leslie Caron; Carmady, Alex Dreier; Kincaid, Mitchell Ryan; Melchior, Gordon Pinsent; Bernie Oakman, Charles McGraw; Leo, Richard Loo; Selma, Gloria Grahame; Sal Sachese, Royal Dano; Zeno, Walter Burke; Angel Carter, Marianne McAndrew; Smoke, Scat Man Crothers; Waxwell, Lal Baum; Binder Ransin, Charles Shull; Rudy, John Mitchum; Bogardy, James Sikking; Salesgirl, Vickery Turner; Captain of Security Guard, Ray Kellogg; Asst. Station Master, Ernest Lawrence; Shoe Shine Boy, Eugene Jackson; Taxi Driver No. 1, Eddie Marks; Taxi Driver No. 2, Frederick Stanley II.

491 CHANGE OF HABIT. (Universal-1970). Dr. John Carpenter, Elvis Presley; Sister Michelle, Mary Tyler Moore; Sister Irene, Barbara McNair; Sister Barbara, Jane Elliot; Mother Joseph, Leora Dana; Lieut. Moretti, Edward Asner; The Banker, Robert Emhardt; Father Gibbons, Regis Toomey; Rose, Doro Merande; Lily, Ruth McDevitt; Bishop Finley, Richard Carlson; Julio Hernandez, Nefti Millet; Desiree, Laura Figueroa; Amanda, Lorena Kirk.

492 CHANGE OF MIND. (Cinerama-1969). David Rowe, Raymond St. Jacques; Margaret Rowe, Susan Oliver; Elizabeth Dickson, Janet MacLachlan; Sheriff Webb, Leslie Nielsen; Roger Morrow, Donnelly Rhodes; Tommy Benson, David Bailey; Scupper, Andre Womble; Rose Landis, Clarisse Taylor; Bill Chambers, Jack Creley; Angela Rowe, Cosette Lee; Judge Forrest, Larry Reynolds; Nancy, Hope Clarke; Howard Culver, Rudy Challenger; Chief Enfield, Henry Ramer; Mayor Farrell, Franz Russell; Governor LaTourette, Joseph Shaw; Attorney Nash, Sydney Brown; Dr. Bornear, Tony Kamreither; Dr. Kelman, Ron Hartmann; Judge Stanton, Murray Westgate; Reporters, Guy Sanvido, Chuck Samata, Can MacDonald and Joseph Wynn; Charles Elder, Horace Bailey, Buddy Ferens, Don Crawford, Pat Collins, Sean Sullivan, Vivian Reis, Ellen Flood, Danny McIlravey, Keith Williams, Clarence Haynes.

493 CHANGES. (Cinerama-1969). Kent, Kent Lane; Julie, Michele Carey; Bobbi, Manuela Thiess; Kent's Father, Jack Albertson; Kent's Mother, Maris Fehr; Kristine, Marcia Strassman; Kent's Roommate, Tom Fielding; Kent's Friend, Bill Kelley; Negro Man, Kenneth Washington; Kim Weston, Sam Chew Jr., Doug Dowell, Sherri Mitchel, Doug Bell, Sammy Vaughn, Buddy Hart, Grant Conroy, Cindy Mitchum, Terry Garr, Monica Petersen, Sammy Tanner, Christopher Hayden, John Moio, Clarice Gillis, Jesus Alonzo Jr., Katherine Victory, Vincent George.

494 CHAPPAQUA. (Regional-1967). Doctor Benoit, Jean-Louis Barrault; Russel Harwick, Conrad Rooks; Opium Jones, William S. Burroughs; Messiah, Allen Ginsberg; Sun God, Ravi Shankar; Water Woman, Paula Pritchett; Peyote Eater, Ornette Coleman; Guru, Swami Satchidananda; The Prophet, Moondog; Sacrificed One, Jill Lator; The Connection, John Esam; The Fugs, Rita Renoir, Jacques Seiler, Sophie Steboun, Peter Orlovsky, France Cremieux, Penny Brown, Moustique, Elder Wilder, Pascal Aubier, Rene Serisier.

495 THE CHARGE OF THE LIGHT BRIGADE. (United Artists-1968). Lord Cardigan, Trevor Howard; Captain Lewis Nolan, David Hemmings; Clarissa Morris, Vanessa Redgrave; Lord Raglan, John Gielgud; Lord Lucan, Harry Andrews; Mrs. Duberly, Jill Bennett; Paymaster Captain, Peter Bowles; Captain Morris, Mark Burns; Sir George Brown, Howard Marion Crawford; General Airey, Mark Dignam; and Alan Dobie, Willoughby Goddard, T. P. McKenna, Michael Miller, Corin Redgrave, Norman Rossington, Ben Aris, Micky Baker, John Carney, Leo Britt, Helen Cherry, Christopher Chittell, Ambrose Coghill, Chris Cunningham, Georges Douking, Clive Endersby, Andrew Faulds, Derek Fuke, John Hallam, Barbara Hicks, Ben Howard, Rachel Kempson, Declan Mulholland, Roger Mutton, Valerie Newman, Roy Pattison, Dino Shafeek, John Treneman, Colin Vancao, Peter Woodthorpe, Donald Wolfit.

496 CHARLES, DEAD OR ALIVE. (New Yorker-1972). Charles De, Francois Simon; Paul, Marcel Robert; Adeline, Marie-Clair Dufour; Pierre De, Andre Schmidt; Marianne De, Maya Simon; Germaine, Michele Martel; Jo Escoffier, Walter Schochli, Jean-Pierre Moriaud, Jean-Luc Bideau, Francis Reusser, Janine Christoffe, Martine Simon, Pierre Verdan, Antoine Bordier, Lilliane Bovard.

497 CHARLEY AND THE ANGEL. (Buena Vista-1973). Charley Appleby, Fred MacMurray; Nettie Appleby, Cloris Leachman; The Angel, Harry Morgan; Ray Ferris, Kurt Russell; Leonora Appleby, Kathleen Cody; Willie Appleby, Vincent Van Patten; Rupert Appleby, Scott Kolden; Pete, George Lindsey; Banker, Edward Andrews; Buggs, Richard Bakalyan; Sadie, Barbara Nichols; Policeman, Kelly Thordsen; Dr. Sprague, Liam Dunn; Felix, Larry D. Mann; Police Chief, George O'Hanlon; Miss Partridge, Susan Tolsky; Frankie Zuto, Mills Watson; Derwood Moseby, Ed Begley Jr.; Susie, Christina Anderson; Driver, Roy Engel; Girl in Sadie's Palace, Pat Delany; News Reporter, Bob Hastings; Policeman #2, Jack Griffin.

498 CHARLEY-ONE-EYE. (Paramount-1973). Black Man, Richard Roundtree; Indian, Roy Thinnes; Bounty Hunter, Nigel Davenport; Officer's Wife, Jill Pearson; Mexican Driver, Aldo Sambrell; Mexican Leader, Rafael Albaicin; Tony, Alex Davion; Bob, Johnny Sekka; Penelope, Madeline Hinde; Richard,

Patrick Mower; Chris, Imogen Hassall; Holstrom, Edward Woodward; Honeydew, William Mervyn; Colonel, David Lodge.

499 CHARLEY VARRICK. (Universal-1973). Charley Varrick, Walter Matthau; Molly, Joe Don Baker; Sybil Fort, Felicia Farr; Harman Sullivan, Andy Robinson; Maynard Boyle, John Vernon; Jewell Everett, Sheree North; Mr. Garfinkle, Norman Fell; Honest John, Benson Fong; Howard Young, Woodrow Parfrey; Sheriff Bill Horton, William Schallert; Nadine Varrick, Jacqueline Scott; Mrs. Taff, Marjorie Bennett; Rudy Sanchez, Rudy Diaz; Steele, Colby Chester; Highway Deputy, Charlie Briggs; Miss Ambar, Priscilla Garcia; Mr. Scott, Scott Hale; Boy, Charles Matthau; Miss Vesta, Hope Summers; Beverly, Monica Lewis; Clerk, Jim Nolan; Tom, Tom Tully; Randolph, Albert Popwell; Jessie, Kathleen O'Malley; Jana, Christina Hart; Van Sickle, Craig Baxley; Taxi Driver, Al Dunlap; Chinese Hostess, Virginia Wing; Murph, Donald Siegel.

500 CHARLIE BUBBLES. (Regional-1968). Charlie Bubbles, Albert Finney; Smokey Pickles, Colin Blakely; Lottie Bubbles, Billie Whitelaw; Eliza, Liza Minelli; Jack Bubbles, Timothy Garland; Accountant, Richard Pearson; Gerry, John Ronane; Agent, Nicholas Phipps; Solicitor, Peter Sallis; Mr. Noseworthy, Charles Lamb; Mrs. Noseworthy, Margery Mason; Maud, Diana Coupland; Airman, Alan Lake; Woman in Cafe, Wendy Padbury; Nanny, Susan Engles; Waiter in Hotel, Joe Gladwin; Head Waiter, Charles Hill; Policeman, Albert Shepherd; Bill, Ted Norris; Herbert, Brian Mosley; Receptionist, Rex Boyd.

501 CHARLIE, THE LONESOME COUGAR. (Buena Vista-1967). Jess Bradley, Ron Brown; Potlatch, Brian Russell; Jess's Fiance, Linda Wallace; Farmer, Jim Wilson; Mill Manager, Clifford Peterson; Chief Engineer, Lewis Sample; Mill Hand, Edward C. Moller; Narrator, Rex Allen.

502 CHARLOTTE'S WEB. (Paramount-1973). Voices of: Charlotte, Debbie Reynolds; Templeton, Paul Lynde; Wilbur, Henry Gibson; Narrator, Rex Allen; Mrs. Arable, Martha Scott; Old Sheep, Dave Madden; Avery, Danny Bonaduce; Geoffrey, Don Messick; Lurvy, Herb Vigran; The Goose, Agnes Moorehead; Fern Arable, Pam Ferdin; Mrs. Zuckerman/Mrs. Fussy, Joan Gerber; Homer Zuckerman, Robert Holt; Arable, John Stephenson; Henry Fussy, William B. White.

503 CHARLY. (Cinerama-1968). Charly Gordon, Cliff Robertson; Alice Kinian, Claire Bloom; Dr. Anna Straus, Lilia Skala; Dr. Richard Nemur, Leon Janney; Bert, Dick Van Patten; Joey, William Dwyer; Gimpy, Ed McNally; Paddy, Dan Morgan; Hank, Barney Martin; Mrs. Apple, Ruth White; Eddie, Frank Dolan; Convention Speaker, Ralph Nelson.

504 CHARRO! (National General-1969). Jess Wade, Elvis Presley; Tracy, Ina Balin; Vince, Victor French; Sara Ramsey, Barbara Werle; Marcie, Lynn Kellogg; Billy Roy, Solomon Sturges; Opie Keetch, Paul Brinegar; Gunner, James Sikking; Heff, Harry Landers; Lt. Rivera, Tony Young; Sheriff Ramsey, James Almanzar; Mody, Charles H. Gray; Lige, Rodd Redwing; Martin Tilford, Gary Walberg; Gabe, Duane Grey; Henry Carter, J. Edward McKinley; Jerome Selby, John Pickard; Will Joslyn, Robert Luster; Christa, Christa Lang; Harvey, Robert Karnes.

505 CHARULATA. (1965). Madhabi Mukherjee, Sailen Mukherjee, Soumitra Chatterjee.

506 THE CHASE. (Columbia-1966). Sheriff Calder, Marlon Brando; Anna Reeves, Jane Fonda; Bubber Reeves, Robert Redford; Val Rogers, E. G. Marshall; Ruby Calder, Angie Dickinson; Emily Stewart, Janice Rule; Mrs. Reeves, Miriam Hopkins; Mary Fuller, Martha Hyer; Damon Fuller, Richard Bradford; Edwin Stewart, Robert Duvall; Jason Rogers, James Fox; Diana Hyland, Henry Hull, Jocelyn Brando, Katherine Walsh, Lori Martin, Marc Seaton, Paul Williams, Clifton James, Malcolm Atterbury, Nydia Westman, Joel Fluellen, Steve Ihnat, Maurice Manson, Bruce Cabot, Steve Whittaker, Pamela Curran, Ken Renard.

507 CHASTITY. (American International-1969). Chastity, Cher; Diana Midnight, Barbara London; Eddie, Stephen Whittaker; To-my, Tom Nolan; Cab Driver, Danny Zapien; First Truck Driver, Elmer Valentine; Salesman, Burke Rhind; Husband, Richard Armstrong; Master of Ceremonies, Joe Light; Church Lady, Dolly Hunt; Second Truck Driver, Jason Clarke.

508 CHATO'S LAND. (United Artists-1972). Pardon Chato, Charles Bronson; Quincey Whitmore, Jack Palance; Nye Buell, Richard Basehart; Joshua Everette, James Whitmore; Jubal Hooker, Simon Oakland; Elias Hooker, Ralph Waite; Earl Hooker, Richard Jordan; Martin Hall, Victor French; Harvey Lansing, William Watson; Gavin Malechie, Roddy McMillan; Brady Logan, Paul Young; George Dunn, Lee Patterson; Will Coop, Rudy Ugland; Mexican Scout, Raul Castro; Chato's Woman, Sonia Rangan; Jacob Meade, Clive Endersby; Edna Malechie, Rebecca Wilson; Shelby Hooker, Verna Harvey; Moira Logan, Sally Adez; Ezra, Peter Dyneley; Bartender, Hugh McDermott; Celestino Gonzalez, Florencio Amarilla, Louise Amarilla, Roland Grand.

509 CHE! (20th Century-Fox-1969). Ernesto "Che" Guevara, Omar Sharif; Fidel Castro, Jack Palance; Ramon Valdez, Cesare Danova; Faustino Morales, Robert Loggia; Guillermo, Woody Strode; Anita Marquez, Barbara Luna; Goatherd, Frank Silvera; Captain Vasquez, Albert Paulsen; Tania Guitterez Bauer, Linda Marsh; Felipe Munoz, Tom Troupe; Willy, Rudy

Diaz; Rolando, Perry Lopez; Pablo Rojas, Abraham Sofaer; Colonel Salazar, Richard Angarola; Celia Sanchez, Sarita Vara; Raul Castro, Paul Bertoya; Antonio, Sid Haig; Juan Almeida, Adolph Caesar; Hector, Paul Picerni; Camilo Cinefuegos, Ray Martell; Captain Flores, Valentin De Vargas; Guide, Miguel Suarez; Sergeant Terraza, Jess Franco.

510 CHECKMATE. (JER-1973). Madame Chang, An Tsan Hu; Pepper, Diana Wilson; Mercer, Don Draper; Snow, J. J. Coyle; Alex, Caren Kaye; Jogger, Kurt Mann; Andre, Reg Roland; Boris, Ion De Hondol.

511 THE CHEERLEADERS. (Cinemation-1973). Jeannie, Stephanie Fondue; Claudia, Denise Dillaway; Bonnie, Jovita Bush; Debbie, Debbie Lowe; Susie, Sandy Evans; Patty, Kim Stanton; Jon, Richard Meatwhistle; Norm, John Jacobs; Novi, Raoul Hoffnung; Coach, Patrick Wright; Isabel, Terry Teague; Daddy, Jack Jonas; Mom, Jay Lindner; Vinnie, John Bracci; Sal, William Goldman; Waiter, Bill Lehrke.

512 THE CHELSEA GIRLS. (Film-Makers' Distribution Center-1966). Nico, Gerard Malanga, Bridgit, International Velvet, Marie Mencken, Ingrid Superstar, Eric Anderson, Mario Montez, Pope Ondine, Mary Might.

513 CHERRY, HARRY, AND RAQUEL. (Russ Meyer-1969). Raquel, Larissa Ely; Cherry, Linda Ashton; Harry, Charles Napier; Enrique, Bert Santos; Mr. Franklin, Franklin H. Bolger; Soul, Astrid Lillimor.

514 THE CHEYENNE SOCIAL CLUB. (National General-1970). John O'Hanlan, James Stewart; Harley Sullivan, Henry Fonda; Jenny, Shirley Jones; Opan Ann, Sue Ane Langdon; Pauline, Elaine Devry; Barkeep, Robert Middleton; Marshal Anderson, Arch Johnson; Willowby, Dabbs Greer; Carrie Virginia, Jackie Russell; Annie Jo, Jackie Joseph; Sara Jean, Sharon DeBord; Nathan Potter, Richard Collier; Charlie Bannister, Charles Tyner; Alice, Jean Willes; Corey Bannister, Robert J. Wilke; Pete Dodge, Carl Reindel; Dr. Foy, J. Pat O'Malley; Dr. Carter, Jason Wingreen; Clay Carroll, John Dehner; Barkeep, Hal Baylor; Mae, Charlotte Stewart; Ranch Foreman, Alberto Morin; Deuter, Myron Healey; Kohler, Warren Kemmerling; Yancy, Dick Johnstone; Cook, Phil Mead; Scared Man, Hi Roberts; Teamster, Ed Pennybacker; Hansen, Red Morgan; Bannister Gang, Dean Smith, Bill Hicks, Bill Davis, Walt Davis, John Welty.

515 No entry.

516 CHILDISH THINGS. (Filmworld-1969). Tom, Don Murray; Pat, Linda Evans; Jennings, David Brian; Angelique, Angelique Pettyjohn; Kelly, Don Joslyn; Gypsy, Gypsy Boots; Rod, Rod Lauren; Preacher, Leroy Jenkins; Simmons, Logan

Ramsey; Fighter, Erik Holland; Jack, Jack Griffin; Gril, Valerie Brooke; Peanut Man, Gene LaBelle; Carousel Man, Ed Bennett; Ex-Fighter, Seaman Glass; Last Fighter, George Atkinson; Gene, Peter Tenen; Sharon, Claire Kelly.

517 CHILDREN SHOULDN'T PLAY WITH DEAD THINGS. (Gemini-1972). Alan, Alan Armsby; Anya, Anya Ormsby; Val, Valerie Mamches; Terry, Jane Daly; Jeff, Jeffrey Gillen; Paul, Paul Cronin; Roy, Roy Engleman; Emerson, Bob Filep; Winns, Alecs Baird; "Orville the Awful," Seth Sklarey.

517a CHILD'S PLAY. (Paramount-1972). Jerome Malley, James Mason; Joseph Dobbs, Robert Preston; Paul Reis, Beau Bridges; Father Mozian, Ronald Weyand; Father Griffin, Charles White; Father Penny, David Rounds; Mrs. Carter, Kate Harrington; Sheppard, Jamie Alexander; O'Donnell, Brian Chapin; Jennings, Bryant Fraser; Wilson, Mark Hall Haefeli; Banks, Paul O'Keefe; Medley, Robert D. Randall; Class President, Robbie Reed; Students, Paul Alessi, Anthony Barletta, Kevin Coupe, Christopher Hoag, Stephen McLaughlin; Travis, Christopher Man; Shea, Tom Leopold; McArdie, Julius Lo Iacono.

518 CHINA IS NEAR. (Royal-1968). Vittorio, Glauco Mauri; Elena, Elda Tattoli; Carlo, Paolo Graziosi; Giovanna, Daniela Surina; Camillo, Pierluigi Apra; Rospo the Toad, Alessandro Haber; Giacomo, Claudio Trionfi; Clotilde, Laura De Marchi; Furio, Claudio Cassinelli; Don Pino, Rossano Jalenti.

519 CHINATOWN. (Paramount-1974). J. J. Gittes, Jack Nicholson; Evelyn Mulwray, Faye Dunaway; Noah Cross, John Huston; Escobar, Perry Lopez; Yelburton, John Hillerman; Hollis Mulwray, Darryll Zwerlind; Ida Sessions, Diane Ladd; Mulvihill, Roy Jenson; Man With Knife, Roman Polanski; Loach, Dick Bakalyan; Walsh, Joe Mantell; Duffy, Bruce Glover; Sophie, Nandu Hinds; Lawyer, James O'Reare; Evelyn's butler, James Hong; Maid, Beulah Quo; Gardener, Jerry Fujikawa; Katherine, Belinda Palmer; Mayor Bagby, Roy Roberts; Councilmen, Noble Willingham and Elliott Montgomery.

520 THE CHINESE IN PARIS. (Cine Qua Non-1974). Regis, Jean Yanne; Gregoire, Michel Serrault; Stephanie, Nicole Calfan; Montebert, Jacques Francois; Fou Yen, Kyozo Magatzuka; Lefranc, Georges Wilson; Madeleine, Macha Meril; President, Bernard Blier; Friend, Daniel Prevost.

521 LA CHINOISE. (Leacock Pennebaker-1968). Veronique, Anne Wiazemsky; Guillaume, Jean-Pierre Leaud; Yvonne, Juliet Berto; Henri, Michel Semeniako; Kirilov, Lex De Bruijn; Himself, Francis Jeanson.

522 CHISUM. (Warner Bros.-1970). John Chisum, John Wayne;

Lawrence Murphy, Forest Tucker; Dan Nodeen, Christopher George; James Pepper, Ben Johnson; Pat Garrett, Glenn Corbett; Sheriff Brady, Bruce Cabot; Alex McSween, Andrew Prince; Tunstall, Patric Knowles; Evans, Richard Jaeckel; Sue McSween, Lynda Day; Patton, John Agar; Neemo, Lloyd Battista; Morton, Robert Donner; Justice Wilson, Ray Teal; Dolan, Edward Faulkner; Bowdre, Ron Soble; Baker, John Mitchum; Dudley, Glenn Langan; Gov. Axtell, Alan Baxter; Delgado, Alberto Morin; Jeff, William Bryant; Ben, Pedro Armendariz Jr.; O'Folliard, Christopher Mitchum; White Buffalo, Abraham Sofaer; Riker, Gregg Palmer; Billy the Kidd, Geoffrey Deuel; Sally Chisum, Pamela McMyler.

523 CHITTY CHITTY BANG BANG. (United Artists-1968). Caractacus Potts, Dick Van Dyke; Truly Scrumptious, Sally Ann Howes; Grandpa Potts, Lionel Jeffries; Baron Bomburst, Gert Frobe; Baroness Bomburst, Anna Quayle; Toymaker, Benny Hill; Lord Scrumptious, James Robertson Justice; Child Catcher, Robert Helpmann; Jemima Potts, Heather Ripley; Jeremy Potts, Adrian Hall; Blonde, Barbara Windsor; Admiral, Davy Kaye; Alexander Dore, Bernard Spear, Stanley Unwin, Peter Arne, Desmond Llewelyn, Victor Maddern, Arthur Mullard, Ross Parker, Gerald Campion, Felix Felton, Monti De Lyle, Totti Truman Taylor, Larry Taylor, Max Bacon, Max Wall, John Heawood, Michael Darbyshire, Kenneth Maller, Gerald Taylor, Eddie Davis.

524 CHLOE IN THE AFTERNOON. (Columbia-1972). Frederic, Bernard Verley; Chloe, Zouzou; Helene, Francoise Verley; Gerard, Daniel Ceccaldi; Fabienne, Malvina Penne; Martine, Babette Ferrier; Madame M, Frederique Hender; Monsieur M, Claude-Jean Philippe; Landlady, Sylvanine Charlet; Client, Daniel Malat; Nurse, Suze Randall; Traveller, Tina Michelino; Friend in Cafe, Jean-Louise Livi; Salesman, Pierre Nunzi; Saleswoman, Irene Skobline; Student, Sulvia Badesco; Women in Dream Sequence, Francoise Fabian, Aurora Cornu, Marie-Christine Barrault, Haydee Politoff, Laurence De Monaghan and Beatrice Romand.

525 CHOSEN SURVIVORS. (Columbia-1974). Raymond Couzins, Jackie Cooper; Steven Mayes, Alex Cord; Gordon Ellis, Richard Jaeckel; Peter Macomber, Bradford Dillman; Luis Cabral, Pedro Armendariz Jr.; Alana Fitzgerald, Diana Muldaur; Woody Russo, Lincoln Kilpatrick; Carrie Draper, Gwen Mitchell; Lenore Chrisman, Barbara Babcock; Kristin Lerner, Christina Moreno; Claire Farraday, Nancy Rodman; Mary Louise Borden, Kelly Lange.

526 CHRISTA. (American International-1971). Christa, Birte Tove; Derek, Clinton Greyn; Torben, Baard Ove; Andre, Daniel Gelin; Michael, Gastone Rosilli; Umberto, Cyrus Elias.

527 THE CHRISTIAN LICORICE STORE. (National General-1971).

Franklin, Beau Bridges; Cynthia, Maud Adams; Jonathan, Gilbert Roland; Monroe, Alan Arbus; Texas, Anne Randall; Joseph, Monte Hellman; Mary, Jaclyn Hellman; Tennis opponent, "Butch" Bucholtz; P. C., Walter Barnes; Smallwood, McLean Stevenson; McGhee, Howard Storm; Robin, Greg Mullavey; Assistant director, Larry Gelman; Mime, Louis De Farra; Evans, Gary Rose; Reporters, Billy James, Rusty Durrell; Hostess, Dawn Cleary; Starlets, Joanna Phillips, Barbara Leigh; Texas Man, James Jeter; Parking Lady, Nina Varela; Tall sailor, Bruce Graziano; Short sailor, Harold Keller; Mercedes girl, Toni Clayton; Themselves, Dido and Jean Renoir.

528 THE CHRISTINE JORGENSEN STORY. (United Artists-1970). George/Christine, John Hansen; Aunt Thora, Joan Tompkins; Tom, Quinn Redeker; Father, John W. Himes; Mother, Ellen Clark; Jess, Rod McCary; Estabrook, Will Kuluva; Dr. Dahlman, Oscar Beregi; Dolly, Lynn Harper; George at 7, Trent Lehman; Dolly as a child, Pamelyn Ferdin; Pastor, Bill Erwin; Tani, Joyce Meadows; Angela, Sondra Scott; Jack, Don Pierce; Loretta, Elaine Joyce; George as a child, Eddie Frank; Mrs. Whalstrom, Dee Carroll; Whalstrom, Peter Bourne.

529 THE CHRISTMAS KID. (Producers Releasing Organization-1967). Joe Novak, Jeffrey Hunter; Mike Culligan, Louis Hayward; Mayor Carrillo, Gustavo Rojo; Marie Lefleur, Perla Cristal; Judge Perkins, Luis Prendes; Dr. Fred Carter, Reginald Gilliam; Jud Walters, Fernando Hilbeck; John Novak, Jack Taylor; Percy Martin, Eric Chapman; Luke Acker, Dennis Kilbane; Pete Prima, Russ Stoddard; Sheriff Anderson, Carl Rapp; Karl Humber, Guillermo Mendez; Burt Froelich, Alvaro De Luna; Marika Novak, Alejandra Nilo.

530 THE CHRISTMAS THAT ALMOST WASN'T. (Childhood-1966). Phineas T. Prune, Rossano Brazzi; Sam Whipple, Paul Tripp; Mrs. Santa Claus, Lidia Brazzi; Santa Claus, Alberto Rabagliati; Jonathan the Bookkeeper, Mischa Auer; Mr. Prim, Sonny Fox; Blossom, John Karlsen.

531 THE CHRISTMAS TREE. (Continental-1969). Laurent, William Holden; Catherine, Virna Lisi; Verdun, Andre Bourvil; Pascal, Brook Fuller; Marinette, Madeleine Damien; Vernet, Friedrich Ledebur; The Doctor, Mario Feliciani.

532 CHROME AND HOT LEATHER. (American International-1972). T. J., William Smith; Mitch, Tony Young; Casey, Michael Haynes; Al, Peter Brown; Jim, Marvin Gaye; Hank, Michael Stearns; Susan, Kathy Baumann; Sheriff Lewis, Wes Bishop; Ned, Herb Jeffries; Sweet Willy, Bob Pickett; Lt. Reardon, George Carey; Captain Barnes, Marland Proctor; Kathy, Cheri Moor; Helen, Ann Marie; Sgt. Mack, Robert Ridgely; NCO Club Bartender, Lee Parrish; Gabe, Larry Bishop.

533 CHRONICLE OF A SUMMER. (Pathe Contemporary-1965). Main Participants, Jean Rouch, Edgar Morin, Marceline, Angelo, Marilou, Jean-Pierre; Factory Workers, Jean, Jacques; Students, Regis, Celine, Jean-Marc, Nadine, Landry, Raymond; Office Workers, Jacques, Simone; Artists, Henri, Madi, Catherine; Model, Sophie.

534 CHUBASCO. (Warner Bros. -7 Arts-1969). Sebastian Marinho, Richard Egan; Chubasco, Christopher Jones; Bunny Marinho, Susan Strasberg; Angela, Ann Sothern; Captain Laurindo, Simon Oakland; Theresa Marinho, Audren Totter; Nick Kassel, Preston Foster; Matt, Peter Whitney; Judge North, Edward Binns; Benito, Joe De Santis; Frenchy, Norman Alden; Les, Stuart Moss; Juno, Ron Rich; Police Sergeant, Milton Frome; Aunt Mary, Toni Gerry.

535 CHUKA. (Paramount-1967). Chuka, Rod Taylor; Sgt. Otto Hahnsbach, Ernest Borgnine; Colonel Stuart Valois, John Mills; Veronica Kleitz, Luciana Paluzzi; Trent, James Whitmore; Helena Chavez, Angela Dorian; Major Benson, Louis Hayward; Private Spivey, Michael Cole; Captain Carrol, Hugh Reilly; Slim, Barry O'Hara; Baldwin, Joseph Sirola; Hanu, Marco Antonio; Lieut. Daly, Gerald York; Indian Girl, Herlinda Del Carmen; Stage Driver, Lucky Carson.

536 CIAO! MANHATTAN. (Maron-1973). Susan, Edie Sedgewick; Butch, Wesley Hayes; Mummy, Isabel Jewell; Geoffrey, Geoff Briggs; Paul, Paul America; Charla, Jane Holzer; Dr. Braun, Roger Vadim; Verdecchio, Jean Margouleff.

537 THE CINCINNATI KID. (MGM-1965). The Cincinnati Kid, Steve McQueen; Lancey Howard, Edward G. Robinson; Melba, Ann-Margret; Shooter, Karl Malden; Christian Rudd, Tuesday Weld; Lady Fingers, Joan Blondell; Slade, Rip Torn; Pig, Jack Weston; Yeller, Cab Calloway; Hoban, Jeff Corey.

538 CINDERELLA LIBERTY. (20th Century-Fox-1973). John Baggs Jr., James Caan; Maggie Paul, Marsha Mason; Forshay, Eli Wallach; Doug, Kirk Calloway; Master at Arms, Burt Young; Alcott, Bruce Kirby Jr.; Miss Watkins, Allyn Ann McLerie; Executive Officer, Dabney Coleman; Dr. Osgood, Fred Sadoff; Drunken Sailor, Allan Arbus; Dental Corpsman, Jon Korkes; Lewis, Don Calfa; Sam, Paul Jackson; Sailor #1, David Proval; Cook, Ted D'Armss; Fleet Chick, Sally Kirkland; Nurse, Diane Schenker; Seaman #1, James Bigham; Seaman #2, Wayne Hudgins; Wave, Rita Joelson Chidester; Yeoman, Knight Landesman; Hot Dog Beggar, Spike Africa; Young Sailor, Chris F. Prebazac; Messboy, David Norfleet; Woman, Sara Jackson.

539 CINERAMA'S RUSSIAN ADVENTURE. (United Roadshow-1966). Narrator, Bing Crosby.

540 CIRCLE OF LOVE. (Walter Reade-Sterling-1965). The Prostitute, Marie Dubois; The Soldier, Claude Giraud; The Maid, Anna Karina; Her Friend, Valerie Lagrange; The Young Man, Jean-Claude Brialy; The Married Woman, Jane Fonda; The Husband, Maurice Ronet; The Midinette, Catherine Spaak; The Author, Bernard Noel; The Actress, Francine Berge; The Young Officer, Jean Sorel.

541 CISCO PIKE. (Columbia-1972). Cisco Pike, Kris Kristofferson; Sue, Karen Black; Officer Leo Holland, Gene Hackman; Jesse Dupre, Harry Dean Stanton; Merna, Viva; Lynn, Joy Bang; Music Store Owner, Roscoe Lee Browne; Mexican Man, Chuy Franco; Lawyer, Severn Darden; Suspicious Customer, Herb Weil; Buffalo, Antonio Fargas; Rex, Douglas Sahm; Recording Engineer, Don Sturdy; Sim Valensi, Alan Arbus; Reed, Hugh Romney; Motorcycle Officer, Frank Hotchkiss; Narc, James Oliver; Mouse, Nawana Davis; Waitress, Timothy Near; Swimming Lady, Lorna Thayer; Jack, William Traylor.

542 CITY OF FEAR. (Allied Artists-1965). Paul Maxwell, Terry Moore, Marisa Mell, Albert Lieven, Pinkas Braun, Zsu Zaa Banki, Birgit Heilberg, Marie Rohm.

543 CLAIRE'S KNEE. (Columbia-1971). Jerome, Jean-Claude Brialy; Aurora, Aurora Cornu; Laura, Beatrice Romand; Claire, Laurence De Monaghan.

544 CLAMBAKE. (United Artists-1967). Scott Heyward, Elvis Presley; Diane Carter, Shelley Fabares; Tom Wilson, Will Hutchins; James Jamison III, Bill Bixby; Duster Heyward, James Gregory; Sam Burton, Gary Merrill; Ellie, Amanda Harley; Sally, Suzie Kaye; Gloria, Angelique Pettyjohn; Gigi, Olga Kaye; Olive, Arlene Charles; Mr. Hathaway, Jack Good; Doorman, Hal Peary; Race Announcer, Sam Riddle; Cigarette Girl, Sue England; Lisa, Lisa Slagle; Bartender, Lee Krieger; Crewman, Melvin Allen; Waiter, Herb Barnett; Bell Hop, Steve Cory; Barasch, Robert Lieb; Ice Cream Vendor, Red Vest.

545 CLARENCE THE CROSS-EYED LION. (MGM-1965). Dr. Marsh Tracy, Marshall Thompson; Julie Harper, Betsy Drake; Paula Tracy, Cheryl Miller; Rupert Rowbotham, Richard Haydn; Carter, Alan Caillou; Gregory, Maurice Marsac.

546 CLASS OF '44. (Warner Bros. -1973). Hermie, Gary Grimes; Oscy, Jerry Houser; Benjie, Oliver Conant; Fraternity President, William Atherton; Marty, Sam Bottoms; Julie, Deborah Winters; Professor, Joe Ponazecki; Principal, Murray Westgate; Grade Advisor, Marion Waldman; Valedictorian, Mary Long; Mrs. Gilhuly, Marcia Diamond; Editor, Jeffrey Cohen; Assistant Editor, Susan Marcus; First Proctor, Lamar Criss; Second Proctor, Michael A. Hoey; Father, Dan

McDonald; Mother, Jan Campbell.

547 CLASS OF '74. (Crest-1972). Heather, Pat Woodell; Carla, Marki Bey; Maggie, Sandra Currie; Gabriella, Barbara Caron; Dave, Phillip Terry; Marsha, Lynn Cartwright; Wally, Chris Beaumont; John, Gary Clarke; Carol, Luanne Roberts; Shelly, Hal Hindey; Xavier, Ronald Lawrence; Stephan, Bob Kresting; Lisa, Lisa Caron; Freshman, Cynthia Hull.

548 CLAUDINE. (20th Century-Fox-1974). Claudine, Diahann Carroll; Roop, James Earl Jones; Charles, Lawrence Hilton-Jacobs; Charlene, Tamu; Paul, David Kruger; Patrice, Yvette Curtis; Francis, Eric Jones; Lurlene, Socorro Stephens; Owen, Adam Wade.

549 CLAY PIGEON. (MGM-1971). Frank Redford, Telly Savalas; Tallin, Robert Vaughn; Police Captain, John Marley; Freedom Lovelace, Burgess Meredith; Simon, Ivan Dixon; Joe Ryan, Tom Stern; Free Clinic Doctor, Jeff Corey; Angeline, Marilyn Akin; Saddle, Marlene Clark; Tracy, Belinda Palmer; Jason, Mario Alcade, Pat McCormack, James Dobson, George Wallace, Renee Tetro, Mark Thomas, Marly Stone, John Quincy Durant, Don Carter, Michael Gwynne, Janet Wood, Don Hansen, Leonard D'John, Ellen Blake, Frank Mitchell, John White, Merie Earl, Andrew Parks, Lee Anthony, Ronald Knight, Alan Braunstein, J. P. Cranshaw, Jerry Brooks; Chief MacGregor, Peter Lawford.

550 CLEOPATRA JONES. (Warner Bros. -1973). Cleopatra, Tamara Dobson; Reuben, Bernie Casey; Mommy, Shelley Winters; Tiffany, Brenda Sykes; Doodlebug, Antonio Fargas; Purdy, Bill McKinney; Crawford, Dan Frazer; Kert, Stafford Morgan; Andy, Mike Warren; Johnson Boys, Albert Popwell, Caro Kenyatta; Mrs. Johnson, Esther Rolle; Mommy's Hoods, Paul Koslo, Joseph A. Tornatore; Chauffeur, Hedley Mattingly; Doodlebug's Hoods, George Reynolds, Theodore Wilson; Snake, Christopher Joy; Maxwell, Keith Hamilton; Annie, Angela Gibbs; Lt., John Garwood; Mommy's Assistant, John Alderman.

551 THE CLIMAX. (Lopert-1967). Sergio Masini, Ugo Tognazzi; Marisa Malagugini, Stefania Sandrelli; Giulia Masini, Renee Longarini; Adela Baistrocchi, Mario Grazia Carmassi; Michele, Gigi Ballista; Colassanti, Sergio Fincato; Riccardo Masini, Marco Della Giovanna; Caputo, Ildebrando Santafe; Filiberto Malagugini, Riccardo Billi; Mr. Malagugini, Carlo Bagno; Mrs. Malagugini, Lina Lagalla; Bruno, Stefano Cierchie; Nini, Constantino Bramini; Luisa, Cinzia Sperapani; Mita, Mimosa Gregoretti; Head Clinic Doctor, Giorgio Bianchi; Nurse, Giovanna Lenzi.

552 CLIMAX. (Sherpix-1971). Kate, Lesley Conners; Perry, Richard Patrick; Erica, Susan Shaw; CeCe, Marie Ario; Bud,

Rick Livermore; Adriene, Maxine Langtree; Henry, Jeff Patton; Daphney, Julie Douglas; Norman, Ivan Beaudell.

553 A CLOCKWORK ORANGE. (Warner Bros. -1971). Alex, Malcolm McDowell; Mr. Alexander, Patrick Magee; Mrs. Alexander, Adrienne Corri; Deltold, Aubrey Morris; Georgie, James Marcus; Dim, Warren Clarke; Pete, Michael Tarn; Mum, Sheila Raynor; Dad, Philip Stone; Cat Lady, Miriam Karlin; Chaplain, Godfrey Quigley; Chief Guard, Michael Bates; Stage Actor, John Clive; Dro. Brodsky, Carl Duering; Tramp, Paul Farrell; Lodger, Clive Francis; Prison Governor, Michael Gover; Dr. Branum, Madge Ryan; Conspirator, John Savident; Minister, Anthony Sharp; Psychiatrist, Pauline Taylor; Conspirator, Margaret Tyzack; and Steven Berkoff, Lindsay Campbell, David Prowse, Barrie Cookson, Jan Adair, Gaye Brown, Peter Burton, John J. Carney, Vivienne Chandler, Richard Connaught, Prudence Drage, Carol Drinkwater, Lee Fox, Cheryl Grunwald, Gillian Hills, Craig Hunter, Shirley Jaffe, Barbara Scott, Virginia Weatherell, Neil Wilson, Katya Wyeth.

554 THE CLONES. (Filmmakers International-1973). Michael Greene, Gregory Sierra, Otis Young, Susan Hunt, Stanley Adams, Barbara Burgdorph, John Barrymore Jr.

555 CLOPORTES. (International Classics-1966). Alphonse, Lino Ventura; Edmond, Charles Aznavour; Catherine, Irina Demick; Arthur, Maurice Biraud; Rouquemoute, Georges Geret; Tonton, Pierre Brasseur; Gertrude, Francoise Rosay; Leone, Annie Fratellini; Omar, Georges Blaness; First Inspector, Francois Mirante; Second Inspector, Francois Dalou; Elizabeth, Patricia Scott; Mme. Clancul, Marie Helene Caste; Lescure, Daniel Ceccaldi; Clancul, Georges Chamarat.

556 CLOSELY WATCHED TRAINS. (Sigma III-1967). Trainee Milos, Vaclav Neckar; Conductor Masa, Jitka Bendova; Stationmaster, Vladimir Valenta; Stationmaster's Wife, Libuse Havelkova; Train Dispatcher Hubeika, Josef Somr; Station Assistant, Alois Vachek; Telegraphist, Jitka Zelenohorska; Councillor Zednicek, Vlastimil Brodsky; Uncle Noneman, Ferdinand Kruta; The Countess, Kveta Fialova; Victoria Freie, Nada Urbankova; Doctor Brabec, Jiri Menzel.

557 CLOUDS OVER ISRAEL. (1966). Dan, Yiftach Spector; Bedouin boy, Ehud Banai; Bedouin woman, Dina Doronne; The infant Sinaia, Hadara Azulai; Enemy pilot, Shaike Levi; Enemy Scout, Itzhak Benyamini; Enemy soldier, Itzhak Barzilai; Enemy jeep soldier, Ygal Alon; Uri, Shimon Israeli.

558 THE CLOWNS. (Levitt-Pickman-1971). The Clowns, Billi, Scotti, Fanfulla, Rizzo, Pistoni, Furia, Reder, Valentini, 14 Colombaioni, Merli, I Martana, Maggio, Sbarra, Carini, Terzo, Vingelli, Fumagalli, Zerbinati, Janigro, Maunsell,

Peverello, Sorrentino, Valdemara, Bevilacqua.

559 CLUE OF THE TWISTED CANDLE. (Lester Schoenfeld-1968). Superintendent Meredith, Bernard Lee; John Lexman/Dr. Griswold, David Knight; Ramon Karadis, Francis De Wolff; Grace Neilson, Colette Wilde; Belinda Holland, Christine Shaw; Sgt. Anson, Stanley Morgan; Police Commissioner, A. J. Brown; Pike Fisher, Richard Caldicott; Manservant, Edmond Bennett; Jock, Simon Lack; Sgt. Butterfield, Anthony Baird; Landlady, Gladys Henson; Finch, Alfred Maron; Viney, Richard Vernon; Secretary, Kenneth Fortescue; Miss Cunningham, Hazel Hughes; Amis, Harry Locke; Brennan, Roy Purcell.

560 C'MON, LET'S LIVE A LITTLE. (Paramount-1967). Jesse Crawford, Bobby Vee; Judy Grant, Jackie De Shannon; Eddie Stewart, Eddie Hodges; Bee Bee Vendemeer, Suzi Kaye; Mrs. Fitts, Patsy Kelly; An' Effel, Ethel Smith; Bo-Bo, Bo Belinsky; Rego, John Ireland Jr.; Jeb Crawford, Don Crawford; Tim Grant, Mark Evans; John W. Grant, Russ Conway; Wendy, Jill Banner; Melinda, Kim Carnes; Joy, Joy Tobin; Balta, Frank Alesia; The Beard, Ken Osmond; Spuko, Tiger Joe Marsh; Jake, Ben Frommer; The Pair Extraordinaire.

561 COAST OF SKELETONS. (Seven Arts-1965). The Insurance Man, Richard Todd; The Texas Tycoon, Dale Robertson.

562 THE COBRA. (American International-1968). Chief Kelly, Dana Andrews; Mike Rand, Peter Martell; Lou, Anita Ekberg; Corinne, Elisa Montes; Stiarkos, Jesus Puente; Hullinger, Peter Dane; Ulla, Luciana Vincenzi; Crane, George Histman; Sadek, Omar Zolficar; King, Giovanni Petrucci; Li Fang, Chang'E; Gamal, Ehsane Sadek.

563 THE COCKEYED COWBOYS OF CALICO COUNTY. (Universal-1970). Charley, Dan Blocker; Sadie, Nanette Fabray; Staunch, Jim Backus; Bester, Wally Cox; Kittrick, Jack Elam; Hanson, Henry Jones; Bartender, Stubby Kaye; Indian Tom, Mickey Rooney; Eddie, Noah Beery; Mrs. Bester, Marge Champion; Rusty, Donald Barry; Fowler, Hamilton Camp; Traveler, Tom Basham; Crazy Foot, Iron Eyes Cody; Dr. Henry, James McCallion; Rev. Marshall, Byron Foulger; Carson, Ray Ballard; Roger Hand, Jack Cassidy.

564 CODE NAME TRIXIE. (Cambist-1973). Judy, Lane Carroll; David, W. G. McMillan; Clank, Harold Wayne Jones; Colonel, Lloyd Hollar; Artie, Richard Liberty; Kathie, Lynn Lowry; Dr. Watts, Richard France; Maj. Rider, Harry Spillman.

565 CODE 7 VICTIM 5. (Universal-1965). Lex Barker, Ronald Fraser, Walter Rilla, Dietmar Schonherr, Gert Van Den Bergh, Howard Davies, Percy Sieff, Gustel Gundelach, Sophia Spentzos, Ann Smyrner, Veronique Vendell.

566 COFFY. (American International-1973). Coffy, Pam Grier; Brunswick, Booker Bradshaw; King George, Robert DoQui; Carter, William Elliott; Vitroni, Allan Arbus; Omar, Sid Haig; McHenry, Barry Cahill; Sugar-Man, Morris Buchanan; Nick, Lee de Broux; Studs, Bob Minor; Aleva, John Perak; Ramos, Ruben Moreno; Priscilla, Carol Lawson; Meg, Linda Haynes; Jeri, Lisa Farringer.

567 COLD SWEAT. (Emerson-1974). Charles Bronson, Liv Ullmann, James Mason, Jill Ireland, Michael Constantine, Jean Topart, Yannick Delulle, Luigi Pistilli.

568 COLD TURKEY. (United Artists-1971). Rev. Clayton Brooks, Dick Van Dyke; Natalie Brooks, Pippa Scott; Mr. Stopworth, Tom Poston; Hiram C. Grayson, Edward Everett Horton; TV Personalities, Bob and Ray; Merwin Wren, Bob Newhart; Mayor Wrappler, Vincent Gardenia; Dr. Proctor, Barnard Hughes; Mrs. Wrappler, Jean Stapleton; Letitia, Barbara Carson.

569 THE COLLECTOR. (Columbia-1965). Freddie Clegg, Terence Stamp; Miranda Grey, Samantha Eggar; Aunt Annie, Mona Washbourne; Neighbor, Maurice Dallimore.

570 COLOR ME DEAD. (Commonwealth-1969). Frank, Tom Tryon; Paula, Carolyn Jones; Bradley, Rick Jason; Marla, Patricia Connolly; Halliday, Tony Ward; Miss Foster, Penny Sugg; Eugene, Reg Gillam; Mrs. Phillips, Margot Reid; Stanley, Peter Sumner; George, Michael Lawrence; Chester, Sandy Harbott.

571 COME BACK BABY. (Film-Makers' Distribution Center-1968). Cal Thacker, John Terry Riebling; Carrie Da Silva, Barbara Teitelbaum; Mike Rubel, Mark Weishaus; Richard Stoney Morgan, Craig Bovia; Stoney's Sister, Barbara Rubel; Carrie's Girlfriend, Mary Anne Seibert; Stoney's Intended Victim, Colette Bablon; Girl in Bed, Jaqueline Uytenbogaart; Girl at Party, Jane Nornick; Boy at Party, Steve Steinhauer; Prostitute, Barbara Riebling; Thief, George Gerdes; Mugging Victim, John McDonald; Streetwalker, Felicia Waynesboro; Policemen, Henry Gribbin, Len Wanetik, Dave Stegstra.

572 COME BACK CHARLESTON BLUE. (Warner Bros. -1972). Gravedigger Jones, Godfrey Cambridge; Coffin Ed Johnson, Raymond St. Jacques; Joe, Peter De Anda; Carol, Jonelle Allen; Caspar, Maxwell Glanville; Her Majesty, Minnie Gentry; Jarema, Dick Sabol; Frank Mago, Leonardo Cimino; Bryce, Percy Rodrigues; Drag Queen, Toney Brealond; Earl J, Tim Pelt; Douglas, Darryl Knibb; Girl Barber, Marcia McBroom; Benjy, Adam Wade; Bubba, Joseph Ray; Cemetery Guard, Theodore Wilson; Streetwalker, Dorothi Fox.

573 COME HAVE COFFEE WITH US. (Altura-1973). Emerenziano, Ugo Tognazzi; Tarsilia, Milena Vukotic; Fortunata, Francesca Romana Coluzzi; Camilla, Angela Goodwin; Caterina, Valentine.

574 COME HOME AND MEET MY WIFE. (Fida-1974). Giulio, Ugo Tognazzi; Vicenzina, Ornella Muti; Giovanni, Michele Placido.

575 COME SPY WITH ME. (20th Century-Fox-1967). Pete Barker, Troy Donahue; Jill Parsons, Andrea Dromm; Walter Ludeker, Albert Dekker; Linda, Lucienne Bridou; Larry Claymore, Mart Hulswit; Samantha, Valerie Allen; Augie, Dan Ferrone; Corbett, Howard Schell; Chance, Chance Gentry; Gunther Stiller, Louis Edmonds; Chris, Kate Aldrich; Pam, Pam Colbert; Kieswetter, Gil Pratley; Pantin, Georges Shoucair; Keefer, Alston Bair; Morgan, Tim Moxon; Karl, Eric Coverly; Brooks, Jack Lewis.

576 THE COMEDIANS. (MGM-1967). Brown, Richard Burton; Martha Pineda, Elizabeth Taylor; Jones, Alec Guinness; Ambassador Pineda, Peter Ustinov; Smith, Paul Ford; Mrs. Smith, Lillian Gish; Concasseur, Raymond St. Jacques; Michel, Zaeks Mokae; Petit Pierre, Roscoe Lee Browne; Joseph, Douta Seck; Cesar, Albia Peters; Mrs. Philipot, Gloria Foster; Angelito, Robin Langford; Henri Philipot, Georg Stanford Brown; Dr. Magiot, James Earl Jones; Marie Therese, Cicely Tyson.

577 COMETOGETHER. (Allied Artists-1971). Tony, Tony Anthony; Lisa, Luciana Paluzzi; Ann, Rosemary Dexter.

578 THE COMIC. (Columbia-1969). Billy Bright, Dick Van Dyke; Mary Gibson, Michele Lee; Cockeye, Mickey Rooney; Frank Powers, Cornel Wilde; Sybil, Nina Wayne; Mama, Pert Kelton; Steve Allen, himself; Ginger, Barbara Heller; Edward G. Englehardt, Ed Peck; Lorraine, Jeannine Riley; First Director, Gavin MacLeod; Miguel, Jay Novello; Doctor, Craig Huebing; Phoebe, Paulene Myers; Armad, Fritz Feld; Lawrence, Jerome Cowan; Woman, Isabell Sanford; Nurse, Jeff Donnell; At Schilling, Carl Reiner.

579 COMING APART. (Kaleidoscope-1969). Joe, Rip Torn; Joy, Megan McCormick; Burn Lady, Lois Markle; Girl with baby carriage, Lynn Swann; Monica, Viveca Lindfors; JoAnn, Sally Kirkland; Friend's Wife, Phoebe Dorin; Amy, Nancy MacKay; Second McCarthy Worker, Julie Garfield; Armand, Kevin O'Connor; Sarabell, Robert Blankshine; Couple at party, Michael McGuire, Darlene Cotton; Dancing Lady, Joanna Vischer; Wife, Jane Marla Robbins.

580 COMPAÑEROS. (Cinerama-1972). Yod, Franco Nero; Vasco, Tomas Milian; John, Jack Palance; Professor Xantos, Fernando

Rey; Lola, Iris Berben; General Mongo, Francisco Bodalo; Zaira, Karin Schubert; Colonel, Edoardo Fajardo; Lieutenant, Gerard Tichy; Captain at Yuma, Lorenzo Robledo; Student, Jesus Fernandez; Luigi Pernice, Alvaro de Luna, Claudio Scarchili, Giovanni Petti, Gianni Pulone.

581 COMPANY OF KILLERS. (Universal-1972). Sam, Van Johnson; Georges, Ray Milland; Nick, Brian Kelly; John, Fritz Weaver; Frank, Clu Gulager; Thelma, Susan Oliver; Edwina, Diana Lynn; Dave, John Saxon; Owen, Robert Middleton; Jaffie, Terry Carter; Maryjane, Anna Capri; Jimmy, Anthony James; Sylvia, Marian Collier; Peterson, Nate Esformes; Luke, Mercer Harris; Marnie, Joyce Jameson; Chick, Gerald Hiken; Dale, Vince Howard; Clarington, Larry Thor; Gloria, Donna Michelle; Patricia, Jeanne Bal.

582 THE COMPUTER WORE TENNIS SHOES. (Buena Vista-1970). A. J. Arno, Cesar Romero; Dexter, Kurt Russell; Dean Higgins, Joe Flynn; Prof. Quigley, William Schallert; Dean Collingsgood, Alan Hewitt; Chillie Walsh, Richard Bakalyan; Annie, Debbie Paine; Pete, Frank Webb; Schuyler, Michael McGreevey; Bradley, Jon Provost; Henry, Frank Welker; Myles, Alexander Clarke; Angelo, Bing Russell; Moderator, Pat Harrington; Little Mac, Fabian Dean; Sigmund Van Dyke, Fritz Feld; Lt. Hannah, Pete Renoudet; J. Reedy, Hillyard Anderson.

583 THE CONCERT FOR BANGLADESH. (20th Century-Fox-1972). Eric Clapton, George Harrison, Leon Russell, Ringo Starr, Bob Dylan, Billy Preston, Ravi Shankar, Klaus Voormann.

584 THE CONCUBINES. (Boxoffice International-1969). Pan Chin Lein, Tomoko Mayama; Wu-Sung, Shikyoku Takashima; Hsi-Men-Ching, Juuzo Itami; Li-Ping-Brh, Ruriko Asari; Chun-Mei, Riko Yurenai; Wu-Ta, Hatsuo Yamatani; Ying, Ko-Hei Tsusaki; Hau, Yuzo Tachikawa.

585 EL CONDOR. (National General-1970). Luke, Jim Brown; Jaroo, Lee Van Cleef; Chavez, Patrick O'Neal; Claudine, Marianna Hill; Santana, Iron Eyes Cody; Dolores, Imogen Hassall; Old Convict, Elisha Cook Jr.; Col. Aguinaldo, Gustavo Rojo; Aguila, Florencio Amarilla; Gen. Hernandez, Julio Pena; Lieutenant, Angel Del Pozo; Julio, Patricio Santiago; Prison Guard Captain, John Clark; Indian, Raul Mendoza Castro; Officer, Rafael Albaicin; Officer for Convicts, George Ross; Chief Mexican Bandit, Ricardo Palacios; Bandits, Charles Stalnaker, Carlos Bravo, Dan Van Husen; Convicts, Peter Lenahan, Art Larkin, Per Barclay.

586 THE CONFESSION. (Paramount-1970). Gerard, Yves Montand; Lise, Simone Signoret; Kohoutek, Gabriele Ferzetti; Smola, Michael Vitold; Boss, Jean Bouise.

587 CONFESSIONS OF A WINDOW CLEANER. (Columbia-1974). Timothy Lea, Robin Askwith; Sidney Noggett, Anthony Booth; Rosie Noggett, Sheila White; Mrs. Lea, Dandy Nichols; Mr. Lea, Bill Maynard; Elizabeth Radlett, Linda Hayden; Inspector Radlett, John Le Mesurier; Mrs. Radlett, Joan Hickson; Richard Wattis, Melissa Stribling, Anita Graham, Sam Kydd, Brian Hall, Christine Donna, Sue Longhurst, Olivia Munday, Judy Matheson, Elaine Baillie, Christopher Owen, Peter Dennis, Marianne Stone, Andee Cromarty, David Rose, Totti Truman Taylor, Frank Sieman, Anika Pavel, Hugo De Vernier, Bruce Wightman, Carole Augustine, Lionel Murton, Peter Fontaine, Jeannie Collings, Claire Russell, Jo Peters, Monika Ringwald, Projai Nicholas, Derek Lord, Robert Longdon.

588 THE CONFORMIST. (Paramount-1971). Marcello, Jean-Louis Trintignant; Giulia, Stefania Sandrelli; Anna Quadri, Dominique Sanda; Nino Seminara, Pierre Clementi; Manganiello, Gastone Moschin.

589 THE CONQUERED CITY. (American International-1966). David Niven, Ben Gazzara, Martin Balsam, Lea Massari, Michael Craig.

590 THE CONQUEROR WORM. (American International-1968). Matthew Hopkins, Vincent Price; Richard Marshall, Ian Ogilvy; Sara, Hilary Dwyer; John Lowes, Rupert Davies; John Stearne, Robert Russell; Oliver Cromwell, Patrick Wymark; Master Coach, Wilfrid Brambell; Captain Gordon, Michael Beint; Trooper Swallow, Nicky Henson; Trooper Harcourt, John Trenaman; Trooper Gifford, William Maxwell; Tony Selby, Beaufoy Milton, John Kidd, Peter Haigh, Hira Talfrey, Ann Tirard, Peter Thomas, Edward Palmer, David Webb, Godfrey James, Paul Dawkins, Jack Lynn, Martin Terry, Lee Peters, David Lyell, Toby Lennon, Maggie Kimberley, Bernard Kay, Gillian Aldham, Paul Ferris, Alf Joint, Morris Segal, Maggie Nolan, Sally Douglas, Donna Reading, Tasma Brereton, Sandy Seager.

591 THE CONQUEST OF THE PLANET OF THE APES. (20th Century-Fox-1972). Caesar, Roddy Mc Dowall; Governor Breck, Don Murray; Lisa, Natalie Trundy; MacDonald, Hari Rhodes; Police Chief Kolp, Severn Darden; Busboy, Lou Wagner; Commission Chairman, John Randolph; Mrs. Riley, Asa Maynor; Hoskyns, H. M. Wynant; Aldo, David Chow; Frank, Buck Kartalian; Policeman, John Dennis; Auctioneer, Gordon Jump; Announcer, Dick Spangler; Zelda, Joyce Haber; Ape With Chain, Hector Soucy; 2nd Policeman, Paul Comi; Armando, Ricardo Montalban.

592 CONRACK. (20th Century-Fox-1974). Jon Voight, Paul Winfield, Hume Cronyn, Madge Sinclair, Tina Andrews, Antonio Fargas, Ruth Attaway, James O'Reare.

593 CONTEST GIRL. (Continental-1966). Ian Hendry, Janette Scott, Ronald Fraser, Edmund Purdom, Jean Claudio, Kay Walsh, Norman Bird, Janina Faye, Tommy Trinder, David Weston, Francis Matthews, Linda Christian.

594 THE CONVERSATION. (Paramount-1974). Harry Caul, Gene Hackman; Stanley, John Cazale; Bernie Moran, Allen Garfield; Mark, Frederic Forrest; Ann, Cindy Williams; Paul, Michael Higgins; Meredith, Elizabeth MacRae; Amy, Teri Garr; Martin Stett, Harrison Ford; Receptionist, Mark Wheeler; The Mime, Robert Shields; Lurleen, Phoebe Alexander; The Director, Robert Duvall.

595 CONVICT STAGE. (20th Century-Fox-1965). Harry Lauter, Donald Barry, Hanna Landy, Jodi Mitchell, Joseph Patridge, Eric Matthews, Walter Reed, Michael Carr, Fred Krone, George Sawaya, Karl MacDonald.

596 COOGAN'S BLUFF. (Universal-1968). Walt Coogan, Clint Eastwood; Det. Lt. McElroy, Lee J. Cobb; Julie Roth, Susan Clark; Linny Raven, Tisha Sterling; James Ringerman, Don Stroud; Mrs. Ringerman, Betty Field; Sheriff McCrea, Tom Tully; Millie, Melodie Johnson; Jackson, James Edwards; Running Bear, Rudy Diaz; David F. Doyle, Louis Zorich, Meg Myles, Marjorie Bennett, Seymour Cassel, Joe Coe, Skip Battyn, Albert Popwell, Conrad Bain, James Gavin, Albert Henderson, James McCallion, Syl Lamont, Jess Osuna, Jerry Summers, Antonia Rey, Marya Henriques.

597 COOL BREEZE. (MGM-1972). Sidney Lord Jones, Thalmus Rasulala; Obalese Eaton, Judy Pace; Bill Mercer, Raymond St. Jacques; Travis Battle, Jim Watkins; Lt. Brian Knowles, Lincoln Kilpatrick; Stretch Finian, Sam Laws; Lark, Margaret Avery; Mona, Pamela Grier; Martha Harris, Paula Kelly; John Battle, Wally Taylor; Roy Harris, Rudy Challenger; Captain Lloyd Harmon, Stewart Bradley; Bus Driver, Edmund Cambridge; Emma Mercer, Royce Wallace; Tinker, Stack Pierce; Lt. Carl Magers, Biff Elliot; Lt. Holster, John Lupton; Raynor, Christopher Joy; Vivian, Tracee Lyles; Officer Matton, Charles Walker; Father Blue, Lee Weaver; Beauty Contestants, Jovita Bush and Linda Sexton and Rita Ford.

598 COOL HAND LUKE. (Warner Bros. -7 Arts-1967). Lucas (Luke) Jackson, Paul Newman; Dragline, George Kennedy; Society Red, J. D. Cannon; Koko, Lou Antonio; Loudmouth Steve, Robert Drivas; The Captain, Strother Martin; Arletta (Luke's Mother), Jo Van Fleet; Carr, Clifton James; Boss Godfrey, Morgan Woodward; Boss Paul, Luke Askew; Rabbitt, Marc Cavell; Blind Dick, Richard Davalos; Boss Shorty, Robert Donner; Tattoo, Warren Finnerty; Babalugats, Dennis Hopper; Bos Kean, John McLiam; Gambler, Wayne Rogers; Tramp, Dean Stanton; Boss Higgins, Charles Tyner; Alibi,

Ralph Waite; Dog Boy, Anthony Zerbe; Dynamite, Buck Kartalian; The Girl, Joy Harmon; Sleepy, James Gammon; Fixer, Joe Don Baker; Sailor, Donn Pearce; Stupid Blondie, Norman Goodwins; Chief, Charles Hicks; John Sr., John Pearce; John Jr., Eddie Rosson; Rush Williams, James Jeter, Robert Luster, Rance Howard, James Bradley, Jr., Cyril Robinson.

599 THE COOL ONES. (Warner Bros. -1967). Tony Krum, Roddy McDowall; Hallie Rodgers, Debbie Watson; Cliff Donner, Gil Peterson; Fred MacElwaine, Phil Harris; Mrs. Miller, Mrs. Elvira Miller; Stanley Krumley, Robert Coote; Dee Dee, Nita Talbot; Howie Snitzer, George Furth; Charlie Forbes, Jim Begg; Manager, James Milhollin; Uncle Steve, Phil Arnold; Sandy, Melanie Alexander; The Bantams, Glenn Campbell, The Leaves, T. J and the Fourmations.

600 THE COP. (Audubon-1971). Inspector, Michel Bouquet; Helene, Francoise Fabian; Barnero, Bernard Fresson; Dan, John Garko; Viletti, Michel Constantin; Lupo, Theo Sarapo; Beausourire, Henri Garcin; Commissioner, Adolfo Celi.

601 COP-OUT. (Cinerama-1968). John Sawyer, James Mason; Angela Sawyer, Geraldine Chaplin; Barney Teale, Bobby Darin; Jo Christophorides, Paul Bertoya; Desmond Flower, Ian Ogilvy; Sue Phillips, Pippa Steel; Peter Hawkins, Bryan Stanton; Colonel Flower, Clive Morton; Harry Hawkins, James Hayter; Mrs. Christophorides, Megs Jenkins; Diana, Lisa Daniely; Mrs. Flower, Moira Lister; Girl at Shooting Range, Yootha Joyce; Old Clerk, John Henderson; Mrs. Plaskett, Rita Webb; Chetham, Canvers Walker; Policeman, Julian Orchard; Inspector Colder, Ivor Dean; Brenda, Marjie Lawrence; Angela (as a child), Lindy Aaron; Library Cleaner, Lucy Griffiths; Charlotte Selwyn; Melinda May, Tom Kempinski, Sheila White, Toni Palmer, Anne Hart, Michael Standing.

602 COPS AND ROBBERS. (United Artists-1973). Tom, Cliff Gorman; Joe, Joe Bologna; Paul Jones, Dick Ward; Eastpole, Shepperd Strudwick; Secretary, Ellen Holly; Patsy, John Ryan; Bandell, Nino Ruggeri; Mary, Gayle Gorman; Grace, Lucy Martin; Hardware Store Owner, Lee Steel; Black Lady, Frances Foster; Thief, Jacob Weiner; Attendants, Arthur Pierce, Martin Cove; Clerk, Jim Ferguson; Wino, Walter Gorney; Rocco, Frank Gio; Ed, Jeff Ossuno; Marty, Joseph Spinell; Harry, George Harris II.

603 CORKY. (MGM-1972). Corky, Robert Blake; His Wife, Charlotte Rampling; Randy, Patrick O'Neal; Billy, Christopher Connelly; Rhonda, Pamela Payton-Wright; Boland, Ben Johnson; Wayne, Laurence Luckinbill; Tobin, Paul Stevens.

604 CORPORATE QUEEN. (Victoria-1969). Crystal, Renay Claire; Edna, Marie Brent; Chino, Tony Vito.

605 THE CORPSE GRINDERS. (Gemini-1972). Dr. Howard Glass, Sean Kenney; Angie Robinson, Monika Kelly; Landau, Sanford Mitchell; Maltby, J. Byron Foster; Caleb, Warren Ball; Cleo, Ann Noble; Monk, Vince Barbi; The Neighbor, Harry Lovejoy; Mr. De Sisto, Earl Burnam; Mrs. Babcock, Zena Foster; Mr. Babcock, Ray Dannis; Tessie, Drucilla Joy; Curt Matson, Charles "Foxy" Fox, Stephen Lester, William Kirschner, George Bowden, Andy Collings, Don Ellis, Mike Garrison, Mary Ellen Burke.

606 THE CORRUPT ONES. (Warner Bros.-1967). Cliff Wilder, Robert Stack; Lily, Elke Sommer; Tina, Nancy Kwan; Joey Brandon, Christian Marquand; Pinto, Werner Peters; Danny Mancini, Maurizio Arena; Kau-Song, Richard Haller; Hugo, Dean Hyde; Chow, Ah-Yue-Lou; Madame Vulcano, Marisa Merlini; Jasmine, Heide Bohlen.

607 CORRUPTION. (Columbia-1968). Sir John Rowan, Peter Cushing; Lynn Nolan, Sue Lloyd; Steve Harris, Noel Trevarthen; Val Nolan, Kate O'Mara; Groper, David Lodge; Mike Orme, Anthony Booth; Terry, Wendy Varnals; Rik, Billy Murray; Kate, Vanessa Howard; Girl in the flat, Jan Waters; Georgie, Phillip Manikum; Sandy, Alexandra Dane; Girl in the train, Valerie Van Ost; Claire, Diana Ashley; Mortuary Attendant, Victor Baring; Girl at the party, Shirley Stelfox.

608 COTTON COMES TO HARLEM. (United Artists-1969). Grave Digger Jones, Godfrey Cambridge; Coffin Ed Johnson, Raymond St. Jacques; Rev. Deke O'Malley, Calvin Lockhart; Iris, Judy Pace; Uncle Bud, Redd Foxx; Bryce, John Anderson; Mabel, Emily Yancy; Calhoun, J. D. Cannon; Billie, Mabel Robinson; Jarema, Dick Sabol; Barry, Theodore Wilson; Casper, Maxwell Glanville; Anderson, Eugene Roche; Early Riser, Van Kirksey; Lo Boy, Cleavon Little; Church Sister, Helen Martin; Hi Jenks, Arnold Williams.

609 COTTONPICKIN' CHICKENPICKERS. (Souther Musical Productions and Southeastern Pictures Corporation-1967). Darby Clyde Fenster, Del Reeves; Jerry Martin, Hugh X. Lewis; Cousin Urie, Sonny Tufts; Deputy Burke, David Houston; Greta, Greta Thyssen; Mailman, Slapsy Maxie Rosenbloom; Viola Zickafoose, Lila Lee; Bird-Dog Berrigan, Tommy Noonan; Deputy Will, Hank Mills; Judge Beale, Philip Hunter; Susie Zickafoose, Margie Bowes; David, David Wilkins; Dreama Sue, J. D. Marshall; Brigit, Birgitta Andersson; Uncle Ned, Ted Lehman; Cousin Elwood, Christian Anderson; Hound-Dog Berrigan, Mel Tillis; Sheriff Mathis, Jack Morey; Liquid Louie Tallfeathers, Buck Bayliss.

610 COULD I BUT LIVE. (Toho-1965). Keiju Kobayashi, Hideko Takamine.

611 COUNT DRACULA. (Crystal-1972). Count Dracula, Christopher

Lee; Professor van Helsing, Herbert Lom; Renfield, Klaus Kinski; Jonathan Harker, Frederick Williams; Mina Harker, Maria Rohm; Lucy Westenra, Soledad Miranda; Dr. Seward, Jack Taylor; Quincey Morris, Paul Muller; Teresa Gimpera.

612 COUNT YORGA, VAMPIRE. (American International-1970). Yorga, Robert Quarry; Hayes, Roger Perry; Paul, Michael Murphy; Michael, Michael Macready; Donna, Donna Anders; Erica, Judith Lang; Brudah, Edward Walsh; Cleo, Julie Conners; Peter, Paul Hansen; Judy, Sybil Scotford; Mother, Marsha Jordan; Vampire, Deborah Darnell; Nurse, Erica Macready.

613 COUNTDOWN. (Warner Bros. -7 Arts-1968). Lee Stegler, James Caan; Mickey Stegler, Joanna Moore; Chiz, Robert Duvall; Jean, Barbara Baxley; Gus, Charles Aidman; Ross, Steve Ihnat; Rick, Michael Murphy; Larson, Ted Knight; Ehrman, Stephen Coit; Dunc, John Rayner; Seidel, Charles Irving; Stevie, Bobby Riha Jr.

614 THE COUNTERFEIT CONSTABLE. (7 Arts-1966). Henri, Robert Dhery; Yvette, Colette Brosset; Yvette's Husband, Ronald Fraser; Herself, Diana Dors; Telephone Operator, Pierre Olaf; Bank Robber, Arthur Mullard; Police Sergeant, Bernard Cribbins; Jean Lefebvre, Robert Rollis, Henri Genes, Catherine Sola.

615 THE COUNTERFEIT KILLER. (Universal-1968). Don Owens, Jack Lord; Angie Peterson, Shirley Knight; Randolph Riker, Jack Weston; Dolan, Charles Drake; Rajeski, Joseph Wiseman; O'Hara, Don Hammer; Ed, Robert Pine; George, George Tyne; Reggie, Cal Bartlett; Keyser, Dean Heyde; Hotel Clerk, L. Q. Jones; Ambulance Driver, David Renard; Plainclothesman, Nicholas Colasanto; Frances, Mercedes McCambridge.

616 COUNTERPOINT. (Universal-1968). Lionel Evans, Charlton Heston; General Schiller, Maximilian Schell; Annabelle Rice, Kathryn Hays; Victor Rice, Leslie Nielsen; Colonel Arndt, Anton Diffring; Lieutenant Long, Linden Chiles; Sergeant Calloway, Pete Masterson; Captain Klingermann, Curt Lowens; Dorothy Neva Patterson; Tartzoff, Cyril Delevanti; Jordon, Gregory Morton; Chaminant, Dan Drazer; Prescott, Ed Peck; Belgian Officer, Ralph Nelson.

617 COUNTESS DRACULA. (20th Century-Fox-1972). Countess Elizabeth Nadasdy, Ingrid Pitt; Captain Dobi, Nigel Green; Imre Toth, Sandor Eles; Julie, Patience Collier; Master Fabio, Maurice Denham; Captain Balogh, Peter Jeffrey; Ilona, Lesley-Anne Down; Bailiff Sergeant, Leon Lissek; Rosa, Jessie Evans; Ziza, Andrea Lawrence; Teri, Susan Brodrick; Clown, Ian Trigger; Gypsy Girl, Nike Arrighi; Janco, Peter May; Priest, John Moore; Cook, Joan Haythorne; Kitchen Maid, Marianne Stone; The Seller, Charles Farrell; Bertha,

Sally Adcock; Pregnant Woman, Anne Stallybrass; Man, Paddy Ryan; Young Man, Michael Cadman; Belly Dancer, Hulya Babus; Gypsy Dancers, Leslie Anderson, Biddy Hearne, Diana Sawday; Boys, Andrew Burleigh, Gary Rich; Circus Midgets, Ismed Hassan and Albert Wilkinson.

618 A COUNTESS FROM HONG KONG. (Universal-1967). Ogden Mears, Marlon Brando; Natascha, Sophia Loren; Harvey Crothers, Sydney Chaplin; Martha, Tippi Hedren; Hudson, Patrick Cargill; Miss Gaulswallow, Margaret Rutherford; John Felix, Michael Medwin; Clark, Oliver Johnston; The Captain, John Paul; The Society Girl, Angela Scoular; An Old Steward, Charles Chaplin; Peter Bartlett, Bill Nagy, Dilys Laye, Angela Pringle, Jenny Bridges, Arthur Gross, Balbina, Anthony Chin, Jose Sukhum Boonlve, Janine Hill, Burnell Tucker, Leonard Trolley, Len Lowe, Francis Dux, Cecil Cheng, Ronald Rubin, Michael Spice, Ray Marlowe, Kervin Manser, Marianne Stone, Lew Luton, Larry Cross, Bill Edwards, Drew Russell, John Sterland, Paul Carson, Paul Tamarin, Carol Cleveland.

619 COUNTRY CUZZINS. (Box Office International-1972). Billie Jo, Rene Bond; LeRoy, John Tull; Jenny, Pamela Princess; Fester, Jack Richisen; Prudence, Ellen Stephens; Jeff, Mark Buckalew; Jeeter, Steven Hodge; Ma, Zena Foster; The Agent, Buck Flower; Melody, Melody Combe; Girl in Maid's Room, Debbie Osborne.

620 A COVENANT WITH DEATH. (Warner Bros. -1967). Ben Lewis, George Maharis; Rosemary, Laura Devon; Eulalia Lewis, Katy Jurado; Bryan Talbot, Earl Holliman; Judge Hochstadter, Arthur O'Connell; Col. Oates, Sidney Blackmer; Harmsworth, Gene Hackman; Dietrich, John Anderson; Rafaela, Wende Wagner; Ignacio, Emilio Fernandez; Parmalee, Kent Smith; Musgrave, Lonny Chapman; Digby, Jose De Vega; Chillingworth, Larry D. Mann; Bruce Donnelly, Whit Bissell; Dr. Shilling, Russell Thorson; Governor, Paul Birch; Willie Wayte, Erwin Neal; Policeman, Robert Dunlap; Louise Talbot, Jadine Vaughn.

621 COVER ME BABE. (20th Century-Fox-1970). Tony, Robert Forster; Melisse, Sondra Locke; Sybil, Susanne Benton; Will, Robert S. Fields; Jerry, Ken Kercheval; Cameraman, Sam Waterston; Steve, Michael Margotta; Derelict, Mike Kellin; Ronnie, Floyd Mutrux; Prostitute, Maggie Thrett; Paul, Jeff Corey; Michael, Regis Toomey; Mother, Mitzi Hoag; Transvestite, Franklin Townsend; Male Puppet, Mello Alexandria; Female Puppet, Linda Howe; Michael Payne, Carmen Argenziano.

622 THE COWARDS. (Jaylo-1970). Philip, John Ross; Joan, Susan Sparling; Peter, Will Patent; Mr. Yates, Thomas Murphy; Father Reis, Philip B. Hall; Mr. Haller, Alexander

Gellman; Mrs. Haller, Edith Briden.

623 THE COWBOYS. (Warner Bros.-1972). Wil Anderson, John Wayne; Jebediah Nighlinger, Roscoe Lee Browne; Long Hair, Bruce Dern; Kate, Colleen Dewhurst; Anse, Slim Pickens; Preacher, Lonny Chapman; Mr. Jenkins, Charles Tyner; Cimarron, A. Martinez; Singing Fats, Alfred Barker Jr.; Four Eyes, Nicolas Beauvy; Steve, Steve Benedict; Slim Honeycutt, Robert Carradine; Weedy, Norman Howell Jr.; Charlie Schwartz, Stephen Hudis; Stuttering Bob, Sean Kelly; Hardy Fimps, Clay O'Brien; Jimmy Phillips, Sam O'Brien; Homer Weems, Mike Pyeatt; Anne Anderson, Sarah Cunningham; Ellen Price, Allyn Ann McLerie; Smiley, Matt Clark; Red Tucker, Wallace Brooks; Pete, Jim Burk; Jake, Larry Finley; Phoebe, Maggie Costain; Howdy, Jerry Gatlin; Okay, Walter Scott; Henry Williams, Dick Farnsworth; Elizabeth, Charise Cullin; Rosemary, Collette Poeppel; Jim's Father, Norman Howell Sr.; Bob's Mother, Margaret Kelley; Ben, Larry Randles; Rustlers, Fred Brookfield, Tap Canutt, Chuck Courtney, Gary Epper, Kent Hays, J. R. Randall, Henry Wills, Joe Yrigoyen.

624 CRACK IN THE WORLD. (Paramount-1965). Stephen Sorensen, Dana Andrews; Maggie Sorensen, Janette Scott; Ted Rampion, Kieron Moore; Sir Charles Eggerston, Alexander Knox.

625 CRAZE. (Warner Bros.-1974). Neal Mottram, Jack Palance; Dolly Newman, Diana Dors; Helena, Julie Ege; Aunt Louise, Edith Evans; Solicitor, Hugh Griffith; Supt. Bellamy, Trevor Howard; Detective Sgt. Wall, Michael Jayston; Sally, Suzy Kendall; Ronnie, Martin Potter.

626 CRAZY JOE. (Columbia-1974). Peter Boyle, Paula Prentiss, Fred Williamson, Charles Cioffi, Rip Torn, Luther Adler, Fausto Tozzi, Franco Lantieri, Eli Wallach, Henry Winkler, Gabriele Torrsi, Guido Leontini, Sam Coppola, Adam Wade, Timothy Halley, Ralph Wilcox, Peter Savage, Robert Riesel, Dan Resin, Nella Dirk.

627 CRAZY PARADISE. (Sherpix-1965). Angelus Goat, Dirch Passer; Thor Goat, Hans W. Petersen; Simon, Ove Sprogoe; Vicar, Paul Hagen; Vicar's wife, Ghita Norby; Bertha Virginius, Bodil Steen; Greta, Lone Hertz; Per Mortensen, Karl Stegner; Reporter, Kjeld Petersen; Betsy Buttock, Elsebeth Larsen.

628 CRAZY QUILT. (Continental-1966). Henry, Rom Rosqui; Lorabelle, Ina Mela; Baby, David Winter; Doctor, S. Maloch Gospe; Minister, George William Meyers; Cyrus, Harry Hunt; Jim, Calvin Kentfield; Dr. Milton Tugwell, Robert Marquis; Big Game Hunter, David Wald; Voice Teacher, Jerry Mander; Fortune Teller, Sonia Berman; Noel, Ellen Frye; Noel (as a

child), Vicki Miller; Falbuck Wheeling, Doug Korty; Narrator, Burgess Meredith.

629 THE CRAZY WORLD OF JULIUS VROODER. (20th Century-Fox-1974). Julius Vrooder, Timothy Bottoms; Nurse Willis, Barbara Seagull; Dr. Passki, Lawrence Pressman; Corky, George Marshall; Splint, Albert Salmi; Vrooder's Parents, Richard A. Dysart, Dena Dietrich; Vrooder's Sister, Debralee Scott; Telephone and Power Executives, Lou Frizzell, Jack Murdock; Alessini, Michael Ivan Cristofer; Rodali, Dewayne Jessie; Chaplain, Andrew Duncan; Detective, Jack Colvin.

630 THE CRAZY WORLD OF LAUREL AND HARDY. (Joseph Brenner Associates-1967). Narrator, Garry Moore; Stan Laurel and Oliver Hardy.

631 LES CREATURES. (New Yorker-1969). Wife, Catherine Deneuve; Writer, Michel Piccoli; Hotel Owner, Eva Dahlbeck; Young Man, Jacques Charrier; Electrician, Nino Castelnuovo; Vamp, Ursula Kubler.

632 THE CREEPING FLESH. (Columbia-1973). James, Christopher Lee; Emmanuel, Peter Cushing; Penelope, Lorna Heilbron; Waterlow, George Benson; Lenny, Kenneth J. Warren.

633 CRESCENDO. (Warner Bros. -1972). Susan, Stefanie Powers; Georges/Jacques, James Olson; Danielle, Margaretta Scott; Lillianne, Jane Lapotaire; Carter, Joss Ackland; Catherine, Kirsten Betts.

634 CRIES AND WHISPERS. (New World-1972). Agnes, Harriet Andersson; Karin, Ingrid Thulin; Maria, Liv Ullmann; Doctor, Erland Josephson; Anna, Kary Sylway; Karin's Husband, George Arlin; Joakin, Henning Moritzen.

635 THE CRIMSON CULT. (American International-1970). Prof. Marsh, Boris Karloff; Morley, Christopher Lee; Robert, Mark Eden; Lavinia, Barbara Steele; Elder, Michael Gough; Radford, Rupert Davies; Eve, Virginia Wetherell.

636 CROMWELL. (Columbia-1970). Oliver Cromwell, Richard Harris; King Charles I, Alec Guinness; Earl of Manchester, Robert Morley; Queen Henrietta Maria, Dorothy Tutin; John Carter, Frank Finlay; Prince Rupert, Timothy Dalton; Earl of Strafford, Patrick Wymark; Hugh Peters, Patrick Magee; Sir Edward Hyde, Nigel Stock; Lord Essex, Charles Gray; Henry Ireton, Michael Jayston; Oliver Cromwell II, Richard Cornish; Ruth Carter, Anna Cropper; Solicitor General, Michael Goodliffe; General Byron, Jack Gwillim; Hacker, Basil Henson; Capt. Lundsford, Patrick Holt; President Bradshaw, Stratford Johns; John Pym, Geoffrey Keen; Richard Cromwell, Anthony May; John Hampden, Ian McCulloch; John

Lilburne, Patrick O'Connell; General Digby, John Paul; Trooper Hawkins, Bryan Pringle; The Speaker, Llewelyn Rees; Prince of Wales, Robin Stewart; Archbishop Rinucinni, Andreevan Gyseghem; Mrs. Cromwell, Zena Walker; Bishop Juxon, John Welsh; Thomas Fairfax, Douglas Wilmer; Henry Cromwell, Anthony Kemp; Mary Cromwell, Stacy Dorning; Bridget Cromwell, Melinda Churcher; Old Man, William George Merritt; Drummer Boy, Gerald Rowland; Elizabeth Cromwell, Josephine Gillick.

637 THE CROOK. (United Artists-1971). Simon, Jean-Louis Trintignant; Janine, Daniele Delorme; Monsieur Gallois, Charles Denner; Martine, Christine Lelouch; Bill, Amidou; Martine's husband, Pierre Zimmer; Charles, Charles Gerard; Madame Gallois, Judith Magre; Inspector, Yves Robert; Daniel Gallois, Vincent Roziere, Sacha Distel.

638 THE CROOKED ROAD. (7 Arts-1965). Richard Ashley, Robert Ryan; Duke of Orgagna, Stewart Granger; Cosima, Nadia Gray; Harlequin, Marius Goring; Carlo, George Coulouris.

639 THE CROSS AND THE SWITCHBLADE. (Gateway-1972). David Wilkerson, Pat Boone; Nicky Cruz, Erik Estrada; Rosa, Jackie Giroux; Little Bo, JoAnn Robinson; Israel, Dino De Filippi; Abdullah, Don Blakely; Big Cat, Gil Frazier; Sergeant Delano, Don Lamond; Mr. Gomez, Sam Capuano; Mingo, Alex Colon; Moonlight, Hector Mercado; Augie, Stew Silver; Mrs. Gomez, Dorothy James; Pusher, David Connel; Angela, Michelle Galjour; Norma, Jackie Cronin; Mary, Virginia Alonso; Bottlecap, Darryl Speer; Chance, Thomas Mooney; Judge, Vincent O'Brien; District Attorney, Jay Devlin; Lawyer, Paul Haney; Pawnbroker, Darrel Adleman; Hugo, Victor Bumbalo; Trial Defendant, Stanley Finesmith; Court Policeman, Sal Christi; Reporter, Andrew T. Murphy; Photographer, Kleg Seth; Mau Mau Deb, Laura Figueroa; Bishop Deb, Jonelle Allen; Policeman, Mark Dawson; Elderly Woman, Dolores Raskin; Heckler, Norman Bly; Bishop, Tim Pelt.

640 CRUCIBLE OF HORROR. (Cannon-1971). Eastwood, Michael Gough; Edith, Yvonne Mitchell; Jane, Sharon Curney; Rupert, Simon Gough; Reid, Olaf Pooley; Gregson, David Butler; Benjy, Nicholas Jones; Servant, Mary Hignett; Gas Station Attendant, Howard Goorney.

641 THE CRUCIFIED LOVERS. (New Line Cinema-1971). Mohei, Kazuo Hasegawa; Osan, Kyrko Kogowa; Otama, Yoko Minamida; Ishun, Eitaro Shindo; Sukeyemon, Sakal Ozawa; Oko, Chieko Naniwa; Genebei, Ichiro Sugai; Doki, Haru Tanaka; Ison, Tatsuya Isheguro.

642 CRUNCH. (American International-1970). Harald Leipnitz, Sybille Maar, Brigitte Skay, Monika Lundi.

643 CRY OF THE BANSHEE. (American International-1970). Lord Whitman, Vincent Price; Oona, Elisabeth Bergner; Lady Patricia, Essy Persson; Mickey, Hugh Griffith; Maureen, Hilary Dwyer; Sarah, Sally Geeson; Roderick, Patrick Mower; Margaret, Pamela Farbrother; Father Tom, Marshall Jones; Harry, Carl Rigg; Burke, Michael Elphick; Sean, Stephen Chase; Bully Boy, Andrew McCullouch; Guest, Robert Hutton; Rider, Godfrey James; Brander, Terry Martin; Timothy, Richard Everett; Witchgirl, Quin O'Hara; Wench, Jan Rossini; Landlord, Gertan Klauber; Party Man, Peter Forest; Party Woman, Joyce Mandre.

644 CRYPT OF THE LIVING DEAD. (Atlas-1973). Andrew Prine, Mark Damon, Teresa Gimpera, Patty Sheppard, Francisco Brana.

645 CUL-DE-SAC. (Sigma III-1966). George, Donald Pleasence; Teresa, Francoise Dorleac; Richard, Lionel Stander; Albert, Jack MacGowran; Christopher, Iaian Quarrier; Christopher's Mother, Renee Houston; Christopher's Father, Geoffrey Sumner; Cecil, William Franklyn; Nicholas, Trevor Delaney; Mrs. Fairweather, Marie Kean; Mr. Fairweather, Robert Dorning; Jacqueline, Jackie Bissett.

646 THE CULPEPPER CATTLE COMPANY. (20th Century-Fox-1972). Ben Mockridge, Gary Grimes; Frank Culpepper, Billy "Green" Bush; Luke, Luke Askew; Dixie Brick, Bo Hopkins; Russ, Geoffrey Lewis; Missoula, Wayne Sutherlin; Thornton Pierce, John McLiam; Pete, Matt Clark; Cook, Raymond Guth; Nathaniel, Anthony James; Tim Slater, Charlie Martin Smith; Mr. Slater, Larry Finley; Old John, Bob Morgan; Mrs. Mockridge, Jan Burrell; Burgess, Hal Needham; Wallop, Jerry Gatlin; Rutter, Bob Orrison; Print, Walter Scott; Cattle Rustler, Royal Dano; Trapper, Paul Harper; Cantina Bartender, Jose Chavez; Doctor, Arthur Malet; Tascosa Bartender, Ted Gehring; One-eyed Horsethief, Gregory Sierra; Spectator, John Pearce; Wounded Man in bar, Dennis Fimple; Piercetown Bartender, William O'Connell; Former Virgin, Lu Shoemaker; Brother Ephraim, Patrick Campbell.

647 CULT OF THE DAMNED. (American International-1969). Astrid, Jennifer Jones; Bogart, Jordan Christopher; Tara, Holly Near; Santoro, Roddy McDowall; Joe, Lou Rawls; Willy, Charles Aidman; Anna, Davey Davison.

648 THE CURSE OF THE FLY. (20th Century-Fox-1966). Henri Delambre, Brian Donlevy; Patricia Stanley, Carole Gray; Martin Delambre, George Baker; Albert Delambre, Michael Graham; Inspector Ronet, Jeremy Wilkins; Inspector Charas, Charles Carson; Tai, Bert Kwouk; Wan, Yvette Rees; Madame Fournier, Rachel Kempson; Judith, Mary Manson; Hotel Manager, Warren Stanhope; Porter, Arnold Bell; The Creature, Stan Simmons.

649 THE CURSE OF THE MUMMY'S TOMB. (Columbia-1965). Terence Morgan, Ronald Howard, Fred Clark, Jeanne Roland, George Pastell, Jack Gwillim, John Paul.

650 CURSE OF THE VAMPIRES. (Marvin-1971). Amalia Guentes, Romeo Vasquez, Eddie Garcia, Johnny Monteiro, Rosario Del Pilar, Mary Walter, Francisco Cruz, Paquito Salcedo, Quiel Mendoza, Andres Benitez, Luz Angeles, Teesie Hernandez, Linda Rivers.

651 CURSE OF THE VOODOO. (Allied Artists-1966). Bryant Haliday, Dennis Price, Lisa Daniely.

652 CUSTER OF THE WEST. (Cinerama-1968). Gen. George Armstrong Custer, Robert Shaw; Elizabeth Custer, Mary Ure; Lieut. Benteen, Jeffrey Hunter; Maj. Marcus Reno, Ty Hardin; Lieut. Howells, Charles Stalnaker; Sgt. Buckley, Robert Hall; Gen. Philip Sheridan, Lawrence Tierney; Chief Dull Knife, Kieron Moore; The Goldminer, Marc Lawrence; Sgt. Mulligan, Robert Ryan.

653 CYCLE SAVAGES. (Trans American-1970). Keeg, Bruce Dern; Romko, Chris Robinson; Lea, Melody Patterson; Sandy, Maray Ayres; Janie, Karen Ciral; Woman, Virginia Hawkins; Marvin, Danny Ghaffouri; Doug, Lee Chandler; Docky, Tom Daly; Walter, Walt Robles; Keeg's Brother, Casey Kasem.

654 CYCLES SOUTH. (DAL Arts-1971). Don Marshall, Vaughn Everly, Bobby Garcia.

655 DADDY'S GONE A-HUNTING. (National General-1969). Cathy Palmer, Carol White; Kenneth Daly, Scott Hylands; Jack Byrnes; Paul Burke; Meg Stone, Mala Powers; Dr. Parkington's nurse, Rachel Ames; FBI Agent Crosley, Barry Cahill; Ilsa, Matilda Calnan; Brenda Frazier, Andrea King; Dr. Blanker, Gene Lyons; Paul Fanning, Ron Masak; Dr. Parkington, Dennis Patrick; FBI Agent Menchell, James Sikking; Inspector Dixon, Harry Holcombe.

656 DAGMAR'S HOT PANTS, INC. (Trans American-1972). Dagmar Anderson, Diana Kjaer; John Blackstone, Robert Strauss; Ingrid Lindberg, Anne Grete; Anne Engstrom, Inger Sundh; Jan Anderson, Tommy Blom; Vivi Eriksen, Anne-Lie Alexandersson; Doktor Adamsen, Karl-Erik Flens; Gunnar Hansen, Lars Soderstrom; Tishoro Suzuki, Bobby Kwan; Sessue Nakajima, Cecil Cheng; Igor Smirnov, Ake Fridell; Vincent Lombardozi, Tor Isedal; Lennart, Ole Soltoft; Lieutenant, Svend Johansen.

657 DAISIES. (Sigma III-1967). Jitka Crhova, Ivana Karbanova, Julius Albert.

658 DAISY MILLER. (Paramount-1974). Annie P. Miller, Cy-

bill Shepherd; Frederick Winterbourne, Barry Brown; Mrs. Miller, Cloris Leachman; Mrs. Costello, Mildred Natwick; Mrs. Walker, Eileen Brennan; Giovanelli, Dulio Del Prete; Randolph Miller, James McMurtry; Charles, Nicholas Jones; Eugenio, George Morfogen.

659 DALEKS--INVASION EARTH 2150 A.D. (Continental-1968). Dr. Who, Peter Cushing; Tom Campbell, Bernard Cribbins; David, Ray Brooks; Wyler, Andrew Keir; Susan, Roberta Tovey; Louise, Jill Curzon; Wells, Roger Avon; Conway, Keith Marsh; RoboMan, Geoffrey Cheshire; Leader RoboMan, Steve Peters; Brockley, Philip Madoc; Thompson, Eddie Powell; Dortmun, Godfrey Quigley; Man on Bicycle, Tony Reynolds; Man With Carrier Bag, Bernard Spear; Young Woman, Sheila Steafel; Old Woman, Eileen Way; Robber, John Wreford; Leader Dalek Operator, Robert Jewell.

660 THE DAMNED. (Warner Bros. -7 Arts-1969). Friederich Bruckmann, Dirk Bogarde; Baroness Sophie von Essenbeck, Ingrid Thulin; Aschenbach, Helmut Griem; Martin von Essenbeck, Helmut Berger; Elisabeth Thallman, Charlotte Rampling; Olga, Florinda Bolkan; Baron Konstantin von Essenbeck, Rene Kolldehoff; Herbert Thallman, Umberto Orsini; Baron Joachim von Essenbeck, Albrecht Shoenhals; Guenther von Essenbeck, Renaud Verley; Governess, Nora Ricci; Lisa Keller, Irina Wanka; Thilde (at 11), Valentina Ricci; Erika (at 8), Karin Mittendorf.

661 A DANDY IN ASPIC. (Columbia-1968). Alexander Eberlin, Laurence Harvey; Gatiss, Tom Courtenay; Caroline, Mia Farrow; Sobakevich, Lionel Stander; Intelligence Chief Fraser, Harry Andrews; Prentiss, Peter Cook; Pavel, Per Oscarsson; Heather Vogler, Barbara Murray; Copperfield, Norman Bird; Flowers, Michael Trubshawe; Nevil, Richard O'Sullivan; Pond, Geoffrey Denton; Ridley, Geoffrey Lumsden; Heston Stevas, James Cossins; Brogue, Calvin Lockhart; Henderson, John Bird; Lake, Geoffrey Bayldon; Greff, Michael Pratt; Hedwig, Monika Dietrich; Quince, Lockwood West; Moon, Arthur Hewlett; Stein, Vernon Dobtcheff; Red Bird, Paulene Stone; Youth, Peter Hutchins; Head Waiter, Andre Charise; Caroline's Mother, Elspeth March.

662 DANGER: DIABOLIK. (Paramount-1968). Diabolik, John Phillip Law; Eva Kent, Marisa Mell; Inspector Ginco, Michel Piccoli; Ralph Valmont, Adolfo Celi; Minister of Finance, Terry-Thomas; Police Chief, Claudio Gora; Sir Harold Clark, Edward Febo Kelleng; Lady Clark, Caterina Boratto; Dr. Vernier, Giulio Donnini; Rose, Annie Gorassini; Renzo Palmer, Mario Donen, Andrea Bosic, Lucia Modugno, Giorgio Gennari, Giorgio Sciolette, Carlo Croccolo, Giuseppe Fazio, Lidia Biondi, Isarco Ravaioli, Federico Boito, Tiberio Mitri, Wolfgang Hillinger.

663 DAREDEVIL IN THE CASTLE. (Frank Lee International-1969). Mohei, Toshiro Mifune; Ai, Kyoko Kagawa; Yodogimi, Isuzu Yamada; Senhime, Yuriko Hoshi; Kobue, Yoshiko Kuga; Hayato, Akihiko Hirata; Tadashi Shimura.

664 THE DARING DOBERMANS. (Dimension-1973). Charles Knox Robinson, Tim Considine, David Moses, Claudio Martinez, Joan Caulfield.

665 DARING GAME. (Paramount-1968). Vic Powers, Lloyd Bridges; Ricardo Balboa, Nico Minardos; President Delgado, Michael Ansara; Kathryn Carlyle, Joan Blackman; Dr. Henry Carlyle, Shepperd Strudwick; General Tovrea, Alex Montoya; Mrs. Carlyle, Irene Dailey; Jonah Hunt, Brock Peters; Larry Sedgewick, Barry Bartle; "Bink" Binkenshpilder, Michael Walker; Reuben, Perry Lopez; Maria, Marie Gomez; Miguel, Oren Stevens.

666 DARK DREAMS. (213 Releasing Organization-1971). Tina Russell, Tim Long, June DuLu, Patrice Deveur, Arlana Blue, Alan Martin, Yoryck Yegno, Darby Lloyd Raines, Kitty Kat.

667 DARK INTRUDER. (Universal-1965). Brett Kingsford, Leslie Nielsen; Robert Vandenburg, Mark Richman; Police Commissioner, Gilbert Green; Evelyn Lang, Judi Meredith; Professor Malaki, Werner Klemperer.

668 DARK OF THE SUN. (MGM-1968). Captain Bruce Curry, Rod Taylor; Claire, Yvette Mimieux; Sergeant Ruffo, Jim Brown; Dr. Reid, Kenneth More; Henlein, Peter Carsten; Surrier, Olivier Despax; Bussier, Andre Morell; Delage, Guy Deghy; President Ubi, Calvin Lockhart; Corporal Kataki, Bloke Modisane; Madame Bussier, Monique Lucas; Mrs. Ubi, Louise Bennett; Captain Hansen, Paul Jantzen; Functionary, Emery J. Ujvari; Belgian Refugee, Alex Gradussov; Adams, David Bauer; Cochrane, Murray Kash; Jansen, Alan Gifford; General Moses, Danny Daniels.

669 DARK PLACES. (Cinerama-1974). Dr. Mandeville, Christopher Lee; Sarah Mandeville, Joan Collins; Edward Foster; Andrew Marr, Robert Hardy; Prescott, Herbert Lom; Alta, Jane Birkin; Old Marr, Carleton Hobbs; Jessica Marr, Jennifer Thanisch; Francis Marr, Michael McVey; Victoria Marr, Jean Marsh.

670 THE DARK SIDE OF TOMORROW. (Able-1970). Denise, Elizabeth Plumb; Adria, Alisa Courtney; Jim, John Aprea; David, Wayne Want; Casey, Marland Proctor; Luan Roberts, Jamie Cooper, Sally Fedem, Linda Hendelman, Vince Romano, Laura Patton, Geretta Taylor, Buss Milburn.

671 DARK STAR. (Jack H. Harris-1974). Doolittle, Brian Narelle; Talby, Andreijah Pahich; Boiler, Carl Kuniholm;

Pinback, Dan O'Bannon.

672 DARKER THAN AMBER. (National General-1970). Travis McGee, Rod Taylor; Vangie/Merrimay, Suzy Kendall; Meyer, Theodore Bikel; Alabama Tiger, Jane Russell; Burk, James Booth; Noreen, Janet MacLachlan; Terry, William Smith; Del, Ahna Capri; Griff, Robert Phillips; Roy, Chris Robinson; Farnsworth, Jack Nagle; Nina, Sherry Faber; Dewey Powell, James H. Frysinger; Manuel, Oswaldo Calvo; Morgue Attendant, Jeff Gillen; Dr. Fairbanks, Miche DeBeausset; Ginny, Judy Wallace; Judson, Harry Wood; Landlady, Marcy Knight; Steward, Don Schoff; Roy's companions, Warren Bauer, Wayne Bauer.

673 DARLING. (Embassy-1965). Dianna Scott, Julie Christie; Robert Gold, Dirk Bogarde; Miles Brand, Laurence Harvey; Malcolm, Ronald Curran; Prince Cesare, Jose Luis de Vilallonga; Tony Bridges, Trevor Bowen; Sean Martin, Alex Scott; Estette Gold, Pauline Yates; Alec Prosser-Jones, Basil Henson; Felicity, Helen Lindsay; Lord Grant, Peter Bayliss; Kurt, Ernest Walder; Allie, Lucille Soong; Gillian, Sidonie Bond; Lady Brentwood, Lydia Sherwood; Charles Glass, David Harrison; Sybil, Ann Firbank; Governess, Helen Stirling.

674 DARLING LILI. (Paramount-1970). Lili Smith, Julie Andrews; Maj. William Larrabee, Rock Hudson; Kurt von Ruger, Jeremy Kemp; Lt. Carstairs (T. C.) Twombley-Crouch, Lance Percival; Major Duvalle, Jacques Marin; Lt. George Youngblood Carson, Michael Witney; Lt. Liggett, Andre Maranne; Bedford, Bernard Kay; Emma, Doreen Keogh; Suzette, Gloria Paul; Kessler, Carl Duering; Kraus, Vernon Dobtcheff; Sgt. Wells, A. E. Gould-Porter; French Generals, Louis Mercier, Laurie Main; Baron von Richthofen, Ingo Mogendorf; von Hindenburg, Niall MacGinnis; Chanteuse, Mimi Monti.

675 THE DARWIN ADVENTURE. (20th Century-Fox-1972). Darwin, Nicholas Clay; Emma, Susan Macready; Henslow, Robert Flemyng; Fitroy, Ian Richardson; Sullivan, Christopher Martin; Huxley, Philip Brack.

676 DAUGHTERS OF DARKNESS. (Gemini-Maron-1971). Elisabeth, Delphine Seyrig; Valerie, Daniele Ouimet; Stefan, John Karlen; Ilona, Andrea Rau; Porter, Paul Esser; Man, Georges Jamin; Butler, Joris Collet; Mother, Fons Rademakers.

677 DAUGHTERS OF SATAN. (United Artists-1972). James Robertson, Tom Selleck; Chris Duarte, Barra Grant; Kitty Rios, Tani Phelps Guthrie; Juana Rios, Paraluman; Dr. Dangal, Vic Silayan; Mrs. Postelwaite, Bobby Greenwood; Andrea, Gina Laforteza; Tommy Tantuico, Ben Rubio; Mortician,

Paquito Salcedo; Guerille, Chito Reyes; Carlos Ching, Vic Diaz.

678 DAY FOR NIGHT. (Warner Bros.-1973). Ferrand, Francois Truffaut; Julie, Jacqueline Bisset; Alphonse, Jean-Pierre Leaud; Severine, Valentina Cortese; Alexandre, Jean-Pierre Aumont; Lilianna, Dani; Stacey, Alexandra Stewart; Bertrand, Jean Champion.

679 A DAY IN COURT. (Ultra-1965). Sophia Loren, Alberto Sordi, Silvana Pampanini, Walter Chiari, Peppino De Filippo, Tania Weber.

680 A DAY IN THE DEATH OF JOE EGG. (Columbia-1972). Bri, Alan Bates; Sheila, Janet Suzman; Freddie, Peter Bowles; Pam, Sheila Gish; Grace, Joan Hickson; Jo, Elizabeth Robillard; The Doctor, Murray Melvin; The Nun, Fanny Carby; The Moonrocket Lady, Constance Chapman; The Midwife, Elizabeth Tyrell.

681 DAY OF ANGER. (National General-1970). Frank, Lee Van Cleef; Scott, Guiliano Gemma; Walter Rilla, Christa Linder, Ennio Balbo, Lukas Ammann, Andrea Boxic, Pepe Calvo, Giorgio Gargiullo, Anna Orso, Hans Otto Alberty, Nino Nini, Virgilio Gazzolo, Eleonora Morana, Benito Stefanelli.

682 THE DAY OF THE DOLPHIN. (Avco Embassy-1973). Dr. Jake Terrell, George C. Scott; Maggie Terrell, Trish Van Devere; Mahoney, Paul Sorvino; Harold DeMilo, Fritz Weaver; David, Jon Korkes; Mike, Edward Herrmann; Maryanne, Leslie Charleson; Larry, John David Carson; Lana, Victoria Racimo; Wallingford, John Dehner; Schwinn, Severn Darden; Dunhill, William Roerick; Mrs. Rome, Elizabeth Wilson; Women at club, Julie Follansbee, Florence Stanley, Brooke Hayward, Pat Englund; Stone, Willie Meyers; Secretary, Phyllis Davis.

683 DAY OF THE EVIL GUN. (MGM-1968). Lorn Warfield, Glenn Ford; Owen Forbes, Arthur Kennedy; Jimmy Noble, Dean Jagger; Captain Jefferson Addis, John Anderson; Sheriff Kelso, Paul Fix; Deleon, Nico Minardos; Sergeant Parker, Dean Stanton; Lydia Yearby, Pilar Pellicer; Willford, Parley Baer; Dr. Eli Prather, Royal Dano; Reverend Yearby, Ross Elliott; Angie Warfield, Barbara Babcock; Storekeeper, James Griffith.

684 DAY OF THE JACKAL. (Universal-1973). "The Jackal," Edward Fox; Lloyd, Terence Alexander; Colonel Rolland, Michel Auclair; The Minister, Alan Badel; Inspector Thomas, Tony Britton; Casson, Dennis Carey; The President, Adrien Cayla-Legrand; Gunsmith, Cyril Cusack; General Colbert, Maurice Denham; Interrogator, Vernon Dobtcheff; Pascal, Jacques Francois; Denise, Olga Georges-Picot; Flavigny,

Raymond Gerome; St. Clair, Barrie Ingham; Caron, Derek Jacobi; Lebel, Michael Lonsdale; Wolenski, Jean Martin; Forger, Ronald Pickup; Colonel Rodin, Eric Porter; Bernard, Anton Rodgers; Colette, Delphine Seyrig; Mallinson, Donald Sinden; Bastien-Thiry, Jean Sorel; Montclair, David Swift; Berthier, Timothy West.

685 THE DAY THE FISH CAME OUT. (International Classics-1967). The Navigator, Tom Courtenay; The Pilot, Colin Blakely; Elias, Sam Wanamaker; Electra, Candice Bergen; Peter, Ian Ogilvy; Dentist, Dimitris Nicolaides; Goatherd, Nicos Alexiou; Mrs. Mavroyannis, Patricia Burke; Fred, Paris Alexander; Frank, Arthur Mitchell; Goatherd's Wife, Marlena Carrere; Mr. French, Tom Klunis; Man in Bed, William Berger; Manolios, C. Papaconstantinou; Travel Agent, Dora Stratou; Director of Tourism, Alexander Lykourezos; Mike, Tom Whitehead; Base Commander, Walter Granecki; Policeman, Demetris Loakimides; Tourists, Lynn Bryant, James Connolly, Assaf Dayan, Robert Killian, Derek Kulai, Alexis Mantheakis, Raymond McWilliams, Michael Radford, Peter Robinson, Grigoris Stefanides, James Smith, Peter Strattul, Costa Timvios and Herbert Zeichner.

686 THE DAY THE SUN ROSE. (Shochiku-1973). Shinkichi, Kinnosuke Nakamura; Kuma, Toshiro Mifune; Ayame, Shima Iwashita; Akamatsu, Yunosuke Ito.

687 THE DAYDREAMER. (Embassy-1966). Chris (Hans Christian Andersen), Paul O'Keefe; Papa Andersen, Jack Gilford; The Pieman, Ray Bolger; Mrs. Klopplebobbler, Margaret Hamilton; and the voices of The Sandman, Cyril Ritchard; The Little Mermaid, Hayley Mills; Father Neptune, Burl Ives; The Sea Witch, Tallulah Bankhead; First Tailor(Brigidier), Terry-Thomas; Second Tailor (Zebro), Victor Borge; The Emperor, Ed Wynn; Big Claus, Robert Harter; Thumbelina, Patty Duke; The Rat, Boris Karloff; The Mole, Sessue Hayakawa; The Singer, Robert Goulet.

688 DAYS AND NIGHTS IN THE FOREST. (Pathe Contemporary-1973). Ashim, Soumitra Chatterjee; Sanjoy, Subhendu Chatterjee; Harinath, Samit Bhanja; Sekhar, Robi Ghose; Aparna, Sharmila Tagore; Jaya, Kaberi Bose; Duli, Simi; Sadashiv, Pahari Sanyal; Atasi, Aperna Sen.

689 DAYTON'S DEVILS. (Commonwealth United Entertainment-1968). Mike Page, Rory Calhoun; Frank Dayton, Leslie Nielsen; Leda Martell, Lainie Kazan; Max Eckhart, Hans Gudegast; Barney Barry, Barry Sadler; Claude Sadi, Pat Renella; Theon Gibson, George Stanford Brown; Sonny Merton, Rigg Kennedy; Captain, Rodolfo Acosta; Hap Holmwood, Danny Stone.

690 DE SADE. (American International-1969). Marquis de Sade,

Keir Dullea; Anne Montreuil, Senta Berger; Mme. de Montreuil, Lili Palmer; Renee de Montreuil, Anna Massey; La Beauvoisin, Sonja Ziemann; Rose Keller, Uta Levka; M. de Montreuil, Herbert Weissbach; Marquis' Mistress, Christiane Kruger; de Sade as a boy, Max Kiebach; The Abbe, John Huston.

691 THE DEAD ARE ALIVE. (National General-1972). Jason, Alex Cord; Myra, Samantha Eggar; Nikos, John Marley; Leni, Nadja Tiller; Stephan, Horst Frank; Inspector Giuranna, Enzo Tarascio; Alberto, Enzo Cerusico; Igor, Carlo De Mejo; Otello, Vladan Milasinovic; Irene; Daniela Surina; Velia, Christiane Von Blank; Vitanza, Mario Maranzana; Minelli, Pier Luigi D'Orazio; Giselle, Wendy D'Olive; Policeman, Ivan Pavicevac.

692 DEAD CERT. (1974). Alan, Scott Antony; Laura Davidson, Judi Dench; Sandy, Michael Williams; Penny, Nina Thomas; Clifford Tudor, Mark Dignam; Lodge, Julian Glover; Joe Nantwich, Joseph Blatchley; Walter, John Bindon; Albert, Dervis Ward; Bill Davidson, Ian Hogg; Sir Cresswell, Bill Fraser; Yuko, Hideo Saito; Sid, Sean Lynch; Mrs. Mervyn, Annie Ross; Sergeant, Nigel Humphries; Gipsy, Frank Gentry; Chemist, Llewellyn Rees; Doctor, Ian Milton; Coroner, Willoughby Gray; Everest, Geoffrey Bateman; Secretary, Joan Crane; Vic Armstrong, Micky Dillon, Tommy Reeves, Richard Graydon, Bronco McLoughlin, John Oaksey.

693 DEAD EYES OF LONDON. (Magna-1966). Joachim Fuchsberger, Karin Baal, Dieter Borsche, Wolfgang Lukschy, Ann Savo, Klaus Kinski, Eddie Arent, Harry Wustenhagen, Ady Berber, Bobby Todd, Ida Ehre, Fritz Schroder-Jahn, Hans Paetsch, Rudolph Fenner.

694 DEAD HEAT ON A MERRY-GO-ROUND. (Columbia-1966). Eli Kotch, James Coburn; Inger Knudson, Camilla Sparv; Eddie Hart, Aldo Ray; Frieda Schmid, Nina Wayne; Milo Stewart, Robert Webber; Margaret Kirby, Rose Marie; Alfred Morgan, Todd Armstrong; Dr. Marion Hague, Marian Moses; Paul Feng, Michael Strong; Miles Fisher, Severn Darden; Jack Balter, James Westerfield; Philip E. Pine, Simon Scott, Ben Astar, Michael St. Angel, Lawrence Mann, Alex Rodine, Albert Nalbandian, Tyler McVey, Roy Glenn, Joey Faye, Mary Young, George Wallace.

695 DEADFALL. (20th Century-Fox-1968). Henry Clarke, Michael Caine; Fe Moreau, Giovanna Ralli; Richard Moreau, Eric Portman; The Girl, Nanette Newman; Salinas, David Buck; Antonio, Carlos Pierre; Fillmore, Leonard Rossiter; Inspector Ballastero, Emilio Rodriguez; Dr. Delgado, Vladek Sheybal; Stresemann, George Ghent; Masseuse, Carmen Dene; Delgado's Receptionist, Geraldine Sherman; Lagranja, Antonio Sanpere; Chauffeur, Reg Howell; Armed Guard, Santiago

Rivera; Bank Manager, Philip Madoc; Symphony Conductor, John Barry; Guitar Soloist, Renata Tarrago.

696 DEADLIER THAN THE MALE. (Universal-1967). Hugh Drummond, Richard Johnson; Irma Eckman, Elke Sommer; Penelope, Sylva Koscina; Carl Petersen Weston, Nigel Green; Grace, Suzanna Leigh; Robert Drummond, Steve Carlson; Sir John Bledlow, Laurence Naismith; Henry Bridgenorth, Leonard Rossiter; King Fedra, Zia Mohyeddin; Boxer, Lee Montague; Chang, Milton Reid; Miss Ashendon, Justine Lord; George Pastell, Virginia North, Yasuko Nagazumi, Didi Sydow, Dervis Ward, John Stone.

697 THE DEADLY AFFAIR. (Columbia-1967). Charles Dobbs, James Mason; Elsa Fennan, Simone Signoret; Dieter Frey, Maximilian Schell; Ann Dobbs, Harriet Andersson; Inspector Mendel, Harry Andrews; Bill Appleby, Kenneth Haigh; Virgin, Lynn Redgrave; Adam Scarr, Roy Kinnear; Adviser, Max Adrian; Samuel Fennan, Robert Flemyng; Director, Corin Redgrave; Harek, Les White; June Murphy, Frank Williams, Rosemary Lord, Kenneth Ives, John Dimech, Julian Sherrier, Petra Markham, Denis Shaw, Maria Charles, Amanda Walker, Sheraton Blount, Janet Hargreaves, Michael Brennan, Richard Steele, Gartan Klauber, Margaret Lacey, Judy Keirn; The Royal Shakespeare Company: David Warner, Michael Bryant, Stanley Leber, Paul Hardwick, Charles Kay, Timothy West, Jonathan Hales, William Dysart, Murray Brown, Paul Starr, Peter Harrison, David Quilter, Terence Sewards, Roger Jones.

698 THE DEADLY BEES. (Paramount-1967). Vicki Robbins, Suzanna Leigh; Manfred, Frank Finlay; Ralph Hargrove, Guy Doleman; Mrs. Hargrove, Catherine Finn; Thompson, John Harvey; Hawkins, Michael Ripper; Compere, Anthony Bailey; Harcourt, Tim Barrett; Coroner, James Cossins; Doctor, Frank Forsyth; Doris Hawkins, Katy Wild; Sister, Greta Farrer; Secretary, Gina Gianelli; Doctor Lang, Michael Gwynn; Agent, Maurice Good; Inspector, Alister Williamson.

699 DEADLY CHINA DOLL. (MGM-1973). Chin, Angela Mao; Pai, Carter Huang; Han, Yen I-feng; Hu, Nan Kung-hsun; Chin, Ke Hsiang-ting.

700 THE DEADLY TRACKERS. (Warner Bros. -1973). Kilpatrick, Richard Harris; Brand, Rod Taylor; Gutierrez, Al Lettieri; Choo Choo, Neville Brand; Schoolboy, William Smith; Jacob, Paul Benjamin; Blacksmith, Pedro Armendariz Jr.; Maria, Isela Varga; Katharine, Kelly Jean Peters.

701 THE DEADLY TRAP. (National General-1972). Jill Hallard, Faye Dunaway; Philip Hallard, Frank Langella; Cynthia, Barbara Parkins; Babysitter, Karen Blaguernon; Organization Man, Maurice Ronet; Inspector Chaneylle, Raymond Gerome;

The Psychiatrist, Gerard Buhr; Cathy Hallard, Michele Lourie; Patrick Hallard, Patrick Vincent; Louise Chevalier, Tener Eckelberry, Massimo Farinelli.

702 DEAF SMITH AND JOHNNY EARS. (MGM-1973). Erasmus "Deaf" Smith, Anthony Quinn; Johnny Ears, Franco Nero; Susie, Pamela Tiffin; General Morton, Franco Graziosi; Hester, Ira Furstenberg; Hoffman, Renato Romano; Adolfo Lastretti, Antonio Faa Di Bruno, Francesca Benedetti, Cristina Airoldi, Romano Puppo, Franca Sciutto, Enrico Casadei, Lorenzo Fineschi, Mario Carra, Georgio Dolfin, Luciano Rossi, Margherita Trentini, Tom Felleghy, Fulvio Grimaldi, Paolo Pierani.

703 DEALING. (Warner Bros. -1972). Susan, Barbara Hershey; Peter, Robert E. Lyons; Murphy, Charles Durning; Sandra, Joy Bang; John, John Lithgow; Annie, Ellen Barber; Musty, Gene Borkan; Receptionist, Ted Williams; Rupert, Desmond Wilson; Emir, Herbert Kerr; Barry, Paul Williams; Buzzy, Buzzy Linhart; Townie Girl, Anitra Walsh; Captain Fry, Tom Harvey.

704 DEAR BRIGITTE. (20th Century-Fox-1965). Professor Robert Leaf, James Stewart; Kenneth, Fabian; Vina Leaf, Glynis Johns; Pandora Leaf, Cindy Carol; Erasmus Leaf, Billy Mumy; Peregrine Upjohn, John Williams; Dr. Volker, Jack Kruschen; The Captain, Ed Wynn; George, Charles Robinson; Dean Sawyer, Howard Freeman; Terry, Jane Wald; Unemployment Office Clerk, Alice Pearce; Argyle, Jesse White; Lt. Rink, Gene O'Donnell; Herself, Brigitte Bardot.

705 DEAR, DEAD DELILAH. (Southern Star-1972). Delilah, Agnes Moorehead; Ray, Will Geer; Morgan, Michael Ansara; Luddy, Patricia Carmichael; Alonzo, Dennis Patrick; Grace, Anne Meacham; Richard, Robert Gentry; Ellen, Elizabeth Eis; Buffy, Ruth Baker; Young Luddy, Ann Gibbs; Marshall, John Marriott.

706 DEAR HEART. (Warner Bros. -1965). Harry Mork, Glenn Ford; Evie Jackson, Geraldine Page; Patrick, Michael Anderson Jr.; June, Barbara Nichols; Frank Taylor, Charles Drake; Daphne Mitchell, Patricia Barry; Phyllis, Angela Lansbury; Miss Tait, Ruth McDevitt; Connie, Neva Patterson; Miss Moore, Alice Pearce; Mr. Cruikshank, Richard Deacon; Zola, Joanna Crawford; Peterson, Peter Turgeon; The Masher, Ken Lynch; Miss Fox, Mary Wickes; Marvin, James O'Rear; Herb, Nelson Olmsted.

707 DEAR JOHN. (Sigma III-1966). John, Karl Julle; Anita, Christina Schollin; Helene, Helena Nilsson; Anita's Brother, Morgan Andersson; Dagny, Synnove Liljeback; Lindgren, Erik Hell; Mrs. Lindgren, Emy Storm; Erwin, Hakan Serner; Elon, Hans Wigren.

708 DEATH CURSE OF TARTU. (Thunderbird International-1967). Ed Tison, Fred Pinero; Julie Tison, Babette Sherrill; Cindy, Mayra Cristine; Johnny, Sherman Hayes; Tommy, Gary Holtz; Joann, Maurice Stewart; Sam Gunter, Frank Weed; Tartu, Doug Hobart; Bill the Indian, Bill Marcos.

709 DEATH IN VENICE. (Warner Bros-1971). Aschenbach, Dirk Bogarde; Hotel Manager, Romolo Valli; Alfred, Mark Burns; Governess, Nora Ricci; Mrs. Aschenbach, Marisa Berensen; Esmeralda, Carol Andre; Tadzio, Bjorn Andresen; His Mother, Silvana Mangano; Singer, Masha Predit; Travel Agent, Leslie French; Barber, Franco Fabrizi; Polish Youth, Sergio Garafanolo; Scapegrace, Luigi Battaglia; Hotel Clerk, Ciro Cristofoletti.

710 DEATH OF A GUNFIGHTER. (Universal-1969). Marshal Frank Patch, Richard Widmark; Claire Quintana, Lena Horne; Lou Trinidad, John Saxon; Lester Locke, Carroll O'Connor; Edward Rosenbloom, David Opatoshu; Andrew Oxley, Kent Smith; Laurie Mills, Jacqueline Scott; Ivan Stanek, Morgan Woodward; Mayor Chester Sayre, Larry Gates; Doc Adams, Dub Taylor; Hilda Jorgenson, Darleen Carr; Dan Joslin, Michael McGreevey; Arch Brandt, Royal Dano; Luke Mills, James Lydon; Mary Elizabeth, Kathleen Freeman; Reverend Rork, Harry Carey Jr.; Angela, Amy Thomson; Will Oxley, Marcer Harris; Father Sweeney, James O'Hara; Paul Hammond, Walter Sande; Phil Miller, Victor French; Chris Hogg, Robert Sorrells; Roy Brandt, Charles Kuenstle; Mexican Woman, Sara Taft.

711 DEATH OF A JEW. (Cine Globe-1973). Shimon, Assaf Dayan; Mehdaloun, Akim Tamiroff; Kassik, Jean Claudio.

712 THE DEATH OF TARZAN. (Brandon-1968). Wolfgang/Tarzan, Rudolf Hrusinsky; Regina, Jana Stepankova; Baron Heinrich von Hoppe, Martin Ruzek; Dr. Foreyt, Vlastimil Hasek; Ring Director, Slavka Budinova; Usher, Ilya Racek; S. A. Man, Miroslav Homolka; Lady with Buckteeth, Nina Popelikova; Baroness, Elena Halkova.

713 DEATH RIDES A HORSE. (United Artists-1969). Bill, John Phillip Law; Ryan, Lee Van Cleef; Wolcott, Luigi Pistilli; Manina, Anthony Dawson; Pedro, Jose Torres; Betsy, Carla Cassola; Vigro, Archie Savage; One-Eye, Mario Brega; Manuel, Gugliemo Spoletini; Sheriff, Giuseppe Castellano; Felicita Fanny, Elena Hall, Nino Vingelli, Giovanni Petrucci, Natale Nazareno, Franco Balducci, Romano Puppo, Carlo Piscane, Ignazio Leone.

714 No entry.

715 DEATH WISH. (Paramount-1974). Paul Kersey, Charles Bronson; Joanna Kersey, Hope Lange; Detective Ochoa,

Vincent Gardenia; Jack Toby, Steven Keats; Sam Kreutzer, William Redfield; Aimes Jainchill, Stuart Margolin; Police Commissioner, Stephen Elliott; Carol Toby, Kathleen Tolan; Hank, Jack Wallace; District Attorney, Fred Scollay; Officer Charles, Robert Kya-Hill; Muggers, Jeff Goldberg, Christopher Logan, Gregory Rozakis.

716 THE DEATHMASTER. (American International-1972). Khorda, Robert Quarry; Pico, Bill Ewing; Rona, Brenda Dickson; Pop, John Fiedler; Esslin, Betty Anne Rees; Monk, William Jordan; Barbado, LeSesne Hilton; Detective, John Lasell; Dancer, Freda T. Vanterpool; Mavis, Tari Tabakin; Kitty Vallacher, Michael Cronin, Charles Hornsby, Olympia Sylvers, Bob Woods, Ted Lynn.

716a DEATHWATCH. (Beverly-1967). Jules, Leonard Nimoy; Greeneyes, Michael Forest; Maurice, Paul Mazursky; Guard, Robert Ellenstein; Emil, Gavin MacLeod.

717 THE DEBUT. (Maron-Gemini-1971). Pasha, Inna Churikova; Valia, V. Telichkina; Katia, T. Stekanova; Arkadi, L. Kuravlev; Pavlik, M. Kononev.

718 THE DECAMERON. (United Artists-1971). Clapelleto, Franco Citti; Andreuccio, Ninetto Davoli; Peronella, Angela Luce; Giotto, Pier Paolo Pasolini; Silvana Mangano.

719 THE DECEASED. (New Yorker-1971). Wife, Fernanda Montenegro; Husband, Ivan Candido; Lover, Paulo Gracindo.

720 DECLINE AND FALL OF A BIRD WATCHER. (20th Century-Fox-1969). The Judge, Felix Aylmer; Potts, Rodney Bewes; Philbrick, Colin Blakely; Flossie Fagan, Patience Collier; Otto Silenus, Roland Curran; Mr. Levy, Kenneth Griffith; Prendergast, Robert Harris; Sir Humphrey Maltravers, Griffith Jones; Maniac, Patrick Magee; Grimes, Leo McKern; Margot Beste-Chetwynde, Genevieve Page; Paul Pennyfeather, Robin Phillips; Cheif Warder, Paul Rogers; Prison Governor, Donald Sinden; Messenger Warder, Kenneth J. Warren; Gallery Warder, Jack Watson; Dr. Fagan, Donald Wolfit.

721 DEEP END. (Paramount-1971). Susan, Jane Asher; Mike, John Moulder-Brown; Lady Client, Diana Dors; Swimming instructor, Karl Michael Vogler; Fiance, Christopher Sandford; Prostitute, Louise Martini; Baths Cashier, Erica Beer.

722 DEEP SLEEP. (Barferd-1973). Willard Butts, Mary Canary.

723 DEEP THROAT. (Aquarius-1972). Linda, Linda Lovelace; Dr. Young, Harry Reems; Helen, Dolly Sharp; Nurse, Carol Connors; Wilbur Wang, William Love; Delivery Boy, Ted Street; Mr. Maltz, Bill Harrison; Mr. Fenster, Bob Phillips; No. 11, John Byron; No. 12, Michael Powers; The Last Man, Al Gork.

724 DEEP THRUST. (American International-1973). Angela Mao, Chang Yi, Pai Ying, June Wu, Anne Liu.

725 THE DEFECTOR. (Seven Arts-1966). Professor James Bower, Montgomery Clift; Counselor Peter Heinzman, Hardy Kruger; CIA Agent Adam, Roddy McDowall; Frieda Hoffman, Macha Meril; Orlovsky, David Opatoshu; Ingrid, Christine Delaroche; Doctor Saltzer, Hannes Messemer; The Major, Karl Lieffen; Tourist-Spy, Jean-Luc Godard.

726 DEFIANCE. (Stu Segall Associates-1974). Cathy, Jean Jennings; Dr. Gabriel, Fred Lincoln; Susan, Day Jason; Cathy's mother, Holly Landis; Cathy's father, Roderick Usher; Miss Caine, Ellen Hill; Dr. Krausse, David Harrison; Male Nurse, Turk Turpin; Admitting Nurse, Dulce Mann; Hospital Orderly, Frank Baker; Tony Marcus, Marc Stevens, Barry Clarke, Sandy Foxx, Hurant, Michael Johns, Tyrone Lowe, Doug Johns, Faith Jones, Mickie Oats, Sal Sanderone, Jaime Gillis, Pam Sanders, Sonny Landham, Alexander Life, Jack Conner.

727 A DEGREE OF MURDER. (Universal-1972). Marie, Anita Pallenberg; Hans P. Hallwachs, Manfred Fischbeck, Warner Enke.

728 A DELICATE BALANCE. (American Film Theatre-1973). Agnes, Katharine Hepburn; Tobias, Paul Scofield; Julia, Lee Remick; Claire, Kate Reid; Harry, Joseph Cotten; Edna, Betsy Blair.

729 DELIVERANCE. (Warner Bros. -1972). Ed Gentry, Jon Voight; Lewis Medlock, Burt Reynolds; Bobby Trippe, Ned Beatty; Drew Ballinger, Ronny Cox; Mountain Man, Billy McKinney; Toothless Man, Herbert "Cowboy" Coward; Sheriff Bullard, James Dickey; Old Man, Ed Ramey; Lonny, Billy Redden; First Griner, Seamon Glass; Second Griner, Randall Deal; First Deputy, Lewis Crone; Second Deputy, Ken Keener; Ambulance Driver, Johnny Popwell; Doctor, John Fowler; Nurse, Kathy Rickman; Mrs. Biddiford, Louise Coldren; Taxi Driver, Pete Ware; Boy at Gas Station, Hoyt J. Pollard; Martha Gentry, Belinha Beatty; Ed's Boy, Charlie Boorman.

730 THE DELUGE. (Film Polski-1974). Kmicic, Daniel Olbrychski; Olenka, Malgorzata Braunek; Wolodyjowski, Tadeusz Lomnicki; Zagloba, Kazimierez Wichniarz; Prince Boguslaw Radziwill, Wladyslaw Hancza; King Jan Kazimierez, Piotr Pawlowski; Chancellor, Hugo Krzyski; Primate, Eugeniusz Luberadzki; Senator, Aleksander Gassowski.

731 LE DEPART. (Pathe Contemporary-1968). Marc, Jean-Pierre Leaud; Michele, Catherine Duport; The Boss, Leon Dory; Marc's Friend, Paul Roland; The Older Woman, Jacqueline Bir; The Maharajah, John Dobrynine; Georges Aubrey,

Lucien Charbonnier, Bernard Graczyk, Maxane, Jacques Cortois, Marthe Dugard.

732 DERBY. (Cinerama-1971). Charlie O'Connell, Eddie Krebs, Mike Snell, Christina Snell, Butch Snell.

733 DESERTER USA. (Kanawha-1969). Bill Jones, Mark Shapiro, John Ashley, Jim Dotson, Steve Gershater, Warren Hamerman, John Toler, Lennart Schlytern.

734 THE DESPERADOS. (Columbia-1969). David Galt, Vince Edwards; Parson Galt, Jack Palance; Jacob Galt, George Maharis; Sheriff, Neville Brand; Laura, Sylvia Syms; Adam Galt, Christian Roberts; Adah, Kate O'Mara.

735 DESPERATE CHARACTERS. (ITC-1971). Sophie, Shirley MacLaine; Otto, Kenneth Mars; Charlie, Gerald O'Loughlin; Claire, Sada Thompson; Leon, Jack Somack; Mike, Chris Gampel; Flo, Mary Ellen Hokanson; Man on subway, Wallace Rooney; Ruth, Rose Gregorio; Young Man, Robert Bauer; Young Girl, Carol Kane; Francis Early, Michael Higgins; Raconteur, Michael McAloney; Saleslady, Elena Karam; Caller, Nick Smith; Hospital Attendant, Robert Delbert; Woman Doctor, Shauneille Ryder; Nurse, Conzalee Ford; Mr. Haynes, Patrick McVey; Tom, L. J. Davis.

736 DESTINATION INNER SPACE. (Magna-1966). Commander Wayne, Scott Brady; Sandra, Sheree North; Dr. Le Satier, Gary Merrill; Hugh, Mike Road; Wende Wagner, John Howard, William Thourly, Biff Elliot, Glen Spies, Richard Niles, Roy Bancroft, Ed Charles Sweeny, Ken Delo, Ron Burke, James Hong.

737 DESTROY ALL MONSTERS. (American International-1969). Captain Katsuo Yamabe, Akira Kubo; Dr. Yoshido, Jun Tazaki; Dr. Otani, Yoshio Tsuchiya; Queen of the Kilaaks, Kyoko Ai; Kyoko, Yukiko Kobayashi; Nishikawa, Kenji Sawara; Dr. Stevenson, Andrew Hughes.

738 DESTROY, SHE SAID. (Grove-1970). Elisabeth, Catherine Sellers; Alissa Thor, Nicole Hiss; Max Thor, Henri Garcin; Stein, Michel Lonsdale; Bernard Alione, Daniel Gelin.

739 THE DESTRUCTORS. (Feature Film Corporation of America-1968). Dan Street, Richard Egan; Charlie Street, Patricia Owens; Dutch Holland, John Ericson; Count Mario Romano, Michael Ansara; Stassa Gertmann, Joan Blackman; Hogan, David Brian; Spaniard, Johnny Seven; King Chou Lai, Khigh Dhiegh; Dr. Frazer, Gregory Morton; Bushnell, John Howard; Barnes, Eddie Firestone; Suzie, Jayne Massey; Michael Dugan, Jim Adams.

740 THE DESTRUCTORS. (American International-1974). Deray,

Michael Caine; Steve Ventura, Anthony Quinn; Brizard, James Mason; Lucianne, Maureen Kerwin; Calmet, Marcel Bozzuffi; Brizard's Mistress, Catherine Rouvel; Briac, Maurice Ronet; Marsac, Andre Oumansky; Rita, Alexandra Stewart.

741 THE DETECTIVE. (20th Century-Fox-1968). Joe Leland, Frank Sinatra; Karen Leland, Lee Remick; Norman MacIver, Jacqueline Bisset; Lieut. Curran, Ralph Meeker; Dave Schoenstein, Jack Klugman; Farrell, Horace McMahon; Dr. Wendell Roberts, Lloyd Bochner; Colin MacIver, William Windom; Felix Tesla, Tony Musante; Robbi Loughren, Al Freeman Jr.; Nestor, Robert Duvall; Pat Henry, Patrick McVey, Dixie Marquis, Sugar Ray Robinson, Renee Taylor, James Inman, Tom Atkins, James Dukas, Norman Rose, Sharon Henesy, Jan Farrand, Marion Brash, Earl Montgomery, Peg Murray, Frank Reiter, Peter York, Mark Dawson, Jose Ridriguez, Tom Gorman, Lou Nelson, Richard Krisher, Jilly Rizzo, Arnold Soboloff, George Plimpton, Phil Sterling, Don Fellows, Paul Larson, Ted Beniades.

742 DETECTIVE BELLI. (Plaza-1970). Belli, Franco Nero; Vera, Florinda Bolkan; Fontana, Adolfo Celi; Sandy, Delia Boccardo; Emmanuelle, Susanna Martinkova; Baldo, Renzo Palmer; Claude, Roberto Bisacco; Mino, Maurizio Bonuglia.

743 DETOUR. (Brandon-1969). Neda, Nevena Kokanova; Boyan, Ivan Andonov.

744 DETROIT 9000. (General-1973). Bassett, Alex Rocco; Williams, Hari Rhodes; Roby, Vonetta McGee; Helen, Ella Edwards; Rev. Markham, Scatman Crothers; Ferdy, Herbert Jefferson Jr.; Capt. Chalmers, Robert Phillips; Clayton, Rudy Challenger; Sam, Ron McIlwain; Ethel, Sally Baker; Oscar, George Skaff; Barbara, June Fairchild; Dilart Heyson, Davis Roberts, Jason Summers, John Nichols, Richard Bourin, Martha Jean Steinberg, Woody Willis, Bob Charlton, Ernie Winstanley, Council Cargle, Doris Ingraham, Ron Khoury, Jerry Dahlman, Whit Vernon, Don Hayes, Herb Weatherspoon, Michael Tylo.

745 THE DEVIL BY THE TAIL. (Lopert-1969). Cesar Maricorne, Yves Montand; Diane, Maria Schell; Georges, Jean Rochefort; Leroy Martin, Jean-Pierre Marielle; La Marquise, Madeleine Renaud; Amelie, Marthe Keller; Jeanne, Clotilde Joano; Monsieur Patin, Claude Pieplu; Charlie, Xavier Gelin; Cookie, Tanya Lopert; Balaze, Jacques Balutin; Schwartz, Pierre Tornade; Madame Passereau, Janine Berdin; Monsieur Passereau, Eddy Roos.

746 THE DEVIL IN LOVE. (Warner Bros.-7 Arts-1968). Belfagor, Vittorio Gassman; Adramalek, Mickey Rooney; Magdalena, Claudine Auger; Lorenzo de Medici, Gabriele Ferzetti; Captain of the Guard, Ettore Manni; Lucretia, Annabella

Incontrera; Innkeeper's Wife, Liana Orfei; The Prince, Luigi Vannucchi; Clarice, Helene Chanel; Aristocrat's Wife, Giorgia Moll; Cardinal Giovanni, Paolo Di Credico.

747 THE DEVIL IN MISS JONES. (Marvin-1973). Justine, Georgina Spelvin; Abaca, John Clemens; Teacher, Harry Reams; Man in the cell, Albert Gork; Marc Stevens, Rick Livermore, Sue Flaken.

748 THE DEVILS. (Warner Bros. -1971). Sister Jeanne, Vanessa Redgrave; Father Grandier, Oliver Reed; Baron de Laubardemont, Dudley Sutton; Ibert, Max Adrian; Madeleine, Gemma Jones; Mignon, Murray Melvin; Father Barre, Michael Gothard; Philippe, Georgina Hale; Adam, Brian Murphy; Richelieu, Christopher Logue; Louis XIII, Graham Armitage; Trincant, John Woodvine; Rangier, Andrew Faulds; Legrand, Kenneth Colley; Sister Judith, Judith Paris; Sister Catherine, Catherine Willmer; Sister Iza, Iza Teller.

749 No entry.

750 DEVIL'S ANGELS. (American International-1967). Cody, John Cassavetes; Lynn, Beverly Adams; Marianne, Mimsy Farmer; Joel-the-Mole, Maurice McEndree; Billy the Kid, Marc Cavell; Louise, Salli Sachse; Tonya, Nai Bonet; Gage, Buck Taylor; Rena, Marianne Kanter; Sheriff Henderson, Leo Gordon; Funky, Buck Kartalian; Robot, John Craig; Roy, Kip Whitman; Leroy, George Sims; Karen, Mitzi Hoag; Royce, Russ Bender; Grog, Wally Campo; Bruno, Dick Anders; Mayor, Paul Mayer; Cane, Lee Wainer; Deputies, Roy Thiel and Ronny Dayton; Store Owner, Henry Kendrick.

751 THE DEVIL'S BRIDE. (20th Century-Fox-1968). Duc de Richleau, Christopher Lee; Mocata, Charles Gray; Tanith, Nike Arrighi; Rex van Ryn, Leon Greene; Simon Aron, Patrick Mower; Countess d'Urfe, Gwen Frangcon-Davies; Marie Eaton, Sarah Lawson; Richard Eaton, Paul Eddington; Peggy Eaton, Rosalyn Landor; Malin, Russell Waters.

752 THE DEVIL'S BRIGADE. (United Artists-1968). Lt. Col. Robert T. Frederick, William Holden; Major Alan Crown, Cliff Robertson; Major Cliff Bricker, Vince Edwards; Lt. Gen. Mark Clark, Michael Rennie; Brig. Gen. Walter Naylor, Dana Andrews; A Lady of Joy, Gretchen Wyler; Pvt. Theodore Ransom, Andrew Prine; Rocky Rockman, Claude Akins; Maj. Gen. Hunter, Carroll O'Connor; Omar Greco, Richard Jaeckel; Jack Watson, Gene Fullmer, Jeremy Slate, Richard Dawson, Tom Stern, Tom Troupe, Luke Askew, Bill Fletcher, Jean-Paul Vignon, Harry Carey, Norman Alden, Don Megowan, Patric Knowles, David Pritchard, Paul Busch, James Craig.

753 THE DEVIL'S DAFFODIL. (Goldstone-1967). Jack Tarling,

William Lucas; Anne Rider, Penelope Horner; Ling Chu, Christopher Lee; Gloria, Ingrid Van Bergen; Raymond Lyne, Albert Lieven; Oliver Milburgh, Marius Goring; Charles, Jan Hendricks; Peter Keene, Colin Jeavons; Jan Putek, Peter Illing; Superintendent Whiteside, Walter Gotell; Sir Archibald, Campbell Singer; Katya, Dawn Beret; Trudy, Bettine de Beau; Gendarme, Lance Percival; Detective, Frederick Bartman; Sluttish Woman, Nancy Nevinson; Maisie, Irene Prador; Mrs. Rider, Grace Denbeigh-Russell; Chinese Girl, Edwina Carroll; Max, Martin Lyder.

754 DEVIL'S DUE. (Norman Arno-1973). Cindy West, Catherine Warren, Lisa Grant, Gus Thomas, Davy Jones, Angel Street, Mac Stevens.

755 THE DEVIL'S 8. (American International-1969). Faulkner, Christopher George; Sonny, Fabian; Billy Joe, Tom Nardini; Cissy, Leslie Parrish; Frank, Ross Hagen; Chandler, Larry Bishop; Bubba, Cliff Osmond; Henry, Robert Doqui; Martin, Ron Rifkin; Bureau, Baynes Barron; Sam, Joseph Turkell; Inez, Lada Edmund Jr.; Hallie, Marjorie Dayne; Burl, Ralph Meeker.

755a DEVILS OF DARKNESS. (20th Century-Fox-1966). Paul Baxter, William Sylvester; Count Sinistre, Hubert Noel; Karen, Carole Gray; Madeline Braun, Diana Decker; Anne Forest, Rona Anderson; Inspector Malin, Peter Illing; Bouvier, Gerard Heinz; Inspector Hardwick, Victor Brooks; Midge, Avril Angers; The colonel, Brian Oulton; Old Gypsy Woman, Marie Burke; The Duchess, Marianne Stone; Dave, Rod McLennan; Keith Forest, Geoffrey Kenion; Derek, Burnell Tucker.

756 THE DEVIL'S OWN. (20th Century-Fox-1967). Gwen Mayfield, Joan Fontaine; Stephanie Bax, Kay Walsh; Alan Bax, Alec McCowen; Sally, Ann Bell; Linda Rigg, Ingrid Brett; Dowsett, John Collin; Valerie, Michele Dotrice; Granny Rigg, Gwen Frangcon-Davies; Ronnie Dowsett, Martin Stephens; Bob Curd, Duncan Lamont; Dr. Wallis, Leonard Rossiter; Mrs. Dowsett, Carmel McSharry; Mrs. Curd, Viola Keats; Mrs. Creek, Shelagh Fraser; Tom, Bryan Marshall.

757 THE DEVIL'S WIDOW. (American International-1972). Michaela, Ava Gardner; Tom, Ian McShane; Janet, Stephanie Beacham; Vicar, Cyril Cusack; Elroy, Richard Wattis; Oliver, David Whitman; Sue, Madeline Smith; Miss Gibson, Fabia Drake; Rose, Sinead Cusack; Caroline, Jennie Hanley; Georgia, Joanna Lumley; Vanna, Pamela Farbrother; Alan, Bruce Robinson; Kate, Rosemary Blake; Michael, Michael Bills; Guy, Peter Henwood; Andy, Heyward Morse; Terry, Julian Barnes; Peter, Oliver Norman; Lottie, Virginia Tingwell.

758 THE DIABOLICAL DR. Z. (U.S. Films-1967). Irma, Mabel

Karr; Philip, Fernando Montes; Nadia, Estella Blain; Dr. Von Zimmer, Antonio J. Escribano; Guy Mairesse, Howard Vernon, Marcello Arroita, Lucia Prado.

759 DIALOGUE. (Lionel Rogosin-1967). Judit Barna, Anita Semjen; Laszlo Horvath, Imre Sinkovits; The Poet, Istvan Sztankai; Miklos Gabor, Zoltan Maklary, Margit Bara, Sandor Pecsi, Mari Torocsik.

760 DIAMONDS ARE FOREVER. (United Artists-1971). James Bond, Sean Connery; Tiffany Case, Jill St. John; Blofeld, Charles Gray; Plenty O'Toole, Lana Wood; Willard Whyte, Jimmy Dean; Saxby, Bruce Cabot; Wint, Bruce Glover; Kidd, Putter Smith; Felix Leiter, Norman Burton; M, Bernard Lee; Q, Desmond Llewelyn; Shady Tree, Leonard Barr; Mrs. Whistler, Margaret Lacey; Miss Moneypenny, Lois Maxwell; Peter Franks, Joe Robinson; Bambi, Donna Garratt; Thumper, Trina Parks; Klaus Hergersheimer, Edward Bishop; Barker, Larry Blake; Dentist, Henry Rowland; Doorman, Nicky Blair; Aide to Mertz, Constantin De Goguel.

761 DIAMONDS OF THE NIGHT. (Impact-1968). First Boy, Antonin Kumbera; Second Boy, Ladislav Jansky; The Woman, Ilse Bischofova.

762 DIARIES, NOTES AND SKETCHES. (FilmMakers-1970). Timothy Leary, Ed Emschwiller, Franz Fuenstler, Jack Smith, Mario Montez, Nico, Edie Sedgwick, Andy Warhol, Judith Malina, Storm de Hirsch, Norman Mailer, Allen Ginsberg, John Lennon, Yoko Ono.

763 DIARY OF A CHAMBERMAID. (International Classics-1965). Celestine, Jeanne Moreau; Joseph, Georges Geret; Monsieur Monteil, Michel Piccoli; Madame Monteil, Francoise Lugagne; Capitaine Mauger, Daniel Ivernel; Monsieur Rabour, Jean Ozenne; The Cure, Jean-Claude Carriere; Rose, Gilberte Geniat; The Sacristan, Bernard Musson; Marianne, Muni; The Judge, Claude Jaeger; Claire, Dominique Sauvage-Dandieux; Madeleine Damien, Geymond Vital, Jean Franval, Marcel Rouze, Jeanne Perez, Andree Tainsy, Francoise Bertin, Pierre Collet, Aline Bertrand, Joelle Bernard, Michelle Dacquid, Marcel Le Floch, Marc Eyraud, and Gabriel Gobin.

764 DIARY OF A MAD HOUSEWIFE. (Universal-1970). Jonathan Balser, Richard Benjamin; George Prager, Frank Langella; Tina Balser, Carrie Snodgress; Sylvie Balser, Lorraine Cullen; Liz Balser, Frannie Michel; Charlotte Rady, Katherine Meskill.

765 DIARY OF A SCHIZOPHRENIC GIRL. (Allied Artists-1970). Anna, Ghislaine D'Orsay; Father, Umbato Raho; Mother, Marija Tosinowsky; Blanche, Margarita Lozano.

766 DIARY OF A SHINJUKU BURGLAR. (Grove-1973). Birdey, Tadanori Tokoo; Umeko, Rie Yokoyama; Molchi Tanabe, Tetsu Takahashi, Kei Sato, Fumio Watanabe, Mitsuhior Toura, Kara Juro.

767 DIARY OF A SWINGER. (Box Office International-1967). Jeannie, Joanna Cunningham; Vivian, Rose Conti; Jim, Biff Field; Ronald Durling, Larry Costner, Al "Bomba" Gilman, Michael-Ann Burns, Jack Benson, Pat Winner, Lena Lamont, Joe Harris, Pat Barrett, Ron Scardera, Rina Baron, Lisa King, Chuck Federico, Darcy Brown.

768 DID YOU HEAR THE ONE ABOUT THE TRAVELING SALES-LADY? (Universal-1968). Agatha Knabenshu, Phyllis Diller; Bertram Webb, Bob Denver; Hubert Shelton, Joe Flynn; Jeanine Morse, Eileen Wesson; Ma Webb, Jeanette Nolan; Pa Webb, Paul Reed; Lyle Chatterton, Bob Hastings; Constable, David Hartman; Clara Buxton, Jane Dulo; Scraggs, Kelly Thordsen; Mr. Duckworth, Charles Lane; Ben Milford, George Neise; Old Soldier, Dallas McKennon; Baggage Man, Herb Vigran; Laundry Man, Lloyd Kino; 1st Salesman, Warde Donovan; 2nd Salesman, Eddie Quillan; 3rd Salesman, Eddie Ness.

769 DIE! DIE! MY DARLING! (Columbia-1965). Mrs. Trefoile, Tallulah Bankhead; Patricia Carroll, Stefanie Powers; Harry, Peter Vaughan; Anna, Yootha Joyce; Joseph, Donald Sutherland; Alan, Maurice Kaufmann; Floria, Gwendolyn Watts; Ormsby, Robert Dorning; Oscar, Philip Gilbert; Talkative Woman, Diane King; Shopkeeper, Winifred Dennis.

770 DIE, MONSTER, DIE! (American International-1965). Boris Karloff, Nick Adams, Freda Jackson, Suzan Farmer, Terence DeMarney, Patrick Magee, Paul Farrell, Leslie Dwyer, Sheila Raynor, Harold Goodwin, Sydney Bromley, Billy Milton.

771 DIGBY, THE BIGGEST DOG IN THE WORLD. (Cinerama-1974). Jeff, Jim Dale; Dr. Harz, Spike Milligan; Janine, Angela Douglas; Jerry, John Bluthal; Tom, Norman Rossington; Dr. Jameson, Milo O'Shea; Billy White, Richard Beaumont; Col. Masters, Dinsdale Landon; Rogerson, Garfield Morgan; Professor Ribart, Victor Spinetti; Ringmaster, Harry Towb; General Frank, Kenneth J. Warren; The Great Manzini, Bob Todd; Assistant, Margaret Stuart; Aunt Ina, Molly Urquart; Dog Home Manager, Victor Maddern; Estate Agent, Frank Thornton; General's Aide, Sandra Caron; Grandfather, Edward Underdown; Army Captain, Ben Aris; Control Operator, Sheila Steafel; Bunny Girl, Clovissa Newcombe; Train Driver, Rob Stewart.

772 DILLINGER. (American International-1973). Dillinger, Warren Oates; Melvin, Ben Johnson; Billie, Michelle Phillips; Anna, Cloris Leachman; Homer, Harry Dean Stanton; Harry,

Geoffrey Lewis; Charles, John Ryan; Baby Face, Richard Dreyfuss; Pretty Boy, Steve Kanaly; Eddie, John Martino; Samuel, Roy Jenson; Big Jim, Read Morgan; Reed, Frank McRae.

773 DINAH EAST. (Emerson-1970). Daniela, Ultra Violet; Alan, Andy Davis; Dinah, Jeremy Stockwell; Jess, Reid Smith; Bobby, Joe Taylor; Tony, Ray Foster; Tank, Matt Bennett; Leland Murray, Margaret Rolph, Victoria Wales, Susan Romen, Kitty Carl, Cal Crenshaw, Steve Shaw.

774 DINGAKA. (Embassy-1965). Tom Davis, Stanley Baker; Ntuku Makwena, Ken Gampu; Marion Davis, Juliet Prowse; Prosecutor, Gordon Hood; Witch Doctor, John Sithebe; Masaba, Paul Makgoba.

775 THE DION BROTHERS. (Columbia-1974). Calvin, Stacy Keach; Rut, Frederic Forrest; Margue, Margot Kidder; Tony, Barry Primus; Carlo, Richard Romanus; Rex, Denny Miller; Bather, Clay Tanner; Gino, Robert Phillips; Mother, Mary L. Honaker.

776 DIONYSUS IN 69. (Sigma III-1970). Remi Barclay, Samuel Blazer, Jason Bosseau, Richard Dia, William Finley, Joan MacIntosh, Vicki May, Patrick McDermott, Margaret Ryan, Richard Schechner, William Shepard, Ciel Smith, Judith Allen, Cara Crosby, Gwendolyn Galsworth, Rozanne Levine, Ron Schenk, Charles Strang.

777 THE DIRT GANG. (American International-1972). Monk, Paul Carr; Snake, Michael Pataki; Jesse, Lee DeBroux; Padre, Jon Shank; Big Beth, Nancy Harris; Biff, T. J. Escott; Stormy, Jessica Stuart; Marty, Tom Anders; Willie, Joe Mosca; Zino, Michael Forest; Dawn, Jo Anne Meredith; Mary, Nanci Beck; Curt, Charles Macaulay; Sidney, Hal England; Jason, Ben Archibek; Station Attendant, William Benedict.

778 THE DIRTIEST GIRL I EVER MET. (American International-1973). Carol, Janet Lynn; Joe, Robin Askwith; Philip, Peter Elliott; Jonathan, Jess Conrad; Strangeways, Stubby Kaye.

779 DIRTY DINGUS MAGEE. (MGM-1970). Dingus Magee, Frank Sinatra; Hoke Birdsill, George Kennedy; Belle, Anne Jackson; Prudence Frost, Lois Nettleton; John Wesley Hardin, Jack Elam; Anna Hotwater, Michele Carey; The General, John Dehner; Reverend Green, Henry Jones; Stuart, Harry Carey Jr.; China Poppy, Marya Christen; Ira Teasdale, Willis Bouchey; Chief Crazy Blanket, Paul Fix; Sergeant, Terry Wilson; Lieutenant, Tom Fadden.

780 THE DIRTY DOZEN. (MGM-1967). Major Reisman, Lee Marvin; General Worden, Ernest Borgnine; Joseph Wladislaw,

Charles Bronson; Robert Jefferson, Jim Brown; Victor Franko, John Cassavetes; Sergeant Bowren, Richard Jaeckel; Major Max Armbruster, George Kennedy; Pedro Jiminez, Trini Lopez; Capt. Stuart Kinder, Ralph Meeker; Col. Everett Dasher Breed, Robert Ryan; Archer Maggott, Telly Savalas; Samson Posey, Clint Walker; General Denton, Robert Webber; Tom Tusby, Ben Carruthers, Stuart Cooper, Robert Phillips, Colin Maitland, Al Mancini, George Roubicek, Thick Wilson, Dora Reisser.

781 THE DIRTY GAME. (American International-1966). Kourlov, Henry Fonda; General Bruce, Robert Ryan; Perego, Vittorio Gassman; Nanette, Annie Girardot; Laland, Bourvil; Dupont, Robert Hossein; Berlin CIA Head, Peter Van Eyck; Natalia, Maria Grazia Buccela.

782 DIRTY HARRY. (Warner Bros. -1971). Harry, Clint Eastwood; Lt. Bressler, Harry Guardino; Chico, Reni Santoni; Mayor, John Vernon; Chief, John Larch; Killer, Andy Robinson.

783 THE DIRTY HEROES. (NMD-1971). Sesamo, Frederick Stafford; Kristina, Daniela Bianchi; General Von Keist, Curt Jurgens; Rollman, Adolfo Celi; Gen Hassler, Helmut Schneider; Petrowsky, Michael Constantine; Marta, Faida Nicols.

784 DIRTY LITTLE BILLY. (Columbia-1972). Billy, Michael J. Pollard; Berle, Lee Purcell; Goldie, Richard Evans; Ben, Charles Aidman; Catherine, Dran Hamilton; Henry, Willard Sage; Jawbone, Josip Elic; Ed, Mills Watson; Len, Alex Wilson; Charlie, Ronnie Graham; Earl, Dick Stahl; Basil, Gary Busey; Orville, Doug Dirksen; Gerta, Cherie Franklin; Harry, Dick Van Patten; Louisiana, Rosary Nix; Young Punk, Frank Welker.

785 DIRTY MARY CRAZY LARRY. (20th Century-Fox-1974). Larry, Peter Fonda; Mary, Susan George; Deke, Adam Roarke; Franklin, Vic Morrow; Donohue, Ken Tobey.

786 DIRTY O'NEIL. (American International-1974). Jimmy O'Neil, Morgan Paull; Lassiter, Art Metrano; Lisa, Pat Anderson; Ruby, Jean Manson; Vera, Katie Saylor; Lou, Raymond O'Keefe; Bennie, Tom Huff; Al, Bob Potter; Clyde, Sam Laws; Mrs. Crawford, Liv Lindeland.

787 THE DIRTY OUTLAWS. (Transvue-1972). Steve, Chip Corman; Katy, Rosemarie Dexter; Lucy, Dana Ghia; Asher, Franco Giornelli; Sam, Piero Lulli; Jonat, Aldo Berti; Giovanni Petrucci, Andrea Scotti, Pino Polidori, Dino Strano, John Bartha, Giorgio Gruden, Antonio Cantafora, Sandro Serafini, Giuseppe Castellani, Claudio Trionfi, G. Luigi Crescenzi.

788 DIRTYMOUTH. (Superior-1971). Lenny Bruce, Bernie Travis; Iris, Courtney Sherman; Lou, Lyn Irwin; Fred, Harry Spillman; Marlene, Miss Sam Teardrop.

789 THE DISCREET CHARM OF THE BOURGEOISIE. (20th Century-Fox-1972). Ambassador, Fernando Rey; Mme. Thevenot, Delphine Seyrig; Mme. Senechal, Stephane Audran; Florence, Bulle Orier; M. Senechal, Jean-Pierre Cassel; Home Secretary, Michel Piccoli; Bishop Dufour, Julien Bertheau; Peasant Girl, Muni.

790 DISK-O-TEK HOLIDAY. (Allied Artists-1966). Peter and Gordon, The Bachelors, The Chiffons, Freddy Cannon, The Vagrans, A Band of Angels, Caroline, Roy, Judy, Casey Paxton, Johnny B. Great, Louise Cordet, The Merseybeats, The Orchids, Freddie and the Dreamers, Jackie and the Raindrops, Millie Small, The Rockin' Ramrods, The Applejacks.

791 DIVORCE AMERICAN STYLE. (Columbia-1967). Richard Harmon, Dick Van Dyke; Barbara Harmon, Debbie Reynolds; Nelson Downes, Jason Robards; Nancy Downes, Jean Simmons; Al Yearling, Van Johnson; Lionel Blandsforth, Joe Flynn; David Grieff, Shelley Berman; Doctor Zenwinn, Martin Gabel; Dede Murphy, Lee Grant; Herself, Pat Collins; Farley, Tom Bosley; Fern Blandsforth, Emmaline Henry; Larry Strickland, Dick Gautier; Mark, Tim Matthieson; Jonathan, Gary Goetzman; Eunice, Eileen Brennan; Jackie, Shelley Morrison; Celia, Bella Bruck; Judge, John J. Anthony.

792 DO NOT DISTURB. (20th Century-Fox-1965). Janet Harper, Doris Day; Mike Harper, Rod Taylor; Vanessa Courtwright, Hermione Baddeley; Paul, Sergio Fantoni; Simmons, Reginald Gardiner; Claire Hackett, Maura McGiveney; Culkos, Aram Katcher; Langsdorf, Leon Askin; Alicia, Lisa Pera; Delegate, Michael Romanoff; Reynard, Albert Carrier; Mrs. Ordley, Barbara Morrison; One-man band, Dick Winslow.

793 DO YOU KEEP A LION AT HOME? (Brandon-1966). Ladislaw Ocenasek, Josef Filip, Olga Machoninova, Jan Brychta.

794 THE DOBERMAN GANG. (Dimension-1972). Eddie Newton, Byron Mabe; Barney Greer, Hal Reed; June, Julie Parrish; Sammy, Simmy Bow; Jojo, Jojo D'Amore; Pet Shop Owner, John Tull; Bank Manager, Jay Paxton; Assistant Manager, John Strong; Sandy, Diane Prior; Real Estate Agent, Clyde Apperson; Janitor, John Hogan; Bank Guard, Charles Vincent.

795 DR. ? COPPELIUS!! (Childhood-1968). Dr. Coppelius, Walter Slezak; Swanhilda/Coppelia, Claudia Corday; Franz, Caj Selling; Brigitta, Eileen Elliott; Spanish Doll, Carmen Rojas; Roman Doll, Veronica Kusmin; Hungarian Dance Champion, Milorad Miskovitch; The Mayor, Luis Prendes; Swanhilda's

Friends, Marcia Bellak, Kathy Jo Brown, Clara Cravey, Kathleen Garrison, Christine Holter, Sharon Kapner; Fran Teatro Del Liceo Ballet; International Cine Ballet.

796 DOCTOR DEATH: SEEKER OF SOULS. (Cinerama-1973). Dr. Death, John Considine; Fred, Barry Coe; Sandy, Cheryl Miller; Greg, Stewart Moss; Thor, Leon Askin; Laura, Jo Morrow; Tana, Florence Marly; Venus, Sivi Aberg; Franz, Jim Boles; Spiritualist, Athena Lorde; Volunteer, Moe Howard; Old Wizard, Robert E. Ball; Old Man, Patrick Dennis-Leigh; TV Watcher, Lin Henson; Girl in phonebooth, Anna Bernard; Alice, Barbara Boles; Harry, Pierre Gonneau; Young man in park, Larry Rogers; Girl with flat tire, Denise Denise; Man at seance, Eric Boles; Man wanting new body, Jeffrey Herman; Man to arrange seance, Leon Williams; Strangler, Larry "Seymour" Vincent.

797 DOCTOR DOLITTLE. (20th Century-Fox-1967). Doctor John Dolittle, Rex Harrison; Matthew Mugg, Anthony Newley; Emma Fairfax, Samantha Eggar; Albert Blossom, Richard Attenborough; Mrs. Blossom, Muriel Landers; Tommy Stubbins, William Dix; General Bellowes, Peter Bull; Sarah Dolittle, Portia Nelson; Lady Petherington, Norman Varden; Willie Shakespeare, Geoffrey Holder.

798 DOCTOR FAUSTUS. (Columbia-1968). Doctor Faustus, Richard Burton; Mephistopheles, Andreas Teuber; Emperor, Ian Marter; Lucifer, David McIntosh; Cornelius, Richard Carwardine; Helen of Troy, Elizabeth Taylor; Empress, Elizabeth O'Donovan; Belzebub, Jeremy Eccles; Valdes, Ram Chopra; Pope, Adrian Benjamin; 1st Scholar, Richard Heffer; 2nd Scholar, Hugh Williams; 3rd Scholar/Lechery, Gwydion Thomas; Cardinal/Pride, Nicholas Loukes; Evil Angel/Knight, Richard Durden-Smith; Wagner, Patrick Barwise; Jeremy Chandler, Angus McIntosh; Ambrose Coghill, Anthony Kaufmann, Julian Wontner, Richard Harrison, Nevill Coghill, Michael Menaugh, John Sandbach, Sebastian Walker, R. Peverello, Maria Aitkien, Valerie James, Bridget Coghill, Petronella Pulsford, Susan Watson, Jacqueline Harvey, Sheila Dawson, Carolyn Bennitt, Jane Wilford.

799 DOCTOR GLAS. (20th Century-Fox-1969). Dr. Glas, Per Oscarsson; Pastor Gregorius, Ulf Palme; Helga Gregorius, Lone Hertz; Markel, Nils Eklund; Eva Martens, Bente Dessau; Klas Recke, Lars Lunoe; Birck, Bendt Rothe; Glas' Father, Ingolf David; Anita, Helle Hertz; Friend at University, Jonas Bergstrom.

800 DR. GOLDFOOT AND THE BIKINI MACHINE. (American International-1966). Dr. Goldfoot, Vincent Price; Craig Gamble, Frankie Avalon; Todd Armstrong, Dwayne Hickman; Diane, Susan Hart; Igor, Jack Mullaney; D. J. Pavney, Fred Clark; Reject No. 12, Alberta Nelson; Motorcycle Cop, Milton

Frome; Newsvendor, Hal Riddle; Girl in nightclub, Kay Elhardt; Guard, William Baskin; Janitor, Vincent L. Barnett; Cook, Joe Ploski; Robots, Patti Chandler, Sally Sachse, Sue Hamilton, Marianne Gaba, Issa Arnal, Pam Rodgers, Sally Frei, Jan Watson, Mary Hughes, Luree Holmes, Laura Nicholson, China Lee, Deanna Lund, Leslie Summers, Kay Michaels, Arlene Charles; Sam and the Ape Men with Diane De Marco.

801 DR. GOLDFOOT AND THE GIRL BOMBS. (American International-1967). Dr. Goldfoot, Vincent Price; Bill Dexter, Fabian; Franco, Franco Franchi; Ciccio, Ciccio Ingrassia; Rosanna, Laura Antonelli; Goldfoot's Assistant, Moana Tahi.

802 DR. JEKYLL AND SISTER HYDE. (American International-1972). Dr. Henry Jekyll, Ralph Bates; Sister Hyde, Martine Beswick; Professor Robertson, Gerald Sim; Howard, Lewis Flander; Susan, Susan Brodrick; Mrs. Spencer, Dorothy Alison; Burke, Ivor Dean; Sgt. Danvers, Paul Whitsun-Jones; Byker, Philip Madoc; Hare, Tony Calvin; Town Crier, Dan Meaden; Betsy, Virginia Wetherell; Street Singer, Julia Wright; Older Policeman, Geoffrey Kenion; Yvonne, Irene Bradshaw; Julie, Anna Brett; Margie, Jackie Poole; Marie, Rosemary Lord; Petra, Petula Portell; Helen, Pat Brackenbury; Emma, Liz Romanoff; Mine Host, Will Stampe; Knife Grinder, Roy Evans; Sailors, Derek Steen and John Lyons; Jill, Jeannette Wild; Young Apprentice, Bobby Parr.

803 DR. PHIBES RISES AGAIN. (American International-1972). Dr. Phibes, Vincent Price; Biederbeck, Robert Quarry; Vulnavia, Valli Kemp; Diana, Fiona Lewis; Captain, Peter Cushing; Mrs. Ambrose, Beryl Reid; Lombardo, Terry-Thomas; Ambrose, Hugh Griffith; Inspector Trout, Peter Jeffrey; Waverly, John Cater; Hackett, Gerald Sim.

804 DR. TERROR'S HOUSE OF HORRORS. (Paramount-1965). Peter Cushing, Christopher Lee, Roy Castle, Donald Sutherland, Neil McCallum, Alan Freeman, Max Adrian, Edward Underdown, Ursula Howells, Peter Madden, Kath Wild, Ann Bell, Sarah Nicholls, Bernard Lee, Jeremy Kemp, Kenny Lynch, Harold Lang, Christopher Carlos, George Mossman, Thomas Baptiste, Tubby Hayes Quintet, Russ Henderson, Michael Gough, Isela Blair, Hedger Wallace, Judy Cornwall, Faith Kent, Brian Hankins, John Martin, Kenneth Kove, Walter Sparrow, Frank Forsyth, Al Mulock, Jennifer Jayne, Frank Barry, Irene Richmond, Laurie Leigh.

805 DR. WHO AND THE DALEKS. (Continental-1967). Dr. Who, Peter Cushing; Ian, Roy Castle; Barbara, Jennie Linden; Susan, Roberta Tovey; Alydon, Barrie Ingham; Temmosus, Geoffrey Toone; Elyon, Mark Petersen; Antodus, John Bown; Ganatus, Michael Coles; Dyoni, Yvonne Antrobus.

806 DOCTOR, YOU'VE GOT TO BE KIDDING! (MGM-1967). Heather Halloran, Sandra Dee; Harlan Wycliff, George Hamilton; Louise Halloran, Celeste Holm; Dick Bender, Bill Bixby; Pat Murad, Dick Kallman; Dan Ruskin, Mort Sahl; Hank Judson, Dwayne Hickman; Joe Bonney, Allen Jenkins; Alex North, Robert Gibbons; Jenny Ribbock, Nichelle Nichols; Miss Reynolds, Charlotte Considine; Cigarette Girl, Allison McKay; Folk Singer, Rica Owen Moore; Themselves, The Wild Affair Trio.

807 DOCTOR ZHIVAGO. (MGM-1965). Yuri Zhivago, Omar Sharif; Lara, Julie Christie; Pasha Antipov, Tom Courtenay; Komarovsky, Rod Steiger; Tonya Gromeko, Geraldine Chaplin; Yevgraf Zhivago, Alec Guinness; Anna Gromeko, Siobhan McKenna; Alexander Gromeko, Ralph Richardson; The Girl, Rita Tushingham; Lara's Mother, Adrienne Corri; Yuri at age of 8, Tarek Sharif; Professor Kurt, Geoffrey Keen; Sasha, Jeffrey Rockland; Katya, Lucy Westmore; Razin, Noel Willman; Liberius, Gerald Tichy; Kostoyed, Klaus Kinski; Petya, Jack MacGowran; Tonya at age of 7, Mercedes Ruiz.

808 DOCTORS' WIVES. (Columbia-1971). Lorrie, Dyan Cannon; Pete, Richard Crenna; Dave, Gene Hackman; Joe, Carroll O'Connor; Della, Rachel Roberts; Amy, Janice Rule; Helen, Diana Sands; Maggie, Cara Williams; D. A., Richard Anderson; Jake, Ralph Bellamy; Mort, John Colicos; Paul, George Gaynes; Elaine, Marian McCargo.

808a DOLLARS. (Columbia-1971). Joe Collins, Warren Beatty; Dawn Divine, Goldie Hawn; Mr. Kessel, Gert Frobe; Attorney, Robert Webber; Sarge, Scott Brady; Candy Man, Arthur Brauss; Major, Robert Stiles; Granich, Wolfgang Kieling; Bodyguard, Robert Herron; Helga, Christiane Maybach; Karl, Hans Hutter; Berta, Monica Stender; Bruno, Horst Hesslein; Fur Coat, Wolfgang Kuhlman; Knife Man, Klaus Tschichan; Customs, Tove Platon, Kirsten Lahman; Stripper, Francoise Blanc; Associated Press, Darrell Armstrong; Stars and Stripes, Walter Trott.

809 A DOLL'S HOUSE. (Paramount-1973). Nora Helmer, Claire Bloom; Torvald Helmer, Anthony Hopkins; Dr. Rank, Ralph Richardson; Krogstad, Denholm Elliott; Kristine Linde, Anna Massey; Anne Marie, Edith Evans; Helen, Helen Blatch; Emmy, Stefanie Summerfield; Ivar, Mark Summerfield; Bob, Kimberley Hampton; Old Woman, Daphne Rigg.

810 A DOLL'S HOUSE. (Tomorrow Entertainment-1973). Nora, Jane Fonda; Torvald, David Warner; Dr. Rank, Trevor Howard; Kristine Linde, Delphine Seyrig; Krogstad, Edward Fox; Anne-Marie, Anna Wing; Olssen, Pierre Oudrey; Ivar, Frode Lien; Emmy, Tone Floor; Bob, Morten Floor; Dr. Rank's Maid, Ingrid Natrud; Helmer's Maid, Freda Krigh; Krogstad's Daughter, Ellen Holm; Krogstad's Son, Dagfinn Hertzberg.

811 No entry.

812 THE DON IS DEAD. (Universal-1973). Don Angelo, Anthony Quinn; Tony, Frederic Forrest; Frank, Robert Forster; Vince, Al Lettieri; Ruby, Angel Tompkins; Orlando, Charles Cioffi; Marie, Jo Anne Meredith; Don Bruno, J. Duke Russo; Mitvh, Louis Zorich; Nella, Ina Balin; Vito, George Skaff; Mike Spada, Robert Carricart; Johnny Tresca, Anthony Charnota; Abe Vigoda, Frank de Kove, Joseph Santos.

813 DON'T CRY WITH YOUR MOUTH FULL. (1974). Annie, Annie Cole; Father, Jean Carmet; Mother, Christiane Chamaret; Grandmother, Helene Dieudonne; Uncle, Daniel Ceccaldi; Aunt, Claudine Paringaux; Sister, Friquette; Alexander, Bernard Menez; Frederic, Frederic Duru.

814 DON'T DRINK THE WATER. (Avco Embassy-1969). Walter Hollander, Jackie Gleason; Marion Hollander, Estelle Parsons; Axel Magee, Ted Bessell; Susan Hollander, Joan Delaney; Krojack, Michael Constantine; Ambassador Magee, Howard St. John; Kilroy, Danny Meehan; Father Drobney, Richard Libertini; Sam, Phil Leeds; Chef, Pierre Olaf; Sultan, Avery Schrieber; Mirik, Mark Gordon; Donald, Dwayne Early; Airline Clerk, Joan Murphy; Mishkin, Martin Danzig; Organgrinder, Rene Constantineau; Getaway Pilot, Howard Morris.

815 DON'T JUST LAY THERE. (Mattis-Pine-1970). Sloan, Weggener; Rock, Don Dyer; Billie, Bridgett; Rusty, Barbara Caron; Eve, Mary Jane Shipper; Lori, Fern Hal Brook; Creighton, Jon Mattisse; Baller, Kathy Hilton; Smokey, Diane Lewis.

816 DON'T JUST STAND THERE! (Universal-1968). Lawrence Colby, Robert Wagner; Martine Randall, Mary Tyler Moore; Sabine Manning, Glynis Johns; Merriman Dudley, Harvey Korman; Kendall Flanagan, Barbara Rhoades; Painter, Vincent Beck; Jean-Jacques, Joseph Perry; Remy, Stuart Margolin; Henri, Emile Genest; Jules, David Mauro; Renee, Penny Santon; Police Inspector, Joe Bernard; Moffat, Herbert Voland; Pascal Decaux, Richard Angarola; Bill Elkins, Otis Young; Gabrielle, Willi Koopman; Bern Hoffman, Gladys Holland.

817 DON'T LOOK BACK. (Leacock-Pennebaker-1967). Bob Dylan, Joan Baez, Donovan.

818 DON'T LOOK IN THE BASEMENT. (Hallmark-1973). Charlotte, Rosie Holotik; Dr. Masters, Ann McAdams; Sam, William Bill McGhee.

819 DON'T LOOK NOW. (Buena Vista-1969). Reginald, Terry-Thomas; Augustin Bouvet, Bourvil; Stanislas Lefort, Louis De Funes; Peter Dunningham, Claudio Brook; Juliette, Marie Dubois; Mayor Achbach, Benno Sterzenbach; Madame Germaine,

Colette Brosset; Sister Marie-Odile, Andrea Parisy; Alan MacIntosh, Mike Marshall; Mother Superior, Mary Marquet; Punch and Judy Operator, Pierre Bertin; Sieghardt Rupp, Paul Preboist, Hans Meyer, Peter Jacob, Rudy Lenoir.

820 DON'T LOOK NOW. (Paramount-1973). Laura Baxter, Julie Christie; John Baxter, Donald Sutherland; Heather, Hilary Mason; Wendy, Clelia Mantana; Bishop Barbarrigo, Massimo Serato; Inspector Longhi, Renato Scarpa; Workman, Georgio Trestini; Hotel Manager, Leopoldo Trieste; Anthony Babbage, David Tree; Mandy Babbage, Ann Rye; Johnny Baxter, Nicholas Salter; Christine Baxter, Sharon Williams; Detective Sabbione, Bruno Cattaneo; Dwarf, Adelina Poerio.

821 DON'T MAKE WAVES. (MGM-1967). Carlo Cofield, Tony Curtis; Laura Colifatti, Claudia Cardinale; Malibu, Sharon Tate; Rod Prescott, Robert Webber; Diane Prescott, Joanna Barnes; Harry Hollard, David Draper; Sam Lingonberry, Mort Sahl; Madame Lavinia, Edgar Bergen; Himself, Jim Backus; Herself, Henny Backus; Ann Elder, Chester Yorton, Marc London, Douglas Henderson, Sarah Selby, Mary Grace Canfield, Dub Taylor, Reg Lewis, Julie Payne, Hollie Haze, Paul Barselow, Eduardo Tirella, George Tyne, Gilbert Green, David Fresco.

822 DON'T RAISE THE BRIDGE, LOWER THE RIVER. (Columbia-1968). George Lester, Jerry Lewis; H. William Homer, Terry-Thomas; Pamela Lester, Jacqueline Pearce; Fred Davies, Bernard Cribbins; Lucille Beatty, Patricia Routledge; Dudley Heath, Nicholas Parsons; Dr. Spink, Michael Bates; Mr. Hartford, Colin Gordon; Dr. Pinto, John Bluthal; Pinto's Nurse, Sandra Caron; Spink's Nurse, Margaret Nolan; Fern Averback, Pippa Benedict; Six-Eyes Wiener, Harold Goodwin; Arab, Henry Soskin; Portuguese Chauffeur, Al Mancini; Digby, John Moore; Zebra Man, John Barrard; Bruce, Robert Lee; Chinese Telephonist, Francesca Tu; Barman, Colin Douglas; Masseuse, Alexandra Dane; Portuguese Waitress, Nike Arrighi; Judy Man, Tatsuo Susuki; Manicurist, Christine Pryor; Heath's Secretary, Mollie Peters; Baseball Umpire, Jerry Paris.

823 DON'T TURN THE OTHER CHEEK. (International Amusement-1974). Eli Wallach, Lynn Redgrave, Franco Nero, Marilu Tolo, Luigi Antonio Guerra, Horst Yanson, Eduardo Fajardo, Jose Moren, Victor Israel, Gisela Hahn, Jose Haspes, Enrique Espinosa, Gunda Hiller, Furio Meniconi, Don Van Husen, Rudy Gaebell, Carla Mancini, Mirko Ellis.

824 DON'T WORRY, WE'LL THINK OF A TITLE. (United Artists-1966). Charlie, Morey Amsterdam; Annie, Rose Marie; Mr. Travis/Police Chief, Richard Deacon; Seed/Samu, Tim Herbert; Mr. Big, Jackie Heller; 1st Guy, Joey Adams; 2nd Guy, Andy Albin; Jim Holliston, Michael Ford; Magda Anders,

January Jones; Olga, Carmen Phillips; Lerowski, Henry Corden; Fat Lady, Peggy Mondo; Fat Man, Percy Helton; The Lover, LaRue Farlow; Mr. Raines, Moe Howard; Chinese Girl, Yau Shan Tung; Girl Student, Arline Hunter; 2nd Student, Annazette; Boy Student, Gregg Amsterdam; Athlete, Darryl Vaughan; Guest Stars, Nick Adams, Cliff Arquette, Carl Reiner, Danny Thomas, Slapsy Maxie Rosenbloom, Steve Allen, Milton Berle, Irene Ryan, Forrest Tucker.

825 DOOMSDAY VOYAGE. (Futurama International-1972). Jason, Joseph Cotten; Wilson, John Gabriel; Katherine, Ann Randall.

826 DOOR-TO-DOOR MANIAC. (American International-1966). Johnny Cash, Donald Woods, Cay Forester, Pamela Mason, Midge Ware, Vic Tayback, Ronnie Howard, Merle Travis, Howard Wright, Norma Varden.

827 DORIAN GRAY. (American International-1970). Dorian, Helmut Berger; Basil, Richard Todd; Henry, Herbert Lom; Sybil, Marie Liljedahl; Gwendolyn, Margaret Lee; Alice, Marie Rohm; Adrienne, Beryl Cunningham; Mrs. Ruxton, Isa Miranda; Esther, Eleonora Rossi Drago; Alan, Renato Romano; James, Stewart Black.

828 DOUBLE INITIATION. (Hollywood International-1970). Lisa, Janet Wass; Carlos, Carlos Tobalina; Psychiatrist, Maria-Pia; Andy, Andy Roth.

829 THE DOUBLE MAN. (Warner Bros. -7 Arts-1968). Dan Slater/Kalmar, Yul Brynner; Gina Ericson, Britt Ekland; Frank Wheatly, Clive Revill; Colonel Berthold, Anton Diffring; Mrs. Carrington, Moira Lister; Bill Edwards, Lloyd Nolan; Max Gruner, George Mikell; Gregori, Brandon Brady; Anna Wheatly, Julia Arnall; Andrew Miller, David Bauer; General, Ronald Radd; Police Chief, Kenneth J. Warren; Halstead, David Healy; Ticket Seller, Frederick Schiller; Man at station, Franklin J. Schaffner.

830 DOUBLE-STOP. (World Entertainment-1968). Jeremiah Sullivan, Mimi Torchin, Anthony Walsh, Patti Fairchild, Billy Kurtz, Barry Gordon, Gino Arditto.

831 DOUBLE TROUBLE. (MGM-1967). Guy Lambert, Elvis Presley; Jill Conway, Annette Day; Gerald Waverly, John Williams; Claire Dunham, Yvonne Romain; Themselves, The Wiere Brothers; Archie Brown, Chips Rafferty; Arthur Babcock, Norman Rossington; Georgie, Monty Landis; Morley, Leon Askin; Iceman, John Alderson; Captain Roach, Stanley Adams; Frenchman, Maurice Marsac; Mate, Walter Burke; Gerda, Helene Winston; Desk Clerk, Monique Lemaire; Themselves, The G. Men.

832 THE DOVE. (Paramount-1974). Robin Lee Graham, Joseph

Bottoms; Patti Ratteree, Deborah Raffin; Lyle Graham, John McLiam; Charles Huntley, Dabney Coleman; Mike Turk, John Anderson; Tom Barkley, Colby Chester; Kenniston, Ivor Barry; Young Fijian, Setoki Ceinaturoga; Minister, Rev. Nikula; Cruise Ship Capt., Apenisa Naigulevu; Tim, John Meillon; Darwin Harbor Master, Gordon Glenwright; S. African Customs Official, Garth Meade; Fred C. Pearson, Peter Gwynne; Mrs. Castaldi, Cecily Polson; License Bureau Clerk, Anthony Fridjon; Reporter, Dale Cutts; Chief Pilot, Jose Augusto De Lima Sampaio e Silva.

833 THE DOWNHILL RACER. (Paramount-1969). David Chappellet, Robert Redford; Eugene Claire, Gene Hackman; Carole Stahl, Camilla Sparv; Machet, Karl Michael Vogler; Creech, Jim McMullan; Brumm, Christian Doermer; American Newspaperwoman, Kathleen Crowley; Mayo, Dabney Coleman; D. K., Kenneth Kirk; Kipsmith, Oren Stevens; Engel, Jerry Dexter; David's father, Walter Stroud; Lena, Carole Carle; Devore, Rip McManus; Tommy, Joe Jay Jalbert; Stiles, Tom J. Kirk; Gabriel, Robin Hutton-Potts; Meier, Heini Schuler; Boyriven, Peter Rohr; Hinsch, Arnold Alpiger; Haas, Eddie Waldburger; Istel, Marco Walli.

834 DRACULA A.D. 1972. (Warner Bros.-1972). Count Dracula, Christopher Lee; Abraham Van Helsing/Professor Van Helsing, Peter Cushing; Jessica Van Helsing, Stephanie Beacham; Johnny Alucard, Christopher Neame; Inspector Murray, Michael Coles; Joe Mitchum, William Ellis; Gaynor, Marsha Hunt; Anna, Janet Key; Bob, Philip Miller; Greg, Michael Kitchen; Sergeant Pearson, David Andrews; Laura, Caroline Munro; Matron, Lally Bowers; Rock Group, Stoneground.

835 DRACULA HAS RISEN FROM THE GRAVE. (Warner Bros.-7 Arts-1969). Count Dracula, Christopher Lee; Monsignor, Rupert Davies; Maria, Veronica Carlson; Zena, Barbara Ewing; Paul, Barry Andrews; Priest, Ewan Hooper; Max, Michael Ripper; Landlord, George A. Cooper; Anna, Marion Mathie; Student, John D. Collins; Farmer, Chris Cunningham; Boy, Norman Bacon; First Victim, Carrie Baker.

836 DRACULA--PRINCE OF DARKNESS. (20th Century-Fox-1966). Dracula, Christopher Lee; Helen Kent, Barbara Shelley; Father Shandor, Andrew Keir; Charles Kent, Francis Matthews; Diana Kent, Suzan Farmer; Alan Kent, Charles Tingwell; Ludwig, Thorley Walters; Klove, Philip Latham; Brother Mark, Walter Brown; Landlord, George Woodbridge; Brother Peter, Jack Lambert; Priest, Philip Ray; Mother, Joyce Hemson; Coach Driver, John Maxim.

837 DRACULA VS. FRANKENSTEIN. (Independent International-1973). Frankenstein, J. Carrol Naish; Groton, Lon Chaney; Dracula, Zandor Vorkov; Rico, Russ Tamblyn; Martin, Jim Davis.

838 THE DRAGON DIES HARD. (American International-1974). Bruce Lee.

839 A DREAM OF KINGS. (National General-1969). Matsoukas, Anthony Quinn; Caliope, Irene Papas; Anna, Inger Stevens; Cicero, Sam Levene; Stavros, Radames Pera; Mother-in-law, Tamara Daykarhanova; Fatsas, Val Avery; Falconis, Peter Mamakos; Fig King, Alan Reed Sr.; Turk, H. B. Haggerty; Telecles, Chris Marks; Javaras, Peter Xantho; Aristotle, Alberto Morin; Zenoitis, Zvee Scooler; Apollo, George Savalas; Toundas, Ernest Sarracino; Herman, Tol Avery; Uncle Louie, Tony Joachim; Hope, Effie Columbus; Faith, Sandra Damato; Young Doctor, James Dobson; Manulis, James Fortunes; Mrs. Cournos, Katherine Theodore; Doctor in church, George Michaelides; Nurses, Lisa Pera, Lisa Moore.

840 THE DREAMER. (Cannon-1970). Eli, Tuvia Tavi; The Girl, Leora Rivlin; Rachel, Berta Litvina; Manager, Shlomo Bar Shavit; Mother, Dvora Keidar; Father, Nathan Kogan.

841 DREAMS OF GLASS. (Universal-1970). Tom, John Denos; Anna, Caroline Barrett; Tom's father, Joe LoPresti; Tom's mother, Margaret Rich; Mrs. Murakoshi, Pat Li.

842 THE DRIFTER. (Filmmakers' Distribution Center-1967). Alan, John Tracy; Renee, Sadja Marr; The Child, Michael Fair; The Musician, Lew Skinner; Club Owner, Ed Randolph; The Waitress, Paula Feiten; The Girl on Horseback, Clair Pelly; The Ticket Taker, Michael Onida.

843 DRIVE, HE SAID. (Columbia-1971). Hector, William Tepper; Olive, Karen Black; Gabriel, Michael Margotta; Coach Bullion, Bruce Dern; Richard, Robert Towne; Conrad, Henry Jaglom.

844 THE DRUMS OF TABU. (PRO-1967). James Philbrook, Seyna Sein, Frank Moran, Frank Fantasia, Benny Deus, Chick Cicarelli, Carl Taberlani, John Sutton, Joseph Han.

845 DUCK, YOU SUCKER. (United Artists-1972). Juan Miranda, Rod Steiger; Sean Mallory, James Coburn; Dr. Villega, Romolo Valli; Adolita, Maria Monti; Santerna, Rik Battaglia; Governor, Franco Graziosi; Guttierrez, Antoine Domingo; Nino, Goffredo Pistoni; Landowner, Roy Bosier; American, John Frederick; Notary, Nino Casale; Priest, Jean Rougeul; Pancho, Vincenzo Norvese; Sebastian, Corrado Solari; Benito, Biacio La Rocca; Pepe, Renato Pontecchi; Peon, Amelio Perlini; Yankee, Michael Harvey; Napoleon, Franco Collace.

846 DUEL AT DIABLO. (United Artists-1966). Jess Remsberg, James Garner; Toller, Sidney Poitier; Ellen Grange, Bibi Andersson; Willard Grange, Dennis Weaver; Lt. McAllister (Scotty), Bill Travers; Sgt. Ferguson, William Redfield; Chata,

John Hoyt; Clay Dean, John Crawford; Major Novak, John Hubbard; Norton, Kevin Coughlin; Tech, Jay Ripley; Casey, Jeff Cooper; Nyles, Ralph Bahnsen; Swenson, Bobby Crawford; Richard Lapp, Armand Alzamora, Alf Elson, Dawn Little Sky, Eddie Little Sky, Al Wyatt, Bill Hart, J. R. Randall, John Daheim, Phil Schumacher, Richard Farnsworth, Joe Finnegan.

847 DUET FOR CANNIBALS. (Grove Press-1969). Francesca, Adriana Asti; Bauer, Lars Ekborg; Tomas, Costa Ekman; Ingrid, Agneta Ekmanner.

848 DUFFY. (Columbia-1968). Duffy, James Coburn; Charles Calvert, James Mason; Stefane Calvert, James Fox; Segolene, Susannah York; Antony Calvert, John Alderton; Bakirgian, Barry Shawzin; Abdul, Marne Maitland; Sea Captain, Guy Deghy; Chief of Police, Andre Maranne; Small Spaniard, Tutte Lemkow; Bonivet, Carl Duering; Belly Dancer, Julie Mendez.

849 DULCIMA. (Cinevision Films Ltd. -1972). Dulcima Gaskain, Carol White; Mr. Parker, John Mills; Gamekeeper, Stuart Wilson; Mr. Gaskain, Bernard Lee; Mrs. Gaskain, Sheila Raynor; Symes; Dudley Foster.

850 THE DUNWICH HORROR. (American International-1970). Nancy, Sandra Dee; Wilbur, Dean Stockwell; Dr. Armitage, Ed Begley; Dr. Cary, Lloyd Bochner; Elizabeth, Donna Baccala; Lavinia, Joanna Moore Jordan; Cora, Talia Coppola; Mrs. Cole, Barboura Morris; Dr. Raskin, Mike Fox; Police Chief: Jason Wingreen; Shateley, Sam Jaffe; Guard, Michael Haynes.

851 DUSTY AND SWEETS MCGEE. (Warner Bros. -1971). Pam, Larry, Clifton Tip Fredell, Kit Ryder, Beverly, Mitch, Armen, Bobby Graham.

852 DUTCHMAN. (Continental-1967). Lula, Shirley Knight; Clay, Al Freeman Jr.; Frank Lieberman, Robert Calvert, Howard Bennett, Sandy McDonald, Denis Peters, Keith James, Devon Hall.

853 DYNAMITE. (Distribpix-1972). Suzy, Marcia Rivers; Harry, Steve Gould; Kay, Dolly Sharp; Usher, Kurt Mann; Converse, Jamie Goodman; Kruger, Leon Oriana; Phoebe, Dee Brown; Uta, Uta Erickson.

854 DYNAMITE CHICKEN. (EYR-1972). The Ace Trucking Company, Joan Baez, The Black Panther Party, Humphrey Bogart, Linda Boyce, Lenny Bruce, Jim Buckley, James Cagney, Linda Calendar, Al Capp, Ron Carey, Cat Mother and the All Night Newsboys, Charon Cohen, Leonard Cohen, The Colwell-Winfield Blues Band, Larry Coryell, John De Coney, Eric Dolphy, Marshall Efron, Jay Garner, Allen Ginsberg, Bob Godfrey, Lionel Goldbart, Al Goldstein, The Groupies,

Tony Hendra, Jimi Hendrix, B. B. King, Al Kooper, Paul Krassner, Tuli Kupferberg, La Rocque Bey School of Dance Theater, Suzenne Landow, John Lennon, Charles Lloyd, Malcolm X, Charlie Manna, The Mattachine Society, Peter Max, Marilyn Monroe, The Muddy Waters Blues Band, Elizanimmo, Pat O'Brien, Michael O'Donoghue, Ondine, Yoko Ono, Eleo Pomare, Richard Pryor, Redstockings, Rhinoceros, Lisa Ryan, Sha-Na-Na, Nina Simone, Sister Feonna, Nick Ulett, The Velvet Underground and Andy Warhol.

855 EAGLE IN A CAGE. (National General-1972). Lord Sissal, John Gielgud; Sir Hudson Lowe, Ralph Richardson; Madame Jacqueline Bertrand, Billie Whitelaw; Napoleon Bonaparte, Kenneth Haigh; General Gourgaud, Moses Gunn; Count Bertrand, Ferdy Mayne; Cipriani, Lee Montague; Betty Balcombe, Georgina Hale; Barry O'Meara, Michael Williams; English Soldier, Hugh Armstrong; Sentry, Athol Coates.

856 EAGLE OVER LONDON. (Cine Globe-1973). Frederick Stafford, Van Johnson, Francisco Rabal, Evelyn Stewart, Luigi Pistilli, Renzo Palmer, Edy Biagetti, Luis Davila, Christian Hay, Jacques Berthier, Teresa Gimpera.

857 EARLY SPRING. (New Yorker-1974). Shoji Sugiyama, Ryo Ikebe; Masako, Chikage Awashima; Chiyo Kaneko, Keiko Kishi; Taizo Aoki, Teiji Takahashi; Kiichi Onodera, Chishu Ryu.

858 THE EARTH DIES SCREAMING. (20th Century-Fox-1966). Willard Parker, Virginia Field, Dennis Price, Vanda Godsell, Thorley Walters, David Spenser, Anna Falk.

859 EARTHQUAKE. (Universal-1974). Graff, Charlton Heston; Remy Graff, Ava Gardner; Patrolman Slade, George Kennedy; Royce, Lorne Greene; Denise, Genevieve Bujold; Miles, Richard Roundtree; Jody, Marjoe Gortner; Dr. Stockle, Barry Sullivan; Dr. Vance, Lloyd Nolan; Rosa, Victoria Principal; Drunk, Walter Mathau; Royce's Secretary, Monica Lewis; Miles' Manager, Gabriel Dell; Slade's Partner, Pedro Armendariz Jr.; Cameron, Lloyd Gough; Mayor, John Randolph; Assistant Seismologist, Kip Niven; Assistant Dam Caretaker, Scott Hylands; Corry Marshall, Tiger Williams; Jody's Hecklers, Michael Richardson, Jesse Vint, Alan Vint.

860 EAST OF SUDAN. (Columbia-1965). Anthony Quayle, Sylvia Sims, Derek Fowlds, Jenny Agutter, Johnny Sekka.

861 EASY COME, EASY GO. (Paramount-1967). Ted Jackson, Elvis Presley; Jo Symington, Dodie Marshall; Dina Bishop, Pat Priest; Judd Whitman, Pat Harrington; Gil Carey, Skip Ward; Madame Neherina, Elsa Lanchester; Captain Jack, Frank McHugh; Lt. Schwartz, Sandy Kenyon; Cooper, Ed Griffith; Lt. Tompkins, Read Morgan; Lt. Whitehead, Mickey

Elley; Vicki, Elaine Beckett; Mary, Shari Nims; Zoltan, Diki Lerner; Artist, Robert Isenberg; Tanya, Kay York.

862 EASY RIDER. (Columbia-1969). Wyatt, Peter Fonda; Billy, Dennis Hopper; Jesus, Antonio Mendoza; The Connection, Phil Spector; Bodyguard, Mac Mashourian; Rancher, Warren Finnerty; Rancher's Wife, Tita Colorado; Stranger on Highway, Luke Askew; Cat Man, Hayward Robillard; Lisa, Luana Anders; Sarah, Sabrina Scharf; Joanne, Sandy Wyeth; Jack, Robert Walker; Mime #1, Robert Ball; Mime #2, Carmen Phillips; Mime #3, Ellie Walker; Mime #4, Michael Pataki; George Hanson, Jack Nicholson; Guard, George Fowler Jr.; Sheriff, Keith Green; Deputy, Arnold Hess Jr.; Customers, Buddy Causey Jr., Duffy Lafont, Blase M. Dawson, Paul Guedry Jr.; Girls, Suzie Ramagos, Elida Ann Hebert, Rose LeBlanc, Mary Kaye Hebert, Cynthia Grezaffi, Colette Purpera; Mary, Toni Basil; Karen, Karen Black; Madame, Lea Marmer; Dancing Girl, Cathe Cozzi; Hookers, Thea Salerno, Anne McClain, Beatriz Monteil, Marcia Bowman; Pickup Truck Riders, Johnny David and David C. Billodeau.

863 THE EAVESDROPPER. (Royal-1966). Janet Margolin, Stathis Giallelis, Lautaro Murua, Leonardo Favio, Nelly Meden, Ignacio de Soroa, Elena Toresina.

864 THE EDGE. (Filmmakers' Distribution Center-1968). Dan Rainer, Jack Rader; Tom Eliot, Tom Griffin; Bill Raskin, Howard Loeb Babeuf; Max Laing, Jeff Weiss; Didi Stein, Anne Waldman Warsch; Peter Stein, Sanford Cohen; Sinclair Davis, Paul Hultberg; Sally Kolka, Catherine Merrill; Michael Warren, Russell Parker; Gerry Toller, Gerald Long; Anne Davis, Theodora Bergery; Randall Kates, Randall Conrad; Connie Barker, Constance Ullman Long; Girl in Bed, Susan Reiner; Mental Patient, Robert Kramer.

865 THE EDUCATION OF SONNY CARSON. (Paramount-1974). Sonny Carson, Rony Clanton; Pigliani, Don Gordon; Virginia, Joyce Walker; Pops, Paul Benjamin; Young Sonny, Thomas Hicks; Moms, Mary Alice; Preacher, Ram John Holder; Lil Boy, Jerry Bell; Benny, Ray Rainbow Johnson; Wolfe, Derrick Champ Ford; Lil John, Roger Hill; Crazy, B. T. Taylor; Willie, Roger Davis; Psychiatrist, Clifton Steere; Western Union Messenger, Dennis Keir; Lil Boy's mother, Linda Hopkins; Parole Board chairman, Mervyn Nelson; Judge, David Kerman.

866 THE EFFECT OF GAMMA RAYS ON MAN-IN-THE-MOON MARIGOLDS. (20th Century-Fox-1972). Beatrice, Joanne Woodward; Matilda, Nell Potts; Ruth, Roberta Wallach; Nanny, Judith Lowry; Floyd, Richard Venture; Mrs. McKay, Carolyn Coates; Junk Man, Will Hare; Caroline, Estelle Omens; Sonny, Jess Osuna; Mr. Goodman, David Spielberg; Janice Vickery, Ellen Dano; Miss Hanley, Lynn Rogers; Charlie, Roger

Serbagi; Apartment Manager, John Lehne; Chris Burns, Michael Kearney; Miss Wyant, Dee Victor.

867 EIGHT ON THE LAM. (United Artists-1967). Henry Dimsdale, Bob Hope; Golda, Phyllis Diller; Jasper Lynch, Jonathan Winters; Ellie Barton, Shirley Eaton; Monica, Jill St. John; Linda Dimsdale, Stacey Maxwell; Steve Dimsdale, Kevin Brody; Mike Dimsdale, Robert Hope; Andy Dimsdale, Glenn Gilger; Dana Dimsdale, Alvis Hope; Lois Dimsdale, Debi Storm; Mark Dimsdale, Michael Freeman; Mr. Pomeroy, Austin Willis; Marty, Peter Leeds.

868 EIGHTEEN IN THE SUN. (Goldstone Film Enterprises-1966). Catherine Spaak, Gianni Garkos, Fabrizio Cappucci, Gianpiero Littera, Luisa Mattioli, Lisa Gastoni, Spiron Focas, Stelvio Rosi, Oliviero Prunas, Franco Giacobini.

869 80 STEPS TO JONAH. (Warner Bros. -1969). Jonah, Wayne Newton; Nonna, Jo Van Fleet; Barney, Keenan Wynn; Tracy, Diana Ewing; Scott, Slim Pickens; R. G. Armstrong; Little Joe, Brandon Cruz; Richard, Teddy Quinn; Velma, Susan Mathews; Pepe, Ira Angustain; Maxon, Dennis Cross; Wilfred, Mickey Rooney; Taggart, Sal Mineo; Hobo, James Bacon; Kim, Erin Moran; Cathy, Michele Tobin; Nina, Lilly Martens; Brian, Butch Patrick; Whitney, Frank Schuller; Self, Jackie Kahane.

870 EL DORADO. (Paramount-1967). Cole Thornton, John Wayne; Sheriff J. J. Harrah, Robert Mitchum; Mississippi, James Caan; Maudie, Charlene Holt; "Doc" Miller, Paul Fix; Deputy Bull Thomas, Arthur Hunnicutt; Joey MacDonald, Michele Carey; Kevin MacDonald, R. G. Armstrong; Bart Jason, Edward Asner; Nelse McLeod, Christopher George; Marina Ghane, John Gabriel, Robert Rothwell, Robert Donner, Adam Roarke, Charles Courtney, Victoria George, Jim Davis, Anne Newman, Diane Strom, Johnny Crawford, Olaf Wieghorst, Anthony Rogers, Dean Smith.

871 EL GRECO. (20th Century-Fox-1967). El Greco, Mel Ferrer; Jeronima, Rosanna Schiaffino; Don Miguel De Las Cuevas, Adolfo Celi; Cardinal Inquisitor, Mario Feliciani; Francisco, Franco Giacobini; Brother Felix, Renzo Giovanpietro; Don Luis, Angel Aranda; Don Diego of Castile, Nino Crisman; Maria, Gabriella Giorgelli; Pignatelli, Giulio Donnini; King Philip II, Fernando Rey; Marquis of Villena, Rafael Rivelles; Prosecutor, John Karlsen; De Agueda, John Francis Lane; Zaida, Rossana Martini; Mother Superior, Maria Marchi; Fencing Master, Franco Fantasia; The Prosecutor, Andrea Bosic; Officer, Bruno Scipioni; Isabel, Rosy Di Pietro; Master of Arms, Giuliano Farnese; Leoni, Ontanoni.

872 EL TOPO. (ABK-1971). El Topo, Alexandro Jodorowsky; Mara, Mara Lorenzio; Woman in black, Paula Romo; Small

woman, Jacqueline Luis; Colonel, David Silva; First Master, Hector Martinez; Second Master, Juan Jose Gurrola; Third Master, Victor Fosado; Fourth Master, Augustin Isunza; Brontis as a child, Brontis Jodorowsky; Brontis as a man, Robert John.

873 ELECTRA GLIDE IN BLUE. (United Artists-1973). John Wintergreen, Robert Blake; Zipper Davis, Billy Green Bush; Harve Poole, Mitchell Ryan; Jolene, Jeannine Riley; Willie, Elisha Cook; Coroner, Royal Dano; Bus Driver, David Wolinski; Bob Zemko, Peter Cetera; Killer, Terry Kath; Pig Man, Lee Loughnane; Loose Lips, Walter Parazaider; Sgt. Ryker, Joe Samsil; L. A. Detective, Jason Clark; Truck Driver, Michael Butler; Ice Cream Girls, Susan Forristal, Lucy Angle Guercio; Zemko's Girlfriend, Melissa Green; Detective, Jim Gilmore; The Beard, Bob Zemko.

874 11 HARROWHOUSE. (20th Century-Fox-1974). Chesser, Charles Grodin; Maren, Candice Bergen; Meecham, John Gielgud; Massey, Trevor Howard; Watts, James Mason; Lady Bolding, Helen Cherry.

875 ELVIRA MADIGAN. (Cinema V-1967). Elvira Madigan, Pia Degermark; Sixten Sparre, Thommy Berggren; Fellow Officer, Lennart Malmen; Little Girl, Nina Widerberg; Cook, Cleo Jensen.

876 THE EMBALMER. (Europix Consolidated-1966). Maureen Brown, Elma Caruso, Jean Mart, Viki Castillo.

877 EMBASSY. (Hemdale-1973). Shannon, Richard Roundtree; Kesten, Chuck Connors; Laure, Marie-Jose Nat; Ambassador, Ray Milland; Dunninger, Broderick Crawford; Gorenko, Max von Sydow; Kadish, David Bauer; Gamble, Larry Cross; Phelan, David Healy; Rylands, Karl Held; Miss Harding, Sara Marshall; Stacy, Dee Pollock; Foreign Minister, Afif Boulos; Leila, Leila Buheiry; Switchboard Operator, Gail Clymer; Man in black, Edmond Rannania; Michel, Mounir Maassri; Roge, Saladin Nader; Tuler, David Parker; Clem, Dean Turner; Clerk, Peter Smith.

878 THE EMBRACERS. (Joseph Brenner-1967). The Girl, Lois Adams; The Boy, Gary Graver; The Alcoholic, Billy Rhodes; The Homosexual, R. J. Gristak; The Man on the Beach, John Romeyn; The "Roommates," Bert Byers, Robert Parr, Tony Tsavidis, Robert Huard.

879-80 No entries.

881 THE EMIGRANTS. (Warner Bros. -1972). Karl Oskar, Max von Sydow; Kristina, Liv Ullmann; Robert, Eddie Axberg; Nils, Svenolof Bern; Marta, Aina Alfredsson; Danjel, Allan

Edwall; Ulrika, Monica Zetterlund; Arvid, Pierre Lindstedt; Jonas Petter, Hans Alfredson; Danjel's Wife, Ulla Smidje; Ulrika's Daughter, Eva-Lena Zetterlund; The Vicar, Gustaf Faringborg; Aron, Ake Friedell; Fina Kajsa, Agneta Prytz; Anders, Halvar Bjork; Kyrkvarden, Arnold Alfredsson; Mans Jakob, Bror Englund; Pastor Jackson, Tom C. Fouts; 2nd Mate, Peter Hoimark; Captain Lorentz, Erik Johansson; Landberg, Staffan Liljander; 1st Mate, Goran Lundin; The Children, Ditte, Lasse and Pelle Martinsson, Annika Nyhammar, Yvonne Oppstedt, Linn Ullmann.

881a EMITAI. (New Yorker-1973). Commandant, Robert Fontaine; Lt., Michel Renaudeau; Colonel, Pierre Blanchard; Villagers, Ibou Camara, Ousmane Camara, Joseph Diatta, Dji Niassebanor, Sibesalang Kalifa.

881b EMMANUELLE. (1974). Emmanuelle, Sylvia Kristel; Marco, Alain Cuny; Jean, Daniel Sarky; Marie Louise, Jeanne Colletin; Bee, Marika Green.

882 EMPEROR OF THE NORTH POLE. (20th Century-Fox-1973). A Number 1, Lee Marvin; Shack, Ernest Borgnine; Cigaret, Keith Carradine; Cracker, Charles Tyner; Hogger, Malcolm Atterbury; Policeman, Simon Oakland; Coaly, Harry Caesar; Yardman's Helper, Hal Baylor; Yardlet, Matt Clark; Gray Cat, Elisha Cook; Dinger, Joe di Reda; Smile, Liam Dunn; Prudence, Diane Dye; Conductor, Robert Foulk; Fakir, James Goodwin; Preacher, Ray Guth; Grease Tail, Sid Haig; Pokey Stiff, Karl Lukas; Yard Clerk, Edward McNally; Stew Bum, John Steadman; Yardman, Vic Tayback; Goundhog, Dave Willock.

883 EMPRESS WU. (Shaw Brothers-1965). Li Li-Hua, Chao Lei, Lo Chi, Chang Chung-wen, Yen Chuan, Lo Wei, Cheung Yingtsoi, Paul Chang Chung, Ting Ning.

883a THE END OF SUMMER. (Toho-1970). Manbei, Ganjiro Nakamura; Akiko, Setsuko Hara; Noriko, Yoko Tsukasa; Fumiko, Michiyo Aratama.

884 END OF THE ROAD. (Allied Artists-1970). Jake, Stacy Keach; Joe, Harris Yulin; Rennie, Dorothy Tristan; Doctor, James Earl Jones; Peggy, Grayson Hall; Sniper/Mrs. Dockey, Ray Brock; School Man, James Coco; Dog Man, Oliver Clark; Miss Banning, June Hutchinson; Dr. Carter, Graham P. Jarvis; Shirley, Maeve McGuire; Chicken Man, Joel Oppenheimer; Finkle, John Pleshette; Dr. Schott, Norman Simpson; Ticket Seller, Joel Wolfe.

885 No entry.

886 THE ENDLESS SUMMER. (Cinema V-1966). Mike Hynson, Robert August.

887 ENGAGEMENT ITALIANO. (Sedgeway-1966). Mario, Rossano Brazzi; Clara, Annie Girardot; Franco, Tony Anthony; Regina, Merisa Merlini; Giuditta Rissone, Silla Bettini, Nino Dal Fabbro, Giorgio Tedeschi.

888 ENGLAND MADE ME. (Cine Globe-1973). Erik Krogh, Peter Finch; Anthony Farrant, Michael York; Kate Farrant, Hildegard Neil; F. Minty, Michael Hordern; Haller, Joss Ackland; Liz Davidge, Tessa Wyatt; Fromm, Michael Sheard; Stein, Bill Baskiville; Reichminster, Dementer Bitenc; Nikki, Mira Nikolic; Hartmann, Vladimir Bacic; Night Club Singer, Maja Papandopulo; Heinrich, Vladan Zivkovic; Maria, Cvetka Cupar.

889 ENOUGH ROPE. (Artkino-1966). Kimmel, Gert Frobe; Ellie, Marina Blady; Corby, Robert Hossein; Walter Saccard, Maurice Ronet; Clara Saccard, Yvonne Furneaux; Mme. Kimmel, Paulette Dubost; Tony, Harry Mayen; Police Commissioner, Jacques Monod.

890 ENTER LAUGHING. (Columbia-1967). Mr. Marlowe, Jose Ferrer; Mrs. Kolowitz, Shelley Winters; Angela, Elaine May; Mr. Foreman, Jack Gilford; Wanda, Janet Margolin; Mr. Kolowitz, David Opatoshu; Marvin, Michael J. Pollard; Harry Hamburger, Don Rickles; Pike, Richard Deacon; Miss B., Nancy Kovack; Mr. Schoenbaum, Herbie Faye; Clark Baxter, Rob Reiner; Spencer Reynolds, Danny Stein; Policeman, Milton Frome; Theatregoer, Lillian Adams; Subway Rider, Mantan Moreland; Butler, Patrick Campbell; Lawyer Peabody, Peter Brocco; David Kolowitz, Rene Santoni.

891 ENTER THE DRAGON. (Warner Bros.-1973). Lee, Bruce Lee; Roper, John Saxon; Williams, Jim Kelly; Han, Shih Kien; Oharra, Bob Wall; Tania, Ahna Capri; Su-Lin, Angela Mao Ying; Mei-Ling, Betty Chung; Braithwaite, Geoffrey Weeks; Bolo, Yang Sze; Parsons, Peter Archer.

892 ENTERTAINING MR. SLOANE. (Continental-1970). Kath, Beryl Reid; Ed, Harry Andrews; Mr. Sloane, Peter McEnery; Kemp, Alan Webb.

893 ERIC SOYA'S "17." Jacob Petersen, Ole Soltoft; Vibeke, Ghita Norby; Miss Rosegod, Lily Broberg; Jacob's Uncle, Ole Monty; Jacob's Aunt, Bodil Steen; Mr. Petersen, Hass Christensen; Hansigne, Susanne Heinrich; Sophie, Lise Rosendahl; Knud, Hugo Herrestrup; Pharmacist, Jorgen Kiil; Girl on Train, Annie Birgit Garde; Provisoren, Ingold David.

894 EROICA. (Amerpole-1966). Dzidzius, Edward Dziewonski; Zosia, Barbara Polomska; Lt. Kolya, Leon Niemczyk; Major, Ignacy Machowski; Colonel Kazimierz Opalinski; Kurzawa, Josef Nowak; Szpakowski, Roman Klosowski; Korwin-Makowski, Mariusz Dmochowski; Dabecki, Bogumil Kobiela; Marianek,

Wojciech Siemion; Turek, Kazimierz Rudzki; Zak, Jozef Kostecki; Krygier, Henryk Bak; Zawistowski, Tadeusz Lomnicki.

895 THE EROTIC ADVENTURES OF ZORRO. (Entertainment Ventures-1973). Don Diego De Vega (Zorro), Douglas Frey; Maria, Robyn Whitting; Helena Bonasario, Penny Boran; Luis Bonasario, Jude Farese; Esteban Valasquez, John Alderman; Rosita, Lynn Harris; Margarita, Michelle Simon; Don Alejandro De Vega, Bruce Gibson; Father Felipe, Sebastian Gregory; Don Manuel, Mike Peratta; Rodriguez, Ernie Dominy; Graciela, Becky Perlman; Estralita, Kathy Hilton; Pablo, Gerard Broulard; Academy Commandant, Allen Bloomfield; Chico, Fermin Castillo Del Muro; Manuel, Cory Brandon; Disfigured Soldier, David Villa; Ortiz, Jesus Valdez; Soldier With Snake, David Friedman; Sgt. Felipio Latio, Robert Cresse.

896 THE EROTIC MEMOIRS OF A MALE CHAUVINIST PIG. (Mature-1973). Georgina Spelvin, Paul Taylor, Tina Russell, Amy Matheau, Helen Madigan, Darby Lloyd Rains, Billy O'Shea.

897 THE EROTIC THREE. (Cannon-1972). Harry, Harry Walker Staff; Erica, Victoria Wilde; Christine, Christine Kelly; The Shadow, Mio Domani.

898 EROTICON. (Adelphia-1971). Bernard Sackett, Al Goldstein, James Buckley, Dr. Albert Ellis, Tommi Ungerer.

899 EROTIKUS. (Hand-in-Hand-1973). Fred Halsted.

900 ESCAPE BY NIGHT. (Allied Artists-1965). Martin Lord, Terence Longdon; Nita Lord, Jennifer Jayne; Doug Roberts, Harry Fowler; Victor Lush, Peter Sallis; Ronald Grey-Simmons, Alan Wheatley; Mrs. Grey-Simmons, Vanda Godsell; Ernie Peel, Arthur Lovegrove; Mrs. Peel, Hilda Fenmore; Sydney Selweyn, Mark Dignam; Inspector, John Arnatt; Danny Watts, Richard Carpenter; George Brett, Stanley Meadows; Mawsley, Robert Brown; Bart Rennison, Tom Bowman; The Intruder, Ray Austen.

901 ESCAPE FROM THE PLANET OF THE APES. (20th Century-Fox-1971). Cornelius, Roddy McDowall; Zira, Kim Hunter; Dr. Lewis Dixon, Bradford Dillman; Dr. Stephanie Branton, Natalie Trundy; Dr. Otto Hasslein, Eric Braeden; The President, William Windom; Milo, Sal Mineo; E-1, Albert Salmi; E-2, Jason Evers; Chairman, John Randolph; Armando, Ricardo Montalban.

902 ESCAPE TO NOWHERE. (Peppercorn-Wormser-1974). Lino Ventura, Lea Massari, Suzanne Flon, Leo Genn, Pierre-Michel Le Conte.

903 ESCAPE TO THE SUN. (Cinevision-1972). Kirsanov, Laurence Harvey; Nina, Josephine Chaplin; Kagan, John Ireland; Sarah, Lila Kedrova; Baburin, Jack Hawkins; Yasha, Yuda Barkan; Romek, Yehuda Efroni; Professor, Peter Capell; Judge, Gila Almagor; Drunk, Clive Revel.

904 EUGENIE. (Distinction-1970). Eugenie, Marie Liljedahl; Mme. Saint-Ange, Maria Rohm; Mirvel, Jack Taylor; Roches, Nino Korda; Hardin, Herbert Fuchs; Father, Paul Muller; Augustin, Anney Kablan; Mother, Marie Luise Ponte; Colette, Colette Giacobino; Maid, Kathy Lagarde; Narrator, Christopher Lee.

905 EVA. (Times Film Corp.-1965). Eva, Jeanne Moreau; Tyvian, Stanley Baker; Francesca, Virna Lisi; Anna Maria, Nona Medici; Pieri, Francesco Rissone; McCormick, James Villiers; The Greek, Alex Revides; The Russian, Lisa Gastoni; The Player, Riccardo Garrone; Branco Malloni, Giorgio Albertazzi.

906 EVE. (Commonwealth United-1968). Eve, Celeste Yarnall; Mike, Robert Walker; Diego, Herbert Lom; John Burke, Fred Clark; Colonel Stuart, Christopher Lee; Conchita, Rosenda Monteros; Pepe, Jean Caffarell; Anna, Maria Rohm; Bruno, Ricardo Diaz.

907 EVEN DWARFS STARTED SMALL. (New Line-1971). Hombre, Helmut Doring; Pepe, Gerd Gickel; Azucar, Ema Gschwentner; Pobrecita, Gisela Hertwig; Territory, Gerhard Marz; Chicklets, Hertel Minkner.

908 AN EVENING WITH THE ROYAL BALLET. (Sigma III-1965). Margot Fonteyn, Rudolf Nureyev, and the Royal Ballet Company.

909 AN EVENT. (Continental-1970). Grandfather, Pavle Vusic; Grandson, Sergio Mimica; Gamekeeper, Boris Dvornik; Friend, Fabijan Sovagovic; Gamekeeper's Wife, Neda Spasojevic.

910 EVERY BASTARD A KING. (Continental-1970). Eileen, Pier Angeli; Roy Hemmings, William Berger; Ralph Cohen, Ohed Kotler; Yehoram, Yehoram Gaon; Foreign Office Man, Ori Levy; Photographer, Reuven Morgan; Woman Officer, Tami Tsifroni; Yossi, Moshe Yanai; The Hagashash Trio.

911 EVERY DAY IS A HOLIDAY. (Columbia-1966). Chica, Marisol; Angel, Angel Peralta; Dancer, Rafael De Crodova; Impresario, Jose Marco Davo; Femme Fatale, Fala Clifton; Manolo, Pedro Mari Sanchez: Jesus Guzman, Jose Sepulveda, Francisco Camoiras, Jose Maria Labernie, Luis Barbero, Toni Canal, Jack Gasins.

912 EVERY LITTLE CROOK AND NANNY. (MGM-1972). Nanny (Miss Poole), Lynn Redgrave; Carmine Ganucci, Victor Mature; Benny Napkins, Paul Sand; Stella, Maggie Blye; Luther, Austin Pendleton; Garbugli, John Astin; Azzecca, Dom DeLuise; Marie, Louise Sorel; Lewis Ganucci, Phillip Graves; Landruncola, Lou Cutell; Truffatore, Leopoldo Trieste; Nonaka, Pat Morita; Lt. Bozzaris, Phil Foster; Willie Shakespeare, Pat Harrington; Dominick, Severn Darden; Jeanette Kay, Katharine Victory; Ida, Mina Kolb; Sarah, Bebe Louie; Bobby, Lee Kafian; Ida's Mother, Sally Marr.

913 EVERYTHING YOU ALWAYS WANTED TO KNOW ABOUT SEX* BUT WERE AFRAID TO ASK. (United Artists-1972). Victor/Fabrizio/Jester/Sperm, Woody Allen; Dr. Bernardo, John Carradine; Sam, Lou Jacobi; Gina, Louise Lasser; The King, Anthony Quayle; The Operator, Tony Randall; The Queen, Lynn Redgrave; Switchboard, Burt Reynolds; Dr. Ross, Gene Wilder; Himself, Jack Barry; The Girl, Erin Fleming; Mrs. Ross, Elaine Giftos; Herself, Toni Hold; Himself, Robert Q. Lewis; Helen, Heather MacRae; George, Sidney Miller; Herself, Pamela Mason; Himself, Regis Philbin; Milos, Titos Vandis; Stomach Operator, Stanley Adams; Brain Control, Oscar Beregi; The Fool's Father, Alan Caillou; Sorcerer, Geoffrey Holder; Sheriff, Dort Clark; The Priest, Jay Robinson; Igor, Ref Chuy; Rabbi Baumel, Baruch Lumet; Football Player, Tom Mack; Sperm, Robert Walden; Bernard Jaffe, H. E. West; Royal Executioner, Inga Neilson.

914 THE EXECUTIONER. (Columbia-1970). John Shay, George Peppard; Sarah Booth, Joan Collins; Polly Bendel, Judy Geeson; Racovsky, Oscar Homolka; Vaughan Jones, Charles Gray; Colonel Scott, Nigel Patrick; Adam Booth, Keith Michell; Philip Crawford, George Baker; Prof. Parker, Alexander Scourby; Butterfield, Peter Bull; Roper, Ernest Clark; Balkov, Peter Dyneley; Anna, Gisela Dali.

915 EXECUTIVE ACTION. (National General-1973). Farrington, Burt Lancaster; Foster, Robert Ryan; Ferguson, Will Geer; Paulitz, Gilbert Green; Halliday, John Anderson; Gunman Chris, Paul Carr; Tim, Colby Chester; Operation Chief Team A, Ed Lauter; Smythe, Walter Brooke; Depository Clerk, Sidney Clute; Stripper, Deanna Darrin; McCadden, Lloyd Gough; Used Car Salesman, Richard Hurst; Man at rifle range, Robert Karnes; Oswald Imposter, James MacColl; Art Mendoza, Joaquin Martinez; Riflemen Team B, Dick Miller, Hunter Von Leer, John Brascia; Jack Ruby, Oscar Oncidi; Sergeant, Tom Peters; Officer Brown, Paul Sorenson; Policeman, Sandy Ward; Technician Team B, William Watson; Gunmen Team A, Richard Bull, Lee Delano.

916 THE EXORCIST. (Warner Bros. -1973). Mrs. MacNeil, Ellen Burstyn; Father Merrin, Max von Sydow; Lt. Kinderman, Lee J. Cobb; Sharon, Kitty Winn; Burke, Jack MacGowran; Father

Karras, Jason Miller; Regan MacNeil, Linda Blair; Father Dyer, Rev. William O'Malley; Karras' Mother, Vasiliki Maliaros; Karras Uncle, Titos Vandis; Bishop, Wallace Rooney; Assistant Director, Ron Faber; President of University, Rev. T. Bermingham.

917 THE EXPERIMENT. (Jaguar-1973). Billy Joe, Mike Stevens; Gary Lee, Joey Daniels; Herm, Gorton Hall; Salesman, Jimmy Hughes; Dave, Tony Ross, Robert Weaver, Eva Faye, David Blair, Peter Thomas.

918 EXPLOSION. (American International-1970). Alan, Gordon Thomson; Richie, Don Stroud; Dr. Neal, Richard Conte; Peter, Robin Ward; Doris, Michele Chicoine; Mr. Evans, Cecil Linder; Timms, Ted Stidder; Susan, Sherry Mitchel; Valerie, Olga Kaya; Kelso, Harry Saunders.

919 EXQUISITE CADAVER. (Wheeler-1973). Parker, Capucine; Esther, Judy Matheson; Teresa, Teresa Gimpera; Husband, Carlos Estrada.

920 THE EXTERMINATING ANGEL. (Altura-1967). Letitia, Silvia Pinal; Senor Nobile, Enrique Rambal; Lucia Nobile, Lucy Gallardo; The Major-Domo, Claudio Brook; Leonora, Bertha Moss; Beatriz, Ofelia Montesco; Eduardo, Xavier Masse; Ana Maynar, Nadia Haro Oliva; Francisco, Xavier Loya; Russell, Antonio Bravo; Jacqueline Andere, Jose Baviera, Augusto Benedico, Luis Beristain, Cesar Del Campo, Rosa Elena Durgel, Enrique Garcia Alvarez, Ofelia Guilmain, Tito Junco, Angel Merino, Patricia Moran, Patricia De Morelos.

921 EXTREME CLOSE-UP. (National General-1973). John, James McMullan; Tom, James A. Watson Jr.; Sally, Kate Woodville; Sylvia, Bara Byrnes; Salesman, Al Checco.

922 AN EYE FOR AN EYE. (Embassy-1966). Talion, Robert Lansing; Benny, Pat Wayne; Ike Slant, Slim Pickens; Bri Quince, Gloria Talbott; Quince, Paul Fix; Trumbull, Strother Martin; Charles, Henry Wills; Jonas, Jerry Gatling; Harry, Rance Howard; Jo-Hi, Clint Howard.

923 EYE OF THE CAT. (Universal-1969). Wylie, Michael Sarrazin; Kassia Lancaster, Gayle Hunnicutt; Aunt Danny, Eleanor Parker; Luke, Tim Henry; Dr. Mills, Laurence Naismith; Poor Dear, Jennifer Leak; Bendetto, Linden Chiles; Bellemondo, Mark Herron; Socialite, Annabelle Garth.

924 EYE OF THE DEVIL. (MGM-1967). Catherine de Montfaucon, Deborah Kerr; Philippe de Montfaucon, David Niven; Pere Dominic, Donald Pleasence; Jean-Claude Ibert, Edward Mulhare; Countess Estelle, Flora Robson; Alain de Montfaucon, Emlyn Williams; Odile, Sharon Tate; Christian de Caray,

David Hemmings; Dr. Monnet, John Le Mesurier; Antoinette de Montfaucon, Suky Appleby; Rennard, Donald Bisset; Jacques de Montfaucon, Robert Duncan; Grandec, Michael Miller.

925 EYE OF THE NEEDLE. (Eldorado-1965). Rosaria, Annette Stroyberg; Toto, Gerard Blain; Nicola, Nino Castelnuovo; Carmelina, Mariangela Giordano; Lawyer Nazzaro, Vittorio Gassman; Lawyer D'Angelo, Gino Carvi; Don Luigino, Umberto Spadaro; Don Salvatore, Ernesto Calindri; Don Calo, Leopoldo Trieste; Don Nene, Ignazio Balsamo; Police Brigadier, Alfredo Varelli; Toto's Mother, Rina Franchetti; Santa, Carla Calo.

926 F.T.A. (American International-1972). Jane Fonda, Donald Sutherland, Len Chandler, Pamela Donegan, Rita Martinson, Holly Near, Paul Mooney, Michael Alaimo, Yale Zimmerman.

927 A FABLE. (MFR-1971). Leader, Al Freeman Jr.; Wife, Hildy Brooks; Husband, James Patterson.

928 THE FABULOUS BASTARD FROM CHICAGO. (Walnut International-1969). Steve, John Alderman; Nancy, Maria Lease; Fats, James Meyers; Maria, Victoria Carbe; Danny, Daryl Colinot; Bambi Allen, Jimmie Johnson, Mike Stringer, Geretta Taylor, Pony Tobias.

929 THE FACE OF FU MANCHU. (7 Arts-1965). Fu Manchu, Christopher Lee; Inspector Smith, Nigel Green; Dr. Petrie, Howard Marion-Crawford; Fu's Daughter, Tsai Chin.

930 FACES. (Continental-1968). Richard Forst, John Marley; Jeannie Rapp, Gena Rowlands; Maria Forst, Lynn Carlin; Chet, Seymour Cassel; Freddie, Fred Draper; Jim McCarthy, Val Avery; Florence, Dorothy Gulliver; Louise, Joanne Moore Jordan; Billy Mae, Darlene Conley; Joe Jackson, Gene Darfler; Stella, Elizabeth Deering; Dave Mazzie, Julie Gambol.

931 THE FACTS OF MURDER. (7 Arts-1965). Inspector Ingrallo, Pietro Germi; Assuntina, Claudia Cardinale; Liliana Banducci, Eleanora Rossi Drago; Diomede, Nino Castelnuovo; Remo Banducci, Claudio Gora; "Dr." Valdarena, Franco Fabrizi; Virginia, Cristina Gaioni; Detective Saro, Saro Urzi.

932 FAHRENHEIT 451. (Universal-1966). Linda/Clarisse, Julie Christie; Montag, Oskar Werner; The Captain, Cyril Cusack; Fabian, Anton Diffring; Man With the Apple, Jeremy Spenser; The Book-Woman, Bee Duffell; TV Announcer, Gillian Lewis; Doris, Ann Bell; Helen, Caroline Hunt; Jackie, Anna Palk; Neighbor, Roma Milne; The Life of Henry Brulard, Alex Scott; Martian Chronicles, Dennis Gilmore; Pride, Fred Cox; Prejudice, Frank Cox; Machiavelli's Prince, Michael Balfour; The Picwick Papers, David Glover; Plato's Dialogues, Judith Drynan; The Jewish Question, Yvonne Blake; Weir of Hermiston,

John Rae; Nephew of Weir of Hermiston, Earl Younger; Male Nurses, Arthur Cox and Eric Mason; TV announcers, Noel Davis and Donald Pickering; Stoneman, Michael Mundell; Chris Williams, Gillian Aldam, Edward Kaye, Mark Lester, Kevin Elder, Joan Francis, Tom Watson.

933 FALSTAFF. (Peppercorn-Wormser-1967). Jack Falstaff, Orson Welles; Doll Tearsheet, Jeanne Moreau; Hostess Quickly, Margaret Rutherford; Henry IV, John Gielgud; Kate Percy, Marina Vlady; Prince Hal, Keith Baxter; Henry Percy, Norman Rodway; Justice Shallow, Alan Webb; Mr. Silence, Walter Chiari; Northumberland, Fernando Rey; Pistol, Michael Aldridge; Poins, Tony Beckley; The Child, Beatrice Welles; Narrator, Ralph Richardson.

934 THE FAMILY. (International Coproduction-1973). Charles Bronson, Telly Savalas, Jill Ireland, Umberto Orsini, Michel Constantin.

935 FAMILY HONOR. (Cinerama-1973). Antony Page, Vera Visconti, James Reyes.

936 THE FAMILY JEWELS. (Paramount-1965). Chauffeur, Everett Peyton, James Peyton, Capt. Eddie Peyton, Julius Peyton, "Buggs" Peyton, Skylock Peyton, Jerry Lewis; Donna Peyton, Donna Butterworth; Dr. Matson, Sebastian Cabot; Lawyer, Jay Adler; Lawyer, Neil Hamilton; Plane Passengers, Marjorie Bennett, Frances Lax, Ellen Corby, Renie Riano, Jesslyn Fax; Circus Clown, Gene Baylos; Pilot, Milton Frome.

937 THE FAMILY WAY. (Warner Bros. -7 Arts-1967). Jenny Piper, Hayley Mills; Ezra Fitton, John Mills; Arthur Fitton, Hywel Bennett; Lucy Fitton, Marjorie Rhodes; Liz Piper, Avril Angers; Molly Thompson, Liz Fraser; Uncle Fred Piper, Wilfred Pickles; Leslie Piper, John Comer; Joe Thompson, Barry Foster; Geoffrey Fitton, Murray Head; Mr. Hutton, Colin Gordon; Mr. Phillips, Robin Parkinson; Eddie, Andrew Bradford; Dora, Lesley Daine; Marriage Counsellor, Ruth Trouncer; Mr. Stubbs, Harry Locke; Maureen O'Reilly, Michael Cadman, Thorley Walters, Hazel Bainbridge, Ruth Gower, Diana Coupland, Fanny Carby, Helen Booth, Margaret Lacey.

938 FANDO AND LIS. (Cannon-1970). Fando, Sergio Klainer; Lis, Diana Mariscal; Maria Teresa Riva, Tamara Garina, Juan Jose Arreola, Rene Rebetez.

939 FANNY HILL. (Pan World Distributing-1965). Fanny, Letitia Roman; Mrs. Brown, Miriam Hopkins; Hemingway, Walter Giller; The Admiral, Alex D'Arcy; Mr. Dinkelspeiler, Helmut Weiss; Charles, Ulli Lommel; Mr. Norbert, Chris Howland; Fiona, Christiane Schmidtmer; Phoebe, Cara Garnett; Grand Duke, Albert Zugsmith.

940 FANNY HILL. (Cinemation-1969). Fanny Hill, Diana Kjaer; Roger Boman, Hans Ernback; Leif Henning, Keve Hjelm; Otto Wilhelmsson, Oscar Ljung; Monika, Tina Hedstrom; Mrs. Schoon, Gio Petre; Charlotte, Mona Seilitz; Hanna, Astrid Bye; Will, Bo Loof; Roger's Father, Gosta Pruzelius; Krafftmann, Hans Lindgren; Kjell Lennartsson, John Harryson, Borje Nyberg, Jan Erik Lindqvist.

941 FANTASTIC VOYAGE. (20th Century-Fox-1966). Grant, Stephen Boyd; Cora Peterson, Raquel Welch; General Carter, Edmond O'Brien; Doctor Michaels, Donald Pleasence; Colonel Donald Reid, Arthur O'Connell; Captain Bill Owens, William Redfield; Doctor Duval, Arthur Kennedy; Jan Benes, Jean Del Val; Communications Aide, Barry Coe; Secret Service Man, Ken Scott; Nurse, Shelby Grant; Technician, James Brolin; Wireless Operator, Brendan Fitzgerald.

942 FANTOMAS. (Lopert-1966). Fantomas, Jean Marais; Fandor, Jean Marais; Commissioner Juve, Louis De Funes; Helene, Mylene Demongeot; Lady Beltham, Marie-Helene Arnaud; Juve's Assistant, Jacques Dynam; Newspaper Editor, Robert Dalban; Chief Inspector, Christian Toma.

943 FAR FROM THE MADDING CROWD. (MGM-1967). Bathsheba Everdene, Julie Christie; Sergeant Frank Troy, Terence Stamp; William Boldwood, Peter Finch; Gabriel Oak, Alan Bates; Fanny Robin, Prunella Ransome; Liddy, Fiona Walker; Henery Fray, Paul Dawkins; Mrs. Hurst, Alison Leggatt; Andrew Randle, Andrew Robertson; Joseph Poorgrass, John Barrett; Julian Somers, Pauline Melville, Vincent Harding, Laurence Carter, Margaret Lacey, Harriet Harper, Denise Coffey, Brian Rawlinson, John Garrie, Marie Hopps, Owen Berry, Michael Beint, Derek Ware, Alba.

944 THE FASCIST. (Embassy-1965). Primo Arcovazzi, The Fascist, Ugo Tognazzi; Professor Bonafe, Georges Wilson; The Thief, Stefania Sandrelli; The Friendly Girl, Mireille Granelli; Bardacci, Gianrico Tedeschi; His Wife, Elsa Vazzoler.

945 FASTER, PUSSYCAT! KILL! KILL! (Eve-1966). Varla, Tura Satana; Rosie, Haji; Billie, Lori Williams; Linda, Susan Bernard; Old Man, Stuart Lancaster; Kirk, Paul Trinka; Vegetable, Dennis Busch; Tommy, Ray Barlow; Attendant, Mickey Foxx.

946 THE FASTEST GUITAR ALIVE. (MGM-1968). Johnny Banner, Roy Orbison; Steve Menlo, Sammy Jackson, Flo Chestnut, Maggie Pierce; Sue Chestnut, Joan Freeman; Charlie Mansfield, Lyle Bettger; Sheriff Max Cooper, John Doucette; Stella, Patricia Donahue; Rink, Ben Cooper; Indian Chief, Ben Lessy; Joe, Douglas Kennedy; Deputy, Len Hendry; 1st Indian, Iron Eyes Cody; 1st Expressman, Sam the Sham;

Emily, Wilda Taylor; Margie, Victoria Carroll; Tanya, Maria Korda; Carmen, Poupee Gamin.

947 FAT CITY. (Columbia-1972). Billy Tully, Stacy Keach; Ernie Munger, Jeff Bridges; Oma, Susan Tyrrell; Faye, Candy Clark; Ruben, Nicholas Colasanto; Babe, Art Aragon; Earl, Curtis Cokes; Lucero, Sixto Rodriguez; Wes, Billy Walker; Bufford, Wayne Mahan; Fuentes, Ruben Navarro.

948 THE FAT SPY. (Magna-1966). Camille, Phyllis Diller; Irving Herman, Jack E. Leonard; Wellington, Brian Donlevy; Junior, Jayne Mansfield; Frankie, Jordan Christopher; Themselves, The Wild Ones; Dodo, Johnny Tillotson; Nanette, Lauree Berger; The Sikh, Lou Nelson; The Mermaid, Toni Lee Shelley; The Secretary, Penny Roman; Special Voices, Adam Keefe; The Treasure Hunters, Chuck Alden, Eddie Wright, Tommy Graves, Tommy Trick, Linda Harrison, Toni Turner, Deborah White, Jill Bleidner, Tracy Vance, Jeanette Taylor.

949 FATHER. (Continental-1967). Tako, Andras Balint; Father, Miklos Gabor; Mother, Klari Tolnay; Tako as a Child, Dani Erdelyi; Anni, Kati Solyom.

950 FATHER OF A SOLDIER. (Artkino-1966). The Father, Sergo Zakariadze; Arkadi, Keto Bochorishvili; Nikolai, Vladimir Privaltsev.

951 FATHOM. (20th Century-Fox-1967). Peter Merriweather, Tony Franciosa; Fathom Harvill, Raquel Welch; Douglas Campbell, Ronald Fraser; Jo-May Soon, Greta Chi; Timothy, Richard Briers; Mike, Tom Adams; Serapkin, Clive Revill; Mr. Trivers, Reg Lye; Mrs. Trivers, Ann Lancaster; Ulla, Elizabeth Ercy; Mehmed, Tutte Lemkow.

952 THE FEAR. (Trans-Lux-1967). Chryssa, Elli Fotiou; Anestis Canalis, Anestis Vlachos; Anna Canalis, Helena Nathanael; Dimitri Canalis, Alexis Damianos; Mrs. Canalis, Mary Chronopoulou; Nicos, Spyros Focas.

953 FEAR IS THE KEY. (Paramount-1973). John, Barry Newman; Sara, Suzy Kendall; Vyland, John Vernon; Jablonski, Dolph Sweet; Royale, Ben Kingsley; Ruthven, Ray McAnally; Larry, Peter Marinker; Larry, Elliott Sullivan; Deputy, Roland Brand; FBI Man, Tony Anholt.

954 FEARLESS FRANK. (American International-1970). Frank, Jon Voight; Plethora, Monique Van Vooren; Lois, Joan Darling; Doctor/Brother/Claude, Severn Darden; Alfred, Anthony Holland; Boss, Lou Gilbert; Cat, Ben Carruthers; Rat, David Steinberg; Screwnose, David Fisher; Needles, Nelson Algren; Stranger, Ken Nordine.

955 THE FEARLESS VAMPIRE KILLERS. (MGM-1967). Professor Abronsius, Jack MacGowran; Sarah, Sharon Tate; Yoine Shagal, Alfie Bass; Count Krolock, Ferdy Mayne; Koukol, Terry Downes; Alfred, Roman Polanski; Rebecca, Jessie Robbins; Magda, Fiona Lewis; Herbert, Ian Quarrier; Village Idiot, Ronald Lacey; Sleigh Driver, Sydney Bromley; Woodcutters, Andre Malandrinos, Otto Di Amant, and Matthew Walters.

956 FELLINI SATYRICON. (United Artists-1970). Encolpius, Martin Potter; Ascyltus, Hiram Keller; Giton, Max Born; Tryphaena, Capucine; Eumolpus, Salvo Randone; Fortunata, Magali Noel; Lichas, Alain Cuny; Suicide Wife, Lucia Rose; Caesar, Tanya Lopert; Robber, Gordon Mitchell; Vernacchio, Fanfulla; Trimalchio, Mario Romagnoli; Oenothea, Donyale Luna; Habinnas, Giuseppe Sanvitale; Oriental Slave Girl, Hylette Adolphe; Suicide Husband, Joseph Wheeler; Cinedo, Genius; Scintilla, Danica La Loggia; Widow of Ephesus, Antonia Pietrosi; Soldier at Tomb, Wolfgang Hillinger; Owner of Garden of Delights, Elio Gigante; Nymphomaniac, Sibil la Sedat; Her Husband, Lorenzo Piani; Her Slave, Luigi Zerbinati; Notary, Vittorio Vittori; Captain of Ship, Carlo Giordana; Proconsul, Marcello DiFolco; Minotaur, Luigi Montefiori; Ariadne, Elisa Mainardi.

957 FELLINI'S ROMA. (United Artists-1972). Himself, Federico Fellini; Fellini, Aged 18, Peter Gonzales; Fellini, as a child, Stefano Majore; The Princess, Pia De Doses; Cardinal Ottaviani, Renato Giovanneli; Young Prostitute, Fiona Florence; Underground Guide, Marne Maitland; Britta Barnes, Angela De Leo, Elisa Mainardi, Stefano Mayore, Galliano Sbarra, Deal Vago, John Francis Lane, Libero Frissi, Alvaro Vitali, Sbarra Adami, Bireno, Anna Magnani, and Gore Vidal.

958 FEMALE ANIMAL. (Cinemation-1970). Angelique, Arlene Tiger; DiMedici, Vassili Lambrinos; Alain, Andre Landzaat; Francesca, Jean Avery; Rafael, Robert Darchi; Juan, Richard Fusco; Marcos, Harold Keith; Carla, Joanne Sopko.

959 THE FEMALE BUNCH. (Gilbreth-1972). Grace, Jenifer Bishop; Russ, Russ Tamblyn; Monty, Lon Chaney Jr.; Sandy, Nesa Renet; Jim, Jeoffrey Land; Waitress, Regina Carrol; Singer, Don Epperson; Mexican Farmer, John Cardos; Barkeeper, Albert Cole; A'Lesha Lee, Jackie Taylor, Lesley MacRae, William Bonner, Bobby Clark.

960 THE FEMALE RESPONSE. (Trans-American-1973). Leona, Raina Barrett; Rosalie, Jacque Lynn Colton; Sandy, Michaela Hope; Andrea, Jennifer Welles; Victoria, Gena Wheeler; Marjorie, Marjorie Hirsch; Gilda, Roz Kelly; Karl, Lawrie Driscoll; Mark, Edmund Donnelly; Gary, Todd Everett; Tom, Richard Wilkins; Rachel, Phyllis MacBride; Ramona, Suzy Mann; Alex, Curtis Carlson; Max, Herb Streicher; Caller,

Anthony Scott Craig; Leland, Richard Lipton.

961 UNE FEMME DOUCE. (New Yorker-1971). She, Dominique Sanda; He, Guy Frangin; Anna, Jane Lobre.

962 LA FEMME INFIDELE. (Allied Artists-1969). Helene, Stephane Audran; Charles, Michel Bouquet; Victor, Maurice Ronet; Michel, Stephen Di Napolo; Inspector, Michel Duchaussoy; Police Detective, Guy Marly; Private Detective, Serge Bento.

963 FEMMES AU SOLEIL. (Albina-1974). Hostess, Juliette Mayniel; Friend, Genevieve Fontanel; Girl, Nathalie Chantrel.

964 FERRY CROSS THE MERSEY. (United Artists-1965). Gerry, Gerry Marsden; Fred, Fred Marsden; Chad, Les Chadwick; Les, Les Maguire; Dodie, Julie Samuel; Colonel Dawson, Eric Barker; Trasler, Deryck Guyler; Mr. Lumsden, George A. Cooper; Miss Kneave, Patricia Lawrence; Aunt Lil, Mona Washbourne; Hanson, T. P. McKenna; Dawson's Butler, Mischa de la Motte; Norah, Margaret Nolan; Art Student, Donald Gee; Art Student, Bernard Sharpe; Dawson's Chauffeur, Keith Smith; Chinese Restaurant Manager, Andy Ho; Cilla Black; The Fourmost; Jimmy Saville; Earl Royce and the Olympics; The Blackwells; The Black Knights.

965 FESTIVAL. (Peppercorn-Wormser-1967). Joan Baez, Bob Dylan, Pete Seeger, Theodore Bikel, Judy Collins.

966 FEVER. (Variety-1971). Isabel Sarli, Armando Bo.

967 FEVER HEAT. (Paramount-1968). Ace Jones, Nick Adams; Sandy Richards, Jeannine Riley; Herbert Herpgruve, Norman Alden; Toad Taplinger, Vaughn Taylor; Ronnie Richards, Daxson Thomas; Loren Peale, Robert Broyles; Al Ruscio, Walt Reno Jr., Skip Nelson, Ron Foreman, Mary Walker, Alvin Meyer, Dwayne Bacon, Arthur Greco, Sharon Baum, Robert McClellan, Art Breese, Gail Miller, Dick Davis, Lon Parsons, John Doughten, Jack Thompson.

968 THE FEVERISH YEARS. (1967). Mirko, Bekim Fehmiu; Maria, Ana Matic; Girl, Dusica Zegarac; Man, Milan Jelic.

969 THE FICKLE FINGER OF FATE. (Producers Releasing Organization-1967). Jerry Parker, Tab Hunter; Winkle, Luis Prendes; Estrala, Gustavo Rojo; Fuentes, Fernando Hilbeck; Jaffe, Ralph Brown; Paco, Pedro Maria Sanchez; Inger, Elsa Skolinstad; Pilar, Patty Sheppard; Maria, Alejandra Milo; Maika, Andrea Lascelles; Jane, May Heatherly.

970 FIDDLER ON THE ROOF. (United Artists-1971). Tevye, Chaim Topol; Golde, Norma Crane; Motel, Leonard Frey; Yente, Molly Picon; Lazar Wolf, Paul Mann; Tzeitel, Rosalind

Harris; Hodel, Michele Marsh; Chava, Neva Small; Perchik, Michael Glaser; Fyedka, Raymond Lovelock; Shprintze, Elaine Edwards; Bielke, Candy Bonstein; Mordchka, Shimen Ruskin; Rabbi, Zvee Scooler; Constable, Louis Zorich; Avram, Alfie Scopp; Nachum, Howard Gorney; Mendel, Barry Dennen; Russian Official, Vernon Dobtcheff; Fruma Sarah, Ruth Madoc; Grandma Tzeitel, Patience Collier; Fiddler, Tutte Lemkow; Shandel, Stella Courtney; Yankel, Jacob Kalich; Beri, Brian Coburn; Hone, George Little; Farcel, Stanley Fleet; Moishe, Arnold Diamond; Rifka, Marika Rivera; Ezekial, Mark Malicz; Sheftel, Aharan Ipale; Sexton, Roger Lloyd Pack; Priest, Vladimir Medar.

971 15 FROM ROME. (McAbee-1968). Vittorio Gassman, Ugo Tognazzi, Marisa Merlini, Michele Mercier, Lando Buzzanca, Luisa Rispoli, Marino Mase, Rick Tognazzi, Franco Castellani, Nina Nini, Angela Portaluri, Rica Dialine.

972 THE FIFTH HORSEMAN IS FEAR. (Sigma III-1968). Dr. Braun, Miroslav Machacek; Music Teacher, Olga Scheinpflugova; Mr. Vesely, Jiri Adamira; Sidlak, Ilja Prachar; Mr. Fanta, Josef Vinklar; Mrs. Vesely, Zdenka Prochazkova; Mrs. Wienerova, Slavka Budinova; The Eccentric, Alexandra Myskova; Police Inspector, Jiri Vrstala.

973 THE FIGHTING PRINCE OF DONEGAL. (Buena Vista-1966). Hugh O'Donnell, Peter McEnery; Kathleen MacSweeney, Susan Hampshire; Henry O'Neill, Tom Adams; Captain Leeds, Gordon Jackson; Lord MacSweeney, Andrew Keir; Sean O'Toole, Donal McCann; Martin, Maurice Roeves; Sir John Perrott, Norman Wooland; Phelim O'Toole, Richard Leech; Troop Sergeant, Peter Jeffrey; Mother, Marie Keen; 1st Officer Powell, Bill Owen; Princess Ineen, Peggy Marshall; Moire, Fidelma Murphy; Moire's Sisters, Moire Ni Grainne and Moire O'Neill; John Forbes Robertson, Patrick Holt, Robert Cawdron, Roger Croucher, Keith McConnell, Inigo Jackson and Peter Cranwell.

974 FIGURES IN A LANDSCAPE. (National General-1971). MacConnachie, Robert Shaw; Ansell, Malcolm McDowell; Helicopter Pilot, Henry Woolf; Helicopter Observer, Christopher Malcolm; The Widow, Pamela Brown; Soldiers, Andrew Bradford, Warwick Sims, Roger Lloyd Pack, Robert East, Tariq Younus.

975 THE FILE ON THE GOLDEN GOOSE. (United Artists-1969). Peter Novak, Yul Brynner; Nick Harrison, Charles Gray; Peter Thompson, Edward Woodward; Sloane, John Barrie; Tina Dell, Adrienne Corri; Collins, Bernard Archard; Reynolds, Ivor Dean; Firenzo, Anthony Jacobs; Franz Mueller, Karel Stepanek; Leeds, Walter Gotell; Smythe, Graham Crowden; Martin, Geoffrey Reed; Stroud, Ken Jones; Ahne, Hilary Dwyer; Debbie, Janet Rossini; Grodie, Joe Cornelius; Moss, Hugh McDermott; Vance, Denis Shaw; Croupier, Ray Marioni;

Bongo Player, Ilario Pedro; Genevieve, Anita Prynne; Laboratory Technician, Philip Anthony; Mary, Paddy Webster.

976 THE FILTHIEST SHOW IN TOWN. (William Mishkin-1973). Dollya Sharp, Harry Reems, Tina Russel, Rudy Hornish, Alexander Sebastian, Judith Resnick, Arlana Blue, Joe Libido, Rudolph Rose, Bernard Erhard, Herbert Manguso, Richard Manchester, Mae Marmy, Rob Kendall, Alan Marlow, Sam Elias, Richard Tenbroke, Don Alter.

977 THE FILTHY FIVE. (William Mishkin-1968). Rita Roman, Anne Linden; Johnny Longo, Matt Garth; Rose White, Jackie Colton; Barney, Nick Orzel; Allison, Maha; Sidney Hart, Gerald Jacuzzo; Billy Delavanti, Mark Jenkins; Ma Delavanti, Maggie Rogers; Brenda Case, Mary Carter; Freakout, Larry Ree; Walter Cash, Haal Borske; Teeny Bopper, Maggie Dominic; Stripper, Selena Robbins.

978 THE FINAL COMEDOWN. (New World-1972). Johnny Johnson, Billy Dee Williams; Imir, Raymond St. Jacques; Billy Joe Ashley, D'Urville Martin; Mr. Freeman, R. G. Armstrong; Rene Freeman, Celia Kaye; Luanna, Pamela Jones; Mrs. Johnson, Maidie Norman; Mr. Johnson, Morris Erby; Michael Freeman, Billy Durkin; Dr. Smalls, Edmund Cambridge.

979 FINDERS KEEPERS. (United Artists-1967). Cliff, Cliff Richard; Colonel Roberts, Robert Morley; Mrs. Bragg, Peggy Mount; Emelia, Viviane Ventura; Burke, Graham Stark; Mr. X, John Le Mesurier; Commander, Robert Hutton; Junior Officer, Gordon Ruttan; Grandma, Ellen Pollock; Air Marshal, Ernest Clark; Pilot, Burnell Tucker; Priest, George Roderick; G. I. Guard, Bill Mitchell; Drunk, Ronnie Brody; The Shadows, Bruce Welch, Hank B. Marvin, Brian Bennett, John Rostill.

980 FINDERS KEEPERS, LOVERS WEEPERS. (Eve-1969). Kelly, Anne Chapman; Paul, Paul Lockwood; Ray, Gordon Wescourt; Cal, Duncan McLeod; Feeny, Robert Rudelson; Claire, Lavelle Roby; Christiana, Jan Sinclair; Joy, Joey Duprez; Nick, Nick Wolcuff; Pam Collins, Vickie Roberts, John Furlong, Michael Roberts.

981 A FINE MADNESS. (Warner Bros.-1966). Samson Shillitoe, Sean Connery; Rhoda Shillitoe, Joanne Woodward; Sydia West, Jean Seberg; Dr. Oliver West, Patrick O'Neal; Dr. Vera Kropotkin, Colleen Dewhurst; Dr. Menken, Clive Revill; Miss Walnicki, Sue Ane Langdon; Dr. Vorbeck, Werner Peters; Daniel K. Papp, John Fiedler; Mrs. Fish, Kay Medford; Mr. Fitzgerald, Jackie Coogan; Mrs. Tupperman, Zohra Lampert; Leonard Tupperman, Sorrell Booke; Bibi Osterwald, Mabel Albertson, Gerald S. O'Loughlin, James Millhollin, Jon Lormer, Harry Bellaver, Ayllene Gibbons.

982 A FINE PAIR. (National General-1969). Captain Mike Harmon, Rock Hudson; Esmeralda Marini, Claudia Cardinale; Roger, Tomas Milian; Chief Wellman, Leon Askin; Mrs. Walker, Ellen Corby; Franz, Walter Giller; Uncle Camillo, Guido Alberti; Vittorio Campanella, Gianni Carnago, Raniero Dorascienzi, Andrea Hesterasy, Umberto Fantoni, Aldo Formisano, Adriano Fraticelli.

983 FINGER ON THE TRIGGER. (Allied Artists-1966). Larry Winton, Rory Calhoun; Adam Hyde, James Philbrook; Hillstrom, Todd Martin; Violet, Silvia Solar; Fred, Brad Talbot; Ed Bannister, Leo Anchoriz; Benton, Jorge Rigaud; McKay, Eric Chapman; O'Brien, Benny Dues; McNamara, Axol Anderson; Tito Garcia, Willy Ellie, John Clarke, Antonio Molino Rojo, Jose Antonio Peral, German Grech, Fernando Bilbao, Sebastian Cavalier.

984 FINIAN'S RAINBOW. (Warner Bros. -7 Arts-1968). Finian McLonergan, Fred Astaire; Sharon McLonergan, Petula Clark; Og, Tommy Steele; Woody Mahoney, Don Francks; Judge Rawkins, Keenan Wynn; Howard, Al Freeman Jr.; Susan the Silent, Barbara Hancock; Buzz Collins, Ronald Colby; Sheriff, Dolph Sweet; District Attorney, Wright King; Henry, Louis Silas; Sharecropper, Brenda Arnau; Passion Pilgrim Gospeleers, Avon Long, Roy Glenn, Jester Hairston.

985 FINNEGANS WAKE. (Brandon-1966). Finnegan (H. C. Earwicker), Martin J. Kelly; Anna Livia Plurabelle (ALP), Jane Reilly; Shem, Peter Haskell; Shaun, Page Johnson; Commentator, John V. Kelleher; Young Shem, Ray Flanagan; Young Iseult, Maura Pryor; Young Shaun, Jo Jo Slavin; Accordion Player, Luke J. O'Malley; Celebrants, Joseph Alderham, Ray Allen, Virginia Blue, Sean Brancato, Joan Campbell, Joe Maher, Paddy Croft, Leonard Frey; Eileen Koch, Janis Markhouse, Kevin O'Leary, Herbert Prah, Jan Thompson, Virginia J. Wallace, Carmen P. Zavick.

986 FINNEY. (Gold Coast-1969). Jim Finney, Robert Kilcullen; Billy, Bill Levinson; Joyce, Joan Sundstrom.

987 THE FIRE WITHIN. (New Yorker-1969). Alain, Maurice Ronet; Lydia, Lena Skerla; Mlle. Farnoux, Yvonne Clech; D'Averseau, Hubert Deschamps; Doctor, Jean-Paul Moulinot; Mrs. Barbinais, Mona Dol; Jeanne, Jeanne Moreau; Moraire, Pierre Moncorbier; Charlie, Rene Dupuy; Milou, Bernard Tiphaine; Dubourg, Bernard Noel; Fanny, Ursula Kubler.

988 FIREBALL 500. (American International-1966). "Fireball" Dave Owens, Frankie Avalon; Jane Harris, Annette Funicello; Sonny Leander Fox, Fabian; Big Jaw Harris, Chill Wills; Charlie Bigg, Harvey Lembeck; Martha Brian, Julie Parrish; Hastings, Doug Henderson; Bronson, Baynes Barron; Joey, Mike Nader; Herman, Ed Garner; Announcer, Vince Scully;

Farmer's Daughter, Sue Hamilton; Herman's Wife, Rene Riano; Man in Garage, Len Lesser; Jobber, Billy Beck; Herman's Friend, Tex Armstrong; Leander Fans, Mary Hughes, Patti Chandler, Karla Conway, Hedy Scott, Jo Collins, Sallie Sachse, Maria McBane, and Linda Bent; The Don Randi Trio Plus One; The Carole Lombard Singers.

989 FIRECREEK. (Warner Bros.-7 Arts-1968). Johnny Cobb, James Stewart; Larkin, Henry Fonda; Evelyn, Inger Stevens; Earl, Gary Lockwood; Whittier, Dean Jagger; Preacher Broyles, Ed Begley; Mr. Pittman, Jay C. Flippen; Norman, Jack Elam; Drew, James Best; Meli, Barbara Luna; Henrietta Cobb, Jacqueline Scott; Leah, Brooke Bundy; Arthur, J. Robert Porter; Willard, Louise Latham; Mrs. Littlejohn, Athena Lord; Fyte, Harry "Slim" Duncan; Aaron, Kevin Tate; Franklin, Christopher Shea.

990 THE FIREMEN'S BALL. (Cinema V-1968). Fire Brigade Commander, Vaclav Stockel; Old Man, Josef Svet; Committee Chairman, Jan Vostrcil; Josef, Josef Kolb; 1st Committee Member, Frantisek Debelka; 2nd Committee Member, Josef Sebanek; 3rd Committee Member, Karel Valnoha; 4th Committee Member, Josef Rehorek; Josef's Wife, Maria Jezkova; Beauty Queen Candidates, Anina Lipoldova, Alena Kvetova, Mila Zelena.

991 THE FIRST CIRCLE. (Paramount-1973). Gleb, Gunthier Malzacher; Simonchka, Elzbieta Czyzewska; Volodin, Peter Steen; Clara, Vera Chekova; Doronin, Ole Ernest; Rubin, Ingolf David; Bobyin, Preben Neergaard; Cheinov, Preben Lerdeorff; Bulatov, Per Bentzon Goldschmidt; Siromakha, Ole Ishoy.

992 FIRST LOVE. (UMC-1970). Alexander, John Moulder-Brown; Sinaida, Dominique Sanda; Father, Maximilian Schell; Mother, Valentina Cortese; Dr. Lushin, Marcus Goring; Princess Zasekina, Dandy Nichols; Lt. Belovzorov, Richard Warwick; Count Malevsky, Keith Bell; Nirmatsky, Johannes Schaaf; Maidanov, John Osborne.

993 THE FIRST TIME. (United Artists-1969). Anna, Jacqueline Bisset; Kenny Leeds, Wes Stern; Mike Decker, Rick Kelman; Tommy Kingsley, Wink Roberts; Charles Leeds, Gerard Parkes; Pamela, Sharon Acker; Grandmother, Cosette Lee; Frankie, Vincent Marino; Joe, Eric Lane; Customs Officer, Murray Westgate; Bartender, Leslie Yeo; Stranger, Guy Sanvido; Elevator Operator, William Barringer; Blonde in Hot-Rod, Gail Carrington.

994 FIRST TIME ROUND. (Kingsway-1972). Sonny, Jason Walker; Ron, Doug Williams; Hank, Eric Martin; Bill, Aaron Bedford; Tony, Joe Markham; Bruce, Dale Carpenter; Lowell, Tim Simon.

995 FIRST TO FIGHT. (Warner Bros. -1967). Jack Connell, Chad Everett; Peggy Sanford, Marilyn Devin; Lt. Col. Baseman, Dean Jagger; Lt. Overman, Bobby Troup; Capt. Mason, Claude Akins; Sgt. Tweed, Gene Hackman; Sgt. Carnavan, James Best; Sgt. Schmidtmer, Norman Alden; Sgt. Maypole, Bob Watson; O'Brien, Ken Swofford; Hawkins, Ray Reese; Karl, Garry Goodgion; Adams, Robert Austin; Sgt. Slater, Clint Ritchie; Pres. F. D. Roosevelt, Stephen Roberts.

996 FISHKE GOES TO WAR. (Moishe Baruch-1972). Fishke, Solo Moshe; Schmil, Paul Smith; Ginger, Gabi Amrani; Commander, Pini Ben-Ari; English Girl, Leora Ramon.

997 FIST IN HIS POCKET. (Peppercorn-Wormser-1968). Alessandro, Lou Castel; Giulia, Paola Pitagora; Augusto, Marino Mase; The Mother, Liliana Gerace; Leone, Pier Luigi Troglio; Lucia, Jean MacNeil; Irene Agnelli, Sandra Bergamini.

998 A FISTFUL OF DOLLARS. (United Artists-1967). Man With No Name, Clint Eastwood; Marisol, Marianne Koch; Ramon Rojo, Gian Maria Volonte; John Baxter, Wolfgang Lukschy; Esteban Rojo, S. Rupp; Benito Rojo, Antonio Prieto; Silvanito, Pepe Calvo; Consuelo Baxter, Margherita Lozano; Julian, Daniel Martin; Rubio, Benny Reeves; Chico, Richard Stuyvesant; Antonia Baxter, Carol Brown.

999 FISTS OF FURY. (National General-1973). Cheng, Bruce Lee; Mei, Maria Yi; Mi's son, Tony Liu; Prostitute, Malalene; Miao Ke Hsiu, Li Quin, Chin Shan, Li Hua Sze.

1000 FITZWILLY. (United Artists-1967). Fitzwilliam, Dick Van Dyke; Juliet Nowell, Barbara Feldon; Victoria Woodworth, Edith Evans; Albert, John McGiver; Mr. Nowell, Harry Townes; Mr. Dunne, John Fiedler; Oberblatz, Norman Fell; Buckmaster, Cecil Kellaway; Byron Casey, Stephen Strimpell; Grimsby, Anne Seymour; Mrs. Mortimer, Helen Kleeb; Oliver, Sam Waterston; Prettikin, Paul Reed; Pierre, Albert Carrier; Simmons, Nelson Olmstead; Adams, Dennis Cooney; Charles, Noam Pitlik; Carland, Antony Eustrel; Cotty, Laurence Naismith; Kitty, Karen Norris; Dolly, Patience Cleveland; Frank, Lew Brown; Goldfarb, Monroe Arnold; Ryan, Bob Willians; Restaurant Owner, Billy Halop.

1001 FIVE BLOODY GRAVES. (Independent International-1971). Ben, Robert Dix; Jim, Scott Brady; Clay, Jim Davis; Boone, John Carradine; Kansas, Paula Raymond; Joe Satago, John Cardos; Althea, Tara Ashton; Dave, Kent Osbourne; Nora, Vicki Volante; Rawhide, Denver Dixon; Horace, Ray Young; Lavinia, Julie Edwards; Driver, Fred Meyers; Little Fawn, Maria Polo; Voice of Death, Gene Raymond.

1002 FIVE CARD STUD. (Paramount-1968). Van Morgan, Dean Martin; Reverend Rudd, Robert Mitchum; Lily Langford, Inger Stevens; Nick Evers, Roddy McDowall; Nora Evers, Katherine Justice; Marshal Dana, John Anderson; Mama Malone, Ruth Springford; Little George, Yaphet Kotto; Sig Evers, Denver Pyle; Joe Hurley, Bill Fletcher; Dr. Cooper, Whit Bissell; Eldon Bates, Ted De Corsia; Rowan, Don Collier; Mace Jones, Roy Jenson; Fred Carson, Boyd Morgan; Stoney, George Rowbotham; The Stranger, Jerry Gatlin; Robert Joy, Louise Lorimer.

1003 FIVE EASY PIECES. (Columbia-1970). Robert Eroica Dupea, Jack Nicholson; Rayette Dipesto, Karen Black; Elton, Billy Bush; Stoney, Fannie Flagg; Betty, Sally Ann Struthers; Twinky, Marlena MacGuire; Recording Engineer, Richard Stahl; Partita Dupea, Lois Smith; Palm Apodaca, Helena Kallianiotes; Terry Grouse, Toni Basil; Waitress, Lorna Thayer; Catherine Van Ost, Susan Anspach; Carl Fidelio Dupea, Ralph Waite; Nicholas Dupea, William Challee; Spicer, John Ryan; Samia Glavia, Irene Dailey.

1004 FIVE FINGERS OF DEATH. (Warner Bros. -1973). Chao, Lo Lieh; Sung, Wang Ping; Yen, Wang Chin-Feng; Han, Nan-Kung Hsun; Meng, Tien Feng; Okada, Chao Hsiung; Meng, Tung Lin.

1005 FIVE GENTS' TRICK BOOK. (Toho-1966). Hisayo Morishige, Asami Kuji, Yoko Tsukasa, Daisuko Kaio, Norihei Miki, Franky Sakal, Junko Ikeuchi, Michiyo Aratama, Reiko Dan.

1006 THE FIVE MAN ARMY. (MGM-1970). Dutchman, Peter Graves; Augustus, James Daly; Mesito, Bud Spencer; Samurai, Tetsuro Tamba; Luis Dominguez, Nino Castelnuovo; Maria, Daniela Giordano; Manuel Estaban, Claudio Gora; Perla, Annabella Andreoli; Gutierrez, Carlo Alighiero; Mexican Officer, Jack Stuart; Carnival Barker, Marc Lawrence; Mexican Spy, Jose Torres; Train Engineer, Marino Mase.

1007 FIVE MILLION YEARS TO EARTH. (20th Century-Fox-1968). Doctor Roney, James Donald; Professor Quatermass, Andrew Keir; Barbara Judd, Barbara Shelley; Colonel Breen, Julian Glover; Sladden, Duncan Lamont; Captain Potter, Bryan Marshall; Howell, Peter Copley; Minister, Edwin Richfield; Police Sergeant Ellis, Grant Taylor; Sergeant Cleghorn, Maurice Good; Watson, Robert Morris; Journalist, Sheila Steafel; Sapper West, Hugh Futcher; Elderly Journalist, Hugh Morton; Vicar, Thomas Heathcote; Abbey Librarian, Noel Howlett; Pub Customer, Hugh Manning; Blonde, June Ellis; Johnson, Keith Marsh; Corporal Gibson, James Culliford; Miss Dobson, Bee Duffell; Electrician, Roger Avon; Technical Officer, Brian Peck; Inspector, John

Graham; Newsvendor, Charles Lamb.

1008 FIVE ON THE BLACK HAND SIDE. (United Artists-1973). Mrs. Brooks, Clarice Taylor; Mr. Brooks, Leonard Jackson; Ruby, Virginia Capers; Gideon, Glynn Turman; Booker T., D'Urville Martin; Gail, Bonnie Banfield; Preston, Richard Williams; Sweetmeat, Sonny Jim; Stormy Monday, Ja'Net Dubois; Marvin, Carl Mikal Franklin.

1009 FIVE THE HARD WAY. (Fantascope-1969). Ross Hagen, Diane McBain, Michael Pataki, Claire Polan, Richard Merrifield, Edward Parrish, Michael Graham, Hoke Howell.

1010 THE FIXER. (MGM-1968). Yakov Bok, Alan Bates; Bibikov, Dirk Bogarde; Marfa Golov, Georgia Brown; Lebedev, Hugh Griffith; Zinaida Lebedev, Elizabeth Hartman; Grubeshov, Ian Holm; Latke, David Opatoshu; Count Odoevsky, David Warner; Raisl Bok, Carol White; Deputy Warden, George Murcell; Priest, Murray Melvin; Berezhinsky, Peter Jeffrey; Ostrovsky, Michael Goodliffe; Proshko, Thomas Heathcote; Father Anastasy, Mike Pratt; Gronfein, Stanley Meadows; Warden, Francis De Wolff; The Tzar, William Hutt; Zhitnyak, David Lodge; Zhenia, Norbert Viszlay.

1011 FLAME OVER VIETNAM. (Producers Releasing Organization-1967). Sister Paula, Elena Barrios; Lazlo, Nose Nietos; Brother Bartholomew, Manolo Moran; Father Elias, Nicolas Perchicot; Selma, Rosita Palomares; The Driver, Vincente P. Avila; Ellison, Felix Defauce; Angela, Maria Martin.

1012 FLAMING FRONTIER. (Warner Bros.-7 Arts-1968). Old Surehand, Steward Granger; Winnetou, Pierre Brice; Judith, Letitia Roman; The General, Larry Pennell; Toby, Mario Girotti; Judge Edwards, Wolfgang Lukschy; Captain Miller, Erik Schumann; Jeremy Wabble, Paddy Fox; Aleksandar Gavric, Vladimir Hedar, Voja Miric, Dusco Janicijevic, Dusan Antonijevic, Hermina Pipinic, Jelena Jovanovic.

1013 THE FLANDERS AND ALCOTT REPORT ON SEX RESPONSE. (Films International-1971). Dr. Leon Flanders, John Dunnigan; Dr. Phyllis Alcott, Sheri Enid.

1014 FLAP. (Warner Bros.-1970). Flapping Eagle, Anthony Quinn; Lobo, Claude Akins; Eleven Snowflake, Tony Bill; Wounded Bear Mr. Smith, Victor Jory; Mike Lyons, Don Collier; Rafferty, Victor French; Storekeep, Rodolfo Acosta; Silver Dollar, Anthony Caruso; Dorothy Bluebell, Shelley Winters; Ann Looking Deer, Susana Miranda; Steve Gray, William Mims; Larry Standing Elk, Rudi Diaz; She'll-Be-Back-Pretty-Soon, Pedro Regas; Harry, J. Edward McKinley; Gus Kirk, Robert Cleaves; Luke Wolf, John War Eagle.

1015 FLAREUP. (MGM-1969). Michele, Raquel Welch; Joe, James Stacy; Alan, Luke Askew; Lt. Manion, Don Chastain; "Sailor," Ron Rifkin; Jerri, Jeane Byron; Lee, Kay Peters; Iris, Pat Delany; Nikki, Sandra Giles; Lloyd, Joe Billings; Jackie, Carol-Jean Thompson; Tory, Mary Wilcox; Sgt. Newcomb, Carl Byrd; Lt. Franklin, Steve Conte; Willows, Tom Fadden; Dr. Connors, Michael Rougas; Technician, David Moses; Gas Station Attendant, Doug Rowe; Security Guard, Gordon Jump; Policeman, Ike Williams.

1016 THE FLAVOR OF GREEN TEA OVER RICE. (New Yorker-1973). Shin Saburi, Michiyo Kogura, Koji Tsuruta, Keiko Tsushima, Kuniko Miyake, Chikaga Awashima, Chishu Ryu, Yuko Mochizuki.

1017 A FLEA IN HER EAR. (20th Century-Fox-1968). Victor Chandebisse/Poche, Rex Harrison; Gabrielle Chandebisse, Rosemary Harris; Henri Tournel, Louis Jourdan; Suzanne de Castilian, Rachel Roberts; Dr. Finache, John Williams; Monsieur Max, Gregoire Aslan; Pierre, Edward Hardwicke; Don Carlos, Georges Descrieres; Antoinette, Isla Blair; Charles, Frank Thornton; Oke Saki, Victor Sen-Yung; Eugenie, Laurence Badie; Olympe, Dominique Davray; Uncle Louis, Olivier Hussenot; Defendant, Estella Blain; Fat Man, Moustache; The Prosecutor, David Horne; Taxi Driver, Roger Carel.

1018 FLESH. (Factory-1968). Joe, Joe Dallesandro; Gerry, Geraldine Smith; Young Man, John Christian; Artist, Maurice Bardell; Boy on Street, Barry Brown; Blonde on Sofa, Candy Darling; Redhead on Sofa, Jackie Curtis; Terry, Geri Miller; David, Louis Waldon; Gerry's Girlfriend, Patti D'Arbanville.

1019 FLESH GORDON. (Mammoth-1974). Flesh Gordon, Jason Williams; Dale Ardor, Suzann Fields; Dr. Flexi Jerkoff, Joseph Judgins; Prof. Gordon, John Hoyt; Professor Wang, William Hunt; Mycle Brandy, Nora Wieternik, Candy Samples, Steven Grummette, Lance Larsen, Judy Ziehm, Donald Harris, Jack Rowe, Mark Fore, Maria Aranoff, Rick Lutze, Sally Alt, Linus Gator, Susan Moore, Pat Hudson, Duane Paulsen, Leonard Goodman, Howard Alexander, Alan Sinclair, Annette Anderson, Shannon West, Patricia Burns, Nancy Ayres, Kathy Foster, Terri Johnson, Linda Shepard, Mary Gavin, Dee Dee Dailies.

1020 FLESHPOT ON 42ND STREET. (William Mishkin-1972). Dusty, Diana Lewis; Cherry, Lynn Flanagan; Bob, Bob Walters; Jimmy, Paul Matthews; Billy, Daniel Deitrich; Dorin McGough, M. A. Whiteside, Joe Powers, Ron Keith, Earle Edgarson, Fred Lincoln, Fred Perisi.

1021 FLIGHT OF THE DOVES. (Columbia-1971). Hawk Dove,

Ron Moody; Finn Dove, Jack Wild; Granny O'Flaherty, Dorothy McGuire; Judge Liffy, Stanley Holloway.

1022 THE FLIGHT OF THE PHOENIX. (20th Century-Fox-1966). Frank Towns, James Stewart; Lew Moran, Richard Attenborough; Captain Harris, Peter Finch; Heinrich Dorfmann, Hardy Kruger; Trucker Cobb, Ernest Borgnine; Crow, Ian Bannen; Sergeant Watson, Ronald Fraser; Dr. Renaud, Christian Marquand; Standish, Dan Duryea; Bellamy, George Kennedy; Gabriele Tinti, Alex Montoya, Peter Bravos, William Aldrich, Barrie Chase.

1023 FLIGHT TO FURY. (Harold Goldman Associates-1967). Joe Gaines, Dewey Martin; Destiny Cooper, Fay Spain; Jay Wickam, Jack Nicholson; Gloria Walsh, Jacqueline Hellman; Lorgren, Vic Diaz; Garuda, Joseph Estrada; Al Ross, John Hackett; Lei Ling, Juliet Prado; Bearded Man, Jennings Sturgeon; Police Inspector, Lucien Pan.

1024 THE FLIM-FLAM MAN. (20th Century-Fox-1967). Mordecai Jones, George C. Scott; Bonnie Lee Packard, Sue Lyon; Curley Treadaway, Michael Sarrazin; Sheriff Slade, Harry Morgan; Mr. Packard, Jack Albertson; Mrs. Packard, Alice Ghostley; Deputy Meshaw, Albert Salmi; Jarvis Bates, Slim Pickens; Lovick, Strother Martin; Tetter, George Mitchell; Super Market Manager, Woodrow Parfrey; First Fertilizer Man, Ray Guth; Second Fertilizer Man, Jay Ose; Doodle Powell, Jesse L. Baker.

1025 FLOATING WEEDS. (Altura-1970). Komajuro, Ganjiro Nakamura; Oyoshi, Haruko Sugimura; Kiyoshi, Hiroshi Kawaguchi; Sumiko, Machiko Kyo; Kayo, Ayako Wakao; Kichinosuke, Koji Mitsui.

1026 FLOWER THIEF. (Filmmakers-1969). Taylor Mead, Turk, Ella, Mikey, Ted, Eric, Bob Kauffman, Phil McKenna.

1027 FLUFFY. (Universal-1965). Daniel Potter, Tony Randall; Janice Claridge, Shirley Jones; Griswald, Edward Andrews; James Claridge, Ernest Truex; Sweeny, Howard Morris.

1028 FLY ME. (New World-1973). Toby, Pat Anderson; Andrea, Lenore Kasdorf; Sherry, Lyllah Torena; Doctor, Richard Young; Toby's Mother, Naomi Stevens; Cab Driver, Richard Miller; Police Chief, Vic Diaz.

1029 THE FLYING MATCHMAKER. (National Showmanship-1970). Kouny Lemel/Max, Mike Burstein; Matchmaker's Daughter, Jermaine Unikowsky; Rich Man's Daughter, Rina Ganor; Matchmaker, Raphel Klatschkin; Rich Man, Shmuel Rodensky; Rebeka, Elisheva Michaeli; Shalmoni, Aharon Meskin; Beralle, Mordechai Arnon; Loksh, Asher Levy; Professor, Hanan Goldblatt; Bullfass, Shlomo Vishinsky; Tzipa, Jetta

Luka; Dr. Fridberg, Ari Kutai.

1030 THE FOLKS AT RED WOLF INN. (Scope III-1972). Policeman, Michael Macready; Pilot, Earl Parker; Pamela, Janet Wood; Edwina, Margaret Avery.

1031 FOLLOW ME. (Cinerama-1969). Claude Codgen, Mary Lou McGinnis, Bob Purvey, Bonnie Hill, Andrea Kermot, Deborah Lee, Ava Zamora.

1032 FOLLOW ME, BOYS! (Buena Vista-1966). Lemuel Siddons, Fred MacMurray; Vida Downey, Vera Miles; Hetty Seibert, Lillian Gish; John Everett Hughes, Charlie Ruggles; Ralph Hastings, Elliott Reid; Whitey, Kurt Russell; Nora White, Luana Patten; Melody Murphy, Ken Murray; Edward White Jr., Donald May; Edward White Sr., Sean McClory; Steve Franken, Parley Baer, William Reynolds, Draig Hill, Tol Avery, Willis Bouchey, John Zaremba, Madge Blake, Carl Reindel, Hank Brandt, Richard Bakalyan, Tim McIntire, Willie Soo Hoo, Tony Regan, Robert B. Williams, Jimmy Murphy, Adam Williams, Dean Moray, Bill Both, Keith Taylor, Rickey Kelman, Gregg Shank, Donnie Carter, Kit Lloyd, Ronnie Dapo, Dennis Rush, Kevin Burchett, David Bailey, Eddie Sallia, Warren Hsieh, Duane Chase, Mike Dodge.

1033 THE FOOL KILLER. (Landau-1965). Milo Bogardus, Anthony Perkins; George Mellish, Edward Albert; Mr. Dodd, Dana Elcar; Dirty Jim Jelliman, Henry Hull; Mrs. Dodd, Salome Jens; Mrs. Ova Fanshawe, Charlotte Jones; Reverend Spotts, Arnold Moss; Blessing Angelina, Sindee Anne Richards; Old Crab, Frances Gaar; Old Man, Wendell Phillips.

1034 FOOLS. (Cinerama-1970). Matthew, Jason Robards; Anais, Katherine Ross; David Appleton, Scott Hylands; Men in Park, Roy C. Jenson, Mark Bramhall; Dog Owner, Marc Hannibal; Private Detective, Robert C. Ferro Jr.; Restaurant Couple, Floy Dean, Roy Jelliffe; Dentist, Charles B. Dorsett; Patient, Laura Ash; Policemen, Robert Rothwell, Michael Davis; Girl in movie, Vera Stough; FBI men, James Burr Johnson, Louis Picetti Jr., Stuart P. Klitsner; Hippies, Robin Menken, Chris Pray, Jack Nance.

1035 FOOLS' PARADE. (Columbia-1971). Mattie Appleyard, James Stewart; "Doc" Council, George Kennedy; Cleo, Anne Baxter; Lee Cottrill, Strother Martin; Johnny Jesus, Kurt Russell; Roy K. Sizemore, William Windom.

1036 FOR A FEW DOLLARS MORE. (United Artists-1967). Man With No Name, Clint Eastwood; Colonel Mortimer, Lee Van Cleef; Indio, Gian Maria Volonte; Old Man Over Railway, Jose Egger; Colonel's Sister, Rosemarie Dexter; Hotel

Managers Wife, Mara Krup; Hunchback, Klaus Kinski; Indio's Gang, Mario Brega, Aldo Sambrell, Luigi Pistilli, Benito Stefanelli; Robert Camardiel, Luis Rodriguez, Panos Papadopulos.

1037 FOR LOVE OF IVY. (Cinerama-1968). Jack Parks, Sidney Poitier; Ivy Moore, Abbey Lincoln; Tim Austin, Beau Bridges; Doris Austin, Nan Martin; Gena Austin, Lauri Peters; Frank Austin, Carroll O'Connor; Billy Talbot, Leon Bibb; Jerry, Hugh Hurd; Harry, Lon Satton; Eddie, Stanley Greene.

1038 FOR PETE'S SAKE. (Columbia-1974). Henry, Barbra Streisand; Pete, Michael Sarrazin; Helen, Estelle Parsons; Fred, William Redfield; Mrs. Cherry, Molly Picon; Nick, Louis Zorich; Loretta, Vivian Bonnell; Bernie, Richard Ward; Judge Hiller, Heywood Hale Broun; Mr. Coates, Joe Maher; Check-out man, Vincent Schiavelli; Loan officer, Fred Struthman; Angelo, Ed Bakey; Dominic, Peter Mamakos; First worker, Norman Marshall; Second cop, Joseph Hardy; Cop in drag, Wil Albert; Loanshark, Jack Hollander; Asst. bank Manager, Gary Pagett; Insurance man, Herb Armstrong; Lady in supermarket, Bella Bruck; Telephone lady, Anne Ramsey; Rocky, Bill McKinney; Drunk driver, Sid Miller; Dog trainer, Lew Burke; Man in theatre, Martin Erlichman.

1039 FOR SINGLES ONLY. (Columbia-1968). Bret Hendley, John Saxon; Anne Carr, Mary Ann Mobley; Helen Todd, Lana Wood; Gerald Pryor, Mark Richman; Nydia Walker, Ann Elder; Lily, Chris Noel; Archibald Baldwin, Marty Ingels; Miss Jenks, Hortense Petra; Jim Allen, Charles Robinson; Bob Merrick, Duke Hobbie; Singer, Dick Castle; Clerk in Bursar's Office, Norman Wells; Pageant Girls, Norma Foster, Maria Korda, Leslie McRae, Dita Nicole; Mr. Parker, Milton Berle.

1040 FORBIDDEN UNDER THE CENSORSHIP OF THE KING. (Lemming-1973). Student, Herb Kaplow; Exhibitionist, Marshall Anker; Student, Bob Lavigne; Girl in theatre, Lee Rey; Mortician, Perry Gerwitz; Dead body, Alana Blue; Ice Cream Girl, Andrea Krangle; Larisa, Leslie Gaye; Ted, Jaime German; Voice, Billy Arrington.

1041 THE FORBIN PROJECT. (Universal-1970). Forbin, Eric Braeden; Cleo, Susan Clark; President, Gordon Pinsent; Grauber, William Schallert; First Chairman, Leonid Rostoff; Fisher, Georg Stanford Brown; Blake, Willard Sage; Kuprin, Alex Rodine; Johnson, Martin Brooks; Angela, Marion Ross; Missile Commander, Dolph Sweet; Secretary of State, Byron Morrow; Peterson, Lew Brown; Secretary of Defense, Sid McCoy; Harrison, Rom Basham; First Scientist, Robert Cornthwaite; Second Scientist, James Hong; Translator,

Sergei Tschernisch.

1042 FORT COURAGEOUS. (20th Century-Fox-1965). Sergeant Lucas, Fred Bier; Captain Howard, Donald Barry; Woman, Hanna Landy; Joe, Harry Lauter; Walter Reed, Michael Carr, George Sawaya, Cheryl MacDonald, Fred Krone, Joseph Patridge.

1043 FORT UTAH. (Paramount-1967). Tom Horn, John Ireland; Linda Lee, Virginia Mayo; Dajin, Scott Brady; Eli Jones, John Russell; Ben Stokes, Robert Strauss; Bo Greer, James Craig; Sam Tyler, Richard Arlen; Scarecrow, Jim Davis; Harris, Donald Barry; Britches, Harry Lauter; Cavalry Lieutenant, Read Morgan; Rafe, Reg Parton; Shirt, Eric Cody.

1044 FORTUNA. (Trans-American-1969). Busaglo, Pierre Brasseur; Margot, Gila Almagor; Fortuna, Ahuva Goren; Simon, Saro Urzi; Pierre, Mike Marshall; Yoseph, Joseph Banai; Haim, Shmuel Oz; Moshe, Abraham Mor; Leon, Avner Hizkyahu; Leon's mother, Miriam Bernstein Cohen; Davidov, Isaac Shilo.

1045 FORTUNE AND MEN'S EYES. (MGM-1971). Smitty, Wendell Burton; Queenie, Michael Greer; Rocky, Zooey Hall; Mona, Danny Freedman.

1046 THE FORTUNE COOKIE. (United Artists-1966). Harry Hinkle, Jack Lemmon; Willie Gingrich, Walter Matthau; Luther "Boom Boom" Jackson, Ron Rich; Mr. Purkey, Cliff Osmond; Sandy, Judi West; Mother Hinkle, Lurene Tuttle; O'Brien, Harry Holcombe; Thompson, Les Tremayne; Charlotte Gingrich, Marge Redmond; Max, Noam Pitlik; Dr. Krugman, Harry Davis; Ann Shoemaker, Maryesther Denver, Lauren Gilbert, Ned Glass, Sig Ruman, Archie Moore, Howard McNear, Bartlett Robinson, Robert P. Lieb, Martin Blaine, Ben Wright, Bill Christopher, Dodie Heath, Herbie Baye, Billy Beck, Judy Pace, Helen Kleeb, Lisa Jill, John Todd Roberts, Keith Jackson, Herb Ellis, Don Reed, Louise Vienna, Bob Doqui.

1047 40 CARATS. (Columbia-1973). Ann Stanley, Liv Ullmann; Peter Latham, Edward Albert; Billy Boyland, Gene Kelly; Maud Ericson, Binnie Barnes; Trina Stanley, Deborah Raffin; J. D. Rogers, Billy Green Bush; Mrs. Margolin, Nancy Walker; Mr. Latham, Don Porter; Mrs. Latham, Rosemary Murphy; Arthur Forbes, Sam Chew Jr.; Mrs. Adams, Natalie Schafer; Gabriella, Claudia Jennings; Polly, Brooke Palance.

1048 40 GUNS TO APACHE PASS. (Columbia-1967). Captain Bruce Coburn, Audie Murphy; Doug Malone, Michael Burns; Corporal Bodine, Kenneth Tobey; Ellen Malone, Laraine

Stephens; Sergeant Walker, Robert Brubaker; Mike Malone, Michael Blodgett; Cochise, Michael Keep; Kate Malone, Kay Stewart; Harry Malone, Kenneth MacDonald; Colonel Reed, Byron Morrow; Fuller, Willard Willingham; Barrett, Ted Gehring; Higgins, James Beck.

1049 THE FOUNTAIN OF LOVE. (Crown International-1969). Alwin, Eddi Arent; Leif, Hans-Jurgen Baumler; Stina, Ann Smyrner; Nils, Sieghardt Rupp; Carl, Hartmuth Hinrichs; Britta, Christa Linder; Brit, Christiane Rucker; Mrs. van Weyden, Marianne Schonauer; Caroline, Helga Marlo; John, Werner Abrolat; Frieda, Emely Reuer.

1050 FOUR CLOWNS. (20th Century-Fox-1970). Stan Laurel, Oliver Hardy, Charley Chase, Buster Keaton.

1051 FOUR FLIES ON GREY VELVET. (Paramount-1972). Robert Tobias, Michael Brandon; Nina Tobias, Mimsy Farmer; Arrosio, Jean-Pierre Marielle; Dalia, Francine Racette; Godfrey, Bud Spencer; Carlo Marosi, Calisto Calisti; Hilda, Marisa Fabbri; Professor, Oreste Lionello; Mirko, Fabrizio Moroni; Andrew, Stefano Sattaflores; Maria, Costanza Spada.

1052 FOUR NIGHTS OF A DREAMER. (New Yorker-1972). Marthe, Isabel Weingarten; Jacques, Guillaume des Forets; Lover, Jean Maurice Monnoyer.

1052a 491. (Janus-1967). Krista, Lars Lind; Nisse, Leif Nymark; Egon, Stig Tornblom; Pyret, Lars Hansson; Inspector, Frank Sundstrom; Jingis, Sven Algotsson; Slaktarn, Torleif Cederstand; Fisken, Bo Andersson; Steva, Lena Nyman; The Preacher, Ake Gronberg; Kajsa, Mona Andersson; The Examiner, Jan Blomberg; German Sailor, Siegfried Wald; German Sailor, Wilhelm Fricks; Policeman, Erik Hell; Policeman, Leif Liljeroth.

1053 FOUR STARS. (Filmmakers' Distribution Center-1967). Nico, International Velvet, Viva, Ivy Nicholson, Edie Sedgewick, Brigit Polk, Alan Midgette, Ondine, Tiger Morse, Ultra Violet, Katrina, Ingrid Superstar.

1054 THE FOX. (Warner Bros. -7 Arts-1968). Jill Banford, Sandy Dennis; Paul Grenfel, Keir Dullea; Ellen March, Anne Heywood; Overseer, Glyn Morris.

1055 FOXY BROWN. (American International-1974). Foxy Brown, Pam Grier; Link Brown, Antonio Fargas; Steve Elias, Peter Brown; Michael Anderson, Terry Carter; Katherine Wall, Kathryn Loder; Judge Fenton, Harry Holcombe; Hays, Sid Haig; Claudia, Juanita Brown; Deb, Sally Ann Stroud; Oscar, Bob Minor.

1056 FRAGMENT OF FEAR. (Columbia-1971). Tom Brett, David Hemmings; Juliet, Gayle Hunnicutt; Lucy Dawson, Flora Robson; Mr. Copsey, Wilfrid Hyde-White; Major Ricketts, Daniel Massey; Mr. Vellacot, Roland Culver; Bardoni, Adolfo Celi; Mrs. Gray, Mona Washbourne; "Bun-face," Mary Wimbush; Priest, Bernard Archard; C. I. D. Superintendent, Glyn Edwards; Sgt. Matthews, Derek Newark; Mr. Nugent, Arthur Lowe; Mrs. Ward-Cadbury, Yootha Joyce; Mrs. Baird, Patricia Hayes; Uncles Stanley, John Rae; Bruno, Angelo Infanti; Miss Dacey, Hilda Barry; Mario, Massimo Sarchielli; C. I. D. Sergeant, Philip Stone; Kenny, Edward Kemp; Joe, Kenneth Cranham; Rocky, Michael Rothwell; Nino, Kurt Christian; Pop Singer, Richard Kerr.

1057 FRANKENSTEIN. (Bryanston-1974). Joe Dallesandro, Udo Kier, Monique Van Vooren, Arno Juerging, Srdjan Zelenovic, Dalila DiLazzaro, Liu Bozizio, Carla Mancini, Marco Liofredi.

1058 FRANKENSTEIN AND THE MONSTER FROM HELL. (Paramount-1974). Baron Frankenstein, Peter Cushing; Simon Helder, Shane Briant; Sarah, Madeline Smith; Monster, Dave Prowse; Asylum Director, John Stratton.

1059 FRANKENSTEIN CONQUERS THE WORLD. (American International-1966). Dr. James Bowen, Nick Adams; Scientist, Tadao Takashima; Woman Doctor, Kumi Mizuno.

1060 No entry.

1061 FRANKENSTEIN CREATED WOMAN. (20th Century-Fox-1967). Baron Frankenstein, Peter Cushing; Christina, Susan Denberg; Dr. Hertz, Thorley Walters; Hans, Robert Morris; Anton, Peter Blythe; Karl, Barry Warren; Johann, Derek Fowlds; Kleve, Alan MacNaughtan; Police Chief, Peter Madden; Hans (as a boy), Stuart Middleton; Prisoner, Duncan Lamont; Priest, Colin Jeavons; New Landlord, Ivan Beavis; Police Sergeant, John Maxim; Mayor, Philip Ray; Jailer, Kevin Flood; Bystander, Bartlett Mullins; Spokesman, Alec Mango.

1062 FRANKENSTEIN MEETS THE SPACE MONSTER. (Allied Artists-1966). Dr. Adam Steele, James Karen; Karen Grant, Nancy Marshall; General Bowers, David Kerman; Princess Marcuzen, Marilyn Hanold; Nadir, Lou Cutell; Colonel Frank Saunders and Frankenstein, Robert Reilly.

1063 FRANKENSTEIN MUST BE DESTROYED! (Warner Bros.-1970). Baron Frankenstein, Peter Cushing; Karl, Simon Ward; Anna, Veronica Carlson; Insp. Frisch, Thorley Walters; Dr. Richter, Freddie Jones; Ella Brandt, Maxine Audley; Police Doctor, Geoffrey Bayldon; Brandt, George Pravda; Mad Woman, Colette O'Neal; Burglar, Harold

Goodwin; Third Guest, Frank Middlemass.

1064 FRANKENSTEIN'S BLOODY TERROR. (Independent-International-1972). Count Waldemar Diansky, Paul Naschy; Countess Janice, Diana Zura; Rudolph, Michael Manza; Dr. Mikelhov, Julian Ugarte; Wandessa, Rossanna Yanni; Aurora De Alba, Jose Nieto, Carlos Casaravilla, Victoriano Lopez, Gualberto Galban.

1065 FRANKIE AND JOHNNY. (United Artists-1966). Johnny, Elvis Presley; Frankie, Donna Douglas; Cully, Harry Morgan; Mitzi, Sue Ane Langdon; Nelli Bly, Nancy Kovack; Peg, Audrey Christie; Blackie, Robert Strauss; Braden, Anthony Eisley; Wilbue, Jerome Cowan; Dancers, Wilda Taylor, Larri Thomas, Dee Jay Mattis, and Judy Chapman.

1066 FRASIER, THE SENSUOUS LION. (LCS-1973). Marvin, Michael Callan; Allison, Katherine Justice; Voice of Frasier, Victor Jory; The Man, Frank de Kova; Bill, Malachi Throne; Chiarelli, Marc Lawrence; Boscov, Peter Lorre Jr.; Dredge, Arthur Space; Worcester, Patrick O'Moore; Minerva, Lori Saunders; Kuback, Joe E. Ross; Marvin's Mother, Fritzi Burr; Motel Manager, A. E. Gould-Porter; Reporter, Ralph James. Editor, Jerry Kobrin; Old Man, John Qualen; Old Lady, Florence Lake; Nurse, Maryesther Denver; Wife in kitchen, Allison McKay; Man in kitchen, Charles Woolfe; Fat Man, John J. Fox; Man in bar, Paul Mousie Garner; Party Host, Frank Biro.

1067 FRAULEIN DOKTOR. (Paramount-1969). Fraulein Doktor, Suzy Kendall; Colonel Foreman, Kenneth More; Dr. Saforet, Capucine; Meyer, James Booth; General Peronne, Alexander Knox; Colonel Mathesius, Nigel Green; Hans Schell, Roberto Bisacco; Cartwright, Malcolm Ingram; Lieut. Hans Ruppert, Giancarlo Giannini; Sgt. Otto Latemar, Mario Novelli; 2nd Lieut., Kenneth Poitevin; Bernhard De Vries, Ralph Nossek, Michael Elphick, Olivera, Andreina Paul, Dilvia Monti, Virginia Bell, Colin Tapley, Gerard Herter, Walter Williams, John Atkinson, Neale Stainton, John Webb, Joan Geary, Aca Stojkovic, Mavid Popovic, Janez Vrhovec, Bata Paskaljevic, Zoran Longinovic, Dusan Bulajic, Miki Micovic, Dusan Djuric, Maggie McGrath.

1068 FREEBIE AND THE BEAN. (Warner Bros.-1974). Bean, Alan Arkin; Freebie, James Caan; Mrs. Meyers, Loretta Swit; Red Meyers, Jack Kruschen; Lt. Rosen, Mike Kellin; Whitey, Paul Koslo; Freebie's Girl, Linda Marsh; Meyers' Chauffeur, John Garwood; District Attorney, Alex Rocco; Bean's Wife, Valerie Harper; Transvestite, Christopher Morley.

1069 THE FRENCH CONNECTION. (20th Century-Fox-1971). Jimmy Doyle, Gene Hackman; Alain Charnier, Fernando

Rey; Buddy Russo, Roy Scheider; Sal Boca, Tony LoBianco; Pierre Nicoli, Marcel Bozzuffi; Henri Devereaux, Frederic De Pasquale; Officer Mulderig, Bill Hickman; Marie Charnier, Ann Rebbot; Joe Weinstock, Harold Gary; Angie Boca, Arlene Farber; Lt. Walter Simonson, Eddie Egan; Maurice La Valle, Andre Ernotte; Officer Klein, Sonny Grosso; Chemist, Pat McDermott; Drug Pusher, Alan Weeks; Lou Boca, Ben Marino; Undercover Agent, Al Fann.

1070 THE FRENCH CONSPIRACY. (Cine Globe-1973). Darien, Jean-Louis Trintignant; Kassar, Michel Piccoli; Sadiel, Gian Maria Volonte; Edith, Jean Seberg; Rouannet, Francois Perier; Garcin, Philippe Noiret; Lempereur, Michel Bouquet; Vigneau, Bruno Cremer; Acconeti, Daniel Ivernel; Howard, Roy Scheider.

1071 FRENZY. (Universal-1972). Richard Blaney, John Finch; Inspector Oxford, Alec McCowen; Bob Rusk, Barry Foster; Brenda Blaney, Barbara Leigh-Hunt; Babs, Anna Massey; Mrs. Oxford, Vivien Merchant; Hetty Porter, Billie Whitelaw; Felix Forsythe, Bernard Cribbins; Johnny Porter, Clive Swift; Sergeant Spearman, Michael Bates; Monica Barling, Jean Marsh; Bob's Mother, Rita Webb; Hall Porter, Jimmy Gardner; Porter's Wife, Elsie Randolph; Mrs. Davison, Madge Ryan; Mr. Salt, George Tovey; Pub Customers, Noel Johnson and Gerald Sim; Sir George, John Boxer; Barmaid, June Ellis; Barman, Bunny May; Hospital Patient, Robert Keegan; Man in Bowler Hat on Waterfront, Alfred Hitchcock.

1072 FRIDAY ON MY MIND. (Continental-1970). Randy, Michael Scott; Ted, Aaron Bedford; Harry, Con Covert; Ray, Allen Rogers; Phil, John Romero; Sandy, Mama Chuck; Lee, Math; Billy, Andy Helman.

1073 FRIEND OF THE FAMILY. (International Classics-1965). Leon (Patate), Pierre Dux; Noel Carradine, Jean Marais; Edith Rollo, Danielle Darrieux; Alexa Rollo, Sylvie Vartan; Veronique Carradine, Anne Vernon; Berthe, Jane Marken.

1074 FRIENDS. (Paramount-1971). Paul, Sean Bury; Michelle, Anicee Alvina; Annie, Pascale Roberts; Pierre, Sady Rebbot; Harrison, Ronald Lewis; Mrs. Gardner, Toby Robins; Lady in bookshop, Joan Hinkson; natives of Camargue, France.

1075 THE FRIENDS OF EDDIE COYLE. (Paramount-1973). Eddie Coyle, Robert Mitchum; Dillon, Peter Boyle; Foley, Richard Jordan; Jackie Brown, Steven Keats; Scalise, Alex Rocco; Artie Van, Joe Santos; Waters, Mitchell Ryan; Coyle's Wife, Helena Carroll; Bank Managers, Peter MacLean, Kevin O'Morrison; Nancy, Carolyn Pickman; Vernon, Marvin Lichterman; Contact Man, James Tolkan; Pete,

Matthew Cowles; Andrea, Margaret Ladd; Wanda, Jane House; The Kid, Michael McCleery; Phil, Alan Koss; Webber, Dennis McMullen; Pale Kid, Jan Egleson; Mrs. Partridge, Judith Ogden Cabot; The Beard, Jack Kehoe; Moran, Robert Anthony; Ames, Gus Johnson; Sauter, Ted Maynard; Ferris, Sheldon Feldner.

1076 FRIGHT. (Allied Artists-1972). Amanda, Susan George; Helen, Honor Blackman; Brian, Ian Bannen; Dr. Cordell, John Gregson; Jim, George Cole; Chris, Dennis Waterman; Tara, Tara Collinson; Police Inspector, Maurice Kaufman; Police Sergeant, Michael Brennan; Constable, Roger Lloyd Pack.

1077 FRITZ THE CAT. (Cinemation-1972). Fritz, Skip Hinnant; Rosetta Le Noire, John McCurry, Judy Engles, Phil Seuling.

1078 FROGS. (American International-1972). Jason Crockett, Ray Milland; Pickett Smith, Sam Elliott; Karen, Joan Van Ark; Clint, Adam Roarke; Bella, Judy Pace; Jenny, Lynn Borden; Maybelle, Mae Mercer; Michael, David Gilliam; Kenneth, Nicholas Cortland; Stuart, George Skaff; Charles, Lance Taylor Sr.; Iris, Holly Irving; Tina, Dale Willingham; Jay, Hal Hodges; Lady in car, Carolyn Fitzsimmons; Young boy in car, Robert Sanders.

1079 FROM EAR TO EAR. (Cinemation-1971). Elisa, Nicole Debonne; Lucile, Solange Pradel; Josine, Daniele Argence; Beatrice, Liliane Bert; Borco, Robert Lombard; Bruno, Jean Gavin; Andre, Alain Doutey.

1080 FROM THE MIXED-UP FILES OF MRS. BASIL E. FRANKWEILER. (Cinema 5-1973). Mrs. Frankweiler, Ingrid Bergman; Claudia, Sally Prager; Jamie, Johnny Doran; Saxonburg, George Rose; Mr. Kincaid, Richard Mulligan; Mrs. Kincaid, Georgann Johnson; Schoolteacher, Madeline Kahn.

1081 THE FRONT PAGE. (Universal-1974). Hildy Johnson, Jack Lemmon; Walter Burns, Walter Matthau; Mollie Malloy, Carol Burnett; Peggy Grant, Susan Sarandon; Sheriff, Vincent Gardenia; Bensinger, David Wayne; Kruger, Allen Garfield; Earl Williams, Austin Pendleton; Murphy, Charles Durning; Schwartz, Herbert Edelman; Dr. Egglehofer, Martin Gabel; Mayor, Harold Gould; City Editor Duffy, John Furlong; Jacobi, Cliff Osmond; McHugh, Dick O'Neill; Keppler, John Korkes; Endicott, Lou Frizzell; Plunkett, Paul Benedict; Jennie, Doro Merande; Wilson, Noam Pitlik.

1082 FRONTIER HELLCAT. (Columbia-1966). Old Surehand, Stewart Granger; Winnetou, Pierre Brice; Annie, Elke Sommer; Martin Baumann, Goetz George; Old Baumann, Walter Barnes; Preston, Sieghardt Rupp; Weller, Mila Balch;

Leader, Renato Baldini; Baker Jr., Mario Girotti; Gordon, Louis Velle; Taddy Fox, Voja Miric, Stole Arandjelovic, Djordje Nenadovic, Georg Mitic, Gordana Cosic, Dusan Bulajic, Dunia Rajter.

1083 FROZEN ALIVE. (Magna-1966). Mark Stevens, Delphi Lawrence, Walter Rilla, Helmuth Weiss, Albert Bessler, Wolfgang Gunther, Sigurd Lohde, John Longden, Marianne Koch, Joachim Hansen, Wolfgang Lukschy.

1084 THE FROZEN DEAD. (Warner Bros.-7 Arts-1967). Dr. Norberg, Dana Andrews; Jean Norberg, Anna Palk; Dr. Ted Roberts, Philip Gilbert; Elsa Tenney, Kathleen Breck; Lubeck, Karel Stepanek; Tirpitz, Basil Henson; Karl Essen, Alan Tilvern; Mrs. Schmidt, Ann Tirard; Prisoner No. 3, Edward Fox; Joseph, Oliver MacGreevy; Inspector Witt, Tom Chatto; Stationmaster, John Moore; Porter, Charles Wade.

1085 FUEGO. (Haven International-1969). Laura, Isabel Sarli; Carlos, Armando Bo; Andrea, Alba Mujica; Zalazar, Roberto Airaldi.

1086 LA FUGA. (International Classics-1966). Piera Fabbri, Giovanna Ralli; Luisa, Anouk Aimee; Andrea Fabbri, Paul Guers; The Psychoanalyst, Enrico Maria Salerno; The Mother, Jone Salinas Musu.

1087 A FULL LIFE. (New Yorker-1972). Junko, Ineko Arima; Ichitaro, Koshiro Harada; Gen-ichi, I. George; Sadakichi, Takahiro Tamura; Harumi, Yukari Ohba; Karashima, Toyozo Yamamoto; Motoko, Miho Nagato; Motchin, Kaori Shima.

1088 FUN AND GAMES. (Audubon-1973). Alice Spivak, David Drew, Bob Hodge, Calvin Culver.

1089 FUNERAL IN BERLIN. (Paramount-1966). Harry Palmer, Michael Caine; Samantha Steele, Eve Renzi; Johnny Vulkan, Paul Hubschmid; Colonel Stok, Oscar Homolka; Ross, Guy Doleman; Mrs. Ross, Rachel Gurney; Hallam, Hugh Burden; Reinhart, Thomas Holtzmann; Kreutzmann, Gunter Meisner; Aaron Levine, Heinz Schubert; Werner, Wolfgang Volz; Otto Rukel, Klaus Jepsen; Artur, Herbert Fux; Benjamin, Rainer Brandt; Monika, Ira Hagen; Brigit, Marte Keller.

1090 FUNERAL PARADE OF ROSES. (New Yorker-1973). Eddie, Peter; Guenvara, Toyosaburo Uchiyama; Tony, Don Madrid; Eddie's Mother, Emiko Azuma; Gonda, Yoshio Tsuchiya.

1091 THE FUNNIEST MAN IN THE WORLD. (Evergreen-1969). Charles Chaplin, Mabel Normand, Chester Conklin, Fatty Arbuckle, Edna Purviance, Ben Turpin, Marie Dressler, Ford Sterling, Stan Laurel, Oliver Hardy.

1092 FUNNY GIRL. (Columbia-1968). Fanny Brice, Barbra Streisand; Nicky Arnstein, Omar Sharif; Rose Brice, Kay Medford; Georgia James, Anne Francis; Florenz Ziegfeld, Walter Pidgeon; Eddie Ryan, Lee Allen; Mrs. Strakosh, Mae Questel; Branca, Gerald Mohr; Keeney, Frank Faylen; Emma, Mittie Lawrence; Mrs. O'Malley, Gertrude Flynn; Mrs. Meeker, Penny Santon; Company Manager, John Harmon; The Ziegfeld Girls, Thordis Brandt, Bettina Brennan, Virginia Ann Ford, Alena Johnston, Karen Lee, Mary Jane Mangler, Inga Neilsen, Sharon Vaughn.

1093 A FUNNY THING HAPPENED ON THE WAY TO THE FORUM. (United Artists-1966). Pseudolus, Zero Mostel; Lycus, Phil Silvers; Erronius, Buster Keaton; Hysterium, Jack Gilford; Hero, Michael Crawford; Philia, Annette Andre; Domina, Patricia Jessel; Senex, Michael Hordern; Miles Gloriosus, Leon Greene; High Priestess, Pamela Brown; Gymnasia, Inga Neilsen; Vibrata, Myrna White; Panacea, Lucianne Bridou; Tintinabula, Helen Funai; Geminae, Jennifer and Susan Baker; Fertilla, Janet Webb.

1094 FUNNYMAN. (1971). Perry, Peter Bonerz; Sue, Sandra Archer; Sybil, Carol Androsky; Jan, Nancy Fish; Vogel, Budd Steinhilber; Sid, Marshall Efron; Heidi, Manuela Ruecker.

1095 THE FURTHER PERILS OF LAUREL AND HARDY. (20th Century-Fox-1968). Stan Laurel and Oliver Hardy; Narrator, Jay Jackson.

1096 FUTZ. (Commonwealth United-1969). Oscar, Seth Allen; Cyprus, John Bakos; Ann, Mari-Claire Charba; Sheriff, Peter Craig; Buford, Jerry Own Cunliffe; Riordon, Johnny Dodd; Marjorie, Beth Porter; Mother Satz, Jeannette Ertelt; Sugford, Fred Forrest; Jeffrey, Clay Haney; Emily, Jane Holzer; Merry, Sally Kirkland; Ned, Victor Lipari; Bill, Michael Warren Powell; Mrs. Loop, Marilyn Roberts; Clay, Sean Shapiro; Father Satz, Rob Thirkield; Dorn, Eric Wildwoode.

1097 FUZZ. (United Artists-1972). Det. Steve Carella, Burt Reynolds; Det. Meyer Meyer, Jack Weston; Det. Bert Kling, Tom Skerritt; Det. Eileen McHenry, Racquel Welch; Deaf Man, Yul Brynner; Det. Arthur Brown, James McEachin; Det. Andy Parker, Steve Ihnat; Det. Hal Willis, Stewart Moss; Lt. Byrnes, Dan Frazer; Sgt. Murchison, Bert Remsen; Patrolman Levine, H. Benny Markowitz; Patrolman Gomez, James Victor; Patrolman Cramer, Roy Applegate; Patrolman Crosby, Tom Lawrence; Police Commissioner Nelson, Norman Burton; Patrolman Marshall, Vince Howard; Patrolman Miscolo, Jake Lexa; Detectives, Britt Leach, Brian Doyle-Murray, Harold Oblong; Telephone Technician, J. S. Johnson; Police Garage Attendant, Harry Eldon Miller;

Mayor's Uniformed Guard, David Dreyer; Mayor's Bodyguard, William Martel; Buck, Peter Bonerz; Ahmad, Cal Bellini; LaBresca, Don Gordon; Pete, Charles Tyner; Jimmy, Gary Morgan; Baby, Charlie Martin Smith.

1098 LE GAI SAVOIR. (EYR-1970). Emile, Jean-Pierre Leaud; Patricia, Juliette Bertho.

1099 GAILY, GAILY. (United Artists-1969). Ben Harvey, Beau Bridges; Queen Lil, Melina Mercouri; Francis X. Sullivan, Brian Keith; Axel P. Johanson, George Kennedy; "Honest" Tim Grogan, Hume Cronyn; Adeline, Margot Kidder; The Governor, Wilfrid Hyde-White; Lilah, Melodie Johnson; Kitty, Joan Huntington; Father Harvey, John Randolph; Mother Harvey, Claudie Bryar; Virgil Harvey, Eric Shea; Grandma Harvey, Merie Earle; Frankie, James Christy; Dr. Lazarus, Charles Tyner; The Stranger, Harry Holcombe; Dunne, Roy Poole; Wally Hill, Clark Gordon; Swami, Peter Brocco; Mrs. Krump, Maggie Oleson; Chauffeur, Nikita Knatz.

1100 GALIA. (Zenith International-1966). Galia, Mireille Darc; Greg, Venantino Venantini; Nicole, Francoise Prevost; Wespyr, Francois Chaumette; Matik, Jacques Riberolles.

1101 GAMBIT. (Universal-1966). Nicole Chang, Shirley MacLaine; Harry Dean, Michael Caine; Ahmad Shahbandar, Herbert Lom; Ram, Roger C. Carmel; Abdul, Arnold Moss; Emil Fournier, John Abbott; Colonel Salim, Richard Angarola; Hotel Clerk, Maurice Marsac.

1102 THE GAMBLER. (Paramount-1974). Alex Freed, James Caan; Hips, Paul Sorvino; Billie, Lauren Hutton; A. R. Lowenthal, Morris Carnovsky; Naomi Freed, Jacqueline Brookes; Carmine, Burt Young; Jimmy, Carmine Caridi; Spencer, Carl W. Drudup; Cowboy, Stuart Margolin; One, Vic Tayback; Pimp, Antonio Fargas; Coach, William Andrews; Howie, Steven Keats; Monique, Starletta De Paur; Bank Officer, James Woods; Monkey, London Lee.

1103 THE GAMBLERS. (UM-1970). Candace, Suzy Kendall; Rooney, Don Gordon; Cozzier, Pierre Olaf; Broadfoot, Kenneth Griffith; Goldy, Stuart Margolin; Kobayashi, Richard Woo; Del Isolla, Massimo Serato; Signora Del Isolla, Faith Domergue; Nono, Tony Chinn.

1104 THE GAME IS OVER. (Royal-1967). Renee Saccard, Jane Fonda; Maxime Saccard, Peter McEnery; Alexandre Saccard, Michel Piccoli; Anne Sernet, Tina Marquand; M. Sernet, Jacques Monod; Mme. Sernet, Simone Valere; Mr. Chou, Ham Chau Luong; Lawyer, Howard Vernon; Maitre d'Hotel, Douglas Read; Guest, Germaine Montero.

1105 GAMES. (Universal-1967). Lisa Schindler, Simone Signoret; Paul Montgomery, James Caan; Jennifer Montgomery, Katharine Ross; Norman Fields, Don Stroud; Harry, Kent Smith; Miss Lillian Beattie, Estelle Winwood; Nora, Marjorie Bennett; Dr. Edwards, Ian Wolfe; Winthrop, Antony Eustrel; Celia, Eloise Hardt; Terry, George Furth; Holly, Carmen Phillips; Count, Peter Brocco; Baroness, Florence Marly; Arthur, Carl Guttenberger; Pharmacist, Pitt Herbert; Detective, Stuart Nisbet; Bookseller, Kendrick Huxham; Masseur, Richard Guizon.

1106 THE GAMES. (20th Century-Fox-1970). Harry Hayes, Michael Crawford; Bill Oliver, Stanley Baker; Scott Reynolds, Ryan O'Neal; Pavel Vendek, Charles Aznavour; Jim Harcourt, Jeremy Kemp; Christine, Elaine Taylor; Sunny Pinturbi, Athol Compton; Kovanda, Fritz Wepper; Kaverly, Kent Smith; Richie Robinson, Sam Elliott; Gilmour, Reg Lye; Mrs. Hayes, Mona Washbourne; Cal Wood, Don Newsome; Vera Vendek, Emmy Werner; Stuart Simmonds, Harvey Hall; Mae Harcourt, June Jago; Kubitsek, Karel Stepanek; Barmaid, Gwendolyn Watts; John, John Alkin; Dr. Tselsura, Dale Ishimoto; Juri Vendek, Alexander Werner; Commentators, Rafer Johnson, Rod Pickering, Adrian Metcalfe.

1107 THE GAMES MEN PLAY. (Joseph Brenner-1968). Wife, Maria Antinea; Prostitute, Amelia Bence; Bride, Elsa Daniel; Secretary, Mirtha Legrand; Teacher, Malvina Pastorina; Industrialist, Jose Cibrian; Ventriloquist, Narciso Ibanez Menta; Columnist, Angel Magana; Taxi Driver, Luis Sandrini; Musician, Enrique Serrano; Maid, Teresa Blasco; Bridegroom, Guillermo Bredeston; Model, Diana Ingro; Lady, Miryan De Urquijo; Muse, Leda Zando; Doctor, Guillermo Battaglia; Police Commissioner, Hector Calcano; Manager, Homero Carpena.

1108 GAMES OF DESIRE. (Times-1968). Nadine Anderson, Ingrid Thulin; Eliot T. Anderson, Paul Hubschmid; Nikos, Nikos Kourkoulos; Elektra, Claudine Auger; Martin, Bernard Verley; Gregor Von Rezzori, Helga Lehner, Inge Book, Helen Vita, Spyros Bakojannis, Eric Helgar, Cecilie Geler.

1109 GAMMERA THE INVINCIBLE. (World Entertainment-1967). Albert Dekker, Brian Donlevy, Diane Findlay, John Baragrey, Dick O'Neill, Eiji Funakoshi, Harumi Kiritachi, Junichiro Yamashita, Yoshiro Uchida, Michiko Sugata, Yoshiro Kitahara, Jun Hamamura.

1110 THE GANG THAT COULDN'T SHOOT STRAIGHT. (MGM-1971). Kid Sally, Jerry Orbach; Angela, Leigh Taylor-Young; Big Momma, Jo Van Fleet; Baccala, Lionel Stander; Mario, Robert De Niro; Big Jelly, Irving Selbst; Beppo, Herve Villechaize.

1111 GANGA ZUMBA. (New Yorker-1972). Antao, Antonio Pitanga; Cipriana, Lea Garcia; Arorba, Eliezer Gomes.

1112 GANJA AND HESS. (Kelly-Jordan-1973). Dr. Hess Green, Duane Jones; Ganja, Marlene Clark; George, Bill Gunn; Rev. Williams, Sam Waymon; Archie, Leonard Jackson; Girl in bar, Candece Tarpley; Dinner Guest, Richard Harrow; Jack, John Hoffmeister; Singer, Betty Barney; Queen of Myrthia, Mabel King; Poetess, Betsy Thurman; Green's Son, Enrico Fales; Pimp, Tommy Lane; Woman with baby, Tara Fields.

1113 THE GARDEN OF DELIGHTS. (Perry-Fleetwood-1971). Antonio, Jose Luis Lopez Vasquez; Luchy, Luchy Soto; Don Pedro, Francisco Pierra; Actress, Charo Soriano; Aunt, Lina Canalejas; Julia, Julia Pena; Nurse, Mayrata O'Wisledo; Nicole, Esperanza Roy; Tony, Alberto Alonso.

1114 THE GARDEN OF THE FINZI-CONTINIS. (Cinema V-1971). Micol, Dominique Sanda; Giorgio, Lino Capolicchio; Alberto, Helmut Berger; Malnate, Fabio Testi; Giorgio's Father, Romolo Valli.

1115 THE GARNET BRACELET. (Artkino-1966). Vera Nikolayevna, Ariadna Shengelaya; Zheltkov, Igor Ozerov; Vasili Lvovich, O. Basilashvili; Nikolai Nikolayevna, V. Strzhelchik; Anna Nikolayevna, N. Malyavina; Gon Friese, Y. Averin; Madam Zarzhitzkaya, O. Zhizneva; Kuprin, G. Gai.

1116 GAS-S-S-S-S! (American International-1970). Coel, Robert Corff; Cilla, Elaine Gifto; Demeter, Pat Patterson; Billy the Kid, George Armitage; Jason, Alex Wilson; Dr. Drake, Alan Braunstein; Carlos, Ben Vereen; Marissa, Cindy Williams; Hooper, Bud Cort; Coralie, Talia Coppola; Marshall, Lou Procopio; Ginny, Jackie Farley; Quant, Phil Borneo.

1117 THE GATLING GUN. (Ellman Enterprises-1973). Woody Strode, Guy Stockwell, Patrick Wayne, Robert Fuller, Barbara Luna, John Carradine.

1118 THE GAY DECEIVERS. (Fanfare-1969). Danny Devlin, Kevin Coughlin; Elliot Crane, Larry Casey; Karen, Brooke Bundy; Leslie Devlin, Jo Ann Harris; Malcolm, Michael Greer; Craig, Sebastian Brook; Colonel Dixon, Jack Starrett; Mr. Devlin, Richard Webb; Mrs. Devlin, Eloise Hardt; Mrs. Conway, Jeanne Baird; Carolyn Marishka; Psychiatrist, Mike Kopscha; Sgt. Kravits, Joe Tornatori; Real Estate Agent, Robert Reese; Duane, Christopher Riordan; Corporal, Doug Hume; Stern, David Osterhout; Sybil, Marilyn Wirt; Freddie, Ron Gans; Dorothy, Rachel Romen; Paul, Tom Grubbs; Bunny, Louise Williams; Sheryl, Randee Lynne; Phil, Meredith Williams; Georgette, Harry Sildoni; Laverne, Lenore Stevens; Jackie, Trigg Kelly; Vince, Tony Epper.

1119 THE GENESIS CHILDREN. (Lyric-1972). Vincent Child, Greg Hill, Peter Glawson, David Johnson, Jack Good, Butch Burr, Max Adams, Bubba Collins, Mike Good.

1120 GENGHIS KHAN. (Columbia-1965). Jamuga, Stephen Boyd; Temujin-Genghis Khan, Omar Sharif; Kam Ling, James Mason; The shah of Khwarezm, Eli Wallach; Bortei, Francoise Dorleac; Shah, Telly Savalas; The Emperor of China, Robert Morley; Geen, Michael Hordern; Katke, Yvonne Mitchell; Sengal, Woody Strode; Subodai, Kenneth Cope; Kassar, Roger Croucher; Jebai, Don Borisenko; Kuchluk, Patrick Holt; Chin Yu, Suzanne Hsaio.

1121 GENTLE GIANT. (Paramount-1968). Tom Wedloe, Dennis Weaver; Ellen Wedloe, Vera Miles; Fog Hanson, Ralph Meeker; Mark Wedloe, Clint Howard; Dink Smith, Huntz Hall; Mike McDonaugh, Charles Martin; Tater Coughlin, Rance Howard; Charlie Mason, Frank Schuller; Swenson, Robertson White; Mate, Ric O'Feldman; James Riddle, Frank Logan, Jerry Newby, Alfred Metz, Levirne De Bord.

1122 THE GENTLE PEOPLE AND THE QUIET LAND. (Commercial-1972). Toss, Patsy McBride; Claude, Reed Apaghian; Jacob, Robert Counsel; Terry, Jeff Warren; Souders, Harold Ayer; Bishop, Charles Knapp; Mrs. Ziegler, Martha Hulley; Little Eli, Philip Kurtz Jr.; Mrs. Souders, Pat Boyer.

1123 THE GENTLE RAIN. (Comet-1966). Bill Patterson, Christopher George; Judy Reynolds, Lynda Day; Nancy Masters, Fay Spain; Gloria, Maria Helena Diaz; Harry Masters, Lon Clark; Girl Friend, Barbara Williams; Hotel Manager, Robert Assumpaco; Jimmy, Herbert Moss; Jewelry Girl, Lorena; Nightclub Girl, Nadyr Fernandes.

1124 GEORGE! (Capital-1972). Jim Paulsen, Marshall Thompson; Walter Clark, Jack Mullaney; Erika Walters, Inge Schoner; Regina, Linda Caroll; Frau Gerber, Ursula Von Wiese; Herr Werner, Hermann Frick; Air Freight Man, Erwin Parker; Boat Owner, Raimund Bucher; Control Tower Operator, Frank Schacher; Ursula, Elisabeth Vonallmen; Monk, Edgar Reiser; 1st Girl Tourist, Brigitte Graubner; 2nd Girl Tourist, Dagmar Balmer; American Tourist, Wallace Bennett; Bell Boy, Jeff Barter.

1125 GEORGIA, GEORGIA. (Cinerama-1972). Georgia Martin, Diana Sands; Mrs. Alberta Anderson, Minnie Gentry; Herbert Thompson, Roger Furman; Bobo, Terry Whitmore; Michael Winters, Dirk Benedict; Diana Kjaer, Lars Eric Berenett, Stig Engstrom, Artie Sheppard, James Thomas Finlay Jr., Andrew Bates Jr., Randolph Henry, Beatrice Wendin, Tina Hedstrom.

1126 GEORGY GIRL. (Columbia-1966). James Leamington, James Mason; Jos, Alan Bates; Georgy Parkin, Lynn Redgrave; Meredith, Charlotte Rampling; Mr. Parkin, Bill Owen; Mrs. Parkin, Clare Kelly; Ellen Leamington, Rachel Kempson; Peg, Denise Coffey; Health Visitor, Dorothy Alison; Hospital Sister, Peggy Thorpe-Bates; Hospital Nurse, Dandy Nichols; Salesman, Terence Soall; Registry Office Clerk, Jolyan Booth.

1127 GERTRUD. (Pathe Contemporary-1966). Gertrud, Nina Pens Rode; Kanning, Bendt Rothe; Gabriel Lidman, Ebbe Rode; Jansson, Baard Owe; Nygren, Axel Strobye; Kanning's Mother, Anna Malberg.

1128 GET CARTER. (MGM-1971). Jack Carter, Michael Caine; Eric, Ian Hendry; Anna, Britt Ekland; Kinnear, John Osborne; Peter, Tony Beckley.

1129 GET ON WITH IT. (Governor-1965). Bob Monkhouse, Kenneth Connor, Shirley Eaton, Eric Barker, Reginald Beckwith, Richard Wattis, Sheena Marsh.

1130 GET TO KNOW YOUR RABBIT. (Warner Bros.-1972). Donald Beeman, Tom Smothers; Mr. Turnbull, John Astin; Paula, Suzanne Zenor; Susan, Samantha Jones; Vic, Allen Garfield; Terrific Looking Girl, Katharine Ross; Mr. Delasandro, Orson Welles; Mrs. Beeman, Hope Summers; Mr. Reese, Jack Collins; Mr. Morris, George Ives; Mr. Weber, Robert Ball; Mr. Wendell, M. Emmet Walsh; Mrs. Wendell, Helen Page Camp; Flo, Pearl Shear; Cop, Timothy Carey; Mr. Beeman, Charles Lane; Mr. Seager, Larry D. Mann; Mrs. Reese, Jessica Myerson; Stewardess, Anne Randall; Police Officer, Bob Einstein; TV Reporter, King Moody; Miss Parsons, Judy Marcione.

1131 GET YOURSELF A COLLEGE GIRL. (MGM-1965). Terry, Mary Ann Mobley; Gary, Chad Everett; Marge, Joan O'Brien; Lynne, Nancy Sinatra; Sue, Chris Noel; Senator, Willard Waterman; Armand, Fabrizio Mioni; Gordon, James Millhollin; Ray, Paul Todd; Donnie, Donnie Brooks; Donna, Hortense Petra; Dean, Dorothy Neumann; Secretary, Marti Barris; Bellboy, Mario Costello; Dave Clark Five, Stan Getz, Jimmy Smith Trio, The Animals, Astrud Gilberto, The Standells, The Rhythm Masters, Roberta Linn, Freddie Bell.

1132 THE GETAWAY. (National General-1972). Doc McCoy, Steve McQueen; Carol McCoy, Ali MacGraw; Jack Benyon, Ben Johnson; Fran Clinton, Sally Struthers; Rudy Butler, Al Lettieri; Cowboy, Slim Pickens; Thief, Richard Bright; Harold Clinton, James Dodson; Laughlin, Dub Taylor; Frank Jackson, Bo Hopkins.

1133 GETTING STRAIGHT. (Columbia-1970). Harry Bailey, Elliott Gould; Jan, Candice Bergen; Dr. Willhunt, Jeff Corey; Ellis, Max Julien; Nick, Robert F. Lyons; Dr. Kasper, Cecil Kellaway; Vandenburg, Jon Lormer; Lysander, Leonard Stone; Wade Linden, William Bramley; Judy Kramer, Jeannie Berlin; Herbert, John Rubinstein; Landlady, Billie Bird; Dr. Greengrass, Richard Anders; Luan, Brenda Sykes; Garcia, Gregory Sierra; Sheila, Jenny Sullivan; Cynthia, Hilarie Thompson; Jake, Harrison Ford; Mrs. Stebbins, Irene Tedrow; Alice Linden, Elizabeth Lane; Roommate, Joanna Serpe; Dean Chesney, Harry Holcombe; Airline Representative, Scott Perry.

1134 GHIDRA, THE THREE-HEADED MONSTER. (Continental-1966). Yosuke Natsuki, Yuriko Hoshi, Kiroshi Koizumi, Takashi Shimura, Em Ito, Yumi Ito.

1135 THE GHOST. (Magna-1966). Barbara Steele, Peter Baldwin, Elio Jotta, Harriet White, Raoul H. Newman, Reginald Price Anderson.

1136 THE GHOST AND MR. CHICKEN. (Universal-1966). Luther Heggs, Don Knotts; Alma Parker, Joan Staley; Mr. Kelsey, Liam Redmond; George Beckett, Dick Sargent; Ollie Weaver, Skip Homeier; Mrs. Maxwell, Reta Shaw; Mrs. Miller, Lurene Tuttle; Nick Simmons, Philip Ober; Police Chief Art Fuller, Harry Hickox; Whitlow, Charles Lane; Jesslyn Fax, Nydia Westman, George Chandler, Robert Cornthwaite, James Begg, J. Edward McKinley, Eddie Quillan, Sandra Gould, James Milhollin, Cliff Norton, Ellen Corby, Jim Boles, Hope Summers, Hal Smith.

1137 GHOST IN THE INVISIBLE BIKINI. (American International-1966). Chuck Phillips, Tommy Kirk; Lili Morton, Deborah Walley; Bobby, Aron Kincaid; Sinistra, Quinn O'Hara; J. Sinister Hulk, Jesse White; Eric Von Zipper, Harvey Lembeck; Vicki, Nancy Sinatra; Lulu, Claudia Martin; Malcolm, Francis X. Bushman; Chicken Feather, Benny Rubin; Princess Yolanda, Bobbi Shaw; Monstro, George Barrows; Shirl, Luree Holmes; Piccola, Piccola Pupa; Alberta, Alberta Nelson; J. D., Andy Romano; Themselves, The Bobby Fuller Four; Reginald Ripper, Basil Rathbone; Myrtle Forbush, Patsy Kelly; Hiram Stokley, Boris Karloff; Cecily, Susan Hart; Ed Garner, Mary Hughes, Patti Chandler, Frank Alexia, Salli Sachse, Sue Hamilton, Myrna Ross, Jerry Brutsche, Bob Harvey, John Macchia, Alan Fife.

1138 GHOSTS--ITALIAN STYLE. (MGM-1969). Maria, Sophia Loren; Pasquale, Vittorio Gassman; Alfredo, Mario Adorf; Sayonara, Margaret Lee; Raffaele, Aldo Giuffre; Professor Santanna, Francesco Tensi; Headless Ghost, Marcello Mastroianni.

1139 GINGER. (Joseph Brenner-1971). Ginger, Cheri Caffaro; Jean, Cindy Barnett; Jimmy, Herb Kerr; Jason, William Grannell; Vicki, Michele Norris; Elizabeth, Lise Mauer; Allison, Herndon Ely; Rex, Duane Tucker; Rodney, Calvin Culver; D. J., David Ross; Brad, Chuck Ames; William, Art Burns; Stanley, Tom Potter.

1140 THE GIRL AND THE BUGLER. (Artkino-1967). Lena Proklova, Rolan Bykov, Victor Belokurov, Lena Zolotuhina, Vitya Kosykh, S. Nikonenko, Olya Semyonova, Vitya Sysoyev.

1141 THE GIRL AND THE GENERAL. (MGM-1967). The General, Rod Steiger; Ada, Virna Lisi; Private Tarasconi, Umberto Orsini.

1142 THE GIRL FROM PETROVKA. (Universal-1974). Oktyabrina, Goldie Hawn; Joe, Hal Holbrook; Kostya, Anthony Hopkins; Minister, Gregoire Aslan; Balletmaster, Anton Dolin; Alexander, Bruno Wintzell; Leonid, Zoran Andric; Judge, Hanna Hertelendy.

1143 THE GIRL-GETTERS. (American International-1966). Tinker, Oliver Reed; Nicola, Jane Merrow; Suzy Barbara Ferris; Lorna, Julia Foster; Larsey, Harry Andrews; Ella, Ann Lynn; Philip, Guy Doleman; Willy, Andrew Ray; Grib, John Porter Davison; Sneakers, Clive Colin Bowler; Sammy, Ian Gregory; David, David Hemmings; Nidge, John Alderton; Ivor, Jeremy Burnham; Michael Mark Burns; James, Derek Nimme; Sylvie, Pauline Munro; Alfred, Derek Newark; Marianne, Stephanie Beaumont; Helga, Talitha Pol; Ingrid, Dora Reisser; Jasmin, Susan Burnet.

1144 GIRL HAPPY. (MGM-1965). Rusty Wells, Elvis Presley; Valerie, Shelley Fabares; Andy, Gary Crosby; Sunny Daze, Nita Talbot; Wilbur, Joby Baker; Deena, Mary Ann Mobley; Big Frank, Harold J. Stone.

1145 THE GIRL IN BLUE. (Cinerama-1974). David Selby, Maud Adams, Gay Rowan, William Osler, Diane Dewey, Michael Kirby, Walter Wakefield, Don Arioli, Valda Dalton, Guy Martin, Michel Maillot, Hanka Poznanska.

1146 THE GIRL ON A MOTORCYCLE. (Claridge-1968). Daniel, Alain Delon; Rebecca, Marianne Faithfull; Raymond, Roger Mutton; Rebecca's Father, Marius Goring; Catherine, Catherine Jourdan; Jean, Jean Leduc; Pump Attendant, Jacques Marin; French Superintendent, Andre Maranne; French Customs Officers, Bari Johnson and Arnold Diamond; German Customs Officer, John G. Heller; German Waitress, Marika Rivera; Students, Richard Blake, Christopher Williams, Colin West and Kit Williams.

1147 THE GIRL WHO COULDN'T SAY NO. (20th Century-Fox-1970). Yolanda, Virna Lisi; Franco, George Segal; Yolanda's Mother, Lila Kedrova; Uncle Egidio, Akim Tamiroff; Paola Pitagora, Felicity Mason, Richard Brill, Jeffrey Copplestone, Vera Nandi.

1148 THE GIRL WHO KNEW TOO MUCH. (Commonwealth-1969). Johnny, Adam West; Revel, Nancy Kwan; Allardice, Robert Alda; Lucky, Buddy Greco; Lt. Crawford, Nehemiah Persoff; Had, David Brian.

1149 THE GIRL WITH HUNGRY EYES. (Boxoffice International-1966). Cathy Crowfoot, Vicky Dee, Shannon Carse, Scott Avery, Oswald Fenwick, Pat Barrington, Vicky Kober, Sharon Smith, Billie Russell, Charlotte Stewart, Frankie O'Brien.

1150 THE GIRL WITH THE HATBOX. (Artkino-1970). Girl, Anna Sten; Boy, Ivan Koval-Samborsky; Wife, Serafina Birman; Stationmaster, Vladimir Fogel; Husband, Pavel Pol.

1151 THE GIRL WITH THREE CAMELS. (Continental-1968). Bobina's Mother, Slavka Budinova; Bobina, Zuzana Ondrouchova; Alfred, Radovan Lukavsky; Josef Pepik, Jan Langsadl; Mother's First Lover, Vladimir Pospisil.

1152 THE GIRLS. (New Line-1972). Liz, Bibi Andersson; Marianne, Harriet Andersson; Gunilla, Gunnel Lindblom; Hugo, Gunnar Bjornstrand; Carl, Erland Josephson; The Doctor, Frank Sundstrom; Bengt, Ake Lindstrom; Thommy, Stig Engstrom; The Director, Ulf Palme; Margaret Weivers, Leif Liljeroth.

1153 GIRLS ARE FOR LOVING. (Continental-1973). Ginger, Cheri Caffaro; Clay, Timothy Brown; Ronnie, Jocelyn Peters; James, Scott Ellsworth; William, Fred Vincent; Mateo, Robert C. Jefferson; Mark, Rod Loomis; Mr. Secretary, Larry Douglas; Neil, Anthony C. Cannon; Jason, William Grannel; Ambassador, Yuki Shimoda.

1154 THE GIRLS ON THE BEACH. (Paramount-1965). Martin West, Noreen Corcoran, Peter Brooks, Michael Love, Alan Jardin, Carl Wilson, Dennis Wilson, Jerry Allison, Jerry Naylor, Sonny Curtis, Arnold Lessing, Linda Marshall, Steven Rogers, Anna Capri, Aron Kincaid, Sheila Bromley, Mary Mitchel, Gale Gerber, Linda Saunders, Mary Kate Denny, Nan Morris, Lana Wood, Pat Deming, Michele Corcoran, Jean Lewis, Joan Conrath, Rick Newton, Lesley Gore, Nancy Spry, Ron Kennedy, Bruno Vesota, Lynn Cartwright, Richard Miller, Leo Gordon, Helen Kay Stephens.

1155 GIRLY. (Cinerama-1970). Girly, Vanessa Howard; New Friend, Michael Bryant; Mumsy, Ursula Howells; Nanny, Pat

Heywood; Sonny, Howard Trevor; Soldier, Robert Swan; Girlfriend, Imogen Hassall; Zoo attendant, Michael Ripper; Friend in Five, Hugh Armstrong.

1156 GIT! (Embassy-1965). Deke, Jack Chaplain; Elaine, Heather North; Finney, Leslie Bradley; Andrew Garrett, Richard Webb; Mrs. Finney, Hannah Landy; T. C. Knox, Emory Parnell; Jed, Joseph Hamilton; District Attorney, Richard Valentine; Police Sergeant, Jeff Burton; Dr. Allen, Sherry Moreland; Sam Lewis, Shug Fisher; Rock, Seldom Seen Sioux.

1157 GIVE HER THE MOON. (United Artists-1970). Gabriel, Philippe Noiret; Broderick, Bert Convy; Dorothy, Dorothy Marchini; Madeleine, Valentina Cortese; Capt. Ragot, Fernand Gravey; Marie, Marthe Keller; Leopold, Jean-Pierre Marielle; Aurore, Didi Perego; Postman, Henri Cremieux; Jean-Jules, Francois Perier.

1158 THE GLASS BOTTOM BOAT. (MGM-1965). Jennifer Nelson, Doris Day; Bruce Templeton, Rod Taylor; Axel Nordstrom, Arthur Godfrey; Ralph Goodwin, John McGiver; Homer Cripps, Paul Lynde; Gen. Wallace Bleecker, Edward Andrews; Edgar Hill, Eric Fleming; Julius Pritter, Dom De Luise; Zack Molloy, Dick Martin; Nina Bailey; Elisabeth Fraser; Mr. Fenimore, George Tobias; Mrs. Fenimore, Alice Pearce; Anna Miller, Ellen Corby; Donna, Dee J. Thompson; Napoleon Solo, Robert Vaughn.

1159 GLASS HOUSES. (Columbia-1972). Victor, Bernard Barrow; Kim, Deirdre Lenihan; Jean, Jennifer O'Neill; Victor's Wife, Ann Summers; Ted, Philip Pine; The Novelist, Clarke Gordon; Gar Campbell, Tom Toner, Lorna Thayer, Logan Ramsey, Maury Hill, Holly Irving, Mary Carver, All Checco, Joan Kaye, Janice Barr, Alma Beltran, Lloyd Kino, James Wellman, Tom J. Halligan, Eve McVeagh, William Cort, Albert Popwell, Laurie Hagen, Robert Karnes, Karen Lind, David Morick, George Berkley, Anita Raffi, Jack Grinnage, Elizabeth Ross, Jack Mattis, John Wyler, Davis Roberts, Chris Carmody, Rhoda Anderson, Pat Walter, Ruth Stanley.

1160 THE GLASS SPHINX. (American International-1968). Professor Karl Nichols, Robert Taylor; Paulette, Anita Ekberg; Jenny, Gianna Serra; Ray, Jack Stuart; Alex, Angel Del Pozo; Theo Jose Truchado; Mirko, Remo De Angelis; Fouad, Emad Hamdy.

1161 GLEN AND RANDA. (UMC-1971). Glen, Steven Curry; Randa, Shelley Plimpton; Sidney, Woodrow Chambliss; Magician, Garry Goodrow; Roy Rox, Robert Holmer, Hubert Powers, William Fratis, Alice Huffman, Ortega Sangster, Richard Frazier, Charles Huffman, Barbara Spiegel, Martha

Furey, Leonard Johnson, Jack Tatarsky, Laura Hawbecker, Lucille Johnson, Dwight Tate, Mary Henry, Matthew Levine, Bud Thompson, Talmadge Holiday, James Nankerius, Winona Tomanoczy, David Woeller.

1162 THE GLORY GUYS. (United Artists-1965). Demas Harrod, Tom Tryon; Sol Rogers, Harve Presnell; Lou Woodward, Senta Berger; Dugan, James Caan; General McCabe, Andrew Duggan; Gregory, Slim Pickens; Hodges, Peter Breck; Mrs. McCabe, Jeanne Cooper; Beth, Laurel Goodwin; Crain, Adam Williams; Gentry, Erik Holland; Marcus, Robert McQueeney; Moyan, Wayne Rogers; Teadway, William Meigs; Mrs. Poole, Alice Backes; Lt. Cook, Walter Scott; Marshall Cushman, Michael Forest; Hanavan, George Ross; Gunsmith, Dal McKennon; Gen. Hoffman, Stephen Chase; Salesman, Henry Beckman; Martin Hale, Michael Anderson, Jr.

1163 THE GLORY STOMPERS. (American International-1968). Chino, Dennis Hopper; Darryl, Jody McCrea; Chris, Chris Noel; Smiley, Jock Mahoney; Jo Ann, Sondra Gale; Paul, Jim Reader; Magoo, Robert Tessier; Doreen, Astrid Warner; Pony, Gary Wood; Monk, Lindsay Crosby; Mouth, Casey Kasem.

1164 THE GNOME-MOBILE. (Buena Vista-1967). D. J. Mulrooney, Walter Brennan; Knobby, Walter Brennan; Jasper, Tom Lowell; Rodney Winthrop, Matthew Garber; Elizabeth Winthrop, Karen Dotrice; Rufus, Ed Wynn; Ralph Yarby, Richard Deacon; Horatio Quaxton, Sean McClory; Violet, Cami Sebring; Dr. Conrad Ramsey, Jerome Cowan; Dr. Scroggins, Charles Lane; Norman Grabowski, Gil Lamb, Maudie Prickett, Ellen Corby, Frank Cady, Hal Baylor, Karl Held, Charles Smith, Byron Foulger, Susan Flannery, Ernestine Barrier, Dee Carroll, William Fawcett, Robert S. Carson, Jack Davis, John Cliff, Mickey Martin, Mark Allen, Alvy Moore, Dale Van Sickle, Parley Baer, Jimmy Murphy, Dee Carroll, Jesslyn Fax, Pamela Gail, Susan Gates, Jacki Ray, Joyce Menges, Susan and Bunn Henning.

1165 THE GO-BETWEEN. (Columbia-1971). Marian-Lady Trimingham, Julie Christie; Ted Burgess, Alan Bates; "Leo" Colston, Dominic Guard; Mrs. Maudsley, Margaret Leighton; Leo Colston, Michael Redgrave; Mr. Maudsley, Michael Gough.

1166 GOD FORGIVES--I DON'T! (American International-1969). Cat, Terence Hill; Bill San Antonio, Frank Wolff; Earp, Bud Spencer; Rose, Gian Rovere; Bud, Jose Manuel Martin.

1167 THE GODFATHER. (Paramount-1972). Don Vito Corleone, Marlon Brando; Michael Corleone, Al Pacino; Sonny Corleone, James Caan; Clemenza, Richard Castellano; Tom Hagen,

Robert Duvall; McCluskey, Sterling Hayden; Jack Woltz, John Marley; Barzini, Richard Conte; Kay Adams, Diane Keaton; Sollozzo, Al Lettieri; Tessio, Abe Vigoda; Connie Rizzi, Talia Shire; Carlo Rizzi, Gianni Russo; Fredo Corleone, John Cazale; Cuneo, Rudy Bond; Johnny Fontane, Al Martino; Mama Corleone, Morgana King; Luca Brazi, Lenny Montana; Paulie Gatto, John Martino; Bonasera, Salvatore Corsitto; Neri, Richard Bright; Moe Greene, Alex Rocco; Bruno Tattaglia, Tony Giorgio; Nazorine, Vito Scotti; Theresa Hagen, Tere Livrano; Phillip Tattaglia, Victor Livrano; Lucy Mancini, Jeannie Linero; Sandra Corleone, Julie Gregg; Mrs. Clemenza, Ardell Sheridan; Spollonia, Simonetta Stefanelli; Fabrizio, Angelo Infanti; Don Tomasino, Corrado Gaipa; Calo, Franco Citti; Vitelli, Saro Urzi.

1168 THE GODFATHER, PART II. (Paramount-1974). Michael, Al Pacino; Tom Hagen, Robert Duvall; Kay, Diane Keaton; Vito Corleone, Robert De Niro; Fredo Corleone, John Cazale; Connie Corleone, Talia Shire; Hyman Roth, Lee Strasberg; Frankie Pentangeli, Michael V. Gazzo; Senator Pat Geary, G. D. Spradlin; Al Neri, Richard Bright; Fanutti, Gaston Moschin; Rocco Lampone, Tom Rosqui; Young Clemenza, B. Kirby Jr.; Genco, Frank Sivero; Young Mama Corleone, Francesca Da Sapio; Mama Corleone, Morgana King; Deanna Corleone, Marianna Hill; Signor Roberto, Leopoldo Trieste; Johnny Ola, Dominic Chianese; Michael's Bodyguard, Amerigo Tot; Merle Johnson, Troy Donahue; Young Tessio, John Aprea; Theresa Hagen, Tere Livrano; Carlo, Gianni Russo; Willi Cicci, Joe Spinell; Vito's mother, Maria Carta; Vitor Andolini (as boy), Oreste Baldini; Don Francesco, Giuseppe Sillato; Don Tommasino, Mario Cotone; Anthony Corleone, James Gounaris; Marcia Roth, Fay Spain; FBI Man 1, Harry Dean Stanon; FBI Man 2, David Baker.

1169 THE GODSON. (Artists International-1972). Jef Costello, Alain Delon; Jane Lagrange, Nathalie Delon; The Inspector, Francois Perier; Valerie, Cathy Rosier; The Gunman, Jacques Leroy; Olivier Rey, Jean-Pierre Posier; Hatcheck Girl, Catherine Jourdan; Wiener, Michel Boisrond; Barman, Robert Favart; Garage Man, Andre Salgues; Policemen, Roger Fradet, Carlo Nell, Robert Rondo, Andre Thorent; Damolini, Georges Casati; Garcia, Jack Leonard; Police Clerk, Jacques Deschamps.

1170 GODSPELL. (Columbia-1973). Jesus, Victor Garber; John/Judas, David Haskell; Jerry, Jerry Sroka; Lynne, Lynne Thigpen; Katie, Katie Hanely; Robin, Robin Lamont; Gilmer, Gilmer McCormick; Joanne, Joanne Jonas; Merrell, Merrell Jackson; Jeffrey, Jeffrey Mylett.

1171 GODZILLA VS. THE SMOG MONSTER. (American International-1972). Doctor Yano, Akira Yamaguchi; Ken Yano, Hiroyuki Kawase; Mrs. Yano, Toshie Kimura; Yukio Keuchi,

Toshio Shibaki; Miki Fujiyama, Keiko Mari.

1172 GO-GO BIGBEAT! (Eldorado-1965). Millie Small, The Animals, Lulu and The Luvvers, The Four Pennies, The Applejacks, The Merseybeats, The Hollies, The Wackers, The Cockneys, Brian Poole and The Tremeloes, The Magil 5, The Swinging Blue Jeans, The Tornadoes, Mods and the Rockers, The Western Theatre Ballet Company, The Cheynes.

1173 GO GO MANIA. (American International-1965). The Beatles, The Animals, Matt Monro, The Nashville Teens, Susan Maughan, The Rockin' Berries, The Honeycombs, Herman's Hermits, The Four Pennies, Peter and Gordon, The Fourmost, Sounds Incorporated, Billy Davis, The Spencer Davis Group, Billy J. Kramer and the Dakotas, Tom Quickly and the Remo Four, Jimmy Savile.

1174 GOIN' DOWN THE ROAD. (Chevron-1970). Peter, Doug McGrath; Joey, Paul Bradley; Betty, Jayne Eastwood; Celina, Gayle Chernin; Nicole, Nicole Morin; Plant Foreman, Pierre La Roche; Girl in record shop, Sheila White.

1175 GOING HOME. (MGM-1971). Harry K. Graham, Robert Mitchum; Jenny, Brenda Vaccaro; Jimmy Graham, Jan-Michael Vincent.

1176 GOLD. (Allied Artists-1974). Rod Slater, Roger Moore; Terry Steyner, Susannah York; Harry Hirschfeld, Ray Milland; Manfred Steyner, Bradford Dillman; Farrell, John Gielgud; Big King, Simon Sabela; Tony Beckley, Bernard Horsfall, Marc Smith, John Hussey, Norman Coombes, George Jackson, Michael McGovern, Andre Maranne, John Bay, Paul Hansard.

1177 GOLDEN NEEDLES. (American International-1974). Dan, Joe Don Baker; Felicity, Elizabeth Ashley; Jeff, Jim Kelly; Winters, Burgess Meredith; Finzie, Ann Sothern; Lin Toa, Roy Chiao; Su Lin, Frances Fong; Kwan, Tony Lee; Lotus, Alice Fong; Claude, Clarence Barnes; Winters' man, Pat Johnson; Bobby, Edgar Justice.

1178 THE GOLDEN VOYAGE OF SINBAD. (Columbia-1974). Sinbad, John Phillip Law; Margiana, Caroline Munro; Koura, Tom Baker; Vizier, Douglas Wilmer; Rachid, Martin Shaw; Hakim, Gregoire Aslan; Haroun, Kurt Christian; Achmed, Takis Emmanuel; Abdul, John D. Garfield; Omar, Aldo Sambrell.

1179 GOLDSTEIN. (Altura-1965). Old Man, Lou Gilbert; Sally, Eileen Madison; Sculptor, Thomas Erhart; Jay, Benito Carruthers; Mr. Nice, Charles Fischer; Doctor, Severn Darden; Aid, Anthony Holland; Nelson Algren, himself.

1180 GONE IN 60 SECONDS. (H. B. Halicki International-1974). H. B. Halicki, Marion Busia, Jerry Daugirda, James McIntyre, George Cole, Ronald Halicki, Markos Kotsikos, Parnelli Jones, Gary Bettenhausen, Jonathan E. Fricke, Hal McClair, J. C. Agajanian, Billy Englehart, Mayor Sak Yamamoto (of Carson, California).

1181 GONE WITH THE WIND. (MGM-1967 Re-release of a 1939 production). Scarlett O'Hara, Vivien Leigh; Rhett Butler, Clark Gable; Ashley Wilkes, Leslie Howard; Melanie Hamilton, Olivia de Havilland; Mammy, Hattie McDaniel; Gerald O'Hara, Thomas Mitchell; Ellen O'Hara, Barbara O'Neil; Frank Kennedy, Caroll Nye; Aunt Pittypat Hamilton, Laura Hope Crews; Doctor Meade, Harry Davenport; Charles Hamilton, Rand Brooks; Belle Watling, Ona Munson; Carreen O'Hara, Ann Rutherford; Brent Tarleton, George Reeves; Stuart Tarleton, Fred Crane; Suellen O'Hara, Evelyn Keyes; Prissy, Butterfly McQueen; Pork, Oscar Polk; Mrs. Merriwether, Jane Darwell; Mrs. Meade, Leona Roberts; Big Sam, Everett Brown; Bonnie Blue Butler, Cammie King.

1182 THE GOOD GUYS AND THE BAD GUYS. (Warner Bros.-7 Arts-1969). Flagg, Robert Mitchum; McKay, George Kennedy; Waco, David Carradine; Carmel, Tina Louise; Grundy, Douglas V. Fowley; Mary, Lois Nettleton; Mayor Wilker, Martin Balsam; Deuce, John Davis Chandler; Ticker, John Carradine; Polly, Marie Windsor; Boyle, Dick Peabody; Mrs. Stone, Kathleen Freeman; Buckshot, Jimmy Murphy; Hawkins, Garrett Lewis; Engineer #2, Nick Dennis.

1183 GOOD MORNING AND GOODBYE! (Eve-1968). Angel, Alaina Capri; Burt, Stuart Lancaster; Stone, Pat Wright; The Catalyst, Haji; Lana, Karen Ciral; Ray, Don Johnson; Herb, Tom Howland; Lottie, Megan Timothy; Betty, Toby Adler; Go Go Dancer, Sylvia Tedemar; Nude, Carol Peters.

1184 THE GOOD, THE BAD AND THE UGLY. (United Artists-1968). Joe, Clint Eastwood; Tuco, Eli Wallach; Setenza, Lee Van Cleef; Aldo Giuffre, Mario Brega, Rada Rassimov, Claudio Scarchilli, Livio Lorenzon, Sandro Sarchelli, Benito Stefanelli, Silvana Bacci, Angelo Novi, Antonio Casale, Al Mulloch, Enzo Petito, Luigi Pistilli, Chelo Alonso.

1185 GOOD TIMES. (Columbia-1967). Themselves, Sonny and Cher; Mr. Mordicus, George Sanders; Warren, Norman Alden; Smith, Larry Duran; Tough Hombre, Kelly Thordsen; Leslie Garth, Lennie Weinrib; Brandon, Peter Robbins; Mordicus' Girls, Edy Williams, China Lee, Diane Haggerty; Lieutenant, James Flavin; Phil Arnold, Hank Worden, Morris Buchanan, Charles Smith, John Cliff, Herk Reardon, Bruce Tegner, Richard Collier, Howard Wright, Joe Devlin, Mike Kopach.

1186 GOODBYE, COLUMBUS. (Paramount-1969). Neil Klugman, Richard Benjamin; Brenda Patimkin, Ali MacGraw; Mr. Patimkin, Jack Klugman; Mrs. Patimkin, Nan Martin; Ron Patimkin, Michael Meyers; Julie Patimkin, Lori Shelle; Carlotta, Royce Wallace; Aunt Gladys, Sylvie Strauss; Doris, Kay Cummings; Don Farber, Michael Nurie; Aunt Molly, Betty Grayson; Uncle Leo, Monroe Arnold; Busboy, Richard Wexler; Sarah Ehrlich, Elaine Swann; Uncle Max, Rubin Schafer; Model, Jackie Smith; John McKee, Bill Derringer; Simp, Mari Gorman; Harriet, Gail Ommerle; Jan Peerce, Max Peerce, Anthony McGowan, Chris Schenkel, David Benedict, Ray Baumel, Delos Smith.

1187 GOODBYE GEMINI. (Cinerama-1970). Jacki, Judy Geeson; Julian, Martin Potter; Harrington-Smith, Michael Redgrave; Clive, Alexis Kanner; Rod, Mike Pratt; Denise Marian Diamond; David, Freddie Jones; Inspector, Peter Jeffrey; Nigel, Terry Scully; Mrs. McLean, Daphne Heard; Minister, Laurence Hardy; Georgiu, Joseph Furst; Taxi driver, Brian Wilde; Myra, Ricky Renee; Audrey, Barry Scott; Stallholder, Hilda Barry; Barman, Jack Connell.

1188 GOODBYE, MR. CHIPS. (MGM-1969). Arthur Chipping, Peter O'Toole; Katherine, Petula Clark; Headmaster, Michael Redgrave; Lord Sutterwick, George Baker; Ursula Mossbank, Sian Phillips; Max Staefel, Michael Bryant; William Baxter, Jack Hedley; Headmaster's Wife, Alison Legatt; Bill Calbury, Clinton Greyn; Mrs. Paunceforth, Barbara Couper; Johnny Longbridge, Michael Culver; Lady Sutterwick, Elspet Gray; General Paunceforth, Clive Morton; Algie, Ronnie Stevens; Sutterwick Jr., John Gugolka; Farley, Tom Owen; David, Michael Ridgway; Pompeii Guide, Mario Maranzana; Tilly, Sheila Steafel; Johnson, Jeremy Lloyd; Mrs. Summersthwaite, Elspeth March; New Boy, Craig Marriott; Price, Jack May; Elder Master, Leo Britt; Policeman, Boyston Tickner; Miss Honeybun, Patricia Hayes; The Boys of Sherbourne School.

1189 GORDON'S WAR. (20th Century-Fox-1973). Gordon, Paul Winfield; Bee, Carl Lee; Otis, David Downing; Roy, Tony King; Spanish Harry, Gilbert Lewis; Luther the Pimp, Carl Gordon; Big Pink, Nathan C. Heard; Mary, Grace Jones; Bedroom Girl, Jackie Page; Caucasian, Charles Bergansky; Bustler, Adam Wade; Dog Salesman, Hansford Rowe; Goose, Warren Taurien; Black Hit Man, Ralph Wilcox; Hotel Proprietor, David Connell; Gordon's wife, Richelle LeNoir; Gray Haired Executive, Michael Galloway.

1190 THE GORGON. (Columbia-1965). Peter Cushing, Christopher Lee, Richard Pasco, Michael Goodliffe, Barbara Shelley.

1191 GOSH! (Tom Scheuer-1974). Alice Goodbody, Sharon Kelly;

Myron Mittleman, Daniel Kauffman; Rex Livingston, Keith McConnell; Manny Spearman, Arem Fisher; J. C. Van Himmel, Norman Field; Roger Merkel, C. D. LaFleure; Arnold Nern, Norman Sheridan; Yvonne, Lorna Thayer; Maurice Millard, William Wanrooy, Vic Caesar, Irving Wasserman, Angela Carnon.

1192 THE GOSPEL ACCORDING TO ST. MATTHEW. (Continental-1966). Jesus Christ, Enrique Irazoqui; Mary (young), Margherita Caruso; Mary (old), Susanna Pasolini; Joseph, Marcello Morante; John the Baptist, Mario Socrate; Peter, Settimo Di Porto; Judas, Otello Sestili; Matthew, Ferruccio Nuzzo; John, Giacomo Morante; Andrew, Alfonso Gatto; Enzo Siciliano, Giorgio Agamben, Guido Cerretani, Luigi Barbini, Marcello Galdini, Elio Spaziani, Rosario Migale, Rodolfo Wilcock, Alessandro Tasca, Amerigo Bevilacqua, Francesco Leonetti, Franca Cupane, Paola Tedesco, Rosana Di Rocco, Elseo Boschi, Natalia Ginsburg, Renato Terra.

1193 GOSPEL ROAD. (20th Century-Fox-1973). Jesus, Robert Elfstrom; Mary Magdalene, June Carter Cash; John the Baptist, Larry Lee; Peter, Paul Smith; Nicodemus, Alan Dater; Child Jesus, Robert Elfstrom Jr.; John, Gelles LaBlanc; Matthew, Terrance Winston Mannock; Judas, Thomas Leventhal; James, John Paul Kay; Thomas, Sean Armstrong; Andrew, Lyle Nicholson; Philip, Steven Chernoff; Nathaniel, Stuart Clark; Thaddeus, Ulf Pollack; Simon, Jonathan Sanders.

1194 GOYOKIN. (Toho-1970). Magobei, Tatsuya Nakadel; Taito, Tetsuro Tamba; Sanmon, Kinnosuka Nakamura; Oriha, Ruriko Asaoka.

1195 GRACE'S PLACE. (L.A.C.-1973). Rebecca Brooke, Jeffrey Hurst, John Westleigh, Jacqueline Penn, Sheila Shelley, Jon Catlin, Dian Chelsea, Nora Escuadero, Grace Tapery, Leon Curiel.

1196 THE GRADUATE. (Embassy-1967). Mrs. Robinson, Anne Bancroft; Benjamin Braddock, Dustin Hoffman; Elaine Robinson, Katharine Ross; Mr. Braddock, William Daniels; Mr. Robinson, Murray Hamilton; Mrs. Braddock, Elizabeth Wilson; Carl Smith, Brian Avery; Mr. Maguire, Walter Brooke; Mr. McCleery, Norman Fell; Lady No. 2, Elizabeth Fraser; Mrs. Singleman, Alice Ghostley; Room Clerk, Buck Henry; Miss De Witt, Marion Lorne; Minister, Harry Holcombe; Night Club Stripper, Lainie Miller.

1197 GRAND PRIX. (MGM-1966). Pete Aron, James Garner; Louise Frederickson, Eva Marie Saint; Jean-Pierre Sarti, Yves Montand; Izo Yamura, Toshiro Mifune; Scott Stoddard, Brian Bedford; Pat Stoddard, Jessica Walter; Nino Barlini, Antonio Sabato; Lisa, Francoise Hardy; Agostini Manetta,

Adolfo Celi; Hugo Simon, Claude Dauphin; Guido, Enzo Fiermonte; Monique Delvaux Sarti, Gencvieve Page; Jeff Jordan, Jack Weston; Wallace Bennett, Donal O'Brien; Children's Father, Jean Michaud; Surgeon, Albert Remy; Mrs. Stoddard, Rachel Kempson; Mr. Stoddard, Ralph Michael; Tim Randolph, Phil Hill; Bob Turner, Graham Hill; Journalist, Bernard Chaier; Sportscasters, Alan Fordney, Anthony Marsh and Tommy Franklin.

1198 GRAND SLAM. (Paramount-1968). Mary Ann, Janet Leigh; Jean-Paul Audry, Robert Hoffman; Prof. James Anders, Edward G. Robinson; Mark Milford, Adolfo Celi; Erich Weiss, Klaus Kinski; Gregg, Georges Rigaud; Agostini Rossi, Ricardo Cucciolla; Setuaka, Jussara; Manager, Miguel Del Castillo.

1199 THE GRAND SUBSTITUTION. (Frank Lee International-1965). Chuang Chi, Li Li-Hua; Chao Wu, Ivy Ling Po; Cheng Ying, Yen Chun; Po Fung, Li Ting; Madam Cheng, Chen Yen-yen.

1200 LA GRANDE BOUFFE. (ABKCO-1973). Marcello Mastroianni, Ugo Tognazzi, Michel Piccoli, Philippe Noiret, Andrea Ferreol.

1201 THE GRAPEDEALER'S DAUGHTER. (Filmmakers-1970). Daughter, Anna Norteus; Bacchus, Walter Gutman; Juicy, Linda Rubera; Paul Rubera, Lucinda Love, David Harting, Paula Tinghe, Charlene Hess, Michael Levy, Marvin Scharfstein, Hanne Weaver, Linda Rubin, Serafina Mafia, Trudy Young, Suzanne Perry, Judy Van Hook.

1202 THE GRASSHOPPER. (National General-1970). Christine, Jacqueline Bisset; Tommy, Jim Brown; Richard, Joseph Cotten; Danny, Corbett Monica; Roosevelt, Ramon Bieri; Jay, Christopher Stone; Buck, Roger Garrett; Buddy, Stanley Adams; Lou, Dick Richards; Eddie, Tim O'Kelly; Libby, Stefanianna Christopherson; Jack, Ed Flanders; Connie, Wendy Farrington; Kyo, Sandi Gaviola; Vicky, Eris Sandy; Timmy, John David Wilder; Manny, Jay Laskay; Larry, Jim Smith; Gigi, Therese Baldwin; Billy, Chris Wong; Ann Marie, Kathalynn Turner; Aaron, William H. Bassett; Walters, Marc Hannibal; Miller's Son, David Duclon.

1203 GRAZIE, ZIA. (AVCO Embassy-1969). Lea, Lisa Gastoni; Alvise, Lou Castel; Stefano, Gabriele Ferzetti; Luisa de Sanctis, Nicoletta Rizzi, Massimo Sarchielli, Anita Dreyer.

1204 GREASER'S PALACE. (Cinema 5-1972). Zoot Suit (Jessy), Allan Arbus; Seaweedhead Greaser, Albert Henderson; The Woman, Elsie Downey; Cholera Greaser, Luana Anders; Lamly Greaser, Michael Sullivan; Vernon, James Antonio;

Coo Coo, George Morgan; Card Man/Ghost, Ron Nealy; Captain Good, Larry Moyer; Smiley, John Paul Hudson; Rope Man, Jackson Haynes; French Padre, Lawrence Wolf; Nun, Alex Hitchcock; Indian, Pablo Ferro; Indian Girl, Toni Basil; Spitunia, Stan Gottlieb; Mr. Spitunia, Herve Villechaize; "Turquoise Skies," Rex King; Gip, Don Smolen; Man with Painting, Joe Madden; Morris, Donald Calfa; Father, Woody Chambliss.

1205 THE GREAT AMERICAN COWBOY. (Sun International-1974). Narrator, Joel McCrea.

1206 THE GREAT BANK ROBBERY. (Warner Bros.-7 Arts-1969). Pious Blue, Zero Mostel; Lyda Kabanov, Kim Novak; Ben Quick, Clint Walker; Slade, Claude Akins; Papa Pedro, Akim Tamiroff; Juan, Larry Storch; Kinkaid, John Anderson; Brother Lilac, Sam Jaffe; Secret Service Agent Fong, Mako; Jeb, Elisha Cook Jr.; Mrs. Applebee, Ruth Warrick; Brother Dismas, John Fiedler; Sheriff, John Larch; Brother Jordan, Peter Whitney; The Great Gregory, Norman Alden; Reverend Sims, Grady Sutton; Square Dance Caller, Homer Garrett; Deputy, Byron Keith; Guards, Bob Steele, Ben Aliza, Mickey Simpson; Glaziers, Guy Wilkerson, Burt Mustin; Commandant, Royden Clark; Janet Clark, Jerry Brown, Chuck O'Brien, Philo McCollough, Fred Krone, Dick Hudkins, Emile Avery, Everett Creach, William Zuckert, Jerry Summers, The Bob Mitchell Boys Choir.

1207 THE GREAT BRITISH TRAIN ROBBERY. (Peppercorn-Wormser-1967). Horst Tappert, Isa Miranda, Hans Cossy, Gunther Neutze, Karl Heinz Hess, Hans Reiser, Rolf Nagel, Harry Engel, Wolfrang Schaerf, Gunther Tabor, Franz Mosthav, Wolfreid Lier, Kurt Conradi, Horst Beck, Paul Edwin Roth, Kai Fischer, Grit Bottcher, Eleonore Schroth, Sylvia Lydi, Seigfried Lowitz, Lothar Grutzner, Dirk Dautzenberg, Albert Hoerrmann.

1208 GREAT CATHERINE. (Warner Bros.-7 Arts-1969). Captain Charles Edstaston, Peter O'Toole; Catherine the Great, Jeanne Moreau; Prince Patiomkin, Zero Mostel; Sir George Gorse, Jack Hawkins; Sergeant, Akim Tamiroff; Dowager Lady Gorse, Marie Lohr; Princess Dashkoff, Marie Kean; Naryshkin, Kenneth Griffith; Claire, Angela Scoular; Varinka, Kate O'Mara; General Pskov, Oliver McGreevy; Grand Duchess, Lea Seidl; Colonel Pugachow, James Mellor; Count Tokhtamysh, Declan Mulholland; Egregyomka, Henry Woolf; Sophia, Catherine Lancaster; Anna Schuvalova, Janet Kelly; Gordon Rollings, Alfred Ravel, Claire Gordon, Sean Barrett, Alf Joint, Reuben Martin, Yuri Borienko, Rupert Evans, Milton Reid, Dinny Powell, Tom Clegg.

1209 THE GREAT GATSBY. (Paramount-1974). Jay Gatsby, Robert Redford; Daisy Buchanan, Mia Farrow; Tom Buchanan,

Bruce Dern; Myrtle Wilson, Karen Black; George Wilson, Scott Wilson; Nick Carraway, Sam Waterston; Jordan Baker, Lois Chiles; Meyer Wolfsheim, Howard Da Silva; Mr. Gatz, Roberts Blossom; Klipspringer, Edward Herrmann; Wilson's Friend, Elliot Sullivan; Gatsby's Bodyguard, John Devlin; Twins, Janet and Louise Arters; Mourner, Tom Ewell.

1210 THE GREAT NORTHFIELD, MINNESOTA RAID. (Universal-1972). Cole Younger, Cliff Robertson; Jesse James, Robert Duvall; Jim Younger, Luke Askew; Clell Miller, R. G. Armstrong; Allen, Dana Elcar; Manning, Donald Moffat; Frank James, John Pearce; Bob Younger, Matt Clark; Charley Pitts, Wayne Sutherlin; Wilcox, Robert H. Harris; Heywood, Jack Manning; Bunker, Elish Cook; Gustavson, Royal Dano; Kate, Mary Robin Redd; Calliopist, Bill Callaway; Jefferson Jones, Arthur Peterson; Chadwell, Craig Curtis; Henry Wheeler, Barry Brown; Doll Woman, Nellie Burt; Drummer, Liam Dunn; Granny Woman, Madeleine Taylor Holmes; Chief Detective, Herbert Nelson; Landlord, Jack Manning; Sheriff, Erik Holland; Clell's Wife, Anne Barton; Maybelle, Marjorie Durant; Singing Whore, Inger Stratton; Nude Girl, Velda J. Hansen; Old Timer, William Challee; Farmer, Robert Gravage.

1211 THE GREAT RACE. (Warner Bros.-1965). Professor Fate/Crown Prince, Jack Lemmon; The Great Leslie, Tony Curtis; Maggie Dubois, Natalie Wood; Max, Peter Falk; Hezekiah, Keenan Wynn; Editor Goodbody, Arthur O'Connell; Mrs. Goodbody, Vivian Vance; Lily Olay, Dorothy Provine; Texas Jack, Larry Storch; Baron von Stuppe, Ross Martin; General Kuhster, George Macready; Frisbee, Marvin Kaplan; Mayor of Boracho, Hal Smith; Sheriff, Denver Pyle.

1212 THE GREAT SIOUX MASSACRE. (Columbia-1965). Joseph Cotten, Darren McGavin, Philip Carey, Julie Sommars, Nancy Kovack, Michael Pate, John Matthews, Don Haggerty, Frank Ferguson, Stacy Harris, Iron Eyes Cody, House Peters Jr., John Napier, William Tannen, Blair Davies, Louise Serpa.

1213 THE GREAT SPY CHASE. (American International-1966). Lagneau, Lino Ventura; Cafarelli, Bernard Blier; Vassilieff, Francis Blanche; Amaranthe, Mireille Darc; Muller, Charles Millot; Rossini, Andre Weber; O'Brien, Jess Hahn; Le Douanier, Jacques Balutin; Le Camionneur, Robert Dalban; Rosalinde, Michele Marceau.

1214 THE GREAT WALL. (Magna-1965). Emperor, Shintaro Katsu; Princess, Fujiko Yamamoto; Crown Prince Tan, Ken Utsui; Hsi Liang, Hiroshi Kawaguchi; Chaing, Ayako Wakao; Li Hei, Kohiro Hongo; Ching Ko, Raizo Ichikawa; Hsu Fu, Ganjiro Nakamura.

1215 THE GREAT WALTZ. (MGM-1972). Johann Strauss Jr., Horst Bucholz; Jetty Treffz, Mary Costa; Baron Tedesco, Rossano Brazzi; Johann Strauss Sr., Nigel Patrick; Anna Strauss, Yvonne Mitchell; Josef Strauss, James Faulkner; Lili Weyl, Vicki Woolf; Emilie Trampusch, Susan Robinson; Karl Frederick Hirsch, George Howe; Donmayer, Lauri Lupino Lane; Karl Haslinger, Michael Tellering; Karl Treffz, Willard Parker; Theresa Strauss, Ingrid Wayland; Olga, Lorna Nathan; Louise, Hermione Farthingale; Caroline Strauss, Elizabeth Muthsam; Hosef Weyl, Franz Aigner; Havemeyer, Helmut Janatsch; Johann Herbeck, Marty Allen; Jacques Offenbach, Dominique Weber; Max Steiner, Guido Wieland; Princess Pauline Metternich, Paola Loew; Emperor Franz Josef, Prince Johannes Schonburg-Hartenstein; The Mike Sammes Singers.

1216 THE GREAT WHITE HOPE. (20th Century-Fox-1970). Jack Jefferson, James Earl Jones; Eleanor, Jane Alexander; Goldie, Lou Gilbert; Tick, Joel Fluellen; Pop Weaver, Chester Morris; Dixon, Robert Webber; Clara, Marlene Warfield; Cap'n. Dan, R. G. Armstrong; Cameron, Hal Holbrook; Mama Tiny, Beah Richards; Scipio, Moses Gunn; Smitty, Lloyd Gough; Fred, George Ebelmy; Frank Brady, Larry Pennell; Pastor, Roy E. Glenn Sr.; Deacon, Bill Walker; French Promoter, Marcel Dolio; El Jefe, Rodolfo Acosta; Sister Pearl, Virginia Capers; Rudy, Rockne Tarkington; Ragosy, Oscar Beregi; Paco, Manuel Padilla Jr.; Hans, Karl Otto Alberty; The Kid, Jim Beattie.

1217 THE GREATEST STORY EVER TOLD. (United Artists-1965). Jesus, Max Von Sydow; Mary, Dorothy McGuire; Joseph, Robert Loggia; John the Baptist, Charlton Heston; James the Younger, Michael Anderson Jr.; Simon the Zealot, Robert Blake; Andrew, Burt Brinckerhoff; John, John Considine; Thaddeus, Jamie Farr; Philip, David Hedison; Nathanael, Peter Mann; Judas Iscariot, David McCallum; Matthew, Roddy McDowall; Peter, Gary Raymond; Thomas, Tom Reese; James the Elder, David Sheiner; Martha of Bethany, Ina Balin; Mary of Bethany, Janet Margolin; Lazarus, Michael Tolan; Simon of Cyrene, Sidney Poitier; Veronica, Carroll Baker; Uriah, Sal Mineo.

1218 THE GREEN BERETS. (Warner Bros.-7 Arts-1968). Col. Mike Kirby, John Wayne; George Beckworth, David Janssen; Sgt. Petersen, Jim Hutton; Sgt. Muldoon, Aldo Ray; Doc McGee, Raymond St. Jacques; Col. Morgan, Bruce Cabot; Col. Cai, Jack Soo; Captain Nim, George Takei; Capt. MacDaniels, Edward Faulkner; Capt. Coleman, Jason Evers; Sgt. Kowalski, Mike Henry; Hamchunk, Craig Jue; Sgt. Griffin, Chuck Roberson; Sgt. Watson, Eddy Donno; Sgt. Parks, Rudy Robins; Collier, Richard "Cactus" Pryor; Vietnamese Singer, Bach Yen; Lieut. Sachs, Frank Koomen; Gen. Ti, William Olds; Sgt. White, Billy Shannon; Sgt.

Lark, Chuck Bail; Viet Cong Soldier, Vincent Cadiente; South Vietnamese Soldier, Yodying Apibal.

1219 THE GREEN SLIME. (MGM-1969). Jack Rankin, Robert Horton; Vince Elliot, Richard Jaeckel; Lisa Benson, Luciana Paluzzi; Jonathan Thompson, Bud Widom; Doctor Halvorsen, Ted Gunther; Captain Martin, Robert Dunham; Lieut. Curtis, David Yorston; Ferguson, William Ross; Cordier, Gary Randolf; Michael, Richard Hylland.

1220 THE GREEN WALL. (Altura-1972). Mario, Julio Aleman; Delba, Sandra Riva; Romulo, Raul Martin; Mother, Lorena Duval; Father, Enrique Victoria; Chief of Jungle Region, Jorje Montero; Director of Colonization, Juan Bautista Font; Escolastico, Escolastico Davila; Friend, Aldo Zignago; Fidel, Esteban Rangifo; Group at Bar, Hernan Romero, Fernando Hilbeck, Alfredo Bastillina, Jorge Castro, Alfredo Morales.

1221 GREETINGS. (Sigma III-1968). Paul Shaw, Jonathan Warden; Jon Rubin, Robert De Niro; Lloyd Clay, Gerritt Graham; Pop Artist, Richard Hamilton; Marina, Megan McCormick; Tina, Bettina Kugel; Photographer, Jack Cowley; Model, Jane Lee Salmons; Bronx Secretary, Ashley Oliver; "Rat" Magazine Vendor, Melvin Marguiles; Divorcee, Cynthia Peltz; Earl Roberts, Peter Maloney; Linda, Ruth Alda; Bookstore Manager, Ted Lescault; Mystic Date, Mona Feit; TV Cameraman from Vietnam, M. Dobish; Richard Landis, Carol Patton, Allen Garfield, Sara-Jo Edlin, Roz Kelly, Ray Tuttle, Lisa Chang, Rex Marshall.

1222 GRIMMS FAIRY TALES FOR ADULTS ONLY. (Cinemation-1970). Snow White, Marie Liljedahl; Cinderella, Eva Rueber-Staier; Queen, Ingrid Van Bergen; Sleeping Beauty, Gaby Fuchs; Evil Sisters, Kitty Gschopf, Evelin Dutree; Hans, Walter Giller; Heinz, Peter Hohberger; Farmer, Hugo Lindinger; Old One, Isolde Stiegler.

1223 THE GRISSOM GANG. (Cinerama-1971). Barbara, Kim Darby; Slim, Scott Wilson; Eddie, Tony Musante; Ma, Irene Dailey; Dave, Robert Lansing; Anna, Connie Stevens.

1224 THE GROUNDSTAR CONSPIRACY. (Universal-1972). Tuxan, George Peppard; John Welles/Peter Bellamy, Michael Sarrazin; Nicole Devon, Christine Belford; Carl Mosely, Cliff Potts; Senator Stanton, James Olson; Frank Gossage, Tim O'Connor; Bender, James McEachin; General Hackett, Alan Oppenheimer; Charlie Kitchen, Roger Dressler; Henshaw, Ty Haller; Dr. Plover, Anna Hagen; Dr. Hager, Hagen Beggs; Zabrinski, John Destry Adams; Dr. Zahl, Milos Zatovic; Technician, Don Granberry; Secretary, Robin Coller; M. P. Sergeant, Bob Meneray; Nicole's Doctor, Ed Collier; M. P. 's, John Mitchell, Richard Sergeant, Martin

Moore; Reporters, Don Vance, William Nunn, Peter Lavender, Barry Cahill.

1225 THE GROUP. (United Artists-1966). Elinor Eastlake, Candice Bergen; Dorothy Renfrew, Joan Hackett; Priss Hartshorn, Elizabeth Hartman; Polly Andrews, Shirley Knight; Kay Strong, Joanna Pettet; Pokey Prothero, Mary-Robin Redd; Libby MacAusland, Jessica Walters; Helena Davison, Kathleen Widdoes; Dr. James Ridgeley, James Broderick; Sloan Crockett, James Congdon; Harald Peterson, Larry Hagman; Gus Leroy, Hal Holbrook; Dick Brown, Richard Mulligan; The Baroness, Lidia Prochnicka; Robert Emhardt, Carrie Nye, Philippa Bevans, Leta Bonynge, Marion Brash, Sarah Burton, Flora Campbell, Bruno Di Cosmi, Leora Dana, Bill Fletcher, George Gaynes, Martha Greenhouse.

1226 GROUP MARRIAGE. (Dimension-1973). Victoria Vetri, Aimee Eccles, Solomon Sturges, Claudia Jennings, Zack Taylor, Jeffrey Pomerantz, Milt Kamen.

1227 GROUPIES. (Maron-1970). Ten Years After, Alvin Lee & Company, Joe Cocker and the Grease Band, Terry Reid, Keith Webb, Peter Shelly, Spooky Tooth, Luther Grosvenor, Dry Creek Road, Miss Harlow, Cynthia P. Caster, Goldie Glitter, Andrea Whips, Patti Cakes, Lixie & Katy

1228 LA GUERRE EST FINIE. (Brandon-1967). Diego, Yves Montand; Marianne, Ingrid Thulin; Nadine, Genevieve Bujold; Jude, Dominique Rozan; Juan, Juan-Francois Remi; Roberto, Paul Crauchet; The Chief, Jean Daste; Narrator, Jorge Semprun; Inspector, Michel Piccoli; Ramon, Jean Bouise; Yvette, Yvette Etievant; Carmen, Francoise Bertin; Gerard Sety, Anouk Ferjac, Annie Farge, Gerard Lartigau, Jacques Rispal, Pierre Leproux, Marie Mergey, Marcel Cuvelier, Roland Monod, Bernard Fresson, Laurence Badie, Jose-Maria Flotats, Catherine De Seynes, Claire Duhamel, Jean Larroquette, Martine Vatel, Roger Pelletier, Antoine Bourseiller, R. J. Chauffard, Antoine Vitez, Jacques Robnard, Paillette.

1229 GUESS WHAT WE LEARNED IN SCHOOL TODAY? (Cannon-1970). Roger, Richard Carballo; Robbie, Devin Goldenberg; Lance, Zachary Haines; Rita, Jane MacLeod; Dr. Whitehorn, Yvonne McCall; Eve, Rosella Olsen; Billie, Stanton Edgehill; Lydia, Diane Moore.

1230 GUESS WHO'S COMING TO DINNER. (Columbia-1967). Matt Drayton, Spencer Tracy; John Prentice, Sidney Poitier; Christina Drayton, Katharine Hepburn; Joey Drayton, Katharine Houghton; Monsignor Ryan, Cecil Kellaway; Mrs. Prentice, Beah Richards; Mr. Prentice, Roy E. Glenn Sr.; Tillie, Isabell Sanford; Hilary St. George, Virginia Christine;

Carhop, Alexandra Hay; Dorothy, Barbara Randolph; Frankie, D'Urville Martin; Peter, Tom Heaton; Judith, Grace Gaynor; Delivery Boy, Skip Martin; Cab Driver, John Hudkins.

1231 GUESTS ARE COMING. (Mitchell Kowal-1967). Mitchell Kowal, Kazimeriz Opalinski, Zagmunt Zintel, Wladyslaw Hancza, Paul Glass, Ryszard Pietruski, Zenon Burbynski, Sylvia Zakrzewska, Wanda Koczewska.

1232 THE GUIDE. (Stratton International-1965). Raju, Dev Anand; Rosie, Waheeda Rehman; Marco, Kishore Sahu; Mother, Leela Chitnis; Gaffur, Anwar Hussein; Velan, K. N. Singh; Dilip, Levy Aaron; Joseph Rashid Khan; Mani, Dilip Dutt; Inspector, Iftikhar; British Correspondent, John Voyantiz; Defense Lawyer, Krisha Dhawan; Velan's Sister, Hazel; Velan's Brother, Satya Dev Duby; Old Man, J. S. Kashyap; TV Reporter, Sheila Burghart.

1233 A GUIDE FOR THE MARRIED MAN. (20th Century-Fox-1967). Paul Manning, Walter Matthau; Ed Stander, Robert Morse; Ruth Manning, Inger Stevens; Irma Johnson, Sue Ane Langdon; Harriet Stander, Claire Kelly; Miss Stardust, Linda Harrison; Jocelyn Montgomery, Elaine Devry; Miss Harris, Jackie Russell; Aline Towne, Eve Brent, Marvin Brody, Majel Barrett, Marian Mason, Tommy Farrell, Jason Wingren, Pat Becker, Fred Holliday, Robert Patten, Dee Carroll, Ray Montgomery, Jackie Joseph, Heather Young, Evelyn King, Nancy De Carl, Warrene Ott, Michael (Prince) Romanoff, Karen Arthur, Mickey Deems, Damian London, Chanin Hale, Julie Tate, George Neise, Tim Herbert, Patricia Sides, Pat McCaffrie, Jimmy Cross, Virginia Wood, Sharyn Hillyer, Lucille Ball, Polly Bergen, Ben Blue, Art Carney, Marty Ingels, Jeffrey Hunter, Louis Nye, Jayne Mansfield, Phil Silvers, Jack Benny, Joey Bishop, Sid Caesar, Wally Cox, Sam Jaffe, Hal March, Carl Reiner, Ann Morgan Guilbert, Terry-Thomas.

1234 GUILT. (Crown International-1967). Hans, Sven Bertil Taube; Gunilla, Helena Brodin; Inga, Tina Hedstrom.

1235 GUMSHOE. (Columbia-1972). Eddie Ginley, Albert Finney; Ellen, Billie Whitelaw; William, Frank Finlay; Mrs. Blankerscoon, Janice Rule; Alison Wyatt, Carolyn Seymour; John Straker, Fulton Mackay; Bookshop Proprietor, George Innes; Jacob De Fries, George Silver; Tommy, Billy Dean; Anne Scott, Wendy Richard; Naomi, Maureen Lipman; Arthur, Neville Smith; Azinge, Oscar James; Joey, Joey Kenyon; Mal, Bert King; Clifford, Chris Cunningham; Labor Exchange Clerk, Ken Jones; Psychiatrist, Tom Kempinski; Kleptomaniac, Harry Hutchinson; Sammy, Sammy Sharples; Artists in Club, Ernie Mack and the Saturated Seven, Jason Kane, The Jacksons, Vicki Day, Scott Christian.

1236-37 No entries.

1238 A GUNFIGHT. (Paramount-1971). Will Tenneray, Kirk Douglas; Abe Cross, Johnny Cash; Nora Tenneray, Jane Alexander; Francisco Alvarez, Raf Vallone; Jenny Simms, Karen Black.

1239 GUNFIGHT IN ABILENE. (Universal-1967). Cal Wayne, Bobby Darin; Amy Martin, Emily Banks; Grant Evers, Leslie Nielsen; Joe Slade, Donnelly Rhodes; Ward Kent, Don Galloway; Ned Martin, Frank McGrath; Cord Decker, Michael Sarrazin; Leann, Barbara Werle; Loop, Johnny Seven; Frank Norton, William Phipps; Ed Scovie, William Mims; Nelson, Robert Sorrells; Sprague, Don Dubbins; Smokey Staub, James McCallion; Frobisher, Bryan O'Byrne.

1240 GUNFIGHTERS OF CASA GRANDE. (MGM-1965). Joe Daylight, Alex Nicol; The Traveler, Jorge Mistral; Doc, Dick Bentley; The Kid, Steve Rowland; Henri, Phil Posner; Maria, Mercedes Alonso; Gitana, Diana Lorys; Pacesita, Maria Granada.

1241 GUNMEN OF THE RIO GRANDE. (Allied Artists-1965). Guy Madison, Madeline Lebeau, Carolyn Davys, Massimo Serato, Gerard Tichy, Fernando Sancho, Olivier Hussenot, D. Michaelis, E. Maran, B. Deus, H. Morrow, X. Das Bolas, A. DeLuna, J. Majan.

1242 GUNN. (Paramount-1967). Peter Gunn, Craig Stevens; Edie, Laura Devon; Jacoby, Edward Asner; Samantha, Sherry Jackson; Mother, Helen Traubel; Fusco, Albert Paulsen; Daisy Jane, Marion Marshall; Tinker, J. Pat O'Malley; "The Bishop," Regis Toomey; Leo Gracey, Dick Crockett; Lazlo Joyce, Charles Dierkof; Corwin, Jerry Douglas; Capt. Brady, Ken Wales; Harry Ross, Gary Lasdun; Archie, George Murdock; Barney, Frank Kreig; Julio Scarlotti, Lincoln Demyan; Scarlotti's Mistress, Chanin Hale; Lieut. Ashford, Ed Peck; Waitress, Jean Carson.

1243 GUNPOINT. (Universal-1966). Chad Luces, Audie Murphy; Uvalde, Joan Staley; Nate Harlan, Warren Stevens; Bull, Edgar Buchanan; Cap, Denver Pyle; Ode, Royal Dano; Nicos, Nick Dennis; Hoag, William Bramley; Ab, Kelly Thordsen; Mark Emerson, David Macklin; Drago, Morgan Woodward; Mitch, Robert Pine; Zack, Mike Ragan.

1243a GUNS FOR SAN SEBASTIAN. (MGM-1968). Leon Alastray, Anthony Quinn; Kinita, Anjanette Comer; Teclo, Charles Bronson; Father Joseph, Sam Jaffe; Felicia, Silvia Pinal; Cayetano, Jorge Martinez De Hoyos; Golden Lance, Jaime Fernandez; Agueda, Rosa Furman; Pedro, Jorge Russek; Vicar General, Leon Askin; Antonito, Jose Chavez; Colonel

Calleja, Ivan Desny; Governor, Fernand Gravey; Father Lucas, Pedro Armendariz Jr.; Magdalena, Aurora Clavel; Diego, Julio Aldama; Luis, Ferrusquilla; Kino, Pancho Cordova; Renaldo, Enrique Lucero; Miguel, Chano Urueta; Capt. Lopez, Noe Murayama; Timoteo, Guillermo Hernandez; Pablo, Carlos Berriochea; Bishop, Francisco Reiguera.

1243b GUNS OF THE MAGNIFICENT SEVEN. (United Artists-1969). Chris, George Kennedy; Keno, Monte Markham; Levi Morgan, James Whitmore; Maximiliano O'Leary, Reni Santoni; Cassie, Bernie Casey; Slater, Joe Don Baker; P. J., Scott Thomas; Colonel Diego, Michael Ansara; Carlos Lobero, Frank Silvera; Emiliano Zapata, Tony Davis; Tina, Wende Wagner; Lt. Prensa, Luis Rivera; Quintero, Fernando Rey; Miguel, Sancho Gracia; Gabriel, Jorge Rigaud; Cesar, Ramon Serrano; Manuel, Vicente Sangiovani.

1244 THE GURU. (20th Century-Fox-1969). Ustad Zafar Khan, Utpal Dutt; Tom Pickle, Michael York; Jenny, Rita Tushingham; Ghazala, Aparna Sen; Girl at the Party, Leela Naidu; Begum Sahiba, Madhur Jaffrey; Mustani, Zohra Seghal; The Guru's Guru, Nana Palsikar; Chris, Barry Foster; Master of Ceremonies, Ismail Merchant; Murad, Saeed Jaffrey; Lady Reporter, Usha Katrak; Howard, Fred Ohringer; Society Hostess, Nargis Cowasji; Snide Guest, Marcus Murch; Tourist, Dorothy Strelsin; Arnold D'Mello, Rafi Ameer; Miss Teen Queen, Soni Aurora; Courtesan, Nadira; Murderer, Pincho Kapoor; Doctor, Shri Agarwal; Classical Singer, Prayag Raaj.

1245 GYPSY GIRL. (Continental-1967). Byrdie White, Hayley Mills; Robin, Ian McShane; Edwin Dacres, Laurence Naismith; Phillip Moss, Geoffrey Bayldon; Mrs. White, Annette Crosbie; Cheeseman, Norman Bird; Bill Slim, Hamilton Dyce; Mrs. Moss, Pauline Jameson; Grandma, Rachel Thomas; Mrs. Rigby, Judith Furse; Mrs. Potts, Anne Blake; Mrs. Cheeseman, June Ellis; Fred Strong, Jack Bligh; Dusty Miller, Len Jones; Harry, Roland Starling; Cathy, Jessica Hobbs; Jabal Jones, Gerald Lawson; Cammellia, Jacqueline Pearce; Camlo, Alan Lake; Blossom, Hira Talfrey; Hubberd, Cyril Chamberlin; Susie, Susan Chatham; Chalky, Robin Crewe; Biddie, Lola Payne; Nell, Nicola Street; Jakey, Stephen Salt; Emm, Joyce Mayhead.

1246 THE GYPSY MOTHS. (MGM-1969). Mike Rettig, Burt Lancaster; Elizabeth Brandon, Deborah Kerr; Joe Browdy, Gene Hackman; Malcolm Webson, Scott Wilson; V. John Brandon, William Windom; Annie Burke, Bonnie Bedelia; Mary, Sheree North; Pilot, Carl Reindel; Stand Owner, Ford Rainey; Dick Donford, John Napier.

1247 HAGBARD AND SIGNE. (Steve Prentoulis-1968). Signe, Gitte Haenning; Hagbard, Oleg Vidov; King Sigvor, Gunnar

Bjornstrand; His Queen, Eva Dahlbeck; Bengrerd, Lisben Movin; Bilvis, Johannes Meyer; Bolvis, Hakan Jahnberg; Hake, Henning Palmer.

1248 HAIL, HERO! (National General-1969). Carl Dixon, Michael Douglas; Albert Dixon, Arthur Kennedy; Santha Dixon, Teresa Wright; Mr. Conklin, John Larch; Senator Murchiston, Charles Drake; Jimmy, Mercer Harris; Becky, Deborah Winters; Frank Dixon, Peter Strauss; Congressman Arcado, Mario Alcalde; Rhetha, Amy Stuart; Tinky, Rene Tetro; Miss Mirabel, Louise Latham; Billy Hurd, John Qualen; Juana, Carmen Zapata; Eleanor Murchiston, Virginia Christine; Molly Adams, Heather Menzies; Carl's Aunts, Dorothy Newman, Marjorie Eaton.

1249 HAIL! MAFIA. (7 Arts-1967). Henry Silva, Jack Klugman, Eddie Constantine, Elsa Martinelli, Micheline Presle, Tener Riggs Eckelberry, Michel Lonsdale, Karl Studer, Ricky Cooper, Daniel O'Brien.

1250 HAIL TO THE CHIEF. (Cine-Globe-1973). President, Dan Resin; Sec. of Health, Richard B. Shull; Attorney General, Dick O'Neill; Rev. Williams, Joseph Sirola; First Lady, Patricia Ripley; Tom, Gary Sandy; Vice President, William Waterman; Burd, K. Callan; Sara, Constance Forslund; Michael, Phil Foster; Mrs. Moloney, Lee Meredith; Reporter, Robert King; Ellinson, Douglas Rutherford; Mrs. Ellinson, Mary Louise Weller; Sister Veronica, Peggy Pope; Professor, Ron Carrol; Sgt. National Guard, Brandon Maggert; Speech Writer, Doyle Newberry; Doctor, Toni Reid; Chief Justice, Ted Gewant; Sgt. Johnson, Jim Nurtaugh; Sgt. Mazzola, Madison Arnold.

1251 HALF A SIXPENCE. (Paramount-1968). Arthur Kipps, Tommy Steele; Ann, Julia Foster; Helen Walsingham, Penelope Horner; Harry Chitterlow, Cyril Ritchard; Pearce, Grover Dale; Kate, Elaine Taylor; Flo, Julia Sutton; Victoria, Sheila Falconer; Buggins, Leslie Meadows; Sid, Christopher Sandford; Mrs. Walsingham, Pamela Brown; Hubert Walsingham, James Villiers; Fat Boy, Gerald Campion; Shalford, Hilton Edwards; Lady Botting, Jean Anderson; Wilkins, Allan Cuthbertson; Laura, Aleta Morrison; Young Ann, Deborah Permenter; Young Kipps, Jeffrey Chandler; Woodrow, Barry Sinclair.

1252 THE HALLELUJAH TRAIL. (United Artists-1965). Col. Thaddeus Gearhart, Burt Lancaster; Cora Massingale, Lee Remick; Capt. Paul Slater, Jim Hutton; Louise Gearhart, Pamela Tiffin; Oracle Jones, Donald Pleasence; Frank Wallingham, Brian Keith; Sgt. Buell, John Anderson; Kevin O'Flaherty, Tom Stern; Five Barrels, Robert J. Wilke; Clayton Howell, Dub Taylor; Interpreter, Noam Pitlik; Newspaper Editor, Whit Bissell; Bartender, Val Avery.

1253 HALLS OF ANGER. (United Artists-1970). Quincy, Calvin Lockhart; Lorraine, Janet MacLachlan; J. T., James A. Watson Jr.; Douglas, Jeff Bridges; Leaky, Bob Reiner; Lerrone, Dewayne Jesse; Sherry, Patricia Stich; Harry, Roy Jenson; Lloyd, John McLiam; McKay, Edward Asner; Stewart, Lou Frizzell; Rita, Helen Kleeb; Fowler, Luther Whitsett; Miss Rowland, Florence St. Peter; Mrs. Taylor, Maye Henderson; Barry Brown, Alex Clark, Paris Earl, Randy Fredericks, Arline Hamlin, Chris Joy, Richard Levin, Kim Manners, Linda Smith, Linda Thomas, Ta-Tanisha, Gary Tigerman, Cal Wilson.

1254 HALLUCINATION GENERATION. (American International-1966). Eric, George Montgomery; Bill, Danny Stone; Lise, Renate Kasche; Denny, Tom Baker; Carol, Marianne Kanter; Stan, Steve Rowland; Eric's Boy, Claude Gersene.

1255 HAMLET. (Lopert-1966). Hamlet, Innokenti Smoktunovsky; King Claudius, Mikhail Nazwanov; Gertrude, Elza Radzin-Szolkonis; Polonius, Yuri Tolubeyev; Ophelia, Anastasia Vertinskaya; Horatio, V. Erenberg; Laertes, C. Oleksenko; Guildenstern, V. Medvedev; Rosencrantz, I. Dmitriev; Fortinbras, A. Krevald; Gravedigger, V. Kolpakor; Actors, A. Chekaerskii, R. Aren, and Y. Berkun.

1256 HAMLET. (Columbia-1969). Hamlet, Nicol Williamson; Horatio, Gordon Jackson; Claudius, Anthony Hopkins, Gertrude, Judy Parfitt; Polonius, Mark Dignam; Laertes, Michael Pennington; Ophelia, Marianne Faithfull; Rosencrantz, Ben Aris; Guildenstern, Clive Graham; Osric, Peter Gale, Player King, John Carney; Player Queen, Richard Everett; Lucianus/Gravedigger, Roger Livesey; Francisco, Robin Chadwick; Priest, Ian Collier; Captain, Michael Elphick; Messenger, Mark Griffith; Court Lady, Anjelica Huston; Courtier, Bill Jarvis; Reynaldo, Roger Lloyd-Pack; First Sailor, John Railton; Barnardo, John Trenaman; Court Lady, Jennifer Tudor.

1257 HAMMER. (United Artists-1972). B. J. Hammer, Fred Williamson; Davis, Bernie Hamilton; Lois, Vonetta McGee; Brenner, William Smith.

1258 HAMMERHEAD. (Columbia-1968). Charles Hood, Vince Edwards; Sue Trenton, Judy Geeson; Hammerhead, Peter Vaughan; Kit, Diana Dors; Andreas/Sir Richard, Michael Bates; Ivory, Beverly Adams; Colonel Condor, Patrick Cargill; Huntzinger, Patrick Holt; Walter Perrin, William Mervyn; Vendriani, Douglas Wilmer; Tracy Reed, Kenneth Cope, Kathleen Byron, Jack Woolgar, Joseph Furst, David Prowse, Earl Younger, Romo Garrara, Maggie Wright, Veronica Carlson, Penny Brahms, Sarah Harden Berg, Windsor Davies, Arthur Gomez, Andrea Malandrinos.

1259 HAMMERSMITH IS OUT. (Cinerama-1972). Jimmie Jean Jackson, Elizabeth Taylor; Hammersmith, Richard Burton; Doctor, Peter Ustinov; Billy Breedlove, Beau Bridges; General Sam Pembroke, Leon Ames; Dr. Krodt, Leon Askin; Henry Joe Fitch, John Schuck; Guido Scartucci, George Raft; Princess, Marjorie Eaton; Kiddo, Lisa Jak; Miss Quim, Linda Gaye Scott; Fat Man, Mel Berger; Oldham, Anthony Holland; Pete Rutter, Brook Williams; Cleopatra, Carl Donn; Duke, Joe Espinoza.

1260 HANDS OF THE RIPPER. (Universal-1972). Dr. John Pritchard, Eric Porter; Anna, Angharad Rees; Laura, Jane Merrow; Michael Pritchard, Keith Bell; Dysart, Derek Godfrey; Mrs. Golding, Dora Bryan; Mrs. Bryant, Marjorie Rhodes; Long Liz, Lynda Baron; Dolly, Marjie Lawrence; Police Inspector, Norman Bird; Madame Bullard, Margaret Rawlings; Mrs. Wilson, Elizabeth Maclennan; Reverend Anderson, A. J. Brown; Catherine, April Wilding; Whores, Anne Clune, Vicki Woolf, Katya Wyeth, Beulah Hughes, and Tallulah Miller; Pleasants, Peter Munt; Police Constable, Philip Ryan; Maid, Molly Weir; Guard, Charles Lamb.

1261 HANG 'EM HIGH. (United Artists-1968). Jed Cooper, Clint Eastwood; Rachel, Inger Stevens; Cap'n Wilson, Ed Begley; Judge Adam Fenton, Pat Hingle; Sheriff Ray Calhoun, Charles McGraw; Madame Sophie, Ruth White; Jennifer, Arlene Golonka; The Preacher, James MacArthur; Miller, Bruce Dern; Stone, Alan Hale Jr.; Prisoner, James Westerfield; The Prophet, Dennis Hopper; Loomis, L. Q. Jones; Hangman, Bert Freed; Francis Duffy, Michael O'Sullivan; Defense Attorney, Todd Andrews; Ben, Rick Gates; Billy Joe, Bruce Scott; Guard, Roy Glenn; Ben Johnson, Jack Ging, Joseph Sirola, Bob Steele, Russell Thorsen, Ned Romero, Jonathan Lippe, Richard Guizon, Mark Lenard, Paul Sorenson, Richard Angarola, Larry Blake, Ted Thorpe, Robert Jones, Barry Chaill, John Wesley, Dennis Dengate, Bill Zukert, Hal England, Robert B. Williams, Tony Di Milo.

1262 No entry.

1263 HANNIBAL BROOKS. (United Artists-1969). "Hannibal" Brooks, Oliver Reed; Packy, Michael J. Pollard; Colonel Von Haller, Wolfgang Preiss; Willi, Helmut Lohner; Vronia, Karin Baal; Padre, James Donald; Kurt, Peter Karsten; Dr. Mendel, Ralf Wolter; Bernard, John Alderton; Sami, Jurgen Draeger; Anna, Maria Brockerhoff; Josef, Fred Haltiner; Stern, Eric Jelde; Kellerman, Ernst Fritz Furbringer; Geordie, John Porter Davison; Von Haller's Sergeant, Til Kiwe; Twilight, Terence Seward; German Captain, Peter Bohlke; 2nd Zoo Keeper, Tei De Maal.

1263a HANNIE CAULDER. (Paramount-1972). Hannie Caulder, Raquel Welch; Thomas Luther Price, Robert Culp; Emmett Clemens, Ernest Borgnine; Rufus Clemens, Strother Martin; Frank Clemens, Jack Elam; Bailey, Christopher Lee; Madame, Diana Dors; The Preacher, Stephen Boyd.

1264 THE HAPPENING. (Columbia-1967). Roc Delmonico, Anthony Quinn; Taurus, George Maharis; Sureshot, Michael Parks; Herby, Robert Walker; Monica, Martha Hyer; Sandy, Faye Dunaway; Fred, Milton Berle; Sam, Oscar Homolka; Inspector, Jack Kruschen; O'Reilly, Clifton James; 1st Motorcycle Officer, Eugene Roche; Arnold, James Randolph Kuhl; 2nd Motorcycle Officer, Luke Askew.

1265 THE HAPPIEST MILLIONAIRE. (Buena Vista-1967). Anthony J. Drexel Biddle, Fred MacMurray; John Lawless, Tommy Steele; Mrs. Cordelia Biddle, Greer Garson; Mrs. Duke, Geraldine Page; Cordy Biddle, Lesley Ann Warren; Angie Duke, John Davidson; Aunt Mary, Gladys Cooper; Mrs. Worth, Hermione Baddeley; Tony Biddle, Paul Peterson; Liv Biddle, Eddie Hodges; Rosemary, Joyce Bulifant; Sgt. Flanagan, Sean McClory; Walter Blakely, Aron Kincaid; Charlie Taylor, Larry Merrill; Aunt Gladys, Frances Robinson; Joe Turner, Norman Grabowski; U. S. Marines, William Wellman Jr., Jim McMullan, and Jim Gurley.

1266 HAPPINESS. (New Yorker-1973). Piotr Zinoviev, Elena Egorova.

1267 THE HAPPINESS CAGE. (Cinerama-1972). Private James Reese, Christopher Walken; Dr. Frederick, Joss Ackland; The Major, Ralph Meeker; Miles, Ronny Cox; Orderly, Marco St. John; Medic, Tom Aldredge; Anna Kraus, Bette Henritze; Nurse Schroeder, Susan Travers; Lisa, Birthe Newmann; Psychiatrist, Claus Nissen.

1268 HAPPY AS THE GRASS WAS GREEN. (Martin-1973). Anna, Geraldine Page; Eli, Pat Hingle; Eric, Graham Beckel; Hazel, Rachel Thomas; Ji, Steve Weaver; Rufus, Elvin Byler; Sarah, Noreen Huber; Ben, John Miller; Menno, Luke Sickles.

1269 HAPPY BIRTHDAY, DAVY. (Zenith-1970). Bob, Chuck Roy; Davy, Larry Neilsen; Balsalm, Richard Fontaine; Sis, Judy Curtis; Butch, Carl Williams; Dick, Jack Reed; Nick, Robin Roberts; Joe, Joe Bell.

1270 HAPPY BIRTHDAY, WANDA JUNE. (Columbia-1971). Harold Ryan, Rod Steiger; Penelope Ryan, Susannah York; Dr. Norbert Woodley, George Grizzard; Herb Shuttle, Don Murray; Looseleaf Harper, William Hickey.

1271 HAPPY DAYS. (Anonymous Releasing Triumvirate-1974).

Georgina Spelvin, Arlana Blue, Cindy West, "Good Guy" Joe O'Brien, Lana Joyce, Sonny Landham, Melissa Evers, Jenny Carlton, Douglas Drew, Curt Gerard, David Hausman, Pat Edwards, Nina Lasko, Raoul Foster, Celine Schneider, Jean Palmer, Harding Harris.

1272 HAPPY END. (Continental-1968). Bedrich, Vladimir Mensik; Julie, Jaroslava Obermaierova; Lothario, Josef Abrham; Father-in-law, Bohuz Zahorsky; Mother-in-law, Stella Zazvorkova; Brunette, Helena Ruzickova; Policeman, Josef Hlinomaz.

1273 THE HAPPY ENDING. (United Artists-1969). Mary Wilson, Jean Simmons; Fred Wilson, John Forsythe; Sam, Lloyd Bridges; Flo, Shirley Jones; Mrs. Spencer, Teresa Wright; Harry Spencer, Dick Shawn; Agnes, Nanette Fabray; Franco, Robert Darin; Helen Bricker, Tina Louise; Marge Wilson, Kathy Fields; Divorcee, Karen Steele; Betty, Gail Hensley.

1274 HAPPY MOTHER'S DAY--LOVE, GEORGE. (Cinema 5-1973). Cara, Patricia Neal; Ronda, Cloris Leachman; Eddie, Bobby Darin; Celia, Tessa Dahl; Johnny, Ron Howard; Crystal, Kathie Browne; Piccolo, Joe Mascolo; Ron, Simon Oakland; Minister, Thayer David; Yolanda, Gale Garnett; Porgie, Roy Applegate; Florence, Jan Chamberlain; Bomber, Gerald E. Forbes; Preacher, Orest Ulan; Mears, Clarence Greene Jeans.

1275 HAPPY NEW YEAR. (AVCO Embassy-1973). Simon, Lino Ventura; Francoise, Francoise Fabian; Charles, Charles Gerard; Jeweler, Andre Falcon; Italian Lover, Silvano Tranquilli; First Intellectual, Claude Mann; Parisian Lover, Frederic De Pasquale; Salesgirl, Bettina Rheims; Madame Felix, Lilo De La Passardiere; Guest Appearance by Mireille Mathieu; Prison Warden, Gerard Sire.

1276 HARD CONTRACT. (20th Century-Fox-1969). John Cunningham, James Coburn; Sheila Metcalf, Lee Remick; Adrianne Bedford, Lilli Palmer; Ramsey Williams, Burgess Meredith; Alexi, Patrick Magee; Michael Carlson, Sterling Hayden; Maurice, Claude Dauphin; Evelyn Carlson, Helen Cherry; Ellen, Karen Black; Belgian Prostitute, Sabine Sun.

1277 THE HARD RIDE. (American International-1971). Phil, Robert Fuller; Sheryl, Sherry Bain; Big Red, Tony Russel; Grady, William Bonner; Father Tom, Marshall Reed; Ralls, Mike Angel; Mike, Biff Elliot; Mooch, Al Cole, Rita, Phyllis Selznick; Jason, R. L. Armstrong; Ted, Robert Swan; Rice, Larry Eisley; Meyers, Frank Charolla; Little Horse, Herman Rudin; Lenny, Alfonso Williams.

1278 THE HARDER THEY COME. (New World-1973). Jimmy

Cliff, Carl Bradshaw, Janet Bartley, Winston Stone, Ras Daniel Hartman, Basil Keane, Bobby Charlton, The Maytals.

1279 HARLOT. (Graffiti-1971). Mary, Fran Spector; Melody, Patty Alexon; 1st Rider, John McGaughtery; 2nd Rider, Bill Pruner; James, Leroy Jones; Miss Gladstone, Judy Angel; Biker, Zeb.

1280 HARLOW. (Magna-1965). Jean Harlow, Carol Lynley; Mrs. Jean Bello, Ginger Rogers; Marino Bello, Barry Sullivan; William Mansfield, Efrem Zimbalist Jr.; Marc Peters, Lloyd Bochner; Jonathan Martin, John Williams; Louis B. Mayer, Jack Kruschen; Ed, Michael Dante; Marie Dressler, Hermione Baddeley; Thelma, Audrey Christie.

1281 HARLOW. (Paramount-1965). Jean Harlow, Carroll Baker; Arthur Landau, Red Buttons; Jack Harrison, Michael Connors; Paul Bern, Peter Lawford; Everett Redman, Martin Balsam; Mama Jean Bello, Angela Lansbury; Marino Bello, Raf Vallone; Richard Manley, Leslie Nielsen; Mrs. Landau, Hanna Landy; Assistant Director, Peter Hansen.

1282 HAROLD AND MAUDE. (Paramount-1971). Maude, Ruth Gordon; Harold, Bud Cort; Mrs. Chasen, Vivian Pickles; Sculptor, Cyril Cusack; Uncle Victor, Charles Tyner; Sunshine, Ellen Geer; Priest, Eric Christmas.

1283 HARPER. (Warner Bros.-1966). Lew Harper, Paul Newman; Mrs. Sampson, Lauren Bacall; Betty Fraley, Julie Harris; Albert Graves, Arthur Hill; Susan Harper, Janet Leigh; Miranda Sampson, Pamela Tiffin; Alan Traggert, Robert Wagner; Dwight Troy, Robert Webber; Fay Estabrook, Shelley Winters; Sheriff Spanner, Harold Gould; Claude, Strother Martin; Puddler, Roy Jensen; Deputy, Martin West; Mrs. Kronberg, Jacqueline De Wit; Felix, Eugene Iglesias; Fred Platt, Richard Carlyle.

1284 THE HARRAD EXPERIMENT. (Cinerama-1973). Philip, James Whitmore; Margaret, Tippi Hedren; Stanley, Don Johnson; Harry, B. Kirby Jr.; Sheila, Laurie Walters; Beth, Victoria Thompson; Wilson, Elliott Street; Barbara, Sharon Taggart; Sidney, Robert Middleton; Jack, Billy Sands; Jeannie, Melody Patterson; Cynthia, Maggie Wellman; Yoga Instructor, Michael Greene; Evan, Ron Kolman; Workmen, Eric Server, Robert C. Ross; The Ace Trucking Company.

1285 THE HARRAD SUMMER. (Cinerama-1974). Stanley Kolasukas, Robert Reiser; Sheila Grove, Laurie Walters; Harry Schacht, Richard Doran; Beth Hillyer, Victoria Thompson; Margaret Tonhausen, Emmaline Henry; Jack Schacht, Bill Dana; Paula Schacht, Jodean Russo; Mrs. Kolasukas, Angela Clarke; Mr. Kolasukas, Tito Vandis; Sam Grove, Walter

Brooke; Diane Schacht, Mimi Saffian; Arnae, Lisa Moore; Brad, James Beach; Britzi, Pearl Shear; Florence, Jane Lambert; Bert Franklin, Marty Allen; Women's Consciousness Group, Sylvia Walden, Chuckie Bradley; Great Grandmother Oliver, Lili Valenty; Dee, Sherry Miles; Marcia, Patrice Rohmer.

1286 HARRY AND TONTO. (20th Century-Fox-1974). Harry, Art Carney; Shirley, Ellen Burstyn; Old Indian, Chief Dan George; Jessie, Geraldine Fitzgerald; Eddie, Larry Hagman; Wade, Arthur Hunnicutt; Burt, Phil Bruns; Norman, Joshua Mostel; Ginger, Melanie Mayron; Elaine, Dolly Jonah; Rivetowski, Herbert Berghof; Leroy, Aron Long; Happy Hooker, Barbara Rhoades; Burt Jr., Cliff De Young.

1287 HARRY IN YOUR POCKET. (United Artists-1973). Harry, James Coburn; Ray, Michael Sarrazin; Sandy, Trish Van Devere; Casey, Walter Pidgeon; Fence, Michael C. Gwynne; First Detective, Tony Giorgio; Second Detective, Michael Stearns; Francine, Sue Mullen; Salesman, Duane Bennet; Mr. Bates, Stanley Bolt; Bellboy, Barry Grimshaw.

1288 HARUM SCARUM. (MGM-1965). Johnny Tyronne, Elvis Presley; Princess Shalimar, Mary Ann Mobley; Aishah, Fran Jeffries; Prince Dragna, Michael Ansara; Zacha, Jay Norvello.

1289 HARVEY MIDDLEMAN, FIREMAN. (Columbia-1965). Harvey Middleman, Gene Trobnick; Lois, Patricia Harty; Harriet, Arlene Golonka; Mrs. Koogleman, Hermione Gingold; Dinny, Will MacKenzie; Mother, Ruth Jaroslow; Dooley, Charles Durning; Mookey, Stanley Handelman; Cindy, Tudy Bordoff; Richie, Neil Rouda.

1290 HAVING A WILD WEEKEND. (Warner Bros.-1965). Steve, Dave Clark; Dinah, Barbara Ferris; Guy, Robin Bailey; Nan, Yootha Joyce; Lenny, Lenny Davidson; Rick, Rick Huxley; Mike, Mike Smith; Denis, Denis Payton; Louis, David Lodge; Zissell, David De Keyser; Beatnik, Ronald Lacey; Grey, Hugh Walters.

1291 HAWAII. (United Artists-1966). Jerusha Bromley, Julie Andrews; Reverend Abner Hale, Max Von Sydow; Rafer Hoxworth, Richard Harris; Reverend Thorn, Torin Thatcher; Alii Nui Malama, Jocelyn La Garde; Kelolo, Ted Nobriga; Keoki, Manu Tupou; Noelani, Elizabeth Logue; Charles Bromley, Carroll O'Connor; Abigail Bromley, Elizabeth Cole; John Whipple, Gene Hackman; Immanuel Quigley, John Cullum; Captain Janders, George Rose; Lou Antonio, Malcolm Atterbury, Dorothy Jeakins, Lokelani S. Scicarell, Diane Sherry, Heather Menzies, Michael Constantine, John Harding, Robert Crawford, Robert Oakley, Henrik Von Sydow, Clas Von Sydow, Bertil Werjefelt.

1292 THE HAWAIIANS. (United Artists-1970). Whip Hoxworth, Charlton Heston; Purity Hoxworth, Geraldine Chaplin; Noel Hoxworth, John Phillip Law; Nyuk Tsin, Tina Chen; Micah Hale, Alec McCowen; Mun Ki, Mako; Milton Overpeck, Don Knight; Fumiko, Miko Mayama; Me Li, Virginia Ann Lee; Queen Liliuokalani, Naomi Stevens; American Minister, Harry Townes; Kai Chung, Khigh Dhiegh; Foo Sen, Keye Luke; Dr. Whipple Sr., James Gregory; Janders, Lyle Bettger; Europe, Winston Charc, Eric Lin Moon Chu; Africa, Michael Leon, Eddie Pang; Asia, Randy Kim, Wayne Chow; America, Victor Young, Jeffrey Chang; Australia, Bill Fong, Cheve Choy; Noel at 6, Jules Martin; Noel at 15, George Paulsin; Mei Li at 8, Tanya Chang; Soo Yong, James Hong, Elizabeth Smith, Chris Robinson, Mark LeBuse, Mathew Fitzgerald, Bruce Wilson, Mary Munday, Mailie McCauley, Alan Naluai, Forrest Wood, Murray Staff, Harry Holcombe, Galen Kam, Herman Wedemeyer, Victor Sen Yung.

1293 THE HAWKS AND THE SPARROWS. (Brandon-1967). The Man/Frate Ciccillo, Toto; The Son/Frate Ninetto, Ninetto Davoli; Femi Benussi, Umberto Bevilacqua, Renato Capogna, Rossana Di Rocco, Pietro Davoli, Cesare Gelli, Vittorio La Paglia, Alfredo Leggi, Renato Montalbano, Mario Pennisi, Lena Lin Solaro, Fides Stagni, Giovanni Tarallo, Vittorio Vittori.

1294 HE WHO RIDES A TIGER. (Sigma III-1968). Peter Rayston, Tom Bell; Joanne, Judi Dench; Superintendent Taylor, Paul Rogers; Mrs. Woodley, Kay Walsh; Orphanage Superintendent, Ray McAnally; The Panda, Jeremy Spenser; Peepers Woodley, Peter Madden; Detective Sgt. Scott, Inigo Jackson; Julie, Annette Andre; Anna, Edina Ronay; Nicolette Pendrell, Grant Lovatt, Ralph Michael, Frederick Piper, Rita Webb, Robin Hughes, Jimmy Gardner, Howard Lang, Naomi Chance, Pat Shakesby, Harry Baird, Margaret Bull, Frank Sieman, The Rapiers.

1295 HEAD. (Columbia-1968). The Monkees, Peter Tork, David Jones, Micky Dolenz, Michael Nesmith; Minnie, Annette Funicello; Lord High n Low, Timothy Carey; Officer Faye Lapid, Logan Ramsey; Swami, Abraham Sofaer; I. Vitteloni, Vito Scotti; Inspector Shrink, Charles Macaulay; Mr. and Mrs. Ace, T. C. Jones; Mayor Feedback, Charles Irving; Black Sheik, William Bagdad; Heraldic Messenger, Percy Helton; Extra, Sonny Liston; Private One, Ray Nitschke; Sally Silicone, Carol Doda; The Critic, Frank Zappa; The Jumper, June Fairchild; Testy True, Terry Garr; Lady Pleasure, I. J. Jefferson; The Big Victor, Victor Mature.

1296 HEAD OF THE FAMILY. (GGP-1973). Paola, Leslie Caron; Marco, Nino Manfredi; Adriana, Claudine Auger;

Romeo, Ugo Tognazzi.

1297 HEAD ON. (Leon-1971). Steve, Michael Witney; Mike, Michael Conrad; Millie, Lori Saunders; Koger, Art Lund; Nadine, Kathleen Freeman; Fred, Mickey Morton.

1298 THE HEART IS A LONELY HUNTER. (Warner Bros.-7 Arts-1968). John Singer, Alan Arkin; Mrs. Kelly, Laurinda Barrett; Blount, Stacy Keach Jr.; Antonapoulos, Chuck McCann; Mr. Kelly, Biff McGuire; Dr. Copeland, Percy Rodriguez; Portia, Cicely Tyson; Bubber Kelly, Jackie Marlowe; Willie, Johnny Popwell; Harry, Wayne Smith; Spirmonedes, Peter Mamakos; Beaudine, John O'Leary; Brannon, Hubert Harper; Mick Kelly, Sondra Locke.

1299 THE HEARTBREAK KID. (20th Century-Fox-1972). Lenny, Charles Grodin; Kelly, Cybil Shepherd; Lila, Jeannie Berlin; Corcoran, Eddie Albert; Mrs. Corcoran, Audra Lindley; Colorado Man, William Prince; Colorado Woman, Augusta Dabney; Cousin Ralph, Mitchell Jason; Entertainer, Art Metrano; Mrs. Kolodny, Marilyn Putnam; Kolodny, Jack Hausman; Pecan Pie Waiter, Erik Lee Preminger; Kelly's Boyfriend, Tim Browne; Flower Girl, Jean Scoppa; Young Boy, Greg Pecque; Mrs. Cantrow, Doris Roberts.

1300 HEAT. (Levitt-Pickman-1972). Joe Davis, Joe Dallesandro; Sally Todd, Sylvia Miles; Jessica Todd, Andrea Feldman; Motel Owner, Pat Ast; Movie Producer, Ray Vestal; Sally's Former Husband, P. J. Lester; His Roommate, Harold Child; Mute, Eric Emerson; Mute's Brother, Gary Koznocha; Hollywood Columnist, John Hallowell; Jessica's Girlfriend, Bonnie Glick; Girl by Pool, Pat Parlemon.

1301 HEAT OF MADNESS. (William Mishkin-1966). Kevin Scott, Alan Wylie, John Burke, Nancy McCormick, Stanley Seidman, Jon Tolliver, Jennifer Llaird, Barbara Ward, Diana Conti, Ann Muench, Sean Spencer, Mark Zalk.

1302 HEAVEN WITH A GUN. (MGM-1969). Jim Killian, Glenn Ford; Madge McCloud, Carolyn Jones; Leloopa, Barbara Hershey; Asa Beck, John Anderson; Coke Beck, David Carradine; Mace, J. D. Cannon; Garvey, Noah Berry; Gus Sampson, Harry Townes; Bart Patterson, William Bryant; Mrs. Patterson, Virginia Gregg; James Griffith, Roger Perry, Claude Woolman, Ed Bakey, Barbara Babcock, James Chandler, Angelique Petty John, Jessica James, Bee Tompkins, Bill Catching, Al Wyatt, Ed McCready, Miss Eddie Crispell and Barbara Dombre.

1303 HEAVY TRAFFIC. (American International-1973). Michael, Joseph Kaufman; Carole, Beverly Hope Atkinson; Angie, Frank DeKova; Ida, Terri Haven; Molly, Mary Dean Lauria; Rosalyn, Jacqueline Mills; Rosa, Lillian Adams.

1304 HEIDI. (Warner Bros.-7 Arts-1968). Heidi, Eva Maria Singhammer; Klara Sesemann, Gertrud Mittermayr; Grandfather, Gustav Knuth; Aunt Dete, Lotte Ledl; Herr Sesemann, Ernst Schroder; Miss Rottenmeier, Margot Trooger; Dr. Klassen, Rolf Moebius; Sebastian, Rudolf Vogel; Peter, Jan Koester.

1305 HELGA. (American International-1968). Helga, Ruth Gassmann; Helga's Husband, Eberhard Mondry; Asgard Hummel, Ilse Zielstorff.

1306 HELL IN THE PACIFIC. (Cinerama-1969). The American Marine Pilot, Lee Marvin; The Japanese Naval Officer, Toshiro Mifune.

1307 HELL ON WHEELS. (Crown International-1967). Marty, Marty Robbins; Del, John Ashley; Sue, Gigi Perreau; Steve, Robert Dornan; Herself, Connie Smith; Themselves, The Stonemans; Moonshiner, Robert Faulk; Moonshiner, Frank Gerstile; Christine Tabbott, Chris Eland, Eddie Crandall.

1308 HELL UP IN HARLEM. (American International-1973). Tommy, Fred Williamson; Papa Gibbs, Julius W. Harris; Helen, Floria Hendry; Sister Jennifer, Margaret Avery; Rev. Rufus, D'Urville Martin; Zach, Tony King; DiAngelo, Gerald Gordon.

1309 THE HELL WITH HEROES. (Universal-1968). Brynie MacKay, Rod Taylor; Elena, Claudia Cardinale; Lee Harris, Harry Guardino; Colonel Wilson, Kevin McCarthy; Mike Brewer, Peter Deuel; Al Poland, William Marshall; Pepper, Don Knight; Pol Guilbert, Michael Shillo; Willoughby, Robert Yuro; Sergeant Shaeffer, Lew Brown; Hans, Wilhelm Von Homburg; Jamila, Tanya Lemani; Chanteuse, Mae Mercer; Inspector Bouchard, Emile Genest; Pierre, Louis De Farra; French Girl, Jacqueline Bertrand; Crespin, Sid Haig; First M. P., Jim Creech; Old Arab, Pedro Regas; The Lookout, David Kurzon; Magid, Naji Gabbay; Urchins, Ric Natoli, Tony Nassour, Ricky Namay, George Samaan, and David Sindaha.

1310 THE HELLBENDERS. (Embassy-1967). Jonas, Joseph Cotten; Claire, Norma Bengell; Ben, Julian Mateos; Jeff, Gino Pernice; Nat, Angel Aranda; Kitty, Maria Martin; The Beggar, Al Mulock; Pedro, Aldo Sambrell; Fort Commander, Enio Girolani; Sheriff, Jose Nieto; Claudio Gora, Julio Pena, Rafael Vaquero, Simon Arriaga, Claudio Scarchilli, Ivan Scatruglia, Alvaro De Luna.

1311 THE HELLCATS. (Crown International-1969). Monte Chapman, Ross Hagen; Linda, Dee Duffy; Sheila, Sharyn Kinzie; Snake, Sonny West; Mr. Adrian, Robert F. Slatzer; Hiney, Eric Lidberg; Rita, Shannon Summers; David Chapman,

Bro Beck; Candy Cave, Diane Ryder; Pepper, Nick Raymond; Dean, Dick Merrifield; Hildy, Hildegard Wendt; Artist, Tony Cardoza; Artists Model, Elena Engstrom; Dee, Irene Martin; Moonfire, Frederic Downs; Sheriff, Noble Kid Chissell; Deputy, Robert Strong; Zombie, Ed Sarquist; Scorpio, Gus Trikonis; Betty, Lydia Goya; Moongoose, Tom Hanson; Scab, Ray Cantrell; Pete, Joe Coffey; Policeman, Eric Tomlin; Attorney, Warren Hammeck; First Detective, Jack Denton; First Senator, Walt Swanner; Second Senator, Bill Reese.

1312 HELLFIGHTERS. (Universal-1969). Chance Buckman, John Wayne; Tish Buckman, Katharine Ross; Greg Parker, Jim Hutton; Madelyn Buckman, Vera Miles; Jack Lomax, Jay C. Flippen; Joe Horn, Bruce Cabot; George Harris, Edward Faulkner; Irene Foster, Barbara Stuart; Colonel Valdez, Edmund Hashim; Amal Bokru, Valentin De Vargas; Madame Loo, Frances Fong; General Lopez, Alberto Morin; Harry York, Alan Caillou; Helen Meadows, Laraine Stephens; Jim Hatch, John Anderson; Dr. Songla, Lal Chand Mehra; Zamora, Rudy Diaz; Gumdrop, Bebe Louie.

1313 No entry.

1314 HELLO, DOLLY! (20th Century-Fox-1969). Dolly Levi, Barbra Streisand; Horace Vandergelder, Walter Matthau; Cornelius Hackl, Michael Crawford; Orchestra Leader, Louis Armstrong; Irene Molloy, Marianne McAndrew; Minnie Fay, E. J. Peaker; Barnaby Tucker, Danny Lockin; Ermengarde, Joyce Ames; Ambrose Kemper, Tommy Tune; Gussie Granger, Judy Knaiz; Rudolph Reisenweber, David Hurst; Fritz, Fritz Feld; Vandergelder's Barber, Richard Collier; Policeman in Park, J. Pat O'Malley.

1315 HELLO DOWN THERE. (Paramount-1969). Fred Miller, Tony Randall; Vivian Miller, Janet Leigh; T. R. Hollister, Jim Backus; Nate Ashbury, Roddy McDowall; Mel Cheever, Ken Berry; Himself, Merv Griffin; Lorrie Miller, Kay Cole; Tommie Miller, Gary Tigerman; Harold Webster, Richard Dreyfuss; Marvin Webster, Lou Wagner; Myrtle Ruth, Charlotte Rae; Mrs. Webster, Henny Backus; Mr. Webster, Bud Hoey; Alan Briggs, Frank Schuller; Dr. Cara Wells, Lee Meredith; Admiral, Bruce Gordon; Sonarman, Harvey Lembeck; Jonah, Arnold Stang; Reilly, Pat Henning; Philo, Jay Laskay; Chief Petty Officer, Charles Martin; Captain, Frank Logan; Radio Man, Andy Jarrell; Secretary, Lora Kaye.

1316 HELLO-GOODBYE. (20th Century-Fox-1970). Harry England, Michael Crawford; Baron De Choisis, Curt Jurgens; Dany, Genevieve Gilles; Evelyne Rosson, Ira Furstenberg; Cole, Lon Satton; Bentley, Peter Myers; Paul, Mike Marshall; Raymond, Didier Haudepin; Joycie, Vivien Pickles;

Monique, Agathe Natanson; Hotel Porter, Georges Bever; Concierge, Denise Grey; Dickie, Jeffry Wickham.

1317 HELL'S ANGELS '69. (American International-1969). Chuck, Tom Stern; Wes, Jeremy Slate; Betsy, Conny Van Dyke; Apache, Steve Sandor; Detective, J. D. Spradlin; Sonny, Sonny Barger; Terry, Terry the Tramp; The Okland Hell's Angels; Bobby Hall, Ray Renard, Michael Michaelian, Bud Ekins, Joe Hooker, Bob Harris, Ric Henry, Danielle Corn, Jerry Randall, Ed Mulder.

1318 HELLS ANGELS ON WHEELS. (U. S. Films-1967). Buddy, Adam Roarke; Poet, Jack Nicholson; Shill, Sabrina Scharf; Abigale, Jana Taylor, Jock; John Garwood; Bull, Richard Anders; Pearl, I. J. Jefferson; Gypsy, James Oliver; Bingham, Jack Starrett; Moley, Gary Littlejohn; Justice of the Peace, Bruno Vesota; Artist, Robert Kelljan; Lori, Kathryn Harrow; Leader of Hells Angels, Sonny Barger.

1319 HELL'S BELLES. (American International-1969). Dan, Jeremy Slate; Tampa, Adam Roarke; Cathy, Jocelyn Lane; Cherry, Angelique Pettyjohn; Gippo, Bill Lucking; Red Beard, Eddie Hice; Meatball, Dick Bullock; Crazy John, Jerry Randall; Rabbit, Jerry Brutsche; Zelda, Kristian Van Buren; Big Sal, Elaine Gefner; Piper, Astrid Warner; Tony, Michael Walker.

1320 HELL'S BLOODY DEVILS. (Independent-International-1970). John Gabriel, Broderick Crawford, Scott Brady, Kent Taylor, Keith Andes, John Carradine.

1320a THE HELLSTROM CHRONICLE. (Cinema V-1971). Dr. Nils Hellstrom, Lawrence Pressman.

1321 HELP! (United Artists-1965). John, John Lennon; Paul, Paul McCartney; Ringo, Ringo Starr; George, George Harrison; Clang, Leo McKern; Ahme, Eleanor Bron; Foot, Victor Spinetti; Algernon, Roy Kinnear; Bhuta, John Bluthal; Superintendent, Patrick Cargill.

1322 HENRY VIII AND HIS SIX WIVES. (Anglo EMI-1973). King Henry VIII, Keith Michell; Thomas Cromwell, Donald Pleasence; Anne Boleyn, Charlotte Rampling; Jane Seymour, Jane Asher; Katherine of Aragon, Frances Cuka; Catherine Howard, Lynn Frederick; Anne of Cleves, Jenny Bos; Catherine Parr, Barbara Leigh-Hunt; Norfolk, Michael Gough; Suffolk, Brian Blessed; Thomas More, Michael Goodliffe; Cranmer, Bernard Hepton; Gardiner, Garfield Morgan; Wolsey, John Bryans; Wriothesley, John Bennett; Fisher, Peter Madden; Mary, Sarah Long; Sir Ralph Ellerker, Michael Godfrey; Warham, Richard Warner; Edward Seymour, Michael Byrne; Thomas Seymour, Peter Clay; Thomas Culpepper, Robin Sachs; Chapuys, Nicholas Amer; Abbot,

Basil Clarke; Smeaton, Damien Thomas; Lady Rochford, Margaret Ward.

1323 HER AND SHE AND HIM. (Rochambeau-1970). Greta, Astrid Frank; Claude, Nicole Debonne; Mathius, Yves Vincent; Jean, Frederick Sakiss.

1324 HERBIE RIDES AGAIN. (Buena Vista-1974). Mrs. Steinmetz, Helen Hayes; Willoughby Whitfield, Ken Berry; Nicole, Stefanie Powers; Mr. Judson, John McIntire; Alonzo Hawk, Keenan Wynn; Judge, Huntz Hall; Chauffeur, Ivor Barry; Lawyer, Dan Tobin; Taxi Driver, Vito Scotti; Lawyer, Raymond Bailey; Doctor, Liam Dunn; Secretary, Elaine Devry; Loostgarten, Chuck McCann; Traffic Commissioner, Richard X. Slattery; Sir Lancelot, Hank Jones; Red Knight, Rod McCary.

1325 HERCULES IN THE HAUNTED WORLD. (Woolner Bros.-1965). Hercules, Reg Park; Deianira, Leonora Ruffo; Lichas, Christopher Lee; Theseus, Giorgio Ardisson; Ida Galli, Ely Draco, Marisa Belli.

1326 HERCULES, SAMSON AND ULYSSES. (MGM-1965). Hercules, Kirk Morris; Samson, Richard Lloyd; Delilah, Liana Orfei; Ulysses, Enzo Cerusico; Seren, Aldo Giuffre.

1327 HERE WE GO ROUND THE MULBERRY BUSH. (Lopert-1968). Jamie McGregor, Barry Evans; Mary Cloucester, Judy Geeson; Caroline Beauchamp, Angela Scoular; Claire, Diane Keen; Audrey, Vanessa Howard; Linda, Adrienne Posta; Paula, Sheila White; Mrs. McGregor, Moyra Fraser; Mr. McGregor, Michael Bates; Mrs. Beauchamp, Maxine Audley; Mr. Beauchamp, Denholm Elliott; Spike, Christopher Timothy; Craig Foster, Nicky Henson; Joe McGregor, Allan Warren; Arthur, Roy Holder; Gordon, George Layton; Bruce, Gareth Robinson; Curtis, Oliver Cotton; Charles Beauchamp, Andrew Hamilton; Cath, Sally Avory; Ingrid, Erika Raffael; Cavan Kendall, Trevor Jones, Gillie Austin, Christopher Mitchell, Pauline Challoner, Mary Griffiths, Stella Kemble, Angela Pleasence, The Spencer Davis Group.

1328 HERE'S YOUR LIFE. (Brandon-1968). Olof, Eddie Axberg; Olivia, Ulla Sjoberg; Lundgren, Gunnar Bjornstrand; Niklas, Per Oscarsson; Larsson, Ulf Palme; Maria, Signe Stade; August, Allan Edwall; August's Wife, Anna Maria Blind; Nicke, Ake Fridell; Kristiansson, Holger Lowenadler; Olof's Stepmother, Gudrun Brost; Olssen, Goeran Lindberg; Johansson, Jan-Erik Lindkvist.

1329 THE HERO. (AVCO Embassy-1972). Eitan, Richard Harris; Nira, Romy Schneider; Nimrod, Kim Burfield; Yasha, Maurice Kaufman; Weiner, Yosi Yadin; Chairman, Shraga Friedman; Teddy, Aviva Marks; Bank Manager, Yossi

Grabber; Eldad, David Heyman; Abraham, Giddion Shemer; Sarah, Sarah Moor.

1330 THE HEROES OF TELEMARK. (Columbia-1966). Dr. Rolf Pedersen, Kirk Douglas; Knut Straud, Richard Harris; Anna, Ulla Jacobsson; Uncle, Michael Redgrave; Arne, David Weston; Major Frick, Anton Diffring; Terboven, Eric Porter; Colonel Wilkinson, Mervyn Johns; Sigrid, Jennifer Hillary; Jensen, Roy Dotrice; Barry Jones, Ralph Michael, Geoffrey Keen, Maurice Denham, Wolf Frees, Robert Ayres, Sebastian Breaks, John Golightly, Alan Howard, Patrick Jordan, William Marlowe, Brook Williams, David Davies, Karel Stepanek, Faith Brook, Elvi Hale, Gerard Heinz, Victor Beaumont, Philo Hauser, George Murcell, Russell Waters, Jan Conrad.

1331 HEROINA. (Royal-1965). Laura, Kitty De Hoyos; Chico, Jaime Sanchez; Marcos, Otto Sirgo; Tito, Jeddu Mascorieto; The Mother, Marta Casanas; The Father, Jose De San Anton; Nina, Nidia Caro; Nick, Felix Monclova; Singer, Olga Guillot.

1332 HEX. (20th Century-Fox-1973). Oriole, Tina Herazo; Acacia, Hilarie Thompson; Old Gunfighter, John Carradine; Whizzer, Keith Carradine; Golly, Mike Combs; Jimbang, Scott Glenn; Giblets, Gary Busey; Chupo, Robert Walker; China, Doria Cook; Duzak, Iggie Wolfington; Elma, Patricia Ann Parker; Elston, Tom Jones; Brother Billy, Dan Haggerty.

1333 HI, MOM! (Sigma III-1970). Jon Rubin, Robert De Niro; Superintendent, Charles Durnham; Joe Banner, Allen Garfield; Pervert in theatre, Abraham Goren; Jeannie Mitchell, Lara Parker; Judy Bishop, Jennifer Salt; Gerrit Wood, Gerrit Graham; Playboy, Nelson Peltz; Pharmacist, Peter Maloney; Co-op Neighbor, William Daley; Newscaster, Floyd L. Peterson; N. I. T. Journal Revolutionaries, Hector Valentin Lino Jr. and Carole Leverett; N. I. T. Journal at Newsstand, Ruth Bocour, Bart De Palma, Arthur Bierman; Be Black, Baby! Troupe, Buddy Butler, David Conell, Milton Earl Forrest, Carolyn Craven, Joyce Griffin, Kirk Kirksey; Audience, Ruth Alda, Carol Vogel, Beth Bowden, Joe Stillman, Joe Fields, Gene Eldman, Paul Milvy.

1334 HICKEY AND BOGGS. (United Artists-1972). Al Hickey, Bill Cosby; Frank Boggs, Robert Culp; Nyona, Rosalind Cash; Edith Boggs, Sheila Sullivan; Nyona's Mother, Isabel Sanford; Lawyer, Lou Frizzell; Nyona's Daughter, T-Ronce Allen; Apartment Manager's Wife, Nancy Howard; Used Car Salesman, Bernard Nedell; Mary Jane, Carmen; Quemando (Prisoner), Louis Moreno; Quemando (Florist), Ron Henrique; Mary Jane's Daughter, Cary Sanchez; Mary Jane's Son, Jason Culp; Mr. Brill, Robert Mandan; Ballard, Michael

Moriarty; Bernie, Bernie Schwartz; Brill's Daughter, Denise Renfro; Papadakis, Vincent Gardenia; Shaw, Jack Colvin; Lt. Wyatt, James Woods; Ted, Ed Lauter; Rice, Lester Fletcher; Farrow, Gil Stuart; Mr. Leroy, Sil Words; Coroner's Assistant, Joe Tata.

1335 HIGH. (Joseph Brenner Associates-1969). Vicky, Astri Thorvik; Tom, Lanny Beckman; Peter Matthews, Joyce Cay, Dennis Payque, Carol Epstein, Doris Cowan, Al Mayoff, Melinda McCracken, Mortie Golum, Janet Amos, Paul Kirby, Jack Epstein, Peter Pyper.

1336 THE HIGH COMMISSIONER. (Cinerama-1968). Scobie Malone, Rod Taylor; Sir James Quentin, Christopher Plummer; Sheila Quentin, Lilli Palmer; Lisa Pretorius, Camilla Sparv; Madame Cholon, Daliah Lavi; Ambassador Townsend, Franchot Tone; Joseph, Clive Revill; Denzil, Lee Montague; Jamaica, Calvin Lockhart; Pallain, Derren Nesbitt; Flannery, Leo McKern; Leeds, Russell Napier; Ferguson, Ken Wayne; Julius, Edric Connor; Edwards, Alan White; Blundell, Peter Reynolds; Pham Chinh, Burt Kwouk; Coburn, Paul Grist; Jackaroo, Charles Tingwell; Rifleman, Jerry Crampton; Cameramen, Tony Selby and Keith Bonnard.

1337 HIGH INFIDELITY. (Magna-1965). Francesco, Nino Manfredi; Raffaella, Fulvia Franco; Ronald, John Philip Law; Giulio, Charles Aznavour; Laura, Claire Bloom; Gloria, Monica Vitti; Tonino, Jean-Pierre Cassel; Paolo, Sergio Fantoni; Cesare, Ugo Tognazzi; Tebaide, Michele Mercier; Reguzzoni, Bernard Blier.

1338 HIGH PLAINS DRIFTER. (Universal-1973). The Stranger, Clint Eastwood; Sarah Belding, Verna Bloom; Callie Travers, Mariana Hill; Dave Drake, Mitchell Ryan; Morgan Allen, Jack Ging; Mayor Jason Hobart, Stefan Gierasch; Lewis Belding, Ted Hartley; Mordecai, Billy Curtis; Stacey Bridges, Geoffrey Lewis; Bill Borders, Scott Walker; Sheriff Sam Shaw, Walter Barnes; Lutie Naylor, Paul Brinegar; Asa Goodwin, Richard Bull; Preacher, Robert Donner; Cole Carlin, Anthony James; Barber, William O'Connell; Jake Ross, John Quade; Townswoman, Jane Aull; Dan Carlin, Dan Vadis; Gunsmith, Reid Cruickshanks; Tommy Morrow, James Gosa; Saddlemaker, Jack Kosslyn; Fred Short, Russ McCubbin; Mrs. Lake, Belle Mitchell; Warden, John Mitchum; Teamster, Carl C. Ptti; Stableman, Chuck Waters; Marshall Jim Duncan, Buddy Van Horn.

1339 HIGH PRIESTESS OF SEXUAL WITCHCRAFT. (Triumvirate-1973). Georgina Spelvin, Rick Livermore, Jean Palmer, Harding Harrison, Marc Stevens.

1340 HIGH RISE. (Maturpix-1973). Tamie Trevor, Geri Miller, Richard Hunt, James Kleeman, Jutta David, Mireille Renaud,

Samantha Whitney.

1341 A HIGH WIND IN JAMAICA. (20th Century-Fox-1965). Chavez, Anthony Quinn; Zac, James Coburn; Mr. Thornton, Nigel Davenport; Mrs. Thornton, Isabel Dean; Emily Thornton, Deborah Baxter; John Thornton, Martin Amis; Laura Thornton, Karen Flack; Harry Thornton, Henry Beltran; Rachel Thornton, Roberta Tovey; Edward Thornton, Jeffrey Chandler; Margaret, Viviana Ventura; Alberto, Benito Carruthers; Captain Marpole, Kenneth J. Warren; Dutch Captain, Gert Frobe; Rosa, Lila Kedrova; Mathias, Dennis Price; Cook, Kenji Takaki; Josephine, Maud Fuller.

1342 THE HILL. (MGM-1965). Joe Roberts, Sean Connery; Sergeant Major, Harry Andrews; Sergeant Williams, Ian Hendry; Sergeant Harris, Ian Bannen; George Stevens, Alfred Lynch; Jackob King, Ossie Davis; Monty Bartlett, Roy Kinnear; Jock McGrath, Jack Watson; Medical Officer, Michael Redgrave; Commandant, Norman Bird.

1343 THE HILLS RUN RED. (United Artists-1967). Jerry Brewster, Thomas Hunter; Mendez, Henry Silva; Getz, Dan Duryea; Ken Seagall, Nando Gazzolo; Mary Ann, Nicoletta Machiavelli; Hattie, Gianna Serra; Tim, Loris Loddi; Horner, Geoffrey Copleston; Stayne, Paolo Magalotti; Federal Sergeant, Tiberio Mitri; First Gambler, Vittorio Bonos; Sancho, Mirko Valentin; Pedro, Guglielmo Spoletini; Burger, Guido Celano; Soldier Mitch, Maura Mannatrizio; Carson, Gian Luigi Crescenzi.

1344 THE HIRED HAND. (Universal-1971). Collings, Peter Fonda; Harris, Warren Oates; Hannah, Verna Bloom; Dan, Robert Pratt; McVey, Severn Darden.

1345 THE HIRED KILLER. (Paramount-1967). Clint Harris, Robert Webber; Tony Lobello, Franco Nero; Mary, Jeanne Valerie; Secchy/Goldstein, Jose Luis de Vallalonga; Andrea Ferri, John Hawkwood; Barry, Michel Bardinet; Gastel, Cec Linder; Lucy, Theodora Bergery; Frank Earl Hammond.

1346 THE HIRELING. (Columbia-1973). Leadbetter, Robert Shaw; Eady Franklin, Sarah Miles; Cantrip, Peter Egan; Mother, Elizabeth Sellars; Connie, Carolin Mortimer; Mrs. Hansen, Patricia Lawrence; Edith, Petra Markham; Davis, Ian Hogg; Doreen, Christine Hargreaves; Lyndon Brook, Alison Leggatt.

1347 HISTORY LESSONS. (New Yorker-1973). Mummilius Spicer, Gottfried Bold; Young Man, Benedikt Zulauf; Peasant, Johann Unterpertinger.

1348 HIT! (Paramount-1973). Nick Allen, Billy Dee Williams; Mike Willmer, Richard Pryor; Barry Strong, Paul Hampton;

Sherry Nielson, Gwen Welles; Dutch Schiller, Warren Kemmerling; Ida, Janet Brandt; Herman, Sid Melton; Carlin, David Hall; Crosby, Todd Martin; Director, Norman Burton; Madame Frelou, Jenny Astruc; Romain, Yves Barsacq; Jean-Baptiste, Jean-Claude Bercq; Bornou, Henri Cogan; Zero, Pierre Collet; Jyras, Paul Mercy; Madame Orissa, Malka Ribovska; Monteca, Richard Saint-Bris; Jeannie Allen, Tina Andrews; Judge, Frank Christi; Boyfriend, Mwako Cumbuka; Esther, Janear Hines; Weasel, Jerry Jones.

1349 HIT MAN. (MGM-1972). Tyrone, Bernie Casey; Gozelda, Pamela Grier; Laural, Lisa Moore; Ivelle, Bhetty Waldron; Sherwood, Sam Laws; Rochelle, Candy All; Zito, Don Diamond; Theotis, Edmund Cambridge; Shag, Bob Harris; Julius, Rudy Challenger; Nita, Tracy Ann King; Leon, Christopher Joy; Baby Huey, Roger E. Mosley.

1350 THE HITCHHIKERS. (Entertainment Ventures-1973). Maggic, Misty Rowe; Benson, Norman Klar; Diane, Linda Avery; Karen, Tammy Gibbs; Jinx, Kathy Stutsman; Brook, Mary Thatcher; Truck Driver, Denny Nichols; Deacon, Ted Ziegler; Store Manager, Efrem Dockter; Doctor, Lou Jefford; Reb, Blue McKenzie; Car Salesman, Lee Morley; Nemo, Jim Sherwood.

1351 HITLER: THE LAST TEN DAYS. (Paramount-1973). Hitler, Alec Guinness; Hoffman, Simon Ward; Krebs, Adolfo Celi; Von Greim, Eric Porter; Hanna, Diane Cilento; Keitel, Gabriele Ferzetti; Eva Braun, Doris Kunstmann; Burgdorf, Joss Ackland; Dr. Stumpfegger, John Barron; Goebbels, John Bennett; Frau Christian, Sheila Gish; Fegelein, Julian Glover; Weidling, Michael Goodliffe; Guensche, John Hallam; Magda Goebbels, Barbara Jefford; Bormann, Mark Kingston; Fraulein Manzialy, Phyllida Law; Fraulein Junge, Ann Lynn; Trude, Angela Pleasence; Wagner, Andrew Sachs; Jodl, Philip Stone; Gebhardt, Timothy West; Voss, William Abney; Boldt, Kenneth Colley; German Officer, James Cossins; Hanske, Philip Locke; Von Below, Richard Fescud; Hewel, John Savident.

1352 HOA BINH. (Transvue-1971). Hung, Phi Lan; Xuan, Huynh Cazenas; Mother, Xuan Ha.

1353 HOFFMAN. (Levitt-Pickman-1971). Hoffman, Peter Sellers; Janet, Sinead Cusack; Tom, Jeremy Bulloch; Mrs. Mitchell, Ruth Dunning; Foreman, David Lodge; Guitarist, Ron Taylor; Kay Hal, Karen Murtagh, Cindy Burrows, Elizabeth Bayley.

1354 HOLD ON! (MGM-1966). Herman, Peter Blair Noone; Karl, Karl Green; Keith, Keith Hopwood; Derek, Derek Leckenby; Barry, Barry Whitwam; Louisa, Shelley Fabares; Cecilie, Sue Ane Langdon; Lindquist, Herbert Anderson;

Dudley, Bernard Fox; Frant, Harry Hickox; Mrs. Page, Hortense Petra; Publicity Man, Mickey Deems; Detective No. 1, Ray Kellog; Detective No. 2, John Hart; Photographer, Phil Arnold.

1355 HOLLYWOOD BABYLON. (Aquarius-1972). Jim Gentry, Myron Griffin, Ashley Phillips, Uschi Digart.

1356 THE HOLY MOUNTAIN. (ABKCO-1974). Alejandro Jodorowsky, Horacio Salina, Juan Ferrara, Adriana Page.

1357 HOMBRE. (20th Century-Fox-1967). John Russell, Paul Newman; Alexander Favor, Fredric March; Cicero Grimes, Richard Boone; Jessie Brown, Diane Cilento; Sheriff Frank Braden, Cameron Mitchell; Audra Favor, Barbara Rush; Billy Lee Blake, Peter Lazer; Doris, Margaret Blye; Henry Mendez, Martin Balsam; Steve Early, Skip Ward; Mexican Bandit, Frank Silvera; Lamar Dean, David Canary; Delgado, Val Avery; Soldier, Larry Ward; Mrs. Delgado, Linda Cordova; Apache, Pete Hernandez; Apache, Merrill C. Isbell.

1358 HOMEBODIES. (AVCO Embassy-1974). Mr. Blakely, Peter Brocco; Miss Emily, Frances Fuller; Mr. Sandy, William Hansen; Mrs. Loomis, Ruth McDevitt; Mattie, Paula Trueman; Mr. Loomis, Ian Wolfe; Miss Pollack, Linda Marsh; Mr. Crawford, Douglas Fowley; Kenneth Tobey, Wesley Lau, Norman Gottschalk, Irene Webster, Nicholas Lewis, Michael Johnson, Alma Du Bus, John Craig, Eldon Quick, William Benedict, Joe De Meo.

1359 THE HOMECOMING. (American Film Theatre-1973). Sam, Cyril Cusack; Lenny, Ian Holm; Teddy, Michael Jayston; Ruth, Vivien Merchant; Joey, Terence Rigby; Max, Paul Rogers.

1360 HOMER. (National General-1970). Homer Edwards, Don Scardino; Mr. Edwards, Alex Nicol; Laurie Grainer, Tisa Farrow; Mrs. Edwards, Lenka Peterson; Hector, Ralph Endersby; Sally, Trudy Young; Mr. Grainger, Arch McDonnell; Mrs. Grainer, Jan Campbell; Eddie Cochran, Tim Henry; Mr. Cochran, Murray Westgate; Mrs. Cochran, Mona O'Hearn; Sheriff, Bob Werner.

1361 L'HOMME SANS VISAGE. (Terra Film-SOAT-1974). The Man, Jacques Champreux; The Woman, Gayle Hunnicutt; Sorbier, Gert Froebe; Martine, Josephine Chaplin; Paul, Ugo Pagliai; Seraphin, Patrick Prejean; Dutreuil, Clement Harari.

1362 HOMO EROTICUS. (CIDIF-1973). Michele, Lando Buzzanca; Mrs. Coco, Rossana Podesta; Coco, Luciano Salce; Marchesa, Adriana Asti; Industrialist, Sylva Koscina; Doctor, Bernard Blier; His Wife, Ira Furstenberg; Maid,

Brigette Skay.

1363 THE HONEY POT. (United Artists-1967). Cecil Fox, Rex Harrison; Mrs. Lone-Star Crockett Sheridan, Susan Hayward; William McFly, Cliff Robertson; Princess Dominique, Capucine; Merle McGill, Edie Adams; Sarah Watkins, Maggie Smith; Inspector, Adolfo Celi; Oscar Ludwig, Herschel Bernardi; Revenue Agent, Cy Grant; Revenue Agent, Frank Latimore; Massimo, Luigi Scavran; Cook, Mimmo Poli; Tailor, Antonio Corevi; Assistant Tailor, Carlos Valles; Volpone, Hugh Manning; Mosca, David Dodimead.

1364 HONEYBABY, HONEYBABY. (Kelly-Jordan-1974). Laura Lewis, Diana Sands; Liv, Calvin Lockhart; Sam, Seth Allen; Skiggy Lewis, J. Eric Bell; Harry, Brian Phelan; Harry's Mother, Bricktop; General Christian Awani, Thomas Baptiste; Mme. Chan, Gay Guilin; Herb, Nabib Aboul Hoson; Makuba, Mr. Sunshine.

1365 HONEYCOMB. (Cine-Globe-1972). Teresa Del Rio, Julia Pena, Maria Elena Flores; Teresa, Geraldine Chaplin; Peter, Per Oscarsson.

1366 THE HONEYMOON KILLERS. (Cinerama-1969). Martha Beck, Shirley Stoler; Ray Fernandez, Tony LoBianco; Janet Fay, Mary Jane Higby; Bunny, Doris Roberts; Delphine Downing, Kip McArdle; Myrtle Young, Marilyn Chris; Mrs. Beck, Dortha Duckworth; Evelyn Long, Barbara Cason; Doris, Ann Harris; Rainelle Downing, Mary Breen, Elsa Raven, Mary Engel, Guy Sorel, Mike Haley, Diane Asselin, Col. William Adams.

1367 No entry.

1368 THE HONKERS. (United Artists-1972). Lew Lathrop, James Coburn; Linda Lathrop, Lois Nettleton; Clete, Slim Pickens; Deborah Moon, Anne Archer; Royce, Richard Anderson; Rita Ferguson, Joan Huntington; Mel Potter, Jim Davis; Jack Ferguson, Ramon Bieri; Bob Lathrop, Ted Eccles; Lowell, Mitchell Ryan; Everett, Wayne McLaren; Sam Martin, John Harmon; Matt Weber, Richard O'Brien; Hat Store Proprietor, Pitt Herbert; Announcer, Chuck Parkinson; Larry Mahan, Himself; Travis, Ross Dollarhyde; Shorty, Jerry Gatlin; Dave, Bobby Hall; Harve, Bud Walls; Waitress, Kitty Sadock.

1368a HONKY. (Jack H. Harris-1971). Sheila, Brenda Sykes; Honky, John Nielson; Sharon, Maia Danziger; Archer, John Lasell; Dr. Smith, William Marshall.

1369 HOOK, LINE AND SINKER. (Columbia-1969). Peter Ingersoll/Fred Dobbs, Jerry Lewis; Dr. Scott Carter, Peter Lawford; Nancy Ingersoll, Anne Francis; Perfecto, Pedro

Gonzalez Gonzalez; Jimmy, Jimmy Miller; Jennifer, Jennifer Edwards; Mrs. Durham, Eleanor Audley; Kenyon Hammercher, Henry Corden; Karlotta Hammercher, Sylvia Lewis; Head Surgeon, Phillip Pine; Foreign Mortician, Felipe Turich; Baby Sitter, Kathleen Freeman.

1370 THE HOOKED GENERATION. (Allied Artists-1969). Daisey, Jeremy Slate; Mark, Steve Alaimo; Acid, John Davis Chandler; Dum Dum, Willie Pastrano; Kelly, Cece Stone.

1371 HORNETS' NEST. (United Artists-1970). Capt. Turner, Rock Hudson; Bianca, Sylva Koscina; Von Hecht, Sergio Fantoni; Maj. Taussig, Jacques Sernas; Schwalberg, Giacomo Rossi Stuart; Col. Jannings, Tom Felleghi; Gen Von Kleger, Andrea Bosic; Gen. Dohrmann, Bondy Esterhazy; Capt. Kreuger, Gerard Herter; Gunther, Hardy Stuart; Col. Weede, Max Turilli; Lt. with Taussig, Raphael Santos; Lt. at village, Viti Caronia.

1372 HORROR CASTLE. (Zodiac-1965). Mary, Rossana Podesta; Max Hunter, Georges Riviere; Erich, Christopher Lee; Selby, Jim Nolan; Marta, Anny Delli Uberti; Doctor, Luigi Severini; Trude, Luciana Milone.

1373 HORROR HOUSE. (American International-1970). Chris, Frankie Avalon; Sheila, Jill Haworth; Gary, Mark Wynter; Inspector, Dennis Price; Kellett, George Sewell; Sylvia, Gina Warwick; Peter, Richard O'Sullivan; Dorothy, Carol Dilworth; Richard, Julian Barnes; Madge, Veronica Doran; Henry, Robin Stewart; Peggy, Jan Holden; Police Sergeant, Clifford Earl; Bradley, Robert Raglan.

1374 THE HORROR OF FRANKENSTEIN. (American Continental-1971). Victor, Ralph Bates; Alys, Kate O'Mara; Wilhelm, Graham James; Elizabeth, Veronica Carlson; Father, Bernard Archard; Grave-robber, Dennis Price; His Wife, Joan Rice; Monster, David Prowse.

1375 THE HORROR OF IT ALL. (20th Century-Fox-1965). Jack Robinson, Pat Boone; Cynthia, Erica Rogers; Cornwallis, Dennis Price; Natalia, Andree Melly; Reginal, Valentine Cyall; Percival, Jack Bligh; Grandpapa, Erik Chitty; Muldoon, Archie Duncan; Young Doctor, Oswald Laurence.

1376 HORROR OF THE BLOOD MONSTERS. (Independent International-1971). Dr. Rynning, John Carradine; Col. Manning, Robert Dix; Valerie, Vicki Volante; Willy, Joey Benson; Lian, Jennifer Bishop; Bryce, Bruce Powers; Bob, Fred Meyers; Linda, Britt Semand.

1377 HORROR ON SNAPE ISLAND. (Fanfare-1972). Evan Brent, Bryant Haliday; Rose Mason, Jill Haworth; Nora Winthorp, Anna Palk; Hamp Gurney, Jack Watson; Adam, Mark

Edwards; Dan Winthorp, Derek Fowlds; Gary, John Hamill; Brom, Gary Hamilton; Penny Read, Candace Glendenning; Lawrence Bakewell, Dennis Price; John Gurney, George Coulouris; Des, Robin Askwith; Mae, Serretta Wilson; Saul Gurney, Fredric Abbott; Michael Gurney, Mark McBride; Det. Supt. Hawk, William Lucas; Dr. Simpson, Anthony Valentine; Nurse, Marianne Stone.

1378 THE HORSE IN THE GRAY FLANNEL SUIT. (Buena Vista-1968). Fred Bolton, Dean Jones; Suzie Clemens, Diane Baker; Archer Madison, Lloyd Bochner; Tom Dugan, Fred Clark; Helen Bolton, Ellen Janov; Charlie Blake, Morey Amsterdam; Ronnie Gardner, Kurt Russell; Aunt Martha, Lurene Tuttle; Harry Townes, Alan Hewitt; Lt. Lorendo, Federico Pinero; Catherine, Florence MacMichael; Mimsey, Joan Marshall; Judy Gardner, Robin Eccles; Sergeant Roberts, Adam Williams; Truck Driver, Norman Grabowski; Lady in Elevator, Nydia Westman; Announcer, Bill Baldwin Sr.

1379 THE HOSPITAL. (United Artists-1971). Dr. Herbert Bock, George C. Scott; Barbara Drummond, Diana Rigg; Drummond, Barnard Hughes; Head Nurse, Nancy Marchand.

1380 THE HOSTAGE. (Crown-International-1968). Davey Cleaves, Danny Martins; Bull, Don O'Kelly; Eddie, Dean Stanton; Otis Lovelace, John Carradine; Steve Cleaves, Ron Hagerty; Carol Cleaves, Jenifer Lea; Miss Mabry, Ann Doran; Sam, Raymond Guth; Selma, Nora Marlowe; Mrs. Primus, Shirley O'Hara; Bartender, Mike McCloskey; Mr. Thomas, Dick Spry; Glenn, Leland Brown.

1381 HOSTILE GUNS. (Paramount-1967). Gid McCool, George Montgomery; Laura Mannon, Yvonne De Carlo; Mike Reno, Tab Hunter; Marshall Willett, Brian Donlevy; Aaron, John Russell; Hank Pleasant, Leo Gordon; R. C. Crawford, Robert Emhardt; Angel, Pedro Gonzalez Gonzalez; Ned Cooper, James Craig; Sheriff Travis, Richard Arlen; Uncle Joe, Emile Meyer; Johnston, Donald Barry; Buck, Fuzzy Knight; Jensen, William Fawcett; Bunco, Joe Brown; Chig, Reg Parton; Tubby, Read Morgan; Alfie, Eric Cody.

1382 THE HOT BOX. (New World-1972). Bunny, Andrea Cagan; Lynn, Margaret Markov; Ellie, Rickey Richardson; Sue, Laurie Rose; Flavio, Carmen Argenziano; Garcia/Major Dubay, Charles Dierkop.

1383 HOT CHANNELS. (Distribpix-1973). Davy Jones, Melanie Daniels, Catharine Warren, M. Tracis, Emmet Gregory, H. Quinlin.

1384 HOT CIRCUIT. (Sherpix-1972). Stripper, Sally Paradise; Salesman, Jack Duquesque; Babysitter, Kit Fox; Adventuress,

Simone Fallique; Woodcutter, Shokan Hill; Nymph, Pris Teen; Producer, Elmo Hassel; Girl Friday, April Lace; Hustler, Jack De Haven; Julie Love, Carol Orange, Mona Lott, Joy Ball, Marylou Wallenstein, Rita Strangworth, Reggie Smith, Crystal Cynk, Phil Luck, Irene Foster, Dana Marlboro.

1385 HOT MILLIONS. (MGM-1968). Marcus Pendleton, Peter Ustinov; Patty Terwilliger, Maggie Smith; Carlton J. Klemper, Karl Malden; Willard C. Gnatpole, Bob Newhart; Caesar Smith, Robert Morley; Customs Officer, Cesar Romero; Nurse, Melinda May; Landlady, Ann Lancaster; Bus Inspector, Frank Tragear; First Charwoman, Julie May; Mrs. Hubbard, Margaret Courtenay; Miss Glyn, Elizabeth Counsell; Second Charwoman, Patsy Crowther; Barber, Carlos Douglas; Louise, Lynda Baron; Agent, Billy Milton; Prison Governor, Peter Jones; Co-Pilot, David Bedard; Elizabeth Hughes, Anne De Vigier, Sally Faulkner, Paul Farrell, Wilfred Carter, Geoffrey Frederick, Betty Duncan, Frank Singuineau.

1386 HOT PANTS HOLIDAY. (AVCO Embassy-1972). Jill, Tudi Wiggins; MacIver, Christopher St. John; Peony, Greer St. John; Marion, Sabra Welles; Myrtle, Bobbie Parker; Robert, Robert Horen; Odette, Odette.

1387 THE HOT ROCK. (20th Century-Fox-1972). Dortmunder, Robert Redford; Kelp, George Segal; Murch, Ron Leibman; Abe Greenberg, Zero Mostel; Greenberg, Paul Sand; Dr. Amusa, Moses Gunn; Lt. Hoover, William Redfield; Sis, Topo Swope; Ma Murch, Charlotte Rae; Warden, Graham P. Jarvis; Bartender Rollo, Harry Bellaver; Happy Hippie, Seth Allen; Cop at Police Station, Robert Levine; Dr. Strauss, Lee Wallace; Albert, Robert Weil; Miasmo, Lynne Gordon; Bird Lady, Frania O'Malley; Otto, Fred Cook; Big Museum Guard, Mark Dawson; Museum Guards, Gilbert Lewis, George Bartenieff; Policemen, Ed Bernard, Charles White, Christopher Guest.

1388 HOT ROD HULLABALOO. (Allied Artists-1966). John Arnold, Arlen Dean Snyder, Kendra Kerr, Val Bisoglio, Ron Cummins, Marsha Mason, Eugene Bua, Robert Paget, William Hunter.

1389 HOT RODS TO HELL. (MGM-1967). Tom Phillips, Dana Andrews; Peg Phillips, Jeanne Crain; Gloria, Mimsy Farmer; Tina Phillips, Laurie Mock; Duke, Paul Bertoya; Ernie, Gene Kirkwood; Jamie Phillips, Tim Stafford; Land Dailey, George Ives; Wife at Picnic, Hortense Petra; Man at Picnic, William Mims; Policeman, Paul Genge; Little Boy, Peter Oliphant; Bill Phillips, Harry Hickox; Charley, Charles P. Thompson; Youth, Jim Hennagan; Combo Leader, Mickey Rooney Jr.

1390 HOT SUMMER WEEK. (Fanfare-1973). Kathleen Cody, Michael Ontkean, Diane Hull, Ralph Waite, John McMurty, Pamela Serpe, Riggs Kennedy.

1391 HOT TIMES. (William Mishkin-1974). Archie, Henry Cory; Ronnie, Gail Lorber; Bette, Amy Farber; Coach-Guru, Bob Lesser; Mughead, Steve Curry; Kate, Clarissa Ainley; Gloria, Bonnie Gondel; Alex Mogulmuph, Jack Baran; La Chochita, Betty Mur; Potemkin the Director, Irving Horowitz.

1392 HOTEL. (Warner Bros. -1967). Peter McDermott, Rod Taylor; Jeanne Rochfort, Catherine Spaak; Keycase, Karl Malden; Warren Trent, Melvyn Douglas; Dupere, Richard Conte; The Duchess, Merle Oberon; Duke of Lanbourne, Michael Rennie; Curtis O'Keefe, Kevin McCarthy; Christine, Carmen McRae; Captain Yolles, Alfred Ryder; Bailey, Roy Roberts; Herbie, Al Checco; Mrs. Grandin, Sheila Bromley; Sam, Harry Hickox; Mason, William Lanteau; Laswell, Ken Lynch; Morgan, Clinton Sundberg; Kilbrick, Tol Avery; Dr. Adams, Davis Roberts; Elliott, Jack Donner; Elevator Operator, Lester Dorr; Mother, Dee Carroll; Daughter, Judy Norton.

1393 HOTEL PARADISO. (MGM-1966). Benedict Boniface, Alec Guinness; Marcelle Cot, Gina Lollobrigida; Henri Cot, Robert Morley; Angelique, Peggy Mount; Anniello, Akim Tamiroff; La Grand Antoinette, Marie Bell; Maxime, Derek Fowldes; Mr. Martin, Douglas Byng; Duke, Robertson Hare; Victoire, Ann Beach; Inspector, Leonard Rossiter; George, David Battley; Turk, Dario Moreno; Georges Feydeau, Peter Glenville.

1394 THE HOUR AND TURN OF AUGUSTO MATRAGA. (New Yorker-1971). Augusto, Leonardo Vilar; His wife, Maria Ribeiro; Bandit Chief, Jofre Soares; Priest, Mauricio Do Valle.

1395 HOUR OF THE GUN. (United Artists-1967). Wyatt Earp, James Garner; Doc Holliday, Jason Robards; Ike Clanton, Robert Ryan; Octavius Roy, Albert Salmi; Horace Sullivan, Charles Aidman; Andy Warshaw, Steve Ihnat; Pete Spence, Michael Tolan; Virgil Earp, Frank Converse; Morgan Earp, Sam Melville; Anson Safford, Austin Willis; Thomas Fitch, Richard Bull; John P. Clum, Larry Gates; Dr. Goodfellow, Karl Swenson; Jimmy Ryan, Bill Fletcher; Frank Stillwell, Robert Phillips; Curly Bill Brocius, Jon Voight; Herman Spicer, William Schallert; Turkey Creek Johnson, Lonnie Chapman; Sherman McMasters, Monte Markham; Texas Jack Vermillion, William Windom; Sanitarium Doctor, Edward Anhalt; Billy Clanton, Walter Gregg; Frank McLowery, David Perna; Tom McLowery, Jim Sheppard; Latigo, Jorge Russek.

1396 HOUR OF THE WOLF. (Lopert-1968). Alma Borg, Liv Ullmann; Johan Borg, Max Von Sydow; Baron von Merkens, Erland Josephson; Corinne von Merkens, Gertrud Fridh; The Baron's Mother, Gudrun Brost; Ernst von Merkens, Bertil Anderberg; Lindhorst, Georg Rydeberg; Heerbrand, Ulf Johanson; Old Lady With Hat, Naima Wifstrand; Kapellmeister Kreisler, Lenn Hjortzberg; Maidservant, Agda Helin; Young Boy, Mikael Rundqvist; Woman in Mortuary, Mona Seilitz; Timino, Folke Sundquist; Veronica Vogler, Ingrid Thulin.

1397 HOURS OF LOVE. (Cinema V-1965). Gianni, Ugo Tognazzi; Maretta, Emmanuele Riva; Leila, Barbara Steele; Ottavio, Umberto D'Orsi; Jolanda, Mara Berni; Mimma, Diletta D'Andrea; Cipriani, Brunelo Rondi, Psychiatrist, Renato Speziali; Roberto, Fabrizio Moroni.

1398 HOUSE IN NAPLES. (UM-1970). Charles, Peter Savage; Joe, Jack LaMotta; Sherry, Sharon Dale; Annette, Theresa Pelati.

1399 HOUSE OF DARK SHADOWS. (MGM-1970). Barnabas, Jonathan Frid; Elizabeth, Joan Bennett; Julia, Grayson Hall; Maggie, Kathryn Leigh Scott; Jeff, Roger Davis; Carolyn, Nancy Barrett; Willie, John Karlen; Roger, Louis Edmonds; Todd, Donald Briscoe; Elliot, Thayer David; Sheriff, Dennis Patrick; David, David Henesy.

1400 HOUSE OF 1,000 DOLLS. (American International-1968). Felix Manderville, Vincent Price; Rebecca, Martha Hyer; Stephen Armstrong, George Nader; Marie Armstrong, Anne Smyrner; Inspector Emil, Wolfgang Kieling; Fernando, Sancho Gracia; Diane, Maria Rohm; Paul, Louis Rivera; Ahmed, Jose Jaspe; Salim, Juan Olaguivel; Abdu, Herbert Fuchs; Madame Viera, Yelena Samarina; Liza, Diane Bond; The Dolls, Andrea Lascelles, Kitty Swan, Loli Munoz, Monique Aime, Carolyn Coo, Sandra Petrelli, Jill Echols, Ursula Janis, Karin Skarreso, Lara Lenti, Marisol Anon.

1401 HOUSE OF WHIPCORD. (1974). Mrs. Wakehurst, Barbara Markham; Justice Bailey, Patrick Barr; Tony, Ray Brooks; Julia, Anne Michelle; Anne Marie de Vernay, Penny Irving; Walker, Sheila Keith; Bates, Dorothy Gordon; Mark Dessart, Robert Tayman; Jack, Ivor Salter; Claire, Judy Robinson; Karen, Karen David; Estelle, Jane Hayward; Denise, Celia Quicke; Barbara, Celia Imrie; Ted, Ron Smerczak; Cavan, David McGillivray; Al, Barry Martin; Henry, Tony Sympson; Henry's Wife, Rose Hill; Ticket Collector, Dave Butler; Police Sergeant, Denis Tinsley; Cyclist, Pete Walker.

1402 THE HOUSE ON CHELOUCHE STREET. (Productions Unlimited-1974). Gila Almagor, Shai Ophir, Yosseph Shiloah,

Michal Bat-Adam, Avner Hiskiahou, Ophir Shalhin.

1403 THE HOUSE ON SKULL MOUNTAIN. (20th Century-Fox-1974). Andrew Cunningham, Victor French; Lorena Christophe, Janee Michelle; Thomas, Jean Durand; Philippe, Mike Evans; Harriet Johnson, Xernona Clayton; Sheriff, Lloyd Nelson; Louette, Ella Woods; Pauline, Mary J. Todd McKenzie; Priest, Don Devendorf; Doctor, Jo Marie; LeDoux, Senator Leroy Johnson.

1404 THE HOUSE THAT CRIED MURDER. (Unisphere-1973). Barbara, Robin Strasser; Father, John Beal; David, Arthur Roberts; Ellen, Ivan Jean Saraceni.

1405 THE HOUSE THAT SCREAMED. (American International-1971). Mme. Fourneau, Lilli Palmer; Theresa, Christina Galbo; Luis, John Moulder-Brown; Irenee, Mary Maude; Mlle. Desprez, Candida Losada; M. Baldie, Tomas Blanco; Catherine, Pauline Challenor; Isabelle, Maribel Martin; Suzanne, Conchita Paredes; Brechard, Victor Israel.

1406 THE HOUSE WITH AN ATTIC. (Artkino-1966). Nellie Mychkova, Sergei Yakovlev.

1407 HOW DO I LOVE THEE. (Cinerama-1970). Stanley Waltz, Jackie Gleason; Elsie Waltz, Maureen O'Hara; Lena Mervin, Shelley Winters; Marion Waltz, Rosemary Forsyth; Tom Waltz (adult), Rick Lenz; Tom at 11, Clinton Robinson; Peter McGurk, Jim McCallian; Art Salerno, Don Sebastian; Dean Bagley, Jack Nagle; Mrs. Bagley, Judy Wallace; Prof. Norman Littlefield, Don Beddoe; Hugo Wellington, J. Edward McKinley; Mrs. Wellington, Templeton Fox; Mrs. Gromulka, Fritzie Burr; Rachel, Marcia Knight; Mother Superior, Olga Varga; Dr. Giroux, Dick Sterling; Old Geezer, Robertson White; Secretary, Harriet Veloshin; French Nurse, Evelyn Turner; French Dentist, Ed Ross; Belly Dancer, Soroya Farah; Bartender, Frank Logan.

1408 HOW I WON THE WAR. (United Artists-1967). Lt. Ernest Goodbody, Michael Crawford; Gripweed, John Lennon; Clapper, Roy Kinnear; Transom, Lee Montague; Juniper, Jack MacGowran; General Grapple, Michael Hordern; Melancholy Musketeer, Jack Hedley; Odlebog, Karl Michael Vogler; Spool, Ronald Lacey; Drogue, James Cossins; Dooley, Ewan Hooper; American General, Alexander Knox; Robert Hardy, Sheila Hancock, Charles Dyer, Bill Dysart, Paul Daneman, Peter Craven, Jack May, Richard Pearson, Pauline Taylor, John Ronane, Norman Chappell, Bryan Pringle, Fanny Carby, Dandy Nichols, Gretchen Franklin, John Junkin, John Trenaman, Mick Dillon, Kenneth Colley.

1409 HOW LOW CAN YOU FALL? (Titanus-1974). Eugenia, Laura Antonelli; Raimondo, Alberto Lionello; Pantasso,

Michele Placido; Henry, Jean Rochefort; Evelyn, Karin Schubert.

1410 HOW MUCH LOVING DOES A NORMAL COUPLE NEED? (Eve-1967). Barney Rickert, Ken Swofford; Sheila Ross, Alaina Capri; Dewey Hoople, Jack Moran; Coral Hoople, Adele Rein; Laurence Talbot, Andrew Hagara; Cracker, Frank Bolger; Babette, Babette Bardot; Dr. Martin Ross, John Furlong.

1411 HOW NOT TO ROB A DEPARTMENT STORE. (Artixo-1965). Marcel, Jean-Claude Brialy; Ida, Marie Laforet; Moune, Sophie Daumier; Justin, Jean-Pierre Marielle; Meloune, Michel Serrault; Leon, Daniel Ceccaldi; Etienne, Albert Remy; Raf, Pierre Clementi; Curly, Roland Blanche; Charles, Renaud Verlay; Limonade, Madeleine Barbulee; Palmoni, Robert Manuel.

1412 HOW SWEET IT IS! (National General-1968). Grif Henderson, James Garner; Jenny Henderson, Debbie Reynolds; Philippe Maspere, Maurice Ronet; Mr. Tilly, Terry-Thomas; The Purser, Paul Lynde; Louis, Marcel Dalio; Mr. Agatzi, Gino Conforti; David Henderson, Donald Losby; Bootsie Wax, Hilarie Thompson; Gloria, Alexandra Hay; Nancy Leigh, Mary Michael; Haskell Wax, Walter Brooke; Vera Wax, Elena Verdugo; Ann Morgan Guilbert, Patty Regan, Vito Scotti, Christopher Ross, Larry Hankin, Larry Riggio, Jack Colvin, Leigh French, Erin Moran, Robert Homel, Jon Silo, Don Diamond, Lenny Kent, Rico Cattani, Nikita Knatz, Bella Bruck, Ogden Talbot, Michael French, Bert Aretsky, Johnny Silver, Penny Marshall, Terri Messina, Patti Braverman, Arlene Parness, Carey Lynn, Erin O'Reilly, Rori Gwynne, Julee Hunter, Peggy Babcock, Mary O'Brien, Susan Meredith, Heather Menzies, Margot Nelson, Marti Litis, Myrna Ross, Jenie Jackson, Sharon Citron, Sheila Leighton, Shiva Rozier, Luana Anders, Barbara E. Fuller, Katherine Darc, Marjorie Dayne, Margie Duncan, Jenny Fridolfs, Bea Bradley, Eve Bruce, Emese Williams, Marilyn White.

1413 HOW TASTY WAS MY LITTLE FRENCHMAN. (New Yorker-1973). Girl, Ana Maria Magalhaes; Frenchman, Arduino Colasanti; Chief, Ital Natur; Eduardo Embassahy, Manfredo Colasanti, Jose Cleber.

1414 HOW TO COMMIT MARRIAGE. (Cinerama-1969). Frank Benson, Bob Hope; Oliver Poe, Jackie Gleason; Elaine Benson, Jane Wyman; Lois Grey, Maureen Arthur; Phil Fletcher, Leslie Nielsen; LaVerne Baker, Tina Louise; Attorney, Paul Stewart; The Baba Ziba, Irwin Corey; Nancy Benson, Joanna Cameron; David Poe, Tim Matthieson; The Comfortable Chair.

1415 HOW TO MURDER YOUR WIFE. (United Artists-1965). Stanley Ford, Jack Lemmon; Mrs. Ford, Virna Lisi; Charles, Terry-Thomas; Harold Lampson, Eddie Mayerhoff; Edna, Claire Trevor; Judge Blackstone, Sidney Blackmer; Tobey Rawlins, Max Showalter; Dr. Bentley, Jack Albertson; District Attorney, Alan Hewitt; Harold's Secretary, Mary Wickes.

1416 HOW TO SAVE A MARRIAGE--AND RUIN YOUR LIFE. (Columbia-1968). David Sloane, Dean Martin; Carol Corman, Stella Stevens; Harry Hunter, Eli Wallach; Muriel Laszlo, Anne Jackson; Thelma, Betty Field; Mr. Slotkin, Jack Albertson; Mary Hunter, Katharine Bard; Eddie Rankin, Woodrow Parfrey; Everett Bauer, Alan Oppenheimer; Marcia Borie, Shelley Morrison; Roger, George Furth; Wally Hammond, Monroe Arnold; Hall Satler, Claude Stroud.

1417 HOW TO SEDUCE A PLAYBOY. (Chevron-1968). Peter Keller, Peter Alexander; Boy Schock, Renato Salvatori; Vera, Antonella Lualdi; Anita Biondo, Scilla Gabel; Sokker, Joachim Fuchsberger; Ginette, Jocelyn Lane; Lucy, Helga Anders; Lucy's Mother, Linda Christian; Coco, Elione Dalmeida; Millie, Christiane Rucker; Emile, Joachim Teege; Director Zwerch, Georg Corten; Schladitz, Otto Ambros.

1418 HOW TO SEDUCE A WOMAN. (Cinerama-1974). Angus Duncan, Angel Tompkins, Heidi Bruhl, Alexandra Hay, Jo Anne Meredith, Judith McConnell, Vito Scotti, Marty Ingels, Janice Carroll, Hope Holiday, Lillian Randolph, Kay Peters, Dita Cobb, James Bacon, Jack Bailey, Fran Ryan, Joe E. Ross, Joe Alfasa, Jackie Brett, Dave Barry, Eve Brent, Herb Vigran, John Craig, Billy Curtis, Billy Frick, Jerry Mann, Marvin Miller, Ilona Wilson, Maurice Dallimore, Eileen McDonough, Angus Duncan Mackintosh, Schoneberg.

1419 HOW TO STEAL A MILLION. (20th Century-Fox-1966). Nicole Bonnet, Audrey Hepburn; Simon Dermott, Peter O'Toole; David Leland, Eli Wallach; Charles Bonnet, Hugh Griffith; De Solnay, Charles Boyer; Grammont, Fernand Gravey; Senor Paravideo, Marcel Dalio; Chief Guard, Jacques Marin; Guard, Moustache; Auctioneer, Roger Treville; Insurance Clerk, Eddie Malin; Marcel, Bert Bertram.

1420 HOW TO STUFF A WILD BIKINI. (American International-1965). Dee Dee, Annette Funicello; Ricky, Dwayne Hickman; B. D., Brian Donlevy; Bwana, Buster Keaton; Peachy Keane, Mickey Rooney; Eric Von Zipper, Harvey Lembeck; Cassandra, Beverly Adams; Bonehead, Jody McCrea; Johnny, John Ashley; Animal, Marianne Gaba; North Dakota Pete, Len Lesser; Dr. Melamed, Arthur Julian; Khola Koku, Bobbi Shaw; Puss, Alberta Nelson; J. D., Andy Romano; John Macchia, Jerry Brutsche, Bob Harvey, Myrna Ross, Alan Fife, Sig Frohlich, Tom Quine, Hollis Morrison, Guy

Hemric, George Boyce, Charlie Reed, Patti Chandler, Mike Nader, Ed Garner, John Fain, Mickey Dora, Brian Wilson, Bruce Baker, Ned Wynn, Kerry Berry, Rick Jones, Ray Atkinson, Ron Dayton, Marianne Gordon, Sheila Stephenson, Rosemary Williams, Sue Hamilton, Tonia Van Deter, Uta Stone, Toni Harper, Michele Barton, Victoria Carroll, Luree Holmes.

1421 HOW TO SUCCEED IN BUSINESS WITHOUT REALLY TRYING. (United Artists-1967). J. Pierpont Finch, Robert Morse; Rosemary Pilkington, Michele Lee; J. B. Biggley, Rudy Valee; Bud Frump, Anthony Teague; Hedy LaRue, Maureen Arthur; Benjamin Ovington, Murray Matheson; Smitty, Kay Reynolds; Mr. Twimble, Sammy Smith; Bratt, John Myhers; Gatch, Jeff De Benning; Miss Jones, Ruth Kobart; George Fenneman, Anne Seymour, Erin O'Brien Moore, Joey Faye, Ellen Verbit, Virginia Sale, Al Nessor, Carol Worthington, Janice Carroll, Patrick O'Moore, Wally Strauss, Ivan Volkman, David Swift, Carl Princi, Dan Tobin, Robert Q. Lewis, John Holland, Paul Hartman, Justin Smith.

1422 HOW TO SUCCEED WITH SEX. (Medford-1970). Jack, Zack Taylor; Sandy, Mary Jane Carpenter; Joan, Bambi Allen; Pam, Victoria Bond; Phyllis, Shawn Devereaux; Peggy, Luanne Roberts; Fred, Keith London; Margaretta, Margaretta Ramsey.

1423 HOWZER. (Uri-1973). Nick, Royal Dano; Mary, Olive Deering; Joe, Virgil Frye; Howzer, Peter Desiante; Debora, Melissa Stocking; Albert, William Gray; Edmund Gilbert, Allyn Ann McLeri, Elaine Partnow, Wonderful Smith, Steven Vaughan, David Dean, Ed Van Nordic.

1424 HUCKLEBERRY FINN. (United Artists-1974). Huck Finn, Jeff East; Jim, Paul Winfield; The King, Harvey Korman; The Duke, David Wayne; Col. Grangerford, Arthur O'Connell; Pap, Gary Merrill; Mrs. Loftus, Natalie Trundy; Widder Douglas, Lucille Benson; Mary Jane Wilks, Kim O'Brien; Susan Wilks, Jean Fay; Jim's Wife, Odessa Cleveland.

1425 HUGO AND JOSEPHINE. (Warner Bros. -7 Arts-1968). Josefin, Maria Ohman; Hugo, Fredrik Becklen; Gudmarsson, Beppe Wolgers.

1426 HUGS AND KISSES. (AVCO Embassy-1968). Eva, Agneta Ekmanner; Max, Sven-Bertil Taube; John, Hakan Serner; Hickan, Lena Granhagen; Photographer, Rolf Larsson; Ingrid Bostrom, Carl Johann Ronn, Peter Cornell.

1427 THE HUMAN DUPLICATORS. (Woolner Bros. -1965). Glenn Martin, George Nader; Gale Wilson, Barbara Nichols;

Professor Dornheimer, George Macready; Lisa, Dolores Faith; Kolos, Richard Kiel; Intelligence Agency Head, Richard Arlen; Austin Welles, Hugh Beaumont; Tommy Leonetti, Lonnie Sattin.

1428 HUNGER. (Sigma III-1968). The Writer, Per Oscarsson; Ylajali, Gunnel Lindblom; Sigrid Horne-Rasmussen; The Pawnbroker, Oswald Helmuth; Ylajali's Siters, Birgitte Federspiel; The Editor, Henki Kolstad; The Beggar, Sverre Hansen; The Man in the Park, Egil Hjort Jensen; The Shop Assistant, Per Theodor Hansen; "The Count," Lars Nordrum; The Painter, Roy Bjornstad.

1429 HUNGER FOR LOVE. (Pathe Contemporary-1973). Leila Diniz, Irene Stefania, Arduino Colasanti, Paulo Porto.

1430 HUNGRY WIVES. (Jack H. Harris-1973). Joan, Jan White; Gregg, Ray Laine; Shirley, Anne Muffly; Nikki, Joedda McClain, Jack, Bill Thunhurst; Marion, Virginia Greenwald; Dr. Miller, Neil Fisher; Sylvia, Esther Lapidus; Gloria, Jean Wechsler; Grace, Shirley Strasser.

1431 THE HUNT. (Trans-Lux-1967). Jose, Ismael Merlo; Paco, Alfredo Mayo; Luis, Jose Maria Prada; Enrique, Emilio Guitierrez Polack; Juan, Fernando Sanchez Polack; Nina, Violetta Garcia.

1432 THE HUNTED SAMURAI. (Toho-1971). Roppeita, Hideki Takahashi; Kyonosuke, Isao Natusyagi; Tarao, Seiichiro Kameishi; Toki, Masako Izumi; Aochi, Yochiro Aoki; Nachi, Shoki Fukae; Jisaku, Kishiro Kawami.

1433 THE HUNTERS ARE THE HUNTED. (Radim-1973). Abram, Martin Sperr; Hannelore, Angela Winkler; Mayor's Wife, Erika Wackernagel; Barbara, Else Quecke; Paula, Hanna Schygulla; Butcher's Wife, Maria Stadler; Priest, Hans Elwenspoek.

1434 THE HUNTING PARTY. (United Artists-1971). Frank, Oliver Reed; Melissa, Candice Bergen; Matthew, Simon Oakland; Brandt, Gene Hackman; Nelson, Ronald Howard; Sam, G. D. Spradlin; Buford, Bernard Kay; Mario, Eugenio Escudero Garcia; Doc, Mitchell Ryan; Hog, L. Q. Jones; Loring, William Watson; Crimp, Rayford Barnes; Collins, Dean Selmier; Owney, Ritchie Adams; Cowboys, Carlos Bravo, Bud Strait; Sheriff, Ralph Brown; Teacher, Marian Collier; Telegrapher, Max Slaten; Mexican, Rafael Escudero Garcia; Priest, Emilio Rodriques; Redhead, Sara Atkinson; Chinese, Francisca Tu; Blonde, Lilibeth Solison; Mexican, Marisa Tovar; Other Girls, Stephanie Pieritz, Christine Larroude.

1435 HURRY SUNDOWN. (Paramount-1967). Henry Warren,

Michael Caine; Julie Ann Warren, Jane Fonda; Rad McDowell, John Phillip Law; Vivian Thurlow, Diahann Carroll; Reeve Scott, Robert Hooks; Lou McDowell, Faye Dunaway; Judge Purcell, Burgess Meredith; Carter Sillens, Jim Backus; Lars Finchley, Robert Reed; Rose Scott, Beah Richards; Rex Ingram, Madeleine Sherwood, Doro Merande, George Kennedy, Frank Converse, Loring Smith, Donna Danton, Luke Askew, Peter Goff, William Elder, Steve Sanders, Dawn Barcelona, David Sanders, Michael Henry Roth, Gladys Newman, Joan Parks, Robert C. Bloodwell, Charles Keel, Kelly Ross, Ada Hall Covington, Gene Rutherford, Bill Hart, Dean Smith.

1436 HURRY UP, OR I'LL BE 30. (AVCO Embassy-1973). George Trapani, John Lefkowitz; Jackie Tice, Linda De Coff; Vince Trapani, Ronald Anton; Flo, Maureen Byrnes; Peter, Danny DeVito; Mr. Trapani, David Kird; Mark Lossier, Frank Quinn; Mrs. Trapani, Selma Rogoff; Ken Harris, George Welbes; Tony, Steve Inwood; Gypsy Girl/Bar Girl, Faith Langford; Audition Girl #1, Samantha Lynche; Miss Walsh, Susan Peretz; Bartender, Bob O'Connell; Gas Station Attendant, Bill Nunnery.

1437 HUSBANDS. (Columbia-1970). Harry, Ben Gazzara; Archie, Peter Falk; Gus, John Cassavetes; Mary Tynan, Jenny Runacre; Pearl Billingham, Jenny Lee Wright; Julie, Noelle Kao; Leola, Leola Harlow; Annie, Meta Shaw; Red, John Kullers; The Countess, Delores Delmar; Diana Mallabee, Peggy Lashbrook; Mrs. Hines, Eleanor Zee; Stuart's Wife, Claire Malis; Annie's Mother, Lorraine McMartin; Ed Weintraub, Edgar Franken; Sarah, Sarah Felcher; Jesus Loves Me, Antoinette Kray; "Jeannie," Gwen Van Dam; "Happy Birthday," John Armstrong; "Normandy," Eleanor Gould; Susanna, Carinthia West; Margaret, Rhonda Parker; Stuart Jackson, David Rowlands; Minister, Joseph Boley; Stuart's Grandmother, Judith Lowry; "Shanghai Lil," Joseph Hardy; Barmaid, K. C. Townsend; Nurses, Anne O'Donnell, Gena Wheeler.

1438 HUSH ... HUSH, SWEET CHARLOTTE. (20th Century-Fox-1965). Charlotte Hollis, Bette Davis; Miriam Deering, Olivia De Havilland; Dr. Drew Bayliss, Joseph Cotten; Velma Cruther, Agnes Moorehead; Harry Willis, Cecil Kellaway; Big Sam Hollis, Victor Buono; Mrs. Jewel Mayhew, Mary Astor; Paul Marchand, William Campbell; Sheriff Luke Standish, Wesley Addy; John Mayhew, Bruce Dern; Foreman, George Kennedy; Taxi Driver, Dave Willock; Boy, John Megna; Newspaper Editor, Frank Ferguson; Gossips, Ellen Corby, Helen Kleeb, and Marianne Stewart.

1439 HYSTERIA. (MGM-1965). Smith, Robert Webber; Dr. Keller, Anthony Newlands; Gina, Jennifer Jayne; Hemmings, Maurice Denham; Denise, Lelia Goldoni; English Girl,

Sandra Boize.

1440 No entry.

1441 I, A LOVER. (Crown International-1968). Peter, Jorgen Ryg; Beatrice, Jessie Flaws; Ole, Axel Strobye; Isak, Ebbe-Langberg; Mr. Pauce, Paul Hagen; Mortensen, Dirch Passer; Sigrid, Kerstin Wartel; Elizabeth, Marie Nylander; Dr. Ulla Pauce, Jeanne Darville; Woman in Office, Sigrid Horne Rasmussen.

1442 I, A MAN. (Andy Warhol-1967). Tom, Tom Baker; First Girl, Cynthia May; Second Girl, Ivy Nicholson; Third Girl, Ingrid Superstar; Fourth Girl, Stephanie Graves; Fifth Girl, Valeria Solanis; Sixth Girl, Bettina Coffin.

1443 I, A WOMAN. (Audubon-1966). Siv Esruth, Essy Persson; Surgeon, Jorgen Reenberg; Heinz, Preben Mahrt; Siv's Fiance, Preben Koerning; Siv's Mother, Tove Maes; Siv's Father, Eric Hell; Lars, Bengt Brunskog; Tough Guy, Frankie Steele.

1444 I, A WOMAN, PART III (THE DAUGHTER). (Chevron-1970). Birthe, Inger Sundh; Stephen, Tom Scott; Lisa, Ellen Faison; Siv, Gun Falk; Leo, Klaus Pagh; Hippie Dancer, Susanne Jagd; Egon, Soren Stromberg; Max, Bent Warburg; Patient, Helli Louise; Older Woman, Tove Bang; Another Older Woman, Tove Maes; Hell's Angel, Benny Hansen; Another, Poul Glargaard; Reporter, John Larsen.

1445 I AM A DANCER. (Anglo-Emi-1973). Rudolf Nureyev, Margot Fonteyn, Carla Fracci, Lynn Seymour, Deanne Bergsma.

1446 I AM A GROUPIE. (Trans American-1970). Sally, Esme Johns; Wes, Billy Boyle; Morrie, Richard Shaw; Detective, Neil Hallett; Dog Handler, Charles Finch; Mooncake Girl, Eliza Terry; Steve, Donald Sumpter; Host, Paul Bacon; Dancer, Lynda Priest; Groupie Thief, Flanagan; Manager, James Beck; Bob, Jimmie Edwards.

1447 I AM CURIOUS BLUE. (Grove-1970). Lena Nyman, Vilgot Sjoman, Borje Ahlstedt, Marie Goranzon, Hans Hellberg, Bim Warne, Gunnel Brostrom, Hanne Sandemose, Frej Lindqvist, Sonja Lindgren, Peter Lindgren, Gudrun Ostbye, Magnus Nilsson, Ulla Lyttkens.

1448 I AM CURIOUS (YELLOW). (Grove-1969). Lena, Lena Nyman; Borje, Borje Ahlstedt; The Director, Vilgot Sjoman; Rune, Peter Lindgren; Rune's Friend, Chris Wahlstrom; Magnus, Magnus Nilsson; Ulla, Ulla Lyttkens; The King, Holger Lowenadler; The Instructor, Anders Ek; The Interpreter, Ollegard Wellton; The Captain, Sven Wollter; Martin

Luther King, Olof Palme, Yevgeni Yevtushenko.

1449 I AM FRIGID ... WHY? (Audubon-1973). Sandra Julien, John Terrade.

1450 I COULD NEVER HAVE SEX WITH ANY MAN WHO HAS SO LITTLE REGARD FOR MY HUSBAND. (Cinema 5-1973). Marvin, Carmine Caridi; Stanley, Andrew Duncan; Laura, Cynthia Harris; Mandy, Lynne Lipton; The DeVrooms, Gail and Martin Stayden; Herb, Dan Greenburg.

1451 I CROSSED THE COLOR LINE. (U.S. Films-1965). Jerry Ellsworth, Richard Gilden; Andrea, Rima Kutner; Rook, Hary Lovejoy; Raymond Estes, Max Julien; Farley, Jackie Deslonde; Lonnie, Jimmy Mack; Carole Ann Rook, Maureen Gaffney; Wallace, William McLennan; Sawyer, Gino De Agustino; Jenkins, Tex Armstrong; Buckley, Byrd Holland; Alex, Whitman Mayo; Ellis Madison, Frances Williams; Sloane, Ray Dennis.

1452 I DEAL IN DANGER. (20th Century-Fox-1966). David March, Robert Goulet; Suzanne Duchard, Christine Carere; Spaulding, Donald Harron; Luber, Horst Frank; Elm, Werner Peters; Gretchen Hoffman, Eva Pflug; Ericka, Christiane Schmidtmer; Von Lindendorf, John Van Dreelan; Richter, Hans Reiser; Baroness, Margit Saad; Eckhardt, Peter Capell; Brunner, Osman Ragheb; Gorleck, John Alderson; Stolnitz, Dieter Eppler; Becker, Dieter Kirchlechner; Dr. Zimmer, Manfred Andrae; Kraus, Alexander Allerson; Submarine Pilot, Paul Glawton.

1453 I DRINK YOUR BLOOD. (Cinemation-1970). Horace, Bhaskar; Sue, Jadine Wong; Molly, Ronda Fultz; Elizabeth Marner-Brooks, George Patterson, Riley Mills, Iris Brooks, John Damon, Richard Bowler, Tyde Kierney, Lynn Lowry, Alex Mann, Bruno Damon, Mike Gentry.

1454 I ESCAPED FROM DEVIL'S ISLAND. (United Artists-1973). Le Bras, Jim Brown; Davert, Christopher George; Jojo, Rick Ely; Zamorra, Richard Rust.

1455 I EVEN MET HAPPY GYPSIES. (Prominent Films-1968). Bora, Bekim Fehmiu; Tisa, Gordana Jovanovic; Mirta, Bata Zivojinovic; Lence, Olivera Vuco; Father Pavle, Mija Aleksic; Nun, Rahela Ferari; Religious Peasant, Severin Bijelic; Bora's Wife, Etelka Filipovski; Toni, Milorad Jovanovic; Sandor, Milivoje Djordjevic.

1455a I. F. STONE'S WEEKLY. (Bruck-1973). Isadore F. Stone.

1456 I LIVE IN FEAR. (Brandon-1967). Klichi Nakajima, Toshiro Mifune; Toyo, Eiko Miyoshi; Yoshi, Togo Haruko; Harada, Takashi Shimura; Takao Yamazaki, Masao Shimizu;

Ichiro, Yutaka Sada; Kimie, Noriko Sengoku; Minoru Chiaki, Kyoko Aoyama, Akemi Negishi, Kichijiro Ueda, Yoichi Tachikawa, Ken Mitsuda Toranosuke Ogawa, Ejiro Tono, Kamatari Fujiwara, Nobuo Nakamura.

1457 I LOVE MY WIFE. (Universal-1970). Dr. Richard Burrows, Elliott Gould; Jody Burrows, Brenda Vaccaro; Helen Donnelly, Angel Tompkins; Frank Donnelly, Dabney Coleman; Grandma Dennison, Joan Tompkins; Dr. Neilson, Leonard Stone; Mrs. Burrows, Helen Westcott; Dr. Korngold, Ivor Francis; Dr. Meyerberg, Al Checco; Nurse Sharon, Joanna Cameron.

1458 I LOVE YOU, ALICE B. TOKLAS! (Warner Bros. -7 Arts-1968). Harold Fine, Peter Sellers; Mrs. Fine, Jo Van Fleet; Nancy, Leigh Taylor-Young; Joyce, Joyce Van Patten; Herbie Fine, David Arkin; Murray, Herb Edelman; Mr. Fine, Salem Ludwig; Guru, Louis Gottlieb; Funeral Director, Grady Sutton; Mrs. Foley, Janet Clark; Mr. Rodriguez, Jorge Moreno; Man in Dress Shop, Ed Peck; Big Bear, Jack Margolis; Love Lady, Eddra Gale; Anita, Carol O'Leary; El Greco, Gary Brown; Mechanic, Sid Clute; Grandfather Rodriguez, Joe Dominguez; Gas Station Attendand, Roy Glenn; Patrolmen, William Bramley and Vincent Howard; Crying Hippie, Robert Miller Driscoll; Crying Hippie's Wife, Karen Mickievic.

1459 I LOVE YOU, I KILL YOU. (New Yorker-1972). Hunter, Rolf Becker; Teacher, Hannes Fuchs; Mayor, Helmut Brasch; Policeman, Thomas Eckelmann; Policeman, Nikolaus Dutsch; Village Girl, Marianne Blomquist; Village Girl, Monika Hansen; Priest, Wolfgang Ebert; Druggist, Stefan Moses.

1460 I LOVE YOU, ROSA. (Leisure Media-1973). Rosa, Michal Bat-Adam; Nessin, Gabi Otterman; Eli, Yosef Shiloah; Rabbi, Avner Chezkiyahu; Jemila, Levana Finkelstein; Nessin grown up, Moshe Tal; Mother, Elisheva Michaeli.

1461 I MARRIED YOU FOR FUN. (AVCO Embassy-1972). Julia, Monica Vitti; Peter, Giorgio Albertazzi; Victoria, Maria Grazia Buccella; Peter's Mother, Italia Marchesini; Juniper, Rosella Como; Englishman, Michael Bardinet; Topaz, Paola Corinti; Manolo, Louis La Torre.

1462 I NEVER SANG FOR MY FATHER. (Columbia-1970). Tom, Melvyn Douglas; Margaret, Dorothy Stickney; Gene, Gene Hackman; Alice, Estelle Parsons; Peggy, Elizabeth Hubbard; Norma, Lovelady Powell; Dr. Mayberry, Daniel Keyes; Marvin Scott, Jon Richards; Rev. Pell, Conrad Bain; Mary, Nikki Counselman; Hostess, Jean Dexter; Nurse 1, Sloane Shelton; Special Nurse, Beverly Penberthy; Nurse 3, Valerie Ogden; Mr. Tucker, Jim Karen, Dr. Jensen, Gene Williams.

1463 I SAW WHAT YOU DID. (Universal-1965). Amy, Joan Crawford; Steve Marak, John Ireland; Libby Mannering, Andi Garrett; Tess Mannering, Sharyl Locke; Kit Austin, Sarah Lane; David Mannering, Leif Erickson; Ellie Mannering, Pat Breslin.

1464 I WALK THE LINE. (Columbia-1970). Sheriff Tawes, Gregory Peck; Alma McCain, Tuesday Weld; Ellen Haney, Estelle Parsons; Carl McCain, Ralph Meeker; Bascomb, Lonny Chapman; Hunnicutt, Charles Durning; Buddy McCain, Freddie McCloud; Clay McCain, Jeff Dalton; Elsie, Jane Rose; Grandpa Tawes, J. C. Evans; Sybil, Margaret A. Morris; Pollard, Bill Littleton; Vogel, Leo Yates; Darlene Hunnicutt, Dodo Denney.

1465 I WANT WHAT I WANT. (Cinerama-1972). Roy/Wendy, Anne Heywood; Father, Harry Andrews; Margaret Stevenson, Jill Bennett; Mr. Waites, Paul Rogers; Frank, Michael Coles; June, Sheila Reid; Shirley, Virginia Stride; Lorna, Jill Melford; Mrs. Parkhurst, Rachel Gurney; Mr. Parkhurst, Anthony Sharpe; Tony, Robin Hawdon; Philip, Philip Bond; Rober Parkhurst, Paul Prescott; Carole, Liza Goddard; Laurie Goode, Deborah Grant, John Baskcombe, Hilda Fenemore.

1466 I WAS ALL HIS. (Casino-1965). Barbara Ruetting, Carlos Thompson, Wolfgang Preiss, Kai Fischer, Seigfried Lowitz, Mario Stadler, Michl Lang, Lina Carstons, Korny Collins, Lukas Ammann.

1467 ICE STATION ZEBRA. (MGM-1968). Cdr. James Ferraday, Rock Hudson; Boris Vaslov, Ernest Borgnine; David Jones, Patrick McGoohan; Capt. Leslie Anders, Jim Brown; Lt. Russell Walker, Tony Bill; Admiral Garvey, Lloyd Nolan; Col. Ostrovsky, Alf Kjellin; Lt. Cdr. Raeburn, Gerald S. O'Laughlin; Lt. Jonathan Hansen, Ted Hartley; Lt. George Mills, Murray Rose; Paul Zabrinczski, Ron Masak; Lt. Edgar Hackett, Sherwood Price; Lt. Mitgang, Lee Stanley; Dr. Jack Benning, Joseph Bernard; Survivors, John Orchard and William O'Connell; Lt. Courtney Cartwright, Michael T. Mikler; Russian Aide, Jonathan Lippe; Wassmeyer, Ted Kristian; Earl McAuliffe, Jim Dixon; Bruce Kentner, Boyd Berlind; Cedric Patterson, David Wendel; Lyle Nichols, Ronnie Rondell; Craig Shreeve, Michael Grossman, Wade Graham, Michael Rougas, Jed Allan, Lloyd Haynes, Buddy Garion, T. J. Escott, Buddy Hart, Gary Downey, Robert Carlson, Don Newsome, Jim Goodwin, Bill Hillman, Dennis Alpert.

1468 THE ICEMAN COMETH. (American Film Theatre-1973). Hickey, Lee Marvin; Harry Hope, Fredric March; Larry Slade, Robert Ryan; Don Parritt, Jeff Bridges; Willie Oban, Bradford Dillman; Hugo Kalmar, Sorrell Booke; Margie,

Hildy Brooks; Pearl, Nancy Juno Dawson; Cora, Evans Evans; Captain Cecil Lewis, Martyn Green; Joe Mott, John McLiam; Chuck Morello, Stephen Pearlman; Rocky Pioggi, Tom Pedi; General Piet Wetjoen, George Voskovec; Moran, Bart Burns; Lieb, Don McGovern.

1469 IDENTIFICATION MARKS: NONE. (New Yorker-1969). Draft Dodger, Jerzy Skolimowski; His Girl, Elzbieta Czysewska; Tadeusz Mins, Jacek Szczek, Andrzej Zarnecki.

1470 THE IDOL. (Embassy-1966). Carol, Jennifer Jones; Marco, Michael Parks; Timothy, John Leyton; Sarah, Jennifer Hilary; Martin Livesy, Guy Doleman; Rosalind, Natasha Pyne; 2nd Woman at Party, Caroline Blakiston; Lewis, Jeremy Bulloch; Barmaid, Fanny Carby; Man at Party, Vernon Dobtcheff; Boy, Michael Gordon; Simon, Gordon Gostelow; Policeman, Ken Haward; Woman at Party, Renee Houston; Rosie, Priscilla Morgan; Mrs. Muller, Edna Morris; Tommy, Peter Porteous; Laborer, Terry Richards; Laborer, Derek Ware; Police Inspector, Jack Watson; Landlady, Rita Webb; Dorothea, Tina Williams.

1471 IF.... (Paramount-1969). Mich Travers, Malcolm McDowell; Johnny, David Wood; Wallace, Richard Warwick; The Girl, Christine Noonan; Rowntree, Robert Swann; Denson, Hugh Thomas; Stephans, Guy Ross; Headmaster, Peter Jeffrey; Matron, Mona Washbourne; Jute, Sean Bury; Housemaster (Mr. Kemp), Arthur Lowe; History Master, Graham Crowden; Chaplain, Geoffrey Chatter; Mrs. Kemp, Mary MacLeod; John Thomas, Ben Aris; General Denson, Anthony Nichols; Bobby Philips, Rupert Webster; Biles, Brian Pettifer; Fortinbras, Michael Cadman; Barnes, Peter Sproule; Keating, Robin Askwith; Classics Master, Charles Lloyd Pack; Pussy Graves, Richard Everett; Peanuts, Philip Bagenal; Cox, Nicholas Page; Fisher, Robert Yetzes; David Griffin, Graham Sharman, Richard Thombleson, Richard Davies, Michael Newport, Charles Sturridge, Martin Beaumont, John Garrie, Tommy Godfrey, Ellis Dale.

1472 IF HE HOLLERS, LET HIM GO! Ellen Whitlock, Dana Wynter; James Lake, Raymond St. Jacques; Leslie Whitlock, Kevin McCarthy; Lily, Barbara McNair; Prosecutor, Arthur O'Connell; Sheriff, John Russell; Thelma Wilson, Ann Prentiss; Carl Blair, Royal Dano; Harry, Steve Sandor; Sally Blair, Susan Seaforth; Police Chief, James Craig; William Lake, Don Newsome; Special Officer, Gregg Palmer; Defense Counsel, James McEachin; Officer, Don Megowan; Jackson, Chet Stratton; Henry Wilson, Edward Schaff; Gas Station Attendant, Kort Flakenberg; Truck Driver, Jason Johnson; Sergeant, Frank Gerstle; Deputy, James H. Drake; Prison Guard, Pepper Martin; Doctor, E. A. Sirianni; Officer, Todd Martin; Judge, Harold J. Kennedy; Chaplain, Jon Lormer; Officer, Ed Cook; Marion, Mimi Gibson.

1473 IF I HAD A GUN. (Ajay-1973). Boy, Marian Bernat; Friend, Josef Graf; Father, Ludevit Kroner; Mother, Emilia Dosekova; Girl, Hana Grissova; B. Hausnerova, M. Furinova, D. Lapunik.

1474 IF IT'S TUESDAY, THIS MUST BE BELGIUM. (United Artists-1969). Samantha Perkins, Suzanne Pleshette; Fred Ferguson, Murray Hamilton; John Marino, Sandy Baron; Jack Harmon, Michael Constantine; Harve Blakely, Norman Fell; Edna Ferguson, Peggy Cass; Bert Greenfield, Marty Ingels; Freda, Pamela Britton; Bo, Luke Halpin; Harry Dix, Aubrey Morris; Irma Blakely, Reva Rose; Shelly Ferguson, Hilary Thompson; Giuseppi, Mario Carotenuto; Mrs. Featherstone, Patricia Routledge; Gina, Marina Berti; Fiat Driver's Wife, Linda Di Felice; German Sergeant, Paul Esser; Dot, Jenny White; Marcel, Roger Six; George, Frank Latimore; Miss Belgium, Sonia Doumen; Miss Germany, Lilian Atterer; Miss Luxembourg, Lucien Krier; Senta Berger, Joan Collins, Donovan, Ben Gazzara, Elsa Martinelli, Robert Vaughn, Catherine Spaak, Virna Lisi, Anita Ekberg, Vittorio De Sica, John Cassavetes, as Themselves.

1475 No entry.

1476 I'LL NEVER FORGET WHAT'S 'IS NAME. (Regional-1968). Jonathan Lute, Orson Welles; Andrew Quint, Oliver Reed; Georgina, Carol White; Gerald Slater, Harry Andrews; Headmaster, Michael Hordern; Louise Quint, Wendy Craig; Josie, Marianne Faithfull; Nicholas, Norman Rodway; Chaplain, Frank Finlay; Maccabee, Harvey Hall; Carla, Ann Lynn; Susannah, Lyn Ashley; Anna, Veronica Clifford; Walter, Edward Fox; Lewis Force, Stuart Cooper; Eldrich, Roland Curran; Bankman, Peter Graves; Michael Cornwall, Mark Burns; Kellaway, Mark Eden; Marian, Josephine Rueg; Vietnamese Girl, Mona Chong; Galloway, Robert Mill; Pinchin, Terence Seward.

1477 I'LL TAKE SWEDEN. (United Artists-1965). Bob Holcomb, Bob Hope; JoJo Holcomb, Tuesday Weld; Kenny Klinger, Frankie Avalon; Karin Grandstedt, Dina Merrill; Erik Carlson, Jeremy Slate.

1477a THE ILLIAC PASSION. (Filmmakers' Cooperative-1968). Film maker and narrator, Gregory Markopoulos; Prometheus, Richard Beauvais; His Conscience, David Beauvais; Narcissus, Robert Alvarez; The Demon or Sprite, Taylor Meade; Echo, Sheila Gary; The Muse, Mrs. Peggy Murray; Hyacinthus, Tom Venturi; Venus, Tally Brown; Adonis, Kenneth King; Ganymede, Gerard Malanga; Orpheus, Jack Smith; Eurydice, Jan Chippman; Poseidon, Andy Warhol; Daedalus, Phillip Klass; Pandora, Margot Brier; Zeus, Paul Swan; Icarus, Wayne Weber; Hades, Carlos Anduze; Moon Goddess, Stella Dundas; Endymion, John Dowd; Apollo, Philip Merker;

Persephone, Beverly Grant; Io, Clara Hoover; Phaeton, Gregory Battcock.

1478 ILLUSION OF BLOOD. (Toho-1968). Iuemon Tamiya, Tatsuya Nakadai; Oiwa, Mariko Okada; Osode, Junko Ikeuchi; Gonbei Naosuke, Kanzaburo Nakamura; Oume, Mayumi Ozora; Omaki, Keiko Awaji; Samon Yotsuya, Yasushi Nagata; Kihei Ito, Eitaro Ozawa; Takuetsu, Masao Mishima.

1479 THE ILLUSTRATED MAN. (Warner Bros.-7 Arts-1969). Carl, Rod Steiger; Felicia, Claire Bloom; Willie, Robert Drivas; Pickard, Don Dubbins; Simmons, Jason Evers; John, Tim Weldon; Anna, Christie Matchett.

1480 IMAGE, FLESH AND VOICE. (Filmmakers-1970). Carolyn Carlson, Emery Hermans.

1481 IMAGES. (Columbia-1972). Cathryn, Susannah York; Hugh, Rene Auberjonois; Rene, Marcel Bozzuffi; Marcel, Hugh Millais; Susannah, Cathryn Harrison.

1482 IMAGO. (Emerson-1970). Carole, Barbara Douglas; Dr. Keith, Morgan Evans; Althea, Victoria Wales; Molly, Jennie Jackson; Barbara, Majila; Dr. Dobbs, Buddy Arett; Peter, Peter Cord; Reagan, Raul Hernandez; Bruce, Dick DeCoit; O'Donnell, Robert Webb; Priest, Parker Herriott; Red, Michael Rae; Tom, Michael Loring; Jay, Harvey Goldstein.

1483 IMITATION OF CHRIST. (Filmmakers-1970). Mother, Brigit Polk; Father, Ondine; Son, Patrick; Maid, Nico; Hobo, Taylor Mead.

1484 THE IMMORTAL STORY. (Fleetwood-1969). Mr. Clay, Orson Welles; Virginia Ducrot, Jeanne Moreau; Elishama Levinsky, Roger Coggio; Paul, Norman Ashley.

1485 L'IMMORTELLE. (Grove-1969). She, Francoise Brion; He, Jacques Doniol-Valcroze; and Guido Celano.

1486 IMPASSE. (United Artists-1969). Pat Morrison, Burt Reynolds; Bobby Jones, Anne Francis; Hanse, Lyle Bettger; Draco, Rodolfo Acosta; Wombat, Jeff Corey; Trev Jones, Clarke Gordon; Mariko Riley, Miko Mayama; Penny, Joanne Dalsass; Jesus Jiminez Riley, Vic Diaz; Pear Blossom, Dely Atay-Atayan; Nakajima, Bruno Punzalan; Maria Bonita, Lily Campillos; Sherry, Shirley Gorospe; Kiling, Bessie Barredo; Interne, Robert Wang; Kuli, Eddie Nicart.

1487 IMPOSSIBLE ON SATURDAY. (Magna-1966). Chaim Silbershatz, Robert Hirsch; Freddy Silbershatz, Robert Hirsch; Frieda Silbershatz, Robert Hirsch; Hans Silbershatz, Robert Hirsch; Carlo Silbershatz, Robert Hirsch; Zwi Silbershatz, Robert Hirsch; Leon Silbershatz, Robert Hirsch; Archibald

Silbershatz, Robert Hirsch; Debrah, Dahlia Friedland; Yankel, Mischa Asherov; Mayor of Jerusalem, Teddy Bilis; Aviva, Geula Nuni; The Sergeant, Yona Levi.

1488 THE IMPOSSIBLE YEARS. (MGM-1968). Jonathan Kingsley, David Niven; Alice Kingsley, Lola Albright; Richard Merrick, Chad Everett; Dr. Herbert Fleischer, Ozzie Nelson; Linda Kingsley, Cristina Ferrare; Bartholomew Smuts, Jeff Cooper; Dean Harvey Rockwell, John Harding; Freddie Fleischer, Rich Chalet; Andy McClaine, Mike McGreevey; Dr. Elliot Fish, Don Beddoe; Abbey Kingsley, Darleen Carr; Mrs. Celia Fish, Louise Lorimer; Mrs. Rockwell, Karen Norris; Miss Hammer, Susan French; Francine, Trudi Ames; Dr. Pepperell, J. Edward McKinley; Dr. Bodey, Ned Wertimer.

1489 IN COLD BLOOD. (Columbia-1967). Dick Hickock, Scott Wilson; Perry Smith, Robert Blake; Alvin Dewey, John Forsythe; Reporter, Paul Stewart; Harold Nye, Gerald S. O'Loughlin; Dick's Father, Jeff Corey; Roy Church, John Gallaudet; Clarence Duntz, James Flavin; Perry's Father, Charles McGraw; Officer Rohleder, James Lantz; Prosecuting Attorney, Will Geer; Herbert Clutter, John McLiam; Bonnie Clutter, Ruth Storey; Nancy Clutter, Brenda C. Currin; Kenyon Clutter, Paul Hough; "Good Samaritan," Vaughn Taylor; Young Reporter, Duke Hobbie; Reverend Post, Sheldon Allman; Mrs. Smith, Sammy Thurman; Herself, Mrs. Sadie Truitt; Myrtle Clare, Teddy Eccles, Raymond Hatton, Mary-Linda Rapelye, Ronda Fultz, Al Christy, Don Sollars, Harriet Levitt, Stan Levitt.

1490 IN ENEMY COUNTRY. (Universal-1968). Colonel Charles Waslow-Carton, Tony Franciosa; Denise Marchois, Anjanette Comer; Lt. Col. Philip Braden, Guy Stockwell; Baron von Wittenberg, Paul Hubschmid; Capt. Ian Peyton-Reid, Tom Bell; Ladislov, Michael Constantine; Rausch, John Marley; General Marchois, Harry Townes; Josef Bartowski, Milton Selzer; Admiral Lloyd Friffis, Patric Knowles; Nicolay, Tige Andrews; General Grieux, Emile Genest; Major Maurice Miral, Lee Bergere; Frau Gulden, Virginia Christine; Pilot, Harry Landers; Co-Pilot, Jim Creech; Polish Boy, Gerald Michenaud; Capek, Eugene Dynarski; Air Marshal Evelyn, Ivor Barry; General Jomar, Simon Scott; Convoy Commander, Paul Busch; Polish Man, Norbert Schiller.

1491 IN HARM'S WAY. (Paramount-1965). Capt. Rockwell Torrey, John Wayne; Cdr. Paul Eddington, Kirk Douglas; Lt. Maggie Haynes, Patricia Neal; Lt. William McConnel, Tom Tryon; Bev McConnel, Paula Prentiss; Ens. Jeremiah Torrey, Brandon De Wilde; Ens. Annalee Dorne, Jill Haworth; Adm. Broderick, Dana Andrews; Calyton Canfil, Stanley Holloway; Cdr. Powell, Burgess Meredith; CINCPAC I Admiral, Franchot Tone; Patrick O'Neal, Carroll O'Connor,

Slim Pickens, James Mitchum, George Kennedy, Bruce Cabot, Barbara Bouchet, Tod Andrews, Larry Hagman, Stewart Moss, Richard Le Pore, Chet Stratton, Soo Young, Dort Clark, Phil Mattingly.

1492 IN LIKE FLINT. (20th Century-Fox-1967). Derek Flint, James Coburn; Cramden, Lee J. Cobb; Lisa, Jean Hale; President Trent, Andrew Duggan; Elisabeth, Anna Lee; Helena, Hanna Landy; Simone, Totty Ames; Carter, Steve Ihnat; Avery, Thomas Hasson; Terry, Mary Michael; Jan, Diane Bond; Denise, Jacki Ray; Russian Premier, Herb Edelman; Yvonne Craig, Buzz Henry, Henry Wills, Mary Meade French, W. P. Lear Sr., Erin O'Brien, Ginny Gan, Eve Bruce, Inge Jaklyn, Faye Farrington, Thordis Brandt, Inga Neilsen, Marilyn Hanold, Pat Becker, Lyzanne La Due, Nancy Stone.

1493 IN SEARCH OF GREGORY. (Universal-1970). Catherine, Julie Christie; Gregory, Michael Sarrazin; Daniel, John Hurt; Max, Adolfo Celi; Nicole, Paola Pitagora; Wardle, Roland Culver; Taxi, Tony Selby; Steward, Jimmy Lynn; Paquita, Violetta Chiarini; Encarna, Gabriella Giorgelli; Giselle, Luisa De Santis; Priest, Ernesto Pagano; Small Boy, Roderick Smith; Old Man, Gordon Gostelow.

1494 IN THE HEAT OF THE NIGHT. (United Artists-1967). Virgil Tibbs, Sidney Poitier; Bill Gillespie, Rod Steiger; Sam Wood, Warren Oates; Mrs. Leslie Colbert, Lee Grant; Purdy, James Patterson; Delores Purdy, Quentin Dean; Eric Endicott, Larry Gates; Webb Schubert, William Schallert; Mama Caleba, Beah Richards; Harvey Oberst, Scott Wilson; Philip Colbert, Jack Teter; Matt Clark, Anthony James, Kermit Murdock, Khalil Bezaleel, Peter Whitney, William Watson, Timothy Scott, Michael LeClaire, Larry D. Mann, Stewart Nisbet, Eldon Quick, Fred Stewart, Arthur Malet, Peter Masterson, Alan Oppenheimer, Philip Garris, Jester Hairston, Clegg Hoyt, Phil Adams, Nikita Knatz, David Stinehart, Buzz Barton.

1495 IN THE NAME OF THE FATHER. (Vides-1971). Angelo, Yves Benayton; Vice Rector, Renato Scarpa; Franco's Mother, Laura Betti; Franco, Aldo Sassi; Salvatore, Lou Castel.

1496 INADMISSIBLE EVIDENCE. (Paramount-1968). Bill Maitland, Nicol Williamson; Anna Maitland, Eleanor Fazan; Liz Eaves, Jill Bennett; Hudson, Peter Sallis; Jones, David Valla; Shirley, Eileen Atkins; Jane Maitland, Ingrid Brett; Joy, Gillian Hills; Mrs. Garnsey, Isobel Dean; Mrs. Anderson, Claire Kelly; Maples, John Normington; Hilda Maples, Patsy Huxter; Wendy Watson, Hilary Hardiman; Mr. Watson, John Savident; Soctt, Rufus Dawson; Peter Maitland, Stephen Martin; Sheila, Penny Bird; Court Clerk, Brian Cleaver;

Plainclothesmen, Martin Ryan Grace and Alan Selwyn; Joseph Tregonino, Lindsay Anderson, Reg Peters, Ron Clarke, Lee Ann Lancaster, Ellis Dale, Debbie Jacobs, Ellen Mann, June Brown, Ishaq Bux, Norma Shebbeare, James Ottaway, Valerie Collier.

1497 THE INBREAKER. (Robert G. Elliott-1974). Chris, Johnny Crawford; Roy, Christopher George; Fisherman, Al Koslik; Muskrat, Jonny Yesno; Carol, Wendy Sparrow; Cannery Manager, Wally MacSween; A Drunk, Gordon Robertson.

1498 THE INCIDENT. (20th Century-Fox-1967). Joe Ferrone, Tony Musante; Artie Connors, Martin Sheen; Private Felix Teflinger, Beau Bridges; Sam Beckerman, Jack Gilford; Bertha Beckerman, Thelma Ritter; Arnold Robinson, Brock Peters; Joan Robinson, Ruby Dee; Bill Wilks, Ed McMahon; Helen Wilks, Diana Van Der Vlis; Harry Purvis, Mike Kellin; Muriel Purvis, Jan Sterling; Douglas McCann, Gary Merrill; Robert Fields, Robert Bannard, Victor Arnold, Donna Mills, Kathleen Smith, Henry Proach, Neal Hynes, Ben Levi, Marty Meyers, Don De Leo, Ted Lowrie, John Servetnik, Ray Cole, Barry Del Rae, Nico Hartos, Macine McCrey, Nina Hansen.

1499 INCIDENT AT PHANTOM HILL. (Universal-1966). Matt Martin, Robert Fuller; Memphis, Jocelyn Lane; Joe Barlow, Dan Duryea; Adam Long, Tom Simcox, Dr. Hanneford, Linden Chiles; Krausman, Claude Akins; O'Rourke, Noah Berry; General Hood, Paul Fix; 1st Hunter, Denver Pyle; Trader, William Phipps; Drum, Don Collier, 2nd Hunter, Mickey Finn.

1500 THE INCREDIBLE TWO-HEADED TRANSPLANT. (American International-1971). Roger, Bruce Dern; Linda, Pat Priest; Ken, Casey Kasem; Cass, Albert Cole; Danny, John Bloom; Max, Berry Kroeger; Andrew, Larry Vincent; Sheriff, Jack Lester; Deputy, Jerry Patterson; Miss Pierce, Darlene Duralia; Station Attendant, Robert Miller; Young Danny, Leslie Cole; Motorcyclists, Ray Thorn, Donald Brody, Mary Ellen Clawsen; Teenagers, Janice Gelman, Mike Espe, Andrew Schneider, Eva Sorensen; Patrolmen, Bill Collins, Jack English; Nurses, Laura Lanza, Carolyn Gilbert.

1501 THE INCREDIBLY STRANGE CREATURES WHO STOPPED LIVING AND BECAME MIXED-UP ZOMBIES. (Hollywood Star-1965). Cash Flagg, Brett O'Hara, Carolyn Brandt, Atlas King, Sharon Walsh, Madison Clarke, Erino Enyo, Jack Brady, Toni Camel, Neil Stillman, Joan Howard, James Bowie, Gene Pollock, Bill Ward, Son Hooker, Steve Clark, Don Snyder, Carol Kay, Teri Randal.

1502 INDIAN PAINT. (Eagle-International-1966). Johnny

Crawford, Jay Silverheels, Robert Crawford Jr., Pat Hogan.

1503 INGA. (Cinemation-1968). Inga, Marie Liljedahl; Greta, Monica Strommerstedt; Einar, Thomas Ungewitter; Karl, Casten Lassen; Frida, Else-Marie Brandt; Segrid, Sissi Kaiser; Dagmar, Anne-Lise Myhrvold.

1504 THE INHERITOR. (Hera-1973). Bart, Jean-Paul Belmondo; Liza, Carla Gravina; Andre, Jean Rochefort; David, Charles Denner; Lauren, Maureen Kerwin; Lambert, Michel Beaune; Schneider, Jean Martin; Editor, Jean De Sailly.

1505 INN OF EVIL. (Toho-1971). Sadahichi, Tatsuya Nakadai; Omitsu, Komaki Kurihara; Ikuzo, Ganuemon Nakamura; Tomijiro, Kei Yamamoto; Yohie, Kei Satoh; Okiwa, Wakako Sakai.

1506 INNOCENT BYSTANDERS. (Paramount-1973). John, Stanley Baker; Miriam, Geraldine Chaplin; Loomis, Donald Pleasence; Blake, Dana Andrews; Joanna, Sue Lloyd; Andrew, Derrin Nesbitt; Aaron, Vladek Sheybal; Omar, Warren Mitchell; Mankowitz, Cec Linder; Zimmer, Howard Goorney; Waiter, J. C. Devlin; Marcus, Ferdy Mayne; Heatherton, Clifton Jones; Azimov, John Collin; Gabril, Aharon Impale; Guard, Yuri Borienko; Daniel, Frank Maher; Zhelkov, Michael Poole; Guard, Tom Bowman.

1507 INSIDE DAISY CLOVER. (Warner Bros.-1966). Daisy Clover, Natalie Wood; Raymond Swan, Christopher Plummer; Wade Lewis, Robert Redford; Baines, Roddy McDowall; The Dealer, Ruth Gordon; Melora Swan, Katharine Bard; Milton Hopwood, Peter Helm; Gloria Goslett, Betty Harford; Harry Goslett, John Hale; Cop, Harold Gould; Old Lady in Hospital, Ottola Nesmith; Cynara, Edna Holland.

1508 INSPECTOR CLOUSEAU. (United Artists-1968). Inspector Jacques Clouseau, Alan Arkin; Lisa Morrel, Delia Boccardo; Superintendent Weaver, Frank Finlay; Sir Charles Braithwaite, Patrick Cargill; Mrs. Weaver, Beryl Reid; Addison Steele, Barry Foster; Clyde Hargreaves, Clive Francis; Bull Parker, John Bindon; Frey, Michael Ripper; Frenchy Le Bec, Tutte Lemkow; Bomber Le Bec, Anthony Ainley; Hoeffler, Wallas Eaton; Geffrion, David Bauer; Shockley, Richard Pearson; Wulf, George Pravda; Bergesch, Eric Pohlmann; Gutch, Geoffrey Bayldon; Innkeeper, Arthur Lovegrove; Meg, Kathya Wyeth; Julie, Tracey Crisp; Peggy, Marjie Lawrence; David, Craig Booth; Nicole, Julie Croft; Stockton, Robert Russell; Policewoman, Susan Engel; Fishmonger, Will Stampe; Nun, Barbara Dana.

1509 INTERLUDE. (Columbia-1968). Stefan Zelter, Oskar Werner; Sally, Barbara Ferris; Antonia Zelter, Virginia Maskell; Lawrence, Donald Sutherland; Mary, Nora Swinburne;

Andrew, Alan Webb; George Selworth, Bernard Kay; Natalie, Geraldine Sherman; TV P. R. Man, John Cleese; TV Director, Humphrey Burton; Mario, Gino Mulvazzi; Mugette De Braie, Robert Lang, Roslyn De Winter, Janet Davies, Sarah Jane Stratton, Simon Davis, Rosalie Westwater, Stephen Plytas, Gay Cameron, Anula Harman, Ernest Fleischmann, Derek Jacobi, Richard Pescud.

1510 THE INTERNECINE PROJECT. (Allied Artists-1974). James Coburn, Lee Grant, Harry Andrews, Ian Hendry, Michael Jayston, Keenan Wynn, Christiane Kruger, Terence Alexander, Philip Anthony, David Swift, Julian Glover, Ray Callaghan, Geoffrey Burridge, Robert Tayman, Judy Robinson, Kevin Scott, John Savident, Richard Cornish, Carrie Kirstein, Richard Marner, Ralph Ball, Brain Tully, Michael Knightingale, Ewan Roberts, Susan Magolier, Mary Larkin.

1511 INTERVAL. (AVCO Embassy-1973). Chris, Robert Wolders; Serena, Merle Oberon; Armando, Claudio Brook; Fraser, Russ Conway; Husband, Charles Bateman; Leonard, Britt Leach; Broch, Peter Von Zerneck; Waiter, Fernando Soler Jr.; Rosalia, Gloria Mestre; Jody, Christina Moreno; Ellie, Betty Lyon; Jackie, Anel.

1512 INTIMACY. (Goldstone Film Enterprises-1966). Jack Ging, Joan Blackman, Nancy Malone, Barry Sullivan, Jackie De Shannon.

1513 INTIMATE LIGHTING. (Altura-1969). Stepa, Vera Kresadlova; Peter, Zdenek Bezusek; Grandfather, Jan Vostrcil; Grandmother, Vlastimila Vlkova; Bambas, Karel Blazek; Marie, Jaroslava Stedra; Pharmacist, Karel Uhlik.

1514 INVASION OF THE BEE GIRLS. (Centaur-1973). Neil Agar, William Smith; Dr. Susan Harris, Anitra Ford; Julie Zorn, Victoria Vetri; Captain Peters, Cliff Osmond; Dr. Henry Murger, Wright King; Herb Kline, Ben Hammer; Nora Kline, Anna Aries; Aldo Ferrara, Andre Phillippe; Stan Williams, Sid Kaiser; Gretchen Grubowsky, Katie A. Saylor; Harriet Williams, Beverly Powers; Harv, Tom Pittman; Joe, William Keller.

1515 INVASION 1700. (Medallion-1965). Jeanne Crain, John Drew Barrymore, Pierre Brice, Akim Tamiroff, Gordon Mitchell.

1516 INVESTIGATION OF A CITIZEN ABOVE SUSPICION. (Columbia-1970). Police Inspector, Gian Maria Volonte; Augusta Terzi, Florinda Bolkan; Plumber, Salvo Randone; Police Commissioner, Gianni Santuccio; Mangani, Arturo Dominici; Biglia, Orazio Orlando; Antonio Pace, Sergio Tramonti; Augusta's Husband, Massimo Foschi; Homicide Functionary, Aldo Rendine.

1517 THE INVITATION. (1974). Michel Robin, Jean-Luc Bideau, Jean Champion, Pierre Collet, Corinne Coderey.

1518 THE IPCRESS FILE. (Universal-1965). Harry Palmer, Michael Caine; Calby, Nigel Green; Ross, Guy Doleman; Jean, Sue Lloyd; Carswell, Gordon Jackson; Radcliffe, Aubrey Richards; Bluejay, Frank Gatliff; Barney, Thomas Baptiste.

1519 IS PARIS BURNING? (Paramount-1966). Consul Raoul Nordling, Orson Welles; Colonel Rol, Bruno Cremer; A Parisienne, Suzy Delair; Parodi, Pierre Dux; Hitler, Billy Frick; Harry Meyen, Hans Messemer, Michel Piccoli, Sacha Pitoeff, Wolfgang Preiss, Michel Berger, Gehrard Borman, Georges Claisse, Germaine De France, Doc Ericson, Michel Etcheverry, Pascal Fardoulis, Bernard Fresson, Ernst Burbringer, Clara Gansard, Rol Fauffin, Georges Geret, Michel Gonzales, Konrad Georg, Klaus Holm, Jean-Pierre Honore, Peter Jakob, Catherine Kamenka, Billy Kearns, Joelle Latour, Michael Lonsdale, Roger Lumont, Maria Machado, Felix Marten, Paloma Matta, Pierre Mirat, Harald Momm, Georges Montant, Russ Moro, Del Negro, Jean Negroni, Alain Pommier, Georges Poujouley, Michel Puterflam, Christian Rode, Serge Rousseau, Michel Sales, Wolfgang Saure, Georges Staquet, Otto Stern, Henia Suchar, Toni Taffin, Pierre Tamin, Jean Valmont, Jo Warfield, Joachim Westhoss, Jean-Pierre Zola; Morandat, Jean-Paul Belmondo; Francoise Labe, Leslie Caron; GI in Tank, George Chakiris; Jacques Chaban-Delmas, Alain Delon; General Omar Bradley, Glenn Ford; Yves Bayet, Daniel Gelin; Marcel Bizien, Yves Montand; General Jacques Leclerc, Claude Rich; General Edwin Sibert, Robert Stack; Major Roger Gallois, Pierre Vaneck; G.I. with Warren, Skip Ward; Charles Monod, Charles Boyer; Lt. Henri Karcher, Jean-Pierre Cassel; Lebel, Claude Dauphin; General George Patton, Kirk Douglas; General Dietrich von Choltitz, Gert Frobe; Intelligence Officer Powell, E. G. Marshall; Sergeant Warren, Anthony Perkins; Cafe Proprietress, Simone Signoret; Claire, Marie Versini.

1520 IS THERE SEX AFTER DEATH. (Abel-Child-1971). Dr. Manos, Buck Henry; Dr. Rogers, Alan Abel; Vince, Marshall Efron; Herself, Holly Woodlawn; Himself, Robert Downey; Dr. Elevenike, Jim Moran; Himself, Rubin Carson; Merkin the Magician, Earle Doud; Announcer, Larry Wolf; Brest School Student, Iris Brooks; Richard Nixon, Jim Dixon; Attorney, Roger Jon Diamond.

1521 ISABEL. (Paramount-1968). Isabel, Genevieve Bujold; Jason, Mark Strange; Uncle Matthew, Gerald Parkes; Eb, Elton Hayes; Viola, Ede Kerr; Herb, Albert Waxman; Herb's Friends, Ratch Wallace, Lynden Bechervaise; Postmaster, Eric Clavering; Fisherman, Rob Hayes; Storekeeper, J.

Donald Dow.

1522 ISLAND AT THE TOP OF THE WORLD. (Buena Vista-1974). Prof. Ivarson, David Hartman; Sir Anthony Ross, Donald Sinden; Captain Brieux, Jacques Marin; Donald Ross, David Gwillim; Freyja, Agneta Echemyr; Gunnar Ohlund, Lasse Kolstad, Erik Silju, Rolf Soder, Torsten Wahlund, Sverre Ousdal, Niels Ninrichsen, Denny Miller, Brendan Dillon, James Almanzar, Ivor Barry, Lee Paul.

1523 ISLAND OF TERROR. (Universal-1967). Dr. Stanley, Peter Cushing; Dr. David West, Edward Judd; Toni Merrill, Carole Gray; Dr. Landers, Eddie Byrne; Constable Harris, Sam Kydd; Mr. Campbell, Niall MacGinnis; Argyle, James Caffrey; Bellows, Liam Caffney; Dunley, Roger Heathcote; Halsey, Keith Bell; Morton, Shay Gorman; Dr. Phillips, Peter Forbes Robertson; Carson, Richard Bidlake; Mrs. Bellows, Joyce Hemson; Helicopter Pilot, Edward Ogden.

1524 ISLAND OF THE BURNING DAMNED. (Maron-1973). Hanson, Christopher Lee; Jeff, Patrick Allen; Angela, Jane Merrow; Mrs. Callan, Sarah Lawson; Dr. Stone, Peter Cushing; Stanley, William Lucas; Mason, Kenneth Cope; Siddle, Jack Bligh.

1525 ISLAND OF THE DOOMED. (Allied Artists-1968). Baron von Weser, Cameron Mitchell; Beth Christiansen, Elisa Montes; David Moss, George Martin; Cora Robinson, Kai Fischer; James Robinson, Ralph Naukoff; Professor Demerist, Hermann Nelson; Myrtle Callahan, Matilde Sampredo; Alfredo, Richard Valle; Baldi, Mike Brendel.

1526 IT. (Warner Bros-7 Arts-1967). Arthur Pimm, Roddy McDowall; Ellen Grove, Jill Haworth; Jim Perkins, Paul Maxwell; Professor Weal, Aubrey Richards; Harold Grove, Ernest Clark; Trimingham, Oliver Johnston; Inspector White, Noel Trevarthen; Wayne, Ian McCulloch; Old Man, Richard Coolden; Miss Swanson, Dorothy Frere; Captain, Tom Chatto; Ellis, Steve Kirby; Boss, Russell Napier; Workman, Frank Sieman; Joe Hill, Brian Haines; First officer, Mark Burns; Second officer, Raymond Adamson; Policeman, Lindsay Campbell, Guard, John Baker; The Golem, Alan Sellers.

1527 IT AIN'T EASY. (Dandelion-1972). Randy, Lance Henriksen; Ann, Barra Grant; Gimma, Bill Moor; Paul, Granville Van Dusen; Charlie, Joseph Maher; "T," Pierrino Mascarino; Jenny, Penelope Allen; Merle, William Schoppert.

1528 IT HAPPENED HERE. (Lopert-1966). Pauline, Pauline Murray; Dr. Fletcher, Sebastian Shaw; Helen Fletcher, Fiona Leland; Honor, Honor Fehrson.

1529 IT HAPPENED IN HOLLYWOOD. (Screw-1973). Felicity Split, Mark Stevens, Al Levitsky, Alan Spitz, Al Goldstein, Richard Sternberger, Jim Buckley, Liz Torres.

1530 IT ONLY HAPPENS TO OTHERS. (GSF-1971). Marcello, Marcello Mastroianni; Catherine, Catherine Deneuve; Xavier, Serge Marquand; Marguerite, Dominique Labourier; Woman in Park, Catherine Allegret; Marcello's mother, Daniele Lebrun; Marc Eyraud, Rosa Chira Magrini, Benoit Ferreux, Marie Trintignant, Edouard Niermans, Michel Gudin, Andree Damant.

1531 IT TAKES ALL KINDS. (Commonwealth-1965). Tony, Robert Lansing; Laura, Vera Miles; Orville, Barry Sullivan; Benji, Sid Melton; J. P., Penny Sugg.

1531a THE ITALIAN CONNECTION. (American International-1973). Luca, Mario Adorf; Dave, Henry Silva; Frank, Woody Strode; Don Vito, Adolfo Celi; Eva, Luciana Paluzzi; Corso, Cyril Cusack.

1532 THE ITALIAN JOB. (Paramount-1969). Charlie Croker, Michael Caine; Bridger, Noel Coward; Lorna, Maggie Blye; Prof. Simon Peach, Benny Hill; Freddie, Tony Beckley; Altabani, Raf Vallone; Beckerman, Rossano Brazzi; Madame Beckerman, Lelia Goldoni; Bill, George Innes; Big William, Harry Baird; Yellow, Robert Powell; Frank, John Forgeham; Arfur, Michael Standing; Rozzer, Derek Ware; Roger, Frank Jarvis; Coco, Stanley Caine.

1533 ITALIANO BRAVA GENTE. (Embassy-1966). Ferro Maria Ferri, Arthur Kennedy; Medical Captain, Peter Falk; Sonja, Tatyana Samoilova; Gabrielli, Raffaele Pisu; Katia, Shanna Prokhorenko; Sermonti, Andrea Checchi; Sanna, Riccardo Cucciolla; Amalfitano, Nino Vingelli; Bazzocchi, Lev Prygunov; Russian Partisan, Grigori Mikhailov; Gino Pernice, Valeri Somov, Boris Kozhukhov, Vincenzo Polizzi, S. Lukyanov, Yuri Nazarov, O. Kaberidze, I. Paramonov, E. Knausmuller.

1534 IT'S A BIKINI WORLD. (Trans American-1967). Delilah Dawes, Deborah Walley; Mike Samson/Herbert Samson, Tommy Kirk; Woody, Bob Pickett; Pebbles, Suzie Kaye; Harvey Pulp, Jack Bernardi; McSnigg, William O'Connell; Daddy, Sid Haig; Boy, Jim Begg; Girl, Lori Williams; Cindy, Pat McGee; The Animals, The Castaways, The Gentrys, The Toys.

1535 IT'S ALIVE. (Warner Bros.-1974). Frank Davies, John Ryan; Leonore Davies, Sharon Farrell; The Professor, Andrew Duggan; Clayton, Guy Stockwell; Lt. Perkins, James Dixon; The Captain, Michael Ansara; The Executive, Robert Emhardt; Charlie, William Wellman Jr.; Chris, Daniel

Holzman.

1536 No entry.

1537 J. C. (AVCO Embassy-1972). J. C., Bill McGaha; David, Hannibal Penny; Miriam, Joanna Moore; Dan, Burr De Benning; Grady, Slim Pickens; Kim, Pati Delany; Rachel, Judy Frazier; Mr. Clean, Max Payne.

1538 J. W. COOP. (Columbia-1972). J. W. Coop, Cliff Robertson; Mama, Geraldine Page; Bean, Christina Ferrare; Jim Sawyer, R. G. Armstrong; Tooter Watson, R. L. Armstrong; Rancher, John Crawford; Billy Sol, Wade Crosby; Big Marge, Marjorie Durant Dye; Warden Morgen, Paul Harper; Motorcycle Cop, Son Hooker; Sheriff, Richard Kennedy; Diesel Driver, Bruce Kirby; Bonnie May, Mary Robin Redd; Rodeo Manager, Claude Stroud; Gas Station Attendant, Wayne Taylor; Hector, Augie Vallejo; Billy Hawkins, Dennis Reiners; Myrtis, Myrtis Dightman; Deacon, Frank Hobbs; Hobue, Billy Hogue; Eddie, Billy Martinelli; Cisco, Clyde W. Maye; Finals Clown, Larry Clavman; Announcers, Les Connelly, Johnnie Jackson, Mel Lambert, Clem McSpadden.

1539 JACK FROST. (Embassy-1966). Nastenka, Natasha Sedykh; Jack Frost, Alexander Khvylya; Ivan, Eduard Isotov; Witch Baba Yaga, Yuri Millyar; Marfushka, Inna Churikova; Step-Mother, Vera Altaiskaya; Old Man, Pavel Pavlenko; Bandit Chieftan, Anatoly Kubatsky.

1540 JACK OF DIAMONDS. (MGM-1967). Jeff Hill, George Hamilton; Ace of Diamonds, Joseph Cotten; Olga, Marie Laforet; Nicolai, Maurice Evans; Von Schenk, Wolfgang Preiss; Helmut, Karl Lieffen; Geisling, Eduard Linkers; Brugger, Alexander Hegarth; Themselves: Carroll Baker, Zsa Zsa Gabor, Lilli Palmer.

1541 JAMILYA. (Artkino-1972). Jamilya, Natalya Arinbasarova; Daniyar, Suimenkul Chkmorov; Seit, Nasredin Dubashev; Mother, A. Jangorozova; Sadyk, A. Kenzhekov; Osmaon, M. Bakhtygireyev; Artist, B. Beishenaliev; Orozmat, N. Kitayev; Narrator, Chinghiz Aitmatov.

1542 JANIS. (Universal-1974). Janis Joplin.

1542a JE T'AIME, JE T'AIME. (New Yorker-1972). Claude Ridder, Claude Rich; Catrine, Olga Georges-Picot; Wiana Lust, Anouk Ferjac; Agnes de Smet, Annie Fargue; Bernard Hannecart, Bernard Fresson; Germaine Coster, Yvette Etievant; Marcelle Hannecart, Irene Tunc; Jan Rouffer, Van Doude; Dr. Haesaerts, Dominique Rozan; Young Woman, Marie-Blanche Vergne; Yves Kerboul, Ray Verhaege, Pierre Barbaud, Alain MacMoy, Vania Vilers, Georges Jamin, Carla Marlier, Claire Duhamel, Annie Bertin, Helene Callot,

Bernard Valdeneige, Jean Martin, Georges Walter, Alan Adair, Ian MacGregor, Jean-Louis Richard, M. Floquet, Pierre Motte, Rene Bazart, Jean Perre, Michele Blondel, Jean Michaud, Ben Danou, Catherine Robbe-Grillet, Alain Robbe-Grillet, Jacques Doniol-Valcroze, Sylvain Dhomme, Francois Regis-Bastide, Francis Lacassin, Jean-Claude Romer, Gerard Lorin, Guilene Pean, Alain Tercinet, Michel Choquet, Jorge Semprun, Billy Fasbender.

1543 JENNIFER ON MY MIND. (United Artists-1971). Marcus, Michael Brandon; Jenny, Tippy Walker; Max, Lou Gilbert; Ornstein, Steve Vinovich; Sergei, Peter Bonerz; Selma, Renee Taylor; Sam, Chuck McCann.

1544 JENNY. (Cinerama-1970). Jenny, Marlo Thomas; Delano, Alan Alda; Kay, Marian Hailey; Mrs. Marsh, Elizabeth Wilson; Mr. Marsh, Vincent Gardenia; Peter, Stephen Strimpell; Woman, Fay Bernardi; Bella Star, Charlotte Rae.

1545 JEREMIAH JOHNSON. (Warner Bros. -1972). Jeremiah Johnson, Robert Redford; Bear Claw, Will Geer; Del Gue, Stefan Gierasch; Crazy Woman, Allyn Ann McLerie; Robidoux, Charles Tyner; Caleb, Josh Albee; Paints His Shirt Red, Joaquin Martinez; Reverend, Paul Benedict; Qualen, Matt Clark; Lebeaux, Richard Angarola; Lt. Mulvey, Jack Colvin; Swan, Delle Bolton.

1546 JEREMY. (United Artists-1973). Jeremy Jones, Robby Benson; Susan Rollins, Glynnis O'Connor; Ralph Manzoni, Len Bari; Cello Teacher, Leonardo Cimino; Susan's Father, Ned Wilson; Jeremy's Father, Chris Bohn; Jeremy's Mother, Pat Wheel; Music Class Teacher, Ted Sorel; Candy Store Owner, Bruce Friedman; Susan's Aunt, Eunice Anderson.

1547 THE JERUSALEM FILE. (MGM-1972). David Armstrong, Bruce Davison; Professor Lang, Nicol Williamson; Nurit, Daria Halprin; Major Samuels, Donald Pleasence; General Mayers, Ian Hendry; Barak, Koya Yair Rubin; Raschid, Zeev Revah; Herzen, David Smader; Altouli, Jack Cohen; Yussof, Isaac Neeman; Captain Ori, Ori Levy; Informer, Arie Elias; Barak's Brother, Itzik Weiss; Raschel, Yona Elian; Alex, Yossi Werzanski; Lieutenant, Johnnie Phillips; Hospital Receptionist, Gabi Eldor; Professor Lang's Secretary, Yael Duryanoff; Officer, Moshe Yanai; Student, Pink Wigoder; Fuad, Ali Mohammad Hassan; Achmed, Samib Mohammad Najib; Security Officer, Salah Darwish.

1548 JESSE JAMES MEETS FRANKENSTEIN'S DAUGHTER. (Embassy-1966). John Lupton, Cal Bolder, Estelita, Narda Onyx, Steven Geray, Raymond Barnes, Felipe Turich, Jim Davis, Rosa Turich, Page Slattery, Dan White, Nestor Paiva.

1549 JESUS CHRIST SUPERSTAR. (Universal-1973). Jesus Christ, Ted Neeley; Judas Iscariot, Carl Anderson; Mary Magdalene, Yvonne Elliman; Pontius Pilate, Barry Dennen; Caiaphas, Bob Bingham; Simon Zealotes, Larry T. Marshall; King Herod, Joshua Mostel; Annas, Kurt Yahgjian; Peter, Philip Toubus; Apostles, Pi Douglass, Jonathan Wynne, Richard Molinare, Jeffrey Hyslop, Robert Lupone, Thommie Walsh, David Devir, Richard Orbach, Shooki Wagner; Women, Darcel Wynne, Sally Neal, Vera Biloshisky, Wendy Maltby, Baayork Lee, Susan Allanson, Ellen Hoffman, Judith Daby, Adaya Pilo, Marcia McBroom, Leeyan Granger, Kathryn Wright, Denise Pence, Wyetta Turner, Tamar Zafria, Riki Oren, Lea Kestin; Priests, Zvulun Cohen, Meir Israel, Itzhak Sidranski, David Rfjwan, Amity Razi, Avi Ben-Haim, Haim Bashi, David Barkan; Roman Soldiers, Steve Boockvor, Peter Luria, David Barkan, Danny Basevitch, Cliff Michaelevski, Tom Guest, Stephen Denenberg, Didi Liekov; Temple Guards, Doron Gaash, Noam Cohen, Zvi Lehat, Moshe Uziel.

1550 THE JESUS TRIP. (EMCO-1971). Sister Anna, Elizabeth "Tippy" Walker; Waco, Robert Porter; Cop, Billy "Green" Bush; Other Police, Robert Tessier, Frank Orsati, Allan Gibbs; Older Nun, Hanna Hertalanda; Gang Members, Diana Ivarson, Virgil Frye, Carmen Argenziano, Wally Strauss, Bebe Louie, Jenny Hecht.

1551 JIG SAW. (Beverly-1965). Jack Warner, Ronald Lewis.

1552 JIGSAW. (Universal-1968). Arthur Belding, Harry Guardino; Jonathan Fields, Bradford Dillman; Helen Atterbury, Hope Lange; Lew Haley, Pat Hingle; Sarah, Diana Hyland; Dr. Edward Arkroyd, Victor Jory; Dr. Simon Joshua, Paul Stewart; Ida, Susan Saint James; Dill, Michael J. Pollard; Arlene Susanne Benton; Building Superintendent, James Doohan; Peter, Donald Mitchell; Arnie, Roy Jenson.

1553 No entry.

1554 JIMI PLAYS BERKELEY. (New Line Cinema-1973). Jimi Hendrix, Mitch Miller, Billy Cox.

1555 JOANNA. (20th Century-Fox-1968). Joanna, Genevieve Waite; Hendrik Casson, Christian Doermer; Gordon, Calvin Lockhart; Lord Peter Sanderson, Donald Sutherland; Beryl, Glenna Forster-Jones; Dominic, David Scheuer; Granny, Marda Vanne; Father, Geoffrey Morris; Margot, Michele Cooke; Inspector, Manning Wilson; Black Detective, Clifton Jones; White Detective, Dan Caulfield; Lefty, Michael Chow; Bruce, Anthony Ainley; Angela, Jane Bradbury; Miranda De Hyde, Fiona Lewis; Teacher, Jayne Sofiano; Nurse, Elizabeth MacLennan; 1st Butler, Richard Hurndall; Maid, Annette Robertson; Married Woman, Jenny Hanley; Art Dealer,

John Gulliver; Bespectacled Woman, Brenda Kempner; Taxi Driver, Peter Porteous; Critic, David Collings; Critic's Wife, Sybilla Kay.

1556 JOE. (Cannon-1970). Melissa Compton, Susan Sarandon; Frank Russo, Patrick McDermott; Kid in Soda Shop, Tim Lewis; Woman in Bargain Store, Estelle Omens; Man in Bargain Store, Bob O'Connell; Bill Compton, Dennis Patrick; Joan Compton, Audrey Caire; Bellevue Nurse, Marlene Warfield; Teeny Boppers, Mary Case & Jenny Paine; Joe Curran, Peter Boyle; American Bartender, Reid Cruikshanks; Man in Bar, Rudy Churney; Mary Lou Curran, K. Callan; TV Newscaster, Robert Emerick; Janine, Gloria Hoye; Sam, Bo Enivel; Bartender at Ginger Man, Patrick O'Neil; Gil Richards, Frank Moon; Phyllis, Jeanne M. Lange; Hippie on Street, Perry Gerwitz; Waiter in Guitar Joint, Morty Schloss; Hippie in Group, Frank Vitale; Poster Shop Proprietor, Al Sentesy; Nancy, Patti Caton; George, Gary Weber; Bob, Claude Robert Simon; Gail, Francine Middleton; Ronnie, Max Couper.

1557 JOE COCKER/MAD DOGS AND ENGLISHMEN. (MGM-1971). Joe Cocker, Leon Russell, Chris Stainton, Carl Radle, Jim Price, Bobby Keys, Jim Gordon, Jim Keltner, Don Preston, Sandy Konikoff, Chuck Blackwell, Rita Coolidge, Claudia Lennear, Donna Washburn, Donna Weiss, Pamela Polland, Nicole Barclay, Matthew Moore, Bobby Jones.

1558 JOE HILL. (Paramount-1971). Joe Hill, Thommy Berggren; Lucia, Ania Schmidt; The Fox, Kelvin Malave; Blackie, Evert Anderson; Cathy, Cathy Smith; Paul, Hasse Persson; Elizabeth, Wendy Geier; Tenor, Franco Molinari.

1559 JOE KIDD. (Universal-1972). Joe Kidd, Clint Eastwood; Frank Harlan, Robert Duvall; Luis Chama, John Saxon; Lamarr, Don Stroud; Helen Sanchez, Stella Garcia.

1560 JOHN AND MARY. (20th Century-Fox-1969). John, Dustin Hoffman; Mary, Mia Farrow; James, Michael Tolan; Ruth, Sunny Griffin; Ernest, Stanley Beck; Hilary, Tyne Daly; Jane, Alix Elias; Fran, Julie Garfield; Dean, Marvin Lichterman; Mags Elliot, Marian Mercer; Minnie, Susan Taylor; John's Mother, Olympia Dukakis; Tennis Player, Carl Parker; Charlie, Richard Clarke; Film Director, Cleavon Little; His Wife, Marilyn Chris; Imaginary Film Director, Alexander Cort; Boy Scout, Kristoffer Tabori.

1561 JOHN GOLDFARB, PLEASE COME HOME. (20th Century-Fox-1965). Jenny Ericson, Shirley MacLaine; King Fawz, Peter Ustinov; John Goldfarb, Richard Crenna; Sakalakis, Scott Brady; Miles Whitepaper, Jim Backus; Heinous Overreach, Fred Clark; Deems Sarajevo, Harry Morgan; Mustafa Gus, Wilfrid Hyde-White; Prince Ammud, Patrick Adiarte;

Samir, Leon Askin; Frinkley, Jerome Cowan; Frobish, Richard Wilson; Maginot, Richard Deacon; Air Force General, Milton Frome; Editor of Strife, Charles Lane; Pinkerton, Jerome Orbach.

1562 JOHNNY CASH! THE MAN, HIS WORLD, HIS MUSIC. (Continental-1970). Johnny Cash, June Carter, Bob Dylan, Mother Maybelle and the Carter Family, Carl Perkins, The Tennessee Trio.

1563 JOHNNY GOT HIS GUN. (Cinemation-1971). Joe Bonham, Timothy Bottoms; Kareen, Kathy Fields; Joe's Mother, Marsha Hunt; Joe's Father, Jason Robards; Christ, Donald Sutherland; Fourth Nurse, Diane Varsi.

1564 JOHNNY HAMLET. (Transvue-1972). Johnny Hamlet, Chip Corman; Horace, Gilbert Roland; Claude, Horst Frank; Gil, Pedro Sanchez; Ross, Enio Girolami; Ophelia, Gabriella Grimaldi; Gertrude, Francoise Prevost; Actress Mother, Stefania Careddu; Polonio, Giorgio Sanmartin; Franco Latini, Manuel Serrano, John Bartha, Franco Leo, Fabio Patella.

1565 JOHNNY MINOTAUR. (Impact-1971). Nikos, Nikos Koulizakis; Johnny, Yiannis Koutsis; Karolos, Chuzzer Miles; Shelley, Shelley Scott; Allen Bole, Billy Bones, Derek, Stavros Georgiakakis, Babis Gnardellis, Charles Haldeman, Dick Johnson, John Kirk, Terry Kouridakis, Stefano, Sotiris Nomikos, Costas Papanikos, Florence Phillips, Jorgos Rantis, Andrea Tagliahue, Lynn Tillman, Yiannia Tsakalozos, The Boys of Chanea.

1566 JOHNNY NOBODY. (Medallion-1965). Father Carey, Nigel Patrick; Miss Floyd, Yvonne Mitchell; Johnny, Aldo Ray; Mulcahy, William Bendix; Prosecuting Counsel, Cyril Cusack; Defending Counsel, Niall MacGinnis; Photographer, Bernie Winters; Brother Timothy, Noel Purcell; Landlord, Eddie Byrne; Postman, Jimmy O'Dea.

1567 JOHNNY RENO. (Paramount-1966). Johnny Reno, Dana Andrews; Nona Williams, Jane Russell; Sheriff Hodges, Lon Chaney; Ed Tomkins, John Agar, Jess Yates, Lyle Bettger; Joe Connors, Tom Drake; Reed, Richard Arlen; Maria Yates, Tracy Olsen; Chief Little Bear, Paul Daniel; Ab Connors, Dale Van Sickle; Jake Reed, Robert Lowery; Bartender, Reg Parton; Indian, Rodd Redwing; Wooster, Charles Horvath; Bellows, Chuck Hicks; Townsman, Edmund Cobb.

1568 JOHNNY TIGER. (Universal-1966). George Dean, Robert Taylor; Doc Leslie Frost, Geraldine Brooks; Johnny Tiger, Chad Everett; Barbara Dean, Brenda Scott; William Billie, Marc Lawrence; Sam Tiger, Ford Rainey; Wendy Dean, Carol Seflinger; Randy Dean, Steven Wheeler; Shalonee, Pamela Melendez; Louise, Deanna Lund.

1569 JOHNNY YUMA. (Clover-1967). Johnny Yuma, Mark Damon; L. J. Carradine, Lawrence Dobkin; Samantha Felton, Rosalba Neri; Pedro, Louis Vanner; Sanchez, Fidel Gonzales; Henchman, Gus Harper; Thomas Felton, Leslie Daniel; Gianni Solaro, Dada Gallotti, Nando Poggi, Frank Liston.

1570 THE JOKERS. (Universal-1967). Michael Tremayne, Michael Crawford; David Tremayne, Oliver Reed; Inspector Marryatt, Harry Andrews; Colonel Gurney Simms, James Donald; Riggs, Daniel Massey; Sir Matthew, Michael Hordern; Eve, Gabriella Licudi; Inge, Lotte Tarp; Harassed Man, Frank Finlay; Lennie, Warren Mitchell; Mrs. Tremayne, Rachel Kempson; Mr. Tremayne, Peter Graves; Sarah, Ingrid Brett; Brian Wilde, Edward Fox, Michael Goodliffe, William Devlin, William Mervyn, William Kendal, Kenneth Colley, Charlotte Curzon, Mark Burns, Brook Williams, Brian Peck, Basil Dignam, John Kidd, Freda Jackson, Nam Munro.

1571 JONATHAN. (New Yorker-1973). Jonathan, Jurgen Jung; Josef, Hans Dieter Jendreyko; Count, Paul Albert Krumm; Thomas, Thomas Astan; Lena's Mother, Ilse Kunkele; Lena, Eleonore Schminke; Professor, Oskar Von Schab; Eleonore, Ilone Grubel.

1572 JONATHAN LIVINGSTON SEAGULL. (Paramount-1973). Jonathan's voice, James Franciscus; Girl's voice, Juliet Mills; Elder's voice, Hal Holbrook; Chang's voice, Philip Ahn; Fletcher's voice, David Ladd; Kimmy's voice, Kelly Harmon; Mother's voice, Dorothy McGuire; Father's Voice, Richard Crenna.

1573 JORY. (AVCO Embassy-1973). Roy, John Marley; Jocko, B. J. Thomas; Jory, Robby Benson; Jack, Brad Dexter; Ethan, Claudio Brook; Carmelita, Patricia Aspillaga; Barron, Todd Martin; Jordan, Ben Baker; Logan, Carlos Cortes; Amy, Linda Purl; Dora, Anne Lockhart; Mrs. Jordan, Betty Sheridan; Evans, Ted Markland; Walker, Quintin Bulnes; Thatcher, John Kelly; Cookie, Eduardo Lopez Rojas.

1574 JOSEPH KILIAN. (1966). Mr. Herold, Karel Vasicek; Girl in Cat Shop, Consuela Morakova; Mr. Kilian, Pavel Bartl.

1575 JOURNEY THROUGH ROSEBUD. (GSF-1972). Frank, Robert Forster; Danny, Kristoffer Tabori; Shirley, Victoria Racimo; Stanley Pike, Eddie Little Sky; Park Ranger, Roy Jenson; Indian Agent, Wright King; Sheriff, Larry Pennell; Hearing Officer, Robert Cornthwaite; John, Steve Shemayme; Stu, Beau Little Sky; Raymond, Lynn Burnette; Mrs. Blackwing, Diane Running; Mrs. Graham, Olive McCloskey; Police Officer, Pat Iyotte.

1576 JOURNEY TO SHILOH. (Universal-1968). Buck Burnett, James Caan; Miller Nalls, Michael Sarrazin; Gabrielle DuPrey, Brenda Scott; Todo McLean, Don Stroud; J. C. Sutton, Paul Petersen; Eubie Bell, Michael Burns; Little Bit Lucket, Michael Vincent; Willie Bill Bearden, Harrison Ford; General Braxton Bragg, John Doucette; Sgt. Mercer Barnes, Noah Berry; Airybelle Sumner, Tisha Sterling; Tellis Yeager, James Gammon; Carter Claiborne, Brian Avery; Colonel Mirabeau Cooney, Clarke Gordon; Collins, Robert Pine; Custis Claiborne, Sean Kennedy; Colonel Boykin, Wesley Lau; Mr. Claiborne, Chet Stratton; Greybeard, Bing Russell; Lane Bradford, Rex Ingram, Charles Lampkin, Myron Healey, Eileen Wesson, Albert Popwell.

1577 JOURNEY TO THE FAR SIDE OF THE SUN. (Universal-1969). John, Ian Hendry; Col. Ross, Roy Thinnes; Jason, Patrick Wymark; Sharon, Lynn Loring; Lise, Loni Von Friedl; Dr. Hassler, Herbert Lom; Mark, George Sewell; Paulo, Franco Derosa; David, Edward Bishop.

1578 JOVITA. (Altura-1970). Agnes, Barbara Lass; Marc, Daniel Orlbrychski; Edouard, Zbigniew Cybulski; Helene, Kalina Jedrusik; Dorota, Anna Pleskaczewska.

1579 JOY HOUSE. (MGM-1965). Marc, Alain Delon; Melinda, Jane Fonda; Barbara, Lola Albright; Loftus, Carl Studer; Harry, Sorrel Booke; Vincent, Andre Oumansky; Rev. Nielson, Arthur Howard; Mick, Nick Del Negro; "Napoleon," Jacques Bezard; Diana, Berett Arcaya.

1580 JOY IN THE MORNING. (MGM-1965). Carl Brown, Richard Chamberlain; Annie McCairy Brown, Yvette Mimieux; Mr. Brown, Arthur Kennedy; Anthony Byrd, Donald Davis; Deane Darwence, Sydney Blackmer; Beverly Karter, Joan Tetzel; Stan Pulaski, Oscar Homolka.

1581 JUD. (Maron-1971). Jud, Jason Robards; Bill, Robert Deman; Shirley, Alix Wyeth; Uncle, Norman Burton; Sunny, Claudia Jennings; Salvadore, Maurice Sherbanee; Vincent, Victor Dunlap; Kathy, Bonnie Bittner.

1582 JUDEX. (Continental-1966). Judex, Channing Pollack; Daisy, Sylva Koscina; Diana Monti, Francine Berge; Jacqueline Favraux, Edith Scob; Favraux, Michel Vitold; Cocantin, Jacques Jouanneau; Morales, Theo Sarapo; De la Rochefontaine, Philippe Mareuil; Kerjean, Rene Genin.

1583 JUDITH. (Paramount-1966). Judith Auerbach, Sophia Loren; Aaron Stein, Peter Finch; Major Lawton, Jack Hawkins; Gustave Schiller, Hans Verner; Rachel, Zharrira Charifai; Nathan, Shraga Friedman; Chaim, Andre Morell; Elie, Frank Wolff; Interrogator, Arnoldo Foa; Yaneck, Joseph Gross; Roger Beaumont, Zipora Peled, Terence

Alexander, Gilad Konstantiner, Daniel Ocko, Roland Bartrop, Peter Burton, John Stacy.

1584 JUGGERNAUT. (United Artists-1974). Fallon, Richard Harris; Capt. Brunel, Omar Sharif; Braddock, David Hemmings; McCleod, Anthony Hopkins; Mrs. Banister, Shirley Knight; Porter, Ian Holm; Corrigan, Clifton James; Social Director, Roy Kinnear; Mrs. McCleod, Caroline Mortimer; 1st Officer, Mark Burns; Buckland, Freddie Jones; Marder, Julian Glover; Azad, Roshan Seth.

1585 JULIET OF THE SPIRITS. (Rizzoli-1965). Giulietta, Giulietta Masina; Husband, Mario Pisu; Susy, Sandra Milo; Mother, Caterina Boratto; Adele, Luisa Della Noce; Sylva, Sylva Koscina; Grandfather, Lou Gilbert; Valentina, Valentina, Valentina Cortese; Dolores, Silvana Jachino; Elena, Elena Fondra; Spanish Gentleman, Jose de Villalonga; Bhishma, Waleska Gert; Bhisma's helpers, Asoka Rubener, Sujata Rubener, Walter Harrison; Russian Teacher, Edoardo Torricella; Lyn-Eyes, Alberto Plebani; Don Raffaele, Felice Fulchignoni; Psychoanalyst, Anne Francine; Family Lawyer, Mario Conocchi; Medium, Genius; Giulietta (as a child), Alba Cancellieri.

1586 JULIETTE DE SADE. (Haven International-1969). Juliette, Maria Pia Conte; Toni, Lea Nanni; Clarissa, Christine Delit; Angela, Angela DeLeo.

1587 JULIUS CAESAR. (American International-1971). Mark Antony, Charlton Heston; Brutus, Jason Robards; Julius Caesar, John Gielgud; Cassius, Richard Johnson; Casca, Robert Vaughn; Octavius Caesar, Richard Chamberlain; Portia, Diana Rigg; Calpurnia, Jill Bennett; Artemidorus, Christopher Lee.

1588 JUMP. (Cannon-1971). Chester Jump, Tom Ligon; Babe, Logan Ramsey; April May, Collin Wilcox-Horne; Ernestine, Sudie Bond; Lester, Conrad Bain; Dutchman, Norman Rose; Enid, Lada Edmund Jr.; Beulah, Bette Craig; Mercy, Vicki Lynn; Ace, Jack Nance; Billy Rae, Ron St. Germain; Starter, Johnny Hicks; Young Boy, James Tallent; The Kentucky Mountain Boys.

1589 THE JUNGLE BOOK. (Buena Vista-1967). Baloo the bear, Phil Harris; Bagheera the panther, Sebastian Cabot; King Louie the ape, Louis Prima; Shere Khan the tiger, George Sanders; Kaa the snake, Sterling Holloway; Colonel Hathi the elephant, J. Pat O'Malley; Mowgli the man cub, Bruce Reitherman; Elephants, Verna Felton, Clint Howard; Vultures, Chad Stuart, Lord Tim Hudson; Wolves, John Abbott, Ben Wright; The Girl, Darleen Carr.

1590 JUNIOR BONNER. (Cinerama-1972). Junior Bonner, Steve

McQueen; Ace Bonner, Robert Preston; Elvira Bonner, Ida Lupino; Buck Roan, Ben Johnson; Curly Bonner, Joe Don Baker; Charmagne, Barbara Leigh; Ruth Bonner, Mary Murphy; Red Terwiliger, Bill McKinney; Nurse Arlis, Sandra Deel; Homer Rutledge, Donald "Red" Barry; Del, Dub Taylor; Burt, Charles Gray; Tim Bonner, Matthew Peckinpah; Nick Bonner, Sundown Spencer; Flashie, Rita Garrison.

1591 JUST BEFORE NIGHTFALL. (Columbia-1974). Stephane Audran, Michel Bouquet, Francois Perier, Jean Carmet, Dominique Zardi, Henri Attal, Paul Temps.

1592 JUST LIKE A WOMAN. (Emerson-1968). Scilla McKenzie, Wendy Craig; Lewis McKenzie, Francis Matthews; John, John Wood; Salesman, Dennis Price; Ellen, Mariam Karlin; Saul, Peter Jones; Von Fischer, Clive Dunn; The Australian, Ray Barrett; Isolde, Sheila Steaffel; TV Floor Manager, Aubrey Woods; Elijah, Barry Fantoni; Lewis' Girl Friend, Juliet Harmer; Singer, Mark Murphy.

1593 JUSTINE. (20th Century-Fox-1969). Justine, Anouk Aimee; Darley, Michael York; Pursewarden, Dirk Bogarde; Melissa, Anna Karina; Nessim Hosnani, John Vernon; Narouz, Robert Forster; Pombal, Philippe Noiret; Cohen, Jack Albertson; Toto, Cliff Gorman; Mountolive, George Baker; Liza, Elaine Church; Memlik Pasha, Michael Constantine; French Consul General, Marcel Dalio; Mnemjian, Michael Dunn; Maskelyne, Barry Morse; Balthazar, Severn Darden; Mrs. Serapamoun, Amapola Del Vando; Proprietor, Abraham Sofaer; Kawwass, Peter Mamakos; Seraphamoun, Stanley Waxman; Woman at Ball, De Ann Mears; Prisoner, Tutte Lemkow.

1594 KALEIDOSCOPE. (Warner Bros. -1966). Barney Lincoln, Warren Beatty; Angel McGinnis, Susannah York; Inspector "Mammy" McGinnis, Clive Revill; Harry Dominion, Eric Porter; Aimes, Murray Melvin; Billy, George Sewell; Dominion Captain, Stanley Meadows; Dominion Porter, John Junkin; Dominion Chauffeur, Larry Taylor; Museum Receptionist, Yootha Joyce; Exquisite Thing, Jane Birkin; Johnny, George Murcell; Leeds, Anthony Newlands.

1595 KANCHENJUNGHA. (Harrison-1966). Indranath Choudhuri, Chabi Biswas; Labanya, Karuna Banerji; Anil, Anil Chatter-Jee; Shankar, Subrata Sen; Tuklu, Indrani Singh; Monisha, Nilima Roy Chowdhury; Bennerji, N. Viswanathan; Jagadish, Pahari Sanyal; Ashoke, Arun Mukherjee; Shibsankar Roy, Vidya Singh.

1596 KANSAS CITY BOMBER. (MGM-1972). Diane (K. C.) Carr, Raquel Welch; Burt Henry, Kevin McCarthy; Jackie Burdette, Helena Kallianiotes; Horrible Hank Hopkins,

Norman Alden; Vivien, Jeanne Cooper; Lovey, Mary Kay Pass; Mrs. Carr, Martine Bartlett; Tammy O'Brien, Cornelia Sharpe; Randy, William Gray Espy; Len, Dick Lane; Dick Wicks, Russ Marin; Walt, Stephen Manley; Rita, Jodie Foster; Old Woman, Georgia Schmidt; Big Bertha Bogliani, Patti (Moo-Moo) Cavin; Fan, Shelly Novack; Fan, Jim Nickerson.

1597 KATERINA ISMAILOVA. (Artkino-1969). Katerina Ismailova, Galina Vishnevskaya; Sergei, Artem Inozemtsev; Boris Ismailova, Alexandre Sokolov; Zinovi Ismailova, Nikolai Boyarsky; Sonetka, T. Gavirolova; Village Drunk, R. Tkachuk.

1598 KAYA, I'LL KILL YOU! (Altura-1969). Kaya, Zaim Muzaferija; Piero, Ugljesa Kojadinovic; Tonko, Antun Nalis; Mare, Jolanda Dacic; Ugo, Izet Hajdarhodzic; Niki, Husein Cokic.

1599 KEEP ON ROCKIN'. (Pennebaker-1973). Chuck Berry, Diddley Richard, Jerry Lee Lewis, Bo Diddley, Janis Joplin, Jimi Hendrix.

1600 KELLY'S HEROES. (MGM-1970). Kelly, Clint Eastwood; Big Joe, Telly Savalas; Crapgame, Don Rickles; Oddball, Donald Sutherland; General Colt, Carroll O'Connor; Moriarty, Gavin MacLeod; Maitland, Hal Buckley; Little Joe, Stuart Margolin; Cowboy, Jeff Morris; Gutowski, Richard Davalos; Petuko, Perry Lopez; Job, Tom Troupe; Willard, Dean Stanton; Fisher, Dick Balduzzi; Babra, Gene Collins; Bellamy, Len Lesser; Colonel Dankhopf, David Hurst; Mitchell, Fred Pearlman; Grace, Michael Clark; Penn, George Fargo; Jonesy, Dee Pollock; Mulligan, George Savalas; German Lieutenant, John Heller; Turk, Shepherd Sanders; Karl Otto Alberty, Ross Elliott, Phil Adams, Hugo De Vernier, Frank J. Garlatta, Harry Goines, David Gross, Sandy Kevin, James McHale, Robert McNamara, Read Morgan, Tom Signorelli, Donald Waugh, Vincent Maracecchi.

1601 KENNER. (MGM-1969). Roy Kenner, Jim Brown; Anasuya, Madlyn Rhue; Henderson, Robert Coote; Saji, Ricky Cordell; Tom Jordan, Charles Horvath; Sandy, Prem Nath; Young Sikh, Kuljit Singh; Mother Superior, Sulochana; Sister Katherine, Ursula Prince; American Friend, Tony North; Ring Referee, Ming Hung; Gym Owner, R. P. Wright; Customs Officer, Nitin Sethi; Young Hindu at Seaman's Associations, Mahendra Jhaveri; Shoe Merchant, G. S. Aasie; Bald Disciple, Ravi Kaant; First Robed Man, Hercules; Second Robed Man, Khalil Amir.

1602 KES. (United Artists-1970). Billy, David Bradley; Mr. Farthing, Colin Welland; Mrs. Casper, Lynne Perrie; Jud, Freddie Fletcher; Mr. Sugden, Brian Glover; Mr. Gryce,

Bob Bowes; Mr. Crossley, Trevor Hasketh; Farmer, Eric Bolderson; Mathematics Teacher, Geoffrey Banks; Librarian, Zoe Sunderland; Mother's Friend, Joe Miller; Comedian at pub, Joey Kaye; Youth Employment Officer, Bernard Atha; MacDowell, Robert Naylor; Milkman, Duggie Brown; Tibutt, David Glover; Billy's Friends, Stephen Crossland, Martin Harley, Frank Norton.

1603 KHARTOUM. (United Artists-1966). General Charles Gordon, Charlton Heston; The Mahdi, Laurence Olivier; Col. J. D. H. Stewart, Richard Johnson; Mr. Gladstone, Ralph Richardson; Sir Evelyn Baring, Alexander Knox; Khaleel, Johnny Sekka; Lord Granville, Michael Hordern; Zobeir Pasha, Zia Mohyeddin; Sheikh Osman, Marne Maitland; General Wolseley, Nigel Green; Lord Hartington, Hugh Williams; Khalifa Abdullah, Douglas Wilmer; Col. Hicks, Edward Underdown; Alec Mango, George Pastell, Peter Arne, Alan Tilvern, Michael Anthony, Jerome Willis, Leila, Ronald Leigh Hunt, Ralph Michael; Narrator, Leo Genn.

1604 KID BLUE. (20th Century-Fox-1973). Bickford Waner, Dennis Hopper; Reese Ford, Warren Oates; Preacher Bob, Peter Boyle; Sheriff "Mean John" Simpson, Ben Johnson; Molly Ford, Lee Purcell; Janet Conforto, Janice Rule; Drummer, Ralph Waite; Mr. Hendricks, Clifton James; Old Coyote, Jose Torvay; Mrs. Evans, Mary Jackson; Mendoza, Jay Varela; Tough Guy, Claude Ennis Starrett Jr.; Wills, Warren Finnerty; Confectionery man, Howard Hessman; Barber, M. Emmet Walsh; Joe Cloudmaker, Henry Smith; Bartender, Bobby Hall; Blackman, Melvin Stewart; Huey, Eddy Donno; Train Robbers, Owen Orr, Richard Rust.

1605 KID RODELO. (Paramount-1966). Kid Rodelo, Don Murray; Nora, Janet Leigh; Joe Harbin, Broderick Crawford; Link, Richard Carlson; Thomas Reese, Jose Nieto; Balsas, Julia Pena; Chavas, Miguel Del Castillo; Cavalry Hat, Jose Villa Sante; Gopher, Alfonso San Felix; Warden, Emilio Rodriguez; Perryman, Fernando Hilbeck; The Doctor, Roberto Rubenstein; Guard, Billy Christmas.

1606 KIDNAPPED. (American International-1971). Alan Breck, Michael Caine; Lord Advocate Grant, Trevor Howard; Captain Hoseason, Jack Hawkins; Ebenezer Balfour, Donald Pleasence; Charles Stewart, Gordon Jackson; Catriona, Vivien Heilbron; David Balfour, Lawrence Douglas.

1607 KILL! (Frank Lee International-1969). Genta, Tatsuya Nakadai; Hanjiro, Etsuji Takahasi; Ayuzawa, Shigeru Kamiyama; Moriuchi, Eijiro Tono; Chino, Yuriko Hosi; Matsuo, Yoshio Tsuchiya; Shoda, Tadao Nakamura; Hideo Amamoto, Ko Hashimoto, Nami Tamura, Akira Kubo.

1608 KILL A DRAGON. (United Artists-1967). Rick, Jack

Palance; Patrai, Fernando Lamas; Vigo, Aldo Ray; Tisa, Alizia Gur; Win Lim, Kam Tong; Ian, Don Knight; Jimmie, Hans Lee; Chunhyang, Judy Dan.

1609 KILL BABY KILL. (Europix Consolidated-1967). Monica Schuftan, Erika Blanc; Dr. Paul Eswai, Giacomo Rossi Stuart; Ruth the Sorceress, Fabienne Dali; Baroness Graps, Gianna Vivaldi; Police Commissioner Kroger, Piero Lulli; Kerl, Max Lawrence; Micaela Esdra, Franca Dominici, Giuseppe Addobbati, Valerio Valeri, Mariella Panfili.

1610 KILL OR BE KILLED. (Rizzoli-1968). Robert Mark, Gordon Mitchell, Elina De Witt, Fabrizio Moroni, Andrea Bosic, Albert Farley, Man Fury, Benjamin May, Tony Rogers, Mary Land.

1611 THE KILLING GAME. (Regional-1968). Pierre Meyraud, Jean-Pierre Cassel; Jacqueline Meyrand, Claudine Auger; Bob Neuman, Michel Duchaussoy; Mme. Neuman, Eleonore Hirt; Ado, Guy Saint Jean; Lisbeth, Anna Gaylor; Nancy, Nancy Holloway.

1612 THE KILLING OF SISTER GEORGE. (Cinerama-1968). June Buckridge, Beryl Reid; Alice "Childie" McNaught, Susannah York; Mercy Croft, Coral Browne; Leo Lockhart, Ronald Fraser; Betty Thaxter, Patricia Medina; Freddie, Hugh Paddick; Ted Baker, Cyril Delevanti; Diana, Sivi Aberg; Floor Manager, William Beckley; Marlene, Elaine Church; Bert Turner, Brendan Dillon; Noel, Mike Freeman; Maid, Maggie Paige; Deputy Commissioner, Jack Raine; Tea Lady, Dolly Taylor; Mr. Katz, Meier Tzelniker; Mrs. Coote, Cicely Walper; Jack Adams, Byron Webster; Mildred, Rosalie Williams; Taxi Driver, Sam Kydd.

1613 KIMBERLEY JIM. (Embassy-1965). Jim Reeves, Madeleine Usher, Clive Parnell, Arthur Swemmer, Tromp Terre Blanche, Vonk De Ridder, Mike Holt, David Van Der Walt, June Neethling, George Moore, Freddie Prozesky, Don Leonard, Morris Blake.

1614 KING AND COUNTRY. (American International-1966). Captain Hargreaves, Dirk Bogarde; Private Hamp, Tom Courtenay; Captain O'Sullivan, Leo McKern; Lieutenant Webb, Barry Foster; Captain Midgley, James Villiers; Colonel, Peter Copley; Lieutenant Prescott, Barry Justice; Padre, Vivian Matalon; Sparrow, Jeremy Spencer; Sykes, James Hunter; Wilson, David Cook, Larry Taylor, Jonah Seymour, Keith Buckley, Arthur Arthure, Cerek Partridge, Brian Tipping, Raymond Brody, Dan Cornwall, Terry Palmer.

1615 A KING IN NEW YORK. (Classic Entertainment-1973). King Shadhov, Charles Chaplin; Ann Kay, Dawn Addams;

The Ambassador, Oliver Johnston; Queen Irene, Maxine Audley; Lawyer Green, Harry Green; Headmaster, Phil Brown; Macabee Seniro, John McLaren; School Superintendent, Allan Gifford; Night Club Vocalist, Shani Wallace; Night Club Vocalist, Jay Nichols; Rupert Macabee, Michael Chaplin; Mr. Cromwell, John Ingram; Mr. Johnson, Sidney James; Prime Minister, Jerry Desmond; Lift Boy, Robert Arden; Comedy Act, Lauri Lupina-Lane, George Truzzi.

1616 KING KONG ESCAPES. (Universal-1968). Commander Nelson, Rhodes Reason; Madame Piranha, Mie Hama; Susan, Linda Miller; Lt. Jiro Nomura, Akira Takarada; Dr. Who, Eisei Amamoto.

1617 KING LEAR. (Altura-1971). King Lear, Paul Scofield; Goneril, Irene Worth; Fool, Jack MacGowran; Duke of Gloucester, Alan Webb; Duke of Albany, Cyril Cusack; Duke of Cornwall, Patrick Magee; Edgar, Robert Lloyd.

1618 KING, MURRAY. (Iconographic-1969). Himself, Murray King; First Starlet, Laura Kaye; Socialite, Gloria Riegger; Second Starlet, Jackie Morris; Girl in Shower, Addie Pezzotta; Masseur, George Koski; Other Girls, Barbara Linden and Nora Lord.

1619 KING OF HEARTS. (Lopert-1967). Pvt. Charles Plumpick, Alan Bates; Generale Geranium, Pierre Brasseur; Le Duc de Trefle, Jean Claude Brialy; Coquelicot, Genevieve Bujold; Colonel Alexander MacBibenbrook, Adolfo Celi; Madame Eglantine, Micheline Presle; La Duchesse, Francoise Christophe; Bishop Daisy, Julien Guiomar; Monsieur Marcel, Michel Serrault; Lieutenant Hamburger, Marc Dudicourt; Colonel Helmut von Krack, Daniel Boulanger.

1620 THE KING OF MARVIN GARDENS. (Columbia-1972). David, Jack Nicholson; Jason, Bruce Dern; Sally, Ellen Burstyn; Jessica, Julia Anne Robinson; Lewis, Benjamin "Scatman" Crothers; Surtees, John Ryan; Lebowitz, Sully Boyar; Frank, Josh Mostel; Bidlack, William Pabst; Nervous Man, Gary Goodrow; Magda, Imogene Bliss; Bambi, Ann Thomas; Spot Operator, Tom Overton; Sonny, Maxwell "Sonny" Goldberg; Messengers, Van Kirksey and Tony King; Agura, Jerry Fujikawa; Fujito, Conrad Yama; Auctioneers, Scott Howard, Henry Foehl; Dancers, Frank Hatchett, Wyetta Turner.

1621 KING OF THE GRIZZLIES. (Buena Vista-1970). Moki, John Yesno; Colonel, Chris Wiggins; Shorty, Hugh Webster; Slim, Jack Van Evers; and Wahb the grizzly bear.

1622 KING RAT. (Columbia-1965). King, George Segal; Lieut. Grey, Tom Courtenay; Peter Marlowe, James Fox; Max, Patrick O'Neal; Lieut. Col. Larkin, Denholm Elliott; Dr.

Kennedy, James Donald; Tex, Todd Armstrong; Col. Smedley-Taylor, John Mills; Col. Jones, Gerald Sim; Maj. McCoy, Leonard Rossiter; Capt. Daven, John Standing; Col. Brant, Alan Webb.

1623 KINGDOM IN THE CLOUDS. (Xerox-1972). Young Lad, Mirceau Breauzu; Princess, Ana Szeles; Prince of Liars, Ion Tugearu; Witch, Carmen Stanescu; Emanoil Petrut, Nicolae Secareanu, Mihai Paladescu, Nicolae Brancomir, Margareta Pogonat, George Mottoi, Eugenia Basanceanu, Zoe Anchel-Stanca, Simona Manda, Corin Constantinescu.

1624 KING'S PIRATE. (Universal-1967). Lt. Brian Fleming, Doug McClure; Mistress Jessica Stephens, Jill St. John; John Avery, Guy Stockwell; Princess Patma, Mary Ann Mobley; Zucco, Kurt Kasznar; Swaine, Richard Deacon; Captain Cullen, Torin Thatcher; Molvina MacGregor, Diana Chesney; Cloudsly, Ivor Barry; Captain Hornsby, Bill Glover; Gow, Woodrow Parfrey; Sparkes, Sean McClory; Collins, Michael St. Clair; Captain Misson, Emile Genest; Captain McTigue, Ted De Corsia; Caraccioli, Alex Montoya.

1625 A KING'S STORY. (Continental-1967). Narrator, Orson Welles; Dame Flora Robson, Patrick Wymark, David Warner, Carleton Hobbs, and the Duke and Duchess of Windsor.

1626 KISS ME, KISS ME, KISS ME! (Extraordinary-1967). Jean Novack, Natalie Rogers; Stan Novack, Don Williams; Eddie, Peter Ratray; Ellen, Joy Martin; Lurlene, Angela Peters; Dominic, Matt Baylor; Ray, Gerald Jacuzzo; Ma, Esther Travers; Mrs. Scilletto, Veronica Radburn; Sal, Nick Orzel; Lou, Alan Sedan; Jimmy, Sean Martin.

1627 KISS THE GIRLS AND MAKE THEM DIE. (Columbia-1967). Kelly, Michael Connors; Susan Fleming, Dorothy Provine; Mr. Ardonian, Raf Vallone; Grace, Margaret Lee; Lord Aldric/James, Terry-Thomas; Sylvia, Nicoletta Machiavelli; Karin, Beverly Adams; British Ambassador, Jack Gwillim; Ringo, Oliver McGreevy; Interpretor, Senya Seyn; Omar, Sandro Dori; Marilu Tolo, Andy Ho, Renato Terra, George Leech, Roland Bartrop, Hans Thorner, Edith Peters, Michael Audley, Nerio Bernardi.

1628 KISS THE OTHER SHEIK. (MGM-1968). Michele, Marcello Mastroianni; Pepita, Pamela Tiffin; Dorothea, Virna Lisi; Arturo Rossi, Luciano Salce; Raimondo Vianello, Lina Valonghi, Lelio Luttazzi, Ennio Balbo, Luciano Bonanni.

1629 THE KLANSMAN. (Paramount-1974). Sheriff Bascomb, Lee Marvin; Breck Stancill, Richard Burton; Deputy Cates, Cameron Mitchell; Loretta Sykes, Lola Falana; Trixie, Luciana Paluzzi; Mayor Hardy, David Huddleston; Nancy Poteet, Linda Evans; Garth, O. J. Simpson; Willy Washington, Spence

Wil-Dee; Bobby Poteet, Hoke Howell; Martha, Eve Christopher; Martha's Husband, Ed Call; Reporters, Morgan Upton, Charles Briggs; Outside Demonstrators, Robert Porter, Gary Catus; Lightning Rod, Larry Williams; Doctor, Bert Williams; Bascomb's Son, Wendell Wellman; Mrs. Bascomb, Susan Brown; Other Rednecks, John Alderson, John Pearce, David Ladd.

1630 THE KNACK--AND HOW TO GET IT. Nancy, Rita Tushingham; Tolen, Ray Brooks; Colin, Michael Crawford; Tom, Donal Donnelly; Dress Shop Owner, William Dexter; Man in Phone Booth, Charles Dyer; Female Teacher, Margot Thomas; Angry Father, John Bluthal; Blonde in Photo Booth, Helen Lennox.

1631 KNIVES OF THE AVENGER. (World Entertainment Corporation-1968). Rurik, Cameron Mitchell; Aghen, Fausto Tozzi; Moki, Luciano Polletin; Karen, Elisa Mitchell; Harald, Jack Stewart.

1632 KOJIRO. (Toho-1968). Kojiro Sasaki, Kikunosuke Onoe; Okinawa Princess, Yoko Tsukasa; Geisha Girl, Mayumi Ozora; Musashi Miyamoto, Tatsuya Nakadai; Lord Tomita, Kenjiro Ishiyama; Pirate Nachimaru, Jotaro Togami; Kabuki Dancer, Keiko Sawai; Jubei Minamiya, Tatsuya Mihashi.

1633 KONA COAST. (Warner Bros. -7 Arts-1968). Captain Sam Moran, Richard Boone; Melissa Hyde, Vera Miles; Kittibelle Lightfoot, Joan Blondell; Kryder, Steve Ihnat; Charlie Lightfoot, Chips Rafferty; Akamai, Kent Smith; Kimo, Sam Kapu Jr.; Mim Lowry, Gina Villines; Tigercat, Duane Eddy; Tate Packer, Scott Thomas; Junior Packer, Erwin Neal; Doris, Doris Erickson; Dee, Gloria Nakea; Kunewa, Lucky Luck; Butler, Kaai Hayes; Macklin, Dr. Thomas Mark; Bartender, Red Kanuha; Sue, Sue Paishon; Crew of the Alika, Dino Kunewa, Earl Perry, Pocho Kanuha, Willie Erickson.

1634 KONGI'S HARVEST. (Tam Communications-1973). Kongi, Wole Soyinka; Oba, Rashidi Onikoyi; Secretary, Femi Johnson; Daodu, Dapo Adelugba; Segi, Nina Baden-Semper; Dr. Gbenga, Orlando Martins.

1635 KOTCH. (Cinerama-1971). Joseph P. Kotcher, Walter Matthau; Erica Herzenstiel, Deborah Winters; Wilma Kotcher, Felicia Farr; Gerald Kotcher, Charles Aidman; Vera Kotcher, Ellen Geer.

1636 KOVACS. (Stone-Galanoy-1971). Ernie Kovacs.

1637 KRAKATOA, EAST OF JAVA. (Cinerama-1969). Captain Chris Hanson, Maximilian Schell; Laura Travis, Diane

Baker; Connerly, Brian Keith; Charley, Barbara Werle; Douglas Rigby, John Leyton; Giovanni Borghese, Rossano Brazzi; Leoncavallo Borghese, Sal Mineo; Danzig, J. D. Cannon; Toshi, Jacqui Chan; Jacobs, Mark Lawrence; Bazooki Man, Geoffrey Holder; Japanese Divers, Sumi Hari, Victoria Young and Midorri Arimoto; Henley, Niall MacGinnis; Jan, Alan Hoskins; Guard, Robert Hall; Peter, Peter Kowalski; Kuan, Joseph Hann.

1638 THE KREMLIN LETTER. (20th Century-Fox-1970). Erika, Bibi Andersson; Ward, Richard Boone; Whore, Nigel Green; Highwayman, Dean Jagger; Sophie, Lila Kedrova; Sweet Alice, Michael MacLiammoir; Rone, Patrick O'Neal; B. A., Barbara Parkins; Potkin, Ronald Radd; Warlock, George Sanders; Puppetmaker, Raf Vallone; Kosnov, Max von Sydow; Bresnavitch, Orson Welles; Grodin, Sandor Eles; Erector Set, Niall MacGinnis; Kitai, Anthony Chinn; Professor, Guy Deghy; Admiral, John Huston; Sonia, Fulvia Ketoff; Negress, Vonetta McGee; Priest, Marc Lawrence; Police Doctor, Cyril Shaps; Rudolph, Christopher Sanford; Mrs. Kazar, Hana-Maria Pravda; Kazar, George Pravda; Mrs. Potkin, Ludmilla Dudarova; Ilya, Dimitri Tamarov; Receptionist, Pehr-Olof Siren; Waiter, Daniel Smid; Dentist, Victor Beaumont; Sacha Carafa, Saara Bannin, Laura Forin, Steve Zacharias.

1639 KWAIDAN. (Continental-1965). First wife, Michiyo Aratama; Second wife, Misako Watanabe; Samurai, Rentaro Mikuni; Hoichi, Katsuo Nakamura; Priest, Takashi Shimura; Samurai, Tetsuo Tamba; Yoshitsune, Yoichi Hayashi; Kannai, Kanyemon Nakamura; Heinai, Noboru Nakaya.

1640 LACOMBE, LUCIEN. (20th Century-Fox-1974). Pierre Blaise, Aurore Clement, Holger Lowenadler, Therese Gieshe, Stephane Bouy, Loumi Iazobesco, Rene Bouloc, Pierre Decazes, Jean Rougerie, Gilbert Rivet, Jacques Rispal.

1641 LADIES AND GENTLEMEN, THE ROLLING STONES. (Dragon Aire-1974). Vocals, Harp, Mick Jagger; Vocals, Guitar, Keith Richard; Guitar, Mick Taylor; Drums, Charlie Watts; Bass, Bill Wyman; Piano, Nicky Hopkins; Sax & Percussion, Bobby Keyes; Trumpet & Trombone, Jim Price; Mystery Piano, Ian Stewart.

1642 LADY CAROLINE LAMB. (United Artists-1973). Lady Caroline Lamb, Sarah Miles; William Lamb, Jon Finch; Lord Byron, Richard Chamberlain; Canning, John Mills; Lady Melbourne, Margaret Leighton; Lady Bessborough, Pamela Brown; Miss Milbanke, Silvia Monti; The King, Ralph Richardson; Duke of Wellington, Laurence Olivier; Government Minister, Peter Bull; Mr. Potter, Charles Carson; Lady Pont, Sonia Dresdel; St. John, Nicholas Field;

Girl in Blue, Felicity Gibson; Apothecary, Robert Harris; Radical Member, Richard Hurndall; Irish Housekeeper, Paddy Joyce; Benson, Bernard Kay; Miss Fairfax, Janet Key; Coachman, Mario Maranzana; ADC to Wellington, Robert Mill; Restaurant Functionary, Norman Mitchell; Murray, John Moffatt; Agent, Trevor Peacock; Mrs. Butler, Maureen Pryor; Lady Holland, Fanny Rowe; Buckham, Stephen Sheppard; Black Pug, Roy Stewart; Admiral, Ralph Truman; Lord Holland, Michael Wilding.

1643 LADY FRANKENSTEIN. (New World-1973). Tanya, Sarah Bay; Baron, Joseph Cotten; Marsh, Paul Muller; Captain, Mickey Hargitay.

1644 LADY ICE. (National General-1973). Andy, Donald Sutherland; Paula, Jennifer O'Neill; Ford, Robert Duvall; Paul, Patrick Magee; Peter, Eric Braeden; Eddy, Jon Cypher.

1645 LADY IN CEMENT. (20th Century-Fox-1968). Tony Rome, Frank Sinatra; Kit Forrest, Raquel Welch; Gronsky, Dan Blocker; Lt. Santini, Richard Conte; Al Mungar, Martin Gabel; Maria Baretto, Lainie Kazan; Hal Rubin, Pat Henry; Paul Mungar, Steve Peck; Audrey, Virginia Wood; Arnie Sherwin, Richard Deacon; Danny Yale, Frank Raiter; Frenchy, Peter Hock; Shev, Alex Stevens; Sandra Lomax, Christine Todd; Sidney, the Organizer, Mac Robbins; The Kid, Tommy Uhlar; Paco, Ray Baumel; McComb, Pauly Dash; The Pool Boy, Andy Jarrell; Himself, Joe E. Lewis.

1646 THE LADY IN THE CAR WITH GLASSES AND A GUN. (Columbia-1970). Dany Lang, Samantha Eggar; Michael Caldwell, Oliver Reed; Philippe, John McEnery; Anita Caldwell, Stephane Audran; Secretary, Billie Dixon; Jean, Bernard Fresson; Highway Policeman, Philippe Nicaud; Manuel, Marcel Bozzuffi; Doctor, Jacques Fabbri; Baptistin, Yves Pignot; Policeman, Jacques Legras; Madam Pacaud, Maria Meriko; Bernard Thorr, Andre Oumansky; Kiki, Martine Kelly; Psychiatrist, Claude Vernier; Barmaid, Monique Melinand; Garage Proprietor, Henri Czarniak; Garage Night Man, Edmond Ardisson; Village Storekeeper, Gilberte Geniat; Hotel Clerk, Roger Lumont; Robert Deac, Lisa Jouvet, Fred Fisher, Raoul Delfosse, Louise Rioton, Jacqueline Porel, Paule Noelle.

1647 THE LADY-KILLER OF ROME. (Manson-1966). Nello Poletti, Marcello Mastroianni; Adalgisa De Matteis, Micheline Presle; Commissioner Palumbo, Salvo Randone; Nicoletta Nogara, Cristina Gajoni; Morello, Andrea Checchi; The Suicide, Mac Roney; Adalgisa's Friend, Max Cartier; Rosa, Giovanna Gagliardo; Enrico Maria Salerno, Bruno Scipioni.

1648 LADY KUNG-FU. (National General-1973). Angela Mao,

Carter Hunning, Pai Wing, Han Jae, Wei Ping Ao, Nancy Sit, Terio Yamane.

1649 LADY L. (MGM-1966). Louise, Sophia Loren; Armand, Paul Newman; Lord Lendale (Dicky), David Niven; Sir Percy, Cecil Parker; Inspector Mercier, Claude Dauphin; Sapper, Marcel Dalio; Amboise Gerome, Phillipe Noiret; Lecoeur, Michel Piccoli; Krajewski, Jean Wiener; Kobeleff, Daniel Emil Fork; Koenigstein, Eugene Deckers; Beala, Jacques Dufilho; Agneau, Tanya Lopert; Pantoufle, Catherine Allegret; Madam, Hella Petri; Prince Otto, Peter Ustinov.

1650 LADY LIBERTY. (United Artists-1972). Maddalena Ciarrapico, Sophia Loren; Michele Bruni, Luigi Proietti; Jock Fenner, William Devane; Dominic, Beeson Carroll; Pasquale, Bill Daprato; Mancuso, Danny De Vito; O'Henry, David Doyle; Wildflower, Charles Bartlett; Wow Girl, Tracy Hotchiner; Wow Boy, Daniel Fortus; Hostess, Irene Signoretti; Stewart, Jack Aaron; Kind Lady, Mary Whelchel; Tim, Richard Libertini; Witty Boy, Adam Reed; Bill, Terry Thompson; Nolan, Alfred Hinckley; Cops, Dennis McMullen, Mark Dawson, Edward Herrmann, Jack Dabdoub, Joel Wolfe, Dick Ensslen, Thomas Murphy, and Robert Cromwell; Teddy, Randy Hines; Policewoman, Elsa Raven; Sally De May, Basil Hoffman, Alex Fisher, Tom Lacy, Darrell Zwerling, Packy McFarland, Alan Feinstein, Garnett Smith, Robert Pickering, Donald Billett, John Gerstad, Dennis Helfend, Peter Landers, Frank Bara, Roger Ochs, Chris Norris, Frank Hamilton, Dutch Miller, Martin Abrams, Peter De Anda, Fred J. Scolley, George Fisher, Candy Darling.

1651 THE LADY OF MONZA. (Tower-1970). Prioress, Anne Heywood; Gian, Antonio Sabato; Arrigoni, Hardy Kruger; Caterina, Carla Gravina; Barca, Tino Carraro; Fuentes, Luigi Pistilli; Benedetta, Margherita Lozano; Ottavia, Annamaria Alegiani; Degnamerita, Angelica Ippolito; Bianca, Maria Michi.

1652 THE LADY ON THE TRACKS. (Royal Films International-1968). Marie, Jirina Bohdalova; Vaclav, Radoslav Brzobohaty; Bedrich, Frantisek Peterka; Katerina, Libuse Geprtova; Mr. Marke, Stanislav Fiser.

1653 LADY SINGS THE BLUES. (Paramount-1972). Billie Holiday, Diana Ross; Louis McKay, Billy Dee Williams; Piano Man, Richard Pryor; Reg Hanley, James Callahan; Harry, Paul Hampton; Jerry, Sid Melton; Mama Holiday, Virginia Capers; Yvonne, Yvonne Fair; Big Ben, Scatman Crothers; Hawk, Robert L. Gordy; Rapist, Harry Caesar; The Doctor, Milton Selzer; Ned Glass, Paulene Myers, Isabel Sanford, Tracee Lyles, Norman Bartold, Clay Tanner, Jester Hairston, Bert Kramer, Paul Micale, Michelle Aller, Byron Kane, Barbara Minkus, Kay Lewis, Helen Lewis, George

Wyner, Shirley Melline, Toby Russ, Larry Duran, Ernie Robinson, Don McGovern, Dick Poston, Charles Woolf, Denise Denise, Lynn Hamilton, Victor Morosco.

1654 LAKE OF DRACULA. (Toho-1973). Akiko, Midori Fujita; Sacki, Choei Takahashi; Natsuoke, Sanae Emi; Mori Kishida.

1655 LANCELOT OF THE LAKE. (1974). Luc Simon, Laura Duke Condominas, Humbert Balsan, Vladimir Antolek-Oresek, Patrick Bernard, Arthur de Montalembert.

1656 LAND RAIDERS. (Columbia-1970). Vince, Telly Savalas; Paul, George Maharis; Martha, Arlene Dahl; Kate, Janet Landgard; Luisa, Jocelyn Lane; Cardenas, George Coulouris; Tanner, Guy Rolfe; Mayfield, Phil Brown; Luisa Montoya, Marcella St. Amant; Carney, Paul Picerni; Rojas, Robert Carricart; Juantez, Gustavo Rojo; Priest, Fernando Rey; Loomis, Ben Tatar; Ace, John Clark; Willis, Charles Stahlnaker; Mrs. Willis, Susan Harvey.

1657 THE LANDLORD. (United Artists-1970). Elgar Enders, Beau Bridges; Marge, Pearl Bailey; Fanny, Diana Sands; Copee, Louis Gossett; Walter Gee, Douglas Grant; Prof. Duboise, Melvin Stewart; Mrs. Enders, Lee Grant; Mr. Enders, Walter Brooke; Susan, Susan Anspach; William Jr., Will McKenzie; Doris, Gretchen Walther; Heywood, Stanley Green; Lanie, Marki Bey.

1657a LAS VEGAS HILLBILLYS. (Woolner Bros. -1966). Ferlin Husky, Jayne Mansfield, Richard Kiel, John Harmon, Sonny James, Del Reeves, Connie Smith, The Duke of Paducah, Mamie Van Doren, Louis Quinn, Don Bowman, Billie Bird, Roy Drusky, Bill Anderson, Wilma Burgess.

1658 THE LAST ADVENTURE. (Universal-1969). Manu, Alain Delon; Roland, Lino Ventura; Letitia, Joanna Shimkus; Pilot, Serge Reggiani; Hans Meyer.

1659 THE LAST AMERICAN HERO. (20th Century-Fox, 1973). Elroy Jackson Jr., Jeff Bridges; Marge, Valerie Perrine; Mrs. Jackson, Geraldine Fitzgerald; Hackel, Ned Beatty; Wayne Jackson, Gary Busey; Elroy Jackson Sr., Art Lund; Burton Colt, Ed Lauter; Kyle Kingman, William Smith II; Morley, Gregory Walcott; Lamar, Tom Ligon; Davie Baer, Ernie Orsatti; Trina, Erica Hagen; Spud, James Murphy; Rick Penny, Lane Smith.

1660 THE LAST CHALLENGE. (MGM-1967). Marshal Dan Blaine, Glenn Ford; Lisa Denton, Angie Dickinson; Lot McGuire, Chad Everett; Squint Calloway, Gary Merrill; Ernest Scarnes, Jack Elam; Marie Webster, Delphi Lawrence; Pretty Horse, Royal Dano; Frank Garrison, Kevin Hagen; Outdoors, Florence Sundstrom; Sadie, Marian Collier;

Harry Bell, Robert Sorrells; Turpin, John Milford; Ballard Weeks, Frank McGrath; Lisa's Maid, Amanda Randolf; Servant, Bill Walker; Girl with Lot, Letitia Paquette; Saloon Hostess, Beverly Hills.

1661 LAST DAYS OF MUSSOLINI. (Paramount-1974). Mussolini, Rod Steiger; Cara Petacci, Lisa Gastoni; Cardinal Schuster, Henry Fonda; Colonel Valerio, Franco Nero; Pedro, Lino Capolicchio.

1662 THE LAST DETAIL. (Columbia-1973). Buddusky, Jack Nicholson; Mulhall, Otis Young; Meadows, Randy Quaid; M.A.A., Clifton James; Young Whore, Carol Kane; Marine O.D., Michael Moriarty; Donna, Luana Anders; Kathleen, Kathleen Miller; Nancy, Nancy Allen; Henry, Gerry Salsberg; Bartender, Don McGovern; Madame, Pat Hamilton; Taxi Driver, Michael Chapman; Sweek, Jim Henshaw; Nichiren Shoshu Members, Derek McGrath, Gilda Radner, Jim Horn, John Castellano.

1663 THE LAST ESCAPE. (United Artists-1970). Capt. Lee Mitche, Stuart Whitman; Sgt. Harry McBee, John Collin; Von Heinken, Pinkas Braun; Lt. Donald Wilcox, Martin Jarvis; Maj. Hessel, Gunther Neutze; Karen, Margit Saad; Maj. Griggs, Patrick Jordon; O'Connell, Johnny Briggs; Maj. Petrov, Harald Dietl; Curt, Andy Pap; Blucher, Gert Vespermann.

1664 LAST FOXTROT IN BURBANK. (Federated-1973). Paul, Michael Pataki; Jeanne, Sherry Denton; Marcel, Simmy Bow; Mrs. Ketchenberg, Sally Marr; Tom, William Quinn.

1665 THE LAST GRENADE. (Cinerama-1970). Grigsby, Stanley Baker; Thompson, Alex Cord; Katherine, Honor Blackman; General Whiteley, Richard Attenborough; Jackson, Rafer Johnson; Mackenzie, Andrew Keir; Coulson, Ray Brooks; Royal, Julian Glover; Mitchell, John Thaw.

1666 THE LAST MERCENARY. (Excelsior-1970). Ray Danton, Pascale Petit, George Rigaud, Carl Mohner, Gunther Stoll.

1667 THE LAST MOVIE. (Universal-1971). Mrs. Anderson, Julie Adams; Thomas Mercado, Daniel Ades; Jonathan, John Alderman; Mayor's Son, Michael Anderson Jr.; Gaffer, Rich Aguilar; Miss Anderson, Donna Baccala; Member of Billy's Gang, Tom Baker; Rose, Toni Basil; Singer, Poupee Bocar; Dance Hall Girl, Anna Lynn Brown; Pat, Rod Cameron; Doctor, Bernard Casselman; Boomman, James Contreras; Stunt Man, Eddie Donno; Mayor, Severn Darden; Prop Man, Lou Donelan; Anderson, Roy Engel; Banker, Warren Finnerty; Sheriff, Peter Fonda; Kansas, Dennis Hopper; Fritz Ford, Sam Fuller, Stella Garcia, Michael Greene, Samya Green, William Gray, Don Gordon; Bud Hassink, George

Hill, Henry Jaglom, Kris Kristofferson, John Phillip Law, Sylvia Miles, Jim Mitchum, Dean Stockwell, Russ Tamblyn, Michelle Phillips.

1668 THE LAST OF SHEILA. (Warner Bros. -1973). Tom, Richard Benjamin; Christine, Dyan Cannon; Clinton, James Coburn; Lee, Joan Hackett; Philip, James Mason; Antony, Ian McShane; Alice, Raquel Welch; Sheila, Yvonne Romain; Vittorio, Pierro Rosso; Serge Citon, Robert Rossi, Elaine Geisinger, Elliot Geisinger, Jack Pugeat, Maurice Crosnier.

1669 LAST OF THE MOBILE HOT-SHOTS. (Warner Bros. -1970). Jeb, James Coburn; Myrtle, Lynn Redgrave; Chicken, Robert Hooks; George, Perry Hayes; Rube, Reggie King.

1670 LAST OF THE RED HOT LOVERS. (Paramount-1972). Barney Cashman, Alan Arkin; Elaine, Sally Kellerman; Bobbi, Paula Prentiss; Jeanette, Rene Taylor; Cashier, Bella Bruck; Charlotte, Sandy Balson; Mel, Frank Loverde; Bert, Burt Conroy; Jesse, Charles Woolf; Mickey, Ben Freedman; Waiters, Buddy Lewis, Mousey Garner; Man with Boxes, Bernie Styles; Truckman's Helper, John Batiste; Girl in Car, Lois Aurino; Men in Coffee Shop, Sully Boyar, J. J. Barry, Paul Larson; Lady in Coffee Shop, Ruth Jaroslow; Cabbie Oliver Steindecker; Parking Lot Attendant, Leonard Parker; Girl on Corner, Leisha Gullisson.

1671 THE LAST OF THE SECRET AGENTS? (Paramount-1966). Marty Johnson, Marty Allen; Steve Donovan, Steve Rossi; J. Frederick Duval, John Williams; Micheline, Nancy Sinatra; Papa Leo, Lou Jacobi; German Colonel, Harvey Korman; Baby May Zoftig, Carmen; Zoltan Schubach, Theo Marcuse; Florence, Connie Sawyer; Harry, Ben Lessy; Remo Pisani, Larry Duran, Wilhelm Von Homburg, Aida Fries, Edy Williams, Phyllis Davis, Don Keefer, Emanuel Thomas, Philip Sascombe, Paul Daniels, Sig Ruman, Ed Sullivan.

1672 LAST OF THE SKI BUMS. (U-M-1969). Ron Funk, Mike Zuettel, Ed Ricks.

1673 THE LAST PICTURE SHOW. (Columbia-1971). Sonny Crawford, Timothy Bottoms; Duane Jackson, Jeff Bridges; Jacy Farrow, Cybill Shepherd; Sam the Lion, Ben Johnson; Ruth Popper, Cloris Leachman; Lois Farrow, Ellen Burstyn; Genevieve, Eileen Brennan; Abilene, Clu Gulager; Billy, Sam Bottoms; Lester Marlow, Randy Quaid.

1674 THE LAST RUN. (MGM-1971). Harry Garmes, George C. Scott; Paul Ricard, Tony Musante; Claudie Scherrer, Trish Van Devere; Monique, Colleen Dewhurst.

1675 THE LAST SAFARI. (Paramount-1968). Casey, Kaz Garas;

Miles Gilchrist, Stewart Granger; Grant, Gabriella Licudi; Jama, Johnny Sekka; Alec Beaumont, Liam Redmond; Refugee, Eugene Deckers; Chongu, David Munyua; Rich, John De Villiers; Game Warden, Wilfred Moore; Mrs. Beaumont, Jean Parnell; Commissioner, Bill Grant; Harry, John Sutton; Gavai, Kipkoske; Chief of Village, Labina; The Masai Tribe Wakamba Tribal Dancers.

1676 THE LAST SHOT YOU HEAR. (20th Century-Fox-1969). Dr. Charles Nordeck, Hugh Marlowe; Eileen, Zena Walker; Anne Nordeck, Patricia Haines; Peter Marriott, William Dysart; General Jowett, Thorley Walters; Mrs. Jowett, Joan Young; Rubens, Lionel Murton; Dodie Rubens, Helen Horton; Nash, John Nettleton; Chambers, John Wentworth; CID Officer, Alistair Williamson; Woman Reporter, Daphne Barker; Pretty Girl, Lynley Laurence; Brash Young Man, Julian Holloway; 1st Reporter, James Mellor; 2nd Reporter, Ian Hamilton; Diver, Shaun Curry; Peter's Colleague, Stephen Moore; Policeman, Job Stewart; Receptionist, Janet Kelly.

1677 LAST SUMMER. (Allied Artists-1969). Sandy, Barbara Hershey; Peter, Richard Thomas; Dan, Bruce Davison; Rhoda, Cathy Burns; Anibal, Ernesto Gonzalez; Mr. Caudell, Peter Turgeon; Town Hoods, Lou Gary, Andrew Krance, and Wayne Mayer.

1678 LAST TANGO IN PARIS. (United Artists-1973). Paul, Marlon Brando; Jeanne, Maria Schneider; Concierge, Darling Legitimus; Tom, Jean-Pierre Leaud; TV Script Girl, Catherine Sola; TV Cameraman, Mauro Marchetti; TV Sound Engineer, Dan Diament; TV Assistant Cameraman, Peter Schommer; Catherine, Catherine Allegret; Monique, Marie-Helene Breillat; Mouchette, Catherine Breillat; Small Mover, Stephane Kosiak; Tall Mover, Gerard Lepennec; Rosa's Mother, Maria Michi; Rosa, Veronica Lazare; Olympia, Luce Marquand; Bible Salesman, Michel Delahaye; Miss Blandish, Laura Betti; Marcel, Massimo Girotti; Prostitute, Giovanna Falletti; Her customer, Armand Ablanalp; Jeanne's Mother, Gitt Magrini; Barge Captain, Jean Luc Bideau; Christine, Rachel Kesterber; President of Tango Jury, Mimi Pinson; Tango Orchestra Leader, Ramon Mendizabal.

1679 THE LAST VALLEY. (Cinerama-1971). The Captain, Michael Caine; Vogel, Omar Sharif; Erica, Florinda Bolkan; Gruber, Nigel Davenport; Father Sebastian, Per Oscarsson; Hoffman, Arthur O'Connell; Inge Hoffman, Madeline Hinde; Pirelli, Yorgo Voyagis; Julio, Miguel Alejandro; Andreas, Christian Roberts; Graf, Ian Hogg; Hansen, Michael Gothard; Korski, Brian Blessed; Vornez, George Innes; Frau Hoffman, Irene Prador; Mathias, Vladek Sheybal; Geddes, John Hallam; Shutz, Andrew McCulloch; Eskesen, Jack Shepherd; Czeraki, Leon Lissek; Svenson, Chris Chittell; Tsaurus, Kurt Christian; Sernen, Mark Edwards.

1680 No entry.

1681 LATE AUTUMN. (New Yorker-1973). The Mother, Setsuko Hara; The Daughter, Yoko Tsukasa; The Uncle, Chishu Ryu; The Daughter's Friend, Mariko Okada; The Young Man, Keiji Sada.

1682 THE LATE LIZ. (Gateway-1972). Liz Addams Hatch, Anne Baxter; James Hatch, Steve Forrest; Gordon Rogers, Jack Albertson; Si Addams, Steve Dunne; Sue Webb, Coleen Gray; Sally Pearson, Joan Hotchkis; Peter Addams, Bill Katt; Alan Trowbridge, Reid Smith; Dr. Murray, Ivor Francis; Howard Borman, Foster Brooks; Laura Valon, Eloise Hardy; Steve Blake, Don Lamond; Logan Pearson, Buck Young; Joe Vito, Lee Delano; Martha, Virginia Capers; Bill Morris, Alvy Moore; Edie Morris, Nancy Hadley; Arthur Bryson, John Baer; Tony Webb, Mark Tapscott; Gladys, Gail Bonney.

1683 LATE SPRING. (New Yorker-1972). Father, Chisu Ryu; Daughter, Setsuko Hara; Aunt, Haruko Sugimura; Friend, Jun Osami.

1684 LATITUDE ZERO. (National General-1970). Capt., Joseph Cotten; Malic, Cesar Romero; Perry, Richard Jaeckel; Lucretia, Patricia Medina; Anne, Linda Haynes; Ken, Akira Takarada; Masson, Masumi Okada; Kroiga, Hikaru Kuroki.

1685 THE LAUGHING POLICEMAN. (20th Century-Fox-1973). Jake Martin, Walther Matthau; Leo Larsen, Bruce Dern; Larrimore, Lou Gossett; Camerero, Albert Paulsen; Lt. Steiner, Anthony Zerbe; Pappas, Val Avery; Kay Butler, Cathy Lee Crosby; Bobby Mow, Mario Gallo; Monica, Joanna Cassidy; Grace Martin, Shirley Ballard; Schwermer, William Hansen; Collins, Jonas Wolfe; Haygood, Paul Koslo; Gus Niles, Lou Guss; Prostitute, Lee McCain; Pimp, David Moody; Rodney, Ivan Bookman; Maloney, Cliff James; Vickery, Gregg Sierra; Riple, Warren Finnerty; Coroner, Mat Clark; Avakian's Brother, Joe Bernard; Maydola, Melvina Smedley; Porno Cashier, Leigh French; Fowler, Jim Clawin; Dave Evans, Tony Costello; Russo, John Francis; Terry, John Vick; Brennan, Wayne Grace; Nurse, Cheryl Christiansen.

1686 LAUGHTER IN THE DARK. (Lopert-1969). Sir Edward More, Nicol Williamson; Margot, Anna Karina; Herve Tourace, Jean-Claude Drouot; Paul, Peter Bowles; Lady Pamela More, Sian Phillips; Brian, Sebastian Breaks; Amelia More, Kate O'Toole; Chauffeur, Edward Gardner; Maid, Helen Booth; Miss Porly, Sheila Burrell; Colonel, Willoughby Goddard; Woman at Gallergy, Mavis Villiers; Girl at gallery, Allison Blair; Girls at Party, Diana Harris, Celia Brook; Art Dealers, Basil Dignam, John Atkinson, Donald

Bissett, John Golightly.

1687 LAW AND DISORDER. (Columbia-1974). Willie, Carroll O'Connor; Cy, Ernest Borgnine; Sally, Ann Wedgeworth; Irene, Anita Dangler; Karen, Leslie Ackerman; Gloria, Karen Black; Elliott, Jack Kehoe; Bobby, David Spielberg; Pete, Joe Ragno; Ken, Pat Corley; Flasher, J. Frank Lucas; Capt. Malloy, Ed Grover; Yablonsky, Pepper Wormser; Chico, Lionel Pina; F. U. Kid, Gary Springer; Jogger, Jay Fletcher; Desk Sgt., Bill Richert; Morris, Jack Stamberger; Frank, Ed Madsen; Eddie, Adam Lessuck; Ralph, Sydney Sherrif; Dr. Richter, Alan Arbus.

1688 LAWMAN. (United Artists-1971). Jered Maddox, Burt Lancaster; Cotton Rayn, Robert Ryan; Vincent Bronson, Lee J. Cobb; Laura Selby, Sheree North.

1689 THE LAWYER. (Paramount-1970). Tony Petrocelli, Barry Newman; Eric P. Scott, Harold Gould; Ruth Petrocelli, Diana Muldaur; Jack Harrison, Robert Colbert; Alice Fiske, Kathleen Crowley; Sgt. Moran, Warren Kemmerling; Judge Crawford, Booth Colman; Charlie O'Keefe, Ken Swofford; F. J. Williamson, E. J. Andre; Paul Harrison, William Sylvester; Andy Greer, Jeff Thompson; Bob Chambers, Tom Harvey; Wyler, Ivor Barry; Melendy Britt, John Himes, Ralph Thomas, Mary Wilcox, Gene O'Donnell, Walter Mathews, Ray Ballard, James McEachin, Robert L. Poyner.

1690 THE LEARNING TREE. (Warner Bros.-7 Arts-1969). Newt Winger, Kyle Johnson; Marcus Savage, Alex Clarke; Sarah Winger, Estelle Evans; Sheriff Kirky, Dana Elcar; Arcella Jefferson, Mira Waters; Uncle Rob, Joel Fluellen; Silas Newhall, Malcolm Atterbury; Booker Savage, Richard Ward; Judge Cavanaugh, Russell Thorson; Miss McClintock, Peggy Rea; Big Mabel, Carole Lamond; Doc Cravens, Kevin Hagen; Chappie Logan, James Rushing; Spikey, Dub Taylor; Jack Winger, Felix P. Nelson; Jake Kiner, George Mitchell; Prissy, Saundra Sharp; Jappy, Stephen Perry; Harley Davis, Don Dubbins; Jon Lormer, Morgan Stern, Thomas Anderson, Philip Roye, Hope Summers, Carter Vinnegar, Bobby Goss, Alfred Jones, Zooey Hall.

1691 THE LEATHER BOYS. (R. Lee Platt-1965). Dot, Rita Tushingham; Reggie, Colin Campbell; Pete, Dudley Sutton; Granny, Gladys Henson; Reggie's Mother, Avice Landon; Reggie's Father, Lockwood West; Dot's Mother, Berry Marsden; Uncle Arthur, Martin Mathews; Boy Friend, Johnny Briggs.

1692 LEFT-HANDED. (Hand-in-Hand-1972). Ray Frank, Robert Rikas, Larry Burns, Teri Reardon, Al Mineo, Alex Marks, Bob Williams, Warren Mans.

1693 THE LEGEND OF FRENCHY KING. (SNC-1973). Frenchy, Brigitte Bardot; Maria, Claudia Cardinale; Marshal, Michael J. Pollard; Sister, Emma Cohen; Aunt, Micheline Presle; France Dougnac, Patty Shepard.

1694 THE LEGEND OF HELL HOUSE. (20th Century-Fox-1973). Florence Tanner, Pamela Franklin; Ben Fischer, Roddy McDowall; Dr. Chris Barrett, Clive Revill; Ann Barrett, Gayle Hunnicutt; Rudolph Deutsch, Roland Culver; Hanley, Peter Bowles.

1695 THE LEGEND OF LYLAH CLARE. (MGM-1968). Lylah Clare/Elsa Brinkmann, Kim Novak; Lewis Zarkan, Peter Finch; Barney Sheean, Ernest Borgnine; Bart Langner, Milton Selzer; Rosella, Rossella Falk; Paolo, Gabriele Tinti; Molly Luther, Coral Browne; Countess Bozo Bedoni, Valentina Cortese; Becky Langner, Jean Carroll; Mark Peter Sheean, Michael Murphy; Young Girl, Lee Meriwether; 1st Legman, James Lanphier; Mike, Robert Ellenstein; Nick, Nick Dennis; Cameraman, Dave Willock; Butler, Peter Bravos; Script Girl, Ellen Corby; Announcer, Michael Fox; 2nd Legman, Hal Maguire; Bedoni's Escort, Tom Patty; Vernon Scott, Vernon Scott; Hairdresser, Queenie Smith; Aerialists, Barbara Ann Warkmeister and Mel Warkmeister; Himself, Sidney Skolsky.

1696 THE LEGEND OF NIGGER CHARLEY. (Paramount-1972). Nigger Charley, Fred Williamson; Toby, D'Urville Martin; Joshua, Don Pedro Colley; Theo, Gertrude Jeanette; Julia, Marcia McBroom; Hill Carter, Alan Gifford; Houston, John Ryan; Dr. Saunders, Will Hussung; Walker, Bill Moor; Shadow, Thomas Anderson; Sheriff, Jerry Gatlin; Sarah Lyons, Tricia O'Neil; Dewey Lyons, Doug Rowe; Nils Fowler, Keith Prentice; Willie, Tom Pemberton; Reverend, Joe Santos; Ollokot, Fred Lerner.

1697 LEMONADE JOE. (Allied Artists-1967). Lemonade Joe, Carl Fiala; Winifred Goodman, Olga Schoberova; Tornado Lou, Veta Fialova; Horace Badman, Miles Kopeck; Doug Badman, Rudy Dale; Grimpo, Joseph Nomaz.

1698 LEO THE LAST. (United Artists-1970). Leo, Marcello Mastroianni; Margaret, Billie Whitelaw; Roscoe, Calvin Lockhart; Salambo, Glenna Forster Jones; Max, Graham Crowden; Hilda, Gwen Davis; David, David DeKeyser; Laszlo, Vladek Sheybal; Jasper, Keefe West; Kowalski, Kenneth J. Warren; Black Preacher, Ram John Holder; Mr. Madi, Thomas Bucson; Mrs. Madi, Tina Solomon; Madi Children, Robert Redman, Malcolm Redman, Robert Kennedy; Blonde Whore, Phyllis McMahon; Black Whore, Princess Patience; Bodyguards, Bernard Boston; Roy Stewart; Wailing Lady, Lucita Lijertwood; Supermarket Manager, Ishaq Bux; Singing Lady, Doris Clark.

1699 LET IT BE. (United Artists-1970). George Harrison, John Lennon, Paul McCartney, Ringo Starr, Yoko Ono.

1700 LET THE GOOD TIMES ROLL. (Columbia-1973). Chuck Berry, Little Richard, Fats Domino, Chubby Checker, Bo Diddley, The Shirelles, The Five Satins, The Coasters, Danny and The Juniors, Bobby Comstock Rock and Roll Band, Bill Haley and The Comets, Richard Nader.

1701 LET'S KILL UNCLE. (Universal-1966). Major Kevin Harrison, Nigel Green; Chrissie, Mary Badham; Barnaby Harrison, Pat Cardi; Sgt. Jack Travis, Robert Pickering; Justine, Linda Lawson; Ketch-man, Reff Sanchez; Steward, Nestor Paiva.

1702 LET'S SCARE JESSICA TO DEATH. (Paramount-1971). Jessica, Zohra Lampert; Duncan, Barton Beyman; Woody, Kevin O'Connor; Girl, Gretchen Corbett.

1703 THE LEXINGTON EXPERIENCE. (Corda-1971). Pacific Gas & Electric.

1704 THE LIBERATION OF L. B. JONES. (Columbia-1970). Oman Hedgepath, Lee J. Cobb; Willie Joe Worth, Anthony Zerbe; Lord Byron Jones, Roscoe Lee Browne; Emma Jones, Lola Falana; Steve Mundine, Lee Majors; Nella Mundine, Barbara Hershey; Sonny Boy Mosby, Yaphet Kotto; Stanley Bumpas, Arch Johnson; Mr. Ike, Chill Wills; Mama Lavorn, Zara Cully; Benny, Favard Nicholas; Henry, Joe Attles; Erleen, Lauren Jones; Mayor, Dub Taylor; Jelly, Brenda Sykes; Grocer, Larry D. Mann; Chief of Police, Ray Teal; Miss Griggs, Eve McVeagh; Miss Ponsella, Sonora McKeller; Blind Man, Robert Van Meter; Driver, Jack Grinnage; Suspect, John S. Jackson.

1705 THE LIBERTINE. (Audubon-1969). Mimi, Catherine Spaak; Dr. DeMarchi, Jean-Louis Trintignant; Family Doctor, Paolo Stoppa; Fabrizio, Renzo Montagnani; Claudia, Fabienne Dali; Mimi's Mother, Nora Ricci; Bookseller, Vittorio Caprioli; Motorist, Gabriele Tinti; Plumber, Venantino Venantini; Maldini, Luigi Proietta; Architect, Luigi Pistilli; Tennis Coach, Philippe Leroy; Dentist, Frank Wolff.

1706 THE LICKERISH QUARTET. (Audubon-1970). The Girl, Silvana Venturelli; The Man, Frank Wolff; The Woman, Erika Remberg; The Boy, Paolo Turco.

1707 LICKITY SPLIT. (MSW-1974). Linda Lovemore, Mark Andrews, Naomi Jason, Max Packs, Sandi Fox, Don Allen, Mary Stuart, Mark Anthony, Leokavidia Olszewski, Cedar Houston, Francis X. Bush, Peches Flambe, Leo Lovelace, Laurie Suesan, Vic Dare.

1708 LIEBELEI. (Elite Tonfilm-1974). Fritz Lobheimer, Wolfgang Liebenelner; Christine Weiring, Magda Schneider; Mitzi Schlager, Luise Ullrich; Theo Kaiser, Willy Eichberger; Hans Weiring, Paul Hoerbiger; Baron Eggerdorff, Gustaf Gruendgens; Baroness Eggerdorff, Olga Tschechowa.

1709 LT. ROBIN CRUSOE, U.S.N. (Buena Vista-1966). Lt. Robin Crusoe, Dick Van Dyke; Wednesday, Nancy Kwan; Chief Tanamashu, Akim Tamiroff; Umbrella Man, Arthur Malet; Captain, Tyler McVey; Pilot, P. L. Renoudet; Co-Pilot, Peter Duryea; Crew Chief, John Dennis; Native Girls, Nancy Hsueh, Victoria Young, Yvonne Ribuca, Bebe Louie, and Lucia Valero.

1710 THE LIFE AND TIMES OF JUDGE ROY BEAN. (National General-1972). Judge Roy Bean, Paul Newman; Lily Langtry, Ava Gardner; Marie Elena, Victoria Principal; Rev. LaSalle, Anthony Perkins; Sam Dodd, Tab Hunter; Grizzly Adams, John Huston; Bad Bob, Stacy Keach; Frank Gass, Roddy McDowall; Rose Bean, Jacqueline Bisset; Tector Crites, Ned Beatty; Bart Jackson, Jim Burk; Nick the Grub, Matt Clark; Whorehouse Lucky Jim, Steve Kanaly; Fermel Parlee, Bill McKinney.

1711 THE LIFE AND TIMES OF XAVIERA HOLLANDER. (Mature-1974). Samantha McClern, Rick Cassidy, John Wadd, Rick Lutz, Paula Stone, Sylvia Reasoner, Betty Hunt, Russel Stover, Bert Finneberg, Larry Laurence, Al Husson, James Walch, John Roach, Marvin Finch and Tad Dood.

1712 LIFE AT THE TOP. (Royal-1965). Joe Lampton, Laurence Harvey; Susan Lampton, Jean Simmons; Norah Hauxley, Honor Blackman; Mark, Michael Craig; Abe Brown, Donald Wolfit; Tiffield, Robert Morley; George Aisgill, Allan Cuthbertson; Mrs. Brown, Ambrosine Phillpots; Sybil, Margaret Johnston; Ralph Hethersett, Ian Shand; Mottram, Nigel Davenport; Graffham, George A. Cooper; Harry Lampton, Paul Anthony Martin; Barbara Lampton, Frances Cosslett; Arthur Wincastle, Charles Lamb; Lord Mayor, Rex Deering.

1713 LIFE LOVE DEATH. (Lopert-1969). Francois Toledo, Amidou; Caroline, Caroline Cellier; Jeanne Toledo, Janine Magnan; Inspector Marchand, Marcel Bozzuffi; Police Officer, Pierre Zimmer; Julie, Catherine Samie; The Mother-in-law, Lisette Bersy; Defense Lawyer, Albert Naud; Partie Civil, Jean Pierre Sloan; Sophie Toledo, Nathalie Durrand; Sylvia Saurel, Denyse Roland, Claudia Morin, Rita Maiden, Pierre Collet, Albert Rajau, Jacques Henry, Jean-Marc Allegre, Colette Taconnat, Jean Collomb, El Cordobes, Robert Hossein, Annie Girardot.

1714 LIFE STUDY. (Nebbia-1973). Angelo, Bartholomew Miro Jr.; Myrna, Frika Peterson; Angela, Ziska; Adrian, Gregory

D'Alessio; Gus, Tom Lee Jones; Grandma, Rosetta Garuffi; John, Anthony Forest; Peggy, Yvonne Sherwell.

1715 LIFE UPSIDE DOWN. (Allied Artists-1965). Charles Denner, Anna Gaylor, Guy Saint Jean, Nicole Guedon, Robert Bousquet.

1716 THE LIGHT AT THE EDGE OF THE WORLD. (National General-1971). Will Denton, Kirk Douglas; Jonathan Kongre, Yul Brynner; Arabella, Samantha Eggar; Virgilio, Jean Claude Drouot; Captain Moriz, Fernando Rey.

1717 THE LIGHT FROM THE SECOND STORY WINDOW. (Jaguar-1973). Lee, David Allen; Chuck, Ray Todd; Big John, Joey Daniels; Movie Star, Jim Cassidy; Karl, Winston Kramer; Alma, Vicki Mills; Richard Lindstrom, Eva Faye, Brad Preston, William Lasky, Felisha Fahr, Richard Lauette, Bob Weaver, Lou Claudio, Greg Phillips, Bob Ratcliffe, Steve Fox, John Mihu.

1718 LIGHTNING BOLT. (Woolner Bros. -1967). Harry Sennet, Anthony Eisley; Patricia, Wandisa Leigh; Rethe, Folco Lulli; Diana Lorys, Maria Caffarel, Ursula Parker, Oreste Palella, Paco Sanz, Renato Montalbano.

1719 LIMBO. (Universal-1972). Sandy Lawton, Kate Jackson; Sharon, Katherine Justice; Phil Garrett; Stuart Margolin; Jane York, Hazel Medina; Mary Kay Buell, Kathleen Nolan; Alan Weber, Russell Wiggins; Margaret Holroyd, Joan Murphy; Joe Buell, Michael Bersell; Kathy Buell, Kim Nicholas; Pete Buell, Ken Kornbluh; Julie Buell, Laura Kornbluh; Colonel Loyd, Richard Callinan; Colonel Gunderson, Charles Martin; General Gibbs, Frank Logan; Ed Baldwin, Andrew Jarrell.

1720 THE LIMIT. (Cannon-1972). Mark, Yaphet Kotto; Jeff, Quinn Redeker; Kenny, Virgil Frye; Judy, Corinne Cole; Big Donnie, Ted Cassidy; Margret, Pamela Jones; Pete, Gary Littlejohn; Delores, Irene Forrest.

1721 THE LION IN WINTER. (AVCO Embassy-1968). King Henry II, Peter O'Toole; Queen Eleanor, Katharine Hepburn; Princess Alais, Jane Merrow; Prince Geoffrey, John Castle; King Philip of France, Timothy Dalton; William Marshall, Nigel Stock; Prince Richard, Anthony Hopkins; Strolling Player, Kenneth Griffith; Bishop, O. Z. Whitehead; Eleanor's Guard, Kenneth Ives; Harry Woolf, Karol Hagar, Mark Griffith.

1722 LIONS LOVE. (Raab-1969). Viva, Jerome Ragni, James Rado, Shirley Clarke, Carlos Clarens, Billie Dixon, Richard Bright, Eddie Constantine.

1723 THE LIQUIDATOR. (MGM-1966). Boysie Oakes, Rod Taylor; Colonel Mostyn, Trevor Howard; Iris MacIntosh, Jill St. John; The Chief, Wilfrid Hyde White; Quadrant, David Tomlinson; Sheriek, Akim Tamiroff; Griffin, Eric Sykes; Corale, Gabriella Licudi; Chekhov, John Le Mesurier; Fly, Derek Nimmo; Young man, Jeremy Lloyd; Janice Benedict, Jennifer Jayne; Assistant, Heller Toren; Frances Anne, Betty McDowall; Betty, Jo Rowbottom; Vicar, Colin Gordon; Jessie, Louise Dunn; Yakov, Henri Cogan; Gregory, Daniel Emilfork; Operations Officer, Scot Finch; Mac, Ronald Leigh-Hunt; Flying Instructor, Richard Wattis; Station Commander, David Langton; Flying Control, Tony Wright; Judith, Susy Kendall; Soldiers, Ken Wayne & Hal Galili.

1724 LISTEN, LET'S MAKE LOVE. (Lopert-1969). Lallo, Pierre Clementi; Aunt Lidia, Beba Loncar; Uncle Carlo, Carlo Caprioli; Giuditta Passani, Edwige Feuillere; Gilberta, Juliette Mayniel; Flavia Menobo, Tanya Lopert; Ida Bernasconi, Claudine Auger; Lallo's Mother, Valentina Cortese; Tassi, Massimo Girotti; Sveva, Martine Malle; Ida's Husband, Roberto Gatto; Mr. Breuner, Mario Meniconi.

1725 THE LITTLE ARK. (National General-1972). Captain, Theodore Bikel; Jan, Philip Frame; Adinda, Genevieve Ambas; Father Grijpma, Max Croiset; Cook, Johan De Slaa; Tandema, Lo Van Hensbergen; Mother Grijpma, Truss Dekker; Miss Winter, Edda Barendis; Lex Schoorel, Heleen Van Meurs, Prince, Ko, Noisette, Monica Achterberg, Wik Jongsma, Manfred De Graff, Renier Heidemann, Jos Bergman, Jeroen Krabbe, Jos Knipscheer, Tim Beekman, John Soer, Maurits Koek, Martin Brozius, Riek Schagen.

1726 LITTLE BIG MAN. (National General-1970). Jack Crabb, Dustin Hoffman; Mrs. Pendrake, Faye Dunaway; Allardyce, T. Merriweather, Martin Balsam; Gen. George A. Custer, Richard Mulligan; Old Lodge Skins, Chief Dan George; Wild Bill Hickok, Jeff Corey; Sunshine, Amy Eccles; Olga, Kelly Jean Peters; Caroline, Carole Androsky; Little Horse, Robert Little Star; Young Bear, Cal Bellini; Shadow That Comes in Sight, Reuben Moreno; Burns Red in the Sun, Steve Shemayne; Historian, William Hickey; Sergeant, James Anderson; Lieutenant, Jesse Vint; Major, Alan Oppenheimer; Rev. Silas Pendrake, Thayer David; Mr. Kane, Philip Kenneally; Captain, Jack Bannon; Young Jack Crabb, Ray Dimas; Adolescent Jack Crabb, Alan Howard; Child, Steve Miranda; Deacon, Lou Cutell; Shotgun Guard, M. Emmett Walsh; Digging Bear, Emily Cho; Cecilia Kootenay, Linda Dyer, Dessie Bad Bear, Len George, Norman Nathan, Helen Verbit, Bert Conway, Earl Rosell, Ken Mayer, Bud Cokes, Rory O'Brien, Tracy Hotchner.

1727 LITTLE CIGARS. (American International-1973). Cleo, Angel Tompkins; Slick, Billy Curtis; Cadillac, Jerry Maren;

Monty, Frank Delfino; Hugo, Emory Souza; Frankie, Felix Silla; Travers, Joe De Santis; Buzz, Todd Susman; Faust, Jon Cedar; Ganz, Phil Kenneally.

1728 LITTLE FAUSS AND BIG HALSY. (Paramount-1970). Halsy Knox, Robert Redford; Little Fauss, Michael J. Pollard; Rita Nebraska, Lauren Hutton; Seally Fauss, Noah Beery; "Mom" Fauss, Lucille Benson; The Photographer, Ray Ballard; Moneth, Linda Gaye Scott; Sylvene McFall, Erin O'Reilly; Rick Nifty, Ben Archibeck.

1729 LITTLE LAURA AND BIG JOHN. (Crown International-1973). John, Fabian Forte; Laura, Karen Black; Laura's Mother, Ivy Thayer; Kenny Miller, Paul Gleason.

1730 LITTLE MALCOLM. (Multicetera-1974). Malcolm Scrawdyke, John Hurt; Wick Blagdon, John McEnery; Irwin Ingham, Raymond Platt; Ann Gedge, Rosalind Ayres; Dennis Charles Nipple, David Warner.

1731 LITTLE MOTHER. (Audubon-1973). Marina, Christiane Kruger; Pinares, Siegfried Rauch; Umberia, Ivan Desny; Riano, Mark Damon; Cardinal, Anton Diffring; Annette, Elga Sorbas.

1732 LITTLE MURDERS. (20th Century-Fox-1971). Alfred Chamberlain, Elliott Gould; Patsy Newquist, Marcia Rodd; Mr. Newquist, Vincent Gardenia; Mrs. Newquist, Elizabeth Wilson; Kenny, Jon Korkes; Mr. Chamberlain, John Randolph; Mrs. Chamberlain, Doris Roberts; Minister, Donald Sutherland; Judge, Lou Jacobi; Detective, Alan Arkin.

1733 THE LITTLE NUNS. (Embassy-1966). Sister Celeste, Catherine Spaak; Elena, Sylva Koscina; Livio Bertana, Amedeo Nazzari; Mother Rachele, Didi Perego; Spugna, Umberto D'Orsi; Damiano, Sandro Bruni; Bertana's Secretary, Annie Gorassini.

1734 THE LITTLE ONES. (Columbia-1965). Ted, Kim Smith; Jackie, Carl Gonzales; Inspector Carter, Dudley Foster; Sergeant Wilson, Derek Newark; Lord Brantley, John Chandos; Ted's Mother, Jean Marlow; Junk Shop Dealer, Derek Francis; Welfare Officer, Cyril Shaps.

1735 THE LITTLE PRINCE. (Paramount-1974). The Pilot, Richard Kiley; The Little Prince, Steven Warner; The Snake, Bob Fosse; The Fox, Gene Wilder; The King, Joss Ackland; The Businessman, Clive Revill; The Historian, Victor Spinetti; The General, Graham Crowden; The Rose, Donna McKechnie.

1736 LIVE A LITTLE, LOVE A LITTLE. (MGM-1968). Greg, Elvis Presley; Bernice, Michele Carey; Mike Landsdown,

Don Porter; Penlow, Rudy Vallee; Harry, Dick Sargent; Milkman, Sterling Holloway; Ellen, Celeste Yarnall; Delivery Boy, Eddie Hodges; Mother, Joan Shawlee; Miss Selfridge, Mary Grover; Receptionist, Emily Banks; Art Director, Michael Keller; Secretaries, Merri Ashley and Phyllis Davis; Perfume Model, Ursula Menzel; Models, Susan Shute, Edie Baskin, Thordis Brandt, Ginny Kaneen, and Gabrielle; Mermaid, Susan Henning; Motorcycle Cops, Morgan Windbeil and Benjie Bancroft.

1737 LIVE AND LET DIE. (United Artists-1973). James Bond, Roger Moore; Kananga/Mr. Big, Yaphet Kotto; Solitaire, Jane Seymour; Sheriff Pepper, Clifton James; Tee Hee, Julius W. Harris; Baron Samedi, Geoffrey Holder; Leiter, David Hedison; Rosie, Gloria Hendry; "M," Bernard Lee; Moneypenny, Lois Maxwell; Adam, Tommy Lane; Whisper, Earl Jolly Brown; Quarrel, Roy Stewart; Strutter, Lon Satton; Cab Driver, Arnold Williams; Mrs. Bell, Ruth Kempf; Charlie, Joie Chitwood; Beautiful Girl, Madeline Smith; Dambala, Michael Ebbin; Sales Girl, Kubi Chaza; Singer, B. J. Arnau.

1738 LIVE FOR LIFE. (United Artists-1967). Robert Colomb, Yves Montand; Candice, Candice Bergen; Catherine Colomb, Annie Girardot; Mereille, Irene Tunc; Jacqueline, Anouk Ferjac; Maid, Uta Taeger; Waiter, Jean Collomb; Photographer, Jacques Portet; Michel, Michel Parbot.

1739 LIVE IN FEAR. (Brandon-1967). Klichi Nakajima, Toshiro Mifune; Toyo, Eiki Miyoshi; Yoshi, Togo Haruko; Takao Yamazaki, Masao Shimizu; Ichiro, Yutaka Sada.

1740 LIVING FREE. (Columbia-1972). Joy Adamson, Susan Hampshire; George Adamson, Nigel Davenport; John Kendall, Geoffrey Keen; Nuru, Peter Lukoye; Madedde, Shane De Louvres; Game Warden Weaver, Edward Judd; Billy Collins, Robert Beaumont; Bank Manager, Nobby Noble; Bank Clerk, Aludin Quershi; Herbert Baker, Charles Hayes; Mrs. Herbert Baker, Jean Hayes; James Kamau.

1741 LIZARD IN A WOMAN'S SKIN. (American International-1972). Carol Hammond, Florinda Bolkan; Inspector Corvin, Stanley Baker; Frank Hammond, Jean Sorel; Edmund Brighton, Leo Genn; Brandon, Alberto De Mendoza; Deborah, Silvia Monti; Hubert, Mike Kennedy; Dr. Kerr, Georges Rigaud; Julia Durer, Anita Strindberg; Jenny, Penny Brown; Joan, Edy Gall; Lowell, Ezio Marano; McKenna, Franco Balducci; Mr. Gordon, Erzsi Paal; Clinic Director, Jean Degrade; Policemen, Gaetano Imbro and Luigi Antonio Guerra.

1742 LOCK UP YOUR DAUGHTERS! (Columbia-1969). Lord Foppington, Christopher Plummer; Hilaret, Susannah York; Mrs. Squeezum, Glynis Johns; Ramble, Ian Bannen; Shaftoe,

Tom Bell; Cloris, Elaine Taylor; Lusty, Jim Dale; Lady Clumsey, Kathleen Harrison; Sir Tunbelly Clumsey, Roy Kinnear; Nell, Georgia Brown; Hoyden, Vanessa Howard; Gossip, Roy Dotrice; Lady Eager, Fenella Fielding; Lord Eager, Paul Dawkins; Mrs. Justice Squeezum, Peter Bayliss; Coupler, Richard Wordsworth; Bull, Peter Butler; Night Watchman, Arthur Mullard; Mr. Justice Worthy, Edward Atienza; La Verole, Michael Darbyshire; Nurse, Patricia Routledge; Bottle, Roy Pember; Earl of Ware, Fred Emney; Nobleman, John Morley; Boswell, Clive Morton; Roger Hammond, Tony Sumpson, Martin Crosbie.

1743 LOLA. (American International-1972). Scott Wardman, Charles Bronson; Lola Londonberry, Susan George; Grandfather, Trevor Howard; Lola's Mother, Honor Blackman; Lola's Father, Michael Craig; Hal, Orson Bean; Scott's Mother, Kay Medford; Scott's Father, Paul Ford; Judge Millington-Draper, Jack Hawkins; Judge Roxburgh, Robert Morley; Mr. Creighton, Lionel Jeffries; Night Club Comedians, Norman Vaughan and Jimmy Tarbuck; Lola's Sister, Polly Williams; Lola's Brother, Anthony Kemp; Felicity, Cathy Jose; Mrs. Finchley, Peggy Aitchison; Secretary, Elspeth March; Client, Eric Chitty; Policemen, Leslie Schofield and Derek Steen; Marty, Gordon Waller; Old Gentleman, Reg Lever; New York Judge, Tony Arpino; Marriage Clerk, Eric Barker; Hotel Receptionist, John Rae; Hotel Waiter, John Wright.

1744 LOLA MONTES. (Brandon-1969). Lola Montes, Martine Carol; Circus Master, Peter Ustinov; King of Bavaria, Anton Walbrook; James, Ivan Desny; Liszt, Will Quadflieg; The Student, Oskar Werner; Mrs. Craigie, Lise Delamare; Maurice, Henri Guisol; Josephine, Paulette Dubost; Lola's Doctor, Willy Eichberger; Beatrice Arnac, Jacques Fayet, Pieral, Friedrich Domin, Gustav Waldau, Werner Finck, Willy Rosner, Daniel Mandaille, Helena Manson.

1745 LOLLY-MADONNA XXX. (MGM-1973). Laban, Rod Steiger; Chickie, Katherine Squire; Thrush, Scott Wilson; Skylar, Timothy Scott; Hawk, Ed Lauter; Finch, Randy Quaid; Zack, Jeff Bridges; Pap, Robert Ryan; Elspeth, Tresa Hughes; Vilum, Paul Koslo; Ludie, Kiel Martin; Seb, Gary Busey; Sister E, Joan Goodfellow; Roonie, Season Hubley.

1746 THE LONERS. (Fanfare-1972). Stein, Dean Stockwell; Julio, Pat Stich; Allan, Todd Susman; Policeman Hearn, Scott Brady; Anabelle, Gloria Grahame; Police Chief Peters, Alex Dreier; Howie, Tim Rooney; Sheriff, Ward Wood; Mrs. Anderson, Hortense Petra; Driver, Richard O'Brien; Stein's Father, Hal Jon Norman; Man in Diner, Duane Grey; Woman in Diner, Jean Dorl; Bridegroom, Stuart Nisbet; Policeman, Larry O'Leno.

1747 LONESOME COWBOYS. (Sherpix-1969). Ramona Alvarez, Viva; The Drifter, Tom Hompertz; Mickey, Louis Waldon; Eric, Eric Emerson; The Nurse, Taylor Mead; Little Joe, Joe Dallesandro; The Sheriff, Francis Francine; Julian, Julian Burroughs.

1748 LONG AGO, TOMORROW. (Cinema 5-1971). Bruce, Malcolm McDowell; Jill, Nanette Newman; Sarah, Georgia Brown; Uncle Bob, Bernard Lee; Rev. Corbett, Gerald Sim.

1749 THE LONG DARKNESS. (Toho-1973). Tetsuro, Go Kato; Shino, Komaki Kurihara; Uasushi Nagata, Kinzo Shin, Kaneko Iwasaki.

1750 THE LONG DAY'S DYING. (Paramount-1968). John, David Hemmings; Tom, Tom Bell; Cliff, Tony Beckley; Helmut, Alan Dobie.

1751 THE LONG DUEL. (Paramount-1967). Sultan, Yul Brynner; Freddy Young, Trevor Howard; Superintendent Stafford, Harry Andrews; Gungaram, Andrew Keir; Jane Stafford, Charlotte Rampling; Champa, Virginia North; McDougal, Laurence Naismith; Governor, Maurice Denham; Tara, Imogen Hassall; Jamadar, Paul Hardwick; Munnu, Antonio Ruiz; Gyan Singh, David Sumner; Pahelwan, Rafiq Anwar; George Pastel, Shivendra Sinha, Zohra Segal, Norman Florence, Dino Shafeek, Kurt Christian, Terry York, Tommy Reeves, Jimmy Lodge, Patrick Newell, Jeremy Lloyd, Terence Alexander, Marianne Stone, Edward Fox, Bakshi Prem, Toni Kanal, Ramon Serrano, Ben Tatar, Aldo Sanbrel, Monisha Bose, Naseem Khan, Shymala Devi, Shirley Sen Guptha, Jamila Massey.

1752 THE LONG GOODBYE. (United Artists-1973). Philip Marlowe, Elliott Gould; Eileen Wade, Nina van Pallandt; Roger Wade, Sterling Hayden; Marty Augustine, Mark Rydell; Dr. Verringer, Henry Gibson; Harry, David Arkin; Terry Lennox, Jim Bouton; Morgan, Warren Berlinger; Jo Ann Eggenweiler, Jo Ann Brody; Hood, Jack Knight; Pepe, Pepe Callahan; Hoods, Vince Palmeri, Arnold Strong; Piano Player, Jack Riley; Colony Guard, Ken Sansom; Bartender, Danny Goldman; Real Estate Lady, Sybil Scotford; Detective Farmer, Steve Coit; Detective, Tracy Harris; Detective Green, Jerry Jones; Clerk, Rodney Moss.

1753 A LONG RIDE FROM HELL. (Cinerama-1970). Mike, Steve Reeves; Mayner, Wayde Preston; Freeman, Dick Palmer; Ruth, Silvana Venturelli; Sheriff, Lee Burton; Shorty, Ted Carter; Prostitute, Rosalba Neri; Roy, Franco Fantasia; Bobcat, Mario Maranzana.

1754 THE LONGEST YARD. (Paramount-1974). Paul Crewe, Burt Reynolds; Warden Hazen, Eddie Albert; Capt. Knauer,

Ed Lauter; Scarboro, Michael Conrad; Caretaker, Jim Hampton; Granville, Harry Caesar; Pop, John Steadman; Unger, Charles Tyner; Guards, Mike Henry, Joe Kapp; Warden's Secretary, Bernadette Peters; Shop Steward, Pepper Martin; Spooner, Ernie Wheelwright; Rotka, Tony Cacciotti; Samson, Richard Kiel; Mawabe, Pervis Atkins; Mason, Dino Washington; Guard Bogdanski, Ray Nitschke; Assistant Warden, Mort Marshall; Melissa, Anitra Ford; Game Announcer, Michael Fox; The Indian, Sonny Sixkiller; Shokner, Bob Tessier.

1755 THE LOOKING GLASS WAR. (Columbia-1970). Leiser, Christopher Jones; The Girl, Pia Degermark; Leclerc, Ralph Richardson; John Avery, Anthony Hopkins; Haldane, Paul Rogers; Susan, Susan George; Johnson, Robert Urquhart; Babs Leclerc, Maxine Audley; Sarah, Anna Massey; Capt. Lansen, Frederick Jaeger; CIA Man, Paul Maxwell; Taylor, Timothy West; Carol, Vivien Pickles; Peerson, Peter Swanwick; Detective, Cyril Shaps; Truck Driver, Michael Robbins; Fritsche, Guy Deghy; Russian Officer, David Scheur; Pine, John Franklin; Taylor's Child, Linda Hedger; Boy, Nicholas Stewart.

1756 LOOT. (Cinevision-1972). Inspector Truscott, Richard Attenborough; Fay, Lee Remick; Dennis, Hywel Bennett; Mr. McLeavy, Milo O'Shea; Hal McLeavy, Roy Holder; Mr. Bateman, Dick Emery; Father O'Shaughnessy, Joe Lynch; Meadows, John Cater; Undertaker, Aubrey Woods; W. V. A. Leader, Enid Lowe; Policewoman, Andonia Katsaros; Bank Manager, Harold Innocent; Vicar, Kevin Brennan; Mrs. McLeavy, Jean Marlow; Doctor, Robert Raglan; Pallbearers, Hal Galili, Douglas Ridley, Adrian Correger and Edwin Finn.

1757 LORD JIM. (Columbia-1965). Jim, Peter O'Toole; Stein, Paul Lucas; The Girl, Dahlia Lavi; The General, Eli Wallach; Cornelius, Curt Jurgens; Gentleman Brown, James Mason; Schomberg, Akim Tamiroff; Marlow, Jack Hawkins; Maris, Ichizo Itami; Du-Ramin, Tatsuo Saito; Robinson, Jack MacGowran; Patna Captain, Walter Gotell; French Officer, Christian Marquand; Brierly, Andrew Keir; Malay, Eric Young; Capt. Chester, Noel Purcell; Moslem Leader, Rafik Anwar; Elder, Marne Maitland; Doctor, Newton Blick; Magistrate, A. J. Brown.

1758 LORD LOVE A DUCK. (United Artists-1966). "Mollymauk" Musgrave, Roddy McDowall; Barbara Ann Greene, Tuesday Weld; Marie Greene, Lola Albright; Bob Barnard, Martin West; Stella Barnard, Ruth Gordon; Weldon Emmett, Harvey Korman; Miss Schwartz, Sarah Marshall; Sally Grace, Lynn Carey; Howard Greene, Max Showalter; Phil Neuhauser, Donald Murphy; Mrs. Butch Neuhauser, Judith Loomis; Dr. Lippman, Joseph Mell; Head Car Salesman, Dan Frazer;

Harry Belmont, Martin Gabel; Inez, Martine Bartlett; Kitten, Jo Collins.

1759 LORDS OF FLATBUSH. (Columbia-1974). Chico Tyrell, Perry King; Stanley Rosiello, Sylvester Stallone; Butchey Weinstein, Henry Winkler; Wimpy Murgalo, Paul Mace; Jane Bradshaw, Susie Blakely; Frannie Malincanico, Maria Smith; Annie Yuckamanelli, Renee Paris.

1760 LORNA. (Eve-1965). Lorna Maitland, Mark Bradley, James Rucker, Hal Hopper, Doc Scortt, James Griffith.

1761 L[OS] A[NGELES] PLAYS ITSELF. (Halsted-1972). Fred Halsted, Himself; Blonde Pickup, Joey Yanichek; Hiker, Jim Frost; Elf, Rick Coates.

1762 THE LOSERS. (Fanfare-1970). Link, William Smith; Capt., Bernie Hamilton; Duke, Adam Roarke; Major, Daniel Kemp; Dirty, Houston Savage; Speed, Gene Cornelius; Limpy, Paul Koslo; Sgt., John Garwood; Kim, Ana Korita; Suriya, Lillian Margarejo; Sama-San, Paraluman; Kowalski, Paul Nuckles; Lt., Ronnie Ross; Screw, Armando Lucero; Charlie, Fran Dinh Hy; Diem, Vic Diaz; Albanian, Alan Caillou; Tac, Paquito Salcedo; Shillick, Von Deming; Inspector, Herman Robles; Chet, Jack Starrett.

1763 LOST COMMAND. (Columbia-1966). Lt. Colonel Raspeguy, Anthony Quinn; Captain Esclavier, Alain Delon; Lt. Mahidi, George Segal; Countess de Clairefons, Michele Morgan; Boisfeuras, Maurice Ronet; Aicha, Claudia Cardinale; Ben Saad, Gregoire Aslan; General Melies, Jean Servais; Merle, Maurice Sarfati; Orsini, Jean-Claude Bercq; Verte, Syl Lamont; Mayor, Jacques Marin; Jean Paul Moulinot, Andres Monreal, Gordon Heath, Simono, Rene Havard, Armand Mestral, Burt Kwouk, Al Mulock, Marie Burke, Aldo Sanbrell, Jorge Rigaud, Roberto Robles, Emilio Carrer, Carmen Tarrazo, Howard Hagan, Mario De Barros, Walter Kelly, Robert Sutton, Simon Benzakein, Hector Quiroga, Felix De Pomes.

1764 THE LOST CONTINENT. (20th Century-Fox-1968). Captain Lansen, Eric Porter; Eva, Hildegard Knef; Unity, Suzanna Leigh; Harry Tyler, Tony Beckley; Dr. Webster, Nigel Stock; First Officer Hemmings, Neil McCallum; Ricaldi, Benito Carruthers; Pat, Jimmy Hanley; Chief, James Cossins; Sarah, Dana Gillespie; Mate, Victor Maddern; Helmsman, Reg Lye; Jonathan, Norman Eshley; Sea Lawyer, Michael Ripper; Sparks, Donald Sumpter; Jason, Alf Joint; Braemar, Charles Houston; Jurri Curri, Shivendra Sinha; El Diablo, Darryl Read; Inquisitor, Eddie Powell; Sergeant, Frank Hayden; Customs Men, Mark Heath and Horace James.

1765 LOST HORIZON. (Columbia-1973). Richard Conway, Peter

Finch; Catherine, Liv Ullman; Sally Hughes, Sally Kellerman; Sam Cornelius, George Kennedy; George Conway, Michael York; Maria, Olivia Hussey; Harry Lovett, Bobby Van; Brother To-Lenn, James Shigeta; High Lama, Charles Boyer; Chang, John Gielgud.

1766 LOST IN THE STARS. (American Film Theatre-1974). Brock Peters, Melba Moore, Raymond St. Jacques, Clifton Davis, Paula Kelly, Paul Rogers, John Williams, Ivor Barry, Harvey Jason, Alan Weeks, H. B. Barnum III, Pauline Myers, Ji-Tu Cumbuka, John Holland, John Hawker, Myrna White, Michael-James Wixted, William Glover.

1767 THE LOST MAN. (Universal-1969). Jason Higgs, Sidney Poitier; Cathy Ellis, Joanna Shimkus; Dennis Laurence, Al Freeman Jr.; Hamilton, Michael Tolin; Eddie Moxy, Leon Bibb; Barnes, Richard Dysart; Photographer, David Steinberg; Sally, Beverly Todd; Orville, Paul Winfield; Reggie Page, Bernie Hamilton; Richard Anthony Williams, Dolph Sweet, Arnold Williams, Virginia Capers, Vonetta McGee, Frank Myers, Lee Weaver, Morris Erby, Doug Johnson, Lincoln Kilpatrick, Johnny Daheim, Sonny Garrison.

1768 LOST SEX. (Chevron-1968). The Master, Hideo Kanze; The Housekeeper, Nobuko Otowa; The Writer Neighbor, Eijiro Tohno; The Young Neighbor, Yoshinobu Ogawa; The Young Neighbor's Wife, Kaori Shima.

1769 THE LOST WORLD OF SINBAD. (American International-1966). Toshiro Mifune, Makoto Staoh, Jun Funando, Ichiro Arishima, Miye Hama, Kumi Mizuno, Eiko Wakabayashi, Mitsuko Kusabue, Tadao Nakamura, Jun Tazaki, Takashi Shimura.

1770 LOTNA. (Pol-Ton-1966). The Lieutenant, Adam Pawlikowski; The Ensign, Jerzy Moes; The Captain, Jerzy Pichelski; The Sergeant-Major Mieczyslaw Loza; Ewa, Bozena Kurowska.

1771 LOVE. (Ajay-1973). Old Lady, Lili Darvas; Luca, Mari Torocsik; Janos, Ivan Darvas.

1772 LOVE A LA CARTE. (Promenade-1965). Adua, Simone Signoret; Piero, Marcello Mastroianni; Milly, Gina Rovere; Lolita, Sandra Milo; Marilyna, Emmanuelle Riva; Ercoli, Claudio Gora; Lawyer, Ivo Garrani; Stefano, Gianrico Tedeschi.

1773 LOVE AFFAIR. (Brandon-1968). Isabela, Eva Ras; Ahmed, Slobodan Aligrudic; Isabela's Friend, Ruzica Sokic; The Postman, Miodrag Andric; Sexologist, Dr. Aleksander Kostic; Criminologist, Dr. Zivojin Aleksic.

1774 LOVE AND ANARCHY. (Steinmann-Baxter-1974). Giancarlo Gianinni, Mariangela Melato, Lina Polito, Eros Pagni, Pina Cei, Elena Fiore.

1775 LOVE AND KISSES. (Universal-1965). Buzzy, Rick Nelson; Jeff Pringle, Jack Kelly; Rosemary, Kristin Nelson; Freddy, Jerry Van Dyke; Nanny, Pert Kelton; Carol, Madelyn Himes; Elizabeth, Sheilah Wells; Officer Jones, Alvy Moore; Stage Manager, Angelo Brovelli; Bobby, Barry Livingston; Assemblyman Potter, Ivan Bonar; Mr. Frisby, Howard McNear; Dancers, Betty Rowland, Nancy Lewis, Anita Mann.

1776 LOVE AND MARRIAGE. (Embassy-1966). Concetto, Lando Buzzanca; Enea, Maria Grazia Buccella; Roro, Umberto D'Orsi; Lady on Yacht, Luciana Angelillo; Marina, Ingeborg Schoener; Giancarlo, Renato Tagliani; Young man in cinema, Steve Forsyth; Fisherman, Marino Mase; Elsa, Eleanora Rossi Drago; Antonio, Aldo Giuffre; Gladys, April Hennessy; Diana, Sylva Koscina; Mario, Philippe Leroy.

1777 LOVE AND PAIN AND THE WHOLE DAMN THING. (Columbia-1973). Lila Fisher, Maggie Smith; Walter Elbertson, Timothy Bottoms; The Duke, Don Jaime de Mora y Aragon; Spanish Gentleman, Emiliano Redondo; Dr. Elbertson, Charles Baxter; Mrs. Elbertson, Margaret Modlin; Melanie Elbertson, May Heatherley; Carl, Lloyd Brimhall; Dr. Edelheidt, Elmer Modlin; Tourist Guide, Andres Monreal.

1778 THE LOVE BUG. (Buena Vista-1969). Jim Douglas, Dean Jones; Carole Bennett, Michele Lee; Peter Thorndyke, David Tomlinson; Tennessee Steinmetz, Buddy Hackett; Havershaw, Joe Flynn; Mr. Wu, Benson Fong; Detective, Joe E. Ross; Police Sergeant, Barry Kelley; Carhop, Iris Adrian; Association President, Andy Granatelli; Ned Glass, Gil Lamb, Nicole Jaffe, Russ Caldwell, P. L. Renoudet, Alan Fordney, Gary Owens, Robert Foulk, Pedro Gonzalez-Gonzalez, Wally Boag, Max Balchowsky, Brian Fong, Stan Duke, Chick Hearn.

1779 LOVE COMES QUIETLY. (Film-Makers International-1974). Barbara Seagull, Sandy van der Linden, Ward De Ravet, Kitty Janssen, Ralph Meeker.

1780 THE LOVE GOD? (Universal-1969). Abner Audubon Peacock, Don Knotts; Lisa LaMonica, Anne Francis; Osborn Tremain, Edmond O'Brien; Darrell Evans Hughes, James Gregory; Eleanor Tremain, Maureen Arthur; Rose Ellen Wilkerson, Maggie Peterson; J. Charles Twilight, B. S. Pully; Miss Love, Jesslyn Fax; Carter Fenton, Jacques Aubuchon; Miss Pickering, Marjorie Bennett; Amos Peacock, Jim Boles; Miss Keezy, Ruth McDevitt; Joe Merkel, Roy

Stuart; Attorney Snow, Herbert Voland; Reverend Wilkerson, James Westerfield; John Hubbard, Bob Hastings, Larry Mc-Cormick, Robert P. Lieb, Willis Bouchey, Herbie Faye, Johnny Seven, Joseph Perry, Jim Begg, Carla Borelli, Nancy Vonniwell, Shelly Davis, Aleshia Lee, Terri Harper.

1781 LOVE HAS MANY FACES. (Columbia-1965). Kit Jordon, Lana Turner; Pete Jordon, Cliff Robertson; Hank Walker, Hugh O'Brian; Margot Eliot, Ruth Roman; Carol Lambert, Stefanie Powers; Irene Talbot, Virginia Grey; Chuck Austin, Ron Husman; Lieut. Riccardo Andrade, Enrique Lucero; Don Julian, Carlos Montalban; Manuel Perez, Jaime Bravo; Maria, Fannie Schiller; Ramos, Rene Dupreyon.

1782 LOVE IN 4 DIMENSIONS. (Eldorado-1965). Carlo Giuffre, Franca Rame, Carlo Bagno, Sylva Koscina, Gastone Moschin, Franca Polesello, Philippe Leroy, Elena Martini, Fabrizio Capucci, Alberto Bonucci, Michele Mercier, Alberto Lionel-lo.

1783 LOVE IS A FUNNY THING. (United Artists-1970). Henri, Jean-Paul Belmondo; Francoise, Annie Girardot; Henri's Wife, Maria-Pia Conte; Francoise's Husband, Marcel Boz-zuffi; Patricia, Farrah Fawcet; Director, Peter Bergman; Paul, Kaz Garas; Passenger, Bill Quinn; Customs Officer, Arturo Dominici; The Dominos, Timothy Blake; Waiter, Jerry Cipperley; Indian, Forster Hood; Sweet Emma, Sweet Emma.

1784 THE LOVE MACHINE. (Columbia-1971). Robin Stone, John Phillip Law; Judith Austin, Dyan Cannon; Gregory Aus-tin, Robert Ryan; Danton Miller, Jackie Cooper; Jerry Nel-son, David Hemmings; Amanda, Jodi Wexler; Cliff Dorne, William Roerick; Ethel Evans, Maureen Arthur.

1785 LOVE ME LIKE I DO. (Hollywood Cinemart-1970). Hus-band, Peter Carpenter; Wife, Dyanne Thorne; Other Man, Paul Fleming; Brunette, Maria de Aragon; Redhead, Lynne Gordon; Pilot, Richard L. Karie; Lawyer, Ralph J. Rose; Chief of Police, Arnold Roberts; Lawyer's Wife, Jacqueline Dalya; Go-Go Girl, Joey Du Prez; Singer, Elaine Hill; Male Dancer, Pedro Dupuy.

1786 LOVE ME--LOVE MY WIFE. (Cimber-1971). Elizabeth, Pier Angeli; Stephen, Glenn Saxon; Alexandra, Colette Des-combe.

1787 THE LOVE MERCHANT. (General Sutdios-1966). Loraine Claire, Jim Chisholm, Joanna Mills, Penni Peyton, Fran-cine Ashley, Annette Godette, Steve Barton, Judson Todd, George Wolfe, Patti Paget, Cleo Nova, Michael Lawrence, Shep Wild, Philip Mason.

1788 LOVE STORY. (Paramount-1970). Jenny Cavilleri, Ali MacGraw; Oliver Barrett IV, Ryan O'Neal; Oliver Barrett III, Ray Milland; Mrs. Barrett, Katherine Balfour; Phil Cavilleri, John Marley; Dean Thompson, Russell Nype; Dr. Shapely, Sydney Walker; Dr. Addison, Robert Modica; Ray, Walker Daniels; Hank, Tom Lee Jones; Steve, John Merensky; Rev. Blauvelt, Andrew Duncan; Doorman, Bob O'Connell.

1789 LOVE, SWEDISH STYLE. (Screencom International-1972). Inga Johanson, Karen Ciral; Dr. Larry Becker, Peter Balakoff; Sterling Phillips, Woody Lee; Eddie, Arne Warda; Mrs. Nolan, Jane Tsentis; Mr. Nolan, Mark Roland; Mrs. Johnson, Rachel English; Mr. Johnson, Marland Proctor; Telephone Man, Phil Hoover; Mr. Goodman, Duke Douglas; Mrs. Goodman, Ginger Madden; Myron Goodman, Ray Dirdoorian; Johnny, John Merenda; Helga, Jeannie Anderson; Vice cop, John Andrews; Tow-Truck Driver, Mike Garrison; Britta, Hilda Wendt; American Tourist, Alex Eliot; Lars, Eric Lidberg; The Judge, Ralph Newton.

1789a THE LOVED ONE. (MGM-1965). Dennis Barlow, Robert Morse; Wilbur Glenworthy/Harry Glenworthy, Jonathan Winters; Aimee Thanatogenos, Anjanette Comer; Mr. Joyboy, Rod Steiger; Joyboy's Mother, Ayllene Gibbons; Dr. J. Jr., Roddy McDowall; Mr. Kenton, Milton Berle; Mrs. Kenton, Margaret Leighton; The Guru Brahmin, Lionel Stander; Sir Francis Hinsley, John Gielgud; Sir Ambrose Abercrombie, Robert Morley; Mr. Starker, Liberace; Guide, Tab Hunter; General Brinkman, Dana Andrews; Immigration Officer, James Coburn; Assistant to the Guru, Bernie Kopell; English Club Official, Alan Napier.

1790 LOVE-IN '72. (Mishkin-1972). Sunny, Linda Southern; Philip Haller, John Ross; Joan Boyd, Susan Sparling; Peter Yates, Will Patent; Howard Yates, Thomas Murphy; Father Reis, Philip B. Hall; Gregory Haller, Alexander Gellman; Nancy Haller, Edith Briden; Terry, Stephen Snow; Jim, George Linjeris; Radical, Spalding Gray; Man at Physical, Kelly Houser; Detective, Larry Hunter; Steven Hilton, Daniel Nugent.

1791 THE LOVE-INS. (Columbia-1967). Dr. Jonathan Barnett, Richard Todd; Larry Osborne, James MacArthur; Patricia Cross, Susan Oliver; Elliot, Mark Goddard; Harriet, Carol Booth; Mario, Marc Cavell; Lamelle, Janee Michelle; Bobby, Ronnie Eckstine; Reverend Spencer, Michael Evans; Mrs. Sacaccio, Hortense Petra; Mr. Henning, James Lloyd; Hippie on LSD, Mario Roccuzzo; Joe Pyne, The Chocolate Watchband, The UFO's, The New Age.

1792 No entry.

1793 LOVELAND. (Illustrated-1973). Carla Montgomery, Burt Allen, Candy Miller, Leslie White, Bill Mantell, Randy Troy, Pamela Patton, Terry Larson, Genie Carson.

1794 A LOVELY WAY TO DIE. (Universal-1968). Jim Schuyler, Kirk Douglas; Rena Westabrook, Sylva Koscina; Tennessee Fredericks, Eli Wallach; Jonathan Fleming, Kenneth Haigh; "Finchley," Martyn Green; Carol, Sharon Farrell; Cook, Ruth White; Feeney, Doris Roberts; Harris, Carey Nairnes; Cooper, John Rogers; Fuller, Philip Bosco; Sean Magruder, Ralph Waite; Mrs. Magruder, Meg Myles; Eric, Gordon Peters; Loren Westabrook, William Roerick; Layton, Dana Elcar; Mrs. Gordon, Dee Victor; Haver, Dolph Sweet; Daley, Lincoln Kilpatrick; Lumson, Alex Stevens; James Lawrence, Conrad Bain; Connor, Robert Gerringer; Harry Samson, John Ryan; The Real Finchley, Jay Barney; Racetrack Announcer, Marty Glickman.

1795 LOVERS AND OTHER STRANGERS. (Cinerama-1970). Hal, Gig Young; Bea, Bea Arthur; Susan, Bonnie Bedelia; Cathy, Anne Jackson; Johnny, Harry Guardino; Mike, Michael Brandon; Frank, Richard Castellano; Jerry, Bob Dishy; Brenda, Marian Hailey; Richie, Joseph Hindy; Donaldson, Anthony Holland; Joan, Diane Keaton; Bernice, Cloris Leachman; Father Gregory, Mort Marshall; Wilma, Anne Meara.

1796 LOVES OF A BLONDE. (Prominent-1966). Andula, Hana Brejchova; Milda, Vladimir Pucholt; Tonda, Antonin Blazejovsky; Milda's Father, Josef Sebanek; Milda's Mother, Milada Jezkova; Jaruska, Jana Novakova; The Major, Jan Vosteil; Vacovsky, Vladimir Mensik.

1797 THE LOVES OF ISADORA. (Universal-1969). Isadora Duncan, Vanessa Redgrave; Gordon Craig, James Fox; Paris Singer, Jason Robards; Sergei Essenin, Ivan Tchenko; Roger, John Fraser; Mrs. Duncan, Bessie Love; Mary Desti, Cynthia Harris; Elizabeth Duncan, Libby Glenn; Raymond Duncan, Tony Vogel; Archer, Wallas Eaton; Pim, John Quentin; Bedford, Nicholas Pennell; Miss Chase, Ronnie Gilbert; Armand, Christian Duvaleix; Raucous Woman, Margaret Courtenay; Hearty Husband, Arthur White; Alicia, Iza Teller; Bugatti, Vladimir Leskovar; Mr. Stirling, John Warner; Russian Teacher, Ina De La Haye; Gospel Billy, John Brandon; Lucinda Chambers, Simon Lutton Davies, Alan Gifford, David Healy, Zuleika Robson, Noel Davies, Arnold Diamond, Anthony Gardner, Sally Travers, Mark Dignam, Robin Lloyd, Constantine Iranski, Lucy Saroyan, Jan Conrad, Hall Galilli, Roy Stephens, Cal McCord, Richard Marner, Stefan Gryss.

1798 THE LOVES OF ONDINE. (Factory Films-1968). Himself, Ondine; Girl in Bed, Viva; "College Wrestler," Joe Dallesandro; Girl on Love Seat, Pepper Davis; Girl on Chair, Ivy

Nicholson; Ondine's Wife, Brigid Polk; Folk Singer, Bill Gary.

1799 LOVIN' MOLLY. (Columbia-1974). Gid, Anthony Perkins; Johnny, Beau Bridges; Molly, Blythe Danner; Mr. Fry, Edward Binns; Sarah, Susan Sarandon; Eddie, Conrad Fowkes; Mr. Tayler, Claude Traverse; Mr. Grinsom, John Henry Faulk.

1800 LOVING. (Columbia-1970). Brooks, George Segal; Selma, Eva Marie Saint; Lepridon, Sterling Hayden; Edward, Keenan Wynn; Nelly, Nancie Phillips; Grace, Janis Young; Will, David Doyle; Marve, Paul Sparer; Willy, Andrew Duncan; Susan, Sherry Lansing; Plommie, Roland Winters; Mr. Kramm, Edgar Stehli; Danny, Calvin Holt; Diane, Mina Kolb; Mrs. Shavelson, Diana Douglas; Al, David Ford; Charles, James Manis; Ted, Mart Hulswitt; Brad, John Fink; Jay, William Duffy; Benny, Irving Selbst; Roger, Martin Friedberg; Lizzie, Lorraine Cullen; Hannah, Cheryl Bucher; Skip, Roy Scheider; Byron, Sab Shimono; Cindy, Eileen O'Neill; Barbie, Diane Davies; Mr. Shavelson, Ed Crowley.

1801 LOVING COUPLES. (Prominent-1966). Agda, Harriet Andersson; Adele, Gunnel Lindblom; Angela, Gio Petre; Aunt Petra, Anita Bjork; Dr. Jacob Lewin, Gunnar Bjornstrand; Mrs. Lewin, Inga Landgre; Stellan, Jan Malmsjo; Ola Landborg, Frank Sundstrom; Mrs. Landborg, Eva Dahlbeck; Bernhard Landborg, Heinz Hopp; Hans Straat, Bengt Brunskog, Toivo Pawlo, Margit Carlqvist, Jan-Erik Lindqvist, Barbro Hjort Af Ornas, Marta Dorff, Lissi Alandh, Ake Gronberg, Hans Sundberg, Stein Lonnert, Axel Fritz, Henrik Schildt, Berit Gustafsson, Lennart Grundtman, Lo Dagerman, Katarina Edefeldt, Nancy Dalunde, Claes Thelander, Lars Grundtman, Dan Landgre, Rebecca Pawlo, Anja Boman, Meta Velander, Borje Mellvig.

1802 LOVING FEELING. (U-M Film Distributors-1969). Suzanne Day, Georgina Ward; Stevee Day, Simon Brent; Carol Taylor, Paula Patterson; Scott, John Railton; Phillip Peterson, Peter Dixon; Christine, Heather Kyd; Jane, Carol Dunningham; Belly Dancer, Sonya Benjamin; Old Man on Beach, Paul Endersby; The Model, Francoise Pasca; Station Sound Mixer, Richard Bartlett; Restaurant Manager, Allen John.

1803 THE LOVING TOUCH. (Medford-1970). Kenneth, Lawrence Montaigne; Valeria, Joanne Meredith; Stacy, Elizabeth Plumb; Marco, Frank Cuva; Attorney, John Vincent.

1804 LUDWIG. (MGM-1973). Ludwig, Helmut Berger; Elizabeth, Romy Schneider; Wagner, Trevor Howard; Cosima Von Bulow, Silvana Mangano; Hoffman, Gert Frobe; Durcheim, Helmut Griem; Queen Mother, Isabella Telezynska; Count von Holstein, Umberto Orsini; Prince Otto, John Moulder Brown;

Sophie, Sonia Petrova; Joseph Kainz, Folker Bohnet; Lila, Adriana Asti; Richard Hornig, Marc Porel; Countess Ida, Nora Ricci; Hans Von Bulow, Mark Burns; Mayor, Maurizio Bonuglia; Alexander Allerson, Bert Bloch, Manfred Furst, Kurt Grosskurt, Anna Maria Hanschke, Gerhard Herter, Jan Linhart, Carla Mancini, Gernot Mohner, Clara Moustawcesky, Alain Naya, Allesandro Perella, Karl Heinz Peters, Wolfram Schaerf, Henning Schluter, Helmut Stern, Eva Tavazzi, Louise Vincent, Gunnar Warner, Karl Heinz Windhorst, Rayka Yurit.

1805 LUDWIG: REQUIEM FOR A VIRGIN KING. (TMS-1974). Harry Baer, Peter Kern, Ingrid Caven, Hanna Kohler, Peter Moland, Siggi Graue, Gunter Kaufmann.

1806 LUMINOUS PROCURESS. (New Line-1972). Pandora, Steven Solberg, Ronald Farrell, Doro Franco, Cherel Fitzpatrick.

1807 LUPO. (Cannon-1971). Lupo, Yuda Barkan; Albert, Gabi Amrani; Mathilda, Esther Greenberg; Mr. Goldwasser, Yuda Efroni; Mrs. Goldwasser, Lia Konig; Rachel, Avirama Golan; Noam, Moti Giladi; Esther, Shoshik Shani; Elimelech, Jacob Ben-Sira; Sgt. -Major Goldberg, Arik Lavi; Marjor, Pinhas Koren; Sgt. Gabriella, Tzipi Zavit; Military Police, Pshik Levi; Ruthie, Naomi Golan; Aliza, Tikva Azziz; Yoske, David Smadar; Adivi, Shlomo Barshavit.

1808 LUST FOR A VAMPIRE. (American Continental-1971). Giles, Ralph Bates; Countess, Barbara Jefford; Janet, Suzanna Leigh; Richard, Macahel Johnson; Mircalla/Carmilla, Yutte Stensgaard; Count, Mike Raven.

1809 LUV. (Columbia-1967). Harry Berlin, Jack Lemmon; Milt Manville, Peter Falk; Ellen Manville, Elaine May; Linda, Nina Wayne; Attorney Goodhart, Eddie Mayerhoff; Doyle, Paul Hartman; Vandergrist, Severn Darden.

1810 MACBETH. (Columbia-1971). Macbeth, Jon Finch; Lady Macbeth, Francesca Annis; Banquo, Martin Shaw; Duncan, Nicholas Selby; Ross, John Stride; Malcolm, Stephen Chase; Donalbain, Paul Shelley; Macduff, Terence Bayler; Lennox, Andrew Laurence; Mentieth, Frank Wylie; Angus, Bernard Archard; Caithness, Bruce Purchase; Fleance, Keith Chegwin; Seyton, Noel Davis; Young Witch, Noelle Rimmington; Blind Witch, Maisie MacFarquhar; First Witch, Elsie Taylor; Cawdor, Vic Abbott; King's Grooms, Bill Drysdale, Roy Jones; Gentlewoman, Patricia Mason; First Minor Thane, Ian Hogg; 2nd Minor Thane, Geoffrey Reed; 3rd Minor Thane, Nigel Ashton; Macduff's son, Mark Dightam; Lady Macduff, Diane Fletcher; Doctor, Richard Pearson; Porter, Sydney Bromley.

1810a McGUIRE, GO HOME. (Continental-1966). Major McGuire, Dirk Bogarde; Haghios, George Chakiris; Juno Kozani, Susan Strasberg; Baker, Denholm Elliott; Skyros, Gregoire Aslan; Emile, Colin Campbell; Dr. Andros, Joseph Furst; Mrs. Andros, Katherine Kath; Prinos, George Pastell; Alkis, Paul Stassino; Colonel Park, Nigel Stock.

1810b McHALE'S NAVY JOINS THE AIR FORCE. (Universal-1965). Capt. Binghamton, Joe Flynn; Ensign Parker, Tim Conway; Lt. Carpenter, Bob Hastings; Christy, Gary Vinson; Tinker, Billy Sands; Virgil, Edson Stroll; Willy, John Wright; Fuji, Yoshio Yoda; Happy Haines, Gavin MacLeod; General Harkness, Tom Tully; Smitty, Susan Silo; Colonel Platt, Henry Beckman; Lt. Wilbur Harkness, Ted Bessell; Madge, Jean Hale; Major Grady, Cliff Norton; Dimitri, Jacques Aubuchon; Admiral Doyle, Willis Bouchey; Vogel, Berkeley Harris; Tresh, Tony Franke; Lt. Wilson, Clay Tanner; Russian Seamen, Jack Bernardi, Norman Leavitt, Joe Ploski, Andy Albin.

1811 MACHIBUSE. (Toho-1971). Toshiro Mifune, Shintaro Katsu, Kinnosuhe Nakamura, Ruriko Saaoka, Yujiro Ishihara.

1812 MACHINE GUN McCAIN. (Columbia-1970). Hank McCain, John Cassavetes; Irene Tucker, Britt Ekland; Charlie Adamo, Peter Falk; Don Francesco, Gabriele Ferzetti; Don Salvatore, Salvo Randone; Jack McCain, Pierluigi Apra; Rosemary Scott, Gena Rowlands; Joni Adama, Florinda Bolkan; Margaret De Marco, Margherita Guzzinati; Abe Stilberman, Stephan Zacharias; Duke Mazzanga, Luigi Pistilli; Joby Cuda, Jim Morrison; Barclay, Claudio Viava; Gennarino Esposito, Ermanno Consolazione; Assunta Esposito, Annabella Andreoli; Chuck Regan, Val Avery; Fred Tecosky, Dennis Sallas; Britten, Jack Ackerman; Pepe, Billy Lee.

1813 MACHO CALLAHAN. (AVCO Embassy-1970). Macho, David Janssen; Alexandra, Jean Seberg; Duffy, Lee J. Cobb; Harry, James Booth; Juan, Pedro Armendariz Jr.; David, David Carradine; Yancy, Bo Hopkins; Senior Officer, Richard Anderson; Girl, Diane Ladd; Jailer, Matt Clark; Mulvey, Richard Evans; McIntyre, Robert Morgan.

1814 THE MACK. (Cinerama-1973). Goldie, Max Julien; Hank, Don Gordon; Slim, Richard Pryor; Lulu, Carol Speed; Olinga, Roger E. Mosley; Pretty Tony, Dick Williams; Jed, William C. Watson; Fatman, George Murdock; Mother, Juanita Moore; Blind Man, Paul Harris; Chico, Kai Hernandez; China Doll, Annazette Chase; Baltimore Bob, Junero Jennings; Sgt. Duncan, Lee Duncan; Announcer, Stu Gilliam; Diane, Sandra Brown; Jesus Christ, Christopher Brooks; Desk Sergeant, Fritz Ford; Hotel Trick, John Vick; Big Woman, Norma McClure; Laughing David, David Mauro; Allen Van, Willie Redman, Frank Ward, Ted Ward, Willie

Ward, Andrew Ward, Roosevelt Taylor, Jay Payton, Terrible Tom, Bill Barnes, Jack Hunter.

1815 MacKENNA'S GOLD. (Columbia-1969). MacKenna, Gregory Peck; Colorado, Omar Sharif; Sergeant Tibbs, Telly Savalas; Inga, Camilla Sparv; Sanchez, Keenan Wynn; Heshke, Julie Newmar; Prairie Dog, Eduardo Ciannelli; Besh, Rudy Diaz; Hachita, Ted Cassidy; Avila, Dick Peabody; Monkey, Robert Phillips; Young Englishman, J. Robert Porter; Laguna, Pepe Callahan; Lieutenant, Duke Hobbie; Old Man, Trevor Bardette; Apache Woman, Madeleine Taylor Holmes; Adams' Boy, John Garfield Jr.; The Pima Squaw, Shelley Morrison; The Editor, Lee J. Cobb; The Storekeeper, Burgess Meredith; Old Adams, Edward G. Robinson; The Preacher, Raymond Massey; Older Englishman, Anthony Quayle; Ben Baker, Eli Wallach; Narrator, Victor Jory.

1815a THE McKENZIE BREAK. (United Artists-1970). Capt. Connor, Brian Keith; Schluetter, Helmut Griem; Maj. Perry, Ian Hendry; Gen. Kerr, Jack Watson; Sgt. Cox, Patrick O'Connell; Neuchl, Horst Janson; Von Sperrle, Alexander Allerson; Kranz, John Abineri; Lt. Hall, Constantin de Goguel; Schmidt, Tom Kepinski; Hochbauer, Eric Allan; Sgt. Bell, Caroline Mortimer; Cpl. Watt, Mary Larkin; Berger, Gregg Palmer; Unger, Michael Sheard; Fullgrabe, Ingo Mogendorf; Dichter, Franz Van Norde; Accomplice, Desmond Perry; Guard Foss, Jim Mooney; Dispatcher, Vernon Hayden; Scots Lassie, Maura Kelly.

1816 THE MACKINTOSH MAN. (Warner Bros.-1973). Rearden, Paul Newman; Mrs. Smith, Dominique Sanda; Sir George Wheeler, James Mason; Mackintosh, Harry Andrews; Slade, Ian Bannen; Brown, Michael Hordern; Soames-Trevelyan, Nigel Patrick; Brunskill, Peter Vaughan; Judge, Roland Culver; Taafe, Percy Herbert; Jack Summers, Robert Land; Gerda, Jenny Runacre; Buster, John Bindon; Prosecutor, Hugh Manning; Malta Police Commissioner, Wolfe Morris; O'Donovan, Noel Purcell; Jervis, Donald Webster; Palmer, Keith Bell; Warder, Niall MacGinnis.

1817 MACON COUNTY LINE. (American International-1974). Chris Dixon, Alan Vint; Jenny, Cheryl Waters; Hamp, Geoffrey Lewis; Carol Morgan, Joan Blackman; Wayne Dixon, Jesse Vint; Deputy Morgan, Max Baer; Deputy, Sam Gilman; Murderers, Timothy Scott, James Gammon; Luke Morgan, Leif Garrett.

1818 McQ. (Warner Bros.-1974). John Wayne, Eddie Albert, Diana Muldaur, Colleen Dewhurst, Clu Gulager, David Huddleston, Jim Watkins, Al Lettieri, Julie Adams, Roger E. Mosley, William Bryant, Joe Tornatore, Richard Kelton, Richard Eastham, Dick Friel, Fred Waugh.

1819 MACUNAIMA. (New Line Cinema-1972). Black Macunaima, Grande Otelo; White Macunaima/Super Mother, Paulo Jose; The Capitalist, Jardel Filho; Ci, Dina Sfat; Jigue, Milton Goncalves; Maanape, Rodolfo Arena; Joana Fomm, Maria Do Rosario, Maria Lucia Dahl, Miriam Muniz, Edi Siqueira, Carmen Palhares, Rafael Carvalho, Carolina Withaker, Hugo Carvana, Zeze Macedo, Wilza Carla, Maria Clara Pellegrino, Maria Leticia, Valdir Onofre, Guaraci Rodrigues, Nazareth Ohana, Tania Marcia, Marcia Tania.

1820 THE MAD BOMBER. (Cinemation-1973). Geronimo, Vince Edwards; William, Chuck Connors; Fromley, Neville Brand; Blake, Hank Brandt; Fromley's Victim, Christina Hart; Martha, Faith Quabius; Mrs. Fromley, Ilona Wilson; Anne, Nancy Honnold.

1821 THE MAD EXECUTIONERS. (Paramount-1965). Hansjorg Felmy, Maria Perschy, Dieter Borsche, Wolfgang Preiss, Chris Howland.

1822 MAD MONSTER PARTY. (Embassy-1967). Frankenstein, Dracula, Werewolf, Creature, Dr. Jekyll & Mr. Hyde, Mummy, Hunchback of Notre Dame, and the talents of Boris Karloff, Phyllis Diller, Ethel Ennis, and Gale Garnett.

1823 THE MAD ROOM. (Columbia-1969). Ellen Hardy, Stella Stevens; Mrs. Armstrong, Shelley Winters; Sam Aller, Skip Ward; Chris, Carol Cole; Nate, Severn Darden; Mrs. Racine, Beverly Garland; George Hardy, Michael Burns; Mandy Hardy, Barbara Sammeth; Mrs. Ericson, Jenifer Bishop; Edna, Gloria Manon; Dr. Marion Kincaid, Lloyd Haynes; Armand Racine, Lou Kane.

1824 MADAME BUTTERFLY. (Rizzoli-1966). Cio Cio San, Kaoru Yachigusa; Suzuki, Michiko Tanaka; Pinkerton, Nicola Filacuridi; Sharpless, Ferdinanco Lidonni; Yamadori, Satoshi Nakamura; Goro, Kiyoshi Takagi; Zio Bonzo, Yoshio Kosugi; The Takarazuka Ballet.

1825 MADAME X. (Universal-1966). Holly Anderson, Lana Turner; Clay Anderson, John Forsythe; Phil Benton, Ricardo Montalban; Dan Sullivan, Burgess Meredith; Estelle, Constance Bennett; Clay Jr. (grown up), Keir Dullea; Clay Jr. (as a child), Teddy Quinn; Christian Torben, John Van Dreelen; Mimsy, Virginia Grey; Michael Spalding, Warren Stevens; Judge, Carl Benton Reid; Dr. Evans, Frank Maxwell; Nurse Riborg, Karen Verne; Carter, Joe De Santis; Combs, Frank Marth; Sgt. Riley, Bing Russell; Manuel Lopez, Teno Pollick; Bromley, Jeff Burton.

1826 MADAME ZENOBIA. (Screencom-1973). Marcia, Tina Russell; John, Derald Delancey; Madame Zenobia, Elizabeth Donovan; Eric, Rick Livermore; Lucy, Inger Kissen; Rocky,

Frank Martin; Clancy, David Jones; Old Man, J. C. Klitz; Heavenly Wench, Claudia Miro.

1827 MADDALENA. (Rand & Co.-1971). Maddalena, Lisa Gaxtoni; Priest, Eric Woofe; Husband, Ivo Garani.

1828 MADE FOR EACH OTHER. (20th Century-Fox-1971). Pandora, Renee Taylor; Giggy, Joseph Bologna; Giggy's Father, Paul Sorvino; Giggy's Mother, Olympia Dukakis; Pandora's Mother, Helen Verbit; Helen's Father, Louis Zorich; Dr. Furro, Norman Shelly.

1829 MADE IN ITALY. (Royal-1967). Bored Socialite, Marina Berti; Her Husband, Claudio Gora; Their Friend, Lionello Pio Di Savola; Fiance, Lando Buzzanca; Fiancee, Yolanda Modio; The Lover, Walter Chiari; The Married Woman, Lea Massari; Defenseless Creature, Virna Lisi; Her Former Sweetheart, Giulio Bosetti; Teenager, Catherine Spaak; Her Beau, Fabrizio Moroni; Lady with Ferrari, Sylva Koscina; Young Man in Fiat, Jean Sorel; Roman Citizen, Nino Manfredi; Young Wife, Rossella Falk; Errant Husband, Alberto Sordi; Attractive Lady, Claudie Lange; Mother, Anna Magnani; Father, Andrea Checchi.

1830 MADE IN PARIS. (MGM-1966). Maggie Scott, Ann-Margret; Marc Fontaine, Louis Jourdan; Herb Stone, Richard Crenna; Irene Chase, Edie Adams; Ted Barclay, John McGiver; Georges, Marcel Dalio; Cecile, Matilda Calnan; Denise Marton, Jacqueline Beer; Attendant, Marcel Hillaire; Elise, Michele Montau; American Bar Singer, Reta Shaw; Count Basie and His Octet, Mongo Santamaria and His Band.

1831 MADE IN U.S.A. (Pathe Contemporary-1967). Paula Nelson, Anna Karina; Richard Widmark, Laszlo Szabo; Donald Siegel, Jean-Pierre Leaud; David Goodis, Yves Alfonso; Edgar Typhus, Ernest Menzer.

1832 MADEMOISELLE. (Lopert-1966). Mademoiselle, Jeanne Moreau; Manou, Ettore Manni; Bruno, Keith Skinner; Anton, Umberto Orsini; Annette, Jane Berretta; Vievotte, Mony Rey; The Priest, Georges Douking; Lisa, Rosine Luguet; Police Sergeant, Gabriel Gobin; Marcel, Pierre Collet; Roger, Jean Gras; Rene, Georges Aubert; Armand, Antoine Marin; Boulot, Gerard Darrieu; Floor Farmer, Charles Lavialle; Robert Larcebeau, Rene Hell, Jacques Chevalier, Claire Ifrane, Denise Peron, Annie Savarin, Valerie Girodias, L. Chevallier, Laure Paillette, Catherine Parquier, Jacques Monod, Paul Barge.

1833 MADHOUSE. (American International-1974). Vincent Price, Peter Cushing, Robert Quarry, Adrienne Corri, Natasha Pyne, Michael Parkinson, Linda Hayden, Barry Dennen, Ellis Dale, Catherine Willmer, John Garrie, Ian Thompson,

Jenny Lee Wright, Julie Crosthwaite, Peter Halliday.

1834 MADIGAN. (Universal-1968). Det. Daniel Madigan, Richard Widmark; Comm. Anthony X. Russell, Henry Fonda; Julia Madigan, Inger Stevens; Det. Rocco Bonaro, Harry Guardino; Chief Insp. Charles Kane, James Whitmore; Tricia Bentley, Susan Clark; Midget Castiglione, Michael Dunne; Barney Benesch, Steve Ihnat; Hughie, Don Stroud; Jonesy, Sheree North; Ben Williams, Warren Stevens; Dr. Taylor, Raymond St. Jacques; Bert Freed, Harry Bellaver, Frank Marth, Lloyd Gough, Virginia Gregg, Toian Machinga, Rita Lynn, Robert Granere, Henry Beckman, Woodrow Parfrey, Dallas Mitchell, Lloyd Haines, Ray Montgomery, Seth Allen, Philippa Bevans, Kay Turner, Diane Sayer, Conrad Bain, Ed Crowley, John McLiam, William Bramley.

1835 MADIGAN'S MILLIONS. (American International-1970). Jason, Dustin Hoffman; Vicky, Elsa Martinelli; Madigan, Cesar Romero.

1836 THE MADWOMAN OF CHAILLOT. (Warner Bros. -7 Arts-1969). Countess Aurelia, Katharine Hepburn; The Broker, Charles Boyer; Dr. Jadin, Claude Dauphin; Josephine, Edith Evans; The Reverend, John Gavin; The General, Paul Henreid; The Commissar, Oscar Homolka; Constance, Margaret Leighton; Gabrielle, Giulietta Masina; Irma, Nanette Newman; Roderick, Richard Chamberlain; The Chairman, Yul Brynner; The prospector, Donald Pleasence; The Ragpicker, Danny Kaye; Police Sergeant, Fernand Gravet; The Folksinger, Gordon Heath; Julius, Gerald Sim.

1837 MAEDCHEN IN UNIFORM. (7 Arts-1965). Manuela von Meinhardis, Romy Schneider; Fraulein von Bernberg, Lilli Palmer; Headmistress, Therese Giehse; Mia, Christine Kaufmann.

1838 MAFIA. (American International-1970). Rosa, Claudia Cardinale; Bellodi, Franco Nero; Mariano, Lee J. Cobb; Pizzuco, Nehemiah Persoff; Parinedu, Sergio Reggani; Catherina, Rosanna Lopapero.

1839 THE MAGIC CHRISTIAN. (Commonwealth-1970). Sir Guy Grand, Peter Sellers; Youngman Grand, Ringo Starr; Aunt Agnes, Isabel Jeans; Aunt Esther, Caroline Balkiston; Klaus, Wilfred Hyde-White; Oxford Coach, Richard Attenborough; Psychiatrist, Leonard Frey; Hamlet, Laurence Harvey; Vampire, Christopher Lee; Warden, Spike Milligan; Slave Priestess, Raquel Welch.

1840 THE MAGIC GARDEN OF STANLEY SWEETHEART. (MGM-1970). Stanley Sweetheart, Don Johnson; Shayne, Linda Gillin; Danny, Michael Greer; Cathy, Diane Hull; Fran, Holly Near; Andrea, Victoria Racimo; Dr. Arthur Osgood, and man in cafe, Brandon Maggart.

1841 THE MAGNIFICENT CONCUBINE. (Frank Lee-1966). Li Li-hua, Yen Chuan, Chao Lei, Li Hsiang-Chun, Yang Chih-ching, Ku Wen-tsung, Ho Pin, Lin Ching, Weng Mu-Lan, Lily Mo Chau.

1842 THE MAGNIFICENT CUCKOLD. (Continental-1965). Maria Grazia Artusi, Claudia Cardinale; Andrea Artusi, Ugo Tognazzi; Corna D'Oro, Bernard Blier; Christiana, Michele Girardon; Belisario, Salvo Randone; Presidente, Jose Luis De Villalonga; Assessore, Gian Maria Volonte; Gabriele, Paul Guers; Doctor, Philippe Nicaud; Wanda, Suzy Andersen; Guest, Alfonso Sansone; 2nd Guest, Ettore Mattia; Brett Halsey, Jean Claudio.

1843 THE MAGNIFICENT SEVEN RIDE! (United Artists-1972). Chris, Lee Van Cleef; Laurie Gunn, Stefanie Powers; Arilla, Mariette Hartley; Noah Forbes, Michael Callan; Skinner, Luke Askew; Pepe Carral, Pedro Armendariz Jr.; Walt Drummond, William Lucking; Hayes, James B. Sikking; Madge Buchanan, Melissa Murphy; Shelly Donavan, Darrell Larson; Scott Elliott, Ed Lauter; Martha, Caroly Conwell; Warden, Jason Wingreen; Mrs. Donavan, Allyn Ann McLerie; Skinner's Woman, Elizabeth Thompson; Jim MacKay, Ralph Waite; De Toro's Woman, Rita Rogers; Bob Allan, Robert Jaffe; Hank Allan, Gary Busey; Juan De Toro, Rodolfo Acosta.

1844 MAGNUM FORCE. (Warner Bros.-1973). Harry Callahan, Clint Eastwood; Lt. Briggs, Hal Holbrook; Early Smith, Felton Perry; Charlie McCoy, Mitchell Ryan; Davis, David Soul; Sweet, Tim Matheson; Grimes, Robert Urich; Astrachan, Kip Niven; Carol McCoy, Christine White; Sunny, Adele Yoshioka.

1845 THE MAGUS. (20th Century-Fox-1968). Maurice Conchis, Anthony Quinn; Nicholas Urfe, Michael Caine; Lily, Candice Bergen; Anne, Anna Karina; Meli, Paul Stassino; Anton, Julian Glover; Kapetan, Takis Emmanuel; Andreas-Priest, George Pastell; Soula, Danielle Noel; German Officer, Jerome Willis; Maria, Ethel Farrugia; Goatherd, Andreas Melandrinos; Second Partisan, George Kafkaris; Party Host, Anthony Newlands; Third Partisan, Stack Constantino; Young Conchis, Roger Lloyd Pack; Captain Wimmel, Corin Redgrave.

1846 MAHLER. (1974). Gustav Mahler, Robert Powell; Alma Mahler, Georgina Hale; Bernhard Mahler, Lee Montague; Max, Richard Morant; Marie Mahler, Rosalie Crutchley; Uncle Arnold, Benny Lee; Aunt Rosa, Miriam Karlin; Angela Down, David Collings, Ronald Pickup, Antonia Ellis, Ken Colley, Arnold Yarrow, Dana Gillespie, Elaine Delmar,

Michael Southgate, Otto Diamant, Gary Rich, Peter Eyre, George Coulouris, Andrew Faulds, David Trevena, Sarah McLellan, Claire McLellan.

1847 MAID IN SWEDEN. (Cannon-1971). Kristina Lindberg, Monika Ekman, Krister Ekman, Per Axel Arosenius, Tina Hedstrom, Vivianne Ojengen, Jim Engelau.

1848 A MAIDEN FOR THE PRINCE. (Royal Films International-1968). Prince Don Vincenzo Gonzaga, Vittorio Gassman; Giulia, Virna Lisi; Ippolito, Philippe Leroy; Duke of Mantova, Tino Buazzelli; Marchesa of Pepara, Maria Grazia Buccella; Marchese Liginio, Vittorio Caprioli; The Matron, Paola Borboni; Margherita Farnese, Anna Maria Guarnieri; Duchess of Mantova, Giusi Raspani Dandolo; Luciano Mandolfo, Esmeralda Ruspoll, Mario Scaccia, Jose Luis De Villalonga, Anna Maria Polani, Claude Lange, Fredo Bianchini, Leopoldo Trieste, Mariangela Giordano.

1849 THE MAIN CHANCE. (Embassy-1966). Potter, Gregoire Aslan; Michael Blake, Edward De Souza; Christine, Tracy Reed; Joe Hayes, Stanley Meadows; Ross, Jack Smethurst; Miller, Bernard Stone; Carter, Will Stampe; Butler, Julian Strange; Chauffeur, Tony Bailey; Madame Rozanne, Joyce Barbour.

1850 MAJIN. (Daiei-1968). Kozasa Hanabusa, Miwa Takada; Tadafumi Hanabusa, Yoshihiko Aoyama; Kogenta, Jun Fujimaki; Samanosuke, Ryutaro Gomi; Gunjuro, Tatsuo Endo.

1851 MAJOR DUNDEE. (Columbia-1965). Major Amos Dundee, Charlton Heston; Capt. Ben Tyreen, Richard Harris; Lieut. Graham, Jim Hutton; Samuel Potts, James Coburn; Tim Ryan, Michael Anderson Jr.; Teresa Santiago, Senta Berger; Sgt. Gomez, Mario Adorf; Aesop, Brock Peters; O. W. Hadley, Warren Oates; Sgt. Chillum, Ben Johnson; R. G. Armstrong, L. Q. Jones, Slim Pickens, Karl Swenson, Michael Pate, John Davis Chandler, Dub Taylor, Albert Carrier, Jose Carlos Ruiz, Aurora Clavell, Begonia Palacios, Enrique Lucero, Francisco Reyguera.

1852 MAKE A FACE. (Sperling-1971). Nina, Karen Sperling; Dr. Davis, Paolo Patti; Stranger, Davis Bernstein; Larry, Nicolas Surovy; George, Joe Horan; Pucci Lady, Jackie Doroshow; Second Stranger, David Franciosi; Delivery Boy, John Chin.

1853 MAKE LIKE A THIEF. (Emerson-1966). Bart Lanigan, Richard Long; Arvo Mald, Ake Lindman; Marja, Pirkko Mannola; Toini, Rose-Marie Precht; Leonard Weston, Juhani Kumpalinen; Helvi, Aulekkki Tarnanen; Gunman, Esko Salamen; Detective, Palmer Thompson.

1854 MAKING IT. (20th Century-Fox-1971). Phil Fuller, Kristoffer Tabori; Betty Fuller, Joyce Van Patten; Yvonne, Marlyn Mason; Wilkie, Bob Balaban; Mallory, Lawrence Pressman; Mrs. Wilson, Louise Latham; Ames, John Fiedler; Debbie, Sherry Miles; Skeeter, Denny Miller; Librarian, Doro Merande.

1855 MALE COMPANION. (International Classics-1966). Antoine, Jean Pierre Cassel; Isabelle, Catherine Deneuve; Balthazar, Jean-Pierre Marielle; Nicole, Irini Demick; Clara, Annie Girardot; Maria, Sandra Milo; Krieg von Spiel, Dalio; The Prince, Jean-Claude Brialy; Grandfather, Andre Luguet; Louisette, Valerie Lagrange; Professor Gaetano, Paolo Stoppa; Benvenuto, Adolfo Celi.

1856 MALE HUNT. (Pathe Contemporary-1965). Fernand, Jean-Paul Belmondo; Tony, Jean-Claude Brialy; Denise, Catherine Deneuve; Sandra, Francoise Dorleac; Isabelle, Micheline Presle; Julien, Claude Rich; Gisele, Marie Laforet; Sophie, Marie Dubois; Monsieur Heurtin, Bernard Blier; Madame Armande, Helen Duc; Papatakes, Francis Blanche; Professor Lartois, Michel Serrault; Flora, Bernadette Lafont; Georgina, Mireille Darc.

1857 MAME. (Warner Bros. -1974). Mame, Lucille Ball; Vera Charles, Beatrice Arthur; Beauregard Burnside, Robert Preston; Patrick, Bruce Davison; Patrick as a boy, Kirby Furlong; Agnes Gooch, Jane Connell; Ito, George Chiang; Sally Cato, Joyce Van Patten; Gloria, Doria Cook; Mr. Upson, Don Porter; Mrs. Upson, Audrey Christie; Mr. Babcock, John McGiver; Pegeen, Bobbi Jordan; Peter, Patrick Laborteaux; Mother Burnside, Lucille Benson; Cousin Fan, Ruth McDevitt; Uncle Jeff, Burt Mustin; Floorwalker, James Brodhead; Stage Manager, Leonard Stone; Ralph Divine, Roger Price; Judge Bregoff, John Wheeler; Fred Kates, Ned Wertimer; Fat Lady, Alice Nunn; Bunny, Jerry Ayres; Midge, Michele Nichols; Boyd, Eric Gordon; Emily, Barbara Bosson.

1858 THE MAN. (Paramount-1972). Douglass Dilman, James Earl Jones; Jim Talley, Martin Balsam; Senator Watson, Burgess Meredith; Noah Calvin, Lew Ayres; Arthur Eaton, William Windom; Kay Eaton, Barbara Rush; Robert Wheeler, Georg Stanford Brown; Wanda, Janet MacLachlan; Wheeler's Lawyer, Martin Brooks; Hugh Gaynor, Simon Scott; South African Consul, Patric Knowles; Webson, Bob Doqui; Ma Blore, Anne Seymour; Secret Service Man, Edward Faulkner; Congressman Hand, Gilbert Green; Reporter Gilbert, Lew Brown; Chief Justice Williams, Philip Bourneuf; Reverend Otis Waldren, Reginald Fenderson; Mrs. Smelker, Elizabeth Ross; Haley, Barry Russo; Pierce, Gary Walberg; Press Secretary, Ted Hartley; Congressman Streller, Lawrence Cook; Congressman Eckworth, Vince Howard;

Congressman Parmel, Leonard Stone; Jack Benny, Howard K. Smith, William Lawrence.

1859 A MAN AND A WOMAN. (Allied Artists-1966). Anne Gauthier, Anouk Aimee; Jean-Louis Duroc, Jean-Louis Trintignant; Pierre Gauthier, Pierre Barouh; Valerie Duroc, Valerie Lagrange; Head Mistress, Simone Paris; Antoine Duroc, Antoine Sire; Francoise Gauthier, Souad Amidou; Jean Louis' Mistress, Yane Barry.

1860 MAN AND BOY. (Levitt-Pickman-1972). Caleb Revers, Bill Cosby; Ivy Revers, Gloria Foster; Sheriff Mossmann, Leif Erickson; Billy Revers, George Spell; Lee Christmas, Douglas Turner Ward; Stretch, John Anderson; Caine, Henry Silva; Atkins, Dub Taylor; Rosita, Shelley Morrison; Nate Hodges, Yaphet Kotto.

1861 A MAN CALLED ADAM. (Embassy-1966). Adam Johnson, Sammy Davis Jr.; Willie Ferguson, Louis Armstrong; Nelson Davis, Ossie Davis; Claudia Ferguson, Cicely Tyson; Vincent, Frank Sinatra Jr.; Manny, Peter Lawford; Himself, Mel Torme; Theo, Lola Falana; Martha, Jeanette Du Bois; Les, Johnny Brown; Leroy, George Rhodes; George, Michael Silva; Bobby Gales, Michael Lipton.

1862 A MAN CALLED DAGGER. (MGM-1968). Dick Dagger, Paul Mantee; Harper Davis, Terry Moore; Rudolph Koffman, Jan Murray; Ingrid, Sue Ane Langdon; Erica, Eileen O'Neill; Joy, Maureen Arthur; Karl Rainer, Leonard Stone; Otto, Richard Kiel; Girl in Auto, Mimi Dillard; Dr. Grulik, Bruno Ve Sota.

1863 A MAN CALLED GANNON. (Universal-1969). Gannon, Tony Franciosa; Jess Washburn, Michael Sarrazin; Beth, Judi West; Matty, Susan Oliver; Capper, John Anderson; Sheriff Polaski, David Sheiner; Amos, James Westerfield; Lou, Gavin MacLeod; Maz, Eddie Firestone; Delivery Rider, Ed Peck; Harry, Harry Davis; Goff, Robert Sorrells; Cass, Terry Wilson; Louisa, Eddra Gale; Ben, Harry Basch; Bo, James Callahan; Ike, Cliff Potter; Mills, Jason Evers; Railroad Lineman, Jack Perkins.

1864 A MAN CALLED HORSE. (National General-1970). Lord John Morgan, Richard Harris; Buffalo Cow Head, Judith Anderson; Batise, Jean Gascon; Yellow Hand, Manu Tupou; Running Deer, Corinna Tsopei; Joe, Dub Taylor; Bent, William Jordan; Ed, James Gammon; Black Eagle, Edward Little Sky; Thron Rose, Lina Marin; Elk Woman, Tamara Garina; He-Wolf, Michael Baseleon; Leaping Buck, Manuel Padilla; Striking Bear, Terry Leonard; Medicine Men, Iron Eyes Cody, Richard Fools Bull, Ben Eagleman.

1865 THE MAN CALLED NOON. (National General-1973). Noon,

Richard Crenna; Rimes, Stephen Boyd; Fan, Rosanna Schiaffino; Judge, Farley Granger; Peg, Patty Shepard; Janish, Angel Del Pozo; Bayles, Howard Ross; Kissling, Aldo Sambrell; Henneker, Jose Jaspe; Lang, Charley Bravo; Brakeman, Ricardo Palacios; Ford, Fernando Hilbeck; Cherry, Jose Canalejas; Charlie, Cesar Burner; Cristobal, Julian Ugarte; Mexican, Barta Barri; Old Mexican, Adolfo Thous; Rancher, Bruce Fischer.

1866 A MAN COULD GET KILLED. (Universal-1966). William Beddoes, James Garner; Aurora-Celeste, Melina Mercouri; Amy Franklin, Sandra Dee; Steve-Antonio, Tony Franciosa; Hatton-Jones, Robert Coote; Dr. Mathieson, Roland Culver; Florian, Gregoire Aslan; Sir H. Frazier, Cecil Parker; Mrs. Mathieson, Dulcie Gray; Politanu, Martin Benson; Zarik, Peter Illing; Ship's Captain, Niall MacGinnis; Inspector Rodriguez, Virgilio Texera; Miss Bannister, Isabel Dean; Osman, Daniele Vargas; Abdul, Nello Pazzafini; Lazlot, George Pastell; Milo, Arnold Diamond; Heinrich, Conrad Anderson; Max, Eric Domain; Carmot, Pasquale Fasciano; Miss Nolan, Ann Firbank.

1867 A MAN FOR ALL SEASONS. (Columbia-1966). Sir Thomas More, Paul Scofield; Alice More, Wendy Hiller; Thomas Cromwell, Leo McKern; King Henry VIII, Robert Shaw; Cardinal Wolsey, Orson Welles; Margaret More, Susannah York; Duke of Norfolk, Nigel Davenport; Rich, John Hurt; William Roper, Corin Redgrave; Matthew, Colin Blakely; Averil Machin, Yootha Joyce; Anne Boleyn, Vanessa Redgrave.

1868 THE MAN FROM BUTTON WILLOW. (United Screen Arts-1965). Voices of Dale Robertson, Howard Keel, Edgar Buchanan, Barbara Jean Wong, Herschel Bernardi, Ross Martin, Verna Felton, Shep Menken, Pinto Colvig, Cliff Edwards, Thurl Ravenscrift, John Hiestand, Clarence Nash, Edward Platt, Buck Buchanan.

1869 MAN FROM COCODY. (American International-1966). Jean Marais, Liselotte Pulver, Philippe Clay, Jacques Morel, Maria Bracia Buccela, Nancy Holloway, Robert Dalban.

1870 MAN FROM DEEP RIVER. (Brenner-1973). Ivan Rassimov, Me Me Lay.

1871 THE MAN FROM O.R.G.Y. AND THE REAL GONE GIRLS. (Cinemation-1970). Steve, Robert Walker; Luigi, Steve Rossi; Vito, Slappy White; Gina, Louisa Moritz; Lynn Carter, Mark Hannibal, Michel Stany, Mary Marx, Jan Bank, Shannon O'Shea.

1872 MAN IN THE DARK. (Universal-1965). Paul, William Sylvester; Anne, Barbara Shelley; Joan, Elizabeth Shepherd;

Ricky, Alex Davion; Mike, Mark Eden; Himself, Ronnie Carroll; Himself, Barry Aldis; Inspector, Frank Forsyth; Chauffeur, Edward Evans; Dancers, Joy Allen, Unity Grimwood, Wendy Martin.

1873 MAN IN THE WILDERNESS. (Warner Bros.-1971). Zachary, Richard Harris; Capt. Henry, John Huston; Coulter, John Bindon; Longbow, Ben Carruthers; Grace, Prunella Ransome; Indian Chief, Henry Wilcoxon; Fogarty, Percy Herbert; Lowrie, Dennis Waterman.

1874 MAN OF LA MANCHA. (United Artists-1972). Don Quixote de la Mancha/Miguel de Cervantes/Alonso Quijana, Peter O'Toole; Dulcinea/Aldonza, Sophia Loren; Sancho Panza, James Coco; Innkeeper/Governor, Harry Andrews; Sanson Carrasco/Duke, John Castle; Pedro, Brian Blessed; Padre, Ian Richardson; Antonia, Julie Gregg; Housekeeper, Rosalie Crutchley; Barber, Gino Conforti.

1875 MAN OF THE YEAR. (Universal-1973). Coco, Rossana Podesta; Michele, Lando Buzzanca; Achille, Luciano Salce; Marchesa, Adriana Asti; Signora Mezzini, Ira Furstenberg; Giusi, Evi Marandi; Pina, Brigitte Skay; Amelia, Angela Luce; Ersilia, Femi Benussi; Ambrogio, Sandro Dori; Pina, Bernard Skay; Dr. Mezzini, Bernard Blier; Carla, Sylva Koscina.

1876 MAN ON A SWING. (Paramount-1974). Cliff Robertson, Joel Grey, Dorothy Tristan, Elizabeth Wilson, George Voskovec, Ron Weyand, Peter Masterson, Lane Smith, Joe Ponazecki, Christopher Allport.

1877 THE MAN OUTSIDE. (Allied Artists-1969). Bill Maclean, Van Heflin; Kay Sebastian, Heidelinde Weis; Rafe Machek, Pinkas Braun; Nikolai Volkov, Peter Vaughan; Charles Griddon, Charles Gray; Judson Murphy, Paul Maxwell; George Venaxas, Ronnie Barker; Dorothy, Linda Marlowe; Brune Parry, Gary Cockrell; Morehouse, Bill Nagy; Austen, Larry Cross; Detective Supt. Barnes, Archie Duncan; Detective Inspector, Willoughby Gray; Detective Sergeant, Christopher Denham; Land lady, Rita Webb; Carole Ann Ford, Carmel MacSharry, John Sterland, Alex Marchevsky, Paul Armstrong, Hugh Elton, Derek Baker, Frank Crawshaw, Roy Sone, Harry Hutchinson, Gabrielie Drake, Carol Kingsley, Martin Terry, Anna Willoughby, Suzanne Owens.

1878 THE MAN WHO FINALLY DIED. (Goldstone Film Enterprises-1967). Joe Newman, Stanley Baker; Dr. Von Brecht, Peter Cushing; Lisa, Mai Zetterling; Inspector Hofmeister, Eric Portman; Brenner, Niall MacGinnis; Hirsch, Nigel Green; Martha, Barbara Everest; Maria, Georgina Ward; The Professor, Harold Scott; Rahn, James Ottoway; Heinrich, Alfred Burke; Helga, Mela White; Minna, Maya Sorell.

1879 THE MAN WHO HAD POWER OVER WOMEN. (AVCO Embassy-1971). Peter, Rod Taylor; Jody, Carol White; Val, James Booth; Angela, Penelope Horner.

1880 THE MAN WHO HAUNTED HIMSELF. (Levitt-Pickman-1971). Pelham, Roger Moore; Eve, Hildegard Neil; Michael, Alastair Mackenzie; James, Hugh Mackenzie; Luigi, Kevork Malikyan; Bellamy, Thorley Walters; Alexander, Anton Rodgers; Julie, Olga Georges-Picot; Psychiatrist, Freddie Jones; Freeman, John Welsh; Barton, Edward Chapman; Mason, Laurence Hardy.

1881 THE MAN WHO LIES. (Grove-1970). Boris, Jean-Louis Trintignant; Maria, Sylvia Breal; Lisa, Dominique Prado; Laura, Suzana Kocurikova; Sylvia, Sylvia Turbova; Jean, Ivan Mistric; A Man, Julius Vasek.

1882 THE MAN WHO LOVED CAT DANCING. (MGM-1973). Jay, Burt Reynolds; Catherine, Sarah Miles; Lapchance, Lee J. Cobb; Dawes, Jack Warden; Dub, Robert Donner; Crocker, George Hamilton; Billy, Bo Hopkins; Iron Knife, Larry Littlebird; Sudie, Nancy Malone; The Chief, Jay Silverheels; Charlie, Jay Varela; Conductor, Owen Bush; Bartender, Larry Finley; Dream Speaker, Sutero Garcia Jr.

1883 THE MAN WITH CONNECTIONS. (Columbia-1970). Claude, Guy Bedos; The Father, Yves Robert; The Mother, Rosy Varte; Corsican Adjutant, Georges Geret; The Lieutenant, Jean-Pierre Marielle; Tania, Zorica Lozic; The Major, Claude Pieplu; Kudierman, Claude Melki; Arlette, Nina Demestre.

1884 THE MAN WITH THE BALLOONS. (Sigma III-1968). Mario, Marcello Mastroianni; Giovanna, Catherine Spaak; William Berger, Antonio Altoviti, Igi Polidoro, Charlotte Folcher, Sonia Romanoff, Ugo Tognazzi.

1885 THE MAN WITH THE GOLDEN GUN. (United Artists-1974). James Bond, Roger Moore; Scaramanga, Christopher Lee; Mary Goodnight, Britt Ekland; Andrea, Maud Adams; Nick Nack, Herve Villechaize; Sheriff Pepper, Clifton James; Hai Fat, Richard Loo; Hip, Soon Taik Oh; Rodney, Marc Lawrence; M, Bernard Lee; Miss Moneypenny, Lois Maxwell; Lazar, Marne Maitland; Q, Desmond Llewellyn; Dancer Saida, Carmen Sautoy.

1886 THE MAN WITH TWO HEADS. (Mishkin-1972). Dr. William Jekyll/Mr. Blood, Denis De Marne; April Conners, Julia Stratton; Mary Ann Marsden, Gay Feld; Carla, Jacqueline Lawrence; Smithers, Berwick Kaler; Oliver Marsden, Bryan Southcombe; Vicky, Jennifer Summerfield.

1887 MANDRAGOLA. (Europix Consolidated-1966). Lucrezia,

Rosanna Schiaffino; Callimaco, Philippe Leroy; Ligurio, Jean Claude Brialy; Fra Timoteo, Toto; Nicia, Romolo Valli; Lucrezia's Mother, Nilla Pizzi; Siro, Armando Bandini.

1888 MANSON. (American International-1973). Charles Manson, Vincent Bugliosi, Patricia Krenwinkle, Leslie Van Houten, Tex Watson, Robert Beausoliel, Steve Grogan, Bruce Davis, Mary Bruner.

1889 MARA OF THE WILDERNESS. (Allied Artists-1966). Ken Williams, Adam West; Mara Wade, Linda Saunders; Jarnagan, Theo Marcuse; Kelly, Denver Pyle; Dr. Frank Wade, Sean McClory; Mrs. Wade, Eve Brent; "Friday," Roberto Contreras; First Pilot, Ed Kemmer; Second Pilot, Stuart Walsh; Mara Wade (Age 7), Lelia Walsh.

1890 MARAT/SADE (THE PERSECUTION AND ASSASSINATION OF JEAN-PAUL MARAT AS PERFORMED BY THE INMATES OF THE ASYLUM OF CHARENTON UNDER THE DIRECTION OF THE MARQUIS DE SADE.) (United Artists-1967). M. Coulmier, Clifford Rose; Mme. Coulmier, Brenda Kempner; Mlle. Coulmier, Ruth Baker; Herald, Michael Williams; Cucurucu, Freddie Jones; Kokol, Hugh Sullivan; Polpoch, Jonathan Burn; Rossignol, Jeannette Landis; Jacques Roux, Robert Lloyd; Charlotte Corday, Glenda Jackson; Jean-Paul Marat, Ian Richardson; Simonne Evrard, Susan Williamson; Marquis de Sade, Patrick Magee; John Steiner, Mark Jones, Morgan Sheppard, John Harwood, Leon Lissek, Henry Mellor, John Hussey, Mary Allen, Guy Gordon, Michael Farnsworth, Tamara Fuerst, Maroussia Frank, Sheila Grant, Michael Percival, Lyn Pinkney, Carol Raymont, Heather Canning, Jennifer Tudor, Timothy Hardy, Stanford Trowell, Patrick Gowers, Richard Callinan, Michael Gould, Nicholas Moes, Rainier Schuelein.

1891 MARCO MEN. (NMF-1971). Harry, Tom Tryon; Sonia, Laura Guerrieri; Marcos, Jose Bodalo; Sonia, Ana Castor; Mirko Ellis, Jesus Puente, Richard Deacon.

1892 MARCO THE MAGNIFICENT. (MGM-1966). Marco Polo, Horst Bucholz; Kublai Khan, Anthony Quinn; Ackerman, Orson Welles; Emir Alaou, Omar Sharif; Woman With Whip, Elsa Martinelli; The Old Man, Akim Tamiroff; Achmed, Gregoire Aslan; Nazam, Robert Hossein; Marco's Father, Massimo Girotti; Spinello, Folco Lulli; Gogatine, Lee Sue Moon; Nicolo de Vicenza, Jacques Monod; Marco's Uncle, Mica Orlovic; Taha, Mansoureh Rihai.

1893 MARJOE. (Cinema V-1972). Marjoe Gortner.

1894 MARK OF THE DEVIL. (Hallmark-1972). Count Cumberland, Herbert Lom; Baron Christian von Meru, Udo Kier;

Vanessa, Olivera Vuco; Albino, Reggie Nalder; Chief Executioner, Herbert Fux; Michael Maien, Gaby Fuchs, Doris Von Danwitz, Dorothea Carrera, Ingeborg Schoener, Johannes Buzalski, Gunther Clemens, Adrian Hoven, Marlies Peterson.

1895 MARLOWE. (MGM-1969). Philip Marlowe, James Garner; Mavis Wald, Gayle Hunnicutt; Lt. Christy French, Carroll O'Connor; Dolores Gonzales, Rita Moreno; Orfamay Quest, Sharon Farrell; Mr. Crowell, William Daniels; Sonny Steelgrave, H. M. Wynant; Grant W. Hicks, Jackie Coogan; Sgt. Fred Beifus, Kenneth Tobey; Winslow Wong, Bruce Lee; Chuck, Christopher Cary; Oliver Hardy, George Tyne; Julie, Corinne Camacho; Dr. Vincent Lagardie, Paul Stevens; Orrin Quest, Roger Newman; Gumpshaw, Read Morgan; Haven Clausen, Warren Finnerty.

1896 MAROC 7. (Paramount-1968). Simon Grant, Gene Barry; Claudia, Elsa Martinelli; Louise Henderson, Cyd Charisse; Raymond Lowe, Leslie Phillips; Inspector Barrada, Denholm Elliott; Michele Craig, Alexandra Stewart; Professor Bannen, Eric Barker; Freddie, Angela Douglas; Vivienne, Tracy Reed; Suzie, Maggie London; Penny, Penny Riley; Alexa, Ann Norman; Hotel Receptionist, Lionel Blair; Police Officer, Paul Danquah; Abdullah, Tom Lee; Consuela, Anne Padwick; Pablo, Richard Montez; Hotel Manager, Roger Good; Young Photographer, Anthony Bygraves; Tony, Robert Mill.

1897 MAROONED. (Columbia-1969). Charles Keith, Gregory Peck; Jim Pruett, Richard Crenna; Ted Dougherty, David Janssen; Clayton Stone, James Franciscus; Buzz Lloyd, Gene Hackman; Celia Pruett, Lee Grant; Teresa Stone, Nancy Kovack; Betty Lloyd, Mariette Hartley; Public Affairs Officer, Scott Brady.

1898 THE MARRIAGE CAME TUMBLING DOWN. (Royal Films International-1968). Grandfather, Michel Simon; Marie Jericho, Maria Dubois; Jacques Jericho, Yves Lefebvre; Agathe, Thalie Fruges; Remy, Serge Gainsbourg; La Duchesse, Mary Marquet; Jeanne, Jeanne Helia.

1899 MARRIAGE ON THE ROCKS. (Warner Bros.-1965). Dan Edwards, Frank Sinatra; Valerie, Deborah Kerr; Ernie Brewer, Dean Martin; Miguel Santos, Cesar Romero; Jeannie, Hermione Baddeley; Jim Blake, Tony Bill; Tracy Edwards, Nancy Sinatra; David Edwards, Michel Petit; Lisa, Davey Davison; Shad Nathan, John McGiver; Lola, Joi Lansing.

1900 A MARRIED COUPLE. (Aquarius-1970). Billy and Antoinette Edwards.

1901 THE MARRIED WOMAN. (Royal-1965). Charlotte, Macna Meril; The Lover, Bernard Noel; The Husband, Philippe Leroy; The Professor, Roger Leenhardt; The Maid, Margaret Le Van; The Physician, Georges Liron.

1902 MARRY ME! MARRY ME! (Allied Artists-1969). Claude Avram, Claude Berri; Isabelle Schmoll, Elisabeth Wiener; Marthe, Regine; Madame Schmoll, Luisa Colpeyn; Monsieur Schmoll, Gregoire Aslan; Helen, Prudence Harrington; 2nd English Teacher, Betsy Blair; Monsieur Avram, Gabriel Jabbour; Madame Avram, Estera Galion.

1903 MARTYRS OF LOVE. (New Line Cinema-1969). The Junior Clerk, Petr Kopriva; The Girl, Marta Kubisova; 1st Girl in Nightclub, Jitka Cerhova; 2nd Girl in Nightclub, Ivana Karbanova; Himself, Lindsay Anderson; Anastasia, Hana Kuberova; The Singer, Karel Gott; The Captain, Jan Klusak; The Tramp, Vladimir Preclik; Orphan Rudolph, Josef Konicek; The Girl, Denisa Dvorakova.

1904 MARY JANE. (American International-1968). Phil Blake, Fabian; Ellie Holden, Diane McBain; Jerry Blackburn, Michael Margotta; Jordan Bates, Kevin Coughlin; Susan Hoffman, Patty McCormack; Herbie Mueller, Phil Vandervort; Chuck Poe (The Raven), Steve Cory; Dick Marsh, Robert Lipton; Arthur Ford (Mayor), Henry Hunter; Frenchy, Tom Nolan; Toby, Bruce Mars; George, Ronn Dayton; Ben, David Meo; Maynard Parlow, Booth Colman; Otis Mosley, Baynes Barron; Harry Braxton, Russ Bender; Rober Campbell, Ivan Bonar; Larry Kane, Carl Gottlieb; Kirby, Peter Madsen.

1905 MARY, QUEEN OF SCOTS. (Universal-1971). Mary, Vanessa Redgrave; Queen Elizabeth, Glenda Jackson; James Stuart, Patrick McGoohan; Henry, Lord Darnley, Timothy Dalton; Lord Bothwell, Nigel Davenport; William Cecil, Trevor Howard; Robert Dudley, Daniel Massey; David Riccio, Ian Holm.

1906 MASCULINE FEMININE. (Royal-1966). Paul, Jean-Pierre Leaud; Madeleine, Chantal Goya; Elisabeth, Marlene Jobert; Robert, Michel Debord; Catherine, Catherine-Isabelle Duport; Lavinia, Eva-Britt Strandberg; Actor, Birger Malmsten; Brigitte Bardot, Antoine Bourseiller.

1907 M*A*S*H. (20th Century-Fox-1970). Hawkeye, Donald Sutherland; Trapper Joe, Elliott Gould; Duke, Tom Skerritt; Maj. Hot Lips, Sally Kellerman; Maj. Frank Burns, Robert Duvall; Lt. Dish, Jo Ann Pflug; Dago Red, Rene Auberjonois; Col. Henry Blake, Roger Bowen; Radar O'Reilly, Gary Burghoff; Sgt. Major Vollmer, David Arkin; Spearchucker, Fred Williamson; Me Lay, Michael Murphy; Ho-Jon, Kim Atwood; Cpl. Judson, Tim Brown; Indus Arthur, John Schuck,

Ken Prymus, Dawne Damon, Carl Gottlieb, Tamara Horrocks, G. Wood, Bobby Troup, Bud Cort, Danny Goldman, Corey Fischer.

1908 MASQUERADE. (United Artists-1965). David Fraser, Cliff Robertson; Colonel Drexel, Jack Hawkins; Sophie, Marisa Mell; Sarrassin, Michel Piccoli; Dunwoody, Bill Fraser; Prince Jamil, Christopher Witty; Paviot, Tutte Lemkow; El Mono, Jose Burgos; Benson, Charles Gray; John Le Mesurier, Roger Delgado, Jerold Wells, Felix Aylmer, Denis Bernard, Ernest Clark, David Nettheim, Anthony Singleton, Norman Fisher, Eric Blyth, James Mossman.

1909 MASSACRE IN ROME. (National General-1973). Kappler, Richard Burton; Father Pietro, Marcello Mastroianni; Maelzer, Leo McKern; Dollmann, John Steiner; Father Pancrazio, Robert Harris; Elena, Della Boccardo.

1910 No entry.

1911 MASTER OF HORROR. (U.S. Films-1966). Narciso Ibanez Menta, Carlos Estrada, Ines Moreno, Narciso Ibanez Serrador, Mercedes Carreras, Lillian Valmar.

1912 THE MASTER TOUCH. (Warner Bros.-1974). Wallace, Kirk Douglas; Anna, Florinda Bolkan; Marco, Giuliano Gemma; Detective, Rene Koldehoff; Miller, Wolfgang Preiss.

1913 MATCHLESS. (United Artists-1967). Perry (Matchless) Liston, Patrick O'Neal; Arabella, Ira Furstenberg; Andreanu, Donald Pleasence; Hank Norris, Henry Silva; Tipsy, Nicoletta Machiavelli; General Shapiro, Howard St. John; Colonel Coolpepper, Sorrell Booke; Hogdon, Tiziano Cortini; Hypnotizer, Valeri Inkijinov; O-Chin, Andy Ho; O'Lan, Elizabeth Wu; Li-Hunang, M. Mishiku; O-Chin's Doctor, Jacques Herlin.

1914 MATCHLESS. (Australian Film Institute-1974). Cynthia, Sally Balke; Annie, Denise Otto; Victor, Allan Penney.

1915 THE MATTEI AFFAIR. (Paramount-1973). Enrico Mattei, Gian Maria Volonte; Journalist, Luigi Equarzina; McHale, Peter Baldwin; Journalist, Renato Romano; Minister, Franco Graziosi; Engineer, Gianfranco Ombuen; Official of Inquiry Commission, Elio Jotta; Mrs. Mattei, Edda Ferronao; Bertuzzi, Luciano Colitti.

1916 A MATTER OF DAYS. (Royal-1969). Francoise, Thalle Fruges; Pavel, Vit Olmer; Father, Milan Mach; Jean Louis, Philippe Baronnet; Philippe, Michel Ducrocq; Stasek, Josef Cap; Maite, Valerie Vienne.

1917 A MATTER OF INNOCENCE. (Universal-1968). Polly Barlow, Hayley Mills; Robert Hook, Trevor Howard; Amaz, Shashi Kapoor; Mrs. Innes-Hook, Brenda De Banzie; Rick Preston, Dick Patterson; Lorelei, Kalen Lui; Miss Gudgeon, Patricia Routledge; Critch, Peter Bayliss; Mrs. Barlow, Dorothy Alison; Ambrose, David Prosser.

1918 MAURIE. (National General-1973). Maurice, Bernie Casey; Jack, Bo Swenson; Dorothy, Janet MacLachlan; Carol, Stephanie Edwards; Rosie, Paulene Myers; Stokes, Bill Walker; Mrs. Stokes, Maidie Norman; Dr. Stewart, Curt Conway; Oscar, Jitu Cumbuka; Lida, Lori Busk; Milton, Tol Avery; Chris Schenkel.

1919 MAYA. (MGM-1966). Hugh Bowen, Clint Walker; Terry Bowen, Jay North; One-Eye, L. S. Johar; Raji, Sajid Kahn; Gammu Ghat, Jairaj; Sheela, Sonia Sahni; Village Spokesman, Ullas; Raji's Father, Nana Palshikar; One-Eye's Daughter, Uma Rao; Station Master, Madhusdan Pathak.

1920 MAYERLING. (MGM-1969). Crown Prince Rudolf, Omar Sharif; Baroness Maria Vetsera, Catherine Deneuve; Emperor Franz-Josef, James Mason; Empress Elizabeth, Ava Gardner; Edward, Prince of Wales, James Robertson Justice; Countess Larisch, Genevieve Page; Count Josef Hoyos, Ivan Desny; Crown Princess Stephanie, Andrea Parisy; Mizzi Kaspar, Fabienne Dali; Mortiz Szeps, Maurice Teynac; Bratfisch, Moustache; Loschek, Bernard Lajarrige; Lisl Stockau, Veronique Vendell; Count Taafe, Charles Millot; Count Karolyi, Roger Pigaut; Baroness Helen Vetsera, Mony Dalmes; Lyne Chardonnet, Alain Saury, Irene Von Meyendorff, Jean-Claude Bercq, Jacques Berthier, Howard Vernon, Jean-Michel Rouziere, Roger Lumont, Jacqueline Lavielle, Jacques Dorfmann, Anthony Stuart, Pierre Verneti, Richard Larke, Fred Vellaca, The Grand Ballet Classique De France.

1921-23 No entries.

1924 ME. (Altura-1970). Francois, Michael Terrazon; Mme. Minguet, Marie Louise Thierry; Minguet, Rene Thierry; Josette, Pierrette Deplanque; Raoul, Henri Puff; Simone, Linda Gutemberg; Roby, Raoul Billery.

1925 ME AND MY BROTHER. (New Yorker-1969). Himself, Julius Orlovsky; Julius Orlovsky, Joseph Chaikin; The Psychiatrist, John Coe; Allen Ginsberg, Allen Ginsberg; Himself, Peter Orlovsky; Peter Orlovsky, Seth Allen; The Social Worker, Virginia Kiser; Herself, Nancy Fish; An Actress, Cynthia McAdams; The Photographer, Roscoe Lee Browne.

1926 ME, NATALIE. (National General-1969). Natalie Miller, Patty Duke; David Harris, James Farentino; Uncle Harold, Martin Balsam; Miss Dennison, Elsa Lanchester; Shirley Norton, Salome Jens; Mrs. Miller, Nancy Marchand; Betty Simon, Deborah Winters; Stanley Dexter, Ronald Hale; Morris, Bob Balaban; Harvey Belman, Matthew Cowles; Mrs. Schroder, Ann Thomas; Tony, Al Pacino; Hester, Catherine Burns; Natalie (7 years old), Robyn Morgan; Surviving Brother, Dan Keyes; Attorney, Peter Turgeon; Plastic Surgeon, Milt Kamen; Arnold, Ross Charap; Mrs. Simon, Dortha Duckworth; Mr. Simon, Milo Boulton; Max, Dennis Allen; Freddie, Robert Frink; Betty Simon (10 years old), Melinda Blachley.

1927 MEAN STREETS. (Warner Bros.-1973). Johnny Boy, Robert De Niro; Charlie, Harvey Keitel; Tony, David Proval; Teresa, Amy Robinson; Michael, Richard Romanus; Giovanni, Cesare Danova; Mario, Vic Argo; Boy with gun, Robert Carradine; Diane, Jeannie Bell; Cop, D'Mitch Davis; Drunk, David Carradine; Joey, George Memmoli; Oscar, Murray Mosten; Sammy, Ken Sinclair; Soldier, Harry Northup; Jewish Girl, Lois Waldon; Jimmy, Lenny Scaletta; Benton, Robert Wilder.

1928 MEAT RACK. (Sherpix-1970). J.C., David Calder; Jean, Donna Troy; Mother, Jan Stratton; Father, Bob Romero; Ken, Steve Ferris; J. C. Child, Ronald Ebbert; Preacher, Alan Dye; Photographer, Rodney Wheelock; Housewife, Anne Muckerman; Man on Beach, Roland Trupp; Transvestite, Pat Monclair.

1929 THE MECHANIC. (United Artists-1972). Arthur Bishop, Charles Bronson; Harry McKenna, Keenan Wynn; Steve McKenna, Jan-Michael Vincent; Prostitute, Jill Ireland; Louise, Linda Ridgeway; Syndicate Head, Frank DeKova; Cam, Kevin O'Neal; Bathtub Girl, Linda Grant; Librarian, Louise Fitch; Yamoto, Takayuki Kubota; Kori, Hank Hamilton; Aikido Master, Hiroyasu Fujishima; Rifle Range Attendant, Michael Hinn; Intern, James Davidson; Policeman, Lindsay H. Crosby; Bikini Waitress, Christine Forbes; Priest, Father Amando De Vincenzo; Butler, Ferald Saunderson Peters; Chickin Lickin Driver, Ernie Orsatti; Gang Leader, J. N. Roberts; Garden Party Woman, Sara Taft; Garden Party Man, John Barclay; Bodyguards, Alan Gibbs, Frank Orsatti.

1930 MEDEA. (New Line-1971). Medea, Maria Callas; Jason, Giuseppi Gentile; Centaur, Laurent Terzieff; Glauce, Margereth Clementi.

1931 MEDIUM COOL. (Paramount-1969). John Cassellis, Robert Forster; Eileen Horton, Verna Bloom; Gus, Peter

Bonerz; Ruth, Marianna Hill; Harold Horton, Harold Blankenship; Frank Baker, Sid McCoy; Dede, Christine Bergstrom; Pennybaker, Robert McAndrew; News Director Karlin, William Sickingen; Rich Lady, Beverly Younger; Social Worker, Marrian Walters; Plainclothesman, Edward Croke; Blonde in Car, Sandra Ann Roberts; Newscaster, Doug Kimball; Gun Clinic Manager, Peter Boyle; Secretary, Georgia Tadda; Buddy, Charles Geary; Jeff Donaldson, Richard Abrams, Felton Perry, Val Grey, Bill Sharp, Robert Paige, Walter Bradford, Russell Davis, Livingston Lewis, Barbara Jones, John Jackson, Simone Zorn, Madeleine Marcou, Mickey Pallas, James Jacobs, Spence Jackson, Dorien Suhr, Kenneth Whitener, Lynn Erlich, Lester Brownlee, Morris Bleckman, Wally Wright, Sam Venturo, George Boulet, Connie Fleischauer, Mary Smith, Nancy Noble.

1932 MEET ME IN MOSCOW. (Cinemasters International-1966). Alena, Galina Polskikh; Volodya, Alexi Loktev; Kolya, Nikita Mikhalkov; Sasha, Yevgeni Steblov; Man in the Park, Roland Bykov.

1933 MELINDA. (MGM-1972). Frankie J. Parker, Calvin Lockhart; Terry Davis, Rosalind Cash; Melinda, Vonetta McGee; Mitch, Paul Stevens; Tank, Rockne Tarkington; Gregg Van, Ross Hagen; Dennis Smith, Renny Roker; Floria, Judyann Elder; Charles Atkins, Jim Kelly; Marcia, Jan Tice; Lt. Daniels, Lonne Elder; Detective, Edmund Cambridge; Young Man, George Fisher; Rome, Allen Pinson; Rome's Servant, Joe Hooker; Bank Man, Jack Manning; Hood, Gene LeBell; Sgt. Adams, Gary Pagett; Washington, Khalil Bezaleel; Bank Woman, Nian Roman; Jean, Jeanie Bell; Karate Group, Earl Maynard, Dori Dixon, Douglas C. Lawrence, Evelyne Cuffee, Peaches Jones.

1934 MELODY. (Levitt-Pickman-1971). Ornshaw, Jack Wild; Daniel, Mark Lester; Melody, Tracy Hyde; Mrs. Latimer, Sheila Steafel; Mr. Latimer, Keith Barron; Headmaster, James Cossins; Mr. Perkins, Roy Kinnear; Mrs. Perkins, Kate Williams.

1935 MEMORIES OF UNDERDEVELOPMENT. (Tricontinental-1973). Serge, Sergio Corrieri; Elena, Daisy Granados; Noemi, Eslinda Nunez; Laura, Beatriz Ponchora.

1936 MEMORIES WITHIN MISS AGGIE. (1974). Aggie, Deborah Ashira; Richard, Patrick Farrelly; Aggie I, Kim Pope; Aggie II, Mary Stuart; Aggie III, Darby Lloyd Rains; Boyfriend I, Eric Edwards; Boyfriend II, Harry Reems; Voyeur, Leo Zorba; Ralph Herman, Christopher Kersen, Rolf Beck.

1937 MEMORY OF US. (Cinema Financial of America-1974). Betty, Ellen Geer; Motel Manager, Will Geer; Brad, Jon Cypher; Iris, Barbara Colby; John, Robert Hogan; Stella,

Charlene Polite; Lisa, Joyce Easton; Housekeeper, Rose Marie; Betty's Children, Robbie Rist, Ann Elizabeth Beesley; Winston, Peter Brown.

1938 THE MEPHISTO WALTZ. (20th Century-Fox-1971). Myles Clarkson, Alan Alda; Paula Clarkson, Jacqueline Bisset; Duncan Ely, Curt Jurgens; Roxanne, Barbara Parkins; Bill Delancey, Bradford Dillman; Dr. West, William Windom; Maggie West, Kathleen Widdoes; Abby Clarkson, Pamelyn Ferdin.

1939 THE MERCENARY. (United Artists-1970). Bill, Franco Nero; Eufemio, Tony Musante; Ricciolo, Jack Palance; Columba, Giovanna Ralli; Alfonso, Eduardo Fajardo; Studs, Bruno Corazzari; Hudo, Remo De Angeles; Larkin, Joe Camel; Pepote, Franco Giacobini; Elias, Vicente Roca; Mexican, Jose Riesgo; Mexican, Angel Ortiz; Sgt., Fernando Villena; Vigilante, Tito Garcia; Notary, Angel Alvarez; Mayor, Juan Cazalilla; Capt., Guillermo Mendez; Innkeeper, Jose Zalde; Ramon, Alvaro DeLuna; Juan, Jose Antonio Lopez; Marco Milo Quesada; Mateo, Raf Baldassarre; Pablo, Jose Canalejas; Simon, Simon Arriaga; Ramirez, Jose Ma Aguinaco; Antonio, Paco Nieto.

1940 THE MERCHANT OF FOUR SEASONS. (New Yorker-1973). Irmgard, Irm Hermann; Erna, Hanna Schygulla; Hans, Hans Hirschmuller; Harry, Kurt Scheydt; Kurt's Wife, Andrea Schober.

1941 THE MERMAID. (Lee-1966). Ching Miao, Au-yang Sha-Fei, Yang Tse-ching, Chiang Kuang-chao, Yeh Ching, Chen Yuen-hua, Tung Di, Li Yuen-chung.

1942 THE MERRY WIVES OF WINDSOR. (Sigma III-1966). Sir John Falstaff, Norman Foster; Mistress Ford, Colette Boky; Mistress Page, Mildred Miller; Mr. Ford, Igor Gorin; Mistress Ann, Lucia Popp; Fenton, Ernst Schutz; Master Page, Edmond Hurshell; Ballerina, Rosella Hightower.

1943 MICHAEL AND HELGA. (American International-1969). Michael, Felix Franchy; Helga, Ruth Gassmann; Young Mother, Elfi Rueter; Doctor, Hildegard Linden; Christian, Christian Margulies; Father (1st Family), Christian Fredersdorf; Mother (1st Family), Ursula Mellin; Father (2nd Family), Jochel Piel; Mother (2nd Family), Lisa Ravel; Sonja Lindorf, Elke Hart, Sabine Dall, Claus Hoeft, Peter Bach, Ulla Best.

1944 MICKEY ONE. (Columbia-1965). Mickey One, Warren Beatty; Castle, Hurd Hatfield; Jenny, Alexandra Stewart; Berson, Teddy Hart; Fryer, Jeff Corey; The Artist, Kamatari Fujiwara; Ruby, Franchot Tone.

1945 MIDAS RUN. (Cinerama-1969). Mike Warden, Richard

Crenna; Sylvia Giroux, Anne Heywood; John Pedley, Fred Astaire; Wister, Roddy McDowall; Henshaw, Ralph Richardson; Dodero, Cesar Romero; Aldo Ferranti, Adolfo Celi; Crittenden, Maurice Denham; Wells, John Le Mesurier; Carabinieri, Aldo Bufi Landi; Co-Pilot, Fred Astaire Jr.; Giroux, Jacques Sernas; Mark Dietrich, Karl Otto Alberty; Pfeiffer, George Hartman; Mrs. Pfeiffer, Caroline De Fonseca; The Dean, Robert Henderson; Pilot, Stanley Baugh; Gordon, Bruce Beeby.

1946 MIDDLE OF THE WORLD. (1974). Olimpia Carlisi, Philippe Leotard, Juliet Berto, Jacques Denis.

1947 MIDNIGHT COWBOY. (United Artists-1969). Ratso Rizzo, Dustin Hoffman; Joe Buck, Jon Voight; Cass, Sylvia Miles; Mr. O'Daniel, John McGiver; Shirley, Brenda Vaccaro; Towny, Barnard Hughes; Sally Buck, Ruth White; Annie, Jennifer Salt; Woodsy Niles, Gil Rankin; Little Joe, Gary Owens & T. Tom Marlow; Ralph, George Eppersen; Cafeteria Manager, Al Scott; Mother on the Bus, Linda Davis; Old Cow-Hand, J. T. Masters; The Old Lady, Arlene Reeder; Rich Lady, Georgann Johnson; Jackie, Jonathan Kramer; TV Bishop, Anthony Holland; The Young Student, Bob Balaban; Freaked-Out Lady, Jan Tice; Bartender, Paul Benjamin; Vegetable Grocers, Peter Scalia and Vito Siracusa; Peter Zamagias, Arthur Anderson, Viva, Gastone Rossilli, Ultra Violet, Paul Jabara, International Velvet, William Dorr, Cecilia Lipson, Taylor Mead, Paul Morrisey, Paul Jasmin, Joan Murphy, Al Stetson.

1948 THE MIDNIGHT MAN. (Universal-1974). Jim Slade, Burt Lancaster; Linda, Susan Clark; Quartz, Cameron Mitchell; Clayborne, Morgan Woodward; Sheriff Casey, Harris Yulin; Quartz' Wife, Joan Lorring; Deputy Sheriff, Richard Winterstein; Bar Owner, William Splawn; Natalie Clayborne, Catherine Bach; Robbery Gang, Ed Lauter, Mills Watson, Bill Hicks; Natalie's Boyfriend, William Lancaster; Psychologist, Robert Quarry; Janitor, Charles Tyner; Prof. Mason, Lawrence Dobkin; Artist, Peter Dane; Robbers' Friend, Eleanor Ross.

1949 MIDNIGHT PLOWBOY. (Boxoffice International-1973). John Tull, Nancee, Debbie Osborne, Christie Anna, Jack Richesim.

1950 THE MIKADO. (Warner Bros.-1967). The Mikado, Donald Adams; Nanki-Poo, Philip Potter; Ko-Ko, John Reed; Pooh-Bah, Kenneth Sandford; Pish-Tush, Thomas Lawlor; Go-To, George Cook; Yum-Yum, Valerie Masterson; Pitti-Sing, Peggy Ann Jones; Peep-Bo, Pauline Wales; Katisha, Christine Palmer; Chorus, Glyn Adams, Neville Grave, John Hugill, Peter Lodwick, Gordon Mackenzie, James Marsland, Ralph Mason, Alfred Oldridge, Clifford Parkes, Anthony

Raffell; David Rayson, John Webley, Howard Williamson, Katherine Dyson, Marcia Glossop, Abby Hadfield, Beti Lloyd-Jones, Susan Maisey, Jennifer Marks, Marian Martin, Norma Millar, Alison Parker, Abigail Ryan, Vera Ryan, Anne Sessions, Anna Vincent.

1951 THE MILITARISTS. (Toho-1973). Tojo, Keiju Kobayashi; Goro, Yuzo Kayama; Pilot, Toshio Kurosawa; So Yamaura, Tatsuya Mihashi, Toshiro Mifune.

1952 THE MILKY WAY. (UM-1970). Pierre, Paul Frankeur; Jean, Laurent Terzieff; Cape, Alain Cuny; Virgin Mary, Edith Scob; Jesus, Bernard Verley; French Clergyman, Francois Maistre; Brigadier, Claude Cerval; Mother Superior, Muni; Maitre d', Julien Bertheau; Mrs. Garnier, Ellen Bahl; Marquis, Michel Piccoli; Teacher, Agnes Capri; Inquisitor, Michel Etcheverry; Devil, Pierre Clementi; Jesuit, Georges Marchal; Jansenite, Jean Piat; Rodolph, Denis Manuel; Francois, Daniel Pilon; L'Eveque, Claudio Brook; Spanish Clergyman, Julien Guiomar; Innkeeper, Marcel Peres; Prostitute, Delphine Seyrig.

1953 THE MILLION EYES OF SU-MURU. (American International-1967). Tommy Carter, Frankie Avalon; Nick West, George Nader; Su-Muru, Shirley Eaton; Colonel Baisbrook, Wilfrid Hyde-White; President Boong, Klaus Kinski; Louise, Patti Chandler; Mikki, Salli Sachse; Ema, Ursula Rank; Zoe, Krista Nell; Helga, Marie Rohm; Inspector Koo, Paul Chang; Kitty, Essie Huang; Colonel Medika, Jon Fong; The Su-Muru Guard, Denise Davreux, Jill Hamilton, Christine Lok, Louise Lee, Margaret Cheung, Lisa Gray, Mary Cheng.

1954 THE MIND OF MR. SOAMES. (Columbia-1970). John Soames, Terence Stamp; Dr. Bergen, Robert Vaughn; Dr. Maitland, Nigel Davenport; Thomas Fleming, Christian Roberts; Joe Allan, Donal Donnelly; Davis, Norman Jones; Nicholls, Dan Jackson; Naomi, Vickery Turner; Jenny Bannerman, Judy Parfitt; Richard Bannerman, Scott Forbes; Inspector Moore, Joe McPartland; Girl on Train, Pamela Moseiwitsch; Sgt. Clifford, Billy Cornelius; Guard, Jon Croft; Ticket Seller, Esmond Webb; Pub Owner, Bill Pilkington; Barmaid, Kate Bimchy; Old Man in Car, Joe Gladwin; Schoolteacher, Tony Caunter; TV Floor Manager, Eric Brooks.

1955 MINGUS. (Film-Makers-1968). Charles McPherson, Lonnie Hillyer, Walter Bishop, John Gilmore, Danny Richmond, Charles Mingus.

1956 THE MINI-SKIRT MOB. (American International-1968). Lon, Jeremy Slate; Shayne, Diane McBain; Connie, Sherry Jackson; Edie, Patty McCormack; Jeff Logan, Ross Hagen;

Spook, Harry Dean Stanton; L. G., Ronnie Rondell.

1957 MINNESOTA CLAY. (Harlequin-1966). Minnesota Clay, Cameron Mitchell; Fox, Georges Riviere; Estella, Ethel Rojo; Nancy, Diana Martin; Scratchy, Anthony Ross; Ortiz, Fernando Sancho; Andy, Alberto Cevenini; Jonathan, Antonio Casas; Lt. Evans, Julia Pena; Tubbs, Nando Poggi; Millicet, Joe Kamel; Gino Pernice, Madelaine Deheco.

1958 MINNIE AND MOSKOWITZ. (Universal-1971). Minnie, Gena Rowlands; Moskowitz, Seymour Cassel; Zelmo Swift, Val Avery; Morgan Morgan, Tim Carey.

1959 A MINUTE TO PRAY, A SECOND TO DIE. (Cinerama-1968). Clay McCord, Alex Cord; Roy Colby, Arthur Kennedy; Governor Lem Carter, Robert Ryan; Laurinda, Nicoletta Machiavelli; Kraut, Mario Brega; Cheap Charley, Renato Romano; Fred Duskin, Gianpiero Albertini; Father Santana, Daniel Martin; Dr. Chase, Enzo Fiermonte; Seminole, Pedro Canalejas; Butler, Franco Lantieri; Fuzzy, Osiride Peverello; El Bailarin, Jose Manuel Martin; Sein, Antonio Molina Rojo; Ruby, Rosa Palomar; Barber, Paco Sanz; Sid, Paolo Magalotti; Zack, Massimo Sarchielli; Clay (as a boy), Ottaviano Dell-Acqua; Ruby's Son, Alberto Dell' Acqua; Jonas, Antonio Vico.

1960 THE MINX. (Cambist-1969). Louise, Jan Sterling; Henry, Robert Rodan; John, Michael Beirne; Benjamin, Ned Cary; Terry, Shirley Parker.

1961 THE MIRACLE OF LOVE. (Times Film Corporation-1969). Biggi Freyer, Regis Vallee, Katarina Haertel, Wilfred Gossler, Fred Tummler, Matthias Grimm, Ortrud Grossman.

1962 MIRAGE. (Universal-1965). David, Gregory Peck; Sheila, Diane Baker; Ted Caselle, Walter Matthau; Charles Calvin, Walter Abel; Major Crawford, Leif Ericson; Josephson, Kevin McCarthy; Mrs. Frances Calvin, Anne Seymour; Lester, Jack Weston; Willard, George Kennedy; Bo, House B. Jameson; Dr. Broden, Robert H. Harris; Joe Trutle, Neil Fitzgerald; Lieut. Franken, Hari Rhodes; Benny, Syl Lamont; Irene, Eileen Baral; Group Leader, Franklin B. Cover.

1963 MISSION BATANGAS. (Manson-1969). Chip Corbett, Dennis Weaver; Joan Barnes, Vera Miles; Colonel Turner, Keith Larsen; Pol Salcedo, Vic Diaz, Fred Galang, Helen Thompson, Bruno Punzalan, Tony Dungan, Ernesto La Guardia.

1964 MISSION MARS. (Allied Artists-1968). Mike Blaiswick, Darren McGavin; Nick Grant, Nick Adams; Duncan, George De Vries; Edith Blaiswick, Heather Hewitt; Cliff Lawson, Michael De Beausset; Alice Grant, Shirley Parker; Russian

Astronaut, Bill Kelly; Chuck (Radio Operator), Chuck Zink; Simpson, Ralph Miller; Doctor, Art Barker; Lawson's Aide, Monroe Myers.

1965 MISSION STARDUST. (Times-1969). Thora, Essy Persson; Maj. Perry Roan, Lang Jeffries; Kress, John Karelsen; Rotkin, Pinkas' Braun; Capt. Bull, Luis Davila.

1966 MISSISSIPPI MERMAID. (United Artists-1970). Louis Durand, Jean-Paul Belmondo; Julie Roussel, Catherine Deneuve; M. Comolli, Michel Bouquet; Berthe Roussel, Nelly Borgeaud.

1967 MR. BROWN. (Andrieux-1972). George, Al Stevenson; Clarissa, Judith Elliotte; Mike, Tyrone Fulton; Pauline Chew Morgan, Ted Harris, Peggy Toy, Jeannine Altobelli, Chuckie Bradley, Billy Green Bush, Bert Kramer, Charles Mott, Christopher Cannon, Charles Douglas, Cheryl Carter, Charles Jackson, Johnny Jingles, Christopher Mock, Michael Elliotte, Wednesday Lea Packer.

1968 MISTER BUDDWING. (MGM-1966). Mister Buddwing, James Garner; The Blonde, Jean Simmons; Fiddle, Suzanne Pleshette; Janet, Katharine Ross; Gloria, Angela Lansbury; Shabby Old Man, George Voskovec; Mr. Schwartz, Jack Gilford; 1st Cab Driver, Joe Mantell; Hank, Raymond St. Jacques; Dan, Ken Lynch; Policeman, Beeson Carroll; 2nd Cab Driver, Billy Halop; Counterman, Michael Hadge; Printer, Charles Seel; Tony, John Tracy; Chaufferu, Bart Conrad; Dice Players, Wesley Addy, Romo Vincent, Nichelle Nichols, John Dennis, Kam Tong, James O'Rear, Rafael Campos, Pat Li, Rikki Stevens.

1969 MISTER FREEDOM. (Grove-1970). Dr. Freedom, Donald Pleasence; Marie, Delphine Seyrig; Mr. Freedom, John Abbey; Moujik-Man, Philippe Noiret; Marie Rouge, Catherine Rouvel; Christ-man, Samy Frey; Dick, Jean Claude Drouot; Mr. Drugstore, Serge Gainsbourg.

1970 MR. MAJESTYK. (United Artists-1974). Vince Majestyk, Charles Bronson; Frank Renda, Al Lettieri; Nancy Chavez, Linda Cristal; Wiley, Lee Purcell; Bobby Kopas, Paul Koslo; Gene Lundy, Taylor Lacher; Det. Lt. McAllen, Frank Maxwell; Larry Mendoza, Alejandro Rey; Deputy Harold Ritchie, Jordon Rhodes.

1971 MISTER MOSES. (United Artists-1965). Joe Moses, Robert Mitchum; Julie Anderson, Carroll Baker; Robert, Ian Bannen; Reverend Anderson, Alexander Knox; Ubi, Raymond St. Jacques; Chief, Orlando Martins; Parkhurst, Reginald Beckwith.

1972 MRS. BARRINGTON. (Monarch-1974). Mrs. Barrington,

Kim Pope; Eloise, Ida Klein; Roberto, David Hausman; Ralph or James, Marlow Ferguson; David Kirk, Jack Sylva, Jennifer Welles, Jeffrey Hurst, Rebecca Brooke, Guy Thomas, Chris Jordan, Eric Edwards, Steve Tucker, Joseph Corral, Paul Giacobbe.

1973 MRS. BROWN, YOU'VE GOT A LOVELY DAUGHTER. (MGM-1968). Herman Tulley, Peter Noone; Barry, Barry Whitwam; Keith, Keith Hopwood; Karl, Karl Green; Derek, Derek Leckenby; George Brown, Stanley Holloway; Mrs. Brown, Mona Washbourne; Percy, Lance Percival; Grandma, Marjorie Rhodes; Tulip, Sheila White; Judy Brown, Sarah Caldwell; Swothard, Hugh Rutcher; Clive Wingate, Drewe Henley; Tulip's Mother, Avis Bunnage; Oakshott, John Sharp; Pub Singer, Nat Jackley; Rita Webb, Billy Milton, Dermot Kelly, Tom Kempinski, Lynda Baron, Joan Hickson, Iris Sadler, Pamela Cundell, Paul Farrell, Michelle Cook, James Myers, Margery Manners.

1974 MRS. POLLIFAX--SPY. (United Artists-1971). Mrs. Pollifax, Rosalind Russell; Farrell, Darren McGavin; Berisha, Nehemiah Persoff; Nexdhet, Harold Gould; Perdido, Albert Paulsen; Lulash, John Beck; Carstairs, Dana Elcar.

1975 MIXED COMPANY. (United Artists-1974). Kathy, Barbara Harris; Pete, Joseph Bologna; Liz, Lisa Gerritsen; Mary, Arianne Heller; Joe, Stephen Honanie; Freddie, Haywood Nelson; Rob, Eric Olson; Quan, Jina Tan; Al, Tom Bosley; Marge, Dorothy Shay; Miss Berquist, Ruth McDevitt; Krause, Bob G. Anthony; Walt Johnson, Ron McIlwain; The Doctor, Roger Price; Milton, Keith Hamilton; Police Sergeant, Jason Clark; Police Officer, Charles J. Samsill; Basketball player, Jophery Clifford Brown; Announcer, Rodney Hundley; Referee, Darell L. Garretson; Santa Claus, Calvin Brown; Voice of Phoenix Suns, Al McCoy; The Phoenix Suns.

1976 MODEL SHOP. (Columbia-1969). Lola, Anouk Aimee; George Matthews, Gary Lockwood; Gloria, Alexandra Hay; Barbara, Carol Cole; Portly Man, Severn Darden; Gerry, Tom Fielding; Fred, Neil Elliot; Model No. 1, Jacqueline Miller; Model No. 2, Anne Randall; David, Duke Hobbie; Rob, Craig Littler; Girl Hippie, Hilarie Thompson; Secretary, Jeanne Sorel; Tony, Jon Lawson; Bearded Hippie, David Mink; Jay, Jay Ferguson; Allan, John Hill; Gas Station Attendant, Fred Willard; Short-Order Cook, Ken Prymus.

1977 MODESTY BLAISE. (20th Century-Fox-1966). Modesty Blaise, Monica Vitti; Willie Garvin, Terence Stamp; Gabriel, Dirk Bogarde; Sir Gerald Tarrant, Harry Andrews; Paul Hagan, Michael Craig; Melinda, Scilla Gabel; Nicole, Tina Marquand; McWhirter, Clive Revill; Mrs. Fothergill, Rosella Falk; Crevier, Joe Melia; Walter, Lex Schoorel; Paco,

Sylvan; Hans, Jon Bluming; Enrico, Roberto Bisacco; Basilio, Sara Urzi; Friar, Giuseppe Paganelli; Minister, Alexander Knox.

1978 MOLLY AND LAWLESS JOHN. (Producers Distributing Corporation-1972). Molly, Vera Miles; Johnny, Sam Elliott; Deputy, Clu Gulager; Sheriff, John Anderson; Dolly, Cynthia Myers.

1979 THE MOLLY MAGUIRES. (Paramount-1970). James McParlan, Richard Harris; Jack Kehoe, Sean Connery; Mary Raines, Samantha Eggar; Davies, Frank Finlay; Frazier, Art Lund; Frank McAndrew, Anthony Costello; Dan Dougherty, Anthony Zerbe; Father O'Connor, Phillip Bourneuf; Mrs. Frazier, Frances Heflin; Mrs. Kehoe, Bethel Leslie; Mrs. McAndrew, Susan Goodman; Old Man, Brendan Dillon; Jenkins, John Alderson; Bartender, Malachy McCourt; Gomer James, Peter Rogan; Franklin Gowen, William Clune; Gen. Charles Albright, Phillip Richards; Girl at Football Game, Karen Machon.

1980 MOMENT TO MOMENT. (Universal-1966). Kay Stanton, Jean Seberg; Daphne, Honor Blackman; Mark, Sean Garrison; Neil Stanton, Arthur Hill; DeFargo, Gregoire Aslan; Timmy, Peter Robbins; Singer, Donald Woods; Hendricks, Walter Reed; Travel Agency Clerk, Albert Carrier; Albie, Lomax Study; Givet, Richard Angarola.

1981 MONA. (Sherpix-1971). Mona, Fifi Watson; Mother, Judy Angel.

1982 MONDO MOD. (Timely Motion Picture-1967). Narrator, Humble Harve; Sam the Soul, The Inspirations, The Group.

1983 MONDO TRASHO. (Film Makers-1970). Mary Vivian Pearce.

1984 No entry.

1985 THE MONEY JUNGLE. (Commonwealth United Entertainment-1968). Blake Heller, John Ericson; Peggy Lido, Lola Albright; Treva Saint, Leslie Parrish; Lt. Dow Reeves, Nehemiah Persoff; Harvey Sheppard, Charles Drake; Paul Kimmel, Kent Smith; Harry Darkwater, Don Rickles; Michael Forest, Mark Roberts, Edy Williams, Marilyn Devin, Jim Adams, Leslie McRae, Dale Monroe, Dodie Warren, Dub Taylor, Tex Armstrong, John Cliff, George De Normand, Byrd Holland, Richard Norris, Ed Parker.

1986 MONEY, MONEY, MONEY. (Cinerama-1973). Lino, Lino Ventura; Jacques, Jacques Brel; Simon, Charles Denner; Johnny Hallyday, Johnny Hallyday; Charlot, Charles Gerard; Aldo, Aldo Maccione; Nicole, Nicole Courcel; Femme de

L'Ambassadeur, Prudence Harrington; L'Ambassadeur, Andre Falcon; L'Avocat General, Gerard Sire; Avocat de la Defense, Yves Robert; Fils de Lino, Xavier Gelin; Ernesto Juarez, Jean-Louis Bunuel; Michel Alet, Madly Bamy, Sophie Boudet, Annie Ho, Annie Kerani.

1987 MONEY TALKS. (United Artists-1972). Allen Funt, Muhammad Ali, Henny Youngman, Juliet Funt, Ira Koslow.

1988 THE MONEY TRAP. (MGM-1966). Joe Baron, Glenn Ford; Lisa Baron, Elke Sommer; Rosalie Kenny, Rita Hayworth; Dr. Horace Van Tilden, Joseph Cotten; Pete Delanos, Ricardo Montalban; Matthews, Tom Reese; Detective Wolski, James Mitchum; Aunt, Argentina Brunetti; Mr. Klein, Fred Essler; Father, Eugene Iglesias; Daughter, Teri Lynn Sandoval.

1989 MONIQUE. (AVCO Embassy-1970). Monique, Sibylla Kay; Jean, Joan Alcorn; Bill, David Sumner; Edward, Jacob Fitz-Jones; Susan, Nicola Brown; Harriet, Davilia O'Connor; Girl, Carolanne Hawkins; Richard, Howard Bawlinson.

1990 THE MONITORS. (Commonwealth United-1969). Harry, Guy Stockwell; Barbara, Susan Oliver; Max, Avery Schreiber; Mona, Sherry Jackson; Tersh, Shepperd Strudwick; General, Keenan Wynn; President, Ed Begley; Col. Stutz, Larry Storch; Alan Arkin, Adam Arkin, Xavier Cugat, Barbara Dana, Everett Dirkson, Stubby Kaye, Fred Kaz, Lynn Lipton, Jackie Vernon.

1991 MONKEYS, GO HOME! (Buena Vista-1967). Father, Maurice Chevalier; Hank Dussard, Dean Jones; Maria Riserau, Yvette Mimieux; Marcel Cartucci, Bernard Woringer; Emile Paraulis, Clement Harari; Yolande Angelli, Yvonne Constant; Mayor Gaston Lou, Marcel Hillaire; Olive Merchant, Jules Munshin; Grocer, Alan Carney; Cafe Owner, Maurice Marsac; Sidoni Riserau, Darleen Carr; Cabinet Maker, Peter Camlin.

1992 THE MONKEY'S UNCLE. (Buena Vista-1965). Merlin Jones, Tommy Kirk; Jennifer, Annette; Judge Holmsby, Leon Ames; Mr. Dearborne, Frank Faylen; Darius Green 3rd, Arthur O'Connell; Leon, Leon Tyler; Norman, Norman Grabowski; Professor Shattuck, Alan Hewitt.

1993 THE MONSTER OF LONDON CITY. (Producers Releasing Corporation-1967). Richard Sand, Hansjoerg Felmy; Ann Morlay, Marianne Koch; Dr. Morley Greely, Dietmar Schoenherr; Dorne, Hans Nielsen; Betty Ball, Chariklia Baxevanos; Sir George, Fritz Tillmann; Horrlick, Walter Pfeil; Teddy Flynn, Peer Schmidt; Maylor, Kurd Pieritz; Housekeeper, Elsa Wagner; Maid, Adelheid Hinz; Assistant, Gerda Blisse; Detective, Manfred Grothe; Helen Capstick,

Kai Fischer; Evelyn Nichols, Gudrun Schmidt.

1994 MONTE WALSH. (National General-1970). Monte Walsh, Lee Marvin; Martine Bernard, Jeanne Moreau; Chet Rollins, Jack Palance; Shorty, Mitch Ryan; Cal Brennan, Jim Davis; Sonny Jacobs, Bear Hudkins; Sunfish Perkins, Ray Guth; Petey Williams, John McKee; Dally Johnson, Michael Conrad; Sugar Wyman, Tom Heaton; Hat Henderson, G. D. Spradlin; Skimpy Eagans, Ted Gehring; Jumpin' Joe Joslin, Bo Hopkins; Rufus Brady, Matt Clark; Powder Kent, Billy Green Bush; Mary Eagle, Allyn Ann McLerie; Fightin' Joe Hooker, John McLiam; Marshal, Leroy Johnson; Colonel Wilson, Eric Christmas; Doctor, Charles Tyner; Card Cheat, Jack Colvin; Bartender, William Graeff Jr.; Farmer, John Carter; Old Man, Guy Wilkerson; Proprietor, Roy Bancroft; Cowboys, Dick Farnsworth, Fred Waugh.

1995 MOON ZERO TWO. (Warner Bros.-1970). Kemp, James Olson; Clem, Catherina Von Schell; Hubbard, Warren Mitchell; Liz, Adrienne Corri; Karminski, Ori Levy; Whitsun, Dudley Foster; Harry, Bernard Besslaw; Space Captain, Neil McCallum; Smith, Joby Blanshard; First Card Player, Michael Ripper; Second Card Player, Robert Tayman; Barman, Sam Kydd; The Gojos, The Gojos.

1996 MOONLIGHTING WIVES. (Craddock Films-1968). Mrs. Joan Rand, Diane Vivienne; Nancy Preston, Joan Nash; Al Jordan, John Aristedes; Belly Dancer, Fatima; Chris Roberts, Tina Marie, Shariaya Lee, Joe Santos, Jackie Farrel, Jody Lynn, Lisa Lillot, Bill Sullivan, Joe Jenckes, Sue Gibson, George Windship.

1997 THE MOONSHINE WAR. (MGM-1970). Frank Long, Patrick McGoohan; Taulbee, Richard Widmark; Son Martin, Alan Alda; Dual Meaders, Lee Hazlewood; Aaron, Joe Williams; Sheriff Baylor, Will Geer; Lizann, Melody Johnson; Miley, Suzanne Zenor; Mr. Worthman, Max Showalter; Stamper, Harry Carey Jr.; Boyd Caswell, Richard Peabody; Tourist, Claude Johnson; Tourist's Wife, Terry Garr; Waitress, Patricia Sauers.

1998 MOONWALK ONE. (NASA-1972). Narrator, Laurence Luckinbill.

1999 MOONWOLF. (Allied Artists-1966). Carl Mohner, Ann Savo, Helmut Schmid.

2000 MORE. (Cinema V-1969). Estelle, Mimsy Farmer; Stefan, Klaus Grunberg; Wolf, Heinz Engelmann; Charlie, Michel Chanderli; Cathy, Louise Wink; Henry, Henry Wolf.

2001 MORE DEAD THAN ALIVE. (United Artists-1969). "Killer" Cain, Clint Walker; Ruffalo, Vincent Price; Monica Alton,

Anne Francis; Billy Eager, Paul Hampton; Luke Santee, Mike Henry; Rafe Karma, Craig Littler; Sheree, Beverly Powers; Linus Carson, Clarke Gordon; Warden, William Woodson.

2002 MORE THAN A MIRACLE. (MGM-1967). Isabella, Sophia Loren; Prince Ramon, Omar Sharif; Princess Mother, Dolores Del Rio; Monzu, Georges Wilson; Brother Joseph, Leslie French; First Witch, Carlo Pisacane; Devout Princess, Marina Malfatti; Impatient Princess, Anna Nogara; Greedy Princess, Rita Forzano; Vain Princess, Rosemary Martin; Superstitious Princess, Carlotta Barilli; Haughty Princess, Fleur Mombelli; Infant Princess, Anna Liotti; Spanish Groom, Chris Huerta; Village Priest, Pietro Carloni; Elderly Monk, Giovanni Tarallo; Prince's Chamberlain, Renato Pinciroli; Prior, Giacomo Furia; Head Witches, Gladys Dawson, Kathleen St. John, and Beatrice Greack; Street Urchins, Pasquale Di Napoli, Francesco Coppola, Salvatore Ruvo, Vincenzo Danaro, Luciano Di Mauro, Luigi Criscuolo, and Francesco Lo Como.

2003 MORGAN! (Cinema V-1966). Leonie Delt, Vanessa Redgrave; Morgan Delt, David Warner; Charles Napier, Robert Stephens; Mrs. Delt, Irene Handl; Mr. Henderson, Newton Blick; Mrs. Henderson, Nan Munro; Policeman, Bernard Bresslaw; Wally, Arthur Mullard; Counsel, Graham Crowden; Second Counsel, Peter Cellier; Judge, John Rae; Best Man, Angus MacKay.

2004 MORIANNA. (Mondial Films-1968). Rita, Lote Tarp; Verner Vade, Anders Henriksson; Anna Vade, Eva Dahlbeck; Inspector Durell, Olle Andersson; Ragnar, Erik Hell; Bengt, Ove Tjernberg; Monica, Ella Henriksson; Jonas, Valter Norman; Agda, Elsa Prawitz; Lisa, Anne Thorstensson; Valter Velin, Tor Isedal; Miss Nilsson, Elisabet Oden; Boris, Heinz Hopf.

2005 THE MORNING AFTER. (Mature-1972). Sammy Cole, Jean Parker, David Marcus, Richard Zunt, Linda Shall, Thomas Strangle, Nessa Trou, Steve Dario, Susan Condo.

2006 MORO WITCH DOCTOR. (20th Century-Fox-1965). Jock Mahoney, Margia Dean, Pancho Magalona, Paraulman, Mike Parsons, Vic Diaz, Nemia Velasco, Bruno Punzalan, Jay Ilagan.

2007 MOSQUITO SQUADRON. (United Artists-1970). Quint, David McCallum; Beth, Suzanne Neve; Scott, David Buck; Douglas, David Dundas; Penrose, Dinsdale Landen; Hufford, Charles Gray; Father Bellague, Michael Anthony; Lt. Schack, Vladek Sheybal; Resistance Leader, Gordon Sterne; Maj. Kemble, Robert Urquhart; Neale, Bryan Marshall; Clark, Michael Latimer; Wiley, Nicky Henson; Pilot Officers, Brian

Grellis, George Layton; Flight Sgts., John Landry, Derek Steen.

2008 THE MOST BEAUTIFUL AGE. (Grove-1970). Hanzlik, Jan Stockl; Kulharkova, Anna Pisarikova; Vranova, Hana Brejchova; Vosta, Josef Sebanek; Ada, Ladislav Adam; Franta, Jiri Halek; Professor, Vladimir Smeral; Susan, Vera Kresadlova.

2009 MOTOR PSYCHO. (Eve-1965). Stephen Oliver, Haji, Alex Rocco, Holle K. Winters, Joseph Cellini, Thomas Scott, Coleman Francis, Sharron Lee, Steve Masters, Arshalouis Alvasian, F. Rufus Owens, E. E. Meyer, George Costello, Richard Brummer.

2010 MOUCHETTE. (Cinema Ventures-1968). Mouchette, Nadine Nortier; Mother, Marie Cardinal; Father, Paul Herbert; Mathieu, Jean Vimenet; Arsene, J. C. Guilbert.

2011 MOVE. (20th Century-Fox-1970). Hiram Jaffe, Elliott Gould; Dolly, Paula Prentiss; Girl, Genevieve Waite; Mounted Patrolman, John Larch; Oscar, Joe Silver; Dr. Picker, Graham Jarvis; Peter, Ron O'Neal; Andrea, Garrie Beau; Doorman, David Burns; Keith, Richard Bull; Mrs. Katz, Mae Questal; Gupta, Aly Wassil; Brown Package, John Wheeler; Detective Sawyer, Rudy Bond; Jeanine, Yvonne D'Angiers; Miss Landry, Amy Thomson; Rabbi, Roger Bowen; New Tenant, Stanley Adams.

2012 MOVIE STAR, AMERICAN STYLE. (Famous Players Corporation-1967). Joe Horner, Robert Strauss; Dr. Horatio, Del Moore; Skippy Roper, T. C. Jones; Honey Bunny, Paula Lane; Dr. Oscar Roscoe, Steve Drexel; Barry James, Steven Rogers; David Erickson, Richard Clair; Miranda Song, Jill Darling; Movie Queen, Cara Garnett; Countess, Sandra Lynn; Harvey Homantash, Peter Van Boorn; Crash Dramm, Ned York; Midget Photographer, Frank Delfino; Miss Fee, Juliet Picaud; Director, Albert Zugsmith.

2013 MOVING. (Poolemar-1974). Casey Donovan, Val Martin, Burt Edouards, Kurt Gerard, Peter Fisk, Tom Wright.

2014 MOZAMBIQUE. (7 Arts-1966). Brad Webster, Steve Cochran; Ilona Valdez, Hildegarde Neff; Commarro, Paul Hubschmid; Christina, Vivi Bach; Da Silva, Martin Benson; Henderson, Dietmar Schoenherr; The Arab, Gert Van Den Bergh; Carl, George Leech.

2015 MUHAIR. (Haven-1970). Eva, Isabel Sarli; Jose, Armando Bo; Mario, Victor Bo; Simon, Mario Lozano.

2016 THE MUMMY'S SHROUD. (20th Century-Fox-1967). Sir Basil Walden, Andre Morell; Stanley Preston, John Phillips,

Paul Preston, David Buck; Barbara Preston, Elizabeth Sellars; Claire, Maggie Kimberley; Longbarrow, Michael Ripper; Harry, Tim Barrett; Inspector Barrani, Richard Warner; Hasmid, Roger Delgado; Haiti, Catherine Lacey; Prem, Dickie Owen; Pharaoh, Bruno Barnabe; Pharaoh's Wife, Toni Gilpin; Kah-to-Bey, Toolsie Persaud; The Mummy, Eddie Powell; The Curator, Andreas Malandrinos.

2017 MUNSTER, GO HOME. (Universal-1966). Herman Munster, Fred Gwynne; Lily Munster, Yvonne De Carlo; Grandpa, Al Lewis; Eddie Munster, Butch Patrick; Marilyn, Debbie Watson; Lady Effigie Munster, Hermione Gingold; Freddy Munster, Terry-Thomas; Grace Munster, Jeanne Arnold; Roger Moresby, Robert Pine; Cruikshank, John Carradine; Squire Moresby, Bernard Fox; Joey, Richard Dawson; Millie, Maria Lennard; Herbert, Cliff Norton; Mrs. Moresby, Diana Chesney; Alfie, Arthur Malet; Hennesy, Ben Wright.

2018 MURDER A LA MOD. (Aries Documentaries-1968). Karen, Margo Norton; Tracy, Andra Akers; Christopher, Jared Martin; Otto, William Finley; Wiley, Ken Burrows; Policeman, Lorenzo Catlett; Jennifer Salt, Melanie Mander, Laura Stevenson.

2019 THE MURDER CLINIC. (Europix Consolidated-1968). Dr. Robert Vance, William Berger; Claudine, Francoise Prevost; Lizabeth, Mary Young; Laura, Delphi Maurin; Fred, Max Dean; Sheena, Harriet White; Philippe Hersent, Grant Laramy, Ann Sherman, William Gold, Anne Field, Patricia Carr.

2020 MURDER CZECH STYLE. (Royal-1968). Frantisek, Rudolf Hrusinsky; Alice, Kveta Fialova; Assistant Manager, Vaclav Voska; Emil, Vladimir Mensik; Bindrova, Vera Uzelacova; Jindriska, Libuse Svormova; The Dandy, Vyacheslav Irmanov.

2021 THE MURDER GAME. (20th Century-Fox-1966). Steve Baldwin, Ken Scott; Marie Aldrich, Marla Landi; Chris Aldrich, Trader Faulkner; Peter Shanley, Conrad Phillips; Larry Lindstrom, Gerald Sim; Inspector Telford, Duncan Lamont; Mrs. Potter, Rosamund Greenwood; Rev. Francis Hood, Victor Brooks; Sir Colin Chalmers, Ballard Berkeley; Arthur Gillett, Jimmy Gardner; Dr. Knight, Peter Bathurst; Secretary, Jennifer White; Radio Announcer, Frank Thornton; Landlady, Gretchen Franklyn; Parkhill, John Dunbar; Croupier, Clement Freud; Police Sergeant, Derek Partridge; Prosecutor, John Richmond.

2022 MURDER IN MISSISSIPPI. (Tiger-1965). Sheilla Britton, Sam Stewart, Derek Crane, Lou Stone, Martin St. John, John Steel, Wayne Foster, Dick Stone, Otis Young, Irv Seldin, Frank Philadelphia.

2023 MURDER MOST FOUL. (MGM-1965). Jane Marple, Margaret Rutherford; Driffold Cosgood, Ron Moody; Detective Inspector Craddock, Charles Tingwell; Mrs. Thomas, Megs Jenkins; Ralph Summers, Ralph Michael; Justice Crosby, Andrew Cruikshank; Bill Hanson, James Bolam; Mr. Stringer, Stringer Davis; Sheila Upward, Francesca Annis; Eva McConigall, Allison Seebohm; Theatrical Agent, Dennis Price, Constable Wells, Terry Scott.

2024 MURDER ON THE ORIENT EXPRESS. (Paramount-1974). Hercule Poirot, Albert Finney; Mrs. Hubbard, Lauren Bacall; Bianchi, Martin Balsam; Greta, Ingrid Bergman; Countess Andrenyi, Jacqueline Bisset; Pierre, Jean Pierre Cassel; Col. Arbuthnott, Sean Connery; Beddoes, John Gielgud; Princess Dragomiroff, Wendy Hiller; McQueen, Anthony Perkins; Mary Debenham, Vanessa Redgrave; Hildegarde, Rachel Roberts; Ratchett, Richard Widmark; Count Andrenyi, Michael York; Hardman, Colin Blakely; Doctor, George Coulouris; Fiscarelli, Denis Quilley; Concierge, Vernon Dobtcheff; A.D.C., Jeremy Lloyd; Chief Attendant, John Moffatt.

2025 THE MURDERED HOUSE. (Creative Film Services-1974). Norma Bengell, Tete Medina, Carlos Kroeber, Nelson Dantas, Rubens Araujo, Augusto Lourenco.

2026 MURDERERS' ROW. (Columbia-1966). Matt Helm, Dean Martin; Suzie, Ann-Margret; Julian Wall, Karl Malden; Coco Duquette, Camilla Sparv; MacDonald, James Gregory; Lovey Kravezit, Beverly Adams; Dr. Norman Solaris, Richard Eastham; Ironhead, Tom Reese; Billy Orcutt, Duke Howard; Guard, Ted Hartley; Captain Devereaux, Marcel Hillaire; Miss January, Corinne Cole; Dr. Rogas, Robert Terry; Dino, Desi and Bill; The Slaygirls, Mary Jane Mangler, Amedee Chabot, Luci Ann Cook, Marilyn Tindall, Dee Duffy, Jan Watson, Dale Brown, Mary Hughes, Lynn Hartoch, Rena Horton, Barbara Burgess.

2027 MURDERS IN THE RUE MORGUE. (American International-1972). Cesar Charron, Jason Robards; Marot, Herbert Lom; Madeleine Charron, Christine Kaufmann; Inspector Vidocq, Adolfo Celi; Madeleine's Mother, Lilli Palmer; Genevre, Maria Perschy; Pierre, Michael Dunn; Hunchback, Jose Calvo; Aubert, Peter Arne; Theater Manager, Werner Umberg; Actor, Luis Rivera; Lucie, Virginia Stach; Jacques, Dean Selmeir; Luigi Orsini, Marshall Jones; Gabrielle, Rosalind Elliot; Orsini's Assistants, Ruth Platt and Xan Das Bolas; Mme. Adolphe, Maria Martin; Members of Repertory Company, Rafael Hernandez, Pamela McInnes, Sally Longley.

2028 MURMUR OF THE HEART. (Walter Reade-1971). Clara, Lea Massari; Laurent, Benoit Ferreux; Father, Daniel Gelin;

Marc, Marc Winocourt; Thomas, Fabien Ferreus; Father Henri, Michel Lonsdale; Augusta, Ave Ninchi.

2029 MURPH THE SURF. (Caruth C. Byrd-1974). Allan Kuhn, Robert Conrad; Jack Murphy, Don Stroud; Ginny Eaton, Donna Mills; Sharon Kagel, Robyn Millan; Max "The Eye," Luther Adler; Avery, Paul Stewart; Arnie Holcomb, Morgan Paull; Hopper Magee, Ben Frank; Sgt. Bernasconi, Burt Young; Sgt. Terwilliger, Pepper Martin; Buffy Dee, Don Matheson, Lindsay Crosby, Mimi Saffian, Nancy Conrad, Jess Barker, Al Bordigi, Lloyd McLinn, Mel Stevens, Harvey Levine, Harriet Haindl, Kip King, Caruth C. Byrd, Joe Mell, Oak R. Gentry, Herb Vigran.

2030 MURPHY'S WAR. (Paramount-1971). Murphy, Peter O'Toole; Hayden, Sian Phillips; Brezan, Philipe Noiret; Lauchs, Horst Janson.

2031 THE MUSIC LOVERS. (United Artists-1971). Tchaikovsky, Richard Chamberlain; Nina, Glenda Jackson; Rubenstein, Max Adrian; Count Anton Chiluvsky, Christopher Gable; Modeste, Kenneth Colley; Madame Von Meck, Izabella Telezynska.

2032 THE MUTATION. (Columbia-1974). Dr. Nolter, Donald Pleasence; Lynch, Tom Baker; Brian, Brad Harris; Hedi, Julie Ege; Burns, Michael Dunn; Tony, Scott Antony; Lauren, Jill Haworth; Bridget, Olga Anthony; Prostitute, Lisa Collings.

2033 MUTINY IN OUTER SPACE. (Allied Artists-1965). Towers, William Leslie; Faith Montaine, Dolores Faith; Connie, Pamela Curran; Col. Cromwell, Richard Garland; Dr. Hoffman, James Dobson; Webber, Carl Crow; Harold Lloyd Jr., Ron Stokes, Robert Palmer, Gabriel Curtis, Glenn Langan.

2034 MY BLOOD RUNS COLD. (Warner Bros.-1965). Ben Gunther, Troy Donahue; Julie Merriday, Joey Heatherton; Julian Merriday, Barry Sullivan; Harry Lindsay, Nicolas Coster; Aunt Sarah, Jeanette Nolan; Sheriff, Russell Thorson; Lansbury, Ben Wright; Mrs. Courtland, Shirley Mitchell; Henry, Howard McNear; Mayor, Howard Wendell; Mr. Courtland, John Holland; Owen, John McCook.

2035 MY FAIR BABY. (Arrow-1973). Noelle Karel, Bill Morgen, Michelle Magazine, Lou Steisel, Bruce Mortimer, Paul Munsinger.

2036 MY HUSTLER. (Film-Makers' Distribution Center-1967). Blonde Hustler, Paul America; Balding Man, Ed Wiener; Second Hustler, S. P. Farry; Beach Girl, Jeanne Vieve.

2037 MY LOVER, MY SON. (MGM-1970). Francesca, Romy

Schneider; Robert, Donald Houston; James, Dennis Waterman; Julie, Patricia Brake; Sidney, Peter Sallis; Parks, William Dexter; Miss Clarkson, Alexandra Bastedo; Macer, Mark Hawkins; Prostitute, Maggie Wright; Mrs. Woods, Janet Brown; Woods, Tom Chatto; Chidley, Michael Forrest; Barman, Peter Gilmore; Receptionist, Rosalie Horner; Judge, Arthur Howard; Kenworthy's Friend, Chrissie Shrimpton; Kenworthy, David Warbeck; Park's Assistant, Robert Wilde.

2038 MY NAME IS NOBODY. (Universal-1974). Nobody, Terence Hill; Jack Beauregard, Henry Fonda; Sullivan, Jean Martin; Sheriff, Pedro Lulli.

2039 MY NIGHT AT MAUD'S. (Pathé-1970). Jean-Louis, Jean-Louis Trintignant; Maud, Francois Fabian; Francoise, Marie-Christine Barrault; Vidal, Antoine Vitez; Leonide Kogan, Anne Dubot, Guy Leger.

2040 MY OLD MAN'S PLACE. (Cinerama-1971). Walter, Arthur Kennedy; Sgt. Flood, Mitchell Ryan; Jimmy, William Devane; Trubee, Michael Moriarty.

2041 MY SIDE OF THE MOUNTAIN. (Paramount-1969). Sam Gribley, Ted Eccles; Bando, Theodore Bikel; Miss Turner, Tudi Wiggins; Mr. Gribley, Frank Perry; Mrs. Gribley, Peggi Loder; Daughter No. 1, Gina Dick; Daughter No. 2, Karen Pearson; Little Boy, Danny McIlravey; Mrs. Fielder, Cosette Lee; Hunter No. 1, Larry Reynolds; Hunter No. 2, Tom Harvey; Hunter No. 3, Paul Herbert; First Boy, Ralph Endersby; Second Boy, George Allan; Ranger, Patrick Pervion.

2042 MY SISTER, MY LOVE. (Sigma III-1967). Jacob, Per Oscarsson; Charlotte, Bibi Andersson; Alsmeden, Jarl Kulle; Count Schwartz, Gunnar Bjornstrand; Ebba Livin, Tina Hedstrom; Mrs. Kuller, Berta Hall; Mrs. Kuller's Son, Ake Lindstrom; Pastor Storck, Rune Lindstrom; Mrs. Storck, Sonya Hedenbratt; Dressmaker, Gudrun Ostby.

2043 MY SWEET CHARLIE. (Universal-1970). Marlene Chambers, Patty Duke; Charles Roberts, Al Freeman Jr.; Treadwell, Ford Rainey; Mr. Larrabee, William Hardy; Mrs. Larrabee, Chris Wilson; Grady, Noble Willingham; Sheriff, Dave Ward.

2044 MY UNCLE ANTOINE. (Gendon-1972). Uncle Antoine, Jean Duceppe; Carmen, Lynde Champagne; Aunt Cecile, Olivette Thibault; Fernand, Claude Jutra; Benoit, Jacques Gagnon; Joe Poulin, Lionel Villeneuve; Madame Poulin, Helene Loiselle; Poulin Children, Mario Dubuc, Lise Brunelle, Alain Legendre, Serge Evers, and Robin Marcous; Alexandrine, Monique Mercure; The Big Boss, Georges

Alexander; The Priest, Rene Salvatore Catta; The Foreman, Jean Dubost; Carmen's Father, Benoit Marcoux; Maurice, Dominique Joly; The Engaged Couple, Lise and Michel Talbot; A Client, Simeon Dallaire; The Helper, Sydney Harris; Euclide, Roger Garand.

2045 MY WIFE'S HUSBAND. (Lopert-1965). Fernand, Fernandel; Andre, Bourvil; Christiane, Claire Maurier; Serrazin, Henry Vilbert; Maximin, Michel Galabru; Pellatan, Andrex; Mme. Rose, Mag Avril; Louise, Evelyne Selena; Marinette, Laurence Ligueres; The Mayor, Henri Arius; Espinasse, Gaston Rey; Carlotti, Ardisson; Gervasoni, Andre Tomasi; Gerda, Anna Maria Carriere; Fernand's Nephew, Roger Bernard.

2046 MYRA BRECKINRIDGE. (20th Century-Fox-1970). Leticia, Mae West; Buck Loner, John Huston; Myra, Raquel Welch; Young Man, Rex Reed; Mary Ann, Farrah Fawcett; Dr. Montag, Roger C. Carmel; Rusty, Roger Herren; Charlie Flager Jr., George Furth; Irving Amadeus, Calvin Lockhart; Doctor, Jim Backus; Surgeon, John Carradine; Coyote Bill, Andy Devine; Kid Barlow, Grady Sutton; Charlei Flager Sr., Robert Lieb; Chance, Skip Ward; Bobby Dean Loner, Kathleen Freeman; Tex, B. S. Pully; Jeff, Buck Kartalian; Vince, Monty Landis; Stud, Tom Selleck; Student, Peter Ireland; Mario, Nelson Sardelli.

2047 THE MYSTERY OF THUG ISLAND. (Columbia-1966). Guy Madison, Peter Van Eyck, Giacomo Rossi Stuart, Ivan Desny, Inge Schoener, Giulia Rubini, Nando Poggi.

2048 NAKED AMONG THE WOLVES. (Lopert-1967). Kramer, Erwin Geschonneck; Bochow, Gerry Wolff; Bogorski, Viktor Awdjuschko; Hofel, Armin Muller-Stahl; Kropinski, Krystyn Woicik; Pippig, Fred Delmare; Peter Strum, Boleslaw Plotnicki, Wolfram Handel, Fred Ludwig, Gerd Ehlers.

2049 NAKED ANGELS. (Favorite-1969). Art Jenoff, Felicia Guy, Leonard Coates, Tedd King, Bruce Sunkees, Cory Fischer, Sahn Berti, Howard Lester, Joe Kasey, Glenn Lee, Penelope Sprerris, Carol Ries.

2050 THE NAKED APE. (Universal-1973). Lee, Johnny Crawford; Cathy, Victoria Principal; Arnie, Dennis Olivieri.

2051 THE NAKED BRIGADE. (Universal-1965). Diana Forsythe, Shirley Eaton; Christo, Ken Scott; Katına, Mary Chronopoulou; Major Hamilton, John Holland; Athena, Sonia Zoidou.

2052 NAKED CHILDHOOD. (1968). Francois, Michel Tarrazon; Simone, Linda Gutemberg; Roby, Raoul Billerey; Josette, Pierrette Deplanque; Mme. Minguet, Marie-Louise Thierry; M. Minguet, Rene Thierry; Raoul, Henri Putt; Meme, Marie

Marc; Letillon, Maurice Coussoneau.

2053 THE NAKED COUNTESS. (Crown International-1973). Ursula Blauth, W. G. Luckschy, Elke Hart, Michael Cromer.

2054 THE NAKED KISS. (Allied Artists-1965). Kelly, Constance Towers; Griff, Anthony Eisley; Grant, Michael Dante; Candy, Virginia Grey; Mac, Patsy Kelly; Miss Josephine, Betty Bronson; Buff, Marie Devereux; Dusty, Karen Conrad; Rembrandt, Linda Francis; Edna, Barbara Perry; Mike, Walter Mathews; Bunny, Betty Robinson; Kip, Gerald Michenaud; Peanuts, Christopher Barry; Tim, George Spell; Angel Face, Patty Robinson; Officer Sam, Neyle Morrow.

2055 THE NAKED PREY. (Paramount-1966). The Man, Cornel Wilde; The Second Man, Gert Van Der Berg; Warrior Leader, Ken Gampu; Safari Overseer, Patrick Mynhardt; Little Girl, Bella Randels.

2056 THE NAKED RUNNER. (Warner Bros.-7 Arts-1967). Sam Laker, Frank Sinatra; Martin Slattery, Peter Vaughan; Colonel Hartman, Derren Nesbitt; Karen Gisevius, Nadia Gray; Ruth, Toby Robins; Anna, Inger Stratton; Cabinet Minister, Cyril Luckham; Ritchie Jackson, Edward Fox; Joseph, J. Dubin-Behrmann; Patrick Laker, Michael Newport.

2057 THE NAME OF THE GAME IS KILL. (Fanfare-1968). Symcha Lipa, Jack Lord; Mickey Terry, Susan Strasberg; Diz Terry, Collin Wilcox; Nan Terry, Tisha Sterling; Mr. & Mrs. Terry, T. C. Jones; Sheriff Fred Kendall, Mort Mills; The Doctor, Marc Desmond.

2058 NAMU, THE KILLER WHALE. (United Artists-1966). Hank Donner, Robert Lansing; Joe Clausen, John Anderson; Kate Rand, Lee Meriwether; Deke, Richard Erdman; Lisa Rand, Robin Mattson; Burt, Joe Higgins; Nick, Michael Shea; Carrie, Clara Tarte; Charlie, Edwin Rochelle.

2059 NANAMI. (Golden Eagle-1969). Shun, Akio Takahashi; Nanami, Kuniko Ishii; Foster Father, Koji Mitsui; Foster Mother, Kazuko Fukuda; Bearded Man, Minoru Yuasa; Gang Leader, Shinatora; Psychiatrist, Ichiro Kimura; Algebra, Haruo Asano.

2060 THE NANNY. (20th Century-Fox-1965). Nanny, Bette Davis; Joey, William Dix; His Mother, Wendy Craig; His Father, James Villiers; Aunt Pen, Jill Bennett; Bobbie, Pamela Franklin; Dr. Medman, Jack Watling; Dr. Wills, Alfred Burke; Dr. Beamaster, Maurice Denham.

2061 NAPOLEON AND SAMANTHA. (Buena Vista-1972). Danny, Michael Douglas; Grandfather, Will Geer; Police Chief, Arch

Johnson; Napoleon Wilson, Johnny Whitaker; Samantha, Jodie Foster; Mr. Gutteridge, Henry Jones; The Clown, Vito Scotti; Desk Sergeant, John Crawford; Clerk, Mary Wickes; Gertrude, Ellen Corby; Mark, Rex Holman; Gary, Claude Johnson; Pete, John Lupton; John Ortega, Monty Margetts.

2062 NASHVILLE REBEL. (American International-1966). Arlin Grove, Waylon Jennings; Wesley Lang, Gordon Oas-Heim; Molly Morgan, Mary Frann; Margo Powell, Ce Ce Whitney; As Themselves, Tex Ritter, Sonny James, Faron Young, Porter Wagoner, Henny Youngman, Wilburn Brothers, Loretta Lynn, Cousin Jody, Archie Campbell.

2063 NAVAJO JOE. (United Artists-1967). Navajo Joe, Burt Reynolds; Marvin "Vee" Duncan, Aldo Sanbrell; Estella, Nicoletta Machiavelli; Maria, Tanya Lopert; Rattigan, Fernando Rey; Barbara, Franca Polesello; Geraldin, Lucia Modugno; Lynne, Pierre Cressoy; Chuck, Nino Imparato; Sancho, Alvaro De Luna; Honor, Valeria Sabel; Clay, Mario Lanfranchi; Jeffrey, Lucio Rosato; Monkey, Simon Arriaga; El Gordo, Cris Huerta; El Cojo, Angel Ortiz; Reagan, Fianni Di Stolfo; Blackwood, Angel Alavarez; Bandits, Rafael Albaicin and Lorenzo Robledo.

2064 NAVAJO RUN. (American International-1966). Mathew Whitehawk, Johnny Seven; Luke Grog, Warren Kemmerling; Sarah Grog, Virginia Vincent; Jesse Grog, Ron Soble.

2065 THE NAVY VS. THE NIGHT MONSTERS. (Realart-1966). Lt. Nora Hall, Mamie Van Doren; Lt. Charles Brown, Anthony Eisley; Woman Scientist, Pamela Mason; Petty Officer Fred Twining, Bill Gray; Ensign Rutherford Chandler, Bobby Van; Dr. Arthur Beecham, Walter Sande; Edward Faulkner, Phillip Terry.

2066 NAZARIN. (Altura-1968). Nazarin, Francisco Rabal; Andara, Rita Macedo; Beatriz, Marga Lopez; The Church Thief, Ignacio Lopez Tarso; Chanfa, Ofelia Guilmain; The Parracide, Luis Acedes Castaneda; El Pinto, Noe Murayama; La Prieta, Rosenda Monteros; Ujo, The Dwarf, Jesus Fernandez; Ada Carrasco, Antonio Bravo, Augora Molina, David Reynoso.

2067 NECROMANCY. (Cinerama Releasing Corporation-1972). Mr. Cato, Orson Welles; Lori Brandon, Pamela Franklin; Priscilla, Lee Purcell; Frank Brandon, Michael Ontkean; Jay, Harvey Jason; Georgette, Lisa James; Nancy, Sue Bernard; Cato's Son, Terry Quinn.

2068 NED KELLY. (United Artists-1970). Ned Kelly, Mick Jagger; Mrs. Kelly, Clarissa Kaye; Joe Byrne, Mark McManus; Supt. Nicholson, Ken Goodlet; Judge Barry, Frank Thring; George King, Bruce Barry; Mr. Scott, Tony Bazell; Dan Kelly, Allen Bickford; Sgt. Steele, Robert Bruning;

McInnes, Alexander Cann; Curnow, David Copping, Maggie Kelly, Diane Craig; Father O'Shea, Gerry Duggan; Steve Hart, Geoff Gilmour; Mrs. Devine, Anne Harvey; Wild Wright, Serge Lazareff; Grace Kelly, Alexi Long; Kate Kelly, Susan Lloyd; Capt. Standish, Nigel Lovell; Living, Clifford Neate; Mrs. Scott, Jessica Noad; Fitzpatrick, Martyn Sanderson; Aaron Sherritt, Ken Shorter; McIntyre, Lindsay Smith; Tom Lloyd, Peter Sumner; Mrs. Jones, Doreen Warburton; Caitlyn, Janne Wesley.

2069 NEGATIVES. (Continental-1968). Theo, Peter McEnery; Reingard, Diane Cilento; Father, Maurice Denham; Vivien, Glenda Jackson; The Dealer, Steven Lewis; Auctioneer, Norman Rossington.

2070 THE NELSON AFFAIR. (Universal-1973). Lady Hamilton, Glenda Jackson; Lord Nelson, Peter Finch; Captain Hardy, Michael Jayston; Lord Minto, Anthony Quayle; Lady Nelson, Margaret Leighton; George Matcham Jr., Dominic Guard; George Matcham Sr., Nigel Stock; Catherine Matcham, Barbara Leigh-Hunt; Lord Barham, Roland Culver; Admiral Villeneuve, Andre Maranne; Rev. William Nelson, Richard Mathews; Sarah Nelson, Liz Ashley; Capt. Blackwood, John Nolan.

2071 THE NEPTUNE FACTOR. (20th Century-Fox-1973). Blake, Ben Gazzara; Leah, Yvette Mimieux; Andrews, Walter Pidgeon; Mack, Ernest Borgnine; Captain, Chris Wiggins; Bob, Donnelly Rhodes; Norton, Ed McGibbon; Hal, J. Reynolds; Stephens, David Yorston; Bradley, Stuart Gillard; Mounton, Mark Walker; Thomas, Kenneth Pogue; Sub Captain, Frank Perry; Hobbs, Dan MacDonald; Briggs, Leslie Carlson; Warrant Officer, David Renton; Dobson, Joan Gregson; Hawkes, Dave Mann; Anita, Kay Fujiwara; Radio Officer, Richard Whelan.

2072 NEVADA SMITH. (Paramount-1966). Max Sand (Nevada Smith), Steve McQueen; Tom Fitch, Karl Malden; Jonas Cord, Brian Keith; Bill Bowdre, Arthur Kennedy; Pilar, Suzanne Pleshette; Father Zaccardi, Raf Vallone; Neesa, Janet Margolin; Warden, Howard Da Silva; Big Foot, Pat Ingle; Jesse Coe, Martin Landau; Paul Fix, Gene Evans, Josephine Hutchingson, John Doucette, Val Avery, Sheldon Allman, Lyle Bettger, Bert Freed, David McLean, Steve Mitchell, Merritt Bohn, Sandy Kenyon, Ric Roman, John Lawrence, Stanley Adams, George Mitchell, John Litel, Ted De Corsia.

2073 NEVER A DULL MOMENT. (Buena Vista-1968). Jack Albany, Dick Van Dyke; Leo Joseph Smooth, Edward G. Robinson; Sally Inwood, Dorothy Provine; Frank Boley, Henry Silva; Melanie Smooth, Joanne Moore; Florian, Tony Bill; Cowboy Schaeffer, Slim Pickens; Ace Williams, Jack

Elam; Rinzy Tobreski, Ned Glass; Bobby Macoon, Richard Bakalyan; Francis, Mickey Shaughnessy; Fingers Felton, Philip Coolidge; Museum Director, James Millhollin; Prop Man, Johnny Silver; Tony Preston, Anthony Caruso; Lenny, Paul Condylis; 1st TV Actor, Dick Winslow; 2nd TV Actor (Police Captain Jacoby), Bob Homel; Sexy Girl, Jackie Russell; Sam, Rex Dominick; Police Lt., Ken Lynch; Matron, Eleanor Audley; Police Chief Grayson, Tyler McVey; Museum Guards, John Cliff and John Dennis; Police Photographer, Jerry Paris,

2074 NEVER TOO LATE. (Warner Bros.-1965). Harry Lambert, Paul Ford; Kate Clinton, Connie Stevens; Edith Lambert, Maureen O'Sullivan; Charlie Clinton, Jim Hutton; Grace Kimbrough, Jane Wyatt; Dr. Kimbrough, Henry Jones; Mayor Crane, Lloyd Nolan.

2075 THE NEW CENTURIONS. (Columbia-1972). Sgt. Kilvinski, George C. Scott; Roy Fehler, Stacy Keach; Dorothy Fehler, Jane Alexander; Gus, Scott Wilson; Lorrie, Rosalind Cash; Sergio, Erik Estrada; Whitey, Clifton James; Milton, Richard Kalk; Sgt. Anders, James Sikking; Alice, Beverly Hope Atkinson; Phillips, Burke Byrnes; Wilma, Isabel Sanford; Johnson, William Atherton; Gladstone, Peter De Anda; Galloway, Ed Lauter; Sgt. Runyon, Dolph Sweet; Landlord, Stefan Gierasch; Martha, Carol Speed; Helen, Tracee Lyles; Lumberjack, Michael Lane; Rebecca Fehler, Debbie Fresh; Truck Driver, Roger E. Mosley; Woodrow Gandy, Read Morgan; Bethel, Charles H. Gray; Ranatti, Michael De Lano; Drunk Mother, Adriana Shaw; Young Mexican Man, Pepe Serna; Silverpants, Bea Thompkins; Young Black Man, Billy Hicks.

2076 THE NEW LAND. (Warner Bros.-1973). Karl Oskar, Max von Sydow; Kristina, Liv Ullmann; Robert, Eddie Axberg; Jonas Petter, Hans Alfredson; Anders Mansson, Halvar Bjork; Danjel, Allan Edwall; Samuel Nojd, Peter Lindgren; Arvid, Pierre Lindstedt; Petrus Olausson, Oscar Ljung; Judit, Karin Nordstrom; Pastor Torner, Per Oscarsson; Fina-Kajas, Agneta Prytz; Ulrika, Monica Zetterlund; Mario Vellejos, Georg Anaya; The Doctor, Ed Carpenter; Mr. Abbott, Larry Clementson; Pastor Jackson, Tom C. Fouts.

2077 A NEW LEAF. (Paramount-1971). Henry Graham, Walter Matthau; Henrietta Lowell, Elaine May; Andrew McPherson, Jack Weston; Harold, George Rose; Beckett, William Redfield; Uncle Harry, James Coco; Sharon Hart, Renee Taylor.

2078 THE NEW LIFE STYLE. (Dot-1970). Walter, Horst Tappert; Renata, Renata Van Holt; Alexy, Alexy Burg; Ava, Jennifer Stone.

2079 THE NEW YORK EXPERIENCE. (Trans-Lux-1973). Robin

King, Maggi Thrall, Bill Alton, Ed Barth, Scott Beach, Bibi Besch, Rick Cimino, George Coe, Fay DeWitt, Dena Dietrich, Paul Dooley, Bob Kaliban, Deborah May, Jesse Osborn, Charlotte Rae, James Ray, Guy Sorel, and the people of New York City.

2080 THE NEWCOMERS. (Ander-1972). Mary, Linda Marena; David, David Strange; Richard, Irving Stein; John, L. Arnet; Peachie, Anne Sargent; Pam, Amanda Benchley; Cathy, Cathy O'Hara; Buck, Alan Randall; Girl in Film, Brit Waugh; Boy in Film, Roger Denley.

2081 THE NEWCOMERS. (Melody-1973). Georgina Spelvin, Harry Reams, Marc Stevens, Tina Russell, Derald Delancey, Cindy West, Davey Jones, Naomi Riis.

2082 NEWMAN'S LAW. (Universal-1974). Vince Newman, George Peppard; Garry, Roger Robinson; Reardon, Eugene Roche; Eastman, Gordon Pinsent; Dellanzia, Abe Vigoda; Falcone, Louis Zorich; Frank Acker, Michael Lerner; Jimenez, Victor Campos; Quist, Mel Stewart; Beutel, Jack Murdock; Hinney, David Spielberg; Jaycee, Theodore Wilson; Sharon, Pat Anderson; Clement, Regis J. Cordic; Edie, Marlene Clark; Assistant Coroner, Kip Niven; Immigration Man, Richard Bull; Spink, Howard Platt; Conrad, Dick Balduzzi; Matron, Penelope Gillette; First Assistant, Kirk Mee; Real Estate Agent, Don Hanmer; Gino, Antony Carbone; Jude Farese, Stack Pierce, Jack Emel, Donald Newsome, Titos Vandis, Wilbert Gowdy, Louis J. DiFonzc, Dea St. Lamont.

2083 NEXT. (Maron-Gemini-1971). Neil, Alberto De Mendoza; Julie, Edwige Fenech; Carol, Cristina Airoldi; George, George Hilton; Jean, Ivan Rassimov.

2084 A NICE GIRL LIKE ME. (AVCO Embassy-1969). Candida, Barbara Ferris; Savage, Harry Andrews; Aunt Mary, Gladys Cooper; Ed, Bill Hinnant; Freddie, James Villiers; Aunt Celia, Joyce Carey; Pierre, Christopher Guinee; Miss Grimsby, Fabia Drake; Madame Dupont, Irene Prador; Vicar, Eric Chitty; Miss Charter, Totti Truman Taylor; Museum Attendant, John Serret; Dover Customs Man, John Clive; Miss Garland, Ann Lancaster; Labor Ward Sister, Shelagh Wilcox; Labor Ward Nurse, Sue Whitman; Post Natal Clinic Doctor, Douglas Wilmer; Marie, Carol Gilles; Pensione "Mama," Madge Brindley; Customs Officer, John Gurnsey.

2085 NICHOLAS AND ALEXANDRA. (Columbia-1971). Nicholas, Michael Jayston; Alexandra, Janet Suzman; Alexis, Roderic Noble; Olga, Ania Marson; Tatiana, Lynne Frederick; Marie, Candace Glendenning; Anastasia, Fiona Fullerton; Grand Duke Nicholas, Harry Andrews; Queen Mother Marie Fedorovna, Irene Worth; Rasputin, Tom Baker.

2086 THE NICKEL RIDE. (20th Century-Fox-1974). Cooper, Jason Miller; Sarah, Linda Haynes; Paddie, Victor French; Carl, John Hillerman; Turner, Bo Hopkins; Bobby, Richard Evans; Larry, Brendan Burns; Paulie, Lou Frizzell; Jeannie, Jeanne Lange; Elias, Bart Burns; Chester, Harvey Gold; Tonozzi, Mark Gordon.

2087 THE NIGHT BEFORE. (Hand-in-Hand-1973). Hank, Coke Hennessy; Paul, Michael Cade; Messenger, Jamal Jones; Tim, Nick Kastroff; Cyclist, Alexis Knight; Bill, Bob Plummer, Pete, Bill Yort; Dancers, Tim Clark, Jeffrey Etting.

2088 NIGHT CALL NURSES. (New World-1972). Barbara, Patricia T. Byrne; Janis, Alana Collins; Sandra, Mittie Lawrence; Dr. Bramlett, Clint Kimbrough; Jude, Felton Perry; Sampson, Stack Pierce; Kyle Toby, Richard Young.

2089 THE NIGHT DIGGER. (MGM-1971). Maura, Patricia Neal; Mother, Pamela Brown; Billy, Nicholas Clay; Mrs. McMurtrey, Jean Anderson; Bolton, Graham Crowden.

2090 THE NIGHT EVELYN CAME OUT OF THE GRAVE. (Phase One-1972). Lord Alan Cunningham, Anthony Steffen; Susan, Erika Blanc; Gladys, Marina Malfatti; George, Rod Murdock; Giacomo Rossi Stuart, Umberto Raho, Roberto Maldera, Joan C. Davies.

2091 NIGHT GAMES. (Sandrews-1966). Irene, Ingrid Thulin; Jan, Keve Khelm; Jan (as a boy), Jorgen Lindstrom; Mariana, Lena Brundin; Aunt Astrid, Naima Wifstrand; Homosexual, Rune Lindstrom; Monica Zetterlund, Lauritz Falk, Christian Bratt.

2092 NIGHT OF DARK SHADOWS. (MGM-1971). Quentin, David Selby; Angelique, Lara Parker; Tracy, Kate Jackson; Carlotta, Grayson Hall; Alex, John Karlen; Claire, Nancy Barrett; Gerard, James Storm; Laura, Diana Millay; Gabriel, Christopher Pennock; Rev. Strack, Thayer David; Sarah, Monica Rich; Mrs. Castle, Clarisse Blackburn.

2093 NIGHT OF THE COBRA WOMAN. (New World-1972). Joanna, Joy Bang; Lena, Marlene Clark; Duff, Roger Garrett; Sgt. Merkle, Slash Marks; Lope, Vic Diaz.

2094 THE NIGHT OF THE FOLLOWING DAY. (Universal-1969). Bud, Marlon Brando; Leer, Richard Boone; Vi, Rita Moreno; The Girl, Pamela Franklin; Wally, Jess Hahn; Gendarme/Fisherman, Gerard Buhr; The Father, Hughes Wanner; Bartender, Jacques Marin.

2095 THE NIGHT OF THE GENERALS. (Columbia-1967). General Tanz, Peter O'Toole; Major Grau, Omar Sharif; Corporal Hartmann, Tom Courtenay; General Kahlenberge,

Donald Pleasence; Ulrike, Joanna Pettet; Inspector Morand, Philippe Noiret; Rommel, Christopher Plummer; General von Seidlitz-Gabler, Charles Gray; Eleanore von Seidlitz-Gabler, Coral Browne; Colonel Sandauer, John Gregson; Otto, Nigel Stock; Juliette, Juliette Greco; Yves Brainville, Sacha Pitoeff, Charles Millot, Raymond Gerome, Veronique Vendell, Pierre Mondy, Eleonore Hirt, Nicole Courcel, Jenny Orleans, Gerard Buhr, Michael Goodliffe, Gordon Jackson, Patrick Allen.

2096 THE NIGHT OF THE GRIZZLY. (Paramount-1966). Jim Cole, Clint Walker; Angela Cole, Martha Hyer; Jed Curry, Keenan Wynn; Wilhelmina Peterson, Nancy Kulp; Charlie Cole, Kevin Brodie; Hazel Squires, Ellen Corby; Hank, Jack Elam; Tad Curry, Ron Ely; Duke Squires, Med Flory; Cass Dowdy, Leo Gordon; Sam Potts, Don Haggerty; Cal Curry, Sammy Jackson; Gypsy Cole, Victoria Paige Meyerink; Meg, Candy Moore; Cotton Benson, Regis Toomey.

2097 NIGHT OF THE LEPUS. (MGM-1972). Roy, Stuart Whitman; Gerry, Janet Leigh; Cole, Rory Calhoun; Elgin, DeForest Kelley; Sheriff, Paul Fix; Amanda, Melanie Fullerton; Jackie, Chris Morrell; Jud, Chuck Hayward; Frank, Henry Wills; Mildren, Francesca Jarvis; Dr. Leopold, William Elliott; Prof. Dirkson, Robert Hardy; Deputy, Richard Jacome; Housekeeper, Inez Perez; Walker, G. Leroy Gaintner; Major White, Evans Thornton; Dispatcher, I. Stanford Jolley; Leslie, Robert Gooden; Truck Driver, Walter Kelley; Doctor, Frank Kennedy; Cutler, Don Starr; Arlen, Peter O'Crotty; Officer, Phillip Avenetti; Priest, Russell Morrell; Wife in Car, Donna Gelgur; Husband in car, Stephen de France; Children in car, Sherry Hummer, Rick Hummer; TV Newscaster, Jerry Dunphy.

2098 NIGHT OF THE LIVING DEAD. (Continental-1968). Barbara, Judith O'Dea; Johnny, Russell Streiner; Ben, Duane Jones; Harry, Karl Hardman; Tom, Keith Wayne; Judy, Judith Ridley; Helen, Marilyn Eastman; Karen, Kyra Schon.

2099 THE NIGHT OF THE SCARECROW. (1974). Maria do Grotao, Rejane Madeiros; Ze do Cao, Jose Pimentel; Ze Tulao, Gilson Moura; The Scarecrow, Alceu Valenca; Colonel, Emmanuel Cavalcanti; Dragon, Fatima Batista; Josue, Luis Gomes Correa; Severino, Geraldo Azevedo; Bento, Jorge Mello; Terencio, Mario de Jacob; Juca, Jose Maximo.

2100 THE NIGHT OF THE SEAGULL. (Toho-1970). Mie Hama, Jin Nakayama, Megumi Matsumoto, Jitsuko Yoshimura, Natsuko Kahara.

2101 THE NIGHT PORTER. (United Artists-1974). Max, Dirk Bogarde; Lucia, Charlotte Rampling; Klaus, Philippe Leroy; Voglet, Gabriele Ferzetti; Countess, Isa Miranda; Bert,

Amedeo Amadio; Stumm, Giuseppi Addobbati.

2102 THE NIGHT THEY RAIDED MINSKY'S. (United Artists-1968). Raymond Paine, Jason Robards; Rachel Schpitendavel, Britt Ekland; Chick Williams, Norman Wisdom; Professor Spats, Bert Lahr; Trim Houlihan, Forrest Tucker; Jacob Schpitendavel, Harry Andrews; Louis Minsky, Joseph Wiseman; Vance Fowler, Denholm Elliott; Billy Minsky, Elliott Gould; Candy Butcher, Jack Burns; Mae Harris, Gloria LeRoy; Scratch, Eddie Lawrence; Duffy, Dexter Maitland; Speakeasy Singer, Lillian Hayman; Pockets, Dick Libertini; Judith Lowery, Will B. Able, Herbie Faye, Joe E. Marks, Chanin Hale, Mike Elias, Frank Shaw, Fats Thomas, Reno Pesauri, Ernestine Barrett, Kelsey Collins, Marilyn D'Honau, Kathryn Doby, Jo Ann Lehmann, Dorothea MacFarland, Billie Mahoney, Carolyn Wood, June Eve Story, Helen Wood, Rudy Vallee.

2103 NIGHT TRAIN TO MUNDO FINE. (Hollywood Star-1966). Coleman Francis, Anthony Cardoza, Harold Saunders, John Carradine, John Morrison, George Prince, Lanell Cado, Tom Hanson, Julian Baker, Charles Harter, Elaine Gibford, Bruce Love, Nick Raymond.

2104 THE NIGHT VISITOR. (UMC-1971). Salem, Max Von Sydow; Inspector, Trevor Howard; Esther, Liv Ullmann; Dr. Jenks, Per Oscarsson; Clemens, Rupert Davies; Dr. Kemp, Andrew Keir; Pop, Arthur Hewlett; Carl, Jim Kennedy; Emmie, Hanne Bork; Tokens, Bjorn Watt Boolsen; Britt, Lottie Freddie.

2105 THE NIGHT WALKER. (Universal-1965). Irene Trent, Barbara Stanwyck; Barry Morland, Robert Taylor; The Dream, Lloyd Bochner; Joyce, Judith Meredith; Howard Trent, Hayden Rorke; Hilda, Rochelle Hudson; Manager, Marjorie Bennett; Malone, Jess Barker; Pat, Pauelle Clark; Gardener, Tetsu Komai.

2106 NIGHT WATCH. (AVCO Embassy-1973). Ellen Wheeler, Elizabeth Taylor; John Wheeler, Laurence Harvey; Sarah Cooke, Billie Whitelaw; Appleby, Robert Lang; Tony, Tony Britton; Inspector Walker, Bill Dean; Sergeant Norris, Michael Danvers-Walker; Dolores, Rosario Serrano; Secretary, Pauline Jameson; Girl in car, Linda Hayden; Carl, Kevin Colson; Florist, Laon Maybanke.

2107 THE NIGHTCOMERS. (AVCO Embassy-1972). Peter Quint, Marlon Brando; Miss Jessel, Stephanie Beacham; Mrs. Grose, Thora Hird; Master of the House, Harry Andrews; Flora, Verna Harvey; Miles, Christopher Ellis; New Governess, Anna Palk.

2108 NIGHTMARE CASTLE. (Allied Artists-1967). Muriel/Jenny,

Barbara Steele; Dr. Stephen Arrowsmith, Paul Miller; Solange, Helga Line; Dr. Derek Joyce, Lawrence Clift; David, Rik Battaglia; Jonathan, John McDouglas.

2109 NIGHTMARE IN THE SUN. (Zodiac-States Rights-1965). Ursula Andress, John Derek, Aldo Ray, Arthur O'Connell, Lurene Tuttle, George Tobias, Douglas Fowley, John Marley, Bill Challe, Michael Petit, James Waters, John Sebastian, Sammy Davis Jr., Allyn Joslyn, Keenan Wynn, Chick Chandler, Richard Jaeckel.

2110 THE NINE LIVES OF FRITZ THE CAT. (American International-1974). Skipp Hinnant, Reva Rose, Bob Holt, Dick Whittington, Robert Ridgley, Fred Smoot, Luke Walker, Peter Leeds, Louisa Moritz, Larry Moss, Stanley Adams, Joan Gerber, Pat Harrington Jr., Jim Johnson, Carol Androsky, Jay Lawrence, Pynn Roman, Ralph James, Eric Monte, Glynn Turman, Ron Knight, Gloria Jones, Renny Roker, Peter Hobbs, Buddy Aret, John Hancock, Chris Graham, Felton Perry, Anthony Mason, Serena Grant.

2111 1900. (Paramount-1974). Burt Lancaster, Robert De Niro, Dominique Sanda, Stefania Sandrelli, Gerard DePardieu, Donald Sutherland, Sterling Hayden, Laura Betti, Anna-Maria Gherardi, Alida Valli.

2112 90 DEGREES IN THE SHADE. (Landau-Unger-1966). Alena, Anne Heywood; Vorell, James Booth; Kurka, Rudolf Krusinski; Mrs. Kurka, Ann Todd; Bazant, Donald Wolfit.

2113 99 and 44/100% DEAD. (20th Century-Fox-1974). Harry Crown, Richard Harris; Uncle Frank, Edmond O'Brien; Big Eddie, Bradford Dillman; Buffy, Ann Turkel; Dolly, Constance Ford; Tony, David Hall; Baby, Kathrine Baumann; Clara, Janice Heiden; Marvin "Claw" Zuckerman, Chuck Connors.

2114 99 WOMEN. (Commonwealth United-1969). Leonie, Maria Schell; Natalie, Luciana Paluzzi; Thelma, Mercedes McCambridge; The Governor, Herbert Lom; Marie, Maria Rohm; Zoe, Rosalba Neri; Rosalie, Valentine Godoy; Helga, Elisa Montes, Maria Perschy.

2115 NO BLADE OF GRASS. (MGM-1970). John Custance, Nigel Davenport; Ann Custance, Jean Wallace; Roger Burnham, John Hamill; Mary Custance, Lynne Frederick; David Custance, Patrick Holt; Pirrie, Anthony May; Clara, Wendy Richard; Davey, Nigel Rathbone.

2116 NO DRUMS, NO BUGLES. (Cinerama-1971). Ashby Gatrell, Martin Sheen; Gallie Gatrell, Davey Davison; Lieutenant, Rod McCary; Sarah, Denine Terry.

2117 NO MORE EXCUSES. (Rogosin-1968). Private Stewart Thompson, Robert Downey; Himself, Allen Abel; President Garfield, Lawrence Wolf; Charles Guiteau, Prentice Wilhite; Mrs. Garfield, Linda Diesem; Chinese Girl, Amy Eckles; Rapist-Priest, Don Calfa; Fat Woman/Prostitute, Paula Morris.

2118 NO WAY TO TREAT A LADY. (Paramount-1968). Christopher Gill, Rod Steiger; Kat Palmer, Lee Remick; Morris Brummel, George Segal; Mrs. Brummel, Eileen Heckart; Inspector Haines, Murray Hamilton; Mr. Kupperman, Michael Dunn; Alma Mulloy, Martine Bartlett; Belle Poppie, Barbara Baxley; Sylvia Poppie, Doris Roberts; Mrs. Fitts, Irene Dailey; Mrs. Himmel, Ruth White; Detective Monaghan, Val Bisoglio; Lieut. Dawson, David Doyle; Sadie, Kim August; Himself, Vincent Sardi; Priest, Tom Ahearne; Policeman, Glenn Kezer.

2119 NOBODY WAVED GOODBYE. (Cinema V-1965). Peter, Peter Kastner; Julie, Julie Biggs; Father, Claude Rae; Sister, Toby Tarnow; Mother, Charmion King; Boyfriend, Ron Taylor; Patrolman, Robert Hill; Sergeant, Jack Beer; Probation Officer, John Sullivan; Julie's Mother, Lynne Gorman; Interviewer, Ivor Barry; Waitress, Sharon Bonin; Landlord, Norman Ettlinger; Lot Supervisor, John Vernon.

2120 NOBODY'S PERFECT. (Universal-1968). Doc Willoughby, Doug McClure; Tomiko Momoyama, Nancy Kwan; Capt. Mike Riley, James Whitmore; Boats McCafferty, David Hartman; Walt Purdy, Gary Vinson; Toshi O'Hara, James Shigeta; Johnny Crane, Steve Carlson; Hamner, George Furth; Gondai-San, Keye Luke; Marci Adler, Jill Donohue; Lt. Large, Bea Bradley; Mr. Bayless, James Creech; Watanabe, Jerry Fujikawa; John Abelard, Edward Faulkner; Terry Abelard, Marion Collier.

2121 NONE BUT THE BRAVE. (Warner Bros. -1965). Maloney, Frank Sinatra; Capt. Bourke, Clint Walker; Lt. Blair, Tommy Sands; Sgt. Bleeker, Brad Dexter; Keller, Tony Bill; Lt. Kuroki, Tatsuya Mihashi; Sgt. Tamura, Takeshi Kato; Cpl. Craddock, Sammy Jackson; Cpl. Ruffino, Richard Bakalyan; Pvt. Johnson, Rafer Johnson; Pvt. Dexter, Jimmy Griffin; Pvt. Searcy, Christopher Dark; Pvt. Hoxie, Don Dorrell; Pvt. Magee, Phil Crosby; Pvt. Waller, John H. Young; Swensholm, Roger Ewing; Hirano, H. Suguro; Cpl. Fujimoto, K. Sahara.

2122 NORWOOD. (Paramount-1970). Norwood, Glen Campbell; Rita, Kim Darby; Joe, Joe Namath; Yvonne, Carol Lynley; Grady, Pat Hingle; Marie, Tisha Sterling; Bill, Dom DeLuise; Vernell, Leigh French; Kay, Meredith MacRae; Wayne, Sammy Jackson; Ratner, Billy Curtis; Grandma, Merie Earle; Mr. Reese, Jack Haley Sr. ; Jeeter, Jimmy

Boyd; Uncle Lonnie, David W. Huddleston; Bus Passenger, Edith Atwater; Remley, Gil Lamb; Mrs. Remley, Cass Daley; Timon, Joe Oakie; Ernestine, Virginia Caper; Pete, Jay Ripley.

2123 NOT MINE TO LOVE. (Edward Meadows-1969). Eli, Odded Kotler; Shuy, Shuy Osherov; Noa, Judith Soleh; Shuy's Father, Misha Asherov; Zvi, Illy Gorlitzky; Yael, Germaine Unikovsky; Neighbor, Stella Avni; Neighbor's Husband, Baruch David; Yael's Mother, Shoshana Duer; Yael's Father, Nissan Yatir.

2124 NOT ON YOUR LIFE. (Pathe Contemporary-1965). Jose Luis, Nino Manfredi; Carmen, Emma Panella; Amedeo, Jose Isbert; Antonio, Jose Luis Lopez Vazquez; Alvarez, Angel Alvarez; Prison Warden, Guido Alberti; Esterfania, Maria Luisa Ponte; Ignacia, Maruja Isbert; First Sacristan, Felix Fernandez; Second Sacristan, Alfredo Landa; Organist, Jose Luis Coll.

2125 NOT WITH MY WIFE, YOU DON'T! (Warner Bros. -1966). Tom Ferris, Tony Curtis; Julie Ferris, Virna Lisi; "Tank" Martin, George C. Scott; General Parker, Carroll O'Connor; General Walters, Richard Eastham; Sgt. Gilroy, Eddie Ryder; Sgt. Dogerty, George Tyne; Doris Parker, Ann Doran; Nurse Sally Ann, Donna Danton; Lillian Walters, Natalie Core.

2126 NOW YOU SEE HIM, NOW YOU DON'T. (Buena Vista-1972). Dexter Riley, Kurt Russell; A. J. Arno, Cesar Romero; Dean Higgins, Joe Flynn; Timothy Forsythe, Jim Backus; Professor Lufkin, William Windom; Mr. Sampson, Edward Andrews, Richard Schuyler, Michael McGreevey; Cookie, Richard Bakalyan; Debbie Dawson, Joyce Menges; Dean Collingsgood, Alan Hewitt; Sgt. Cassidy, Kelly Thordsen; Alfred, Neil Russell; Ted, George O'Hanlon; Golfer, John Myhers; Secretary, Pat Delany; TV Announcer, Frank Aletter; Driver, Robert Rothwell; Mr. Burns, Dave Willock; Myles, Frank Welker; Slither Roth, Jack Bender; Henry Fathington, Mike Evans; Druffle, Ed Begley Jr.; Roadblock Officer, Paul Smith; Professional Golfers, Billy Casper and Dave Hill.

2127 THE NUDE RESTAURANT. (Andy Warhol-1967). The Waitress, Viva; Harmonica Player, Taylor Mead; Painted Man, Louis Waldron; Man in Tub, James Davis; Girl in Tub, Brigitte Polk; Draft Dodger, Julian Burroughs; Silent Man, Allen Midgette.

2128 NO. 96. (Cash-Harmon and 0-10 Network-1974). Aldo Godolfus, Johnny Lockwood; Roma Godolfus, Philippa Baker; Dorrie Evans, Pat McDonald; Herb Evans, Ron Shand; Don Finlayson, Joe Hasham; Norma Whittaker, Sheila Kennelly;

Les Whittaker, Gordon McDougall; Jack Sellars, Tom Oliver; Vera Collins, Elaine Lee; Lucy Sutcliffe, Elisabeth Kirkby; Alf Sutcliffe, James Elliott; Arnold Feather, Jeff Kevin; Flo Patterson, Bunney Brooke; Maggie Cameron, Bettina Welch.

2129 NUMBER ONE. (United Artists-1969). Ron "Cat" Catlan, Charlton Heston; Julie Catlan, Jessica Walter; Richie Fowler, Bruce Dern; Coach Jim Southerd, John Randolph; Ann Marley, Diana Muldaur; Harvey Hess, Bobby Troup; Dr. Tristler, G. D. Spradlin; Kelly Williams, Richard Elkins; Walt Chaffee, Mike Henry; Deke Coleman, Ernie Barnes; Robin, Steve Franken; Ed Davis, Bart Burns; Attendant, Forrest Wood; Dr. Overstreet, George Sperdakos; Roy Nelson, Roy Jenson; Himself, Al Hirt; Themselves, The New Orleans Saints.

2130 THE NUN. (Altura-1971). Suzanne, Anna Karina; Mme. de Chelles, Liselotte Pulver; Mme. de Moni, Micheline Presle; Soeur Ste. Christine, Francine Barge; Dan Morel, Francisco Rabal.

2131 A NUN AT THE CROSSROADS. (Universal-1970). Sister Maria, Rosanna Schiaffino; Pierre, John Richardson; Lisa, Mara Cruz; Father Raymond, Angel Picazo; Sister Blanche, Paloma Valdes; Mother Claire, Lily Murati; Nangu, Lex Monson; Madeleine, Margot Cottens; Michel, Andres Mejuto; Isaku, Willie P. Elie; Yvonne, Claudia Gravy; Jean, Lorenzo Terzon; Mother Superior, Maria Fernanda Ladron Guevara; Officer, Antonio Pica; Sister Genevieve, Alicia Altabella; Sister Marcella, Portifia Sanchis; Sister Herminia, Matilde Munoz Sampedro; Sister Lucille, Petra Lacey.

2132 O BRAVO GUERREIRO. (New Yorker-1971). Miguel, Paulo Cesar Pereio; Augusto, Mario Lago; Frota, Italo Rossi; Clara, Maria Lucia Dahl; Virgilio, Cezar Ladeiro; Pericles, Paulo Gracindo.

2133 O LUCKY MAN! (Warner Bros. -1973). Mick, Malcolm McDowell; Sir James/Monty, Ralph Richardson; Duff/Johnson/Munda, Arthur Lowe; Gloria/Mme. Paillard/Mrs. Richards, Rachel Roberts; Patricia, Helen Mirren; Tea Lady/Neighbor, Dandy Nichols; Neighbor/Usher/Sister Hallet, Mona Washbourne; Factory Chairman/Prison Governor, Peter Jeffrey; Stewart/Millar/Meths Drinker, Graham Crowden; Jenkins/Interrogator/Salvation Army Major, Philip Stone; Himself, Alan Price; Stone/Steiger/Executive/Warder, Wallas Eaton; M. C. /Warner/Male Nurse, Warren Clarke; Barlow/Superintendent, Bill Owen; Oswald, Edward Judd; Mrs. Naidu, Pearl Nunez; Mary Ball/Vicar's Wife, Mary Macleod; William/Interrogator/Released Prisoner, Michael Bangerter; Duke of Belminster/Captain/Power Station Technician, Michael Medwin.

2133a OSS 117--MISSION FOR A KILLER. (Embassy-1966). OSS 117, Frederick Stafford; Anna Maria Sulza, Mylene Demongeot; Leandro, Raymond Pellegrin; Consuela 1, Perrette Pradier; Consuela 2, Annie Andersson; Carlos, Francois Maistre; Miguel, Jacques Riberolles; Clark, Yves Furet; Karl, Guy Delorme; Ludwig, Jean-Pierre Janic; Thomas Ellis, Claude Carliez.

2134 THE OBLONG BOX. (American International-1969). Julian Markham, Vincent Price; Dr. Neuhartt, Christopher Lee; Sir Edward Markham, Alastair Williamson; Elizabeth Markham, Hilary Dwyer; Samuel Trench, Peter Arne; N'Galo, Harry Baird; Mark Norton, Carl Rigg; Tom Hackett, Maxwell Shaw; Ruddock, Michael Balfour; Weller, Godfrey James; Joshua Kemp, Rupert Davies; Sally Baxter, Sally Geeson; Hawthorne, Ivor Dean; Uta Levka, James Mellor, Danny Daniels, John Barrie, Hira Talfrey, John Wentworth, Betty Woolfe, Martin Terry, Anne Clune, Jackie Noble, Ann Barass, Jan Rossini, Zeph Gladstone, Tara Fernando, Tony Thawnton, Anthony Bailey, Richard Cornish, Colin Jeavons, Andreas Melandrinos, Edgar Wallace, Martin Wyldeck, Oh! Ugunde Dancers.

2135 OBSESSION. (O.R.P.-1968). "You," Mathia Henrikson; Leni, Maude Adleson; The other man, Lars Lind; German Tourist, Guy De La Berg; Andreas, Johannes Blind.

2136 THE ODD COUPLE. (Paramount-1968). Felix Ungar, Jack Lemmon; Oscar Madison, Walter Matthau; Vinnie, John Fiedler; Murray, Herbert Edelman; Roy, David Sheiner; Speed, Larry Haines; Cecily Pigeon, Monica Evans; Gwendolyn Pigeon, Carole Shelley; Waitress, Iris Adrian; Sports Writer, Heywood Hale Broun; Hotel Clerk, John C. Becher.

2137 THE ODESSA FILE. (Columbia-1974). Peter Miller, Jon Voight; Eduard Roschmann, Maximilian Schell; Mrs. Miller, Maria Schell; Sigi, Mary Tamm; Klaus Wenzer, Derek Jacobi; Simon Weisenthal, Shmuel Rodensky; Marx, Martin Brandt; Magazine Publisher Hoffman, Werner Bruhns; Killer Mackensen, Klaus Lowitsch; Oster, Kurt Meisel; Mrs. Wenzer, Elizabeth Neumann-Viertel; Werner Deilman, Ernst Schroder; Police Official Kunik, Gunter Strack; Franz Bayer, Noel Willman; Israeli Intelligence Leader, Peter Jeffrey; Landlord, Hans Wyprachtiger; Karl Braun, Gunnar Miller; Dr. Schultz Schmidt, Hans Canineberg; Medal Shop Owner, Til Kiwe.

2138 OEDIPUS THE KING. (Universal-1968). Oedipus, Christopher Plummer; Tiresias, Orson Welles; Jocasta, Lilli Palmer; Creon, Richard Johnson; Messenger, Cyril Cusack; Shepherd, Roger Livesey; Chorus Leader, Donald Sutherland; King Laius, Freidrich Ledebur; Official, Alexia Mantheakis; Priest, Demos Starenios; Antigone, Oenone Luke;

Ismene, Cressida Luke; Chorus Members, Costas Themos, Paul Roche, Minos Argyrakis, Takis Emmanouel and George Dialegmenos; Jocasta's Handmaidens, Mary Xenoudaki, Jenny Damianopoulou and Diana J. Reed.

2139 THE OFFENSE. (United Artists-1973). Johnson, Sean Connery; Cartwright, Trevor Howard; Maureen, Vivien Merchant; Baxter, Ian Bannen; Jessard, Derek Newark; Panton, John Hallam; Cameron, Peter Bowles; Lawson, Ronald Radd; Hill, Anthony Sagar; Lambeth, Howard Goorney; Garrett, Richard Moore; Janie, Maxine Gordon.

2140 THE OFFICE PICNIC. (Tom Cowan-1974). Clyde, John Wood; Mara, Kate Fitzpatrick; Peter, Phillip Deamer; Mrs. Rourke, Patricia Kennedy; Elly, Gay Steele; The Boss, Ben Gabriel; Paddy, Max Cullen.

2141 OH, CALCUTTA! (Cinemation-1972).

2142 OH DAD, POOR DAD, MAMA'S HUNG YOU IN THE CLOSET AND I'M FEELIN' SO SAD. (Paramount-1967). Madame Rosepettle, Rosalind Russell; Jonathan, Robert Morse; Rosalie, Barbara Harris; Commodore Roseabove, Hugh Griffith; Dad, Jonathan Winters; Airport Commander, Lionel Jeffries; Hawkins, Cyril Delavanti; Breckenduff, Hiram Sherman; Moses, George Kirby; The Other Woman, Janis Hansen.

2143 OH! THOSE MOST SECRET AGENTS! (Allied Artists-1966). Franco Franchi, Ciccio Ingrassia, Ingrid Schoeller, Arnoldo Tieri, Annie Gorassini, Carla Calo, Poldo Bendanti.

2144 OH! WHAT A LOVELY WAR. (Paramount-1969). Field Marshal Sir Douglas Haig, John Mills; Stephen, Dirk Bogarde; French Colonel, Jean-Pierre Cassel; Count Leopold von Berchtold, John Gielgud; President Poincare, Ian Holm; Sir Edward Grey, Ralph Richardson; General Sir Henry Wilson, Michael Redgrave; Music Hall Star, Maggie Smith; Lady Haig, Phyllis Calvert; General von Moltke, John Clements; Emperor Franz Josef, Jack Hawkins; Kaiser Wilhelm II, Kenneth More; Sir John French, Laurence Olivier; Sylvia Pankhurst, Vanessa Redgrave; Eleanor, Susannah York; Grandpa, John Rae; Mother, Mary Wimbush; Bertie, Corin Redgrave; George, Maurice Roeves; Jack, Paul Shelley; Freddie, Malcolm McFee; Harry, Colin Farrell; Betty, Angela Thorne; Flo, Wendy Allnutt; Dickie, Kim Smith; Emma (age 4), Kathleen Wileman; Emma (age 8), Charlotte Attenborough; Tsar Nicholas II, Paul Daneman; French Singer, Pia Colombo; Fritz, Christian Doermer; Woodrow Wilson, Frank Forsyth; Lenin, John Gabriel; Italian Military Attache, Anthony Morton; Lady Grey, Meriel Forbes; Nurses at Station, Nanette Newman and Juliet Mills; Recruiting Sergeant, David Lodge; Archduke Franz Ferdinand,

Wensley Pithey.

2145 OHAYO. (Shochiku Films of America-1966). The Elder Brother, Koji Shidara; The Young Brother, Masahiko Shimazu; Their Father, Chisu Ryu; Their Mother, Kuniko Miyake; Their Aunt, Yoshiko Kuga; Their Teacher, Keiji Sada; Tatsuzo, Haruo Tanaka; Kikue, Haruko Sugimura.

2146 OKAY BILL. (Four Star Excelsior-1971). Bill, Bob Brady; Nancy, Nancy Salmon; Zachary, Gordon Felio; Roz, Roz Kelly.

2147 OKLAHOMA CRUDE. (Columbia-1973). Mase, George C. Scott; Lena, Faye Dunaway; Cleon, John Mills; Hellman, Jack Palance; Marion, William Lucking; Wilcox, Harvey James; Wobbly, Ted Gehring; Massive Man, Cliff Osmond; Jimmy, Rafael Campos; Lawyer, Woodrow Parfrey; Bloom, John Hudkins; Bliss, Harvey Parry; Dulling, Bob Herron; rucker, Jerry Brown; Moody, Jim Burk; Walker, Henry Wills; C. R. Miller, Hal Smith; Indian, Cody Bearpaw; Stapp, James Jeter; Deke Watson, Larry D. Mann; Farmer, John Dierkes; Hobo 1, Karl Lukas; Hobo 2, Wayne Storm; Cook, Billy Varga.

2148 THE OLDEST PROFESSION. (VIP-1968). Britt, Michele Mercier; Braque, Enrico Maria Salerno; Man from the Sea, Gabriele Tinti; Dimitilla, Elsa Martinelli; Flavius Caesar, Gaston Moschin; Mademoiselle Mimi, Jeanne Moreau; Philibert, Jean-Claude Brialy; Constable, Jean Richard; Nini, Raquel Welch; Banker, Martin Held; Catherine, France Anglade; Nadia, Nadia Gray; Doctor, Francis Blanche; Space Traveler, Jacques Charrier; Miss Conversation, Anna Karina; Miss Physical Love, Marilu Tolo; Bellboy, Jean-Pierre Leaud.

2149 THE OLIVE TREES OF JUSTICE. (Pathe Contemporary-1967). Jean, Pierre Prothon; His Father, Jean Pelegri; His Mother, Marie Decaitre; Cousin Louise, Hugette Poggi.

2150 OLIVER! (Columbia-1968). Fagin, Ron Moody; Nancy, Shani Wallis; Bill Sikes, Oliver Reed; Mr. Bumble, Harry Secombe; Oliver, Mark Lester; The Magistrate, Hugh Griffith; Mrs. Sowerberry, Hylda Baker; The Artful Dodger, Jack Wild; Mr. Brownlow, Joseph O'Connor; Mr. Sowerberry, Leonard Rossiter.

2151 THE OMEGA MAN. (Warner Bros. -1971). Neville, Charlton Heston; Matthias, Anthony Zerbe; Lisa, Rosalind Cash; Dutch, Paul Kosto; Zachary, Lincoln Kilpatrick; Richie, Eric Laneuville.

2152 ON A CLEAR DAY YOU CAN SEE FOREVER. (Paramount-1970). Daisy Gamble, Barbra Streisand; Dr. Marc Chabot,

Yves Montand; Dr. Mason Hume, Bob Newhart; Warren Pratt, Larry Blyden; Dr. Conrad Fuller, Simon Oakland; Tad Pringle, Jack Nicholson; Robert Tentrees, John Richardson; Mrs. Fitzherbert, Pamela Brown; Winnie Wainwhistle, Irene Handl; Prince Regent, Roy Kinnear; Divorce Attorney, Peter Crowcroft; Prosecuting Attorney, Byron Webster; Mrs. Hatch, Mabel Albertson; Lord Percy, Laurie Main; Hoyt III, Kermit Murdock; Muriel, Elaine Giftos; Pelham, John Le Mesurier; Diana Smallwood, Angela Pringle; Clews, Leon Ames; Millard, Paul Camen; Wytelipt, George Neise; Preston, Tony Colti.

2153 ON HER BED OF ROSES. (Famous Players Corporation-1966). Ronald Warren, Sandra Lynn, Barbara Hines, Dr. Lee Gladden, Ric Marlow, Regina Gleason, Lovey Song, Richard Clair, Pat Barrington, Elaine Poulos, Sarah Nade, Richard Tretter, Karen Arney, Pamela Woolman, Ned York.

2154 ON HER MAJESTY'S SECRET SERVICE. (United Artists-1969). James Bond, George Lazenby; Tracy, Diana Rigg; Blofeld, Telly Savalas; Irma Bunt, Ilse Steppat; Draco, Gabriele Ferzetti; Grunther, Yuri Borienko; Campbell, Bernard Horsfall; Sir Hilary Bray, George Baker; "M," Bernard Lee; Miss Moneypenny, Lois Maxwell; "Q," Desmond Llewelyn; Ruby, Angela Scoular; Nancy, Catherina Von Schell; Casino Guest, Bessie Love; Toussaint, Geoffrey Cheshire; Che Che, Irvin Allen; Raphael, Terry Mountain; Klett, Bill Morgan; Felsen, Les Crawford; Braun, George Cooper; Gumpold, James Bree; Olympe, Virginia North; Manuel, Brian Worth.

2155 ON MY WAY TO THE CRUSADES, I MET A GIRL WHO... (Warner Bros.-7 Arts-1969). Guerrando da Montone, Tony Curtis; Boccadoro, Monica Vitti; Sultan of Bari, Hugh Griffith; Drogone, John Richardson; Duke of Padolfo, Ivo Garrani; Marculfo, Nino Castelnuovo; Bertuccio, Franco Sportelli, Hermit, Lauro Gazzolo.

2156 ONCE A THIEF. (MGM-1965). Eddie Pedak, Alain Delon; Kristine Pedak, Ann-Margret; Mike Vido, Van Heflin; Walter Pedak, Jack Palance; James Sargatanas, John Davis Chandler; Lieutenant Kebner, Jeff Corey; Cleve Shoenstein, Tony Musante; Frank Kane, Steve Mitchell; Luke, Zekial Marko; Kathy Pedak, Tammy Locke; John Ling, Tuki Shimoda; Drummer, Russell Lee.

2157 ONCE BEFORE I DIE. (Goldstone Film Enterprises-1966). Ursula Andress, John Derek, Rod Lauren, Richard Jaeckel, Ron Ely.

2158 ONCE UPON A SCOUNDREL. (Carlyle Films-1974). Zero Mostel, Katy Jurado, Tito Vandis, Priscilla Garcia, A. Martinez.

2159 ONCE UPON A TIME IN THE WEST. (Paramount-1969). Frank, Henry Fonda; Jill McBain, Claudia Cardinale; Cheyenne, Jason Robards; The Man (Harmonica), Charles Bronson; Brett McBain, Frank Wolff; Morton, Gabriele Ferzetti; Sheriff, Keenan Wynn; Sam, Paolo Stoppa; Wobbles, Marco Zuanelli; Barman, Lionel Stander; Knuckles, Jack Elam; Member of Frank's Gang, John Frederick; Stony, Woody Strode; Timmy, Enzio Santianello; Harmonica sa s Boy, Dino Mele; Benito Stefanelli, Salvo Basile, Aldo Berti, Luigi Ciavarro, Spartaco Conversi, Marilu Carteny, Marco Zuanelli, Livio Andronico.

2160 ONCE YOU KISS A STRANGER. (Warner Bros. -7 Arts-1969). Jerry, Paul Burke; Diana, Carol Lynley; Lee, Martha Hyer; Peter, Peter Lind Hayes; Mike, Philip Carey; Lt. Gavin, Stephen McNally; Dr. Haggis, Whit Bissell; Sharon, Elaine Devry; Aunt Margaret, Kathryn Givney; Johnny, Jim Raymond; Announcer, George Fenneman; Raymond, Orville Sherman; Harriet, Maura McGiveney; Lee's Mother, Ann Doran.

2161 THE ONE AND ONLY, GENUINE, ORIGINAL FAMILY BAND. (Buena Vista-1968). Grandpa Bower, Walter Brennan; Papa Bower, Buddy Ebsen; Joe Calder, John Davidson; Alice Bower, Lesley Ann Warren; Mama Bower, Janet Blair; Sidney Bower, Kurt Russel; Ernie Stubbins, Steve Harmon; Charlie Wrenn, Richard Deacon; Mr. Wampler, Wally Cox; Lulu Bower, Debbie Smith; Mayo Bower, Robby Riha; Nettie Bower, Smitty Wordes; Rose Bower, Heidi Rook; Quinn Bower, Jon Walmsley; Laura Bower, Pamelyn Ferdin; Frank, John Craig; Mr. Henry White, William Woodson.

2162 ONE BRIEF SUMMER. (Cinevision-1972). Susan Long, Felicity Gibson; Mark Stevens, Clifford Evans; Jennifer Stevens, Jennifer Hilary; Elizabeth, Jan Holden; Bill Denton, Peter Egan; Mrs. Shaw, Fanny Carby; Hayward, Richard Vernon; Mrs. Hayward, Helen Lindsay; John Robertson, Basil Moss; Peter, David Leland; Lambert, Brian Wilde; Lockwood West, Neville Marten, Keith Smith, Susan Harvey, Carolyn Seymour, Robert Wilde, Virginia Balfour, Moira Foot, Pauline Challoner.

2163 ONE BY ONE. (Trans-International-1974). Stacy Keach, Peter Revson, Jackie Stewart, Francois Devert, Mike Hailwood, The Grand Prix Drivers of the World.

2164 ONE DAY IN THE LIFE OF IVAN DENISOVICH. (Cinerama-1971). Tom Courtenay, Alfred Burke.

2165 THE ONE EYED SOLDIERS. (United Screen Arts-1967). Richard Owne, Dale Robertson; Gava Berens, Luciana Paluzzi; Harold Schmidt, Guy Deghy; Colonel Ferrer, Andrew Faulds; Caporelli the Dwarf, Mila Avramovic; The Mummer,

Dragi Nikol; Dr. Charles Berens, Boza Drinic.

2166 100 RIFLES. (20th Century-Fox-1969). Lyedecker, Jim Brown; Sarita, Raquel Welch; Yaqui Joe, Burt Reynolds; General Verdugo, Fernando Lamas; Grimes, Dan O'Herlihy; Von Klemme, Hans Gudegast; Humara, Michael Forest; Sergeant Paletes, Aldo Sambrell; Girl in Hotel, Soledad Miranda; Padre Francisco, Alberto Dalbes; Lopez, Carlos Bravo; Sarita's Father, Jose Manuel Martin.

2167 ONE IS A LONELY NUMBER. (MGM-1972). Amy Brower, Trish Van Devere; Howard Carpenter, Monte Markham; Gert Meredith, Janet Leigh; Joseph Provo, Melvyn Douglas; Madge Frazier, Jane Elliot; Sherman Cooke, Jonathan Lippe; Morgue Attendant, Mark Bramhall; James Brower, Paul Jenkins; Frawley King, A. Scott Beach; Arnold Holzgang, Henry Leff; "King Lear," Dudley Knight; Pool Manager, Maurice Argent; Hardware Clerk, Thomas McNallan; "Earl of Gloucester," Joseph Spano; Ronnie Porter, Kim Allen; Employment Office Clerk, Peter Fitzsimmons; Marvin Friedlander, Christopher Brooks.

2168 ONE LITTLE INDIAN. (Buena Vista-1973). Clint, James Garner; Doris, Vera Miles; Mark, Clay O'Brien; Capt. Stewart, Pat Hingle; Chaplain, Andrew Prine; Sgt. Raines, Morgan Woodward; Martha, Jodie Foster; John Doucette, Robert Pine, Bruce Glover, Ken Swofford, Jay Silverheels, Walter Brooke, Rudy Diaz, John Flinn, Tom Simcox, Lois Red Elk, Hal Baylor, Terry Wilson, Paul Sorensen, Read Morgan, Jim Davis.

2169 $1,000,000 DUCK. (Buena Vista-1971). Prof. Albert Dooley, Dean Jones; Katie Dooley, Sandy Duncan; Finley Hooper, Joe Flynn; Fred Hines, Tony Roberts; Rutledge, James Gregory; Dr. Gottlieb, Jack Kruschen.

2170 ONE MILLION YEARS B.C. (20th Century-Fox-1967). Tumak, John Richardson; Sakana, Percy Herbert; Akhoba, Robert Brown; Nupondi, Martine Beswick; Tohana, Malya Nappi; Ulla, Yvonne Horner; Young Rock Man, Richard James; Rock Man, Frank Hayden; Loana, Raquel Welch; Ahot, Jean Wladon; Sura, Lisa Thomas; Payto, William Lyon Brown; Shell Man, Terence Maidment; Shell Girl, Micky De Rauch.

2171 ONE MORE TIME. (United Artists-1970). Charlie Salt, Sammy Davis Jr.; Chris Pepper, Peter Lawford; Billie, Esther Anderson; Miss Tomkins, Maggie Wright; Inspector, Leslie Sands; Mander, John Percy Herbert; Jenson, Bill Maynard; Wilson, Dudley Sutton; Dennis, Glyn Owen; Kim, Lucille Soong; Candler, Anthony Nichols; Belton, Allan Cuthbertson; Magistrate, Cyril Luckham; Priest, Moultrie Kelsal; General, Julian D'Albie; Lady Turpington-Mellish,

Gladys Spencer; Claire, Joanna Wake; Salt & Pepper Club Girls, Juliette Bora, Florence George, Amber Dean Smith, Lorraine Hall, Carmel Stratton, Thalma Neal.

2172 ONE MORE TRAIN TO ROB. (Universal-1971). Harker Fleet, George Peppard; Kate, Diana Muldaur; Timothy X. Nolan, John Vernon; Toy, France Nuyen; Jim Steve Sandor; Yung, Soon-Taik Oh; Monte, John Doucette; Conductor, George Chandler; Louella, Marie Windsor; Big Nellie, Joan Shawlee; Red, Harry Carey; Slim, Timothy Scott; Bert, Hal Needham; Skinner, Jim Burk; Deputy, Ben Cooper; Sen, Guy Lee; Herbert, Ray Dimas; Cora May, Pamela McMyler; Eli, Merlin Olsen; Luke, Phil Olsen.

2173 ONE NIGHT AT DINNER. (International-1971). Michel, Jean-Louis Trintignant; Max, Tony Musante; Nina, Florinda Bolkan; Giovanna, Annie Girardot; Ric, Lino Capolicchio.

2174 ONE OF OUR SPIES IS MISSING. (1966). Napoleon Solo, Robert Vaughn; Illya Kuryakin, David McCallum; Mr. Waverly, Leo G. Carroll; Sir Norman Swickert, Maurice Evans; Madame De Sala, Vera Miles; Joanna Sweet, Ann Elder; Jordin, Bernard Fox; Lorelei Lancer, Dolores Faith; Do Do, Anna Capri; Alexander Gritsky, Harry Davis; Wanda, Yvonne Craig; Olga, Monica Keating; Fleeton, Cal Bolder; Texan, Robert Easton; Phillip Bainbridge, James Doohan; Corvy, Ollie O'Toole; Steward, Antony Eustrel; Cat Man, Richard Peel; Pet Shop Owner, Barry Bernard.

2175 ONE ON TOP OF THE OTHER. (GGP-1973). Susan, Marisa Mell; George, Jean Sorel; Jane, Elsa Martinelli; Detective, John Ireland; Henry, Alberto De Mendoza; Benjamin, Jean Sobieski; Sister in law, Faith Domergue.

2176 ONE SPY TOO MANY. (MGM-1966). Napoleon Solo, Robert Vaughn; Illya Kuryakin, David McCallum; Alexander, Rip Torn; Tracey Alexander, Dorothy Provine; Mr. Waverly, Leo G. Carroll; Maude Waverly, Yvonne Craig; Kavon, David Opatoshu; Paviz, David Sheiner; Princess Nicole, Donna Michelle; General Bon-Phouma, Leon Lontoc; Colonel Hawks, Robert Karnes; Claxon, Clarke Gordon; Prince Phanong, James Hong; Ingo Lindstrum, Cal Bolder; Receptionist, Carole Williams; President Sing-Mok, Teru Shimada; General Man-Phang, Arthur Wong; Farrell, Robert Gibbons.

2177 1,000 CONVICTS AND A WOMAN. (American International-1971). Angela Thorne, Alexandra Hay; Paul Floret, Sandor Eles; Carl, Harry Baird; Warden Thorne, Neil Hallett.

2178 1001 DANISH DELIGHTS. (Cambist-1973). Count Axel, Dirch Passer; Baron Joachim, Axel Strobye; Inspector, Lone Hertz; Julie, Judy Gringer; Margaretha, Gertie Jung.

2179 ONE WAY PENDULUM. (Lopert-1965). Mr. Groomkirby, Eric Sykes; Defense Counsel, George Cole; Sylvia, Julia Foster; Kirby, Jonathan Miller; Mrs. Gantry, Peggy Mount; Mrs. Groomkirby, Alison Leggatt; Aunt Mildred, Mona Washbourne; Judge, Douglas Wilmer; Stan, Kenneth Farrington; Det. Inspector Barnes, Glyn Houston; Prosecuting Counsel, Graham Crowden; Clerk of the Court, Walter Horsburgh; Usher, Frederick Piper; Policeman, Vincent Harding; Voice of the Gormless, Tommy Bruce.

2180 ONE WAY WAHINI. (Allied Artists-1965). Joy Harmon, Anthony Eisley, Adele Claire, David Whorf, Edgar Bergen, Lee Kreiger, Ken Mayer, Harold Fong, Alvy Moore, Aime Luce, Ralph Nanalei.

2181 THE ONLY GAME IN TOWN. (20th Century-Fox-1970). Fran, Elizabeth Taylor; Joe Grady, Warren Beatty; Lockwood, Charles Brasswell; Tony, Hank Henry; Woman With Purple Wig, Olga Valery.

2182 ONLY THE WIND. (Casino-1965). Freddy Quinn, Gustav Knuth, Cordula Trantow, Gottfried Herbe, Gudrun Schmidt, Helmut Oeser.

2183 THE ONLY WAY HOME. (Regional-1972). Orval, Bo Hopkins; Marcia, Beth Brickell; Billy Joe, Steve Sandor; Philip, G. D. Spradlin; Boss, Walt Jones; Bobby, Jack Isaacs; Orval's Mother, Jean Abney; Henderson, Maurice Eaves; Custodian, Stanley Zenor; Deliveryman, Tom Kroutil; Waitress, Jane Hall; Car Salesman, Lynn Hickey; Cowboy, Beverly Osborne; Motorist, Edgar Springer; Little Boy, Matthew Smith; Boy's Mother, Ida B.; Drunk Lady, Jo Peters; Model, Linda Capetta; Waitress, Louise Chester; Gunshop Clerk, Clyde Martin; Proprietress, Nancy Harris; Billy Joe's Wife, Francine Shed; Uncle John, George Clow; Barfly, Joseph Taft; Driver, Ross Cummings; Driver's Wife, Mary Gordon Taft; Marcia's Mother, Anne Ault; Workman, George Keyes.

2184 ONLY WHEN I LARF. (Paramount-1968). Silas, Richard Attenborough; Bob, David Hemmings; Liz, Alexandra Stewart; Spencer, Nicholas Pennell; Diana, Melissa Stribling; Gee Gee Gray, Terence Alexander; Awana, Cedric Connor; General Sakut, Clifton Jones; Ali Lin, Calvin Lockhart; Spider, Brian Grellis; Jones, David Healy; Poster, Alan Gifford.

2185 ONLY YOU KNOW, AND I KNOW. (Shoeshine-1971). Piano Teacher, Patrice Barnett; Stripper, Josephine Mitchell; Sportswoman, Peaches Harden; Girl with car, Carol Sanders; Mechanic, Philadelphia Frank; Actress, Dolce Mann; Hardy, Hardy Harrison; Pornographer, Michael Merlin.

2186 OPEN SEASON. (Columbia-1974). Ken, Peter Fonda; Nancy, Cornelia Sharpe; Greg, John Phillip Law; Art, Richard Lynch; Martin, Albert Mendoza; Wolkowski, William Holden.

2187 OPERATION C.I.A. (Allied Artists-1965). Burt Reynolds, Kieu Chinh, John Hoyt, Danielle Aubry, Cyril Thomson, John Laughinghouse, Frank Estes, Chaiporn, Michael Schwiner, Robert Gulbranson, Janet Russell, Santi.

2188 OPERATION CROSSBOW. (MGM-1965). Nora, Sophia Loren; John Curtis, George Peppard; Professor Lindemann, Trevor Howard; Boyd of M.I. 6, John Mills; Duncan Sandys, Richard Johnson; Robert Henshaw, Tom Courtenay; Phil Bradley, Jeremy Kemp; Bamford, Anthony Quayle; Frieda, Lilli Palmer; Ziemann, Paul Henreid; Helmut Dantine, Barbara Ruetting, Richard Todd, Sylvia Syms, John Fraser, Maurice Denham, Patrick Wymark, Moray Watson, Richard Wattis, Allan Cuthbertson, Robert Brown.

2189 OPERATION KID BROTHER. (United Artists-1967). Neil Connery, Neil Connery; Maya, Daniela Bianchi; Thair Beta, Adolfo Celi; Mildred, Agata Flori; Commander Cunningham, Bernard Lee; Alpha, Anthony Dawson; Max, Lois Maxwell; Yachuco, Yachuco Yama; Kurt, Guido Lollobrigida; Juan, Franco Giacobini; Ward Jones, Nando Angelini; Gamma, Mario Soria; Lotte, Anna Maria Noe.

2190 OPERATION LEONTINE. (Macmillan Audio Brandon-1973). Leontine, Francoise Rosay; Rita, Marlene Jobert; Fred, Andre Pousse; Charles, Bernard Blier; Casmir, Robert Dalban; Ruffin, Paul Frankeur; Tiburce, Claude Rollet.

2191 OPERATION SNAFU. (American International-1965). Horace Pope, Alfred Lynch; Pedlar Pascoe, Sean Connery; Mr. Bascombe, Cecil Parker; Mr. Cooksley, Stanley Holloway; Flora McNaughton, Eleanor Summerfield; Mrs. Cooksley, Kathleen Harrison; Trowbridge, Wilfrid Hyde White; Sergeant Buzzer, Alan King.

2192 OPHELIA. (New Line Cinema-1974). Alida Valli, Andre Jocelyn, Juliette Mayniel, Claude Cerval, Robert Burnier, Jean-Louis Maury, Sacha Briquet, Serge Bento, Liliane David, Pierre Vernier.

2193 THE OPTIMISTS. (Paramount-1973). Sam, Peter Sellers; Liz, Donna Mullane; Mark, John Chaffey; Bob Ellis, David Daker; Chrissie Ellis, Marjorie Yates; Ellis Baby, Katyana Kass; Dog's Home Secretary, Patricia Brake; Park Keeper, Michael Graham Cox; Park Policeman, Bruce Purchase; Dustmen, Bernie Searl, Tommy Wright; Mrs. Bonini, Pat Ashton; Laundry Ladies, Pat Becket, Daphne Lawson, Candyce Jane Brandl, Hilary Pritchard.

2194 THE ORGANIZATION. (United Artists-1971). Virgil Tibbs, Sidney Poitier; Valerie Tibbs, Barbara McNair; Jack Pecora, Gerald S. O'Loughlin; Mrs. Morgan, Sheree North.

2195 THE OSCAR. (Embassy-1966). Frank Fane, Stephen Boyd; Kay Bergdahl, Elke Sommer; Kappy Kapstetter, Milton Berle; Sophie Cantaro, Eleanor Parker; Kenneth H. Regan, Joseph Cotten; Laurel Scott, Jill St. John; Hymie Kelly, Tony Bennett; Trina Yale, Edie Adams; Barney Yale, Ernest Borgnine; Grobard, Ed Begley; Orrin C. Quentin, Walter Brennan; Sheriff, Broderick Crawford; Network Executive, James Dunn; Steve Marks, Peter Lawford; Sam, Jack Soo; Cheryl Barker, Jean Hale; Edith Head, Hedda Hopper, Frank Sinatra, Nancy Sinatra, Merle Oberon, Bob Hope.

2196 No entry.

2197 OTHELLO. (Warner Bros.-1966). Othello, Laurence Olivier; Iago, Frank Finlay; Desdemona, Maggie Smith; Emilia, Joyce Redman; Cassio, Derek Jacobi; Roderigo, Robert Lang; Brabantio, Anthony Nicholls; Duke of Venice, Harry Lomax; Bianca, Sheila Reid; Gratiano, Michael Turner; Kenneth MacKintosh, Edward Hardwicke, Roy Holder, David Hargreaves, Malcolm Terris, Terence Knapp, Keith Marsh, Tom Kempinski, Nicholas Edmett, William Hobbs, Trevor Martin.

2198 THE OTHER. (20th Century-Fox-1972). Ada, Uta Hagen; Alexandra, Diana Muldaur; Niles Perry, Chris Udvarnoky; Holland Perry, Martin Udvarnoky; Aunt Vee, Norma Connolly; Angelini, Victor French; Winnie, Loretta Leversee; Uncle George, Lou Frizzell; Mrs. Rowe, Portia Nelson; Torrie, Jenny Sullivan; Rider, John Ritter; Mr. P. C. Pretty, Jack Collins; Chan-yu, Ed Bakey; Russell, Clarence Crow.

2199 THE OTHER ONE. (Continental-1967). Anne, Malka Ribovska; Andre, Philippe Noiret; Julien, Marc Cassot; Remoulin, Christian Alers; Simone, Francoise Prevost; Serebriakov, Claude Dauphin.

2200 THE OTHER SIDE OF JOEY. (Jaguar-1972). Erik Kahnler, Gordon Harris, Elliott Crawford, William Maxwell, James Fuller.

2201 OTHON. (1971). Plautine, Anne Brumagge; Othon, Adriano Apra; Galba, Ennio Lauricella; Camille, Olimpia Carlisi; Vinius, Anthony Pensabene; Martian, Jean-Claude Biette; Lacus, Jubarithe Semaran.

2202 No entry.

2203 OTLEY. (Columbia-1969). Gerald Arthur Otley, Tom

Courtenay; Imogen, Romy Schneider; Sir Alec Hadrian, Alan Badel; Hendrickson, James Villiers; Johnston, Leonard Rossiter; Albert, James Bolam; Lin, Fiona Lewis; Philip Proudfoot, Freddie Jones; Jeffcock, James Cossins; Rollo, James Maxwell; Eric Lambert, Edward Hardwicke; Curtis, Ronald Lacey; Jean, Phyllida Law; Hewitt, Geoffrey Bayldon; Bruce, Frank Middlemass; Miles, Damian Harris; Paul, Robert Brownjohn; Landlady, Maureen Toal; Larry, Barry Fantoni; Tony, Bernard Sharpe; Constable, Paul Angelis; Ground Steward, David Kernan; Ground Stewardess, Sheila Steafel; News Agent, Katherine Parr; Dietician, Kathleen Helm; Ron Owen, Stella Tanner, Jonathan Cecil, Georgina Simpson, Norman Shelley, John Savident, Ken Parry, Robin Askwith, Kevin Bennett, Kenneth Cranham, Robert Gillespie, Donald McKillop, The Herd, Jimmy Young, Pete Murray.

2204 OUR MAN FLINT. (20th Century-Fox-1966). Derek Flint, James Coburn; Cramden, Lee J. Cobb; Gila, Gila Golan; Malcolm Rodney, Edward Mulhare; Dr. Schneider, Benson Fong; Gina, Gianna Serra; Anna, Sigrid Valdis; Leslie, Shelby Grant; Sakito, Helen Funai; Gruber, Michael St. Clair; Dr. Krupov, Khys Williams; American General, Russ Conway; WAC, Ena Hartman; American Diplomat, William Walker; Dr. Wu, Peter Brocco.

2205 OUR MOTHER'S HOUSE. (MGM-1967). Charlie Hook, Dirk Bogarde; Elsa Hook, Margaret Brooks; Diana Hook, Pamela Franklin; Hubert Hook, Louis Sheldon Williams; Dunstan Hook, John Gugolka; Jiminee Hook, Mark Lester; Gerty Hook, Sarah Nicholls; Willy Hook, Gustav Henry; Louis, Farnham Wallace; Mother, Annette Carell; Mrs. Quayle, Yootha Joyce; Doreen, Edina Ronay; Mr. Halbert, Anthony Nicholls; Miss Bailey, Claire Davidson; Bank Clerk, Gerald Sim; Girl Friend, Diana Ashley; Mr. Moley, Garfield Morgan; Woman Client, Faith Kent; Man Client, John Arnatt; Motorcyclist, Jack Silk.

2206 OUR TIME. (Warner Bros.-1974). Abby, Pamela Sue Martin; Muffy, Betsy Slade; Michael, Parker Stevenson; Malcolm, George O'Hanlon Jr.; Headmaster, Roderick Cook; Mrs. Pendleton, Edith Atwater; Miss Picard, Marijane Maricle; Nurse, Meg Wyllie; Buzzy, Michael Gray.

2207 OUT OF IT. (United Artists-1969). Russ, Jon Voight; Paul, Barry Gordon; Christine, Lada Edmund Jr.; Barbara, Gretchen Corbett; Steve, Peter Grad.

2208 OUT OF SIGHT. (Universal-1966). Homer, Jonathan Daly; Sandra, Karen Jensen; Marvin, Carole Shelyne; Greg, Robert Pine; Mr. Carter, Forrest Lewis; Scuba, Wende Wagner; Wipeout, Maggie Thrett; Tuff Bod, Deanna Lund; The Girl from FLUSH, Rena Horten; Big D, John Lawrence;

Mousie, Jimmy Murphy; Huh, Norman Grabowski; FLUSH Assistant, Billy Curtis; Mike, Deon Douglas; M.C., Bob Eubanks; Madge, Pamela Rodgers; Janet, Vicki Fee; Tom, Coby Denton; John Stamp, John Lodge; Gary Lewis and the Playboys, Freddie and the Dreamers, Dobie Gray, The Turtles, The Astronauts, The Knickerbockers.

2209 THE OUT-OF-TOWNERS. (Paramount-1970). George Kellerman, Jack Lemmon; Gwen Kellerman, Sandy Dennis; TV Man, Sandy Baron; Woman in Police Station, Anne Meara; Man in Plane, Robert Nichols; Airline Stewardess, Ann Prentiss; Murray, Graham Jarvis; Boston Cab Driver, Ron Carey; Officer Meyers, Phil Bruns; Cuban Diplomat, Carlos Montalban; Boston Lost & Found, Billy Dee Williams; Hotel Night Clerk, Anthony Holland; Hotel Day Clerk, Paul Dooley; Boston Agent, Robert King; Waiter on Train, Johnny Brown; Police Sergeant, Dolph Sweet; Police Officer, Jack Crowder; Looters, Jon Korkes, Robert Walden; Boston Baggage Man, Richard Libertini; Man in Phone Booth, Bob Bennett; Attendant, Ray Ballard; Porter, A. P. Westcott; Cleaning Woman, J. French; Sweeper, B. Paipert; Washroom Lady, Meredith Vincent; Redcap, Maxwell Glanville; Airline Stewardess, Mary Norman.

2210 OUT ONE SPECTRE. (Sunchild-1974). Thief, Juliet Berto; Director, Michel Lonsdale; Lawyer, Francoise Fabian; Writer, Bernadette Lafont.

2211 OUTBACK. (United Artists-1972). Doc Tydon, Donald Pleasence; John Grant, Gary Bond; Jock Crawford, Chips Rafferty; Janette Hynes, Sylvia Kay; Dick, Jack Thompson; Joe, Peter Whittle; Tim Hynes, Al Thomas; Charlie, John Meillon; Atkins, John Armstrong; Jarvis, Slim De Grey; Receptionist, Maggie Dence; Joe the Cook, Norman Erskine; Controllers, Owen Moase and John Calleen; Charlie Jones, Buster Fiddess; Stubbs, Tex Foote; Stockman, Colin Hughes; Van Driver, Jacko Jackson; Robyn, Nancy Knudsen; Joyce, Dawn Lake; Higgins, Harry Lawrence; Pig Eyes, Bob McDarra; Poker Player, Carlo Marchini; Miner, Liam Reynolds.

2212 THE OUTFIT. (MGM-1973). Macklin, Robert Duvall; Bett, Karen Black; Cody, Joe Don Baker; Mailer, Robert Ryan; Menner, Timothy Carey; Chemey, Richard Jaeckel; Buck's Wife, Sheree North; Frank, Felice Orlandi; Madge, Marie Windsor; Alma, Jane Greer; Doctor, Henry Jones; Rita, Joanna Cassidy; First Man, Tom Reese; Carl, Elisha Cook; Buck, Bill McKinney; Herself, Anita O'Day; Packard, Archie Moore; Accountant, Tony Young; Hit Man, Roland LaStarza; Ed, Edward Ness; Bob, Roy Roberts; Parking Attendant, Toby Anderson; Amos, Emile Meyer; Al, Roy Jenson; Bartender, Philip Kenneally; Sinclair, Bern Hoffman; Gas Attendant, John Steadman; Payoff Man, Paul Genge; Jim,

Francis DeSales; Bookie, James Bacon; Butler, Army Archerd; Himself, Tony Trabert.

2213 THE OUTLAWS IS COMING. (Columbia-1965). Larry, Larry Fine; Moe, Moe Howard; Curley Joe, Joe De Rita; Kenneth Cabot, Adam West; Annie Oakley, Nancy Kovack; Trigger Mortis, Mort Mills; Rance Roden, Don Lamond; Sunstroke Kid, Rex Holman; Abernathy/Doctor/Colonel, Emil Sitka; Charlie Horse, Henry Gibson; Murray Alper, Tiny Brauer, Joe Bolton, Bill Camfield, Hal Fryar, Johnny Giner, Wayne Mack, Ed T. McDonnell, Bruce Sedley, Paul Shannon, Sally Starr.

2214 OUTSIDE IN. (Robbins International-1972). Ollie, Darrel Larson; Chris, Heather Manzies; Bernard, Dennis Olivieri; Bink, John Bill; Mrs. Wilson, Peggy Deury; Uncle Albert, Logan Ramsey.

2215 THE OUTSIDE MAN. (United Artists-1973). Lucian, Jean-Louis Trintignant; Nancy, Ann-Margret; Lenny, Roy Scheider; Jackie, Angie Dickinson; Jane, Georgia Engel; Anderson, Felice Orlandi; Antoine, Michel Constantin; Karl, Carlo De Mejo; Alex, Umberto Orsini; Second Hawk, Carmine Argenziano; Butler, Rice Cattani; Victor, Ted Corsia; Hitchiker, Edward Greenberg; Salesgirl, Philippa Harris; Eric, Jackie Haley; Department Store Manager, John Hillerman; First Hawk, Jon Korkes; Rosie, Connie Kreski; Desk Clerk, Ben Piazza; Miller, Alex Rocco; Make-up Girl, Talia Shire; Paul, Lionel Vitrant.

2216 THE OVERCOAT. (Cinemasters International-1965). Akaky Akakyevich, Roland Bykov; Petrovich, Y. Tolubeyev; Petrovich's Wife, A. Yezhkina; Landlady, Y. Ponsova.

2217 THE OWL AND THE PUSSYCAT. (Columbia-1970). Doris, Barbra Streisand; Felix, George Segal; Barney, Robert Klein; Dress Shop Proprietor, Allen Garfield; Eleanor, Roz Kelly; Rapzinsky, Jacques Sandelescu; Weyderhaus, Jack Manning; Mrs. Weyderhaus, Grace Carney; Miss Weyderhaus, Barbara Anson; Theatre Cashier, Kim Chan; Coatcheck Man, Stan Gottlieb; Old Man Neighbor, Joe Madden; Old Woman Neighbor, Fay Sappington; Barney's Girl, Evelyn Land; Man in Bar, Dominic T. Barto; Gang in Car, Marshall Ward, Tom Atkins, Stan Bryant.

2218 P. J. (Universal-1968). P. J. Detweiler, George Peppard; William Orbison, Raymond Burr; Maureen Preble, Gayle Hunnicutt; Police Chief Waterpack, Brock Peters; Billings Browne, Wilfrid Hyde-White; Jason Grenoble, Jason Evers; Betty Orbison, Coleen Gray; Linette Orbison, Susan Saint James; Shelton Quell, Severn Darden; Elinor Silene, H. Jane Van Duser; Sonny Silene, George Furth; Lita, Barbara Dana; Charlie, Herbert Edelman; Poppa, John Qualen; Police

Lieutenant, Bert Freed; Thorson, Ken Lynch; Landlord's Agent, Jim Boles; Jackie, Arte Johnson; Calypso Singer, King Charles MacNiles; Ape, Don H. B. Haggerty; Mrs. Thorson, Kay Farrington; Greavy, Lennie Bremen.

2219 THE P.O.W. (Dossick-1973). Howie, Howard Jahre; Rudy, Rudy Hornish; Wendy, Wendy Messier; Manuel, Manuel Sicart; Marcia, Marcia Davis; Shelley, Shelley Kaplan; Patty, Joanna Lee Dossick.

2220 PACIFIC VIBRATIONS. (American International-1971). Jock Sutherland, Rolf Aurness, Corky Carroll, Tom Stone, Mike Tabeling, Rick Griffin, Spyder Wills, Chuck Dent, Mike Murpus, Bill Hamilton, David Huuhiwa, Merv Larson, Jeff Hakman, Angie Feno, Brad McCaul, Mickey Dora, Steve Bigler.

2221 THE PAD (AND HOW TO USE IT). (Universal-1966). Bob, Brian Bedford; Doreen, Julie Sommars; Ted, James Farentino; Lavinia, Edy Williams; Beatnik, Nick Navarro; Fat Woman on Bus, Pearl Shear; Waitress, Barbara London; Girl on Phone, Barbara Reid; Larry, Rober Bacon; Ralph, Don Conreaux.

2222 PADDY. (Allied Artists-1970). Harry Redmond, Milo O'Shea; Paddy, Des Cave; Maureen, Dearbhla Molloy; Breeda, Judy Cornwell; Larry, Donald LeBlanc; Mrs. Doyle, Lillian Rappel; Cahill, Desmond Perry; Ma, Marie O'Donnell; Billy, Vincent Smith; Josie, Ita Darcy; Butcher's Apprentice, Desmond Ellis; Duncan Stuart, Dominic Roche; Tony Deugan, Clive Geraghty; Graveyard Priest, Alec Doran; Liz O'Boyle, Mary Larkin; Mrs. Hays, Pat Layde; Willie Egan, John Kananagh; Watchbox, John Molloy; Priest, William Foley; Barney, Brendan Dunne; Mary, Mary Jo Kennedy; Jack, Mark Mulholland; Mrs. Kearney, Maureen Toal; Ireneee, Peggy Cass; Taxi Driver, Danny Cummings.

2223 PAINT YOUR WAGON. (Paramount-1969). Ben Rumson, Lee Marvin; Fardner, Clint Eastwood; Elizabeth, Jean Seberg; Rotten Luck Willie, Harve Presnell; Mad Jack Duncan, Ray Walston; Horton Fenty, Tom Ligon; Parson, Alan Dexter; Horace Tabor, William O'Connell; Haywood Holbrook, Ben Baker; Mr. Fenty, Alan Baxter; Mrs. Fenty, Paula Trueman; Atwell, Robert Easton; Foster, Geoffrey Norman; Steve Bull, H. B. Haggerty; Joe Mooney, Terry Jenkins; Schermerhorn, Karl Bruck; Jacob Woodling, John Mitchum; Sarah Woodling, Sue Casey; Indian, Eddie Little Sky; Higgins, Harvey Parry; Wong, H. W. Ginn; Frock-Coated Man, William Mims; Hennessey, Roy Jenson; Clendennon, Pat Hawley.

2224 PAMELA, PAMELA YOU ARE... (Distribpix Inc. -1968). Pamela Browning, Elaine Edwards; Cal Miller, Paul Hardy;

Susan Browning, Mary Lindsay; Felix Browning, Sherman Lloyd; Charles, Henry Andrews; Evelyn, Margaret Ann Cathell; Nazi, Paul Zayas; Secretary, Barbara Ellen.

2225 THE PANIC IN NEEDLE PARK. (20th Century-Fox-1971). Bobby, Al Pacino; Helen, Kitty Winn; Hotchner, Alan Vint; Hank, Richard Bright; Chico, Kiel Martin.

2226 PANIC IN THE CITY. (Commonwealth United Entertainment-1968). Dave Pomeroy, Howard Duff; Dr. Paula Stevens, Linda Cristal; James Kincade, Stephen McNally; August Best, Nehemiah Persoff; Myra Pryor, Anne Jeffreys; Dr. Paul Cerbo, Oscar Beregi; Steadman, Gregory Morton; Goff, Dennis Hopper; George Barrows, John Hoyt, Steve Franken, Wesley Lau, Jim Adams, Hank Brandt, Eddie Firestone, John Pickard, Cal Currens, Jann Watson, Elaine Beckett, Stanley Clements, Walter Reed, Leon Lontoc, Deanna Lund, Edith Loder, Wendy Stuart, Robert Terry, Bee Tompkins, Michael Farrell, Eilene Jannsen, Jim Kline, William Tannen, Dodie Warren, Rush Williams, Douglas Evans, Maurice Wells, James Seay, Al Shafran, Renee Redman, Tex Armstrong, Walter Scott, George Sawaya.

2227 PAPER CHASE. (20th Century-Fox-1973). Hart, Timothy Bottoms; Susan, Lindsay Wagner; Kingsfield, John Houseman; Ford, Graham Beckel; Anderson, Edward Herrmann; O'Connor, Bob Lydiard; Bell, Craig Richard Nelson; Kevin, James Naughton; Asheley, Regina Baff; Toombs, David Clennon; Moss, Lenny Baker.

2228 PAPER LION. (United Artists-1968). George Plimpton, Alan Alda; Kate, Lauren Hutton; Himself, Sugar Ray Robinson; Himself, Frank Gifford; Himself, Vincent Lombardi; Oscar Barnes, David Doyle; Susan, Ann Turkel; The Detroit Lions' Coaching Staff & Team; Coath Joe Schmidt, John Gordy, Pat Studstill, Alex Karras, Mike Lucci, Roger Brown.

2229 PAPER MOON. (Paramount-1973). Moses Pray, Ryan O'Neal; Addie Loggins, Tatum O'Neal; Trixie Delight, Madeline Kahn; Deputy Hardin, John Hillerman; Imogene, P. J. Johnson; Floyd, Burton Gilliam; Leroy, Randy Quade; Widow Huff, Dorothy Forster; Miss Ollie, Jessie Lee Fulton; Minister, Jim Harrell; Minister's Wife, Lila Waters; Robertson, Noble Willingham; Gas Station Attendant, Bob Young; Station Master, Jack Saunders; Widow Pearl Morgan, Liz Ross; Widow Marie Bates, Yvonne Harrison; Lawman, Ed Reed; Dorothy Price, Eleanor Bogart, Lana Daniel, Herschel Morris, Dejah Moore, Ralph Coder, Harriet Ketchum, Desmond Dhooge, Kenneth Hughes, George Lillie, Floyd Maheney, Randy Arnold, Vernon Schwanke, Dennis Beden, Hugh Gillin, Art Ellison, Rosemary Rumbley.

2230 PAPILLON. (Allied Artists-1973). Papillon, Steve McQueen; Dega, Dustin Hoffman; Indian Chief, Victor Jory; Julot, Don Gordon; Leper Colony Chief, Anthony Zerbe; Maturette, Robert Deman; Clusiot, Woodrow Parfrey; Dr. Chatal, George Coulouris; Lariot, Bill Mumy; Zoraima, Ratna Assan; Warden Barrot, William Smithers; Antonio, Gregory Sierra; Mother Superior, Barbara Morrison; Nun, Ellen Moss; Butterfly Trader, Don Hammer; Commandant, Dalton Trumbo.

2231 PARADES. (Cinerama-1972). "Baby" Novik, Russ Thacker; Sergeant Hook, Brad Sullivan; Potofski, Lewis J. Stadlen; Captain Jinks, David Doyle; Mother, Dorothy Chace; Filmmaker "T," Anthony Holland; Filmmaker "S," Joseph R. Sicari; Wexley, Russell Horton; Chaplain, Andrew Duncan; Brahmberg, James Catusi; Chicano, Erik Estrada; Barrymore, Michael Heit; Crazyhorse, Tim Riley; Dimedropper, Michael McGowan; Wild One, Robert Capece; Blackass, Don Blakely; Murray, John Pleshette; Togo, Sab Shimono; Nurse, Ruth McKinney; Bertha, Madeline Lee; Mildred, Alice Whitfield; Jane, Peggy Whitton.

2232 PARADISE, HAWAIIAN STYLE. (Paramount-1966). Rick Richards, Elvis Presley; Judy Hudson (Friday), Suzanna Leigh; Danny Kohana, James Shigeta; Jan Kohana, Donna Butterworth; Lani, Marianna Hill; Pua, Irene Tsu; Lehua, Linda Wong; Joanna, Julie Parrish; Betty Kohana, Jan Shepard; Donald Belden, John Doucette; Moki, Philip Ahn; Mr. Cubbertson, Grady Sutton; Andy Lowell, Don Collier; Mrs. Barrington, Doris Packer; Mrs. Belden, Mary Treen; Peggy Holdren, Gigi Verone; Blonde Applicant, Shanon Hale.

2233 THE PARALLAX VIEW. (Paramount-1974). Joseph Frady, Warren Beatty; Editor Rintels, Hume Cronyn; Austin Tucker, William Daniels; Lee Carter, Paula Prentiss; Sheriff, Kelly Thorsden; Deputy, Earl Hindman; Former FBI Agent, Kenneth Mars; Parallax Corp. Rep., Walter McGinn; Senator Hammond, Jim Davis; Senator Carroll, Bill Joyce; Assassin, Bill McKinney; Tucker's Aide, William Jordan; Commission Spokesmen, Stacy Keach Sr. and Ford Rainey.

2234 PARANOIA. (Commonwealth United-1969). Kathryn West, Carroll Baker; Peter Donovan, Lou Castel; Eva, Colette Descombes; Brian Sanders, Tino Carraro; Teresa, Lilla Brignone; Martino, Franco Pesce; Police Inspector, Jacques Stany; Kathryn's Aunt, Sara Simoni; Gaetano Imbro, Calisto Calisti, Mario Rosiello, Alberto Cocchi.

2235 PARIS IN THE MONTH OF AUGUST. (Trans-Lux-1968). Henri Plantin, Charles Aznavour; Patricia Seagrave, Susan Hampshire; Gogaille, Michel De Re; Civadusse, Daniel Ivernel; Peter, Alan Scott; Simone Plantin, Etchika Choureau; Bouvreuil, Jacques Marin; Concierge, Helena Manson; Model,

Dominique Davray; Leonce Corne, Andre Certes, Marcel Charvey, Bernard Musson, Ann Lewis, Dominique Zardi, Henri Attal, Joelle Cazal, Amarande, Max Amyl, Jean Sylvere, Patricia Aznavour.

2236 PART-TIME WORK OF A DOMESTIC SLAVE. (1974). Alexandra Kluge, Franz Bronski, Sylvia Gartmann, Traugott Buhre, Ursula Diriches, Walter Flamme, Ulrike Laurenze, Ortrud Teichart, Alfred Edel, Arno Rogeenbuck, W. Petermann, Michael Hanemann, Roland Wiegenstein.

2237 THE PARTY. (United Artists-1968). Hrundi V. Bakshi, Peter Sellers; Michele Monet, Claudine Longet; Rosalind Dunphy, Marge Champion; Levinson, Steve Franken; Alice Clutterbuck, Fay McKenzie; Fred Clutterbuck, J. Edward McKinley; Princess Helena, Sharron Kimberly; Wyoming Bill Kelso, Denny Miller; C. S. Divot, Gavin MacLeod; Davey Kane, Buddy Lester; Janice Kane, Corinne Cole; Molly Clutterbuck, Kathe Green; Congressman Dunphy, Tom Quine; June Warren, Carol Wayne; Gore Pontoon, Timothy Scott; Bernard Stein, Al Checco; Wiggy, Elianne Nadeau; Harry, James Lanphier; Bradford, Jerry Martin; Stella D'Angelo, Danielle De Metz; Wells, Dick Crockett; Maid, Frances Davis; Cook, Allen Jung; Film Director, Herb Ellis.

2238 THE PARTY'S OVER. (Allied Artists-1967). Moise, Oliver Reed; Carson, Clifford David; Nina, Catherine Woodville; Libby, Ann Lynn; Melina, Louise Sorel; Geronimo, Mike Pratt; Tutzi, Maurice Browning; Phil, Jonathan Burn; Hector, Roddy Maude-Roxby; Fran, Annette Robertson; Countess, Mildred Mayne; Ada, Alison Seebohm; Almoner, Barbara Lott; Ben, Eddie Albert.

2239 PASSAGES FROM JAMES JOYCE'S FINNEGANS WAKE. (Grove Press-1967). Finnegan, Martin J. Kelly; Anna Livia Plurabelle, Jane Reilly; Shem, Peter Haskell; Shaun, Page Johnson; Commentator, John V. Kelleher; Young Shem, Ray Flanagan; Young Iseult, Maura Pryor; Young Shaun, Jo Jo Slavin; Accordian Player, Luke J. O'Malley; Joseph Alderham, Ray Allen, Virginia Blue, Sean Brancato, Joan Campbell, Paddy Croft, Leonard Frey, Eileen Koch, Joe Maher, Janis Markhouse, Kevin O'Leary, Herbert Prah, Jan Thompson, Virginia J. Wallace, Carmen P. Zavick.

2240 THE PASSION OF ANNA. (United Artists-1970). Anna Fromm, Liv Ullmann; Eva, Bibi Andersson; Andreas Winkelman, Max Von Sydow; Elis Vergerus, Erland Josephson; Johan Andersson, Erik Hell; Verner, Sigge Furst; Verner's Wife, Svea Holst; Katarina, Annika Kronberg; Johan's Sister, Hjordis Pettersson; First Policeman, Lars-Owe Carlberg; Second Policeman, Brian Wikstrom; Barbro Hiort af Ornas, Malin Ek, Britta Brunius, Brita Oberg, Marianne Karlbeck,

Lennart Blomkvist.

2241 PAT GARRETT AND BILLY THE KID. (MGM-1973). Pat Garrett, James Coburn; Billy the Kid, Kris Kristofferson; Sheriff Kip McKinney, Richard Jaeckel; Mrs. Baker, Katy Jurado; Lemuel, Chil Wills; Governor Wallace, Jason Robards; Alias, Bob Dylan; Ollinger, R. G. Armstrong; Eno, Luke Askew; Poe, John Beck; Holly, Richard Bright; J. W. Bell, Matt Clark; Maria, Rita Coolidge; Howland, Jack Dodson; Alamosa Bill, Jack Elam; Paco, Emilio Fernandez; Maxwell, Paul Fix; Black Harris, L. Q. Jones; Sheriff Baker, Slim Pickens; Silva, Jorge Russek; Bowdre, Charlie Martin Smith; Luke, Harry Dean Stanton; Mrs. Horrell, Claudia Bryar; Norris, John Chandler; Denver, Mike Mikler; Ida, Aurora Clavel; Ruthie, Rutanya Alda; Rupert, Walter Kelley; O'Folliard, Rudy Wurlitzer; Cody, Elisha Cook Jr.; Horrell, Gene Evans; Josh, Dub Taylor.

2242 A PATCH OF BLUE. (MGM-1965). Gordon Ralfe, Sidney Poitier; Rose-Ann D'Arcey, Shelley Winters; Selina D'Arcey, Elizabeth Hartman; Ole Pa, Wallace Ford; Mark Ralfe, Ivan Dixon; Sadie, Elisabeth Fraser; Mr. Faber, John Qualen.

2243 PATTON. (20th Century-Fox-1970). Gen. George S. Patton Jr., George C. Scott; Gen. Omar N. Bradley, Karl Malden; Capt. Chester B. Hansen, Stephen Young; Brig. Gen. Hobart Carver, Michael Strong; Gen Bradley's Driver, Cary Loftin; Moroccan Minister, Albert Dumortier; Lt. Gen. Harry Bufford, David Bauer; Col. Gen. Alfred Jodl, Richard Muench; Capt. Oskar Steiger, Siegfried Rauch; Field Marshal Sir Bernard L. Montgomery, Micael Bates; Soldier Who Gets Slapped, Tim Considine.

2244 PAUL AND MICHELLE. (Paramount-1974). Michelle Latour, Anicee Alvina; Paul Harrison, Sean Bury; Garry, Keir Dullea; Ronald Lewis, Catherine Allegret, Georges Beller, Anne Lonnberg, Sara Stout, Steve Gilbert, Anthony Clarke, Peggy Frankston, Peter Graves, Toby Robins, Andre Maranne, Jenny Arasse, Michel Garland, Elizabeth Kaza, Albert Simono, Sylvie Joly, Robert Favart, Carine Vogel, Lucy Arnold, Jacqueline Fogt, Jack Berard, Guy Harly.

2245 THE PAWNBROKER. (Ely Landau-1965). Sol Nazerman, Rod Steiger; Marilyn Birchfield, Geraldine Fitzgerald; Rodriguez, Brock Peters; Jesus Ortiz, Jaime Sanchez; Ortiz' Girl, Thelma Oliver; Tessie, Marketa Kimbrell; Mende, Baruch Lumet; Philosopher, Juano Hernandez; Ruth, Linda Geiser; Bertha, Nancy R. Pollock; Raymond St. Jacques, John McCurry, Charles Dierkop, Eusebia Cosme, Warren Finnerty, Jack Ader, Marianne Kanter.

2246 PAYDAY. (Cinerama-1973). Maury Dann, Rip Torn;

Mayleen, Ahna Capri; Rosamond, Flayne Heilveil; Clarence, Michael C. Gwynne; Tally, Jeff Morris; Chauffeur, Cliff Emmich; Ted, Henry O. Arnold; Bridgeway, Walter Bamberg; Sandy, Linda Spatz; Galen Dann, Eleanor Fell; Mama Dann, Clara Dunn; Disk Jockey, Earle Trigg; Restaurant Manager, Mike Edwards; Highway Policeman, Winton McNair.

2247 PAYMENT IN BLOOD. (Columbia-1968). Stuart, Edd Byrnes; Colonel Blake, Guy Madison; Manuela, Louise Barrett; Chamaco, Enzo Girolami; Ryk Boyd, Mario Donen, Rosella Bergamonti, Alfred Aysanoa, Attillio Severini, Marco Mariani, Ariana Facchetti, Giulio Maculani, Mirella Pamphilio, Piero Vida.

2248 THE PEACE KILLERS. (Transvue-1971). Rebel, Clint Ritchie; Kristy, Jess Walton; Alex, Paul Prokop; Jeff, Michael Ontkean; Black Widow, Lavelle Roby; Snatch, Nino Candido; Whitey, Jon Hill; Gadget, Gary Morgan; Cowboy, John Raymond Taylor; Ben, Robert Cornthwaite; Carol, Kres Mersky; Blackjack, Albert Popwell; Joey, Joey Rosendo; Linda, Candace Depuy; Detective, Jack Starr; Hippie, Milt Gold.

2249 THE PEACH THIEF. (Brandon-1969). Lisa, Nevena Kokanova; Ivo Obrenovich, Rade Markovich; The Colonel, Mikhail Mikhailov; The Colonel's Orderly, Vassil Vachev.

2250 THE PEDESTRIAN. (Cinerama-1974). Gustav Rudolf Sellner, Peter Hall, Maximilian Schell, Gila von Weitershausen, Alexander May, Peggy Ashcroft, Elisabeth Bergner, Lil Dagover, Kathe Haack, Johanna Hofer, Elsa Wagner, Francoise Rosay, Manuel Sellner, Dagmar Hirtz, Michael Weinert, Christian Kohlund, Franz Seitz, Herbert Mensching, Peter Moland, Gertrud Bald, Walter Kohut, Margarethe Schell von Noe, Sigfrit Steiner, Fani Fotinou, Gaddi Ben-Artzi, Walter Schmidinger, Walter von Varndal, Silvia Hurlimann, Norbert Schiller, Angela Sa-loker.

2251 PEER GYNT. (Brandon-1965). Peer Gynt, Charlton Heston; Aase, Betty Hanisee; Old Woman, Mrs. Herbert Hyde; Kari, Lucielle Powell; Old Woman, Sue Straub; Aslak, Charles Paetow; Solveig, Kathryne Elfstrom; Haegstad, Morris Wilson; Drunk, George B. Moll; Ingrid, Betty Barton; Mads Moen, Alan Eckhart; Cowherd Girls, Katharine Bradley, Anty Ball, Alice Badgerow; Dovre-King, Roy Eggert Jr.; The Boyg, Francis X. Bushman; Woman in Green, Audrey Wedlock; Woman in Green (now a hag), Sarah Merrill; Ugly Urchin, Alan Heston; Herr Trumpeterstraale, David Bradley; Anitra, Rose Andrews; Mr. MacPherson, Warren McKenzie; Monsieur Ballon, Roy Eggert Jr.; Robert Cooper, Rod Maynard, Jane Wilimovsky, Thomas A. Blair.

2252 PENDULUM. (Columbia-1969). Captain Frank Matthews, George Peppard; Adele Matthews, Jean Seberg; Woodrow Wilson King, Richard Kiley; Deputy Chief Hildebrand, Charles McGraw; Eileen Sanderson, Madeleine Sherwood; Paul Martin Sanderson, Robert F. Lyons; Lt. Smithson, Frank Marth; Liz Tennant, Marj Dusay; Senator Augustus Cole, Paul McGrath; Richard D'Angelo, Stewart Moss; Effie, Isabell Sanford; Det. JJ "Red" Thornton, Dana Elcar; Brooks Elliot, Harry Lewis; Mary Schumacher, Mildred Trares; Myra, Robin Raymond; Mrs. Wilma Elliot, Phyllis Hill; U. S. Attorney Grady Butler, Jock MacKelvie, Judge Kinsella, S. John Launer; Deputy Marshal Jack Barnes, Richard Guizon; Artie, Jack Grimes; Garland, Gene Boland; Detective Jelinek, Logan Ramsey; Detective Hanauer, Douglas Henderson.

2253 PENELOPE. (MGM-1966). Penelope, Natalie Wood; James B. Elcott, Ian Bannen; Dr. Gregory Mannix, Dick Shawn; Lt. Bixbee, Peter Falk; Professor Klobb, Jonathan Winters; Sadaba, Lila Kedrova; Ducky, Lou Jacobi; Mildred, Norma Crane; Major Higgins, Arthur Malet; Bank Manager, Jerome Cowan; Honeysuckle Rose, Arlene Golonka; Miss Serena, Amzie Strickland; Sgt. Rothschild, Bill Gunn; Boom Boom, Carl Ballantine; Store Owner, Iggie Wolfington.

2254 THE PENTHOUSE. (Paramount-1967). Barbara, Suzy Kendall; Bruce, Terence Morgan; Tom, Tony Beckley; Dick, Norman Rodway; Harry, Martine Beswick.

2255 PEOPLE MEET AND SWEET MUSIC FILLS THE HEART. (Trans-Lux-1969). Sofia Petersen, Harriet Andersson; Shalof Hansen, Preben Neergaard; Hans Madsen, Erik Wedersoe; Devah Sorensen, Eva Dahlbeck; Evangeline Hansen, Lone Rode; Mithra, Lotte Horne; Robert Clair de Lune, Georg Rydeberg; Madam Calcura, Elin Reimer; Ramon, Knud Rex; Falconetti, Bent Christensen; Girl of the House, Mona Chong; Girl of the House, Cassandra Mahon; Eske Holme, Ove Rud, Benny Juhlin, Zito Kerras, Lotte Tarp.

2256 THE PEOPLE NEXT DOOR. (AVCO Embassy-1970). Arthur, Eli Wallach; Gerri, Julie Harris; Maxie, Deborah Winters; Artie, Stephen McHattie; David, Hal Holbrook; Tina, Cloris Leachman; Sandy, Don Scardino; Della, Rue McClanahan; Dr. Salazar, Nehemiah Persoff; Dr. Margolin, Mike Kellin; Elliott, Sandy Alexander; Dr. Lauran, Anthony Call; Wally, Mathew Cowles; Prince, Joseph Leon; Jack, Bruce Scott; Blonde Mother, Anita Dangler; Bobby Sandler, Jay Savino, Steve Kanyon, Ron Panvini, The Bead Game.

2257 PERFECT FRIDAY. (Chevron-1970). Britt, Ursula Andress; Dorsett, David Warner; Graham, Stanley Baker; Nanny, Patience Collier; Smith, T. P. McKenna; William, David Waller; Miss Welsh, Joan Benham; Thompson, Julian

Orchard; Janet, Trisha Mortimer; Miss Marsh, Ann Tirard.

2258 PERFORMANCE. (Warner Bros.-1970). Charles, James Fox; Turner, Mick Jagger; Pherber, Anita Pallenberg; Lucy, Michele Breton; Dana, Ann Sidney; Moody, John Bindon; Rosebloom, Stanley Meadows; Lawyer, Allen Cuthbertson; Dennis, Antony Morton; Harry, Johnny Shannon; Joey, Anthony Valentine; Tony, Ken Colley; Chauffeur, John Sterland; Lorraine, Laraine Wickens.

2259 THE PERILS OF PAULINE. (Universal-1967). George, Pat Boone; Pauline, Pamela Austin; Sten Martin, Terry-Thomas; Mr. Coleman, Edward Everett Horton; Thorpe, Hamilton Camp; Mrs. Carruthers, Doris Packer; Consul General, Kurt Kasznar; Frandisi, Vito Scotti; Commissar, Leon Askin; Vizier, Aram Katcher; Prince Benji, Rick Natoli; Pauline's Foster Mother, Jeanne Gerson; Pauline's Foster Father, Joe Higgins; Henry, Keith Taylor; The Gorilla, Max Klevin.

2260 PERSECUTION. (Fanfare-1974). Carrie Masters, Lana Turner; David Masters, Ralph Bates; Paul Bellamy, Trevor Howard; Monique Kalfon, Olga Georges-Picot; Janie Masters, Suzan Farmer; Robert Masters, Patrick Allen; Young David, Mark Weavers.

2261 PERSONA. (Lopert-1967). Nurse Alma, Bibi Andersson; Actress Elisabeth Vogler, Liv Ullmann; Woman Doctor, Margaretha Krook; Mr. Vogler, Gunnar Bjornstrand.

2262 PETE 'N' TILLIE. (Universal-1972). Pete, Walter Matthau; Tillie, Carol Burnett; Gertrude, Geraldine Page; Burt, Barry Nelson; Jimmy Twitchell, Rene Auberjonois; Robbie, Lee H. Montgomery; Mr. Tucker, Henry Jones; Father Keating, Kent Smith; Dr. Willett, Philip Bourneuf; Minister, Whit Bissell; Lucy Lund, Timothy Blake.

2263 PETER RABBIT AND TALES OF BEATRIX POTTER. (MGM-1971). Beatrix Potter, Erin Geraghty; Nurse, Joan Benham; Butler, Wilfred Babbage.

2264 LE PETIT SOLDAT. (West End-1967). Bruno Forestier, Michel Subor; Veronica Dreyer, Anna Karina; Jacques, Henri-Jacques Huet; Paul, Paul Beauvais; Laszlo, Laszlo Szabo.

2265 PETULIA. (Warner Bros.-7 Arts-1968). Petulia Danner, Julie Christie; Archie Bollen, George C. Scott; David Danner, Richard Chamberlain; Barney, Arthur Hill; Polo, Shirley Knight; Mr. Danner, Joseph Cotten; May, Pippa Scott; Wilma, Kathleen Widdoes; Warren, Roger Bowen; Motel Receptionist, Richard Dysart; Nuns, Ruth Kobart and Ellen Geer; Mr. Howard, Lou Gilbert; Mr. Mendoza, Nat

Esformes; Mrs. Mendoza, Maria Val; Oliver, Vincent Arias; Michael, Eric Weiss; Stevie, Kevin Cooper; Intern, Austin Pendleton; Patient, Barbara Colby; Salesman, Rene Auberjonois; Neighbor, Josephine Nichols; Nurse, De Ann Mears; The Grateful Dead, Big Brother and the Holding Company, Members of The Committee, Members of the American Conservatory Theatre.

2266 THE PHANTOM OF FREEDOM. (20th Century-Fox-1974). Husband, Jean-Claude Brialy; Wife, Monica Vitti; Woman, Milena Vukotic; Man, Michel Lonsdale; Inspector, Claude Pieplu; Prefect, Michel Piccoli; Prefect, Julien Bertheau; Sister, Adriana Asti; Innkeeper, Paul Frankeur; Monk, Paul Leperson; Officer, Bernard Verley.

2267 THE PHANTOM OF SOHO. (Producers Releasing Organization-1967). Hugh Patton, Dieter Borsche; Clarinda Smith, Barbara Ruetting; Sir Philip, Hans Sohnker; Joanna, Elisabeth Flickenschildt; Hallam, Peter Vogel; Corinna Smith, Helga Sommerfeld; Dr. Dalmar, Werner Peters; Lord Malhouse, Hans Lielsen; Gilard, Stanislav Ledinek; "Liver-Spot," Otto Waldis; Captain, Hans W. Hamacher; Daddy, Emil Feldmar; Charlis, Harald Sawade.

2268 PHANTOM OF THE PARADISE. (20th Century-Fox-1974). Paul Williams, William Finley, George Memmoli, Harold Oblong, Archie Jahn, Jeffrey Comanor, Gerrit Graham, Jessica Harper.

2269 PHASE IV. (Paramount-1974). Hubbs, Nigel Davenport; Lesko, Michael Murphy; Kendra, Lynne Frederick; Eldridge, Alan Gifford; Clete, Robert Henderson; Mrs. Eldridge, Helen Horton.

2270 PHEDRE. (Altura-1973). Phedre, Marie Bell; Theramene, Jean Chevrier; Theseus, Jacques Dacqmine; Hippolyte, Claud Giraud; Aricie, Tania Torrens; Ismene, Claudia Maurin; Panope, Jean-Noel Sissia; Oenone, Mary Marquet.

2271 THE PHYNX. (Warner Bros. -1970). A. Michael Miller, Ray Chippeway, Dennis Larden, Lonny Stevens, Lou Antonio, Mike Kellin, Michael Ansara, George Tobias, Joan Blondell, Larry Hankin, Teddy Eccles, Ultra Violet, Pat McCormick, Joseph Gazal, Bob Williams, Barbara Noonan, Rich Little, Sue Bernard, Sherry Miles, Ann Morell, Motha, Patti Andrews, Rona Barrett, Edgar Bergen, Busby Berkeley, James Brown, Dick Clark, Xavier Cugat, Cass Daley, Andy Devine, Fritz Feld, Leo Gorcey, Huntz Hall, John Hart, Louis Hayward, George Jessel, Ruby Keeler, Patsy Kelly, Dorothy Lamour, Joe Louis, Guy Lombardo, Trini Lopez, Marilyn Maxwell, Butterfly McQueen, Pat O'Brien, Maureen O'Sullivan, Richard Pryor, Martha Raye, Harold Sakata, Colonel Harland Sanders, Jay Silverheels, Ed

Sullivan, Rudy Vallee, Clint Walker, Johnny Weismuller.

2272 PIAF. (AMLF-1974). Edith Piaf, Brigitte Ariel; Momone, Pascale Christophe; Leple, Guy Trian; Raymond Asso, Pierre Vernier; Julien, Jacques Duby; Madeleine, Anouk Ferjac; Lula, Sylvie Joly; Felix, Yvan Varco.

2273 PICKPOCKET. (New Yorker-1969). Michel, Martin La-Salle; Jeanne, Marika Green; The Inspector, Jean Pelagri; Michel's Mother, Dolly Scal; Jacques, Pierre Leymarie, 1st Accomplice, Kassagi; 2nd Accomplice, Pierre Etaix; Detective, Cesar Gattegno.

2274 PICKUP ON 101. (American International-1972). Obediah, Jack Albertson; Nickie, Lesley Warren; Les, Martin Sheen; Chuck, Michael Ontkean; Cop, Hal Baylor; Pawnshop Owner, George Chandler; Sergeant, Mike Road; Mechanic, Eddie Firestone; Antique Shop Owner, William Mims; First Farm-er, Robert Donner; His Wife, Kathleen Harper; 2nd Farmer, Harold J. Stone; Buck Young, Peggy Stewart, Greg Young, Cynthia Johnson, Don Spruance.

2275 PICTURE MOMMY DEAD. (Embassy-1966). Edward Shel-ley, Don Ameche; Francene Shelley, Martha Hyer; Jessica, Zsa Zsa Gabor; Susan Shelley, Susan Gordon; Anthony, Maxwell Reed; Clayborn, Wendell Corey; Sister Rene, Signe Hasso; Elsie Kornwald, Anna Lee; First Woman, Paule Clark; Second Woman, Marlene Tracy; Third Woman, Steffi Henderson; Father, Robert Sherman; Boy, Kelly Corcoran.

2276 PIE IN THE SKY. (Allied Artists-1965). Suzy, Lee Grant; Brill, Richard Bray; Carl, Michael Higgins; Paco, Roberto Marsach; Brill's Father, Robert Allen; Rose, Sylvia Miles; Farmer's Wife, Ruth Attaway; Farmer, Robert Earl Jones; Rick, Jaime Charlamagne; Artificial Inseminator, Charles Jordan; Preacher, Roscoe Browne; Pickpocket, Rick Colitti; Brill's Sisters, Muriel Franklin, Debby Bliss, Susie Dress-er; Pitchman, Monroe Arnold; Haberdasher, Boris Marsha-lov; Doorman, Spencer Davis; Gas Station Attendant, Fred Feldt; Hot Dog Vendor, Bill Da Prato; Delicatessen Man, Joseph Leberman; Bartender, Milton Luchan; Brill's Brother, Danny Dresser; Truck Driver, Mel Brown.

2277 PIECES OF DREAMS. (United Artists-1970). Gregory, Robert Forster; Pamela, Lauren Hutton; Bishop, Will Geer; Father Paul Schaeffer, Ivor Francis; Monsignor Hurley, Richard O'Brien; Mrs. Lind, Edith Atwater; Gregory's Sis-ter, Mitzi Hoag; Police Sergeant, Rudy Diaz; Leo Rose, Sam Javis; Mrs. Tietgens, Gail Bonney; Mrs. Straub, Helen Westcott; Girl in Bar, Joanne Moore Jordan; Mrs. Rios, Miriam Martinez; Estella, Kathy Baca; Charlie, Eloy Phil Casados; Employment Agency Interviewer, Robert McCoy.

2278 THE PIED PIPER. (Paramount-1972). The Pied Piper, Donovan; The Baron, Donald Pleasence; Gavin, Jack Wild; Franz, John Hurt; Lisa, Cathryn Harrison; Melius, Michael Hordern; Burgermeister, Roy Kinnear; Bishop, Peter Vaughan; Frau Poppendick, Diana Dors; Mattio, Keith Buckley; Otto, Arthur Hewlett; Pilgrim, Peter Eyre; Papal Nuncio, Hamilton Dyce; Friar, Andre Van Gyseghem; Priests, John Falconer and Clive Elliott; Helga, Patsy Puttnam; Kulik, David Netheim; Karl, Paul Hennen; Officer, David Leland; Gretel, Sammie Winmill; Chancellor, John Welsh; Town Crier, Gertan Klauber; Maidservant, Mary McLeod; Burgers, Michael Goldie, Edwin Brown, George Cormack, and Roger Hammond.

2279 PIERROT LE FOU. (Pathe Contemporary-1969). Ferdinand Griffon, Jean-Paul Belmondo; Marianne Renoir, Anna Karina; Marianne's Brother, Dirk Sanders; Man on the Pier, Raymond Devos; Ferdinand's Wife, Graziella Galvni; Gangster, Roger Dutoit; Gangster, Hans Meyer; Dwarf, Jimmy Karoubi; Mme. Staquet, Christa Nell; 2nd Brother, Pascal Aubier; 3rd Brother, Pierre Hanin; Herself, Princess Aicha Abidir; Sailor, Alexis Poliakoff; Himself, Samuel Fuller; Political Exile, Laszlo Szabo; Young Man in Cinema, Jean-Pierre Leaud.

2280 PIGEONS. (Plaza-1971). Jonathan, Jordan Christopher; Jennifer, Jill O'Hara; Winslow, Robert Walden; Jonathan's Mother, Kate Reid; William's Father, William Redfield; Mildred, Lois Nettleton; Tough Lady, Elaine Stritch; Model, Melba Moore.

2281 THE PIGKEEPER'S DAUGHTER. (Box Office International-1972). Moonbeam Swyner, Terry Gibson; Pretty Patty, Patty Smith; Mrs. Swyner, Gina Paluzzi; Jasper Jenkins, John Keith; Salesman, Peter James; Mr. Swyner, Buck Wayner; Wyngate, Paul Stanley; Prince, Nick Armans.

2282 PIGPEN. (New Line Cinema-1974). Jean Pierre Leaud, Anne Wiazemsky, Alberto Lionello, Margherita Lozano, Pierre Clementi, Ugo Tognazzi.

2283 PINK FLAMINGOS. (Saliva-1974). Divine/Babs Johnson, Divine; Raymond Marble, David Lochary; Connie Marble, Mink Stole; Cotton, Mary Vivian Pearce; Mama Edie, Edith Massey; Crackers, Danny Mills; Channing, Channing Wilroy; Cookie, Cookie Mueller; Eggman, Paul Swift; 1st Kidnapped Girl, Susan Walsh; 2nd Kidnapped Girl, Linda Olgeirson.

2284 THE PINK JUNGLE. (Universal-1968). Ben Morris, James Garner; Alison Duquesne, Eva Renzi; Sammy Ryderbeit, George Kennedy; Crowley, Nigel Green; Paul Ortega, Michael Ansara; Stopes, George Rose; Colonel Celaya, Fabrizio Mioni; Sanchez, Vincent Beck; Rodriguez, Val

Avery; Benavides, Robert Carricart; Helicopter Pilot, Victor Millan; Figueroa, Natividad Vacio; Hotel Proprietor, Nacho Galindo; Bellboy, Pepito Galindo; Customs Agent, Thann Wyenn; Hoodlum, Pepe Callahan.

2285 PINK NARCISSUS. (Sherpix-1971). Boy, Bobby Kendall.

2286 THE PINK PUSSY CAT. (Cambist-1967). The Blonde Performer, Libertad Leblanc; The Vice Lord, Nestor Zavarce; His Mistress, Teresa Marti; Francisco Ferrari, Eva Moreno, Jose Jorda.

2287 PINOCCHIO IN OUTER SPACE. (Universal-1965). Buzzy, Rick Nelson; Jeff Pringle, Jack Kelly; Rosemary, Kristin Nelson; Freddy, Jerry Van Dyke; Nanny, Pert Kelton; Carol, Madelyn Himes; Elizabeth, Sheilah Wells.

2288 PIPPI IN THE SOUTH SEAS. (G. G. Communications-1974). Pippi Longstocking, Inger Nilsson; Annika, Maria Perrson; Tommy, Par Sundberg; Capt. Longstocking, Beppe Wolgers; Pirate Boss Blood Sevente, Jarl Borssen; Pirate Boss Knife-Jocke, Martin Ljund.

2289 A PISTOL FOR RINGO. (1966). Ringo, Montgomery Wood; Sancho, Fernando Sancho; Ruby, Hally Hammond; Sheriff, George Martin; Dolores, Mieves Navarro.

2290 PIT STOP. (Distributors International-1969). Grant, Brian Donlevy; Rick, Dick Davalos; Ellen, Ellen McRae; Hawk, Sid Haig; Jolene, Beverly Washburn; Ed, George Washburn.

2291 THE PIZZA TRIANGLE. (Warner Bros. -1970). Oreste, Marcello Mastroianni; Adelaide, Monica Vitti; Nello, Giancarlo Giannini; Uto, Manolo Zarzo; Silvana, Marisa Merlini; Ambleto Di Meo, Hercules Cortes; Dist. Hd. Communist Party, Fernando S. Polak; Adelaide's Friend, Gioia Desideri; Antonia's Son, Juan Diego; Pizza Maker, Bruno Scipioni; Antonia, Josefina Serratosa.

2292 A PLACE CALLED GLORY. (Embassy-1966). Brenner, Lex Barker; Reece, Pierre Brice; Jade Grande, Marianne Koch; Seth Grande, Jorge Rigaud; Jack Vallone, Gerard Tichy; Leader of Homesteaders, Angel Del Pozo; Mayor of Glory City, Santiago Ontanon; Judge of Glory City, Hans Nielsen; Barman, Wolfgang Lukschy; Clerk, Victor Israel.

2293 A PLACE CALLED TODAY. (AVCO Embassy-1972). Carolyn Schneider, Lana Wood; Cindy Cartwright, Cheri Caffaro; Randy Johnson, J. Herbert Kerr Jr.; Ron Carton, Richard Smedley; Steve Smith, Tim Brown; Alex Cartwright, Leo Tepp; Mayor Ben Atkinson, Peter Carew; Doug Gilmore, Howard Zeiden; Mrs. Johnson, Mary Rio Lewis; Black Radical, Woody Carter; White Radical, David Ross; White

Construction Worker, John La Motta; Black Construction Worker, George Fairley; Brian Johnson, Peter Landers, Frederick Warner, Patricia Wright, Sam Gray, Arthur Wenzel, William Boesen, Herman Arbeit, Paul Ladenheim, Art Vasil, Bob Horen, Gunnar Peters, Lynn Lowry, Ann Loveward, John Marriott, James Hainesworth, David Downing, Joe Cirillo, Martin Brent, Franklin Scott, Buddy Davis, Walter Lott, Stephen Harrison.

2294 A PLACE FOR LOVERS. (MGM-1969). Julia, Faye Dunaway; Valerio, Marcello Mastroianni; Maggie, Caroline Mortimer; Griselda, Karin Engh; Esmeralda Ruspoli, Enrico Simonetti, Mirella Pamphili.

2295 PLAGUE OF THE ZOMBIES. (20th Century-Fox-1966). Sir James Forbes, Andre Morell; Sylvia, Diane Clare; Dr. Peter Tompson, Brook Williams; Alice Jacqueline Pearce; Clive Hamilton, John Carson; Harry Denver, Alexander Davion; Sergeant Swift, Michael Ripper; Constable Christian, Dennis Chinnery; Servant, Louis Mahoney; Vicar, Roy Royston; Marcus Hammond, Ben Aris, Jerry Verno, Joylan Booth, Tim Condroy, Bernard Egan, Norman Mann, Francis Willey.

2296 THE PLAINSMAN. (Universal-1966). Wild Bill Hickok, Don Murray; Buffalo Bill Cody, Guy Stockwell; Calamity Jane, Abby Dalton; St. Stiles, Bradford Dillman; Crazy Knife, Henry Silva; Black Kettle, Simon Oakland; Col. George A. Custer, Leslie Nielsen; Lattimer, Edward Binns; Estrick, Michael Evans; Brother John, Percy Rodriguez; Sgt. Womack, Terry Wilson; Abe Ireland, Walter Burke; Louisa Cody, Emily Banks.

2297 PLANET OF BLOOD. (American International-1965). Barry Sullivan, Norma Bengell, Angel Aranda, Evi Marandi, Fernando Villena, Stelio Candelli, Massimo Righi, Mario Morales, Franco Andrei, Ivan Rassimov, Rico Boido, Alberto Cevenini.

2298 PLANET OF THE APES. (20th Century-Fox-1968). George Taylor, Charlton Heston; Cornelius, Roddy McDowall; Dr. Zira, Kim Hunter; Dr. Zaius, Maurice Evans; Assembly President, James Whitmore; Honorious, James Daly; Nova, Linda Harrison; Landon, Robert Gunner; Lucius, Lou Wagner; Dodge, Jeff Burton; Julius, Buck Kartalian; Hunt Leader, Norman Burton; Dr. Galen, Wright King; Minister, Paul Lambert; Female Astronaut, Dianne Stanley.

2299 PLANET OF THE VAMPIRES. (American International-1965). Barry Sullivan, Norma Bengell, Angel Aranda, Evi Marandi, Fernando Villena, Stelio Candelli, Massimo Righi, Mario Morales, Franco Andrei.

2300 THE PLANTATION BOY. (New Yorker-1971). Carlinho, Savio Rolim; Grandfather, Rodolfo Arena; Aunt, Anecy Rocha; Uncle, Geraldo Del Rey; Maria Luisa, Maria Luisa Dahl.

2300a PLAY DIRTY. (United Artists-1969). Captain Douglas, Michael Caine; Cyril Leech, Nigel Davenport; Colonel Masters, Nigel Green; Brigadier Blore, Harry Andrews; Sadok, Aly Ben Ayed; German Nurse, Vivian Pickles; Colonel Homerton, Bernard Archard; Captain Attwood, Daniel Pilon; Kostas Manou, Takis Emmanouel; Kafkarides, Enrique Avila; Boudesh, Scott Miller; Assine, Mohamed Kouka; Mohsen Ben-ab-Dullah, Tony Stambouleih, Patrick Jordan, Mike Stevens, Martin Burland, Bridget Espeet, George McKeenan, Rafael Albaicin, Jose Halufi.

2301 PLAY IT AGAIN, SAM. (Paramount-1972). Allan, Woody Allen; Linda, Diane Keaton; Dick, Tony Roberts; Bogart, Jerry Lacy; Nancy, Susan Anspach; Sharon, Jennifer Salt; Julie, Joy Bang; Jennifer, Viva; Dream Sharon, Mari Fletcher; Girl in Museum, Diana Davila; Discotheque Girl, Suzanne Zenor; Hoods, Michael Greene, Ted Markland.

2302 PLAY IT AS IT LAYS. (Universal-1972). Maria Wyeth, Tuesday Weld; B. Z., Anthony Perkins; Helene, Tammy Grimes; Carter Lang, Adam Roarke; Carlotta, Ruth Ford; Benny Austin, Eddie Firestone; Susannah, Diana Ewing; Larry Kulik, Paul Lambert; Abortionist's Assistant, Chuck McCann; Hypnotist, Severn Darden; Johnny Waters, Tony Young; Les Goodwin, Richard Anderson; The Chickie, Elizabeth Claman; Patsy, Mitzi Hoag; Nelson, Roger Ewing; Apartment Manager, Richard Ryal; Journalist, Tyne Daly; B. Z.'s Lover, Mike Edwards; Frank John Finnegan; Jeanelle, Tracy Morgan; Kate's Nurse, Darlene Conley; Himself, Arthur Knight; Himself, Albert Johnson; T. V. Panelist, Alan Warnick.

2303 PLAY MISTY FOR ME. (Universal-1971). Dave, Clint Eastwood; Evelyn, Jessica Walter; Tobie, Donna Mills; Sgt. McCallum, John Larch; Frank, Jack Ging; Madge, Irene Hervey.

2304 No entry.

2305 THE PLAYGROUND. (Jerand-1965). Tom Smith, Rees Vaughn; Eva, Inger Stratton; Jason Porter, Edmond Ryan; Mrs. Porter, Andrea Blayne; Mary, Loretta Leversee; Mr. Williams, Richard Kilbride; Virginia Williams, Carol White; Mrs. Williams, Marian Blake; Dr. Zimmerman, Sol Schwade; Mrs. Cartwright, Ethel Shutta; Duncan Cartwright, Paul Schmidt; Dr. Ronald, Peter MacLean; Dr. Jacques, Conrad Jameson.

2306 PLAYTIME. (Continental-1973). Mr. Hulot, Jacques Tati; Young Stranger, Barbara Dennek; Young Stranger's Friend, Jacqueline Lecomte; Secretary, Valerie Camille; Eyeglasses Saleswoman, France Rumilly; Customer Stand, France Delahalle; Ladies at Lampost, Laure Paillette, Colette Proust; Mrs. Giffard, Erika Dentzler; Girl at Cloakroom, Yvette Ducreux; Mrs. Schultz' Companion, Rita Maiden; Singer, Nicole Ray.

2307 PLAZA SUITE. (Paramount-1971). Sam Nash, Walter Matthau; Karen Nash, Maureen Stapleton; Jesse Kiplinger, Walter Matthau; Muriel Tate, Barbara Harris; Roy Hubley, Walter Matthau; Norma Hubley, Lee Grant; Mimsey Hubley, Jennie Sullivan; Borden Eisler, Tom Carey; Waiter, Jose Ocasio; Bellhop, Dan Ferrone; Miss McCormack, Louise Sorel.

2308 PLEASE DON'T EAT MY MOTHER! (Box-Office International-1971). Henry Fudd, Buck Kartalian; The New Widow, Rene Bond; The Hooker, Alicia Friedland; Henry's Mother, Lyn Lundgren; Flower Store Owner, Dash Fremont; Lovers, Flora Wiesel, David Curtis, and Adam Blari.

2309 PLEASE STAND BY. (Milton-1972). Freemont, David Peel; Marian, Wendy Appel; Narrator, Alex Bennett; A. J., A. J. Weberman; Judge, Roberts Blossom; Corporal Tuck, Charlie; Hugo, Walter Hadler.

2310 THE PLEASURE GAME. (Eve-1970). Harry, Victor Sandor; Susan, Ann Staunton; David, William Borsella; Jenny, Leah James; Robert, Daniel Ades; Zelda, Angela Martell; Shirley, Erika Von Kessler.

2311 THE PLEASURE GIRLS. (Times Film Corp.-1966). Sally Feather, Francesca Annis; Keith Dexter, Ian McShane; Nikko, Klaus Kinski; Prinny, Mark Eden; Paddy, Tony Tanner; Marion, Rosemary Nicols; Dee, Suzanna Leigh; Angela, Anneke Wills; Cobber, Coleen Fitzpatrick.

2312 THE PLEASURE SEEKERS. (20th Century-Fox-1965). Maggie Williams, Carol Lynley; Fran Hobson, Ann-Margret; Susie Higgins, Pamela Tiffin; Emilio Lacaye, Tony Franciosa; Pete Stenello, Gardner McKay; Dr. Andres Briones, Andre Lawrence; Paul Barton, Brian Keith; Jane Barton, Gene Tierney; Dona Teresa Lacaye, Isobel Elsom; Flamenco Dancer, Antonio Gades; Neighborhood Man, Vito Scotti; Martinez, Raoul De Leon.

2313 THE PLEDGEMASTERS. (Signature-1971). Bruce Gregory, David Knapp, Michael Tremor, James Palmer, Trevor Tiffany, Larry Kennedy.

2314 POCKET MONEY. (National General-1972). Jim Kane,

Paul Newman; Leonard, Lee Marvin; Garrett, Strother Martin; Adelita, Christine Belford; Wife, Kelly Jean Peters; Herb, Fred Graham; Stretch, Wayne Rogers.

2315 POINT BLANK. (MGM-1967). Walker, Lee Marvin; Chris, Angie Dickinson; Yost/Fairfax, Keenan Wynn; Brewster, Carroll O'Connor; Frederick Carter, Lloyd Bochner, Stegman, Michael Strong; Mal Reese, John Vernon; Lynne, Sharon Acker; Hired Gun, James Sikking; Waitress, Sandra Warner; Mrs. Carter, Roberta Haynes; First Citizen, Kathleen Freeman; Carter's Man, Fictor Creatore; Car Salesman, Lawrence Hauben; Girl Customer, Susan Holloway; Penthouse Lobby Guards, Sid Haig and Michael Bell; Receptionist, Priscilla Boyd; Messenger, John McMurtry; Two Young Men in Apartment, Ron Walters, George Stratton; Carter's Secretary, Nicole Rogell; Reese's Guards, Rico Cattani and Roland Lastarza.

2316 POINT OF TERROR. (Crown International-1972). Tony Trelos, Peter Carpenter; Andrea, Dyanne Thorne; Helayne, Lory Hansen; Sally, Paula Mitchell; Fran, Leslie Simms; Martin, Joel Marston; First Wife, Roberta Robson; Barmaid, Dana Diamond; Bartender, Al Dunlap; Detective, Ernest Charles; Priest, Tony Kent.

2317 THE POLICE CONNECTION. (Cinemation-1973). Vince Edwards, Chuck Connors, Neville Brand.

2318 THE POLICEMAN. (Cinema 5-1972). Abraham Azulai, Shay Kophir; His Wife, Zaharira Harifai; The Commandant, Avner Hezkeyahu; The Sergeant, Itzko Rachamimov; The Gang Leader, Josef Shiloach; The Prostitute, Nitza Shaul.

2319 THE POLITICIANS. (Fountain-1970). Sandra, Angela Carnan; Larry, Robert Warner; Karen, Vickie Carbe; Doctor, Douglas Frey; Laurie, Neola Graef; Bud, Vincent Mongol; Susan, Dixie Donovan; Portman, Richard Gonzales; Lisa, Heidi Stohler; Dwight, Robert Copple; Nanci Sheldon, Gil Francassa, Rick Rivera, John B. Lewis, Tony Marasca, Bruce Martin, Vincent Martin, Alex Roseff.

2320 POOR COW. (National General-1968). Joy, Carol White; Dave, Terence Stamp; Tom, John Bindon; Beryl, Kate Williams; Aunt Emm, Queenie Watts; Trixie, Geraldine Sherman; Tom's Mate, James Beckett; Tom's Mate, Billy Murray; Jonny (age 1 1/2), Simon King; Jonny (age 3), Stevie King; Woman in Park, Winnie Holman; Customer in Hairdresser's, Rose Hillier; Solicitor, Ellis Dale; Judge, Gerald Young; Paddy Joyce, Gladys Dawson, Ron Pember, Malcolm McDowell, George Tovey, Will Stampe, Bernard Stone, John Halstead, Peter Claughton, Julie May, Philip Rose, Martin King, Muriel Hunte, James Thornhill, Mo Dwyer, Terry Duggan, Ian Christian, Liza Carrol, Tony Selby, Ray Barron,

Sian Davis, Mike Negal, George Sewell, Chris Gannon, Philip Newman, Alan Selwyn, Wally Patch, Hilda Barry, Joe Palmer.

2321 POPCORN. (Sherpix-1969). Mick Jagger, The Rolling Stones, Jimi Hendrix, Otis Redding, Vanilla Fudge, Bee Gees, Joe Cocker, The Groove, Beach Boys, Twiggy, Sebastian Jorgensen, Emperor Rosko.

2322 POPE JOAN. (Columbia-1972). Joan, Liv Ullmann; Dr. Stevens, Keir Dullea; Dr. Corwin, Robert Beatty; Joan's Mother, Natasa Nicolescu; Joan's Father, Jeremy Kemp; Young Joan, Sharon Winter; Village Woman, Margareta Pogonat; Lord of the Manor, Richard Bebb; Richard, Peter Arne; Elder Monk, Patrick Magee; Second Monk, George Innes; Young Monk, Nigel Havers; Decilia, Lesley-Anne Down; Mother Superior, Olivia De Havilland; Sister Louise, Sheelah Wilcocks; Sister Nunciata, Susan Macready; Andre Morell, Martin Benson, Lorain Bertorelli, Mary Healey, Franco Nero, Kurt Christian, Maximilian Schell, Trevor Howard, Philip Ross, Duncan Lamont, Manning Wilson, Ion Grafini, Katharine Schofield, Carl Bernard, John Arineri, John Shrapnel, Richard Pearson.

2323 POPI. (United Artists-1969). Popi (Abraham Rodriguez), Alan Arkin; Lupe, Rita Moreno; Junior Rodriguez, Miguel Alejandro; Luis Rodriguez, Ruben Figueroa; Harmon, John Harkins; Miss Musto, Joan Tompkins; Pickett, Anthony Holland; Diaz, Arny Freeman; Receptionist, Barbara Dana; Mrs. Cruz, Antonia Rey; Dr. Perle, Arnold Soboloff; Novitas Man, Victor Junquera; Silvia, Gladys Velez; Nurse, Anita Dangler; Old Lady, Judith Lowry.

2324 THE POPPY IS ALSO A FLOWER. (Comet-1967). Night Club Entertainer, Senta Berger; Benson, Stephen Boyd; Colonel Salem, Yul Brynner; Linda, Angie Dickinson; Sup't. Roche, Georges Geret; Tribal Chief, Hugh Griffith; General Bahar, Jack Hawkins; Monique, Rita Hayworth; Lincoln, Trevor Howard; Society Photographer, Jocelyn Lane; Himself, Trini Lopez; Jones, E. G. Marshall; Inspector Mosca, Marcello Mastroianni; Captain Dinonno, Amedeo Nazzari; Tribesmen Leader, Jean-Claude Pascal; Captain, Anthony Quayle; Guest of Marco, Laya Raki; Marco, Gilbert Roland; Martin, Harold Sakata; Dr. Rad, Omar Sharif; Chasen, Barry Sullivan; Dr. Bronovska, Nadja Tiller; Police Analyst, Howard Vernon; Locarno, Eli Wallach; Gilda Dahlberg, Silvia Sorrente, Violette Marceau, Morteza Kazerouni, Luisa Rivelli, Bob Cunningham, Ali Oveisi, Marilu Tolo.

2325 PORTNOY'S COMPLAINT. (Warner Bros. -1972). Alexander Portnoy, Richard Benjamin; The Monkey, Karen Black; Sophie Portnoy, Lee Grant; Jack Portnoy, Jack Somack; Bubbles Girardi, Jeannie Berlin; Naomi, Jill Clayburgh; Dr.

Otto Spielvogel, D. P. Barnes; Lina, Francesca De Sapio; Smolka, Kevin Conway; Mandel, Lewis Stadlen; Hannah Portnoy, Renee Lippin; Girl in Office, Jessica Rains; Woman in Hospital Bed, Eleanor Zee; Inn Clerk, William Pabst; Cab Driver, Tony Brande; Alexander (age 8), Darryl Seamen; Mr. Harero, Mike De Anda; Mrs. Harero, Carmen Zapata.

2326 PORTRAIT OF HELL. (Toho-1972). The Artist, Tatsuya Nakadai; His Daughter, Yoko Naito; The Lord, Kinnosuke Nakamura.

2327 PORTRAIT OF JASON. (Film-Makers' Distribution Center-1967). Jason, Jason Holliday.

2328 PORTRAIT OF LENIN. (Artkino-1967). Maxim Straukh, Anna Lisyanskaya, Antoninia Pavlycheva, Ilona Kusmierska, Krzysztof Kalczynski.

2329 PORTRAITS OF WOMEN. (Allied Artists-1972). Sara, Ritva Vepsa; Lisa, Kirsti Wallasvaara; Ulla, Marianne Holmstrom; Jussi, Aarree Elo; Perti, Jorn Donner; Sven, Henrik Grano; Peter Von Spaak, Jaakko Talaskiva; Producer, Lennart Laurama; Journalist, Helena Makela; Agent, Jukka Sipila; Actress, Heli Sakki; Pupil, Hannu Oravisto.

2330 THE POSEIDON ADVENTURE. (20th Century-Fox-1972). Reverend Frank Scott, Gene Hackman; Mike Rogo, Ernest Borgnine; James Martin, Red Buttons; Nonni Parry, Carol Lynley; Acres, Roddy McDowall; Linda Rogo, Stella Stevens; Belle Rosen, Shelley Winters; Manny Rosen, Jack Albertson; Susan Shelby, Pamela Sue Martin; The Captain, Leslie Nielsen; Chaplain, Arthur O'Connell; Robin, Eric Shea; Linarcos, Fred Sadoff; Nurse, Sheila Mathews; Doctor, Jan Arvan; Purser, Byron Webster; M. C., Bob Hastings; Chief Engineer, John Crawford; Tinkham, Erik Nelson.

2331 THE POSSESSION OF JOEL DELANEY. (Paramount-1972). Norah, Shirley MacLaine; Joel, Perry King; Dr. Reichman, Michael Horden; Charles, Earle Hyman; Ted, Robert Burr; Veronica, Miriam Colon; Erika, Lovelady Powell; Don Pedro, Edmundo Rivera Alvarez; Mrs. Perez, Teodorino Bello; Peter Benson, David Elliott; Tonio Perez, Jose Fernandez; Handsome Seance Subject, Ernesto Gonzales; Mr. Perez, Aukie Herger; Female Bruja, Paulita Inglesias; Carrie Benson, Lisa Kohane; Marta, Marita Lindholm; Sherry, Barbara Trentham; Brady, Peter Turgeon.

2332 THE POSTGRADUATE. (Kariofilms-1970). John Dugan, Bert Lewison, Babs Lewison, Darwin Burke, Randi Sablon, Danny Sillman, Fran Carston, Robert Weaver, Don Jones, Michael Barber, Jane Barber, Candy Bacardi, Linda Bloom, Barry Cornwall, Allan Figaro, Michael Garson, Pamela Garson, Danny Ireland, Eric Van West, Louis Velez, Marcie

Webster, Alan Saunders, Leo Slezak, Bonnie Podrid.

2333 THE POWER. (MGM-1968). Jim Tanner, George Hamilton; Margery Lansing, Suzanne Pleshette; Arthur Nordlund, Michael Rennie; Carl Melniker, Nehemiah Persoff; Talbot Scott, Earl Holliman; Henry Hallson, Arthur O'Connell; Bruce, Aldo Ray; Flora, Barbara Nichols; Sally Hallson, Yvonne De Carlo; N. E. Van Zandt, Richard Carlson; Mark Corlane, Gary Merrill; Grover, Ken Murray; Mrs. Van Zandt, Miiko Taka; Mrs. Hallson, Ceila Lovsky; Mr. Hallson, Vaughn Taylor; Briggs, Lawrence Montaigne; Sylvia, Beverly Hills.

2334 PREHISTORIC WOMEN. (20th Century-Fox-1967). Karl, Martine Beswick; Saria, Edina Ronay; David, Michael Latimer; Amyak, Stephanie Randall; Gido, Carol White; Luri, Alexandra Stevenson; First Amazon, Yvonne Horner; Ullo, Sydney Bromley; Arja, Frank Hayden; Colonel Hammond, Robert Raglan; Mrs. Hammond, Mary Hignett; Head Boy, Louis Mahoney; High Priest, Bari Bonson; Jakara, Danny Daniels; John Steven Berkoff.

2335 PREMONITION. (Transvue-1972). Neal, Carl Crow; Andy, Tim Ray; Baker, Winfrey Hester Hill; Kilkeny, Victor Izay; Janice, Judith Patterson; Jon, Jon Huss; Susan, Cheryl Adams; Michael, Barry Brown; Denise, Michele Fitzsimmons; Ralph, Eddie Patterson; Norm, Doug Digioila; Lotheridge, John Holman; Miss Thorsen, Diana Daves; Drummer, Andy Hare; Frat Brother, Lee Alpert; Man in Cabin, Larry Loveridge; Promoter, Miles Tilton; Shelley Snell, Tom Akers, Alex Del Zoppo, Paul Katz, Joyce Rudolph.

2336 THE PRESIDENT'S ANALYST. (Paramount-1967). Dr. Sidney Schaefer, James Coburn; Don Masters, Godfrey Cambridge; Kropotkin, Severn Darden; Nan Butler, Joan Delaney; Arlington Hewes, Pat Harrington; Old Wrangler, Barry McGuire; Snow White, Jill Banner; Ethan Allan Crocket, Eduard Franz; Henry Lux, Walter Burke; Dr. Lee-Evans, Will Beer; Wynn Quantrill, William Daniels; Jeff Quantrill, Joan Darling; Bing Quantrill, Sheldon Collins; Sullivan, Arte Johnson; First Puddlian, Martin Horsey; Second Puddlian, William Beckley; White House Tourist, Kathleen Hughes.

2337 PRETTY MAIDS ALL IN A ROW. (MGM-1971). Tiger, Rock Hudson; Miss Smith, Angie Dickinson; Surcher, Telly Savalas; Ponce, John David Carson; Proffer, Roddy McDowall; Pooldaski, Keenan Wynn.

2338 PRETTY POISON. (20th Century-Fox-1968). Dennis Pitt, Anthony Perkins; Sue Ann Stepanek, Tuesday Weld; Mrs. Stepanek, Beverly Garland; Azenauer, John Randolph; Bud

Munsch, Dick O'Neill; Mrs. Bronson, Clarice Blackburn; Pete, Joe Bova; Harry, Ken Kercheval; Night Watchman, Parker Fennelly; Mrs. Stepanek's Boy Friend, Paul Larson; Plainclothesmen, Tim Callahan; Burly Man, George Fisher; Cop at Beanery, William Sorrells; Men in Police Station, Dan Morgan, Mark Dawson, and Gil Rogers; Highway Policemen, John Randolph Jones and Maurice Ottinger; First Detective, Tom Gorman; 2nd Detective, Don Fellows; 1st Cop, Bill Fort; 2nd Cop, Ed Wagner; George Ryan's Winslow High-Steppers.

2339 THE PRIEST AND THE GIRL. (New Yorker-1973). Priest, Paulo Jose; Girl, Helena Ignez; Old Man, Mario Lago; Druggist, Fauzi Arap.

2340 THE PRIEST'S WIFE. (Warner Bros. -1971). Valeria Villi, Sophia Loren; Don Marco, Marcello Mastroianni; Maurizio, Venantino Venantini; Jimmy Guitar, Jacques Stany; Valeria's Father, Pippo Starnazza; Monsignor Caldana, Augusto Mastrantoni; Davide Libretti, Giuseppe Maffioli; Valeria's Mother, Miranda Campa; Don Felippo, Gino Cavalieri; Caldana's Secretary, Gino Lazzari; Lucia, Dana Ghia.

2341 PRIME CUT. (National General-1972). Nick Devlin, Lee Marvin; "Mary Ann," Gene Hackman; Clarabelle, Angel Tompkins; Weenie, Gregory Walcott; Poppy, Sissy Spacek; Violet, Janit Baldwin; Shay, William Morey; Delaney, Clint Ellison; Shaughnessy, Howard Platt; O'Brien, Les Lannom; Jake, Eddie Egan; Jake's Girl, Therese Reinch; Reaper Driver, Bob Wilson; Brockman, Gordon Singer; Milk Lady, Gladys Watson; Desk Clerk, Hugh Gillin Jr. ; Mrs. O'Brien, P. Lund; Ox-Eye, David Savage; Farmer Bob, Craig Chapman; Big Jim, Jim Taksas; Freckle Face, Wayne Savagne.

2342 THE PRIME OF MISS JEAN BRODIE. (20th Century-Fox-1969). Jean Brodie, Maggie Smith; Teddy Lloyd, Robert Stephens; Sandy, Pamela Franklin; Gordon Lowther, Gordon Jackson; Miss MacKay, Celia Johnson; Mary McGregor, Jane Carr; Jenny, Diane Grayson; Monica, Shirley Steedman; Miss Campbell, Margo Cunningham; Miss Gaunt, Ann Way; Miss Mackenzie, Isla Cameron; Miss Kerr, Helena Gloag; Miss Alison Kerr, Molly Weir; Emily Carstairs, Lavina Lang; Miss Lockhart, Rona Anderson; Mr. Burrage, John Dunbar; Schoolgirls, Kristen Hatfield, Janette Sattler, Hilary Berlin, Diane Robillard, Jennifer Irvine, Helen Wigglesworth, Gillian Evans, Antonia Moss, Antoinette Biggerstaff.

2343 PRISM. (Corn King-1971). Ben, Paul Geier; Eva, Dale Soules; Sally, Nancy Volkman; Peter, Ozzie Tortora; Larry, Frank Geraci; Heckler, Robert Root.

2344 PRISON GIRLS. (American International-1973). Robin Whitting, Maria Arnold, Angie Monet, Ushi Diagart, Lisa Ashbury, Tracy Handfuss, Jamie McKenna, Ilona Lakes, Claire Bow, Lois Darst, Carol Peters.

2345 PRISON GUARD. (Filmaco-1973). Pepa, Jiri Hrzan; Mother, Vera Tichanokova; Mary, Helen Vershurova; Cervinka, Karel Mares.

2346 THE PRISONER OF SECOND AVENUE. (Warner Bros.-1974). Mel, Jack Lemmon; Edna, Anne Bancroft; Harry, Gene Saks; Pauline, Elizabeth Wilson; Pearl, Florence Stanley; Belle, Macine Stuart; Man Upstairs, Ed Peck; Charlie, Gene Blakely; Psychiatrist, Ivor Francis; Detective, Stack Pierce.

2347 LA PRISONNIERE. (AVCO Embassy-1969). Stanislas Hassler, Laurent Terzieff; Gilbert Moreau, Bernard Fresson; Jose, Elisabeth Wiener; Maguy, Dany Carrel; Sala, Dario Moreno; Maurice, Daniel Riviere.

2348 PRIVATE DUTY NURSES. (New World-1972). Spring, Kathy Cannon; Lola, Joyce Williams; Lynn, Pegi Boucher; Dr. Doug Selden, Joseph Kaufmann; Domino, Dennis Redfield; Dr. Elton, Herbert Jefferson Jr.; Dewey, Paul Hampton; Dr. McClintock, Paul Gleason; Ahmed, George Sawaya; Kirby, Morris Buchanan; Bartender, Cliff Carnell.

2349 THE PRIVATE LIFE OF SHERLOCK HOLMES. (United Artists-1970). Sherlock Holmes, Robert Stephens; Dr. John Watson, Colin Blakely; Mrs. Hudson, Irene Handl; First Gravedigger, Stanley Holloway; Mycroft Holmes, Christopher Lee; Gabrielle Valladon, Genevieve Page; Rogozhin, Clive Revill; Petrova, Tamara Toumanova; Inspector Lestrade, George Benson; Old Lady, Catherine Lacey; Queen Victoria, Mollie Maureen; Von Tirpitz, Peter Madden; Hotel Manager, Robert Cawdron; Cassidy, Michael Elwyn; Cabby, Michael Balfour; Porter, Frank Thornton; Guide, James Copeland; Baggageman, Alex McCrindle; Minister, Kenneth Benda; Wiggins, Graham Armitage; Second Gravedigger, Eric Francis; Carters, John Garrie, Godfrey James; Petrova's Maid, Ina De La Haye; Old Man, Kynaston Reeves; Madame, Anne Blake; Girls, Marilyn Head, Anna Matisse, Wendy Ligham, Penny Brahms, Sheena Hunter; Lady-in-Waiting, Daphne Riggs; Equerry, John Gatrell; Lt. Commander, Phillip Anthony; McKeller, Phillip Ross; Secretary, Annette Kerr; Twins, Tina and Judy Spooner.

2350 THE PRIVATE NAVY OF SGT. O'FARRELL. (United Artists-1968). Master Sergeant Dan O'Farrell, Bob Hope; Nurse Nellie Krause, Phyllis Diller; Lt. Lyman P. Jones, Jeffrey Hunter; Maria, Gina Lollobrigida; Gaby, Mylene Demongeot; Lt. Cdr. Roger Snavely, John Myhers; Calvin

Coolidge Ishimura, Mako; Rear Admiral Stokes, Henry Wilcoxen; Capt. Elwood Prohaska, Dick Sargent; Pvt. George Strongbow, Christopher Dark; Pvt. Johnny Bannon, Michael Burns; Corporal Kennedy, William Wellman Jr.; Marine Private Ogg, Robert Donner; Private Roberts, Jack Grinnage; Private Jack Schultz, William Christopher; Corporal Miller, John Spina.

2351 PRIVATE PARTS. (MGM-1972). Cheryl, Ayn Ruymen; Aunt Martha, Lucille Benson; George, John Ventantonio; Rev. Moon, Laurie Main; Jeff, Stanley Livingston; Jeff's Dad, Charles Woolf; Judy, Ann Gibbs; Mike, Len Travis; Mrs. Quigley, Dorothy Neumann; Policemen, Gene Simms, John Lupton; Artie, Patrick Strong.

2352 PRIVILEGE. (Universal-1967). Steve Shorter, Paul Jones; Vanessa Ritchie, Jean Shrimpton; Alvin Kirsch, Mark London; Julie Jordan, Max Bacon; Martin Crossley, Jeremy Child; Andrew Butler, William Job; Professor Tatham, James Cossins; Marcus Hooper, Frederick Danner; Freddie K., Victor Henry; Leo Stanley, Arthur Pentelow; Squit, Steve Kirby; Bishop of Essex, Michael Barrington; Bishop of Cornwall, Edwin Fink; Bishop of Surrey, John Gill; Bishop of Hersham, Norman Pitt; Bishop of Rutland, Alba; Reverend Jeremy Tate, Malcolm Rogers; Miss Crawford, Doreen Mantle; TV Director, Michael Graham; The Runner Beans, George Bean Group.

2353 THE PRODUCERS. (Embassy-1968). Max Bialystock, Zero Mostel; Leo Bloom, Gene Wilder; Lorenzo St. Du Bois (LSD), Dick Shawn; Franz Liebkind, Kenneth Mars; First Old Lady, Estelle Winwood; Roger De Bris, Christopher Hewett; Carmen Giya, Andreas Voutsinas; Ulla, Lee Meredith; Eva Braun, Renee Taylor; Production Tenor, Michael Davis; N. Y. Times Critic, John Zoller; Woman at Window, Madlyn Cates; Bartender, Frank Campanella; Auditioning Hitlers, Arthur Rubin, Zale Kessler, Bernie Allen, Rusty Blitz, Anthony Gardell; Old Ladies, Mary Love, Amelie Barleon, Nell Harrison, Elsie Kirk; German Officer in Play, Barney Martin; Showgirl, Diana Eden; Lead Dancers, Tucker Smith and David Evans.

2354 THE PROFESSIONALS. (Columbia-1966). Bill Dolworth, Burt Lancaster; Henry Rico Fardan, Lee Marvin; Hans Ehrengard, Robert Ryan; Captain Jesus Raza, Jack Palance; Maria Grant, Claudia Cardinale; J. W. Grant, Ralph Bellamy; Jacob Sharp, Woody Strode; Ortega, Joe De Santis; Fierro, Rafael Bertrand; Padilla, Jorge Martinez De Hoyos; Chiquita, Maria Gomez; Revolutionary, Jose Chavez; Revolutionary, Carlos Romero; Banker, Vaughn Taylor.

2355 THE PROFITEER. (Belial-1974). Baroness Bezzi, Valeria Moriconi; Servant, Al Cliver; Parsifal, Giancarlo Mariangeli;

Tersa, Janet Agren.

2356 PROJECT X. (Paramount-1968). Hagen Arnold, Christopher George; Karen Summers, Greta Baldwin; Dr. Crowther, Henry Jones; Gregory Gallea, Monte Markham; Colonel Holt, Harold Gould; Lee Craig, Phillip E. Pine; Dr. Tony Verity, Lee Delano; Colonel Cowen, Ivan Bonar; Dr. George Tarvin, Robert Cleaves; Major Tolley, Charles Irving; Sybil Dennis, Sheila Bartold; Stover, Patrick Wright; Overseer, Maryesther Denver; Sen Chiu, Keye Luke; Hicks, Ed Prentiss.

2357 THE PROJECTED MAN. (Universal-1967). Professor Steiner, Bryant Haliday; Dr. Pat Hill, Mary Peach; Dr. Blanchard, Norman Wooland; Christopher Mitchell, Ronald Allen; Inspector Davis, Derek Farr; Sheila Anderson, Tracey Crisp; Latham, Derrick De Marney; Professor Lembach, Gerard Heinz; Harry, Sam Kydd; Steve, Terry Scully; Gloria, Norma West; Dr. Wilson, Frank Gatliff.

2358 THE PROJECTIONIST. (Maron-1971). Projectionist/Flash, Chuck McCann; The Girl, Ina Balin; Renaldi/The Bat, Rodney Dangerfield; Candy Man/Scientist, Jara Kohout; Friendly Usher, Harry Hurwitz; TV Pitchman, Robert Staats; Premiere Announcer, Robert King.

2359 PROLOGUE. (Vaudeo-1970). Jesse, John Robb; Karen, Elaine Malus; David, Gary Rader; Allen, Peter Cullen; Neil, Christopher Cordeaux; Karen's Father, Henry Gamer; Judge, Victor Knight; Newscaster, Robert Girolami; Janitor, Frank Edwards; Themselves, Abbie Hoffman, William Burroughs, Jean Genet, Dick Gregory, Allen Ginsberg.

2360 PROMISE AT DAWN. (AVCO Embassy-1970). Nina Kacew, Melina Mercouri; Romain (25-30), Assaf Dayan; Romain (at 15), Didier Haudepin; Romain (at 9), François Raffoul; Aniela, Despo; Igor Igorevitch, Jean Martin; M. Serusier, Fernand Gravey; Madame Mailler, Jacqueline Porel; Louison, Carol Cole; Romain's Wren Friend, Julie Dassin; Mariette, Marina Nestora.

2361 PROMISE HER ANYTHING. (Paramount-1966). Harley Rummel, Warren Beatty; Michele O'Brien, Leslie Caron; Dr. Peter Brock, Bob Cummings; Mrs. Luce, Hermione Gingold; Sam, Lionel Stander; Rusty, Asa Maynor; Ange, Keenan Wynn; Dr. Brock's Mother, Cathleen Nesbitt; John Thomas, Michael Bradley; Woman in Pet Shop, Bessie Love; Riggs O'Hara, Mavis Villiers, Hal Galili, Warren Mitchell, Sydney Tafler, Ferdy Mayne, Margaret Nolan, Vivienne Ventura, Anita Sharp Bolster, George Moon, Charlotte Holland, Chuck Julian, Michael Chaplin.

2362 PROSTITUTION. (Stratford-1965). Etchika Choreau, Evelyn Dassas, Alain Lionel, Jean Werner, Alicia Buttierez,

Ann Darden, Rita Cadillac, Gabrille Robinne, Victor Guyay, Robert Dalban, Carl Eich, Raoul Dantes.

2363 THE PROUD AND THE DAMNED. (Prestige-1972). Will, Chuck Connors; Ike, Aron Kincaid; Alcalde, Cesar Romero; Ramon, Jose Greco; Hank, Henry Capps; Billy, Peter Ford; Jeb, Smoky Roberds; Maria, Maria Grimm; Dancer, Nana Lorca; Mila, Anita Quinn; Juan, Conrad Parkham; Chico, Alvaro Ruiz; Gen. Martinez, Andre Marquis; Lt., Pacheco; Padre, Ignacio Gomez; Aide, Ernesto Uribe; Innkeeper, Rey Vasquez; Rollo, Bernardo Herrera; and Los Caballeros de Villa de Leyva.

2364 PRUDENCE AND THE PILL. (20th Century-Fox-1968). Prudence Hardcastle, Deborah Kerr; Gerald Hardcastle, David Niven; Henry Hardcastle, Robert Coote; Elizabeth, Irina Demick; Grace Hardcastle, Joyce Redman; Geraldine Hardcastle, Judy Geeson; Dr. Allan Huart, Keith Michell; Lady Roberta Bates, Edith Evans; Tony Bates, David Dundas; Rose, Vickery Turner; Ted, Hugh Armstrong; Chemist, Peter Butterworth; Woman in Tea Shop, Moyra Fraser; Gerald's Secretary, Annette Kerr; Race Track Official, Harry Towb; Chemist's Assistant, Jonathan Lynn.

2365-66 No entries.

2367 PSYCHO-CIRCUS. (American International-1967). Gregor, Christopher Lee; Inspector Elliott, Leo Genn; Barberini, Anthony Newlands; Carl, Heinz Drache; Eddie, Eddi Arent; Manfred, Klaus Kinski; Gina, Margaret Lee; Natasha, Suzy Kendall; Sir John, Cecil Parker; Mason, Victor Maddern; Mario, Maurice Kaufmann; Manley, Lawrence James; Jackson, Tom Bowman; Mr. Big, Skip Martin; Red, Fred Powell; Negro, Gordon Petrie; Hotel Porter, Henry Blakely; Armed Van Guard, Dennis Blakely; Fourth Man, George Fisher; Speedboat Men, Peter Brace and Roy Scammel; Security Men, Geoff Silk and Keith Peacock.

2368 THE PSYCHOPATH. (Paramount-1966). Inspector Holloway, Patrick Wymark; Mrs. Von Sturm, Margaret Johnston; Mark Von Sturm, John Standing; Frank Saville, Alexander Knox; Louise Saville, Judy Huxtable; Donald Loftis, Don Borisenko; Dr. Glyn, Colin Gordon; Martin Roth, Thorley Walters; Victor Ledoux, Robert Crewdson; Morgan, Tim Barrett; Tucker, Frank Forsyth; Mary, Olive Gregg; Biggs, Harold Lang; Reinhardt Klermer, John Harvey; Cigarette Girl, Greta Farrer.

2368a PSYCH-OUT. (American International-1968). Jennie Davis, Susan Strasberg; Dave, Dean Stockwell; Stoney, Jack Nicholson; Steve Davis, Bruce Dern; Ben, Adam Roarke; Elwood, Max Julien; Arthur, Robert Kelljan; Warren, Henry Jaglom;

Sadie, Barbara London; Wesley, Tommy Flanders; Pandora, I. J. Jefferson; Greg, Geoffrey Stevens; Plainclothesman, Gary Marshall; Landlady, Beatriz Monteil; Preacher, Ken Scott; Lynn, Linda Gaye Scott; The Strawberry Alarm Clock; The Seeds.

2368b PSYCHOUT FOR MURDER. (Times-1971). Licia, Adrienne La Russa; Daddy, Rossano Brazzi; Mario, Nino Castelnuovo; Giovanna, Paola Pitagora; Francesco, Alberto De Mendoza; Laura, Idelma Carlo; Paterlini, Renzo Petretto; Politician, Nestor Garay.

2369 THE PUBLIC EYE. (Universal-1972). Belinda Sidley, Mia Farrow; Julian Cristoforou, Topol; Charles Sidley, Michael Jayston; Mrs. Sidley, Margaret Rawlings; Miss Framer, Annette Crosbie; Mr. Mayhew, Dudley Foster; Sir Philip Crouch, Michael Aldridge; Mr. Scrampton, Michael Barrington; Parkinson, Neil McCarthy; Lady Crouch, Gabrielle Brune; Wealthy Client, Jack Watling; Writer, David Battley; Bertha, Lucy Griffiths; Dinner Guest, David Hutcheson; Dinner Guest, Joan Henley.

2370 PUFNSTUF. (Universal-1970). Jimmy, Jack Wild; Witchiepoo, Billie Hayes; Boss Witch, Martha Raye; Witch Hazel, Mama Cass.

2371 PULP. (United Artists-1972). Mickey King, Michael Caine; Preston Gilbert, Mickey Rooney; Ben Dinuccio, Lionel Stander; Princess Betty Cippola, Lizabeth Scott; Liz Adams, Nadia Cassini; Miller, Al Lettieri; Mysterious Englishman, Dennis Price; Sotgio, Amerigo Tot; Marcovic, Leopoldo Trieste; Jim Norman, Robert Sacchi; Santana, Joe Zammit Cordina; Chambermaid, Ave Ninchi; Tourists in Restaurant, Werner Hasselman, Louise Lambert; Del Duce, Luciano Pigozzi; Senora Pavone, Maria Quasimodo; Tourists in Coach, Iver Gilborn, Elaine Olcott; Silvana, Janet Agren; Blonde Typist, Christina Gaioni; First Guide, Cyrus Elias; Office Manager, Giulio Donnini; Gilbert's Mother, Cettina Borg Oliver; Cripple, Giuseppe Mallia; Mario, Roy Marmara.

2372 PUNISHMENT PARK. (Sherpix-1971). Captain, Jim Bohan; Sheriff, Van Daniels; Prof. Daly, Frederick Franklyn; Senator, Sanford Golden; Sheriff, Harlan Green; Marshall, Rodger Greene.

2373 PUPPET ON A CHAIN. (Cinerama-1972). Paul Sherman, Sven-Bertil Taube; Maggie, Barbara Parkins; Colonel De Graaf, Alexander Knox; Inspector Van Gelder, Patrick Allen; Meegeren, Vladek Sheybal; Astrid Lemay, Ania Marson; Trudi, Penny Casdagli; The Assassin, Peter Hutchins; Himmy Duclos, Drewe Henley; Herta, Henni Orri; George Lemay, Stewart Lane; Morgenstern, Mark Malicz; Hotel Manager, Michael Mellinger.

2374 THE PURSUIT OF HAPPINESS. (Columbia-1971). William Popper, Michael Sarrazin; Jane Kauffman, Barbara Hershey; Melvin Lasher, Robert Klein; Ruth Lawrence, Sada Thompson; Detective Cromie, Ralph Waite; John Popper, Arthur Hill; Daniel Lawrence, E. G. Marshall; Mrs. Conroy, Maya Kenin; Mrs. O'Mara, Rue McClanahan; Terence Lawrence, Peter White; Holmes, Joseph Attles; Josephine, Beulah Garrick; Mrs. Popper, Ruth White; Judge Vogel, Barnard Hughes; James Moran, David Doyle; George Wilson, Gilbert Lewis; McArdle, Albert Henderson; Defense Attorney Keller, Tom Rosqui; Judge Palumbo, Jack Somack; First Guard, Edward Kovens; Second Guard, Charles Durning; Policeman, Ed Setrakian; Traffic Cop, Ted Beniades; Pilot, William Devane.

2375 PUSS AND KRAM. (1967). Eva, Agneta Ekmanner; John, Hakan Serner; John's Girl, Lena Granhagen; Max, Sven-Bertil Taube.

2376 PUSSYCAT, PUSSYCAT, I LOVE YOU. (United Artists-1970). Fred, Ian McShane; Millie, Anna Calder-Marshall; Grant, John Gavin; Farquardt, Severn Darden; Anna, Joyce Van Patten; Ornella, Beba Loncar; Ottavio, Samy Pavel; Angelica, Katia Christina; Liz, Veronica Carlson; Flavia, Gaby Andre; Franco, Marino Mase; Hesther, Dari Lallou; Dr. Ponti, Ian Trigger; Clerk, Leopoldo Trieste; Amo, Paul Muller; Gwendolyn, Madeline Smith; Director, Maurizio Lucidi; Girl, Josiane Tanzilli.

2377 PUTNEY SWOPE. (Cinema V-1969). Putney Swope, Arnold Johnson; Stanley Gottlieb, Allen Garfield, Archie Russell, Ramon Gordon, Bert Lawrence, Joe Engler, David Kirk, Don George, Buddy Butler, Vincent Hamill, Tom Odachi, Ching Yeh, Spunky-Funk Johnson, Joe Fields, Norman Schreiber, Bob Staats, Alan Abel, Sol Brawerman, Ben Israel, Mel Brooks, Louise Heath, Barbara Clarke, Catherine Lojacono, Johnjohn Robinson, Charles Buffum, Ron Palombo, Wendy Appel, Antonio Fargas, Geegee Brown, Vance Amaker, Al Green, Chuck Ender, Anthony Chisholm, Walter Jones, Khaula Bakr, Melvia, Annette, Andrea Marshall.

2378 PUZZLE OF A DOWNFALL CHILD. (Universal-1970). Lou Andreas Sand, Faye Dunaway; Aaron, Barry Primus; Pauline Balba, Viveca Lindfors; Dr. Galba, Barry Morse; Mark, Roy Scheider; Barbara Casey, Ruth Jackson; Dr. Sherman, John Heffernan; Psychiatrist, Sydney Walker; Davy Bright, Clark Burckhalter; Peggy McCavage, Shirley Rich; Falco, Emerick Bronson; First Man in Bar, Joe George; First Doctor, John Eames; Mr. Wong, Harry Lee; Joan, Jane Halleran; Neighbor, Susan Willis; T. J. Brady, Barbara Carrera; George, Sam Schacht.

2379 THE PYX. (Cinerama-1973). Elizabeth, Karen Black; Jim, Christopher Plummer; Pierre, Donald Pilon; Keerson, Jean-Louis Roux; Meg, Yvette Brind'Amour; Superintendent, Jacques Godin; Herbie, Lee Broker; Jimmy, Terry Haig; Worther, Robin Gammell; Sandra, Louise Rinfret.

2380 QUACKSER FORTUNE HAS A COUSIN IN THE BRONX. (UMC-1970). Quackser Fortune, Gene Wilder; Zazel Pierce, Margot Kidder; Betsy Bourke, Eileen Colgan; Mr. Fortune, Seamus Ford; Mrs. Fortune, May Ollis; Kathleen Fortune, Liz Davis; Vera Fortune, Caroline Tully; Damien, Paul Murphy; Tom Maguire, David Kelly; Mike, Tony Doyle; Tim, John Kelly; Men in Pub, Liam Sweeney & Robert Somerset & Danny Cummings; Charlady, Julie Hamilton; Coal Merchant, Cecil Sheehan; Blacksmith, Charles Byrne; Attendant, Brendan Mathews; Walter, Robert Carrickford; Woman, Lillian Rapple; Student, Jeremy Jones; Hall Porter, John Hoey; Policeman, Martin Crosbie; Elaine Boland, Marjorie McHenry; Man at Foundry, Patrick Smyth.

2381 QUADROON. (Presidio-1972). Coral, Kathrine McKee; Caleb, Tim Kincaid; Antoine, Robert Priest; Celeste, Madelyn Sanders; Dupree, George Lupo; Aunt Nancy, Marinda French; Jacques, Bill McGhee; Felix, David Snow.

2382 QUE HACER. (Impact-1973). Suzanne, Sandra Archer; Martin, Richard Stahl; Hugo, Pablo de la Barra; Simon, Anibal Reyna; Osvaldo, Lucho Alarcon; Padre, Jorge Yanez.

2383 THE QUEEN. (Grove Press-1968). Flawless Sabrina, Jack Doroshow; Miss Philadelphia, Harlow (Richard Finochio); Miss Manhattan, Crystal; Miss Boston, Sonya; Miss New Jersey, Emory; Miss Chicago, Alfonse; The Judges, Andy Warhol, Edie Sedgwick, Terry Southern, Larry Rivers; Guest Appearance, Mario Montez.

2384 QUEEN OF BLOOD. (American International-1966). John Saxon, Judi Meredith, Florence Marly, Don Eitner, Robert Porter, Forrest Ackerman, Basil Rathbone, Dennis Hopper, Robert Boon, Virgil Frye, Terry Lee.

2385 THE QUEENS. (Royal-1968). Sabina, Monica Vitti; Giani, Enrico Maria Salerno; First Motorist, Franco Balducci; Second Motorist, Renzo Giovanpietro; Armenia, Claudia Cardinale; Dr. Aldini, Gastone Moschin; Elena, Raquel Welch; Luigi, Jean Sorel; Claudia, Pia Lindstrom; Alberto, Massimo Fornari; Marta, Capucine; Giovanni, Alberto Sordi; The Professor, Anthony Steel; Countess Rattazzi, Olga Villi; The Priest, Gigi Ballista; The Guest, Nino Marchetti.

2386 QUEST FOR LOVE. (Rank-1971). Ottilie, Joan Collins; Colin, Tom Bell; Tom, Denholm Elliott; Sir Henry, Laurence Naismith; Jennifer, Lyn Ashley; Geraldine, Juliet

Harmer; Jimmy, Neil McCallum.

2387 QUICK, BEFORE IT MELTS. (MGM-1965). Pete Santelli, George Maharis; Oliver Cromwell Cannon, Robert Morse; Tiare Marshall, Anjanette Comer; Vice Admiral, James Gregory; Harvey T. Sweigert, Howard St. John; Mikhail Drozhensky, Michael Constantine; George Snell, Norman Fell; Diana Grenville-Wells, Janine Gray; Sharon Sweigert, Yvonne Craig; Leslie Folliott, Bernard Fox; Orville Bayleaf, Conland Carter; Ben Livingston, Richard Lepore; Prison Guard, Hal Baylor; Ham Operator, Doodles Weaver; Shaggy Type, Frank London; Scientist, Nelson Olmstead; Military Men, Tom Vize, John Dennis, Hugh "Slim" Langtry, Fletcher Allen, Davis Roberts, Dale Malone.

2388 QUIET DAYS IN CLICHY. (Grove-1970). Paul Faljean, Louise White, Wayne Rodda, Ulla Lemvigh-Mueller.

2389 A QUIET PLACE IN THE COUNTRY. (Lopert-1970). Leonardo, Franco Nero; Flavia, Vanessa Redgrave; Attilio, Georges Geret; Wanda, Gabriella Grimaldi; Wanda's Mother, Madeleine Damien; Egle, Rita Calderoni; Egle's Friend, Renato Menegotto; Asylum Attendant, John Francis Lane; Medium, David Maunsell; Villagers, Mirta Simionato, Graziella Simionato, Camillo Besenson, Constantine De Luca, Marino Pagiola, Piero De Franceschi, Otello Cazzola, Arnaldo, Momo, Sara Momo, Guilia Menin.

2390 THE QUILLER MEMORANDUM. (20th Century-Fox-1966). Quiller, George Segal; Pol, Alec Guinness; Oktober, Max Von Sydow; Inge, Senta Berger; Gibbs, George Sanders; Weng, Robert Helpmann; Gibbs' Associate, Robert Flemyng; Hengel, Peter Carsten; Headmistress, Edith Schneider; Hassler, Gunther Meisner; Jones, Robert Stass; Grauber, Ernst Walder; Oktober's Men, Philip Madoc and John Rees.

2391 A QUIXOTE WITHOUT LA MANCHA. (Columbia-1970). Justo, Cantinflas; Arvide, Angel Garaza; Angelica, Lupita Ferrer; Sarita, Susana Salvat; Police Commander, Eduardo Alcaraz; Alberto, Carlos Fernandez; Store Owner, Luis Manuel Pelayo; Judge, Carlos Riquelme; Tenant House Owner, Victor Alcocer.

2392 R. P. M. (Columbia-1970). Perez, Anthony Quinn; Rhoda, Ann-Margret; Rossiter, Gary Lockwood; Dempsey, Paul Winfield; Thatcher, Graham Jarvis; Hewlett, Alan Hewitt; Brown, Ramon Bieri; Rev. Blauvelt, John McLiam; Dean Cooper, Don Keefer; Perry Howard, Donald Moffat; Coach McCurdy, Norman Burton; Tyler, John Zaremba; Estella, Inez Pedroza; Students, Ted Bracci, Linda Meiklejohn, Bruce Fleischer, David Ladd, John David Wilder, Bradjose, Raymond Cavaleri, Henry Brown Jr., Frank Alesia, Robert Carricart Jr.

2393 RABBIT, RUN. (Warner Bros.-1970). Rabbit, James Caan; Ruth, Anjanette Comer; Tothero, Jack Albertson; Lucy, Melodie Johnson; Angstrum, Henry Jones; Mrs. Springer, Carmen Mathews; Margaret, Virginia Vincent; Mrs. Smith, Nydia Westman; Nelson as a Child, Marc Anthony Van Der Nagel; Mrs. Angstrum, Josephine Hutchinson; Springer, Don Keefer; Mrs. Tothero, Margot Stevenson; Miriam, Sondra Scott; Barney, Ken Kercheval; Janice, Carrie Snodgress; Jack Eccles, Arthur Hill.

2394 THE RABBLE. (Frank Lee International-1968). Kanzaburao, Somegoro Ichikawa; Midori, Yuriko Hoshi; Makie, Mayumi Ozora.

2395 RACHEL, RACHEL. (Warner Bros.-7 Arts-1968). Rachel Cameron, Joanne Woodward; Nick Kazlik, James Olson; Mrs. Cameron, Kate Harrington; Calla Mackie, Estelle Parsons; Reverend Wood, Geraldine Fitzgerald; Niall Cameron, Donald Moffatt; Preacher, Terry Kiser; Hector Jonas, Frank Corsaro; Leighton Barrow, Bernard Barrow; Rachel (as a child), Nell Potts; James, Shawn Campbell; Verla, Violet Dunn; Lee Shabab, Izzy Singer; Nick (as a child), Tod Engle; Bartender, Bruno Engl; Beatrice Pons, Dorothea Duckworth, Simm Landres, Connie Robinson, Sylvia Shipman, Larry Fredericks, Wendell MacNeal.

2396 RACING FEVER. (Allied Artists-1965). Joe Morrison, Dave Blanchard, Charles G. Martin, Barbara Biggart, Maxine Carroll, Ruth Nadel.

2397 RAGE. (Columbia-1967). Doc Reuben, Glenn Ford; Perla, Stella Stevens; Pancho, David Reynoso; Antonio, Armando Silvestre; Blanca, Ariadna Welter; Fortunato, Jose Elias Moreno; Maria, Dacia Gonzalez; Old Man, Pancho Cordova; His Wife, Susana Cabrera; Bus Driver, David Silva; Pedro, Quintin Bulnes; Jose, Valentin Trujillo.

2398 RAGE. (Warner Bros.-1972). Dan Logan, George C. Scott; Dr. Caldwell, Richard Basehart; Major Holliford, Martin Sheen; Dr. Spencer, Barnard Hughes; Chris Logan, Nicolas Beauvy; Colonel Franklin, Paul Stevens; Major Reintz, Stephen Young; Colonel Nickerson, Kenneth Tobey; Major Cooper, William Jordan.

2399 A RAGE TO LIVE. (United Artists-1965). Grace Caldwell, Suzanne Pleshette; Sidney Tate, Bradford Dillman; Roger Bannon, Ben Gazzara; Jack Hollister, Peter Graves; Amy Hollister, Bethel Leslie; Dr. O'Brien, James Gregory; Mrs. Caldwell, Carmen Mathews; Mrs. Bannon, Ruth White; Brock Caldwell, Linden Chiles; Charlie Jay, Mark Goddard.

2400 THE RAGMAN'S DAUGHTER. (Penelope Films-1974). Simon

Rouse, Victor Tennant, Patrick O'Connell, Leslie Sands, Rita Howard, Brenda Peters, Brian Murphy, Jane Wood.

2401 RAID ON ROMMEL. (Universal-1971). Foster, Richard Burton; Mackenzie, John Colicos; Major Tarkington, Clinton Greyn; Rommel, Wolfgang Preiss; Vivi, Danielle De Metz; Schroeder, Karl Otto Alberty; Conscientious Objector, Christopher Cary; Garth, John Orchard; Reilly, Brook Williams; Brown, Greg Mullavey; Admiral, Ben Wright; Wembley, Michael Sevareid; Tank Sergeant, Chris Anders.

2402 RAIDERS FROM BENEATH THE SEA. (20th Century-Fox-1965). Bill Harper, Ken Scott; Dottie Harper, Merry Anders; Tucker, Russ Bender; Purdy, Booth Colman; Buddy, Garth Benton; Walter Maslow, Stacey Winters, Ray Dennis, Larry Barton, Roger Creed.

2403 THE RAILROAD MAN. (Continental-1965). Andrea Marcocci, Pietro Germi; Sara Marcocci, Luisa Della Noce; Giulia, Sylva Koscina; Sandrino, Edoardo Nevola; Marcello, Carlo Giuffre; Liverani, Saro Urzi; Renato, Renato Speziali.

2404 THE RAILWAY CHILDREN. (Universal-1971). Mother, Dinah Sheridan; Perks, Bernard Cribbins; Old Gentleman, William Mervyn; Father, Iaian Cuthbertson.

2405 THE RAIN PEOPLE. (Warner Bros. -7 Arts-1969). Jimmie "Killer" Kilgannon, James Caan; Natalie Ravenna, Shirley Knight; Gordon, Robert Duvall; Rosalie, Marya Zimmet; Mr. Alfred, Tom Aldredge; Ellen, Laurie Crewes; Ellen's Father, Andrew Duncan; Ellen's Mother, Margaret Fairchild; Beth, Sally Gracie; Lou, Alan Manson; Vinny Ravenna, Robert Modica.

2406 RAMPAGE AT APACHE WELLS. (Columbia-1966). Stewart Granger, Pierre Brice, Harald Leipnitz, Macha Meril.

2407 RAMPARTS OF CLAY. (Cinema V-1971). Rima, Leila Schenna.

2408 RAPTURE. (International Classics-1965). Agnes, Patricia Gozzi; Joseph, Dean Stockwell; Larbaud, Melvyn Douglas; Karen, Gunnel Lindblom; Genevieve, Sylvia Kay.

2409 THE RARE BREED. (Universal-1966). Sam Burnett, James Stewart; Martha Price, Maureen O'Hara; Alexander Bowen, Brian Keith; Hilary Price, Juliet Mills; Jamie Bowen, Don Galloway; Charles Ellsworth, David Brian; Deke Simons, Jack Elam; Jeff Harter, Ben Johnson; Ed Mabry, Harry Carey Jr.; Juan, Perry Lopez; Alberto, Larry Domasin; Taylor, Alan Caillou.

2410 RASCAL. (Buena Vista-1969). Willard North, Steve Forrest; Sterling North, Bill Murphy; Theo North, Pamela Toll; Miss Whalen, Bettye Ackerman; Mrs. Satterfield, Elsa Lanchester; Garth Shadwick, Henry Jones; Cy Jenkins, John Fiedler; Rev. Thurman, Jonathan Daly; Mr. Pringle, Herbert Anderson; Miss Pince-nez, Maudie Prickett; Walter Dabbitt, Richard Erdman; Norman Bradshaw, Steve Carlson; Constable Stacey, Robert Emhardt; Narrator, Walter Pidgeon.

2411 RASPUTIN--THE MAD MONK. (20th Century-Fox-1966). Rasputin, Christopher Lee; Sonia, Barbara Shelley; Dr. Zargo, Richard Pasco; Ivan, Francis Matthews; Vanessa, Suzan Farmer; Peter, Nicholas Pennell; Tsarina, Renee Asherson; Innkeeper, Derek Francis; Patron, Alan Tilvern; The Bishop, Joss Ackland; The Abbott, John Welsh; Tsarvitch, Robert Duncan; Court Physician, John Bailey.

2412 RAT PFINK AND BOO BOO. (Craddock-1966). Carolyn Brandt, Vin Saxon, Titus Moede, George Caldwell, Mike Kannon, James Bowie, Keith Wester, Mary Jo Curtis, Romeo Barrymore, Dean Danger, Kogar.

2413 THE RATS ARE COMING! THE WEREWOLVES ARE HERE! (Mishkin-1972). Monica Mooney, Hope Stansbury; Diana, Jacqueline Skarvellis; Mortimer Mooney, Noel Collins; Phoebe Mooney, Joan Ogden; Pa Mooney, Douglas Phair; Malcolm Mooney, Berwick Kaler; Gerald, Ian Innes.

2414 THE RAVAGERS. (Hemisphere-1965). John Saxon, Bronwyn Fitzsimons, Fernando Poe Jr.

2415 RAVEN'S END. (New Yorker-1970). Anders, Thommy Berggren; Father, Keve Hjelm; Mother, Emy Storm; Sixten, Engvar Hirdwall; Elsie, Christina Framback; Neighbor, Agneta Prytz.

2416 RAW MEAT. (American International-1973). Inspector Calhoun, Donald Pleasence; Det. Rogers, Norman Rossington; Stratton-Villers, Christopher Lee; Alex, David Ladd; The Woman, June Turner; Patricia, Sharon Gurney; The Man, Hugh Armstrong; Manfred, James Cossins; Insp. Richardson, Clive Swift; Alice, Heather Stoney; Dr. Bacon, Hugh Dickson; Inspector, Jack Woolgar; Lif Operator, Ron Pember; Constable, Colin McCormack and Gary Winkler; Publican, James Culliford; Prostitute, Suzanne Winkler; Tunnel Workers, Gerry Crampton, Terry Plummer, Gordon Petrie.

2417 A REASON TO LIVE, A REASON TO DIE! (K-Tel-1974). James Coburn, Telly Savalas, Bud Spencer.

2418 REBEL ROUSERS. (Four Star Excelsior-1970). Cameron

Mitchell, Jack Nicholson, Bruce Dern, Diane Ladd.

2419 REBELLION. (Toho-1968). Isaburo Sasahara, Toshiro Mifune; Yogoro, Takeshi Kato; Ichi, Yoko Tsukasa; Bunzo, Tatsuyoshi Ebara; Suga, Michiko Otsuka; Lord Matsudaira, Tatsuo Matsumura; Chamberlain Yanase, Masao Mishima; Stewart Takahashi, Shigeru Koyama; Kotani, Isao Yamagata; Tatewaki Asano, Tatsuya Nakadai.

2420 THE RECKONING. (Columbia-1969). Michael, Nicol Williamson; Joyce, Rachel Roberts; John, Paul Rogers; Hilda, Zena Walker.

2421 THE RED ANGEL. (Daiei-1971). Nurse, Ayako Wakao; Doctor, Shinsuke Ashida; Pvt. Orihara, Yasuke Kawazu; Pvt. Sakamoto, Jotaro Senba.

2422 RED BEARD. (Frank Lee International-1968). Dr. Nilde (Red Beard), Toshiro Mifune; Dr. Noboru Yasumoto, Yuzo Kayama; Dr. Handayu Mori, Yoshio Tsuchiya; Otoyo, Terumi Niki; Sahachi, Tsutomu Yamazaki; Osuki, Reiko Dan; Mental Patient, Ryoko Kagawa; Masae, Yoko Naito, Okumi, Akemi Negishi; Rokusuke, Kamatari Fujiwara; Onaka, Miyuki Kuwano; Tokubei Izumiya, Takashi Shimura; Goheiji, Eijiro Tono; Genzo Tsugawa, Tatsuyoshi Ehara; Masae's Father, Ken Mitsuda; Yasumoto's Mother, Kinuyo Tanaka; Yasumoto's Father, Chishu Ryu; Chobo, Yoshitaka Zushi.

2423 RED DESERT. (Rizzoli-1965). Giuliana, Monica Vitti; Corrado Zeller, Richard Harris; Ugo, Carlo Chionetti; Linda, Xenia Valderi; Emilia, Rita Renoir; Max, Aldo Grotti; Valerio, Valerio Bartoleschi; Workman, Giuliano Missirini; Workman's Wife, Lili Rheims; Emanuela Pala Carboni, Bruno Borghi, Beppe Conti, Giulio Cotignoli, Giovanni Lolli, Hiram Mino Madonia, Arturo Parmiani, Carla Ravasi, Ivo Scherpiani, Bruno Scipioni.

2424 RED DRAGON. (Woolner Bros. -1967). Michael Scott, Stewart Granger; Carol, Rosanna Schiaffino; Smoky, Harald Juhnke; Norman, Paul Klinger; Blanche, Margit Saad; Pierre Milot, Sieghardt Rupp; Harris, Paul Dahlke; Helga Sommerfeld, Franco Fantasia, Suzanne Roquette, Chitra Ratana, Horst Frank.

2425 RED LANTERNS. (Times-1965). Jenny Karezi, Mary Chronopoulou, Alexandra Ladikou, George Foondas, Phaedon Georgitsis, Manos Katrakis, Despo Diamantidou.

2426 RED LINE 7000. (Paramount-1965). Mike, James Caan; Julie, Laura Devon; Holly, Gail Hire; Linday, Charlene Holt; Ned, John Robert Crawford; Gabrielle, Marianna Hill; Dan, James Ward; Pat, Norman Alden.

2427 RED LION. (Toho-1971). Gonzo, Toshiro Mifune; Hanzo, Etsushi Takahishi; Tomi, Shima Iwashita.

2428 RED PSALM. (Macmillan Audio Brandon-1973). Andrea Drahota, Lajos Balazsovits, Andras Balint, Gyongyi Buros, Jozsef Madaras, Tibor Molnar, Tibor Orban, Bertalan Solti.

2429 RED SKY AT MORNING. (Universal-1971). Josh Arnold, Richard Thomas; Marcia Davidson, Catherine Burns; Steenie Moreno, Desi Arnaz Jr.; Frank Arnold, Richard Crenna; Ann Arnold, Claire Bloom; Jimbob Buel, John Colicos; Romeo Bonino, Harry Guardino; John Cloyd, Strother Martin; Amadeo Montoya, Nehemiah Persoff.

2430 RED SUN. (National General-1972). Link, Charles Bronson; Cristina, Ursula Andress; Kuroda, Toshiro Mifune; Gauche, Alain Delon; Pepita, Capucine; Ambassador, Satoshi Nakamoura; Bart Barry, Lee Burton, Tony Dawson, John Hamilton, George W. Lycan, Luke Merenda, Jo Nieto, Jules Pena, Monica Randall, Hiroshi Tanaka, John Vermont.

2431 THE RED TENT. (Paramount-1971). Amundsen, Sean Connery; Valeria, Claudia Cardinale; Lundborg, Hardy Kruger; Nobile, Peter Finch; Romagna, Massimo Girotti; Zappi, Luigi Vannucchi; Biagi, Mario Adorf; Malmgren, Edward Marzevuc; Viglieri, Boris Kmelnizki; Troiani, Juri Solomin; Behounek, Jiri Vizbor; Mariano, Donatas Banionis; Cecioni, Otar Koberidze; Samoilovich, Grigori Gaj; Chuknovsky, Nikita Mikhalkov; Kolka, Nicolai Ivanov.

2432 RED TOMAHAWK. (Paramount-1967). Captain Tom York, Howard Keel; Dakota Lil, Joan Caulfield; Columbus Smith, Broderick Crawford; Ep Wyatt, Scott Brady; Elkins, Wendell Corey; Telegrapher, Richard Arlen; Bill Kane, Tom Drake; Sal, Tracey Olsen; Lieut. Drake, Ben Cooper; Bly, Donald Barry; 3rd Prospector, Reg Parton; Wu Sing, Gerald Jann; 2nd Prospector, Roy Jenson; 1st Prospector, Dan White; Samuels, Henry Wills; Townsman, Saul Gross.

2433 THE REDEEMER. (Empire-1966). Luis Alvarez, Maruchi Fresno, Virgilio Texeira, Manuel Monroy, Jose Marco Davo, Carlos Casaraville, Antonio Vilar, Felix Acaso, Heve Donay, Jacinto San Emeterio, Macdonald Carey.

2434 REFINEMENTS IN LOVE. (Hollywood International-1971). Hostess, Liz Renay.

2435 A REFLECTION OF FEAR. (Columbia-1973). Michael, Robert Shaw; Anne, Sally Kellerman; Katherine, Mary Ure; Marguerite, Sondra Locke; McKenna, Mitchell Ryan; Hector, Gordon DeVol; Voice of Aaron, Gordon Anderson; Peggy, Victoria Risk; Aaron, Leonard John Crofoot; Kevin, Michael

St. Clair; Coroner, Liam Dunn; Nurse, Michelle Marvin; Mme. Caraquet, Michele Montau.

2436 REFLECTIONS IN A GOLDEN EYE. (Warner Bros.-7 Arts-1967). Leonora Penderton, Elizabeth Taylor; Lieut. Colonel Morris Langdon, Brian Keith; Anacleto, Zorro David; Captain Weincheck, Irvin Dugan; Major Weldon Penderton, Marlon Brando; Alison Langdon, Julie Harris; Stables Sergeant, Gordon Mitchell; Susie, Fay Sparks; Private Williams, Robert Forster.

2437 THE REIVERS. (Cinema Center-1969). Boon Hoggenbeck, Steve McQueen; Carrie, Sharon Farrell; Boss McCaslin, Will Geer; Mr. Binford, Michael Constantine; Ned McCaslin, Rupert Crosse; Lucius McCaslin, Mitch Vogel; Maury McCaslin, Lonny Chapman; Uncle Possum, Juano Hernandez; Butch Lovemaiden, Clifton James; Miss Reba, Ruth White; Dr. Peabody, Dub Taylor; Alison McCaslin, Allyn Ann McLerie; Hannah, Diane Shalet; Phoebe, Diane Ladd; Sally, Ellen Geer; May Ellen, Pat Randall; Edmonds, Charles Tyner; Aunt Callie, Vinnette Carroll; Minnie, Gloria Calomee; Sarah, Sara Taft; Otis, Lindy Davis; Uncle Ike, Raymond Guth; Cousin Zack, Shug Fisher; Walter Clapp, Logan Ramsey; Joe Poleymus, Jon Shank; Mrs. Possum, Ella Mae Brown; Mary Possu, Florence St. Peter; Van Tosch, John McLiam; Doyle, Lou Frizzell; Ed, Roy Barcroft.

2438 RELATIONS. (Cambist-1971). Sonja, Gertie Jung; Papa, Bjorn Puggaard Muller; Egon, Paul Glargard; Rigmor, Dorthea Ross.

2439 THE RELUCTANT ASTRONAUT. (Universal-1967). Roy Fleming, Don Knotts; Buck Fleming, Arthur O'Connell; Major Fred Gifford, Leslie Nielsen; Ellie Jackson, Joan Freeman; Mrs. Fleming, Jeanette Nolan; Donelli, Jesse White; Plank, Frank McGrath; Rush, Paul Hartman; Blonde in Bar, Joan Shawlee; Bert, Guy Raymond; Aunt Zana, Nydia Westman; Cervantes, Robert Simon; Ned, Burt Mustin; Moran, Robert Pickering; Waitress, Ceil Cabot; Secretary, Fay De Witt; Bus Driver, Fabian Dean.

2440 A REPORT ON THE PARTY AND THE GUESTS. (Sigma III-1968). The Host, Ivan Vyskocil; Rudolph, Jan Klusak; Josef, Jiri Nemec; Eva, Zdenka Skvorecka; Frantisek, Pavel Bosek; Marta, Helena Pajskova; Karel, Karel Mares; The Wife, Jana Pracharova; The Husband, Evald Schorm.

2441 THE REPTILE. (20th Century-Fox-1966). Noel William, Ray Barrett, Michael Ripper, Marne Maitland, David Baron, Charles Lloyd Pack, George Woodbridge, Harold Goldblatt, John Laurie, Jacqueline Pearce, Jennifer Daniel.

2442 REPULSION. (Royal Films International-1965). Catherine Deneuve, Yvonne Furneaux, Ian Hendry, Patrick Wymark, John Fraser.

2443 REQUIEM FOR A GUNFIGHTER. (Embassy-1965). Rod Cameron, Stephen McNally, Mike Mazurki, Olive Sturgess, Tim McCoy, Johnny Mack Brown, Bob Steele, Lane Chandler, Raymond Hatton.

2444 REQUIEM FOR MOZART. (Artkino-1967). Innokenti Smoktunovsky, Pyotr Clebov, Am Milbert, and the voices of Sergei Lemeshev and Alexander Pirogov.

2445 THE RESTLESS NIGHT. (Casino-1965). Bernard Wicki, Ulla Jacobson, Hansjorg Felmy, Ann Savo, Erik Schuman, Werner Hinz, Werner Peters.

2446 RESURRECTION. (Artkino-1966). Tamara Syomia, Yevgeni Matveyev, Nina Samsonova.

2447 RESURRECTION OF EVE. (Mitchell Bros. -1973). Eve, Nancy Weich; Eve, Mimi Morgan; Eve, Marilyn Chambers; Frank, Matthew Armon; Johnnie, Johnnie Keyes; Mother, Bentley Christmas; Phil, Dale Meador; Nurses, Debbie Marinoff, Dozy Edmundson; Dallas, June Richards; Pam, Pam Francis; Manager, Binky Bish.

2448 THE RESURRECTION OF ZACHARY WHEELER. (Vidtronics-1971). Harry, Leslie Nielsen; Sen. Wheeler, Bradford Dillman; Dr. Redding, James Daly; Dr. Johnson, Angie Dickinson; Hugh, Robert J. Wilke; Dwight, Jack Carter; Jake, Don Haggerty; Jim Healy, Lou Brown, Pat O'Moore, Richard Schuyler, Richard Simmons, Ruben Moreno, Peter Mamakos, Jill Jaress, Jim Healey, Lee Giroux.

2449 LE RETOUR D'AFRIQUE. (New Yorker-1973). Francoise, Josee Destoop; Vincent, Francois Marthouret; Emilio, Juliet Berto; Girl, Anne Wiazemsky.

2450 RETURN FROM THE ASHES. (United Artists-1965). Stanislaus Pilgrim, Maximilian Schell; Fabienne, Samantha Eggar; Dr. Michele Wolf, Ingrid Thulin; Dr. Charles Bovard, Herbert Lom; Prostitute, Talitha Pol.

2451 THE RETURN OF COUNT YORGA. (American International-1972). Count Yorga, Robert Quarry; Cynthia Nelson, Mariette Hartley; Dr. David Baldwin, Roger Perry; Jennifer, Yvonne Wilder; Reverend Thomas, Tom Toner; Lt. Madden, Rudy De Luca; Tommy, Philip Frame; Professor Rightstat, George Macready; Bill Nelson, Walter Brooke; Brudah, Edward Walsh; Sgt. O'Connor, Craig Nelson; Jason, David Lampson; Ellen, Karen Houston; Mrs. Nelson, Helen Baron; Mitzi Carthay, Jesse Wells; Joe, Mike Pataki; Witch,

Corinne Conley; Michael Farmer, Allen Joseph; Claret Farmer, Peg Shirley; Laurie Greggs, Liz Rogers; Jonathan Greggs, Paul Hansen.

2452 THE RETURN OF MR. MOTO. (20th Century-Fox-1965). Mr. Moto, Henry Silva; Jonathan Westering, Terence Langdon; Maxine Powell, Suzanne Lloyd; Wasir Hussein, Marne Maitland; Dargo, Martin Widdeck; Inspector Halliday, Manley Morgan; Ginelli, Peter Zander; McCallister, Gordon Tanner; Shahardar, Harold Kasket; Chief Inspector Marlow, Richard Evans; Chapel, Dennis Holmes; Rogers, Ian Fleming; Belly Dancer, Sonia Benjamin.

2453 RETURN OF SABATA. (United Artists-1972). Sabata, Lee Van Cleef; Clyde, Reiner Schone; Maggie, Annabelle Incontrera; Jeremy Sweeney, Gianni Rizzo; McIntock, Gianpiero Albertini; Jackie, Jacqueline Alexandre; Bronco, Pedro Sanchez; Angel, Nick Jordan; Acrobat, Karis Vassili; McIntock's Henchman, Annibal Venturi; Bouncer, Benito Vasconi; Saloon Girl, Sylvia Alba; Hershel Kerrona, Miguel Vascez, Ernesto Hayes, Steffen Zacharias, Maria Pia Giancarlo, Janos Bartha, Gunther Stoll, Carmelo Reade, Vittorio Fanfoni.

2454 RETURN OF THE DRAGON. (Bryanston-1974). Tang Lung, Bruce Lee; Kuda, Chuck Norris; Chen Ching Hua, Nora Miao; Uncle Wang, Huang Chung Hsun; Ah K'ung, Chin Ti; Boss, Jon T. Benn; Robert, Robert Wall; Liu Yun, Chu'eng Li, Little Unicorn, Ch'eng Pin Chih, Ho Pich, Wei Ping Au, Huang Jen Chih, Mali Sha.

2455 RETURN OF THE SEVEN. (United Artists-1966). Chris, Yul Brynner; Vin, Robert Fuller; Chico, Julian Mateos; Colbee, Warren Oates; Manuel, Jordan Christopher; Frank, Claude Akins; Luis, Virgilio Texera; Lorca, Emilio Fernandez; Lopez, Rudy Acosta; Petra, Elisa Montes; Priest, Fernando Rey.

2456 REVENGE. (Rank-1971). Carol, Joan Collins; Jim, James Booth; Harry, Ray Barrett; Rose, Sinead Cusack; Lee, Tom Marshall; Seely, Kenneth Griffith; Jill, Zuleika Robson; Priest, Angus Mackay; Brewery Driver's Mate, Ronald Clarke; George, Patrick McAlinney; Jacko, Artro Morris; Inspector, Donald Morley; Undertaker, Martin Carroll; Pub Customer, Richard Holden; Brewery Driver, Geoffrey Hughes; Sales Representative, Basil Lord; Sgt., Barry Andrews.

2457 REVENGE OF THE GLADIATORS. (Paramount-1965). Roger Browne, Scilla Gabel, Giacomo Rossi Stuart, Danielle Vargas, Gordon Mitchell, Germano Longo.

2458 THE REVENGERS. (National General-1972). John Benedict, William Holden; Hoop, Ernest Borgnine; Job, Woody

Strode; Elizabeth Reilly, Susan Hayward; Quiberon, Roger Hanin; Zweig, Rene Koldehoff; Chamaco, Jorge Luke; Cholo, Jorge Martinez De Hoyos; Free State, Arthur Hunnicutt; Tarp, Warren Vanders; Arny, Larry Pennell; Whitcomb, John Kelly; Lieutenant Mercer, Scott Holden; Morgan, James Daughton; Mrs. Benedict, Lorraine Chanel; Warden, Raul Prieto.

2459 THE REVOLUTIONARY. (United Artists-1970). "A," Jon Voight; Helen, Jennifer Salt; Leonard II, Seymour Cassel; Despard, Robert Duvall; Ann, Collin Wilcox-Horne; Professor, Lionel Murton; Mayor, Reed De Rouen; A's Father, Stanhope; A's Mother, Mary Barclay; N.C.O., Richard Pendry; Nurse, Alexandra Berlin; Girl, Julie Garfield; Mrs. Peret, Libby Glenn; Lady Guest, Tucker McGuire; Sid, Alan Tilvern; Judge, Reginald Cornish; Gansard, Bill Nagy; Speaker, Earl Cameron; Sergeant, Kenneth J. Warren; Man Guest, Tommy Duggan.

2460 THE REWARD. (20th Century-Fox-1965). Scott Swenson, Max von Sydow; Sylvia, Yvette Mimieux; Frank Bryant, Efrem Zimbalist Jr.; Captain Carbajal, Gilbert Roland; Sargento Lopez, Emilio Fernandez; Joaquin, Henry Silva; Luis, Nino Castelnuovo; Patron, Rodolfo Acosta; El Veijo, Julian Rivero; Indian Boy, Rafael Lopez.

2461 THE RIBALD TALES OF ROBIN HOOD. (Adam-1969). Robin, Ralph Jenkins; Lady Sallyforth, August Carver; Maid Marian, Dee Lockwood; Prince John, Lawrence Adams; Sheriff, C. S. Poole; James Brand, Wendel Swink, Eddie Nova, Bami Allen, Paul Smith, Terry Sands, Scott Sizemore, Barbara Sanders.

2462 RICHARD. (Billings Associates-1972). Richard, Richard M. Dixon; Young Richard, Dan Resin; Young Pat, Lyon Lepton; Guardian Angel, Mickey Rooney; Plastic Surgeon, John Carradine; Himself, Richard M. Nixon; Advisers, Hazen Gifford, Hank Garrett, Paul Forrest.

2463 RIDE BEYOND VENGEANCE. (Columbia-1966). Jonas Trapp, Chuck Connors; Brooks Durham, Michael Rennie; Jessie, Kathryn Hays; Mrs. Lavender, Joan Blondell; Bonnie Shelley, Gloria Grahame; Dub Stokes, Gary Merrill; Johnsy Boy Hood, Bill Bixby; Elwood Coates, Claude Akins; Hanley, Paul Fix; Maria, Marrisa Mathes; Vogan, Harry Harvey Sr.; Bartender, William Bryant; Pete, Jamie Farr; Mexican Boy, Larrie Domasin; Drunk, William Catching; Census Taker, James MacArthur; Narrator, Arthur O'Connell; Aunt Gussie, Ruth Warrick; Mr. Kratz, Buddy Baer; Tod Wisdom, Frank Gorshin; Hotel Clerk, Robert Q. Lewis.

2464 RIDE THE HIGH WIND. (Feature Film Corporation of American-1968). Mike Gregory, Darren McGavin; Helena

Hansen, Maria Perschy; Karl Du Val, Albert Lieven; Maria Du Val, Alison Seebohm; Jack Dillon, Michael McGovern; Major Dillon, John Hayter; Brian O'Shaughnessy, Fiona Fraser, Michael Todd, Valerie Miller, Jan Fenn, Eric Egan, Geoffrey Morris.

2465 THE RIDE TO HANGMAN'S TREE. (Universal-1967). Guy Russell, Jack Lord; Matt Stone, James Farentino; Nevada Jones, Don Galloway; Lillie Malone, Melodie Johnson; Steve Carlson, Richard Anderson; Jeff Scott, Robert Yuro; Sheriff Stewart, Ed Peck; Corbett, Paul Reed; Ed Mason, Richard Cutting; Keller, Bing Russell; Teresa Moreno, Virginia Capers; Blake, Robert Sorrells; T. L. Harper, Robert Cornthwaite; Indian, Fabian Dean.

2466 RIDER ON THE RAIN. (AVCO Embassy-1970). Mellie, Marlene Jobert; Dobbs, Charles Bronson; Juliette, Annie Cordy; Nicole, Jill Ireland; Tony, Gabriele Tinti; Toussaint, Jean Gaven; Passenger, Marc Mazza; Tania, Corinne Marchand; Armand, Jean Piat; Hostess, Marika Green; Madeline Legauff, Ellen Bahl; Station Master, Marcel Peres.

2467 RIGHT ON! (Concept East-1971). The Original Last Poets, Gylan Kain, David Nelson, Felipe Lucano.

2468 RING OF BRIGHT WATER. (Cinerama-1969). Graham Merrill, Bill Travers; Mary MacKenzie, Virginia McKenna; Colin Wilcox, Peter Jeffrey; Storekeeper, James Clark; Mrs. Flora Elrich, Helena Gloag; Lighthouse Keeper, W. H. D. Joss; Bus Driver, Roddy McMillan; Mrs. Sarah Chambers, Jean Taylor-Smith; Road Mender, Archie Duncan; Fisherman, Kevin Collins; Guard, John Young; Sleeping Car Attendant, James Gibson; Herman, Michael O'Halloran; Frank, Philip McCall; Fishmonger, Christopher Benjamin; Pet Stall Girl, Phillipa Gail; Barmaid, June Ellis; Ticket Seller, Tommy Godfrey.

2469 RINGS AROUND THE WORLD. (Columbia-1967). John Shawcross, Don Ameche.

2470 RIO LOBO. (National General-1970). Cord McNally, John Wayne; Pierre Cordona, Jorge Rivero; Shasta, Jennifer O'Neill; Phillips, Jack Elam; Ketcham, Victor French; Maria Carmen, Susana Dosamantes; Tuscarora, Chris Mitchum; Sheriff Hendricks, Mike Henry; Dr. Jones, David Huddleston; Sheriff Cronin, Bill Williams; Lt. Harris, Edward Faulkner; Amelita, Sherry Lansing; Bitey, Dean Smith; Whitey, Robert Donner; Riley, Jim Davis; Lt. Forsythe, Peter Jason; Whitey's Henchmen, Robert Rothwell, Chuck Courtney, George Plimpton.

2471 RIOT. (Paramount-1969). Cully Briston, Jim Brown; Red Fletcher, Gene Hackman; Joe Surefoot, Ben Carruthers;

Bugsy, Mike Kellin; Grossman, Gerald O'Loughlin; "Big Mary" Sheldon, Clifford David; Jake, Bill Walker; "Gertie," Ricky Summers; Murray, Michael Byron; Deputy Warden Fisk, Jerry Thompson; Homosexual, M. Gerri; Homosexual, John Neiderhauser; The Warden, Warden Frank A. Eyman.

2472 RIOT ON THE SUNSET STRIP. (American International-1967). Lt. Walt Lorimer, Aldo Ray; Andy, Mimsy Farmer; Sgt. Tweedy, Michael Evans; Liz-Ann, Laurie Mock; Grady, Tim Rooney; Flip, Gene Kirkwood; Marge, Hortense Petra; Helen Tweedy, Anna Mizrahi; Herby, Schuyler Hayden; Bill Baldwin, Dick Winslow, Tony Benson, Frank Alesia, Jim Lefebvre, Pat Renella, Forrest Lewis, The Enemies, John Hart, The Chocolate Watch Band, The Longhairs, Deborah Travis, George E. Carey, The Standelles, Al Ferrara.

2473 RIP-OFF. (Alliance-1972). Michael, Don Scardino; Steve, Ralph Endersby; Cooley, Michael Kukelewich; Richie, Peter Gross; Sue, Sue Helen Petrie; Dunken, Hugh Webster; Mrs. Dunken, Maxine Miller; Nancy, Teddy Moore.

2474 THE RISE AND FALL OF THE WORLD AS SEEN FROM A SEXUAL POSITION. (Meyer-1972). Carol Doda, Arthur Meyer, Neil Prussel, Roger Larson, Ricky and Janine, Kitty Newman, Ruth Weis, Patrick Foley, Richard Foley, Marcelaine Robbins, Jerry Bissell, Lynn James, Nancy Wang, The Cockettes.

2475 THE RISE OF LOUIS XIV. (Brandon-1970). Louis XIV, Jean-Marie Patte; Colbert, Raymond Jourdan; Mazarin, Silvagni; Anne, Katharine Renn; Mme. de Plessis, Dominique Vincent; Fouquet, Pierre Barrat; Le Tellier, Fernand Fabre; Louise, Francoise Ponty; Marie-Therese, Joelle Laugeois; D'Artagnan, Maurice Barrier; Father Joly, Andre Dumas.

2476 RIVALS. (AVCO Embassy-1972). Christine Sutton, Joan Hackett; Peter Simon, Robert Klein; Jaime Sutton, Scott Jacoby; Mary, Jeanne Tanzy; Douglas, Gen Hayes; Madge, Phoebe Dorin; Child Psychiatrist, James Karen; Tony, Randy Digeronimo; Phil, Frank Fiore; Bob, Bill Herndon; Calloux, William Shust; Rabbi, Leib Lensky; Mrs. Sturgess, Viola Swayne; Salesman, Noel Craig; Matron, Iris Whitney; Stunt Girl, Ann Miles; Policemen, Ben Wilson and Robert Kya-Hill.

2477 RIVERRUN. (Columbia-1970). Jeffries, John McLiam; Sarah, Louise Ober; Dan, Mark Jenkins; Sarah's Mother, Josephine Nichols.

2478 THE ROAD HUSTLERS. (American International-1968). Noah Reedy, Jim Davis; Earl Veasey, Scott Brady; Matt Reedy, Bruce Yarnell; Mark Reedy, Bob Dix; Nadine, Victoria

Carroll; Sheriff Estep, Andy Devine; Helen, Sue Raney; Luke Reedy, Christian Anderson; Hagar, Ted Lehmann; Chandler, John Cardos; Hays, Bill McKinney; Bassett, Bill MacDowell; Eskie, Jack Lester; Deke, Sid Lawrence; Martha Lu, Monica Davis; Ted, Derek Hughes; Nelly, Marshall Lockhart; Imhoff, Jim Quick; Harrison, Jack Morey.

2479 ROAD TO SALINA. (AVCO Embassy-1971). Billie, Mimsy Farmer; Jonas, Robert Walker; Mara, Rita Hayworth; Warren, Ed Begley; Charlie, Bruce Pecheur; Sheriff, David Sachs; Linda, Sophie Hardy; Rocky, Marc Porel.

2480 ROBBERY. (Embassy-1967). Paul Clifton, Stanley Baker; Kate Clifton, Joanna Pettet; Inspector Langdon, James Booth; Robinson, Frank Finlay; Frank, Barry Foster; Dave, William Marlowe; Jack, Clinton Greyn; Ben, George Sewell; Don, Michael McStay; Freddy, Patrick Jordan; 7th Robber, Ken Farrington; Squad Chief, Glyn Edwards; Detective Inspector, Anthony Sweeney; Constable, David Pinner; Prison Contact, Frank Williams; Car Lot Owner, Barry Stanton; School Teacher, Rachel Herbert; CID Chief on Track, Michael David; Martin Wyldeck, Malcolm Taylor, Linda Marlowe, Roger Booth.

2481 ROBBY. (Bluewood-1968). Robby, Warren Raum; Friday, Ryp Siani; Horton Crandall and Lloyd Woodruff, John Garces; Janet Woodruff, Rita Elliot; Simmons, John Woodbridge; Chauffeur, Ralph C. Bluemke.

2482 ROBIN HOOD. (Buena Vista-1973). Voice of the Rooster, Roger Miller; Voice of Robin Hood, Brian Bedford; Voice of Maid Marian, Monica Evans; Voice of Little John, Phil Harris; Friar Tuck, Andy Devine; Lady Kluck, Carole Shelley; Prince John, Peter Ustinov; Sir Hiss, Terry-Thomas; Sheriff, Pat Buttram; Trigger, George Lindsey; Nutsy, Ken Curtis.

2483 ROMANCE OF A HORSETHIEF. (Allied Artists-1971). Stoloff, Yul Brynner; Kifke, Eli Wallach; Naomi, Jane Birkin; Zanvill, Oliver Tobias; Estusha, Lainie Kazan; Shloime, David Opatoshu.

2484 ROME WANTS ANOTHER CAESAR. (1974). Daniel Olbrychsky, Hiram Keller, Lino Troisi, Gino Lavagetto, Luigi Montini, Guido Lollobrigida, Jose De Vega, Renato Baldini.

2485 ROMEO AND JULIET. (Embassy-1966). Juliet, Margot Fonteyn; Romeo, Rudolf Nureyev; Mercutio, David Blair; Tybalt, Desmond Doyle; and Artists of the Royal Ballet.

2486 ROMEO AND JULIET. (Paramount-1968). Romeo, Leonard Whiting; Juliet, Olivia Hussey; Friar Laurence, Milo O'Shea;

Tybalt, Michael York; Mercutio, John McEnery; The Nurse, Pat Heywood; Lady Capulet, Natasha Parry; Lord Capulet, Paul Hardwick; Prince of Verona, Robert Stephens; Balthazar, Keith Skinner; Gregory, Richard Warwick; Count Paris, Roberto Bisacco; Benvolio, Bruce Robinson; Sampson, Dyson Lovell; Abraham, Ugo Barbone; Lord Montague, Antonio Pierfederici; Lady Montague, Esmeralda Ruspoli; Peter, Roy Holder; Friar John, Aldo Miranda; Page to Tybalt, Dario Tanzini; Rosaline, Paola Tedesco; The Chorus, Murray Head; Prologue and Epilogue Narrator, Laurence Olivier.

2487 THE ROOMMATES. (GFC-1973). Pat Woodell, Marki Bey, Roberta Collins, Laurie Rose, Christina Hart.

2488 ROOMMATES. (Pantages-1971). Henry, Dan Mason; Solly, Harvey Marks; Sandy, Barbara Press; Rhoda, Theon Banos; Martin, Allen Garfield; Bookmaster, Rick Wessler; Madison, Stanley Brock.

2489 ROPE OF FLESH. (Eve-1965). Hal Hopper, Lorna Maitland, Antoinette Cristiani, John Furlong, Stu Lancaster, Rena Horten, Princess Livingston, Sam Hanna, Nick Wolcuff, Frank Bolger, Lee Ballard, Mickey Foxx, F. Rufus Owens.

2490 A ROSE FOR EVERYONE. (Royal International-1967). Rosa, Claudia Cardinale; The Doctor, Nino Manfredi; Paolo, Mario Adorf; Basilio, Akim Tamiroff; Lino, Lando Buzzanca; Silvano, Luis Pellegrini; Sergio, Milton Rodriguez; Nino, Oswaldo Loureiro; Floreal, Jose Lewgoy; Ze Amoro, Grande Othelo; Nilse, Celia Bilar; Donna Natalia, Laura Soares.

2491 ROSELAND. (Boxoffice International-1973). Adam, E. Kerrigan Prescott; Bosch, Christopher Brooks; Princess Moon, Peggy Browne; Watkins, Karen Ingenthron; Sistine Skate, Victor Alter; Gosamer Girl, Carla Li Brizzi; Father Finney, Pierre Henri Delattre; Nico, Terry Wills; Miss Higgen, Andrea Schmidt; Narrator, H. K. Bauer.

2492 ROSEMARY'S BABY. (Paramount-1968). Rosemary Woodhouse, Mia Farrow; Guy Woodhouse, John Cassavetes; Minnie Castevet, Ruth Gordon; Roman Castevet, Sidney Blackmer; Hutch, Maurice Evans; Dr. Sapirstein, Ralph Bellamy; Terry, Angela Dorian; Laura-Louise, Patsy Kelly; Mr. Nicklas, Elisha Cook; Dr. Hill, Charles Grodin; Elise Dunstan, Emmaline Henry; Joan Jellico, Marianne Gordon; Shand, Phil Leeds; Mrs. Gilmore, Hope Summers; Tiger, Wendy Wagner; Grace Cardiff, Hanna Landy; Guy's Agent, Gordon Connell; Nurse, Janet Garland; Pregnant Woman, Joan Reilly; Voice of Donald Baumgart, Tony Curtis; Man at Telephone Booth, William Castle; Coven Members, Walter Baldwin, Charlotte Boerner, Sebastian Brooks, Ernest Harada,

Natali Masters, Elmer Modlin, Patricia O'Neal, Robert Osterloh, Almira Sessions, Bruno Sidar.

2493 ROSIE! (Universal-1968). Rosie Lord, Rosalind Russell; Daphne Shaw, Sandra Dee; Oliver Stevenson, Brian Aherne; Mildred Deever, Audrey Meadows; David Wheelwright, James Farentino; Edith Shaw, Vanessa Brown; Cabot Shaw, Leslie Nielsen; Mae, Margaret Hamilton; Patrick, Reginald Owen; Nurse, Juanita Moore; Mrs. Peters, Virginia Grey; Willetts, Dean Harens; Lawyer, Richard Derr; First Detective, Harry Hickox; Second Detective, Eddie Ness; Telephone Man, Hal Lynch; Old Lady, Ann Doran; Psychiatrist, Than Wyenn; Judge, Walter Woolf King; Pianist, Ronald Chisholm; Sedalia, Doris Lloyd; Taxi Driver, Ron Stokes; Joseph, Gene Roth; Secretary, Kathleen O'Malley; Florist, Doodles Weaver.

2494 ROTTEN TO THE CORE. (Cinema V-1965). The Duke, Anton Rodgers; Sara, Charlotte Rampling; Hunt, Eric Sykes; Lieutenant Vine, Ian Bannen; "Countess," Avis Bunnage; Lenny, Kenneth Griffith; Jelly, Dudley Sutton; Scapa, James Beckett; Anxious, Victor Maddern; Prisoner Governor, Raymond Huntley.

2495 ROUGH MAGIC. (New Yorker-1972). Ferdinand, Dieter Engel; Leira, Leila Knox; Milana, Linda Blackwell; Jonathan Hill, Jan Moore.

2496 ROUGH NIGHT IN JERICHO. (Universal-1967). Alex Flood, Dean Martin; Dolan, George Peppard; Molly Lang, Jean Simmons; Ben Hickman, John McIntire; Yarbrough, Slim Pickens; Jace, Don Galloway; Torrey, Brad Weston; Ryan, Richard O'Brien; Claire, Carol Anderson; Simms, Steve Sandor; Harvey, Warren Vanders; McGivern, John Napier.

2497 ROUND TRIP. (Continental-1967). Marc Daumel, Venantino Venantini; Ellen Tracy, Ellen Faison; Larry, Larry Rivers; Diana Evremont, Joan Thornton; Clarice, Clarice Rivers; Jacques, Jacques Kaplan; Sheila, Sheila Clarke.

2498 THE ROUND UP. (Altura-1969). Janos Gajdor, Janos Gorbe; Kabai, Tibor Molnar; Torma, Gabor Agardy; Kabai's Son, Andras Kozak; Veszelka, Zoltan Latinovits; 1st Interrogator, Istvan Avar; 2nd Interrogator, Lajos Oze; Bela Barsi, Janos Koltai, Attila Nagy, Jozsef Madarss, Rudolf Somogyvari, Zoltan Basilides.

2499 THE ROUNDERS. (MGM-1965). Ben Jones, Glenn Ford; Howdy Lewis, Henry Fonda; Mary, Sue Ane Langdon; Sister, Hope Holiday; Jim Ed Love, Chill Wills; Vince Moore, Edgar Buchanan; Agatha Moore, Kathleen Freeman; Meg Moore, Joan Freeman; Bull, Denver Pyle; Tanner, Barton

Maclane; Ariee, Doodles Weaver; Mrs. Norson, Allegra Varron.

2500 ROWDYMAN. (Crowley-1973). Will, Gordon Pinsent; Andrew, Frank Converse; Stan, Will Geer; Ruth, Linda Gorenson; Constable, Ted Henley; Mary, Estelle Wall; Bill, Stuart Gillard; Walt, Austin Davis; Woman on Train, Dawn Greenhaigh.

2501 THE ROYAL HUNT OF THE SUN. (National General-1969). Pizarro, Robert Shaw; Atahuallpa, Christopher Plummer; De Soto, Nigel Davenport; Estete, Michael Craig; Young Martin, Leonard Whiting; Valverde, Andrew Keir; King Carlos V, James Donald; Candia, William Marlowe; Diego, Percy Herbert; DeNizza, Alexander Davion; Felipillo, Sam Krauss.

2502 RUBY. (Bartlett-1971). Ruby, Ruth Hurd; Clifford, Phillip Webber; Singer, Danny Kosow; Girl, Susan Peters; Mother, Joanie Andrews; Father, George Bartlett.

2503 THE RULING CLASS. (AVCO Embassy-1972). Jack, 14th Earl of Gurney; Peter O'Toole; Bishop Lampton, Alastair Sim; Tucker, Arthur Lowe; 13th Earl of Gurney, Harry Andrews; Lady Claire Gurney, Coral Browne; Dr. Herder, Michael Bryant; McKyle, Nigel Green; Sir Charles Gurney, William Mervyn; Grace Shelly, Carolyn Seymour; Dinsdale Gurney, James Villiers; Hugh Burden, Graham Crowden, Kay Walsh, Patsy Byrne, Joan Cooper, James Grout, Margaret Lacey, James Hazeldine, Hugh Owens, Griffith Davies, Oliver, Henry Woolf, Neil Kennedy, Julian D'Albie, Llewellyn Rees, Ronald Adam, Kenneth Benda, Declan Mulholland, Cyril Appleton, Leslie Schofield.

2504 RUN, ANGEL, RUN. (Fanfare-1969). Angel, William Smith; Lauri, Valerie Starrett; Ron, Gene Shane; Pappy, Lee De Broux; Space, Eugene Cornelius; Chic, Paul Harper; Turk, Earl Finn; Duke, Bill Bonner; Dan Felton, Dan Kempt; Flo Felton, Ann Fry; Meg Felton, Margaret Markov; Felton Children, Brian Rapp, Jennifer Starrett, Jeb Adams; Roger, Lou Robb; Elmo, Homer Thurman; Harry, Augustin Roberts; Stan, Stanford Morgan; Maggy, Rachel Romen; Estelle, Joy Wilkerson; Doctor, Wally Berns.

2505 RUN, APPALOOSA, RUN. (Buena Vista-1966). Adele Palacios, Wilbur Plaugher, Jerry Gatlin, Walter Cloud, Ray Patnaude.

2506 RUN FOR YOUR WIFE. (Allied Artists-1967). Riccardo Vanzi, Ugo Tognazzi; Nicole, Marina Vlady; Nita, Rhonda Fleming; Jenny, Juliet Prowse; Louise, Graziella Granata; Carlo, Carlo Mazzone; Teenager, Ruth Laney; Mary, Sharon Obeck; Call Girl, Cherie Latimer.

2507 RUN LIKE A THIEF. (Feature Film Corporation of America-1968). Johnny Dent, Kieron Moore; Mona Shannon, Ina Balin; Willy Gore, Keenan Wynn; Colonel Romero, Fernando Rey; Piet De Jonge, Charles Regnier; Abel Baker, Victor Maddern; Sancho Gracia, Luis Rivera, Scott Miller, Bobby Hall, Vicente Roca, Mike Brendel.

2508 RUN, RUN, JOE. (Pacific Theatres-1974). Keith Carradine, Tom Skerritt, Sybil Danning, Cyril Cusack, Marcello Mando, Pepe Calvo, Enzo Monteduro, Emilio Messina, Tito Garcia.

2509 RUN WILD, RUN FREE. (Columbia-1969). Philip Ransome, Mark Lester; The Moorman, John Mills; Ellen Ransome, Sylvia Syms; James Ransome, Gordon Jackson; Reg, Bernard Miles; Diana, Fiona Fullerton.

2510 RUNAWAY GIRL. (Laurel Films and United Screen Arts-1966). Lili St. Cyr, Jock Mahoney, Ron Hagerthy, Laurie Mitchell, Booth Colman, Laurindo Almeida, Robert Shayne, June Jocelyn Lisa Pons, Shary Layne, Susan Carnell, Dusty Enders, Sandra Phelps, Anne Graves.

2511 RUSH TO JUDGMENT. (Impact-1967). Mark Lane.

2512 RUSS MEYER'S VIXEN. (Eve-1969). Vixen, Erica Gavin; Niles, Harrison Page; Jud, Jon Evans; O'Banion, Michael O'Donnell; Tom, Garth Pillsbury; Janet King, Vincene Wallace; Dave King, Robert Aiken; Mountie, Peter Carpenter; Girl, Jackie Illman; Gas Attendant, John Furlong.

2513 THE RUSSIANS ARE COMING! THE RUSSIANS ARE COMING! (United Artists-1966). Walt Whittaker, Carl Reiner; Elspeth Whittaker, Eva Marie Saint; Rosanov, Alan Arkin; Link Mattocks, Brian Keith; Norman Jonas, Jonathan Winters; The Captain, Theodore Bikel; Fendall Hawkins, Paul Ford; Alice Foss, Tessie O'Shea; Kolchin, John Phillip Law; Alison, Andrea Dromm; Luther Grilk, Ben Blue; Pete Whittaker, Sheldon Golomb; Annie Whittaker, Cindy Putnam; Lester Tilly, Guy Raymond; Charlie Hinkson, Cliff Norton; Oscar Maxwell, Dick Schaal; Mr. Porter, Philip Coolidge; Irving Christiansen, Don Keefer; Parker Fennelly, Doro Merande, Vaughn Taylor, Johnnie Whitaker, Danny Klega, Ray Baxter, Paul Verdier, Nikita Knatz, Constantine Baksheef, Alex Hassilev, Milos Milos, Gino Gottarelli.

2514 RYAN'S DAUGHTER. (MGM-1970). Charles Shaughnessy, Robert Mitchum; Father Collins, Trevor Howard; Rosy, Sarah Miles; Randolph Doryan, Christopher Jones; Michael, John Mills; Tom Ryan, Leo McKern; Tim O'Leary, Barry Foster; McCardle, Archie O'Sullivan; Mrs. McCardle, Marie Kean; Maureen, Evin Crowley; Corporal, Barry Jackson; Driver, Douglas Sheldon; Bernard, Ed O'Callaghan;

Paddy, Philip O'Flynn; Joseph, Niall O'Brien; Peter, Owen O'Sullivan; O'Keefe, Niall Toibin; Sean, Emmet Bergin; Storekeeper, May Cluskey; Old Woman, Annie Dalton.

2515 SABATA. (United Artists-1970). Sabata, Lee Van Cleef; Banjo, William Berger; Carrincha, Pedro Sanchez; Indio, Nick Jordan; Jane, Linda Veras; Stengal, Franco Ressel; Fergusson, Antonio Gradoli; Oswald, Robert Hundar; Judge O'Hara, Gianni Rizzo; Slim, Spanny Convery; Sharky, Marco Zuanelli; McCallum, Gino Marturano; Frankie, Joseph Mathews; Cutty, Franco Ukmar; Jumping Kid, Bruno Ukmar; Father Brown, Rodolfo Lodi; False Father Brown, Alan Collins; Logan, Vittorio Andre; Rocky Bendato, Romano Puppo; Daniel, Andrea Aureli; Captain, Franco Marletta; Sheriff, John Bartha; Nickols, Charles Tamblyn.

2516 SABOTEUR: CODE NAME--MORITURI. (20th Century-Fox-1965). Robert Crain, Marlon Brando; Captain Mueller, Yul Brynner; Esther, Janet Margolin; Colonel Statter, Trevor Howard; Kruse, Martin Benrath; Donkeyman, Hans Christian Blech; Dr. Ambach, Wally Cox; Branner, Max Haufler; Milkereit, Rainer Penkert; Baldwin, William Redfield.

2517 SACCO AND VANZETTI. (UMC-1971). Vanzetti, Gian Maria Volonte; Sacco, Riccardo Cucciolla; Moore, Milo O'Shea; Katzman, Cyril Cusack; Committeewoman, Rosanna Fratello; Judge, Geoffrey Keen; Thompson, William Prince; Newspaperman, Claude Mann.

2518 A SAFE PLACE. (Columbia-1971). Susan/Noah, Tuesday Weld; Magician, Orson Welles; Mitch, Jack Nicholson; Fred, Philip Proctor; Bari, Gwen Welles; Larry, Dov Lawrence; Maid, Fanny Birkenmaier; Girl in Rowboat, Rhonda Alfaro; Susan at 5, Sylvia Zapp; Friends, Jennifer Walker, Francesca Hilton, Julie Robinson, Jordon Hahn; Roger Garrett, Richard Finnochio, Barbara Flood.

2519 THE SAILOR FROM GIBRALTAR. (Lopert-1967). Anna, Jeanne Moreau; Alan, Ian Bannen; Sheila, Vanessa Redgrave; Noori, Zia Moyheddin; Legrand, Hugh Griffith; Louis of Mozambique, Orson Welles; Postcard Vendor, Umberto Orsini; Eolo, Erminio Spalla; Carla, Eleanor Brown; Girl at Dance, Gabriella Pallotta; Man on Train, Arnoldo Foa; Jeannot, Claudio De Renzi; Fausto Tozzi, John Hurt, Theodor Roubanis, Brad Moore, Massimo Sarchielli, Guglielmo Spoletini, Wolfgang Hillinger.

2520 THE ST. VALENTINE'S DAY MASSACRE. (20th Century-Fox-1967). Al Capone, Jason Robards; Peter Gusenberg, George Segal; Bugs Moran, Ralph Meeker; Myrtle, Jean Hale; Jack McGurn, Clint Ritchie; Sorello, Frank Silvera; Wienshank, Joseph Campanella; Scalisi, Richard Bakalyan; May, Bruce Dern; Patsy Lolorado, Michele Guayini; Harold

J. Stone, Kurt Krueger, Paul Richards, Joseph Turkel, Milton Frome, Mickey Deems, John Agar, Celia Lovsky, Tom Reese, Jan Merlin, Gus Trikonis, Alex D'Arcy, Reed Hadley, Charles Dierkop, Tom Signorelli, Rico Cattani, Alex Rocco, Leo Gordon, Mary Grace Canfield, Daniel Ades, Richard Krisher.

2521 LA SALAMANDRE. (New Yorker-1972). Rosemonde, Bulle Ogier; Pierre, Jean-Luc Bideau; Paul, Jacques Denis; Narrator, Anne-Marie Michel; Suzanne, Veronique Alain; Paul's Wife, Marblum Jequier.

2522 SALESMAN. (Maysles Film-1969). "The Badger," Paul Brennan; "The Gipper," Charles McDevitt; "The Rabbit," James Baker; "The Bull," Raymond Martos; Sales Manager, Kennie Turner; Theological Consultant, Melbourne I. Feltman; Motel Maid, Margaret McCarron.

2523 SALLAH. (Palisades International-1965). Topol, Geula Noni, Gila Almogor, Arik Einstein, Shraga Friedman, Zaharira Harifai, Nathan Meisler, Shaika Levi, Esther Greenberg, Mordecai Arnon.

2524 SALT AND PEPPER. (United Artists-1968). Charles Salt, Sammy Davis Jr.; Christopher Pepper, Peter Lawford; Inspector Carbbe, Michael Bates; Marianne Renaud, Ilona Rodgers; Colonel Woodstock, John Le Mesurier; Sergeant Walters, Graham Stark; Colonel Balsom, Ernest Clark; Mai Ling, Jeanne Roland; Club Secretary, Robert Dorning; Dove, Robertson Hare; Foreign Secretary, Geoffrey Lumsden; William Mervyn, Llewellyn Rees, Mark Singleton, Michael Trubshawe, Francisca Tu, Oliver MacGreevy, Peter Hutchins, Jeremy Lloyd, Sean Lynch, Ivor Dean, Brian Harrison, Harry Hutchinson, Max Faulkner, Beth Rogan, Rifat Shenel, Calvin Lockhart, Nicholas Smith, Susan Blair, Christine Pocket, Cassandra Mowan, Joe Wadham.

2525 SALT OF THE EARTH. (Independent Productions Corp.-1965). Rosaura Revueltas, Juan Chacon, Will Geer, Mervyn Williams, Herman Waldman, Frank Talevera, Mary Lou Castillo, Clinton Jencks, Virginia Jencks.

2526 SALTO. (Kanawha-1966). Kowalski-Malinowski, Zbigniew Cybulski; The Host, Gustaw Holoubek; Helena, Marta Lipinska; Decylia, Irena Laskowska; The Poet, Wojcjech Siemion; Blumenfeld, Wlodzimierez Borunski; The Captain, Zdzislaw Maklakiewicz; The Drunkard, Andrzej Lapicki.

2527 THE SALZBURG CONNECTION. (20th Century-Fox-1972). William Mathison, Barry Newman; Anna Bryant, Anna Karina; Johann Kronsteiner, Klaus-Maria Brandauer; Elissa Lang, Karen Jensen; Chuck, Joe Maross; Felix Zauner, Wolfgang Preiss; Grell, Helmut Schmid; Anton, Udo Kier;

Lev Benedescu, Michael Haussermann; Newhart, Whit Bissell; Large Man, Raoul Retzer; Trudi Seidl, Elisabeth Felchner; Rugged Man, Bert Fortell; Anton's Companion, Alf Beinell; Richard Bryant, Patrick Jordan; Tour Guide, Edward Linkers; American Tourist, Gene Moss; Stocky Men, Karl Otto Alberty and Rudolf Bary; Waitress, Christine Buchegger; The Wiener Spatzen Boys' Choir.

2528 SAM WHISKEY. (United Artists-1969). Sam Whiskey, Burt Reynolds; O. W. Bandy, Clint Walker; Jedidiah Hooker, Ossie Davis; Laura Breckinridge, Angie Dickinson; Fat Henry Hobson, Rick Davis; The Fisherman, Del Reeves; Mint Supt. Perkins, William Schallert; The Mint Inspector, Woodrow Parfrey; Anthony James, Bud Adler, Ayllene Gibbons, Amanda Harley, Tracey Roberts, Virgil Warner, William Boyett, Sidney Clute, Chubby Johnson, John Damler.

2529 SAMBIZANGA. (New Yorker-1973). Domingos, Domingos Oliviera; Maria, Elisa Andrade; Zito, Dino Abelino; Petelo, Jean M'Vondo; Chico, Benoit Moutsila; Miguel, Talagongo; Bebiana, Henriette Meya; Les Ombres.

2530 SAMURAI (Part 2). (Toho-1967). Toshiro Mifune, Koji Tsuruta, Sachio Sakai, Akihiko Hirata, Yu Fujiki, Daisuke Kato, Eijiro Tono, Kuninori Kodo, Kaoru Yachigusa, Misuko Mito.

2531 SAMURAI (Part 3). (Toho-1967). Toshiro Mifuni, Koji Tsuruta, Kaoru Yachigusa, Michiko Saga, Mariko Okada.

2532 SAMURAI ASSASSIN. (Tojo-Mifune-1965). Niino, Toshiro Mifune; Kurihara, Keiju Kobayashi; Okiku, Michiyo Aratama; Kukihime, Michiyo Aratama; Hoshino, Yunosuke Ito; Lord Li, Koshiro Matsumoto; Yoe, Nami Tamura; Mitsu, Kaoru Yachigusa.

2533 THE SAND PEBBLES. (20th Century-Fox-1966). Jake Holman, Steve McQueen; Frenchy, Richard Attenborough; Captain Collins, Richard Crenna; Shirley Eckert, Candice Bergen; Maily, Marayat Andriane; Po-Han, Mako; Mr. Jameson, Larry Gates; Ensign Bordelles, Charles Robinson; Stawski, Simon Oakland; Harris, Ford Rainey; Bronson, Joe Turkel; Crosley, Gavin MacLeod; Shanahan, Joseph Di Reda; Major Chin, Richard Loo; Franks, Barney Phillips; Restorff, Gus Trikonis; Perna, Shepherd Sanders; Farren, James Jeter; Jennings, Tom Middleton; Cho-Jen, Paul Chinpae; Chien, Tommy Lee; Mama Chunk, Beulah Quo; Victor Shu, James Hong; Haythron, Stephen Jahn; Wilsey, Jay Alan Hopkins, Steve Ferry, Ted Fish, Loren Janes, Glenn Wilder.

2534 THE SANDPIPER. (MGM-1965). Laura Reynolds, Elizabeth Taylor; Dr. Edward Hewitt, Richard Burton; Claire

Hewitt, Eva Marie Saint; Cos Erikson, Charles Bronson; Ward Hendricks, Robert Webber; Larry Brant, James Edwards; Judge Thumpson, Torin Thatcher; Walter Robinson, Tom Drake; Danny Reynolds, Morgan Mason.

2535 SANDRA. (Royal-1966). Sandra, Claudia Cardinale; Andrew, Michael Craig; Gianni, Jean Sorel; The Mother, Marie Bell; Gilardini, Renzo Ricci; Pietro Fornari, Fred Williams; Fosca, Amalia Troiani.

2536 SANDRA, THE MAKING OF A WOMAN. (Mini-1970). Monica Gayle, Daryll Largo, Raymond Zona, Jean Clark, James Ritter, Bobbie Seasons, Ronald Mowry, Desiree Trayle, Crack Laird, Keel Smythe, Bobbie Martin.

2537 SANDS OF BEERSHEBA. (Landau-Unger-1966). Susan, Diane Baker; Daoud, David Opatoshu; Dan, Tom Bell; Salim, Paul Stassino; Naima, Didi Ramati; Nuri, Theodore Marcuse; Ayub, Wolfe Barzell.

2538 SANDS OF THE KALAHARI. (Paramount-1965). O'Brien, Stuart Whitman; Bain, Stanley Baker; Grace, Susannah York; Grimmelman, Harry Andrews; Bondarahkai, Theodore Bikel; Sturdevant, Nigel Davenport.

2539 SANTEE. (Crown International-1973). Santee, Glenn Ford; Jody, Michael Burns; Valerie, Dana Wynter; John Crow, Jay Silverheels; Harry Townes, John Larch, Robert Wilke, Bob Donner, Taylor Lacher, Lindsay Crosby, Charles Courtney, X. Brand, John Hart, Ross McCubbin, Robert Mellard.

2540 THE SARAGOSSA MANUSCRIPT. (Amerpole Enterprise-1972). Alfons van Worden, Zbigniew Cybulski; Hermit, Kazimierz Opalinski; Moorish Princess, Inga Cembrzynska; Moorish Princess, Joanna Jedryka; Van Worden's Father, Slowomir Linder; Van Worden's Mother, Miroslawa Lombardo; Spanish Nobleman, Aleksander Fogiel; Pascheco, Franciszek Pieczka; Pascheco's Father, Ludwig Benoit; Camilla, Barbara Krafftowna.

2541 SASUKE AGAINST THE WIND. (Bijou-1973). Sasuke, Kohil Takahashi; Mitsuaki, Matsuhiro Toura; Okiwas, Misako Watanabe; Jinnai, Seiji Miyaguchi; Yashiro, Yasunori Irikawa; Genga, Minoru Hotaka; Sakon, Tetsuro Tanha; Omiyo, Jitsuko Yoshimura.

2542 THE SATAN BUG. (United Artists-1965). Lee Barrett, George Maharis; Dr. Hoffman, Richard Basehart; Ann, Anne Francis; The General, Dana Andrews; Veretti, Edward Asner; Donald, Frank Sutton; Michaelson, John Larkin; Cavanaugh, Richard Bull; Martin, Martin Blaine; Reagan, John Anderson; Mason, Russ Bender; Johnson, Hari Rhodes;

Raskin, John Clarke; Tesserly, Simon Oakland; Dr. Ostrer, Harold Bould; Dr. Yang, James Hong.

2543 SATAN'S SADISTS. (Independent-International-1970). Anchor, Russ Tamblyn; Charles, Scott Brady; Lew, Kent Taylor; Firewater, John Cardos; Willie, Robert Dix; Johnny, Gary Kent; Acid, Greydon Clark; Gina, Regina Carrol; Tracy, Jackie Taylor; Muscle, William Bonner; Romero, Bobby Clark; Nora, Evelyn Frank; Carol, Yvonne Stewart; Jan, Cheryl Anne; Rita, Randee Lynn; Lois, Bambi Allen; Ben, Breck Warwick.

2544 SATURDAY NIGHT IN APPLE VALLEY. (Emerson-1965). Phil Ford, Mimi Hines, Cliff Arquette, Shanton Granger, Joan Benedict, Marvin Miller, Anthony Dexter.

2545 SAUL AND DAVID. (Rizzoli-1968). King Saul, Norman Wooland; David, Giani Garko; Abigail, Luz Marquez; Akhinoam, Elisa Cegani; Mikol, Pilar Clemens; Abner, Virgilio Texera; Jonathan, Anthony J. Mayans; Samuel, Carlos Casaravilla; David (as a boy), Marco Paoloetti; Goliath, Stefy Lang; Joab, Paolo Gozlino; Abdon, Dante Maggio.

2546 SAVAGE! (New World-1973). James Inglehart, Carol Speed, Lada Edmund, Jr., Sally Jordan, Ken Metcalf, Rossana Ortiz, Vic Diaz, Eddie Gutierrez, Harley Paton, Marie Saunders, Aura Aurea.

2547 THE SAVAGE IS LOOSE. (Campbell Devon-1974). George C. Scott, Trish Van Devere, John David Carson, Lee H. Montgomery.

2548 SAVAGE MESSIAH. (MGM-1972). Sophie Brezeska, Dorothy Tutin; Henri Gaudier, Scott Antony; Gosh Boyle, Helen Mirren; Angus Corky, Lindsay Kemp; M. Gaudier, Michael Gough; Lionel Shaw, John Justin; Mayor, Aubrey Richards; Museum Attendant, Peter Vaughan; Thomas Buff, Ben Aris; Mme. Gaudier, Eleanor Fazan; Mr. Saltzman, Otto Diamant; Pippa, Susanna East; Tart, Maggy Maxwell; Mavis Coldstream, Imogen Claire; Kate, Judith Paris; Major Boyle, Robert Lang.

2549 SAVAGE PAMPAS. (Comet-1967). Captain Martin, Robert Taylor; Padron, Ron Randell; Sergeant Barril, Marc Lawrence; Carreras, Ty Hardin; Rucu, Rosenda Monteros; Camila, Felicia Roc; Lieut. del Rio, Angel Del Pozo; Santiago, Mario Lozano; Petizo, Enrique Avila; Carmen, Laura Granados; Alfonso, Milo Quesada; Pepe, Hector Quiroga; Isidro, Juan Carlos Galvan; El Gato, Charles Fawcett; Chicha, Julio Pena; General Chavez, Jose Pieto; Luis, Jose Jasp; Vigo, Jose Maria Cafarell; Chiquito, Lucia Prado; Priest, Barta Barry; Magnolia, Pastora Ruiz; Carlos, Sancho Grazia; Old Man, George Rigaud; Lucy, Isabel Pisano;

Mimi, Laya Raki.

2550 THE SAVAGE SEVEN. (American International-1968). Johnnie Little Hawk, Robert Walker; Joint, Larry Bishop; Kisum, Adam Roarke; Maria Little Hawk, Joanna Frank; Stud, John Garwood; Grey Wolf, Max Julien; Bull, Richard Anders; Eddie, Duane Eddy; Taggert, Chuck Bail; Fillmore, Mel Berger; Seely, Billy Rush; Running Buck, John Cardos; Nancy Susannah Darrow; Bruno, Beach Dickerson; Fat Jack, Eddy Dono; Stunt Man, Alan Gibbs; Tommy, Fabian Gregory; Lansford, Gary Kent; Dogface, Gary Littlejohn; Tina, Penny Marshall; Walt, Walt Robles.

2551 THE SAVAGE WILD. (American International-1970). Gordon, Gordon Eastman; Red, Carl Spore; Maria, Maria Eastman; Arlo, Arlo Curtis; Jim, Jim Timiaough; Bob, Robert Wellington Kirk; John, John Payne; Cha-Lay, Charles Abou; Brother, Alex Dennis; Charley, Charley Davis; Pilot, Wilber O'Brian.

2552 SAVAGES. (Angelika-1972). Julian, Lewis J. Stadlen; Carlotta, Anne Francine; Otto, Thayer David; Cecily, Susie Blakely; Andrew, Russ Thacker; Emily, Salome Jens; Lady Cora, Margaret Brewster; Sir Harry, Neil Fitzgerald; Zia, Eva Saleh; Iliona, Ultra Violet; Leslie, Kathleen Widdoes; James, Sam Waterston; Archie, Martin Kove; Forest Girl, Asha Puthili; Penelope, Paulita Sedgwick.

2553 SAVE THE CHILDREN. (Paramount-1973). Marvin Gaye, The Staple Singers, The Temptations, The Chilites, The Main Ingredient, The O'Jays, Isaac Hayes, Zulema, Cannonball Adderly Quintet, Albertina Walker, Push Mass Choir, Loretta Oliver, James Cleveland, Bill Withers, Curtis Mayfield, Sammy Davis Jr., Roberta Flack, Quincy Jones, Gladys Knight & The Pips, Jerry Butler, Brenda Lee Eager, Ramsey Lewis, Nancy Wilson, The Jackson Five, Jackie Verdell, Jesse Jackson.

2554 SAVE THE TIGER. (Paramount-1973). Harry Stoner, Jack Lemmon; Phil Greene, Jack Guilford; Myra, Laurie Heineman; Fred, Norman Burton; Janet Stoner, Patricia Smith; Charlie Robbins, Thayer David; Meyer, William Hansen; Rico, Harvey Jason; Ula, Liv Von Linden; Margo, Lara Parker; Jackie, Eloise Hardt; Dusty, Janina; Sid, Ned Glass; Cashier, Pearl Shear; Tiger Petitioner, Bliff Elliott; Taxi Driver, Ben Freedman; Receptionist, Madeline Lee.

2555 SAY HELLO TO YESTERDAY. (Cinerama-1971). Woman, Jean Simmons; Boy, Leonard Whiting; Woman's Mother, Evelyn Laye; Woman's Husband, John Lee.

2556 SAY IT WITH FLOWERS. (1974). Jacques, Fernando Rey; Francoise, Delphine Seyrig; Ursula, Rocio Durcal; Jean-

Claude, John Moulder-Brown; Gerard, Francis Blanche; Comolli, Julien Guiomar; Hilde, Maria Perschy; Klaus, Frederic Mitterand; Inspector, Jean Becker.

2557 SCALAWAG. (Paramount-1973). Peg, Kirk Douglas; Jamie, Mark Lester; Brimstone/Mudhook, Neville Brand; Don Aragon, George Eastman; Velvet, Don Stroud; Lucy-Ann, Lesley Anne Down; Fly Speck, Danny DeVito; Barfly the Parrot, Mel Blanc; Sandy, Phil Brown; Rooster, Davor Antolic; Beanbelly, Stole Arandjelovic; Blackfoot, Fabijan Sovagovic; Beau, Shaft Douglas.

2558 THE SCALPHUNTERS. (United Artists-1968). Joe Bass, Burt Lancaster; Kate, Shelley Winters; Jim Howie, Telly Savalas; Joseph Winfield Lee, Ossie Davis; Two Crows, Armando Silvestre; Yuma, Dan Vadis; Jed, Dabney Coleman; Frank, Paul Picerni; Ramon, Nick Cravat; Scalphunters, John Epper, Jack Williams, Chuck Roberson, Tony Epper, Agapito Roldan, Gregorio Acosta and Marco Antonio Arzate; Scalphunters' Women, Angela Rodriguez, Amelia Rivera, Alicia De Lago; Kiowas, Nestor Dominguez, Francisco Oliva, Benjamin Ramos, Raul Martinez, Enrique Tello, Jose Martinez, Rodolfo Toledo, Jose Salas, Cuco Velazquez, Alejandro Lopez, Raul Hernandez, Pedro Aguilar.

2559 SCANDALOUS JOHN. (Buena Vista-1971). John McCanless, Brian Keith; Paco Martinez, Alfonso Arau; Amanda, Michele Carey; Jimmy Whitaker, Rick Lenz; Hector Pippin, Harry Morgan; Whitaker Senior, Simon Oakland.

2560 SCARECROW. (Warner Bros.-1973). Max, Gene Hackman; Lion, Al Pacino; Coley, Dorothy Tristan; Frenchy, Ann Wedgeworth; Riley, Richard Lynch; Darlene, Eileen Brennan; Annie, Penny Allen; Mickey, Richard Hackman; Skipper, Al Cingolani; Woman in Camper, Rutanya Alda.

2561 SCARECROW IN A GARDEN OF CUCUMBERS. (New Line-1972). Eve Harrington/Rhett Butler, Holly Woodlawn; Mary Poppins, Tally Brown; Ninotchka, Suzanne Skillen; Margo Channing, Yafa Lerner; Walter Mitty, David Margulies; Blanche DuBois, Jennifer Laird; Baby and Jane Hudson, Katherine and Margaret Howell; Marjorie Morningstar, Jane Kutler; Joe Buck, Sonny Boy Hayes; Noel Airman, Michael Sklar; Ratzo Rizzo, Joe Malanga; Stanley Kowalski, Johnny Jumpup; Megg Winters, Joe Palmieri, Dori Brenner, Judy Martin.

2562 SCARLET CAMELLIA. (Shiro Kido-1973). Oshino, Shima Iwashita; Kihei, Yoshi Kato; Osono, Sachiko Hidari; General, Elli Okada; Aoki, Go Kato.

2563 SCARS OF DRACULA. (American Continental-1971). Dracula, Christopher Lee; Simon, Dennis Waterman; Sarah,

Jenny Hanley; Paul, Christopher Matthews; Klove, Patrick Troughton; Priest, Michael Gwynn; Julie, Wendy Hamilton; Tania, Anouska Hempel; Alice, Delia Lindsay; Burgomaster, Bob Todd; Wagonmaster, Toke Townley; Landlord, Michael Ripper; 1st Officer, David Lealand; 2nd Officer, Richard Durden; Farmer, Morris Bush; Landlord's Wife, Margot Boht; Fat Young Man, Clive Barrie.

2564 THE SCAVENGERS. (Aquarius-1971). Jonathon Bliss, Maria Lease, Michael Divoka, Roda Spain, John Riazzi, Wes Bishop, Bruce Kemp, Sanford Mitchell, Tom Siegel, Jody Berry, Paul Wilmouth, Ushi Digart, James E. McIarty, Claudia Siefried, Karen Swanson, Warren James, Paul Hunt, James K. Shea, Freddy Mizrahi, Ben Adams, Tom Bowden Jr., Fig Blackman, Ben Cadlett, Robert Jones, James Gorden.

2565 SCENES FROM A MARRIAGE. (Cinema 5-1974). Marianne, Liv Ullmann; Johan, Erland Josephson; Katarina, Bibi Andersson; Peter, Jan Malmsjo; Eva, Gunnel Lindblom.

2566 SCHLOCK. (Jack H. Harris-1973). Saul Kahan, Joseph Piantadosi, Eliza Garrett, Eric Allison, Enrica Blankey, Charles Villiers, John Chambers.

2567 SCHOOL FOR SEX. (Toho-1967). Taeko, Kyoko Kishida; Senkichi, Tsutomu Yamazaki; Yuki Nakagawa, S. Yamamura.

2568 SCORE. (Audubon-1973). Elvira, Claire Wilbur; Eddie, Calvin Culver; Betsy, Lynn Lowry; Jack, Gerald Grant; Mike, Carl Parker.

2569 SCORPIO. (United Artists-1973). Cross, Burt Lancaster; Laurier, Alain Delon; Zharkov, Paul Scofield; McLeod, John Colicos; Susan, Gayle Hunnicutt; Filchock, J. D. Cannon; Sarah, Joanne Linville; Pick, Melvin Stewart; Zemetkin, Vladek Sheybal; Anne, Mary Maude; Thief, Jack Colvin; Harris, James Sikking; Morrison, Burke Byrnes; Mitchell, William Smithers; Lang, Shmuel Rodensky; Heck, Howard Morton; Helen, Celeste Yarnall; Malkin, Sandor Eles; Novins, Frederick Jaeger; Dor, George Mikell; Man in Hotel, Robert Emhardt.

2570 SCORPIO 70. (Lake-1970). Layne, Jennifer Welles; Glenn, Stacey Michaels; Bill, Michael Hanes; Janet, Iris Brooks; Dorothy, Hollis Solomon; Pete, Blaine Quincy; Christina, Jessica Stuart; Captain, Larry Hunter; Lt., Whitey Wayne; Sailor, Jud Phillips; Crewman, Robin Elliot.

2571 SCREAM AND SCREAM AGAIN. (American International-1970). Dr. Browning, Vincent Price; Fremont, Christopher Lee; Benedek, Peter Cushing; Sylvia, Judy Huxtable; Bellaver, Alfred Marks; Keith, Michael Gothard; Ludwig, Anthony

Newlands; Schweitz, Peter Sallis; Strickland, David Lodge; Jane, Uta Levka; David, Christopher Matthews; Helen, Judi Bloom; Det. Joyce, Clifford Earl; Kingsmill, Kenneth Benda; Konratz, Marshall Jones.

2572 SCREAM BLACULA SCREAM. (American International-1973). Mamuwalde, William Marshall; Lisa, Pam Grier; Justin, Don Mitchell; Sheriff, Michael Conrad; Willis, Richard Lawson; Denny, Lynne Moody; Maggie, Beverly Gill; Ragman, Bernie Hamilton; Elaine, Barbara Rhoades; Gloria, Jenee Michelle; Doll Man, Don Blackman; Prof. Walston, Van Kirksey; Louis Arnold Williams.

2573 A SCREAM IN THE STREETS. (Box-Office International-1972). Ed Haskell, John Kirkpatric; Bob Streeter, Frank Bannon; Policewoman, Rosie Stone; Rapist, Brandy Lyman; Linda York, Con Covert, Tony Scaponi, Pat O'Connor, Terry Woolman, Irving Parham, Mike Doty, Erick Norden, Phil Kaufman, Brink Brydon, Linda Vale, Morgan Tyler, Lauralie Hart, Flora Wiesel, Bobby Angelle, Michael Lee, Eddy Doty, Susan Norden, Dan Foley, Wes Young.

2574 SCREAM OF THE DEMON LOVER. (New World-1971). Baron, Jeffrey Chase; Ivana, Jennifer Hartley; Inspector, Ronald Grey; Agostina Belli, Mariano Videl Molina, Christiana Galloni, Antonio Gimenez Escribano, Enzo Fisichella.

2575 SCROOGE. (National General-1970). Scrooge, Albert Finney; Marley's Ghost, Alec Guinness; Ghost of Christmas Past, Edith Evans; Ghost of Christmas Present, Kenneth More; Nephew, Michael Medwin; Fezziwig, Laurence Naismith; Bob Cratchit, David Collings; Tom Jenkins, Anton Rodgers; Isabel, Suzanne Neve; Mrs. Cratchit, Frances Cuka; Portly Gentlemen, Derek Francis and Roy Kinnear; Nephew's Wife, Mary Peach; Ghost of Christmas Yet to Come, Paddy Stone; Mrs. Fezziwig, Kay Walsh; Nephew's Friend, Gordon Jackson; Tiny Tim, Richard Beaumont; Toy Shop Owner, Geoffrey Bayldon; Women Debtors, Molly Weir, Helena Gloag; Punch and Judy Man, Reg Lever; Well Wisher, Keith March; Party Guest, Marianne Stone.

2576 THE SEA GULL. (Warner Bros. -7 Arts-1968). Trigorin, James Mason; Nina, Vanessa Redgrave; Arkadina, Simone Signoret; Konstantin, David Warner; Sorin, Harry Andrews; Dorn, Denholm Elliott; Polina, Eileen Herlie; Medvedenko, Alfred Lynch; Shamraev, Ronald Radd; Masha, Kathleen Widdoes; Yakov, Frej Lindqvist; Housemaid, Karen Miller.

2577 THE SEA PIRATE. (Paramount-1967). Robert Surcouf, Gerard Barray; Margaret Carruthers, Antonella Lualdi; Lord Blackwood, Terence Morgan; Marie Catherine, Genevieve Casile; Nicholas, Frank Oliveras; Captain Fell, Armand Mestral; Kernon, Gerard Tichy; Gameray, Alberto

Cevinini; Napoleon, Gianni Esposito; The Jailer, Fernando Sancho.

2578 SEASIDE SWINGERS. (Embassy-1965). John Leyton, Mike Sarne, Freddie and The Dreamers, Ron Moody, Liz Fraser, Grązina Frame, Susan Baker, Jennifer Baker, The Mojos, Nicholas Parsons, Richard O'Sullivan, Michael Ripper, Hazel Hughes, Tony Daines, Peter Gilmore, Charles Lloyd Pack, Patrick Newell, Gaby Vargas, Coral Morphew, Nicola Riley, Marion Grimaldi, The Leroys.

2579 SEBASTIAN. (Paramount-1968). Sebastian, Dirk Bogarde; Becky Howard, Susannah York; Elsa Shahn, Lilli Palmer; Head of Intelligence, John Gielgud; Carol Fancy, Janet Munro; Miss Elliott, Margaret Johnston; General Phillips, Nigel Davenport; Toby, Ronald Fraser; Security Head Jameson, John Ronane; Tilly, Susan Whitman; Pamela, Ann Beach; Naomi, Ann Sidney; Ginny, Veronica Clifford; Randy, Jeanne Roland; Joan, Lyn Pinkney; Thelma, Louise Pernell; American, Donald Sutherland; TV Disc Jockey, Alan Freeman; Chess Player, Charles Lloyd Pack; The UG Girl, Portland Mason.

2580 THE SECOND BEST SECRET AGENT IN THE WHOLE WIDE WORLD. (Embassy-1966). Charles Vine, Tom Adams; Henrik Jacobsen, Karel Stephanek; Julia Lindberg, Veronica Hurst; Masterman, Peter Bull; Rockwell, John Arnatt; Walter Pickering, Francis De Wolff; Tetchnikov, Felix Felton; Russian Commissar, George Pastell; Computer Center Girl, Judy Hustable; Army Officer, Harry Hope; Maltby, Denis Holmes; Wilson, Billy Milton; Carole Blake, Tony Wall, Oliver MacGreevy, Stuart Saunders, Paul Tann, Shelagh Booth, John Evitts, Robert Marsden, Mona Chong, Michael Godfrey, Julian Strange, Claire Gordon, J. B. Dubin-Behrmann, Sarah Maddern.

2581 THE SECOND COMING OF SUZANNE. (Barry Film-1974). Suzanne, Sondra Locke; Artist, Paul Sand; Filmmaker, Jared Martin; Clavius, Richard Dreyfuss; TV Commentator, Gene Barry.

2582 SECONDS. (Paramount-1966). Antiochus Wilson, Rock Hudson; Nora Marcus, Salome Jens; Arthur Hamilton, John Randolph; The Old Man, Will Geer; Mr. Ruby, Jeff Corey; Dr. Innes, Richard Anderson; Charlie Evans, Murray Hamilton; Dr. Morris, Karl Swenson; Davalo, Khigh Dhiegh; Emily Hamilton, Frances Reid; John, Wesley Addy; Texan, John Lawrence; Elisabeth Fraser, Dody Heath, Robert Brubaker, Dorothy Morris, Barbara Werle, Frank Campanella, Edgar Stehli, Aaron Magidow, De De Young, Francoise Ruggieri, Thom Conroy, Ned Young, Kirk Duncan, William Richard Wintersole, Tina Scala.

2583 LE SECRET. (Valoria-1974). David, Jean-Louis Trintignant; Julia, Marlene Jobert; Thomas, Philippe Noiret; Claude, Jean-Francois Adam; Greta, Solange Pradel.

2584 SECRET AGENT FIREBALL. (American International-1966). Robert Fleming, Richard Harrison; Liz, Dominique Boschero; Elena, Wanda Guida; Taxi-Driver, Alcide Borik; Russian Agent, Jim Clay; Russian Agent, Alan Collins; Audrey Fisher, Clement Harari, Carrol Brown, Franklin Fred, Jean Ozenne, F. Unger.

2585 SECRET AGENT SUPER DRAGON. (United Screen Arts-1966). Bryan Cooper (Super Dragon), Ray Danton; Charity Farrell, Marisa Mell; Cynthia Fulton, Margaret Lee; Baby Face, Jess Hahn; Fernand Lamas, Carlo D'Angelo; Verna, Adriana Ambesi; Professor Kurge, Marco Guglielmi; Elizabeth, Solvi Stubing; Coleman, Gerhard Haerter; Dumont, Jacques Herlin.

2586 SECRET CEREMONY. (Universal-1968). Leonora, Elizabeth Taylor; Cenci, Mia Farrow; Albert, Robert Mitchum; Hannah, Peggy Ashcroft; Hilda, Pamela Brown.

2587 THE SECRET LIFE OF AN AMERICAN WIFE. (20th Century-Fox-1968). The Movie Star (Charlie), Walter Matthau; Victoria Layton, Anne Jackson; Tom Layton, Patrick O'Neal; Suzie Steinberg, Edy Williams; Howard, Richard Bull; Herb Steinberg, Paul Napier; Jimmy, Gary Brown; Jean-Claude, Albert Carrier; Peter Layton, Todd Baron; Susan Layton, Christy Hall.

2588 THE SECRET OF BLOOD ISLAND. (Universal-1965). Barbara Shelley, Jack Hedley, Charles Tingwell, Bill Owen, Peter Welch, Lee Montague, Edwin Richfield, Michael Ripper, Patrick Wymark, Philip Latham, Glyn Houston, Ian Whittaker, John Southworth, David Saire, Peter Craze, Henry Davies.

2589 THE SECRET OF MAGIC ISLAND. (Embassy-1965).

2590 THE SECRET OF MY SUCCESS. (MGM-1965). Violet Lawson, Stella Stevens; Baroness von Lukenburg, Honor Blackman; Marigold Murado, Shirley Jones; Arthur Tate, James Booth; Inspector Hobart/Baron von Lukenburg,/President Esteda/Earl of Aldershot, Lionel Jeffries; Mrs. Tate, Amy Dolby; Mrs. Pringle, Joan Hickman.

2591 THE SECRET OF SANTA VITTORIA. (United Artists-1969). Italo Bombolini, Anthony Quinn; Rosa Bombolini, Anna Magnani; Caterina Malatesta, Virna Lisi; Sepp Von Prum, Hardy Kruger; Tufa, Sergio Franchi; Babbaluche, Renato Rascel; Fabio, Giancarlo Giannini; Angela, Patricia Valturri; Gabriella, Valentina Cortese; Luigi Lunghetti, Eduardo Ciannelli;

Vittorini, Leopoldo Trieste.

2592 SECRET SCROLLS. (Toho-1968). Tasaburo, Toshiro Mifune; Senshiro, Koji Tsuruta; Yujime, Yoshiko Kuga; Oki, Kyoko Kagawa; Rika, Mariko Okada; Lord Yagyu, Denjiro Okochi; Jubei, Jotaro Togami; Tomonori, Akihiko Hirata; Matajuro, Senjaku Namamura; Iyemitsu, Hanshiro Iwai; Fugetsusai, Eijiro Tono; The Princess, Nobuke Otawa.

2593 THE SECRET SEVEN. (MGM-1966). Leslio, Tony Russel; Lydia, Helga Line; Axel, Massimo Serato; Rabirio, Gerard Tichy; Kadem, Renato Baldini; Rubio, Livio Lorenzon; Baxo, Barta Barry; Luzar, Joseph Marco; Gular, Kriss Huerta; Nakasser, Gianni Solaro; Aristocratic, Francesco Sormano; Mother, Emma Baron; Ario, Pedro Mari; Panuzio, Tomas Blanco; Aristocratic, Renato Montalbano.

2594 THE SECRET WAR OF HARRY FRIGG. (Universal-1968). Harry Frigg, Paul Newman; Countess Di Montefiore, Sylva Koscina; General Armstrong, Andrew Duggan; General Pennypacker, Tom Bosley; General Mayhew, John Williams; General Cox-Roberts, Charles D. Gray; Lt. Col. Ferrucci, Vito Scotti; General Rochambeau, Jacques Roux; Major von Steignitz, Werner Peters; General Prentiss, James Gregory; Lt. Rossano, Fabrizio Mioni; Sgt. Pozzallo, Johnny Haymer; Captain Stanley, Norman Fell; Stockade Commandant, Buck Henry; Lt. Gruber, Horst Ebersberg; M. P. Sergeant, Richard X. Slattery; Major, George Ives.

2595 SECRET WORLD. (20th Century-Fox-1969). Wendy, Jacqueline Bisset; Florence, Giselle Pascal; Philippe, Pierre Zimmer; Olivier, Marc Porel; Francois, Jean-Francois Maurin; Gustave, Paul Bonifas; Malevar, Guy D'Avout; Norbert, Jacques Riberolles; Eliane, Judith Magre; Monique, Chantal Goya; Alain, Yves Lefebvre.

2596 THE SEDUCERS. (Cinemation-1970). Mudy, Maud DeBelleroche; Aldo, Maurizio Bonuglia; Ulla, Edwige Fenech; Tony, Ruggero Miti; Paula, Rosalba Neri; Fisherman, Salvatore Puntillo; Peasant, Ewa Thulin.

2597 THE SEDUCTION OF INGA. (Cinemation-1972). Inga Dahlman, Marie Liljedahl; Stig Tillstrom, Lennart Lindberg; Rolf Andersson, Tommy Blom; Greta Tillstrom, Inger Sundh; Lothar Olafson, Lennart Norbach; Lissi Alandh, Harriet Ayres.

2598 SEE NO EVIL. (Columbia-1971). Sarah, Mia Farrow; Betty Rexton, Dorothy Alison; George Rexton, Robin Bailey; Sandy Rexton, Diane Grayson.

2599 THE SEED OF MAN. (SRL-1970). Marco Margine, Anna Wiazemski, Annie Girardot, Rada Rassimov, Maria Teresa

Piaggio, Milva Frosini, Angela Pagano.

2600 SEIZURE. (American International-1974). Edmund Blackstone, Jonathan Frid; Queen of Evil, Martine Beswick; Charlie, Joe Sirola; Nicole Blackstone, Christina Pickles; The Spider, Herve Villechaize; Eunice, Anne Meacham; Serge, Roger De Koven; Mark, Troy Donahue; Mikki, Mary Woronov; Jackal, Henry Baker.

2601 SENSO. (Fleetwood-1968). Contessa Livia Serpieri, Alida Valli; Lieut. Franz Mahler, Farley Granger; Marquis Roberto Ussoni, Massimo Girotti; Count Serpieri, Heinz Moog; Laura, Rina Morelli; Prostitute, Marcella Mariani; Bohemian Officer, Christian Marquand; Colonel Kleist, Tonio Selwart; Patriot, Sergio Fantoni; Commander at Venetian Square, Cristoforo De Hartungen; Meucci, Tino Bianchi; Wife of Austrian General, Marianna Leibl; Ernst Nadherny, Goliarda Sapienza.

2602 A SEPARATE PEACE. (Paramount-1972). Finny, John Heyl; Gene, Parker Stevenson; Leper, Peter Brush; Brinker, Victor Bevine; Chet, Scott Bradbury; Bobby, John E. A. MacKenzie.

2603 SEPARATION. (Continental-1968). Jane, Jane Arden; The Husband, David De Keyser; The Woman, Ann Lynn; The Lover, Iain Quarrier; The Old Man, Terence De Marney; Peter Thomas, Donald Sayer, Kathleen Saintsbury, Theo Aygar, Malou Pantera, Ann Norman, Neil Holms, Joy Bang, Leslie Linder, Fay Brook.

2604 SERAFINO. (Royal-1970). Serafino, Adriano Celentano; Lidia, Ottavia Piccolo; Uncle, Saro Urzi; Asmara, Francesca Romana Coluzzi; Armido, Benjamin Lev; Silio, Nazareno Natale; Rocco, Giosue Ippolito; Armida, Ermelinda De Felice; Gesuina, Nerina Montagnani; Lucia, Luciana Turina; Lawyer, Oreste Palella.

2605 THE SERGEANT. (Warner Bros.-7 Arts-1968). M/Sgt. Albert Callan, Rod Steiger; Pvt. Tom Swanson, John Phillip Law; Solange, Ludmila Mikael; Captain Loring, Frank Latimore; Pop Henneken, Elliott Sullivan; Corporal Cowley, Ronald Rubin; Aldous Brown, Philip Roye; Sgt. Komski, Jerry Brouer; Solange's Brother-in-law, Gabriel Gascond; Nightclub Singer, Memphis Slim.

2606 SERGEANT DEADHEAD. (American International-1965). Sergeant Deadhead/Sergeant Donovan, Frankie Avalon; Col. Lucy Turner, Deborah Walley; Admiral Stoneham, Cesar Romero; Gen. Rufus Fogg, Fred Clark; Captain Weiskopf, Gale Gordon; Lieut. Comdr. Talbott, Reginald Gardiner; Lt. Kinsey, Eve Arden.

2607 SERGEANT RYKER. (Universal-1968). Sgt. Paul Ryker, Lee Marvin; Capt. David Young, Bradford Dillman; Ann Ryker, Vera Miles; Maj. Whitaker, Peter Graves; Gen. Amos Bailey, Lloyd Nolan; Capt. Appleton, Murray Hamilton; Sgt. Max Winkler, Norman Fell; Col. Arthur Merriam, Walter Brooke; Pres. of Court Martial, Francis De Sales; Corp. Jenks, Don Marshall; Maj. Kitchener, Charles Aidman.

2608 THE SERPENT. (AVCO Embassy-1973). Vlassov, Yul Brynner; Allan Davies, Henry Fonda; Philip Boyle, Dirk Bogarde; Berthon, Philippe Noiret; Tavel, Michael Bouquet; Lpeke, Martin Held; Computer Programming Chief, Farley Granger; Annabel Lee, Virna Lisi; Deval, Guy Trejan; Suzanne, Marie Dubois; Interrogator, Robert Alda.

2609 SERPICO. (Paramount-1973). Frank Serpico, Al Pacino; Chief Green, John Randolph; Tom Keough, Jack Kehoe; Captain McClain, Biff McGuire; Laurie, Barbara eda-Young; Leslie, Cornelia Sharpe; Bob Blair, Tony Roberts; D.A., Allan Rich; Rubello, Norman Ornellas; Lombardo, Ed Grover; Captain Tolkin, Gene Gross; Steiger, James Tolkin; Berman, Lewis J. Stadlen; Gilbert, John Lehne; Gallagher, M. Emmet Walsh; Daley, George Ede; Commissioner Delaney, Charles White; Pasquale, John Medici; Peluce, Al Henderson; Malone, Hank Garrett; Joey, Damien Leake; Potts, Joe Bova; Watterman, John Stewart; Barto, Ed Crowley; Larry, Woodie King; Smith, Nathan George; Palmer, Bernard Barrow; Mr. Serpico, Sal Carollo; Mrs. Serpico, Mildred Clinton; Corsaro, Richard Foronjy; Brown, Alan North.

2610 A SESSION WITH THE COMMITTEE. (Commonwealth United-1969). The Committee: Peter Bonerz, Gary Goodrow, Jessica Myerson, Melvin Stewart, Barbara Bosson, Carl Gottlieb, Christopher Ross, Don Sturdy.

2611 SEVEN DWARFS TO THE RESCUE. (Childhood-1965). Rossana Podesta, Roberto Risso, Georges Marchal, Ave Ninchi, Salvatore Furmari, Francesco Gatto, Ulisse Lorenzelli, Mario Mastriantonio, Giovanni Solinas, Arturo Tosi, Domenico Tosi.

2612 SEVEN GOLDEN MEN. (Warner Bros.-7 Arts-1969). Giorgia, Rossana Podesta; Albert, Philippe Leroy; Adolf, Gastone Moschin; Aldo, Gabriele Tinti; Bank Manager, Jose Suarez; August, Giampiero Albertini; Anthony, Dario De Grassi; Alfonso, Manuel Zarzo; Alfred, Maurice Poli; Police Chief, Ennio Balbo; Radio Ham, Alberto Bonucci; Renzo Palmer, Renato Terra, Juan Cortez, Gianni Di Benedetto, Juan Luis Gagliardo.

2613 SEVEN GUNS FOR THE MACGREGORS. (Columbia-1968).

Gregor MacGregor, Robert Wood; David MacGregor, Manny Zarzo; Peter MacGregor, Nick Anderson; Kenneth MacGregor, Paul Carter; Mark MacGregor, Julio Perez Tabernero; Johnny MacGregor, Saturno Cerra; Dick MacGregor, Albert Waterman; Rosita Carson, Agata Flori; Santillana, Leo Anchoriz; Miguel, Fernando Sancho; Peria, Perla Cristal; Alastair MacGregor/Harold MacGregor, Harold Cotton; Mamie MacGregor, Anne-Marie Noe; Annie MacGregor, Margaret Horowitz; Justice Garland, Raphael Bardem; Sheriff, Antonio Molino Rojo; Crawford, Cris Huerta.

2614 THE SEVEN MINUTES. (20th Century-Fox-1971). Mike, Wayne Maunder; Maggie, Marianne McAndrew; Elmo, Philip Carey; Luther, Jay C. Flippen; Faye, Edy Williams; Constance, Yvonne De Carlo.

2615 THE SEVEN UPS. (20th Century-Fox-1973). Buddy Manucci, Roy Scheider; Vito, Tony Lo Bianco; Max Kalish, Larry Haines; Barilli, Victor Arnold; Mingo, Jerry Leon; Ansel, Ken Kercheval; Moon, Richard Lynch; Bo, Bill Hickman; Bruno, Ed Jordan; Bobby, David Wilson; Lt. Hanes, Robert Burr; Gilson, Rex Everhart; Festa, Matt Russo; Coltello, Lou Polan; Toredano, Joe Spinell; Henry Parten, William Shust; Mickey Parten, Roger Serbagi; Sara Kalish, Frances Chaney; Chef, Louis Yaccarino; Besta's Son, Benedetto Marino; Fitz, Tom Signorelli; Fat Man, Thomas Rand; Nurse, Adeline Leonard; Barber, Frank Mascetta; Mrs. Pugliese, Mary Multari.

2616 SEVEN WOMEN. (MGM-1966). Dr. D. R. Cartwright, Anne Bancroft; Emma Clark, Sue Lyon; Agatha Andrews, Margaret Leighton; Miss Binns, Flora Robson; Jane Argent, Mildred Dunnock; Florrie Pether, Betty Field; Mrs. Russell, Anna Lee; Charles Pether, Eddie Albert; Tunga Khan, Mike Mazurki; Lean Warrior, Woody Strode; Miss Ling, Jane Chang; Kim, Hans William Lee; Coolie, H. W. Gim; Chinese Girl, Irene Tsu.

2617 1776. (Columbia-1972). John Adams, William Daniels; John Hancock, David Ford; Benjamin Franklin, Howard Da Silva; John Dickinson, Donald Madden; James Wilson, Emory Bass; Thomas Jefferson, Ken Howard; Richard Henry Lee, Ronald Holgate; Roger Sherman, Rex Robbins; Oliver Wolcott, Peter Forster; Samuel Huntington, Fred Downs; Lewis Morris, Howard Caine; Robert Livingston, John Myhers; Francis Lewis, Richard McMurray; Edward Rutledge, John Cullum; William H. Bassett, Jonathan Moore, William Engle, Barry O'Hara, William Hansen, Ray Middleton, Leo Leyden, Patrick Hines, Heber Jentzsch, Andy Albin, Charles Rule, Jack De Mave, Jordan Rhodes, Roy Poole, James Noble, Richard O'Shea, Fred Slyter, Daniel Keyes, John Holland, Ralston Hill, Stephen Nathan, William Duell, Mark Montgomery, Blythe Danner, Virginia Vestoff.

2618 THE SEVENTH CONTINENT. (U-M-1968). Yellow Girl, Iris Vrus; White Boy, Tomislav Pasaric; Black Boy, Abdulaie Seck; White Boy's Mother, Hermina Pipinic; White Boy's Father, Demeter Bitenc; Yello Girl's Father, Oudy Rachmat Endang; General, Mikulas Huba; General's Wife, Karla Chadimova; Expert at Conference, Victor Starcic; Diplomat, Vanja Drach.

2619 A SEVERED HEAD. (Columbia-1971). Antonia Lynch-Gibbon, Lee Remick; Palmer Anderson, Richard Attenborough; Martin Lynch-Gibbon, Ian Holm; Honor Klein, Claire Bloom; Georgie Hands, Jennie Linden.

2620 SEX AND THE SINGLE GAY. (Bizarre-1970). Ross Judd Jr., Larry Lynn, Chico Rodriguez, William King, Jimmie Michaels, Gerald Strickland, Chris Markham, Judy Coleman, Ron Dilly, Paul Bach, John Marino.

2621 SEX FREAKS. (Rainbow Distributors-1974). John Holmes, Rich Cassidy, Joan Morrissey, Robert Chatham, Tine Hakansson, Leona Raphael, Noelle Cooper, Dirk Lenz, Viola James.

2622 LE SEX SHOP. (Peppercorn-Wormser-1973). Claude, Claude Berri; Isabelle, Juliet Berto; Lucien, Jean-Pierre Marielle; Jacqueline, Nathalie Delon; Karin, Beatrice Romand.

2623 THE SEX THIEF. (International Amusement-1974). Emily Barrow, Jenny Westbrook; Grant Henry, David Warbeck; Constable, Henry Rayner; Herbert Barrow, Gerald Taylor; Sergeant Plinth, Michael Armstrong; Inspector Smith, Terence Edmond; Judy Marvin, Diane Keen; Guy Hammond, Christopher Neil; Jacobi, Harvey Hall; Angie, Gloria Walker; Porky Prescott, Christopher Biggins; Wesleydale, Christopher Mitchell; Crabshaw, Eric Deacon; Florinda Prescott, Susan Glanville; Jezebel, Linda Coombes; Guido, David Landor; First Reporter, David Landor; Second Reporter, James Aubrey; Salesgirl, Brenda Rae; Barman, Anthony May; Doorman, Derek Martin; Stripper, Val Penny; Jeweller, Dave Carter; Auctioneer, Neville Barber; Chauffeur, Michael Hannah.

2624 SHADOW HUNTERS. (Toho-1973). Yujiro Ishihara, Ryohei Uchida, Mikio Narita, Ruriko Asaoka.

2625 SHADOW OF EVIL. (7 Arts-1966). O.S.S. 117, Kerwin Mathews; Dr. Sinn, Robert Hossein; Lila, Pier Angeli; Eva, Dominique Wilms; Sonsak, Akom Mokranond; Prasit, Sing Milintrasai; Leasock, Henri Virlogeux; Gamil Ratib, Jacques Mauclair.

2626 SHADOWS OF FORGOTTEN ANCESTORS. (Artkino-1967).

Ivan Nikolaichuk, Larisa Kadochnikova, Titiana Bestayeva, Spartak Bagashvili.

2627 SHAFT. (MGM-1971). John Shaft, Richard Roundtree; Bumpy, Moses Gunn; Vic Androzzi, Charles Cioffi; Ben Buford, Christopher St. John; Ellie Moore, Gwen Mitchell; Tom Hannon, Lawrence Pressman.

2628 SHAFT IN AFRICA. (MGM-1973). John Shaft, Richard Roundtree; Amafi, Frank Finlay; Aleme, Vonetta McGee; Jazar, Neda Arneric; Wassa, Debebe Eshetu; Sassari, Spiros Focas; Perreau, Jacques Herlin; Ziba, Jho Jhenkins; Oyo, Willie Jonah; Piro, Adolfo Lastretti; Colonel Gondar, Marne Maitland; Osiat, Frank McRae; Prostitute, Zenebech Tadesse; Ramila's Son, A. V. Falana; Williams, James E. Myers; Zubair, Nadim Sawalha; Kopo, Thomas Baptiste; Shimba, Jon Chevron; Vanden, Glynn Edwards; Emir Ramila, Cy Grant; Cusset, Jacques Marin; Sadi, Nick Zaran; Angelo, Aldo Sambrell.

2629 SHAFT'S BIG SCORE! (MGM-1972). John Shaft, Richard Roundtree; Bumpy Jonas, Moses Gunn; Willy, Drew Bundini Brown; Gus Mascola, Joseph Mascolo; Rita, Kathy Imrie; Johnny Kelly, Wally Taylor; Captain Bollin, Julius W. Harris; Arna, Rosalind Miles; Pascal, Joe Santos; Al, Angelo Nazzo; Johnson, Don Blakely; Junior Gillis, Melvin Green Jr.; Preacher, Thomas Anderson; Old Lady, Evelyn Davis; Kelly's Hood No. 1, Richard Pittman; Cal Asby, Robert Kya-Hill; Mascola's Hood, Thomas Brann; Harrison, Bob Jefferson; Cooper, Dan P. Hannafin; Caretaker, Jimmy Hayeson; Detective Salmi, Henry Ferrentino; Rip, Frank Scioscia; Cabaret Dancer, Kitty Jones; Foglio, Gregory Reese; Mascola's Girl, Marilyn Hamlin; John Foster, Joyce Walker, Gordon Parks.

2630 SHAKESPEARE WALLAH. (Walter Reade-Sterling-1966). Sanju, Shashi Kapoor; Lizzie Buckingham, Felicity Kendal; Manjula, Madhur Jaffrey; Mr. Buckingham, Geoffrey Kendal; Mrs. Buckingham, Laura Liddell; The Maharaja, Utpal Dutt; Didi, Parveen Paul; Bobby, Jim Tyler; Sharmaji, Prayag Raaj; Guptaji, Pincho Kapoor; Aslam, Partap Sharma; The Headmaster's Brother, Hamid Sayani; The Director, Sudershan; Mrs. Bowen, Jennifer Kapoor.

2631 THE SHAKIEST GUN IN THE WEST. (Universal-1968). Jesse W. Heywood, Don Knotts; Penelope Cushings, Barbara Rhoades; Matthew Basch, Jackie Coogan; Reverend Zachary Grant, Donald Barry; Olive, Ruth McDevitt; Mr. Remington, Frank McGrath; Welsh, Terry Wilson; Swanson, Carl Ballantine; Wong, Pat Morita; Arnold the Kid, Robert Yuro; Dr. Friedlander, Herbert Voland; Violet, Fay De Witt; Pop McGovern, Dub Taylor; Celia, Hope Summers; Indian Chief, Dick Wilson; Sheriff, Ed Peck; Huggins, Ed Faulkner;

Sheriff Tolliver, Arthur Space; Phelps, Gregory Mullavey; Benny Rubin, Dorothy Neuman, E. J. Andre.

2632 SHALAKO. (Cinerama-1968). Shalako, Sean Connery; Countess Irina Lazaar, Brigitte Bardot; Bosky Fulton, Stephen Boyd; Sir Charles Daggett, Jack Hawkins; Frederick Von Hallstatt, Peter Van Eyck; Lady Daggett, Honor Blackman; Chato, Woody Strode; Mako, Eric Sykes; Henry Clarke, Alexander Knox; Elena, Valerie French; Rojas, Julian Mateos; Buffalo, Donald Barry; Chato's Father, Rodd Redwing; Loco, "Chief" Tug Smith; Hans, Hans De Vries; Pete Wells, Walter Brown; Marker, Charles Stalnaker; Luther, Bob Cunningham; Hockett, John Clark; Johnson, Bob Hall.

2633 SHAME. (Lopert-1968). Eve Rosenberg, Liv Ullmann; Jan Rosenberg, Max Von Sydow; Colonel Jacobi, Gunnar Bjornstrand; Filip, Sigge Furst; Mrs. Jacobi, Birgitta Valberg; Lobelius, Hans Alfredson; Oswald, Ingvar Kjellson; Jacobi's Son, Raymond Lundberg.

2634 SHAME, SHAME, EVERYBODY KNOWS HER NAME. (J.E.R.-1970). Susan, Karen Carlson; Diane, Getti Miller; Vic, Augustus Sultatos; Tony, Tony Seville; Go-Go Dancer, Rita Bennett; Roy, Dennis Johnson; Motley, Tyrus Chesney; George, John Harrison; Jim, Vic Vallaro; Carol, Karil Daniels; Photographer, Jahn Cardoza; Marvin, Stuart Coffee.

2635 THE SHAMELESS OLD LADY. (Continental-1966). Madame Berthe, Sylvie; Rosalie, Malka Ribovska; Pierre, Victor Lanoux; Albert, Etienne Bierry; Gaston, Francois Maistre; Simone, Pascale De Boysson; Victoire, Lena Delanne; Rose, Jeanne Hardeyn; Charles, Jean-Louis Lamande; Robert, Robert Bousquet; Lucien, Andre Jourdan; Ernest, Armand Meffre; Charlot, Pierre Decazes; Alphonse, Jean Bouise; Dufour, Andre Thorrent.

2636 SHAMUS. (Columbia-1973). McCoy, Burt Reynolds; Alexis, Dyan Cannon; Col. Hardcore, John Ryan; Lt. Promuto, Joe Santos; Dottore, Giorgio Tozzi; Hume, Ron Weyand; Springy, Larry Block; Bolton, Beeson Carroll; The Kid, Kevin Conway; Bookstore Girl, Kay Frye; Johnnie, John Glover; Schnook, Merwin Goldsmith; First Woman, Melody Santangelo; Irving Selbst, Alex Wilson, Tony Amato Jr., Lou Martell, Marshall Anker, Bert Bertram, Jimmy Kelly, Alisha Fontaine, Mickey Freeman, Capt. Arthur Haggerty, Tommy Lane, Ric Mancini, Norman Marshall, Fat Thomas Rand, Frank Silvera, Alex Stevens, Steven Vignari, Mark Weston, Glenn Wilder, Charles Picerni, Tony Amato Sr.

2637 SHANKS. (Paramount-1974). Marcel Marceau, Tsilla Chelton, Philippe Clay, Cindy Eilbacher, Larry Bishop, Giff Manard, Phil Adams, Helena Kallianiotes, Read Morgan, Lara Wing.

2638 SHARK. (Excelsior-1970). Caine, Burt Reynolds; Mallare, Barry Sullivan; Doc, Arthur Kennedy; Anna, Silvia Pinal; Barok, Enrique Lucero; Smoky, Charles Berriochoa; Latalla, Manuel Alvarado; Asha, Emilia Stuart.

2639 SHATTERHAND. (Goldstone Film Enterprises-1968). Lex Barker, Pierre Brice, Daliah Lavi, Guy Madison, Ralf Wolter, Bill Ramsey, Gustavo Rojo, Rik Battaglia, Kitti Mattern, Alain Tissier, Charles Fawcett, Nikola Popovic, Mirko Ellis, Burschi Putzgruber.

2640 SHE. (MGM-1965). Ayesha, Ursula Andress; Leo Vincey, John Richardson; Major Holly, Peter Cushing; Job, Bernard Cribbins; Ustane, Rosenda Monteros; Billali, Christopher Lee; Haumeid, Andre Morell.

2641 SHE AND HE. (Brandon-1967). Naoko, Sachiko Hidari; Ikona, Kikuji Yamashita; Husband, Eiji Okada; Blind Girl, Mariko Igarashi.

2642 THE SHE BEAST. (Europix Consolidated-1966). Barbara Steele, John Karlsen, Ian Ogilvy, Mal Welles, Richard Watson, Jay Riley, Ed Randolph.

2643 SHE FREAK. (Sonney Amusement Enterprises-1967). Jade Cochran, Claire Brennan; Blackie Fleming, Lee Raymond; Pat Mullings, Lynn Courtney; Steve St. John, Bill McKinney; Mr. Babcock, Van Teen; Shortie, Felix Silla; Olga, Marsha Drake; Greasy, Claude Smith; Max, Bobby Matthews; Pretty Boy, Bill Bagdad; Advance Man, Ben Moore; Customer in Cage, David Boudrot; Snake Charmer, Madame Lee.

2644 SHENANDOAH. (Universal-1965). Charlie Anderson, James Stewart; Sam, Doug McClure; Jacob, Glenn Corbett; James, Patrick Wayne; Jennie, Rosemary Forsyth; Boy, Philip Alford; Ann, Katharine Ross; Nathan, Charles Robinson; John, James McMullan; Henry, Tim McIntire; Gabriel, Eugene Jackson Jr.; Dr. Witherspoon, Paul Fix; Pastor Bjoerling, Denver Pyle.

2645 THE SHEPHERD GIRL. (Frank Lee-1965). Hsiu Hsiu, Julie Yeh Feng; Liu Ta-lung, Kwan Shan; Ku, Yang Chi-ching; Tiger Tseng, Chy Mu; Yao Teh-pao, Chiang Kuang-chao; Hsiao Tsul, Li Ting; Widow Chu, Ouyang Sha-fei; Wei, Lin Feng.

2646 SHINBONE ALLEY. (Allied Artists-1971). Archy, voice of Eddie Bracken; Mehitabel, voice of Carol Channing; Tyrone T. Tattersall, voice of John Carradine; Big Bill, voice of Alan Reed, Sr.

2647 SHIP OF FOOLS. (Columbia-1965). Dr. Schumann, Oskar Werner; Captain Thiele, Charles Korvin; La Condesa,

Simone Signoret; Mary Treadwell, Vivien Leigh; Tenny, Lee Marvin; Rieber, Jose Ferrer; Glocken, Michael Dunn; Jenny, Elizabeth Ashley; David, George Segal; Pepe, Jose Greco; Lowenthal, Heinz Ruhmann; Frau Hutten, Lilia Skala; Amparo, Barbara Luna; Lizzi, Christine Schmidtmer; Freytag, Alf Kjellin; Lieutenant Heebner, Werner Klemperer; Graf, John Wengraf; Frau Schmidt, Olga Fabian.

2648 SHOCK TROOPS. (United Artists-1969). Jean, Jean-Claude Brialy; Cazal, Bruno Cremer; Kerk, Jacques Perrin; Thomas, Gerard Blain; Groubac, Claude Brasseur; The Extra Man, Michel Piccoli; Lucien, Pierre Clementi; Moujon, Francois Perier; Passevin, Charles Vanel; Philippe, Paolo Fratini; Solin, Michel Creton; Ouf, Claude Brosset; Paco, Nino Segurini; Lecocq, Med Hondo; Girl, Julie Dassin.

2649 THE SHOES OF THE FISHERMAN. (MGM-1968). Kiril Lakota, Anthony Quinn; Father David Telemond, Oskar Werner; Cardinal Rinaldi, Vittorio De Sica; The Elder Pope, John Gielgud; Chiara, Rosemary Dexter; Piotr Llyich Kamenev, Laurence Olivier; George Faber, David Janssen; Cardinal Leone, Leo McKern; Dr. Ruth Faber, Barbara Jefford; Igor Bounin, Frank Finlay; Gelasio, Arnoldo Foa; Chairman Peng, Burt Kwouk.

2650 SHOOT IT: BLACK, SHOOT IT: BLUE. (Levitt-Pickman-1974). Herbert G. Rucker, Michael Moriarty; Lamont, Eric Laneuville; Ring, Paul Sorvino; Garrity, Earl Hindman; Stacy, Linda Scruggs; Buddy, Bruce Kornbluth; Sal, Anthony Harnotta; Teacher, Fred Burrell; Hattie, Lynda Wescott; Wardell, Val Pringle; Mark S. Johnson, Buck Buchanan; George, George DiCenzo; Molly McGreevy, Michael Shannon, Joella Deffenbaugh, John Quastler, Art Ellison, Gilbert Milton, Bob Phillips, Cecil Burton, Linda McGuire, Irene Ballinger, LeRoy Vaughn, Don Peterson, Tom Turner, Ronnie Sellers.

2651 SHOOT LOUD, LOUDER ... I DON'T UNDERSTAND. (Embassy-1967). Alberto Saporito, Marcello Mastroianni; Tania Mottini, Raquel Welch; Pasquale Cimmaruta, Guido Alberti; Carlo Saporito, Leopoldo Trieste; Aunt Rosa Cimmaruta, Tecla Scarano; Uncle Nicola, Eduardo De Filippo; Elvira Cimmaruta, Rosalba Grottesi; Aniello Amitrano, Paolo Ricci; Mrs. Amitrano, Regina Bianchi; Chief Police Inspector, Franco Parenti; Beautiful Woman, Angela Luce; Lieut. Bertolucci, Silvano Tranquilli; Matilde Cimmaruta, Pina D'Amato; Marshal Bagnacavallo, Carlo Bagno; Maid, Pia Morra; Luigi Cimmaruta, Gino Minopoli; Deputy Police Inspector, Alberto Bugli; Carmelo Vitiello, Ignazio Spalla.

2652 SHOOT OUT. (Universal-1971). Clay Lomax, Gregory Peck; Juliana, Pat Quinn; Bobby Jay, Robert F. Lyons; Alma, Susan Tyrrell; Trooper, Jeff Corey.

2653 THE SHOP ON MAIN STREET. (Prominent Films-1966). Tono Brtko, Josef Kroner; Rosalie Lautmann, Ida Kaminska; Evelina Brtko, Hana Slivkova; Marcus Kolbotsky, Franktisek Zvarik; Rose Kolkotska, Helena Zvarikova; Imro Kuchar, Martin Holly; Katz, Martin Gregor.

2654 SHOWDOWN. (Universal-1973). Chuck, Rock Hudson; Billy, Dean Martin; Kate, Susan Clark; Art, Donald Moffat; P. J., John McLiam; Martinez, Charles Baca; Clem, Jackson Clem; Perry, Ben Zeller; Earl, John Richard Gill; Jack, Philip L. Mead; Girl, Rita Rogers; Big Eye, Vic Mohica; Joe, Raleigh Gardenhire; Pook, Ed Begley Jr.; Rawls, Dan Boydston.

2655 SHOWDOWN FOR ZATOICHI. (Daiei-1968). Zatoichi, Shintaro Katsu; Jumonji, Mikio Narita; Enoshimeya, Chizu Hayashi; Otane, Kaneko Iwasaki; Tomonoshin, Gaku Yamamoto.

2656 THE SHUTTERED ROOM. (Warner Bros.-7 Arts-1968). Mike Kelton, Gig Young; Susannah Kelton, Carol Lynley; Ethan, Oliver Reed; Aunt Agatha, Flora Robson; Zebulon, William Devlin; Tait, Bernard Kay; Emma, Judith Arthy; Luther, Robert Cawdron; Aunt Sarah, Celia Hewitt; Village Girl, Ingrid Bower; Peter Porteous, Anita Anderson, Clifford Diggins.

2657 THE SICILIAN CLAN. (20th Century-Fox-1970). Vittorio Manalese, Jean Gabin; Roger Sartet, Alain Delon; Inspector LeGoff, Lino Ventura; Jeanne Manalese, Irina Demick; Tony Nicosia, Amedeo Nazzari; Jack, Sydney Chaplin; Maria Manalese, Elise Cegani; Theresa, Karen Blanguernon; Sergio Manalese, Marc Porel; Aldo Manalese, Yves Lefebvre; Luigi, Philippe Baronnet; Stamp Expert, Leopoldo Trieste; Roberto, Cesar Chauveau; Monique Sartet, Danielle Volle; Pilot, Ed Meeks, Rovel, Jacques Duby.

2658 SIDDHARTHA. (Columbia-1973). Siddhartha, Shashi Kapoor; Kamala, Simi Garewal; Govinda, Romesh Sharma; Kamaswami, Pincho Kapoor; Vasudeva, Zul Vellani; Siddhartha's Father, Amrik Singh; Siddhartha's Mother, Shanti Hiranand; Siddhartha's Son, Kunal Kapoor.

2659 SIGN OF THE VIRGIN. (Brandon-1969). Stan, Josef Cap; Jana, Jaroslava Obermaierova; Veleba, Vladimir Pucholt; Beiman, Jiri Wimmer; Capt. Pazourek, Ilja Prachar; Lt. Brezina, Jiri Adamira; Lt. Tonselser, Rudolf Jelinek.

2660 SIGNPOST TO MURDER. (MGM-1965). Molly Thomas, Joanne Woodward; Alex Forrester, Stuart Whitman; Dr. Mark Fleming, Edward Mulhare; The Vicar, Alan Napier; Mrs. Barnes, Joyce Worsley; Supt. Bickley, Leslie Denison; Dr. Graham, Murray Matheson; Officer Rogers, Hedley

Mattingly; Auntie, Carol Veazie.

2661 SILENCE. (Cinema Financial of America-1974). Crazy Jack, Will Geer; Barbara, Ellen Geer; Al, Richard Kelton; Eric, Ian Geer Flanders; Sheriff, Craig Kelly; Deputy, Sam Robustelli; Car Thieves, Tad Greer, Raleigh Geer.

2662 THE SILENCERS. (Columbia-1966). Matt Helm, Dean Martin; Gail, Stella Stevens; Tina, Daliah Lavi; Tung-Tze, Victor Buono; Wigwam, Arthur O'Connell; Sam Gunther, Robert Webber; MacDonald, James Gregory; Barbara, Nancy Kovack; Andreyev, Roger C. Carmel; Sarita, Cyd Charisse; Lovey Kravezit, Beverly Adams; Richard Devon, David Bond, John Reach, Robert Phillips, John Willis, Frank Gerstle, Grant Woods, Patrick Waltz.

2663 SILENT RUNNING. (Universal-1972). Freeman Lowell, Bruce Dern; Wolf, Cliff Potts; Barker, Ron Rifkin; Keenan, Jesse Vint; The Drones, Mark Persons, Steven Brown, Cheryl Sparks, Larry Whisenhunt.

2664 SIMON, KING OF THE WITCHES. (Fanfare-1971). Simon, Andrew Prine; Linda, Brenda Scott; Turk, George Paulsin; Rackum, Norman Burton; Hercules, Gerald York; Michael C. Ford, Ultra Violet, Lee J. Lambert, William Martel, Angus Duncan, Richard Shepard, Richard Ford Grayling, Allyson Ames, Harry Rose, Mike Kopcha, John Yates, Jerry Brooks, Ray Galvin, Buck Holland, David Vaile, Helen Jay, Art Hern, John Hart, Sharon Berryhill.

2665 SIMON OF THE DESERT. (Altura-1969). Simon, Claudio Brook; The Temptress, Silvia Pinal; The Mother, Hortensia Santovena; Brother Matias, Enrique Alvarez Felix; Mutilated One, Enrique Del Castillo; Dwarf, Jesus Fernandez Martinez; Priest, Francisco Reiguera; Priest, Luis Aceves Castaneda; Priest, Antonio Bravo Sanchez; Enrique Garcia Alvarez, Eduardo MacGregor.

2666 SINDERELLA AND THE GOLDEN BRA. (Manson-1965). Suzanne Sybele, Bill Gaskin, David Duffield, Sid Lassick, Patricia Mayfield, June Faith, Joan Lemo, Gerald Strickland, John Bradley, Kay Hall, Althea Currier, Jackie DeWitt, Justine Scott, Lisa Carole, Beverly Frankell, Donna Anderson.

2667 SINFUL DAVEY. (United Artists-1969). Davey Haggart, John Hurt; Annie, Pamela Franklin; Constable Richardson, Nigel Davenport; MacNab, Ronald Fraser; Duke of Argyll, Robert Morley; Jean Carlisle, Fidelma Murphy; Duchess of Argyll, Maxine Audley; Penelope, Fionnuala Flanagan; Sir James Graham, Donal McCann; Captain Douglas, Allan Cuthbertson; Yorkshire Bill, Eddie Byrne; Boots Simpson, Niall MacGinnis; Jock, Noel Purcell; Mary, Judith Furse; Andrew,

Francis De Wolff; Baliff of Stirling, Paul Farrell; Warden McEwan, Geoffrey Golden; Dr. Gresham, Leon Collins; Billy the Goat, Mickser Reid; Bobby Rae, Derek Young; George Bagrie, John Franklyn; Mary Kidd, Eileen Murphy.

2668 THE SINFUL DWARF. (Boxoffice International-1973). Anne Sparrow, Tony Eades, Clara Keller, Torben, Werner Hedman, Gerda Madsen, Dale Robinson.

2669 THE SINGING NUN. (MGM-1966). Sister Ann, Debbie Reynolds; Father Clementi, Ricardo Montalban; Mother Prioress, Greer Garson; Sister Cluny, Agnes Moorehead; Robert Gerarde, Chad Everett; Nicole Arlien, Katharine Ross; Himself, Ed Sullivan; Sister Mary, Juanita Moore; Dominic Arlien, Ricky Cordell; Mr. Arlien, Michael Pate; Fitzpatrick, Tom Drake; Mr. Duvries, Larry D. Mann; Marauder, Charles Robinson; Sister Michele, Monique Montaigne; Sister Elise, Joyce Vanderveen; Sister Brigitte, Anne Wakefield; Sister Gertrude, Pam Peterson; Sister Martha, Marina Koshetz; Sister Therese, Nancy Walters; Sister Elizabeth, Violet Rensing; Sister Consuella, Inez Pedroza.

2670 SISTERS. (American International-1973). Danielle Breton, Margot Kidder; Gracie Collier, Jennifer Salt; Joseph Larch, Charles Durning; Emil Breton, Bill Finley; Philip Woode, Lisle Wilson; Mr. McLennen, Barnard Hughes; Mrs. Collier, Mary Davenport; Detective Kelley, Dolph Sweet.

2671 SITTING TARGET. (MGM-1972). Harry Lomart, Oliver Reed; Pat Lomart, Jill St. John; Birdy Williams, Ian McShane; Inspector Milton, Edward Woodward; Marty Gold, Frank Finlay; MacNeil, Freddie Jones; Maureen, Jill Townsend; Gun Dealer, Robert Beatty; Soapy Tucker, Tony Beckley; Prison Warder Accomplice, Mike Pratt; Prison Warder One, Robert Russell; Prison Warder Two, Joe Cahill; Gun Dealer's Bodyguard, Robert Ramsey; Girl in Truck, Susan Shaw; Lomart Neighbor, June Brown; Irate Mother, Maggy Maxwell.

2672 SITUATION HOPELESS--BUT NOT SERIOUS. (Paramount-1965). Herr Wilhelm Frick, Sir Alec Guinness; Lucky, Michael Connors; Hank, Robert Redford; Edeltraud, Anita Hoefer; Lissie, Mady Rahl; Herr Neusel, Paul Dahlke; QM Master Sergeant, Frank Wolff; Sergeant, John Briley; Wanda, Elisabeth Von Molo.

2673 SIX IN PARIS. (New Yorker-1969). Katherine, Barbara Wilkind; Jean, Jean-Francois Chappey; Raymond, Jean-Pierre Andreani; Odile, Nadine Ballot; The Husband, Barbet Schroeder; The Stranger, Gilles Queant; The Prostitute, Micheline Dax; Leon, Claude Melki; Jean-Marc, Jean-Michel Rouziere; The Victim, Marcel Gallon; Monica, Joanna

Shimkus; Roger, Philippe Hiquilly; Ivan, Serge Davri; The Wife, Stephane Audran; The Husband, Claude Chabrol; The Boy, Gilles Chusseau; The Maid, Dinah Saril.

2674 SKEZAG. (Soho Cinema-1971). Wayne Shirley, Louis "Sonny" Berrios, Angel Sanchez.

2675 THE SKI BUM. (AVCO Embassy-1971). Johnny, Zalman King; Samantha, Charlotte Rampling; Burt, Joseph Mell; Liz, Dimitra Arless.

2676 SKI FEVER. (Allied Artists-1969). Brian, Martin Milner; Susan, Claudia Martin; Karen, Vivi Bach; Toni, Dietmar Schoenherr; Franz, Toni Sailor; Dominique, Dorit Dom; Max, Kurt Grosskurth; MacDoodle, Curt Bock.

2677 SKI PARTY. (American International-1965). Todd Armstrong, Frankie Avalon; Craig Gamble, Dwayne Hickman; Linda, Deborah Walley; Barbara, Yvonne Craig; Pevney, Robert Q. Lewis; Freddie Carter, Aron Kincaid; James Brown and the Famous Flames; Lesley Gore.

2678 SKIDOO. (Paramount-1969). Tony Banks, Jackie Gleason; Flo Banks, Carol Channing; "God," Groucho Marx; Angie, Frankie Avalon; A Tower Guard, Fred Clark; Leech, Michael Constantine; The Man, Frank Gorshin; Stash, John Phillip Law; The Senator, Peter Lawford; The Warden, Burgess Meredith; Captain Garbaldo, George Raft; Hechy, Cesar Romero; "Blue Chips" Packard, Mickey Rooney; The Professor, Austin Pendleton; Darleen Banks, Alexandra Hay; Luna, Arnold Stang, Doro Merande, Phil Arnold, Slim Pickens, Robert Donner, Richard Kiel, Tom Law, Jaik Rosenstein, Stacy King, Renny Roker, Roman Gabriel, Harry Nilsson, William Cannon, Stone Country, Orange County Ramblers.

2679 SKIN GAME. (Warner Bros.-1971). Quincy, James Garner; Jason, Louis Gossett; Ginger, Susan Clark; Naomi, Brenda Sykes; Plunkett, Edward Asner.

2680 THE SKIN GAME. (William Mishkin-1966). Ronald Howard, Jess Conrad, Peter Gray, David Graham, Melody O'Brian, Peter Hager, Lawrence Taylor, Anne Martin, John Scott, Jane Wilde.

2681 THE SKULL. (Paramount-1965). Peter Cushing, Patrick Wymark, Christopher Lee, Nigel Green.

2682 SKULLDUGGERY. (Universal-1970). Douglas, Burt Reynolds; Sybil, Susan Clark; Kreps, Roger C. Carmel; Vancruysen, Paul Hubschmid; Pop, Chips Rafferty; Buffington, Alexander Knox; Topazia, Pat Suzuki; Spofford, Edward Fox; Eaton, Wilfrid Hyde-White; Attorney General, William

Marshall; Judge Draper, Rhys Williams; Dr. Figgins, Mort Marshall; Tee Hee, Michael St. Clair; Smooth, Booker Bradshaw; Epstein, John Kimberley; Officer, James Henry Eldridge; Motel Manager, Totty Ames; Commentator, James Bacon; Kauni, Gilbert Senior; Siria, Clarence Harris; Chief, Burnal "Custus" Smith; Spigget, John Woodcock; Mimms, Newton D. Arnold; Rev. Holzapple, Wendell Baggett; Naylor, Mike Preece; Papuan, Charles Washburn; Worker, Cliff Bell Jr.; Russian Delegate, Alex Gradussov; Reporter, Jim Alexander; Berle Tanen, Saul David; Associate Judge, Bernard Pike; Israeli Delegate, Eddie Fuchs.

2683 THE SKY PIRATE. (FilmMakers-1970). Joe, Michael McClanathan; Charlie, Claudia Leacock; Norman, Frank Meyer; Shy Lady, Margaret Kramer; Pepe, Lorenzo Mans; Sarah, Zelda Keiser; Uptight Girl, Francesca Annis; Carmen, Rainy Michaelyan.

2684 SKYJACKED. (MGM-1972). Henry O'Hara, Charlton Heston; Angela Thacher, Yvette Mimieux; Jerome K. Weber, James Brolin; Sgt. Ben Puzo, Claude Akins; Mrs. Clara Shaw, Jeanne Crain; Elly Brewster, Susan Dey; Gary Brown, Roosevelt Grier; Harriet Stevens, Mariette Hartley; Senator Arne Lindner, Walter Pidgeon; John Bimonte, Ken Swofford; Lovejoy Wells, Leslie Uggams; Harold Shaw, Ross Elliott; Peter Lindner, Nicholas Hammond; Sam Allen, Mike Henry; William Reading, Jayson William Kane; Jane Burke, Toni Clayton; Walter Burke, John Hillerman; Hazel Martin, Kelley Miles; Robert Grundig, John Fiedler; Mrs. O'Hara, Maureen Connell; First Class Passengers, Ed Connelly, Forrest Wood; Stanley Morris, Wesley Lau; Cosmetic Sales Girl, Jennifer Shaw; Thompson, Jack Denbo; Bonanza Pilot, Roy Engel; Hunter, Joe Canutt; Bronson, Grahame Pratt; Russian Leader, Genadii Biegouloff; Airline Attendant, Craig Shreeve; Weber's Mother, Lorna Thayer; Weber's Father, Daniel White; General, William Martel.

2685 THE SLAMS. (MGM-1973). Curtis, Jim Brown; Iris, Judy Pace; Stambell, Roland Bob Harris; Jackson, Paul E. Harris; Capiello, Frank de Kova; Glover, Ted Cassidy; Macey, Frenchia Guizon; Flood, John Dennis; Zack, Jac Emel; Warden, Quinn Redeker; Mother, Betty Coles; Cohalt, Robert Phillips; Saddler, Jan Merlin.

2686 SLAUGHTER. (American International-1972). Slaughter, Jim Brown; Ann Cooper, Stella Stevens; Dominick, Rip Torn; Harry Bastoli, Don Gordon; A. W. Price, Cameron Mitchell; Kim Walker, Marlene Clark; Morelli, Robert Phillips; Jenny, Marion Brash; Felice, Norman Alfe; Little Al, Eddie LoRusso.

2687 SLAUGHTERHOUSE-FIVE. (Universal-1972). Billy Pilgrim, Michael Sacks; Paul Lazzaro, Ron Leibman; Derby, Eugene

Roche; Valencia, Sharon Gans; Montana Wildhack, Valerie Perrine; Wild Bob Cody, Roberts Blossom; Lionel Merble, Sorrell Booke; Weary, Kevin Conway; Stanley, Gary Waynesmith; Rumford, John Dehner; Hobo, Stan Gottlieb; Robert, Perry King; German Leader, Friedrich Ledebur; Young German Guard, Nick Belle; Eliot Rosewater, Henry Bumstead; Billy's Mother, Lucille Benson; Lily, Gilmer McCormick; Barbara, Holly Near; Campbell, Richard Schaal; German Guard Group 2, Karl Otto Alberty; Englishman, Tom Wood.

2688 SLAUGHTER'S BIG RIPOFF. (American International-1973). Slaughter, Jim Brown; Duncan, Ed McMahon; Reynolds, Brock Peters; Kirk, Don Stroud; Marcia, Gloria Hendry; Joe, Richard Williams; Burtoli, Art Metrano; Noria, Judy Brown; Crowder, Russ Martin; Arnie, Eddie LoRusso; Mrs. Duncan, Jackie Giroux; Pratt, Tony Brubaker; Leo, Gene LeBell; Chin, Fuji; Harvey, Russ McGinn.

2689 SLAVES. (Continental-1969). Nathan Mackay, Stephen Boyd; Cassy, Dionne Warwicke; Luke, Ossie Davis; Jericho, Robert Kya-Hill; Esther, Barbara Ann Teer; Emmeline, Adline King; Zacharious, Oscar Paul Jones; Luther, James Heath; Julia, Eva Jessye; Holland, David Huddleston; Shadrach, Julius Harris; Mrs. Stillwell, Nancy Coleman; Arthur Stillwell, Shepperd Strudwick; New Orleans Lady, Gale Sondergaard; Mrs. Bennett, Marilyn Clark.

2690 SLEEPER. (United Artists-1973). Miles Monroe, Woody Allen; Luna, Diane Keaton; Erno, John Beck; Dr. Nero, Marya Small; Dr. Orva, Bartlett Robinson; Dr. Melik, Mary Gregory; Rainer, Chris Forbes; Dr. Dean, Peter Hobbs; Jeb, Spencer Milligan; Sears, Stanley Ross; Janus, Whitney Rydbeck.

2691 THE SLEEPING BEAUTY. (Royal-1966). Princess Aurora, Alla Sizova; Prince Desire, Yuri Soloviev; Wicked Fairy, Natalia Dudinskaya; Lilac Fairy, Irini Bazhenova; Blue Bird, Natalia Makarova; Blue Bird, Sergei Vykulov; King, Vsevolod Ukhov; Queen, O. Zabotkina; Master of Ceremonies, V. Riazanov; Princess Florine, M. Makasova; Blue Bird, V. Panov; and the Corps de Ballet of the Leningrad Kirov Ballet.

2692 THE SLEEPING CAR MURDER. (7 Arts-1966). Inspector Grazzi, Yves Montand; Eliane Darres, Simone Signoret; Le Patron, Pierre Mondy; Bambi, Catherine Allegret; Georgette Thomas, Pascale Roberts; Daniel, Jacques Perrin; Cabourg, Michel Piccoli; Eric, Jean-Louis Trintignant; Bob, Charles Denner; Jean-Lou, Claude Mann; Madame Grazzi, Nadine Alari.

2693 THE SLENDER THREAD. (Paramount-1965). Alan Newell,

Sidney Poitier; Mrs. Inga Dyson, Anne Bancroft; Dr. Coburn, Telly Savalas; Mark Dyson, Steven Hill; Chris Dyson, Greg Jarvis; Detective Judd Ridley, Edward Asner; Marion, Indus Arthur; Sgt. Harry Ward, Paul Newlan; Charlie, Dabney Coleman; Doctor, H. M. Wynant; Patrolman Steve Peters, Robert Hoy; Medical Technician, Jason Wingreen; Mrs. Thomas, Marjorie Nelson; Arthur Foss, Steven Marlo; Al McCardle, Lane Bradford; Edna, Janet Dudley; Dr. Alden Van, John Napier.

2694 SLEUTH. (20th Century-Fox-1972). Andrew Wyke, Laurence Olivier; Milo Tindle, Michael Caine; Inspector Doppler, Alec Cawthorne; Marguerite, Margo Channing; Detective Sergeant Tarrant, John Matthews; Police Constable Higgs, Teddy Martin.

2695 SLIPSTREAM. (Pacific Rim-1974). Mike Mallard, Luke Askew; Kathy, Patti Oatmar; Allec, Eli Rill; Terry, Scott Hylands; Hitch, Danny Friedman.

2696 SLITHER. (MGM-1973). Dick Kanipsia, James Caan; Barry Fenaka, Peter Boyle; Kitty Kopetzky, Sally Kellerman; Mary Fenaka, Louise Lasser; Vincent J. Palmer, Allen Garfield; Harry Moss, Richard B. Shull; Man With Ice Cream, Alex Rocco; Farmer in Truck, Seamon Glass; Highway Patrolman, Wayne Storm; Band Singer, Diane Darrin; Buddy, Stuart Nisbet; Bingo Player, Edwina Gough; Man in Men's Room, Al Dunlap; Short Order Cook, James Joseph; Bingo Caller, Virginia Sale; Man at Phone Booth, Alex Henteloff; Jogger, Len Lesser; Man With Camera, Garry Goodrow.

2697 SLOGAN. (Royal-1970). Serge Gainsbourg, Jane Birkin, Andrea Parisy, Daniel Gelin, Henri-Jacques Huet, Juliet Berto, Pierre Doris.

2698 SLOW RUN. (Film-Makers' Distribution Center-1968). Narrator, Saul Rubinek; Bruce Gordon, David Flower, Heather Sim, Jane Amsten, Pat Jones, Rita Stein, Melvyn Green.

2699 SMASHING TIME. (Paramount-1967). Brenda, Rita Tushingham; Yvonne, Lynn Redgrave; Tom Wabe, Michael York; Charlotte Brilling, Anna Quayle; Mrs. Gimble, Irene Handl; Bobbie Mome-Rath, Ian Carmichael; Toni, Toni Palmer; Jeremy Tove, Jeremy Lloyd; Cape Boss, Arthur Mullard; Tramp, Sydney Bromley; Hall Porter, Howard Marion Crawford; 1st Exquisite, Murray Melvin; 2nd Exquisite, Paul Danquah; Tove's Secretary, Valerie Leon; Gossiping Customer, Adele Strong; Man in Cafe No. 6, Jerold Wells; Dominic, Peter Jones; Irishman, George A. Cooper; 1st Waiter, Ronnie Stevens; Sweenie Todd, John Clive; Disc Jockey, Mike Lennox; Clive Sword, Bruce Lacey; Custard-pie Vicar, Cardew Robinson; The Caretaker, David Lodge; 2nd Waiter,

Ray Mackin; Demolished Old Lady, May Dalby; The Snarks, The Tomorrow.

2700 SMIC, SMAC, SMOC. (GSF-1971). Catherine, Catherine Allegret; Midou, Amidou; Jeannot, Jean Collomb; Charlot, Charles Gerard; The Blindman, Francis Lai; Handcuffed Hoodlum, Claude Lelouch.

2701 SMITH! (Buena Vista-1969). Smith, Glenn Ford; Norah, Nancy Olson; Judge, Dean Jagger; Vince Heber, Keenan Wynn; Walter Charlie, Warren Oates; Ol' Antoine, Chief Dan George; Gabriel Jimmyboy, Frank Ramirez; Mr. Edwards, John Randolph; Albie, Christopher Shea; Peterpaul, Ricky Cordell.

2702 SMOKY. (20th Century-Fox-1966). Clint, Fess Parker; Julie, Diana Hyland; Maria, Katy Jurado; Fred, Hoyt Axton; Jeff, Robert Wilke; Gordon, Armando Silvestre; Manuel, Jose Hector Galindo; Pepe, Jorge Martinez de Hoyos; Abbott, Ted White; Cowboys, Chuck Roberson, Robert Terhune, Jack Williams.

2703 THE SMUGGLERS. (New Yorker-1969). Francois Vatel, Monique Thieiet, Johnny Monteilhet, Albert Juross, Paul Martin, Bernard Cazassua, Luc Moullet, Gerard Tanguy, Patrick Huber.

2704 SNOW JOB. (Warner Bros.-1972). Christian Biton, Jean-Claude Killy; Monica Scotti, Daniele Gaubert; Bob Skinner, Cliff Potts; Enrico Dolphi, Vittorio De Sica; Simonelli, Lelio Luttazzi; Lorraine Borman, Delia Boccardo; Vito, Umberto D'Orsi.

2705 SNOWBALL EXPRESS. (Buena Vista-1972). Johnny Baxter, Dean Jones; Sue Baxter, Nancy Olson; Jesse McCord, Harry Morgan; Martin Ridgeway, Keenan Wynn; Richard Baxter, Johnny Whitaker; Wally Perkins, Michael McGreevey; Double L. Dingman, George Lindsey; Chris Baxter, Kathleen Cody; Miss Wiggington, Mary Wickes; Mr. Fowler, David White; Mr. Carruthers, Dick Van Patten; Miss Obelvie, Alice Backes; Naomi Voight, Joanna Phillips; Mr. Manescue, John Myhers.

2706 SO LONG, BLUE BOY. (Maryon-1973). Ed, Arthur Franz; Isaiah, Rick Gates; Julie, Neile Adams McQueen; Dean, Richard Rowley; Cathy, Pamela Collins; Martha, Anne Seymour; Eli, Richard McMurray; Buck, Henry Brandon.

2707 LE SOCRATE. (New Yorker-1969). Le Socrate, Pierre Luzan; Lemay, R. J. Chauffard; Sylvie, Martine Brochard; Pierre, Stephane Fay; Adam, Jean-Pierre Sentier.

2708 SOCRATES. (New Yorker-1971). Socrates, Jean Sylvere; Xanthippe, Anne Caprile; Crito, Ricardo Palacios; Appollodorus, Beppi Mannaiuolo.

2709 SOFI. (Golden Bear-1968). The Clerk, Tom Troupe.

2710 SOL MADRID. (MGM-1968). Sol Madrid, David McCallum; Stacey Woodward, Stella Stevens; Emil Dietrich, Telly Savalas; Jalisco, Ricardo Montalban; Dano Villanova, Rip Torn; Harry Mitchell, Pat Hingle; Capo Riccione, Paul Lukas; Captain Ortega, Michael Ansara; First Hood, Perry Lopez; Scarpi, Michael Conrad; Chief Danvers, Robert Rockwell; Refinery Engineer, Merritt Bohn; Woman in Cantina, Madge Cameron; Cantina Operator, Shep Sanders; 2nd Dietrich Gunman, Henry Escalante; 3rd Dietrich Gunman, George Sawaya; Joe Brighton, Ken Del Conte; Old Field Foreman, Robert McNamara; Stacey's Dance Partner, Tony Barbario.

2711 SOLDIER BLUE. (AVCO Embassy-1970). Cresta Marybelle Lee, Candice Bergen; Pvt. Honus Gant, Peter Strauss; Isaac, Donald Pleasence; Col. Iverson, John Anderson; Spotted Wolf, Jorge Rivero; Capt. Battle, Dana Elcar; Pvt. Menzies, James Hampton; Sgt. O'Hearn, Mort Mills; Lt. McNair, Bob Carraway; Lt. Spingarn, Martin West; Running Fox, Jorge Russek; Kiowa Brave, Marco Antonio Arzate; Lt. Mitchell, Ron Fletcher; Mrs. Long, Barbara Turner; Indian Woman, Aurora Clavell.

2712 SOLEIL-O. (New Yorker-1973). Robert Liensol, Theo Legitimus, Gabriel Glissand, Gregoire Germain, Maboussolo, Bernard Fresson, Gilles Segal.

2713 SOLOMON KING. (Sal/Wa-1974). Solomon King, Sal Watts; Maney King, "Little Jamie" Watts; Princess Oneeba, Claudia Russo; Albert, Felice Kinchelow; Samaki Miller, Samaki Bennett; O'Malley, Louis Zito; Abdulla, Bernard B. Burton; Hassan, Richard Scarso; Tito Fuentes, Himself.

2714 SOME CALL IT LOVING. (CineGlobe-1973). Robert, Zalman King; Scarlett, Carol White; Jennifer, Tisa Farrow; Jeff, Richard Pryor; Angelica, Veronica Anderson; Doctor, Logan Ramsey; Cheerleader, Brandy Herred; Nurse, Pat Priest; Mortician, Ed Rue; Bartender, Joseph De Meo.

2715 SOME GIRLS DO. (United Artists-1971). Hugh, Richard Johnson; Helga, Daliah Lavi; Pandora, Beba Loncar; Carl, James Villiers; #7, Vanessa Howard; Flicky, Sydney Rome; Mortimer, Maurice Denham; Miss Mary, Robert Morley; Carruthers, Ronnie Stevens; #9, Virginia North; Angela, Adrienne Posta; Lady Manderley, Florence Desmond.

2716 SOME KIND OF A NUT. (United Artists-1969). Fred Amidon, Dick Van Dyke; Rachel Amidon, Angie Dickinson; Pamela Anders, Rosemary Forsyth; Bunny Erickson, Zohra Lampert; Gardner Anders, Elliot Reid; Baxter Anders, Steve

Roland; Otis Havemeyer, Dennis King; Dr. Sara, Pippa Scott; Mr. Suzumi, Peter Brocco; George Toyota, Roberto Ito; Mr. Defoe, Peter Turgeon; Dr. Ball, Harry Davis; Cab Driver, Benny Baker; Samantha, Lucy Saroyan; 1st Vice Pres., Roy Roberts; 2nd Vice President, Jonathan Hole; Larry, Ned Wertimer; Dr. Abrams, Danny Crystal; Mrs. Boland, Connie Gilchrist; Bank Guard, Milo Boulton; Himself, Heywood Hale Broun.

2717 SOME OF MY BEST FRIENDS ARE... (American International-1971). Tanny, Tom Bade; Clint, David Baker; Kenny, Paul Blake; Terry, Gary Campbell; Miss Untouchable, Carleton Carpenter; Eric, Robert Christian; Karen/Harry, Candy Darling; Leo, Jeff David; Pete, Alan Dellay; Phil, Nick Denoia; Lloyd, Dan Drake; Howard, David Drew; Gable, Jim Enzel; Ernie, Tommy Fiorello; Helen, Fannie Flagg; Al, Joe George; Scott, Gil Berard; Michael, Uva Harden; Lita, Rue McClanahan; Jose, Hector Martinez; Mrs. Nabour, Peg Murray; Tim, Dick O'Neil; Louis, Larry Reed; Jim, Gary Sandy; Barrett, Lou Steele; Giggling Gertie, Clifton Steere; Sadie, Sylvia Syms; Nebraska, Joe Taylor; Marvin, Ben Yaffee.

2718 SOMEONE BEHIND THE DOOR. (GSF-1971). The Stranger, Charles Bronson; Laurence, Anthony Perkins; Frances, Jill Ireland.

2719 SOMETHING BIG. (National General-1971). Joe Baker, Dean Martin; Colonel Morgan, Brian Keith; Mary Anna Morgan, Honor Blackman; Dover MacBride, Carol White; Jesse Bookbinder, Ben Johnson; Johnny Cobb, Albert Salmi; Tommy MacBride, Don Knight; Polly Standall, Joyce Van Patten.

2720 SOMETHING FOR EVERYONE. (National General-1970). Countess Herthe von Ornstein, Angela Lansbury; Conrad Ludwig, Michael York; Helmuth von Ornstein, Anthony Corlan; Annaliese Pleschke, Heidelinde Weis; Mrs. Pleschke, Eva-Maria Meineke; Mr. Pleschke, John Gill; Lotte von Ornstein, Jane Carr; Bobby, Despo; Klaus, Wolfrid Lier; Father Georg, Walter Janssen; Rudolph, Klaus Havenstein.

2721 SOMETIME SWEET SUSAN. (Variety-1974). Susan, Shawn Harris; Mark, Harry Reems; Bill, Neil Flanagan; Leslie, Sarah Nicholson; Johnny, Craig Baumgarten; Nurse Carrie, Kirsten Steen; Father, Rod Loomis; Mother, Carole Holland; Orderly, Tom Skowron; Rapist No. 1, James Gillis; Rapist No. 2, Alex Mann.

2722 SOMETIMES A GREAT NOTION. (Universal-1971). Hank, Paul Newman; Henry, Henry Fonda; Viv, Lee Remick; Leeland, Michael Sarrazin; Joe Ben, Richard Jaeckel.

2723 SON OF A GUNFIGHTER. (MGM-1966). Johnny, Russ Tamblyn; Deputy Fenton, Kieron Moore; James Ketchum, James Philbrook; Don Fortuna, Fernando Rey; Pilar, Maria

Granada; Morales, Aldo Sambrell; Pecos, Antonio Casas; Esteban, Barta Barri; Sheriff, Ralph Browne; Fuentes, Andy Anza; Joaquin, Fernando Hilbeck.

2724 THE SONG AND THE SILENCE. (Cloverhouse-1969). Rivkeh Shlomo, Annita Koutsouveli; Rabbi Shlomo, Harry Rubin; Fievel, Jim Murphy; Mrs. Shlomo, Nana Austin; Channaleh, Mary Antoianette; David Shlomo, Jonathan Scott; Principal, Harry Leshner; Matchmaker, Felix Fiebich.

2725 SONG OF NORWAY. (Cinerama-1970). Edvard Grieg, Toralv Maurstad; Nina Grieg, Florence Henderson; Therese Berg, Christina Schollin; Rikard Nordraak, Frank Porretta; Bjornsterne Bjornson, Harry Secombe; Berg, Robert Morley; Krogstad, Edward G. Robinson; Mrs. Bjornson, Elizabeth Larner; Engstrand, Oscar Homolka; Frederick Jaeger, Henry Gilbert, Richard Wordsworth, Bernard Archard, Susan Richards Chitty, John Barrie, Wenke Foss, Ronald Adam, Aline Towne, Nan Munro, James Hayter, Erik Chitty, Manoug Parikian, Richard Vernon, Ernest Clark, Eli Lindtner.

2726 SONNY & JED. (K-Tel-1974). Jed, Thomas Milian; Sonny, Susan George; Franciscus, Telly Savalas; Linda, Rossana Yanny; Aparacito, Franco Giacobini; Garcia, Eduardo Fajardo; Merril, Herbert Fux; Donna Aparacity, Laura Betti; Arcuri Francesco, Alvaro De Luna.

2727 SONS AND MOTHERS. (Artkino-1967). Mother, Elena Fadeyeva; Vladimir, Rodion Nakhapetov; Oulianov, Danili Sagal; Anna, Nina Menichkova; Alexander, Guennady Tchertov; Olga, Nina Vikovskaia; Dmitry, A. Bogoslavsky.

2728 SONS OF GOOD EARTH. (Frank Lee International-1967). Peter Chen Ho, Betty Loh Tih, King Chuan, Julia Hsin, Chen Yen Yeh.

2729 THE SONS OF KATIE ELDER. (Paramount-1965). John Elder, John Wayne; Tom Elder, Dean Martin; Matt Elder, Earl Holliman; Bud Elder, Michael Anderson Jr.; Mary Gordon, Martha Hyer; Morgan Hastings, James Gregory; Sheriff Wilson, Paul Fix; Dave Hastings, Dennis Hopper; Deputy Sheriff Latta, Jeremy Slate; Undertaker Syselman, John Doucette.

2730 THE SORCERERS. (Allied Artists-1968). Professor Monserrat, Boris Karloff; Estelle Monserrat, Catherine Lacey; Mike, Ian Ogilvy; Nicole, Elizabeth Ercy; Alan, Victor Henry; Audrey, Susan George; Laura, Dani Sheridan; Inspector Matalon, Ivor Dean; Detective, Peter Fraser; Meier Tzelniker, Bill Barnsley, Martin Terry, Gerald Campion, Alf Joint.

2731 THE SOUL OF NIGGER CHARLEY. (Paramount-1973). Charley, Fred Williamson; Toby, D'Urville Martin; Elena, Denise Nicholas; Sandoval, Pedro Armendariz Jr.; Marcellus, Kirk Calloway; Ode, George Allen; Colonel Blanchard, Kevin Hagen; Sergeant Foss, Michael Cameron; Roy, Johnny Greenwood; Collins, James Garbo; Anita, Nai Bonet; Fred, Robert Minor; Woods, Fred Lerner; Lee, Joe Henderson; Walker, Dick Farnsworth; Aben, Tony Brubaker; Donovan, Boyd Red Morgan; Vet. Al Hassan; Mexicans, Ed Hice, Henry Wills; Pedro, Phil Avenetti.

2732 SOUL SOLDIER. (Fanfare-1972). Private Armstrong, Rafer Johnson; Sergeant Hatch, Lincoln Kilpatrick; Trooper Eli Brown, Robert DoQui; Julie, Janee Michelle; Colonel Grierson, Cesar Romero; Mrs. Grierson, Barbara Hale; 1st Sergeant Robertson, Isaac Fields; Private Adams, Otis Taylor; Isabel, Isabel Sanford; Walking Horse, Robert Dix; Kayitah, Bobby Clark; Captain Carpenter, Steve Drexel; The Butler, Byrd Holland; Private Washington, Bill Collins; The Signifier, John Fox; Lieutenant Bigelow, Russ Nannarello Jr.; Troopers of the 10th Cavalry, Bernard Brown, Clarence Comas, Donald Diggs, Jeff Everett, Cal Fields, Perry Fluker, Noah Hobson, Earl Humphrey, De Vaughn LaBon, Rod Law, Jim Pace, John Nettles, and Eric Richmond.

2733 SOUND OF HORROR. (Europix Consolidated-1967). Pete, James Philbrook; Professor Andre, Arturo Fernandez; Maria, Soledad Miranda; Sofia, Ingrid Pitt; Antonio Casas, Jose Bodalo, Lola Gaos, Francisco Piquer.

2734 THE SOUND OF MUSIC. (20th Century-Fox-1965). Maria, Julie Andrews; Captain Von Trapp, Christopher Plummer; The Baroness, Eleanor Parker; Max Detweiler, Richard Haydn; Mother Abbess, Peggy Wood; Leisl, Charmian Carr; Louisa, Heather Menzies; Friedrich, Nicolas Hammond; Kurt, Duane Chase; Brigitta, Angela Cartwright; Marta, Debbie Turner; Gretl, Kym Karath; Sister Margaretta, Anna Lee; Sister Berthe, Portia Nelson; Herr Zeller, Ben Wright; Rolfe, Daniel Truhitte; Frau Schmidt, Norma Varden; Franz, Gil Stuart; Sister Sophia, Marni Nixon; Sister Bernice, Evadne Baker; Baroness Ebberfeld, Doris Lloyd.

2735 SOUNDER. (20th Century-Fox-1972). Rebecca Morgan, Cicely Tyson; Nathan Lee Morgan, Paul Winfield; David Lee Morgan, Kevin Hooks; Mrs. Boatwright, Carmen Mathews; Ike, Taj Mahal; Sheriff Young, James Best; Josie Mae Morgan, Yvonne Jarrell; Earl Morgan, Eric Hooks; Harriet, Sylvia "Kuumba" Williams; Camille Johnson, Janet MacLachlan; Mr. Perkins, Teddy Airhart; The Preacher, Reverend Thomas N. Phillips; The Judge, Judge William Thomas Bennett; Court Clerk, Inez Durham; Clarence, Spencer Bradford; Mrs. Clay, Myrl Sharkey.

2736 THE SOUTHERN STAR. (Columbia-1969). Dan, George Segal; Erica, Ursula Andress; Planett, Orson Welles; Karl, Ian Hendry; Matakit, Johnny Sekka; Jose, Michael Constantine; Andre, George Geret; Louis, Sylvain; Todd, Charles Lamb; Michael, Guy Delorme; Kramer, Harry Andrews.

2737 SOYLENT GREEN. (MGM-1973). Thorn, Charlton Heston; Shirl, Leigh Taylor-Young; Simonson, Joseph Cotten; Tab, Chuck Connors; Hatcher, Brock Peters; Martha, Paula Kelly; Sol Roth, Edward G. Robinson; Gilbert, Stephen Young; Kulozik, Mike Henry; Priest, Lincoln Kilpatrick; Donovan, Roy Jenson; Charles, Leonard Stone, Santini, Whit Bissell; Exchange Leader, Celia Lovsky; Mrs. Santini, Jane Dulo; Usher, Dick Van Patten; Brady, Tim Herbert; Wagner, John Dennis; Bandana Woman, Jan Bradley; New Tenant, Carlos Romero.

2738 THE SPECTRE OF EDGAR ALLAN POE. (Cinerama-1974). Edgar Allan Poe, Robert Walker; Dr. Grimaldi, Cesar Romero; Dr. Forest, Tom Drake; Lisa, Carol Ohmart; Lenore, Mary Grover; Grimaldi's Assistant, Mario Milano; Night Nurse, Karen Hartford; Lisa's Brother, Dennis Fimple; Poe's Publisher, Paul Bryar; Jonah, Frank Packard; Sarah, Marsha Mae Jones.

2739 SPEEDWAY. (MGM-1968). Steve Grayson, Elvis Presley; Susan Jacks, Nancy Sinatra; Kenny Donford, Bill Bixby; R. W. Hepworth, Gale Gordon; Ellie Esterlake, Victoria Meyerink; Abel Esterlake, William Schallert; Paul Dado, Ross Hagen; Juan Medala, Poncie Ponce; Birdie Kebner, Carl Ballantine; Lloyd Meadow, Robert Harris; Debbie Esterlake, Michele Newman; Carrie Esterlake, Courtney Brown; Billie Esterlake, Dana Brown; Annie Esterlake, Patti Jean Keith; Lori, Charlotte Considine; Mary Ann, Beverly Hills; Billie Joe, Christopher West; Mike, Carl Reindel; Dumb Blonde, Gari Hardy; Dado's Crew, Ward Ramsey, Robert James, Gary Littlejohn, Ralph Adano, Tom McCauley.

2740 THE SPIDER'S STRATAGEM. (New Yorker-1973). Giulio Brogi, Alida Valli, Tino Scotti, Pippo Campanini, Franco Giovanelli, Allen Midgett.

2741 THE SPIKES GANG. (United Artists-1974). Harry Spikes, Lee Marvin; Will Young, Gary Grimes; Les Richter, Ron Howard; Tod Mayhew, Charlie Martin Smith; Kid White, Arthur Hunnicutt; Jack Bassett, Noah Beery; Will's Father, Marc Smith.

2742 SPINOUT. (MGM-1966). Mike McCoy, Elvis Presley; Cynthia Foxhugh, Shelley Fabares; Diana St. Clair, Diane McBain; Les, Deborah Walley; Susan, Dodie Marshall; Curly, Jack Mullaney; Lt. Tracy Richards, Will Hutchins;

Philip Short, Warren Berlinger.

2743 THE SPIRIT IS WILLING. (Paramount-1968). Ben Powell, Sid Caesar; Kate Powell, Vera Miles; Steve Powell, Barry Gordon; Uncle George, John McGiver; Felicity Twitchell, Cass Daley; Jenny/Priscilla/Carol, Jill Townsend; Dr. Frieden, John Astin.

2744 SPIRITS OF THE DEAD. (American International-1969). Countess Frederica, Jane Fonda; Claude, Carla Marlier; Countess' Advisor, James Robertson Justice; Philippe, Philippe Lemaire; Second Guest, Andreas Voutsinas; Baron Wilhelm, Peter Fonda; Friend of Countess, Francoise Prevost; First Guest, Annie Duperrey; Hugues, Serge Marquand; Page, Audoin De Bardot; du Lissier, Douking; Giuseppina, Brigitte Bardot; Wilson, Alain Delon; Young Girl, Katia Cristina; Hans, Umberto D'Orsi; The Professor, Daniele Vargas; The Priest, Renzo Palmer; Toby Dammit, Terence Stamp; Priest, Salvo Randone; 1st Director, Fabrizio Angeli; 2nd Director, Ernesto Colli; Child, Marina Yaru; Television Commentator, Anna Tonietti; 1st Interviewer, Eleardo Ward; 2nd Interviewer, Paul Cooper; Antonia Pietrosi, Rick Boyd.

2745 THE SPLIT. (MGM-1968). McClain, Jim Brown; Ellie McClain, Diahann Carroll; Gladys, Julie Harris; Bert Clinger, Ernest Borgnine; Lt. Walter Brill, Gene Hackman; Harry Kifka, Jack Klugman; Marty Gough, Warren Oates; Herb Sutro, James Whitmore; Dave Negli, Donald Sutherland; Jackie, Jackie Joseph; Detective, Harry Hickox; Jenifer, Joyce Jameson; Mason, Warren Vanders.

2746 SPOILS OF THE NIGHT. (William Mishkin-1969). Tatsuo Unemiya, Mako Midori, Reiko Ohara, Akiyo Kubo.

2747 THE SPOOK WHO SAT BY THE DOOR. (United Artists-1973). Dan, Lawrence Cook; Dahomey Queen, Paula Kelly; Joy, Janet League; Dawson, J. A. Preston; Do-Daddy, Paul Butler; Stud, Don Blakely; Pretty Willie, David Lemieux; General, Byron Morrow; Carstairs, Jack Aaron; Senator, Joseph Mascolo; Willa, Beverly Gill; Calhoun, Bob Hill; Perkins, Martin Golar; Policeman, Jeff Hamilton; Old Woman, Margaret Kromgols; Security Officer, Tom Alderman; Colonel, Stephen Ferry; Doris, Kathy Berk; Boy Guardsman, Stephen Ferry II; Shorty, Anthony Ray; Jackson, Harold Johnson; Commentator, Frank Lesley; Mrs. Duncan, Audrey Stevenson; Stew, John Charles; Ponciano Olayta Jr., Sidney Eden, Colostine Boatwright, Johnny Williams, Cora Williams, Bobbie Gene Williams.

2748 THE SPORTING CLUB. (AVCO Embassy-1971). Vernor, Robert Fields; James, Nicolas Coster; Janey, Maggie Blye; Earl, Jack Warden.

2749 THE SPOTS ON MY LEOPARD. (Falcon American-1974). Robbie, Mark Hopley; Kati, Karen de Kock; Robbie's Father, Dale Cutts; Robbie's Mother, Erica Rogers; Miss Baker, Bess Finney; Mr. Mantz, Denis Smith; Liz, Van Dunlop; Lulu, Delia Sheppard; Philip, Johan Swanepoet.

2750 SPREE. (United Producers-1967). Vic Damone, Jayne Mansfield, Juliet Prowse, Mickey Hargitay, Constance Moore, Clara Ward Singers, Rozana Tapajos, Barklay Shaw.

2751 SPY IN YOUR EYE. (American International-1966). Bert Morris, Brett Halsey; Paula Krauss, Pier Angeli; Colonel Lancaster, Dana Andrews; Boris, Gastone Moschin; Tania Beryl, Mario Valdemarin, Tino Bianchi, Aldo De Francesco, Renato Baldini, Marco Guglielmi, Luciana Angiolillo.

2752 THE SPY WHO CAME IN FROM THE COLD. (Paramount-1965). Alec Leamas, Richard Burton; Nan Perry, Claire Bloom; Fiedler, Oskar Werner; Mundt, Peter Van Eyck; Peters, Sam Wanamaker; Defense Attorney, George Voskovec; Smiley, Rupert Davies; Control, Cyril Cusack; Ashe, Michael Hordern; President of Tribunal, Beatrix Lehmann.

2753 THE SPY WITH A COLD NOSE. (Embassy-1966). Dr. Francis Trevellyan, Laurence Harvey; Princess Natasha Romanova, Daliah Lavi; Stanley Farquhar, Lionel Jeffries; Wrigley, Eric Sykes; British Ambassador, Eric Portman; Pond-Jones, Denholm Elliott; Russian Premier, Colin Blakely; Elsie Farquhar, June Whitfield; Belly Dancer, Nai Bonet; American General, Paul Ford; Professor, Peter Bayliss; Chief of M.I. 5, Robert Flemyng; Night Club Hostess, Geneveve; Nurse, Norma Foster; Lady Blanchflower, Renee Houston; Braithwaite, Michael Trubshawe; Miss Marchbanks, Amy Dalby; M.I. 5 Commander, Robin Bailey.

2754 THE SPY WITH MY FACE. (MGM-1965). Napoleon Solo, Robert Vaughn; Serena, Senta Berger; Illya Kuryakin, David McCallum; Alexander Waverly, Leo G. Carroll; Darius Two, Michael Evans; Sandy Wister, Sharon Farrell; Arsene Coria, Fabrizio Mioni; Kitt Kittridge, Donald Harron; Namana, Bill Cunn; Taffy, Jennifer Billingsley; Director, Paula Raymond; Nina, Donna Michele; Doctor, Harold Gould; Wanda, Nancy Hsueh; Maggie, Michele Carey; Clerk, Paul Siemion; Waiter, Jan Arvin.

2755 SPYS. (20th Century-Fox-1974). Bruland, Donald Sutherland; Griff, Elliott Gould; Sybil, Zouzou; Martinson, Joss Ackland; Hessler, Shane Rimmer; Russian Spy Chief, Vladek Sheybal; Defector, Michael Petrovitch; Revolutionaries, Xavier Gelin, Pierre Oudry; Lafayette, Jacques Marin; Lippet, Kenneth Griffith.

2756 SQUARES. (Plateau International-1972). Austin, Andrew

Prine; Chase, Gilmer McCormick; Ruth's Parents, Harriet Medin, Jack Mather; State Policeman, William Wintersole; Woman in Restaurant, Sam Christopher.

2757 SSSSSSS. (Universal-1973). Dr. Stoner, Strother Martin; David, Dirk Benedict; Kristine, Heather Menzies; Daniels, Richard B. Shull; Kogen, Tim O'Connor; Sheriff, Jack Ging; Kitty, Kathleen King; Steve, Reb Brown; Deputy, Ted Grossman; Old Man, Charles Seel; Tourist, Ray Ballard; Jock, Brendan Burns; Jock 2, Rich Beckner; Hawkers, James Drum, Ed McCready, Frank Kowalski, Ralph Montgomery, Michael Masters; Arvin, Charlie Fox; Seal Boy, Felix Silla; Tim, Nobel Craig; Kootch Dancer, Bobbi Kiger; Attendant, J. R. Clark; Clerk, Chip Potter.

2758 STACEY! (New World-1973). Anne Randall, Marjorie Bennett, Anitra Ford, Alan Landers, James Westmoreland, Cristina Raines, Nicholas Georgiade, Richard Le Pore, John Alderman, Eddie Ryder, Madelaine Peterson, Michael Keep, Miki Garcia.

2759 STAGECOACH. (20th Century-Fox-1966). Dallas, Ann-Margret; Mr. Peacock, Red Buttons; Hatfield, Michael Connors; Ringo, Alex Cord; Doc Boone, Bing Crosby; Mr. Gatewood, Bob Cummings; Curly, Van Heflin; Buck, Slim Pickens; Mrs. Lucy Mallory, Stephanie Powers; Luke Plummer, Keenan Wynn; Matt Plummer, Brad Weston; Lt. Blanchard, Joseph Hoover; Mr. Haines, Oliver McGowan; Billy Picker, David Humphreys Miller; Trooper, Bruce Mars; Sergeant, Brett Pearson; Woman, Muriel Davidson; Ike Plummer, New Wynn; Townsman, Norman Rockwell; Sgt. Major, Edwin Mills; Bartender, Hal Lynch.

2760 STAIRCASE. (20th Century-Fox-1969). Charlie Dyer, Rex Harrison; Harry Leeds, Richard Burton; Harry's Mother, Cathleen Nesbitt; Charlie's Mother, Beatrix Lehmann; Jack, Stephen Lewis; Policeman, Neil Wilson; Postman, Gordon Heath; Miss Ricard, Avril Angers; Cub Mistress, Shelagh Fraser; Matron, Gwen Nelson; Nurse, Pat Heywood; Gravedigger, Dermot Kelly; Drag Singers, Rogers and Starr.

2761 THE STALKING MOON. (National General-1969). Sam Varner, Gregory Peck; Sarah Carver, Eva Marie Saint; Nick Tana, Robert Forster; Boy, Noland Clay; Ned, Russell Thorson; Major, Frank Silvera; Purdue, Lonny Chapman; Stationmaster, Lou Frizell; Sgt. Rudabaugh, Henry Beckman; Dace, Charles Tyner; Doctor, Richard Bull; Rachel, Sandy Wyeth; Julio, Joaquin Martinez; Stage Driver Shelby, Red Morgan; Salvaje, Nathaniel Narcisco.

2762 STAND UP AND BE COUNTED. (Columbia-1972). Sheila Hammond, Jacqueline Bisset; Yvonne Kellerman, Stella Stevens; Gary McBride, Steve Lawrence; Eliot Travis, Gary

Lockwood; Karen Hammond, Lee Purcell; Lou Kellerman, Hector Elizondo; Mabel Hammond, Anne Francine; Gloria Seagar, Madlyn Rhue; Jerry Kamanski, Alex Wilson; Playboy Speaker, Michael Ansara; Herself, Dr. Joyce Brothers; Sadie, Jessica Rains; Tracy, Meredith Baxter; Harley Burton, Greg Mullavey; Agnes, Nancy Walker; Sophie, Edith Atwater; Ruth, Jeff Donnel; Sarah, Kathleen Freeman; Shelley Morrison, Marsha Metrinko.

2763 STANLEY. (Crown International-1972). Tim Ochopee, Chris Robinson; Richard Thompkins, Alex Rocco; Craig Denning, Steve Alaimo; Susie Thompkins, Susan Carroll; Bob Wilson, Mark Harris.

2764 STAR! (20th Century-Fox-1968). Gertrude Lawrence, Julie Andrews; Richard Aldrich, Richard Crenna; Noel Coward, Daniel Massey; Sir Anthony Spencer, Michael Craig; Charles Fraser, Robert Reed; Arthur Lawrence, Bruce Forsyth; Jack Roper, John Collin; David Holtzman, Richard Karlan; Andre Charlot, Alan Oppenheimer; Rose, Beryl Reid; Billy Carleton, Lynley Laurence; Jack Buchanan, Garrett Lewis; Jeannie Banks, Elizabeth St. Clair; Pamela, Jenny Agutter; Ben Mitchell, Anthony Eisley; Alexander Woollcott, Jock Livingston; Dan, J. Pat O'Malley; Bert, Harvey Jason; Jerry Paul, Damian London; Cesare, Richard Angarola; Dorothy, Matilda Calnan; Lord Chamberlain, Lester Matthews.

2765 STAR SPANGLED GIRL. (Paramount-1971). Amy Cooper, Sandy Duncan; Andy Hobart, Tony Roberts; Norman Cornell, Todd Susman; Landlady, Elizabeth Allen.

2766 STARDUST. (Columbia-1974). Jim Maclaine, David Essex; Mike, Adam Faith; Porter Lee Austin, Larry Hagman; Danielle, Innes Des Longchamps; Jeanette, Rosalind Ayres; Colin Day, Marty Wilde; TV Interviewer, Edd Byrnes; J. D. Clover, Keith Moon; Alex, Dave Edmunds; Johnny, Paul Nicholas; Stevie, Karl Howman; Felix Hoffman, Rick Lee Parmentier; Kevin, Peter Duncan; Harrap, John Normington; Brian, James Hazeldine; Ralph Woods, Dave Daker; Keith Nolan, Anthony Naylor; Sally Potter, Charlotte Cornwall.

2767 START THE REVOLUTION WITHOUT ME. (Warner Bros.-1970). Claude/Philippe, Gene Wilder; Charles/Pierre, Donald Sutherland; King Louis, Hugh Griffith; Jacques, Jack MacGowran; Queen Marie, Billie Whitelaw; Duke d'Escargot, Victor Spinetti; Orson Welles, Helen Fraser, Ewa Aulin, Harry Fowler, Rosalind Knight, Murray Melvin, Ken Parry, Jacques Maury, Maxwell Shaw, Graham Stark, Barry Lowe, George A. Cooper, Michael Rothwell, Denise Coffey.

2768 STATE OF SIEGE. (Cinema 5-1973). Philip Michael Santore, Yves Montand; Captain Lopez, Renato Salvatori; Carlos Ducas, O. E. Hasse; Hugo, Jacques Weber; Este, Jean-Luc

Bideau; Mrs. Philip Santore, Evangeline Peterson; Minister of Internal Security, Maurice Teynac; Woman Senator, Yvette Etievant; Minister of Foreign Affairs, Harald Wolff; President of the Republic, Nemesio Antunes; Deputy Fabbri, Andre Falcon; Fontana, Mario Montilles; Lee, Jerry Brouer; Journalist, Jean-Francois Gobbi; Spokesman for Internal Security, Eugenio Guzman; Dean of Law Faculty, Maurice Jacquemont; Romero, Roberto Navarette; Student, Gloria Lass; Manuel, Alejandro Cohen; Alicia, Martha Contreras.

2769 THE STATUE. (Cinerama-1971). Alex, David Niven; Rhonda, Virna Lisi; Ray, Robert Vaughn; Pat, Ann Bell; Joachim, Mircha Carven; Harry, John Clees; Dunhill, Bettine Milne; Sanders, Derek Francis.

2770 STAVISKY. (Cinemation-1974). Alexandre Stavisky, Jean-Paul Belmondo; Arlette Stavisky, Anny Duperey; Baron Raoul, Charles Boyer; Borelli, François Perier; Montalvo, Roberto Bisaco; Dr. Mezy, Michel Lonsdale; Bonny, Claude Rich; Henriet, Gigi Balista.

2771 STAY AWAY, JOE. (MGM-1968). Joe Lightcloud, Elvis Presley; Charlie Lightcloud, Burgess Meredith; Glenda Callahan, Joan Blondell; Annie Lightcloud, Katy Jurado; Grandpa, Thomas Gomez; Hy Slager, Henry Jones; Bronc Hoverty, L. Q. Jones; Mamie Callahan, Quentin Dean; Mrs. Hawkins, Anne Seymour; Lorne Hawkins, Angus Duncan; Congressman Morrissey, Douglas Henderson; Frank Hawk, Michael Lane; Mary Lightcloud, Susan Trustman; Mike Bowers, Warren Vanders; Bull Shortgun, Buck Kartalian; Connie Shortgun, Maurishka; Marlene Standing Rattle, Caitlin Wyles.

2772 THE STEAGLE. (AVCO Embassy-1971). Harold, Richard Benjamin; Tall Guy, Chill Wills; Rita, Cloris Leachman.

2773 STEEL ARENA. (L-T-1973). Dusty Russell, Gene Drew, Buddy Love, Dutch Schnitzer, Bruce Mackey, Laura Brooks.

2774 STEELYARD BLUES. (Warner Bros.-1973). Iris, Jane Fonda; Veldini, Donald Sutherland; Eagle, Peter Boyle; Duval, Garry Goodrow; Frank, Howard Hesselman; The Kid, John Savage; Zoo Official, Richard Schaal; Black Man in Jail, Melvin Stewart; Police Captain, Morgan Upton; Fire Commissioner, Roger Bowen; Health Inspector, Howard Storm; Savage Rose, Jessica Myerson; Rocky, Dan Barrows; Pool Hall Waitress, Nancy Fish; Bar Waitress, Lynn Bernay; Rookie Cop, Edward Greenberg.

2775 STEFANIA. (Chancellor-1968). Stefania, Zoe Laskari; George, Spyros Fokas; Stefania's Stepfather, Viron Pallis; Armagos, Spyros Kalagyrou; Directress, Tasso Kavadia.

2776 THE STEPMOTHER. (Crown International-1972). Frank

Delgado, Alejandro Rey; Inspector Darnezi, John Anderson; Margo Delgado, Katherine Justice; Dick Hill, Larry Linville; Sonja Hill, Marlene Schmidt; Police Chief, Duncan Macleod; Nude, Claudia Jennings; Petro, David Renard; Steve Delgado, Rudy Jerrera Jr.; Petro's Girlfriend, Priscilla Garcia; Housekeeper, Margarite Garcia.

2777 STEPPENWOLF. (Peter J. Sprague-1974). Harry, Max von Sydow; Hermine, Dominique Sanda; Pablo, Pierre Clementi; Maria, Carla Romanelli; Aztec, Roy Bosier; Goethe, Alfred Baillou; Gustav, Niels-Peter Rudolph; Franz, Helmut Furnbacher; Loering, Charles Regnier; Mr. Hefte, Eduard Linkers; Dora, Sylvia Reize.

2778 THE STERILE CUCKOO. (Paramount-1969). Mary Anne (Pookie) Adams, Lisa Minnelli; Jerry Payne, Wendell Burton; Charlie Schumaker, Tim McIntire; Landlady, Elizabeth Harrower; Pookie's Father, Austin Green; Nancy Putnam, Sandra Faison; Roe, Chris Bugbee; Helen Upshaw, Jawn McKinley; Fred M. Lerner, A. Frederick Gooseen.

2779 THE STEWARDESSES. (Sherpix-1970). Samantha, Christina Hart; Tina, Paula Erikson; Jo, Angelique De Moline; Colin, Michael Garrett; Capt., William Basil; Cappy, Jerry Litvanoff; Kathy, Kathy Ferrick; Wendy, Janet Wass; Donna Stanley, Patricia Fein, Beth Shields, Monica Gayle, Robert Keller, Andy Roth, John Barcado, Gordon White, Barry Shoenborn, Alicia Taggart.

2780 STICKS AND STONES. (Filmteam-1970). Peter, Craig Dudley; Buddy, J. Will Deane; Jimmy, Jimmy Foster; Guru, Robert Case; Danny, Danny Landau; Lou, Maureen Sadusk; Irving, Wyn Shaw; June, Kim Pope; Bobby, Robert Nero; Feranando, Fernando Ascencio; George, Gene Edwards; Gary, Gary Bennet.

2781 STIGMA. (Cinerama-1972). Dr. Calvin Crosse, Philip M. Thomas; Bill Waco, Harlan Cary Poe; D. D. Whitehead, Josie Johnson; Sheriff Whitehead, Peter H. Clune; Jeremy, William Magerman; Tassie, Connie Van Ess; Himself, "Cousin" Bruce Morrow; Joe, Richard Geisman; "B" Girl, Raina Barrett; Homosexual, Carter Courtney; Rhoda, Rhonda Fuller; Kathleen, Kathy Joyce; Jeanie, Jean Parker; Choir Leader, Edwin Mills; Ed, Jim Grace.

2782 STILETTO. (AVCO Embassy-1969). Count Cesare Cardinali, Alex Cord; Illeana, Britt Ekland; George Baker, Patrick O'Neal; Emilio Matteo, Joseph Wiseman; Ahn Dessje, Barbara McNair; Frank Simpson, John Dehner; Tonio, Titos Vandis; Don Andrea, Eduardo Ciannelli; Bennett, Roy Scheider; Hannibal Smith, Lincoln Kilpatrick; Mann, Louis Elias; Macy, Luke Andreas; Franchini, Dominic Barto; Edwards, James Tolka; Rosa, Amaru; Blonde at Casino, Michaelina Marten.

2783 THE STING. (Universal-1973). Henry Gondorff, Paul Newman; Johnny Hooker, Robert Redford; Doyle Lonnegan, Robert Shaw; Lt. Snyder, Charles Durning; Singleton, Ray Walston; Billie, Eileen Brennan; Kid Twist, Harold Gould; Niles, John Heffernan; FBI Agent, Dana Elcar; Erie Kid, Jack Kohoe; Loretta, Dimitra Arliss.

2784 STING OF DEATH. (Thunderbird International-1967). John Hoyt, Joe Morrison; Karen Richardson, Valerie Hawkins; Egon, John Vella; Dr. Richardson, Jack Nagle; Louise, Sandy Lee Kane; Jessica, Deanna Lund; First Girl, Barbara Paridon; Donna, Lois Etelman; Ruth, Judy Lee; Susan, Blanche Devreaux; The Monster, Doug Hobart; Sheriff, Robert Stanton; First Boy, Tony Gulliver; 2nd Boy, Ron Pinchbeck; 3rd Boy, John Castle; Singer, Neil Sedaka.

2785 STOLEN KISSES. (Lopert-1969). Antoine Doinel, Jean-Pierre Leaud; Fabienne Tabard, Delphine Seyrig; Monsieur Tabard, Michel Lonsdale; Christine Darbon, Claude Jade; Monsieur Henri, Harry Max; Monsieur Darbon, Daniel Ceccaldi; Madame Darbon, Claire Duhamel; Catherine, Catherine Lutz; Monsieur Vidal, Andre Falcon; Julien, Paul Pavel; The Stranger, Serge Rousseau.

2786 THE STONE KILLER. (Columbia-1973). Torrey, Charles Bronson; Vescari, Martin Balsam; Lorenz, David Sheiner; Daniels, Norman Fell; Mathews, Ralph Waite; Armitage, Eddie Firestone; J. D., Walter Burke; Lipper, David Moody; Psychiatrist, Charles Tyner; Langley, Paul Koslo; Lawrence, Stuart Margolin; Hart, John Ritter; Police Chief, Byron Morrow; Jumper, Jack Colvin.

2787 THE STOOLIE. (Jama-1972). Roger, Jackie Mason; Sheila, Marcia Jean Kurtz; Alex, Dan Frazer; Marco, Richard Carballo; Police Chief, Gigi Gaus; Gas Station Proprietor, William McCutcheon; Nightclub Singer, Anne Marie; Sheriff, Burt Harris; Cousin Ralphie, Jerome Rudolph; Josip Elic, Reid Cruikshank, Leonard York.

2788 STOP THE WORLD--I WANT TO GET OFF. (Warner Bros.-1966). Littlechap, Tony Tanner; Evie/Anya/Ara/Ginnie, Millicent Martin; Susan, Leila Croft; Jane, Valerie Croft; Little Littlechap, Neil Hawley; Georgina Allan, Natasha Ashton, Carlotta Barlow, Sandra Burville, Christy Carroll, Vivyen Dunbar, Margaret Frost, Liz Gold.

2789 THE STORY OF A THREE DAY PASS. (Sigma III-1968). Turner, Harry Baird; Miriam, Nicole Berger; Hotelman, Christian Marin; Peasant, Pierre Doris.

2790 STORY OF A WOMAN. (Universal-1970). Karin, Bibi Andersson; David, Robert Stack; Bruno, James Farentino; Liliana, Annie Girardot; Woman, Didi Perego; Prof. Ferrara,

Mario Nascimbene.

2791 STRANDED. (Compton-1965). Juleen Compton, Gary Collins, Gian Pietro Calasso, Alkis Yanakis.

2792 THE STRANGE AFFAIR. (Paramount-1968). Peter Strange, Michael York; Det. Sgt. Pierce, Jeremy Kemp; Fredericka, Susan George; Daddy Quince, Jack Watson; Supt. Kingley, George A. Cooper; Inspector Evans, Arturo Morris; Charley Small, Barry Fantoni; Defense Attorney, Nigel Davenport; Aunt Mary, Madge Ryan.

2793 STRANGE BEDFELLOWS. (Universal-1965). Carter Harrison, Rock Hudson; Toni Vincente, Gina Lollobrigida; Richard Bramwell, Gig Young; Harry Jones, Edward Judd; Assistant Mortician, Terry-Thomas; Carter's Taxi Driver, Arthur Haynes; J. L. Stevens, Howard St. John; Aggressive Woman, Nancy Kulp; Toni's Taxi Driver, David King; Mavis, Peggy Rea; Petracini, Joseph Sirola; Jolly Woman, Lucy Landau; Policeman, Bernard Fox; Mrs. Stevens, Edith Atwater.

2794 THE STRANGE EXORCISM OF LYNN HART. (Classic Films-1974). Marc Lawrence, Jesse Vint, Paul Hickey, Jim Antonio, Toni Lawrence, Katherine Ross, Iris Korn, Walter Barnes, Eric Holland, William Michael, Bone Adams, Larry Hussman, Don Skylar.

2795 THE STRANGE VENGEANCE OF ROSALIE. (20th Century-Fox-1972). Rosalie, Bonnie Bedelia; Virgil, Ken Howard; Fry, Anthony Zerbe.

2796 THE STRANGER. (Paramount-1967). Arthur Meursault, Marcello Mastroianni; Marie Cardona, Anna Karina; Lawyer, Bernard Blier; Examining Magistrate, Georges Wilson; Priest, Bruno Cremer; Judge, Pierre Bertin; Director of Home, Jacques Herlin.

2797 A STRANGER IN TOWN. (MGM-1968). The Stranger, Tony Anthony; Aguila, Frank Wolff; Cica, Yolanda Modio; Maruka, Gia Sandri.

2798 A STRANGER KNOCKS. (Trans-Lux-1965). The Woman, Birgitte Federspiel; The Stranger, Preben Lerdorff Rye; Man From Village, Victor Montell.

2799 THE STRANGER RETURNS. (MGM-1968). The Stranger, Tony Anthony; En Plein, Dan Vadis; Good Jim, Daniele Vargas; The Prophet, Marco Guglielmi; Caroline, Jill Banner.

2800 STRANGERS. (Aquarius-1972). Paul, Michael Simon; Andrea, Michele Simon; Chip, Quentin James; Buddy, Adam

Richards; Susan, Lisa Marie.

2801 STRATEGY OF TERROR. (Universal-1969). Lt. Matt Lacey, Hugh O'Brian; Karen Lownes, Barbara Rush; Mr. Harkin, Neil Hamilton; Jacques Serac, Frederick O'Neal; Wally Pitt, Willy Corry; Richard, Harry Townes; John, Jan Merlin; Tippo, Eric Morris; Victor Prelling, Mort Mills; Mrs. Sallett, Jocelyn Brando; David Lewis, Jeff Cooper, Leonard Stone, Val Avery, Byron Morrow, Seven Hugo Borg, Norman Palmer, Clark Howat, Gil Stuart, Steve London, Tom Gilleran.

2802 STRAW DOGS. (Cinerama-1972). David Sumner, Dustin Hoffman; Amy Sumner, Susan George; Tom Hedden, Peter Vaughan; Major Scott, T. P. McKenna; Charlie Venner, Del Henney; Scutt, Ken Hutchison; Reverend Hood, Colin Welland; Cawsey, Jim Norton; Janice, Sally Thomsett; Riddaway, Donald Webster; Bobby Hedden, Len Jones; Bertie Hedden, Michael Mundell; John Niles, Peter Arne; Harry Ware, Robert Keegan; Mrs. Hedden, June Brown; Emma Hedden, Chloe Franks; Mrs. Hood, Cherina Mann; Henry Niles, David Warner.

2803 THE STRAWBERRY STATEMENT. (MGM-1970). Simon, Bruce Davison; Linda, Kim Darby; Coxswain, Bud Cort; George, Murray MacLeod; Coach, Tom Foral; Organizer Elliott, Bob Balaban; Swatch, Michael Margotta; Dr. Benton, Israel Horovitz; Chairman, James Kunen; Clipboard Girl, Jeannie Berlin; Telephone Girl, Carol Bagdasarian; Students, Jon Hill, Jess Walton, Andrew Parks; Filing Room Girl, Kristin Van Buren; Lucas, Booker Bradshaw; Tim, Drew Eshelman.

2804 STREET GANGS OF HONK KONG. (Cinerama-1974). Shen Chang, Wang Chung; Huang Lan, Lili Li; Teng Fen-Ni, Betty Pei Ti; Shen Chang's Father, Lu Ti; Lan Chen Chuan, Tung Lin; Ta Hsiung, Fan Mei Sheng.

2805 THE STREET IS MY BEAT. (Emerson-1966). Della Martinson, Shary Marshall; Phil Demarest, Todd Lasswell; Mr. Martinson, John Harmon; Mrs. Martinson, Ann MacAdams; Johnny Gibson, Tom Irish.

2806 THE STUD FARM. (McAbee-1969). Gary, Gary Yuma; Wayne, Wayne Douglas; Sam, Paul Daniels; Clarence, Joe Dante; House Manager, Ken Craig; Sheldon, Jac Zacha.

2807 THE STUDENT TEACHERS. (New World-1973). Susan Damante, Brooke Mills, Brenda Sutton, Nora Heflin, Dick Miller, John Kramer, James Millhollin, Johnny Ray McGhee, Rich Duran, Douglas D. Anderson, Bob Harris, Charles Dierkop, Jac Emel, Tom Mohler.

2808 A STUDY IN TERROR. (Columbia-1966). Sherlock Holmes, John Neville; Doctor Watson, Donald Houston; Lord Carfax, John Fraser; Doctor Murray, Anthony Quayle; Mycroft Holmes, Robert Morley; Annie Chapman, Barbara Windsor; Angela, Adrienne Corri; Inspector Lestrade, Frank Finlay; Sally, Judi Dench; Prime Minister, Cecil Parker; Singer, Georgia Brown; Duke of Shires, Barry Jones.

2809 SUB ROSA RISING. (Sherpix-1971). Narrator, Allan Jones.

2810 THE SUBJECT WAS ROSES. (MGM-1968). Nettie Cleary, Patricia Neal; John Cleary, Jack Albertson; Timmy Cleary, Martin Sheen; Nightclub M. C., Don Saxon; Woman, Elaine Williams; Man in Restaurant, Grant Gordon.

2811 SUBMARINE X-1. (United Artists-1969). Lt. Cdr. John Bolton, James Caan; Vice Admiral Redmayne, Rupert Davies; Lt. Davies, David Sumner; Lt. Gogan, William Dysart; Sub Lt. Pennington, Norman Bowler; C. P. O. Barquist, Brian Grellis; Leading Seaman Quentin, Paul Young; Sub Lt. Willis, John Kelland; C. P. O. Knowles, Kenneth Farrington; Redmayne's Flag Officer, George Roubicek; Sub Lt., Keith Alexander.

2812 SUBTERFUGE. (Commonwealth United-1969). Donovan, Gene Barry; Anne, Joan Collins; Redmayne, Richard Todd; Langley, Tom Adams; Donetta, Suzanna Leigh; Goldsmith, Michael Rennie; Shevik, Marius Goring; Pannell, Scott Forbes; Kitteridge, Colin Gordon.

2813 SUBURBAN ROULETTE. (Argent-1968). Ilene Fisher, Elizabeth Wilkinson; Ron Elston, Ben Moore; Ione Rolnick, Tony McCabe, Vickie Miles, Thomas Wood.

2814 SUBURBAN WIVES. (Scotia International-1973). Sara, Eva Whishaw; Irene, Maggie Wright; John, Peter May; His Boss, Barry Linehan; Jean, Nicola Austine; Sheila, Claire Gordon; Bookmaker, James Donnelly; Kathy, Heather Chasen; Her Husband, Dennis Hawthorne; Secretary, Gabrielle Drake; Yokki, Yokki Rhodes; Instructor, Ian Sinclair; Carole, Jane Cardew; Photographer, Robin Culver; Mavis, Pauline Pearl; Sara's Husband, Richard Thrope; Husband's Friend, Brian Miller; Jill, Sidonie Bond; Her Husband, Timothy Parkes; Helen, Mia Martin.

2815 SUBURBIA CONFIDENTIAL. (Cambist-1966). George Cooper, John Andrews, James Jeans, John Bealy, Eastman Price, Lou Ojena, Mark Crowe, Elena Clayton, Barbara Corey, Phil Brian, Don Jones, Didi Seider, Brandi, Lolita Williams, Jade Green.

2816 IL SUCCESSO. (Embassy-1965). Giulio Ceriani, Vittorio Gassman; Laura Ceriani, Anouk Aimee; Sergio, Jean-Louis

Trintignant; Grassi, Leopoldo Trieste; The Maid, Cristina Gajoni; The Fascist-Capitalist, Umberto D'Orsi; Giulio's Father, Filippo Scelzo; Giulio's Brother In Law, Gastone Moschin; Diana, Grazia Maria Spina.

2817 SUCCUBUS. (Trans American-1969). Lorna, Janine Reynaud; Bill Mulligan, Jack Taylor; Kapp, Howard Vernon; Pierce, Michel Lemoine.

2818 SUCH A GORGEOUS KID LIKE ME. (Columbia-1973). Camille, Bernadette Lafont; Murene, Claude Brasseur; Arthur, Charles Denner; Sam, Guy Marchand; Stanislas, Andre Dussollier; Clovis, Philippe Leotard; Helene, Anne Kreis; Isobel, Gilbert Geniat; Florence, Daniel Girard.

2819 SUCH GOOD FRIENDS. (Paramount-1971). Julie Messinger, Dyan Cannon; Dr. Timmy Spector, James Coco; Miranda Graham, Jennifer O'Neill; Cal Whiting, Ken Howard; Mrs. Wallman, Nina Foch; Richard Messinger, Laurence Luckinbill.

2820 THE SUCKER. (Royal-1967). Antoine Marechal, Bourvil; Leopold Saroyan, Louis De Funes; La Souris, Walter Chiari; Stutterer, Venantino Venantini; Ursula, Beba Loncar; Gina, Daniella Rocca; Lino, Lando Buzzanca; Maurel, Jose-Luis de Villalonga.

2821 SUDDEN TERROR. (National General-1971). Ziggy, Mark Lester; Colonel, Lionel Jeffries; Pippa, Susan George; Tom, Tony Bonner; Galleria, Jeremy Kemp; Paul, Peter Vaughan; Victor, Peter Bowles.

2822 SUDDENLY, A WOMAN! (PMK-1968). Gudrun, Laila Andersson; Manne, Jorgen Buckhoj; Mr. Hollund, Poul Reichardt; Mr. Rossen, Nils Asther; Mrs. Brunn, Brigitte Federspiel; Mrs. Hollund, Elsa Kourani; Office Girl, Yvonne Ingdal; Dancer, Constance.

2823 SUGAR COOKIES. (General Film-1973). Max, George Shannon; Camilla, Mary Woronov; Alta-Julie, Lynn Lowry; Helene, Monique Van Vooren; Dola, Maureen Byrnes; Gus, Daniel Sadur; Roderick, Ondine; Secretary, Jennifer Welles; Oliver, Anthony Pompei; Det. Schwartz, Reid Cruickshanks; Det. Joe, Thomas Mahony.

2824 SUGAR HILL. (American International-1974). Marki Bey, Robert Quarry, Don Pedro Colley, Richard Lawson, Betty Anne Rees, Zara Culley, Larry D. Johnson, Charles Robinson, Rick Hagood.

2825 THE SUGARLAND EXPRESS. (Universal-1974). Lou Jean Poplin, Goldie Hawn; Captain Tanner, Ben Johnson; Officer Slide, Michael Sacks; Clovis Poplin, William Atherton;

Officer Mashburn, Gregory Walcott; Baby Langston, Harrison Zanuck.

2826 SULLIVAN'S EMPIRE. (Universal-1967). John Sullivan Jr., Martin Milner; Patrick Sullivan, Linden Chiles; Kevin Sullivan, Don Quine; Juan Clemente, Clu Gulager; John Sullivan Sr., Arch Johnson; Doris Wheeler, Karen Jensen; Amando, Bernie Hamilton; Rudi Andujar, Lee Bergere; Inspector Huante, Than Wyenn; Miss Wingate, Jeanette Nolan; Driver, Miguel De Anda; Clerk, Ken Renard; 2nd Girl, Marianne Gordon; 3rd Girl, Eileen Wesson; Boy, Mark Miranda; Carlos, Ruben Moreno; Ramona, Nadine Nardi; Chico, Robert De Coy; Bartender, Pepe Callahan; Pilot, Peter Pascal; Sergio Mendes and Brazil '66.

2827 SUMMER OF '42. (Warner Bros.-1971). Dorothy, Jennifer O'Neill; Hermie, Gary Grimes; Oscy, Jerry Houser; Benjie, Oliver Conant; Aggie, Katherine Allentuck; Miriam, Christopher Norris; Druggist, Lou Frizzell.

2828 SUMMER RUN. (Lighthouse-1974). Harry Ross, Andy Parks; Kristina, Tina Lund; Felix Zipper, Dennis Redfield; Sam, Gail Joy; Debbie, Judith Nugent; Juliet, Juliet Berto; Leon Capetanos, Froda Rassmussen, John Broderick, Phyllis Altenhaus.

2829 SUMMER WISHES, WINTER DREAMS. (Columbia-1973). Rita Walden, Joanne Woodward; Harry Walden, Martin Balsam; Mrs. Pritchett, Sylvia Sidney; Anna, Dori Brenner; Fred Goody, Win Forman; Betty Goody, Tresa Hughes; Joel, Peter Marklin; Bobby Walden, Ron Rickards; Waitress, Charlotte Oberley; Mrs. Bimberg, Minerva Pious; Grandmother, Helen Ludlam; Grandfather, Grant Code; Mr. Goldblatt, Sol Frieder; Student in Theatre, Gaetano Lisi; Mrs. Pat Hungerford, Nancy Andrews; Carl Hurlbutt, Lee Jackson; Chauffeur, David Thomas; Nurse, Marian Swan; Dancer in Dream, Dennis Wayne.

2830 SUMMERTIME KILLER. (AVCO Embassy-1973). Kiley, Karl Malden; Ray, Christopher Mitchum; Tonia, Olivia Hussey; Lazaro, Raf Vallone; Michele, Claudine Auger.

2831 SUMMERTREE. (Columbia-1971). Jerry, Michael Douglas; Herb, Jack Warden; Vanetta, Brenda Vaccaro; Ruth, Barbara Bel Geddes; Marvis, Kirk Callaway; Tony, Bill Vint; Bennie, Jeff Siggens; Don, Rob Reiner; Draft Lawyer, William Smith; Ginsberg, Garry Goodrow; Shelly, Dennis Clark Fimple; Girl in Dorm, June Fairchild; Man in Conservatory, Richard Stahl.

2832 SUNDAY BLOODY SUNDAY. (United Artists-1971). Alex Greville, Glenda Jackson; Dr. Daniel Hirsh, Peter Finch; Bob Elkin, Murray Head; Mrs. Greville, Peggy Ashcroft;

Mr. Harding, Tony Britton; Mr. Greville, Maurice Denham; Answering Service, Bessie Love; Alva Hodson, Vivian Pickles.

2833 SUNFLOWER. (AVCO Embassy-1970). Giovanna, Sophia Loren; Antonio, Marcello Mastroianni; Mascia, Ludmilla Savelyeva; Soviet Woman Official, Galina Andreeva; Antonio's Mother, Anna Carena; Giovanna's Second Husband, Germano Longo; Woman in Sunflower Field, Nadia Cerednichenko; Returning Veteran, Glauco Onorato; Russian-Italian Worker, Silvano Tranquilli; Prostitute, Marisa Traversi; Russian Ministry Official, Gunar Zilinkski; Giovanna's Baby, Carlo Ponti Jr.

2834 SUNSCORCHED. (Feature Film Corporation of America-1968). Sheriff Jess Kinley, Mark Stevens; Abel Dragna, Mario Adorf; Anna-Lisa, Marianne Koch; Luke, Frank Oliveras; Charlie, Antonio Iranzo; Oscar Pellicer, Vivian Dodds, Julio Pena, Albert Bessler, Mario Via, Jesus Puche, Luis Rivera, Felipe Pena.

2835 THE SUPER COPS. (United Artists-1974). Ron Leibman, David Selby, Sheila E. Frazier, Pat Hingle, Dan Frazer, Joseph Sirola, Arny Freeman, Bernard Kates, Alex Colon, Charles Turner, Ralph Wilcox, Al Fann, David Greenberg, Robert Hantz, Norman Bush, Arthur French, Tamu, Hector Troy, Charles White, Ralph Strait, Joseph P. McCartney, Pat Corley, Albert Henderson, Barton Heyman.

2836 SUPER FLY. (Warner Bros.-1972). Youngblood Priest, Ron O'Neal; Eddie, Carl Lee; Georgia, Sheila Frazier; Scatter, Julius W. Harris; Fat Freddie, Charles McGregor; Dealer, Nate Adams; Cynthia, Polly Niles.

2837 SUPER FLY T.N.T. (Paramount-1973). Priest, Ron O'Neal; Dr. Lamine Sonko, Roscoe Lee Browne; Georgia, Sheila Frazier; Jordan Gaines, Robert Guillaume; Matty Smity, Jacques Sernas; Lefevre, William Berger; Customs Man, Roy Bosler; George, Silvio Nardo; Lisa, Olga Bisera; Rik, Rik Boyd; Rand, Dominic Barto; General, Minister Dem; Riding Instructress, Jeannie McNeill; Pilot, Dan Davis; Crew Chief, Luigi Orso; Photographer, Ennio Catalfamo; Warehouse Custodian, Francesco Rachini.

2838 SUPERBEAST. (United Artists-1972). Alix, Antoinette Bower; Bill, Craig Littler; Stewart, Harry Lauter; Diaz, Vic Diaz; Vigo, Jose Romulo; Cleaver, John Garwood; Dr. Rojas, Manny Oheda.

2839 SUPERCHICK. (Crown International-1973). Joyce Jillson, Louis Quinn, Tony Young, Thomas Reardon, Timothy Wayne Brown.

2840 SUPERDAD. (Buena Vista-1974). Charlie McCready, Bob Crane; Sue McCready, Barbara Rush; Bart, Kurt Russell; Cyrus Hershberger, Joe Flynn; Wendy McCready, Kathleen Cody; Stanley, B. Kirby Jr.; Klutch, Joby Baker; Ira Hershaw, Dick Van Patten; Judith Lowry, Ivor Francis, Jonathan Daly, Naomi Stevens, Nicholas Hammond, Jack Manning, Jim Wakefield, Ed McCready, Larry Gelman, Steve Dunne, Allison McKay, Leon Belasco, Sarah Fankboner.

2841 SUPPORT YOUR LOCAL GUNFIGHTER. (United Artists-1971). Latigo Smith, James Garner; Patience Barton, Suzanne Pleshette; Jug Mag, Jack Elam; Jenny, Joan Blondell; Taylor Barton, Harry Morgan; Goldie, Marie Windsor; Ez, Henry Jones; Colonel Ames, John Dehner; Swifty Morgan, Chuck Connors.

2842 SUPPORT YOUR LOCAL SHERIFF. (United Artists-1969). Jason McCullough, James Garner; Prudy Perkins, Joan Hackett; Pa Danby, Walter Brennan; Mayor Olly Perkins, Harry Morgan; Jake, Jack Elam; Joe Danby, Bruce Dern; Preacher Henry Jackson, Henry Jones; Fred Johnson, Walter Burke; Luke Danby, Dick Peabody; Tom Danby, Gene Evans; Thomas Devry, Willis Bouchey; Mrs. Danvers, Kathleen Freeman; Bar Girl, Gayle Rogers; Gunfighter, Richard Hoyt; Bordello Girl, Marilyn Jones.

2843 SUPPOSE THEY GAVE A WAR AND NOBODY CAME? (Cinerama-1970). Shannon Gambroni, Tony Curtis; Nace, Brian Keith; Sheriff, Ernest Borgnine; Ramona, Suzanne Pleshette; Sgt. Jones, Ivan Dixon; Billy Joe Davis, Tom Ewell; Capt. Myerson, Bradford Dillman; Mr. Kruft, Arthur O'Connell; Major Purvis, John Fiedler; Colonel Flanders, Don Ameche; Bob Emhardt, Maxine Stuart, Christopher Mitchum, Pamela Britton, Grady Sutton, Clifford Norton, Jeanne Bates, Eddie Firestone, William Bramley, Sam G. Edwards, Buck Young, Paul E. Sorensen, David Cass, John Lasell, Dorothy Green, Pamela Branch, Janet E. Clark, Jean Argyle, Monty Margetts, Paula Stewart, Carolyn Williamson, Stanley W. Barrett, John James Bannon, Vincent Howard.

2844 THE SWAPPERS. (Trans American-1970). Paul, James Donnelly; Leonard, Larry Taylor; Ellen, Valerie St. John; Cliff, Dennis Hawthorne; Sheila, Bunty Garland; Carol, Sandra Satchwith; Marion, Fiona Fraser; Jean, Joan Hayward.

2845 SWEDISH WEDDING NIGHT. (Royal-1965). Hilmer Westlund, Jarl Kulle; Siri Westlund, Lena Hansson; Hildur Palm, Christina Schollin; Victor Palm, Edvin Adolphson; Irma Palm, Catrin Westerlund; Hilma Palm, Isa Quensel; Rudolph Palm, Tor Isedal.

2846 THE SWEET BODY OF DEBORAH. (Warner Bros.-7 Arts-1969). Deborah, Carroll Baker; Marcel, Jean Sorel; Robert, George Hilton; Susan, Evelyn Stewart; Philip, Luigi Pistilli; Police Commissioner, Michel Bardinet; Telephone Man, Renato Montalbano; Telephone Clerk, Mirella Panfili; Doctor, Domenico Ravenna.

2847 SWEET CHARITY. (Universal-1969). Charity Hope Valentine, Shirley MacLaine; Vittorio Vitale, Ricardo Montalban; Nickie, Chita Rivera; Big Daddy, Sammy Davis Jr.; Oscar Lindquist, John McMartin; Helene, Paula Kelly; Ursula, Barbara Bouchet; Herman, Stubby Kaye; Mr. Nicholsby, Alan Hewitt; Charlie, Dante D'Paulo; Dancer-Rhythm of Life, John Wheeler; Man in Fandango Ballroom, John Craig; Woman on Tandem, Dee Carroll; Man on Tandem, Tom Hatten; Young Woman on Bridge, Sharon Harvey; Young Man on Bridge, Charles Brewer; Maitre D', Richard Angarola; First Cop, Henry Beckman; 2nd Cop, Jeff Burton.

2848 SWEET GEORGIA. (Box Office International-1972). Georgia, Marsha Jordan; Virginia, Barbara Mills; Big T, Gene Drew; Cal, Chuck Lawson; Leroy, Bill King Jr.; Jack, Al Wilkins.

2849 SWEET JESUS, PREACHER MAN. (MGM-1973). Holmes Lee, Roger E. Mosley; Martelli, William Smith; Sills, Michael Pataki; Eddie, Tom Johnigarn; Joey, Joe Tornatore; Sweetstick, Damu King; Beverly, Marla Gibbs; Deacon, Sam Laws; George, Phil Hoover; Roy, Paul Silliman; Detroit Charlie, Chuck Lyles.

2850 SWEET LIGHT IN A DARK ROOM. (Promenade-1966). Hana, Dana Smutna; Pavel, Ivan Mistrik; Mother, Jirina Sejbalova; Grandfather, Frantisek Smolik; Mlle. Kubiasova, Blanka Bohdanova; Votja, Jiri Kodet; Alena, Eva Mrazova.

2851 SWEET LOVE, BITTER. (Film 2 Associates-1967). Richie "Eagle" Stokes, Dick Gregory; David Hillary, Don Murray; Della, Diane Varsi; Keel Robinson, Robert Hooks; Candy, Jeri Archer; Girl in Bar, Barbara Davis.

2852 SWEET NOVEMBER. (Warner Bros.-7 Arts-1968). Sara Deever, Sandy Dennis; Charlie Blake, Anthony Newley; Alonzo, Theodore Bikel; Clem Batchman, Burr De Benning; Richard, Sandy Baron; Carol, Marj Dusay; Gordon, Martin West; Mrs. Schumacher, Virginia Vincent; Digby, King Moody; Sam Naylor, Robert Gibbons.

2853 THE SWEET RIDE. (20th Century-Fox-1968). Collie Ransom, Tony Franciosa; Denny McGuire, Michael Sarrazin; Vickie Cartwright, Jacqueline Bisset; Choo-Choo Burns, Bob Denver; Mr. Cartwright, Michael Wilding; Thumper, Michele Carey; Martha, Lara Lindsay; Lt. Atkins, Percy Rodriguez; Mrs. Cartwright, Norma Crane; Brady Caswell, Warren

Stevens; Texan, Pat Buttram; Barry Green, Michael Forest; Parker, Lloyd Gough; Big Jane, Stacy King; Tennis Girl, Corinna Tsopei; Mr. Clean, Charles Dierkop; Psychiatrist, Arthur Franz; Surfer/Cyclist, Seymour Cassel; Sgt. Solomon, Paul Condylis; Scratch, Ralph Lee; Diablo, Lou Procopio; Linda Gamble and Sam Chew Jr.

2854 SWEET SAVIOUR. (Trans World-1971). Moon, Troy Donahue; Sandra, Renay Granville; Faith, Francine Middleton; Ruth, Talie Cochrane; Bull, Matt Greene; Fritzi, Tobi Marsh; Maggie, Lee Terri; Carol, Joie Addison; Chris, Mark Curran; Folk Singer, Alan Waters; Pretzel Man, Perry Gewirtz; Elsa, Joy Campbell; Maggie's Friend, Michelle Norris.

2855 SWEET SKIN. (Times Film Corporation-1966). Krista Nico, Darry Cowl, Jean Tissier, Renee Passeur, Dany Saval, Jean Sobieski, Umberto Orsini, Alice Cocea.

2856 SWEET SUGAR. (Dimension-1973). Phyllis Davis, Timothy Brown, Pam Collins, Angus Duncan, Ella Edwards, Jackie Giroux, Cliff Osmond, Albert Cole, Jim Houghton, Daryl Severns, James Whitworth.

2857 SWEET SUZY. (Signal 166-1973). Susan, Anouska Hempel; Walker, David Warbeck; Overseer, Percy Herbert; Joshua, Milton McCollin; Isaiah, Thomas Baptiste; Daladier, Bernard Boston; Slave, Vikki Richards; Walker's Brother, Dave Prowse.

2858 SWEET SWEETBACK'S BAADASSSSS SONG. (Cinemation-1971). The Black Community, Simon Chuckster, John Dullaghan, Hubert Scales, West Gale, Niva Rochelle, Rhetta Hughes, Nick Ferrari, Ed Rue, Johnny Amos, Lavelle Roby.

2859 THE SWIMMER. (Columbia-1968). Ned Merrill, Burt Lancaster; Shirley Abbott, Janice Rule; Julianne Hooper, Janet Landgard; Donald Westerhazy, Tony Bickley; Muffie, Alva Celauro; Peggy Forsburgh, Marge Champion; Mrs. Halloran, Nancy Cushman; Matron at Biswangers' Pool, Lisa Daniels; Howard Graham, Charles Drake; Howie Hunsacker, Bill Fiore; Ticket Seller, John Garfield Jr.; Guest at the Bunkers Pool, John Gerstad; Sylvia Finney, Rose Gregorio; Chauffeur, Bernie Hamilton; Betty Graham, Kim Hunter; Mr. Halloran, House Jameson; Jack Finney, Jimmy Joyce; Kevin Gilmartin, Michael Kearney; Enid Bunker, Marilyn Langner; Bunkers' Party Guest, Ray Mason; Stu Forsburgh, Richard McMurray; Lillian Hunsacker, Jan Miner; Cynthia, Diana Muldaur; Vernon, Keri Oleson; Joan, Joan Rivers; Mrs. Hammar, Cornelia Otis Skinner; Henry Biswanger, Dolph Sweet; Grace Biswanger, Louise Troy; Helen Westerhazy, Diana Van Der Vlis.

2860 THE SWIMMING POOL. (AVCO Embassy-1970). Jean-Paul, Alain Delon; Marianne, Romy Schneider; Harry, Maurice Ronet; Penelope, Jane Birkin.

2861 THE SWINGER. (Paramount-1966). Kelly Olsson, Ann-Margret; Ric Colby, Tony Franciosa; Sir Hubert Charles, Robert Coote; Aunt Cora, Nydia Westman; Sergeant Hooker, Horace McMahon; Warren, Lance Le Gault; Mrs. Olsson, Mary La Roche; Mr. Olsson, Milton Frome; Karen Charles, Yvonne Romain; Sammy Jenkins, Craig Hill; Himself, Clete Roberts; Sally, Myrna Ross; Sir Hubert's Secretary, Corinne Cole; Police Captain, Bert Freed; Jack Happy, Romo Vincent.

2862 SWINGERS' PARADISE. (American International-1965). Johnnie, Cliff Richard; Lloyd Davis, Walter Slezak; Jenny, Susan Hampshire; Mood Musicians, Hank B. Marvin, Bruce Welch, Brian Bennett, John Rostill; Jerry, Melvyn Hayes; Edward, Richard O'Sullivan; Barbara, Una Stubbs; Miguel, Joseph Cuby; Douglas Leslie, Derek Bond; Senior Sheik, Scotsman, Harold, Gerald Harper.

2863 THE SWINGIN' STEWARDESSES. (Hemisphere-1972). Eveline Traeger, Kathrin Heberle, Raphael Britten, Ingrid Steeger, Margaret Siegel, Detlev Heyse, Bernd Wilcevsky.

2864 A SWINGIN' SUMMER. (United Screen Arts-1965). James Stacy, William Wellman Jr., Quinn O'Hara, Martin West, Mary Mitchell, Robert Blair, Raquel Welch, Allan Jones, Lili Kardell, Diane Bond, Diane Swanson, Irene Sale, Kathy Francis, Laurie Williams, The Righteous Brothers, The Rip Chords, Donnie Brooks, Gary Lewis and The Playboys, Jody Miller.

2865 THE SWINGING CHEERLEADERS. (Centaur-1974). Kate, Jo Johnston; Andrea, Rainbeaux Smith; Mary Ann, Colleen Camp; Lisa, Rosanne Katon; Buck, Ron Hajek; Prof. Thorpe, Jason Sommers; Ron, Ian Sander; Mr. Putnam, George Wallace; Coach Turner, Jack Denton; Belski, John Quade; Ryan, Bob Minor; Jessica Thorpe, Mae Mercer; Dion Lane, Hanke Rolike, Fred Schweiwiller, Jodi Carlson, Gary Schneider, Sandy Dempsey, Candy All.

2866 SWORD OF ALI BABA. (Universal-1965). Ali Baba, Peter Mann; Amara, Jocelyn Lane; Abou, Peter Whitney; Hulagu Khan, Gavin MacLeod; Prince Cassim, Frank Puglia; Pindar, Frank McGrath; Yusuf, Greg Morris; Baba, Frank De Kova; Captain of Guard, Morgan Woodward.

2867 THE SWORD OF DOOM. (Toho-1967). Ryunosuke Tsukue, Tatsuya Nakadai; Toranosuke Shimada, Toshiro Mifune; Hyoma Utsuki, Yuzo Kayama; Ohama, Michiyo Aratama.

2868 THE SWORD OF EL CID. (Eldorado-1965). Chantel Debert, Roland Carey, Sandro Moretti, Iliana Grimandi, Ray Myles, Jeff Russel.

2869 SWORD OF VENGEANCE. (Toho-1973). Tomisaburo Wakayama, Fumio Watanabe, Yunosuka Ito, Shigeru Tsuyuguchi, Tomoko Mayama.

2870 SWORDS OF DEATH. (Toho-1971). Musashi, Kinnosuke Nakamura; Baiken, Rentaro Mikuni; Wife, Hideko Okiyama.

2871 SYLVIA. (Paramount-1965). Sylvia West, Carroll Baker; Alan Macklin, George Maharis; Jane Phillips, Joanne Dru; Frederic Summers, Peter Lawford; Irma Olanski, Viveca Lindfors; Oscar Stewart, Edmond O'Brien; Jonas Karoki, Aldo Ray; Mrs. Argona, Ann Sothern; Bruce Stamford III, Lloyd Bochner; Lola Diamond, Paul Gilbert; Big Shirley, Nancy Kovack.

2872 SYMPATHY FOR THE DEVIL. (New Line Cinema-1970). Mick Jagger, Brian Jones, Keith Richard, Charlie Watts, Bill Wyman, Anne Wiazemski, Ian Quarrier, Frankie Dymon Jr.

2873 SYMPHONY FOR A MASSACRE. (7 Arts-1965). Paoli, Charles Vanel; Jabeke, Jean Rochefort; Valoti, Claude Dauphin; Clavet, Michel Auclair; Moreau, Jose Giovanni; Helene Valoti, Daniela Rocca; Madeleine Clavet, Michele Mercier.

2874 SYNANON. (Columbia-1965). Chuck Dederich, Edmond O'Brien; Ben, Chuck Connors; Joaney, Stella Stevens; Zankie Albo, Alex Cord; Reid, Richard Conte; Betty Coleman, Eartha Kitt; Mary, Barbara Luna; Chris, Alejandro Rey; Hopper, Richard Evans; Vince, Gregory Morton; Arline, Chanin Hale; Pruddy, Casey Townsend; Bob Adamic, Larry Kert; Pete, Bernie Hamilton; Joe Mann, Mark Sturges; The Greek, Lawrence Montaigne; Carla, Patricia Huston; Arnold Ross, John Peterson, James Middleton, Anthony Daddio, Candy Latson, Dan Spaccarelli, Herb Rosen, William Crawford, Charles Haden.

2875 T. R. BASKIN. (Paramount-1971). T.R., Candice Bergen; Jack, Peter Boyle; Larry, James Caan; Dayle, Marcia Rodd; Kathy, Erin O'Reilly.

2876 TAFFY AND THE JUNGLE HUNTER. (Allied Artists-1965). Jacques Bergerac, Manuel Padilla, Shary Marshall, Hari Rhodes, Taffy, Margo.

2877 THE TAKE. (Columbia-1974). Sneed, Billy Dee Williams; Chief Berrigan, Eddie Albert; Danny James, Frankie Avalon; Oscar, Sorrell Booke; Nancy, Tracy Reed; Dolek, Albert Salmi; Manso, Vic Morrow; Tallbear, A. Martinez;

Benedetto, James Luisi.

2878 TAKE A GIRL LIKE YOU. (Columbia-1970). Jenny, Hayley Mills; Patrick, Oliver Reed; Julian, Noel Harrison; Martha, Sheila Hancock; Dick, John Bird; Wendy, Aimi MacDonald; Graham, Ronald Lacey; Anna, Geraldine Sherman.

2879 TAKE IT ALL. (Lopert-1966). Johanne, Johanne; Claude, Claude Jutra; The Mother, Tania Fedor; Victor, Victor Desy; The Priest, Guy Hoffmann; Monique, Monique Joly; Barbara, Monique Mercure; Nicolas, Patrick Straram; An Actor, François Tasse.

2880 TAKE THE MONEY AND RUN. (Cinerama-1969). Virgil Starkwell, Woody Allen; Louise, Janet Margolin; Fritz, Marcel Hillaire; Miss Blaire, Jacquelyn Hyde; Jake, Lonny Chapman; Al, Jan Merlin; Chain Gang Warden, James Anderson; Fred, Howard Storm; Vince, Mark Gordon; Frank, Micil Murphy; Joe Agneta, Minnow Moskowitz; The Judge, Nate Jacobson; Farm House Lady, Grace Bauer; Mother Starkwell, Ethel Sokolow; Father Starkwell, Henry Leff; Psychiatrist, Don Frazier; Michael Sullivan, Mike O'Dowd; The Narrator, Jackson Beck.

2881 THE TAKING OF PELHAM ONE TWO THREE. (United Artists-1974). Lt. Garber, Walter Matthau; Blue, Robert Shaw; Green, Martin Balsam; Grey, Hector Elizondo; Brown, Earl Hindman; Mayor's Aide, Tony Roberts; Motorman, Denny Doyle; Dispatcher, Dick O'Neill; Mayor, Lee Wallace; Supervisor, Tom Pedi; Lt. Patrone, Jerry Stiller; Patrolman James, Nathan George; Commissioner, Rudy Bond; Borough Commander, Kenneth McMillan; Insp. Daniels, Julius Harris.

2882 TAKING OFF. (Universal-1971). Lynn Tyne, Lynn Carlin; Larry Tyne, Buck Henry; Jeannie Tyne, Linnea Heacock; Margot, Georgia Engel; Tony, Tony Harvey; Ann Lockston, Audra Lindley; Ben Lockston, Paul Benedict; Schiavelli, Vincent Schiavelli; Jamie, David Gittler.

2883 TALES FROM THE CRYPT. (Cinerama-1972). The Crypt Keeper, Ralph Richardson; Guide, Geoffrey Bayldon; Joanne Clayton, Joan Collins; Richard Clayton, Martin Boddney; Maniac, Oliver MacGreevy; Carol Clayton, Chloe Franks; Carl Maitland, Ian Hendry; Mrs. Maitland, Susan Denny; Susan, Angie Grant; Maitland's Son, Paul Clere; Maitland's Daughter, Sharon Clere; Tramp, Frank Forsyth; James Elliot, Robin Phillips; Grimsdyke, Peter Cushing; Edward Elliot, David Markham; Mr. Ramsay, Edward Evans; Mrs. Carter, Ann Sears; Mrs. Phelps, Irene Gawne; Mrs. Davies, Kay Adrian; Police Sgt., Clifford Earl; Vicar, Manning Wilson; Postman, Dan Caulfield; Mr. Baker, Robert Hutton;

Mrs. Carter's Daughter, Melinda Clancy; Mrs. Phelps' Son, Stafford Medhurst; Mrs. Davies' Son, Carlos Baker; Ralph Jason, Richard Greene; Charles Gregory, Roy Dotrice; Enid Jason, Barbara Murray; Pallbearer, Peter Thomas; Detective, Hedger Wallace; William Robers, Nigel Patrick; George Carter, Patrick Magee; Attendant, Tony Wall; Cook, Harry Locke.

2884 TALES THAT WITNESS MADNESS. (Paramount-1973). Nicholas, Jack Hawkins; Tremayne, Donald Pleasence; Mother, Georgia Brown; Father, Donald Houston; Paul, Russell Lewis; Tutor, David Wood; Ann/Beatrice, Suzy Kendall; Timothy, Peter McEnery; Moving Men, Richard Connaught, Neil Kennedy; Polly, Beth Morris; Uncle Albert, Frank Forsyth; Bella, Joan Collins; Brian, Michael Jayston; Auriol, Kim Novak; Kimo, Michael Petrovitch; Ginny, Mary Tamm; Vera, Lesley Nunnerley; Keoki, Leon Lissek; Malia, Zohra Segal.

2885 THE TALL BLOND MAN WITH ONE BLACK SHOE. (Cinema V-1973). Francois, Pierre Richard; Milan, Bernard Blier; Toulouse, Jean Rochefort; Christine, Mireille Darc; Maurice, Jean Carmet; Paulette, Colette Castel; Perrache, Paul Le Person; Botrel, Jean Obe; Georghiu, Robert Castel; M. Boudart, Robert Caccia; Poucet, Jean Saudray.

2886 THE TALL WOMEN. (Allied Artists-1967). Mary Ann, Anne Baxter; Ursula, Maria Perschy; Gus McIntosh, Gustavo Rojo; Katy, Rosella Como; Betty, Adriana Ambesi; Perla, Pearl Cristal; Dorothy, Maria Mahor; Bridgette, Christa Linder; Pope, Luis Prendes.

2887 THE TAMARIND SEED. (AVCO Embassy-1974). Judith Farrow, Julie Andrews; Feodor Sverdlov, Omar Sharif; Jack Loder, Anthony Quayle; Fergus Stephenson, Dan O'Herlihy; Margaret Stephenson, Sylvia Syms; General Golitsyn, Oscar Homolka; George MacLeod, Bryan Marshall; Richard Paterson, David Baron; Rachel Paterson, Celia Bannerman; Colonel Moreau, Roger Dann; Sandy Mitchell, Sharon Duce; Major Stukalov, George Mikell; Anna Skriabina, Kate O'Mara; Dimitri Memenov, Constantin de Goguel; KGB Agents, John Sullivan, Terence Plummer, Leslie Crawford; Igor Kalinin, Alexei Jawdokimov; Embassy Section Head, Janet Henfry.

2888 THE TAMING. (Times Film Corporation-1968). Tom Mannix, Lindsey Bowen; Rita, Liz Stevens; Barbra Forrest, Sharon Church; Marco, Sam Stewart.

2889 THE TAMING OF THE SHREW. (Columbia-1967). Katharina, Elizabeth Taylor; Petrucchio, Richard Burton; Grumio, Cyril Cusack; Baptista, Michael Hordern; Lucentio, Michael York; Bianca, Natasha Pyne; Tranio, Alfred Lynch; Gremio, Alan Webb; Hortensio, Victor Spinetti; Pedant, Vernon

Dobtcheff; Biondello, Roy Holder; Priest, Giancarlo Cobelli; Curtis, Gianni Magni; Nathaniel, Alberto Bonucci; Gregory, Lino Capolicchio; Philip, Roberto Antonelli; Vincentio, Mark Dignam; Haberdasher, Anthony Garner; Tailor, Ken Parry; Widow, Bice Valori.

2890 TAMMY AND THE MILLIONAIRE. (Universal-1967). Tammy, Debbie Watson; Uncle Lucius, Frank McGrath; Grandpa, Denver Pyle; Dwayne, Whitt, George Furth; John Brent, Donald Woods; Lavinia Tate, Dorothy Green; Peter Tate, David Macklin; Gloria Tate, Linda Marshall; Steven Brent, Jay Sheffield; Dewey M. McKinley, Teddy Quinn; Sybelline Tate, Bella Bruck; The Mailman, Andy Albin; Billy Joe Morgan, Craig Hundley; Governor Alden, Roy Roberts; Grundy Tate, Jeff York.

2891 TARGETS. (Paramount-1968). Byron Orlok, Boris Karloff; Bobby Thompson, Tim O'Kelly; Jenny, Nancy Hsueh; Robert Thompson Sr., James Brown; Kip Larkin, Sandy Baron; Ed Loughlin, Arthur Peterson; Charlotte Thompson, Mary Jackson; Ilene Thompson, Tanya Morgan; Marshall Smith, Monty Landis; Sammy Michaels, Peter Bogdanovich; Drive-In Manager, Paul Condylis; Salesman, Mark Dennis; Salesman (1st gunshop), Stafford Morgan; Chauffeur, Daniel Ades.

2892 TARZAN AND THE GREAT RIVER. (Paramount-1967). Tarzan, Mike Henry; Captain Sam Bishop, Jan Murray; Pepe, Manuel Padilla Jr.; Dr. Ann Phillips, Diana Millay; Barcuna, Rafer Johnson; Professor, Paulo Grazindo.

2893 TARZAN AND THE JUNGLE BOY. (Paramount-1968). Tarzan, Mike Henry; Nagambi, Rafer Johnson; Myrna Claudel, Alizia Gur; Buharu, Steve Bond; Ken Matson, Ed Johnson; Eric Brunik, Ronald Gans.

2894 TARZAN AND THE VALLEY OF GOLD. (American International-1967). Tarzan, Mike Henry; Sophia Renault, Nancy Kovack; Vinaro, David Opatoshu; Ramel, Manuel Padilla Jr.; Mr. Train, Don Megowan; Perez, Enrique Lucero; Talmadge, Eduardo Noriega; Voss, John Kelly; Manco, Francisco Riquerio; Ruiz, Frank Brandstetter; Romulo, Carlos Rivas; Rodriguez, Jorge Beirute; Antonio, Oswald Olvera.

2895 TARZANA, THE WILD GIRL. (Ellman Enterprises-1973). Ken Clark, Beryl Cunningham, Franca Polsello, Frank Ressel, Andrew Ray.

2896 TARZAN'S DEADLY SILENCE. (National General-1970). Tarzan, Ron Ely; Jai, Manuel Padilla Jr.; Colonel, Jock Mahoney; Marshak, Woodrow Strode; Chico, Gregorio Acosta; Officer, Rudolph Charles; Ruana, Michelle Nicols; Metusa, Robert Doqui; Akaba, Kenneth W. Washington; Boru, Lupe Garnica; Okala, Jose Chaves; Tabor, Virgil Richardson.

2897 A TASTE OF HELL. (Boxoffice International-1973). Barry, John Garwood; Maria, Lisa Lorena; Jack, William Smith; Major, Vic Diaz; Captain, Lloyd Kino; Tomas, Angel Buenaventura; Mario, Ruben Rustia.

2898 TASTE THE BLOOD OF DRACULA. (Warner Bros. -1970). Dracula, Christopher Lee; William Hargood, Geoffrey Keen; Martha Hargood, Gwen Watford; Alice Hargood, Linda Hayden; Samuel Paxton, Peter Sallis; Lucy Paxton, Isla Blair; Jonathan Secker, John Carson; Jeremy Secker, Martin Jarvis; Paul Paxton, Anthony Corlan; Lord Courtley, Ralph Bates; Weller, Roy Kinnear.

2899 TAXI FOR TOBRUK. (7 Arts-1965). Captain von Stegel, Hardy Kruger; Samuel Goldman, Charles Aznavour; Theo, Lino Ventura; Paolo, German Cobos; François, Maurice Biraud.

2900 A TEAR IN THE OCEAN. (Levitt-Pickman-1973). Edi, Alexandre Stere; Bynie, Dominique Rollin; Roman, Armand Abplanalp; Rabbi, Henri Glaeser; Yanouch, Dominique Zardi; Mendel, Jacques Brafman; Commandant, Frantz Wolf; Jadwiga, Diane Lepvrier.

2901 TEARS OF HAPPINESS. (Mutual Film Enterprises-1974). Manuel, Sosie Kodjian; S. Sepian, Levon Yergat, Jon Kouzouyan.

2902 TEENAGE COWGIRLS. (Kairio-1973). Johnny Wadd, Teresa Gillies, Felice Karr, Roberta Hine, Harold Banover.

2903 TEENAGE MOTHER. (Cinemation-1968). Arlene Taylor, Arlene Sue Farber; Duke Markell, Frederick Riccio; Erica Petersen, Julie Ange; Tony Michaels, Howard Le May; Mr. Taylor, George Peters.

2904 THE TELEPHONE BOOK. (Rosebud-1971). Alice, Sarah Kennedy; Smith, Norman Rose; Caller 1, James Harder; Eyemask, Jill Clayburgh; Narrator, Ondine; Har Poon, Barry Morse; Whip Woman, Ultra Violet; Dancer, Geri Miller; Analyst, Roger C. Carmel; Man in Bed, William Hickey; Mugger, Matthew Tobin; Caller 2, David Dozer.

2905 TELL ME IN THE SUNLIGHT. (Movie-Rama-1967). Dave, Steve Cochran; Julie, Shary Marshall; Barber, Jay Robinson; Alex, Dave Bondu; Chata, Patricia Wolf; Tony, George Hopkins; Rocky, Rockne Tarkington; Dr. Franklin, Harold Franklin; Airport Attendant, Hamish Mackay; Princess Naga, Lucille; Pickpocket, George Roberts; Carol, Jill Walden; Pepe, Oliver Nissick.

2906 TELL ME LIES. (Continental-1968). Mark, Mark Jones; Pauline, Pauline Munro; Bob, Robert Lloyd; Eric Allan,

Mary Allen, Jeremy Anthony, Hugh Armstrong, Noel Collins, Ian Hogg, John Hussey, Glenda Jackson, Marjie Lawrence, Joanne Lindsay.

2907 TELL ME THAT YOU LOVE ME, JUNIE MOON. (Paramount-1970). Junie Moon, Liza Minnelli; Arthur, Ken Howard; Warren, Robert Moore; Mario, James Coco; Gregory, Kay Thompson; Beach Boy, Fred Williamson; Jesse, Ben Piazza; Solana, Emily Yancy; Guiles, Leonard Frey; Minnie, Clarice Taylor; Sidney Wyner, James Beard; Ramona, Julia Bovasso; Lila, Gina Collins; Mother Moon, Barbara Logan; Nurse Oxford, Nancy Marchand; Nurse Holt, Lynn Milgrim; Joebee, Ric O. Feldman; Artist, James D. Pasternak.

2908 TELL THEM WILLIE BOY IS HERE. (Universal-1969). Coop, Robert Redford; Lola, Katharine Ross; Willie Boy, Robert Blake; Liz Arnold, Susan Clark; Calvert, Barry Sullivan; Frank Wilson, Charles McGraw; Benby, Charles Aidman; Hacker, John Vernon; Finney, Shelly Novack; Tom, Ned Romero; Sam Wood, John Daheim; Meathead, Lee DeBroux; Le Marie, George Tyne; Johnny Hyde, Steve Shemayme; Third Man, John Hudkins; Chino, Jerry Velasco.

2909 TEN DAYS' WONDER. (Levitt-Pickman-1972). Theo Van Horn, Orson Welles; Helene Van Horn, Marlene Jobert; Charles Van Horn, Anthony Perkins; Paul Regis, Michael Piccoli; Ludovic, Guido Alberti; One Eyed Old Man, Ermando Casanova; Receptionist, Mathilde Ceccarelli; Child Charles, Eric Frisdal; Child Helene, Aline Montovani and Corinne Koeningswarter; Pawnbroker, Giovanni Sciuto; Police Officer, Vittorio Sanipoli; Little Girl on Train, Fabienne Gaugloff; Charles' Mother, Tsilla Chelton.

2910 TEN FROM YOUR SHOW OF SHOWS. (Continental-1973). Sid Caesar, Imogene Coca, Carl Reiner, Louis Nye, Howard Morris, Dorothy Patten, Jack Russell, Ray Drakely, Eleanor Williams, Swen Swenson, Ed Herlihy.

2911 TEN LITTLE INDIANS. (7 Arts-1966). Hugh Lombard, Hugh O'Brian; Ann Clyde, Shirley Eaton; Mike Raven, Fabian; General Mandrake, Leo Genn; William Blore, Stanley Holloway; Frau Grohmann, Marianne Hoppe; Judge Cannon, Wilfrid Hyde-White; Ilona Bergen, Daliah Lavi; Dr. Armstrong, Dennis Price; Herr Grohmann, Mario Adorf.

2912 10 RILLINGTON PLACE. (Columbia-1971). John Reginald Christie, Richard Attenborough; Beryl Evans, Judy Geeson; Timothy John Evans, John Hurt; Mrs. Ethel Christie, Pat Heywood; Alice, Isobel Black.

2913 10:30 P.M. SUMMER. (Lopert-1966). Maria, Melina Mercouri; Claire, Romy Schneider; Paul, Peter Finch; Rodrigo

Palestra, Julian Mateos; Judith, Isabel Maria Perez; Rodrigo's Wife, Beatriz Savon.

2914 TENCHU. (Japanese Film Exchange-1972). Izo, Shintaro Katsu; Hampeita, Tatsuya Nakadai; Shimbei, Yukio Mishima; Ryoma, Yujiro Ishihara; Onimo, Mitsuko Baisho.

2915 THE TENDER MOMENT. (Maron-1971). Olivier, Renaud Verley; Frederique, Nathalie Delon; Enrico, Robert Hossein; Jean-Pierre, Bernard Lecoq; Christine, Katia Cristina.

2916 TENDER SCOUNDREL. (Embassy-1967). Tony Marechal, Jean-Paul Belmondo; Baroness Minna Strasshofer, Nadja Tiller; Muriel, Mylene Demongeot; Lord Swift, Robert Morley; Veronique, Stefania Sandrelli; Germaine, Maria Pacome; Beatrice Dumonceaux, Genevieve Page; Dumonceaux, Philippe Noiret; Bob, Jean-Pierre Marielle; Josette, Ellen Bahl; Marjorie, Micheline Dax; Stranger from the Ritz, Michele Girardon; Madame Aline, Paula Dehelly; Captain Otto Hanz, Peter Carsten; Haberdasher, Ivan Desny.

2917 THE TENDER WARRIOR. (Safari-1971). Cal, Dan Haggerty; Sammy, Charles Lee; Pa, Liston Elkins.

2918 THE 10TH VICTIM. (Embassy-1965). Marcello Polletti, Marcello Mastroianni; Caroline Meredith, Ursula Andress; Olga, Salvo Randone; Lawyer, Massimo Serato; Professor, Salvo Randone; The Victim, Evi Rigano; Rudi, Milo Quesada; Lidia, Luce Bonifassy; Relaxatorium Girl, Anita Sanders; Chet, Mickey Knox; Cole, Richard Armstrong; Martin, Walter Williams; Chinese Assailant, George Wang.

2919 TEOREMA. (Continental-1969). The Visitor, Terence Stamp; The Wife, Silvana Mangano; The Husband, Massimo Girotti; The Daughter, Anne Wiazemsky; The Maid, Laura Betti; The Son, Andres Jose Cruz; Angelino, Ninetto Davoli; Alfonso Gatto, Adele Cambria, Carlo De Mejo, Soublette.

2920 THE TERMINAL MAN. (Warner Bros. -1974). Harry Benson, George Segal; Dr. Ross, Joan Hackett; Dr. Ellis, Richard Dysart; Dr. Morris, Michael C. Gwynne; Dr. McPherson, Donald Moffat; Angela, Jill Clayburgh; Gerhard, Matt Clark; Detective, Norman Burton; Priest, Ian Wolfe; Police Guards, Gene Borkan, Burke Byrnes.

2920a TERROR IN THE CITY. (Allied Artists-1966). Suzy, Lee Grant; Brill, Richard Bray; Carl, Michael Higgins; Paco, Roberto Marsach; Brill's Father, Robert Allen; Rose, Sylvia Miles; Rick, Jaime Charlamagne; Farmer, Robert Earl Jones; Farmer's Wife, Ruth Attaway; Artificial Inseminator, Charles Jordan; Preacher, Roscoe Browne; Pickpocket, Rick Colitti; Brill's Sister, Muriel Franklin; Pitchman, Monroe Arnold.

2921 TERROR IN THE WAX MUSEUM. (Cinerama-1973). Flexner, Ray Milland; Burns, Broderick Crawford; Julia, Elsa Lanchester; Inspector, Maurice Evans; Laurie, Shani Wallis; Dupree, John Carradine; Fowley, Louis Hayward; Southcott, Patric Knowles; Sgt. Hawks, Mark W. Edwards; Mme. Yang, Lisa Lu; Karkov, Steven Marlo; Constable, Ben Wright; Charwoman, Matilda Calnan; Charwoman, Peggy Stewart; Constable, Leslie Thompson; Meg, Nicole Shelby.

2922-23 No entries.

2924 TERROR-CREATURES FROM THE GRAVE. (Pacemaker Pictures-1967). Cleo, Barbara Steele; Morgan, Richard Garret; Kovaks, Walter Brandt; Corinne, Marilyn Mitchell; Dr. Nemek, Alfred Rice; Kurt, Alan Collins; Louise, Tilde Till.

2925 THE TERRORNAUTS. (Embassy-1967). Dr. Joe Burke, Simon Oates; Sandy Lund, Zena Marshall; Joshua Yellowless, Charles Hawtrey; Mrs. Jones, Patricia Hayes; Ben Keller, Stanley Meadows; Dr. Henry Shore, Max Adrian; Burke, Frank Barry; Danny, Richard Carpenter; Nick, Leonard Cracknell; Robot Operator, Robert Jewell; Uncle, Frank Forsyth; Gendarme, Andre Maranne.

2925a TERRY WHITMORE, FOR EXAMPLE. (Grove-1969). Terry Whitmore.

2926 TEXAS ACROSS THE RIVER. (Universal-1966). Sam Hollis, Dean Martin; Don Andrea Baldasar, Alain Delon; Phoebe Ann Naylor, Rosemary Forsyth; Kronk, Joey Bishop; Lonetta, Tina Marquand; Captain Stimpson, Peter Graves; Chief Iron Jacket, Michael Ansara; Yellow Knife, Linden Chiles; Lieutenant Sibley, Andrew Prine; Yancy, Stuart Anderson; Morton, Roy Barcroft; Willet, George Wallace; Mr. Naylor, Don Beddoe; Turkey Shoot Boss, Kelly Thordsen; Emma, Nora Marlowe; Gabe, John Harmon; Medicine Man, Dick Farnsworth.

2927 THE TEXAS CHAIN SAW MASSACRE. (Bryanston-1974). Sally, Marilyn Burns; Jerry, Allen Danziger; Kirk, William Vail; Franklin, Paul A. Partain; Pam, Teri McMinn; Hitchhiker, Edwin Neal; Old Man, Jim Siedow; Leatherface, Gunnar Hansen; Grandfather, John Dugan.

2928 THE TEXICAN. (Columbia-1966). Audie Murphy, Broderick Crawford, Diana Lorys, Luz Marquez, Antonio Casas, Molino Rojo, Aldo Sambrell, Antonio Peral, Jorge Rigaud, Martha May, Juan Carlos Torres, Gerard Tichy, Luis Induni, Helga Genth.

2929 THANK HEAVEN FOR SMALL FAVORS. (International

Classics-1965). Georges Lachesnaye, Bourvil; Inspector, Francis Blanche; Raoul, Jean Poiret; Lachesnaye Pere, Jean Yonnel; Inspector Bridoux, Jean Tissier; Bishop, Jean Galland; Francoise, Veronique Nordey; Raillargaud, Marcel Peres; Juliette, Solange Certain; Aunt Claire, Denise Perronne; Prefect of Police, Bernard Lavalette.

2930 THANK YOU ALL VERY MUCH. (Columbia-1969). Rosamund Stacey, Sandy Dennis; George, Ian McKellen; Lydia, Eleanor Bron; Roger, John Standing; Joe, Michael Coles; Sister Harvey, Rachel Kempson; Mrs. Stacey, Peggy Thorpe-Bates; Mr. Stacey, Kenneth Benda; Mike, Roger Hammond; Octavia, Sarah Whalley; Miss Guernsey, Shelagh Fraser; Dr. Prothero, Maurice Denham; Beatrice, Deborah Stanford; Sister Bennett, Margaret Tyzack.

2931 THANOS AND DESPINA. (Grove-1970). Despina, Olga Carlatos; Thanos, Georges Dialegmenos; Yankos, Lambros Tsangas; Katina, Elli Xanthaki; Vlahopoulos, Carroussos.

2932 THAT DARN CAT. (Buena Vista-1965). Patti Randall, Hayley Mills; Zeke Kelso, Dean Jones; Ingrid Randall, Dorothy Provine; Gregory Benson, Roddy McDowall; Dan, Neville Brand; Mrs. MacDougall, Elsa Lanchester; Mr. MacDougall, William Demarest; Iggy, Frank Gorshin; Supervisor Newton, Richard Eastham; Margaret Miller, Grayson Hall; Ed Wynn, Mr. Hofstedder; Canoe, Tom Lowell; Drive In Manager, Richard Deacon; Landlady, Iris Adrian.

2933 THAT FUNNY FEELING. (Universal-1965). Joan, Sandra Dee; Tom, Bobby Darin; Harvey, Donald O'Connor; Audrey, Nita Talbot; Luther, Larry Storch.

2934 THAT MAN BOLT. (Universal-1973). Bolt, Fred Williamson; Griffiths, Byron Webster; Dominique, Miko Mayama; Samantha, Teresa Graves; Kumada, Satoshi Nakamura; Carter, John Orchard; Connie, Jack Ging; Spider, Ken Kazama; De Vargas, Vassili Lambrinos.

2935 THAT MAN FLINTSTONE. (Columbia-1966). Voices of Alan Reed, Mel Blanc, Jean Vander Pyl, Gerry Johnson, Don Messick, Janet Waldo, Paul Frees, Harvey Korman, John Stephenson, June Foray.

2936 THAT MAN GEORGE. (Allied Artists-1968). George, George Hamilton; Lila, Claudine Auger; Travis, Alberto De Mendoza; Vibert, Daniel Ivernel; Jose, Tiberio Murgia; Jorge Rigaud, Giacomo Furia.

2937 THAT MAN IN ISTANBUL. (Columbia-1966). Tony Maecenas, Horst Bucholz; Kenny, Sylva Koscina; Bill, Mario Adorf; Elisabeth, Perette Pradier; Schenck, Klaus Kinsky; Bogo, Alvaro De Luna; Brain, Gustavo Re; CIA Chief,

Georges Rigaud; Josette, Christine Mercier; Charley, Gerard Tichy; Jonny, Augustin Gonzales.

2938 THAT TENDER TOUCH. (World Premiere-1969). Terry, Sue Bernard; Marsha, Bee Tompkins; Ken, Rick Cooper; Wendy, Phae Dera; Dodie, Margaret Read; Jane, Victoria Hale; Paul, Richard St. John; Irene, Tania Lemani; Jim, Roger Helfond; Joe, Joe Castagna.

2939 THAT TENNESSEE BEAT. (20th Century-Fox-1966). Merle Travis, Minnie Pearl, Sharon De Bord, Dolores Faith, Jim Reader, Earl Richards, Cecil Scaife, Rink Hardin, The Statler Brothers, Stony Mountain Cloggers, Boots Randolph, Pete Drake.

2940 THAT WOMAN. (Globe-1968). Alexandra Borovski, Eva Renzi; Siegbert Lahner, Harald Peipnitz; Joachim Steigenwald, Paul Hubschmid; Timo, Umberto Orsini; Hildchen Volker, Elga Stass.

2941 THAT'LL BE THE DAY. (Walter Reade-1974). David Essex, Rosemary Leach, Ringo Starr, James Booth, Billy Fury, Keith Moon, Rosalind Ayres.

2942 THAT'S ENTERTAINMENT. (United Artists-1974). Fred Astaire, Bing Crosby, Gene Kelly, Peter Lawford, Liza Minnelli, Donald O'Connor, Debbie Reynolds, Mickey Rooney, Frank Sinatra, James Stewart, Elizabeth Taylor.

2943 THEATRE OF BLOOD. (United Artists-1973). Edward Lionheart, Vincent Price; Edwina Lionheart, Diana Rigg; Peregrine Devlin, Ian Hendry; Trevor Dickman, Harry Andrews; Miss Chloe Moon, Coral Browne; Oliver Larding, Robert Coote; Solomon Psaltery, Jack Hawkins; George Maxwell, Michael Hordern; Horace Sprout, Arthur Lowe; Meredith Merridew, Robert Morley; Hector Snipe, Dennis Price; Mrs. Psaltery, Diana Dors; Mrs. Sprout, Joan Hickson; Mrs. Maxwell, Renee Asherson; Rosemary, Madeline Smith; Inspector Boot, Milo O'Shea; Sgt. Dogge, Eric Sykes; Agnes, Brigid Eric Bates; Police Photographer, Tony Calvin; Policemen, Bunny Reed, Peter Thornton.

2944 THERE IS NO 13. (Unset-1974). George Thomas, Mark Damon; Eleven, Margaret Markov; Older George, Harvey Lembeck; Number Twelve, Jean Jennings; Dr. Honneycutt, Lee Moore; Mr. A., Reuben Schafer; Rosie, Bonnie Inch.

2945 THERE WAS A CROOKED MAN. (Warner Bros.-1970). Paris Pitman Jr., Kirk Douglas; Woodward Lopeman, Henry Fonda; Dudley Whinner, Hume Cronyn; Missouri Kid, Burgess Meredith; Mr. Lomax, Arthur O'Connell; Warden LeGoff, Martin Gabel; Cyrus McNutt, John Randolph; Coy Cavendish, Michael Blodgett; Madame, Claudia McNeil;

Tobaccy, Alan Hale; Whiskey, Victor French; Mrs. Bullard, Lee Grant; Prostitute, Jeanne Cooper; Ah-Ping Woo, C. K. Yang; Skinner, Bert Freed; Colonel Wolff, Gene Evans; Edwina, Pamela Hensley; Miss Brundage, Barbara Rhoades.

2946 THERE WAS AN OLD COUPLE. (Artkino-1967). Old Man, Ivan Marin; Old Woman, Vera Kuznetsova; Valentin, Griory Martinyunk; Nina, Ludmila Maximova.

2947 THERE'S A GIRL IN MY SOUP. (Columbia-1970). Robert Danvers, Peter Sellers; Marion, Goldie Hawn; Andrew, Tony Britton; Jimmy, Nicky Henson; John, John Comer; John's Wife, Diana Dors; Julia, Gabrielle Drake; Caroline, Geraldine Sherman; Lady Heather, Judy Campbell; Clare, Nicola Pagett; Nigel, Christopher Cazenove; Reporters, Robin Parkinson, Roy Skelton; Nigel's Girlfriend, Caroline Seymour; Leguestier, Raf De La Torre; Salesman, Constantin De Goguel; Hotel Manager, Thorley Walters; Floor Waiter, Georges Lambert; Concierge, Andre Charisse; Lift Attendant, John Serret; Woman in Lift, Avril Angers; Gilly, Ruth Trouncer.

2948 THERE'S ALWAYS VANILLA. (Cambist-1972). Ray Laine, Judith Streiner, Johanna Lawrence, Richard Ricci, Roger McGovern, Ron Jaye, Bob Wilson, Louise Sahene, Christopher Priore, Robert Trow.

2949 THERESE AND ISABELLE. (Audubon-1968). Therese, Essy Persson; Isabelle, Anna Gael; Therese's Mother, Barbara Laage; Mlle. LeBlanc, Anne Vernon; M. Martin, Maurice Teynac; Pierre, Remy Longa; The Madame, Simone Paris; Mlle. Germain, Suzanne Marchellier; Renee, Nathalie Nort; Agnes, Darcy Pulliam; Martine, Martine LeClerc; Francoise, Bernadette Stern.

2950 THESE ARE THE DAMNED. (Columbia-1965). Simon Wells, Macdonald Carey; Joan, Shirley Anne Field; Freya, Viveca Lindfors; Bernard, Alexander Knox; King, Oliver Reed; Major Holland, Walter Gotell; Captain Gregory, James Villiers.

2951 THEY CALL HER ONE EYE. (American International-1974). Frigga, Christina Lindberg; Tony, Heinz Hopf; Lesbian, Despina Tomazani.

2952 THEY CALL ME MR. TIBBS. (United Artists-1970). Virgil Tibbs, Sidney Poitier; Rev. Logan Sharpe, Martin Landau; Valerie Tibbs, Barbara McNair; Rice Weedon, Anthony Zerbe; Captain Marden, Jeff Corey; Herbert Kenner, David Sheiner; Mealie, Juano Hernandez; Marge Garfield, Norma Crane; Woody Garfield, Edward Asner; Sgt. Deutsch, Ted Gehring; Puff, Beverly Todd; Joy Sturges, Linda Towne; Andrew, George Spell; Gineer, Wanda Spell.

2953 THEY CALL ME TRINITY. (AVCO Embassy-1972). Trinity, Terence Hill; Bambino, Bud Spencer; Major Harriman, Farley Granger; Jonathan, Steffen Zacharias; Tobias, Dan Sturkie; Sarah, Gisela Hahn; Judith, Elena Pedemonte; Weasel, Ezio Marano; Timid, Luciano Rossi; Peone, Michele Spaeara; Mezcal, Remo Capitani; Michele Cimarosa, Ugo Sasso, Riccardo Pizzuti, Gigi Bonos.

2954 THEY CAME FROM BEYOND SPACE. (Embassy-1967). Dr. Curtis Temple, Robert Hutton; Lee Mason, Jennifer Jayne; Farge, Zia Mohyeddin; Richard Arden, Bernard Kay; Monj, Michael Gough; Allan Mullane, Geoffrey Wallace; Stilwell, Maurice Good.

2955 THEY CAME TO ROB LAS VEGAS. (Warner Bros. -7 Arts-1969). Tony Vincenzo, Gary Lockwood; Anne, Elke Sommer; Skorsky, Lee J. Cobb; Douglas, Jack Palance; Leroy, George Geret; Salvatore, Gustavo Re; Merino, Daniel Martin; Gino Vincenzo, Jean Servais; The Boss, Roger Hanin; Clark, Maurizio Arena; Mass, Armand Mestral; Cooper, Fabrizio Capucci; Baxter, Enrique Avila.

2956 THEY MIGHT BE GIANTS. (Universal-1971). Dr. Watson, Joanne Woodward; Justin Playfair, George C. Scott; Wilbur Peabody, Jack Gilford; Blevins Playfair, Lester Rawlins; Grace, Kitty Winn; Daisy, Rue McClanahan.

2957 THEY ONLY KILL THEIR MASTERS. (MGM-1972). Abel Marsh, James Garner; Kate, Katharine Ross; Dr. Watkins, Hal Holbrook; Captain Streeter, Harry Guardino; Mrs. Watkins, June Allyson; John, Christopher Connelly; Walter, Tom Ewell; Lee Campbell, Peter Lawford; George, Edmond O'Brien; Ernie, Arthur O'Connell; Gloria, Ann Rutherford; Malcolm, Art Metrano; The Mayor, Harry Basch; Diana, Jenifer Shaw; Mallory, Jason Wingreen; Mrs. DeCamp, Norma Connolly; Doctor, Robert Nichols; State Trooper, David Westberg; Jenny Campbell, Lee Pulford; Harry, Roy Applegate; Rosa, Alma Lenor Beltran.

2958 THEY SHOOT HORSES, DON'T THEY? (Cinerama-1969). Gloria Beatty, Jane Fonda; Robert Syverton, Michael Sarrazin; Alice, Susannah York; Rocky, Gig Young; Sailor, Red Buttons; Ruby, Bonnie Bedelia; Rollo, Michael Conrad; James, Bruce Dern; Turkey, Al Lewis; Joel, Robert Fields; Cecil, Severn Darden; Shirl, Allyn Ann McLerie; Jackie, Jacquelyn Hyde; Mario, Felice Orlandi; Max, Art Metrano; Lillian, Gail Billings; Agnes, Maxine Greene; Nurse, Mary Gregory; College Boy, Robert Dunlap; Jiggs, Paul Mantee; Mrs. Layden, Madge Kennedy; Doctor, Tim Herbert; Trainers, Tom McFadden and Noble "Kid" Chissell.

2959 THE THIEF OF PARIS. (Lopert-1967). Georges Randal, Jean-Paul Belmondo; Charlotte, Genevieve Bujold; Genevieve,

Marie Dubois; Cannonier, Charles Denner; Ida, Françoise Fabian; Abbot Lamargelle, Julien Guiomar; Roger La Honte, Paul Le Person; Renee, Martine Sarcey; Broussaille, Marlene Jobert; Marguerite, Bernadette Lafont; Madeleine Damien, Christian Lude, Fernand Guiot, Marc Dudicourt, Jacqueline Staup, Christian De Tilliere, Jacques David, Roger Crouzet, Jacques Debarry, Paul Vally, Anne Germon.

2960 THE THIEF WHO CAME TO DINNER. (Warner Bros. -1973). Webster, Ryan O'Neal; Laura, Jacqueline Bisset; Dave, Warren Oates; Jackie, Jill Clayburgh; Henderling, Charles Cioffi; Deams, Ned Beatty; Zukovsky, Austin Pendleton; Cynamite, Gregory Sierra; Ted, Michael Murphy; Laxker, John Hillerman; Insurance Man, Alan Oppenheimer; Mrs. Donner, Margaret Fairchild; Tom, Jack Manning; Sgt. Del Conte, Richard O'Brien; Rivera, George Morfogen.

2961 THIEVES LIKE US. (United Artists-1974). Keith Carradine, Shelley Duvall, John Schuck, Bert Remsen, Louise Fletcher, Ann Latham, Tom Skerritt, Al Scott, John Roper, Mary Waits, Rodney Lee Jr., William Watters, Joan Tewkesbury, Dr. Edward Fisher, Josephine Bennett, Howard Warner, Eleanor Matthews, Pam Warner, Suzanne Majure, Walter Cooper, Lloyd Jones.

2962 THE THING WITH TWO HEADS. (American International-1972). Maxwell Kirshner, Ray Milland; Jack Moss, "Rosey" Grier; Dr. Fred Williams, Don Marshall; Dr. Philip Desmond, Roger Perry; Lila, Chelsea Brown; Patricia, Kathy Baumann; Thomas, John Dullaghan; Donald, John Bliss; Police Lieutenant, Bruce Kimball; Miss Mullen, Jane Kellem; Sgt. Hacker, Lee Frost; Dr. Smith, Wes Bishop; Police Sergeant, Roger Gentry; Nurse, Britt Nilsson; Gorilla, Rick Baker; Policeman, Phil Hoover; Medical Salesman, Rod Steel; Prison Guard, Michael Viner.

2963 THE THINGS OF LIFE. (Columbia-1970). Helene, Romy Schneider; Pierre, Michel Piccoli; Catherine, Lea Massari; Francois, Jean Bouise; Pig-Truck Driver, Boby Lapointe; Truck Driver, Herve Sand; Pierre's Father, Henri Nassiet; Bertrand, Gerard Lartigau; Helen's Mother, Marcelle Arnold; Helen's Father, Jean-Pierre Zola.

2964 30 IS A DANGEROUS AGE, CYNTHIA. (Columbia-1968). Rupert Street, Dudley Moore; Oscar, Eddie Foy Jr.; Louise Hammond, Suzy Kendall; Herbert Greenslade, John Bird; Jock McCue, Duncan Macrae; Mrs. Woolley, Patricia Routledge; Victor, Peter Bayliss; Hon. Gavin Hopton, John Wells; Mr. Woolley, Harry Towb; Capt. Gore-Taylor, Jonathan Routh; Horst Cohen Jr., Ted Dicks; Paul, Nicky Henson; Doctor, Clive Dunn; Registrar, Frank Thornton; TV Announcer, Derek Farr; Irish Story Teller, Michael MacLiammoir.

2965 36 HOURS. (MGM-1965). Major Jefferson Pike, James Garner; Major Walter Gerber, Rod Taylor; Anna Hedler, Eva Marie Saint; Otto Schack, Werner Peters; Col. Peter MacLean, Alan Napier; Elsa, Cecilia Lovsky; Ernst, John Banner; Gen. Allison, Russell Thorson; Lt. Col. Ostermann, Oscar Beregi; Capt. Abbott, Ed Gilbert; Corporal Kentner, Carl Held; Kraatz, Martin Kosleck; Charwoman, Marjorie Bennett; German Guard, Sig Ruman; German Soldiers, Henry Rowland and Otto Reichow; German Agent, Hilda Plowright; Denker, Walter Friedl; Lamke, Joseph Mell.

2966 THIS IS A HIJACK. (Fanfare-1973). Christie, Adam Roarke; Dominic, Neville Brand; Scott, Jay Robinson; Diane, Lynn Borden; Phillips, Milt Kamen; Latımer, John Alderman; Mrs. Phillips, Sandy Balson; Pierce, Sam Chew; Champ, Don Pedro Colley; Sheriff, Dub Taylor; Mrs. Pierce, Carol Lawson; Scott's Girl, Jackie Giroux; Banker, Barney Phillips; Latimer's Girl, Patricia Winters.

2967 THIS MAN MUST DIE. (Allied Artists-1970). Charles Thenier, Michael Duchaussoy; Paul, Jean Yanne; Helen Lanson, Caroline Cellier; Jeanne, Lorraine Rainer; Philippe, Marc DiNapoli; Jacques Ferrand, Guy Marly; Anna, Anouk Ferjac; Martin Thenier, Stephane DiNapoli.

2968 THIS PROPERTY IS CONDEMNED. (Paramount-1966). Alva Starr, Natalie Wood; Owen Legate, Robert Redford; J. J. Nichols, Charles Bronson; Hazel Starr, Kate Reid; Willie Starr, Mary Badham; Knopke, Alan Baxter; Sidney, Robert Blake; Johnson, John Harding; Salesman, Dabney Coleman; Jimmy Bell, Ray Hemphill; Charlie Steinkamp, Brett Pearson; Tom, Jon Provost; Hank, Quentin Sondergaard; Max, Michael Steen; Lindsay Tate, Bruce Watson; Tiny, Bob Random; Railroad Conductor, Nick Stuart.

2969 THIS SAVAGE LAND. (Universal-1969). Ben Pride, Barry Sullivan; Kip, Kelly Corcoran; Timothy, Andrew Prine; Grandma, Katherine Squire; Grandpa, Charles Seel; Elizabeth, Kathryn Hayes; Elizabeth's Father, Roy Roberts; Stacey, John Drew Barrymore; Chance, Glenn Corbett.

2970 THIS SPECIAL FRIENDSHIP. (Pathe Contemporary-1967). Georges De Sarre, Francis Lacombrade; Alexandre Motier, Didier Haudepin; Father Superior, Lucien Nat; Father Lauzon, Louis Seigner; Father Trennes, Michel Bouquet; Lucien Rouvere, Francois Leccia.

2971 THE THOMAS CROWN AFFAIR. (United Artists-1968). Thomas Crown, Steve McQueen; Vicky Anderson, Faye Dunaway; Eddy Malone, Paul Burke; Erwin Weaver, Jack Weston; Carl, Yaphet Kotto; Benjy, Todd Martin; Dave, Sam Melville; Abe, Addison Powell; Arnie, Sidney Armus; Curley,

Jon Shank; Don, Allen Emerson; Ernie, Harry Cooper; Bert, John Silver; Gwen, Astrid Heeren; Sandy, Biff McGuire; Miss Sullivan, Carol Corbett; John, John Orchard; Jamie MacDonald, Gordon Pinsent; Danny, Patrick Horgan; Honey Weaver, Peg Shirley; Jimmy Weaver, Leonard Caron; Booth Guard, Richard Bull; Cash Room Guards, Paul Rhone and Victor Creatore; Paul Verdier, James Rawley, Charles Lampkin, Ted Behring, Nikita Knatz, Nora Marlowe, Carole Kelly, Michael Shillo, Tom Rosqui, Judy Pace, Patty Regan.

2972 THOMASINE AND BUSHROD. (Columbia-1974). Bushrod, Max Julien; Thomasine, Vonetta McGee; Bogardie, George Murdock; Jomo, Glynn Turman; Pecoloa, Juanita Moore; Joel Fluellen, Jackson D. Kane, Bud Conlan, Kip Allen, Ben Zeller, Herb Robins, Harry Luck, Jason Bernhard, Paul Barby, Scott Britt, Geno Silva, John Gill, Dave Burleson, James Sargeant, Leigh Potter.

2973 THOROUGHLY MODERN MILLIE. (Universal-1967). Millie Dillmount, Julie Andrews; Dorothy Brown, Mary Tyler Moore; Muzzy Van Hossmere, Carol Channing; Jimmy Smith, James Fox; Mrs. Meers, Beatrice Lillie; Trevor Graydon, John Gavin; Number One, Jack Soo; Number Two, Pat Morita; Tea, Philip Ahn; Miss Flannery, Cavada Humphrey; Anthony Dexter, Lou Nova, Michael St. Clair, Albert Carrier, Victor Rogers, Lizabeth Hush, Herbie Faye, Ann Dee, Buddy Schwab, Jay Thompson, Todd Mason.

2974 THOSE CALLAWAYS. (Buena Vista-1965). Cam Calloway, Brian Keith; Liddy Calloway, Vera Miles; Bucky Calloway, Brandon De Wilde; Alf Simes, Walter Brennan; Ed Parker, Ed Wynn; Bridie Mellot, Linda Evans; Dell Fraser, Philip Abbott; Jim Mellot, John Larkin; Doane Shattuck, Parley Baer; Nigosh, Frank De Kova; E. J. Fletcher, Roy Roberts; Ernie Evans, John Qualen; Whit Turner, Tom Skerritt; Charley Evans, Paul Hartman; Nat Perkins, Russell Collins; Ollie Gibbons, John Davis Chandler; Phil Petrie, Chet Stratton; Sarah Mellot, Renee Godfrey.

2975 THOSE DARING YOUNG MEN IN THEIR JAUNTY JALOPIES. (Paramount-1969). Chester Schofield, Tony Curtis; Betty, Susan Hampshire; Sir Cuthbert Ware-Armitage, Terry-Thomas; Perkins, Eric Sykes; Schnickel, Gert Frobe; Major Digby Dawlish, Peter Cook; Lt. Kit Barrington, Dudley Moore; Monsieur Dupont, Bourvil; Count Levinovitch, Jack Hawkins; Otto, Peer Schmidt; Walter Chiari, Lando Buzzanca, Mireille Darc, Marie Dubois, Nicoletta Machiavelli, Jacques Duby, Hattie Jacques, Darren Nesbitt, Nicholas Phipps, William Rushton, Michael Trubshawe, Richard Wattis, Walter Williams, Joe Wadham, Roy Scammel, Dinny Powell, Frank Henson, Mark Boyle, Jeff Silk.

2976 THOSE DIRTY DOGS. (Cinema Financial of America-1974).

Chadwell, Stephen Boyd; Korano, Johnny Garko; Younger, Howard Ross; Angelo Sanchez, Simon Andrew; Washington Smith, Harry Baird; Miss Adams, Theresa Gompers; General Mueller, Daniel Vargas.

2977 THOSE FANTASTIC FLYING FOOLS. (American International-1967). Phineas T. Barnum, Burl Ives; Gaylord Sullivan, Troy Donahue; Professor Van Bulow, Gert Frobe; Sir Harry Washington Smythe, Terry-Thomas; Angelica, Hermione Gingold; Madelaine, Daliah Lavi; Sir Charles Dillsworthy, Lionel Jeffries; Duke of Barset, Dennis Price; Warrant Officer, Stratford Johns; Grundle, Graham Stark; General Tom Thumb, Jimmy Clitheroe; Henri, Edward De Souza; Bulgeroff, Klaus Kinski; Queen Victoria, Joan Sterndale Bennett; Electra, Judy Cornwell; Anna, Renate Holt; Puddleby, Derek Francis; Scotland Yard Man, Allan Cuthbertson.

2978 THOSE MAGNIFICENT MEN IN THEIR FLYING MACHINES (OR HOW I FLEW FROM LONDON TO PARIS IN 25 HOURS AND 11 MINUTES). (20th Century-Fox-1965). Orvil Newton, Stuart Whitman; Patricia Rawnsley, Sarah Miles; Richard Mays, James Fox; Count Emilio Ponticelli, Alberto Sordi; Lord Rawnsley, Robert Morley; Colonel Manfred Von Holstein, Gert Frobe; Pierre Dubois, Jean-Pierre Cassel; Courtney, Eric Sykes; Sir Percy Ware-Armitage, Terry-Thomas; Brigitte/Ingrid/Marlene/Francoise/Yvette/Betty, Irina Demick; Popperwell, Tony Hancock; Benny Hill, Yujiro Ishihara, Flora Robson, Karl Michael Vogler, Sam Wanamaker, Eric Barker, Fred Emney, Gordon Jackson, Davy Kaye, John Le Mesurier, Jeremy Lloyd, Zena Marshall, Millicent Martin, Eric Pohlman, Marjorie Rhodes, Norman Rossington, William Rushton.

2979 A THOUSAND CLOWNS. (United Artists-1965). Murray, Jason Robards; Sandra, Barbara Harris; Arnold, Martin Balsam; Nick, Barry Gordon; Leo, Gene Saks; Albert, William Daniels.

2980 THE THOUSAND PLANE RAID. (United Artists-1969). Col. Greg Brandon, Christopher George; Wac Lt. Gabrielle Ames, Laraine Stephens; Gen. Cotten Palmer, J. D. Cannon; RAF Wing Commander Trafton Howard, Gary Marshall; Leslie Hardwicke, Michael Evans; Lt. Archer, Ben Murphy; Maj. Varga, James Gammon; Sgt. Kruger, Gavin MacLeod; Richman, Scott Thomas; Quimby, Tim McIntire; Douglas, Bo Hopkins; Worchek, Henry Jaglom; Jacobi, Noam Pitlik; Gen. Conway, Barry Atwater; Middleton, John Carter; Railla, Charles Dierkop; Waist Gunner, Mac McLaughlin; Waist Gunner, Wayne Sutherlin; Turret Gunner, Philip Proctor; Navigator, Larry Perkins; Bombardier, Carl Reindel.

2981 THREE. (United Artists-1969). Marty, Charlotte Rampling; Bert, Robie Porter; Taylor, Sam Waterston; Claude, Pascale

Roberts; Liz, Edina Ronay; Ann, Gilliam Hills; Silvano, Mario Cotone; Gloria, Patrizia Giammei.

2982 THREE. (Impact-1967). Milos, Velimir-Bata Zivojinovic; Man, Ali Raner; Woman, Senka Veletanlic-Petrovic; Partisan, Voja Miric.

2983 THREE BITES OF THE APPLE. (MGM-1967). Stanley Thrumm, David McCallum; Carla Moretti, Sylva Koscina; Miss Sparrow, Tammy Grimes; Harvey Tomlinson, Harvey Korman; Remo Romano, Domenico Modugno; The Doctor, Aldo Fabrizi; Francesca Bianchini, Mirella Maravidi; Croupier, Riccardo Garrone; Gladys Tomlinson, Avril Angers; Teddy Farnum, Claude Alliotti; Gussie Hagstrom, Freda Bamford; Alfred Guffy, Arthur Hewlett; Peg Farnum, Alison Frazer; Bernhard Hagstrom, Cardew Robinson; Winifred Batterly, Ann Lancaster; Joe Batterly, John Sharp; Birdie Guffy, Maureen Pryor; The Yodeler, Edra Gale.

2984 THREE GUNS FOR TEXAS. (Universal-1968). Reese Bennett, Neville Brand; Chad Cooper, Peter Brown; Joe Riley, William Smith; MacMillan, Martin Milner; Capt. Parmalee, Philip Carey; Cleetus Grogan, Albert Salmi; Running Antelope, Cliff Osmond; Wily G. Tinney, Michael Conrad; Linda Little Trees, Shelley Morrison; John Abbott, Ralph Manza, Richard Devon, Dub Taylor.

2985 THREE HUNDRED YEAR WEEKEND. (Cinerama-1971). Marshall, Michael Tolan; Nancy, Sharon Laughlin; Hal, Roy Cooper; Wynter, Gabriel Dell; Carole, Mel Dowd; Rockne, Bernard Ward; Jean, Dorothy Lyman; Tom, William Devane; Dr. Roland, James Congdon; Joy, Carole Demas.

2986 THREE IN THE ATTIC. (American International-1969). Paxton Quigley, Christopher Jones; Tobey Clinton, Yvette Mimieux; Eunice, Judy Pace; Jan, Maggie Thrett; Dean Nazarin, Nan Martin; Selma, Reva Rose; Jake, John Beck; Mr. Clinton, Richard Derr; Mrs. Clinton, Eve McVeagh; Flo, Honey Alden; Wilfred, Thomas F. Ahearne.

2987 3 INTO 2 WON'T GO. (Universal-1969). Steve Howard, Rod Steiger; Frances Howard, Claire Bloom; Ella Patterson, Judy Geeson; Belle, Peggy Ashcroft; Jack Roberts, Paul Rogers; Janet, Lynn Farleigh; Marcia, Elizabeth Spriggs; Beth, Sheila Allen.

2988 THREE LIVES. (Impact-1971). Mallory, Mallory Millet-Jones; Lillian, Lillian Shreve; Robin, Robin Mide.

2989 THE THREE MUSKETEERS. (20th Century-Fox-1974). D'Artagnan, Michael York; Athos, Oliver Reed; Constance Bonancieux, Raquel Welch; Aramis, Richard Chamberlain;

Porthos, Frank Finlay; O'Reilly, Frank Finlay; Cardinal Richelieu, Charlton Heston; Milady de Winter, Faye Dunaway; Rochefort, Christopher Lee; Anne of Austria, Geraldine Chaplin; Louis XIII, Jean-Pierre Cassel; M. Bonancieux, Spike Milligan; Planchet, Roy Kinnear; Felton, Michael Gothard; Eugenie, Sybil Danning; Beatrice, Gitty Djamal; Duke of Buckingham, Simon Ward; Kitty, Nicole Calfan; Treville, Georges Wilson; Jussac, Angel Del Pozo; Richelieu's Spy, Rodney Bewes; 1st Musketeer, Ben Aris; D'Artagnan's Father, Joss Ackland; D'Artagnan's Mother, Gretchen Franklyn; Captain, Francis De Wolff; Swordsman at Inn, William Hobbs.

2990 3 ON A COUCH. (Columbia-1966). Christopher Pride and Warren, Ringo Rutherford, Heather, Jerry Lewis; Dr. Elizabeth Acord, Janet Leigh; Susan Manning, Mary Ann Mobley; Anna Jacques, Gila Golan; Mary Lou Mauve, Leslie Parrish; Dr. Ben Mizer, James Best; Murphy, Kathleen Freeman; The Drunk, Buddy Lester; The Ambassador, Renzo Cesana; The Attache, Fritz Feld; Jesslyn Fax, Renie Riano.

2991 THE THREE SISTERS. (Brandon-1969). Olga, Lyubov Sokolva; Masha, Margarita Volodina; Irina, Tatyana Malchenko; Andrei, Leonid Gubanov; Natalya, Alla Larionova; Vershinin, Lev Inanov; Kuligan, Leonid Gallis; Chebutykin, Konstantin Sorokin; Tusenbach, Oleg Strizhenov; Solyony, Vladimir Druzhnikov.

2992 THREE THE HARD WAY. (Allied Artists-1974). Jimmy Lait, Jim Brown; Jagger Daniels, Fred Williamson; Mister Keyes, Jim Kelly; Wendy Kane, Sheila Frazier; Monroe Feather, Jay Robinson; Charley, Charles McGregor; Keep, Howard Platt; Dr. Fortrero, Richard Angarola; Link, David Chow; Eva, Marian Collier; House, Junero Jennings; Lt. Di Nisco, Alex Rocco; Boy, Corbin Bernsen; Girl, Renie Radich; Nurse, Janice Carroll; Chicago Girl, Angelyn Chester; Norman Evans, Pamela Serpe, Marie O'Henry, Irene Tsu, Robert Cleaves, Roberta Collins, Lance Taylor, Jeanie Bell, Victor Brandt, Mario Roccuzzo, Don Gazzaniga, Fred Cash, Sam Gooden, Ralph Johnson, Reggie Torian.

2993 THREE TOUGH GUYS. (Paramount-1974). Father Charlie, Lino Ventura; Lee Stevens, Isaac Hayes; Joe Snake, Fred Williamson; Fay Collins, Paula Kelly; Captain Ryan, William Berger; Bishop, Luciano Salce; Mike Petralia, Vittorio Sanipoli; Tequila, Jacques Herlin; Bartender, Jess Hahn; Anne Lombardo, Lorella De Luca; Tony Red, Thurman E. Scott.

2994 THREESOME. (Howard Mahler-1970). Judy Brown, Marianne Tholsted, Joergen Kiil.

2995 THE THRILL KILLERS. (Hollywood Star-1965). Cash Flagg, Liz Renay, Brick Bardo, Carolyn Brandt, Ron Burr, Garay Kent, Herb Robins, Keith O'Brien, Laura Benedict, Erina Enyo, Atlas King, Titus Moede, George J. Morgan.

2996 THUMB TRIPPING. (AVCO Embassy-1972). Gary, Michael Burns; Chay, Meg Foster; Lynn, Mariana Hill; Jack, Burke Byrnes; Diesel, Mike Conrad; Smitty, Bruce Dern; Simp, Larry Hankin; Thelma, Joyce Van Patten; Sandra, Anna Aries; Sol, Don Sturdy; Danny, Jason Goodrow; Judy, Nevada Spencer; Donald, Sundown Spencer; Ed, Ed Greenberg; Eric, Eric Butler.

2997 THUNDER ALLEY. (American International-1967). Francie Madsen, Annette Funicello; Tommy Callahan, Fabian; Annie Blaine, Diane McBain; Eddie Sands, Warren Berlinger; Pete Madsen, Jan Murray; Mac Lunsford, Stanley Adams; Babe, Maureen Arthur; Harry Wise, Michael T. Mikler; Leroy, Mike Bell; Dom, Kip King.

2998 THUNDERBALL. (United Artists-1965). James Bond, Sean Connery; Domino, Claudine Auger; Emilio Largo, Adolfo Celi; Fiona, Luciana Paluzzi; Felix Leiter, Rik Van Nutter; M, Bernard Lee; Paula, Martine Beswick; Count Lippe, Guy Doleman; Patricia, Molly Peters; Q, Desmond Llewelyn; Moneypenny, Lois Maxwell; Foreign Secretary, Roland Culver.

2999 THUNDERBOLT AND LIGHTFOOT. (United Artists-1974). Thunderbolt, Clint Eastwood; Lightfoot, Jeff Bridges; Red Leary, George Kennedy; Goody, Geoffrey Lewis.

3000 THX-1138. (Warner Bros. -1971). THX, Robert Duvall; SEN, Donald Pleasence; LUH, Maggie McOmie; SRT, Don Pedro Colley.

3001 A TIA TULA. (United International-1965). Tula, Aurora Batista; Ramiro, Carlos Estrada; Tulita, Mari Loli Cabo; Ramirin, Carlos Sanchez Jimeniz; Emilio, Chiro Bermejo; Pedro Alvarez, Jose Prada; Uncle Pedro, Manuel Granada; Juanita, Enriqueta Carballeira.

3002 ... TICK ... TICK ... TICK.... (MGM-1970). Jimmy Price, Jim Brown; John Little, George Kennedy; Mayor Jeff Parks, Fredric March; Julia Little, Lynn Carlin; Bengy Springer, Don Stroud; Mary Price, Janet MacLachlan; Bradford Wilkest, Richard Elkins; D. J. Rankin, Clifton James; John Braddock, Bob Random; Deputy Joe Warren, Mills Watson; George Harley, Bernie Casey; H. C. Tolbert, Anthony James; Junior, Dub Taylor; Ernest Anderson, Karl Swenson, Barry Cahill, Anne Whitfield, Bill Walker, Dan Frazer, Leonard O. Smith, Renny Roker, Roy E. Glenn Sr., George Cisar, Paulene Myers, Dino Washington,

Calvin Brown, Beverly Taylor.

3003 TICKLE ME. (Allied Artists-1965). Lonnie Beale, Elvis Presley; Pam Merritt, Jocelyn Lane; Vera Radford, Julie Adams; Stanley Potter, Jack Mullaney; Brad Bentley, Edward Faulkner; Deputy Sturdivant, Bill Williams; Estelle Penfield, Merry Anders.

3004 LA TIERRA PROMETIDA. (Tricontinental-1974). Jose Duran, Nelson Villagra; Traje Cruzado, Marcelo Gaete; Don Fernando, Rafael Benavente; Virgin of the Carmen, Mireye Kulcheesky; Train Engineer, Anibal Reyna; Carmen Buono, Pedro Alvarez, and the inhabitants of Santa Cruz, Colchagua.

3005 THE TIGER AND THE PUSSYCAT. (Embassy-1967). Francesco Vincenzini, Vittorio Gassman; Carolina, Ann-Margret; Esperia Vincenzini, Eleanor Parker; Delia, Caterina Boratto; Luisella, Eleanora Brown; Pinella, Antonella Steni; Taxio, Fiorenzo Fiorentini; Luca, Giambattista Salerno; Monsignor, Jacques Herlen; Company President, Luigi Vanucchi.

3006 THE TIGER MAKES OUT. (Columbia-1967). Ben Harris, Eli Wallach; Gloria Fiske, Anne Jackson; Jerry Fiske, Bob Dishy; Leo, John Harkins; Mrs. Kelly, Ruth White; Mr. Kelly, Roland Wood; Beverly, Rae Allen; Miss Lane, Sudie Bond; Mr. Ratner, David Burns; Pawnbroker, Jack Fletcher; Mrs. Ratner, Bibi Osterwald.

3007 TIKO AND THE SHARK. (MGM-1966). Tiko, Al Kauwe; Diana, Marlene Among; Tiko (as a child), Denis Pouira; Diana (as a child), Diane Samsoi; Cocoyo, Roau.

3008 TIL SEX DO US PART. (Astro-1974). Solveig Ternstron, Borje Ahlstedt, Margaretha Bystrom, Frej Lindquist, Jan-Olaf Strandberg, and members of the Royal Swedish Opera Company.

3009 A TIME FOR DYING. (Etoile-1971). Cass, Richard Lapp; Nellie, Anne Randall; Jesse James, Audie Murphy; Judge, Victor Jory; Mamie, Beatrice Kay; Billy, Bob Random; Ed, Peter Brocco; Seth, Burt Mustin.

3010 A TIME FOR KILLING. (Columbia-1967). Captain Charles Wolcott, Glenn Ford; Blue Lake, Paul Petersen; Billy Cat, Timothy Carey; Sgt. Cleehan, Kenneth Tobey; Corp Paddy Darling, Richard X. Slattery; Lt. Shaffer, Harrison J. Ford; Owelson, Kay E. Kuter; Emily Biddle, Inger Stevens; Major Dorrit Bentley, George Hamilton; Sgt. Luther Liskell, Max Baer; Lt. Prudessing, Todd Armstrong; Lt. Frist, Duke Hobbie; Stedner, Marshall Reed.

3011 A TIME IN THE SUN. (Universal-1970). Princess, Grynet

Molvig; Gunnar, Lars Passgard; Pirjo, Monica Nielsen; Doctor, Birgitta Valberg; Obstetrician, Tore Lindwall; Chum, Heinz Spira; Clergyman, Axel Duberg.

3012 TIME LOST AND TIME REMEMBERED. (Continental-1966). Cass, Sarah Miles; Hogan, Cyril Cusack; Dr. Matthew Langdon, Julian Glover; Colin Foley, Sean Caffrey; Barkeeper, Marie Kean; Kate, Eve Belton.

3013 TIME OF INDIFFERENCE. (Continental-1966). Leo, Rod Steiger; Carla Ardengo, Claudia Cardinale; Lisa, Shelley Winters; Maria Grazia Ardengo, Paulette Goddard; Michele Ardengo, Tomas Milian.

3014 TIME OF ROSES. (Cinema Dimensions-1970). Saara, Ritva Vepsa; Raimo, Arto Tuominen; Anu, Tarja Markus.

3015 A TIME TO SING. (MGM-1968). Grady Dodd, Hank Williams Jr.; Amy Carter, Shelley Fabares; Kermit Dodd, Ed Begley; "Shifty" Barker, Charles Robinson; Luke Harper, D'Urville Martin; Vernon W. Carter, Donald Woods; Clara, Clara Ward; Dr. Cartwright, Harold Ayer; First M.C., Dick Haynes; Second M.C., Gene Gentry; Themselves, The X-L's.

3016 'TIS PITY SHE'S A WHORE. (Euro International-1973). Annabella, Charlotte Rampling; Giovanni, Oliver Tobias; Soranzo, Fabio Testi; Bonaventura, Antonio Falsi.

3017 TO BE A CROOK. (Comet-1967). Jean-Pierre, Jean-Pierre Kalfon; Amidou, Amidou; Pierre, Pierre Barouh; Jacques, Jacques Portet; Martine, Janine Magnan; Reporter's Voice, Gerard Sire; Stand-in, Annette Karsenti; Cafe Owner, Yane Barry.

3018 TO BE FREE. (Magarac-1972). Carole, Barbara Douglas; Dr. Keith, Morgan Evans; Althea, Victoria Wales; Bruce, Dick Decoit; Molly, Jenie Jackson; Dr. O'Donnell, Robert Webb; Peter, Peter Cord; Rehan, Paul Hernandez; Barbara, Najila; Dobbs, Bubby Arett.

3019 TO COMMIT A MURDER. (Cinerama-1970). Charles, Louis Jourdan; Gertrud, Senta Berger; Sphax, Edmond O'Brien; Rhome, Bernard Blier; Decil, Fabrizzio Capucci; Moranez, Giuseppe Addobatti.

3020 TO DIE OF LOVE. (MGM-1972). Daniele Guenot, Annie Girardot; Gerard Leguen, Bruno Pradal; Monsieur Leguen, Francois Simon; Madame Leguen, Monique Melinand; Therese, Nathalie Nell; Marc, Nicolas Dumayet; The Examining Magistrate, Claude Cerval; Madame Jaias, Marcelle Ranson; Madame Jaias Senior, Helene Dieudonne; Renee, Edith Loria; Decile, Marianick Revillon; The Snake, Marie-Helene Breillat; Head of the Clinic, Jean Marconi.

3021 TO FIND A MAN. (Columbia-1972). Rosalind, Pamela Martin; Andy, Darren O'Connor; Frank, Lloyd Bridges; Betty, Phyllis Newman; Dr. Hargrave, Tom Ewell; Mr. Katchaturian, Tom Bosley; Pete, Miles Chapin; Rick, Schell Rasten; Modesta, Antonia Rey.

3022 TO INGRID MY LOVE, LISA. (Cannon-1969). Lisa, Gun Falck; Ingrid, Gunilla Iwanson; Nils, Heinz Hopf.

3023 TO KILL A CLOWN. (20th Century-Fox-1972). Maj. Ritchie, Alan Alda; Lily Frischer, Blythe Danner; Timothy Frischer, Heath Lamberts; Stanley, Eric Clavering.

3024 TO LOVE OPHELIA. (Cineriz-1974). Federica, Françoise Fabian; Orlando, Renato Pozzetto; Ofelia, Giovanna Ralli; Fruscione, Alberto De Mendoza; Santona, Didi Perego; Spartaco, Maurizio Arena.

3025 TO SIR, WITH LOVE. (Columbia-1967). Thackeray, Sidney Poitier; Pamela Dare, Judy Geeson; Denham, Christian Roberts; Gillian Blanchard, Suzy Kendall; Barbara Pegg, Lulu; Mrs. Evans, Faith Brook; Potter, Christopher Chittell; Mr. Weston, Geoffrey Bayldon; Clinty, Patricia Routledge; Moira Jackson, Adrienne Posta; Mr. Florian, Edward Burnham; Mrs. Joseph, Rita Webb; Miss Phillips, Fiona Duncan; Seales, Anthony Villaroel; Fernman, Grahme Charles.

3026 TO TRAP A SPY. (MGM-1966). Napoleon Solo, Robert Vaughn; Illya Kuryakin, David McCallum; Angela, Luciana Paluzzi; Elaine May Donaldson, Patricia Crowley; Vulcan, Fritz Weaver; Mr. Allison, Will Kuluva; Ashumen, William Marshall; Soumarin, Ivan Dixon; Gracie Ladovan, Victoria Shaw; Lancer, Miguel Landa; Alfred Ghist, Eric Berry; Del Floria, Mario Siletti; Nobuk, Rupert Crosse.

3027 TOBRUK. (Universal-1967). Major Donald Craig, Rock Hudson; Captain Kurt Bergman, George Peppard; Colonel John Harker, Nigel Green; Lt. Max Mohnfeld, Guy Stockwell; Sgt. Major Tyne, Jack Watson; Alfie, Norman Rossington; Dolan, Percy Herbert; Henry Portman, Liam Redmond; Cheryl Portman, Heidy Hunt; Sgt. Krug, Leo Gordon; Corporal Bruckner, Robert Wolders; Lt. Boyden, Anthony Ashdown; Curt Lowens, Henry Rico Cattani, Peter Coe, Lawrence Montaigne, Robert Hoy, Phil Adams, Ronnie R. Rondell.

3028 TODAY WE KILL ... TOMORROW WE DIE! (Cinerama-1971). Bill, Montgomery Ford; O'Bannion, Bud Spencer; El Fego, Tatsuya Nakadai; Colt, William Berger; Jeff, Wayde Preston; Bunny, Stanley Gordon.

3029 THE TODD KILLINGS. (National General-1971). Skipper,

Robert F. Lyons; Billy, Richard Thomas; Roberta, Belinda Montgomery; Mrs. Todd, Barbara Bel Geddes; Amata, Sherry Miles; Haddie, Joyce Ames; Norma, Holly Near; Sam, James Broderick; Mrs. Roy, Gloria Grahame; Mrs. Mack, Fay Spain; Fred, Edward Asner; Detective, Michael Conrad.

3030 TOGETHER BROTHERS. (20th Century-Fox-1974). H. J., Ahmad Nurradin; Tommy, Anthony Wilson; A. P., Nelson Sims; Mau Mau, Kenneth Bell; Monk, Owen Pace; Gri Gri, Kim Dorsey; Mr. Kool, Ed Bernard; Billy Most, Lincoln Kilpatrick; Dr. Johnson, Glynn Turman; Vega, Richard Yniguez; Francine, Angela Gibbs; Strokes McGee, Mwako Cumbuka; Mama Wes, Frances Williams; Maria, Craig Campfield; Rev. Brown, Bessie Griffin; Sugar, Lynne Holmes; Armstrong, Danny Big Black; Alice Martin, Gloria Calomee; Police Detective, Howard Picard; Matthew, Charles Lemons; Chicano, Joe Zapata; Clutie, Leah Ward; Desk Officer, William Dagg; Nurse, Roberta Ester; Harry, Ernest Boyd; Policeman, John Jennings; Dude, Lane Mitchell.

3031 TOGETHER FOR DAYS. (Olas-1973). Gus, Clifton Davis; Shelley, Lois Chiles; Calvin, Northern Calloway; Phil, Leonard Jackson; Karen, Gisela Caldwell; Jerry, Woodie King; Miriam, Liz Wright; Doug, Ben Jones; Sister Sonji, Andrea Frye; Big Bubba, Gilbert Lewis; Stan, Sam Jackson; Hanratty, Brooke Clift.

3032 TOKOLOSHE. (Artist International-1973). Boy, Saul Pelle; Blind Man, Sidney James; Zulu Chief, Chief Butulezei; Thief, Cy Sacks; Witchdoctor, Jimmy Sabe.

3033 TOKYO STORY. (New Yorker-1972). Shukishi Hirayama, Chishu Ryu; Tomi Hirayama, Chiyeko Higashiyama; Koichi, So Yamamura; Fumiko, Kuniko Miyake; Shige, Haruko Sugimura; Kurazo, Nobuo Nakamura; Noriko, Kyoko Kagawa; Noriko, Setsuko Hara; Keiso, Shiro Osaka.

3034 TOM. (Four Star International-1973). Jim, Greydon Clark; Makinba, Tom Johnigarn; Lt. Stans, Aldo Ray; Sgt. Berry, Jock Mahoney; Nancy, Jacquelin Cole; Bobbie, Bambi Allen; Tina, Pamela Corbett.

3035 TOM SAWYER. (United Artists-1973). Tom Sawyer, Johnny Whitaker; Aunt Polly, Celeste Holm; Muff Potter, Warren Oates; Huckleberry Finn, Jeff East; Becky Thatcher, Jodie Foster; Widder Douglas, Lucille Benson; Mister Dobbins, Henry Jones; Judge Thatcher, Noah Keen; Clayton, Dub Taylor; Doc Robinson, Richard Eastham; Constable Clemens, Sandy Kenyon; Cousin Sidney, Joshua Hill Lewis; Cousin Mary, Susan Joyce; Ben Rogers, Steve Hogg; Billy Fisher, Sean Summers; Joe Jefferson, Kevin Jefferson; Saloon Girl, Page Williams; Injun Joe, Kunu Hank; Blacksmith, James A. Kuhn; Prosecuting Attorney, Mark Lynch;

Small Boy, Jonathan Taylor; Girl, Anne Voss.

3036 TOMB OF LIGEIA. (American International-1965). Verdon Fell, Vincent Price; Ligeia/Lady Rowena, Elizabeth Shepherd; Christopher, John Westbrook; Kenrick, Oliver Johnston;, Lord Trevanion, Derek Francis.

3037 TOMB OF TORTURE. (Trans-Lux-1966). Annie Albert, Thony Maky, Elizabeth Queen, Mark Marian.

3038 TOMORROW. (Filmgroup-1972). Jackson Fentry, Robert Duvall; Sarah Eubanks, Olga Bellin; Mrs. Hulie, Sudie Bond; Isham Russell, Richard McConnell; Lawyer Douglas, Peter Masterson; Pap Fentry, William Hawley; Preacher Whitehead, James Franks; Sarah's Child, Johnny Mask; Dick Dougherty, Effie Green, Ken Lindley, R. M. Weaver, Billy Summerford, Thomas C. Coggin.

3039 TONIO KROGER. (Pathe Contemporary-1968). Tonio Kroger, Jean-Claude Brialy; Lisaveta Iwanovna, Nadja Tiller; Konsul Kroger, Werner Hinz; Frau Kroger, Anaid Iplicjian; Herr Seehaase, Rudolf Forster.

3040 TONY ROME. (20th Century-Fox-1967). Tony Rome, Frank Sinatra; Ann Archer, Jill St. John; Lt. Santini, Richard Conte; Diana Pines, Sue Lyon; Rita Kosterman, Gena Rowlands; Rudolph Kosterman, Simon Oakland; Adam Boyd, Jeffrey Lynn; Vic Rood, Lloyd Bochner; Ralph Turpin, Robert J. Wilke; Donald Pines, Richard Krisher; Sally Bullock, Virginia Vincent; Fat Candy, Joan Shawlee; Langley, Lloyd Gough; Oscar, Babe Hart; Mrs. Langley, Timpleton Fox; Packy, Rocky Graziano; Irma, Elizabeth Fraser; Nimmo, Buzz Henry; Catleg, Shecky Greene; Lorna, Jeanne Cooper; Henrik Ruyter, Harry Davis; Sam Boyd, Stanley Ross; Georgia McKay, Deanna Lund; Maitre d'Hotel, Mike Romanoff; Photo Girl, Tiffany Bolling.

3041 TOO LATE THE HERO. (Cinerama-1970). Pvt. Tosh Hearne, Michael Caine; Lt. Sam Lawson, Cliff Robertson; Capt. John G. Nolan, Henry Fonda; Pvt. Thornton, Ian Bannen; Lt. Col. Thompson, Harry Andrews; Capt. Hornsby, Denholm Elliott; Pvt. Campbell, Ronald Fraser; Cpl. McLean, Lance Percival; Sgt. Johnstone, Percy Herbert; Pvt. Rafferty, Michael J. Parsons; Signalman Scott, Harvey Jason.

3042 TOP OF THE HEAP. (Fanfare-1972). George Lattimer, Christopher St. John; Singer, Paula Kelly; Viola Lattimer, Florence St. Peter; Bobby Gelman, Leonard Kuras; Captain Walsh, John Alderson; Tim Cassidy, Patrick McVey; Nurse Swenson, Ingeborg Sorensen; Hip Passenger, Ron Douglas; Valerie Lattimer, Almeria Quinn; George's Mother, Beatrice Webster; African Dancer, Essie McSwine; Club Owner, Jerry

Jones; Bouncer, Willie Harris; Man With Knife, Tiger Joe Marsh; Dope Dealer, John McMurtry; Bus Driver, Raymond O'Keefe; Rookie Policeman, Brian Cutler; Young Hooker, Angela Seymour.

3043 TOPAZ. (Universal-1969). Michael Nordstrom, John Forsythe; Andre Devereaux, Frederick Stafford; Nicole Devereaux, Dany Robin; Rico Parra, John Vernon; Juanita de Cordoba, Karin Dor; Jacques Granville, Michel Piccoli; Henri Jarre, Philippe Noiret; Michele Picard, Claude Jade; François Picard, Michel Subor; Philippe Dubois, Roscoe Lee Browne; Boris Kusenov, Per-Axel Arosenius.

3044 TORA! TORA! TORA! (20th Century-Fox-1970). Admiral Kimmel, Martin Balsam; Admiral Yamamoto, Soh Yamamura; Henry Stimson, Joseph Cotton; Commander Genda, Tatsuya Mihashi; Lt. Colonel Bratton, E. G. Marshall; Lt. Commander Fuchida, Takahiro Tamura; Admiral Halsey, James Whitmore; Admiral Nagumo, Eijiro Tono; Lt. Commander Kramer, Wesley Addy; Ambassador Nomura, Shogo Shimada; Lt. Commander Thomas, Frank Aletter; Prince Konoye, Koreya Senda; Frank Knox, Leon Ames; Admiral Yoshida, Junya Usami; Captain John Earle, Richard Anderson; Foreign Minister Matsuoka, Kazuo Kitamura; General George C. Marshall, Keith Andes; Admiral Stark, Edward Andrews; Lieutenant Kaminsky, Neville Brand; Mrs. Kramer, Leora Dana; General Tojo, Asao Uchida; Cordell Hull, George Macready; Major Truman Landon, Norman Alden; Captain Theodore Wilkinson, Walter Brooke; Lieutenant George Welch, Rick Cooper; Doris Miller, Elven Havard; Miss Ray Cave, June Dayton; Colonel Edward F. French, Richard Erdman; Cornelia, Jeff Donnell; General Short, Jason Robards.

3045 TORN CURTAIN. (Universal-1966). Professor Michael Armstrong, Paul Newman; Sarah Sherman, Julie Andrews; Countess Kuchinska, Lila Kedrova; Heinrich Gerhard, Hans Joerg Felmy; Herman Gromek, Wolfgang Kieling; Ballerina, Tamara Toumanova; Professor Karl Manfred, Gunther Strack; Professor Gustav Lindt, Ludwig Donath; Mr. Jacobi, David Opatoshu; Dr. Koska, Gisela Fischer; Farmer, Mort Mills; Farmer's Wife, Carolyn Conwell; Freddy, Arthur Gould-Porter; Fraulein Mann, Gloria Gorvin.

3046 TORSO. (Joseph Brenner-1974). Jane, Suzy Kendall; Dani, Tina Aumont; Roberto, Luc Meranda; Franz, John Richardson; Stefano, Roberto Bisacco; Katia, Angela Covello; Ursula, Carla Brait; Carol, Cristina Airoldi; Flo, Patricia Adiutori.

3047 TORTURE GARDEN. (Columbia-1968). Ronald Wyatt, Jack Palance; Dr. Diablo, Burgess Meredith; Carla Hayes, Beverly Adams; Lancelot Channing, Peter Cushing; Dorothy

Endicott, Barbara Ewing; Colin Williams, Michael Bryant; Colin's Uncle, Maurice Denham; Leo Winson, John Standing; Bruce Benton, Robert Hutton; Eddie Storm, John Phillips; Gordon Roberts, Michael Ripper; Dr. Heim, Bernard Kay; Nurse Parker, Catherine Finn; Miss Chambers, Ursula Howells; Doctor, Niall MacGinnis; Fairground Barker, Timothy Bateson; Mike Charles, David Bauer; Millie, Nicole Shelby; Atropos, Clytie Jessop; Constable, Michael Hawkins; Edgar Allan Poe, Hedger Wallace; Roy Stevens, James Copeland, Roy Godfrey, Geoffrey Wallace, Norman Claridge, Barry Low.

3048 THE TOUCH. (Cinerama-1971). Karin, Bibi Andersson; David, Elliott Gould; Dr. Andreas, Max Von Sydow; Sara, Sheila Reid; Karin's Mother, Barbro Hiort of Ornas; Anders, Staffan Hallerstam; Agnes, Maria Nolgard.

3049 A TOUCH OF CLASS. (AVCO Embassy-1973). Steve Blackburn, George Segal; Vicki Allessio, Glenda Jackson; Walter Menkes, Paul Sorvino; Gloria Blackburn, Hildegard Neil; Wendell Thompson, Cec Linder; Patty Menkes, K. Callan; Marsha Thompson, Mary Barclay; Cecil, Michael Elwyn; Night Hotel Manager, Nadim Sawalha; Derek, Ian Thompson; Miss Ramos, Eve Karpf; Dr. Alvarez, David De Keyser; Dora French, Gaye Brown.

3050 THE TOUCHABLES. (20th Century-Fox-1968). Sadie, Judy Huxtable; Melanie, Esther Anderson; Busbee, Marilyn Rickard; Samson, Kathy Simmonds; Christian, David Anthony; Ricki, Ricki Starr; Twyning, James Villiers; Kasher, John Ronane; Lillywhite, Harry Baird; Denzil, Michael Chow; Interviewer, Joan Bakewell; Quayle, William Dexter; Glubb, Roy Davies; March, Danny Lynch; Bruno, Bruno Elrington.

3051 TOUGH. (Dimension-1974). Dion Gossett, Renny Roker, Sandy Reed, Rich Holmes, Christopher Towns, Detra Piernas, Philip Hadler, David Shafer.

3052 TOUT VA BIEN. (New Yorker-1973). He, Yves Montand; She, Jane Fonda; Factory Manager, Vittorio Caprioli; Delegate, Jean Pignol; Frederic, Pierre Ondry; Genevieve, Illizabeth Chauvin; Lucien, Eric Chartier; Leon, Yves Gabrielli.

3053 TOWER OF SCREAMING VIRGINS. (Maron-1972). Marguerite, Terry Torday; Captain Bouridan, Jean Piat; Blanche, Uschi Glas; Orsini, Frank Olivier (Armando Francioli); Jeanne, Veronique Vendell; Catherine, Marie-Agne Anies; Fluerette, Dada Gallotti; Honore De La Tour, Rudolf Forster; Karlheim Fiege, George Markos, Franz Rudnik, Jorg Pleva, Rolf Becker, Jacques Herlin, Werner Fliege.

3054 THE TOWERING INFERNO. (20th Century-Fox-1974). Fire

Chief O'Hallorhan, Steve McQueen; Doug Roberts, Paul Newman; Jim Duncan, William Holden; Susan, Faye Dunaway; Harlee Claiborne, Fred Astaire; Patty Simmons, Susan Blakely; Simmons, Richard Chamberlain; Lisolette, Jennifer Jones; Security Chief Jernigan, O. J. Simpson; Senator Parker, Robert Vaughn; Bigelow, Robert Wagner; Lorrie, Susan Flannery; Mayor, Jack Collins; Mayor's Wife, Sheila Mathews; Construction Chief, Norman Burton; Mrs. Albright, Carol McEvoy; Albright Children, Michael Lookinland, Carlene Gower; Engineer, Olan Soule; Pilots, LCDR Norman Hicks and LTJG Thomas Karnahan.

3055 A TOWN CALLED HELL. (Scotia International-1971). Robert Shaw, Stella Stevens, Martin Landau, Telly Savalas, Michael Craig, Dudley Sutton, Al Lettieri, Aldo Sambrell, Fernando Rey.

3056 TOWN TAMER. (Paramount-1965). Dana Andrews, Terry Moore, Pat O'Brien, Lon Chaney, Bruce Cabot, Lyle Bettger, Coleen Gray, Barton MacLane, Richard Arlen, Richard Jaeckel, Philip Carey, DeForrest Kelley, Sonny Tufts, Roger Torres, James Brown, Richard Webb, Jeanne Cagney, Don Barry, Bob Steele.

3057 THE TOY BOX. (Boxoffice International-1972). Donna, Ann Myers; Ralph, Neal Bishope; "The Benevolent Man," Evan Steele; Deborah Osborne, Lisa Goodman, Marie Arnold, Steve Moon, T. E. Brown, Marsha Jordan, Ralph Dale, Kathie Hilton, Karen Hutt, Jack King, Nancey Freese, Casey Larrain, Patti Mendosa.

3058 TOYS ARE NOT FOR CHILDREN. (Maron-1972). Jamie, Marcia Forbes; Edna, Fran Warren; Phillip, Peter Lightstone; Charlie, Harlan Cary Poe; Pearl, Evelyn Kingsley; Eddie, Luis Arroyo; Jamie as a girl, Tiberia Mitri; John, Jack Cobb; Max, N. J. Osrak.

3059 TRACK OF THUNDER. (United Artists-1968). Bobby Goodwin, Tom Kirk; Gary Regal, Ray Stricklyn; Maxwell Carstairs, H. M. Wynant; Shelley Newman, Brenda Benet; Mrs. Goodwin, Faith Domergue; Georgia Clark, Majel Barrett; Mr. Regal, Chet Stratton; Bowser Smith, James Dobson; Mr. Bigelow, Paul Crabtree; Colonel Lee, Sam Tarpley; Bob Stewart, Maurice Dembsky, Leslie Jameson, Bob Smith, Ed Livingston, Horace Wood, Carol Doughty, Don Gregory, Chuck Doughty.

3060 TRADER HORN. (MGM-1973). Trader Horn, Rod Taylor; Nicole, Anne Heywood; Emil, Jean Sorel; Sinclair, Don Knight; Apaque, Ed Bernard; Malugi, Stack Pierce; Medford, Erik Holland; Alfredo, Robert Miller Driscoll; Red Sun, King Solomon III; Blue Star, Willie Harris; Umbopa, Caro Kenyatta; Dancer, Oliver Givens; Schmidt, Curt Lowens;

German Officer, John Siegfried.

3061 TRADER HORNEE. (Entertainment Ventures-1970). Hornee, Buddy Pantsari; Jane, Elisabeth Monica; Max, John Alderman; Tender Lee, Lisa Grant; Doris, Christine Murray; Kenya, Brandon Duffy; Algona, Deek Sills; Fletcher Davies, Neal Henderson, Andrew Herbert, Debbie Douglas, Ed Rogers, Ben Cadlett, Chuck Wells, Bill Babcock.

3062 TRAFFIC. (Columbia-1972). Mr. Hulot, Jacques Tati; Public Relations Girl, Maria Kimberly; Truck Driver, Marcel Fraval; Managing Director of ALTRA, H. Bostel; Dutch Garage Proprietor, Tony Kneppers.

3063 THE TRAIN. (United Artists-1965). Labiche, Burt Lancaster; Colonel von Waldheim, Paul Scofield; Christine, Jeanne Moreau; Papa Boule, Michel Simon; Miss Villard, Suzanne Flon; Herren, Wolfgang Preiss; Von Lubitz, Richard Munch; Didont, Albert Remy; Pesquet, Charles Millot; Jacques, Jacques Marin; Spinet, Paul Bonifas; Schmidt, Jean Bouchaud.

3064 THE TRAIN ROBBERS. (Warner Bros. -1973). Lane, John Wayne; Mrs. Lowe, Ann-Margret; Grady, Rod Taylor; Jesse, Ben Johnson; Calhoun, Christopher George; Ben Young, Bobby Vinton; Sam Turner, Jerry Gatlin; Pinkerton Man, Ricardo Montalban.

3065 TRAITOR'S GATE. (Columbia-1966). Gary Raymond, Albert Lieven, Margot Trooger, Klaus Kinski, Catherina Von Schell, Eddie Arent.

3066 THE TRAMPLERS. (Embassy-1966). Temple Cordeen, Joseph Cotten; Lon Cordeen, Gordon Scott; Hoby Cordeen, James Mitchum; Edith Wickett, Ilaria Occhini; Charley Garvey, Franco Nero; Bess Cordeen, Emma Vannoni; Longfellow Wiley, Georges Lycan; Alice Cordeen, Muriel Franklin; Jim Hennessy, Aldo Cecconi; Pete Wiley, Franco Balducci; Fred Wickett, Claudio Gora; Paine Cordeen, Romano Puppo; Bert Cordeen, Dario Michaelis; Adrian Cordeen, Ivan Scratuglia; Mrs. Temple Cordeen, Carla Calo.

3067 TRANS-EUROPE-EXPRESS. (Trans American-1968). Elias, Jean-Louis Trintignant; Eva, Marie-France Pisier; Franck, Charles Millot; Lorentz, Christian Barbier; Hotel Maid, Nadine Verdier; Cabaret Singer, Clo Vanesco; Agent, Daniel Emilfork; Inspector, Henri Lambert; Director, Alain Robbe-Grillet; Producer, Sammy Helfon; Script Girl, Catherine Robbe-Grillet; Raoul Guylad, Salkin, Ariane Sapriel, Gerard Palaprat, Paul Louyet, Rezy Norbert, Virginie Vignon.

3068 TRANSPORT FROM PARADISE. (Impact-1967). Lowenbach,

Zdenek Stepanek; Murmelstaub, Cestmir Randa; Herz, Ilja Pracher; Binde, Jiri Vrstala; Holler, Jaroslav Raner; Roubicek, Ladislav Pesek.

3069 THE TRAP. (Continental-1968). Eve, Rita Tushingham; Jean La Bete, Oliver Reed; The Trader, Rex Sevenoaks; The Trader's Wife, Barbara Chilcott; The Trader's Daughter, Linda Goranson; Clerk, Blain Fairman; Preacher, Walter Marsh; Baptiste, Jo Golland.

3070 TRASH. (Andy Warhol-1970). Joe Dallesandro, Jane Forth, Holly Woodlawn, Michael Sklar, Gerri Miller, Andrea Feldman, Bruce Pecheur, Johnny Patton, Diane Podlewski, Bob Dallesandro.

3071 THE TRAVELING EXECUTIONER. (MGM-1970). Jonas Candide, Stacy Keach; Gundred Hezallerliebst, Mariana Hill; Jimmy, Bud Cort; Doc Prittle, Graham Jarvis; Piquant, James J. Sloyan; Warden Brodski, M. Emmet Walsh; Lawyer, John Bottoms; Stanley Mae, Ford Rainey; Gravey Combs, James Greene; Priest, Sammy Reese; Willy Hezzalerliebst, Stefan Gierasch; La Follette, Logan Ramsey; Virgil, Charles Tyner; Lynn, William Mims; Jake, Val Avery; Sheriff, Walter Barnes; Zak, Charles Briggs; Woman Passerby, Claire Brennen; Alice Thorn, Scottie MacGregor; First Child, Tony Fraser; Second Child, Martine Fraser; Madam, Lorna Thayer; Roscoe, Pat Patterson.

3072 TRAVELS WITH MY AUNT. (MGM-1972). Aunt Augusta, Maggie Smith; Henry, Alec McCowen; Wordsworth, Lou Gossett; Visconti, Robert Stephens; Tooley, Cindy Williams; Crowder, Robert Flemyng; Dambreuse, Jose Luis Lopez Vazquez; Mario, Raymond Gerome; Hakim, Daniel Emilfork; Crowder's Man, John Hamill; Detective, David Swift.

3073 TREASURE ISLAND. (National General-1972). Long John Silver, Orson Welles; Jim, Kim Burfield; Squire Trelawney; Billy Bones, Lionel Stander; Blind Pew, Paul Muller; Mrs. Hawkins, Maria Rohm; Dr. Livesey, Angel Del Pozo; Merry, Michel Garland; Capt. Smollett, Rik Battaglia; Ben Gunn, Jean Lefebvre.

3074 THE TREASURE OF MAKUBA. (Producers Releasing Organization-1967). Coogan, Cameron Mitchell; Maroa, Maria Cruz; Mary, Jessie Paradise; Hank, Todd Martin; Pat, Al Mulock; Tony, Joseph Luis Lluch; Duval, Pastor Serrador; Chief Moala, Felix Noble; Ling, Walter Zamudio.

3075 TREASURE OF SAN GENNARO. (Paramount-1968). Dudu, Nino Manfredi; Maggie, Senta Berger; Jack, Harry Guardino; Concettina, Claudine Auger; Don Vincenzo, Toto; Sciascillo, Mario Adorf; Frank, Frank Wolff; Agony, Ugo Fangareggi; The Captain, Dante Maggio; The Cardinal, Giovanni Bruti;

The Baron, Pinuccio Ardia.

3076 TREASURE OF SILVER LAKE. (Columbia-1965). Lex Barker, Herbert Lom, Gotz-George, Pierre Brice.

3077 THE TREE. (Robert Guenette-1969). Bucky Gagnon, Jordan Christopher; Sally Dunning, Eileen Heckart; Stuey, George Rose; Detective McCarthy, James Broderick; Mrs. Gagnon, Ruth Ford; Alex, Fred J. Scollay; Lorry, Gale Dixon; Jim Wisiewski, Alan Landers; Terry, Kathy Ryan; Detective Gorman, Ed Griffith; Joe, Tom Ahearne; 1st Boy on Bicycle, Glenn Scimonelli; 2nd Boy on Bicycle, Alan Zemel; Delivery Boy, Billy King; Waiter, Ben Gerard.

3078 THE TRIAL OF BILLY JACK. (Taylor-Laughlin-1974). Billy Jack, Tom Laughlin; Jean Roberts, Delores Taylor; Doc, Victor Izay; Carol, Teresa Laughlin; Posner, Riley Hill; Sheriff Cole, Sparky Watt; Nat'l. Guardsman, William Wellman Jr.; Michelle, Michelle Wilson; Joanne, Geo Anna Sosa; Lynn, Lynn Baker; Blue Elk, Gus Greymountain; Patsy Littlejohn, Sacheen Littlefeather; Danny, Michael Bolland; Grandfather, Jack Stanley; Rolling Thunder, Sandra Ego; Trinidad Hopkins, Marianne Hall, Jason Clark, Johnny West, Buffalo Horse, Dennis O'Flaherty, Bong Soo Han, Michael J. Shingezane.

3079 TRIAL OF JOAN OF ARC. (Pathe Contemporary-1965). Joan of Arc, Florence Carrez; Bishop Cauchon, Jean-Claude Fourneau; Jean Lemaitre (Inquisitor), Marc Jacquier; Jean Beaupere, Roger Honorat; Jean de Chatillon, Jean Gillibert; D'Estivet, Andre Regnier; Frere Isambart de la Pierre, Michel Herubel; Frere Martin Ladvenu, Philippe Dreux; Nicolas de Houppeville, Jean Darbaud; Warwick, E. R. Pratt; Englishman, Michael Williams; Bishop of Winchester, Harry Sommers; English Priest, Donald O'Brien; Jean Lohier, Gerard Zingg; Tiphaine, Andre Maurice; Guillaume Erard, Robert Mimet; Pierre Morice, Yves Leprince.

3080 THE TRIAL OF THE CATONSVILLE NINE. (Cinema V-1972). Marjorie Melville, Gwen Arner; Father Daniel Berrigan, Ed Flanders; John Hogan, Barton Heyman; Witness, Mary Jackson; George Mische, Richard Jordan; Mary Moyland, Nancy Malone; Thomas Melville, Donald Moffat; Prosecutor, Davis Roberts; David Darst, Leon Russom; Judge, William Schallert; Defense, David Spielberg; Thomas Lewis, Peter Strauss; Father Philip Berrigan, Douglass Watson.

3081 TRICK BABY. (Universal-1973). Carlson, Jan Leighton; Parkview Clerk, Byron Sanders; Vincent, Dick Boccelli; Doc, Jim Mapp; Bartender, Ronald Carter; Hookers, Celeste Creech, Deloris Brown-Harper; Aunt Rose, Jacqueline Weiss; Priest, Father James Kelly.

3082 TRILOGY. (Allied Artists-1969). Miss Miller, Mildred Natwick; Miriam, Susan Dunfee; Miss Lake, Carol Gustafson; Emily, Robin Ponterio; Nina, Beverly Ballard; Mrs. Connolly, Jane Connell; Man in Theatre, Frederic Morton; Man in automat, Richard Hamilton; Woman in Automat, Phyllis Eldridge; Mr. Connolly, Brooks Rogers; Mary O'Meaghan, Maureen Stapleton; Ivor Belli, Martin Balsam; Woman, Geraldine Page; Buddy, Donnie Melvin; Aunts, Lavinia Cassels, Christine Marler; Haha, Josip Elic; Woman in Car, Lynn Forman; Storekeeper, Win Forman.

3083 TRINITY IS STILL MY NAME. (AVCO Embassy-1973). Trinity, Terence Hill; Bambino, Bud Spencer; Father, Harry Carey Jr.; Mother, Jessica Dublin; Pioneer, Yanti Somer; Sheriff, Enzo Tarascio; Padre, Pupo De Luca.

3084 THE TRIP. (American International-1967). Paul Groves, Peter Fonda; Sally Groves, Susan Strasberg; John, Bruce Dern; Max, Dennis Hopper; Glenn, Salli Sachse; Lulu, Katherine Walsh; Flo, Barboura Morris; Alexandra, Caren Bernsen; Cash, Dick Miller; Waitress, Luana Anders; Al, Tommy Signorelli; Wife, Mitzi Hoag; Nadine, Judy Lang; Helena, Barbara Renson; Go-Go Girls, Susan Walters and Frankie Smith.

3085 THE TRIP. (1974). Adriana, Sophia Loren; Cesar, Richard Burton; Antonio, Ian Bannen; Doctor, Renato Pinciroli; Notary, Daniele Pitani; Mother, Barbara Leonard; Armando Gill, Sergio Bruni; Rinaldo, Ettore Geri; Clementina, Olga Romanelli.

3086 TRIPLE CROSS. (Warner Bros.-7 Arts-1967). Eddie Chapman, Christopher Plummer; Baron von Grunen, Yul Brynner; The Countess, Romy Schneider; Distinguished Civilian, Trevor Howard; Colonel Steinhager, Gert Frobe; Paulette, Claudine Auger; Lt. Keller, Harry Meyen; Leo, Georges Lycan; Bergman, Gil Barber; Major von Leeb, Jean-Claude Bercq; Sgt. Thomas, Jean Claudio; General Dalyrumple, Robert Favart; Raymond, Bernard Fresson; Losch, Clement Harrari; Lisbon Embassy Official, Howard Vernon; German Col.-General, Francis De Wolff; Commander Braid, Jess Hahn; Resistance Leader, Jean-Marc Bory; Hubert Noel, Jean Bertrand.

3087 TRIPLE ECHO. (Altura-1973). Alice, Glenda Jackson; Barton, Brian Deacon; Sergeant, Oliver Reed; Subaltern, Anthony May; Stan, Gavin Richards; Christine, Jenny Lee Wright; Shopkeeper, Daphne Heard.

3088 TRIPLE IRONS. (National General-1973). Pa, Li Ching; Lei, David Chiang; Feng, Ti Lung; Lung, Ku Feng; Chen, Chen Hsing; Chin, Wang Chung; Ho, Cheng Lei.

3089 TRISTANA. (Maron-1970). Tristana, Catherine Deneuve; Horacio, Franco Nero; Don Lope, Fernando Rey; Saturna, Lola Gaos; Don Cosme, Antonio Casas; Saturno, Jesus Fernandez; Don Ambrosio, Vicente Soler; Professor, Sergio Mendizabal; Bellringer, Jose Valvo; Girl, Mary Paz Pondal; Bourgeois, Candida Losada; Dr. Miquis, Fernando Cebrian; Don Candido, Juanjo Menendez.

3090 TROG. (Warner Bros.-1970). Dr. Brockton, Joan Crawford; Sam, Michael Gough; Ann, Kim Braden; Leader, David Griffin; and John Hamill, Joe Cornelius, Bernard Kay, Thorley Walters.

3091 TROIKA. (Emerson-1969). Fredric Hobbs, Nate Thurmond, Gloria Rossi, Morgan Upton, Richard Faun, Parra O'Siochain.

3092 THE TROJAN WOMEN. (Cinerama-1971). Hecuba, Katharine Hepburn; Andromache, Vanessa Redgrave; Cassandra, Genevieve Bujold; Helen, Irene Papas; Talthybius, Brian Blessed; Menelaus, Patrick Magee; Atsyanax, Alberto Sanz.

3093 TROPIC OF CANCER. (Paramount-1970). Henry Miller, Rip Torn; Fillmore, James Callahan; Mona, Ellen Burstyn; Carl, David Bauer; Ginette, Laurence Ligneres; Van Norden, Phil Brown; Vite Cheri, Dominique Delpierre; Ranji, Stuart de Silva.

3094 TROPICAL ECSTACY. (Haven-1970). Minica, Isabel Sarli; Jose, Armando Bo; Pedro, Egidio Eccio.

3095 TROPICS. (New Yorker-1969). Miguel, Joel Barcelos; Maria, Janira Santiago; Graciele, Graciele Campos; Batista, Batista Campos; Black Man, Antonio Pitanga; Julio, Roque Aranjo; Maria Euridice, Maria Euridice; The Doctor, Giorgio Poppi.

3096 TROUBLE MAN. (20th Century-Fox-1972). Mr. "T," Robert Hooks; Chalky Price, Paul Winfield; Pete Cockrell, Ralph Waite; Captain Joe Marks, William Smithers; Cleo, Paula Kelly; Mr. Big, Julius W. Harris; Jimmy, Bill Henderson; Preston, Vince Howard; Buddy, Larry Cook; Chi, Akili Jones; Pindar, Rick Ferrell; Collie, Stack Pierce; Sam Edmund Cambridge, Bobby Fleton Perry; Frank, Wayne Storm; Macy, Virginia Capers; Pool Shark, James Earl Brown; Leroy, Jita Hadi; Policewoman, Tracy Reed; Sgt. Koeppler, John Crawford.

3097 THE TROUBLE WITH ANGELS. (Columbia-1966). Mother Superior, Rosalind Russell; Mary Clancy, Hayley Mills; Sister Celestine, Binnie Barnes; Rachel Devery, June Harding; Mrs. Phipps, Gypsy Rose Lee; Sister Clarissa, Mary Wickes; Sister Constance, Camilla Sparv; Uncle George,

Kent Smith; Sister Barbara, Margalo Gillmore; Sister Elizabeth, Portia Nelson; Marvel-Ann, Barbara Hunter; Mr. Devery, Pat McCaffrie; Mr. Gottschalk, Jim Boles; Sister Liguori, Marge Redmond; Dolores Sutton, Marjorie Eaton, Barbara Bell Wright, Bernadette Withers, Vicky Albright, Patty Gerrity, Vicki Draves.

3098 THE TROUBLE WITH GIRLS. (MGM-1969). Walter Hale, Elvis Presley; Charlene, Marlyn Mason; Betty, Nicole Jaffe; Nita, Sheree North; Johnny, Edward Andrews; Drewcott, John Carradine; Caro, Anissa Jones; Morality, Vincent Price; Maude, Joyce Van Patten; Willy, Pepe Brown; Harrison, Dabney Coleman; Mayor, Bill Zuckert; Perper, Pitt Herbert; Clarene, Anthony Teague; Constable, Med Flory.

3099 TRUCK STOP WOMEN. (LT Films-1974). Rose, Claudia Jennings; Anna, Lieux Dressler; Smith, John Martino; Curly, Dennis Fimple; Trish, Dolores Dorn; Mac, Gene Drew; Seago, Paul Carr; Tina, Jennifer Burton; Sheriff, Eric Nord.

3100 TRUCK TURNER. (American International-1974). Truck Turner, Isaac Hayes; Harvard Blue, Yaphet Kotto; Jerry, Alan Weeks; Annie, Annazette Chase; Gator, Paul Harris; Dorinda, Nichelle Nichols; Nate, Sam Laws.

3101 TRUE GRIT. (Paramount-1969). Rooster Cogburn, John Wayne; Le Boeuf, Glen Campbell; Mattie Ross, Kim Darby; Emmett Quincy, Jeremy Slate; Ned Pepper, Robert Duvall; Moon, Dennis Hopper; Goudy, Alfred Ryder; Col. G. Stonehill, Strother Martin; Tom Chaney, Jeff Corey; Capt. Boots Finch, Ron Soble; Lawyer Daggett, John Fiedler; Judge Parker, James Westerfield; Sheriff, John Doucette; Barlow, Donald Woods; Mrs. Floyd, Edith Atwater; Dirty Bob, Carlos Rivas; Mrs. Bagby, Isabel Boniface; Chen Lee, H. W. Gim; Frank Ross, John Pickard; Mrs. Ross, Elizabeth Harrower; Yarnell, Ken Renard; Harold Parmalee, Jay Ripley; Farrell Parmalee, Kenneth Becker.

3102 TRUNK TO CAIRO. (American International-1966). Mike Merrick, Audie Murphy; Professor Schlieben, George Sanders; Helga Schlieben, Marianne Koch; Yasmin, Gila Almagor; Captain Gabar, Joseph Yadin; Hadassa, Elana Eden; Ephraim, Zalman; Christina, Tikva Mor.

3103 THE TRUTH ABOUT SPRING. (Universal-1965). Spring Tyler, Hayley Mills; Tommy Tyler, John Mills; William Ashton, James MacArthur; Cark, Lionel Jeffries; Cleary, Niall Mac Ginnis; Sellers, Harry Andrews; Skelton, David Tomlinson.

3104 THE TRYGON FACTOR. (Warner Bros. -7 Arts-1969). Supt. Cooper-Smith, Stewart Granger; Trudy Emberday, Susan Hampshire; Hubert Hamlyn, Robert Morley; Livia

Emberday, Cathleen Nesbitt; Sister General, Brigitte Horney; Sophie, Sophie Hardy; Sir John, James Robertson Justice; Sister Clare, Diane Clare; Luke Emberday, James Culliford; Detective Thompson, Allan Cuthbertson; Dice, Colin Gordon; Nailer, Yuri Borienko; Pasco, Conrad Monk; Sergeant Chivers, Russell Waters; White Nun, Caroline Blakiston; Black Nun, Richardina Jackson; Guide, John Barrett; Bank Manager, Jeremy Hawk.

3105 THE TSAR'S BRIDE. (Artkino-1966). Raissa Nedashkovskaya, Natalya Rudnaya, Otar Koberidze.

3106 TSCHAIKOVSKY. (Artkino-1972). Innokenti Smoktunovsky.

3107 TURKISH DELIGHT. (1974). Monique van de Ven, Rutger Hauer, Tonny Huurdeman, Wim van den Brink, Dolf de Vries, Hans Boskamp, Dick Scheffer, Manfred de Graaf.

3108 TURN ON TO LOVE. (Haven International-1969). Janice, Sharon Kent; Gerard, Richard Michaels; Rico, Luigi Mastoianni.

3109 THE TWELVE CHAIRS. (UMC-1970). Vorobyaninov, Ron Moody; Ostap Bender, Frank Langella; Father Fyodor, Dom DeLuise; Tikon, Mel Brooks; Young Woman, Bridget Brice; Curator, Robert Bernal; Engineer Bruns, David Lander; Nikolai Sestrin, Andreas Voutsinas.

3110 THE 25TH HOUR. (MGM-1967). Johann Moritz, Anthony Quinn; Suzanna, Virna Lisi; Defense Counsel, Michael Redgrave; Nicolai Dobresco, Gregoire Aslan; Strul, Marcel Dalio; Trajan, Serge Reggiani; Captain Brunner, Drewe Henley; Photographer, Paul Maxwell; Goldenberg, George Roderich; Prosecutor, Alexander Knox.

3111 TWILIGHT PEOPLE. (Dimension-1972). Matt Farrell, John Ashley; Steinman, Pat Woodell; Steinman, Jan Merlin; The Panther Woman, Pam Grier; Pereira, Eddie Garcia; The Antelope Man, Ken Metcalfe; Dr. Gordon, Charles Macaulay; Pereira, Eddie Garcia; The Bat Man, Tony Gonsalvez; The Ape Man, Kim Ramos; The Wolf Woman, Mona Morena.

3112 TWINS OF EVIL. (Universal-1972). Frieda Gellhorn, Madeleine Collinson; Maria Gellhorn, Mary Collinson; Gustav Weil, Peter Cushing; Katy Weil, Kathleen Byron; Dietrich, Dennis Price; Franz, Harvey Hall; Ingrid Hoffer, Isobel Black.

3113 A TWIST OF SAND. (United Artists-1969). Geoffrey Pearce, Richard Johnson; Julie Chambois, Honor Blackman; Harry Riker, Jeremy Kemp; Johann, Peter Vaughan; David Garland, Roy Dotrice; Patrol Boat Commander, Guy Doleman;

Patrol Boat Lieutenant, James Falkland; Seekert, Jack May; Flag Officer, Kenneth Cope; Elton, Tony Caunter; Admiral Tringham, Clifford Evans.

3114 TWISTED NERVE. (National General-1969). Susan Harper, Hayley Mills; Martin Durnley, Hywel Bennett; Joan Harper, Billie Whitelaw; Enid Durnley, Phyllis Calvert; Henry Durnley, Frank Finlay; Gerry Henderson, Barry Foster; Shashi Kadir, Salmaan Peer; Sir John Forrester, Thorley Walters; Philip Harvey, Christian Roberts; Superintendent Dakin, Timothy West; Mrs. Clarke, Gretchen Franklin; Inspector Goddard, Clifford Cox.

3115 TWITCH OF THE DEATH NERVE. (Hallmark-1973). Claudine Auger, Claudio Volonto, Ana Maria Rosati, Laura Betti, Luigi Pistilli, Brigitte Skay.

3116 "2." (Chevron-1969). Siv Holm, Gio Petre; Hans Holm, Lars Lunde; Mrs. Holm, Hjordis Petterson; Svendsen, Bertel Lauring; Leo, Klaus Pagh.

3117 TWO. (1974). Ellen, Sarah Venable; Steven, Douglas Travis; Irate Driver, Clifford Villeneuve; Doctor, Ray Houle; Hardware Customer, Florence Hadley; Husband, William Green; Wife, Thelma Green; Bank Teller, Sylvia Harman; Guard, Elwyn Miller; Man in Bank, Jack Dykeman; Chief of Police, Stanley McIntire; Policeman, Fred Gilbert; Postal Clerk, Winston Merrill.

3118 TWO ENGLISH GIRLS. (Janus-1972). Claude Roc, Jean-Pierre Leaud; Anne Brown, Kika Markham; Muriel Brown, Stacey Tendeter; Mrs. Brown, Sylvia Marriott; Mme. Roc, Marie Mansart; Diurka, Philippe Leotard; Ruta, Irene Tunc; Mr. Flint, Mark Petersen; Palmist, David Markham; Claude's Business Agent, Georges Delerue; Art Dealer, Marcel Bergert; Monique de Monferrand, Annie Miller; Claude's Secretary, Christine Pelle; Jeanne, Jeanne Lobre; Muriel as a Child, Anne Levaslot; Clarisse, Sophie Jeanne; Taxi Driver, Rene Gaillard; Friend in Cafe, Sophie Baker; Narrator, Francois Truffaut.

3119 TWO FOR THE ROAD. (20th Century-Fox-1967). Joanne Wallace, Audrey Hepburn; Mark Wallace, Albert Finney; Cathy Manchester, Eleanor Bron; Howard Manchester, William Daniel; Maurice Dalbret, Claude Dauphin; Francoise Calbret, Nadia Grey; David, Georges Descrieres; Ruth, Gabrielle Middleton; Caroline, Kathy Chelimsky; Michelle, Carol Van Dyke; Simone, Karyn Balm; Mario Verdon, Roger Dann, Irene Hilda, Dominique Joos, Libby Morris, Yves Barsacq, Helene Tossy, Jean-Francoise Lalet, Albert Michel, Jackie Bisset, Joanna Jones, Judy Cornwell, Sofia Torkeli, Patricia Viterbo, Olga George Picot, Clarissa Hillel.

3120 TWO GENTLEMEN SHARING. (American International-1969). Roddy, Robin Phillips; Jane, Judy Geeson; Andrew McKenzie, Hal Frederick; Caroline, Esther Anderson; Phil, Norman Rossington; Ethne, Hilary Dwyer; Mrs. Ashby-Kydd, Rachel Kempson; Amanda, Daisy Mae Williams; Marcus, Sam John Holder; Charles, Earl Cameron; Helen, Shelagh Fraser; Mr. Pater, David Markham; Mrs. Pater, Avice Landon; Philip Stone, Elspeth March, Thomas Baptiste, Linbert Spencer, Tommy Ansar.

3121 TWO HUNDRED MOTELS. (United Artists-1971). Themselves, The Mothers of Invention; Rance, Theodore Bikel; Larry, Ringo Starr; Hot Nun, Keith Moon; Lonesome Cowboy, Jimmy Carl Black; Jeff, Martin Lickert; Groupies, Janet Ferguson, Lucy Offerall; Interviewer, Pamela Miller; Don Preston, Motorhead Sherwood, Mark Volman, Howard Kaylan, Ian Underwood, Aynsley, George Duke, Jim Pons, Frank Zappa.

3122 TWO-LANE BLACKTOP. (Universal-1971). Driver, James Taylor; G.T.O., Warren Oates; Girl, Laurie Bird; Mechanic, Dennis Wilson; Station Attendant, David Drake; Station Mechanic, Richard Ruth; Hot rod driver, Rudolph Wurlitzer; Driver's girl, Jaclyn Hellman; Texas hitchhiker, Bill Keller; Oklahoma, H. D. Stanton; Policemen, Don Samuels and Charles Moore; Boswell Attendant, Tom Green.

3123 TWO MULES FOR SISTER SARA. (Universal-1970). Sara, Shirley MacLaine; Hogan, Clint Eastwood; Colonel Beltran, Manolo Fabregas; General LeClaire, Alberto Morin; First American, Armando Silvestre; Second American, John Kelly; Third American, Enrique Lucero; Juan, David Estuardo; Juan's Mother, Ada Carrasco; Juan's Father, Poncho Cordoba; Horacio, Jose Chavez.

3124 THE TWO OF US. (Cinema V-1968). Gramps, Michel Simon; Claude, Alain Cohen; Granny, Luce Fabiole; Victor, Roger Carel; Maxime, Paul Preboist; Claude's Father, Charles Denner; Claude's Mother, Zorica Lozic; Teacher, Jacqueline Rouillard; Raymonde, Aline Bertrand; Suzanne, Sylvine Delannoy; Marco Perrin, Elizabeth Rey.

3125 TWO ON A GUILLOTINE. (Warner Bros.-1965). Melinda Duquesne, Connie Stevens; Cassie Duquesne, Connie Stevens; Val Henderson, Dean Jones; Duke Duquesne, Cesar Romero; Buzz Sheridan, Parley Baer; Dolly Bast, Virginia Gregg; Ramona Ryerdon, Connie Gilchrist; Carl Vickers, John Hoyt; Carmichael, Russell Thorson.

3126 TWO OR THREE THINGS I KNOW ABOUT HER. (New Yorker-1970). Juliette, Marina Vlady.

3127 TWO PEOPLE. (Universal-1973). Evan, Peter Fonda;

Deirdre, Lindsay Wagner; Barbara, Estelle Parsons; Fitzgerald, Alan Fudge; Gilles, Philippe March; Mrs. McCluskey, Frances Sternhagen; Marcus, Brian Limac; Ron, Geoffrey Horne.

3128 2001: A SPACE ODYSSEY. (MGM-1968). David Bowman, Keir Dullea; Dr. Heywood Floyd, William Sylvester; Frank Poole, Gary Lockwood; Moonwatcher, Daniel Richter; Smyslov, Leonard Rossitter; Elena, Margaret Tyzack; Halvorsen, Robert Beatty; Michaels, Sean Sullivan; Mission Controller, Frank Miller; Poole's Father, Alan Gifford; Stewardess, Penny Brahms; Stewardess, Edwina Carroll; The Voice of Hal, Douglas Rain; Edward Bishop, Mike Lovell, Peter Delman, Dany Grover, Brian Hawley, Glenn Beck.

3129 2000 YEARS LATER. (Warner Bros. -7 Arts-1969). Charles Goodwyn, Terry-Thomas; Evermore, Edward Everett Horton; The Director, Pat Harrington; Cindy, Lisa Seagram; Gregorius, John Abbott; The Senator, Tom Melody; Miss Forever, Myrna Ross; Tomorrow's Leader, Monti Rock III; Superdude, Murray Roman; The Piston Kid, Michael Christian; The Disc Jockey, Casey Kasem; Mercury's Voice, Bert Tenzer; Himself, Rudi Gernreich; Milton Parsons, Buddy Lewis, Tony Garner.

3130 TWO WEEKS IN SEPTEMBER. (Paramount-1968). Cecile, Brigitte Bardot; Vincent, Laurent Terzieff; Philippe, Jean Rochefort; McClintock, James Robertson Justice; Dickinson, Michael Sarne; Patricia, Georgina Ward; Monique, Carole Lebel; Chantal, Annie Nicolas; Dickinson's Assistant, Murray Head.

3131 THE UGLY DACHSHUND. (Buena Vista-1966). Mark Garrison, Dean Jones; Fran Garrison, Suzanne Pleshette; Dr. Pruitt, Charlie Ruggles; Officer Carmody, Kelly Thordsen; Mel Chadwick, Parley Baer; Kenji, Mako; Judge, Charles Lane; Mr. Toyama, Robert Kino.

3132 THE UGLY ONES. (United Artists-1968). Luke Chilson, Richard Wyler; Jose Gomez, Tomas Milian; Eden, Ella Karin; Mario Brega, Glenn Foster, Lola Gaos, Hugo Blanco, Ricardo Canales.

3133 ULYSSES. (Continental-1967). Molly Brown, Barbara Jefford; Leopold Bloom, Milo O'Shea; Stephen Dedalus, Maurice Roeves; Buck Mulligan, T. P. McKenna; Simon Dedalus, Martin Dempsey; May Goulding Dedalus, Sheila O'Sullivan; Haines, Graham Lines; Jack Power, Peter Mayock; Gerty MacDowell, Fionnuala Flanagan; Bella Cohen, Anna Manahan; Maureen Toal, Maureen Potter, Chris Curran, Maire Hastings, Eddie Golden, Joe Lynch, Ruadhan Neeson, Biddie White-Lennon, Meryl Gourley, Ann Rowan, Rosaleen Linehan, Robert Carlisle Jr., O. Z. Whitehead, Cecil Sheridan,

Geoffrey Golden.

3134 ULZANA'S RAID. (Universal-1972). McIntosh, Burt Lancaster; Lt. Garnett DeBuin, Bruce Davison; Ke-Ni-Tay, Jorge Luke; Sergeant, Richard Jaeckel; Ulzana, Joaquin Martinez; Captain Gates, Lloyd Bochner; Rukeyser, Karl Swenson; Major Cartwright, Douglass Watson; Mrs. Riordan, Fran Hamilton; Corporal, John Pearce; Mrs. Rukeyser, Gladys Holland; Mrs. Ginsford, Margaret Fairchild; Ginsford, Richard Bull; Steegmeyer, Otto Reichow; Horowitz, Dean Smith.

3135 THE UNCLE. (Lenart-1966). David, Rupert Davies; Addie, Brenda Bruce; Gus, Robert Duncan; Wayne, William Marlowe; Sally, Ann Lynn; Tom, Christopher Arris; Mr. Ream, Maurice Denham; Mary Ream, Helen Fraser; Emma, Barbara Leake; Jamie, John Moulder-Brown; Susie, Jane Ratcliffe.

3136 UNCLE VANYA. (Artkino-1972). Uncle Vanya, Innokenty Smoktunovsky; Astrov, Sergei Bondarchuk; Serebryskov, Vladimir Zeldin; Sonya, Irina Kupchenko; Yelena, Irina Miroshnichenko; Mother, Irina Anisimova-Wolf; Telyepin, Nikolai Pastukov.

3137 AN UNCOMMON THIEF. (Artkino-1967). Innokenty Smoktunovsky, Oleg Efremov, Lubov Dobrzhanskaya, Olga Aroseva, Andrei Mironov, Anatoli Papanov, Tatyana Gavrilova, Georgi Zhenov, Eugene Evstigneyev, Sergei Kulagin, Victoria Radunskaya.

3138 UNDER MILK WOOD. (Altura-1973). Voice, Richard Burton; Rosie, Elizabeth Taylor; Capt. Cat, Peter O'Toole; Myfanwy, Glynis Johns; Mrs. Pugh, Vivien Merchant; Mrs. Ogmore, Sian Phillips; Mog, Victor Spinetti; Voice, Ryan Davies; Gossamer, Angharad Rees; Waldo, Ray Smith; Polly, Ann Beach; Pugh, Talfryn Thomas; Lily, Meg Wynn Owen.

3139 UNDERGROUND. (United Artists-1970). Dawson, Robert Goulet; Yvonne, Danielle Gaubert; Boule, Lawrence Dobkin; Stryker, Carl Duering; Hessler, Joachim Hansen; Xavier, Roger Delgado; Moravin, Alexander Peleg; Menke, George Pravda; Sgt. in Bistro, Leon Lissek; Panzer Sergeant, Harry Brooks Jr.; Condon, Sebastian Breaks.

3140 THE UNDERTAKER AND HIS PALS. (Howco-1967). Robert Lowery, Ray Dennis.

3141 UNDERWORLD INFORMERS. (Continental-1965). Chief Inspector Johnnoe, Nigel Patrick; Charlie Ruskin, Colin Blakely; Maisie, Margaret Whiting; Bertie Hoyle, Derren Nesbitt; Leon Sale, Frank Finlay; Jim Ruskin, John Cowley; Superintendent Bestwick, Harry Andrews; Mary Johnnoe,

Catherine Woodville.

3142 UNHOLY ROLLERS. (American International-1972). Karen, Claudia Jennings; Stern, Louis Quinn; Mickey, Betty Anne Rees; Greg, Alan Vint; Donna, Candice Roman; Nick, Jay Varela; Beverly, Charlene Jones; Marshall, Joe E. Tata; Angie, Maxine Gates; Mother, Kathleen Freeman; Doctor, John Harmon; Horace, John Mitchell; Duane, Dennis Redfield; Referees; Carl Rizzo and Mike Miller; Guard, John Steadman.

3143 THE UNINHIBITED. (Peppercorn-Wormser-1968). Jenny, Melina Mercouri; Pascal Regnier, James Mason; Vincent, Hardy Kruger; Daniel Regnier, Didier Haudepin; Serge, Renaud Verley; Nadine, Martine Ziguel; Nora, Keiko Kishi; Reginald, Maurice Teynac; Orange, Karin Mossberg; Tom, Jose Maria Monpin; Bryant, Louis Inouni.

3144 UNMAN, WITTERING AND ZIGO. (Paramount-1971). John Ebony, David Hemmings; Headmaster, Douglas Wilmer; Gary Garthingale, Anthony Haygarth; Silvia Ebony, Carolyn Seymour; Mr. Winstanley, Hamilton Dyce; Mrs. Winstanley, Barbara Lott; Stretton, Donald Gee.

3145 UNSTRAP ME. (Hawk Serpent-1968). Walter Gutman, Janine Soderhjelm, Donna Kerness, Lucinda Love, Frank Meyer, Hannah Weaver, Floraine Connors, Iris Holtzman, George Segal, Helen Segal, Lucien Boujema, Inga Nyrod, Lea Bobey, Hope Morris, Francis Liebowitz, Doris Zeitlen, Corky Cristians, Dorian West.

3146 UP FROM THE BEACH. (20th Century-Fox-1965). Sgt. Edward Baxter, Cliff Robertson; PFC. Harry Devine, Red Buttons; Lili Rolland, Irina Demick; Mayor, George Chamarat; Lili's Grandmother, Francoise Rosay; Dupre, Raymond Bussieres; Barrelmaker, Fernand Ledoux; Commandant German Wehrmacht, Marius Goring; Artillery Colonel, Slim Pickens; Beachmaster, James Robertson-Justice; M. P. Major, Broderick Crawford; Marie, Louise Chevalier; Seamstress, Germain Delbat; Clarisse, Paula Dehelly; Trombonist, Gabriel Gobin.

3147 UP IN THE CELLAR. (American International-1970). Colin, Wes Stern; Pat, Joan Collins; Maurice, Larry Hagman; Harlene, Judy Pace; Hugo, David Arkin; Tracy, Nira Barab.

3148 UP THE DOWN STAIRCASE. (Warner Bros.-7 Arts-1967). Sylvia Barrett, Sandy Dennis; Paul Barringer, Patrick Bedford; Henrietta Pastorfield, Eileen Heckart; Beatrice Schracter, Ruth White; Sadie Finch, Jean Stapleton; Dr. Bester, Sorrell Booke; McHabe, Roy Poole; Ella Friedenberg, Florence Stanley; The Mother, Vinnette Carroll; Miss Gordon, Janice Mars; Loretta Leversee, Robert Levine, Elena

Karam, Frances Sternhagen, Candace Culkin, Salvatore Rosa, Lew Wallach, Maria Landa; Joe Ferone, Jeff Howard; Alice Blake, Ellen O'Mara; Jose Rodriguez, Jose Rodriguez; Ed Williams, John Fantauzzi.

3149 UP THE JUNCTION. (Paramount-1968). Polly, Suzy Kendall; Peter, Dennis Waterman; Rube McCarthy, Adrienne Posta; Sylvie McCarthy, Maureen Lipman; Terry, Michael Gothard; Mrs. McCarthy, Liz Fraser; Winny, Hylda Baker; Charlie, Alfie Bass; Pauline, Linda Cole; Rita, Doreen Herrington; Lil, Jessie Robins; Edith, Ruby Head.

3150 UP THE MACGREGORS. (Columbia-1968). Gregor MacGregor, David Bailey; Rosita Carson, Agata Flori; Maldonado, Leo Anchoriz; Donovan, Roberto Camardiel; Dick MacGregor, Cole Kitosh; Peter MacGregor, Nick Anderson; Kenneth MacGregor, Paul Carter; Mark MacGregor, Julio Perez Tabernero; David MacGregor, Hugo Blanco.

3151 UP THE SANDBOX. (National General-1972). Margaret Reynolds, Barbra Streisand; Paul Reynolds, David Selby; Mrs. Yussim, Jane Hoffman; Mr. Yussim, John C. Becher; Fidel Castro, Jacobo Morales; Vicki, Iris Brooks; Dr. Bowden, Barbara Rhodes.

3152 UP TO HIS EARS. (Lopert-1966). Arthur Lempereur, Jean-Paul Belmondo; Alexandrine Pinardel, Ursula Andress; Suzy, Maria Pacome; Alice Ponchabert, Valerie Lagrange; Cornelius, Jess Hahn; Mr. Goh, Valery Inkijinoff; Leon, Jean Rochefort.

3153 THE UPPER HAND. (Paramount-1967). Paulo Berger, Jean Gabin; Charles Binaggio, George Raft; Walter, Gert Frobe; Irene, Nadja Tiller; Lili Princesse, Mireille Darc; Mike Coppolano, Claudio Brook; Giulio, Claude Brasseur; Commissioner Noel, Daniel Ceccaldi; Rene, Claude Cerval; Lea, Dany Dauberson; Girl, Christa Lang.

3154 UPTIGHT. (Paramount-1968). B.G., Raymond St. Jacques; Laurie, Ruby Dee; Kyle, Frank Silvera; Tank Williams, Julian Mayfield; Clarence, Roscoe Lee Browne; Jeannie, Janet MacLachlan; Johnny Wells, Max Julien; Mama Wells, Juanita Moore; Teddy, Michael Baseleon; Street Speaker, Tobert Doqui; Alma, Ketty Lester.

3155 UPTOWN SATURDAY NIGHT. (Warner Bros.-1974). Steve Jackson, Sidney Poitier; Wardell Franklin, Bill Cosby; Geechie, Harry Belafonte; The Reverend, Flip Wilson; Sharp Eye Washington, Richard Pryor; Sarah Jackson, Rosalind Cash; Congressman Lincoln, Roscoe Lee Browne; Leggy Peggy, Paula Kelly; Madame Zenobia, Lee Chamberlin; Geechie's Henchman, Johnny Sekka; Slim's Henchmen, Lincoln Kilpatrick and Don Marshal; Irma Franklin, Ketty

Lester; Little Seymour, Harold Nicholas; Silky Slim, Calvin Lockhart.

3156 UTAMARO AND HIS FIVE WOMEN. (New Yorker-1972). Kitagawa, Monnosuke Bando; Okita, Kinuyo Tanaka; Kotaro Bando, Kiroko Kowasaki; Kinnasuke Takamatsu, Toshiro Izuka, Masso Hori.

3157 THE VALACHI PAPERS. (Columbia-1972). Joseph Valachi, Charles Bronson; Salerto, Mario Pilar; Johnny Beck, Fred Valleca; Little Augie, Giacomino De Michelis; Warden, Arny Freeman; Federal Agent Ryan, Gerald S. O'Loughlin; Vito Genovese, Lino Ventura; Dominick Petrilli, Walter Chiari; Charles "Lucky" Luciano, Angelo Infanti; Maria Valachi, Jill Ireland.

3158 VALDEZ IS COMING. (United Artists-1971). Bob Valdez, Burt Lancaster; Gay, Susan Clark; Tanner, Jon Cypher; El Segundo, Barton Heyman.

3159 VALI. (Film-Makers-1967). Vali Myers, Rudi Rappold, Caroline Thompson, Diane Rochlin.

3160 VALLEY OF BLOOD. (Mica-1973). Penny DeHaven, Ernie Ashworth, Zeke Clements, Wayne Forsythe, Rita Cristinziano, Joseph Turner.

3161 THE VALLEY OF GWANGI. (Warner Bros. -7 Arts-1969). Tuck Kirby, James Franciscus; T. J. Breckenridge, Gila Golan; Champ Connors, Richard Carlson; Professor Bromley, Laurence Naismith; Lope, Curtis Arden; Tia Zorina, Freda Jackson; Carlos dos Orsos, Gustavo Rojo; Rowdy, Dennis Kilbane; Bean, Mario De Barros; Dwarf, Jose Burgos.

3162 VALLEY OF MYSTERY. (Universal-1967). Wade Cochran, Richard Egan; Ben Barstow, Peter Graves; Rita Brown, Lois Nettleton; Francisco Rivera, Fernando Lamas; Pete Patton, Joby Baker; Danny O'Neill, Harry Guardino; Joan Simon, Julie Adams; Dr. Weatherly, Alfred Ryder; Connie Lane, Karen Sharpe; Margalo York, Lisa Gaye; Ann Dickson, Barbara Werle; Dino Doretti, Lee Patterson; Manuel Sanchez, Rodolfo Acosta; Charles Kiley, Douglas Kennedy; Jim Walker, Don Stewart; Spence Atherton, Leonard Nimoy; Juan Hidalgo, Tony Patino; Dr. John Quincy, Otis Young; Forrest Hart, George Tyne; Indian Boy, Larry Domasin; M'tu, Eddie Little Sky; Immigration Inspector, William Phipps.

3163 VALLEY OF THE DOLLS. (20th Century-Fox-1967). Anne Welles, Barbara Parkins; Neely O'Hara, Patty Duke; Lyon Burke, Paul Burke; Jennifer North, Sharon Tate; Tony Polar, Tony Scotti; Mel Anderson, Martin Milner; Kevin

Gillmore, Charles Drake; Ted Casablanca, Alex Davion; Miriam, Lee Grant; Miss Steinberg, Neomi Stevens; Henry Bellamy, Robert H. Harris; First Reporter, Jacqueline Susann; Director, Robert Viharo; Man in Hotel Room, Mikel Angel; Man in Bar, Barry Cahill; Claude Chardot, Richard Angarola; MC, Joey Bishop; MC at Grammy Awards, George Jessel; Helen Lawson, Susan Hayward.

3164 VAMPIRE CIRCUS. (20th Century-Fox-1972). Gypsy Woman, Adrienne Corri; Professor Mueller, Laurence Payne; Burgermeister, Thorley Walters; Anton Kersh, John Moulder-Brown; Dora, Lynne Frederick; Gerta Hauser, Elizabeth Seal; Emil, Anthony Corlan; Dr. Kersh, Richard Owens; Anna Mueller, Domini Blythe; Hauser, Robin Hunter.

3165 THE VAMPIRE DOLL. (Toho-1972). The Girl, Yukiko Kobayashi; The Mother, Yoko Manakaze.

3166 THE VAMPIRE LOVERS. (American International-1970). Carmilla, Ingrid Pitt; Laura, Pippa Steele; Emma, Madelein Smith; General, Peter Cushing; Morton, George Cole; Countess, Dawn Addams; Governess, Kate O'Mara; Baron, Douglas Wilmer; Carl, John Finch; Vampire, Kirsten Betts; Renton, Harvey Hall; Fretchen, Janet Key; Landlord, Charles Farrell; Doctor, Ferdy Mayne.

3167 VANISHING POINT. (20th Century-Fox-1971). Kowalski, Barry Newman; Super Soul, Cleavon Little; Prospector, Dean Jagger; Vera, Victoria Medlin; Young Cop, Paul Koslo; Older Cop, Bob Donner; Angel, Timothy Scott; Nude Rider, Gilda Texter; First Male Hitch-hiker, Anthony James; Second Male Hitch-hiker, Arthur Malet.

3168 VARIETY LIGHTS. (Pathe Contemporary-1965). Checco Dal Monte, Peppino De Filippo; Liliana, Carla Del Poggio; Melina Amour, Giulietta Masina; Adelmo Conti, Folco Lulli; Johnny John Kitzmiller; Remo, Dante e Maggio; La Rosa, Carlo Romano; Valeria del Sole, Gina Mascetti; Theatre Owner, Checco Durante; Bill, Joe Falletta.

3169 THE VAULT OF HORROR. (Cinerama-1973). Rogers, Daniel Massey; Donna, Anna Massey; Clive, Mike Pratt; Old Waiter, Erik Chitty; Waiter, Jerold Wells; Maitland, Michael Craig; Alex, Edward Judd; Tom, Robin Nedwell; Jerry, Geoffrey Davies; Gravedigger, Arthur Mullard; Sebastian, Curt Jurgens; Inez, Dawn Addams; Indian Girl, Jasmina Hilton; Fakir, Ishaq Bux; Critchit, Terry-Thomas; Eleanor, Glynis Johns; Jane, Marianne Stone; Wilson, John Forbes-Robertson; Moore, Tom Baker; Diltant, Denholm Elliott; Breedley, Terence Alexander; Gaskill, John Witty.

3170 THE VELVET VAMPIRE. (New World-1971). Lee, Michael Blodgett; Susan, Sherry Miles; Diane, Celeste

Yarnall; Juan, Jerry Daniels; Carl, Gene Shane; Cliff, Paul Prokop; Amos, Sandy Ward; Cliff's Girlfriend, Chris Woodley; Biker, Bob Thessier.

3171 THE VENETIAN AFFAIR. (MGM-1967). Bill Fenner, Robert Vaughn; Sandra Fane, Elke Sommer; Claire Connor, Felicia Farr; Robert Wahl, Karl Boehm; Giulia Almeranti, Luciana Paluzzi; Dr. Pierre Vaugirous, Boris Karloff; Mike Ballard, Roger C. Carmel; Frank Rosenfeld, Edward Asner; Jan Aarvan, Joe De Santis; Russo, Fabrizio Mioni; Neill Carlson, Wesley Lau; Goldsmith, Bill Weiss.

3172 THE VENGEANCE OF FU MANCHU. (Warner Bros.-7 Arts-1968). Fu Manchu, Christopher Lee; Inspector Ramos, Tony Ferrer; Ling Tang, Tsai Chin; Nayland Smith, Douglas Wilmer; Dr. Lieberson, Wolfgang Kieling; Maria Lieberson, Susanne Roquette; Dr. Petrie, Howard Marion Crawford; Mark Weston, Noel Trevarthen; Rudy Moss, Horst Frank; Kurt, Peter Carsten; Ingrid, Maria Rohm; Jasmin, Mona Chong.

3173 THE VENGEANCE OF SHE. (20th Century-Fox-1968). King Killikrates, John Richardson; Carol, Olinka Berova; Philip Smith, Edward Judd; George Carter, Colin Blakely; Sheila Carter, Jill Melford; Harry Walker, George Sewell; Kassim, Andre Morell; Zo-Tor, Noel Willman.

3174 VENOM. (Peppercorn-Wormser-1968). Per, Soeren Stromberg; Susanne, Sisse Reingaard; Henrike Steen, Poul Reichhardt; Mrs. Steen, Astrid Villaume; Sonjo, Judy Gringer; Frau Jacobsen, Grethe Morgensen.

3175 VENUS IN FURS. (American International-1970). Jimmy, James Darren; Rita, Barbara McNair; Wanda, Maria Rohm; Ahmed, Klaus Kinski; Kapp, Dennis Price; Olga, Margaret Lee; Inspector, Adolfo Lastretti.

3176 THE VERDICT. (1974). Teresa, Sophia Loren; Leguen, Jean Gabin; Lannelongue, Henri Garcia; Verlac, Julien Bertheau; Andre, Michel Albertini; Annie, Muriel Catala.

3177 A VERY CURIOUS GIRL. (Regional-1970). Gaston Duvalier, Georges Geret; Hippolyte, Jacques Masson; Marie, Bernadette LaFont; Pepe, Marcel Peres; Julien, Henry Czarniak; Irene, Claire Maurier.

3178 A VERY HANDY MAN. (Rizzoli-1966). Liola, Ugo Tognazzi; Tuzza Azzara, Giovanna Ralli; Simone Palumbo, Pierre Brasseur; Mita, Anouk Aimee; Aunt Geas, Elisa Cegani.

3179 A VERY NATURAL THING. (New Line-1974). David, Robert Joel; Mark, Curt Gareth; Jason, Bo White; Alan, Jay Pierce; Hughey, Barnaby Rudge; Gary, Anthony McKay;

Valerie, Marily Meyers; Minister, A. Bailey Chapin; Michel Kell, Sheila Rock, Linda Weitz, Robert Grillo, Kurt Brandt, George Diaz, Deborah Trowbridge, Jesse Trowbridge.

3180 A VERY SPECIAL FAVOR. (Universal-1965). Paul, Rock Hudson; Lauren, Leslie Caron; Michel, Charles Boyer; Etienne, Walter Slezak; Arnold, Dick Shawn; Harry, Larry Storch; Mickey, Nita Talbot; Mother Plum, Norma Varden; Pete, George Furth; Claude, Marcel Hillaire; Rene, Jay Novello; Bartender, Stafford Repp.

3181 VICE AND VIRTUE. (MGM-1965). Juliette, Annie Girardot; Justine, Catherine Deneuve; Schondorff, Robert Hossein; Von Bamberg, Otto Hasse; Hans, Philippe Lemaire; Ivan, Serge Marquand; Helena, Luciana Paluzzi; Manuela, Valeria Ciangottini; Hoech, Georges Poujouly; Astrologer, Michel De Re; S. S. Doctor, Paul Degauff.

3182 LA VIE DE CHATEAU. (Royal-1967). Marie, Catherine Deneuve; Jerome, Philippe Noiret; Father, Pierre Brasseur; Mother, Mary Marquet; French Officer, Henri Garcin; German Officer, Carlos Thompson.

3183 THE VIKING QUEEN. (20th Century-Fox-1967). Justinian, Don Murray; Salina, Carita; Maelgan, Donald Houston; Octavian, Andrew Keir; Beatrice, Adrienne Corri; Tiberion, Niall MacGinnis; King Priam, Wilfrid Lawson; Talia, Nicola Pagett; Catus, Percy Herbert; Tristram, Patrick Troughton; Fergus, Sean Caffrey; Osiris, Denis Shaw; Merchant, Philip O'Flynn; Nigel, Brendan Mathews; Fabian, Gerry Alexander; Benedict, Patrick Gardiner; Dalan, Paul Murphy; Old Man, Arthur O'Sullivan; Shopkeeper, Cecil Sheridan.

3184 VILLA RIDES. (Paramount-1968). Pancho Villa, Yul Brynner; Lee Arnold, Robert Mitchum; Fina Gonzalez, Grazia Buccella; Fierro, Charles Bronson; Urbina, Robert Viharo; Captain Ramirez, Frank Wolff; General Huerta, Herbert Lom; President Madero, Alexander Knox; Emilita, Diana Lorys; Luis Gonzalez, Robert Carricart; Man in Barber Shop, John Ireland; Girl in Restaurant, Jill Ireland; Lupita Gonzalez, Regina De Julian; Herrera, Andres Monreal.

3185 VILLAGE OF THE GIANTS. (Embassy-1965). Tommy Kirk, Johnny Crawford, Ronny Howard, The Beau Brummels, Freddy Cannon, Mike Clifford, Joy Harmon, Bob Random, Tisha Sterling, Charla Doherty, Tim Rooney, Kevin O'Neal, Gail Gilmore, Toni Basil, Hank Jones, Jim Begg, Vicki London, Joseph Turkel.

3186 VILLAIN. (MGM-1971). Vic, Richard Burton; Wolfe, Ian McShane; Bob, Nigel Davenport; Gerald, Donald Sinden; Venetia, Fiona Lewis.

3187 VINCENT, FRANÇOIS, PAUL ... AND THE OTHERS. (1974). Vincent, Yves Montand; François, Michel Piccoli; Paul, Serge Reggiani; Jean, Gerard Depardieu; Catherine, Stephane Audran; Lucie, Marie Dubois; Julia, Antonella Lualdi; Colette, Catherine Allegret; Marie, Ludmilla Mikael; Jacques, Umberto Orsini.

3188 LE VIOL. (Freena Films-1968). Marianne Pescourt, Bibi Andersson; Walter, Bruno Cremer; Henri Pescourt, Frederic De Pasquale; The Maid, Katerina Larsson.

3189 THE VIOLENT FOUR. (Paramount-1968). Cavallero, Gian Maria Volonte; Inspector Basevi, Tomas Milian; Prostitute, Margaret Lee; Telephone Victim, Carla Gravina; Notarnicola, Don Backy; Rovoletto, Ezzio Sancrotti; Lopez, Raymond Lovelock; Piva, Piero Mazarella.

3190 THE VIOLENT ONES. (Feature Film Corporation of America-1967). Manuel Vega, Fernando Lamas; Lucas Barnes, David Carradine; Mike Marain, Tommy Sands; Joe Vorzyck, Aldo Ray; Dolores, Lisa Gaye.

3191 THE VIRGIN AND THE GYPSY. (Chevron-1970). Yvette, Joanna Shimkus; Gypsy, Franco Nero; Mrs. Fawcett, Honor Blackman; Major, Mark Burns; Rector, Maurice Denham; Grandma, Fay Compton; Cissie, Kay Walsh; Lucille, Harriett Harper; Fred, Norman Bird; Gypsy's Wife, Imogen Hassall; Leo, Jeremy Bulloch; Bob, Roy Holder; Ella, Margo Andrew; Mary, Janet Chappell; Cook, Helen Booth; Thomas, Laurie Dale; Gypsy Grandmother, Lulu Davies.

3192 THE VIRGIN SOLDIERS. (Columbia-1970). Phillipa Raskin, Lynn Redgrave; Brigg, Hywel Bennett; Sgt. Driscoll, Nigel Davenport; R. S. M. Raskin, Nigel Patrick; Sgt. Wellbeloved, Jack Shepherd; Mrs. Raskin, Rachel Kempson; Lucy, Tsai Chin; Col. Pickering, Michael Gwynn; Lt. Col. Browning, Jolyon Jackley; Cutler, Keith Nicholls; Lantry, Geoffrey Hughes; Tasker, Don Hawkins; Villiers, Wayne Sleep; Foster, Gregory Phillips; Sandy Jacobs, Peter Kelly.

3193 THE VIRGIN WITCH. (Joseph Brenner-1973). Christine, Anne Michelle; Betty, Vicky Michelle; Johnny, Keith Buckley; Sybil, Patricia Haines; Peter, James Chase; Mrs. Wendell, Paula Wright; Gerald, Neil Hallett.

3194 THE VISCOUNT. (Warner Bros. -1967). Clint de la Roche, Kerwin Mathews; Ricco Barone, Edmond O'Brien; Lili, Jane Fleming; Claudia, Yvette Lebon; Billette, Jean Yanne; Marco, Fernando Rey; Tania, Maria Latour; Manuel, John Martin; Vincento, Alain Saury.

3195 VISIT TO A CHIEF'S SON. (United Artists-1974). Anthropologist, Richard Mulligan; Tribal Leader, Johnny Sekka;

Anthropologist's Son, John Philip Hogdon; Tribal Chief's Son, Jesse Kinaru.

3196 THE VISITORS. (United Artists-1972). Harry Wayne, Patrick McVey; Martha Wayne, Patricia Joyce; Bill Schmidt, James Woods; Tony Rodriquez, Chico Martinez; Mike Nickerson, Steve Railsback.

3197 LA VISTA. (Promenade-1966). Pina, Sandro Milo; Adolfo, François Perier; Cucaracha, Mario Adorf; Chiaretta, Angela Minervini; Renato, Gaston Moschin; Nella, Didi Perego.

3198 VIVA LA MUERTE. (Raab-1971). Aunt, Anouk Ferjac; Father, Ivan Henriques; Mother, Nuria Espert; Boy, Mahdi Chaouch; Girl, Jazia Klibi.

3199 VIVA MARIA. (United Artists-1965). Maria I, Jeanne Moreau; Maria II, Brigitte Bardot; Flores, George Hamilton; Madame Diogene, Paulette Dubost; Werther, Gregor von Rezzori; Rodolfo, Poldo Bendani; Rodriguez, Carlos Lopez Moctezuma.

3200 THE VIXENS. (Stratford-1969). Betty, Anne Linden; Anne, Mary Kahn; Bob, Peter Burns; Alan, Steven Harrison; Judy, Claudia Bach; Harold, Robert Raymond; Inspector, Hector Elizondo.

3201 VON RYAN'S EXPRESS. (20th Century-Fox-1965). Col. Joseph L. Ryan, Frank Sinatra; Maj. Eric Fincham, Trevor Howard; Gabriella, Raffaella Carra; Sergeant Baslick, Brad Dexter; Captain Oriani, Sergio Fantoni; Orde, John Leyton; Costanzo, Edward Mulhare; Maj. Von Klemment, Wolfgang Preiss; Private Ames, James Brolin; Colonel Gort, John Van Dreelen; Battaglia, Adolfo Celi; Italian Train Engineer, Vito Scotti; Corporal Giannini, Richard Bakalyan; Captain Stein, Michael Goodliffe; Sergeant Dunbar, Michael St. Clair.

3202 THE VULTURE. (Paramount-1967). Eric Lutyens, Robert Hutton; Professor Koniglich, Akim Tamiroff; Brian Stroud, Broderick Crawford; Trudy Lutyens, Diane Clare; The Vicar, Philip Friend; Jarvis, Patrick Holt; Ellen West, Annette Carell; The Sexton, Edward Caddick; Edward Stroud, Gordon Sterne; Police Sup't. Wendell, Keith McConnell; Nurse, Margaret Robertson.

3203 W. (Cinerama-1974). Katie Lewis, Twiggy; Ben Lewis, Michael Witney; Charles Jasper, Eugene Roche; William Caulder, Dirk Benedict; Arnie Felson, John Vernon; Lt. Whitfield, Michael Conrad; Investigator, Alfred Ryder; Betty, Carmen Zapata.

3203a WR--MYSTERIES OF THE ORGANISM. (Cinema V-1971).

Milena, Milena Dravic; Jagoda, Jagoda Kaloper; Vladimir, Ivica Vidovic; Radmilovic, Zoran Radmilovic; Guerilla Poet, Tuli Kupferberg; Transvestite, Jackie Curtis; Stalin, Michael Gelovani.

3204 WACO. (Paramount-1966). Waco, Howard Keel; Jill Stone, Jane Russell; Ace Ross, Brian Donlevy; Preacher Sam Stone, Wendell Corey; Dolly, Terry Moore; Joe Gore, John Smith; George Gates, John Agar; Deputy Sheriff O'Neill, Gene Evans; Sheriff Billy Kelly, Richard Arlen; Scotty Moore, Ben Cooper; Patricia West, Tracy Olsen; Bill Rile, DeForest Kelley; Ma Jenner, Anne Seymour.

3205 WAIT UNTIL DARK. (Warner Bros.-7 Arts-1967). Susy Hendrix, Audrey Hepburn; Roat, Alan Arkin; Mike Talman, Richard Crenna; Sam Hendrix, Efrem Zimbalist, Jr.; Carlino, Jack Weston; Lisa, Samantha Jones; Gloria, Julie Herrod; Shatner, Frank O'Brien; The Boy, Gary Morgan.

3206 WAITING FOR CAROLINE. (Lopert-1969). Caroline, Alexandra Stewart; Marc, François Tasse; Peter, Robert Howay; Emily, Sharon Acker; Stephen, William Needles; Lally, Aileen Seaton; Simard, Paul Guevremont; Jean-Pierre, Daniel Gadouas; Mme. Simard, Lucie Poitras.

3207 WAKE UP AND DIE. (Rizzoli-1968). Luciano Lutring, Robert Hoffman; Yvonne Lutring, Lisa Gastoni; Inspector Moroni, Gian Maria Volonte; Claudio Volonte, Renato Nicolai.

3208 WALK, DON'T RUN. (Columbia-1966). William Rutland, Cary Grant; Christine, Samantha Eggar; Steve Davis, Jim Hutton; Julius P. Haversack, John Standing; Aiko Kurawa, Miiko Taka; Yuri Andreyovitch, Ted Hartley; Dimitry, Ben Astar; Police Captain, George Takei; Mr. Kurawa, Teru Shimada; Mrs. Kurawa, Lois Kiuchi.

3209 WALK IN THE SHADOW. (Continental-1966). John Harris, Michael Craig; Dr. James Brown, Patrick McGoohan; Pat Harris, Janet Munro; Hart Jacobs, Paul Rogers; Mrs. Gordon, Megs Jenkins; Teddy's Mother, Maureen Pryor; Mr. Gordon, John Barrie; Mapleton, Basil Dignam; Clyde, Leslie Sands; Duty Sister, Ellen McIntosh; Teddy's Father, Frank Finlay; Harvard, Michael Aldridge; Ruth Harris, Lynn Taylor; Teddy, Freddy Ramsey; John's Counsel, Michael Bryant; Crown Counsel, Norman Wooland; John's Father, Malcolm Keen; Vicar, Maurice Colebourne; Marshall, John Welsh.

3210 A WALK IN THE SPRING RAIN. (Columbia-1970). Will Cade, Anthony Quinn; Libby Meredith, Ingrid Bergman; Roger Meredith, Fritz Weaver; Ellen, Katherine Crawford; Boy, Tom Fielding; Ann Cade, Virginia Gregg; Bucky,

Mitchell Silverman.

3211 A WALK WITH LOVE AND DEATH. (20th Century-Fox-1969). Claudia, Anjelica Huston; Heron, Assaf Dayan; Robert, Anthony Corlan; Sir Meles, John Hallam; Pilgrim Leader, Robert Lang; Priest, Guy Deghy; Mad Monk, Michael Gough; Captain, George Murcell; Gypsy, Eileen Murphy; Father Superior, Anthony Nicholls; St. Jean, Joseph O'Connor; Robert the Elder, John Huston; Whoremaster, John Franklin; Knight, Francis Heim; Melvin Hayes, Barry Keegan, Nicholas Smith, Antoinette Reuss, Gilles Segal.

3212 WALKABOUT. (20th Century-Fox-1971). Girl, Jenny Agutter; Brother, Lucien John; Aborigine, David Gumpilil.

3213 THE WALKING STICK. (MGM-1970). Leigh Hartley, David Hemmings; Deborah Dainton, Samantha Eggar; Jack Foil, Emlyn Williams; Erica Dainton, Phyllis Calvert; Douglas Dainton, Ferdy Mayne; Arabella Dainton, Francesca Annis; Sarah Dainton, Bridget Turner; Ted Sandymount, Dudley Sutton; Bertie Irons, John Woodvine.

3214 WALKING TALL. (Cinerama-1973). Buford Pusser, Joe Don Baker; Pauline Pusser, Elizabeth Hartman; Sheriff Al Thurman, Gene Evans; Grandpa Pusser, Noah Beery; Luan Paxton, Brenda Benet; Prentiss Parley, John Brascia; Grady Coker, Bruce Glover; Buel Jaggers, Arch Johnson; Obra Eaker, Felton Perry; Arno Purdy, Richard X. Slattery; Callie Hacker, Rosemary Murphy; Margie Ann, Lynn Borden; Lutie McVeigh, Ed Call; Sheldon Levine, Sidney Clute.

3215 WALL OF FLESH. (Provocative-1969). Dan Machuen, Lita Coleman, Marianne Provost.

3216 THE WALLS OF HELL. (Hemisphere Pictures-1965). Lieut. Jim Sorenson, Jock Mahoney; Nardo, Fernando Poe Jr.; Papa, Mike Parsons; Tina Sorenson, Cecillia Lopez; Joker, Oscar Roncal; The Captain, Vance Skarstad; Murray, Paul Edwards Jr.; The Major, Claude Wilson; The Guerrillas, Ely Ramos Jr., Angel Buenaventura.

3217 WANDA. (Bardene International-1971). Wanda, Barbara Loden; Dennis, Michael Higgins; Dennis' Father, Charles Dosinan; Soldier, Frank Jourdano; Girl in Roadhouse, Valerie Manches.

3218 THE WANDERER. (Leacock Pennebaker-1969). Yvonne de Galais, Brigitte Fossey; Augustin Meaulnes, Jean Blaise; Francois Seurel, Alain Libolt; Frantz de Galais, Alain Noury; Valentine Blondeau, Juliette Villard; Ganache, Christian De Tiliere.

3219 WAR AND PEACE. (Continental-1968). Natasha Rostova, Ludmila Savelyeva; Andrei Bolkonsky, Vyacheslav Tihonov; Countess Rostova, Hira Ivanov-Golovko; Sonya Rostova, Irina Gubanova; Maria Bolkonsky, Antonia Shuranova; Pierre Bezuhov, Sergei Bondarchuk; Count Rostova, Victor Stanitsin; Nikolai Rostova, Oleg Tabakov; Nikolai Bolkonsky, Anatoly Ktorov; Liza Bolkonsky, Anastasia Vertinskaya; Nikolai Kodin, Seryozha Yermilov, Boris Smirnov, Irina Skobtseva, Vasily Lanovoi, Eleg Yefremov, N. Tolkachev, Yelena Tyapkina, K. Polivikova, Eduard Martsevich.

3220 THE WAR BETWEEN MEN AND WOMEN. (National General-1972). Peter Wilson, Jack Lemmon; Terry Kozlenko, Barbara Harris; Stephen Kozlenko, Jason Robards; Howard Mann, Herb Edelman; Linda Kozlenko, Lisa Gerritsen; David Kozlenko, Moosie Drier; Dr. Harris, Severn Darden; Caroline Kozlenko, Lisa Eilbacher; Mrs. Schenker, Lucille Meredith; Elderly Woman, Ruth McDevitt; Florist Delivery Man, Joey Faye; Man, Alan DeWitt; Minister, John Zaremba; Bernie, Rick Gates.

3221 WAR GODS OF THE DEEP. (American-International-1965). The Captain, Vincent Price; Ben Harris, Tab Hunter; Jill Tregellis, Susan Hart; Harold Tiffin Jones, David Tomlinson.

3222 WAR ITALIAN STYLE. (American International-1967). General Von Kassler, Buster Keaton; Frank, Franco Franchi; Joe, Ciccio Ingrassia; Lt. Inge Schultze, Martha Hyer; General Zacharias, Fred Clark.

3223 THE WAR LORD. (Universal-1965). Chrysagon, Charlton Heston; Bors, Richard Boone; Bronwyn, Rosemary Forsyth; Priest, Maurice Evans; Drado, Guy Stockwell; Odins, Niall MacGinnis; Frisian Prince, Henry Wilcoxon; Marc, James Farentino; Volc, Sammy Ross; Piet, Woodrow Parfrey; Holbracht, John Alderson; Tybald, Allen Jaffe; Rainault, Michael Conrad; Dirck, Dal Jenkins; Boy Prince, Johnny Jensen; Chrysagon Man, Forrest Wood; Old Woman, Belle Mitchell.

3224 THE WAR OF THE ZOMBIES. (American International-1966).. John Drew Barrymore, Susi Andersen, Ettore Manni, Ida Galli, Philippe Hersent, Mino Doro, Ivano Staccioli, Matilde Calnan, Giulio Maculani.

3225 WAR PARTY. (20th Century-Fox-1965). Johnny Hawk, Michael T. Mikler; Sarah, Davey Davison; Sgt. Chaney, Donald Barry; Nicoma, Laurie Mock; Dennis Robertson, Fred Krone, Michael Carr, Guy Wilkerson, Charles Horvath.

3226 THE WAR WAGON. (Universal-1967). Taw Jackson, John Wayne; Lomax, Kirk Douglas; Levi Walking Bear, Howard

Keel; Billy Hyatt, Robert Walker; Wes Catlin, Keenan Wynn; Pierce, Bruce Cabot; Kate, Valora Noland; Hoag, Gene Evans; Lola, Joanna Barnes; Hammond, Bruce Dern; Terry Wilson, Don Collier, Sheb Wooley, Ann McCrea, Emilio Fernandez, Frank McGrath, Chuck Roberson, Red Morgan, Hal Needham, Perla Walter.

3227 WARKILL. (Universal-1968). Col. John Hannegan, George Montgomery; Phil Sutton, Tom Drake; Pedring, Conrad Parham; Dr. Fernandez, Eddie Infante; Willy, Henry Duval; Mike Harris, Paul Edwards; Major Hashiri, Bruno Punzalan; Sgt. Johnson, David Michael.

3228 A WARM DECEMBER. (National General-1973). Matt Younger, Sidney Poitier; Catherine, Esther Anderson; Stefanie, Yvette Curtis; Henry Barlow, George Baker; Myomo, Johnny Sekka; George Oswandu, Earl Cameron; Marsha Barlow, Hilary Crane; Burberry, John Beardmore.

3229 WARM IN THE BUD. (FilmMakers-1970). Mortiz, Robert Mont; Melchior, Dean Stricklin; Martha, Toni Hamilton; Ernst, Bruce Johnson; Hanchen, John Goetz; Wendla, Mary Rivard; Ilse, Nuala Willis; Otto, John Carmody; George, Barry Peterson.

3230 WARNING SHOT. (Paramount-1967). Sgt. Tom Valens, David Janssen; Capt. Roy Klodin, Ed Begley; Sgt. Ed Musso, Keenan Wynn; Frank Sanderman, Sam Wanamaker; Alice Willows, Lillian Gish; Liz Thayer, Stefanie Powers; Mrs. Doris Ruston, Eleanor Parker; Walter Cody, George Grizzard; Calvin York, George Sanders; Perry Knowland, Steve Allen; Paul Jerez, Carroll O'Connor; Joanie Valens, Joan Collins; Orville Ames, Walter Pidgeon; Police Surgeon, John Garfield Jr.; Bob Williams, Jerry Dunphy, Vito Scotti, Romo Vincent, Jean Carson, Donald Curtis, Brian Dunne, Norma Clark.

3231 WATCHED. (Penthouse-1974). Mike Mandell/Sonny, Stacy Keach; Gordon Rankey, Harris Yulin; The Informer, Bridget Pole; The Blonde, Turid Aarstd; Hitchhiker, Valerie Parker.

3232 WATERHOLE NO. 3. (Paramount-1967). Lewton Cole, James Coburn; Sheriff John Copperud, Carroll O'Connor; Billie Copperud, Margaret Blye; Sgt. Henry Foggers, Claude Akins; Hilb, Timothy Carey; Deputy, Bruce Dern; Lavinia, Joan Blondell; Captain Shipley, James Whitmore; Ben, Harry Davis; Doc Quinlen, Roy Jenson; Hotel Clerk, Robert Cornthwaite; Corporal Blyth, Jim Boles.

3233 WATERLOO. (Paramount-1971). Napoleon, Rod Steiger; Wellington, Christopher Plummer; Louis XVIII, Orson Welles; General Picton, Jack Hawkins; Duchess of Richmond, Virginia McKenna; Marshal Ney, Dan O'Herlihy; Sir William

Ponsonby, Michael Wilding; Lord Uxbridge, Terence Alexander; Pvt. O'Connor, Donal Donnelly; Lord Gordon, Rupert Davies; Marshal Soult, Ivo Garrani; General Drouot, Gianni Garko; Cambronne, Eughenj Samoilov; William De Lancey, Ian Ogilvy; Marshal Blucher, Sergei Zakhariadze.

3234 WATERMELON MAN. (Columbia-1970). Jeff Gerber, Godfrey Cambridge; Althea Gerber, Estelle Parsons; Townsend, Howard Caine; Bus Driver, D'Urville Martin; Counterman, Mantan Moreland; Erica, Kay Kimberly; Dr. Wainwright, Kay E. Kuter; Burton Gerber, Scott Garrett; Janice Gerber, Erin Moran; Johnson, Irving Selbst.

3235 WATTSTAX. (Columbia-1973). Richard Pryor, The Dramatics, Staple Singers, Kim Weston, Jimmy Jones, Rance Allen Group, William Bell, Louise McCord, Debra Manning, Eric Mercury, Freddy Robinson, Lee Sain, Ernie Hines, Little Sonny, Newcomers, Eddie Floyd, Tempress, Frederick Knight, The Emotions, Bar Kays, Albert King, Little Milton, Johnnie Taylor, Mel and Tim, Carla Thomas, Rufus Thomas, Luther Ingram, Isaac Hayes, Ted Lange, Elizabeth Cleveland.

3236 WAY OUT. (Premier Presentations-1967). Frankie, Frank Rodriguez; Jim, James Dunleavy; Anita, Sharyn Jimenez; Jerry, Jerry Rutkin.

3237 WAY ... WAY OUT. (20th Century-Fox-1966). Peter Mattemore, Jerry Lewis; Eileen Forbes, Connie Stevens; Harold Quonset, Robert Morley; Hoffman, Dennis Weaver; Schmidlap, Howard Morris; Igor, Dick Shawn; General Hallenby, Brian Keith; Anna Sablova, Anita Ekberg; Ponsonby, William O'Connell; Esther Davenport, Bobo Lewis; Russian Delegate, Milton Prame; Deuce, Alex D'Arcy; Peggy, Linda Harrison; Ted Robertson, James Brolin.

3238 THE WAY WE LIVE NOW. (United Artists-1970). Lionel, Nicholas Pryor; Rosalind, Linda Simon; Amelia, Joanna Miles; Laurie, Pat McAneny; Martha, Rebecca Darke; Lincoln, Sydney Walker.

3239 THE WAY WE WERE. (Columbia-1973). Katie, Barbra Streisand; Hubbell, Robert Redford; J. J., Bradford Dillman; Carol Ann, Lois Chiles; George Bissinger, Patrick O'Neal; Paula Reisner, Viveca Lindfors; Rhea Edwards, Allyn Ann McLerie; Brooks Carpenter, Murray Hamilton; Bill Verso, Herb Edelman; Vicki Bissinger, Diana Ewing; Pony Dunbar, Sally Kirkland; Peggy Vanderbilt, Marcia Mae Jones; Actor, Don Keefer; El Morocco Captain, George Gaynes; Army Corporal, Eric Boles; Ashe Blonde, Barbara Peterson; Army Captain, Roy Jenson; Rally Speaker, Brenda Kelly; Frankie McVeigh, James Woods; Jenny, Connie Forslund; Dr. Short, Robert Gerringer; Judianne, Susie Blakely;

Airforce, Ed Power; Dumb Blonde, Suzanne Zenor; Guest, Dan Seymour.

3240 THE WAY WEST. (United Artists-1967). Senator William J. Tadlock, Kirk Douglas; Dick Summers, Robert Mitchum; Lije Evans, Richard Widmark; Rebecca Evans, Lola Albright; Johnnie Mack, Michael Witney; Mercy McBee, Sally Field; Amanda Mack, Katherine Justice; Sam Stubby Kaye; Michael Moynihan, William Lundigan; Turley, Paul Lukather; Roy Barcroft, Jack Elam, Patric Knowles, Ken Murray, John Mitchum, Nick Cravat, Harry Carey Jr., Roy Glenn, Michael McGreevey, Connie Sawyer, Anne Barton, Eve McVeagh, Peggy Stewart.

3241 WE ARE ALL NAKED. (Citel-USA-1970). Stranger, Alain Saury; Father, Jacques Normand; Son, Gerard Desailes; Little Girl, Isabelle Pierson; Worker, Georges Beauvilliers; Crony, Max Montavon; Young Seaman, Rene Roussel; Old Seaman, Boniface.

3242 WE STILL KILL THE OLD WAY. (Lopert-1968). Paolo Laurana, Gian Maria Volonte; Luisa Roscio, Irene Papas; Rosello, Gabriele Ferzetti; Professor Roscio, Salvo Randone; Arturo Manno, Luigi Pistilli; The Priest, Mario Scaccia; Lauranna's Mother, Laura Nucci; Parliament Member, Leopoldo Trieste.

3243 WEB OF FEAR. (Comet-1967). Constance, Michele Morgan; Pascale, Dany Saval; Hugo, Simon Andreu; Marie-Cecile, Maria Pacome; Student, Claude Rich; Georges Rigaud, Carlos Casaravilla.

3244 WEDDING IN BLOOD. (New Line Cinema-1974). Stephane Audran, Michel Piccoli, Claude Pieplu, Clothilde Joano, Eliana de Santis, Francois Robert, Daniel Lecourtois, Pipo Merisi.

3245 WEDDING IN WHITE. (AVCO Embassy-1973). Jim, Donald Pleasence; Jeannie, Carol Kane; Mary, Doris Petrie; Sandy, Leo Phillips; Jimmy, Paul Bradley; Billy, Doug McGrath; Sarah, Christine Thomas; Dollie, Bonnie Carol Case.

3246 WEDDING NIGHT. (American International-1970). Groom, Dennis Waterman; Bride, Tessa Wyatt; Girl Friend, Alexandra Bastedo.

3247 THE WEDDING PARTY. (Ajay-1969). Josephine Fish, Jill Clayburgh; Charlie, Charles Pfluger; Mrs. Fish, Valda Setterfield; Mr. Fish, Raymond McNally; Phoebe, Jennifer Salt; Reverend Oldfield, John Braswell; Celeste, Judy Thomas; Nanny, Sue Ann Converse; Baker, John Quinn; Decil, Robert De Nero; Alistair, William Finley.

3248 THE WEDNESDAY CHILDREN. (Venture-1973). Mrs. Miller, Marji Dodril; Miller, Donald E. Murray; Scott, Tom Kelly; Mrs. Berlow, Carol Cary; Fenton, Al Miskell; Minister, Robert D. West.

3249 WEDNESDAY'S CHILD. (Cinema V-1972). Janice, Sandy Ratcliff; Mr. Baildon, Bill Dean; Mrs. Baildon, Grace Cave; Tim, Malcolm Tierney; Barbara, Hilary Martyn; Dr. Donaldson, Michael Riddall.

3250 WEEKEND. (Grove Press-1968). Corinne, Mireille Darc; Roland, Jean Yanne; F. L. S. O. Leader, Jean-Pierre Kalfon; His Moll, Valerie Lagrange; Saint-Just/Man in Phone Booth, Jean-Pierre Leaud; F. L. S. O. Member, Yves Beneyton; Pianist, Paul Gegauff; Joseph Balsamo, Daniel Pommereulle; Gros Poucet, Yves Afonso; Emily Bronte/Girl in Farmyard, Blandine Jeanson; Cook, Ernest Menzer; Tractor Driver, Georges Staquet; Girl in Car Crash/F. L. S. O. Member, Anne Wiazemsky; Marie-Madeleine, Virginie Vignon; Hitchhiker, Jean Eustache; Monsieur Jojot, Isabelle Pons.

3251 WEEKEND AT DUNKIRK. (20th Century-Fox-1966). Sergeant Maillat, Jean-Paul Belmondo; Jeanne, Catherine Spaak; Pinot, Georges Geret; Father Pierson, Jean-Pierre Marielle; Dhery, Pierre Mondy; Helene, Marie Dubois; Alexander, François Perier; Atkins, Kenneth Haigh; Robinson, Ronald Howard; The Burnt Man, Nigel Stock.

3252 WEEKEND, ITALIAN STYLE. (Marvin Films-1968). Enrico Marletti, Enrico Maria Salerno; Giuliana Marletti, Sandra Milo; Sergio, Jean Sorel; Signora Dominici, Daniela Bianchi; Valdameri, Trini Alonso; Swedish Vamp, Alicia Brandet; Count Bellanca, Lelio Luttazzi; Pasqualino, Raffaele Pisu; Ferri, Leopoldo Trieste.

3253 WEEKEND MURDERS. (MGM-1972). Barbara, Anna Moffo; Inspector Grey, Lance Percival; Sgt. Thorpe, Gastone Moschin; Isabelle, Evelyn Stewart; Anthony, Peter Baldwin; Ted, Giacomo Rossi Stuart; Georgie, Christopher Chittell; Aunt Gladys, Marisa Fabbri; Pauline, Beryl Cunningham; Lawrence, Quinto Parmeggiana; Maid, Orchidea De Santis; Valet, Robert Hundar; Stranger, Franco Borelli.

3254 WEEKEND OF FEAR. (JD-1966). Micki Malone, Kenneth Washman, Tory Alburn, Ruth Trent, Dianne Danford, James Vaneck, Kurt Donsbach, Jill Banner.

3255 WELCOME HOME, SOLDIER BOYS. (20th Century-Fox-1972). Danny, Joe Don Baker; Shooter, Paul Koslo; Kid, Alan Vint; Fatback, Elliott Street; Broad, Jennifer Billingsley; Sheriff, Billy Green Bush; Francis Rapture, Geoffrey Lewis; Lydia, Francine York; Mike, Timothy Scott; Father, Lonny Chapman; Danny's Mother, Florence MacMichael;

Ruby, Damienne Oliver; Charlene, Luanne Roberts.

3256 WELCOME KOSTYA! (Artkino-1965). Kostya, Vitya Kosikh; Camp Director, Evgeni Yevstigneye; The Informer, Lida Smirnova; Camp Nurse, Ava Aleinikova.

3257 WELCOME TO ARROW BEACH. (Warner Bros. -1974). Jason Henry, Laurence Harvey; Grace Henry, Joanna Pettet; Deputy Rakes, Stuart Whitman; Sheriff H. Bingham, John Ireland; Ginger, Gloria Leroy; Alex Heath, David Macklin; Felice, Dody Heath; Robbin Stanley, Meg Foster.

3258 WELCOME TO HARD TIMES. (MGM-1967). Will Blue, Henry Fonda; Molly Riordan, Janice Rule; Man from Bodie, Aldo Ray; Zar, Keenan Wynn; Adah, Janis Paige; Ezra Isaac Maple, John Anderson; Jenks, Warren Oates; Jessie, Fay Spain; Brown, Edgar Buchanan; Alfie, Denver Pyle; Michael Shea, Arlene Golonka, Lon Chaney, Royal Dano, Alan Baxter, John Birch, Dan Ferrone, Paul Fix, Elisha Cook, Kalin Liu, Ann McCrea, Bob Terhune, Ron Burke.

3259 WELCOME TO THE CLUB. (Columbia-1971). Andrew, Brain Foley; Gen. Strapp, Jack Warden; Fairfax, Andy Jarrell; Harrison, Kevin O'Connor.

3260 WEREWOLF OF WASHINGTON. (Diplomat-1973). Jack, Dean Stockwell; President, Biff McGuire; Attorney General, Clifton James; Cmdr. Salmon, Beeson Carroll; Marion, Jane House; Dr. Kiss, Michael Dunn; Hippy, Barbara Siegel; Foreign Minister, Stephen Cheng.

3261 WEREWOLVES ON WHEELS. (Fanfare-1971). Adam, Stephen Oliver; High Priest, Severn Darden; Helen, D. J. Anderson; Tarot, Deuce Berry; Bill, Billy Gray; Movie, Gray Johnson; Scarf, Barry McGuire; Mouse, Owen Orr; Shirley, Anna Lynn Brown; Gas Station Operator, Leonard Rogel.

3262 WESTWORLD. (MGM-1973). Gunslinger, Yul Brynner; Peter Martin, Richard Benjamin; John Blane, James Brolin; Medieval Knight, Norman Bartold; Chief Supervisor, Alan Oppenheimer; Medieval Queen, Victoria Shaw; Banker, Dick Van Patten; Arlette, Linda Scott; Technician, Steve Franken; Black Knight, Michael Mikler.

3263 WHAT ABOUT JANE? (Sherpix-1972). Emily Smith, John Christian, Martha Strawberry, Lee Parsons.

3264 WHAT AM I BID? (Emerson-1967). Pat Hubbard, LeRoy Van Dyke; Beth Hubbard, Kristin Nelson; Maggie Hendricks, Stephanie Hill; Mike Evans, Bill Craig; Bus Ticket Clerk, Leland Murray; Clem, Bill Benedict; Captain Harrigan, Robert Boylan; Tractor Salesman, Andy Davis; Concert Fan,

Muriel Landers; Fenster, Sid Rushakoff; Publisher, J. B. Towner; Hal Cook, Jack McCall.

3265 WHAT BECAME OF JACK AND JILL? (20th Century-Fox-1972). Jill, Vanessa Howard; Gran, Mona Washbourne; Johnny (Jack), Paul Nicholas; Dickson, Peter Copley; Dr. Graham, Peter Jeffrey; Frankie, Patricia Fuller; Mr. Trouncer, George A. Cooper; Woman in Street, Renee Roberts; Dickson's Secretary, Lillian Walker; Jehovah's Witness, Angela Down; Vicar, George Benson.

3266 WHAT DID YOU DO IN THE WAR, DADDY? (United Artists-1966). Lt. Christian, James Coburn; Capt. Cash, Dick Shawn; Capt. Oppo, Sergio Fantoni; Gina Romano, Giovanna Ralli; Sgt. Rizzo, Aldo Ray; Major Pott, Harry Morgan; General Bolt, Carroll O'Connor; Kastorp, Leon Askin; Benedetto, Henry Rico Cattani; Romano, Jay Novello; Federico, Vito Scotti; Vittorio, Johnny Seven.

3267 WHAT DO I TELL THE BOYS AT THE STATION? (August-1972). Barry, William C. Reilly; Sheila, Anita Morris; Maxine, Sloane Shelton.

3268 WHAT DO YOU SAY TO A NAKED LADY? (United Artists-1970). Girl in Elevator, Joie Addison; Girl on Ladder, Laura Huston; Tailor, Martin Meyers; Girl who is not raped, Karil Daniels; Inter-racial couple, Donna Whitfield, Richard Roundtree; Girl in Keyhole, Susanna Clemm; Male Model, Norman Manzon; Lecturer, Joan Bell.

3269 WHAT EVER HAPPENED TO AUNT ALICE? (Cinerama-1969). Mrs. Claire Marrable, Geraldine Page; Mrs. Alice Dimmock, Ruth Gordon; Harriet Vaughn, Rosemary Forsyth; Mike Darrah, Robert Fuller; Miss Tinsley, Mildred Dunnock; Julia Lawson, Joan Huntington; George Lawson, Peter Brandon; Jim Vaughn, Michael Barbera; Mr. Bentley, Peter Bonerz; Sheriff Armijo, Richard Angarola; Elva, Claire Kelly; Dottie, Valerie Allen; Juan, Martin Garragla; Olin, Jack Bannon; Warren, Seth Riggs; Telephone Man, Lou Kane.

3270 WHATEVER HAPPENED TO MISS SEPTEMBER? (808 Pictures-1973). Tina Russell, Nick Harley, Jason Russell, Marc Stevens, Hardy Harrison, Marcello Bonino, Eric Edwards, Ultra Max, Kathy May, Mary Madigan, Janis King, Jean Jeffries.

3271 WHAT'S GOOD FOR THE GOOSE. (National Showmanship-1969). Timothy, Norman Wisdom; Nikki, Sally Geeson; Margaret, Sally Bazely; Meg, Sarah Atkinson; Frisby, Terence Alexander.

3272 WHAT'S NEW PUSSYCAT? (United Artists-1965). Fritz Fassbender, Peter Sellers; Michael James, Peter O'Toole;

Carol Werner, Romy Schneider; Renee Lefebvre, Capucine; Liz, Paula Prentiss; Victor Shakapopolis, Woody Allen; Rita, Ursula Andress; Fassbender's Wife, Edra Gale; Jacqueline, Catherine Schaake; Carol's Father, Jess Hahn; Carol's Mother, Eleanor Hirt.

3273 WHAT'S SO BAD ABOUT FEELING GOOD? (Universal-1968). Pete, George Peppard; Liz, Mary Tyler Moore; J. Gardner Monroe, Dom De Luise; The Mayor, John McMartin; Conrad, Nathaniel Frey; Dr. Shapiro, Charles Lane; Gertrude, Jeanne Arnold; Murgatroyd, George Furth; Aida, Susan Saint James; Barney, Don Stroud; Sgt. Gunty, Morty Gunty; Officer Ponazecki, Joe Ponazecki; Capt. Wallace, Frank Campanella; First Mate, Arny Freeman; TV Newscaster, Martin O'Hara; Roger, John Ryan; Phil, Cleavon Little; Sybil, Emily Yancy; The Sack, Gillian Spencer; Sam, Donald Hotten; Board Member, Robert Moore; Mrs. Schwartz, Thelma Ritter.

3274 WHAT'S THE MATTER WITH HELEN? (United Artists-1971). Adelle Bruckner, Debbie Reynolds; Helen Hill, Shelley Winters; Lincoln Palmer, Dennis Weaver; Sister Alma, Agnes Moorehead.

3275 WHAT'S UP, DOC? (Warner Bros.-1972). Judy Maxwell, Barbra Streisand; Howard Bannister, Ryan O'Neal; Eunice Burns, Madeline Kahn; Hugh Simon, Kenneth Mars; Frederick Larrabee, Austin Pendleton; Harry, Sorrell Booke; Fritz, Stefan Gierasch; Mrs. Van Hoskins, Mabel Albertson; Mr. Smith, Michael Murphy; Baliff, Graham Jarvis; Judge, Liam Dunn; Mr. Jones, Phil Roth; Mr. Kaltenborn, John Hillerman; Rudy, George Morfogen; Professor Hosquith, Randy Quaid; Arresting Officer, M. Emmet Walsh; Banquet Receptionist, Eleanor Zee; Delivery Boy, Kevin O'Neal; Room Service Waiter, Paul Condylis; Jewel Thieves, Fred Scheiwiller, Carl Saxe, and Jack Perkins; Druggist, Paul B. Kililman; Mr. Jones' Driver, Gil Perkins; Mrs. Hosquith, Christa Land; Musicologists, Stan Ross and Peter Paul Eastman; Larrabee's Brother, Eric Brotherson.

3276 WHAT'S UP, TIGER LILY? (American International-1966). Phil Moscowitz, Tatsuya Mihashi; Terri Yaki, Mie Hana; Wuki Yaki, Akiko Wakayabayashi; Shepherd Wong, Tadao Nakamuru; Wing Fat, Susumu Kurobe; Narrator-Host, Woody Allen.

3277 WHEN DINOSAURS RULED THE EARTH. (Warner Bros.-1971). Sanna, Victoria Vetri; Tara, Robin Hawdon; Kingsor, Patrick Allen; Khaku, Drewe Henley; Kane, Sean Caffrey; Ulido, Magda Konopka; Ayak, Imogen Hassall; Ammon, Patrick Holt; Rock Girl, Jan Rossini; Yani, Carol-Anne Hawkins; Omah, Maria O'Brien; Sand Mother, Connie Tilton; Rock Mother, Maggie Lynton; Fisherman, Jimmy Lodge;

Hunters, Billy Cornelius, Ray Ford.

3278 WHEN EIGHT BELLS TOLL. (Cinerama-1971). Philip, Anthony Hopkins; Sir Arthur, Robert Morley; Charlotte, Nathalie Delon; Sir Anthony, Jack Hawkins.

3279 WHEN THE BOYS MEET THE GIRLS. (MGM-1966). Ginger, Connie Francis; Danny, Harve Presnell; Tess, Sue Ane Langdon; Phin, Frank Faylen; Bill, Fred Clark; Sam, Joby Baker; Kate, Hortense Petra; Lank, Stanley Adams; Pete, Romo Vincent; Delilah, Susan Holloway; Stokes, Russ Collins; Dean of Cody, William T. Quinn; Herman's Hermits, Louis Armstrong, Liberace, Davis and Reese, Sam the Sham and the Pharoahs.

3280 WHEN THE LEGENDS DIE. (20th Century-Fox-1972). Red Dillon, Richard Widmark; Tom Black Bull, Frederic Forrest; Mary Redmont, Luana Anders; Meo, Vito Scotti; Young Tom Black Bull, Tillman Box; Dr. Wilson, Herbert Nelson; Blue Elk, John War Eagle; Tex Walker, John Gruber; Superintendent, Garry Walberg; Gas Station Attendant, Jack Mullaney; Benny Grayback, Malcolm Curley; Sam Turner, Roy Engel; Neil Swenson, Rex Holman; Cowboy, Mel Gallagher; Angie, Sondra Pratt; George, Evan Stevens; Harold, Verne Muehlstedt; Old Man, John Renforth; Teacher, Rhoda Stevens; Carl Salesman, Mel Flock; Mom, Joyce Davis; Waitress, Terry Hutchison.

3281 WHEN WOMEN HAD TAILS. (Film Ventures International-1973). Senta Berger, Giuliano Gemma, Frank Wolff, Paolo Borboni, Lando Buzzanca.

3282 WHERE ANGELS GO--TROUBLE FOLLOWS! (Columbia-1968). Mother Simplicia, Rosalind Russell; Sister George, Stella Stevens; Sister Celestine, Binnie Barnes; Sister Clarissa, Mary Wickes; Sister Rose Marie, Dolores Sutton; Rosabelle, Susan Saint James; Marvel Ann Clancy, Barbara Hunter; Patty, Alice Rawlings; Hilarie, Hilarie Thompson; Devon, Devon Douglas; Tanya, Ellen Moss; Father Chase, Van Johnson; Mr. Clancy, William Lundigan; Mr. Farriday, Robert Taylor; Motorcycle Leader, Michael Christian; Cyclist, Jon Hill; Jud Farriday, John Findletter.

3283 WHERE DOES IT HURT? (Cinerama-1972). Albert Hopfnagel, Peter Sellers; Alice, Jo Ann Pflug; Lester, Rick Lenz; Dr. Zerny, Harold Gould; Nurse Throttle, Hope Summers; LaMarr, Eve Bruce; Mrs. Mazzini, Kathleen Freeman; Katzen, Norman Alden; Hinkley, Keith Allison; Oscar, William Elliot; Dr. Kincaid, Jeanne Byron.

3284 WHERE EAGLES DARE. (MGM-1969). John Smith, Richard Burton; Lt. Morris Schaffer, Clint Eastwood; Mary Ellison, Mary Ure; Vice-Admiral Rolland, Michael Hordern;

Col. Wyatt-Turner, Patrick Wymark; Cartwright-Jones, Robert Beatty; Col. Kramer, Anton Diffring; Olaf Christiansen, Donald Houston; Rechmarshall Rosemeyer, Ferdy Mayne; Torrance-Smythe, Neil McCarthy; Peter Barkworth, William Squire, Brook Williams, Victor Beaumont, Ingrid Pitt, Vincent Ball, Derren Nesbitt, Richard Beale.

3285 WHERE IT'S AT. (United Artists-1969). A. C. Smith, David Janssen; Andy Smith, Robert Drivas; Diana Mayhew, Rosemary Forsyth; Molly Hirsch, Brenda Vaccaro; Willie the Dealer, Don Rickles; Betty Avery, Warrene Ott; Phyllis Horrigan, Edy Williams; Ralph, Vince Howard; and the voices of The Committee.

3286 WHERE THE BULLETS FLY. (Embassy-1967). Charles Vine, Tom Adams; Felicity Moonlight, Dawn Addams; Seraph, Tim Barrett; Angel, Michael Ripper; Minister, Joe Baker; Train Conductor, Wilfred Brambell.

3287 WHERE THE RED FERN GROWS. (Doty-Dayton-1974). Grandpa, James Whitmore; Mother, Beverly Garland; Father, Jack Ging; Sheriff, Lonny Chapman; Billy, Stewart Petersen; Alice, Jill Clark; Sara, Jeanna Wilson.

3288 WHERE THE SPIES ARE. (MGM-1966). Dr. Jason Love, David Niven; Vikki, Francoise Dorleac; Col. MacGillivray, John Le Mesurier; Peter Rosser, Cyril Cusack; Farouk, Eric Pohlmann; Josef, Richard Marner; Simmias, Paul Stassino; 1st Agent, George Pravda; Mr. Kahn, Reginald Beckwith; Assassin, George Mikell; Nigel Davenport, Gabor Baraker, Ronald Radd, Noel Harrison, Alan Gifford, Bill Nagy, Geoffrey Bayldon, Derek Partridge, Robert Raglan, Riyad Gholmieh, Muhsen Samrani, Basil Dignam, Gordon Tanner.

3289 WHERE WERE YOU WHEN THE LIGHTS WENT OUT? (MGM-1968). Margaret Garrison, Doris Day; Waldo Zane, Robert Morse; Ladislaw Walichek, Terry-Thomas; Peter Garrison, Patrick O'Neal; Roberta Lane, Lola Albright; Radio Announcer, Steve Allen; Tru-Blu Lou, Jim Backus; Man With a Razor, Ben Blue; Conductor, Pat Paulsen.

3290 WHERE'S JACK? (Paramount-1969). Jack Sheppard, Tommy Steele; Jonathan Wild, Stanley Baker; Edgworth Bess, Fiona Lewis; Lord Chancellor, Alan Badel; Blueskin, Dudley Foster; Leatherchest, Noel Purcell; Tom Sheppard, William Marlowe; Lady Darlington, Sue Lloyd; King, Harold Kasket; Lord Mayor, Cardew Robinson; Ballad Singer, Esmond Knight; Rev. Wagstaff, Eddie Byrne.

3291 WHERE'S POPPA? (United Artists-1970). Gordon Hocheiser, George Segal; Mrs. Hocheiser, Ruth Gordon; Louise, Trish Van Devere; Sidney Hocheiser, Ron Leibman; First

Policeman, Tom Atkins; Secretary, Florence Tarlow; First Woman, Jane Hoffman; Capable Woman, Helen Martin.

3292 WHICH WAY TO THE FRONT? (Warner Bros.-1970). Brendan, Jerry Lewis; Finkel, John Wood; Hackle, Jan Murray; Bland, Steve Franken; Love, Dack Rambo; Colonico, Robert Middleton; Lincoln, Willie Davis; Mayor's Wife, Kaye Ballard; General Buck, Harold J. Stone; Hitler, Sidney Miller; Schroeder, Paul Winchell; Dock Master, Joe Besser.

3293 WHIRLPOOL. (Cinemation-1970). Theo, Karl Lanchbury; Tulia, Vivian Neves; Sara, Pia Anderson; Johanna Hegger, Andrea Grant, Edwin Brown, Ernest Jenning, Larry Dann, Alan Charles, Barrie Craine.

3294 WHIRLWIND. (Toho-1968). Lord Akashi, Toshiro Mifune; Jubei, Somegoro Ichikawa; Kozato, Yuriko Hoshi; The Witch, Kumi Mizuno.

3295 THE WHISPERERS. (Lopert-1967). Mrs. Ross, Edith Evans; Archie, Eric Portman; Girl Upstairs, Nanette Newman; Conrad, Gerald Sim; Mrs. Noona, Avis Bunnage; Charlie, Ronald Fraser; Official, Leonard Rossiter; Mr. Weaver, Kenneth Griffith; Earl, Harry Baird; Almoner, Margaret Tyzack; Prostitute, Clare Kelly; Andy, Robert Russell.

3296 THE WHITE DAWN. (Paramount-1974). Billy, Warren Oates; Daggett, Timothy Bottoms; Portagee, Lou Gossett; Sarkak, Simonie Kopapik; Kangiak, Joanasie Salomonie; Nevee, Pilitak; Sowniapik, Munamee Sake.

3297 WHITE LIGHTNING. (United Artists-1973). Gator McKlusky, Burt Reynolds; Lou, Jennifer Billingsley; Sheriff Connors, Ned Beatty; Roy Boone, Bo Hopkins; Dude Watson, Matt Clark; Martha Culpepper, Louise Latham; Maggie, Diane Ladd; Big Bear, R. G. Armstrong; Deputy, Conlan Carter; Pa McKluskey, Dabbs Greer; Superintendent Simms, Lincoln Demyan; Skeeter, John Steadman; Ma McKluskey, Iris Korn; Jenny, Stephanie Burchfield; Louella, Barbara Muller; Harvey, Robert Ginnaven; Sister Linda Fay, Fay Martin; Treasury Agents, Richard Allin, Bill Bond.

3298 WHITE SISTER. (Columbia-1973). Sister Germana, Sophia Loren; Annibale Pezzi, Adriano Celentano; Chief Physician, Fernando Rey; Guido, Juan Luis Galiardo; Libyan Brigadiere, Luis Marin; Dr. Arrighi, Giuseppe Maffioli; Dr. Filippini, Sergio Fasanelli.

3299 WHITE VOICES. (Rizzoli-1965). Meo, Paolo Ferrari; Carolina, Sandra Milo; Teresa, Graziella Granata; Lorenza, Anouk Aimee; Matteuccio, Vittorio Caprioli; Maria, Jeanne

Valerie; Ascanio, Philippe Leroy; Guilia, Barbara Steele; Oropreenobbi, Leopoldo Trieste; Eugenia, Jacqueline Sassard; Marchionne, Claudio Gora.

3300 WHO IS HARRY KELLERMAN AND WHY IS HE SAYING THOSE TERRIBLE THINGS ABOUT ME? (National General-1971). Georgie, Dustin Hoffman; Allison, Barbara Harris; Dr. Moses, Jack Warden; Leon, David Burns; Irwin, Dom DeLuise; Margot, Betty Walker; Gloria, Rose Gregorio; Sid, Gabriel Dell.

3301 WHO KILLED MARY WHAT'S 'ERNAME? (Cannon-1971). Mickey, Red Buttons; Della, Alice Playten; Christine, Sylvia Miles; Alex, Sam Waterston; Malthus, Dick Williams; Val, Conrad Bain.

3302 WHO KILLED TEDDY BEAR? (Magna-1965). Sal Mineo, Juliet Prowse, Jan Murray, Elaine Stritch, Margot Bennett, Dan Travanty, Diana Moore, Frank Campanella, Bruce Glover, Tom Aldredge, Rex Everhart, Alex Fisher, Stanley Beck, Casey Townsend.

3303 WHO SAYS I CAN'T RIDE A RAINBOW! (Transvue-1971). Barney, Jack Klugman; Mary Lee, Norma French; Angel, Reuben Figueroa; David, David Mann.

3304 WHO SLEW AUNTIE ROO? (American International-1972). Rosie Forrest, Shelley Winters; Christopher, Mark Lester; Mr. Benton, Ralph Richardson; Inspector Willoughby, Lionel Jeffries; Clarine, Judy Cornwell; Albie, Michael Gothard; The Pigman (Mr. Harrison), Hugh Griffith; Katy, Chloe Franks; Miss Henley, Rosalie Crutchley; Miss Wilcox, Marianne Stone; Katherine, Charlotte Sayce; Peter, Richard Beaumont; Dr. Mason, Pat Heywood.

3305 WHO'S AFRAID OF VIRGINIA WOOLF? (Warner Bros.-1966). Martha, Elizabeth Taylor; George, Richard Burton; Nick, George Segal; Honey, Sandy Dennis.

3306 WHO'S MINDING THE MINT? (Columbia-1967). Harry Lucas, Jim Hutton; Verna, Dorothy Provine; Luther Burton, Milton Berle; Ralph Randazzo, Joey Bishop; Willie Owens, Bob Denver; Pop Gillis, Walter Brennan; Captain, Victor Buono; Avery Dugan, Jack Gilford; Mario, Jamie Farr; Samson Link, David J. Stewart.

3307 WHO'S THAT KNOCKING AT MY DOOR? (Joseph Brenner Associates-1969). The Girl, Zena Bethune; J.R., Harvey Keitel; Joey, Lennard Kuras; Salvatore Gaga, Michael Scala; Sally's Girl Friend, Wendy Russell; Mountain Guide, Philip Carlson; Gunman at Stag Party, Robert Uricola; Iggy & Radio Announcer, Bill Minkin; Susan, Susan Wood; Rosie, Marissa; Rapist, Harry Northrup; J.R.'s Mother, Catherine

Scorsese.

3308 WHY. (Hallmark Releasing Corporation-1972). Giuseppe Di Noi, Alberto Sordi; Ingrid Di Noi, Elga Andersen; Lino Banfi, Giuseppe Anatrelli, Tano Cimarosa, Antonio Casagrande, Nino Formicola.

3309 WHY BOTHER TO KNOCK. (7 Arts-1965). Bill Ferguson, Richard Todd; Lucille, Nicole Maurey; Ingrid, Elke Sommer; Stella, June Thorburn; Maggie Shoemaker, Judith Anderson; Giulio, Rik Battaglia; Harry, Dawn Beret; Perry, Scot Finch; Mother, Eleanor Summerfield; Father, John Le Mesurier; Rolsom, Colin Gordon; Ian, Kenneth Fortescue; Fred, Ronald Fraser; Al, Tom Duggan; Colonel, Michael Shepley; Spinster, Joan Sterndale-Bennett; Neighbor, Kynaston Reeves; Taxi Driver, John Laurie; Waiter, Warren Mitchell.

3310 WHY ROCK THE BOAT? (Columbia-1974). Harry Barnes, Stuart Gillard; Ronny Waldron, Ken James; Julia Martin, Tiiu Leek; Philip L. Butcher, Henry Beckman; Fred O'Neill, Budd Knapp; Herb Scannell, Sean Sullivan; Isobel Scannell, Patricia Gage; Señor Gomez, Ruben Moreno.

3311 THE WICKED DREAMS OF PAULA SCHULTZ. (United Artists-1968). Paula Schultz, Elke Sommer; Bill Mason, Bob Crane; Klaus, Werner Klemperer; Oscar, Leon Askin; Herbert Sweeney, Joey Forman; Kessel, Fritz Feld.

3312 WICKED, WICKED. (MGM-1973). Rick, David Bailey; Lisa, Tiffany Bolling; Jason, Randolph Roberts; Sgt. Ramsey, Scott Brady; Hank, Edd Byrnes; Dolores, Diane McBain; Manager, Roger Bowen; Lenore, Madeleine Sherwood; Genny, Indira Danks; Engineer, Arthur O'Connell; Bill, Jack Knight; Housekeeper, Patsy Garrett; Day Clerk, Robert Nichols; Owen, Kirk Bates; Organist, Maryesther Denver.

3313 THE WICKER MAN. (Warner Bros. -1974). Sergeant Howie, Edward Woodward; Willow, Britt Ekland; Miss Rose, Diane Cilento; Librarian, Ingrid Pitt; Lord Summerisle, Christopher Lee; Broome, Roy Boyd; School Master, Walter Carr; Alder MacGreagor, Lindsay Kemp; Old Fisherman, Kevin Collins; Harbour Master, Russell Waters; Daisy, Leslie Mackie; May Morrison, Irene Sunter; Oak, Ian Campbell; Old Gardener/Gravedigger, Aubrey Morris; T. H. Lennox, Donald Eccles; Rowan Morrison, Geraldine Cowper.

3314 THE WIFE SWAPPERS. (Eagle-1970). Paul, James Donnelly; Leonard, Larry Taylor; Ellen, Valerie St. John; Cliff, Denys Hawthorne.

3315 THE WILD AFFAIR. (Goldstone Film Enterprises-1966). Nancy Kwan, Terry-Thomas, Jimmy Logan, Bud Flanagan,

Gladys Morgan, Betty Marsden, Paul Whitsun-Jones, David Sumner, Donald Churchill, Joyce Blair, Victor Spinetti, Bessie Love, Joan Benham.

3316 THE WILD ANGELS. (American International-1966). Heavenly Blues, Peter Fonda; Mike, Nancy Sinatra; Loser, Bruce Dern; Joint, Lou Procopio; Bull Puckey, Coby Denton; Frankenstein, Marc Cavell; Dear John, Buck Taylor; Medic, Norm Alden.

3317 THE WILD BUNCH. (Warner Bros. -7 Arts-1969). Pike Bishop, William Holden; Dutch Engstrom, Ernest Borgnine; Deke Thornton, Robert Ryan; Sykes, Edmond O'Brien; Lyle Gorch, Warren Oates; Angel, Jaime Sanchez; Tector Gorch, Ben Johnson; Mapache, Emilio Fernandez; Coffer, Strother Martin; T. C. , L.Q. Jones; Crazy Lee, Bo Hopkins; Mayor Wainscoat, Dub Taylor.

3318 THE WILD CHILD. (United Artists-1970). Victor, Jean-Pierre Cargol; Professor Pinel, Jean Daste; Jean Itard, Francois Truffaut; Madame Guerin, Francoise Seigner; Remy, Paul Ville; Monsieur Lemeri, Claude Miler; Madame Lemeri, Annie Miler.

3319 THE WILD COUNTRY. (Buena Vista-1971). Jim, Steve Forrest; Thompson, Jack Elam; Virgil, Ronny Howard; Two Dog, Frank De Kova; Kate, Vera Miles.

3320 THE WILD EYE. (American International-1968). Paolo, Philippe LeRoy; Barbara Bates, Delia Boccardo; Valentino, Gabriele Tinti.

3321 WILD IN THE STREETS. (American International-1968). Mrs. Flatow, Shelley Winters; Max Frost, Christopher Jones; Sally Leroy, Diane Varsi; Senator Allbright, Ed Begley; John Fergus, Hal Holbrook; Stanley X, Richard Pryor; Mary Fergus, Millie Perkins; Max Jacob Flatow Sr. , Bert Freed; Billy Cage, Kevin Coughlin; Abraham, Larry Bishop; Buiji Ellie, May Ishihara.

3322 WILD 90. (Supreme Mix-1968). The Prince, Norman Mailer; Cameo, Buzz Farber; 20 Years, Mickey Knox; Margie, Beverly Bentley; Kid Cha Cha, Jose Torres; Lillian, Mara Lynn; Lieutenant, Dick Adler.

3323 WILD ON THE BEACH. (20th Century-Fox-1965). Frankie Randall, Sherry Jackson, Jackie and Gayle, The Astronauts, Sonny and Cher.

3324 THE WILD PACK. (American International-1972). Bullet, Kent Lane; Dora, Tisha Sterling; Professor, John Rubinstein; No Legs, Butch Patrick; Dry Turn, Mark De Vries; Lollypop, Peter Nielsen; Father Jose Pedro, Alejandro Rey;

Dalvah, Eliana Pittman.

3325 THE WILD RACERS. (American International-1968). Jo-Jo Quillico, Fabian; Katharine, Mimsy Farmer; Charlie, Alan Haufret; British Girl, Judy Cornwall; Manager, David Landers; Jo-Jo's Partner, Warwick Sims.

3326 THE WILD REBELS. (Crown International-1967). Rod Tillman, Steve Alaimo; Banjo, Willie Pastrano; Jeeter, John Vella; Linda, Bobbi Byers; Fats, Jeff Gillen; Lt. Dorn, Watler R. Philbin; Detective, Robert Freund; Walt Simpson, Seymour A. Eisenfeld; First Man, Phil Longo; Bartender, Milton Smith; College Boys, Kurt Nagler, Steve Geller, Chris Martell, Gary Brady; Nori, Nora Alonzo.

3327 WILD ROVERS. (MGM-1971). Ross Bodine, William Holden; Frank Post, Ryan O'Neal; Walter Buckman, Karl Malden; Sada Billings, Lynn Carlin; John Buckman, Tom Skerritt; Paul Buckman, Joe Don Baker; Nell Buckman, Leora Dana; Joe Billings, James Olson.

3328 THE WILD SCENE. (Four Star Excelsior-1970). Richard Tate, Alberta Nelson, Gary Pillar, Anita Eubank.

3329 WILD SEED. (Universal-1965). Michael Parks, Celia Kaye, Ross Elliott, Woodrow Chambliss, Rupert Crosse, Eva Novak, Norman Burton, Merritt Bohn, Anthony Lettier.

3330 WILD, WILD PLANET. (MGM-1967). Mike Halstead, Tony Russell; Connie, Lisa Gastoni; Nurmi, Massimo Serato; Jake, Franco Nero; Ken, Charles Justin; General, Enzo Fiermonte; Maitland, Umberto Raho.

3331 WILD WILD WINTER. (Universal-1966). Ronnie, Gary Clarke; Susan, Chris Noel; Burt, Don Edmonds; Sandy, Suzie Kaye; Perry, Les Brown Jr.; Dot, Vicky Albright; Dean, Jim Wellman; John, Steve Franken; Benton, Steve Rogers; The Bear, Loren James; Jay and the Americans, Beau Brummels, Dick and Dee Dee, The Astronauts, Jackie and Gayle.

3332 WILL PENNY. (Paramount-1968). Will Penny, Charlton Heston; Catherine Allen, Joan Hackett; Preacher Quint, Donald Pleasence; Blue, Lee Majors; Rafe Quint, Bruce Dern; Alex, Ben Johnson; Ike Wallerstein, Slim Pickens; Catron, Clifton James; Dutchy, Anthony Zerbe; Horace Greeley Allen, Jon Francis; Boetius Sullivan, Roy Jenson; Anse Howard, G. D. Spradlin; Jennie, Quentin Dean.

3333 WILLARD. (Cinerama-1971). Willard Stiles, Bruce Davison; Henrietta Stiles, Elsa Lanchester; Al Martin, Ernest Borgnine; Joan, Sondra Locke; Brandt, Michael Dante; Charlotte Stassen, Jody Gilbert; Alice, Joan Shawlee.

3334 WILLY McBEAN AND HIS MAGIC MACHINE. (Magna-1965). Willy McBean, Larry Mann, Billie Richards, Alfie Scopp, Paul Ligman, Bunny Cowan.

3335 WILLY WONKA AND THE CHOCOLATE FACTORY. (Paramount-1971). Willy Wonka, Gene Wilder; Grandpa Joe, Jack Albertson; Charlie, Peter Ostrum; Augustus Gloop, Michael Bollner; Mrs. Gloop, Ursula Reit.

3336 WINDFLOWERS. (Film-Makers' Distribution Center-1968). Paul Ramsey, John Kramer; Julie, Pola Chapelle; 1st FBI Agent, William Traylor; 2nd FBI Agent, Reathel Bean; Publisher, Maxton Latham; Newspaper Reporter, James Hunter; Driver, Edward Rishon; Police Captain, Dave Tice; Police Rookie, Todd Everett; Student, Roger Briant.

3337 THE WINDSPLITTER. (POP-1971). Bobby Joe, Jim McMullan; Buford, Paul Lambert; Jenny, Joyce Taylor; Louis, I. Van Charles; R. T., Richard Everett; Mr. Smith, Jim Sedlow; Mrs. Smith, Chris Wilson; Annie, Anne Layne; John Martin, Carter Smith, Ray O'Leary, Ruth Roberts, Greg Ford, Lee Ryan, Mahlon Foreman, Tobe Hooper.

3338 THE WINNER. (Gilmor-Kingsley-1966). Abdoulaye Faye, Marcel Bruchard, Milou Pladner, Luce Vidi, Yasumiko Michele Morgan, Jean-Paul Belmondo.

3339 WINNING. (Universal-1969). Frank Capua, Paul Newman; Elora, Joanne Woodward; Charley, Richard Thomas; Luther Erding, Robert Wagner; Leo Crawford, David Sheiner; Larry Morechek, Clu Gulager; Les Battineau, Barry Ford; Sam Jagin, Bob Quarry; Miss Redburne 200, Eileen Wesson; The Girl, Toni Clayton; Eshovo, Charles Steel.

3340 WINTER A-GO-GO. (Columbia-1965). James Stacy, William Wellman Jr., Beverly Adams, Anthony Hayes, Jill Donohue, Tom Nardini, Duke Hobbie, Julie Parrish, Nancy Czar, Linda Rogers, Judy Parker, Bob Kanter, Walter Maslow, H. T. Tsiang, Buck Holland, The Reflections, Carey Foster, Cheryl Hurley, Arlene Charles.

3341 WINTER KEPT US WARM. (Film-Makers' Distribution Center-1968). Doug, John Labow; Peter, Henry Tarvainen; Bev, Joy Tepperman; Sandra, Janet Amos; Artie, Ian Ewing; Larry, Larry Greenspan; Hall Porter, Sol Mendelson; House Don, George Appleby.

3342 WINTER WIND. (Grove-1970). Marko, Jacques Charrier; Maria, Marina Vlady; Ilona, Eva Swann; Markovics, Mozsef Madaras.

3343 WISE GUYS. (Universal-1969). Hector, Bourvil; Laurent, Lino Ventura; Jackie, Marie Dubois; Mick, Jean-Claude

Rolland.

3344 A WITCH WITHOUT A BROOM. (Producers Releasing Organization-1967). Garver Logan, Jeffrey Hunter; Marianna, Maria Perschy; Cayo, Gustavo Rojo; Octavia, Pearl Cristal; Don Ignacio, Reginald Gillam; Wurlitz the Wizard, Al Mulock; Yolanda, Katherine Ellison.

3345 WITCHCRAFT. (20th Century-Fox-1965). Morgan Whitlock, Lon Chaney; Bill Lanier, Jack Hedley; Tracy Lanier, Jill Dixon; Helen Lanier, Viola Keats; Malvina Lanier, Marie Ney; Todd Lanier, David Weston; Vanessa Whitlock, Yvette Rees; Amy, Diane Clair; Myles Forrester, Barry Linehan; Forrester's Secretary, Marianne Stone; Nurse, Hilda Fenemore.

3346 THE WITCHES. (Lopert-1969). Silvana Mangano, Annie Girardot, Francisco Rabal, Massimo Girotti, Elsa Albani, Helmut Steinberger, Alberto Sordi, Toto, Ninetto Davoli, Pietro Tordi, Clint Eastwood, Armando Bottin, Gianni Gori, Paolo Gozlino, Angelo Santi.

3347 THE WITCHMAKER. (Excelsior-1969). Luther, John Lodge; Dr. Hayes, Alvy Moore; Tasha, Thordis Brandt; Victor, Anthony Eisley; Maggie, Shelby Grant; Student, Robyn Millan; Student, Tony Benson; Jessie #1, Helene Winston; Jessie #2, Warene Ott; Boatman, Burt Mustin; Patty, Kathy Lynn; Goody, Sue Nancy Crawford.

3348 WITH SIX YOU GET EGGROLL. (National General-1968). Abby McClure, Doris Day; Jake Iverson, Brian Keith; Maxine Scott, Pat Carroll; Stacey Iverson, Barbara Hershey; Herbie Fleck, George Carlin; Housekeeper, Alice Ghostley; Flip McClure, John Findlater; Mitch McClure, Jimmy Bracken; Jason McClure, Richard Steele; Harry Scott, Herbert Voland; Cleo, Elaine Devry; Calico, Lord Nelson.

3349 WITHOUT A STITCH. (VIP-Sherpix-1970). Lilian, Anne Grete; Petersen, Ib Mossin; Henry, Niels Borksand; Britta, Ki-Jo Feza; Goran, Niels Dybeck.

3350 WITHOUT APPARENT MOTIVE. (20th Century-Fox-1972). Stephane Carella, Jean-Louis Trintignant; Sandra Forest, Dominique Sanda; Julien Sabirnou, Sacha Distel; Jocelyne Rocca, Carla Gravina; Francis Palombo, Paul Crauchet; Juliette Vaudreuil, Laura Antonelli; Perry Rupert-Foote, Jean-Pierre Marielle; Helene Vallee, Stephane Audran; Di Bozzo, Pierre Dominique; Hans Kleinberg, Erich Segal; Commissioner, Jean-Jacques Delbo.

3351 WOMAN AND TEMPTATION. (Prentoulis-1969). Sandra, Isabel Sarli; Joseph, Armando Bo; Chuck, Victor Bo; Shorty,

Oscar Valicelli; The Crazy One, Juan Jose Miguez; The Other One, Anibal Pardeiro.

3352 A WOMAN ON FIRE. (Commonwealth United-1970). Clara, Françoise Prevost; Giancarlo, Gianni Macchia; Silvio, Michel Bardinet; Marina, Monica Strebel.

3353 WOMAN TIMES SEVEN. (Embassy-1967). Paulette, Maria Teresa, Linda, Edith, Eve, Marie, Jeanne, Shirley MacLaine; Jean, Peter Sellers; Jeannine, Catherine Samie; Annette, Elspeth March; Husband, Rossano Brazzi; Second Prostitute, Judith Magre; Italian, Vittorio Gassman; Scotsman, Clinton Greyn; Husband, Lex Barker; Woman in Market, Elsa Martinelli; Psychiatrist, Robert Morley; Husband, Patrick Wymark; Rival, Adrienne Corri; Fred, Alan Arkin; Handsome Stranger, Michael Caine; Friend, Anita Ekberg; Husband, Philippe Noiret.

3354 A WOMAN UNDER THE INFLUENCE. (Faces International-1974). Nick Longhetti, Peter Falk; Mabel Longhetti, Gena Rowlands; Tony Longhetti, Matthew Cassel; Angelo Longhetti, Matthew Laborteaux; Maria Longhetti, Christina Grisanti; Mama Longhetti, Katherine Cassavetes; Martha Mortensen, Lady Rowlands; George Mortensen, Fred Draper; Garson Cross, O. G. Dunn; Harold Jensen, Mario Gallo; Doctor Zepp, Eddie Shaw; Vito Grimaldi, Angelo Grisanti; Bowman, James Joyce; Clancy, John Finnegan; Willie Johnson, Hugh Hurd; Billy Tidrow, Leon Wagner; Joseph Morton, John Hawker; James Turner, Sil Words; Angela, Elizabeth Deering; Tina, Jackie Peters; Principal, Elsie Ames.

3355 THE WOMAN WHO WOULDN'T DIE. (Warner Bros. -1965). Raymond Garth, Gary Merrill; Alice Taylor, Jane Merrow; Ellen Garth, Georgina Cookson; Dick Corbett, Neil McCallum; Christine, Rachel Thomas.

3356 WOMEN IN CAGES. (New World-1972). Jeff, Jennifer Gan; Sandy, Judy Brown; Stoke, Roberta Collins; Alabama, Pamela Grier; Theresa, Sofia Moran; Acosta, Bernard Bonnin; Rudy, Charlie Davao; Jorge, Paquito Diaz; Lorca, Nick Cayari; Juana, Marissa Delgado.

3357 WOMEN IN CELL BLOCK 7. (Aquarius-1974). Hilda, Anita Strinberg; Daniela, Eva Czemeys; Chief Matron, Olga Bisera; Gisa, Jane Avril; Napolitana, Valeria Fabrizi; Musumeci, Paola Senatore; Inspector Weil, Roger Browne; Gerda, Jenny Tamburi; Mama S, Christina Baioni.

3358 WOMEN IN LOVE. (United Artists-1970). Rupert Birkin, Alan Bates; Gerald Crich, Oliver Reed; Gudrun Brangwen, Glenda Jackson; Ursula Brangwen, Jennie Linden; Hermione Roddice, Eleanor Bron; Thomas Crich, Alan Webb; Loerke, Vladek Shcybal; Mrs. Crich, Catherine Willmer; Winifred

Crich, Sarah Nicholls; Laura Crich, Sharon Gurney; Lupton, Christopher Gable; Tom Brangwen, Michael Gough; Anna Brangwen, Norma Shebbeare; Contessa, Nike Arrighi; Minister, James Laurenson; Palmer, Michael Graham Cox; Barber, Leslie Anderson; Miner 1, Barrie Fletcher; Miner 2, Brian Osborne; Loerke's Friend, Richard Heffer; Salsie, Richard Fitzgerald; Maestro, Michael Garratt.

3359 WOMEN IN REVOLT. (Andy Warhol-1972). Candy, Candy Darling; Jackie, Jackie Curtis; Holly, Holly Woodlawn; Duncan, Duncan MacKenzie; Marty, Marty Kove; Candy's Father, Maurice Braddell; Max Morris, Michael Sklar; Johnny Minute, Johnny Kemper; Mrs. Fitzpatrick, Sean O'Meara; Jane, Jane Forth.

3360 WOMEN OF THE PREHISTORIC PLANET. (Realart-1966). Admiral King, Wendell Corey; Commander Scott, Keith Larsen; Doctor, John Agar; Linda, Irene Tsu; Paul Gilbert, Merry Anders, Suzie Kaye.

3361 WONDER WOMEN. (General-1973). Dr. Tsu, Nancy Kwan; Mike, Ross Hagen; Linda, Maria De Aragan; Laura, Roberta Collins; Paulson/Lorenzo, Tony Lorea; Gregorius, Sid Haig; Lapu, Vic Dias; Vera, Claire Hagen; Maggie, Shirley Washington; Gail, Gail Hansen.

3362 WOODSTOCK. (Warner Bros. -1969). Joan Baez, Joe Cocker, Country Joe and the Fish, Crosby, Stills, Nash and Young, Arlo Guthrie, Richie Havens, Jimi Hendrix, Santana, John Sebastian, The Who.

3363 THE WORLD IS JUST A "B" MOVIE. (Robinson-1971). Jonathan, James Christopher; Harry, Robert Lincoln Robb; Gandalf, Riki Ferguson; Alice, Georgina Clegg; Speaker, Willie Harris; Mitch, Walter Jones; Jerry Charburn, Pigeon Darbo, Uschi Digaid, Eleanor Dixson, Monica Gayle, Mike Hall, Hans Ludermilk.

3364 THE WORLD OF HANS CHRISTIAN ANDERSEN. (United Artists-1971). Uncle Oley, Chuck McCann; Hans, Hetty Galen; Elisha/Kitty Kat/Little Boy/Match Girl, Corinne Orr; Karen, Sidney Filson.

3365 THE WORLD OF SPORT FISHING. (Allied Artists-1972). Ernest Borgnine, Joe Brooks, Bing Crosby, Ken Curtis, Curt Gowdy, Phil Harris, Van Heflin, Gordie Howe, Jack Nicklaus, Lee Wulff.

3366 THE WORLD'S GREATEST ATHLETE. (Buena Vista-1973). Coach Archer, John Amos; Nanu, Jan-Michael Vincent; Gazenga, Roscoe Lee Browne; Milo, Tim Conway; Jane, Dayle Haddon; Landlady, Nancy Walker; Maxwell, Billy DeWolfe; Leopold, Danny Goldman; Don Pedro Colley, Vito

Scotti, Liam Dunn, Ivor Francis, Leon Askin, Howard Cosell, Frank Gifford, Jim McKay, Bud Palmer, Bill Toomey

3367 WOUNDED IN ACTION. (Myriad-1966). Steve Marlo, Maura McGiveney, Leopoldo Salcedo, Mary Humphrey, Albert Quinton, Victor Izay.

3368 No entry.

3369 THE WRATH OF GOD. (MGM-1972). Van Horne, Robert Mitchum; Thomas De La Plata, Frank Langella; Senora De La Plata, Rita Hayworth; Colonel Santilla, John Colicos; Jennings, Victor Buono; Emmet Keogh, Ken Hutchinson; Chela, Paula Pritchett; Jurado, Gregory Sierra; Moreno, Frank Ramirez; Nacho, Enrique Lucero.

3370 THE WRECKING CREW. (Columbia-1969). Matt Helm, Dean Martin; Linka Karensky, Elke Sommer; Freya Carlson, Sharon Tate; Yu-Rang, Nancy Kwan; Count Contini, Nigel Green; Lola Medina, Tina Louise; MacDonald, John Larch; Karl, John Brascia; Kim, Weaver Levy.

3371 THE WRESTLER. (Entertainment Ventures-1974). Frank Bass, Edward Asner; Debbie, Elaine Giftos; Mike Bullard, Verne Gagne; Betty Bullard, Sarah Miller; Odd Job, Harold Sakata; Mobster, Sam Menecker; Bartender, Hardboiled Haggerty; Dusty Rhodes, Dick Murdoch, The Crusher, The Bruiser, Lord James Blears, Billy Graham.

3372 THE WRONG BOX. (Columbia-1966). Masterman Finsbury, John Mills; Joseph Finsbury, Ralph Richardson; Michael, Michael Caine; Morris, Peter Cook; John, Dudley Moore; Julia, Nanette Newman; Detective, Tony Hancock; Dr. Pratt, Peter Sellers; Peacock, Wilfrid Lawson; Patience, Thorley Walters; Cecily Courtneidge, Irene Handl, Gerald Sim, Norman Bird, Tutte Lemkow, Peter Graves, Norman Rossington.

3373 WUSA. (Paramount-1970). Rheinhardt, Paul Newman; Geraldine, Joanne Woodward; Rainey, Anthony Perkins; Farley, Laurence Harvey; Bingamon, Pat Hingle; Philomene, Cloris Leachman; Bogdanovich, Don Gordon; Marvin, Michael Anderson Jr.; Girl, Leigh French; Clotho, Moses Gunn; King Wolyoe, Bruce Cabot; Roosevelt Berry, B. J. Mason.

3374 WUTHERING HEIGHTS. (American International-1971). Catherine, Anna Calder-Marshall; Heathcliff, Timothy Dalton; Mr. Earnshaw, Harry Andrews; Mrs. Linton, Pamela Browne; Nellie, Judy Cornwell; Mr. Linton, James Cossins; Mrs. Earnshaw, Rosalie Crutchley.

3375 X Y & ZEE. (Columbia-1972). Zee Blakeley, Elizabeth Taylor; Robert Blakeley, Michael Caine; Stella, Susannah

York; Gladys, Margaret Leighton; Gordon, John Standing; Rita, Mary Larkin; Gavin, Michael Cashman; Head Waiter, Gino Melvazzi; Oscar, Julian West; Shaun, Hilary West.

3376 THE YEAR OF THE CANNIBALS. (American International-1970). Antigone, Britt Ekland; Tiresias, Pierre Clementi; Ismene, Delia Boccardo; Ismene's Fiance, Marino Mase; Haimon, Tomas Milian.

3377 YEAR OF THE HORSE. (Dienstag-Orkin-1966). Gabriel Mason, Bradley Joe, Alvin Lum, Mary Mon Toy, Lorraine Wong, Mr. and Mrs. Thom, Mary Hui, Peter Wond, Dick Hanover, Burt Harris.

3378 YEAR OF THE WOMAN. (1973). Sandra Hochman, Liz Renay, Florynce Kennedy, Art Buchwald, Warren Beatty, Shirley MacLaine, Gloria Steinem, Shirley Chisholm, Norman Mailer, Bella Abzug.

3379 YEAR ONE. (talnoleggio-1974). Alcide De Gasperi, Luigi Vannucchi; Romana De Gasperi, Dominique Darel; Giornalista, Rita Calderoni; Francesca De Gasperi, Valeria Sabel.

3380 THE YELLOW ROLLS-ROYCE. (MGM-1965). Mrs. Gerda Milett, Ingrid Bergman; Marquess of Frinton, Rex Harrison; Mae Jenkins, Shirley MacLaine; Paolo Maltese, George C. Scott; Stefano, Alain Delon; Marchioness of Frinton, Jeanne Moreau; Davich, Omar Sharif; Ferguson, Wally Cox; Joey, Art Carney; Norwood, Roland Culver.

3381 YELLOW SUBMARINE. (United Artists-1968). John, John Clive; Paul, Geoffrey Hughes; George, Peter Batten; Ringo/Chief Blue Meanie, Paul Angelus; Lord Mayor/Nowhere Man, Dick Emery; Old Fred, Lance Percival.

3382 YESTERDAY GIRL. (1967). Anita G., Alexandra Kluge; Pichota, Gunther Mack; Mrs. Pichota, Eva Marie Meineke; Judge, Hans Korte.

3383 YO YO. (Magna-1967). Millionaire, Pierre Etaix; Yo Yo, Pierre Etaix; Yo Yo as a child, Philippe Dionnet; Isolina, Claudine Auger.

3384 YOG--MONSTER FROM SPACE. (American International-1971). Taro, Akira Kubo; Ayako, Atsuko Takahashi; Kyoichi, Yoshio Tsuchiya; Makoto, Kenji Sahara; Rico, Noritake Saito; Saki, Yukiko Kobayashi.

3385 YOLANTA. (Artkino-1966). Yolanta, Natalya Rudnaya; King Rene, Fyodor Nikitin; Vaudemont, Yuri Perov; Duke Robert, Alexander Belyavsky; Eon-Hakkia, Pyotor Glebov; Martha, Valentina Ushakova.

3386 YOU CAN'T WIN 'EM ALL. (Columbia-1970). Adam, Tony Curtis; Josh, Charles Bronson; Aila, Michele Mercier; Osman Boy, Gregoire Aslan; Col. Elci, Fikret Hakan; Capt. Enver, Salih Guney; Reese, Tony Bonner.

3387 YOU ONLY LIVE TWICE. (United Artists-1967). James Bond, Sean Connery; Aiki, Akiko Wakabayashi; Tiger Tanaka, Tetsuro Tamba; Kissy Suzuki, Mie Hama; Osato, Teru Shimada; Helga Brandt, Karin Dor; M, Bernard Lee; Miss Moneypenny, Lois Maxwell; Q, Desmond Llewelyn; Henderson, Charles Gray; Chinese Girl, Tsai Chin; U. S. President, Alexander Knox; President's aide, Robert Hutton.

3388 YOU ONLY LOVE ONCE. (Sigma III-1969). Clara, Karen Blanguernon; Julie, Leslie Bedos; Patrice, Frederic de Pasquale; Roger, Jean Moussy; Rene, Victor Lanoux; Charles, Rene Goliard.

3389 YOU'LL LIKE MY MOTHER. (Universal-1972). Francesca Kinsolving, Patty Duke; Mrs. Kinsolving, Rosemary Murphy; Kenny, Richard Thomas; Kathleen, Sian Barbara Allen; Red Cooper, Dennis Rucker.

3390 YOUNG AMERICANS. (Columbia-1967). The Young Americans.

3391 YOUNG APHRODITES. (Janus-1967). Tsakalos, Takis Emmanouel; Arta, Eleni Prokopiou; Skymnos, Vangelis Joannides; Chloe, Cleopatra Rota; Erster Hirte, Anestis Vlachos.

3392 YOUNG BILLY YOUNG. (United Artists-1969). Kane, Robert Mitchum; Lily Belloit, Angie Dickinson; Billy Young, Robert Walker; Jesse Boone, David Carradine; John Behan, Jack Kelly; Frank Boone, John Anderson; Evvie Cushman, Deana Martin; Charlie, Paul Fix; Kane's Son, Chris Mitchum; Mexican Officer, Rodolfo Acosta.

3393 YOUNG CASSIDY. (MGM-1965). John Cassidy, Rod Taylor; Mrs. Cassidy, Flora Robson; Archie, Jack MacGowran; Ella, Sian Phillips; Tom, T. P. McKenna; Sara, Julie Ross; Michael, Robin Summer; Mick Mullen, Philip O'Flynn; Nora, Maggie Smith; Daisy Battles, Julie Christie; Bessie Ballynoy, Pauline Delaney; Lady Gregory, Edith Evans; W. B. Yeats, Michael Redgrave; Murphy, Harry Brogan; Foreman, Arthur O'Sullivan; Constable, Tom Irwin.

3394 A YOUNG COUPLE. (Trans World-1971). Veronique, Anna Gael; Gilles, Alain Libolt; Ariane, Anny Duperey; Charles, Jean-Francois Calve; Alex, Christian Kerville; Janine, Corinne Lapolitaine.

3395 YOUNG DILLINGER. (Allied Artists-1965). John Dillinger, Nick Adams; Pretty Boy Floyd, Robert Conrad; Elaine, Mary

Ann Mobley; Professor Hoffman, Victor Buono; Homer Van Meter, Dan Terranova; Dr. Wilson, John Hoyt.

3396 YOUNG FRANKENSTEIN. (20th Century-Fox-1974). Dr. Frankenstein, Gene Wilder; Monster, Peter Boyle; Igor, Marty Feldman; Elizabeth, Madeline Kahn; Frau Blucher, Cloris Leachman; Inga, Teri Garr; Inspector Kemp, Kenneth Mars; Herr Falkstein, Richard Haydn; Mr. Hilltop, Liam Dunn; Blind Man, Gene Hackman.

3397 YOUNG FURY. (20th Century-Fox-1965). Rory Calhoun, Virginia Mayo, Lon Chaney, John Agar, Richard Arlen, Linda Foster, Merry Anders, Joan Huntington, Jody McCrea, Rex Bell Jr., William Wellman Jr., Reg Parton, William Bendix, Preston Pierce, Robert Biheller.

3398 THE YOUNG GIRLS OF ROCHEFORT. (Warner Bros.-7 Arts-1968). Delphine Garnier, Catherine Deneuve; Solange Garnier, Francoise Dorleac; Etienne, George Chakiris; Bill, Grover Dale; Andy Miller, Gene Kelly; Yvonne, Danielle Darrieux; Maxence, Jacques Perrin; Simon Dame, Michel Piccoli; Judith, Pamela Hart; Esther, Leslie North.

3399 THE YOUNG LORD. (Beta-1970). Luise, Edith Mathis; Wilhelm, Donald Grove; Barrat, Loren Driscoll; Secretary, Barry McDaniel; Sir Edgar, Otto Graf; Begonia, Vera Little; Frau Hasentraffer, Lisa Otto.

3400 THE YOUNG LOVERS. (MGM-1965). Eddie Slocum, Peter Fonda; Pam Burns, Sharon Hugueny; Tarragoo, Nick Adams; Debbie, Deborah Walley; Mrs. Burns, Beatrice Straight; Prof. Schwartz, Malachi Throne; Dr. Shoemaker, Kent Smith; Prof. Reese, Joseph Campanella.

3401 THE YOUNG NURSES. (New World-1973). Kitty, Jean Manson; Joanne, Ashley Porter; Michelle, Angela Gibbs; Donahue, Zack Taylor; Ken, Jack La Rue Jr.; Fairbanks, William Joyce; Policeman, Richard Miller; Patient, Sally Kirkland; Krebs, Allan Arbus; Nurse, Mary Doyle.

3402 THE YOUNG RUNAWAYS. (MGM-1968). Shelly Allen, Brooke Bundy; Dewey Norson, Kevin Coughlin, Raymond Marquis Allen, Lloyd Bochner; Deanie Donford, Patty McCormack; Mrs. Donford, Lynn Bari; Mr. Donford, Norman Fell; Joanne, Quentin Dean; Terry, Richard Dreyfuss; Freddie, Dick Sargent; Sgt. Joe Collyer, James Edwards; Loch Riccano, Ken Del Conte; Mrs. Morse, Hortense Petra.

3403 THE YOUNG SINNER. (United Screen Arts-1965). Tom Laughlin, Stephanie Powers, William Wellman Jr., Robert Angelo, Linda March, Roxanne Heard, Jack Starrett, Ed Cook, Chris Robinson, James Stacy.

3404 THE YOUNG, THE EVIL AND THE SAVAGE. (American International-1968). Inspector Duran, Michael Rennie; Richard, Mark Damon; Lucille, Eleanor Brown; Jill, Sally Smith; Denise, Pat Valturri; Miss Clay, Ludmilla Lvova; DeBrazzi, Alan Collins; Detective Gabon, Frank De Rosa.

3405 YOUNG TORLESS. (Kanawha-1968). Torless, Matthieu Carriere; Basini, Marian Seidowsky; Reiting, Alfred Dietz; Beineberg, Bernd Tischer.

3406 THE YOUNG WARRIORS. (Universal-1967). Sgt. Cooley, James Drury; Pvt. Hacker, Steve Carlson; Pvt. Guthrie, Jonathan Daly; Pvt. Foley, Robert Pine; Riley, Michael Stanwood; Lippincott, Jeff Scott; Sgt. Wadley, Norman Fell; The Lieutenant, Kent McWhirter.

3407 YOUNG WINSTON. (Columbia-1972). Winston Churchill, Simon Ward; Lord Randolph, Robert Shaw; Lady Jennie, Anne Bancroft; Dr. James Welldon, Jack Hawkins; George Buckle, Ian Holm; David Lloyd George, Anthony Hopkins; General Bindon Blood, Patrick Magee; Captain Haldane, Edward Woodward; General Herbert Kitchener, John Mills; Captain (35th Sikhs), Peter Cellier; Mrs. Everest, Pat Heywood; Lord Salisbury, Laurence Naismith.

3408 A YOUNG WORLD. (Lopert-1966). Anne, Christine Delaroche; Carlo, Nino Castelnuovo; Mary, Tanya Lopert; Woman, Madeleine Robinson; Doctor, Georges Wilson; Boss, Pierre Brasseur.

3409 YOUR CHEATIN' HEART. (MGM-1965). Hank Williams, George Hamilton; Audrey Williams, Susan Oliver; Shorty Younger, Red Buttons; Fred Rose, Arthur O'Connell.

3410 YOUR THREE MINUTES ARE UP. (Cinerama-1973). Charlie, Beau Bridges; Mike, Ron Liebman; Betty, Janet Margolin; Mrs. Wilk, Kathleen Freeman; Mr. Kellogg, David Ketchum; Dr. Claymore, Stu Nisbet; Eddie Abruzzi, Read Morgan; Teenage Driver, Jennifer Ashley; Sugar, Sherry Bain; Gas Station Operator, Paul Barselou.

3411 YOU'RE A BIG BOY NOW. (7 Arts-1967). Bernard Chanticleer, Peter Kastner; Barbara Darling, Elizabeth Hartman; Margery Chanticleer, Geraldine Page; Miss Thing, Julie Harris; I. H. Chanticleer, Rip Torn; Richard Mudd, Michael Dunn; Raef, Tony Bill; Amy, Karen Black.

3412 YOU'RE LYING. (Grove Press-1973). Lasse, Stig Engstrom; Bjorn, Borge Ahlstedt; Mother, Siff Rund; Himself, Vilgot Sjoman.

3413 YOURS, MINE AND OURS. (United Artists-1968). Helen North, Lucille Ball; Frank Beardsley, Henry Fonda; Darrel Harrison, Van Johnson; The Doctor, Tom Bosley; Frank's

Date, Louise Troy; Larry, Ben Murphy; The North Children, Jennifer Leak, Kevin Burchett, Kimberly Beck, Mitchell Vogel, Margot Jane, Eric Shea, Gregory Atkins, Lynnell Atkins; The Beardsley Children, Timothy Matthieson, Gilbert Rogers, Nancy Roth, Gary Goetzman, Suzanne Cupito, Holly O'Brien, Michel Tobin, Maralee Foster, Tracy Nelson, Stephanie Oliver.

3414 YOU'VE GOT TO BE SMART. (Producers Releasing Organization-1967). Nick Sloane, Tom Stern; Jerry Harper, Roger Perry; Connie Jackson, Gloria Castillo; Miss Hathaway, Mamie Van Doren.

3415 YOU'VE GOT TO WALK IT LIKE YOU TALK IT OR YOU'LL LOSE THAT BEAT. (JER-1971). Carter, Zalman King; Herby, Allen Garfield; Susan, Suzette Green; Wino, Richard Pryor; Ad Agency Head, Bob Downey; Singer in Men's Room, Liz Torres; Girl in Park, Roz Kelly.

3416 Z. (Cinema V-1969). The Deputy, Yves Montand; Helene, Irene Papas; Examining Magistrate, Jean-Louis Trintignant; Manuel, Charles Denner; Nick, The Witness, George Geret; The Journalist, Jacques Perrin; The Public Prosecutor, Francois Perier; Matt, Bernard Fresson; The General, Pierre Dux; The Colonel, Julien Guiomar; Vago, Marcel Bozzufi; Nick's Sister, Magali Noe, Yago, Renato Salvatori; Pirou, Jean Bouise; Pierre, Jean-Pierre Miquel; Dumas, Guy Mairesse; Shoula, Clotilde Joano.

3417 Z. P. G. (Paramount-1972). Russ McNeil, Oliver Reed; Carole McNeil, Geraldine Chaplin; George Borden, Don Gordon; Edna Borden, Diane Cilento; Dr. Herrick, David Markham; Mary Herrick, Sheila Reid; Dr. Mallory, Aubrey Woods; President, Bill Nagy.

3418 ZABRISKIE POINT. (MGM-1970). Mark, Mark Frechette; Daria, Daria Halprin; Cafe Owner, Paul Fix; Lee Allen's Associate, G. D. Spradlin; Lee Allen, Rod Taylor; Kathleen, Kathleen Cleaver; Morty, Bill Garaway.

3419 ZANDY'S BRIDE. (Warner Bros. -1974). Zandy Allan, Gene Hackman; Hannah Lund, Liv Ullmann; Ma Allan, Eileen Heckart; Maria Cordova, Susan Tyrrell; Mal Allan, Sam Bottoms; Frank Gallo, Joe Santos.

3420 ZARDOZ. (20th Century-Fox-1974). Sean Connery.

3421 ZATOICHI. (Daiei-1968). Zatoichi, Shintaro Katsu: Omitsu, Shiho Fujimura; Jingoro, Ryuzo Shimada; Ohisa, Reiko Fujiwara.

3422 ZATOICHI AT LARGE. (Toho-1973). Shintaro Katsu, Hisaya Morishige, Naoko Otani, Etsushi Takahashi, Rentaro Mikuni.

3423 ZATOICHI MEETS YOJIMBO. (Bijou-1971). Yojimbo,

Toshiro Mifune; Zatoichi, Shintaro Katsu; Courtesan, Ayako Wakao; Stonecutter, Kanjuro Arashi; Elder, Osamu Takizawa.

3424 ZATOICHI'S CANE SWORD. (Daiei-1971). Shintaro Katsu, Shino Fujimura, Yeshihiro Aoyama, Makoto Fujita, Eijiro Tono.

3425 ZEBRA IN THE KITCHEN. (MGM-1965). Chris Carlyle, Jay North; Dr. Del Hartwood, Martin Milner; Branch Hawksbill, Andy Devine; Isobel Moon, Joyce Meadows; Adam Carlyle, Jim Davis; Anne Carlyle, Dorothy Green; Wilma Carlyle, Karen Green; Councilman Pew, Vaughn Taylor; Sgt. Freebee, John Milford; Councilman Lawrence, Tris Coffin; Chief of Police, Merritt Bohn.

3426 ZERO IN THE UNIVERSE. (Film-Makers' Distribution Center-1966). Zero, Jock Livingston; Steinmetz, George Bartenieff; Vivian, Pam Badyk; Peep, George Moorse; Dubois, Rob Du Mee; Gillomovitch Mullendorf, Henke Raaff; The Major, Louis Lehmans.

3427 ZIGZAG. (MGM-1970). Paul R. Cameron, George Kennedy; Jean Cameron, Anne Jackson; Mario Gambretti, Eli Wallach; Asst. District Attorney Gates, Steve Ihnat; Morrie Bronson, William Marshall; Lt. Max Hines, Joe Maross; Harold Tracey, Dana Elcar; Adam Mercer, Walter Brooke; Sheila Mangan, Anita O'Day.

3428 ZITA. (Regional-1968). Annie, Joanna Shimkus; Aunt Zita, Katina Paxinou; Yvette, Suzanne Flon; Simon, Jose Maria Flotats; Bernard, Paul Crauchet; Boni, Bernard Fresson; James, Med Hondo; The Spaniard, Roger Ibanez; The Sergeant, Jacques Rispal.

INDEX